T0323342

Bond Pricing and Yield-Curve Modelling

A Structural Approach

This book provides the theoretical foundations (no-arbitrage, convexity, expectations, affine modelling) for a treatment of government bond markets; presents and critically discusses the wealth of empirical findings that have appeared in the literature in the last decade; and introduces the 'structural' models that are used by central banks, institutional investors, sovereign wealth funds, academics and advanced practitioners to model the yield curve, to answer policy questions, to estimate the magnitude of the risk premium, to gauge market expectations and to assess investment opportunities. The book weaves precise theory with up-to-date empirical evidence to build, with the minimum mathematical sophistication required for the task, a critical understanding of what drives the government bond market.

Riccardo Rebonato is Professor of Finance at the EDHEC Business School and the EDHEC Risk Institute and holds the EDHEC PIMCO Research Chair. He has been Global Head of Fixed Income and FX Analytics at PIMCO and Head of Research, Risk Management and Derivatives Trading at several major international banks. He has previously held academic positions at Imperial College and Oxford University, and has been a board director for the International Swaps and Derivatives Association (ISDA) and the Global Association of Risk Professionals (GARP). He currently sits on the board of The Nine Dots Prize. He is the author of several books and articles in finance and risk management, including *Portfolio Management under Stress* (2004).

Bond Pricing and Yield-Curve Modelling

A Structural Approach

Riccardo Rebonato
EDHEC Business School
EDHEC Risk Institute

CAMBRIDGE
UNIVERSITY PRESS

University Printing House, Cambridge CB2 8BS, United Kingdom

One Liberty Plaza, 20th Floor, New York, NY 10006, USA

477 Williamstown Road, Port Melbourne, VIC 3207, Australia

314–321, 3rd Floor, Plot 3, Splendor Forum, Jasola District Centre, New Delhi - 110025, India

79 Anson Road, #06-04/06, Singapore 079906

Cambridge University Press is part of the University of Cambridge.

It furthers the University's mission by disseminating knowledge in the pursuit of
education, learning, and research at the highest international levels of excellence.

www.cambridge.org
Information on this title: www.cambridge.org/9781107165854
DOI: 10.1017/9781316694169

© Riccardo Rebonato 2018

First published 2018

Printed in the United Kingdom by Clays, St Ives plc

A catalogue record for this publication is available from the British Library

ISBN 978-1-107-16585-4 Hardback

Cambridge University Press has no responsibility for the persistence or accuracy of
URLs for external or third-party internet websites referred to in this publication
and does not guarantee that any content on such websites is, or will remain,
accurate or appropriate.

To the memory of my father, to my wife and to my son, with thanks.

Contents

Acknowledgements

I owe a great debt of gratitude to a number of friends and colleagues. First and foremost, an anonymous referee has produced the most thorough and constructively critical review of an earlier draft of this manuscript that I have ever received in my publishing career. If he or she had written this book, I am sure it would have been far better than what I managed to produce. Luckily (for me) he or she didn' t. Thank you.

My ex-colleagues at PIMCO have been a constant source of inspiration, illumination, challenge and insight. I have benefitted greatly from illuminating discussions with (in alphabetical order) Mr Mukundan Deverajan, Dr Soraya Kazziha, Mr Ravi Mattu, Dr Vasant Naik, Dr Niels Pedersen, Dr David Pottinton, Dr Vlad Putiatyn, Dr Wendong Qu, Mr Jeremy Rosten, Mr Ivan Saroka and Dr Chelsea Wang. These ex-colleagues have been generous with their time and suggestions beyond what is reasonable to expect.

Among friends, Dr Andrei Liasenko has shown great interest in several early drafts of the manuscript, corrected small and not-so-small mistakes and suggested a far more elegant (and, the reader will be happy to hear, simpler) proof for an important result in Chapter 33. Ms Jean Whitmore has made use of her unfailing good judgment to suggest ways in which an earlier version of the work could be improved.

Professors Francis Diebold, Michael Dempster, Rene Garcia, Lionel Martinelli and Raman Uppal have provided very useful comments. Prof Paolo Veronesi has pointed me in the direction of important material which has found its way into the book.

Several of my students, both from EDEHC and from my previous academic affiliation (The Mathematical Finance Department at Oxford University), have provided a springboard for discussing the ideas presented in this book. In particular, I would like to thank Dr Daniela Villegas, Dr Tramback, Dr Taku Hatano and Dr Alexey Eherekinski.

I have benefited greatly from discussion with Dr Taylor Spears, and with the delegates at the Global Derivatives conferences delegates in Amsterdam (2014–2015) and Budapest (2016).

The editors at Cambridge University Press have displayed an enthusiasm for the project that has delighted – and surprised – me, all the more because this is my second book with them. Special thanks go to Mr Chris Harrison for his help and guidance, Ms Karen Maloney for her enthusiasm and the production team for their endless patience. I am truly touched.

My father and my wife have given me all the support I could have wished for the project. My eight-year-old son has forgiven me, I hope, for not playing with him as much as I would have otherwise; perhaps he has been so understanding because he has had a chance to build a few thousand paper planes with the earlier drafts of this book.

Despite all this help and encouragement, and despite the care I have devoted to this work, I am sure that many errors still lurk in its 750-plus pages. It goes without saying that I am fully responsible for these errors; but I will say so nonetheless.

Symbols and Abbreviations

LATIN SYMBOLS

A_t^T = A scalar that enters the expression for P_t^T, ie, for the price at time t of a zero-coupon bond of maturity T, as in $P_t^T = e^{A_t^T + (B_t^T)^{\mathrm{T}} x_t}$

B_t^T = A vector that enters the expression for P_t^T, ie, for the price at time t of a zero-coupon bond of maturity T, as in $P_t^T = e^{A_t^T + (B_t^T)^{\mathrm{T}} x_t}$

$BEI_{t,T}$ = Break-even inflation at time t for maturity T

c_t = Consumption at time t

$Conv_t^T$ = Time-t convexity of a T-maturity (discount) bond

$$D = \sum_{i=1,n} \omega_i \left(B_t^{T_i}\right) \left(B_t^{T_i}\right)^{\mathrm{T}}$$

Dur_t^T = Time-t duration of a T-maturity (discount) bond

EI_t^T = Time-t expected inflation per unit time over the period $[t, T]$

f_t^T = Value at time t of an instantaneous forward rate expiring at time T

$F_t^{T,T+\tau}$ = Value at time t of a discrete forward rate expiring at time T and covering a notional borrowing/lending period of length τ

$\{l_i\}$ = Eiegenvalues of the reversion-speed matrix

m_{t+1} = Stochastic discount factor for time $t + 1$

$M_t = \beta u'(c_t)$ stochastic discount factor in continuous time

p_t^T = Log price at time t of a zero-coupon bond of maturity T

p_s = Probability of reaching state s

P_t^T = Price at time t of a zero-coupon bond of maturity T

$P_{t,T}^R$ = Price at time t of a real zero-coupon bond of maturity T

$q_t \equiv \log Q_t$

Q_t = Value of the price process at time t

r_t = Value of the short rate at time t

r_t^R = Value of the real short rate at time t

r_f = Riskless rate

ret_t^T = Annualized return from investing in the T-maturity discount bond

R^f = Gross one-period riskless return

$\underline{S}$ = Volatility matrix for an affine model

S_t = Time-t price of a generic security

sp_s = State price at time s
SR = Sharpe Ratio
$u(c_t)$ = Utility for consumption at time t
W = Initial wealth
x_t = A scalar or a vector that denotes the state variables in an affine model
$xret_t^T$ = Annualized *excess* return from investing in the T-maturity discount bond
y_t^T = Yield at time t of a zero-coupon bond of maturity T
$y_t^{nom,T}$ = Nominal yield at time t of a zero-coupon bond of maturity T
$y_t^{real,T}$ = Real yield at time t of a zero-coupon bond of maturity T

GREEK SYMBOLS

$\alpha_t^T = -\frac{1}{T-t}A_t^T$: One of the two quantities that links yields to state variables for affine models, as in $y_t^T = \alpha_t^T + \left(\beta_t^T\right)^{\mathsf{T}} x_t$

$\beta_t^T = -\frac{1}{T-t}A_t^T$: One of the two quantities that links yields to state variables for affine models, as in $y_t^T = \alpha_t^T + \left(\beta_t^T\right)^{\mathsf{T}} x_t$

β = Time impatience term in the stochastic discount factor: $m_{t+1} = \beta\frac{u'(c_{t+1})}{u'(c_t)}$
κ = Reversion speed in a one-dimensional mean-reverting process
θ = Reversion level (vector or scalar) for an affine model
$\Theta_t^T \equiv \left(\frac{Q_t^T}{Q_t^t}\right)^{-1}$
λ = Market price of risk
Λ = Matrix of eigenvalues of the reversion-speed matrix
$\mu_r^{\mathbb{P}(\mathbb{Q})}$ = Drift in the real-world (risk-neutral) measure of the short rate
v_0 = The price of a security today
π_s = State-price deflator
$\pi_t^{real,T}$ = Real state-price deflator
σ_P = Bond price volatility
σ_r = Volatility of the short rate
$\sigma_{y_t^T}$ = Volatility of a yield of expiry T
$\tau \equiv T - t$
ω_i = The ith weight in a portfolio

FRAKTUR AND CALLIGRAPHIC SYMBOLS

$\mathfrak{CP}$ = Convexity of a portfolio
$\mathfrak{Cp}_t^T$ (*Vasicek*) = Bond price convexity in the Vasicek model
$\mathfrak{Cy}_t^T$ (*Vasicek*) = Yield convexity in the Vasicek model
$\mathrm{Ci}_{t,T}$ = Convexity term in the expression for break-even inflation in the real-world measure
$\mathrm{Ci}_{t,T}^{\mathbb{Q}}$ = Convexity term in the expression for break-even inflation in the risk-neutral measure

$\mathrm{Ci}_{t,T}^{\mathbb{T}} = $ Convexity term in the expression for break-even inflation in the risk-neutral measure

$\mathcal{K} = $ Reversion speed matrix for an affine model

$\mathcal{L}_t^T = $ Liquidity component in the decomposition of break-even inflation:
$$BEI_{t,T} = \mathbb{E}\left(I_t^T\right)^{\mathbb{P}} + \mathcal{P}_t^T + \mathcal{L}_t^T$$

$\mathcal{M}_t^N = $ The Ratio of the nominal stochastic discount factors: $\mathcal{M}_t^N = \frac{\pi^N(T)}{\pi^N(t)}$

$\mathcal{N}\left(\mu, \sigma^2\right) = $ Normal distribution with mean, μ, and variance, σ^2

$\mathcal{P}_t^T = $ Risk premium required by an investor in order to bear inflation risk

$\mathbb{P} = $ Real-world measure

$\mathbb{Q} = $ Risk-neutral measure

$\mathbb{S} = $ Subjective measure

$\mathcal{S}_\tau = $ The Set of all the possible future states at time τ

$\mathbb{T} = $ Terminal measure

PART I

THE FOUNDATIONS

CHAPTER 1

What This Book Is About

> It is not my intention to detain the reader by expatiating on the variety, or the importance of the subject, which I have undertaken to treat; since the merit of the choice would serve to render the weakness of the execution still more apparent, and still less excusable. But [...] it will perhaps be expected that I should explain, in a few words, the nature and limits of my general plan.
> Edward Gibbon, *The Decline and Fall of the Roman Empire*[1]

1.1 MY GOAL IN WRITING THIS BOOK

In this book I intend to look at yield-curve modelling from a 'structural' perspective.[2] I use the adjective *structural* in a very specific sense, to refer to those models which are created with the goal of *explaining* (as opposed to *describing*) the yield curve. What does 'explaining' mean? In the context of this book, I mean accounting for the observed yields by combining the expectations investors form about future rates (and, more generally, the economy) and the compensation they require to bear the risk inherent with holding default-free bonds. (As we shall see later, there is a third 'building block', ie, convexity.)

This provides one level of explanation, but one could go deeper. So, for instance, the degree of compensation investors require in order to bear 'interest-rate risk' could be derived ('explained') in more fundamental terms from the strategy undertaken by a rational, risk-averse investor who is faced with a set of investment opportunities and wants to maximize her utility from consumption

---

[1] From the Prologue.

[2] A note on terminology. In the term-structure literature the adjective 'structural' is often applied to those models that are based on a specification of the economy – a specification that may go all the way down to preferences, utility maximization and equilibrium. I use the term 'equilibrium models' to refer to these descriptions. We shall only dip our toes in these topics in Chapter 15. For those readers who already understand the meaning of the expression, structural models in this book are those that straddle the $\mathbb{P}$- (real-world) and $\mathbb{Q}$- (risk-neutral) measures. If this does not make much sense at the moment, all will be revealed.

in a multiperiod economy. I will sketch with a broad brush the main lines of this fundamental derivation, but will not pursue this line of argument in great detail. The compensation exacted by investors for bearing market risk (the 'market price of risk') will instead be empirically related (say, via regressions) either to combinations of past and present bond prices and yields, or to past history and present values of macroeconomic variables.

Another way to look at what I try to do in this book is to say that I *describe* the market price of risk in order to *explain* the yield curve. If one took a more 'fundamental' approach, one could try to *explain* the market price of risk as well, but would still have to *describe* something more basic, say, the utility function. Sooner or later, all scientific treatments hit against this hard descriptive core; even theoretical physics is not immune to the curse, or blessing, of having to describe. See, in this respect, the Section 7 of this chapter.

In keeping with the quote that opens this chapter, I will not dwell on why yield curve modelling is important – after all, if the reader were not convinced of this, she probably would not be reading these words. Still, one may well ask, 'Why write a book on *structural* yield-curve modelling?' The answer is that since the mid-2000s there have been exciting developments in the theoretical and empirical understanding of the yield curve dynamics and of risk premia. The 'old' picture with which many of us grew up is now recognized to be in important respects qualitatively wrong. To go from the old to the new class of models requires a rather substantial piece of surgery, not a face-lift, but it is well worth the effort.

Unfortunately, the existing literature on these exciting new topics is somewhat specialized and uses elegant but, to the uninitiated, rather opaque and forbidding-sounding concepts (such as the state-price deflator or the stochastic discount factor). Gone is the simplicity with which even a relative newcomer could pick up Vasicek's paper and, with a good afternoon's work, understand what it was about.

It is therefore my intention to 'translate' and introduce these exciting new developments using the simplest mathematical tools that allow me to handle correctly (but not rigorously) the material at hand. In doing so, I will always trade off a pound of mathematical rigour for an ounce of intuition.

I will also try to explain the vocabulary of the 'new language', and rederive in the simplest possible way the old (and probably familiar) no-arbitrage results using the modern tools. This will both deepen the reader's understanding and enable her to read the current literature.

In addition to expectations and risk premia, there is a third important determinant to the shape of the yield curve, namely 'convexity'. In Part V explain in detail what convexity is, and why it is, in some sense, unique. (In a nutshell, to extract the risk premium you just have to be patient and will be 'fairly' rewarded for your patience; to earn convexity, you have to work very, very hard.) For the moment, the important point is that in the treatment I present in this book these three building blocks (expectations, risk premia, and convexity), together with the principle of no-arbitrage, explain all that there is to know about the yield curve.[3]

1.2 WHAT MY ACCOUNT LEAVES OUT

Is it true that, once we account for expectations, risk premia and convexity, there is really nothing else to the dynamics of credit-risk-free yield curves, at least at the level of description that we have chosen? Of course it isn't. To understand what is left out some historical perspective may help.

The current modelling approach places the Expectation Hypothesis at its centre. This does not mean that 'only expectations matter', but that the only (or the main) deviations from expectations come from risk premia (and the neglected relation, convexity). As Fontaine and Garcia (2015) state '[w]hat distinguishes modern literature is the emphasis on interest rate risk as the leading (or sole) determinant of the risk premium.'[4] As a result 'sources of risk premium other than interest rate risk found a refuge in undergraduate textbooks while the academic agenda leapt forward, developing an array of sophisticated yet tractable no-arbitrage models.'[5]

So what is left behind by the expectations–risk premia–convexity triad?

To begin with, I devote little attention to liquidity, which can become very important, especially in periods of market distress.[6] However, in most market conditions the securities I deal with in this book – US Treasury bonds, German Bunds, UK gilts – are among the most liquid instruments available to investors. Liquidity, one can therefore argue, should be relatively unimportant in a reasonable hierarchy of important factors.[7] If the reader is interested in liquidity-specific issues (such as the pricing of on-the-run versus off-the-run Treasury bonds), the approach of Fontaine and Garcia (2008) discussed in some detail

---

[3] As noted earlier, I will mention briefly the links between my building blocks and more fundamental macroeconomic and monetary-economics concepts (see Chapters 3 and 15), but I will do so simply to give the reader a qualitative understanding of the form a more fundamental approach to yield curve modelling would take.

[4] p. 463.   [5] ibid., pp. 463–464.

[6] In Chapter 18 I present a general pricing methodology that will allow the reader to build her own affine model, DIY-style. Using this toolkit, there is nothing to stop the reader from introducing a factor called 'liquidity', equip it with the necessary parameter paraphernalia (reversion speed, reversion level, volatility, etc) and plug it in the multipurpose affine framework that I develop in Chapter 18. By construction, her 'fits' will be at least as good, and probably better, than before she introduced the 'liquidity' factor. However, it is not easy to find a 'principled' way to assign the correct explanatory contribution to this factor: are we really modelling liquidity, or have we just over-parametrized our model?

[7] Of the models that we explore in Part VII, two deal with liquidity. One is the D'Amico, Kim and Wei (2010) approach, which deals with nominal and *real* rates, explicitly models liquidity – and the authors make the point that the inclusion of this factor is important in order to have a correct estimation of the model parameters and a convincing description of inflation expectations. Dollar-denominated inflation-linked bonds were, especially in the early years after their introduction, far less liquid that their nominal Treasury counterparts, and a strong case can therefore be made for an explicit modelling of liquidity.

in Chapter 32, is very useful.[8] When it comes to government bonds, however, it must be kept in mind that a bond-specific maturity factor presents a serious challenge for traditional (and frictionless) no-arbitrage models, which are built on the assumption that all bonds are created exactly equal, once their return and risk characteristics are properly taken into account.[9]

The other main possible missing ingredient from the description presented in this book is market segmentation – the idea that classes of investors, such as pension funds, might have preferred 'habitats' (maturity ranges) where they 'like to' invest. According to proponents of segmentation, by so doing, these investors create an imbalance of supply and demand that arbitrageurs either do not manage to eliminate, or do eliminate, but by taking risk, for which compensation – and hence risk premium – is exacted.[10] According to researchers such as Vayanos and Vila (2009), the compensation for the risky activities of pseudo-arbitrageurs then leaves a detectable signature in the shape of a risk-premiuma contribution to various yields. Readers interested in the topic of segmentation are referred to Vayanos and Vila (2009) for a theoretical treatment along these lines, and Chen et al. (2014) for an empirical discussion of the maturity preference exhibited by insurance firms.

These topics, and other sources of imperfections such as the zero bound of rates, are well treated in Fontaine and Garcia (2015) – the title of their chapter ('Recent Advances in Old Fixed Income Topics: Liquidity, Learning, and the Lower Bound') gives a good flavour of what the reader can find in their work. As mentioned, we look at liquidity in Chapter 32, and we deal with the zero bound in Chapter 19. We do not deal with market segmentation, and only cursorily with learning-related issues; see, however, the opening sections of Chapter 28.

1.3 AFFINE MODELS

Let's therefore assume that we are happy with our identification of the three building blocks (expectations, risk premia and convexity) and of the glue

---

I also deal with liquidity in Chapter 32, which is devoted to the Diebold and Rudebusch approach. The treatment is based on the insight by Fontaine and Garcia (2008), and can be applied to other liquidity-unaware models as well.

[8] 'On-the-run' bonds are freshly-minted, newly-issued Treasury bonds. They enjoy special liquidity, and therefore yield several basis points less (are more expensive) than earlier-issued ('off-the-run') Treasury bonds of similar maturity. This on-the-run/off-the-run spread can become significantly larger in periods of market distress, when liquidity becomes very sought after.

[9] As Fontaine and Garcia (2008) write, 'a structural specification of the liquidity premium raises important challenges. The on-the, run-premium is a real arbitrage opportunity unless we explicitly consider the cost of shorting the more expensive bond, or, alternatively, the benefits accruing to a bondholder from a lower repo rate. These features are absent from the current crop of term-structure model' (pp. 9–10).

[10] As Fontaine and Garcia (2015) point out, liquidity and segmentation need not be looked at as totally different sources of friction or inefficiency because '[t]he clientele demand for new and old bonds is similar in spirit to the view that investors have "preferred habitats"' and '[t]he clientele demand may be scattered across bond maturities, but it can also be scattered across the illiquidity spectrum' (p. 472).

(noarbitrage) that holds them together. What we need next is a way to combine these ingredients in a coherent and logically consistent manner. This is what a model does, and this is why a large part of this book is devoted to discussing models of the yield curve. *Which* models, though?

Because of their unsurpassed intuitional appeal and their analytical tractability, I deal mainly with a popular class of structural models – the affine class.[11] In order to give a transparent understanding of how these models weave together these three building blocks to determine the shape of the yield curve, I will start my discussion from the simplest incarnation of affine models – the Vasicek (1977) model.[12]

The Vasicek model is unparalleled for the intuitive understanding it affords, and it is for this reason that I introduce it, perhaps unwisely, very early in the book – even, that is, before dealing with the theoretical underpinnings of term-structure modelling. Quite simply, I want the reader to have a vivid, if, at this point, probably imprecise, picture of what we will be talking about more precisely and more abstractly in the later parts of the book, when more complex, and more opaque, models come to the fore.

In general, I strongly encourage the reader who feels her intuition beginning to fail her when looking at the more complex models to adopt ruthlessly the strategy of *reductio ad Vasicek*, ie, to ask herself, 'What is the equivalent of this concept/formalism/result in the Vasicek model?' She is encouraged to do so, not because the Vasicek model is perfect, but because it lays bare with great clarity the mechanics and intuition behind more complex affine models.

For all the virtues of the Vasicek model, recent empirical evidence suggests that the explanation of risk premia Vasicek-family models afford is *qualitatively* wrong. Since the risk premium constitutes the explanatory bridge between expectations and observed prices, and since the Vasicek approach is the progenitor of all the more recent affine models, this does not seem to bode well for affine structural approaches to term-structure modelling.

Luckily, the same empirical evidence also suggests how the first-generation, Vasicek-like, affine models can be modified and enriched. I therefore present in Part VI of this book what we now know about term premia, and in Part VII how these empirical findings can be incorporated in the new-generation affine models.

---

[11] See, for instance, Dai and Singleton (2000) for a systematic calssification of affine models, and Duffee (2002) for a discussion of *essentially* affine models – loosely speaking, models which remain affine both in the real-world and in the pricing measures. Good reviews of affine models can be found in Bloder (2001), who also deals with Kalman filter estimation methods, and Piazzesi (2010). Extensions to stochastic affine-volatility models are found in Longstaff and Schwartz (1992) and Balduzzi et al. (1996).

[12] I must make very clear from the start that I will deal in this book with *Gaussian* affine models, which are far simpler than the square-root models of the Cox–Ingersoll–Ross (1985a, b) family. Admittedly, Gaussian affine models do allow for negative rates, but recent experience suggests that this should be considered more of a virtue than a blemish. (At the time of this writing, Germany just issued short-dated government bonds with a negative yield.)

Speaking of affine models means that we require a special type of relationship between yields and the state variables. But how should we choose these variables? As we shall discuss towards the end of the book, from a very abstract point of view, and as long as some quantities are exactly recovered by the different models, the choice of variables makes very little difference. In practice, however, this choice informs the statistical estimation techniques used in the calibration, the degree of 'structure' on the dynamics of the state variables (via the condition of no-arbitrage), the parsimony of the model and the user's ability to understand and interpret the model. Section 1.5 of this introductory chapter makes these statements more precise. First, however, we want to look a bit more carefully at the various types of yield curve models, so that the reader can clearly see what we are going to deal with and what we will not touch upon. Probably, the reader should not throw away her book receipt before reading the next section.

1.4 A SIMPLE TAXONOMY

There are many different types of term-structure models. They are different in part because they have been created with different purposes in mind and in part because they look at the same problem from different angles. A reasonable taxonomy may look as follows.

1. *Statistical models* aim to *describe* how the yield curve moves. Their main workhorses here are the Vector Auto-Regressive (VAR) models, which are often employed to forecast interest rates and to estimate the risk premium as the difference between the forward and the forecasted rates. This task sounds easy, but, as I discuss later in the book, the quasi-unit-root nature of the level of rates (and many more statistical pitfalls) makes estimations based purely on time-series analysis arduous, and the associated 'error bars' embarrassingly large. See, eg, the discussion in Cochrane and Piazzesi (2008).[13]

   In the attempt to improve on this state of affairs, no-arbitrage structural models, which add *cross-sectional* information to the time-series data, come to the fore. *In this book we shall take a cursory and instrumental look at statistical models, mainly to glean statistical information about one important ingredient of our structural models, ie, the market price of risk.*

   The important thing to stress is that statistical models fit observed market yield curves well and have good predictive power but lack a strong theoretical foundation, because, by themselves, they cannot guarantee absence of arbitrage among the predicted yields. Their strengths and weaknesses are therefore complementary to those of the no-arbitrage models discussed in the text that follows: these are theoretically sound, but sometimes poor at fitting the market yield

---

[13] See, in particular, the discussion of their Panel 1 on p. 2 of their paper.

covariance structure and the observed yield curves, and worse at predicting their evolution. See, in this respect, the discussion in Diebold and Rudebusch (2013)[14] and Section 1 in Chapter 32.

One of the underlying themes developed in this book is the attempt to marry the predictive and fitting virtues of statistical models with the theoretical solidity of the no-arbitrage models. Chapters 32, 33 and 34 should be read in this light.

2. *Structural no-arbitrage models* (of which the Vasicek (1977) and Cox–Ingersoll–Ross (1985a, b) are the earliest and best-known textbook examples) make assumptions about how a handful of important driving factors behave; they ensure that the no-arbitrage condition is satisfied; and they derive how the three components that drive the yield curve (expectations, risk premia and convexity) should affect the shape of the yield curve. The no-arbitrage conditions ensure that the derived prices of bonds do not offer free lunches. As I explain in footnote 1, I speak of structural no-arbitrage models when they straddle the physical (real-world, $\mathbb{P}$) and risk-neutral ($\mathbb{Q}$) measures – as opposed to restricted no-arbitrage models that are formulated only in the $\mathbb{Q}$ measure.

   The distinction is important for at least two reasons. First, if we want to understand how bond prices are formed based on expectations and risk aversion, we cannot look at just one measure: market prices are compatible with an infinity of different combinations of expectations and market prices of risk.

   The second reason is subtler. It is well known that if we only look at the risk-neutral ($\mathbb{Q}$) measure three factors (as we shall see, the first three principal components) explain the movements in prices extremely well. However, if we also want to explain excess returns (risk premia) we may have to use more variables (perhaps up to five, according to Cochrane and Piazzesi (2005, 2008), Adrian, Crump and Moench (2013) and Hellerstein (2011)).[15] The message here is that variables virtually irrelevant in one measure may become important when the two measures are linked. More about this later. *Structural no-arbitrage models constitute the class of models this book is about.*

3. *'Snapshot' models* (such as the Nelson–Siegel (1987) model, or the many splines models of which Fisher, Nychka and Zervos's (1995) is probably the best known) are cross-sectional devices to *interpolate* prices or yields of bonds that we cannot observe, given a set of prices or yields that we *can* observe.[16] They also produce as a by-product the model yields of the bonds we *do* observe. If supplemented with

---

[14] p. 76.

[15] See in this respect the discussion on p. 140 of Cochrane and Piazzesi (2005) and on p. 3 of Hellerstein (2011).

[16] For two early, but still valid, evaluations of yield-curve estimation models, see Bliss (1997) and Anderson et al. (1996).

the ubiquitous but somewhat ad hoc assumption that the residuals (the differences between the model and the market prices) are mean reverting, these models give practitioners suggestions about whether a given observed bond yield (hence, price) is 'out of line' with a reasonable smooth interpolation of where it should lie.[17] Liquidity corrections such as those discussed in Fontaine and Garcia (2008) can be very important in these 'cheap/dear' analyses.

Apart from the smoothness-based assessment of the relative cheapness or dearness of different bonds, snapshot models are extremely important for structural affine models because they assume the existence of a continuum of discount bonds. So the output of snapshot models (a snapshot discount function) is the input to structural models.

In general, there is no deep meaning to the parameters of fitted snapshot models. However, some recent developments have given a time-series, dynamic interpretation to their parameters, and married them with Principal Component Analysis. (See, eg, (Diebold and Rudebusch, 2013).) So, these latest developments combine features of structural, statistical and snapshot models. We shall revisit this approach later in the chapter.

4. *Derivatives models* (eg, the Heat–Jarrow–Morton (1992), the Brace–Gatarek–Musiela (1997), the Hull and White (1990), the Black–Derman–Toy (1990), …) are based on *relative* pricing and on the enforcement of no-arbitrage. Because of this, they strongly rely on first-order cancellation of errors (between the derivative they are designed to price and the hedging instruments used to build the riskless or minimum-variance portfolio; see the discussion in Nawalha and Rebonato (2011)). Therefore they do not strive to provide a particularly realistic description of the underlying economic reality. After the first generation (Vasicek (1977), Cox et al. (1985a,b), derivatives models squarely set up camp in the risk-neutral $\mathbb{Q}$ measure, and affect a disdainful lack of interest for risk premia. I do not deal with this class of models in this book.

1.5   THE CHOICE OF VARIABLES*

1.5.1   Latent versus Observable Variables

As mentioned previously, an important theme that recurs throughout the book is that the choice of the type of state variable is a very important, and often

---

[17] Snapshot models are also important because all structural models use as their building blocks discount bonds, which are not traded in the market but which make mathematical analysis (immensely) easier. The output of snapshot models (the discount curve) is therefore the input to structural models.

neglected, aspect of term-structure modelling. In this section I aim to give a first explanation of why this is the case. This is only part of the story, as the plot will thicken in Chapters 27 and 29. A health warning: this section requires an understanding of modelling issues and of mathematical formalism that is introduced in the body of the book. Consequently, it may be rather opaque at the moment and, as the saying goes, can be skipped on a first reading without loss of continuity.[18] These readers can then come back to this section after reading Chapters 27 and 29.

Every model comes equipped with a number of parameters (*constant*[19] quantities that describe the plumbing of the model – say, the volatility of the short rate or the speed with which a variable returns to its reversion level), and a, usually much smaller, number of state variables, ie, quantities that, according to the model, should vary *stochastically* during the life of a bond.

What is a parameter and what is a state variable is a modelling choice, not a fact of nature: for instance, in one affine model (say, the Vasicek) the volatility of the short rate may play the role of a parameter; in another (say, the Longstaff and Schwartz (1992) model) it may become a state variables; ditto for the reversion level. So, the choice of what to treat as a fixed building block and what to model as a stochastic variable reflects a messy trade-off between richness of the description, ability to estimate the model parameters,[20] analytical tractability, parsimony of the model and the aesthetic sensitivity of the modeller.

The difficult choices faced by the model developer are not limited to the state-variable/parameter dichotomy. She will also have to choose the nature of the state variables. Two main routes are open here: the latent-variable and the specified-variable approaches.

With the first approach the modeller will start from some latent (unspecified) variables and impose that these variables (whatever their meaning) should follow a particular process; she will impose a simple link (typically an affine transformation) between the latent variables and some observable variables; and she will then estimate indirectly the statistical properties (the parameters) of the latent variables, usually by econometric analysis (say, using Kalman filter techniques) of the time series of the observable quantities. The D'Amico, Kim and Wei (2010) model, that we study in Chapter 31, is a prime and popular example in this mould.

The beauty of the latent-variable approach is that we do not make any assumptions (which could, of course, be wrong) about what 'really' drives the yield curve. The drawback likewise is that do not make any assumptions (right

---

[18] Sections marked with an asterisk can be skipped on a first reading.

[19] Parameters may have a deterministic time dependence, but in this case the 'meta-parameters' of the deterministic function of time become the constant quantities.

[20] Whenever a parameter is 'promoted' to a state variable, it receives as a dowry its own set of process parameters: so, for instance, the moment we allow the volatility to become stochastic, we are immediately faced with the problem of assigning the volatility of volatility, its drift and the correlation between the shocks to the volatility and the shocks to the yield curve.

or wrong as they may be) about what 'really' drives the yield curve. This has several unpleasant consequences.

To begin with, it is difficult to restrict, on the basis of our understanding of the meaning of the variables we use, the number of the admissible values for the model parameters. The price to pay for enforcing a Newtonian *hypotheses-non-fingo* attitude to the choice of variables is the risk of overparametrization: once p observable variables and their q lags are added to m latent variables one has to deal with $(p + m)(pq + m)$ parameters, which can quickly add up to $O(10^1)$ if not $O(10^2)$ 'degrees of freedom'.[21] As Johnny von Neumann pointed out, '[w]ith four parameters I can fit an elephant, and with five I can make it wiggle his trunk'.[22] As Mayer, Khairy and Howard (2010) prove, this is no empty boast, and Figure 1.1 shows how they indeed achieved the feat with four (complex) parameters.

The second problem with latent-variable approaches is that they do not lend themselves to easy 'sanity checks'. For instance, if we estimate a reversion level of the short rate, after making the appropriate adjustments for risk aversion, we can assess if this roughly squares with past experience and future expectations. Or, from the estimated reversion-speed coefficient for the target rate, we can impute, again after adjusting for risk, a half-life for the short rate, and assess whether this is reasonable.[23] But how are we to make these semi-quantitative sanity checks for the reversion level or reversion speed of a variable whose meaning we do not specify?

One can rebut: surely, a latent-variable model provides a mapping (a 'dictionary') capable of translating latent variables into observables. If this is the case, does it really make much of a difference whether we work with latent or observable variables, as long as we can go to our model dictionary and translate from one set of variables to the next? Can't we do our sanity checks after looking up the variable translation in our dictionary?

Indeed, it would make little difference if there were a unique correspondence between sets of acceptable values for the observable variables and combinations of latent variables. However, more often than not, very different combinations of latent variables can give rise to observable quantities in very similar ranges, as shown in the lower half of Figure 1.2. If we find ourselves in the case depicted in the lower half of the figure, which of the latent-variable bubbles (all converging into the same region of acceptability for the observable variables)

---

[21] The Ang and Piazzes: ((2003)) model, with its 2 observable variables, their associated 12 lags, and the 3 latent factors requires 135 parameters for the pricing kernel to be defined. Similarly, the Gaussian QMLE affine model discussed in Diebold and Rudebusch (2013) comes equipped with 139 parameters eager to be estimated: in their words, this is 'a challenging if not absurd situation' (pp. 37–38).

[22] Quoted in Mayer et al. (2010).

[23] Some lazy people say 'After adjusting for risk (ie, after moving from one measure to the other) 'anything can happen to the drift, and the risk-neutral drift could become anything '. This is emphatically not true, and this is where a 'principled' structural approach to term-structure modelling makes a difference. In reality, any transformation from the real-world to term-structure the risk-neutral measure implies a price of risk function that can and should be interrogated for plausibility, and for consistency with the empirical information. (Much) more about this later.

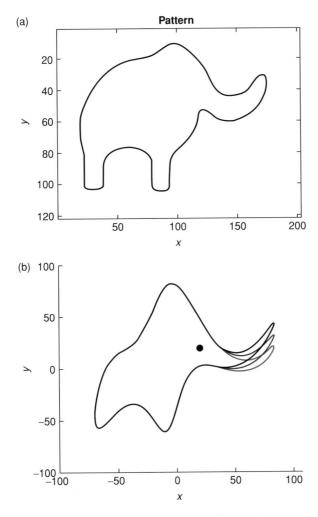

Figure 1.1 (a) As shown, it is indeed possible to draw an elephant with four (complex parameters). (b) With a fifth, Mayer et al. (2010) can both locate its right eye, and make it wiggle its trunk.

are we going to choose? In essence, the problem is the following: we have some observable variables (such as, say, market yields or yield volatilities) that we use to calibrate our model. We are interested in some not directly observable quantities (such as, say, expectations or risk premia). In the upper half of Figure 1.2 we then have two sets of values for latent variables. One set maps to 'good' values for the observable quantities to which we 'fit' our model and the other to 'bad' values. The two sets make different predictions for the quantities we are actually interested in gaining information about (say, the risk premia), but it is not difficult to choose which set of values for the latent variables we should choose: the upper one, that maps into the 'good' region for the fitting observables.

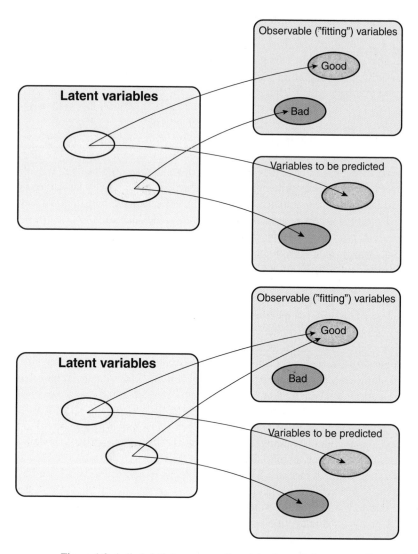

Figure 1.2 A 'helpful' (upper panel) and 'awkward' (lower panel) mapping from latent variables to observables and predicted quantities. See the text for a discussion.

The situation is trickier in the lower half of Figure 1.2: now two very different combinations (sets) of values for the latent variables map into the same region of acceptability for the observable quantities. However, they give rise to very different predictions for the future values of the variables-which, after all, is what we are interested in obtaining. Which set should we choose?

So much for (some of) the problem one faces using latent variables. Not everything is problem-free, however, when we use identifiable state variables. We have two distinct sets of problem here: the spanning problem and the constraint problem. Let's look at both in turn.

1.5.2 The Spanning Problem*

The first requisite of a successful set of state variables is that they should span the changes in the yield curve. But there is an additional requirement: if we are interested in a structural description, we must also include variables that describe the risk premia. There is no a priori reason why the two sets of variables should coincide – ie, that the variables that 'span' the yield curve variations should also account for the market price of risk.

What does this mean in practice? Every term-structure model establishes a mapping between the state variables and the observable yields. Suppose that, as is the case for affine models, this link is linear. Also suppose that, departing from the latent-variable approach, we have specified the exact nature of our state variables. For instance, if we took a macrofinancial approach, we may have chosen as state variables a set of macroeconomic quantities; or perhaps we may require our state variables to be some of the yield-curve principal components.[24] Now, roughly speaking, a good spanning is achieved when, given the mapping afforded by the model, the model-produced variability in the observable yields 'looks like' the yield variability observed in reality.

Whether this turns out to be the case strongly depends on the variables we have chosen. And, with specified-variable models, just throwing in more and more variables is no guarantee that we are going to fare any better. To explain why this may be the case, let's consider a contrived example. Suppose that a modeller decided that what drives the yield curve is real economic activity – and nothing else. On the face of it, the claim sounds somewhat audacious, but not absurd. Suppose also that the same modeller established that changes in real economic activity are associated with[25] changes in the slope, but not the level, of the yield curve. (Again, I am not saying that any of this is true: I am just explaining what 'spanning' means.) Armed with this insight, the modeller decides to use real economic activity as *the* driver of the yield curve. Then it is clear that changes in real economic activity, given the mapping allowed by the model, will generate a change only in the slope, but not in the level, of the yield curve. But this is not what we observe in reality, where changes in the level usually dominate slope changes. Here, the chosen state variable did not adequately span the observed changes in what we want to describe.

The example was obviously far from realistic, but the problem of ensuring that state variables chosen a priori do span changes in the yield curve is a real one. The model we propose in Chapter 35 suggests one possible solution to this problem.

There is another aspect to the spanning problem. If we are interested purely in pricing – and, therefore, not in a structural description that weaves together expectations and risk premia – the only spanning requirement is that the chosen variables should be able to account for the observed variability in the observed *market* yields. Recall, however, that market yields are made up of an

---

[24] We explain what principal components are in Chapter 6.
[25] And *fully* reflected in – see the end of the section about this important point.

expectation and a risk-premium component.[26] If we are interested in modelling risk premia as well, it is not obvious that 'just' knowing about the present and past prices (yields) can give us the optimal information set for the prediction of excess returns. It may very well be – and indeed, Ludvigson and Ng (2009) show that it *is* the case – that macroeconomic variables have explanatory power over and above what is embedded in the prices. This raises an important question, that we discuss towards the end of the book: does the traditional affine modelling setting allow a simple 'augmentation' of the yield-curve–based state variables to include the *full* information provided by the macro quantities? Can we do this in theory? Can we do so in practice? Understanding this point would require too long a detour at this stage, but it is important to keep this *caveat* in mind for later discussion.

1.5.3   The Constraint Problem*

As mentioned previously, there is a second problem when one uses non-latent (specified) variables – the 'constraint' problem. To understand the nature of this problem, a good place to start is with the work by Dai and Singleton (2000). In an important paper published at the beginning of the new millennium, they produced a very general classification of affine models and they obtained the following result. Start from N state variables (factors), x_t, and impose that they should follow a diffusive process of the form[27]

$$dx_t = a(x_t)\,dt + \sqrt{b(x_t)}dz_t. \tag{1.1}$$

As for the "drift' and 'variance' coefficients', $a(x_t)$ and $\underline{b}(x_t)$, they can depend on the state variables, $\vec{x}_t$, but only in a linear (or, rather, affine[28]) fashion

$$\text{drift} = a_0 + a_1 x_t,$$
$$\text{variance} = b_0 + b_1 x_t. \tag{1.2}$$

Now, if the short rate, r_t, can be written as a linear combination of these N factors plus a constant,

$$r_t = c_0 + c_1^{\mathrm{T}} x_t, \tag{1.3}$$

then Dai and Singleton (2000) show that the bond prices, P_t^T, can always be written as exponentially affine functions of the factors, ie, as a function of the form

$$P_t^T = e^{A_t^T + \left(\vec{B}_t^T\right)^{\mathrm{T}} \vec{x}_t}. \tag{1.4}$$

---

[26] And, of course, a convexity contribution as well.
[27] We have not introduced our notation yet, and the reader may at this stage be unfamiliar with the matrix formulation of a mean-reverting process – or may not have seen a mean-reverting process at all. We ask the reader to 'go with the flow' for the moment and promise that all we be explained in due course. In particular, we define and explain the matrix notation in detail in Chapter 17.
[28] We discuss the difference between linear and affine function in Chapter 18.

Note that, apart from the short-rate requirement that $r_t = c_0 + c_1^{\mathrm{T}} x_t$, the factors can be totally general. However, we know[29] that the time-t yield for maturity T is defined as

$$y_t^T = -\frac{1}{T-t} \log P_t^T. \tag{1.5}$$

By taking the logarithm of the expression for the bond price (Equation (1.4)), we see that in affine models yields always have this very simple form:

$$y_t^T = u_t + \overrightarrow{g}^T \overrightarrow{x} \tag{1.6}$$

for some row vector $\overrightarrow{g}^T$.

Now, in specified-variable approaches, the modeller assigns a priori the link between the state variables and the yields. Let this assigned relationship be of the form

$$y_t^T = \phi_t + \overrightarrow{\Phi}^T \overrightarrow{x}. \tag{1.7}$$

For instance, Duffie and Kan (1996) simply identify the factors with the yields themselves ($\phi_t = 0$ and $\Phi_t = I$). More interestingly, as we have seen, macro-financial models link the observable yields (or linear functions thereof) to macroeconomic observables via some structural models. Or, again, we may use as state variables some special combinations of yields, such as their principal components. See, eg, the approaches described in Chapters 33 and 34.

In general, modifying the terminology in Saroka (2014), let's call *specified-variable models*[30] all models in which the loadings ϕ_t and Φ_t are assigned *a priori* by the modeller on the basis of her knowledge of (or prejudices about) how the world works.

Now, as we saw earlier, working with non-latent factors has obvious important advantages. However, even leaving to one side the spanning problem alluded to above, Equations (1.6) and (1.7) immediately suggest that working with prespecified factors must bring about strong issues of internal consistency: indeed, once absence of arbitrage is imposed, any exogenous, a priori specification of the loadings ϕ_t and Φ_t must imply a relationship between yields-as-by-products of the model (Equation (1.6)) and yields-as-specified-by-the-modeller (1.7). This means that, for consistency, we must have

$$\phi_t = u_t \tag{1.8}$$

$$\Phi_t = g_t^T. \tag{1.9}$$

As we shall see, this can place severe restrictions on the admissible stochastic behaviour of the state variables.[31]

Let's give a concrete example. Suppose that we choose to work with principal components as state variables – a natural enough choice (which we pursue in Chapter 33) given how much we know about the principal components obtained

---

[29] See Chapter 2.

[30] Saroka (2014) calls them *observable affine-factor models*.

[31] This topic is discussed in detail in Joslin, Singleton and Zhu (2011).

from the covariance matrix of yield curve changes. (Why work with specified variables unless we know a lot about them, after all?) As principal components are a particular linear combination of yields, our principal component–based model would certainly fall in the specified-variable model category.

Given this choice of principal components as state variables, let's now evolve them to some future time, τ. These future values of the state variables determine the future bond prices via Equation (1.4). And, as we have seen, in an affine setting future bond prices require future yields to be a linear (affine, really) function of the state variables – see again Equation (1.6).

But remember that we have required our state variables to be principal components. We have not defined principal components yet, but at this stage we can just say that they are some special (and fixed!) linear combinations of yields – such as the linear combinations in Equation (1.7). But if this is the case, the econometrically determined coefficients that link at all times yields and principal components must be linked to the model coefficients that give yields as linear functions of log prices! Achieving this internal consistency, as we shall see, is not a trivial task.

This is another way to look at the same problem. In an affine framework, we may then *like* to require that each principal component should display a nice and simple mean-reverting behaviour.[32] For instance, we may want to impose that, as each principal component moves away from its own reversion level, it is attracted back towards it by a 'spring' of appropriate strength, and that the strength of this mean-reversion is unaffected by what the other principal components are doing.[33]

We may well *like* to impose this simple behaviour, but the internal consistency constraints mentioned above and discussed in detail in Chapter 33 (see also Rebonato, Saroka and Putyatin (2017) and Saroka (2014)) tell us that it is not in our gift to do so.

In sum, if the reader is still with us, the message of this section is that the problem with specified-variable models is general: by specifying the variables, we add constraints to their dynamics over and above the no-arbitrage restrictions. These constraints come from imposing Equations (1.6) and (1.7). Taken together, these two sets of equations will dictate part of the dynamics of the state variables. So, we *can* choose principal components (or any other set of specified variables) as state variables, *or* we can choose (latent) state variables and assign a nice and simple mean-reverting behaviour (in the $\mathbb{Q}$-measure). What we *cannot* do is choose principal components (or any other set of specified variables) as state variables *and* impose that they should follow a 'nice and simple' mean-reverting behaviour (in the $\mathbb{Q}$-measure).

I must stress here that there is nothing special about principal components in this impossibility result. Once we have made a priori the modelling choice

---

[32] We should add 'in the $\mathbb{Q}$ measure'. Please bear with us and go with the flow for the moment.

[33] The situation we are describing here corresponds to a diagonal reversion-speed matrix. For readers not familiar with mean-reverting (Ornstein–Uhlenbeck) processes, we give a first intuitive presentation in Chapter 8, and a more thorough treatment in Chapters 15 to 17 and 33.

of Equation (1.7), ie, once, on the basis of our domain knowledge, we choose to assign the link between the yields and the state variables, we lose part of our ability to assign the precise nature of their dynamics.

All of this may sound rather abstract at this stage, but it will, hopefully, become clearer when we deal with the various models.

1.6   WHY DO WE NEED NO-ARBITRAGE MODELS AFTER ALL?

Before getting started in earnest we have to answer one more important question.

I said that a substantial part of this book is devoted to term-structure models. What's so good about models, and about *no-arbitrage* models in particular? Suppose that our main interest is in predicting future rates, or in decomposing yields into the three components of expectations, term premia and convexity. Why can't we just rely on statistical regularities, as uncovered by careful econometric analysis, to extract this information?

To be even more concrete, suppose that we look at the strategy of investing in an n-year maturity bond, funding it with a 1-year-maturity bond, selling the $n - 1$-maturity bond after one year, and repaying our loan. (This is what excess return studies essentially investigate.) We want to know in what configurations of the yield curve (level, slope, curvature), or in what states of the economy, we expect this strategy to be profitable. Why are statistical models not enough to answer this question? If no arbitrage opportunities are indeed found in the market, surely the observed market prices should reflect this. To the extent that econometric estimation reveals these regularities, the no-arbitrage conditions should automatically be present in the estimated models.[34] Granted, by themselves statistical models may not explain a lot, but, as far as detecting empirical regularities, surely they should be unsurpassed. Or are they?

One could take an even more provocative stance. Unless one determines the market price of risk from an equilibrium asset model and from the utility function of the representative investor – a feat that, for the purpose of predicting excess returns, very few modellers are brave enough to attempt – one has to take a rather uninspiring two-step approach: first one must estimate risk premia by extracting empirical information about excess returns and/or the real-world behaviour of rates (say, their reversion levels, their reversion speeds, if any, etc). Then one has to pour this empirical content into the often-funny-shaped vessel of the model. (I describe the model as a funny-shaped vessel because one can carry out this exercise in translation of information only in the rather restricted way that any given model allows.)

So, a cynic may say, the model purely regurgitates the empirical econometric information it has been fed, and can only do so imperfectly: it is a halting and

---

[34] Diebold and Rudebusch (2013, Section 1.5.3, p. 16 and passim) ask the question: 'Is the Imposition of No-Arbitrage Useful?': 'if reality is arbitrage-free, and if a model provides a very good description of reality, then imposition of no-arbitrage would presumably have little effect.'

stuttering rendition of lines it has 'learnt by heart', not arrived at itself. (The lines are 'learnt by heart' because we almost certainly eschewed the utility-function-based approach.)

There is more than a grain of truth in these objections. Still, I think that there is value in a disciplined and skeptical use of models. Of course, a model affords an *understanding* of how reality works that no purely-data-driven statistical analysis can afford. But I believe that a model can tell us something useful even if we are interested only in prediction. As I think that my case for the importance of models can be better made after reviewing the actual model performance than in the abstract, I will defer the 'argument for the defence' to the last chapter of the book. This 'existential' question, however, should be kept vividly in mind by the critical reader.[35]

1.7   STAMP COLLECTING AND SHALLOW VERSUS DEEP EXPLANATIONS

I said in the opening paragraphs of this chapter that my goal is to present a *structural* approach to yield-curve modelling. Having said that, it is good to keep in mind that the boundaries between descriptive and structural approaches are a bit arbitrary, and that what we may proudly call 'structural' in this book could be regarded as 'descriptive' by a hard-core financial economist. To understand this point, let's consider again for a moment one important component of yield-curve modelling, the explanation of excess returns.

We can start from the observation that term premia seem to be time varying. If we stop here, we are clearly just describing. After carrying out some clever regressions, however, we may find that, say, the slope of the yield curve 'explains' a large portion of these time-varying excess returns. We may feel better, because we are now able to explain the time variation of excess returns in terms of something else: term premia are high when the curve is steep, and low when it is flat or inverted. But why is it so?

Perhaps we can relate the slope of the yield curve to the business cycle. This sounds encouraging. But this new explanation just moves the goal posts: why should the slope of the yield curve be linked to the business cycle?

---

[35] I stress that what I provide in Chapter 31 is *my* explanation of why models are useful. For a different discussion of the need for no-arbitrage ('cross-sectional') restrictions, see Piazzesi (2010), p. 695 and passim. Ang and Piazzesi (2003) also discuss from an econometric perspective how imposing no-arbitrage helps the out-of-sample prediction of yields. In particular, Piazzesi (2010, pp. 694–695) mentions among the five reasons for using no-arbitrage models the problem of the 'missing bond yields', ie, yields for 'odd' maturities whose value can be recovered using a no-arbitrage model from a small set of reference yields. As Piazzesi (2010) points out, this can be important for markets with sparse reference points (such as energy markets), but this is unlikely to be a major consideration for the government bond markets of most G7 economies. Piazzesi (2010, p. 695) also mentions the advantage of having consistency between the time series and the cross-sectional yield equations, and the ability to split an observed yield into its expectation and term-premium components. Regarding the last split, it should be pointed out that the same split can also be achieved by a statistical analysis of excess returns.

Perhaps we can come up with a compelling story about state-dependent (in this case, business-cycle–dependent) degrees of risk aversion. Or perhaps we can look at how other asset classes behave (co-vary) during different phases of the business cycle, and argue that in some parts of the business cycle bonds act as effective diversifiers.[36] Or whatever. Also this, however, does not provide the 'final' answer to the series of new questions that every new explanation opens up.

The point here is that even the most 'structural' approaches sooner or later end up hitting against a hard descriptive wall. Perhaps the goal of most scientific enquiries is to make this collision occur later rather than sooner. Physicists used to say that, outside their domain, everything is just stamp collecting. This may well be true, but physicists, too, at some point, must begin to collect stamps.

This important reminder is to put in perspective what we are trying to do in this book. First, we do not want to stop at a 'shallow' explanation of bond behaviour, an explanation which is but a small step away from the most basic observations. ('Bonds are exposed to the risk of rates going up' is one such shallow explanation.) Like good physicists, we want to delay at least for a while the moment when we begin collecting stamps. At the same time, we must keep in mind that the idea of reaching the 'ultimate' explanation is futile, and that we will stop somewhere halfway between an eighteenth-century-like specimen collection of 'curios' and the Grand Unified Theory.

1.8 THE IDEAL READER AND PLAN OF THE BOOK

> "And what is the use of a book," thought Alice, "without pictures or conversations in it?"
>
> *Alice's Adventures in Wonderland*, L. Carroll

Who is the ideal reader of this work? The stock-in-trade recommendation for a writer is to imagine the 'ideal reader' peeking over her (that is, the writer's) shoulder as she writes. This is all well and good, but in this case of limited help, because the ideal reader I have in mind will change significantly from the first pages of the book to its last chapters. How so?

Of course, I hope that, towards the later chapters of the book, the reader will have become progressively more familiar and comfortable with some simple mathematical techniques that I will introduce as we go along, and with which she may have not been familiar from the start. But, more importantly, I as well hope that she will have also become subtler and more sophisticated in her thinking about term-structure modelling. This changing reader will therefore have to deploy not just a wider and wider set of mathematical tools, but also a progressively subtler and deeper mode of financial reasoning.

---

[36] On the important topic of the stock-bond correlation, see the good paper by Johnson et al. (2015).

The tone of the book, and the level of mathematical sophistication will therefore change, and become somewhat more demanding, in the later parts if the book. I have always chosen, however, the path (or the shortcut) of least mathematical resistance, and, given a choice, I have invariably chosen the mathematically simplest (yet correct) way to present the topic at hand.

As a consequence, I think that an undergraduate student, an MBA student, an MSc student or a quantitatively conversant investment professional should certainly be able to follow the arguments and the derivations presented in the book. However, I believe that also a graduate student, a proficient 'quant' or an academic will find in the book a fresh perspective, and something to agree or disagree with. I hope, in sum, that this book will make the novice think, and the expert think again.[37] Above all, I have strived to provide the precise tools with which all readers can reproduce the results presented in the body of the work, and tinker with their own variations on the affine theme.

The book is therefore organized as follows.

In Part I (which contains this introduction) I lay the foundations of the book: I state what the topic is, I explain my goal and my strategy, I define my notation, I introduce some mathematical tools, and I present some topics (such as some rudiments of Monetary Economics) that will appear over and over again in the body of the work. Chapters 4 and 5 are particularly important in Part I, because they give the first introduction to the risks to which a bond is exposed and the compensations investors can exact for bearing these risks. It is here that the real-world and risk-neutral measures make their first appearance.

Part II is devoted to presenting two of the three building blocks of term-structure building, namely, expectations and convexity. Convexity will be revisited in greater detail in Part V, but, in keeping with my general strategy, I have chosen to offer early on a taste of the main course. As another amuse bouche, I present at this early stage (Chapter 8) an incomplete, but hopefully inspiring, first look at the Vasicek model.

In Part III I introduce the glue that holds together the three building blocks, namely the conditions of no-arbitrage. I do so from a variety of perspectives, with different levels of sophistication, and for different types of assets (ie, nominal and real bonds). In particular, I present and derive the no-arbitrage conditions using both the traditional (Partial Differential Equation [PDE]–based) approach and the modern language based on the stochastic discount factor and the pricing kernel.

With all of the building blocks in place, and the conditions of arbitrage thoroughly explained, I return in Part IV to the Vasicek model (Chapter 16), with a simple derivation of its salient results, and a deeper discussion of its strengths and weaknesses than what was presented in Chapter 8. By the end of Chapter 16 the reader will have understood not only how to 'solve' the Vasicek model, but also the reason why, despite it being so dearly loved by modellers who prize parsimony and simplicity, it can take us only on part of our journey, and why more complex approaches will be needed.

---

[37] Paraphrased from Jackson (2015, p. 9).

In this part of the book I also present a generalization to many state variables of the results obtained in Chapter 16 for the Vasicek model. Chapter 17 provides a gentle introduction to the notation and the techniques presented in Chapter 18. In this latter chapter general pricing results are presented that the reader will be able to apply to virtually all the models that she will come across – or that she may care to create herself. Chapter 19 closes Part IV with a discussion of the shadow rate – a topic of salient relevance especially, but not only, during times of ultra-low rates.

In Part V I return to the topic of convexity, and I present in this part of the book both theoretical and empirical results.

Part VI, which deals with excess returns, is very important, because it presents the bridge between the real-world and the risk-neutral description. The particular bridge we have chosen in order to cross this chasm is the empirical study of excess returns, to which we devote no fewer than seven chapters. I present in this part of the book a detailed critical discussion of the traditional (eg, Fama and Bliss, 1987) and of the modern (eg, Cochrane and Piazzesi, 2005; Cieslak and Povala, 2010a) return-predicting factors. Once these empirical results are presented, the reader will also understand another important short-coming of simple Vasicek-like models when it comes to a structural account of yield curve modelling – in a nutshell, why the Vasicek form of the market price of risk is *qualitatively* wrong.

Now that the case for progressing beyond the simple Vasicek framework has been fully made, in Part VII I present and critically discuss a number of models that, to different extents and from different perspectives, attempt to overcome the limitations of the simple Vasicek-like models discussed in Parts I to VI. This is no encyclopaedia of Gaussian affine models (no such thing can exist); rather, it is a presentation of models organized in such a way as to answer, in turn, some of the questions raised by the analysis in Parts I to VI.

By the end of Part VII the inquisitive ideal reader will, indeed, have changed a lot, and should be ready for experimenting with her own version of a Gaussian affine model in order to deal with the specific problems she may face. This is, indeed, what several of my Oxford students have chosen to do after reading early drafts of this book.

To conclude, a few words about the figures. In the hope that even Alice may find in this book something to interest her, I have given special care to the many pictures that complement the text. These are not meant as decoration for an otherwise dull page, but, with their captions, are an integral part of the story the book tells. The reader will find her efforts well rewarded if she spends almost as much time examining the graphs and their descriptions as reading the text. However, sorry, Alice, I have not been able to put a lot of conversations in my book.

CHAPTER 2

Definitions, Notation and a Few Mathematical Results

Boswell: "He says plain things in a formal and abstract way, to be sure; but his method is good: for to have clear notions about any subject, we must have recourse to analytick arrangement."

Johnson: "Sir, it is what every body does, whether they will or not. But sometimes things can be made darker by a definition. I see a cow. I define her, *Animal quadrupes ruminans*. But a goat ruminates, and a cow may have no horns. *Cow* is plainer."

Boswell (1791) – *The Life of Samuel Johnson*[1]

2.1 THE PURPOSE OF THIS CHAPTER

This is not going to be a chapter that will set pulses racing, but it is a useful one. In it we define the financial quantities that we are going to use in the book, we fix our vector notation and we try to clarify possible sources of notational confusion.

We also present (in the appendices at the end of the chapter) some elementary mathematical results that we shall use throughout the book.

2.2 THE BUILDING BLOCKS

2.2.1 Arbitrage

For the purposes of this book, an arbitrage is a strategy that is too good to be true – and, therefore, one that in an efficient market does not exist.

A bit more precisely, one says that a strategy is an arbitrage if it costs nothing to set up, if it never produces a negative payoff, and if in at least one possible state of the world it produces a strictly positive payoff.

It pays to look at the definition carefully. First we require that the strategy should cost nothing to set up. Very often, when we buy an asset and sell another to crystallize the value of an arbitrage strategy, the resulting portfolio will not

---

[1] p. 791.

be self-financing – which means that the proceeds from the sale of the asset we are shorting will not exactly match the cost of the asset we want to buy. This means that we must either borrow or lend some money. Since the interest on the borrowing or lending up to the end of the investment horizon of the strategy must be locked in for the strategy to be an arbitrage (why?), this means that we must buy or sell a discount bond. The price of this discount bond is the 'balancing item' that makes the initial set-up cost of the portfolio equal to zero.

Now we have set up our portfolio. For this portfolio to qualify as a possible arbitrage strategy (the necessary-condition part), we want to make sure that our strategy will never lose any money.

Finally, to make sure that what we have set up is indeed an arbitrage strategy, we want to stipulate that, at least in some states of the world, we will make *some* money – no matter how little.

Can we change the composition of the portfolio between the set-up time and the investment horizon? Yes, provided that all we are doing at the intermediate time t is a reshuffling of the time-t wealth among the three components: the asset we have bought, the asset we we have sold and the bond. This is what we mean when we say that the strategy must be self-financing.

Note that we do not require that an arbitrage strategy should always make money. Even if we make money only in an extremely unlikely state of the world (and we never lose money in any other state of the world), we still have an arbitrage. A free lottery ticket for El Gordo is an arbitrage.

Exercise 1 *Consider two zero-cost strategies. At time 1 there are three states of the world, ω_1, ω_2 and ω_3. The probability of ending in any one of the state is $\frac{1}{3}$.*

The first strategy pays \$1,000,000 in state ω_1, \$0 in state ω_2 and $-\$0.0001$ in state ω_3.

The second strategy pays \$0 in state ω_1, \$0 in state ω_2 and \$0.0001 in state ω_3.

Which strategy is an arbitrage? Which one would you prefer to enter at no cost? How much would you pay to enter the first lottery? What about the second?

An arbitrage strategy in itself is not necessarily more desirable than another, no-arbitrage, strategy. Exercise 1 should have convinced you that this is the case – unless, of course, you can scale up the free-lunch strategy to any size you want.

2.2.2 Pseudo-Arbitrage

True perfect arbitrage is very rare. More often than not, the investor who believes she has entered a risk-less arbitrage strategy is simply failing to recognize (or to price) some sources of risk or some costs (perhaps in terms of capital or balance sheet utilization) that the strategy entails. This does not mean, however, that, in the absence of strict arbitrage opportunities, everything is perfectly priced. Some strategies may be risky, but the risk inherent in their implementation may be more handsomely rewarded than the risk associated with other deals or strategies.

What does that mean? How does one compare the risk incurred in, say, a convertible-stock arbitrage strategy with the risk of a duration-neutral portfolio? What are the common units of risk that allow us to say that strategy A is more risky than strategy B? Risk, as risk managers say, is not a number: it is a four-letter word.

One common proxy for risk is the variance of returns of the strategy. However, we may have strategies with the same variance and the same expected return, but still with very different distributional properties. To the extent that investors react differently to same-return, same-variance, but different-skewness and different-kurtosis (and different-higher-moments) distributions, we cannot describe the riskiness of a strategy just by looking at its variance. Whether investors do care about the higher moments of a distribution *after we control for the return and variance*, and, if they do, how much, is an empirical, not a theoretical question. If they do, then a pure variance-based description of risk is inadequate, in the sense that it tells only part of the story.

In principle, we do not have to choose arbitrary mixtures of variance, skewness, kurtosis and, who knows, even higher moments to describe risk. If we believe that a given utility function describes well the investors' preferences for more rather than less and their aversion to risk, then maximizing the expected utility (subject to the chosen constraints) automatically gives the best trade-off between the expected gains and the accompanying risk. The nice feature of variance as a handy proxy for risk stems from the fact that, if returns are normally distributed, or if the utility function is well approximated by a quadratic one, then minimizing the variance is exactly the same as maximizing the utility.

We know well, of course, that neither of these two conditions is met in practice. However, before dismissing with an impatient wave of the hand the quadratic-approximation starting point as useless, the reader would do well to read Markowitz (1959/1991), and, perhaps, also Rebonato and Denev (2013).

For all this, variance is a common and reasonable proxy for risk – the longer the investment horizons, the more so.[2] Therefore the ratio of the expected (excess) return from a strategy to its standard deviation ('risk') is a very informative statistic. The more common incarnation of this statistic is the Sharpe Ratio (Sharpe, 1994),[3] to which we now turn.

---

[2] Why is this the case? Ultimately, it is because of the central limit theorem, which says that if we add many independent and identically distributed draws (in our case, price increments) from any reasonable distribution, the distribution of the sum asymptotically approaches a Gaussian as we add more and more elements to the sum.

[3] Sharpe (1994) describes well the Sharpe Ratio. However, the concept was introduced in Sharpe (1966).

2.2.3 Sharpe Ratios

If – at least for a certain set of strategies – variance captures well the investors' behavioural response to uncertainty (ie, if variance is a good proxy for risk), then a good indicator of whether a deal is 'better' than another is the Sharpe Ratio, SR, defined as the ratio of the *excess* return from a strategy, $(R - r_f)$, to its standard deviation:

$$SR \equiv \frac{R - r_f}{\sigma}. \tag{2.1}$$

Given what we have said about risk and variance, the measure looks reasonable enough. However, note that, when we use the Sharpe Ratio, each strategy is looked at in isolation, not in the context of the market portfolio: diversification does not appear. The picture of the investment world implied by the Sharpe Ratio is therefore that of a one-factor economy, ie, of an economy in which all assets are shocked by a single common risk factor. Sharpe Ratios fail to capture the important feature that some strategies may perform well and others poorly in states of the world when investors 'feel poor': nobody, for instance, would buy fire insurance on their house by looking at the Sharpe Ratio of the strategy, but I recommend that you do.

If, for these and other reasons, one found the Sharpe Ratio statistic too crude, one could make use of an asset-pricing model (such as the CAPM, the Arbitrage Pricing model, etc). However, without being too wedded to a specific model, it makes intuitive sense that strategies with a Sharpe Ratio that is too good to be true, are, well, too good to be true. Indeed, this is one of the crucial messages behind the no-too-good-deal approach by Cochrane and Saa-Requejo (1999), which I encourage the interested reader to look at in detail (perhaps after studying Part III).

Why should one be suspicious of strategies with over-optimistic Sharpe Ratios? In essence, it is for the same reason why one should be surprised to find arbitrage strategies: a strategy with a Sharpe Ratio which is 'too high' entices investors to pursue it. By doing so, they reduce its attractiveness, and, as a result, tend to equalize the Sharpe Ratios (once other sources of risk are accounted for) across different strategies. So, strategies with excessively good Sharpe Ratios are unlikely to remain available for long. The more liquid the market, the more suspicious one should be of cheap, if not free, lunches.[4]

This search, exploitation and, ultimately, elimination of deals that are 'too good' goes on all the time, but there are limits to pseudo-arbitrage (also referred to as risky arbitrage), and these are well discussed in Shleifer (2000). These hindrances to engaging in risky arbitrage can be state dependent: for instance, during periods of market turmoil risk capital devoted to pseudo-arbitrage may

---

[4] For a discussion of 'astronomically high' Sharpe ratios in over-fitted models of the Treasury market, see Duffee (2010): '[l]arge Sharpe ratios are evidence of overfitting, thus the ratios can be used as an informal specification test. Similarly, more realistic models can be estimated by imposing a constraint on allowable Sharpe Ratios' (p. 1).

become scarce, and therefore Sharpe Ratios for different assets (calculated as they are without taking capital or balance-sheet constraints into account) can get more out of line with each other than in normal market conditions.

The important point here is that, much as textbooks focus on absence of riskless arbitrage, pseudo-arbitrage strategies are far more commonly adopted in the market than pure arbitrage ones. It is risky arbitrage, not risk-less arbitrage, that determines the finer (and more interesting) relationship between the prices of different assets – and, in our universe, between the prices of different bonds. Pure arbitrage by itself provides pricing bounds that are often too loose to be useful. It is the search for slightly-too-good deals that makes markets tick.

2.2.4   Bond Prices and Yields

Bonds are our fundamental building blocks, so this is a good place to start our discussion of the securities in our economy. In this book we will almost exclusively deal with discount bonds. Discount bonds are purchased at time t for \$$X$, and pay \$1 at their maturity. We denote the time-t price of a T-maturity discount bond by P_t^T.

Often people say that discount bonds do not pay coupons. One can indeed look at discount bonds this way, but I find it more helpful to think of a discount bond as an instrument that returns at maturity the purchase price (say, \$$X$) plus a single fixed coupon given by \$$(1 - X)$. With a discount bond, the coupon is (notionally) accumulated and reinvested over the life of the bond.

Discount bonds are not actively traded in the market. What is actively traded are coupon bonds, which pay a periodic (say, annual) fixed coupon, *coup*, and return the notional (face value) at maturity. Note that, since the timing and the periodicity of the coupon payments are chosen in such a way that the last coupon payment coincides with the bond maturity, the actual last payment of a coupon bond is its face value plus the last coupon.

Let's go back to discount bonds. If we denote the time-t yield of a T-maturity discount bond by y_t^T, we have

$$P_t^T = e^{-y_t^T(T-t)} \tag{2.2}$$

or, equivalently,

$$y_t^T = -\frac{1}{T-t} \log P_t^T. \tag{2.3}$$

Following market conventions, in this book we sometimes express a yield as a percentage (ie, as, say, 4%), but more often than not we write it just as a number – so, instead of 4% we prefer to write 0.04. When we talk about yields (and, occasionally, about volatilities) we often call a hundredth of a percentage point a 'basis point'.

Since the price today of a discount bond is the value of a unit payment at maturity, we will show that the price P_t^T also plays the role of a discount factor, ie, of the quantity that transform a future (time-T) certain payoff, $payoff^T$, (not necessarily a unit payment) into its present value today:

$$PV(x^T) = payoff^T P_t^T. \tag{2.4}$$

Note, however, that in order to use the formula in Equation (2.4) to present-value cashflows, the payments $payoff^T$ must be the same in every state of the world at time T.

This condition (identical payments in every state of the world at a given time) applies to the coupons and the final maturity repayment of a nominal riskless bond. So, if we have the prices of discount bonds maturing on the coupon and maturity dates of a nominal bond, we can immediately recover the time-t price of a T-maturity coupon bond bearing coupons $coup_i$ at times t_i, as follows:

$$PC_t^T = \left[\sum_{i=1,N} coup_i \times P_t^{T_i} \right] + 1 \times P_t^{T_N}. \tag{2.5}$$

We defined above the yield, y_t^T, of a discount bond. The yield (gross redemption yield), GRY_t^T, at time t of a coupon bond[5] of maturity T is a different beast: it is the single number such that (for annual bonds)

$$PC_t^T = \left[\sum_{i=1,N} coup_i \times Z_i \right] + 1 \times Z_N \tag{2.6}$$

with

$$Z_i = \frac{1}{(1 + GRY_t^T)^i}. \tag{2.7}$$

Note carefully that the sums in Equations (2.5) and (2.6) add up to the same values, but, in general, the GRY-derived pseudo-discount factors Z_i are not equal to the real discount factors, $P_t^{T_i}$.

Exercise 2 *Establish the relationship between a continuously compounded and a discretely compounded yield, when the discrete compounding frequency is not necessarily annual.*

Exercise 3 *When would the quantities Z_i and $P_t^{T_i}$ all be exactly the same? (The answer 'For a one-period bond' does not count as an answer.)*

If coupon, and not discount, bonds are actively traded, why base our treatment on the latter instead of the former?

First, the mathematics of discount bonds is infinitely simpler and 'elegant'. There is no 'inversion formula', for instance, linking the (gross redemption) yield of a coupon bond to its price, while the yield of a discount bond is obtained from its price just by taking the logarithm, dividing by the bond maturity, and changing the sign. See again Equation (2.3).

---

[5] For the sake of simplicity, we assume that the coupon-paying frequency is annual.

Second, for a coupon bond, 'yield' is an awkward concept. For instance, two coupon bonds with the same maturity but different coupons will in general have different gross redemption yields, *even if they are both fairly priced*. So, observing that one coupon bond has a higher yield than another bond with the same maturity but a different coupon does not mean that the former is a better deal than the latter.

Exercise 4 *Suppose that a yield curve is upward sloping. Consider two bonds maturing at the same time T. The first carries a coupon $coup_1$ and the second a coupon $coup_2$, with $coup_1 > coup_2$. They are both fairly priced. Clearly, they will trade at different prices. But will they have the same gross redemption yield? If not, which bond will have the higher gross redemption yield?*

More generally, as Schaefer (1977) showed decades ago, discounting cash flows from different coupon bonds using the gross redemption yield means using different discount factors to present-value cash flows from different bonds that occur at the same point in time – while one would like to do exactly the opposite, ie, one would like to use identical *security-independent* discount factors for all cash flows occurring at the same point in time. Indeed, note the subtle but important difference between Equations (2.5) and (2.6): in Equation (2.6) the discount rate, GRY_t^T, is the same at every point in time; however, in Equation (2.5) the yield associated with each discount factor is in general different (and equal to $-\frac{1}{T_i - t} \log P_t^{T_i}$) for every payment.

Because of all of this, the reader should always assume that i) we refer to discount bonds unless we explicitly say the opposite, and ii) we always refer to the yield of a discount bond instead of the gross redemption yield of a coupon bond.

If we deal with discount bonds, speaking of its price or of its yield obviously conveys exactly the same information. This being the case, we could in principle specify as primitive a process for yields or a process for bond prices. In principle this is perfectly equivalent, but discount bonds must be worth \$1 at maturity, which poses some clumsy restrictions on the bond process.[6] Also, it is intuitive that a 30-year discount bond would be a lot more volatile (display a much greater price variability) than a 3-month discount bond, *even if yields of all maturities all had exactly the same volatility*. This is one of the reasons why modelling yields makes a lot more sense than modelling directly bond prices.

Another reason for modelling yields rather than prices is that, by speaking of yields of (discount) bonds we focus on what is essential (how much the bonds yield) and abstract from what is inessential (the deterministic flow of time) in a way that we cannot do if we work with bond prices: if I tell you that the yield of a 1-year bond is 1% and the yield of a 30-year bond is 5% you immediately grasp something about how differently the two bonds yield that you would not

---

[6] For readers who know what a Brownian bridge is, Ball and Torous (1983) tried to model the bond process as a Brownian bridge. This was a nice idea, but with unpleasant consequences for the drift. We need not concern ourselves with this problem.

if I told you that the price of the former is \$0.99004 and the price of the latter is \$0.22313. For readers familiar with options, using yields instead of bond prices is similar to using 'implied volatilities' instead of call or put prices when dealing when options.

Yet another, related, reason for choosing yield-like quantities as the variables to model is that a bond price is a beast whose behaviour changes dramatically as its maturity changes: as we said, we expect, for instance, the price volatility of a 2-day-maturity bond to be much, much smaller than the price volatility of a 30-year bond. Yields (and 'rates' in general), although still variable, do not tend to change for deterministic reasons like the passage of time. Their variability contains the 'interesting' stochastic factors that we want to capture, not the 'boring' observation that another day has gone by.

2.2.5 Duration and Convexity

The time-t duration, Dur_t^T, of a T-maturity (discount) bond is defined as minus the derivative with respect to the yield of the bond price, divided by the bond price:

$$Dur_t^T = -\frac{1}{P_t^T}\frac{dP_t^T}{dy_t^T}. \tag{2.8}$$

Given the definition of yield, we have

$$Dur_t^T = -\frac{1}{P_t^T}\frac{dP_t^T}{dy_t^T} = \frac{1}{P_t^T}P_t^T(T-t) = T-t. \tag{2.9}$$

A duration-neutral portfolio of bonds is a combination of long and short positions in bonds such that the total duration is zero. Such a special portfolio is conceptually important, because, if the yield curve moved exactly in parallel, then the value of the portfolio would not change (to first order).

The expression just given is valid irrespective of how many factors shock the yield curve. In a multifactor world it is customary to call the derivative of a bond price with respect to each of the factors, $\{x_i\}$, as its factor-specific duration, Dur_i:

$$Dur_i^T = \frac{1}{P_t^T}\frac{\partial P_t^T}{\partial x_t}. \tag{2.10}$$

Note that, when we do so, the sign is usually taken to be positive.

The time-t convexity, $Conv_t^T$, of a T-maturity (discount) bond tells us by how much the duration changes when the yield changes. More precisely, it is given by

$$Conv_t^T = \frac{1}{P_t^T}\frac{d^2P_t^T}{d\left(y_t^T\right)^2} = (T-t)^2. \tag{2.11}$$

Exercise 5 *On any given day it can perfectly happen that the yield curve (ie, all the yield of the bonds in the market) will move up or down exactly in parallel. However, if we knew in advance that this is the only possible mode of deformation of the yield curve, we would have an arbitrage. Show that this is the case, by looking carefully at the definition of arbitrage and of convexity. Hint: a zero-duration portfolio will exactly keep its value for a parallel move in the yield curve to first order. What can you say about the second-order term?*

Duration and convexity are perfect descriptions (at least to second order) of the changes in the price of a bond in a universe where all yields always move in parallel. Actual yields don't.[7] We shall see in the rest of the book how these two concepts (duration and convexity) can be extended to a more complex, and more realistic, non-parallel-yield-moves world.

2.2.6 Forward Rates

A very important concept is that of forward rate. The time-t continuously compounded instantaneous forward rate of expiry T, f_t^T, is defined by

$$f_t^T = -\frac{\partial \log P_t^T}{\partial T}. \tag{2.12}$$

It is the instantaneous borrowing/lending rate that one can 'lock-in' by going long/short at time t a discount bond of maturity P_t^T and selling/buying at the same time a discount bond of maturity $P_t^{T+\epsilon}$ (where ϵ is an infinitesimally small positive maturity mismatch). Note carefully that we have not said that this is the 'expected' future borrowing or lending rate. It is a *forward* rate, not a *future* rate.[8]

Exercise 6 *Spell out clearly how the locking-in strategy works, and show that any value for the instantaneous forward rate other than that given by Equation (2.12) would give rise to an arbitrage. You may find easier to answer the question for the discrete case (see later) and then take the appropriate limit.*

Using the fundamental theorem of calculus, and the initial condition, $P_T^T = 1$, using Equation (2.12) one can immediately write

$$P_t^T = e^{-\int_t^T f_t^s ds}. \tag{2.13}$$

In the limit as the maturity T approaches time t, the forward rate approaches the time-t instantaneous short rate:

$$r_t = \lim_{T \to t} f_t^T. \tag{2.14}$$

---

[7] It is not just that they don't in practice. When we study convexity, we will understand that, under penalty of arbitrage, they cannot be expected to move in parallel.

[8] Not in the real-world measure, anyway.

It is important to look carefully at Equation (2.13). First of all, there is not a single expectation in sight. All the quantities needed to compute the bond price, ie, all the instantaneous forward rates, are known *today* from *today*'s yield curve. The integration is over *same-time* instantaneous forward rates of *different* maturities. The reason for belabouring this point is that we will encounter in the following a deceptively similar relationship:

$$P_t^T = \mathbb{E}\left[e^{-\int_t^T r_s ds}\right]. \tag{2.15}$$

In this equation there *is* an expectation, and the integral to obtain *the time-t* bond price is over *future* (and, therefore, today-unknown) values of the instantaneous short rate. Considerable grief has come to erstwhile happy individuals and to their families by confusing Equations (2.13) and (2.15).

Instantaneous forward rates are theoretically elegant, but they are not traded in practice. What *are* traded are contracts based on discretely compounding forward rates, $F_t^{T,T+\tau}$. This is the borrowing/lending rate that one can 'lock-in' by going long at time t a discount bond of maturity P_t^T and selling at the same time a discount bond of maturity $P_t^{T+\tau}$, where τ is now a finite tensor (say, 3 or 6 months). Again, note that I have not said that $F_t^{T,T+\tau}$ is the *expected* future borrowing/lending rate for 3 or 6 months. It is easy to show that

$$F_t^{T,T+\tau} = \left(\frac{P_t^T}{P_t^{T+\tau}} - 1\right)\frac{1}{\tau}. \tag{2.16}$$

Exercise 7 *Derive Equation (2.16), and spell out in detail the long/short strategy that allows you to borrow with certainty in the future at the forward rate.*

2.3 LOG PRICES AND LOG RETURNS

When we study excess returns we will often make use of log bond prices, p_t^T:

$$p_t^T = \log P_t^T. \tag{2.17}$$

In econometric analysis one works in discrete time, and the 'time step' between consecutive observations is often taken to be a year. Then the time-t, n-maturity log price is then written as p_t^n.

The discrete-time, continuously compounded forward rate, f_t^n, and the yield, y_t^n, are then given by

$$f_t^n = p_t^{t+n-1} - p_t^{t+n} \tag{2.18}$$

and

$$y_t^n = -\frac{1}{n}p_t^{t+n}, \tag{2.19}$$

respectively.

The expression p_t^{t+n} is almost invariably shortened as p_t^n.

If one starts with the 'boundary condition' $p_t^{t+0} = 0$, one can readily obtain

$$p_t^{t+n} = -\left(\sum_{i=1,n} f_t^i\right) \quad \text{for} \quad n = 1, 2 \ldots \tag{2.20}$$

Equation (2.20) will be useful when we look at excess returns (see Chapter 23, Section 5).

The percentage return, $PercRet_t$, from a holding a bond from time t to time $t + 1$ is given by

$$PercRet_t = \frac{P_{t+1}^{T-1} - P_t^T}{P_t^T}. \tag{2.21}$$

Remembering that $\log(1 + x) \simeq x$, as long $P_{t+1}^{T-1} - P_t^T$ as is 'small', this is approximately equal to

$$PercRet_t \simeq \log\left(P_{t+1}^{T-1}\right) - \log\left(P_t^T\right). \tag{2.22}$$

One therefore defines log returns, $LogRet_t$, as

$$LogRet_t \equiv \log\left(P_{t+1}^{T-1}\right) - \log\left(P_t^T\right) = p_{t+1}^{T-1} - p_t^T. \tag{2.23}$$

2.4 DIMENSIONAL ANALYSIS

One last thing before closing the chapter: dimensional analysis. This is a topic that is not frequently found in books about matters financial, but that can be of great help when checking whether an equation makes sense at all. Those readers who come from a physics background will nod in understanding; those who don't may looked puzzled at the beginning, but will be better and wiser persons by the end of the section.

Every term in an equation is either a pure number or indicates a quantity that is measured in some units. Units refer to a particular dimension. Now, one can choose for units kilograms, pounds or, if one is feeling really awkward, even stones, but they all refer to the same dimension, 'mass'. The units are arbitrary (you can define your own if you like), but the dimensions depend on the problem at hand. The two important things to remember with dimensional analysis 101 are

1. we can only add together or equate terms of the same dimensions – it is the old saying about apples and oranges; and
2. the argument of a logarithm, an exponent, a sine or a cosine must always be pure number.

So, bond prices could be considered pure numbers, but I like to think of their natural units as dollars (or euros, or pounds sterling, or whatever, as long as they are units of money).

Rates and yields are money per unit time. In this book we measure time in years. So, a rate $r = 0.03$ means that you get \$0.03 every year, and has units of $[\$][t]^{-1}$.

When we write an equation such as

$$dr_t = \mu_r dt + \sigma_r dz_t \qquad (2.24)$$

we know (see Appendix 2C) that dz_t has dimensions of $[t]^{\frac{1}{2}}$. Since the term $\sigma_r dz_t$ is a contributor to dr_t, it must have the same dimensions as dr, that is, $[\$][t]^{-1}$. From this follows that the volatility, σ_r, must have dimensions $[\$][t]^{-\frac{3}{2}}$.

Careful, though: this does not mean that *all* volatilities have dimensions $[\$][t]^{-\frac{3}{2}}$. We obtained this result only because we were considering the volatility *of a rate*. Take the following equation for a bond price:

$$\frac{dP_t}{P_t} = \mu_{P_t} dt + \sigma_{P_t} dz_t. \qquad (2.25)$$

Now, dz_t always has dimensions of $[t]^{\frac{1}{2}}$. However, the left-hand side is a pure number (it is the ratio of two \$-like quantities). Therefore σ_{P_t} has dimensions $[t]^{-\frac{1}{2}}$.

From this it follows that a Sharpe Ratio, *SR*, defined as the ratio

$$SR = \frac{\mu - r}{\sigma}, \qquad (2.26)$$

is not a pure number, and therefore depends on the units and on the investment horizon. We can see it directly: the numerator (which is the difference of two yield-like quantities) has dimensions of $[t]^{-1}$, but the denominator has dimensions of $[t]^{-\frac{1}{2}}$, so that *SR* has dimensions $[t]^{\frac{1}{2}}$. This is why we always conventionally fix an investment horizon (one year, unless we say otherwise) when we report a Sharpe Ratio. And this is also why unscrupulous hedge fund managers like to quote Sharpe Ratio for funny investment horizons.

Finally, take an equation like

$$dr_t = \kappa (\theta - r_t) dt + \sigma_r dz_t. \qquad (2.27)$$

The term in round brackets on the right-hand sign, $(\theta - r_t)$, has the same dimensions as the left-hand side, r_t (because one of its two additive terms is the short rate itself). Therefore the product κdt must be a pure number; this in turn means that the dimensions of the reversion speed, κ, must be $[t]^{-1}$. This is important, because we will encounter throughout the book terms like $e^{\kappa t}$. As we said, whatever appears as the argument of an exponent (or of a sine, a cosine or any trigonometric function) must always be a pure number. If we get anything else, (say, $e^{\kappa \sqrt{t}}$), we know for sure that we have made a mistake, and that we have to retrace our steps.

Exercise 8 *What are the dimensions of θ in Equation (2.27)?*

Exercise 9 *If we had a stochastic-volatility model, what would the dimensions be of the volatility of the volatility?*

2.5 APPENDIX 2A: VECTORS AND MATRICES

2.5.1 Definition

In the following we will often find it very convenient to use vector and matrix notation. For our purposes, we do not necessarily require, as physicists do, a (column) vector to be a collection of numbers that change under a change of coordinates in the same way as the components of a position vector do. We simply define it to be a collection of numbers arranged in a column.

When there can be ambiguity between vectors and plain numbers (or matrices), we denote a vector by decorating it with an arrow on top, like this: $\vec{\theta}$. When ambiguity can arise, we shall also write a matrix with an underscore, as $\underline{A}$. This notation will be useful, because, when we deal with affine models, for more than one factor we will almost invariably use vector notation. The first time we do so, we will show in painful detail the precise correspondence between the more abstract vector notation and the familiar component-by-component notation. After that, we will never look back, and always use vector notation. As we shall soon see, the initial pain is well worth the effort.

The symbolic vector notation is immensely useful when we develop our equations, but when we finally want some final answer we will have to choose some particular coordinates. Once a set of coordinates is chosen, the components of a vector usually will be denoted by an index. So, if $\vec{x}$ is a three-dimensional vector, its three coordinate-system-dependent components will be x_1, x_2, and x_3. Usually, we will position the index as a subscript, but, if it gets a bit crowded downstairs, we will happily move the index to the superscript position, as in x^i.[9] Now, when it comes to matrices, physicists often like to place the column index in the superscript position, and to write the row index as a subscript. We won't. Instead we will always indicate the coordinate-system-dependent components of the matrix as a_{ij}, where the first index denotes the row and the second the column. The upstairs/downstairs notation is great if you do tensor calculus (but we won't); the row-first, column-second convention is great when you translate equations into computer code (and this we will).

Now, start from any set of orthogonal coordinates and perform a rigid rotation. All the components (of a vector or a matrix) will in general change, which is annoying. There are some quantities, however, that are more 'fundamental' than others, in the sense that they do not change when we change coordinates. For instance, the components of a vector will in general change:

$$
\begin{bmatrix} \theta_1 \\ \theta_2 \\ \dots \\ \theta_n \end{bmatrix} \implies \begin{bmatrix} \theta_1' \\ \theta_2' \\ \dots \\ \theta_n' \end{bmatrix},
\tag{2.28}
$$

---

[9] In case you were wondering, the position of the index should never be interpreted to indicate a contravariant or covariant vector.

but the (square of the) length of the vector, $s^2(\theta)$, does not change under a rotation of axes:

$$s^2 = \sum_{k=1,n} (\theta_k)^2 = \sum_{k=1,n} (\theta'_k)^2 . \tag{2.29}$$

We denote the square of the length of a vector θ by

$$s^2(\theta) = \langle \theta, \theta \rangle . \tag{2.30}$$

The length itself is denoted by $\|\theta\|$, and is equal to

$$\|\theta\| = \sqrt{\langle \theta, \theta \rangle}. \tag{2.31}$$

Also the angle, ϕ, between any two vectors, $\overrightarrow{c}$ and $\overrightarrow{b}$, does not depend on our arbitrary choice of coordinates. The angle is implicitly defined by

$$\overrightarrow{c} \cdot \overrightarrow{b} = \sum c_k d_k = \left\| \overrightarrow{c} \right\| \left\| \overrightarrow{b} \right\| \cos(\phi) . \tag{2.32}$$

2.5.2 Transformations of Vectors

Given a set of coordinates, we say that a set of numbers arranged as in $\begin{bmatrix} \theta_1 \\ \theta_2 \\ \cdots \\ \theta_n \end{bmatrix}$

characterizes a (column) vector. If we pre-multiply this vector by an $n \times n$ matrix, A, we obtain another (column) vector, $\overrightarrow{b}$:

$$A\overrightarrow{\theta} = \overrightarrow{b} \tag{2.33}$$

$$\begin{bmatrix} a_{11} & a_{12} & \cdots & a_{12} \\ a_{21} & a_{22} & \cdots & \\ \cdots & & & \\ a_{n1} & & & a_{nn} \end{bmatrix} \begin{bmatrix} \theta_1 \\ \theta_2 \\ \cdots \\ \theta_n \end{bmatrix} = \begin{bmatrix} b_1 \\ b_2 \\ \cdots \\ b_n \end{bmatrix} \tag{2.34}$$

with

$$b_1 = \sum a_{1k} \theta_k \tag{2.35}$$

$$b_2 = \sum a_{2k} \theta_k \tag{2.36}$$

$\cdots$

$$b_n = \sum a_{nk} \theta_k. \tag{2.37a}$$

We can therefore think of the matrix as an operator, transforming the original vector, $\overrightarrow{\theta}$, into another vector, $\overrightarrow{b} = A\overrightarrow{\theta}$, whose components are linear combinations of the original variables given by Equations (2.35) to (2.37a).

We mentioned quantities such as the length of a vector that do not change when we perform a rotation of coordinates, and we presented earlier some vector invariants (their length and the angle between any two vectors).[10] With rotations, there are two important invariants also when it comes to matrices, namely their determinant and their trace.[11] The trace is particularly important in the context of mean-reverting processes because, as we shall see, it is linked to the sum of the strengths of mean reversions (the diagonal elements of the reversion-speed matrix).

If the determinant of a square matrix, A, is non-zero, then there always exists another matrix, called the inverse, denoted by A^{-1}, such that

$$AA^{-1} = A^{-1}A = I \tag{2.38}$$

with I equal to the identity matrix,

$$I = \begin{bmatrix} 1 & 0 & \dots & 0 \\ 0 & 1 & \dots & \\ \dots & & & \\ 0 & 0 & & 1 \end{bmatrix}. \tag{2.39}$$

If we look at matrices as operators on vectors, we can ask ourselves which operations they can perform. In general, they can effect rotations, reflections, dilations and magnifications, or combinations thereof. (See Pettofrezzo, 1978/1966 for a friendly introduction, Chapter 3 in particular.) Reflections and rotation are carried out by special, norm- and angle-preserving, matrices, ie, orthogonal matrices, to which we now turn.

2.5.3　Orthogonal Matrices

If matrix A is such that $AA^T = I$, then we say that matrix A is orthogonal.

An orthogonal matrix preserves the length of vectors. This means that, if A is orthogonal, and $A\theta$ is the new vector that we obtain by operating with the matrix operator A on the original vector, θ, then

$$\langle \theta, \theta \rangle = \langle A\theta, A\theta \rangle. \tag{2.40}$$

Orthogonal matrices also preserve the angle between two vectors: if A is orthogonal, then

$$\langle b, c \rangle = \langle Ab, Ac \rangle. \tag{2.41}$$

We will not go into this, but in three dimensions, matrices that do not change the length of vectors are associated with the symmetries (rotations, reflections) of 3-D space.

---

[10] More generally, this invariance is preserved also by reflections, but we are not interested in reflections in what follows.

[11] The trace is the sum of the diagonal elements of a square matrix.

We simply state without proof that[12], if matrix A is orthogonal *and* the determinant of A is equal to 1,

$$\det(A) = 1,$$

then the operation carried out by the matrix A on the vector $\vec{\theta}$ is just a rotation.[13] These will be the orthogonal transformations we will be mainly interested in.

If an n-dimensional square matrix A is orthogonal, with elements a_{ij}, then we have for the sums along columns and rows:

$$\sum_{i=1,n} a_{ij}^2 = 1 \tag{2.42}$$

and

$$\sum_{j=1,n} a_{ij}^2 = 1. \tag{2.43}$$

We will repeatedly use the result that the columns of an orthogonal matrix are normalized ($\sum_{i=1,n} a_{ij}^2 = 1$) and orthogonal to each other (for any j and k, $\sum_{i=1,n} a_{ij}a_{ik} = 0$). They form a possible basis in $\mathbb{R}^n$.

2.5.4 Row Vectors

Given any set of (column) vectors, say, $\vec{v}$, there exists a (dual) space of row vectors,[14] that we denote by $\left(\vec{v}\right)^{\mathrm{T}}$: so, to each column vector, $\vec{v}$,

$$\vec{v} = \begin{bmatrix} v_1 \\ v_2 \\ \dots \\ v_n \end{bmatrix} \tag{2.44}$$

---

[12] We are being a bit sloppy here: a vector, θ, and a linear operator, $\mathcal{A}$, are abstract, coordinate-independent entities, and the action of the latter on the former should be indicated by $\mathcal{A}\theta$. Once we choose a coordinate system (a particular basis in the vector space), then we may represent the abstract vector, θ, as a column of numbers, $\vec{\theta}$, and the abstract operator, $\mathcal{A}$, as a matrix of numbers, A, and we may stipulate that the action of the latter on the former should be given by the usual rules of matrix multiplication. The point is that vectors are what they are, and do not care about the systems of coordinates we may choose to represent them. In the following we will gloss over this distinction, but it does not hurt to keep it in mind.

[13] For an orthogonal matrix, the determinant can only be ± 1. In two dimensions, if $\det(A) = 1$ we are dealing with a rotation, and if $\det(A) = -1$ we have a reflection. In three dimensions, if $\det(A) = 1$ we are certainly dealing with a rotation, but if $\det(A) = -1$ we *certainly* do not have a pure rotation, but we could have either a pure reflection or a combination of rotations and reflections.

[14] For a good discussion of the dual space inhabited by 'dual' (covariant) vectors, see Lam (2015), p. 63 and passim. Fortunately or unfortunately, depending on the reader's disposition, we shall not have to concern ourselves with the distinction between contravariant and covariant vectors.

we can associate a row vector, $\left(\vec{v}\right)^{\mathrm{T}}$:

$$\left(\vec{v}\right)^{\mathrm{T}} = \begin{bmatrix} v_1 & v_2 & \ldots & v_n \end{bmatrix}. \tag{2.45}$$

We then immediately recognize, by using the familiar rules of matrix multiplication, that the length (squared) of the vector defined previously (an invariant) is just given by

$$s^2 = \left(\vec{v}\right)^{\mathrm{T}} \vec{v}. \tag{2.46}$$

In general, the expression $\left(\vec{g}\right)^{\mathrm{T}} \vec{h}$ (where the two vectors are, of course, of the appropriate dimensions) produces just a number, ie, a quantity that will not change even if we change our coordinates. Looking at Equation (2.32) we see that this number is given by

$$\vec{c} \cdot \vec{b} = \sum c_k b_k = \left(\vec{c}\right)^T \vec{b} = \left\| \vec{c} \right\| \left\| \vec{b} \right\| \cos{(\phi)}. \tag{2.47}$$

By the way, for readers familiar with quantum mechanics notation, the relationship between the 'usual' (column) vectors, $\vec{v}$, and the 'awkward' (row) vectors, $\left(\vec{v}\right)^{\mathrm{T}}$, is exactly the same as between bras and kets. And precisely as in quantum mechanics, operators, A, operate on row vectors from the right:

$$\left(\vec{g}\right)^{\mathrm{T}} = \left(\vec{f}\right)^{\mathrm{T}} A \tag{2.48}$$

and on column vectors from the left

$$A\left(\vec{g}\right) = \left(\vec{f}\right). \tag{2.49}$$

As for the expression $\left[\left(\vec{f}\right)^{\mathrm{T}} A \right] \left[B\vec{q} \right]$, it just represents a number, k:

$$\left[\left(\vec{f}\right)^{\mathrm{T}} A \right] \left[B\vec{\theta} \right] = \left(\vec{g}\right)^{T} \vec{b} = k. \tag{2.50}$$

2.5.5   Exponential of a Matrix

Finally, we recall the definition of the exponential of a matrix. If A is an $n \times n$ matrix, then e^A is an $n \times n$ matrix given by

$$e^A = I + \frac{1}{n!} \sum_{n=1,\infty} A^n. \tag{2.51}$$

(In this expression we assume, of course, that the infinite sum will converge.) Equation (2.51) is a perfect definition of the exponential of a matrix, and is useful to prove theorems involving matrix exponentiation, but for actual computations is close to useless. We will present some essential properties of the exponential of a matrix and how to handle in practice matrix exponentiation in Appendix 2A of Chapter 18.

2.6 APPENDIX 2B: MEAN-REVERTING AND AR(1) PROCESSES

2.6.1 The Ornstein–Uhlenbeck Process

Consider the following continuous-time process (which is known as the Ornstein-Uhlenbeck process, as a mean-reverting diffusion process, or, more compactly, as a mean-reverting diffusion):

$$dx_t = \underbrace{\kappa\,(\theta - x_t)\,dt}_{\text{mean-reverting term}} + \underbrace{\sigma\,dz_t}_{\text{stochastic term}} \, , \qquad (2.52)$$

with dz_t the time-t increment of a Brownian motion. We discuss the properties of mean-reverting diffusion process in Chapter 8. For the moment we simply note that Equation (2.52) 'says' that a variable, x_t, is attracted to its reversion level, θ, with a strength that is proportional to a reversion-speed strength (the quantity κ), and to how distant the variable is from its reversion level (the quantity $(\theta - x_t)$). Absent the stochastic term, $\sigma\,dz_t$, the quantity x_t would approach monotonically and exponentially its reversion level, θ. It is the exponential term that allows moves away from the reversion level, and the 'crossing' of the reversion level.

We can discretize the process (2.52) as

$$x_{t+1} - x_t = \kappa\theta\,\Delta t - \kappa x_t\,\Delta t + \sigma\sqrt{\Delta t}\,\epsilon_t$$
$$\implies x_{t+1} = \kappa\theta\,\Delta t + x_t\,(1 - \kappa\,\Delta t) + \sigma\sqrt{\Delta t}\,\epsilon_t \qquad (2.53)$$

with

$$\epsilon_t \tilde{} \mathcal{N}(0, 1). \qquad (2.54)$$

As we shall see in the next subsection, this discretization shows clearly the parallels between an Ornstein–Uhlenbeck process and a simple autoregressive ($AR(1)$) process. See later.

A few words on the volatility, σ. Since we almost invariably deal with Gaussian models, the volatilities are 'absolute' or 'normal' (not percentage) volatilities. So, we write a volatility as $\sigma_r = 0.0120$, never as $\sigma_r = 1.2\%$. As for yields, we often refer to one hundredth of a 0.01 volatility as a 'basis point volatility'. So, we sometimes say 'the volatility of the short rate is 120 basis points' instead of writing $\sigma_r = 0.0120$. The important thing to remember is that, whatever units we may want to express volatilities in, they will always have the dimensions of $[\$][t]^{-\frac{3}{2}}$. This would not be the case if we used a different (but still affine) model, such as the one by Cox, Cox, Ingersoll and Ross (1985a,b).

Suppose now that the time-t value of the process is x_t, and that this value does not coincide with the reversion level, θ . If we neglect the stochastic term, how quickly does the process halve its distance to θ? It is easy to show (see Chapter 8) that the 'half-life', $H(\kappa)$, (as this time is called) is given by

$$H(\kappa) = \frac{\log 2}{\kappa}.$$ (2.55)

In arriving at this result we have neglected the stochastic term; ie, we have assumed that the process (2.52) was actually of the form

$$dx_t = \kappa \left(\theta - x_t\right) dt.$$ (2.56)

One can show that one obtains the same result if one deals with the full process (2.52), but one is interested in the *expected* time for the distance $|\theta - x_t|$ to be halved.

Exercise 10 *Prove this result using the information provided in Appendix 2C.*

2.6.2   The AR(1) Process

Let's now move to discrete time, and let's consider the trusted work-horse of time-series analysis, the autoregressive, order-1, $AR(1)$, process[15]

$$x_{t+1} = \mu + x_t \phi + \nu \eta_{t+1}$$ (2.57)

with

$$\eta_{t+1} \tilde{} \mathcal{N}(0, 1).$$ (2.58)

Note that Equation (2.57) is just a regression, with the values of the variable at time t as independent variables (the 'right-hand' variables) and the values of the variable at time $t + 1$ as the dependent variables (the 'left-hand' variables). Then ϕ is the slope and μ the intercept.

The parameter ϕ is important, because it determines the stability of the process: if $|\phi < 1|$, the system is stable, and the further back in time a disturbance has occurred, the less it will affect the present. Random walks are a special case of this, where $\phi = 1$: yesterday's increment does not affect in any way today's increment. Full memory is therefore retained of any shock that occurred in the past. As the shock 'persists' (in expectation), an $AR(1)$ process with $\phi = 1$ is said to be *persistent*.

If $|\phi > 1|$ the system is unstable, which is a less scary way to say that it blows up.

One can show that the (theoretical) mean, m, of the AR(1) process x_t is given by

$$m = \frac{\mu}{1 - \phi},$$ (2.59)

---

[15] If the reader needs a refresher on basic time-series analysis, see, eg, Chatfield (1989) for a student-friendly treatment, or Hamilton (1994) for a very thorough exposition (see Chapters 3 to 5 for AR processes).

its (theoretical) variance, $Var(x_t)$, is given by

$$Var(x_t) = \frac{v^2}{1 - \phi^2} \tag{2.60}$$

and that the (theoretical) serial correlation, $corr_n$, between realizations n periods apart is given by

$$corr_n = \phi^n. \tag{2.61}$$

Finally, for future reference we state without proof that the time-t expectation of the process x_t i steps ahead of time t, $E_t[x_{t+i}]$, is given by

$$E_t[x_{t+i}] = \phi^i x_t + \frac{1 - \phi^i}{1 - \phi} \mu. \tag{2.62}$$

Exercise 11 *Derive Equation (2.62) and show that it coincides with Equation (2.59) when time i goes to infinity.*

2.6.3 Parallels between AR(1) Processes and the Ornstein–Uhlenbeck Process

With these properties and definitions under the belt, we can establish a parallel between a discrete $AR(1)$ process and the discrete-time versions of the continuous-time mean-reverting process (2.52). We go back to the discretization of the Ornstein–Uhlenbeck process obtained earlier:

$$x_{t+1} = \kappa\theta\,\Delta t + x_t\,(1 - \kappa\,\Delta t) + \sigma\sqrt{\Delta t}\epsilon_t.$$

Comparing this expression with the definition of a discrete-time $AR(1)$ process, this means that a discretized Ornstein–Uhlenbeck process is just a special $AR(1)$ process with

$$\mu = \kappa\theta\,\Delta t \tag{2.63}$$

$$\phi = (1 - \kappa\,\Delta t) \tag{2.64}$$

$$v^2 = \sigma^2\Delta t. \tag{2.65}$$

Given a time series (x_t) the parameters of the $AR(1)$ process can be estimated by regressing the left-hand variable (the 'y' variable), x_{t+1}, against the right-hand variable (the 'x' variable, the regressor), x_t. Once again, the independent variable (the regressor) is the lagged left-hand variable: the intercept will give μ, and the slope will give ϕ.

In principle, using Equations (2.63) to (2.65) we can then relate the regression slope, the intercept and the variance of the error to the parameters of the mean-reverting, continuous-time process, (2.52). In practice, this brute-force approach usually requires some tender loving care before it can be made to yield reasonable results, but we won't go into this here.

In the rest of the book we will eclectically and opportunistically move from the continuous-time and the discrete-time ($AR(1)$) formulations of a process so as best to serve our needs.

2.7   APPENDIX 2C: SOME RESULTS FROM STOCHASTIC CALCULUS

We present without proof some results from stochastic calculus that we will use when we switch from a discrete-time to a continuous-time treatment. For readers who do not like seeing rabbits being pulled out of hats, a non-scary introduction to stochastic calculus is given in Klebaner (2005). And for those more demanding readers who do not want to take any shortcuts, and for whom only the best will do, Karatzas and Shreve (1988) is the place to go. It is so good that one day I will finish it myself.[16]

2.7.1   Ito's Lemma

Suppose that a stochastic variable, x_t, follows this process:

$$dx_t = \mu(x_t, t)dt + \sigma(x_t, t)dz_t, \tag{2.66}$$

where dz_t is the increment of a Brownian motion: $E[dz_t] = 0$ and $Var[dz_t] = dt$. Purists will say that Equation (2.66), which is often referred to as a Stochastic Differential Equation, is just a short-hand notation, because only the equivalent integral form (the Ito integral)[17] is properly defined. However, for our purposes it will do just fine.

Consider now a function, y_t, of the stochastic quantity, x_t, that evolves according to Equation (2.66): $y_t = f(x_t)$. Let's assume that the function $f(x_t)$ can be differentiated twice with respect to x_t and at least once with respect to time. What will the process for the variable y_t look like?

Ito's Lemma gives us the answer: given the process for the state variable in Equation (2.66), the process of the new variable, y_t, will have the following form:

$$dy_t = \left[\frac{\partial y_t}{\partial t} + \frac{\partial y_t}{\partial x_t}\mu(x_t, t) + \frac{1}{2}\frac{\partial^2 y_t}{\partial x_t^2}\sigma^2(x_t, t) \right] dt + \frac{\partial y_t}{\partial x_t}\sigma(x_t, t)\, dz_t. \tag{2.67}$$

For readers who are familiar with 'traditional', but not stochastic, calculus, the only surprising term is the 'convexity' term $\frac{1}{2}\frac{\partial^2 y_t}{\partial x_t^2}\sigma^2(x_t, t)$.

---

[16] Just to warn the reader: 'It has been our goal to write a systematic and thorough exposition of this subject, *leading in many instances to the frontiers of knowledge*' (p. vii, emphasis added).

[17] The integral form of Equation (2.66) is $x_t = x_0 + \int_0^t \mu(x_s, s)ds + \int_0^t \sigma(x_s, s)dz_s$. The first bit, $\int_0^t \mu(x_s, s)ds$, is just a 'regular' (time) integral; it is the second component, $\int_0^t \sigma(x_s, s)dz_s$ (ie, the Ito integral) that is a bit trickier. Again, see Klebaner (2005), Chapter 4, and Section 4.1 in particular, for a relatively gentle introduction.

What if the 'new' variable, y_t, had been a (twice-differentiable) function of n variables, x_t^i, $i = 1, 2, \ldots, n$? Then Ito's Lemma generalizes as follows:

$$
dy_t = \left[\frac{\partial y_t}{\partial t} + \sum_i \frac{\partial y_t}{\partial x_t^i} \mu(x_t, t) + \frac{1}{2} \sum_{iij} \frac{\partial^2 y_t}{\partial x_t^i \partial x_t^j} \sigma_i \sigma_i \rho_{ij} \right] dt
$$
$$
+ \sum_i \frac{\partial y_t}{\partial x_t^i} \sigma_i dz_t^i, \tag{2.68}
$$

where ρ_{ij} denote the correlations between the ith and the jth state variable.

2.7.2 Stochastic-Calculus Rules for $dp_t dx_t$

With respect to the one-dimensional case, the only significant difference in Equation (2.68) comes from the terms $\sigma_i \sigma_i \rho_{ij}$. Where do these correlations come from?

To understand their origin, consider two diffusive stochastic processes, x_t and p_t. Let the process for a second quantity, p_t, be given by

$$
dp_t = \mu_p(p_t, t)dt + \sigma_p(p_t, t)dw_t. \tag{2.69}
$$

Here dw_t is the increment of another Brownian motion, correlated with degree of correlation ρ with dz_t. Sometimes (for instance when we calculate variances or correlations), we may want to calculate the product $dx_t dp_t$:

$$
dp_t dx_t = [\mu_x(x_t, t) dt + \sigma_x(x_t, t) dz_t] [\mu_p(p_t, t) dt + \sigma_p(p_t, t) dw_t].
$$

When we take expectations, the following heuristic rules are then useful to keep track of the order of differentials:

$$
dt dt = 0 \tag{2.70}
$$

$$
dz dt = 0 \tag{2.71}
$$

$$
dz dw = \rho dt. \tag{2.72}
$$

So, the correlations ρ_{ij} in Equation (2.68) come the product of stochastic terms of the form $\left[\sigma_i dz_t^i \right] \left[\sigma_j dz_t^j \right]$. As anticipated, we will use these relationships when we calculate the covariance between two processes of the type (2.66). For instance, by using the cheat sheet of Equations (2.70) to (2.72), we immediately obtain for the covariance between the two processes:

$$
\begin{aligned}
\text{cov}\left[dx_t^1, dx_t^2 \right] &\equiv E\left[dx_t^1 dx_t^2 \right] \\
&= E\left[[\mu^1(x_t, t) dt + \sigma^1(x_t^1, t) dz_t] \right. \\
&\quad \left. \times [\mu^2(x_t, t) dt + \sigma^1(x_t^2, t) dz_t] \right] \\
&= \sigma^1(x_t^1, t) \sigma^2(x_t^2, t) \rho dt. \tag{2.73}
\end{aligned}
$$

2.7.3 Expectations of Ito Integrals

Another useful result is the following.[18] Let's integrate over time (from time t to time T) the diffusive process for x_t. What we have is called an Ito integral, I_t^T,

$$I_t^T = \int_t^T dx_s = \int_t^T \mu(s)\,ds + \sigma(x_s, s)\,dz_s. \tag{2.74}$$

Its value at time T is not known at time t, because it will depend on the path followed by dz_s from time t to time T. However, its expectation *is* known at time t, and is given by

$$E_t\left[I_t^T\right] = E_t\left[\int_t^T \mu(s)\,ds + \sigma(x_s, s)\,dz_s\right] = \int_t^T \mu(s)\,ds \tag{2.75}$$

because, for any $\sigma(x_s, s)$,

$$E_t\left[\int_t^T \sigma(x_s, s)\,dz_s\right] = 0. \tag{2.76}$$

The Normal Case

From this we can obtain some interesting results. Take a process, x_t. If its drifts and volatilities are of the form

$$\mu(x_t, t) = \mu(t) \tag{2.77}$$

$$\sigma(x_t, t) = \sigma(t) \tag{2.78}$$

(ie, they do not depend on the state variable), then the future, time-T, value of the state variable, x_T, given its value, x_t, at time t is given by

$$x_T = x_t + \int_t^T \mu(s)\,ds + \widehat{\sigma}_t^T \sqrt{T-t}\,\epsilon \tag{2.79}$$

with ϵ the draw from a standard normal distribution,

$$\epsilon \tilde{} \mathcal{N}(0, 1) \tag{2.80}$$

and $\widehat{\sigma}_t^T$ denotes the mean-square-root of the volatility:

$$\widehat{\sigma}_t^T \equiv \sqrt{\frac{1}{T-t}\int_t^T \sigma^2(s)\,ds}. \tag{2.81}$$

As for the (conditional) expectation of the process, $\mathbb{E}[x_T|x_t]$, from the preceding result about the expectation of an Ito integral we have

$$\mathbb{E}[x_T|x_t] = x_t + \int_t^T \mu(s)\,ds. \tag{2.82}$$

---

[18] See Klebaner (2005), p. 94.

The Lognormal Case

If the drifts and volatilities are instead of the form

$$\mu\,(x_t, t) = x_t \mu\,(t) \tag{2.83}$$

$$\sigma\,(x_t, t) = x_t \sigma\,(t) \tag{2.84}$$

then the process is called a lognormal or geometric diffusion and we can write for it the following Stochastic Differential Equation[19]:

$$\frac{dx_t}{x_t} = \underbrace{\mu\,(t)\,dt}_{\text{drift}} + \underbrace{\sigma\,(t)\,dz_t}_{\text{stochastic term}} \tag{2.85}$$

which has a solution of the following form:

$$x_T = x_t e^{\int_t^T [\mu(s) - \frac{1}{2}\sigma^2(s)]ds} e^{\int_t^T \sigma(s)dz_s}. \tag{2.86}$$

The expectation $\mathbb{E}_t\,[x_T]$ is given by

$$\mathbb{E}_t\,[x_T] = x_t e^{\int_t^T \mu(s)ds} \tag{2.87}$$

because it can be shown that

$$\mathbb{E}_t\left[e^{\int_t^T -\frac{1}{2}\sigma^2(s)ds} e^{\int_t^T \sigma(s)dz_s} \right] = 1. \tag{2.88}$$

2.7.4 The Ito Isometry

Finally, when we calculate variances over a finite time span we are sometimes led to evaluate expression of the type $\mathbb{E}_t\left(\left[\int_t^T \sigma(x_s, s)dz_s \right]^2 \right)$. The following result (Ito isometry) holds[20]:

$$\mathbb{E}_t\left(\left[\int_t^T \sigma\,(x_s, s)\,dz_s \right]^2 \right) = \int_t^T \mathbb{E}_t\left[\sigma\,(x_s, s)^2 \right]ds. \tag{2.89}$$

Note carefully: we started with the expectation of the square of the integral of a stochastic quantity (the value of the path-dependent integral, $\int_t^T \sigma\,(x_s, s)\,dz_s$) and we ended with the integral of the expectation of the square of the 'volatility'.

If the volatility does not depend on the stochastic variable, $\sigma\,(x_s, s) = \sigma\,(s)$, this gives

$$E_t\left(\left[\int_t^T \sigma\,(x_s, s)\,dz_s \right]^2 \right) = \int_t^T \sigma\,(x_s, s)^2\,ds, \tag{2.90}$$

which says something even more amazing, namely that the time-t expectation of $\left[\int_t^T \sigma\,(x_s, s)\,dz_s \right]^2$ is a deterministic quantity, and that this quantity is just equal to the 'variance delivered' from time t to time T. This property means

---

[19] See Klebaner (2005), p. 224. [20] See Klebaner (2005), p. 94.

that there are no 'lucky' paths, and that, for a Brownian process, *along each and every path*, no matter how short or how long, the variance is always known at the outset. This is the property upon which replication strategies for derivatives pricing are built, but we will not go into that.

2.7.5   Risk-less Portfolios

To conclude, one more very important result, that we will use both to derive the no-arbitrage conditions in the traditional (Partial Differential Equation–based) approach, and in our treatment of convexity. Suppose that we have n factors (n state variables), x_t^i, $i = 1, 2, \ldots, n$, and that they all follow Brownian processes of the type

$$\frac{dx_t^i}{x_t^i} = \mu \left(x_t^i, t \right) dt + \sigma \left(x_t^i, t \right) dz_t, \quad i = 1, 2 \ldots, n. \tag{2.91}$$

(Note that we have allowed both the drifts and the volatilities to depend on all the state variables.) For short we call these processes 'multidimensional diffusions'.

The prices of bonds will depend on these state variables and, via Ito's Lemma, we know that they will be diffusions as well.

It can be shown that, in this setting, it is always possible to combine $n + 1$ bonds with clever weights to create a portfolio which behaves totally deterministically. This means that by dint of constructing the clever portfolio, we will have killed (locally) its stochastic behaviour. (In the derivatives world normally one has a 'special' asset – the 'option' – and one hedges its stochastic behaviour using n hedging instruments. It amounts to exactly the same thing; it is just a matter of perspective.) In continuous time, to remain riskless the portfolio will, of course, require continuous rebalancing. To prove this result, Björk (2004) is a good place to go.[21] We will show in detail in several parts of the book how the riskless portfolio can be constructed when the bond prices come from factors that follow a multidimensional diffusion.

What if the 'volatilities' ($\sigma \left(x_t^i, t \right)$) were stochastic not just because of their dependence on the n state variables, x_t^i, but because they are shocked by other, independent, sources of uncertainty? If there are m such additional sources of *diffusive* uncertainty, then we can still form a risk-less portfolio (we can still 'hedge' one bond using lots of other bonds), but the portfolio will be made up of $n + m + 1$ bonds. We will not need this result in the rest of the book, but there are affine models, such as the Longstaff and Schwartz (1992) model, for which this becomes relevant. Another time.

---

[21] See Chapters 6 to 8 in particular.

CHAPTER 3

Links among Models, Monetary Policy and the Macroeconomy

3.1 THE PURPOSE OF THIS CHAPTER

In our treatment we do not provide a macroeconomic or monetary-economics foundation of yield curve modelling. In this sense, our approach is therefore 'reduced-form': we acknowledge that deeper drivers (say, expected inflation, or the output gap) than the variables we use (say, the short rate, or the slope of the yield curve) affect the yield curve; but, for a variety of reasons, in our modelling we choose to make use of the latter, less fundamental, variables instead of the fundamental ones.

Why would we want to do so? Perhaps because they are more easily observable (estimating the slope of the yield curve requires a Bloomberg terminal; assessing the output gap is a tad more difficult). Perhaps because they synthetically embed a lot of information about the more fundamental variables (much as the temperature of a gas 'contains' information about the velocities of its molecules). Perhaps because they give rise to a simpler analytical treatment (we will show, for instance, that bond prices are given by expectations of a function of the path of the short rate). More generally, whenever one uses a reduced-form approach, one has a rough idea of the link between the fundamental variables and the phenomenon at hand, but one despairs of one's ability to connect all the modelling dots from the former to the latter. One therefore takes a number of judicious shortcuts through the toughest hairpin turns, hoping that one will still land in the right direction.

Even if we embrace a high-level, reduced-form approach it is still very useful to have at least an approximate picture of the links between the reduced-form variables that we use and the more fundamental variables that drive the yield curve. Providing this link is the task undertaken in this chapter. As we do so, we also present the first extension of the simple Vasicek model that we will encounter in Chapter 10.

3.2   THE MONETARY CHANNELS

> Accordingly we find that in every kingdom, into which money begins to flow
> in greater abundance than formerly, everything takes on a new face; labour
> and industry gain life; the merchant becomes more enterprising, and even the
> farmer follows his plough with greater alacrity and attention...
>
> David Hume, *'On Money', Political Discourses* (1752)

In most Western economies, central banks have the mandate to keep price inflation under control: changes in the price level should be small, smooth and positive. In addition, most central banks also pursue, explicitly or implicitly, the
goal of encouraging macroeconomic conditions conducive to economic growth.
For instance, most central banks directly or indirectly try to ensure that the
economy grows at its productive potential.[1]

One of the latent variables they monitor in this context is the elusive output
gap, ie, the difference between what the economy could produce at a given point
in time if all its factors of production (labour, plants, etc) were fully utilized,
and what it actually does produce. For instance, during a recession factories
may be working at half-shift, full-time workers may have been substituted by
part-timers and unwanted inventories may be building up. In this environment
a stimulus in demand can increase production without stoking up inflationary
pressure. (It is clear that the same increase in demand would have a very different effect if the economy were already firing on all cylinders.)

Since, at least in the short run, demand can be affected by the level of rates
(just think of the effect on your spending of the borrowing rate of the credit card
you carry in your wallet), the point here is that the output gap can be influenced
(albeit with 'long and variable' lags) by monetary actions.

Modern central bankers tend to communicate the thinking behind their
actions – and sometimes even provide explicit 'forward guidance' – so that
economic agents can not only observe their current policy, but also form expectations about their future monetary interventions. Post Lucas, modern economic
theory places great emphasis on the rational expectations of investors. Indeed,
in modern economic theory a feedback loop is established between today's
macroeconomic variables (say, inflation, or real growth), the current monetary
policy to adjust these variables, the expectations about the effect of today's
policies on future macroeconomic variables, the expectations of future monetary actions and so on. It all (quickly) becomes rather complicated, but, for our
purposes, the important thing to keep in mind is that, after adjusting for risk
premia and convexity, bond yields are just given by the expected path of the
short rate that central bankers will determine in the future in order to fulfil their
mandates. Therefore we can say that the main variables directly or indirectly

---

[1] For a good and insightful, yet discoursive, discussion of the roles and mandates of central banks,
see, eg, Davies and Green (2010), Chapters 1 to 5 in particular.

set or influenced by the monetary authorities that affect the evolution of the yield curve are[2]:

1. the actually observed current risk-less overnight borrowing rate;
2. the near-term target set by central bankers for this borrowing rate;
3. the expectations ('managed' by the monetary authorities) of how this target will change over time;
4. the speed (Naik (2002) says 'the aggressiveness') with which the monetary authorities intend to bring the current rate to its desired target;
5. risk premia.

Risk premia, of course, are not set by the central bankers. However, the clarity with which they communicate their intentions, and their credibility in controlling inflation expectations, play an important part in determining the degree of uncertainty in the future path of the economy, and hence the compensation investors want to exact for this uncertainty.

To put some flesh on the bones, we can cast our mind to the economic and monetary environment that prevailed in the United States (and, with some important differences, in Europe) during the Great Repression (the years from 2010 to the second part of the 2010s). Central bankers in the United States and in Europe not only brought the target rate to unprecedentedly low levels; they also gave clear indications that rates would remain exceptionally low for an extended period. At the same they communicated that, although this 'exceptional' period could last for a long time, it should nonetheless be regarded as an 'extended aberration', after which rates would return to more normal levels.

Starting with early summer of 2013 the US monetary authorities (Bernanke was at the time the chairman of the Fed) therefore began engaging in the delicate task of adjusting expectations about when the 'tapering'[3] would begin – ie, about the speed with which the target rate would change.

Needless to say, the uncertainty attending to the reading of the tea leaves of the central bankers' pronouncements affected risk premia – indeed, according to some models the increase of risk premia in this period accounts for the lion's share of the observed changes in market yields: we shall discuss at length in Chapter 31 and passim the extent to which we can trust these conclusions, but this is a different story.

Why dwell on this episode of monetary intervention? Because we can easily recognize in the episode itself and in the accompanying changes in the yield curve all the five ingredients outlined earlier. More precisely, during this period in making their estimates about future yields, investors

---

[2] We follow closely the treatment in Naik (2002).

[3] The word 'tapering' refers to the slowing down of the purchases of long-maturity assets in which the monetary authorities engaged in the wake of the protracted post-2009 slowing down of the economy, when the traditional means of lowering short-rate rates became ineffective.

- observed the risk-less overnight rate;
- made assumptions that the near-term target would not change for a long(ish) but not infinite period;
- speculated as to when the target might be changed;
- formed and revised opinions about how quickly the Fed would move when the time came; and
- fretted and worried a lot about getting some, or most, or all of these predictions, assessments and guesses wrong – which, of course, is the bit where the risk premium part comes in.

How much they fretted, worried and reviewed their assessments can be easily read in the recorded movements of the 10-year yield from the late Spring to early autumn of 2013 – an episode that we discuss in some detail in Chapter 5.

So, yes, it is indeed the case that, as Naik (2002) says, '[t]he expected future path of the central bank target rates combined with a risk premium for holding interest-rate sensitive securities are the most important considerations in pricing government bonds.'

One thing, however, is recognizing the variables that drive the yield curve. Another is modelling them. It is to this task that we turn in the next section.

3.3   A MODELLING FRAMEWORK

One of the best-known empirical rules to link the administered short rate with macroeconomic variable is the Taylor rule, which belongs to the class of feed-back rules. With these rules

> the central bank's policy interest rate responds to movements in a small number of macroeconomic factors, such as the current amount of labor market slack and the deviation of the rate of inflation from its target. The precise definitions of these factors and the magnitudes of their response coefficients can be chosen to provide the best obtainable outcome with respect to policy-maker objectives for a specific macroeconomic model, or they can be chosen to provide good outcomes across a range of plausible models.
>
> (Brayton, Laubach and Reifschneider, 2014)[4]

Traditional (backward-looking) Taylor rules state that the target rate should be a function of the expected inflation and of the output gap. (By the way, I

---

[4] p. 1. Feedback rules are not the only approach by means of which central banks seek guidance to set rates. Another approach is the optimal-control monetary policy. See Brayton et al. (2014) for a simple discussion. Optimal-control models are far more complex (the FRB/US optimal control model currently in use contains approximately 60 stochastic equations, 320 identities and 125 exogenous variables) and hence more difficult to calibrate and more prone to model error. In contrast, '[s]imple feedback rules are relatively easy to understand and communicate to the public, and potentially robust to uncertainty about the structure of the macroeconomy' (ibid, p. 1). Despite being less robust, optimal-control approaches can be desirable in atypical macroeconomic conditions – such as the conditions prevailing in the wake of the Great Recession, as discussed in English, Lopez-Salido and Tetlow (2013).

say 'rules' rather than 'rule' because several variations have appeared of the original version by Taylor (1993)). In the original paper the target rate was assumed to be given by

$$TR_t = i_{t-1} + \theta_1\left(i_{t-1} - i^T\right) + \theta_2\frac{y_{t-1} - y^*}{y_{t-1}} + (TR_t - i_t)^*, \tag{3.1}$$

where TR_t is the the target rate set by the central bank for time t, i_t is inflation at time t, i^T is the inflation target rate, $\frac{y_t - y^*}{y_t}$ is the percentage deviation of the time-t output from its natural level, y^*, and $(TR_t - i_t)^*$ is the target *real* (as opposed to nominal) rate. Recall that, in this equation, we have information about quantities at time $t - 1$ and we want to determine the target rate for time t. In Taylor's original paper the 'reversion speed' constants θ_2 and θ_2 were both set at 0.5, but the precise values should be obtained from regression analysis.[5]

How can one interpret this formula? Equation (3.1) is expressed in terms of the control variable, ie, of the target rate, which is the quantity that policymakers can influence. However, the economic content of the Taylor rule can be seen more clearly by re-writing Equation (3.1) as follows:

$$\underbrace{(TR_t - i_t)^*}_{\text{target real rate}} = \underbrace{(TR_t - i_{t-1})}_{\text{current real rate}} \underbrace{-\theta_1\left(i_{t-1} - i^T\right)}_{\text{inflation excess}}$$

$$\underbrace{-\theta_2\frac{y_{t-1} - y^*}{y_{t-1}}}_{\text{output gap}}. \tag{3.2}$$

Equation (3.2) shows clearly that the goal is to set the official nominal rate so as to obtain a target real rate (the term $(TR_t - i_t)^*$) consistent both with the inflation target (the term $\left(i_{t-1} - i^T\right)$) and the 'natural' rate of (real) growth for the economy (the term $\frac{y_{t-1} - y^*}{y_{t-1}}$).

So, the level of the current real rate is given by $(TR_t - i_{t-1})$. In general, it may not be optimal. It must therefore be adjusted for two effects: the first is how much current inflation is about target: this is the term $\left(i_{t-1} - i^T\right)$; the second is how much current output is above its target: this is the term $\frac{y_{t-1} - y^*}{y_{t-1}}$. For instance, if either the inflation or the output we observe are below their targets, the quantities $\left(i_{t-1} - i^T\right)$ and $\frac{y_{t-1} - y^*}{y_{t-1}}$ will pull the target rate downwards.

Figures 3.1 and 3.2 show the extent to which the shape of the yield curve is indeed influenced by expectations about inflation and the output gap. (Of course, we do not have direct access to expectations, but we assume that investors 'learn' about inflation and the spare capacity in the economy by estimating a long-term moving average of past realizations. The specifics of the this learning algorithm are briefly explained in Chapter 27, in the context of the Cieslak and Povala (2010a) approach.) Of particular interest is the

---

[5] See, eg, Bain and Howells (2003/2009), Chapter 8, p. 244 and passim for a discussion of the Taylor rule.

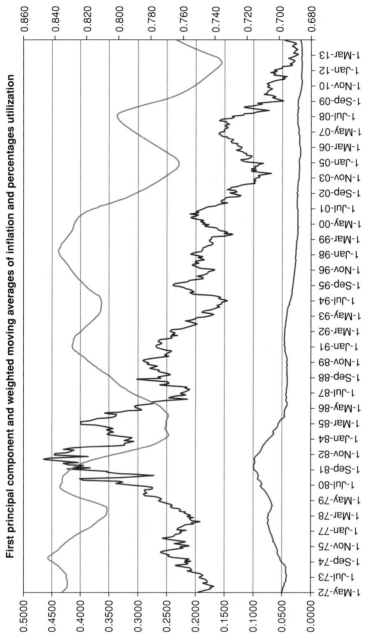

Figure 3.1 Times series of the first principal component of the yield curve – roughly, its level – (purple line), and weighted moving averages of inflation (red bottom line) and capacity utilization (blue top smooth line). The data for the inflation and the capacity utilization are extracted from the FRED® (Federal Reserve Economic Data) data base, codes TCU (Percent of Capacity) and CPIL-FESL (Consumer Price Index for All Urban Consumers: All Items Less Food and Energy). Note the overall decline of rates with inflation, and, at least after the mid 1980s, the approximate coincidence between the level of rates (as proxied by the first principal component) and the capacity utilization.

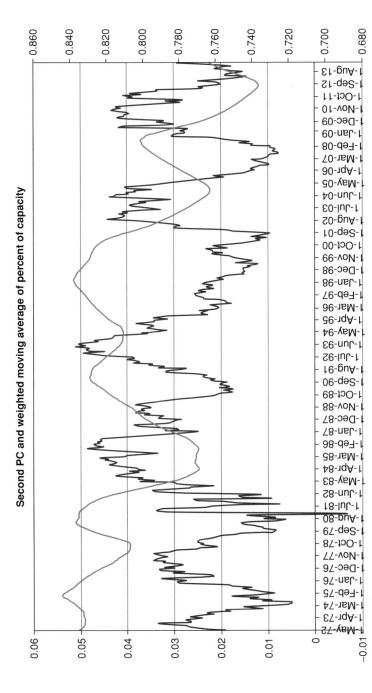

Figure 3.2 Times series of the second principal component of the yield curve – roughly, its slope – (purple line), and weighted moving average of capacity utilization (blue smooth line). The data for the inflation are extracted from the FRED® (Federal Reserve Economic Data) database, code CPILFESL (Consumer Price Index for All Urban Consumers: All Items Less Food and Energy). Note the strong anticorrelation between the slope of the yield curve (as proxied by the second principal component) and the capacity utilization.

pronounced anticorrelation between the second principal component of the yield curve (its 'slope') and the capacity utilization: when the utilization is high, the monetary authorities raise the short rate(s), thereby flattening the yield curve; conversely, when there is a lot of spare capacity in the economy the central bank cuts the short rate(s), and, by doing so, causes the yield curve to steepen. We shall discuss in detail the relevance of this when we look at excess returns (Part VI).

Going back to Equation (3.2), apart from the specific values for the model coefficients, the important thing to note is that in the backward-looking Taylor rule the target rate depends on 'backward-looking' quantities that are all known at time t: the time-$(t-1)$ inflation, i_{t-1} (which appears twice) and the time-$(t-1)$ output gap, y_{t-1}. Forward-looking versions of the Taylor rule shift the focus from what has happened in the past to what is expected to happen in the future. Indeed, Svensson (1997) observes that 'inflation targeting' should really mean 'inflation forecast targeting'. More generally, modern versions put the emphasis on *expectations* of inflation and output gap. This is eminently sensible but, of course, estimating expectations is far more difficult than recording current statistics about the economy (even when the statistic in question is as difficult to measure as the output gap).

The approach by Judd and Rudebusch Judd and Rudebusch (1998) and Clarida, Gali and Gertler (1999) belongs to the more modern, forward-looking, expectation-oriented Taylor school. The following quote from Gurkaynak et al. (2007) illustrates clearly the importance attributed by central bank policymakers to inflation expectations:

> One measure that is of particular interest is the five-year forward five-year inflation compensation[6] rate (also known as the five-year five-year forward breakeven inflation rate), because it has been explicitly mentioned by a number of Fed policymakers in their speeches. The behaviour of this measure is often taken as a gauge of the Fed's inflation-fighting credibility. *Policymakers seem to look to this measure to help judge whether near-term inflation pressures are working their way into longer-term expectations.* The concern is that such leakage would create a more persistent inflation problem that would then be costly to reverse.[7]

3.4 THE MONETARY ACTIONS: A SIMPLE MODEL

In the light of the preceding discussion, following Naik (2002), (who is in turn inspired by the work by Clarida, Gali and Gertler (2000)), we take the target rate at time t, TR_t, to be given by a weighted average of time-t expectations

---

[6] This is the inflation that would make the yield of an inflation-linked bond equal to the yield from a nominal bond. See Chapter 4 for a discussion.

[7] pp. 12–13, emphasis added. As the authors are well aware of, the forward break-even inflation also contains a real-rate risk premium and a liquidity premium. See their footnote 11, and Section 5 of their paper.

of inflation ($E_t[i_{t \to t+q}]$) and output gap ($E_t[OG_{t+q}]$) over the period from t to $t + q$.[8] So

$$TR_t = a + bE_t \left[i_{t \to t+q} \right] + cE_t \left[OG_{t+q} \right].$$ (3.3)

So much for the target rate. However, Equation (3.3) defines the official rate set by the central bank, not the actual short rate, r_t, which is brought to the desired target level only by means of monetary operations.[9] How quickly the short rate is brought to the target comes down to the 'aggressiveness' of the central bankers referred to above. In discrete time one can therefore write

$$r_{t+1} = \phi r_t + (1 - \phi)TR_t + \gamma \varepsilon$$ (3.4)

$$\varepsilon \sim \mathcal{N}(0, 1).$$

Equation (3.4) says that tomorrow's short rate, r_{t+1}, is a (linear) combination of today's short rate, r_t, of the target rate the central bankers have set today, TR_t, plus the ubiquitous noise term, $\gamma \varepsilon$. The smaller the coefficient ϕ, the quicker the approach of the actual short rate to the target rate (ie, in the terminology we have used above, the more 'aggressive' central bankers are). Readers familiar with time-series analysis and its continuous-time counterparts, will recognize Equation (3.4) as an instance of of $AR(1)$ (auto-regressive, order 1) process, which maps in continuous time onto a simple (Ornstein–Uhlenbeck) mean-reverting process. See the discussion in Chapter 2. The important point here is that the reversion speed to the target rate is, in the 'big picture of things', very high and is therefore unlikely to affect the behaviour of long yields. More about this later.

What about the behaviour of the target rate itself? Naik (2002) suggests that, *locally* (ie, 'today'), it should be attracted to a reversion level, but that this reversion level may in turn be varying over time. To be concrete, during the Zero-Interest-Rate Period (ZIRP) of the 2010s, the target rate may have been very low, and may be attracted to a very low reversion level; however, this 'local' reversion level may not be the long-term one, but may revert, with its own speed, to a more 'normal' reversion level.

This nested dynamics of mean reversions can therefore be described in continuous time by the following joint equations:

$$dTR_t = \kappa_{TR} \left(\theta_t - TR_t \right) dt + \sigma_{TR} dz_t^{TR}$$ (3.5)

$$d\theta_t = \kappa_\theta \left(TR_\infty - \theta_t \right) dt + \sigma_\theta dz_t^\theta,$$ (3.6)

---

[8] Empirical analysis finds a good agreement between the forward-looking version of the Taylor rule and the actual target rates set by several central banks. In particular, Judd and Rudebusch (1998), divide the period in their study in three sub-periods, corresponding to the chairmanships of Burns, Volker and Greenspan. They find the best agreement between theory and reality for the Greenspan period, with over- and undershoots, respectively, in the Burns and Volker periods, respectively. For a discussion, see Bain and Howell (2003/2009), pp. 245–246.

[9] For a thoughtful and realistic undergraduate-level description of monetary operations see, eg, Bain and Howells (2003/2009), Chapter 9 in particular. Chapters 10, 11 and 12 discuss monetary policy in the United Kingdom, the European Union and the United States.

where θ_t is the 'local', time-varying reversion level of the target rate, and TR_∞ is its ultimate, long-term, level of attraction. The first equation should describe medium-term (cyclical) behaviour, while the last equation should be a description of long-term (secular) evolution of rates.

Again, it is important to note that, if the model is well specified, the reversion speeds, κ_{TR} and κ_θ, should after calibration turn out rather different, with $\kappa_{TR} > \kappa_\theta$, and with associated half-lives a few years and many years (and possibly decades), respectively. If we associated a reversion speed, κ_r, to the short rate as well (see Appendix A), we therefore have a hierarchy of time scales, with

$$\kappa_r >> \kappa_{TR} > \kappa_\theta \tag{3.7}$$

and with half lives, HL_r, HL_{TR}, and HL_θ in years, approximately,

$$HL_r = 0.1 \tag{3.8}$$

$$HL_{TR} = 1 - 5 \tag{3.9}$$

$$HL_\theta = 10 - 20. \tag{3.10}$$

In words: the short rate should revert very quickly to the target rate; the target rate should revert more slowly, but still relatively quickly to the time-varying (stochastic) reversion level; and the latter should be attracted extremely slowly to an asymptotic level TR_∞.

As we shall discuss in later chapters, such a description may be 'too rich' (and the attending model overparametrized): indeed, given the very fast reversion speed of the short rate to the target level, for yields other than the very-short-maturity ones specifying a full mean-reverting behaviour associated with the reversion of the short rate, and endowing it with an extremely high reversion speed to its target, may be a bit of 'luxury'. In general, very high reversion speeds, as we shall see, quickly 'kill' the effect of the associated volatility, as the fast-reverting variable is forced to 'hug' its reversion level. So, it may be reasonable to dispose of the γ ('volatility') term in Equation (3.4).

Or perhaps we can get rid of the fast reversion process altogether, and set, at any point in time t, $r_t = TR_t$. (We shall, indeed, explore a model of this form in Chapter 30.) For the moment, however, we prefer to lay out a rather general framework and leave the pruning for later.

3.5   CALIBRATING REDUCED-FORM MODELS

The last temptation is the greatest treason:
To do the right deed for the wrong reason.
Murder in the Cathedral – T. S. Eliot

3.5.1   General Considerations

In the previous sections I have sketched with a broad brush how one can arrive at a reduced-form class of monetary-policy-inspired mean-reverting models of the evolution of the yield curve. Why 'reduced form'? Because the parameters of the model are not arrived ab initio, but by means of a 'calibration' procedure. 'Calibrating' a model means making use of time-series statistical information and (more frequently) of cross-sectional market information (such as contemporaneous prices and yields) to impute what the model parameters should be. It must be stresses that, more often than not, the model parameters cannot be directly estimated. The calibration proceeds via the estimation of some model quantity (say a yield, or a yield volatility), which is a function of the unknown parameters; and the varying of the parameters until a satisfactory match is obtained between the model quantity and the associated market observable.

It sounds simple enough; but what does 'satisfactory' mean? It pays to look at this deceptively simple aspect of modelling in detail, because it is fundamental, yet error-prone, and because we will encounter it over and over again in our treatment. The discussion that follows mainly refers to models with identifiable (as opposed to 'latent') variables.

Broadly speaking, a reduced-form model is calibrated by following four distinct steps. Following them carefully is the road to reduced-form-modelling joy; skipping the second step is the road to perdition.

1. First we write down the descriptive equations (eg, 'this term should be mean-reverting'; 'this term should be stochastic, and this deterministic'; etc). Note that several still-to-be-determined parameters will appear in the descriptive equations that we have written down.
2. Next, we use whatever understanding we have about how the model should qualitatively behave to establish some qualitative relationships among, or restrictions on, the model parameters (eg, *'if the reduced-form model is in its essence correct* this reversion speed, or volatility, should be higher than that one'; or *'if the reduced-form model is in its essence correct* this parameter should be positive'; or, *'if the reduced-form model is in its essence correct* the volatility of this factor should be smaller (or larger) than the volatility of that factor; etc). In doing so, we must pay attention to whether the quantities we assume to know are in the $\mathbb{P}$ or in the $\mathbb{Q}$ measure.
3. Then, we establish a link between the parameters of the reduced-form model and some model-produced quantities (eg, the *model* yield curve, the *model* yield volatilities, the *model* covariance matrix, etc) that we can relate to market observables – see later.
4. Next we compare the model-produced quantities in step 3 with their market counterparts (eg, the *market* yield curve, the *market* yield volatilities, the *market* swaption matrix, etc).
5. Finally we 'calibrate' the model. By this we mean that we vary the model parameters, *within the bounds allowed by the constraints established in the second phase*, so as to produce via the link established in phases 3 and 4 as close a match as possible between the observable

and predicted quantities (eg, between the model and the market yield curve, or between the model and the market yield volatilities).

Many inexperienced modellers skip the second phase and rush to the calibration phase (phases 4 and 5). In the derivatives pricing world, the not-too-flattering term reserved for these hasty modellers is 'Shift F9 monkeys'. The term is unkind, but apposite: if one searches over an unrestricted parameters space and one obtains a good 'fit' (ie, if phase 4 works well), but the 'optimal' parameters thus determined make no sense with the 'story' one started with,[10] then the agreement between predictions and reality should be considered a fluke, and the model should not be used for prediction with any more confidence than one would grant to the predictions produced by the extrapolation of a cubic spline. Given *any* model, no matter how bad, the more parameters one has at one's disposal, the easier, and less meaningful, it becomes to get a good unconstrained fit.

3.5.2   Assessing the Quality of the Calibration Process

Of course, it would be beautiful if the calibration 'naturally' found values for the parameters consistent with our story even if we searched over the unrestricted parameters space. When this happens we get a warm feeling of satisfaction and, in the rare cases when this happens to me, I have to fight a strong temptation to switch off the computer and go home for the rest of the afternoon lest I spoil a beautiful day. Simultaneously obtaining a good fit *and* a solution consistent with the financial story we started with *without trying to do so* is a strong indication that our model does capture correctly the essence of the problem at hand. The model is telling us that we are on to something.

Getting a good fit with a constrained search is clearly second best, especially if the quality of the fit is not greatly degraded by the imposition of the parameter constraints: yes, our model admits of different solutions that would give rise to perhaps slightly better agreement with what we know already, but which clash with our understanding of how the world works. We know that we have to resist the siren calls of the beautiful fit, and we must discard the 'incongruous' solutions. On the basis of this pruning we also know how to choose among the various predictions for the quantities that we do *not* know about, and that we are interested in. Needless to say, it is only the predictions associated with the not-so-well-fitting-but-financial-story-consistent solutions that we should (tentatively) trust. The reader can at this point profitably revisit Figure 1.2 in Chapter 1.

A distant third best is getting a good fit to our benchmark quantities, but with implausible parameters, and a poor fit with the restricted parameters. We may still decide to limp along with the poorly fitting parameters, but we have been

---

[10] Where the 'story', of course, is also made up of a reasonable specification of the market price of risk.

warned that there is something wrong with our modelling. We must, however, make a call as to whether these blemishes are merely unpleasant or near-fatal. Above all, we must at all costs resist the temptation of the good fit with implausible parameters. As Thomas Becket reminds us, *this* is the greatest treason, because a good fit can be, by itself, a strong temptation but a bad reason for accepting a poor model parametrization.

Finally, we may well fail to get a decent fit to the market quantities no matter how much we change and torture the free parameters. Arguably, this is not as bad as it seems, and our efforts have not necessarily been all in vain: indeed, we have learnt something useful, namely that there is a fundamental problem in our conceptualization of the problem at hand. We are now possibly sadder, but wiser, individuals.

This discussion also makes clearer the issue of parsimony and of the optimal number of parameters. In ab initio models, the number of parameters is really neither here nor there, because the parameters are fixed by the theory employed. In reduced-form models, instead, each parameter is to some extent 'free-floating', and provides some wiggle room, which can produce a spurious agreement between predictions and reality.

This is true, but not all parameters are created equal. The more restrictions one can impose on a parameter, the less room it has got left to wiggle, and the more it begins to resemble a fixed (ab initio–like) parameter. Adding highly-restricted parameters can actually reduce the solution space. So, for a similar quality of fit to the observable quantities, a seven-parameter model can be more parsimonious (or, at least, more 'principled') than a four-parameter model if the seven parameters of the former are strongly constrained, and the four parameters of the latter are free to roam the real line. All of this may sound rather hand-waving, but it can be made acceptably precise. Unfortunately, we have no time for it.

3.5.3 State Variables versus Model Parameters

One last word. Reduced-form models – and, indeed, *any* model – come equipped with parameters and state variables. Variables, well, vary. However, almost invariably reduced-form models require the estimation of the initial values of the state variables – initial values which are just numbers. (For instance, the model may have the short rate as a state variable, and will require the value of the short rate *today* to get started.) Very often the initial values of the state variables are jointly estimated with the fixed parameters in the calibration process. All the considerations made relating to parameters about imposing as many restrictions on these quantities as one can still apply. (If, in mid-2014, we obtained a beautiful fit to the yield curve using an initial value of the short rate of 14%, we were clearly up to no good.) However, there is an important additional check that should be, but seldom is, carried out. This works as follows.

By carrying out the calibration procedure day after day we obtain a time series of the initial values, ie, the calibration-day value(s) of the state variable(s). After collecting a long history of these calibrated initial values, we therefore have a time series of the state variables at hand. We should then ask the question: is this time series of the state variable(s) obtained from the repeated calibration process consistent with the behaviour we posited for the state variable(s)? If we assumed that the short rate was, say, mean reverting, do we observe a mean-reverting behaviour in the fitted time series of initial values of the short rate? Does it have the right volatility? The right reversion speed?[11]

As I said, this test is difficult and requires great care (often, as we shall see, the comparison has to be carried out 'across measures') before standard statistical rejection tests can be used. Statistical analysis is also 'polluted' by those pesky model parameters that, once determined, should remain exactly the same until the end of time, and yet invariably want to change (but hopefully not too much) from day to day. However, the gold standard test of the congruence between the posited and the calibrated behaviour of the state variables can add a lot to our confidence that the modelling approach we have embraced is well-founded.

A related, and statistically sounder, approach is described in Pearson and Sun (1994), which shows how to 'invert' an affine model (ie, how to obtain the values of the state variables from the market and model yields) in order to estimate the *conditional* density implied by a given affine model. Once a density conditional on a given state of the world (a given configuration of the state variables) has been obtained, one can calculate the evolution of the term structure through time. And once these conditional projections have been made, one can test the empirical performance of the model – hence the considerable potential appeal of their approach.[12] Alas, their article has been more widely quoted than used in practice.

In the treatment that follows I will try to be faithful to the four-step credo outlined earlier. This book also intends to enable readers to modify and create their own reduced-form models. Those who will choose to do so will find that, as advertised, the path to modelling joy winds its way through *all* the four steps discussed previously. The fifth test (ie, the test of model consistency described in this sub-section) is then the pot of gold at the end of the rainbow.

---

[11] If the state variable is directly linked to an observable quantity to which the model is fitted (such as the short rate), the test will not tell us much new, because, if the daily fit is decent, we will in essence recover the market time series of the short rate. However, the test becomes very informative if we deal with a more 'opaque' quantity, such as, say, the reversion level of the short rate.

[12] See the discussion on their p. 1285.

CHAPTER 4

Bonds: Their Risks and Their Compensations

4.1 THE PURPOSE OF THIS CHAPTER

In this chapter we look at the risks to which bonds are exposed. Risk comes from not knowing for certain how things will pan out. Therefore saying that we are going to look at the risks to which bonds are exposed is the same as saying that we are going to consider those *stochastic* drivers that affect the prices of bonds.

The price of bonds is also affected by non-stochastic quantities, such as the residual time to maturity, or their coupons. However, these deterministic quantities are perfectly known, and investors demand no 'uncertainty compensation'. We are interested in the risks to which a bond is exposed, because it is for risk, and for risk only, that investors can ask compensation.

This chapter is therefore important for two different but related reasons. The first is rather obvious: if we want to pursue a *structural* approach to yield curve modelling, a clear understanding of the nature of the risks to which bonds are exposed is essential. For instance, if we speak of risk premia, it is important to understand what risk investors get compensated for taking, and why the bearing of certain risks should command a greater or smaller compensation than the bearing of others.

The second reason for looking at the ultimate sources of risk in some detail is a bit subtler. We may or we may not choose as state variables the risk factors. It may seem reasonable to do so, but sometimes considerations such as analytical tractability, or availability of empirical knowledge, will point in the direction of state variables other than the 'ultimate' risk factors that drive the yield curve. Using these 'convenient coordinates' is fine, as long as we understand clearly which risk factors 'really' drive the yield curve, and the nature of the 'mapping' from these 'true' risks to our chosen state variables.

We shall see in this chapter that the risks to which a (perfectly liquid and creditworthy) bond is exposed are inflation and real-rate risk. In order to understand the compensation that investors can expect for bearing these risks, we give a first 'informal' presentation in Section 4.3 of risk-neutral and real-world expectations. The reason for doing so is that the link between the real-world and the risk-neutral probabilities is directly linked to the two sources of risk mentioned earlier, and to investors' aversions to these risks.

4.2 NOMINAL RATES, INFLATION AND REAL RATES: A QUALITATIVE DISCUSSION

An investor has just bought a risk-less (nominal) discount bond.[1] To make the discussion concrete, let's suppose that she has bought a 5-year bond for a yield of 4.50%. What keeps her awake at night?

4.2.1 Inflation Risk

We said that she has bought a *discount* bond. Discount bonds are normally described as coupon-less. However, a more useful perspective is to look at a discount bond as an instrument that repays at maturity what the investor paid today, plus a 'rolled-up' coupon equal to the difference between $1 and the purchase price. So, if the investor bought a 5-year discount bond yielding 4.5%, this means that she paid today $0.79852, and that she will get back in five years' time her initial investment ($0.79852), plus a 'rolled-up' single final coupon of $0.20148 = $(1 − 0.79852). The investment yields 4.5% (continuously compounded) because $1 \times e^{-0.045 \times 5} = 0.79852$.

Our investor presumably likes to consume, not to collect coins. However, the (nominal) bond she has bought promises to deliver with certainty a fixed amount of coins, not of consumer goods. Therefore the investor does not know how many goods the fixed amount she will receive at maturity will buy. How much she will be able to consume depends on the realized inflation between bond purchase and maturity. So, the first (but, as we shall see in future chapters, not necessarily the foremost) source of risk to which a fixed-rate investor is exposed is *inflation risk*.

Suppose that the inflation over the next 5-year period were known *with certainty* at the time of the bond purchase. If the known average inflation over the 5-year period had been 4.5%, in real (ie, inflation-adjusted) terms, the purchasing power of $1 in year 5 would be exactly the same as the purchasing power of $0.79852 today. Would this be a fair price for the discount bond?

By paying $0.79852 today to buy the discount bind, the investor would have delayed for five years the same consumption for no compensation. This does not look like a good deal. Because of impatience (our preference for a slice of cake today rather than *the same* slice of cake in 5 years' time), if the investor accepted a 4.5% nominal return, the certain inflation over the investment period she factored in her calculations must have been less than 4.5%. Perhaps she reckoned that the certain inflation over the life of the bond was going

---

[1] In this section we neglect all other assets in the economy, ie, we neglect how the bond in the investor's portfolio may interact with, say, the credit or equity assets she also owns. The treatment in this section, in other words, is equivalent to placing ourselves in a one-factor economy.

to be 2%, in which case the 'remaining' 2.5% would fully reflect the investor's impatience.

So far we have dealt with a certain future inflation. Assuming that we know inflation with certainty, however, is hardly realistic. Let's relax this assumption, and speak instead of 'expected inflation'. Once expectations come in, uncertainty and risk aversion come to the fore. Just as our investor would not accept entering for nothing into a 50–50 bet to win or lose a year's salary, she will also require an inducement to accept a bet on inflation risk. So, if she expects (actuarially, in the real-world measure) inflation to be, say, 2%, she will 'skew' (risk-adjust) her inflation estimate, and price the bond as if the projected inflation were higher, say, 2.5%. The difference between the actuarially expected inflation and the inflation she uses to price the bond is the *inflation risk premium*.

The more investors are uncertain about inflation, the more inflation risk premium they will demand. For the same estimate of expected inflation, a higher inflation uncertainty will translate into higher nominal yields because of the greater inflation risk premium. In the last decades the central banks of most G7 countries have gained independence from government interference and have become more credible about their commitment to keeping inflation under control. It has therefore been widely argued that uncertainty about inflation has decreased, and so therefore have inflation risk premia and nominal yields. This is part of the 'Great Moderation' narrative of the 2000s.

Expected inflation and the inflation risk premium are therefore the first two components of the yield of a bond – and the easiest ones to understand.

4.2.2 Real-Rate Risk

Let's now look again at the components of the all-in yield of the bond, 4.5%. With a yield of 4.5% our investor was granted by the market a compensation for inflation (actuarially expected to be 2%), a compensation for the uncertainty about inflation (an inflation risk premium of 0.5%), and an extra 2%. This 'extra 2%' is a real return – it is 'real' because it is a return on top of inflation (inflation expectation and inflation risk premium).

This compensation (the *real* return), however, is not fixed, but also changes over time. As with everything that is uncertain, the investor first will have to form an estimate of this expected real rate; and then, since she is risk averse, she will ask for some compensation on top of her actuarial estimate for this source of risk as well.

While the uncertainty about inflation (and hence the inflation risk premium) is a familiar and intuitive concept, the idea of an expected real rate of return, and of a real-rate risk premium may cause some difficulty. To see more clearly into the matter, let's consider a different risk-less discount bond, a *real* (inflation-linked) discount bond.[2] This instrument repays at maturity the initial investment

---

[2] The economics of real rates are briefly treated in Section 15.6.3.

grossed up by the *realized* (not expected or risk-adjusted) inflation, plus an extra bit. Note that, since this different instrument pays the realized inflation over the investment period (plus a bit), the investor is no longer exposed to inflation risk. The 'extra bit' is a real return, ie, some extra amount of consumption the investor will enjoy at the end. The magnitude of this extra return is stipulated today.

Now, given the way the instrument is designed, with a real (inflation-linked) bond the investor is fully insulated from inflation risk. But this does not mean that she is insulated against *all* risks. Tomorrow's investors may be luckier, because the market might price 'consumption impatience' more attractively, and offer a greater amount *of consumption* at bond maturity – a higher *real* return. If between today and tomorrow the real rate of return over the life of the bond goes up, tomorrow's investor will pay less than today's buyer for the same inflation-protected bond, ie, for the same terminal consumption bundle.

Why should the real rate of return change between today and tomorrow? In the long run, the (real) returns to all financial assets (including bonds) must reflect the (real) returns on capital investment.[3] *If the saving rate is constant*, slower (faster) economic growth will yield a lower (higher) marginal product of capital, and, ultimately, lower (higher) return from all securities (stocks and bonds).[4] So, changes in the real rate ultimately reflects different market expectations about long-term economic growth. Needless to say, these projected rates of real economic growth are very uncertain, and therefore attract a risk premium.

The important thing to understand is that with a real (inflation-linked) bond the investor is now perfectly insulated against inflation risk, and cannot, therefore, ask for an inflation risk premium. But, if there is uncertainty about the real rate of return, she is still exposed to real-rate risk and can therefore demand a compensation for bearing this risk, in the form of a real-rate risk premium. This is the only risk premium that can be embedded in the price of a real discount bond,[5] as its variability in real terms can come only from the variability in the real rate of return.

4.2.3 Putting the Pieces Together

Putting all the pieces together we have therefore identified four components to the yield of a nominal bond:

---

[3] The interested reader can gain a better appreciation of these important topics (the Solow growth model) from Acemoglu (2008). See Chapter 2 in particular. The treatment is very good, if a bit heavy going.

[4] The caveat 'if the savings rate is constant' is important, because if savings decline as growth slows (and vice versa) this will at least partially offset the lower growth. As Diamond (1999), points out '[s]ince growth has fluctuated in the past, the long term stability in real rates of return to capital supports the notion of an offsetting savings effect', p. 3. This was written in 1999. It must be said, however, that real rates have since significantly fallen.

[5] Again, we are neglecting liquidity risk. See, however, Chapter 31 for a discussion of the different degree of liquidity of real and nominal bonds.

1. the expected inflation;
2. the risk premium for the uncertainty in inflation;
3. the real rate of return;
4. the risk premium for the uncertainty in the real rate.

Clearly, a nominal bond is exposed to all four sources of risk, but a real (inflation-linked) bond only to the last two.

So, perhaps the observed all-in yield of 4.50% was made up of 2.00% of expected inflation, of 0.50% of inflation risk premium, of 1.25% of real return and of 0.75% of risk premium for the uncertainty in the real return. Being able to carry out this decomposition is one of the main goals of a structural explanation of the yield curve dynamics. In general, after buying her nominal discount bond, the investor will hurt if inflation goes up, if the inflation risk premium goes up, if the real rate increases or the if real-rate risk premium increases. After buying her real discount bond, the investor will suffer if the real rate increases or if the real-rate risk premium increases.

Is that it? Of course it isn't. In our explanation of the observed yield of a bond we have left out, to begin with, convexity and liquidity. And, since convexity depends on volatility, and future volatility is also imperfectly known, one could argue that we should take into account also a volatility risk premium. Also liquidity is uncertain, and so, for all we know, it may command a risk premium as well. And so on.

The point is that whenever there is an uncertain risk factor that influences a price, a risk premium may have to be taken into account. Whether we choose to model these factors and their attending 'risk premia' – or, more to the point, whether investors do demand compensation for bearing these risks – is a different matter.[6]

This is where the art of modelling comes in, ie, in the ability to draw a line and to say 'This is in, and this is out'. There is no correct answer, and no hard-and-fast rule. What is on the 'in' side of the line and what lies on the other depends on many factors, not least what one is analysing: if one is interested in the behaviour of on- against off-the-run Treasuries, perhaps liquidity *is* the most important factor – and, by observing what happens in situations of distress to the on-the-run-off-the-run spread, perhaps one *should* look at the liquidity risk premium as well. In the treatment we present in this book, the components in the four bullet points above are certainly 'inside the line', and so is convexity. Liquidity is mainly outside,[7] and the volatility risk premium is totally outside.

'Wait a minute', you may say. 'You have been saying from the first page of this book that one of the important components of market yields is the expectation about the future path of rates. Surely, if we expect rates to go up, the bond price goes down. Isn't this another risk factor?'

---

[6] As we shall see, empirically we tend to observe that investors seek compensation for changes in level of yields, but not for a steepening or flattening of the yield curve. So, a 'stylized fact' about risk premia is that the first principal component attracts a risk compensation, but the second and third do not.

[7] But see the treatment in the last section of Chapter 32.

Of course it is, but the question is: why did we expect rates to go up? Was it because our inflation expectation increased? Or because we became more uncertain about inflation? Because we thought that the real rate may be higher in the future? Or because we realized that we understood less about the real rate than we thought (and we were therefore less confident about its range of variability)? All these factors can make 'rates go up'.

Hopefully, these qualitative considerations are useful to frame the issue of the risks to which a bond is exposed. We now move to a simple, but more precise, treatment. Before doing so, however, we must introduce some important concepts related to risk aversion. More precisely, we want to show how risk aversion can be thought of as altering our perceptions of the probabilities of good and bad events.

4.3 REAL-WORLD AND RISK-NEUTRAL PROBABILITIES: THE MARKET PRICE OF RISK

We will encounter real-world and risk-neutral probabilities throughout the book. This is the first time we tackle this important concept. We place this gentle introduction here because the link between risk-neutral and real-world probabilities stems directly from risk, and from aversion to risk – which, insofar as risk relates to bonds, is exactly the topic of this chapter.

To start with, real-world probabilities are the probabilities of states of the world that can be estimated using all the historical and model-driven information at our disposal about the world and its history. This information is made up of past prices, of course, but of a lot of other things as well – for instance, past information about the states of the economy, the output of the models of the economy that we build, etc.[8]

It is generally assumed that, since everyone observes the same public data, and everybody can avail themselves of the same statistical tools to analyse them, and of the same theoretical constructs to interpret them, everybody will agree on the real-world probabilities. The assumption is very common not because it is particularly easy to swallow, but because it makes life very easy. It belongs up there with frictionless planes and point masses.

So much for real-world probabilities. What about risk-neutral probabilities? To understand what they are, we start from the assumption that investors are risk averse, which means that they prefer $1,000 with certainty to a bet with an expectation of $1,000. For our discussion it is important to note that being risk-averse towards risky bets today also means that investors prefer to consume one cake a month for a year, rather than 12 cakes in March, and to starve

---

[8] One should distinguish here between the real-world probabilities just described (the 'econometrician's probabilities') and the subjective probabilities held by an investor. These may, but need not, coincide. We will deal with this topic in Chapter 28, but for the moment we gloss over the distinction, so as not to complicate matters too much.

on all the other months of the year. This is true at least for 'common' utility functions.[9]

When investors look at investments, they consider their payoffs in different states of the world. In some states of the world investors already feel rich (can consume a lot) for reasons that have nothing to do with the performance of the investment they are looking at. In other states of the world a given investment may perform very well when everything else is going to hell in a handbasket – think for instance of US Treasuries, which promise to pay very little in good states of the world but can perform very well during financial crises.

All of this is to say that what investors care about is not how well a particular investment will perform in the various future states of the world in isolation, but how much this investment will allow them *consume* in the future, and how well it will help them smooth out their consumption streams (avoid feast and famine). As a consequence, they will not look at an investment, such as a bond, in isolation, but as a component as their portfolio, which will contain equities, credit-risky bonds, real estate, etc. This is the reason why, given the same actuarial odds, paying for house insurance is a lousy investment if you do not own a house, but a splendid one if you do.

This must always be kept in mind when looking at the risk compensation for bonds, even if, as we are about to do, for illustrative purposes we often neglect the big picture and we pretend that bonds are the only game in town.

4.3.1 Introducing the $\mathbb{P}$ and $\mathbb{Q}$ Measures

So, suppose that we have observed that, given its value today, r_i, the short rate can move up or down over the next interval Δt with equal probability to two possible values, r_{i+1}^{up} and r_{i+1}^{down}, according to the following law:

$$r_{i+1}^{up} = r_i + \kappa(\theta - r_i)\Delta t + \sigma\sqrt{\Delta t} \tag{4.1a}$$

$$r_{i+1}^{down} = r_i + \kappa(\theta - r_i)\Delta t - \sigma\sqrt{\Delta t}. \tag{4.2}$$

As we have seen in Chapter 2, this is a simple discretization of a mean-reverting process, but the details of the process are not important right now. What is a bit more important for future discussion is that the 'drift' term (the term in Δt) contains the state variable.

We can easily evaluate the expectation today of value of the short rate at the time $i + 1$ as

$$E^{\mathbb{P}}[r_{i+1}|r_i] = 0.5 \times [r_i + \kappa(\theta - r_i)\Delta t + \sigma\sqrt{\Delta t}]$$
$$+ 0.5 \times [r_i + \kappa(\theta - r_i)\Delta t - \sigma\sqrt{\Delta t}]$$
$$= r_i + \kappa(\theta - r_i)\Delta t. \tag{4.3}$$

---

[9] See the discussion in Section 13.4 on the double role of the coefficient of risk aversion.

Note that, in order to evaluate this expectation, we have used the real-world probabilities ($\frac{1}{2}$ and $\frac{1}{2}$ for both states). To remind ourselves of this, we have added a superscript sign, $\mathbb{P}$,[10] to the expectation operator. Remember: an expectation operator tells us to carry out certain operations *given a set of probabilities*. Unless we specify the probabilities ($\frac{1}{2}$ and $\frac{1}{2}$ for both states in this case), saying that we take an expectation does not mean much.

Suppose now that the investor has to make a bet on the outcome of the short rate in one period's time. More precisely, the bet is such that, if the state r_{i+1}^{up} prevails, the investor will receive $S_{up} = e^{-r_{i+1}^{up}\Delta t}$, but if the *down* state she will receive $S_{down} = e^{-r_{i+1}^{down}\Delta t}$. So, the expected payoff, $E^{\mathbb{P}}[Payoff(bet)]$, from the bet is

$$\mathbb{E}^{\mathbb{P}}[Payoff(bet)] = 0.5 \times (S_{up} + S_{down}). \tag{4.4}$$

Now, this is the real-world expectation of the payoff from the bet. Remember, however, that the investor is risk averse. This means that she will not enter the bet just for its actuarial value. One natural way to account for this is to say that she will want a positive compensation over and above the actuarial expectation to enter the bet. Call this compensation H.

How can the investor account for this risk preference in the framework just described? She can pretend that she is risk neutral, but that an additional negative payoff, $-H$, attaches to the actual payoffs in both states of the world. If this is the case, the real-world ($\mathbb{P}$-distribution) expectation of the bet will now become $0.5 \times (S_{up} + S_{down}) - H$ and she would therefore be willing to pay only $\$[0.5 \times (S_{up} + S_{down}) - H]$ in order to get the outcome from the bet – which is what she wanted to do in the first place.

We can formalize this as follows:

$$\mathbb{E}^{\mathbb{P}}[Payoff(bet)] = p^{up} \times [S_{up} - H] + p^{down} \times [S_{down} - H]$$
$$= 0.5 \times [S_{up} - H] + 0.5 \times [S_{down} - H]$$
$$= 0.5 \times (S_{up} + S_{down}) - H. \tag{4.5}$$

Note that H has the dimensions of $\$$.

This is very natural, but there is another way to look at the same problem. We could also say that the payoffs are the true ones (ie, S_{up} and S_{down}, without any adjustment H), but, because of her risk aversion, the investor will give a higher probability to the bad state of the world (and therefore, of course, a lower probability to the good state).

To fix ideas, let's assumes that she sets $\tilde{p}^{up}$ and $\tilde{p}^{down} = (1 - \tilde{p}^{up})$ for the *up* and *down* probabilities, respectively. We have appended a tilde to the probability symbols to remind ourselves that these are not the actuarial, real-world probabilities.

---

[10] Why $\mathbb{P}$? Probably becausue it refers to the *P*hysical (real-world) measure. Why $\mathbb{Q}$ then for risk-neutral expectations? I can only imagine that it is because it is the letter after P.

These two probabilities define a new probability distribution, which we denote by $\mathbb{Q}$.[11] Of course, whichever way we choose to describe things, what the investor demands to enter the risky bet does not change. For the two descriptions to be equivalent, we want the expectation with the 'funny' probabilities and the real payoffs to give the same value as the expectation with the real-world probabilities, and the funny (risk-adjusted) payoffs ($S_{up,down} - H$). What does this imply about the 'funny' probabilities $\widetilde{p}^{up}$ and $\widetilde{p}^{down}$?

To answer the question, let's take the expectation of the payoff with respect to this new probability distribution. We have:

$$\mathbb{E}^{\mathbb{Q}}[Payoff(bet)] = \widetilde{p}^{up} S_{up} + \widetilde{p}^{down} S_{down}. \tag{4.6}$$

As we have seen, however, no matter how we choose to describe the set-up, the investor is always willing to pay at most $0.5 \times (S_{up} + S_{down}) - H$ up-front to enter this bet. So we can write

$$\widetilde{p}^{up} S_{up} + \widetilde{p}^{down} S_{down} = p^{up} \times [S_{up} - H] + p^{down} \times [S_{down} - H]$$

$$= 0.5 \times (S_{up} + S_{down}) - H. \tag{4.7}$$

For the two expectations to give the same value ($0.5 \times (S_{up} + S_{down}) - H$) we must have

$$\widetilde{p}^{up} = \frac{1}{2} - \frac{H}{S_{up} - S_{down}} \tag{4.8}$$

and, of course,

$$\widetilde{p}^{down} = \frac{1}{2} + \frac{H}{S_{up} - S_{down}}. \tag{4.9}$$

Exercise 12 *Check that using the risk-neutral probabilities (4.8) and (4.9) and the real payoffs (ie, S_{up} and S_{down}), one gets the correct up-front value of $0.5 \times (S_{up} + S_{down}) - H$.*

The quantities in Equations (4.8) and (4.9) are the so-called risk-neutral probabilities, and the distribution associated with them is called the risk-neutral probability distribution (measure), which is labelled by $\mathbb{Q}$: if we use these 'funny' probabilities the investor can use the same payoffs as in the real world, pretend that she is risk neutral (ie, not ask for the extra compensation, H), and she will correctly account for the inducement she wants over the actuarial price in order to enter the risk bet.

There are several interesting observations. First of all, the state we have denoted by *up* (with payoff S_{up}) denotes the state of the world where the short rate has gone up and the one-period bond at time 1 ($e^{-r_{i+1}^{up} \Delta t}$) has therefore done poorly. This means that $S_{up} - S_{down} < 0$, and therefore the probability of the

---

[11] Textbooks in financial economics refer to $\mathbb{Q}$ as the risk-neutral 'measure'. Saying 'measure' is not the same as saying 'probability distribution', but for our purposes we can gloss over the differences.

'bad' state, $\widetilde{p}^{up}$, is *greater* than the real-world probability, $\frac{1}{2}$. This result is general: the risk-neutral probabilities can be regarded as 'pessimistic' probabilities, ie, probabilities that put extra weight on the bad states of the world. Lengwiler (2004) puts it nicely:

> Risk-neutral probabilities are pessimistic. Suppose that the [investor] is risk averse. Then the risk-neutral distribution is pessimistic in the sense that it puts excessive weight on low-income states [...], and little weight on high-income states. [...] The intuitive reason why the risk-neutral probability must be pessimistic is as follows. One can evaluate a risky situation either by computing the excess return, using the best guesses one has about the probabilities of the different states of the world, and then subtracting a premium for bearing the risk; or simply by considering its expected payoffs, just as a risk-neutral agent would do, but using distorted probabilities that exaggerate the probabilities of bad outcomes.

4.3.2   Introducing the Market Price of Risk

Next, let's look more closely into the risk adjustment quantity, H. We go back to the definitions of r_{i+1}^{up} and r_{i+1}^{down} (Equations (4.1a) and (4.2)):

$$r_{i+1}^{up} = r_i + \kappa(\theta - r_i)\Delta t + \sigma\sqrt{\Delta t} \qquad (4.10a)$$

$$r_{i+1}^{down} = r_i + \kappa(\theta - r_i)\Delta t - \sigma\sqrt{\Delta t}. \qquad (4.11)$$

To make the algebra easier, let's linearize the payoffs S_{up} and S_{down}, and substitute the expressions for r_{i+1}^{up} and r_{i+1}^{down} to give

$$S_{up} = e^{-r_{i+1}^{up}\Delta t} \simeq 1 - r^{up}\Delta t = 1 - \underbrace{[r_i + \kappa(\theta - r_i)\Delta t + \sigma\sqrt{\Delta t}]}_{r_{i+1}^{up}}\Delta t$$

$$(4.12)$$

and

$$S_{down} = e^{-r_{i+1}^{down}\Delta t} \simeq 1 - r^{down}\Delta t$$

$$= 1 - \underbrace{[r_i + \kappa(\theta - r_i)\Delta t - \sigma\sqrt{\Delta t}]}_{r_{i+1}^{down}}\Delta t. \qquad (4.13)$$

Therefore[12]

$$S_{up} - S_{down} = -2\sigma\,\Delta t^{\frac{3}{2}}. \qquad (4.14)$$

---

[12] Where does the strange exponent $\frac{3}{2}$ come from? Recall that σ is the volatility of a rate, and that a rate has dimensions of $[\$][time]^{-1}$. Therefore the dimensions of σ are $[\$][time]^{-\frac{3}{2}}$. So, the product $\sigma\,\Delta t^{\frac{3}{2}}$ just gives a result in dollars, as it should, given the right-hand side. I did tell you that the dimensional analysis introduced in Chapter 2 was going to be useful!

But we have derived above that

$$\tilde{p}^{up} = \frac{1}{2} - \frac{H}{S_{up} - S_{down}}, \tag{4.15}$$

and therefore

$$\tilde{p}^{up} = \frac{1}{2} + \frac{H}{2\sigma \Delta t^{\frac{3}{2}}}. \tag{4.16}$$

(Remember that the payoff in the 'up' state is worse than the payoff in the 'down' state, and therefore $S_{up} - S_{down}$ is negative!)

Now, the probabilities $\tilde{p}^{up}$ and $\tilde{p}^{down}$ are 'funny', but they still have to be probabilities, ie, non-negative quantities between 0 and 1. This puts an upper limit to the compensation, H, that the investor can demand, because $\tilde{p}^{up} \leq 1$:

$$H \leq \sigma \Delta t^{\frac{3}{2}}. \tag{4.17}$$

It is easy to see the financial justification for this upper bound. The investor cannot be too greedy: if she asked as compensation for bearing risk more than $\sigma \Delta t^{\frac{3}{2}}$, it would be for her a heads-I-win-tails-you-lose situation, as she would always make money on her bet.

Expression (4.16) must hold true for any combination of $\sigma \Delta t^{\frac{3}{2}}$. Therefore Equation (4.16) also shows that the compensation, H, must be not just any function of the volatility, but a *linear* function of $\sigma \Delta t^{3/2}$; otherwise, for a choice of time step Δt, there could be volatilities for which the funny probability $\tilde{p}^{up}$ would exceed 1.

One more thing and then we are (almost) done for the time being. Consider the expression for expectation over the *up* and *down* states of the short rate calculated with the funny probabilities. We get

$$\mathbb{E}^{\mathbb{Q}}[r_{i+1}|r_i] = \underbrace{\left(\frac{1}{2} + \frac{H}{2\sigma \Delta t^{\frac{3}{2}}}\right)}_{\tilde{p}^{up}} \times \underbrace{[r_i + \kappa(\theta - r_i)\Delta t + \sigma \sqrt{\Delta t}]}_{r^{up}}$$

$$+ \underbrace{\left(\frac{1}{2} - \frac{H}{2\sigma \Delta t^{\frac{3}{2}}}\right)}_{\tilde{p}^{down}} \times \underbrace{[r_i + \kappa(\theta - r_i)\Delta t - \sigma \sqrt{\Delta t}]}_{r^{down}}$$

$$= [r_i + \kappa(\theta - r_i)\Delta t] + \frac{H}{\Delta t}. \tag{4.18}$$

Now, recall that H has the dimensions of money ($\$$), and that it is the dollar compensation we obtained for bearing risk over the arbitrary time step Δt. We are more interested in the compensation per unit time. So one can write $H = m\Delta t$, for some yield-like quantity, m, which has dimensions of $\$[t]^{-1}$. Therefore we can go back to using the real-world probabilities as long as we write

$$r_{i+1}^{up} = r_i + \kappa(\theta - r_i)\Delta t + m + \sigma \sqrt{\Delta t} \tag{4.19}$$

$$r_{i+1}^{down} = r_i + \kappa(\theta - r_i)\Delta t + m - \sigma \sqrt{\Delta t}. \tag{4.20}$$

Furthermore, since we have established that H must be proportional to $\sigma \Delta t^{\frac{3}{2}}$, let's write the compensation *per unit time*, m, as $\lambda \sigma$. Then we can rewrite the expressions for r_{i+1}^{up} and r_{i+1}^{down} (with some prescience)[13] as

$$r_{i+1}^{up} = r_i + \kappa(\theta - r_i)\Delta t + \lambda \sigma \Delta t + \sigma \sqrt{\Delta t} \tag{4.21}$$

$$r_{i+1}^{down} = r_i + \kappa(\theta - r_i)\Delta t + \lambda \sigma \Delta t - \sigma \sqrt{\Delta t}. \tag{4.22}$$

We can give a nice – if, at this stage, rather heuristic – interpretation to the term $\lambda \sigma \Delta t$. Let's recapitulate 'where it came from': the term H was the compensation (in dollars!) for bearing the risk associated with the bet over the period Δt. We defined the compensation per unit time as m. Since we have established that H had to be proportional to the volatility, σ, then so does the compensation per unit time, m. If we denote the proportionality constant by λ, we get for the compensation term, H, the expression $\lambda \sigma \Delta t$. This compensation term, $\lambda \sigma \Delta t$, is proportional to the time step, Δt, and is proportional to the risk per unit time step, which is just σ. Therefore we can aptly regard the term λ as the compensation for risk per unit time and per unit risk. *It is the 'market price' for bearing the risk associated with the bet in question.*

It is intuitively clear that this new quantity, the market price of risk, will be related to the risk premia of yields of different maturities. We will see the precise relationship between the market price of risk and risk (term) premia in chapters to come.

One last thing. In discrete time steps it is just as convenient to work with symmetric ($\frac{1}{2}$ and $\frac{1}{2}$) or skewed probabilities. However, when we move to the continuous-time limit, it will be immensely more convenient to work with a standard (ie, no-drift) Brownian motion. Equations (4.21) and (4.22) show that we can still work with the convenient symmetric probabilities ($\frac{1}{2}$ and $\frac{1}{2}$), as long as we push the deformation of the distribution into the drift term $\lambda \sigma$.

Exercise 13 *Show that, if λ is a constant, one can rewrite Equations (4.21) and (4.22) as $r_{i+1}^{up,down} = r_i + \kappa \left(\theta' - r_i\right)\Delta t \pm \sigma\sqrt{\Delta t}$. Obtain the expression for θ'.*

Exercise 14 *Repeat the exercise in the (affine) case when λ is of the form $a + br_i$. What changes now in addition to θ? Obtain an expression for the quantities that change.*

As I said, we will revisit this topic extensively throughout the book, and the reader should take the treatment of risk aversion presented above as a foretaste of things to come. The important messages for the moment are the following:

- Risk aversion can be accounted for by skewing the probabilities appropriately, and then valuing the payoffs without any explicit risk correction (the risk correction has gone into the funny probabilities) as if the investor were risk neutral.

---

[13] In Equation (4.21) the quantity λ must have dimensions of $[t]^{-\frac{1}{2}}$.

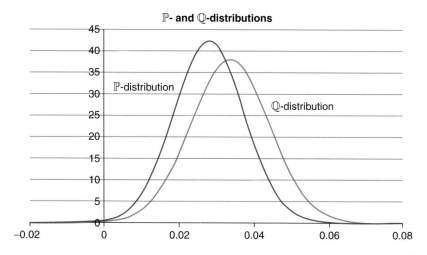

Figure 4.1 A $\mathbb{P}$-distribution and the corresponding deformed $\mathbb{Q}$-distribution. The first moment of the $\mathbb{Q}$-distribution is higher than the first moment of the $\mathbb{P}$-distribution; and the variance of the $\mathbb{Q}$-distribution is higher than the variance of the $\mathbb{P}$-distribution.

- Deforming the probabilities means that the distribution of outcomes for the state variable(s) – the short rate in the preceding example – will change. We start from a set of probabilities that we collectively denote by $\mathbb{P}$ and we produce a new set, which we call $\mathbb{Q}$. When we value assets (such as bonds) we always take expectations using the 'pessimistic' $\mathbb{Q}$ probabilities (which include, but hide, risk aversion).
- If the degree of risk aversion is independent of the state of the world, then the $\mathbb{Q}$-distribution will just be shifted by a rigid amount (in the 'pessimistic' direction) with respect to the $\mathbb{P}$-distribution. However, in general, ie, when the compensation for risk depends on the state of the world, *the whole $\mathbb{P}$-distribution, not just its first moment*, is changed by the introduction of risk aversion.
- Deforming the distribution can be equivalently achieved by working with asymmetric probabilities (which is a pain), or with symmetric probabilities (which is convenient) as long as we push the risk correction into the term $\lambda \sigma \, \Delta t$. This term that re-symmetrizes the probabilities is a *drift* term. This drift term can be a constant or can be state dependent. In the latter case it will deform the higher moments of the $\mathbb{P}$-distribution – as mentioned in the third bullet point.

All of this is shown in Figure 4.1, which displays a $\mathbb{P}$-distribution and the corresponding deformed $\mathbb{Q}$-distribution. As we have seen, in order to compensate for risk aversion, the pessimistic probabilities put more weight on bad states of the world. In the case we have been looking at this means that the first moment of the $\mathbb{Q}$-distribution is higher than the first moment of the $\mathbb{P}$-distribution, but also that the variance of the $\mathbb{Q}$-distribution is higher than the variance of the $\mathbb{P}$-distribution. Differences between the $\mathbb{P}$ and $\mathbb{Q}$ both in the mean and the variance could be obtained for a risk compensation whose magnitude per unit risk depended on the state variable, r_t. More about this later.

4.4   AN IMPORTANT FIRST RESULT: BOND PRICES AS $\mathbb{Q}$-EXPECTATIONS

We are now in a good position to obtain a first important expression for the price of a discount bond.

Consider again the two realizations of the short rate that gave rise to the payoff of the bet. Since the rate on which the bet was based was uncertain, the quantity to guess in the bet cannot have been the short rate prevailing today, r_0: everyone can observe that one. Let's say that it was the rate prevailing from time Δt to time $2\Delta t$, and let's call it r_1. To be clear: the rate r_0 (known today) spans the period from 0 to Δt; the rate r_1 (not known today) refers to the period from time Δt to time $2\Delta t$.

Consider now a two-period discount bond. This will pay \$1 with certainty at time $2\Delta t$. We know its terminal value, but what is the value of that payment today? Discounting from time Δt to today is easy: we can just use the rate r_0. But what about discounting from time $2\Delta t$ to time Δt? If the economy was in the 'up' state we should of course discount by r_1^{up}, and by r_1^{down} if it was in the 'down' state. Since we don't know in which state the economy will be, we must take an expectation over the different ways of discounting. And, to take uncertainty into account, a risk-averse investor should take the expectation using the 'funny', not the real-world, probabilities.

This means that the present value of the certain \$1 paid at time 2 is given by

$$
\begin{aligned}
P_0^2 &= e^{-r_0 \Delta t} \times \left[\widetilde{p}_{up} e^{-r_1^{up} \Delta t} + \widetilde{p}_{down} e^{-r_1^{down} \Delta t} \right] \\
&= \mathbb{E}_0^{\mathbb{Q}} \left[e^{-r_0 \Delta t} e^{-r_1 \Delta t} \right] \\
&= \mathbb{E}_0^{\mathbb{Q}} \left[e^{-\sum_{i=0,1} r_i \Delta t} \right].
\end{aligned}
\tag{4.23}
$$

It is then easy to see that, as we go to the continuous limit and we extend the bond maturity, we get

$$
P_0^T = \mathbb{E}_0^{\mathbb{Q}} \left[e^{-\int_0^T r_s ds} \right].
\tag{4.24}
$$

This is a very important result, as it relates today's price of a discount bond to the funny-probability expectation (the $\mathbb{Q}$-measure expectation) of the exponential of (minus) the path of the short rate from today to the maturity of the bond. We shall revisit (and re-express) this condition in the rest of the book.

By the way, for those readers who are familiar with asset pricing and with changes of measures, the same result can be obtained in one line, by choosing as numeraire, N_t, the money-market account, defined by $N_t = e^{\int_0^t r_s ds}$. Invoking the fact that the relative price, $\frac{P_t^T}{N_t}$, must be a martingale, one gets:

$$\frac{P_0^T}{N_0} = P_0^T = \mathbb{E}^{\mathbb{Q}} \left[\frac{P_T^T}{N_T} \right] = \mathbb{E}^{\mathbb{Q}} \left[\frac{P_T^T}{e^{\int_0^T r_s ds}} \right] = \mathbb{E}^{\mathbb{Q}} \left[\frac{1}{e^{\int_0^T r_s ds}} \right]$$

$$= \mathbb{E}^{\mathbb{Q}} \left[e^{-\int_0^T r_s ds} \right]. \tag{4.25}$$

For those readers who do not know (yet) what a martingale is, the heuristic derivation presented earlier is less elegant, but more transparent, and, for our current purposes, just as good.

4.5 THE PRICE PROCESS AND ITS EXPECTATIONS

This chapter is about the risks to which a bond is exposed. Inflation risk is clearly one of these sources of risk. We shall see that, when looking at the part of the yield of a bond that comes from the compensation for inflation, the concept of break-even inflation is very useful. We need one more ingredient, however, in order to discuss break-even inflation properly, namely, we have to describe the process for the prices, Q_t. For simplicity we can think of the economy as producing one single good, and of Q_t as the price of this one good at time t.

4.5.1 The General Case

In nominal terms, the log of the price of the one good in the economy grows as

$$d \log Q_t = e i_t dt + \sigma_{i,r} dz + v_i dw, \tag{4.26}$$

where ei_t is the *expected* inflation over the next time step at time t, and we have allowed for two orthogonal shocks, one that 'loads onto' nominal rates and inflation ($\sigma_{i,n} dz$), and one orthogonal to it ($v_i dw$). The second shock is typically introduced to account for short-run inflation variations not captured (not 'spanned') by movements in the yield curve.[14] We keep this slightly more cumbersome formalism for future applications, but nothing much would change in what immediately follows if we had a single shock.

A lurid health warning at this point: if we really want to identify the integral of the term $ei_t dt$ with *expected* inflation, as we will, we should have really written

$$\frac{dQ_t}{Q_t} = e i_t dt + \sigma_{i,r} dz + v_i dw,$$

---

[14] See D'Amico, Kim and Wei (2010), p. 8.

not

$$d \log Q_t = ei_t dt + \sigma_{i,r} dz + v_i dw. \tag{4.27}$$

The two expressions differ by a bothersome, but small(ish) and conceptually not-very-important, convexity term (see Chapter 10). For the sake of simplicity, in this section we work with Equation (4.26), but we promise that will be more careful when we revisit the topic later on.

Integrating both sides of Equation (4.26) from t to T we get

$$\log \left(\frac{Q_T}{Q_t} \right) = \int_t^T ei_s ds + \int_t^T \sigma_{i,r} dz_s + \int_t^T v_i dw_s. \tag{4.28}$$

Now, taking expectations and dividing by $(T - t)$, the inflation per unit time expected at time t for horizon T, EI_t^T, is given by

$$\begin{aligned}
EI_t^T &= \frac{1}{T-t} \mathbb{E}_t \left[\log \left(\frac{Q_T}{Q_t} \right) \right] \\
&= \frac{1}{T-t} \mathbb{E}_t \left[\int_t^T ei_s ds + \int_t^T \sigma_{i,r} dz_s + \int_t^T v_i dw_s \right] \\
&= \frac{1}{T-t} \mathbb{E}_t \left[\int_t^T ei_s ds \right].
\end{aligned} \tag{4.29}$$

(In obtaining this result we have used the result mentioned in Chapter 2 that the expectation of on Ito integral – ie, of a quantity like $\int_t^T \sigma_{i,r} dz_s$ – is always zero.)

Why have we kept the expectation on the right-hand side, where we have what looks like an innocent integral over time? Because, in general, the expected inflation will be a function of the state variables of our model: $ei_s = ei(x_s)$. This makes sense: changes in the economy will change our inflation expectations. We do not know what values our state variables (and hence the yield curve and the economy) will have at a future time s, but, conditional on this information, we are saying that we know today what expectations about inflation we will form at time s. We (conditionally) know what we will expect.

4.5.2 The Affine Case

As it happens, very often we will make the assumption that the expected inflation is not just any function, but an *affine* function of the state variable(s):

$$ei(x_s) = \alpha + \beta x_s. \tag{4.30}$$

If this is the case, and if we impose, as we shall invariably do in this book, that the state variables follow a mean-reverting process, then so will the expected inflation. This implies that we will be able to write

$$dei_t = \kappa_{ei}(\theta_{ei} - ei_t)dt + \sigma dB_t. \tag{4.31}$$

If this is the process for the expected inflation, it is easy to derive the value of the expected inflation at a future time T, given its value at time t (which is just what we need in Equation (4.29) to carry out the expectation.) Indeed we will carry out this calculation in Chapter 14. For the moment, we simply note that, when $T = t + dt$, we have

$$\frac{1}{dt} \mathbb{E} \left[\log \left(\frac{Q_{t+dt}}{Q_t} \right) \right] = ei_t \tag{4.32}$$

and therefore, apart from a convexity term, ei_t is exactly the instantaneous *expected* inflation per unit time.

Finally, integrating Equation (4.26) between time t and a generic future time T we have

$$\log \left(\frac{Q_T}{Q_t} \right) = \int_t^T ei_s ds + \int_t^T \sigma_{i,r} dz_s + \int_t^T v_i dw_s$$

$$\implies Q_T = Q_t e^{\int_t^T ei_s ds + \sigma_{i,r} dz_s + v_i dw_s}. \tag{4.33}$$

We call the quantity $\log(\frac{Q_T}{Q_t})$ the realized cumulative inflation from time t to time T.

In writing these equations we have been uncharacteristically coy about whether we are taking a real-world expectation or a risk-neutral expectation. This is an important question, but a proper discussion will have to be deferred until we have introduced the conditions of no arbitrage for real bonds in Chapter 14.

4.6 NOMINAL RATES, INFLATION AND REAL RATES: DEFINITIONS

Suppose that in the market two different types of securities exist, nominal and real bonds.[15] If I invest \$1 at time t in a T-maturity nominal bond I get with certainty the amount \$$\frac{1}{P_t^{nom,T}}$ at maturity, T.

The nominal yield from the nominal bond, y_t^T, is given by

$$y_t^{nom,T} = -\frac{1}{T-t} \log P_t^{nom,T}. \tag{4.34}$$

Similarly we can define the real yield of a real bond as

$$y_t^{real,T} = -\frac{1}{T-t} \log P_t^{real,T}. \tag{4.35}$$

---

[15] In the market, 'real' bonds are often referred to as 'inflation-linked' bonds. (Evans (1998) distinguishes between real bonds and inflation-linked bonds according to whether there is an indexation lag or not. We do not deal with this practically important, but messy and theoretically irrelevant, issue.) This is fine, but confusion creeps in when they are also called 'inflation bonds', because, with this sloppy choice of words, a real bond is an inflation bond – not helpful. To avoid confusion, in this book we shall interchangeably speak of real or inflation-linked bonds, but never of inflation bonds.

This suggests that we can also define a new quantity, the time-t, maturity-T break-even inflation, $BEI_{t,T}$, by the relationship

$$BEI_{t,T} \equiv y_t^{nom,T} - y_t^{real,T}. \tag{4.36}$$

Now, we can define anything we want, but the interesting question is the following: is the break-even inflation we just defined equal to the expected inflation, EI_t^T, that we defined at the end of the previous section? The answer is: 'it depends'. If the expectation is taken in the real-world measure, then we will show that

$$BEI_{t,T} = \left(EI_t^T\right)^{\mathbb{P}} + \mathcal{P}_t^T, \tag{4.37}$$

where $\mathcal{P}_t^T$ is the real premium required by an investor in order to bear real-rate risk. (We have written $\left(EI_t^T\right)^{\mathbb{P}}$ to remind ourselves that we took the expectation in the real-world measure.) Would then be the case that

$$BEI_{t,T} =? = \left(EI_t^T\right)^{\mathbb{Q}} \tag{4.38}$$

if we took the expectation in the risk-neutral measure? Not quite, as we will show that another correction term is needed to make the relation an equality.

Is there some way, then, to take the expectation of the growth of the price process such that

$$BEI_{t,T} = \left(EI_t^T\right)^{\mathbb{X}}? \tag{4.39}$$

(Which means: is there *some* measure, $\mathbb{X}$, under which break-even inflation is equal to the expectation of the growth of the price process?) The answer is, *yes*, but, again, we will have to wait until Chapter 14 to understand how to find this measure.

CHAPTER 5

The Risk Factors in Action

5.1 THE PURPOSE OF THIS CHAPTER

The discussion about risk factors presented in the previous chapter may have seemed a bit abstract. In this chapter we therefore put some empirical flesh on the theoretical bones. We do so by looking in some detail at the US yield curve after the Great Recession, and in the summer of 2013 in particular. The reason for doing so is that what happened in this period gives a clear illustration of 'risk factors in action'.

In Chapter 4 we argued that expectations about inflation and real rates, and the attending risk factors, are in principle all embedded in the observed bond yields. Can we say something more precise? For instance, are investors currently reaping a greater compensation for bearing inflation risk, or real-rate risk? Has the ratio of the inflation-to-real-rate risk compensation changed over time?

To answer these questions we examine the joint evidence coming from recent changes in prices of nominal and real Treasury bonds. We will draw the conclusion that, in the twenty-first century, real rates and real-rate premia have been the main drivers of yield curve changes. (This may not have been the case in periods such as the 1970s when inflation was a major concern, but, unfortunately, we do not have real-bond data for that period to test this hypothesis.)

5.2 EXPECTATIONS AND RISK PREMIA DURING AN IMPORTANT MARKET PERIOD

5.2.1 An Account of What Happened

Economics and finance are plagued by the fact that controlled and repeatable experiments are hardly, if ever, possible. Fortunately, sometimes market conditions and external events occur in combinations not too dissimilar from what a keen experimentalist would have set up if she had been allowed to play God. If we want to understand the interplay between expectations and risk premia

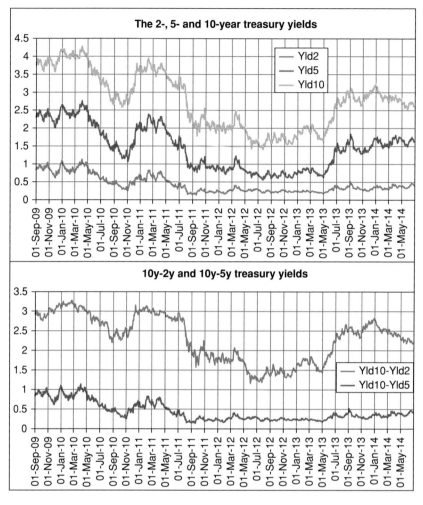

Figure 5.1 The behaviour from September 2009 to June 2014 of the 2-year, 5-year and 10-year nominal yields of Treasuries, as proxied by the 2.5% Treasury maturing 15 May 2024, the 1 5/8% Treasury maturing 30 June 2019, and the 0 1/2% Treasury maturing 30 June 2016. The bottom half of the graph shows the difference between the 10-year proxy yield and the 5-year and the 2-year proxy yields, respectively.

(both for real and for nominal rates), the summer of 2013 provided one of these rare 'real-life laboratory experiments'.

To understand why, let's begin by looking at Figure 5.1, which shows the 10-year, 5-year and 2-year Treasury yields. The first (rather obvious) observation is that, as a response to monetary actions in the wake of the Great Recession of 2007–2009, all these nominal Treasury yields came down (bonds became more expensive) very significantly from late 2009 until early summer of 2013.

Looking at the same figure, we also note a particularly pronounced drop in yields in the second half of 2011. It was in this period that the then-Chairman of the Fed, Ben Bernanke, indicated that rates would remain low for an extended period of time. After this announcement all yields declined, but the fall was particularly pronounced for short-dated yields: the 2-year rate, for instance, declined to approximately a quarter of a percentage point, and remained almost constant at this level until the early summer of 2013. Not only that: note also how the 2-year yield barely showed the up-and-down round trip displayed by the 5- and 10-year yields in the spring of 2012.

This behaviour for the 2-year rate is consistent with an explanation in terms of *expectations*. More precisely, if the words of the Fed were to be believed, the period of rate repression would certainly extend well beyond two years; since yields are (approximately) risk-adjusted averages of expected paths of the short rate, it is then natural to explain the behaviour of the 2-year yield as driven by the *expectation* that the short rate (say, the Fed funds) would remain constant and low.

Note also that, to the extent that investors fully believed in the commitment by the Fed to keep rates low for an extended period of time, there would be no uncertainty about the path of the Fed funds over the short term. No uncertainty means no compensation for uncertainty, and no risk premium. We would therefore expect hardly any term premia to attach to yields up to, approximately, two years.

Why were the 5- and 10-year yields not as constant during this period? If there was uncertainty about the timing of the switch from the exceptionally accommodative monetary conditions to more normal rates, this would be reflected in the 5-year and, in a more pronounced fashion, in the 10-year yield. So, their behaviour *could* be explained, at least in part, in terms of changing expectations about the timing of monetary actions. Note, however, that, the moment we say that investors were *uncertain* about the path of rates beyond, say, a two-year horizon, we immediately bring into play the possibility of a risk premium attaching to this degree of uncertainty.

This was the state of affairs, when, in late May 2013 the then-Chairman of the Fed made a statement about the 'tapering' of the accommodative monetary conditions that had been put in place in the prior two years.[1]

His comments were understood at the time to mean that the market had overestimated the duration of the exceptionally accommodative monetary conditions. Immediately after this announcement, longer-dated yields moved up, with the 10-year yield increasing by almost 100 basis points in a relatively short period of time. Several weeks later, Chairman Bernanke clarified the meaning of his May statement, and suggested that the market may have misinterpreted what he meant when he referred to the speed of the 'tapering'. Longer-dated

---

[1] As a matter of fact, the 'tapering' language actually appeared in the question-and-answer session after Chairman Bernanke's testimony. In the testimony itself the word 'taper' does not appear at all. See Bernanke (2013).

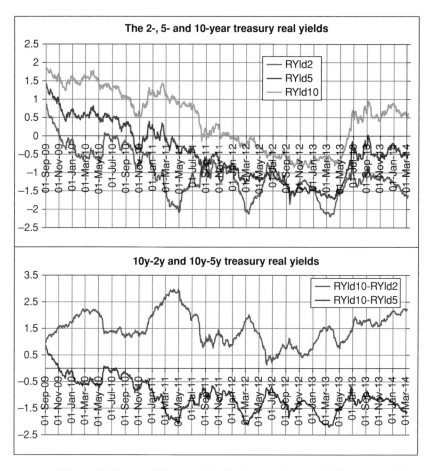

Figure 5.2 Same as Figure 5.1 for the 2-year, 5-year and 10-year real yields of Treasuries, as proxied by the 0 5/8% Treasury (TIPS) maturing 15 January 2024, the 0 1/8% Treasury maturing 15 April 2019 and the 0 1/8% Treasury maturing 15 April 2016. Also in this case the period shown covers September 2009 to June 2014.

yields promptly came down, although not nearly as much as they had gone up in late May. See again Figure 5.1.

The picture becomes more interesting if we couple information about nominal yields (that incorporate information about expectations and risk premia for inflation and real rates) with information about real yields (that incorporate information about expectations and risk premia only for real rates). See Figure 5.2.

What can we deduce from these figures? First of all, we note a pattern of protracted decline/sharp increase/modest decline for the 2-, 5- and 10-year *real* yields similar to what observed for nominal yields. This points to the

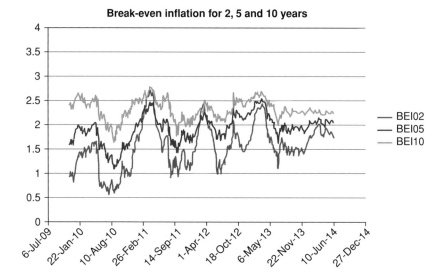

Figure 5.3 The break-even inflation for the 2- (blue curve), 5- (red curve) and 10-year yields (green curve) from the data by Gurkaynak, Sack and Wright (2000, 2006).

first observation that real yields (ie, expectations thereof, plus the associated risk premium) certainly played a role in explaining the observed changes in nominal yields.

By taking the difference between the nominal and the real yields we can also look at the break-even inflation – which, we must remember, reflects both the expectations about future inflation and the associated risk premium. This quantity is shown in Figure 5.3 for the zero-coupon data from Gurkaynak et al. (2000, 2006). If we fix our attention on the 10-year break-even inflation, we see that the increase in break-even inflation after the Bernanke tapering speech (late May 2013) was by less than 50 basis points, while the increase in the nominal rate was by more than 100 basis points. Break-even inflation, as we have seen in Section 4.6, reflect inflation expectations and inflation risk premia. So, a change in either the expectations about, or in the risk premium associated with, the real rate must have played an important role in the observed increase in nominal yields.

5.2.2 Possible Explanations of What Happened

How can one account for this complex behaviour? By making reference to the Bernanke 'tapering speech', I hinted earlier at the plausibility of an expectation-driven explanation in the 2009–2013 period. But this is neither a full account of what happened, nor, indeed, the only way to understand the observed behaviour of yields. For instance, did the decrease in yields in the pre–May

2013 period occur because inflation expectations decreased? Or because the monetary authorities, in their attempt to stimulate the then-still-ailing economy, endeavoured and committed to bring down *real* rates for an extended period whatever the inflation would turn out to be?[2] There was a lot of talk at the time of the investors' 'hunger for yield'. This can be understood, for instance, in terms of the need by institutional players with fixed nominal liabilities, or who had made high-real-rate promises, to invest in riskier securities. Of course, if expectations do not change, by doing so they would bring down the attached risk premia. Was then this 'hunger for yield' responsible for risk premia becoming so compressed as to become negative? And what was the part played in this by a reduction in the inflation risk premium (over and above a reduction in inflation expectations)? Had the inflation risk premium all but disappeared simply because it was felt at the time that central banks had won their credibility stripes in their two-decade-long fight against inflation, and could now be 'trusted'?

The range of possible explanations then became even wider after May 2013, as lack of clarity about what the Fed 'really meant' with the 'tapering language' increased uncertainty, and therefore, arguably, risk premia. So, did investors think that rates would go up more quickly than had been previously anticipated? Or did the sudden increase in the summer of 2013 occur because investors became more uncertain about real rates, and the associated risk premia suddenly increased? (The latter, by the way, is the explanation offered by some popular structural models, which we will discuss in Chapters 31 to 34.)

And one must not forget that, in their attempts to stimulate an ailing world economy, at the time central banks were engaging in complex forms of money-printing – an activity that, in normal economic conditions is very likely to stoke up inflation. Were investors becoming sufficiently uncertain about inflation to demand a higher risk premium? If so, the fall in inflation *expectations* would have had to be truly dramatic to account for the observed market yields.

The point here is that expectations of course matter, but risk premia matter too. And the uncertainty, which is at the root of risk premia, is both about inflation and about real rates. We can all spin stories about 'inflation expectations' or 'declining real yields' faster than we can say 'state-dependent risk premia', but, if we want to engage in something firmer than fireside story-telling, it is essential to check whether the output of our mythopoiesis squares with what the empirical evidence, and the models that organize this evidence, tell us. We will discuss what the models and statistical analysis have to say about these events in later parts of the book.

Of course, we don't have to accept the exact decomposition between expectations and risk premia that a model produces,[3] but, if we reject what a model

---

[2] It is not surprising that this may have been the case. As explained in Chapter 15, this lowering of real rates is, after all, the main goal of the monetary authorities in periods of sluggish growth.

[3] Indeed, in Chapter 31 we discuss in detail why the model outputs about risk premia for the 2010–2015 period should be looked at with greater-than-usual suspicion.

says, we should make sure that we can articulate in a coherent fashion the reason why we think that 'this time it's different'.

This is easier said than done. We are all familiar with expectations, so much so that we almost cannot stop ourselves from forming views about how things will unfold. We can also tap into information sources by looking at what pundits say, by reading the minutes of central bankers who provide 'forward guidance', by looking at the professional surveys, etc. All of this information is expectations based and expectations focussed. What we are less comfortable with are risk premia, which may seem sometimes like glorified 'balancing items' to reconcile expected and observed yields. We neglect them, however, at our peril.

During the period 2012–2014, most estimates were pointing to negative or barely positive risk premia both for nominal and for real bonds. In the late 1990s similar estimates suggested risk premia of the order of 3%. And during periods of very high inflation, the inflation risk premium might have been of the same order of magnitude as the expected inflation itself. (We just don't know, because Treasury real bonds were not in issuance at the time.) These are very big differences indeed.

Does it matter whether a given change in the observed yields is due to changes in expectations or in the risk premia? If risk premia are not constant (and the overwhelming empirical evidence points to the conclusion that they are not), it certainly does matter for a bond investor, who would like to know whether, at a given point in time, she is being handsomely or meagerly compensated for taking inflation and real-rate risk on board. Risk premia do not matter in derivatives pricing (which rely on supposedly perfect hedging), but become all-important for investing.

If risk premia matter so much, how can we try to *measure* these ethereal quantities? We will answer this question precisely in Part VI of this book, but, for the moment, it is useful to give a first intuitive answer.

5.3 HOW CAN WE ESTIMATE RISK PREMIA?

Let's for the moment make the assumption that the risk premia are constant – as mentioned earlier and as we shall discuss at length in Part VI and Chapter 8 (see Section 8.6 in particular), this is *not* a good assumption, but it will keep the discussion simple for the moment.

Consider the following strategy, which is an example of the excess-return-extracting strategies discussed in detail in Chapter 23. An investor buys an n-year discount *real* (ie, inflation-linked) bond, and funds it by selling a 1-year discount real bond. After one year, she unwinds her position and records her profit or loss. She does so for 100 years. She keeps a tally of her cumulative profit or loss.

At the end of each investment period she is not exposed to realized inflation, because both bonds in her portfolio are exposed to the same realized inflation that occurred over each investment period of one year. If, over the long run, her buy-long-fund-short strategy earns her a compensation, this can therefore be due only to the real-rate risk premium. Let's write this number down on a piece of paper.

Now, during the same 100-year period the patient investor has also entered a similar buy-long-fund-short strategy, but with *nominal* bonds: she buys an *n*-year discount *nominal* bond, and funds it by selling a 1-year discount nominal bond. After one year, she unwinds her position and records her profit or loss. At the end of her century of investing she looks at the profit per annum that she has earned. Since nominal bonds are exposed to real-rate risk, some of this profit must come from the real-rate risk premium. But there should be another compensation on top of it: the inflation risk premium. Which of the two, the real-rate or the inflation risk premium, is larger is an empirical question, which we shall address in Section 5.5.

The point of this thought-experiment is that, at least in theory, by looking at the excess returns earned by the buy-long-fund-short strategies applied to real and nominal bonds we can measure and decompose both risk premia. We shall see in Part VI of this book how closely we can carry out this decomposition in practice.

5.4   DIFFERENT TYPES OF RISK PREMIA

In Chapter 4 we looked briefly at the monetary economics background to yield-curve dynamics. In Chapter 15 we will establish some links with micro- and macroeconomics. In all of these treatments, risk premia come to the fore, because we associate them with the compensation an investor would require because of her uncertainty about, say, expected inflation, the output gap or the level of real economic activity.

The first risk premium (the inflation risk premium) can be easily recognized in the discussion we have presented in this chapter. But what about the uncertainty about, say, the output gap? The output gap certainly informs the monetary decisions of central bankers, and therefore bond prices. If investors (and central bankers) are uncertain about the future output gap, should there be an 'output-gap risk premium'? And, since a 'new' risk premium has just popped up apparently out of thin air, are more surprises waiting in the wings? What about a risk premium for, say, uncertain real activity? How many types of risk premia are *really* there?

As we discussed earlier in this chapter, *every* source of uncertainty that affects prices carries with it a possible compensation. (We mentioned, for instance, compensation for uncertain volatility and the liquidity risk premia.) We must be careful, however, not to double count. 'Risks', and the associated risk premia, do not necessarily nicely decompose in a unique manner. Depending on how we look at the drivers of the dynamics of the yield curve, we can identify different, or, rather, partly overlapping, sources of risk. In a reduced-form description, for instance, one may identify 'level' risk ('duration') and slope risk. But one can ask oneself: what makes the level and slope of the yield curve change? One factor is certainly expectations about future rate increases.

And why do we expect rates to increase or decrease? Perhaps because we expect the monetary authorities to react either to perceived inflationary pressure or to a widening or narrowing output gap. So, level and slope risk on the one hand, and output-gap risk on the other, although not exactly 'the same thing', are clearly related, as Figure 5.4 clearly shows.[4] (The correlation in levels between the two time series is a respectable 52.2%.) The point is that prima facie very different sources of risk may not be not independent, but can 'overlap' depending on the type of description that we employ. In modelling terms, depending on our choice of state variables.

Of course, just as there are apparently different, but ultimately equivalent, sources of risk, so there are also different, but equivalent, ways of parsing risk premia: we can think in terms of compensation for inflation risk and of compensation for real rate risk, as we have done in this chapter; or of compensation for uncertainty in the target rate, the short rate, the reversion level etc; or, if one used different state variables, one may have compensation for uncertainty in output gap and in the real economic growth.

All these quantities are linked, and, to some extent, choosing one type of description instead of another it is like using, say, spherical instead of cylindrical coordinates: there is nothing fundamental about the choice, but, as anyone knows who has tried to solve the problem of planetary motion in Cartesian coordinates, a good choice of coordinates can make all the difference between a happy and a miserable life. The important thing is that the variables we have chosen should 'span' all the (important) risks that affect the yield curve. See in this respect the discussion in Section 1.5.2 in Chapter 1, and in more detail, in Chapter 29.

Why did we qualify the statement in the previous paragraph with the words 'to some extent'? Because macrofinancial sources of risk may not be necessarily 'translatable' into risks associated with yield-curve variables – such as yields, forward rates, principal components, etc. If we switch from Cartesian to spherical coordinates we do not leave anything by the wayside. This is not necessarily true if we decide to use sources of risk associated only with yield curve variables. We will discuss this important point in detail in Chapter 27, where we discuss the work by Ludvigson and Ng (2009), but it is important to alert the reader to this important caveat at this early stage.

Be as it may, in this book we mainly, but not exclusively, adopt a reduced-form approach (for instance, we often choose as our 'coordinates' the level, slope and curvature of the yield curve); at times, we may choose more fundamental variables, such as the market price of risk itself (see Chapter 35);

---

[4] 'Real Potential GDP, Real Nominal GDP, and the Natural Rate of Unemployment are figures taken directly from the [Congressional Budget Office]'s 'Key Assumptions in CBO's Projection of Potential Output' table. These numbers reflect the quarterly historical and projected estimates of potential GDP and the NAIRU, or nonaccelerating inflation rate of unemployment. The nominal output gap is a Bloomberg-calculated value that uses the CBO data as the Potential GDP source and GDP CUR$ Index as the nominal GDP source. Positive output gap numbers indicate over-utilization, and negative numbers reflect under-utilization' (Bloomberg, 2014).

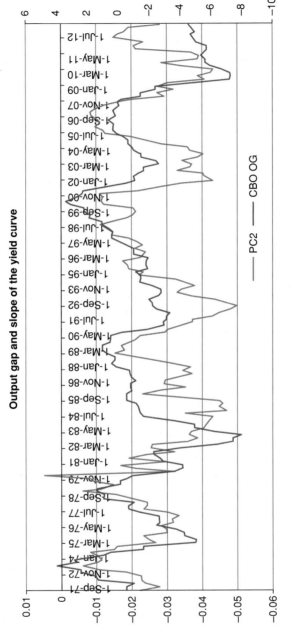

Figure 5.4 The output gap in the economy (right-hand *y*-axis, curve labelled CBO OG) and the second principal component (the slope) of the yield curve (left-hand *y*-axis, curve with crosses labelled PC2) for the period 1971–2013.

Table 5.1 *The R^2 statistic from regressing the 10-year nominal yield against the 10-year break-even inflation, the 10-year real yield and the VIX index for the period 2 Jan 04–24 Jun 14 (left-hand column) and from regressing the 10-year break-even inflation against the 10-year nominal yields, the 10-year real yields and the VIX index, also for the period 2 Jan 04–24 Jun 14 unless otherwise indicated, (right-hand column). All regressions in levels (not differences). All regression coefficients are very strongly significant, all at least at the 95% confidence level, and most at the 99%.*

R^2 (Nominal yields) (2 Jan 04–24 Jun 14)	R^2 (BEI)
Nominal vs. BEI = 8.3%	BEI vs. Nominal = 8.3%
Nominal vs. Real = 87.5%	BEI vs. VIX = 56.5%
Nominal vs. VIX = 1.3%	BEI vs. Real = 0.0%
	BEI vs. VIX (Jun 04–Jan 08) = 0.0%
	BEI vs. VIX (Jun 10–Jun 14) = 18.9%

and sometimes, as we shall see, we may use latent (unspecified, unidentifiable) variables. It is important, however, to keep in the back of our mind the fundamental link between the variables we choose to use, and the more fundamental drivers discussed in the previous chapter. As we do so, we must always ask ourselves whether we have done enough to capture, *one way or another*, the main economic risks that affect the yield curve.

5.5 WHAT ARE INVESTORS COMPENSATED FOR?

5.5.1 Decomposition of the Risk Premium

We will look at risk premia and excess returns in detail in Part VI, but we can already begin to gather some clues in order to answer one the central questions addressed in this book: have investors in the twenty-first century required more compensation for real risk, or inflation risk?

To venture a first answer, we can start from the observation that a nominal yield is given by the sum of the corresponding real yield and the break-even inflation. This is just an 'accounting identity' and conveys nothing very profound, since we define the break-even inflation as the difference between two market observable quantities, the nominal and the real yield.

The question, however, becomes more interesting when we move from a static to a dynamic perspective, and ask ourselves whether changes in nominal yields can be best accounted for by changes in real yields or in the break-even inflation. We can try to answer this question because the real yield can be estimated from a set of instruments (TIPS bonds) that isolate one of the two sources of risk to which nominal yields are exposed.

To carry out this decomposition, we can regress nominal yields against the break-even inflation and the real yield. The result are shown in Table 5.1.

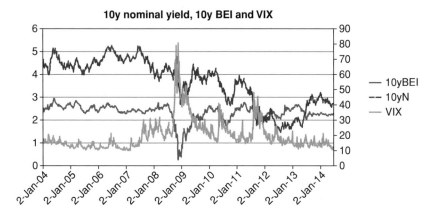

Figure 5.5 Time series of the 10-year nominal yield, 10-year break-even inflation and of the VIX index for the 2-Jan-2004–24 Jun-2014 period.

These regressions suggest several interesting observations. (See also Figure 5.5.) First of all, it is clear from Table 5.1 that, at least during the period under consideration, the level of the nominal rates was driven by the real rate (R^2 of 87.5%), not by the break-even inflation (R^2 of only 8.35%). The picture may have been very different in the 1970s, but, alas, TIPS had not been issued at the time. These results should be looked at together with the analysis (discussed in Chapter 25, Section 25.9) of the split of the nominal risk premium into its real-rate and inflation components. As we shall see, we find that since the early 2000s most of the risk premium is attributable to real-rate risk.

The second interesting observation is the strong dependence between the break-even inflation and the VIX. We note that the dependence is negative: when uncertainty (proxied by the VIX) increases, the break-even inflation decreases.

To understand this relationship, we have to enrich the definition of break-even inflation presented in Equation (4.37). As we will derive in Chapter 14 and in Chapter 31, break-even inflation is actually the sum of real-world inflation expectations, $\mathbb{E}(I_t^T)^{\mathbb{P}}$, of inflation risk premium, $\mathcal{P}_t^T$ and of a TIPS liquidity component, $\mathcal{L}_t^T$:

$$BEI_{t,T} = \mathbb{E}\left(I_t^T\right)^{\mathbb{P}} + \mathcal{P}_t^T + \mathcal{L}_t^T. \tag{5.1}$$

Now, in conditions of market turmoil we expect two things to happen: uncertainty will increase (driving up risk premia), and liquidity will deteriorate (reducing the liquidity contribution to the break-even inflation, $\mathcal{L}_t^T$).[5] A quick-and-ready proxy for market turmoil is the VIX index, often luridly

---

[5] Why so? Because when liquidity deteriorates, the price of the relatively less liquid TIPS goes down relative to the nominal Treasury bonds, which means that 'less future inflation' is required for TIPS to give the same return as the nominal bonds. This in turn means that the breakeven inflation as a whole, and the liquidity component, $\mathcal{L}_t^T$, in particular, will decrease.

referred to in the financial press as the 'fear index'. And, indeed, when we regress the break-even inflation against the VIX we get a very high R^2 (56.5%).

So, we know that there is a dependence between the break-even inflation and the degree of market turmoil. But why?

When markets become unsettled investors may become more fearful, and they may demand greater compensation for taking risk. During the same unsettled times, however, also liquidity deteriorates. Is the dependence of break-even inflation on the VIX then realized because of a change in the risk aversion (reflected in the risk premium, $\mathcal{P}_t^T$) or in the liquidity factor, $\mathcal{L}_t^T$? We can answer this question because nominal Treasury bonds respond to inflation risk but are virtually immune to liquidity risk[6], while inflation-linked bonds are insulated from inflation risk, but respond (negatively) to serious liquidity shocks.

The first part of the question can then be stated as follows: during periods of turmoil i) inflation risk premia may increase, ii) real-rate risk premia may increase and iii) liquidity may deteriorate. Which is true?

If uncertainty were to increase the inflation risk premium or the real-rate risk premium, we would see this dependence filtering through to the nominal yields. However, we do not see this (see the regressions on the left panel of Table 5.1).

If, instead, during periods of turmoil changes in yields of inflation-linked bonds were due mainly to a deterioration in liquidity, and nominal bonds acted as safe-havens, we would see no dependence between nominal yields and the turmoil proxy (the VIX) – and indeed we don't – but a clear dependence between the VIX index and the inflation-linked bonds (and we do – see the regressions in the right-hand column.)

However, things are a bit more nuanced. If we exclude the Lehman period and its aftermath, the correlation between BEI and VIX drops to very small values. This seems to indicate that liquidity (proxied by the VIX) affects the prices of TIPS only in periods of major dislocations. We discuss this important point in the section that follows.

5.5.2 'Which' Liquidity Are TIPS-Investors Compensated For?

D'Amico, Kim and Wei (2010) reach conclusions similar to the ones we reached in the previous sub-section, and also point to liquidity as the extra factor to which TIPS, but not Treasuries, are exposed. However, there is liquidity and liquidity.

There is a run-of-the-mill, garden-variety reduction in liquidity, which manifests itself in somewhat higher transaction costs for some instruments (say, TIPS) than for others (say on-the-run Treasuries) in choppy, but still close-to-normal market conditions; and there is the very severe reduction in liquidity (inability to trade in meaningful size without incurring punitive bid-offer spreads) that sets in during period of exceptional market

---

[6] If anything, they may even enjoy a liquidity and quality premium during periods of serious crisis.

dislocations. Which 'type of liquidity' is more significantly affecting the break-even inflation?

To answer this question, we ran the regression of the break-even inflation for the period before, but excluding, the 2008 Lehman event (2 June 2004/30 Dec 2007), and for the period after, but again excluding, the same event (2 Jan 2010/24 June 2014). The idea is that the pre- and post-Lehman periods reflect 'normally choppy' market conditions, while, in this respect the Lehmans events stand in a class of their own.

As the table shows, the correlation between break-even liquidity and our turmoil proxy (which is strong for the whole period) is totally absent in the pre-Lehman period, and markedly weaker (18.9%) in the post-Lehman period than for the whole sample.

Now, there is ample evidence (see, for instance the discussion in D'Amico et al. (2010)) that the TIPS market became progressively deeper and better established in the years after its introduction – which is what happens for virtually every successful market. So, if run-of-the-mill lack of liquidity affected the TIPS yields, then we should arguably see a greater correlation with our liquidity proxy in the first portion of the data. If anything (and if the level of the VIX is a good proxy for poor liquidity), we observe the opposite.

If we add to this the very high correlation between the VIX and the break-even inflation when the Lehman period is included, we are led to conclude that it is the 'major-stress liquidity shocks', and not the progressive improvement in the run-of-the-mill liquidity, that affect the break-even inflation.

In sum, the analysis in this section suggests that, in the 2004–2014 period

- the main factor in the reduction in the nominal yields has been a reduction in real yields;
- if there is a substantial risk premium to nominal yields, this should be attributable mainly to a real-risk, not an inflation, risk premium; and
- break-even rates are strongly affected by liquidity – as it appears, especially so during periods of high market turmoil.

5.6 WHAT IS AND WHAT IS NOT A *TRUE* RISK PREMIUM

In the economy that we sketched with a broad brush in the previous sections of this chapter, and that we will revisit in greater detail in Chapter 9, the only reason for the existence a 'wedge' between the market yields and the expectation over the paths of the short rate is the degree of risk aversion of the investors in the economy.[7] In this picture the market price of risk is truly the price the market assigns *to risk*.[8]

---

[7] To be a bit more precise, we shall show in Chapter 15 that a positive risk premium is a compensation for getting good payoffs in states of the world when we feel rich, and poor payoffs when we would most like to have some extra cash. A negative risk premium attaches to a security that pays well in bad states of the world, and badly when the economy as a whole does well.

[8] Again, to be a bit more precise, it is linked to the covariance between the payoff of a security and our expected consumption growth – see footnote 11 in Section 15.5 of Chapter 15.

Suppose that we establish, perhaps via surveys, or on the basis of the forward guidance provided by central bankers (as embodied, for instance, the Fed 'blue dots' discussed in Chapter 35), what the expectations of real rates and inflation are. We also observe the market yields. In the sublunar world that we inhabit (as opposed to the stylized economy in which we build our models) we then observe a difference between these expectations and the market yields. Can we really say that this difference is due only to a compensation for inflation and real-rate risk?

The question is far from academic: in the second half of 2014, for instance, the path of the target rate projected by the Fed to various horizons was stubbornly above the corresponding market yields. Was it then the case that in the latter part of 2014 investors became risk-lovers? Or, perhaps, in this period did investors consider Treasury bonds to be such a good hedge against equity risk that they were prepared to pay an insurance premium for the protection they were hoped to afford? Or were there factors other than risk aversion at play that could explain the (in this case negative) difference between yields and expectations? And, if so, what could these factors be?

To answer the question, we can look at long-term yields, which fell significantly in all major bond markets in 2004–2005, just as the Fed, under the direction of the then-chairman Alan Greenspan, was *raising* the policy rates. As Joyce, Kaminska and Lildholdt (2008) say, "[t]his phenomenon was famously described as a 'conundrum'. Several explanations have been put forward to explain the conundrum. Some point to a reduced perception of risk, and a reduced risk aversion, due to the macroeconomic stability of the period. (This, by the way, is the type of explanation a structural model would readily 'understand'.) Other explanations, however, offer themselves, such as 'the portfolio inflows into bonds from Asian central banks', the 'strong demand from pension funds', the 'search for yield, which could have driven up the demand for riskier but higher yielding assets'.[9]

More generally, it is generally agreed (see, eg, Kim and Wright (2005)) that risk premia in US Treasuries fell broadly during the 2000s. Did this happen because investors cared less about risk, or because they perceived less risk to be on the horizon? Or, if we look for different explanations, what could these other risk-premia-reducing factors be?

Kim and Wright (2005)[10] mention a few.

1. The first explanation points to demand for Treasuries from foreign high-growth, high-saving countries. The purchase of Treasuries by the Chinese monetary authorities is a point in case. This is the 'savings glut' explanation.

2. Another explanation points to the regulatory demands (in the United States, the United Kingdom and Europe) that pension funds should better match their liabilities with fixed-income products.

---

[9] Joyce et al. (2008), p. 3.   [10] p. 3 and passim.

3. Low long-term yields could be explained by a reduced appetite from corporates in Western economies for capital spending relative to their profits: as a smaller proportion of the profits are invested, a larger fraction is saved, contributing to the 'savings glut'.
4. As the baby-boom generation approached and entered retirement in the first decade of the new century, it is plausible that their portfolios should have been progressively tilted towards fixed-income products at the expenses of 'riskier' equity holdings.

Whatever the true cause, Kim and Wright (2005) point out that

> …term premium estimates […] should be thought of as "catch-all" measures that combine all of these effects and *indeed anything else that might affect the price of Treasury securities other than expected future monetary policy…*[11]

Does it matter where the quantity we call risk premia 'really' comes from? It does not, if we simply want to *describe* the yield curve. However, it does matter if we want to understand, predict, or intervene. We explain why in the next section.

5.7 DOES IT MATTER IF A RISK PREMIUM IS 'REALLY' A RISK PREMIUM?

Let's start from intervening. This can take at least two forms. One is investing (see later). The other is through the conduct of monetary policy.

For the latter, understanding whether an observed difference between observed market yields and their expectations is 'really' a risk premium – and, if it is, for which perceived risk investors are seeking compensation – obviously matters a lot. As Joyce et al. (2008) point out

> [u]nderstanding the causes of low long real rates matters for monetary policy makers, not least because different explanations have correspondingly different implications for monetary conditions. If, for example, low real rates are due to lower investor risk aversion, the response of monetary policy may differ from the scenario where they reflect expectations of weaker long-term growth. There are also implications regarding the risks of long rates reverting to more normal, higher levels. For example, if low long real rates reflect a temporary rather than a permanent shock, there is a greater risk of a sharp upward adjustment in borrowing rates, which would be disruptive for the real economy.

And, of course, the parsing of the expectations-versus-risk-premium tea leaves affects the conduct of monetary policy (ie, affects where the 'short rate' will be). As we show in Chapters 11 and 12, today's bond prices are linked to the expectation of the path of future rates. So the bond prices that central bankers observe today to distil risk premia and expectations embed the investors' expectations of where the future short rate will be. The same central bankers therefore

---

[11] Ibid., p. 5, emphasis added.

base, at least in part, their decision of where to move the short rate by taking their cue from where the bond prices are. There is a nice reflexivity here...

Let's then take the perspective of an investor. As we will show in Chapter 15, according to finance theory an asset can provide a positive risk premium (have a positive Sharpe Ratio) only if it pays well in states of the world in which investors already feel rich. We will prove this result, but the intuition about why this should be the case is simple: assume the reverse, ie, assume that an asset paid handsomely in these states of the world in which we feel poor. If it did, it would act as an insurance policy. With insurance policies, we typically pay above the odds for peace of mind; we don't invest in them to become rich.

Now, if all assets with positive Sharpe Ratios had positive Sharpe Ratios because of 'true' risk premia, then they would all pay well roughly at the same time, ie, when the investor feels rich already. At least in a one-factor economy, the investor could not create a 'diversified portfolio' of positive-Sharpe-Ratio, true-risk-premium assets.

If the positive Sharpe Ratio, however, originated not from a 'true' risk premium, but from any of the possible market frictions, then there is no longer any reason why these 'friction-affected' assets should all pay handsomely in the good states of the world. Which means that it should be possible to form diversified portfolios of positive-Sharpe-Ratio sub-portfolios, with the overall portfolio enjoying an even better Sharpe Ratio (thanks to diversification). Needless to say, saying that it would be possible does not mean that it would be easy.

It gets more interesting. Positive Sharpe Ratios due to frictions, imperfection, anomalies and other monsters of Nature can in principle be 'arbitraged away' if enough shrewd and unconstrained arbitrageurs can put their minds (or, rather, their money) to it. Positive Sharpe Ratio portfolios where the positive Sharpe Ratio is due to 'true' risk premia cannot be arbitraged away. Why? Because they are fully consistent with arbitrage in the first place: nothing will wash away the original sin that these portfolios pay well when we feel rich already; that, as a result, we do not pay much for these fair-weather assets; and that it is just the fact that we do not pay very much for them that depresses their prices and grants them a higher yield.

So, with Kim and Wright, we too call 'risk premia' the differences between the market yields and the expectations of the paths of the future short rate (wherever these differences come from), but we must keep in mind that this catch-all term can have many different explanations, which suggest different predictions and interventions – some of which our models know nothing about: like Horatio, we must always keep in mind that there are more things in heaven and earth than are dreamt of in our philosophy.

CHAPTER 6

Principal Components: Theory

Parlare oscuramente lo sa fare ognumo, ma chiaro pochissimi.[1]
— Galileo Galilei

6.1 THE PURPOSE OF THIS CHAPTER

Principal Component Analysis (PCA) is a well-known technique used to reduce the dimensionality of multidimensional problems. When it comes to term-structure modelling, it is well known that the principal components obtained by orthogonalizing the covariance matrix (of yields or forward rates) afford a synthetic yet 'rich' description of the yield curve. Principal components are also loved by practitioners because they lend themselves to an appealing intuitive interpretation as the 'level', 'slope' and 'curvature' of the yield curve.

Beside being of intrinsic descriptive interest, principal components (or their proxies) are also important because several affine modelling approaches use them (or their proxies) as their state variables. Furthermore, as we shall see in Part VI, one principal component (the 'slope') by itself explains a lot about excess returns.

In this chapter we therefore explain what principal components are. In the next, we present what is known empirically about them (looking at the covariance matrix both of levels and of differences). We explore important issues such as their persistence, and we highlight how this feature is linked to the quasi-unit-root nature of rates. We look both at nominal and at real yields.

6.2 WHAT ARE PRINCIPAL COMPONENTS?

6.2.1 The Axis Rotation

There so many excellent introductions to Principal Component Analysis[2] that we feel that it is really unnecessary to reinvent this particular wheel and give

[1] Anybody can speak obscurely, with clarity exceedingly few.
[2] For a student-friendly introduction see, eg, Chatfield and Collins (1980, 1989); for a thorough treatment, see Campbell, Lo and McKinley (1996); the paper that introduced the interpretation of

a self-contained presentation here. However, it may still be useful to try and explain the intuition behind Principal Component Analysis and to discuss the two distinct functions that this mathematical technique fulfills – both in general, and in term-structure modelling applications. Unfortunately, these distinct roles are frequently confused.

The first reason why principal components are used is that they allow a significant reduction of redundancy. This reduction is obtained by forming combinations of the original variables to create new variables that behave in a simpler and more 'informative' manner. (What 'redundancy' and 'informative' mean will become apparent in the following).

The second reason for using principal components is the removal of noise.

To understand both of these aspects of Principal Component Analysis consider a yield curve, described by a large number, N, of yields, y_i, $i = 1, \ldots N$. Suppose that a modeller records exactly the daily changes in all the yields. She diligently does so day after day. By doing so, she will have a perfectly faithful record of the changes that the (discrete, but very-finely-sampled) yield curve has experienced on those days. After some time (say, a few months), she cannot help forming the impression that she has been wasting a lot of her time. Take for instance her birthday, 3 April: on that day she recorded the following changes (in basis points) for the yields of maturities from 24 to 29 years (see Figure 6.1):

$$
\begin{bmatrix}
y_{24} & 3.1 \\
y_{25} & 3.2 \\
y_{26} & 3.1 \\
y_{27} & 3.3 \\
y_{28} & 3.3 \\
y_{29} & 3.4
\end{bmatrix} . \qquad (6.1)
$$

For all her efforts, she can't help feeling that if she had recorded that all the yields of maturity from 24 to 29 years moved by 3.22 basis points (the average of the recorded values) she would have saved herself a lot of time, and lost little information.

Then the researcher decides to look at the data a bit more carefully, and she plots the changes against yield maturity. See again Figure 6.1. Perhaps, by squinting hard, one can see an upward trend in the data. The change in the 26-year yield, however, does not fit well with the trend story. Perhaps it was a noisy data point. Being a conscientious modeller, the researcher runs a regression, and finds an R^2 of almost 80%. On this very small sample, the slope coefficient (ie, the coefficient b in the regression $a + bT$) has a t statistic of 3.75, and therefore it is likely that there is indeed an upward trend in the data.

Short of transcendental meditation, with one single record there is not much more that the researcher can do. However, if she has access to the equivalent

the first three principal components in a term-structure context as 'level', 'slope' and 'curvature' is Litterman and Scheinkman (1991).

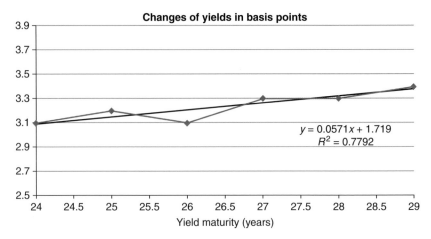

Figure 6.1 The recorded changes in the yields of maturity from 24 to 29 years, the associate regression line, with its intercept (1.719), slope (0.0571) and R^2 (0.7792).

changes for many days, she can do something better: she can construct a matrix of (empirical) covariances in yield changes and study this quantity.

A covariance matrix is in itself a synthetic description of a much larger quantity of data[3] and therefore in general entails a considerable loss of information when compared to all the original data; however, it is still a rather unwieldy beast: for 30 yields, the matrix will contain $\frac{30^2-30}{2} + 30$ distinct elements.

Exercise 15 *Why is the number of distinct elements of an $n \times n$ covariance matrix equal to $\frac{n^2-n}{2} + n$?*

Can she do better than staring at (or analyzing) this rather forbidding square matrix in its entirety?

This is where Principal Component Analysis offers some help. With this technique one creates some clever linear combinations, $\{x\}$, of the original data:

$$x_i = \sum_{j=1.30} c_{ij} y_j. \qquad (6.2)$$

These linear combinations have an important property, best understood if we restrict the attention to two yields only. See Figure 6.2, which records the

---

[3] Why? Because, if we have N observations of a vector of n variables (with $N \gg n$), each element, cov_{ij}, of the covariance matrix is obtained from the N terms $\left(x_k^i - \bar{x}^i\right)\left(x_k^j - \bar{x}^j\right), k = 1, 2, \ldots N.$

Unless we are up to no good, N should always be (much) larger than the $\frac{n^2-n}{2} + n$ distinct elements of the covariance matrix, and therefore from the $\frac{n^2-n}{2} + n$ elements of the covariance matrix we cannot reconstruct the $N \times n$ numbers in the N n-dimensional vectors $\left(x_k^i - \bar{x}^i\right)$. See Excercise 15.

daily changes in the two of the yields in question. Every point in the scatterplot corresponds to a realization of the change in the first yield (whose numerical value can be read as the Δy_1-coordinate of that point), and a realization of the change in the second yield (whose numerical value can be read as the y-coordinate of that same point). On the two axes, Δy_1 and Δy_2, we have projected the cloud of points, to obtain two marginal distributions. We note that the variance of the changes in yield 2 are a bit less than the variance of the changes in yield 1, but, apart from that, the two marginal distributions look quite similar.

Let's now rotate the axes in a skillful way, as we have done in Figure 6.3, and let's project the scatterplot again in the direction of the two new axes, to obtain the new marginal distributions. We stress that we are still dealing exactly with the same data, and only the axes have changed (they have been rotated). Note also that we have spoken of a *rotation* of axes (no stretching). Therefore we know from Chapter 2 that the matrix (the set of numbers c_{ij} in Equation (6.2)) that carries out the transformation to the new clever variables (the $\{x\}$) is a rotation matrix, with a determinant equal to $+1$.

After this length-preserving transformation the two marginal distributions look very different: the variation along the new first axis, x_1, clearly shows that along this new direction is where 'all the action is'; the variation along the second axis has now become a side show.

What do the transformed variables look like? In this simple case they may be given by a transformation such as the following:

$$dx_1 = \frac{1}{\sqrt{2}}dy_1 + \frac{1}{\sqrt{2}}dy_2 \tag{6.3}$$

$$dx_2 = \frac{1}{\sqrt{2}}dy_1 - \frac{1}{\sqrt{2}}dy_2. \tag{6.4}$$

Note that the two new variables, dx_1 and dx_2, are made up of the original variables multiplied by some coefficients. Looking at the coefficients, we can see that the first variable turns out being proportional to the average move in the yield curve. If, as the modeller indeed observed in the preceding example, a parallel move in the yields is the dominant mode of deformation of the yield curve, the change in the first variable (the first principal component) will convey most of the information about how all the yield curve moved on any day. One number (the change in x_1) will convey almost as much information as 2 numbers (the changes in y_1 and y_2). This is what we meant when we said that the new variables are more informative: if we look at both principal components we get an equivalent transformation of the original data; but if decide to keep only one principal component, in the case at hand the first new variable contains the 'essence' of the yield curve deformation.

Note also that if we take the sum of the squares of the coefficients, and we add either along rows or columns, we always obtain 1: again, this is because the transformation c is just a rotation.

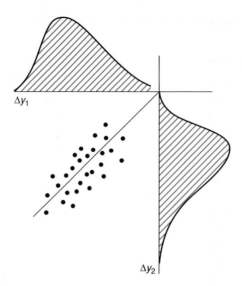

Figure 6.2 The daily changes in the two yields. Every point corresponds to a realization of the change in the first yield (given by the x-coordinate of that point) and a realization of the change in the second yield (given by the y-coordinate of that same point). On the two axes, x and y, we have projected the cloud of points, to obtain two marginal distributions.

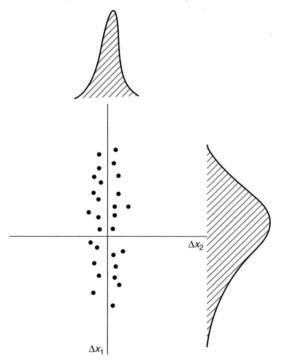

Figure 6.3 The same data as in Figure 6.3, but after rotating the axes. Also in this case, the data have been projected along the two axes to obtain the marginal distributions. Note the very different variances of the two marginal distributions.

6.2.2 The Signal and the Noise

What about the noise? Now the modeller has to decide whether the much narrower variation in the second variable conveys (less-important, but still-significant) information, or is just an effect of measurement noise.

If she decides that it is noise, then in this simple example *all* the signal in the data is captured by the change in the first principal component. If, beside the parallel-move signal there is no additional information, by neglecting the second principal component all she is throwing away is measurement error.

If she decides instead that the second transformed variable (the second principal component) conveys less important, but nonetheless still valuable, information she can make a modelling choice as to whether keeping the second variable is essential for her study or not.

In the case of two yields, all of this seems rather underwhelming. However, if we have, say, 30 yields, the picture changes dramatically. If the variation in the original 30 yields is indeed captured well by two or three new variables, then we *have* obtained a dramatic reduction in dimensionality.

Now, for two variables only, there are no advantages, other than aesthetic ones, in using the two original variables, or the two transformed variables (the principal components.) On the other hand, if we use only one transformed variable we throw away both the noise and whatever information may have been contained in the second variable.

With two variables, it's a tough and invidious choice. But with many variables we can do something more nuanced: we can split the decision of how many variables really matter for our application from the decision of what is signal and what is unwanted noise. For instance, we may ascertain that three principal components do contain information, but, perhaps to keep our model simple, we may decide that we will work with only two. When we do this drastic culling we do two things at the same time: first, we clean the data from noise; second, we achieve a more synthetic, albeit less complete, description of the original signal.

Where do we place the noise boundary when we have 30 variables? There is no hard-and-fast rule. We can look at the variance of the marginal distribution of the nth transformed variable, obtained by projecting the 30-dimensional scatterplot along one of the 30 orthogonal axes (easy to say, less easy to draw – hence the choice of two variables for my artistic efforts in Figures 6.2 and 6.3. Michelangelo could have handled three variables, but only as a ceiling fresco). In practice, when the variance becomes 'too small' we say that either we do not care, or it is noise. This, however, is not the full story: more about this at the end of the section.

6.3 HOW MANY PRINCIPAL COMPONENTS DO WE NEED FOR YIELDS?

Traditional wisdom holds that, if we look at changes in market yields (ie, if we work in the risk-neutral, $\mathbb{Q}$, measure), one principal component is a bit skimpy, two components are often adequate, and three are all that one really needs. However, if we look at excess returns (risk premia) some recent studies of the market price of risk (Cochrane and Piazzesi, 2005, 2008; Adrian, Crump and Moench, 2013) suggest that up to four or five principal components may convey useful predictive information. One must trust, of course, that these higher-order principal components reflect some subtle aspects of the signal, and not just noise. How can this be, when the conventional wisdom has always been that three principal components do a 98+%-good job at describing the behaviour of yields?

One possible explanation is that three principal components may well be all that is needed for a description of market yields. However, it may be still the case that extra principal components are indeed needed if one want to capture in the econometrically most complete manner both the observed yields *and* the risk premia. Whether using yield-curve–based variables (such as yields or principal components) is indeed the most efficient way to do so is a different and rather subtle story, that we will discuss at length in Section 27.4 and in Chapter 29. However, the important message here is that the number of principal components that 'tell (almost) all the story' depends on the story that we want to tell, ie, on the specific problem at hand.

6.4   FIRST CONCLUSIONS

Let's summarize our reasoning.

First of all, Principal Component Analysis works well when the signal-to-noise ratio is high. Whether this is true or not depends on the application at hand. For instance, in his good tutorial on Principal Component Analysis Shlens (2009) says: 'Measurement noise in any data set must be low or else, no matter the analysis technique, no information about a signal can be extracted'.[4] However, wishful thinking should not cloud our appreciation of what is signal and what is noise. It is *not* true that, when the variance of a principal component (of one of the transformed variables) is small we are safe in assuming that we are dealing with noise. Whether we are or not depends on the nature of the phenomenon at hand and on the quality of our data collection, not on the size of the variance. This often-forgotten fact should be engraved on the keyboard of any statistician and econometrician.

Second, PCA works well when there is a lot of redundancy in the original data. For linear systems, this means that it works well when the original data are strongly correlated (as yields are). What does 'redundancy' mean? With high redundancy, if you tell me the realization of one variable (say, the change in the 26-year yield), I have a sporting chance of guessing pretty accurately the realization of another variable (say, the change in the 27-year yield).[5] The variable transformation that PCA carries out

---

[4] p. 4.

[5] Note in passing how the noise must be small relative to the signal for my guess to be accurate.

creates variables with *no* redundancy, in the sense that knowledge of the realization of one variable (say, the level of the yield curve) makes one none the wiser as to the realization of the second variable (say, it slope). See again Figure 6.3.

Third, if the second new variable (principal component) is less important than the first (and the third less than the second, and so on), then one can 'throw' away these higher principal components, *even if they are not noise*, and lose little in the accuracy of the description.

What does it mean that a transformed variable is 'less important than another'? If all variables impact the something we are interested in with a similar 'elasticity', then a variable that varies less (which has a smaller variance) will be less important – simply by virtue of the fact that, despite having a similar impact as the first 'per unit shock', it varies over a more limited range of values. Look again at Equations (6.3) and (6.4): a *unit* change in either variable produces a change in the yield curve which is just as large. The 'elasticity' of the quantity we are interested in (the magnitude of the deformation[6] of the yield curve) is the same for the two principal components. However, *empirically* we find that the second principal component varies much less than the first (see Figure 6.3), and therefore it is not reasonable to assign a unit change to both. It is only in this sense that, *for the application at hand*, one variable matters more than the other.

Note again however, that 'importance' is intimately linked to the application at hand. The first principal component is what matters most if we are interested in how the yield curve as a whole moves. However, as we shall see, the second principal component matters more than the first when it comes to determining risk premia and the market price of risk. Despite the fact that the second principal component varies far less than the second, in the case of the market price of risk if we throw the slope away we throw away the signal. The variance of a variable is a good indicator of its importance *only if all the variables act on what we are interested in on an equal footing*. This is important, but also often forgotten.

6.5 SOME MATHEMATICAL RESULTS

In this section we present without proof some of fundamental results about Principal Component Analysis. The reader is referred to Chatfield and Collins (1980, 1989), Campbell, Lo and McKinley (1996) and Litterman and Scheinkman (1991) for the derivations and the gory details.

Take a real symmetric matrix, A, of dimensions $[n \times n]$ and of rank r. Saying that a matrix is of rank r means that r of the column vectors from which it is built up are linearly independent. In our applications we will almost invariably consider matrices of full rank, ie, such that $r = n$.

---

[6] We can use as a proxy of the deformation of the yield curve the sum of the absolute values of the changes in the various yields.

Any real symmetric matrix, A, can be orthogonalized. This means that it is always possible to re-express A as

$$A = V \Lambda V^{\mathrm{T}}, \tag{6.5}$$

where Λ is a diagonal matrix that contains the r distinct eigenvalues, λ_i, of A:

$$\Lambda = \mathrm{diag}\,[\lambda_i] \tag{6.6}$$

and V is an orthogonal matrix, ie, a matrix such that its transpose is equal to its inverse:

$$V^T = V^{-1}. \tag{6.7}$$

The matrix V is made up of r distinct and orthogonal and normalized (orthonormal) eigenvectors, $\vec{v}_i$:

$$V = \begin{bmatrix} \uparrow & \uparrow & & \uparrow \\ \vec{v}_1 & \vec{v}_2 & \cdots & \vec{v}_r \\ \downarrow & \downarrow & & \downarrow \end{bmatrix}. \tag{6.8}$$

The fact that each vector, $\vec{v}_i$, is an *eigen*vector means that

$$A\vec{v}_i = \lambda_i \vec{v}_i, \qquad i = 1, 2, \ldots r, \tag{6.9}$$

ie, when the original matrix, A, operates on the eigenvector, $\vec{v}_i$, it returns the same eigenvector back, multiplied by a constant. This constant is the ith eigenvalue.

Saying that the eigenvectors are all orthogonal to each other means that

$$\vec{v}_j^{\mathrm{T}} \vec{v}_i = 0 \quad \text{if } i \neq j. \tag{6.10}$$

Saying that they are normalized means that

$$\vec{v}_i^T \vec{v}_i = 1. \tag{6.11}$$

(Note carefully that the expression $\vec{v}_j^{\mathrm{T}}$ indicates an $[1 \times r]$ *row* vector, which, when multiplied using the matrix multiplication rules by the $[r \times 1]$ *column* vector, $\vec{v}_j$, gives a scalar. The operation is also known as a contraction, or an inner product. If this is not clear, please see Chapter 2 again, because this notation will recur over and over again.)

Consider now the case when the matrix A is the covariance matrix between n variables y_i. The transformed variables, ie, the principal components, x_i, are given by

$$x_i = \sum_{j=1,n} \left(v_{ij} \right)^{\mathrm{T}} y_j, \tag{6.12}$$

or, in matrix notation,

$$\vec{x} = \underline{V}^{\mathrm{T}} \vec{y}. \tag{6.13}$$

Of course, because of orthogonality,

$$\vec{y} = \underline{V} \vec{x}. \tag{6.14}$$

If the first eigenvector (the first column of V) is made up of almost identical elements, then the first principal component will be proportional to an average of the original variables. See again Equation (6.3); it will describe the 'level' of the original variables.

If the second eigenvector (the second column of V) is made up of positive (negative) elements in the top half and negative (positive) elements in the second half, and all these elements become smaller as they approach the centre of the vector, then the second principal component will be a good proxy for the 'slope' of the original variables. See again Equation (6.4).

Finally, if a matrix is orthogonal, the absolute value of its determinant is 1. If the determinant is $+1$, when this matrix is regarded as an operator, it is a rotation: it produces no stretching of, and no reflection about, the original axes.

CHAPTER 7

Principal Components: Empirical Results

> We must improve our concrete experience of persons and things
> into the contemplation of general rules and principles; but without
> being grounded in individual facts [...] we shall end as we began,
> in ignorance.
>
> – William Hazlitt, *On Reason and Imagination*[1]

7.1 THE PURPOSE OF THIS CHAPTER

In Chapter 6 we explained what principal components are, and why (and when) they are useful.

In this chapter we present some empirical results about the principal components obtained from the covariance matrix of changes in yields. The data we present clearly show the high degree of redundancy in the whole set of yield-change data.

Readers are probably already familiar with the principal-component results obtained using nominal yields (or forward rates). However, in this chapter we present some results that are less widely discussed (such as the mean-reverting properties of principal components), but which are greatly relevant for some of the modelling approaches we present in Part VII. In the second part of the chapter we then present similar results for real rates and break-even inflation.

Beside being of intrinsic interest, all these results provide a motivation for the modelling choices discussed in Chapters 32 and 33, and a foundation for the discussion of the reversion-speed matrix in the real-world and the risk-neutral measures.

7.2 NOMINAL RATES

7.2.1 Descriptive Features

Most readers will probably already be familiar with the Principal-Component results for nominal yields, and therefore in this section we move at a rather brisk

---

[1] From Hazlitt (2000), p. 410.

space, and simply recall that the first three eigenvectors lend themselves to the usual interpretation – a 'level', 'slope' and 'curvature'. Figure 7.1, which shows the first three eigenvectors (the first three principal components) obtained from orthogonalizing the covariance matrix of yield curve levels (upper panel L) or differences (lower panel D) for maturities out to 20 years, gives a justification for this interpretation. As well known, the first eigenvalue by itself explains more than 90% of the observed variance, the first two eigenvalues account for about 95%, and, depending on the currency and the time period under study, one can explain close to 98–99% of the yield curve variance using three principal components.[2]

Should one use the covariance matrix of levels or of differences? It depends on the application at hand. If we are interested, say, in hedging, then it is the covariance between *changes* in various yields that matters most. If we want to understand how quickly, say, the slope of the yield curve will revert to its 'natural' reversion level, then we should look at the covariance matrix extracted from levels.

The principal components shown in Figure 7.1 have been obtained by orthogonalizing the covariance matrix (of levels or differences). One could orthogonalize the correlation matrix as well, of course; however, by so doing one is discarding useful volatility information – information that is essential if we want, for instance, to neutralize one portion of the yield curve by taking positions in another portion. In order to gain an intuitive understanding of the link between the various yields, however, the correlation matrix provides a more vivid picture of 'what is going on'. This is what is shown in Figure 7.2 for the same data (levels) from which Figure 7.1 has been obtained.

A remark in closing this sub-section. Much has been made of how convenient and insightful it is to read first three principal components in terms of the level, slope and curvature. We would more readily challenge motherhood and apple pie than this cherished interpretation. However, lest the reader endows this interpretation with too deep a financial meaning, it pays to remember that these three shapes are, to a very large extent, dictated by the need to make the three eigenvectors orthogonal to each other. Indeed, Chatfield and Collins (1980, 1989) find a qualitatively very similar level/slope/curvature pattern in the analysis of almost any data set – indeed, even in the analysis of criminological data.[3] So, yes, the yield curve changes are well described by changes in levels, slope and curvature, but so are many other quantities that have nothing to do with yields (such as, it seems, criminal behaviour). Indeed, in 30-plus years of working with principal components with a variety of data derived from sources as unrelated as neutron scattering and yield curves, I do not recall a single case in which I have *not* found a level/slope/curvature pattern for the first

---

[2] These results are for *changes* in yields. For levels, the explanatory power of the first eigenvalues is considerably higher, with the first principal component by itself accounting for 98.6% of the observed variance.

[3] p. 73 and passim.

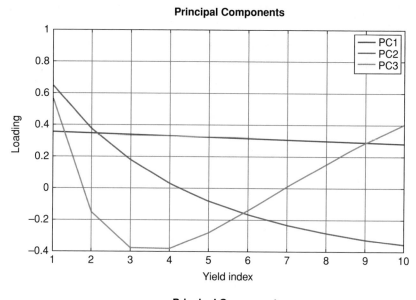

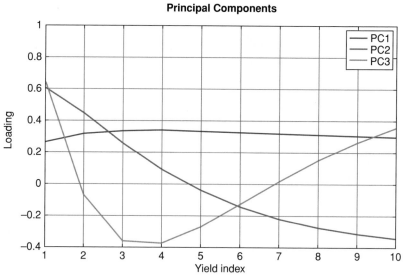

Figure 7.1 The first three eigenvectors (the first three principal components) obtained from orthogonalizing the covariance matrix of yield curve levels (top) or differences (bottom). Note the similarity of the shapes. The data, from Gurkaynak, Sack and Wright (2000) and in Gurkaynak, Sack and Wright (2006), cover the period 17 August 1971–24 June 2014.

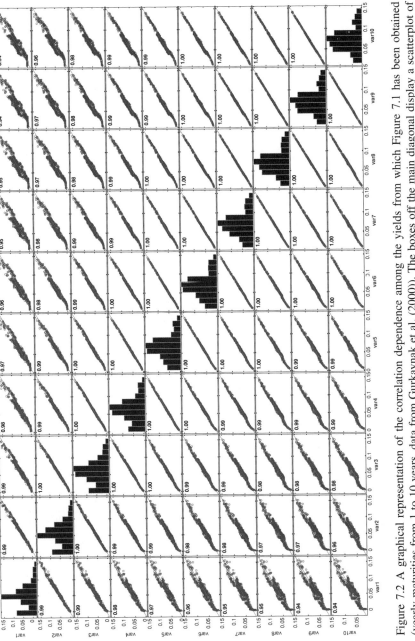

Figure 7.2 A graphical representation of the correlation dependence among the yields from which Figure 7.1 has been obtained (yearly maturities from 1 to 10 years, data from Gurkaynak et al. (2000)). The boxes off the main diagonal display a scatterplot of the realizations of the *i*th and the *j*th yields. Note that, as we move to higher and higher yields, the scatterplots cluster more and more tightly along the 45-degree line. The boxes down the main diagonal show a histogram of the yield realizations.

principal components, *at least when all the variables have been positively correlated.*[4] Which simply suggests we are mainly observing a mathematical fact, rather than a sign from a Higher Being.

7.2.2 Mean-Reverting Properties – Each PC in Isolation

As we have seen in Chapter 6, given a set of N yields, y_i^t, $i = 1, 2,..., N$, and the associated first n eigenvectors, we can obtain the new, transformed variables, x_i^t, $i = 1, 2,..., n$, by the linear transformation

$$\underbrace{\overrightarrow{x^t}}_{n \times 1} = \underbrace{V^T}_{n \times N} \underbrace{\overrightarrow{y^t}}_{N \times 1} . \tag{7.1}$$

What do the time series of these linear transformations – the principal components[5] – look like? Figures 7.3 to 7.5 show their behaviour from the early 1970s to the mid-2010s.[6] Since the first principal component is approximately proportional to the level of the yield curve, it is not surprising that it should decline markedly after the Volker, inflation-slaying rate hikes of the late 1970s. The other principal components display no such trend behaviour, and a very different level of persistence.

What do we mean by persistence? Take a stochastic process that follows a random walk without any mean reversion (and, for simplicity, without any drift, although this is not essential for the argument). Suppose that, at time $\hat{t}$, a shock

---

[4] Chatfield and Collins (1980, 1989, p. 72) discuss the orthogonalization of a correlation matrix given by

$$\begin{bmatrix} 1 & 0.4 & 0.4 & 0.4 \\ & 1 & 0.4 & 0.4 \\ & & 1 & 0.4 \\ & & & 1 \end{bmatrix}$$

and find the first eigenvector to be given by $a_1^T = [0.50, 0.50, 0.50, 0.50]$. They then present the very different correlation matrix

$$\begin{bmatrix} 1 & 0.9 & 0.3 & 0.3 \\ & 1 & 0.4 & 0.4 \\ & & 1 & 0.9 \\ & & & 1 \end{bmatrix}$$

and work out that the first eigenvector is given by $a_1^T = [0.48, 0.52, 0.50, 0.50]$. Once again, pronounced differences in the correlation matrix produce small differences in the first eigenvector. As long as the all the variables are all positively correlated, the 'level' answer is almost baked into the correlation question.

[5] Rather confusingly, the term 'principal component' is often used to denote both the eiegenvectors of the covariance matrix and the transformed variables, $\{x\}$. Usually the context makes the meaning clear. When there is scope for ambiguity, we use the term 'eigenvectors' to denote the columns of the orthogonalizing matrix, V.

[6] Yields of maturities from 1 to 20 years were used for the exercise. The yields were taken from the Fed-provided database in Gurkaynak, Sack and Wright (2007).

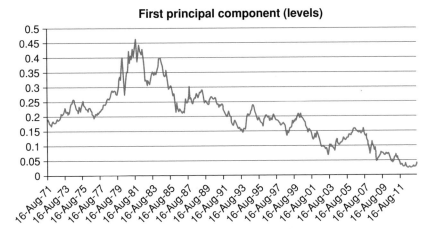

Figure 7.3 Time series of the first principal component obtained from orthogonalizing the covariance matrix of US$ yields (levels) obtained from the Fed data in Gurkaynak et al. (2000) for the period 17 August 1971–24 June 2014.

arrives that displaces the level of the random walk. This shock could be a run-of-the-mill, 'normal' shock, or an exceptional one, perhaps due to a structural break. If the process displays no mean reversion, the effect of this shock, small or large, will be permanent. More precisely, for a drift-less random walk with no mean reversion, the expectation of the future level of the random for any future time τ taken 1 second before and 1 second after the time-$\hat{t}$ shock will differ exactly by the magnitude of the shock itself. In this sense the shock will *persist*, and the process will retain memory of it forever.

Consider instead the case when the process displays a strong mean reversion. Suppose, again, that it experiences the same time-$\hat{t}$ shock. It is easy to see that,

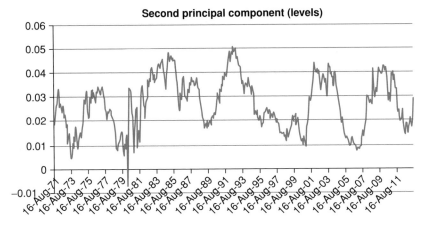

Figure 7.4 Same as Figure 7.3 for the second principal component.

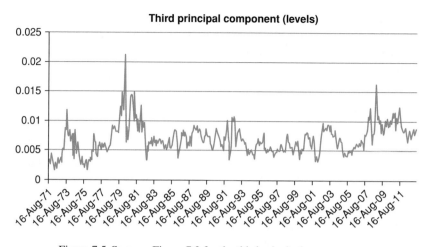

Figure 7.5 Same as Figure 7.3 for the third principal component.

by virtue of the pull to the mean-reversion level, the process will progressively 'forget' about the shock, and the expectation of the level of the process for $\tau \gg \hat{t}$ will be virtually unaffected by the magnitude of the time-$\hat{t}$ shock. It is also easy to see that, the stronger the mean reversion, the more quickly the process will 'forget about' the shock. A mean-reverting process, in other terms, displays a persistence which is inversely related to the strength of the mean reversion.

Why does this matter? As we shall see, when working with affine models one of the ways to build a bridge between the risk-neutral and the real-world measure is first to measure the reversion level in the risk-neutral world by fitting (cross-sectionally) to prices, and then to estimate statistically the reversion level in the risk-neutral measure. As we shall soon see in Chapter 8 – and as we shall discuss at much greater length in the rest of the book – the difference between the two reversion levels is related to the market price of risk, which, in turn, is just the bridge between the two measures that is needed for a structural description.

Suppose now that the modeller has chosen principal components as state variables. If one could easily determine the reversion level of the first principal component in the real world, then one could easily estimate the market price of risk. Why doesn't everyone pursue this estimation route?

To understand why, let's look again at Figures 7.3 to 7.5. Given the approximate interpretation of the first principal component as being proportional to the average level of rate, the first time series gives an indication as to whether rates as a whole tend to wander in rates space without any moorings (whether they are random walks) or, if they do not, what degree of persistence (what reversion speed) they display.

Let's look first at Figure 7.3. The first casual observation is that, at least over 40 years, rates do not seem to have wandered off to plus or minus infinity.

There seems to be *some* degree of mean reversion to a, possibly time-varying, but finite, level. At the same time, we would be hard pressed to point with any degree of accuracy either to the reversion level to which the average level of rates seems to be attracted, or to the reversion speed. From the mid-1980s to 2014, in particular, the average level of rates seems to have been drifting relentlessly down. Casual inspection therefore suggests that the reversion speed must be very weak indeed.

The picture changes radically when we look at Figure 7.4 and, even more so, at Figure 7.5. Looking at the second principal component, if we draw a line somewhere between the levels of 0.2 and 0.3, we can be pretty confident that there is where the real-world reversion level should lie.

What about the reversion speed? It is more difficult to have an intuitive feel for this quantity. However, we can think in terms of half-life of a shock, ie, of the time horizon over which we can expect a given shock to have halved in magnitude. As we have discussed in Chapter 2, if HL denotes the half-life, and κ the reversion speed, the precise formula is

$$HL = \frac{\log(2)}{\kappa}. \tag{7.2}$$

Inverting the temporal yardstick provided by Equation (7.2), we can go back to Figure 7.4, and, after noticing that it takes a small number of years for a shock to halve in magnitude, we can venture a guess for the reversion speed of, say, 0.2 to 0.4.

The same message is conveyed with even greater clarity by Figure 7.5: now the level of mean reversion is even easier to identify, and the half-life seems to be of the order of several months, rather than a few years, pointing to a very strong reversion speed, of magnitude close to 1. Persistence is now very small.[7]

From the perspective of a yield curve modeller, this state of affairs is unfortunate to say the least. We have a situation where what we can measure accurately doesn't matter much, and what we cannot measure with any precision matters a lot. More precisely, as we shall discuss at length in Part VI, investors mainly want to be compensated for bearing *level* risk.[8] In an affine setting, this means that it is the real-world reversion level of the first principal component that will

---

[7] To be more precise, when we carry out a log-likelihood estimation of the parameters of one continuous-time Ornstein–Uhlenbeck process for each principal component taken separately, we obtain reversion levels of 0.0224, 0.0277 and 0.0070, respectively, and reversion speeds of 0.0016, 0.433 and 1.8265. These correspond to half-lives of 433, 1.602 and 0.379 years, respectively.

[8] One has to be careful here, and distinguish between what investors get compensated for, and the magnitude of the compensation per unit risk. The empirical evidence presented in Part VI suggests that the magnitude (and perhaps even the sign!) of the market price of risk strongly depends on the *slope* of the yield curve. This is the compensation per unit risk. The risk in question, the same empirical studies then show, is the risk associated with a change in the level of rates. More about this later.

be altered in going from the real-world to the risk-neutral measure. Alas, of the three real-world reversion levels, this is just the one that is most difficult to estimate. If you get the real-world reversion level of rates wrong, then your market price of risk will be wrong, and your deduction of 'market expectations' will be wrong.[9] This, in essence, is at the heart of what is called the 'unit-root problem' with rates, where 'unit-root' is another term (whose origin and precise meaning need not concern us here) for infinite persistence.[10]

Finally, it will be useful for future comparison with model predictions to obtain the autocorrelation functions *for the levels* of the first three principal components. These are shown in Figure 7.6 for lags out to 100 business days. As is well known, the rate at which the autocorrelation function decays is directly proportional to the reversion speed (high reversion speed, fast decay). Once again the vastly different speeds of mean reversion are well reflected in the rates of decay of the autocorrelation functions: note in particular that after 100 business days, the autocorrelation is still above 95% for the first principal component, but has fallen below 60% for the third.

It will be important to keep these considerations in mind when we look at the across-measure calibration of affine models (and, therefore, at the estimation of risk premia and real-world expectations). For the moment we turn our attention to real rates and break-even inflation rates.

7.2.3   The Joint Mean-Reverting Behaviour of Principal Components

In the previous section we looked at the mean-reverting behaviour of each principal component in isolation using the nominal yield US Treasury data from

---

[9] If one assumes the generating process for the three principal components to be a simple mean-reverting process – as discussed in Chapter 10 – a maximum-log-likelihood estimation of its parameters produces reasonable values for the second and third principal components, with reversion levels of 0.0277 and 0.0070, respectively, and reversion speeds of 0.4328 and 1.826, respectively. The reversion speeds correspond to half-lives of 1.6 and 0.38 years. However, applying the same log-likelihood maximization to the time series of the first principal component gives difficult-to-interpret results for the reversion speed, with a half-life extending to decades.

[10] If you really want to know, a simple definition of a unit-root process is as follows. Consider a discrete-time stochastic auto-regressive process of order p: $x_t = a_1 x_{t-1} + a_2 x_{t-2} + \ldots a_p x_{t-p} + \epsilon_t$, with ϵ_t the usual zero-mean, constant-variance, iid process. Build the characteristic equation $y^p - y^{p-1} a_1 - y^{p-2} a_2 \ldots - a_p = 0$. It is a polynomial of order p in the variable y, with coefficients $\{1, a_1, a_2, \ldots, a_p\}$. Now, if $x = 1$ is a root of the characteristic equation (ie, if it is a solution of the equation), then the process is said to be *unit root*. This is important, because if the process is unit root, then it is not stationary. Fortunately, if the root has single multiplicity (in which case the process is said to be *integrated of order 1*) it is enough to take differences once in order to get a stationary process. If the root has multiplicity r, then one has to take differences of differences of differences...$r - 1$ times in order to get a stationary process. In most financial time series it is enough to differentiate once in order for the resulting process to become stationary.

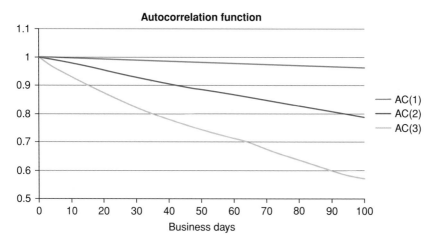

Figure 7.6 The autocorrelation functions for the levels of first three principal components (labelled AC(1), AC(2) and AC(3) for the first, second and third principal component) for lags out to 100 business days. Same data as for Figure 7.1.

Gurkaynak et al. (2000).[11] Doing so was tantamount to assuming that in the real-world measure the reversion speed matrix, $\mathcal{K}$, should be of the diagonal form:

$$
\begin{bmatrix} dx_1 \\ dx_2 \\ dx_3 \end{bmatrix} = \begin{bmatrix} k_{11} & 0 & 0 \\ 0 & k_{22} & 0 \\ 0 & 0 & k_{33} \end{bmatrix} \left(\begin{bmatrix} \theta_1 \\ \theta_2 \\ \theta_3 \end{bmatrix} - \begin{bmatrix} x_1 \\ x_2 \\ x_3 \end{bmatrix} \right) dt
$$

$$
+ \begin{bmatrix} s_{11} & 0 & 0 \\ 0 & s_{22} & 0 \\ 0 & 0 & s_{33} \end{bmatrix} \begin{bmatrix} dz_1 \\ dz_2 \\ dz_3 \end{bmatrix}. \tag{7.3}
$$

But what do we actually empirically know about this reversion-speed matrix in the real-world measure? Can we reliably estimate the full matrix, without having to assume that it should be diagonal?

To get a feel for the data, first we show in Figure 7.7 the correlation plot for the first three principal components. Looking at the off-diagonal plots, we observe some residual structure (the elements ρ_{12} and ρ_{31}, for instance, clearly display localized periods of almost deterministic dependence of the second and third principal component on the first[12]), but no obvious overall linear dependence is apparent. See the figure caption for a discussion. As we shall see, the full picture is far more complex (and interesting).

---

[11] This section is notationally – although not conceptually – a bit more demanding than the chapters in Parts I to III. The reader who finds the vector-and-matrix notation of this section at the moment a bit forbidding may want to look at Chapters 17 and 18 first.

[12] These almost deterministically linked points correspond to the post-2009 period.

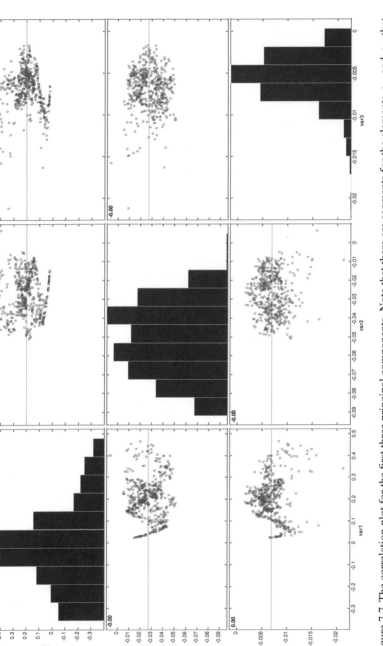

Figure 7.7 The correlation plot for the first three principal components. Note that there are segments for the elements ρ_{12} and ρ_{31} that display an almost perfect deterministic dependence between level and slope and level and curvature. These segments correspond to the post-2009 data. In this period short-maturity yield were 'pinned' to be close to zero by the actions and guidance of the monetary authorities. Therefore, one end of the yield curve being pinned, an increase in rates must be associated with an increase in slope. Furthermore, as the uncertainty in the speed of monetary normalization (the 'tapering' speed) mainly affected the medium-maturity

To answer more precisely the preceding question, we discretize Equation (7.3), and obtain

$$\vec{x}_{t+1} = \vec{x}_t + \left(\underline{K}\vec{\theta} - \underline{K}\vec{x} \right) \Delta t + \epsilon_t$$

$$\implies \vec{x}_{t+1} = \left(\underline{I} - \underline{K}\Delta t \right) \vec{x}_t + \underline{K}\vec{\theta} \, \Delta t + \epsilon_t. \qquad (7.4)$$

This shows that we can estimate the reversion-speed matrix, $\underline{K}$, and the reversion-level vector, $\vec{\theta}$, from the slopes and the intercepts, respectively, of the regression of the vector $\vec{x}_{t+1}$ (the left-hand variable), against the vector $\vec{x}_t$, (the right hand variables). More precisely, for each principal component, r, we can estimate

$$x_{t+1}^r = x_t^r - \sum_{j=1,3} k_{rj} x_t^j \Delta t + \sum_{j=1,3} k_{rj} \theta_t^j \Delta t + \epsilon_t^r. \qquad (7.5)$$

So, for instance, for $r = 2$, this can be rearranged to give

$$x_{t+1}^2 = \underbrace{(-\kappa_{21}\Delta t)x_t^1}_{\text{slope 1}} + \underbrace{(1 - \kappa_{22}\Delta t)x_t^2}_{\text{slope 2}} + \underbrace{(-\kappa_{31}\Delta t)x_t^3}_{\text{slope 3}}$$

$$+ \underbrace{(\kappa_{21}\theta_1\Delta t + \kappa_{22}\theta_2\Delta t + \kappa_{23}\theta_3\Delta t)}_{\text{intercept}}$$

$$+ \underbrace{\epsilon_t^{(2)}}_{\text{residual}}. \qquad (7.6)$$

This equation clearly shows that, when it comes to estimating the reversion-speed properties of the second and third principal components, the difficult-to-determine reversion-speed coefficients of the highly persistent first principal component do not matter.[13] This means that we do not have to worry about 'contamination issues', and that we can have a lot of confidence in the behaviour of the higher principal components.

What does this analysis yield? We show the results for the estimated reversion-speed matrix, $\widehat{K}$, in Table 7.1.

The first and third principal components present little surprises. However, the behaviour of the 'slope' principal component is more complex than one might have anticipated, and can be summarized as follows:

$$\Delta x_2 = \left[0.58 \left(\underbrace{\theta_2}_{0.027} - x_2 \right) - 1.94 \left(\underbrace{\theta_3}_{-0.007} - x_3 \right) \right] \Delta t. \qquad (7.7)$$

This equation says that when the yield curve is steeper than 2.7% it will revert to this level; but it also says that as the yield curve becomes more curved (the third principal component more *negative*) the yield curve tends to become steeper.

---

[13] To determine the reversion level one has to solve a 3 × 3 system, in which the reversion-speed elements associated with the first principal component do appear.

Table 7.1 *The reversion-speed matrix, $\widehat{\mathcal{K}}$, estimated using the regression described in the text for $\Delta t = 1$ month and $\Delta t = 2$ months (numbers in parentheses). Those coefficients that were not significantly different from zero at the 99% confidence level were set exactly to zero for clarity of presentation. The non-zero coefficients were all significant well above the 99% confidence level. The half lives associated with the diagonal elements were 10 years, 1.2 years and 0.4 year, respectively. The mean-reverting behaviour of the second principal component, however, must be interpreted more carefully. See the text for a discussion.*

$\widehat{\mathcal{K}} =$	0.079 (0.065)	0	0
	0	0.58 (0.58)	−1.94 (−1.96)
	0	0	1.68 (1.71)

How big is the effect of the curvature on the slope? By itself, the reversion coefficient, κ_{23}, seems large (-1.94); however, as Figure 7.5 shows, the third principal component strays from its reversion level very little (because its reversion speed is very high), so the term $(\theta_3 - x_3)$ tends to be small. How significant is the combined effect of a large coefficient times a small movement? To quantify the effect we have calculated the mean absolute deviation of the slope from its reversion level (ie, the term $avg(|\theta_2 - x_2|)$), and of the curvature from its reversion level (ie, the term $avg(|\theta_3 - x_3|)$). We obtain

$$\text{avg}(|\theta_2 - x_2|) = 0.0090$$
$$\text{avg}(|\theta_3 - x_3|) = 0.0020. \tag{7.8}$$

As expected, we find $\text{avg}(|\theta_3 - x_3|) < \text{avg}(|\theta_2 - x_2|)$. However, when we multiply these average values by their respective reversion speed elements, we find that the curvature contributes an average pull of approximately 3 basis points per month, while the slope contributes an average pull of 4.5 basis points per month. The curvature effect is therefore not negligible: when the yield curve is more curved, it tends to become steeper. What can this effect be due to?

To answer this question we have created a simple proxy for the time-varying volatility of the yield curve by calculating the volatility of the first principal component, and we have then regressed this volatility estimate against the curvature principal component. The results are shown in Figures 7.8 and 7.9: the two quantities are significantly correlated, with an R^2 of 0.20. In itself, the R^2 is rather underwhelming. However, note from Figure 7.8 that the relationship between the third principal component and the yield curve volatility becomes clear and strongly positive during periods of high volatility.

How are we to interpret this positive correlation between the third principal component and the yield curve volatility? And how are these quantities related to the slope of the yield curve?

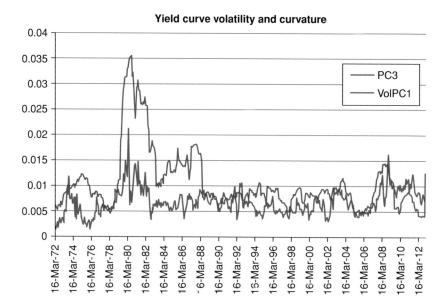

Figure 7.8 The time series of the volatility of the first principal component (rolling window of 15 monthly observations) (curve labelled VolPC1) and the third principal component (curve labelled PC3). The first principal components were obtained using yield out to 10 years.

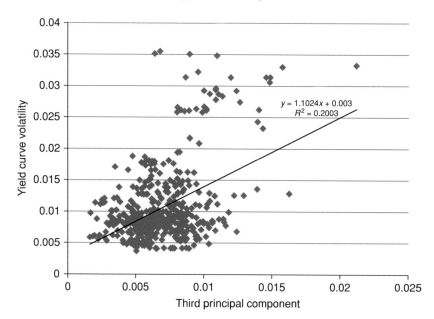

Figure 7.9 Same data as in Figure 7.8, but displayed in scatterplot form, with a regression line fitted to the data.

Answering the first question is easier: as we show in Chapters 10 and 20, when volatility increases, the value of convexity increases (quadratically), and long yields are pulled downwards more. So, this is a rather clear convexity-related effect.

What about the link with the slope? Here the explanation becomes more tentative. One can argue along the following lines. First of all, we note that the yield curve tends to steepen when the economy enters a recession or is in the last stages of a spent expansion. This is a well-established fact. (See the empirical evidence presented in Chapter 25.) It is then plausible to argue that the early-recessionary cuts in rates that steepen the yield curve are associated with periods of greater uncertainty and increased risk aversion. If this is correct, then the volatility should increase, and so should the convexity effect that 'pulls down' long yields and increases the curvature of the yield curve.

We shall discuss at length the business-cycle properties of the slope of the yield curve in Part VI, but for the moment we simply stress the empirical findings we have discussed in this sub-section:

1. as the yield curve becomes steeper, it also tends to become more curved; and
2. the yield curve tends to become more curved in periods of high volatility.

7.3   REAL RATES AND BREAK-EVEN INFLATION

In this section we focus on the principal components for real yields and break-even inflation, both for levels and for changes in levels. The real yields and the break-even inflations from the US Treasuries (nominal bonds and Treasury Inflation Protected Securities (TIPS)) market used in the analysis were obtained from the Fed data in Gurkaynak et al. (2000, 2006).

As with any time-series analysis, looking at what actually happened to the untransformed quantities of interest is always an excellent starting point. We therefore show in Figures 7.10 and 7.11 the real yields and the break-even inflation rates for the 10 years from 2004 to 2014.

Looking at both charts, the events in the middle of the time series obviously call for an explanation. In both cases, the sudden variations in levels (of real yields or of break-even inflations) correspond to the immediate aftermath of the 2008 Lehman default. We must keep in mind that the real yields and the break-even inflation that we display are the corresponding $\mathbb{Q}$-measure quantities, ie, they 'contain' risk premia. In this case, it is fair to say that they also contained a liquidity component (and possibly liquidity premia), and, indeed, D'Amico, Kim and Wei (2010) make a convincing case of the importance of a liquidity factors in order to explain the behaviour of TIPS.

The important point is that, if it is always imprudent to read directly from market-implied quantities the corresponding 'market expectation', doing so becomes outright meaningless in situations of market distress. *If* market risk premia (and liquidity) were constant, interpreting changes in yields and

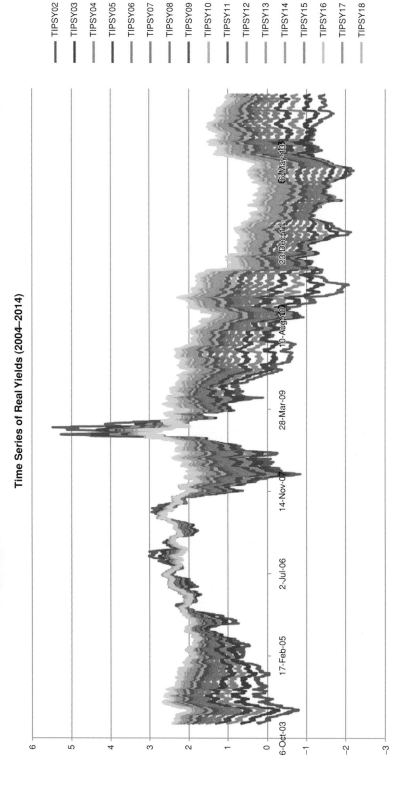

Figure 7.10 The time series of the real US$ yields of different maturities (from 2 to 18 years) obtained from the Fed data in Gurkaynak et al. (2000) for the period 2 Jan 04–24 Jun 14. The strong variation in the middle of the time series corresponds to the aftermath of the 2008 Lehman default.

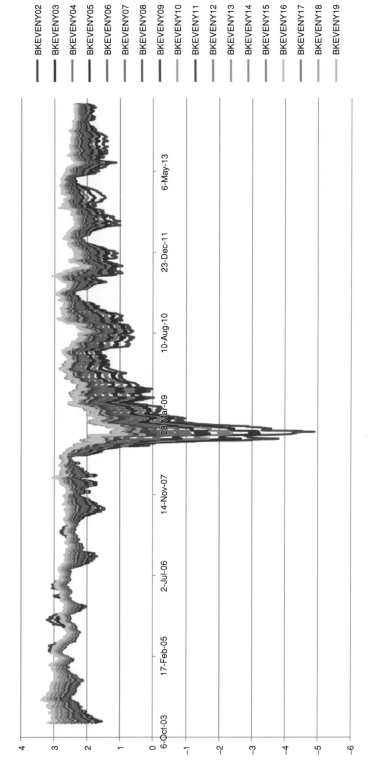

Figure 7.11 Same as Figure 7.10 for the break-even inflation.

inflation as changes in the respective expectations could be justified. However, as the discussion in the chapters at the end of this book highlights, the assumption of constant risk premia can be very seriously misleading – the more so when one looks at turbulent periods.

So, it would be rash to conclude from looking at Figure 7.11 then in the aftermath of the Lehman default investors 'expected' inflation over the next two years to be -5%. Admittedly, in those troubled days investors feared that a deep recession may be incumbent. The possibility of a significant decline in inflation therefore *was* on everybody's mind, and it is plausible that inflation expectations did fall at the beginning of the Great Recession. However, as investors were entering virtually unchartered territory, their uncertainty about future inflation increased as well. This factor by itself would have made break-even inflation rates *even lower*.[14] But recall that break-even inflation is obtained by combining the prices of TIPS and the prices of nominal bonds. Any differential in liquidity between the two asset classes may have played an even larger role in that instance. Without a proper model, or a well-constructed statistical analysis, we just cannot tell.

This also suggests something else. If we want to use techniques such as principal components for predictive, and not just descriptive, purposes (if we want, that is, to understand how yields will co-move tomorrow, not just how they co-moved in the past), then our choice of the 'patch' of historical data to use becomes essential. For predictive purposes, what we need is a conditional estimate, where we would like to condition on the current state of the world. See Rebonato and Denev (2013) for more than you probably wanted to know about this point.

Finally, saying 'predicting' in the abstract is close to vacuous, unless one specifies for what purpose the prediction is made (ie, without specifying the 'penalty function' incurred by the forecaster if she gets her prediction wrong). So, for a risk manager interested in stress events, neglecting the middle of the time series would probably be insane. For a modeller who today saw no clouds on the horizon, and who wanted to make a forecast about what will happen next month, it would probably be wise. Again, the interested reader can follow the much deeper, or at least lengthier, discussion of these issues in Rebonato and Denev (2013) and in the references therein.

Now that we have a good qualitative understanding of what actually happened to real yields and break-even inflation in the period under study, we can begin the Principal Component Analysis proper of real and breakeven rates. To

---

[14] Why? Think, suggestively if not accurately, of break-even inflation as the future realized inflation needed to make an investor today indifferent between investing in a nominal or in a real (inflation-linked) bond. So, if the real yield promised by the inflation-linked bond is 2% and the yield of the nominal bond is 3.5%, one can approximately gauge that an expected inflation of 1.5% would make the two instruments equally attractive. Now, if, *for whatever reason*, the price of an inflation-protected bond goes down relative to the price of a same-maturity nominal bond, its (real) yield will go up. Therefore 'less future inflation' is required for nominal and inflation-linked bonds to be equivalent. We stress that this argument is intuitively appealing, but far from precise. The reader is invited to explain why so. (Hint: think of liquidity and of risk premia.)

Covariance matrix (real yields) – differences

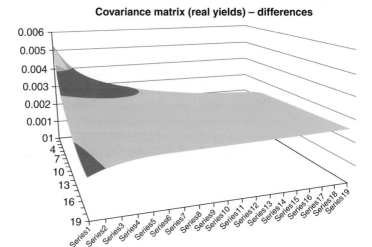

Figure 7.12 The covariance matrix of differences in real yields for maturities from 2 to 20 years for the period 2 Jan 2004–24 Jun 2014. Because of seasonality effects at the short end, the first yield is the 2-year real yield. We therefore have 19 data series. The covariance on the z-axis is multiplied by 10^4.

this effect, first we show in Figures 7.12 and 7.13 the covariance matrices (level and differences) for the real yields.

In the case of real yields, the first three principal components have the usual shape, and lend themselves to the usual interpretation as level, slope and curvature, both in the case of levels and in the case of differences. The similarity of the principal components in the two cases is shown in Figure 7.14. The most

Covariance matrix (real yields) – levels

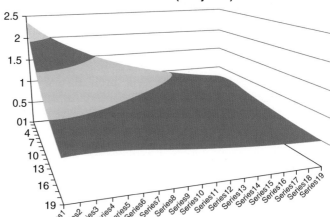

Figure 7.13 Same as Figure 7.12 for levels of real yields instead of differences.

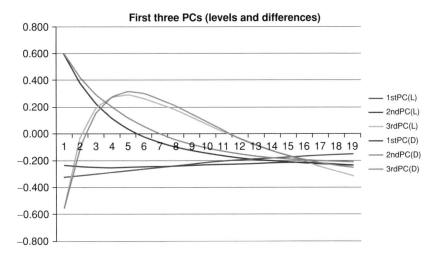

Figure 7.14 The first three principal components from the orthogonaliza-tion of the covariance matrix for levels (curves labelled $1stPC(L)$, $2ndPC(L)$ and $3rdPC(L)$), and differences (curves labelled $1stPC(D)$, $2ndPC(D)$ and $3rdPC(D)$) of real yields.

noteworthy feature is how flat the first principal component is (both for lev-els and differences), suggesting that the volatilities of the real yields must be very similar for different maturities. This is confirmed by Figure 7.15, which compares the absolute volatilities for real yields and break-even inflations.

If the shape of the eigenvectors is very similar for levels and differences, the amount of variance explained by the first n principal components changes

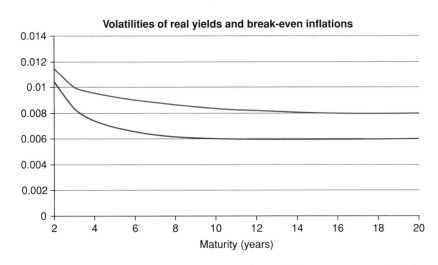

Figure 7.15 The absolute volatilities of real yields (upper curve) and of the break-even inflations (lower curve) for maturities from 2 to 20 years.

Table 7.2 *The percentage of the total variance explained by the first n (n = 1, 2 ... 5) principal components (left column) for the case of levels (second column) and differences (third column) for real yields.*

n of PCs	Levels (%)	Differences (%)
1	94.5	86.2
2	99.7	96.7
3	100.0	98.9
4	100.0	99.8
5	100.0	100.0

significantly between the two cases, as shown in Table 7.2. This, of course, is to be expected.

We can repeat the same exercise for break-even inflation. The results are similar (see Figure 7.16 and Table 7.3).

7.4 CORRELATION BETWEEN NOMINAL, INFLATION AND REAL PRINCIPAL COMPONENTS

We expect little correlation between the time series of the first and second principal components, both for real and nominal rates. But what can we say about the correlation between (changes in) levels of real rates and (changes in) levels

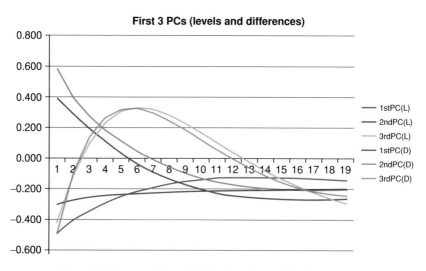

Figure 7.16 Same as Figure 7.14 for break-even inflations.

Table 7.3 *The percentage of the total variance explained by the first n (n = 1, 2 . . . 5) principal components (left column) for the case of levels (second column) and differences (third column) for break-even inflations.*

n of PCs	Levels (%)	Differences (%)
1	95.3	81.5
2	99.2	94.3
3	99.7	98.1
4	100.0	99.6
5	100.0	100.0

of nominal rates? What about the correlation between (changes in) slope (level) of real rates and (changes in) levels (slope) of nominal rates?

The time series (obtained from the same data sources) for the first and second principal components of changes are shown in Figure 7.17. The correlations in the changes of the principal components are then shown in Table 7.4.

As anticipated, the empirical correlation between the slope and levels of the same variables are small. However, it is clear that the levels of the real and of the nominal rates are very strongly correlated (76.3%) – as they should also be, since the nominal rate is the sum of the real rate and of inflation: it would

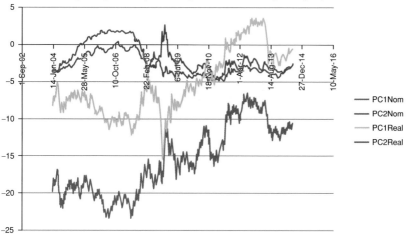

Figure 7.17 The time series of the first two principal components obtained from the covariance matrix of changes in nominal yields (curves labelled PC1Nom and PC2Nom), and real yields (curves labelled PCReal and PC2Real). Note that the units of the quantities on the y-axis in this graph are such that a rate of, say, 3% has a value of 3.

Table 7.4 *The correlation between the first two nominal and real principal components obtained using the data in Gurkaynak et al. (2000, 2006)*

	PC1Nom	PC2Nom	PC1Real	PC2Real
PC1Nom	1	−0.041	0.763	0.239
PC2Nom	−0.041	1	−0.120	0.547
PC1Real	0.763	−0.120	1	−0.017
PC2Real	0.239	0.547	−0.017	1

be close to independent only if all the changes in nominal rates came from changes in inflation, and the real rate were almost constant. Table 7.4, and, indeed, Figure 7.17 show, that it is not. *If anything, if we exclude the aftermath of the Lehman event, Figure 7.17 suggests that, for the period under study, the bulk of the variation in nominal rates has come from changes in real rates.* See again in this respect the discussion in Chapter 5.

But what about the level and slope extracted from the covariance matrix of the break-even inflation? Will these be uncorrelated with the level and slope of the real rate? Let's look at Figure 7.18 and at Table 7.5.

The largest correlation elements are between the slopes of the real rates and the level and the slope of the break-even inflation rates. Before reading too much into these results, note, however, that, apart from the Lehman period, the slope of the break-even inflation is almost constant. Since all principal components change a lot during the turbulent window that starts in September 2008,

First two principal components (real and inflation, changes)

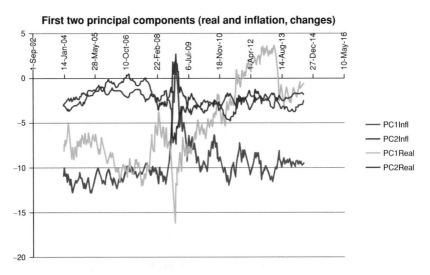

Figure 7.18 Same as Figure 7.17, for real yields and break-even inflation.

Table 7.5 *The correlation between the first two principal components of break-even inflation and the first two principal components of real yields obtained using the data in Gurkaynak et al. (2000)*

	PC1Infl	PC2Infl	PC1Real	PC2Real
PC1Infl	1	0.009	−0.192	0.390
PC2Infl	0.009	1	0.183	−0.452
PC1Real	−0.192	0.183	1	−0.017
PC2Real	0.390	−0.452	−0.017	1

the resulting correlation coefficients are, to a large extent, a function of what happened during this particular period.

Similarly, note that, apart from the Lehman window, the level component of (changes in) break-even inflation appears strongly mean-reverting around a level of −10, while the level of (changes in) the real rates declines monotonically after the Lehman default.

Why look at these quantities in such detail? Because this analysis can give us an indication of which variables are most informative if we want a parsimonious description of real and nominal yields. If we have to use a single variable, the levels of nominal rates or of real rates provide very similar information. If we can afford to use two variables, the level of, say, real rates and the level of inflation provide an acceptable synthetic description, while remaining close to uncorrelated. Finally, there isn't much to choose between the slope of real rates or the slope of the break-even inflation when it comes to the choice of the best candidate for the third factor.

Needless to say, one can throw any pair of independent variables (ie, nominal and real rates, or real and inflation rates, or nominal and inflation rates) into the covariance pot, turn the handle, obtain the principal components and rest assured that the resulting linear combinations of the original variables will be the most informative combination possible, given the data at hand. However, what is gained in informational efficiency[15] may be lost in clarity of understanding of what the resulting factors actually 'are'.

Exercise 16 *Get hold of the data in Gurkaynak et al. (2000, 2006), obtain the principal components for a pair of independent variables of your choice (eg, nominal and real rates, or real and inflation rates, or nominal and inflation rates), obtain the principal components, and interpret the resulting 'level', 'slope', etc in terms of the original variables.*

---

[15] There is a gain in informational efficiency in the sense that, for the same number of explanatory variables, with the combined principal components one explains most of the observed variance.

PART II

THE BUILDING BLOCKS: A FIRST LOOK

In Part I of the book we gathered some of the tools we will need for the journey ahead, and have taken a peek at some of the topics we will encounter in the rest of the book.

Our goal in this part of the book is to introduce the simplest affine model, ie, the Vasicek one. By way of preparation, we begin to look more precisely in Chapters 8 and 9 at two of our building blocks of yield curve dynamics, namely, expectations (in Chapter 8) and convexity (in Chapter 9). The purpose of these two chapters is to explain in the simplest possible setting how affine models in general deal with these two aspects.[1]

When we move to the Vasicek model (in Chapter 10) our goal will focus on building the reader's intuition, and on showing in the simplest possible way how affine models and mean-reversion 'work'. There will be precious few derivations in this chapter.

As discussed in the Introduction, the decomposition of the yield curve as made up of contributions from expectations, risk premia and convexity is at the heart of how the material is organized in this book. It pays, therefore, to have a picture of how these three components affect the yield curve. I have tried to show this pictorially in Figure 8.1. To build this picture I have placed myself in the simple Vasicek-like setting we discuss in Chapter 8, and I have assumed that the short rate starts from a value of 0.5% today, and reverts, in the real world, to the fixed reversion level of 3.5%.

In the top left-hand panel I have shown the real-world expectation contribution to the shape of the yield curve for three different speeds of asymptotic approach (reversion speeds) from 'today's' value of the short rate (0.5%) to the reversion level (3.5%).

---

[1] Since expectations and convexity are only two components of the chosen explanatory triad, logically Chapter 4, which gives a first introduction to risk premia, should have belonged to this part of the book. However, in one of the many structural compromises I have decided to make, I chose to place it in Part I because otherwise references to risk premia that appear in other chapters of Part I would have been obscure or imprecise.

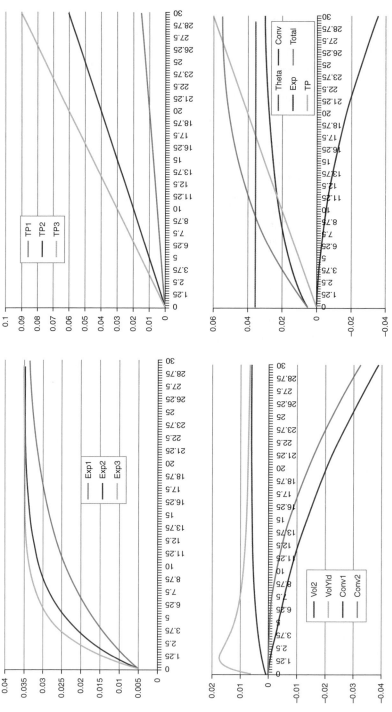

Figure 8.1 The three contributions to the yield curve: expectations (top left), term premia (top right), convexity (bottom left corner), combined to obtained the full yield curve (the curve with crosses labelled Total). The short rate was assumed to start from a value of 0.5% today, and to revert, in the real world, to the fixed reversion level of 3.5%.

As we have seen see in Chapters 4 and 5, the risk aversion of investors will superimpose a risk premium on top of these 'naked' (real-world) expectations. This is shown in the top right-hand panel. The important thing to notice is that risk premia add a contribution to yields which is to a good approximation linear in maturity. The three curves, labelled TP1, TP2 and TP3 show what the additions to the yields may be for three different degrees of risk aversion. The curves have been drawn in such a way to represent a plausible range of risk compensation. (As we shall see, the risk compensation is not constant over time, but we leave these complications for later.)

The bottom left-hand panel then shows two different patterns of volatilities for yields of different maturities, shown in curves VolYld and Vol2. Different volatilities will give rise to different convexity contributions. For zero reversion speed, convexity, as we discuss in detail in Chapter 10, would depend on the *square* of the maturity and the *square* of the yield volatility. With non-zero reversion speeds, its behaviour becomes more complex, but, for the moment, we don't have to worry about these subtler effects.

Convexity comes from the non-linear dependence of prices on yields: the average of bond price changes for a symmetric up and down move in yields is positive. This is a 'good thing', for which investors are ready to pay good money. This pushes prices up and yields down. That is why the contribution to the yield curve from convexity is negative, and, for zero reversion speed, quadratic. Therefore it matters little at the short end, but more and more as the maturity of the yield increases. Again, I have chosen a plausible range of parameters to obtain these curves.

All the different pieces are put together in the bottom right-hand panel which shows

- the asymptotic reversion level (the straight line labelled 'Theta');
- the central of the three expectation contributions – this is the curve labelled 'Exp', which constitutes the backbone of the yield curve;
- the central of the risk-premium contributions – this is the curve labelled 'TP';
- the lower of the two convexity contributions – this is the curve labelled 'Conv'; and
- the resulting yield curve, given by the superposition of the three contributions – this is the curve with crosses labelled 'Total'.

Note how expectations dominate the short end; how term premia become dominant in the belly of the curve; and how expectations cease to be important at the very long end, when the *quadratic* convexity contribution takes over from the linear term premia.

It will be very important to keep this picture in mind – and the different magnitudes of the three distinct contributions we have discussed in different portions of the yield curve – in the next chapters, and throughout the book.

CHAPTER 8

Expectations

Prediction is very difficult, especially about the future.

Niels Bohr

8.1 THE PURPOSE OF THIS CHAPTER

This chapter deals with expectations. Expectations about what? At a very general level, about the future paths of all the state variables that describe our model. But, ultimately, the expectations that 'matter most' are expectations about the future paths of the short rate. Why so? Because, as we will see, yields are convexity-adjusted path averages of the short rate.

Speaking of expectations, however, does not make much sense unless the measure (roughly speaking, the probability distribution) under which the expectation is taken is clearly specified. Therefore in the text that follows we look below at expectations of the short rate both under the real-world and under the risk-neutral measures.

Building on this, we provide a first heuristic argument to show that a bond price is the expectation in the risk-neutral measure of the exponential of (minus) the path of the short rate from evaluation time to maturity. At this stage we do not introduce with any degree of precision of conditions of the no-arbitrage – obtaining these will be the topic of Part III, which is by far the most heavy-going of the book. However, exactly because Part III is rather abstract and in parts more demanding, we believe that building as early as possible a good intuition of the bond-as-expectation result will put the reader in good stead when the going gets, if not necessarily tougher, certainly more abstract.

We then focus on affine models, and we show how expectations can be specified with these models. We conclude the chapter with a word of caution against overconfident fitting of the expectation part of affine models to bond prices.

8.2 LINKING EXPECTATIONS WITH NO-ARBITRAGE

We have argued that if we just assign expectations, term premia and convexity in what we happen to think is a 'plausible' and 'reasonable' way, there is no guarantee that the resulting bond prices will be free of arbitrage. That is why we will spend four chapters in Part III to derive the conditions of no-arbitrage from several different angles.

This is all well and good. But how can we translate the rather abstract conditions that we will obtain in precise modelling prescriptions? How can one obtain the price of a bond in such a way that we can rest assured that it will be arbitrage-free? Of course, we don't want to have to deal with an *ad hoc* equation for each individual bond. We would like to link bond prices to what we (claim we) know about the process(es) of our state variable(s). But how shall we do so?

8.2.1 A One-Factor World

To see how this works in practice, let's carry out a thought experiment. We are at time t and want to price a bond of maturity T. Let's consider the simple case when we have a single state variable, and this is the short rate. Suppose that we have estimated to our heart's content the properties in the real world of the short-rate process. Armed with this knowledge, we can then create (perhaps using a Monte Carlo simulation) many paths of the short rate. Along each of these paths, we start with $1 and accrue (ie, keep on reinvesting) this initial wealth at the short rate from time t to time T. (What we have created, by the way, is the money market account, but we need not concern ourselves with this for the moment.)

Once we get to the end, along each path we will have accrued $\$\left(\exp \int_t^T r_s ds\right)$.

Now, we started with $1 and ended with $\$\left(\exp \int_t^T r_s ds\right)$ by the end of a given path. With discount bonds it is more customary to receive $1 at the end. Let's suppose that, with some prescience, we had invested $\$\left(\exp - \int_t^T r_s ds\right)$ at the beginning (time t) to get $1 at maturity time (time T). We can't do this in real life, but, after each path reaches the end, we can always adjust ex post the starting point of our simulation so as to ensure that this condition is realized along each and every path.

So, as we wanted, getting $1 at the end is just the pay-off of a discount bond. But what should its price today be?

Recall that, in order to get $1 at the maturity along the different paths of the short rate, we had to invest different initial amounts. One plausible solution for the price would seem to be to average (using the real-world probabilities) these initial investment amounts:

$$P_t^T = ? = E^{\mathbb{P}}\left[e^{-\int_t^T r_s ds}\right]. \tag{8.1}$$

(Note carefully that I have decorated the expectation sign with the superscript sign $\mathbb{P}$ to emphasize that we have evolved the short rate using the parameters we have estimated in the real world.)

Associating the price of the bond today with the average amount I have to invest in a money market account in order to obtain the bond payoff sounds plausible. However, If I buy a discount bond, I pay P_t^T today, and receive $1 at time T *with certainty*. But if I invest $E^{\mathbb{P}}\left[\exp - \int_t^T r_s ds\right]$ dollars today, and carry out the interest-accruing strategy outlined earlier, I will get $1 at time T only *on average*. Exactly as we saw in the one-period example in Chapters 4 and 5 (and as we will discuss in detail in Part III), why should we accept even odds on a risky prospect? We need an extra compensation for taking on the risk. But what should a 'fair compensation' be?

For the moment, let us just accept the following statements as plausible (at least in a one-factor world).

First, we describe the process for a discount bond by the following equation:

$$\frac{dP_t^T}{P_t^T} = \mu_{P^T} dt + \sigma_{P^T} dz_t. \tag{8.2}$$

Then, to get started, we are going to say that different bonds can be expected to be more profitable than others. For instance, it is in general reasonable to expect that a 10-year bond should yield more than a 3-month one – if it did not, why accept a greater 'duration' risk? So, it is reasonable to require that $\mu_{P^{T_1}} > \mu_{P^{T_2}}$, if $T_1 > T_2$. And the shorter the maturity of the bond, of course, the closer its yield should be to the riskless rate:

$$\lim_{T \to 0} \mu_{P^T} = r. \tag{8.3}$$

Next we are going to say that different bonds can be more volatile than others. Again, we expect the 30-year bond to be more volatile than the 3-month bond.

We combine these plausible conditions by stating that the relationship between the expected return on a bond, μ_{P^T}, its volatility, σ_{P^T}, and the short rate should be such that the excess return from a T-maturity bond, $\mu_P - r$, should just be a multiple of its volatility, σ_{P^T}. This means that we must have

$$-\lambda_r = \frac{\mu_P - r}{\sigma_P}, \tag{8.4}$$

where λ_r is a universal constant. (Don't worry about the negative sign for the moment.) We shall prove that this is indeed the case in Section 12.2. So far, we are just *proposing* that how much more one bond is expected to return over the riskless rate must be proportional to its volatility; and that the ratio of the excess return to the volatility should be a universal proportionality constant, the same for all bonds. We stress that, so far, we have presented a plausible argument, not a proof.

If we accept this, we can easily solve for μ_P to give

$$\mu_P = r - \lambda_r \sigma_P. \tag{8.5}$$

Remembering our Ito's Lemma, and thinking of a bond as a function of *the* factor (the short rate), we have

$$P_t^T = f(r_t).$$ (8.6)

Since the volatility of the bond is given by

$$\sigma_P = \frac{\partial P_t^T}{\partial r}\sigma_r.$$ (8.7)

Equation (8.2) implies that

$$\mu_P = r - \frac{1}{P_t^T}\lambda_r\sigma_P = r - \lambda_r\frac{1}{P_t^T}\frac{\partial P_t^T}{\partial r}\sigma_r,$$ (8.8)

where σ_r is the volatility of our short-rate factor.

But we also know that the drift of a bond is linked to the volatility and drift of the state variable (the short rate, in this case) by Ito's Lemma:

$$\mu_P = \left[\frac{\partial P_t^T}{\partial t} + \frac{\partial P_t^T}{\partial r}\mu_r^{\mathbb{P}} + \frac{1}{2}\frac{\partial^2 P_t^T}{\partial r^2}\sigma_r^2\right],$$ (8.9)

where $\mu_r^{\mathbb{P}}$ is the drift in the real-world measure of the short rate.

Equating expressions (8.9) and (8.8) we obtain

$$\frac{1}{P_t^T}\left[\frac{\partial P_t^T}{\partial t} + \frac{\partial P_t^T}{\partial r}\mu_r^{\mathbb{P}} + \frac{1}{2}\frac{\partial^2 P_t^T}{\partial r^2}\sigma_r^2\right] = r - \lambda_r\frac{1}{P_t^T}\frac{\partial P_t^T}{\partial r}\sigma_r.$$ (8.10)

This in turn means that

$$\frac{1}{P_t^T}\left[\frac{\partial P_t^T}{\partial t} + \frac{\partial P_t^T}{\partial r}\left(\mu_r^{\mathbb{P}} + \lambda_r\sigma_r\right) + \frac{1}{2}\frac{\partial^2 P_t^T}{\partial r^2}\sigma_r^2\right] = r.$$ (8.11)

We can look at this result in two equivalent ways.

The first interpretation goes as follows. Start with the process for the bond price, that, as we have seen, we know must be linked to 'some' expectation of the path of the short rate. If we are risk averse, we would not accept to earn the risk-less rate to bear the risk of a T-maturity bond. We want a compensation for doing so, and this compensation is given by $\mu_P = r - \lambda_r\frac{1}{P_t^T}\frac{\partial P_t^T}{\partial r}\sigma_r$. (Remember that the 'duration' $\frac{\partial P_t^T}{\partial r}$ is negative: as yields go up, bond prices go down! Therefore $-\lambda_r\frac{1}{P_t^T}\frac{\partial P_t^T}{\partial r}$ is positive.)

Here is the second way to look at Equation (8.11): we can pretend that over a time step dt we earn 'only' the short rate from holding the risky bond, as long as the process for the short rate is adjusted to 'point higher', by adding the term $\lambda_r\sigma_r$.

Why higher? Because if rates go higher, the bond price today must be lower, and, *for a fixed terminal payment* ($P_T^T = \$1$), the bond yields more. That's where the compensation comes from.

This shows us two important things. The first is that, after we have adjusted for risk, ie, in the risk-neutral measure, the rate of growth of any bond is just the short rate, r. This is just what we found in Chapter 4.

The second is that we can write for the process for the short rate in the pricing measure

$$\mu_r^{\mathbb{Q}} = \mu_r^{\mathbb{P}} + \lambda_r \sigma_r. \tag{8.12}$$

Therefore, going back to the Monte Carlo thought experiment that started this discussion, the thought process we had used was almost correct. It was only 'almost correct' because, in order to calculate the price of the T-maturity bond today, we really have to take the expectation (ie, to calculate and average the 'accrual paths') in the 'risk-neutral measure', ie, we have to take the expectation after adjusting the drift of the short rate from the real-world drift, $\mu_r^{\mathbb{P}}$, to the risk-adjusted drift, $\mu_r^{\mathbb{Q}}$:

$$P_t^T = \mathbb{E}^{\mathbb{Q}}\big[e^{-\int_t^T r_s ds}\big]. \tag{8.13}$$

In terms of our hypothetical Monte Carlo simulation, this simply means that we will have to make the short rate evolve not with the drift we have estimated in the real world, $\mu_r^{\mathbb{P}}$, but with the adjusted drift, $\mu_r^{\mathbb{Q}} = \mu_r^{\mathbb{P}} + \lambda_r \sigma_r$. (This is a good time to revisit Section 4.4.)

And, of course, if we do this for bonds of different maturities, we can rest assured that all the bond prices will allow no arbitrage.

I stress that we have not proven this result (because little more than plausibility could be invoked for the condition $(-\lambda_r = \frac{\mu_P - r}{\sigma_P})$ from which all of this follows. A proper proof will have to wait till Part III, but, in general, plausibility is not a bad place to start with.

8.2.2 Moving to Many Factors

What else happens if we have many factors in our affine model, and perhaps none of these is the short rate itself? Not much, really. Why so? Because one of the requirements for a model to be affine is that the short rate should be given by an affine function of the state variables, like so:

$$r_t = a + \big(\overrightarrow{b}\big)^{\mathrm{T}}\overrightarrow{x}_t, \tag{8.14}$$

where $\overrightarrow{x}_t$ denotes the vector of state variables, a is a constant, and $\big(\overrightarrow{b}\big)^{\mathrm{T}}$ is the transpose of some vector $\overrightarrow{b}$. (As we have seen in Chapter 2, the row-vector-by-column-vector multiplication $\big(\overrightarrow{b}\big)^{\mathrm{T}}\overrightarrow{x}_t$ gives just a number.)

Therefore, whatever our chosen variables, we can always transform them into the short rate, and then the heuristic reasoning presented in the previous sub-section carries on without change.

'Wait a minute', the reader may say at this point, 'if this is the case, why bother with multifactor models? If, ultimately, it matters only what the short rate does, why not use the short rate as the one and only state variable?'

One glib way to answer the question is that, to begin with, we would live in a one-factor world, and therefore all the yields would have to move in the same direction. This is all well and good, but not very illuminating. If we have, say, three state variables, what exactly happens in the multifactor case to the paths of the one and only quantity, the short rate, that ultimately determines the yields? In which way will the paths be different in the multifactor case, so as to make some yields go up and some others go down?

This question can be answered from many angles. Since in this chapter we are dealing with expectations, let's answer it from the expectation perspective. So, let's assume that we live in a two-factor world, and that the affine link between the state variables (x_t^1 and x_t^2) on the one hand and the short rate on the other is given by

$$r_t = a_1 x_t^1 + a_2 x_t^2. \tag{8.15}$$

For instance, if we denote by l_t some 'long yield' we could have

$$x_t^1 = r_t + l_t \tag{8.16}$$

$$x_t^2 = r_t - l_t \tag{8.17}$$

$$a_1 = a_2 = \frac{1}{2} \tag{8.18}$$

and we could interpret the first variable as the level of rates, and the second as the slope of the yield curve. However, nothing hangs on this interpretation. Suppose now that the two state variables follow the same mean-reverting process of the form:

$$dx_t^i = \kappa_i \left(\theta_i - x_t^i \right) dt + \sigma_i dz_t^i \quad i = 1, 2 \tag{8.19}$$

and that variable x_t^1 starts from a level well above its reversion level, and variable x_t^2 from a level well below. See Figure 8.2. Finally let's require that the reversion speed of the second variable should be much greater than the reversion speed of the first. Again, this is not essential, but it will help make the point. We can then look at the expected path of the two state variables, and hence of the short rate (which is just the weighted sum of the two). These expected paths are shown in Figure 8.2.

The important thing to note is that, while the expected paths for the two state variables are monotonic, the resulting path for the short rate is humped. It would not be possible to obtain such a humped path for the short rate with a single-factor affine model with time-independent parameters, because such a model can only produce either a monotonically increasing or a monotonically decreasing expected path. So, yes, it is the case that if we know all the possible paths of the short rate we know everything we need to determine yields and all their properties. However, it is not enough to specify an affine time-independent process for the short rate to obtain the flexibility afforded by a multifactor description.

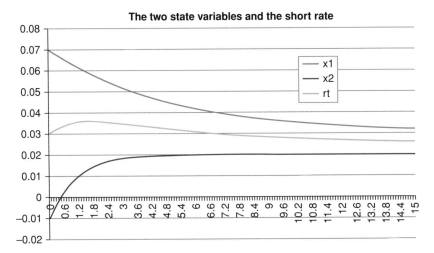

Figure 8.2 The deterministic evolution over a 15-year period horizon of the two state variables whose sum makes up the short rate. The reversion speed for the two variables were chosen to be 0.2 and 0.88 $year^{-1}$, respectively, and the reversion levels 0.03 and 0.02 $year^{-1}$. Note how the expected path for the short rate is humped, despite the monotonic behaviour of the expected paths for the two component state variables.

The problem, of course, is not limited to the expectation part of the process. The reader is invited to extend the reasoning to the volatilities of different-maturity yields.

There is another important reason why multifactor affine models are essentially different from a one-factor short-rate–based model, despite the fact that 'all that matters in the end' are the paths of the short rate. When we say 'all that matters in the end', what we really mean is that 'all that matters in the end *for pricing*' is the distribution of paths of the short rate. This statement is therefore about how we should take expectations in the risk-neutral ($\mathbb{Q}$) measure. But there is more to life – even to the life of a bond investor – than market prices. No theorem says that the risk premium should just be a function of the paths of the short rate. Therefore, if we are interested in a *structural* description (ie, a description that straddles the $\mathbb{Q}$- and $\mathbb{P}$-measures), it may well be that we require quantities that are not 'spanned' by the $\mathbb{Q}$-paths of the short rate. More about this in what follows.

8.3 AN EXAMPLE: A MEAN-REVERTING PROCESS FOR THE SHORT RATE

Let's see all of this in action, and, as we always do when we find our feet, let's go back to the Vasicek model.

Suppose that we have estimated, using historical data, the parameters of the process of the short rate (note the superscript $\mathbb{P}$ attached to the reversion level and to the increment of the Brownian motion):

$$dr_t = \kappa \left(\theta^{\mathbb{P}} - r_t \right) dt + \sigma_r dz_t^{\mathbb{P}}. \tag{8.20}$$

Then, when we run our 'Monte Carlo simulation', we have to augment the drift of the short rate by the term $\lambda \sigma_r$; ie, we have to evolve (note the $\mathbb{Q}$)

$$dr_t = \left[\mu_r^{\mathbb{P}} + \lambda_r \sigma_r \right] dt + \sigma_r dz_t^{\mathbb{Q}} \tag{8.21}$$

and the compensation for risk will be accounted for correctly.

Since

$$\mu_r^{\mathbb{P}} = \kappa \left(\theta^{\mathbb{P}} - r_t \right) \tag{8.22}$$

this just means that we have to adjust the reversion level from $\theta^{\mathbb{P}}$ to $\theta' = \theta^{\mathbb{P}} + \frac{\lambda \sigma_r}{\kappa}$. This is exactly what we shall see in detail in Chapter 10,[1] but, hopefully, we should already have a satisfactory (although still not complete) understanding of the transformation.

In reality, we usually proceed the other way around. At time t we observe the prices P_t^T (so we now are in the risk-neutral measure $\mathbb{Q}$), and we work out which parameters, $\{\kappa, \theta', \sigma_r\}$, for the process of the short rate in the thought-experiment Monte Carlo simulation best reproduce these prices. Note that, by doing this we can only obtain $\theta' = \theta^{\mathbb{P}} + \frac{\lambda \sigma_r}{\kappa}$: we cannot disentangle the real-world reversion level from the risk compensation.

Of course, if we had *independently* estimated $\theta^{\mathbb{P}}$ using statistical data, *then* we could gain access to the risk premium. But this is not an easy task, as we discussed in Chapters 6 and 7, given the quasi-unit-root nature (the high persistence) of rates.

This is all well and good, but does this mean that really we have to run Monte Carlo simulations to get the prices? Luckily, we don't. We will show in Chapter 17 that, if the state variables are affine and follow a mean-reverting process, the expression for the bond price, which in the Vasicek case will be shown to have the form

$$P_t^T = e^{A_t^T + B_t^T r_t}, \tag{8.23}$$

now simply generalizes to

$$P_t^T = e^{A_t^T + \left(B_t^T \right)^{\mathsf{T}} r_t}. \tag{8.24}$$

It both cases we will show that this expression comes exactly from evaluating the expectation (8.13) with some clever mathematics. *Therefore, if we price bonds using Equation (8.24), we are automatically guaranteed that we have woven together expectations, convexity and term premia in an arbitrage-free manner.*

Did we say 'convexity'? What happened to convexity in our thought-experiment Monte Carlo simulation? Where does it comes in?

---

[1] See Section 10.7.

The crucial part is that we carry out an *average over prices*, each of which is given by $\exp \int_t^T r_s ds$. We do not first average over the paths and then take the exponential:

$$P_t^T \neq e^{-(\mathbb{E}^{\mathbb{Q}}[\int_t^T r_s ds])}. \tag{8.25}$$

This makes a difference, and the difference is convexity: when a function does not describe a linear relationship, calculating the average of the function, or the function of the average does not give the same result. (The difference is due to the *Jensen's inequality* that we discuss in detail in Chapter 9.) Whether the difference is positive or negative depends on whether the function is concave or convex. This too will be the topic of the next chapter.

8.4 EXPECTATIONS AND SURVEY DATA

Economists and finance professionals regularly provide their predictions about macroeconomic data and financial quantities. Central bankers also provide 'forward guidance' about the future paths of the rates they directly control. Some of these predictions are formalized in public releases, of which the Fed's 'blue dots' and the Bank of England's 'inflation fans' are probably the best known. These vaticinations and pieces of guidance are pored over by market professionals with the exegetic devotion once afforded to biblical texts.

To the extent that the predictions and the guidance of market experts and of the monetary authorities (respectively) are 'believed' by the market participants, it would therefore seem that real-world expectations should be relatively easy to arrive at.

Of course, whether the projections of the experts are on average 'correct' is neither here nor there: ex ante they should still inform the (possibly very wrong, but unbiased) expectations formed by investors.[2]

Now, it would be clearly foolish to disregard these predictions. However, it is not infrequent to observe market quantities that are difficult to reconcile with the public predictions or guidance. During 2014, for instance, market yields (which are in the $\mathbb{Q}$ measure) were systematically *below* the guidance provided by the Fed's 'blue dots'. So much so that Fed officials expressed their puzzlement as to why 'they were not taken seriously', ie, why their guidance was not heeded.

Of course, the *deus ex machina* of a negative risk premium can always be invoked to reconcile the market yields and the guidance.[3] However, at least another explanation for a discrepancy must be taken into account.

---

[2] Persistent prediction errors could occur systematically, of course only, to the extent that investors did not detect the systematic bias in the predictions of the experts, and did not adjust their views accordingly.

[3] For instance, in December 2014 ex-chairman Bernanke mooted the possibility of a 'negative beta with the equity market' as a possible explanation for the fact that the expectation-related 'blue dots' were found stubbornly above the corresponding market yields. By this he meant that perhaps in late 2014 investors were happy with a negative risk premium because they perceived Treasuries to be a good hedge against equity market moves.

In many surveys the polled expert (economist or central banker) is asked to express a view about *the most likely outcome* for, say, the Fed rates or inflation over a certain horizon. In statistical parlance, asking for the *most likely* outcome means asking for the mode. For a Gaussian distribution, this exactly coincides with the mean and the median and, for a not-too-asymmetric distribution, it will not lie too distant from either. However, it may be that at a particular time deviations from the most likely outcome may be strongly biased (in the real-world, $\mathbb{P}$, measure) either up or down. In this case, the mode and the mean can be very different.

So, for instance, suppose that at time t_0 the distribution in the back of an expert's mind of the possible realizations of a yield is as follows:

- rate at 4.00% with probability 25%
- rate at 3.00% with probability 50%
- rate at 2.00% with probability 25%

Clearly, her 'most likely' value is 3.00%, which also corresponds with the mean of her subjective distribution.

At a later time t_1 the expert changes her mind, and her distribution becomes

- rate at 4.00% with probability 1%
- rate at 3.00% with probability 50%
- rate at 2.00% with probability 49%

Now, if asked about her 'most likely' value the answer would still be 3.00%; however, the mean is now close to 2.5%. If the market shares a similarly shaped distribution as the expert's (ie, if the market thinks that the surprises to the most likely scenario are more likely to be in one direction rather than the other), then the market expectations of the yield will be very different from the mode.

All of this is to say that forward guidance data should, well, *guide* the location of the real-world parameters linked to expectations, but that too rigid a link should be avoided for a variety of reasons, of which the mode/mean difference is an important one.

CHAPTER 9

Convexity: A First Look

9.1 THE PURPOSE OF THIS CHAPTER

In this chapter we look at another of the three building blocks of term-structure modelling, namely convexity.

In Part V we will look in detail at how convexity reveals itself in market yield curves, and we will explore to what extent we can 'capture' its value. For the moment we explain where convexity 'comes from' and explore its links with Jensen's inequality.

We show that it is related to the volatility of (a function of) the state variables: no volatility, no convexity. We also provide an order-of-magnitude estimate of its magnitude. Finally, we show on which parameters of affine models convexity depends – the Vasicek model, as usual, will provide the intuition.

9.2 WHERE DOES CONVEXITY COME FROM?

Take the yield, y_t^T, of a bond of maturity T. This yield will move stochastically over time. Let's assume that an upward yield move by x basis points is just as likely as a downward move by the same amount.

If we accept this equi-probability assumption of same-magnitude up-and-down moves *of yields*, we immediately observe that the moves in the bond price will not display this symmetry: the bond price will move up in price (in correspondence with the *down* move in yield) by more than it declines (in correspondence with the *up* move in the yield). By how much? Let's look at Table 9.1, which shows the initial prices of discount bonds of various maturities from 2 to 30 years (we assumed a flat yield curve at 5.5%), the average prices corresponding to an up-and-down move of 25 basis points, and the difference (in basis points) between the average and the initial value of each price.

Note how the difference between the average of the two prices and the initial price increases as the maturity increases. This is because the relationship between yields and prices is not linear – more precisely, because of Jensen's inequality, that we briefly discuss later.

Table 9.1 *Average up-and-down prices and their differences. The row labelled 'price (0)' shows the initial prices of discount bonds of various maturities from 2 to 30 years (we assumed a flat yield curve at 5.5%). The row labelled 'avg(price)' shows the average prices corresponding to an up-and-down move of 50 basis points. The bottom row, labelled 'diff (bp)', shows the difference (in basis points) between the initial price and the average price.*

Mat (yrs)	2	3	5	7	10	15	20	30
price(0)	0.8958	0.8479	0.7595	0.6805	0.5769	0.4382	0.3329	0.1920
avg(price)	0.8959	0.8480	0.7598	0.6809	0.5777	0.4395	0.335	0.1942
diff (bp)	0.4	1.0	2.4	4.2	7.2	12.3	16.7	21.6

Whatever the origin of this effect, the market 'knows about' this nice feature of long bonds, and, *everything else being equal*, long-dated bonds will command a higher price (a lower yield) than short-dated ones.

Where does the effect come from? We can see it formally from the expansion for the bond price as a function of the yield. Start from

$$P_t^T = e^{-y_t^T(T-t)}. \tag{9.1}$$

We want to use Ito's Lemma to obtain an expression for the increment in the bond price, dP_t^T, once we are given the process for the yield, of the form

$$dy_t^T = \mu_{y_t^T} dt + \sigma_{y_t^T} dz_t. \tag{9.2}$$

As a preparation, recall that

$$\frac{\partial P_t^T}{\partial t} = y_t^T P_t^T \tag{9.3}$$

and that

$$\frac{\partial^2 P_t^T}{\partial (y_t^T)^2} = (T-t)^2 P_t^T. \tag{9.4}$$

Next, assume for simplicity that up-and-down moves are equiprobable:

$$\mathbb{E}[dy_t^T] = 0 \implies \mu_{y_t^T} = 0. \tag{9.5}$$

This assumption is not really necessary, but it simplifies the algebra.

Then we obtain for the percentage increment in the bond price:

$$\begin{aligned}
\frac{\mathbb{E}[dP_t^T]}{P_t^T} &= \frac{1}{P_t^T}\left[\frac{\partial P_t^T}{\partial t}dt + \frac{\partial P_t^T}{\partial y_t^T}\mathbb{E}[dy_t^T] + \frac{1}{2}\frac{\partial^2 P_t^T}{\partial (y_t^T)^2}(dy_t^T)^2 + \ldots\right] \\
&= \left[y_t^T dt + \frac{1}{2}(T-t)^2(dy_t^T)^2 + \ldots\right] \\
&= \left[y_t^T + \frac{1}{2}(T-t)^2(\sigma_{y_t^T})^2 + \ldots\right]dt, \tag{9.6}
\end{aligned}$$

where $\sigma_{y_t^T}$ is the absolute volatility (ie, the basis-point volatility) of the $(T - t)$ maturity yield, and in the last line we have used the relationship

$$\left(dy_t^T\right)^2 = \left(\sigma_{y_t^T} dz_t\right)\left(\sigma_{y_t^T} dz_t\right) = \left(\sigma_{y_t^T}\right)^2 dt. \tag{9.7}$$

Equation (9.6) shows that the expected return gets an extra boost over and above the yield term, y_t^T, by the quantity, $\frac{1}{2}(T - t)^2(\sigma_{y_t^T})^2$, which is always positive.

It also shows that the magnitude of this yield boost depends *quadratically* on the maturity of the discount bond and on the volatility of the yield. The convexity effect should therefore dominate at the long end.

As we said, the market 'knows about' this effect. Investors will therefore pay more for long-dated bonds, pushing down their yields. The shape of the yield curve at the very long end is unlikely to be affected by expectations (do *you* have views as to whether the short rate will be rising or falling in 30 years' time?), but it *will* be affected by the term premium. However, while the contribution from the term premium is approximately linear in maturity, the contribution from convexity is quadratic. In the long run, *Convexitas* (if not *Amor*) *vincit omnia*. This is why all yield curves, sooner or later, should become downward sloping. The very nice paper by Brown and Schaefer (2000) – whose title is *Why Long Term Forward Interest Rates (Almost) Always Slope Downwards* – makes the point very clearly.

Note that we have set $\mathbb{E}[dy_t^T] = 0$. Nothing hangs on this, as long as we are focussing on convexity. Adding a non-zero expectation term simply adds an extra term, but does does not change the discussion in this section: it only makes the algebra messier.

(Much) more about this later.

9.3 THE LINKS BETWEEN CONVEXITY AND JENSEN'S INEQUALITY

The concept of convexity is linked to a very general mathematical result, which goes under the name of Jensen's inequality (Jensen, 1906), and which says the following[1].

Given a random variable, x, for any concave function of x, $f_{\text{conc}}(x)$, the expectation of the function evaluated at x is smaller than the function of the expectation of x:[2]

$$\mathbb{E}[f_{\text{conc}}(x)] \leq f_{\text{conc}}(\mathbb{E}[x]). \tag{9.8}$$

---

[1] The original (1906) paper by Jensen says nothing about expectations. The version of Jensen's inequality used in finance (and statistical physics!) is a probabilistic extension. In this probabilistic extension, since we are talking of expectations, the variable x must be stochastic.

[2] If we assume differentiability at least to second order, a concave function is one for which the second derivative is negative. Conversely, for a convex function. Mathematicians do not like this definition, because, by requiring differentiability, it is unduly restrictive. For our purposes it will do nicely.

The reverse is true for any convex function, f_{conv}:

$$E[f_{\text{conv}}(x)] \geq f_{\text{conv}}(E[x]). \tag{9.9}$$

When the function f is an exponential, the probabilistic form of Jensen's inequality can be proven very simply.[3] This is how it is done.

We want to prove that

$$\mathbb{E}[e^x] \geq e^{\mathbb{E}[x]}. \tag{9.10}$$

Rewrite the left-hand side as

$$\mathbb{E}[e^x] = \mathbb{E}\big[e^{x+\mathbb{E}[x]-\mathbb{E}[x]}\big]. \tag{9.11}$$

(We have just added and subtracted in the exponent the same quantity, $\mathbb{E}[x]$, something that we can always do.) Now, x is a stochastic variable, but $\mathbb{E}[x]$ is a known quantity (a real number), so we can take $e^{\mathbb{E}[x]}$ (which is also a known number) out of the expectation sign, or leave it in, as we please. We choose to do half and half and to write

$$\mathbb{E}\big[e^{x+\mathbb{E}[x]-\mathbb{E}[x]}\big] = \mathbb{E}\big[e^{\mathbb{E}[x]}e^{x-\mathbb{E}[x]}\big] = e^{\mathbb{E}[x]}\mathbb{E}\big[e^{x-\mathbb{E}[x]}\big]. \tag{9.12}$$

Now we are going to expand the exponential inside the expectation sign, recalling that

$$e^x = 1 + x + O(x^2) \tag{9.13}$$

and that

$$e^x > 1 + x. \tag{9.14}$$

Then we have

$$\begin{aligned}
\mathbb{E}[e^x] &= \mathbb{E}\big[e^{x+\mathbb{E}[x]-\mathbb{E}[x]}\big] = e^{\mathbb{E}[x]}\mathbb{E}\big[e^{x-\mathbb{E}[x]}\big] \\
&\geq e^{\mathbb{E}[x]}(\mathbb{E}[1 + x - \mathbb{E}[x]]) = e^{\mathbb{E}[x]}(1 + \mathbb{E}[x] - \mathbb{E}[\mathbb{E}[x]]) \\
&= e^{\mathbb{E}[x]}(1 + \mathbb{E}[x] - \mathbb{E}[x]) = e^{\mathbb{E}[x]}.
\end{aligned} \tag{9.15}$$

Therefore we have shown that

$$\mathbb{E}[e^x] \geq e^{\mathbb{E}[x]}, \tag{9.16}$$

which is what we had set out to do.

9.3.1 A Special but Important Case: Gaussian Random Variables

This is all well and good, but the result we have just obtained does not show clearly an important feature of convexity, ie, the fact that *how much* the exponential of the expectation differs from the expectation of the exponential depends on the volatility (squared) of the underlying stochastic variable.

---

[3] See, eg, Chandler (1987), Section 5.5.

To show that this is indeed the case, we are going to place ourselves in a rather special setting, ie, in the case when the stochastic variable x follows a Brownian process:

$$dx = \mu_x dt + \sigma_x dz. \tag{9.17}$$

To keep things really simple we are also going to assume that the drift, μ_x, and the volatility, σ_x, are both deterministic. We want to compare in this special but important case the two quantities $\mathbb{E}[e^{x_t}]$ and $e^{\mathbb{E}[x_t]}$. To do so we must first get an expression for x_t:

$$x_t = x_0 + \int_0^t \mu_x dt + \int_0^t \sigma_x dz_t. \tag{9.18}$$

(To lighten notation, and without loss of generality, in what follows we set $x_0 = 0$.) So, we want an expression for $\mathbb{E}[e^{\int_0^t \mu_x dt + \int_0^t \sigma_x dz_t}]$ and for $e^{\mathbb{E}[\int_0^t \mu_x dt + \int_0^t \sigma_x dz_t]}$.

Let's start from the second quantity. We know that the expectation of an Ito integral is always zero:

$$\mathbb{E}\left[\int_0^t \sigma_x dz_t\right] = 0. \tag{9.19}$$

Therefore

$$e^{\mathbb{E}[\int_0^t \mu_x dt + \int_0^t \sigma_x dz_t]} = e^{\mathbb{E}[\int_0^t \mu_x dt]} = e^{\int_0^t \mu_x dt}. \tag{9.20}$$

Let's now go back to the first quantity, $\mathbb{E}[e^{\int_0^t \mu_x dt + \int_0^t \sigma_x dz_t}]$. We know[4] that

$$\mathbb{E}\left[e^{-\int_0^t \frac{1}{2}\sigma_x^2 dt + \int_0^t \sigma_x dz_t}\right] = 1, \tag{9.21}$$

and therefore

$$1 = \mathbb{E}\left[e^{-\int_0^t \frac{1}{2}\sigma_x^2 dt \int_0^t \sigma_x dz_t}\right] = e^{-\int_0^t \frac{1}{2}\sigma_x^2 dt} \mathbb{E}\left[e^{\int_0^t \sigma_x dz_t}\right]$$

$$\Rightarrow \mathbb{E}\left[e^{\int_0^t \sigma_x dz_t}\right] = \frac{1}{e^{-\int_0^t \frac{1}{2}\sigma_x^2 dt}} = e^{\int_0^t \frac{1}{2}\sigma_x^2 dt}. \tag{9.22}$$

This means that we can write

$$\mathbb{E}\left[e^{\int_0^t \mu_x dt + \int_0^t \sigma_x dz_t}\right] = \mathbb{E}\left[e^{\int_0^t \mu_x dt} e^{\int_0^t \sigma_x dz_t}\right] = e^{\int_0^t \mu_x dt} \mathbb{E}\left[e^{\int_0^t \sigma_x dz_t}\right]$$

$$= e^{\int_0^t \mu_x dt} e^{\int_0^t \frac{1}{2}\sigma_x^2 dt}, \tag{9.23}$$

where we have used the result in Equation (9.22) to get to the last line. So, in this particular setting, we have ascertained that

$$\mathbb{E}\left[e^{\int_0^t \mu_x dt + \int_0^t \sigma_x dz_t}\right] = e^{\int_0^t \mu_x dt} e^{\int_0^t \frac{1}{2}\sigma_x^2 dt}. \tag{9.24}$$

Now, the multiplicative term $e^{\int_0^t \frac{1}{2}\sigma_x^2 dt}$ is always positive (because it is an exponential) and therefore we not only can say that

$$\mathbb{E}\left[e^{\int_0^t \mu_x dt + \int_0^t \sigma_x dz_t}\right] = \mathbb{E}[e^{x_t}] > e^{\mathbb{E}\left[\int_0^t \mu_x dt + \int_0^t \sigma_x dz_t\right]} = e^{\mathbb{E}[x_t]} \tag{9.25}$$

---

[4] See Chapter 2.

(which we knew already), but we can also see by *how much* it is larger: by the quantity $e^{\int_0^t \frac{1}{2}\sigma_x^2 dt}$.

In general, if Z is a Gaussian random variable, then we have *exactly*

$$\log(\mathbb{E}[e^Z]) = \mathbb{E}[Z] + \frac{1}{2}Var[Z]. \tag{9.26}$$

For any (not-necessarily-Gaussian) random variable, X, the result holds as a (normally very good) approximation:

$$\log(\mathbb{E}[e^X]) \simeq \mathbb{E}[X] + \frac{1}{2}Var[X].$$

This is the important result of this section: when the convex function under consideration is the exponential, the difference between the expectation of the exponential and the exponential of the expectation always depends (exactly or to first order, depending on whether the stochastic variable is Gaussian or not) *on the square of the volatility* of the underlying stochastic variable. Figure 9.1 graphically displays this result.

Exercise 17 *In which part of the proof did we make use of the fact that the drift, μ_x, and the volatility, σ_x, were deterministic functions of time?*

9.4   WHAT DOES CONVEXITY DEPEND ON?

Let's look back at the last line of Equation (9.6). What we are interested in is the convexity term, $\frac{1}{2}(T-t)^2(\sigma_{y_t})^2$. When we do affine term-structure modelling, we start from the process of a set of state variables; we derive the expression for bond prices, and from these we obtain the yields; and finally, using Ito's Lemma we can obtain the yield volatilities, $\sigma_{y_t^T}$, that enter the convexity term.

Now, if convexity is all that we interested in, as long as our chosen model produces, after the transformations just described, what we think are the correct yield volatilities, then we can rest assured that the convexity that comes out of our model is right. Why so? Because, looking again at the last line of Equation (9.6), there is nothing else to convexity. So, if we have on one hand a one-factor model à la Vasicek, and on the other hand a seven-factor affine model with a fantastically complex reversion speed matrix, a volatility matrix to match, and exotic state variables, but we know that the two models produce exactly the same yield volatilities for *all* maturities, then the convexity contribution to the shape of the yield curve the two models provide is exactly the same. Therefore, the question 'What does convexity depend on?' can be equivalently (and more transparently) rephrased as 'What do yield volatilities depend on?'

What do these volatilities do depend on, then? We shall take a first look at convexity in the Vasicek model in Chapter 10. In that simple setting, we shall see that the volatilities of yields of different maturities came from the interplay between the reversion speed, κ (which 'tucks in' the dispersion of the bond prices), and the volatility of the short rate, σ_r (which acts in the direction of spreading them out).

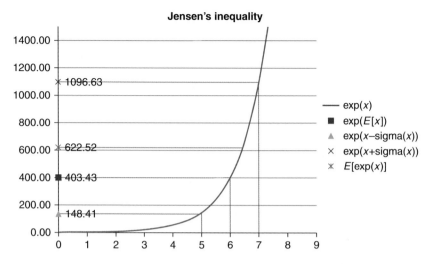

Figure 9.1 Illustration of Jensen's inequality in the case of the exponential function, e^x. The Gaussian variable x has an expectation of 6 and a standard derivation of 1: $E[x] = 6, \sigma[x] = 1$. The values of x at its expectation and one standard deviation above and below the expectation, $E[x] = 6, E[x] + \sigma[x] = 7$ and $E[x] - \sigma[x] = 5$, are marked on the x-axis. On the y-axis the markers show the exponential of the expectation of x, $e^{E[x]} = 403.43$ (red square); the exponential $e^{E[x]+\sigma[x]} = 1096.65$ (the cross); the exponential $e^{E[x]-\sigma[x]} = 148.41$ (the triangle); and the average of the two exponentials evaluated one standard deviation above and below the expectation (the light blue barred cross), $E[e^x] = 622.52$. One immediately sees that $E[e^x] = 622.52 > e^{E[x]} = 403.43$. One can also simply appreciate that the greater the standard deviation (ie, the more spaced the points $E[x] + \sigma[x]$ and $E[x] - \sigma[x]$ on the x-axis), the greater the difference.

The observation can be generalized to multifactor affine models. These, in general, come equipped with a volatility matrix and a reversion-speed matrix. The former specifies how the various factors spread out over time, and how they are correlated; the latter accounts for their mean-reverting behaviour, ie, for how tightly they are tucked in. Together, once we have gone through the Ito's Lemma transformation, these two quantities will uniquely determine the volatilities of different yields. Hence, they will determine convexity.

These simple – and pretty obvious – observations give us a first inkling that perhaps using the heavy machinery of a multifactor affine model can be a cumbersome way to look at convexity – even more so, when we consider that, if we want to recover closely the volatilities of *lots* of yields, our model is very likely to have several factors. Perhaps a statistical approach that focusses on the best forward-looking estimates of yield volatilities might be a better tool to crack the convexity nut. As we shall see, this is exactly the approach we shall explore in detail in Chapter 21. (See, in particular, Section 21.6.)

9.5   WHY CONVEXITY IS DIFFERENT

We prove in excruciating detail in Chapter 24 that, if 'forward rates came true' (ie, if forward rates were unbiased estimates of future rates) there would be no money to be made on average from the systematic strategy of funding oneself at the short end and investing at the long end of the yield curve. As we shall discuss in detail in Chapter 24, saying 'forward rates came true' is just another way of saying that the expectation hypothesis is true.

The empirical evidence that has accumulated over the last 40 years points rather unambiguously to the conclusion that the expectation hypothesis does not hold. To be clear: this does not mean that forward rates contain *no* information about future rates; it simply means that they contain something more, and that this 'something more' is not just noise. As we will discuss in detail, it is, of course, the risk premium.

Now, if the risk premium associated with Treasury bonds is on average positive, an obvious strategy offers itself to the (very) patient investor. She should just fund herself with a short-maturity bond, invest in a long-maturity bond, unwind the zero-cost portfolio when the funding expires, and put in place again an equivalent portfolio with the new short and long bonds available. Wash, rinse, and repeat, really. We discussed this in Chapter 5, and we will look at this strategy in detail in Part VI of this book.

The important point for this discussion is that the investor who engaged in this 'carry' strategy will admittedly suffer pretty unpleasant P&L swings (and Chapter 25 shows how unpleasant these can be), but in the long run she will come out on top, as long as the average risk premium is positive.[5] The reason for this 'easy money' is simply that the risk premium is, well, a 'premium' – ie, an extra compensation – over the actuarially expected ($\mathbb{P}$-measure) future paths of rates. In the context of the discussion of convexity, the point here is that, apart from patience and a strong capitalization, nothing else is required to profit from risk premia.

Convexity is different. If one buys a highly convex bond (and pays for its convexity in terms of a lower yield, ie, a yield lower than if convexity were not factored in the price) and just sits on it, the precious convexity advantage, for which good money has been paid, is dissipated away. As we will show in Chapter 20, 'capturing' the value of convexity requires an active (actually, a *very* active) dynamic strategy, akin to the 'gamma trading' that a delta-neutralized option trader would engage in.

As we have said, convexity does not come for free: when we buy a long-dated bond, its yield will be lower (its price higher) than in the absence of

---

[5] We shall show in Chapters 26 and 27 that, both for nominal and for real yields, the risk premium is positively correlated with the slope of the yield curve. As this changes sign over time, so does the risk premium. However, since the yield curve is, on average, upward sloping, the (unconditional) risk premium is, on average, positive. Of course, by watching the slope of the yield curve, an investor could do better than always buying long-dated bonds and selling short-dated ones, irrespective of the slope signal. However, even this not-so-clever strategy would on average make money.

convexity. The greater the expected future volatility, the lower the yield.[6] So, to get convexity, we are paying up in yield terms. Is convexity good value? It depends on the interplay between the price the market assigns to convexity (linked to today's market's expectation of the future yield volatility) and the future realized volatility of the same yield. It is a tug of war between future realized and current 'implied' volatility.

When the trade-off is presented in these terms, the analogy with the gamma of an option is clear: suppose a trader buys an option (and therefore ends up being long gamma, and 'long' realized volatility[7]) and engages in accurate delta-hedging. Whether she will end up on top by option expiry will depend on whether the future realized volatility will turn out to be greater or smaller than the 'implied' volatility that determined the price for which she bought the option.

This way of looking at convexity also shows that whether an investor can effectively 'capture' the convexity value embedded in the higher bond price to a large extent depends on who the investor is. This is because the value of convexity can be harnessed, if at all, only by pursuing a 'very-high-maintenance' hedging strategy. So, for a buy and-hold, long-only investor, paying for convexity is unlikely to be an attractive proposition. It is akin to buying an out-of-the-money option with zero intrinsic value, and not engaging in delta hedging. We may end up making money (because the option may end up in-the-money), but, if we do, it will be because of the correctness of our directional views, not because of the value of convexity that we bought (possibly cheaply).

What about more active investors? In principle, by immunizing against the sources of risk (by 'delta hedging' in options lingo, or by 'duration hedging' in the language of bond trading), the investor can set out to capture the difference between the realized and the implied volatility: if she thinks that the market implies too low a volatility, she will be 'buying' convexity (ie, she will build a duration-neutral portfolio with positive convexity) and, by rebalancing her positions (ie, by keeping it constantly duration neutral), she will make a little bit of money every time she does so.

How would the investor make money? Because, exactly as an option trader who has bought an option (and is therefore long gamma), she will repeatedly buy low and sell high. The greater the (realized) volatility, the more of these buy-and-sell 'round trips' she will engage in, and the more money she will make.

Vice versa, if she thinks that the implied volatility 'too high', she will build a duration-neutral portfolio which has negative convexity, and she will hope that she will have to rebalance it as rarely as possible. Why so? Because now she is short an option (she is short gamma), and in order to remain duration-neutral she will have to buy when the price has gone up, and sell when it falls.

---

[6] How much lower will the yield be? In a Vasick world, the results derived in Section 3.5 provide the answer.

[7] The expression 'being long realized volatility' means that the trader will benefit more and more the higher the realized volatility will end up being.

'Wait a minute', the attentive reader may say, 'When I sell an option I get a premium up-front, and I hope that the re-hedging costs during the life of the option will eat into only a fraction of this premium. But where is the "premium up-front" when I set up a negative convexity portfolio?' The answer is that, almost invariably, a negative convexity portfolio will offer the trader a 'yield pick-up'. What this exactly means is explained in detail in Chapters 20 and 21. For the moment, the important observation is that this yield pick-up is the exact equivalent of the option premium received for selling an option.

This is all fine in theory. We show in Chapter 20 that life is not quite as simple as that. An investor who enters a simple-minded duration-neutral, long-convexity strategy is likely to see his P&L buffeted even by relatively small residual level and slope exposures. As a consequence, even when this active, but hedging-naive, investor believes that she is entering a pure convexity trade, her P&L is likely to be first-order affected by unwanted residual level and slope risk. So, even the active investor can only hope to 'monetize' convexity if she is willing to craft and rebalance a well-designed and precisely immunized portfolio.

It will, in general, not be enough just to immunize against parallel moves in the yield curve, or even against the first principal component. However, we show in Chapters 20 and 21 that, if the investor insulates carefully her portfolio against level and slope risk; if she chooses advisedly the mix of maturities for the constituent bonds; and if she rebalances her portfolio assiduously and with small transaction costs, then the 'signal' (ie, the convexity-driven P&L) can become significantly larger than the noise (the unhedged residual factor(s)).

9.6 WHY ISN'T CONVEXITY 'ALWAYS GOOD'?

These conclusions seem to fly in the face of conventional wisdom, which places long convexity in the company of motherhood and apple pie. The argument roughly goes as follows. Suppose the investor has entered a duration-neutral position, long, say, a 30-year zero and short a 5-year zero. Suppose also, to focus on the essentials of the example, that the yield curve can only move in parallel.

Now, recall that convexity is the rate of change of duration[8]. Therefore, if rates fall, the long-convexity position will make the investor longer duration, and if they rise, shorter. Being long duration when rates fall and being short duration when they rise is rather nice. Surely, irrespective of whether we actively rebalance or not, this is a state of affairs worth paying for (at least something). Or is it?

The fly in the ointment is that this simple reasoning applies only to the first move. The initial portfolio was duration neutral, but, after the initial parallel shift (up or down, as the case may be), the portfolio will no longer be duration neutral: as we said, convexity is the rate of change of duration, just as, in option

---

[8] If a refresher is needed, see Chapter 2.

language, the 'gamma' (convexity) is the rate of change of the delta (duration). And the crucial point is that, over the next move, the small delta that the portfolio will inherit after the initial move is likely to give rise to larger P&L changes than any convexity contribution. Even a small delta can easily swamp a 'large' convexity.

Of course, the investor can re-immunize her portfolio, but she must do so very actively. If she does not, the long-convexity investor is throwing away the time value of her 'option': every time the yield curve moves up and down and comes back to the same level without the investor having re-hedged her position, she will have thrown away some of the time value of the option she had paid for. In option language, the investor has lost some 'theta' (time decay): she has thrown away some of the time value she paid for.

This brings us back to the same conclusion: reaping the benefit of convexity requires a very active strategy, and sluggishness in rebalancing the portfolio wastes money. Once again, it is like buying an out-of-the money call option, perhaps for a low implied volatility, and failing to delta hedge: the strategy might make money, but, if it does, it will do so only because of a directional move. And, arguably, if one really has directional views, buying out of the money calls or puts is not the best way to express them. One should just buy (or sell) the underlying – or futures, if one is enamoured of leverage.

9.7 WHO SETS THE PRICE OF CONVEXITY? A BIT OF STORY-TELLING

> There are those [...] who, deeming that all truth is contained within certain outlines [...], if you proceed to add colour or relief from individuality, protest against rhetoric as an illogical thing; and if you drop as much as a hint of pleasure or pain [...], raise a prodigious outcry against all appeals to the passions.
> William Hazlitt – *On Reason and Imagination*

In matters financial, engaging in story-telling is every bit as fun as in any other human endeavour, but probably more dangerous: the danger being, of course, that, with enough ingenuity and imagination, we can all too easily concoct just-so stories to explain virtually everything we observe. So, as a rule, I refrain from providing explanations based on 'market colour', and I usually count myself among the curmudgeonly individuals who 'raise a prodigious outcry' against loose financial narratives. I make an exception in this final section, but, as I do so, I must place more numerous, and more luridly painted, health warnings than I normally do. So, this is my foray into mythopoiesis.

The value of convexity becomes apparent only in very-long-dated bonds and swaps. (So far, this is a fact; the story has not begun yet.) In this segment of the yield curve we can expect two classes of players to be active: (i) institutional investors (pension funds, insurance companies), who may have negatively convex long-dated liabilities, and, perhaps for accountancy or regulatory reasons, may want to match their long-dated liabilities with long-dated assets;

(ii) opportunistic, maturity-agnostic arbitrageurs (say, hedge funds), ready to exploit 'mispricings' wherever they occur. (In case you didn't notice, the story is in full swing now.)

We can think of the former as the 'drivers' of the implied value of convexity, and of the latter as the potential 'exploiters' of excessive or insufficient implied convexity. Let's assume that this thumb-nail picture is sufficiently accurate to be useful. What does this imply?

If we look at the institutional investors, these are unlikely to engage in the very active hedging strategies needed to extract the value of convexity. Absent their regulatory constraints and the enticement from matching their liabilities, one could therefore argue that these players are unlikely to pay much for convexity, and long-dated yield would therefore end up being 'too high'.

However, the picture changes when their long-dated (and negatively convex) liabilities are brought into consideration: the desire to match the maturity profile of their liabilities, and to reduce the associated negative convexity,[9] creates a net institutional demand for these long-dated assets. This demand, in turn, is strongly influenced by regulatory changes, which dictate how liabilities should be discounted.

The question then is whether this desire, or regulatory requirement, to hedge their duration and convexity exposure generates 'too much' or 'too little' demand from institutional investors (where 'too much' or 'too little' is to be understood with respect to the fair 'amount of' convexity embedded in the curvature of the term structure of yields). Now, it would be close to a miracle if the complex combination of the regulatory requirements, the internal risk policies, and the total amount and maturity profile of the pension liabilities conjured to create a demand for long-dated bonds that exactly matched the fair value of convexity. In general, one can therefore expect 'mispricing' – ie, one can expect that long-dated yields may be 'too low' or 'too high'.

Now, if the mispricing were sufficiently large, the opportunistic pseudo-arbitrageurs may be enticed to spring into action, thereby reducing – and perhaps fully correcting – the price 'error'. And it may also be expected that these 'hedge-fund-like' players should be active in periods of high liquidity, capacious balance sheets and plentiful assets to manage, and run for the hills in periods of turmoil. If this were true, and if their actions were an important contributor to the fair pricing of convexity, we may observe greater residual opportunities from 'mispriced convexity' in the aftermath of market dislocations (ie, when skittish investors withdraw funds, balance sheets are shrunk, and no asset is liquid enough) . Finally, our story leads us to something that we can test (and that can, albeit very indirectly, corroborate the plot): are convexity-trading opportunities greater in periods of reduced liquidity?

---

[9] Where does the negative convexity of pension providers come from? For accountancy purposes, their liabilities are made equivalent to a short position in some (real or 'virtual') very-long-dated bonds – a short position which possesses negative convexity. Since the pension fund managers are effectively short these virtual super-long bonds, their liability profile is negatively convex.

Indeed, the results we present in Chapter 22 show two things.

First, as already mentioned, the difference (of either sign) between the 'right' and the realized ('implied') convexity value is certainly larger than, but of the same order of magnitude as, the unavoidable noise associated with the strategies required to extract it. This absence of gross trading opportunities suggests that someone out there must be keeping a watchful eye on the fair value of convexity.

Second, the aftermath of the 2008 crisis seems to have provided a window of opportunity for convexity trading. Whether this was due to the retreat of the pseudo-arbitrageurs, to the sudden increase in volatility, to the increased regulatory cost of the balance sheet, or to the change in the convexity of the liabilities, it is difficult to tell. The fact remains that few, if any, dollar bills are likely to be lying in open view on the pavements of Convexity Street. For the dogged and the brave, there may, however, be many dimes and a few quarters.

CHAPTER 10

A Preview: A First Look at the Vasicek Model

> A basic rule of [research]: if the universe hands you a hard problem, try to solve an easier one instead, and hope the simpler version is close enough to the original problem that the universe doesn't object.
>
> Ellenberg (2014), *How Not To Be Wrong*[1]

> My dad once gave me the following advice: "If you have a tough question that you can't answer, first tackle a simple question that you can't answer."
>
> Tegmark (2015), *Our Mathematical Universe*[2]

10.1 THE PURPOSE OF THIS CHAPTER

In this chapter we are going to put the cart before the horse. Out of metaphor, we are going to introduce without any proofs the simplest affine model (the Vasicek model), and show its qualitative behaviour. Methodically minded readers may prefer to go through Chapters 12 to 16 first, and revisit this chapter once the theoretical foundations are firmly in place. Either way, this chapter should not be skipped.

The reason for this unseemly haste in presentation is that the Vasicek model is unsurpassed when it comes to building one's intuition about how affine models work. Whenever we look at more complex models, and our intuition begins to falter, translating the problem in Vasicek-like term (asking the question: '*What would Vasicek do?*') is almost invariably illuminating. We therefore take a first look in this chapter at how the Vasicek model juggles our three fundamental building blocks – expectations, risk premia and convexity – to determine shape of the yield curve.

More generally, keeping the results of this chapter in mind will put some flesh around the dry bones of the theoretical treatment to follow – even if the particular Vasicek flesh may later have to be flayed away to be replaced with the more muscular structure of the later-generation affine models.

---

[1] p. 35.　　[2] p. 18.

10.2 THE VASICEK MODEL

In the Vasicek (1977) model, the full yield curve is driven by a single state variable (a single factor): the short rate. It may seem that, by making this assumption, we are wagging the yield curve dog from its short-end tail. However, if we think of the short rate as closely related to the target rate set by central banks, and of yields as the (risk-premium- and convexity-corrected) expectations of the future paths of the target rate, we see that, as assumptions go, the Vasicek starting point is eminently sensible: in a nutshell, if we know where the short rate is today, and where we expect it to go in the future, we know a lot (if not everything) about how the yield curve will behave.

In the Vasicek model the short rate follows a mean-reverting process. This means that, according to the model, in the real world this single factor is attracted to a constant reversion level, θ, with a strength which is the greater the more distant the factor is from where 'it wants to be' – ie, its constant reversion level.

Why doesn't the factor just settle on its reversion level and stay there forever? (And why isn't the short rate today at the reversion level to begin with?) Because it is also randomly shocked (away or towards the reversion level) by a stochastic component with a constant volatility.

The higher (lower) the short rate has been shocked above (below) the reversion level, the larger the negative (positive) distance $(\theta - r_t)$ will be, and the stronger the reversion pull towards the reversion level, θ.

How much stronger? In the Vasicek model, the strength of the pull to the reversion level is proportional to the distance from it of the short rate. The proportionality constant is aptly called the reversion speed, κ. It can be interpreted as the strength of a spring.

Putting all the pieces together we get:

$$dr_t = \kappa \left(\theta - r_t \right) dt + \sigma_r dz_t^{\mathbb{P}}. \tag{10.1}$$

The superscript $\mathbb{P}$ in Equation (10.1) reminds us that for the moment we are using real-world quantities, with no adjustment for risk. Therefore, we cannot use this equation as it stands to price bonds. To do so, we would have to introduce the risk premium. We shall take a first look into how to do this later in this chapter.

10.3 PROPERTIES OF THE VASICEK MODEL

The Vasicek model has two important strengths: it can be analytically solved and it readily lends itself to a simple intuitive interpretation. In this section we avail ourselves of its analytical tractability to describe its salient properties.

10.3.1 Distributional Properties of the Vasicek Model

Given a process for the short rate of the type (10.1), and given the value of the short rate today, r_0, the future value of the short rate at time t is given by

$$r_t = \left\{ e^{-\kappa(t-t_0)} \right\} r_0 + \left\{ 1 - e^{-\kappa(t-t_0)} \right\} \theta + \sigma_r \int_{t_0}^{t} e^{-\kappa(t-s)} dz_s. \qquad (10.2)$$

For those readers who do not like to see rabbits produced from hats, we show in Appendix 10A how this result can be derived. For the moment let's take it for granted. From this expression it follows that the value of the distribution $\phi(r_t|r_0)$ for the short rate at any future time t is a normal and *stationary* distribution:

$$\phi(r_t|r_0) = \mathcal{N}\left(\mu, s^2 \right). \qquad (10.3)$$

Its (conditional) mean is given by

$$\mu = \left\{ e^{-\kappa(t-t_0)} \right\} r_0 + \left\{ 1 - e^{-\kappa(t-t_0)} \right\} \theta \qquad (10.4)$$

$$= w_k r_0 + (1 - w_k) \theta \qquad (10.5)$$

with

$$w_k = e^{-\kappa(t-t_0)}, \qquad (10.6)$$

and its (conditional) variance is given by

$$s^2 = \frac{\sigma_r^2}{2\kappa} \left\{ 1 - e^{-2\kappa(t-t_0)} \right\}. \qquad (10.7)$$

Exercise 18 *Why? Why is it a normal distribution? The bit about the conditional mean is easy. Derive the expression for the conditional variance.*

What does 'stationary' mean? It means that the variance of the distribution does not grow indefinitely with time. Why doesn't it? Because of the 'tucking-in' effect of the reversion speed. See later.

Some comments are in order. As we said, and as Equation (10.4) shows, the expectation, $\mathbb{E}[r_t|r_0]$, of the short rate at a future time, t, is given by a weighted combination of where the short rate is today, r_0, and its reversion level, θ:

$$\mathbb{E}[r_t|r_0] = \left\{ e^{-\kappa(t-t_0)} \right\} r_0 + \left\{ 1 - e^{-\kappa(t-t_0)} \right\} \theta \qquad (10.8)$$

$$= w_k r_0 + (1 - w_k) \theta, \qquad (10.9)$$

with the weights, w_k and $1 - w_k$, adding up to 1. How quickly the expectation will go to the reversion level depends on the reversion speed, κ. For a given reversion speed, the longer in the future we look, the closer the expectation will be to the reversion level. Figure 10.1 shows the expectation of the future values of the short rate for different initial values of r_0, as a function of the dimensionless parameter $x = \kappa \times t$, when the reversion level is $\theta = 4.5\%$. So, if we want to see the expectation of the short rate 10 years after today when the reversion speed is, say, $\kappa = 0.2$, we just have to look at the value $x = 10 \times 0.2 = 5$. This works because κ and t always appear together as a product, and this product is a pure (dimensionless) number.

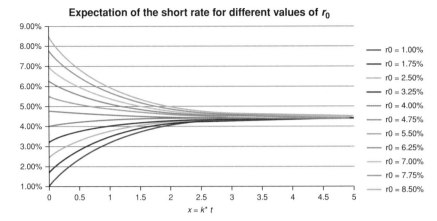

Figure 10.1 Expectation of the future values of the short rate for different initial values of r_0, the short rate 'today', from 1.00% to 8.00%, as a function of the dimensionless parameter, $x = \kappa \times t$, shown on the x-axis. The reversion level, θ, was assumed to be 4.50%.

As mentioned previously, the variance of the short rate, $var\,[r_t|r_0]$, does not grow indefinitely as the horizon time grows, but tends to a finite reversion-speed-dependent asymptotic level, $\left(s^\kappa_{\text{asympt}}\right)^2$, given by

$$\left(s^\kappa_{\text{asympt}}\right)^2 \equiv \frac{\sigma_r^2}{2\kappa}. \tag{10.10}$$

The same weight, w_k, encountered in the expression for the expectation plays a role again in determining how quickly the variance approaches its asymptotic value, because one can write for the variance

$$s^2 = \left(s^\kappa_{\text{asympt}}\right)^2 \left\{1 - w_k^2\right\}. \tag{10.11}$$

This asymptotic level is reached exponentially. Figures 10.2 and 10.3 show the square root of the variance for two typical values of the reversion speed, ie, $\kappa = 0.1$ and $\kappa = 0.8$.

We clearly see from these figures that in both cases the variance does not increase indefinitely. When the speed of mean reversion is strong, the variance 'saturates' very quickly.

Why does the asymptotic variance depends (inversely) on the reversion speed? Because the higher the reversion speed (the stronger the 'spring' that pulls the short rate back towards its reversion level when its strays away from it), the more rates will be 'tucked in', and the less they will behave like a Brownian diffusion – whose variance goes to infinity with time and which, given enough time, will visit all of the available space. This 'tucking in' of the rates effected by the positive reversion speed is arguably the single most important

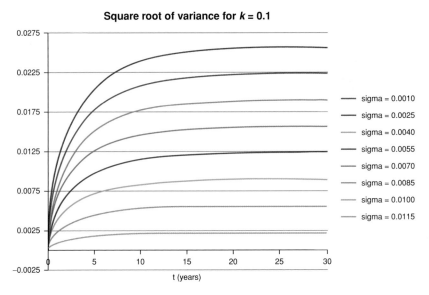

Figure 10.2 Square root of the variance as a function of the projection horizon (*x*-axis, in years), for different values of the absolute short rate volatility from 0.0010 to 0.0115, for a relatively weak reversion ($\kappa = 0.1$).

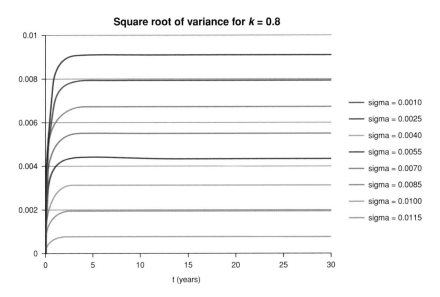

Figure 10.3 Same as Figure 10.2 for a strong reversion speed of $\kappa = 0.8$. Note how the variance now 'saturates' very quickly for all values of the short rate volatility.

feature of Vasicek-like (mean-reverting) models, and affects absolutely everything: expectations, how risk premia are 'distributed' across different maturities, convexity, you name it.

10.3.2 Bond Prices in the Vasicek Model

We will show that the time-t price of a T-maturity discount bond, P_t^T, generated by a process of the form (10.46) is given by

$$P_t^T = e^{A_t^T + B_t^T r_t},$$ (10.12)

with

$$B_t^T = -\frac{1 - e^{-\kappa(T-t)}}{\kappa}$$ (10.13)

and

$$A_t^T = -\left(\theta' - \frac{\sigma_r^2}{2\kappa^2}\right)\left[B_t^T + (T - t)\right] - \frac{\sigma_r^2}{4\kappa}\left(B_t^T\right)^2.$$ (10.14)

(We derive this result in Chapter 16.) Note that in Equation (10.14) there appears a superscript prime (′) decorating the reversion level. This is to remind us that this is not the reversion level in the real world (ie, the reversion level that we could, in principle, determine by means of statistical techniques), but a 'corrected' reversion level, where the correction comes from risk aversion.[3] We will present first and then derive an expression for this correction in what follows.

10.3.3 The Duration in the Vasicek Model

Let's recall now the definition of duration, Dur_t^T, presented in Chapter 2:

$$Dur_t^T = -\frac{1}{P_t^T}\frac{dP_t^T}{dy_t^T}.$$ (10.15)

By looking at Equation (10.12) as a function of r_t, and using Ito's Lemma, it is easy to see that the term B_t^T has an interpretation of (minus) 'duration'[4]:

$$B_t^T = \frac{1}{P_t^T}\frac{\partial P_t^T}{\partial r_t},$$ (10.16)

with the short rate playing the role of the yield in the standard definition. We can be a bit more precise. As we shall see, one of the defining features of affine

---

[3] We have assumed in arriving at Equations (10.13) and (10.14) that the market price of risk is a constant. If it were to depend on the short rate as well, then also the reversion speed, κ, would change. See Exercises 6 and 7 in Chapter 4 and the discussion in Section 10.6 of this chapter.

[4] Duration is always taken to be a positive quantity, measured in years.

models is that all yields should be expressible as an affine function of the state variables. In the case of the Vasicek model the only state variable is the short rate, and therefore the affine conditions for the yields becomes

$$y_t^T = \alpha_t^T + \beta_t^T r_t. \tag{10.17}$$

This also means that

$$dy_t^T = \beta_t^T dr_t, \tag{10.18}$$

and therefore the expression for the yield duration becomes:

$$Dur_t^T = -\frac{1}{P_t^T}\frac{dP_t^T}{dy_t^T} = -\frac{1}{P_t^T}\frac{1}{\beta_t^T}\frac{dP_t^T}{dr_t}. \tag{10.19}$$

Now, from Equation (10.12) we known that

$$P_t^T = e^{A_t^T + B_t^T r_t} \tag{10.20}$$

and, from Equation (10.13), that

$$B_t^T = -\frac{1 - e^{-\kappa(T-t)}}{\kappa}. \tag{10.21}$$

Taking the logarithm of Equation (10.12), and remembering the definition of a yield, one therefore obtains

$$\beta_t^T = \frac{1 - e^{-\kappa(T-t)}}{\kappa(T-t)} \tag{10.22}$$

and, finally,

$$Dur_t^T = -\frac{1}{P_t^T}\frac{1}{\beta_t^T}\frac{dP_t^T}{dr_t} = -\frac{1}{P_t^T}\frac{\kappa\tau}{1 - e^{-\kappa\tau}}\frac{dP_t^T}{dr_t}, \tag{10.23}$$

with

$$\tau \equiv T - t. \tag{10.24}$$

Exercise 19 *Derive Equation (10.22).*

When τ is very small – ie, when the yield maturity is very close to zero – we can expand the exponential to first order only:

$$e^{-\kappa\tau} \simeq 1 - \kappa\tau + O\left(\tau^2\right) \tag{10.25}$$

and therefore we have

$$Dur_t^T = -\frac{1}{P_t^T}\frac{\kappa\tau}{1 - e^{-\kappa\tau}}\frac{dP_t^T}{dr_t} = -\frac{1}{P_t^T}\frac{dP_t^T}{dr_t}, \quad \tau \ll 1. \tag{10.26}$$

This makes sense: a very-short-maturity yield behaves 'almost like' the short rate, and therefore taking a derivative with respect to the short-maturity yield should be almost the same as taking a derivative with respect to the short rate.

When τ is not small, taking a derivative with respect to the short rate is not quite the same as taking a derivative with respect to a yield, because, as we have seen,

$$\frac{d}{dy_t^T} = \frac{1}{\beta_t^T} \frac{d}{dr_t}. \tag{10.27}$$

More precisely, since $\beta_t^T \leq 1$, taking the derivative with respect to the short rate is equivalent to taking the derivative with respect to the τ-maturity yield, times a term (β_t^T), which is almost identical to unity for small τ, and then becomes progressively smaller than one as maturity increases.

As we shall see, when we have many factors in a mean-reverting model, each will contribute a term like B_t^T, and to each factor we will therefore associate an equivalent duration.

The model-specific function B_t^T is very important, and not just because it is the Vasicek equivalent of duration, but also because, as we show in the text that follows, it is linked to convexity. And it also determines how the risk premium associated with each risk factor is apportioned to bonds of different maturities. Even if we did a splendid job at estimating the *risk-factor* risk premia, but our model described poorly how the various-maturity bonds depend on the risk factors, our apportionment of risk premia across the yield curve would be very wrong. And, as we show in the next sub-section, B_t^T enters (via its first-degree cousin, β_t^T) the expression for the volatilities of yields of different maturities. Of course, since the quantity B_t^T, and hence β_t^T, are just a function of the reversion speed, κ, all these features go back (once again), to the 'tucking in' effect of a non-zero reversion speed.

As this quantity is so important, it is useful to get an intuitive feel for its magnitude. We can do so by revisiting the concept of half-life, $H(\kappa)$, that we introduced in Chapter 2. Suppose that the short rate is today a certain distance above or below the reversion level, θ. How long do we expect it will it take for this distance to be halved? The answer is: 'A time $H(\kappa)$, given by $H(\kappa) = \frac{\log 2}{\kappa}$.' So, for $\kappa = 0.1$ the half-life is a bit less than 6 years; for $\kappa = 0.8$ it is a bit more than 10 months; for $\kappa = 0.02$ it is a bit less than 35 years.

Exercise 20 *Given a long but finite time series of rates, what are your hopes of estimating reliably a reversion speed of $\kappa = 0.02$? Simulate a long history (say, 10 years), of a mean-reverting process with a reversion speed of 0.002, and of a pure Brownian motion with the same random draw. Compare the two time series. Could you confidently tell whether the process you are measuring is a Brownian diffusion or a mean-reversion with a reversion speed of $\kappa = 0.02$? What does it mean for the variance of yields?*

Exercise 21 *Instead of the half-life, calculate the third- fourth-, . . ., nth life, ie, the expected time for the process to reduce its current (non-zero) distance* *from the reversion level, θ, to one third, one fourth, $\ldots$, one nth of its original distance.*

10.3.4   Yield Volatilities in the Vasicek Model

We have derived in the preceding text the link between yields and the short rate in the Vasicek model,

$$y_t^T = \alpha_t^T + \beta_t^T r_t. \tag{10.28}$$

It is a very simple step, then, to deduce that the volatility of a T-expiry yield will just be β_t^T times the volatility of the short rate. As we said, since the term β_t^T depends only on the term B_t^T, and this term, in turn, depends only on the reversion speed, yield volatilities (and forward-rate volatilities) will depend only on the reversion speed and the volatility:

$$\sigma_{y_t^T} = \beta_t^T \sigma_r. \tag{10.29}$$

Since we know that the term β_t^T is monotonically decreasing from a value of 1 for $\tau = 0$, we see that the volatilities of yields will always be smaller than or equal to the volatility of the short rate. This is not a very nice feature of the model. We will have a lot more to say about this in Chapter 30.

Note carefully that the reversion level, θ, which influences the expectation contribution to the shape of the yield curve, only enters the term A_t^T, and therefore does not affect yield volatilities.

What the term A_t^T does affect is the shape of the yield curve, which is determined to first order by the interplay between today's value of the short rate and its reversion level (is the expected path of the short rate going to point upwards or downwards?); and, to a lesser extent, by the volatility (via convexity). We shall make use of this partial decomposition when we calibrate complex Vasicek-like models, which come equipped with a multitude of parameters eager to be estimated.

Now that we have built a first understanding of how the Vasicek model behaves, we can go back to our original framework, where we had decomposed the drivers of the yield curve into expectation, risk premium and convexity,[5] and ask the question: 'How do these contributors to the shape of the yield curve appear in the Vasicek model?'

10.4   RATE EXPECTATIONS AND THE SHAPE OF THE VASICEK YIELD CURVE

The Vasicek model can deal with expectations of rates only in a very simple, and actually rather crude, way: given that the short rate today is at value r_0, according to the model it can only be pulled upwards or downwards to a fixed level, θ, according to Equation (10.8). Given the location of the short rate today

---

[5] See the beginning of Part IV for a qualitative picture of how these three components determine the shape of the yield curve.

with respect to the reversion level, θ, the only other degree of freedom we have to modulate our expectations is the strength of the reversion speed, κ. However, as we have seen, this parameter is crucial in determining a host of other things, such as the model duration, the volatility of yields and the value of convexity. Therefore, if one wants to obtain an economically justifiable model, and not a 'snapshot' (fitting) model, one has to handle the reversion-speed parameter with great care.

The observation that the short rate can only be pulled up or down at a greater or lower speed does not mean that the yield curve as a whole has to be monotonically increasing or decreasing – we also have the convexity term to take into account, which can 'bend downward' the long end of the yield curve. However, if we try to fit a yield curve that, because of expectations, has a relatively complex shape, we may well find a decent fit, but we have probably tortured the model parameters so as make them confess under duress to values they really did not want to assume. See later.

The obvious conclusion from this brief analysis is that in the Vasicek model the deterministic component to the yield curve shape coming from expectations is rather crude: it can direct the short rate up or down only from where it is now, and at a speed dictated by the reversion speed, κ, on whose slender shoulders also rests the task of controlling how quickly the asymptotic variance is reached. See Equation (10.11).

This is a first example of the double role played in affine models by the reversion speed, κ: on the one hand, it determines how quickly the short rate will approach its reversion level – and, therefore, the short-term, expectation-driven contribution to the shape of the yield curve; on the other hand, it also controls the volatilities of different yields – see Equation (10.29) – which in turn control convexity and the apportionment of risk premia across the yield curve. This 'double life' of κ creates a problem in affine models: if the reversion speed is optimized together with the other model parameters by fitting to yields of all maturities, the outcome will be an uneasy compromise between getting the convexity or the expectation right. If the reversion speed is instead determined together with the volatility of the short rate by a fit to yield volatilities or to swaption volatilities,[6] the recovery of short-maturity yields is unlikely to be satisfactory.

The problem is not automatically solved by introducing more factors, or more complex affine models. Fortunately, judicious fixes can solve this problem, but these will be presented later.

---

[6] A swaption is an option on a forward swap rate. If we accept that the volatility of yields should not be too different from the volatility of swap rates, then the volatilities of very-short-expiry swaptions can provide a reasonable proxy for the market-implied yield volatility. Why would one want to go through the trouble of extracting the market-implied estimate of a yield volatility when one can calculate it in Excel® in under a minute using the trusted STDEV function? Because the former is forward-looking, and the latter only knows about the past. Careful, though: to the extent that volatility is (perceived to be) stochastic, the 'implied' swaption volatility will also contain a volatility risk premium.

10.5 CONVEXITY IN THE VASICEK MODEL

10.5.1 An Expression for Convexity

So much for expectations. Let us now move to the second building block, convexity.

We will show later that the T-maturity yield, y_t^T, is not equal to the $\mathbb{Q}$-expectation of the average of the path of the short rate from time t to time T. This is because yields are proportional to the logarithm of bond prices, and bond prices, in turn, are the expectation of the exponential of the short rate path,

$$P_t^T = \mathbb{E}^{\mathbb{Q}} \left[e^{-\int_t^T r_s ds} \right],$$ (10.30)

not the exponential of the expectation of the short rate path.

The difference, $\mathfrak{Cp}_t^T$, between the real bond price, P_t^T, and the fictitious price, $\widetilde{P}_t^T$, that would obtain if one could write

$$\widetilde{P}_t^T = e^{-\mathbb{E}^{\mathbb{Q}}\left[\int_t^T r_s ds\right]}$$ (10.31)

is a quantity of interest. This is the 'value of convexity' in price terms. Of even greater interest is the corresponding difference in yields, ie, the 'value of convexity', in yield terms, $\mathfrak{Cy}_t^T$:

$$\mathfrak{Cy}_t^T = y_t^T - \widetilde{y}_t^T \,,$$ (10.32)

where the fictitious yield, $\widetilde{y}_t^T$, is given by

$$\widetilde{y}_t^T = -\frac{1}{T-t} \log \widetilde{P}_t^T \,.$$ (10.33)

Since, if there were no uncertainty (no volatility), there would be no convexity, one can always obtain the value of convexity in yield terms, $\mathfrak{Cy}_t^T$, simply by taking the difference between the yields obtained using the correct expressions (10.13) and (10.14) and the 'virtual' yields that would obtain if in the expression for the A_t^T term the volatility were zero. A quick derivation shows that, for the Vasicek model, the 'value of convexity' in yield terms is given by

$$\mathfrak{Cy}_t^T \,(Vasicek) = \frac{1}{\tau}\sigma_r^2 \left[\frac{-B_t^T - \tau}{2\kappa^2} + \frac{\left(B_t^T\right)^2}{4\kappa} \right]$$ (10.34)

with

$$\tau \equiv T - t$$ (10.35)

Exercise 22 *Derive Equation (10.34).*

Exercise 23 *Prove that, in the limit as κ tends to zero from above, the term* $\mathfrak{Cy}_t^T \,(Vasicek) \equiv y_t^T - \widetilde{y}_t^T$ *is given by*

$$\lim_{\kappa \to 0} \mathfrak{Cy}_t^T \,(Vasicek) \equiv \lim_{\kappa \to 0} \left[y_t^T - \widetilde{y}_t^T \right] = -\frac{1}{6}\sigma_r^2\tau^2$$ (10.36)

Note that, for a reversion speed approaching zero, the Vasicek model behaves almost like a pure Brownian diffusion. By taking the limit as κ tends to zero from above, Equation (10.34) therefore shows that

- 'value of convexity' is always quadratic in the volatility of the factor (in the Vasicek model, the short rate);
- it would also be quadratic in $(T - t)$ if the reversion speed were zero; and
- it will grow less than quadratically for any finite reversion speed, κ (because, for $\kappa > 0$, B_t^T is always smaller than $(T - t)$).

10.5.2   Convexity and the Volatility of Yields

Equation (10.34) can be rewritten as a function of the yield volatilities. Let's derive these quantities first. Recall that the yield, y_t^T, is always given by

$$y_t^T = -\frac{1}{\tau} \log \left(P_t^T \right),\tag{10.37}$$

and, in the Vasicek model, the bond price, P_t^T, is given by

$$P_t^T = \exp \left[A_t^T + B_t^T r_t \right].\tag{10.38}$$

It therefore follows that

$$y_t^T = -\frac{1}{\tau} \log \left(P_t^T \right) = -\frac{1}{\tau} \left[A_t^T + B_t^T r_t \right].\tag{10.39}$$

Now, if the process for the short rate has the form

$$dr_t = \kappa \left(\theta - r_t \right) dt + \sigma_r dz_t\tag{10.40}$$

then a quick application of Ito's Lemma gives for the volatility, $\sigma_{y_t^T}$, of the T-maturity yield,

$$\sigma_{y_t^T} = -\frac{B_t^T}{T - t} \sigma_r.\tag{10.41}$$

And, as we know from Equation (10.13), as τ goes to zero from above, B_t^T goes to zero as τ itself.

Let us now rewrite the expression for the Vasicek convexity (Equation (10.34)) as a function of the yield volatilities that we have just derived. Equation (10.41) and some simple algebra give

$$\mathfrak{Cny}_t^T \ (Vasicek) = \frac{1}{\tau} \sigma_r^2 \left[\frac{-B_t^T - \tau}{2\kappa^2} + \frac{\left(B_t^T \right)^2}{4\kappa} \right]$$

$$= \frac{1}{2\kappa} \left[\sigma_{y_t^T} \frac{\sigma_r}{\kappa} - \frac{\sigma_r^2}{\kappa} + \frac{\tau}{2} \left(\sigma_{y_t^T} \right)^2 \right].\tag{10.42}$$

Exercise 24 *Derive Equation (10.42).*

This expression seems to depend both on yield volatilities ($\sigma_{y_t^T}$ and σ_r) and on the reversion speed, κ. But these quantities are not independent, as B_t^T depends on κ. So, if we managed to choose σ_r and κ in such a way that the model volatilities of *all* the yields coincide with the corresponding market yield volatilities, then we would know that the estimated convexity is perfectly consistent with the market. Which is another way to say that, if our model recovers all the yield volatilities correctly, then the convexity is also correctly recovered.

Of course, with a model of such Spartan simplicity as the Vasicek, the model yield volatilities will not, in general, match the market ones. However, we shall see how this result can be generalized to the case of multifactor affine models.

10.5.3 How Big Should One Expect the Convexity Effect to Be?

Let's do a back-of-the-envelope calculation to estimate the magnitude of the convexity effect in the Vasicek model. Let's assume, for simplicity, a constant yield volatility of 80 basis points (ie, $\sigma_{y_t^T} = 0.0080$). Then for the reversion speed, κ, approaching zero we would have for the 'yield value of convexity', $\mathfrak{Cy}_t^T$, for a 5-, 10-, 20-, 30- and 50-year (discount) bond of 3, 11, 43, 116 and 267 basis points, respectively. To be clear: this means that, in the absence of any mean reversion, the yield of a 50-year bond is 267 basis points lower than it would be in the absence of convexity (for $\sigma_{y_t^T} = 0.0080$). For long maturities this is not a small effect at all!

We have shown that, when the reversion speed is zero, all the yields have the same volatility, and this is just equal to the volatility of the short rate. Using the same volatility is, however, not very reasonable for yields of such different maturities as the ones considered previously. Longer-dated yields should have a lower volatility than shorter-dated ones – the more so, the more rates are mean-reverting: this is the 'tucking in' effect of the reversion speed in action again.

Let's therefore use again the Vasicek model as a guide to get a more realistic feel for the magnitude of the convexity effect when the reversion speed is not zero. As we have shown previously, the volatility, $\sigma_{y_t^T}$, of a yield of maturity $(T - t)$ is given by

$$\sigma_{y_t^T} = -\frac{B_t^T}{T-t}\sigma_r, \tag{10.43}$$

where σ_r is the volatility of the short rate, and B_t^T is the sensitivity of the bond price to the short rate that we encountered previously. (See Figure 10.4.) To get us started, let's set the volatility of the short rate at $\sigma_r = 0.0120$, ie, 120 basis points. (In isolation, this does not seem to be a reasonable value, even in normal – ie, non-monetarily repressed – market conditions, but we have to use this 'fix' with a model as simple as the Vasicek in order to obtain reasonable

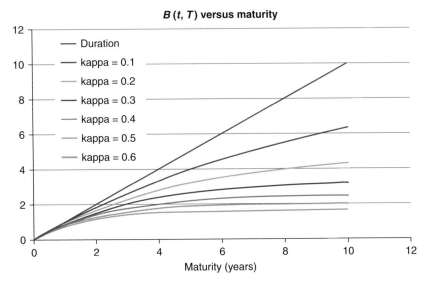

Figure 10.4 The term B_t^1 as a function of maturity (x-axis, in years) for different values of the reversion speed, from $\kappa = 0.1$ to $\kappa = 0.6$. The line labelled Duration shows the term B_t^T when the reversion speed is zero – in which case for a discount bond it corresponds to its maturity, and hence its duration.

results. We will discuss how to correct this blemish the Vasicek model in a more satisfactory way later on.)

With this volatility for the short rate we can display the volatilities of yields of different maturities for different values of the reversion speed, κ. This is done in Figure 10.5.

This gives for the convexity contribution as a function of maturity corresponding to different values of the reversion speed the behaviour shown in Figure 10.6.

For values of the reversion speed that, with this simple model, give reasonable volatilities to long-dated yields (in the region of 50 to 100 basis points), we see again that the contribution convexity makes to very-long-dated yields can be as large as 100 basis points. Not as large as the zero-reversion-speed estimate given earlier suggested, but still a very important component at the (very) long end of the yield curve.

10.5.4 What Is the 'Right' Reversion Speed?

We saw that in the Vasicek model the value of convexity depends very strongly on the value of the reversion speed. For reversion speeds as large as 0.6 (which corresponds to a half-life of a bit more than a year) the convexity contribution to yields is negligible for all maturities. However, for reversion speeds smaller than 0.1 (ie, for half-lives longer than about 7 years), the contribution at the

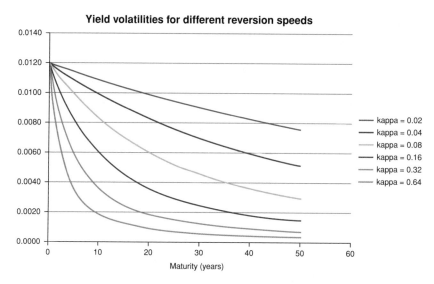

Figure 10.5 Yield volatilities for yields of different maturities (x-axis, in years) for different values of the reversion speed, doubling from $\kappa = 0.02$ to $\kappa = 0.64$. Not that the convexity contribution to the yields is given by the values on the left-hand y-axis for non-zero values of the reversion speed, and by the value son the right-hand y-axis for the zero-κ case.

long end becomes very important. This prompts the question: what is the 'right' value for the reversion speed?

To answer the question, suppose that we decompose yield changes into principal components. (See Chapters 7 and 29.) It is not difficult to calculate the reversion speeds associated with the second and third components. (See, eg,

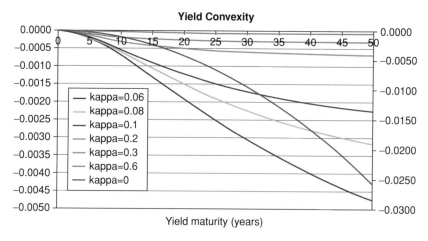

Figure 10.6 Convexity contribution to yields of different maturities (x-axis, in years) for different values of the reversion speed, from $\kappa = 0.04$ to $\kappa = 0.4$.

Diebold and Rudebusch (2013)[7] and the discussion in Chapter 32.) Whatever their precise values, casual inspection shows that the half-life of principal components higher than the first is short, the reversion speed high, and the convexity contribution from the 'slope' and 'curvature' therefore exceedingly modest.

The situation changes radically when we look at the first principal component, whose reversion speed is so low that it is difficult empirically to reject the possibility that it may be a unit-root process (ie, that it may follow a pure diffusion). If this is the case, then the convexity associated with the 'level' can be significant, especially because the volatility associated with the first principal component is much higher than the volatility associated with the second and third.

Of course, we do not have to use principal components to describe the yield curve. However, whatever set of coordinates we may choose, it will still remain the case that at least one of our state variables will display a very low degree of mean reversion, and that it will be the state variable to which the largest volatility is associated.

From this observation, it follows that there will always be a non-negligible convexity contributor to the shape of the yield curve. Note that the result follows from the combination of two facts: the first is that, however we may want to describe the dynamics of the yield curve, one component will always have a (very) low reversion speed; the second is that this slowly reverting component accounts for the lion's share of the yield curve volatility. Neither a high volatility, nor a low reversion speed in isolation is enough to bend the long end of the yield curve downwards to a significant extent. This is the intuition behind Brown and Schaefer's (2000) excellent and clear paper, aptly titled 'Why Long Term Forward Interest Rates (Almost) Always Slope Downwards'.

10.6 THE RISK PREMIUM IN THE VASICEK MODEL

When we look at the return form a bond we will see that introducing risk aversion adds an extra term to the risk-less rate in the expression for the expected return of a bond. When the term structure is driven by the short rate, we will show that the expression for the expected percentage return in the real world from a T-maturity bond becomes:

$$\frac{\mathbb{E}_t\left[P_{t+dt}^{T-dt}\right] - P_t^T}{P_t^T} = \left(r_t + \lambda_r \sigma_P^{T-dt}\right)dt = \left[r_t + \frac{1}{P_t^T}\left(\frac{\partial P_{t+dt}^{T-dt}}{\partial r}\right)\lambda_r \sigma_r\right]dt.$$

$$(10.44)$$

---

[7] See the discussion on their pp. 10–11, and their Table 1.3. For those readers who may not be familiar with the terminology used with time-series analysis, when Diebold and Rudebusch mention a process with 'high persistence', they refer to a process not too dissimilar from a pure Brownian diffusion. The reason for the term is that, if we have a pure diffusion, given a shock, there is no force to bring the Brownian motion towards some level, and the effect of the shock will therefore *persist* forever.

where σ_P^{T-dt} is the volatility of a T-maturity bond, and the quantity λ_r is the market price of risk – as we shall see, this is the compensation per unit risk an investor requires to bear the 'duration' risk associated with a risk factor. Since the 'duration' term $\left(\frac{\partial P_{t+dt}^{T-dt}}{\partial r}\right)$ simply gives the responsiveness of the particular bond to the risk factor (which, in the Vasicek case, is just the short rate), we can heuristically expect (and we will derive in Chapter 9) that the correction to the process for the short rate to account for risk aversion should have the form:

$$dr_t = [\kappa\,(\theta - r_t) + \lambda\sigma_r]\,dt + \sigma_r dz_t^Q. \tag{10.45}$$

But this can be rewritten as

$$dr_t = \kappa\left(\theta + \frac{\lambda\sigma_r}{\kappa} - r_t\right)dt + \sigma_r dz_t^Q \tag{10.46}$$

$$= \kappa\left(\theta' - r_t\right)dt + \sigma_r dz_t^Q \tag{10.47}$$

with

$$\theta' = \theta + \frac{\lambda\sigma_r}{\kappa}. \tag{10.48}$$

This equation can be interpreted in a very intuitive and natural way: adding the risk premium (ie, accounting for risk aversion) changes the reversion level from θ to θ'. This makes sense. If the term premium is positive, the reversion level will be higher, implying that rates will be attracted to a higher level, and the prices of bonds will be lower. As a reflection of aversion to risk, this is a reasonable result. (Compare this with the discussion in Section 4.3, and, in particular, with the quantity H that we will introduce there.)

10.7   THE FUNCTIONAL FORM OF THE MARKET PRICE OF RISK

An important *caveat*. The original Vasicek model assumed the market price of risk, λ, to be a constant. This assumption gives the simple result that the only change in moving from the real world to the risk-neutral world is to alter the reversion level of the short rate.

It is possible, however, to assign a more complex form to the market price of risk, while retaining the analytic tractability (and the affine nature) of the model: we can posit

$$\lambda = \lambda_0 + \lambda_1 r_t, \tag{10.49}$$

ie, we can require that the market price of risk should be a linear (affine) function of the state variable, the short rate, r_t.

Mathematically, it is easy to see what this entails: Equation (10.45) becomes

$$dr_t = [\kappa (\theta - r_t) + \lambda \sigma_r] dt + \sigma_r dz_t^Q \qquad (10.50)$$

$$= [\kappa (\theta - r_t) + (\lambda_0 + \lambda_1 r_t) \sigma_r] dt + \sigma_r dz_t^Q \qquad (10.51)$$

$$= (\kappa - \lambda_1 \sigma_r) \left[\frac{\kappa \theta + \lambda_0 \sigma_r}{\kappa - \lambda_1 \sigma_r} - r_t \right] dt + \sigma_r dz_t^Q \qquad (10.52)$$

$$= \kappa'' \left[\theta'' - r_t \right] dt + \sigma_r dz_t^Q \qquad (10.53)$$

with

$$\kappa'' = \kappa - \lambda_1 \sigma_r \qquad (10.54)$$

$$\theta'' = \frac{\kappa \theta + \lambda_0 \sigma_r}{\kappa - \lambda_1 \sigma_r} = \frac{\kappa \theta}{\kappa - \lambda_1 \sigma_r} + \frac{\lambda_0 \sigma_r}{\kappa - \lambda_1 \sigma_r}. \qquad (10.55)$$

So, the equation has retained the original form, but now both the reversion level and the reversion speed have changed. Do the changes make sense?

Let's look at the reversion speed first. If λ_1 is positive (and if $\lambda = \lambda_0$), Equation (10.54) tells us that the risk-aversion adjusted reversion speed will be lower with a state-dependent than with a constant market price of risk. A lower reversion speed means a smaller 'tucking-in' of the dispersion of rates, ie, a higher variance. It is as if risk-averse investors perceived rates to be less mean-reverting, and hence bonds to be riskier, and therefore demanded higher compensation (higher yields). This makes sense.

What about the new level of mean reversion? Now, when the market price of risk was constant, the risk-adjusted reversion level, θ', was given by

$$\theta' = \theta + \frac{\lambda \sigma_r}{\kappa}. \qquad (10.56)$$

From Equation (10.55), the new reversion level, θ'', ie, the reversion level when the market price of risk depends on the short rate, can be rewritten as

$$\theta'' = \theta \left[\frac{1}{1 - \frac{\lambda_1 \sigma_r}{\kappa}} \right] + \frac{\lambda_0 \sigma_r}{\kappa - \lambda_1 \sigma_r}. \qquad (10.57)$$

Comparing Equations (10.55) and (10.56) we can see that (for positive λ_1) $\theta \left[\frac{1}{1 - \frac{\lambda_1 \sigma_r}{\kappa}} \right]$ must be greater than θ and (if $\lambda = \lambda_0$) $\frac{\lambda_0 \sigma_r}{\kappa - \lambda_1 \sigma_r}$ must be greater than $\frac{\lambda \sigma_r}{\kappa}$. Therefore, θ'' must be greater than θ'. This means that the additional, state-dependent contribution to the market price of risk behaves as if investors were more risk averse, and therefore required the short rate to be attracted to a higher level (θ'' rather than θ').

This analysis assumed, of course, that we have *added* a state-dependent term (ie, to a term of the form $+\lambda_1 r_t$) to the same constant market price of risk ($\lambda = \lambda_0$). More realistically, when we allow for a state dependence of the market price of risk the constant term, λ_0, in the affine equation $\lambda = \lambda_0 + \lambda_1 r_t$ will *not* be the same as our best estimate of a constant market price of risk, λ_0. We will discuss the estimation problems in Chapters 23 to 25.

The distinction between models for which the market price of risk is a constant, and models for which it depends linearly (in an affine manner) on the state variables is important enough to warrant the giving of different names to the two classes. Following Dai and Singleton (2000), affine models for which the market price of risk is a constant (and for which, therefore, in one dimension, the only transformation in moving across measures is to change the reversion level from θ to θ') are called *completely affine models*. Models in which the market price of risk instead depends in an affine manner on the state variables (and for which, therefore, both the reversion level and the reversion speed change) are called *essentially affine models*. See also Saroka (2014)[8] for a discussion of this point. Remembering the names is not very important, but, as we shall see in Chapters 23 and 27, understanding the difference is.

10.8   THE LINK BETWEEN THE MARKET PRICE OF RISK AND THE SHARPE RATIO

The analysis presented in the preceding text can give us no feeling for the order of magnitude for the market price of risk. If we do not have an idea about its plausible magnitude, we will not be able to tell whether a value for the reversion level that we have fitted to the shape of the yield curve is plausible at all. This matters, because, as we have seen, we can get very similar fits to a given market yield curve with very different combinations of reversion speeds, volatilities and reversion levels. In this section we obtain an expression for the Sharpe Ratio in a one-factor world (such as a Vasicek economy). (The more general result in a multifactor case is derived in Section 15.8 in Chapter 15.)

To get an estimate of a plausible range of values for the market price of risk, recall first the expression for the Sharpe Ratio, SR, of a strategy

$$SR = \frac{\mu - r}{\sigma}. \tag{10.58}$$

(For a refresher on the Sharpe Ratio, see Sharpe (1966, 1994).)

Now, μ is the (expected) excess return from a given strategy, and σ is the associated volatility. We can consider our 'strategy' being consistently long a T-maturity bond, and funding it with a very-short-maturity bond. The short bond has very little volatility, and its return must be very close to the short rate, r. Therefore the numerator of Equation (10.58) when applied to the invest-long/fund-short strategy must be very close to the expected return from the long bond minus the short rate (the funding cost). As for the denominator, the volatility of the funding bond is essentially zero, and therefore the volatility of the strategy will be almost equal to the volatility of the long bond. So, the

[8] p. 34.

Sharpe Ratio of the invest-long/fund-short strategy is simply the ratio of the expected excess return of a T-maturity bond to its volatility:

$$SR(P) = \frac{\mu_P - r}{\sigma_P}.$$ (10.59)

We shall see in Chapter 25 that the Sharpe Ratio associated with this strategy is of the order of 0.25. (The two significant figures are not meant to convey an impression of unwarranted precision – I am simply trying to say that the Sharpe Ratios for this 'long-duration' strategies are somewhere between 0.1 and 0.4. Any number in this neighbourhood will do just as well for the reasoning that follows.)

For the sake of simplicity we are going to remain in a one-factor universe, and we assume *the* factor to be the short rate. As we shall see, nothing much hangs on this. To be sure that we don't miss the wood for the trees, we also are going to assume that the market price of risk does not depend on the state variable (the short rate). We are therefore firmly in a Vasicek world.

In this setting we then know that all that changes when we introduce risk aversion is that the reversion level of the short rate will change from θ to θ', with $\theta' = \theta + \Delta\theta = \theta + \frac{\lambda\sigma_r}{\kappa}$.

Now, consider the bond price as a function of *the* state variable, in our case r. Using Ito's Lemma the expected return from holding a T-maturity bond is given by

$$\mathbb{E}_t\left[dP_t^T\right] = \mathbb{E}_t\left[\mu_r \frac{\partial P_t^T}{\partial r_t}dt + \sigma_r \frac{\partial P_t^T}{\partial r_t}dz + \frac{1}{2}\frac{\partial^2 P_t^T}{\partial r_t^2}\sigma_r^2 dt\right]$$

$$= \mu_r \frac{\partial P_t^T}{\partial r_t}dt + \frac{1}{2}\frac{\partial^2 P_t^T}{\partial r_t^2}\sigma_r^2 dt.$$ (10.60)

We have been careless about specifying in which measure we are taking this expectation (and in not decorating the drift of the factor with a label telling us whether we are working in the real or the risk-neutral world). Clearly, if we take the expectation in the real world, then we will have to use $\mu_r^{\mathbb{P}}$; if we take expectations in the risk-neutral world we will use $\mu_r^{\mathbb{Q}}$.

But we know from the preceding discussion that the risk-neutral and the real-world drifts of the short rate differ only by the term $\Delta\theta$, given by

$$\Delta\theta = \theta' - \theta = \frac{\lambda\sigma_r}{\kappa}.$$ (10.61)

Therefore the annualized *excess* return, $xret_t^T$, that the holder of the long bond can expect to make depends on the difference in the drifts, $\mu_r^{\mathbb{Q}} - \mu_r^{\mathbb{P}}$, as the convexity terms, $\frac{1}{2}\frac{\partial^2 P_t^T}{\partial r_t^2}\sigma_r^2 dt$, will cancel out. This gives us

$$xret_t^T = \kappa\,\Delta\theta \frac{\partial P_t^T}{\partial r_t} = \kappa\left[\frac{\lambda\sigma_r}{\kappa}\right]\frac{\partial P_t^T}{\partial r_t}.$$ (10.62)

Why is this true? Because the annualized extra return over the actuarial expectation is just given by $\mu_r^{\mathbb{Q}} - \mu_r^{\mathbb{P}}$, and, in a Vasicek world, this difference is just given by

$$\mu_r^{\mathbb{Q}} - \mu_r^{\mathbb{P}} = \kappa \Delta \theta = \kappa \left[\frac{\lambda \sigma_r}{\kappa} \right].$$

This is therefore the numerator to use in the Sharpe Ratio for our bond-holding strategy.

What about the denominator, ie, the annualized volatility of the strategy? This is just the volatility from holding the T-maturity bond, $\sigma_{P_t^T}$, which, in turn, is given by

$$\sigma_{P_t^T} = \sigma_r \frac{\partial P_t^T}{\partial r_t}.$$

Therefore the Sharpe Ratio is given by

$$SR = \frac{\mu - r}{\sigma} = \frac{xret_t^T}{\sigma} = \frac{\kappa \lambda \frac{\sigma_r}{\kappa} \frac{\partial P_t^T}{\partial r_t}}{\sigma_r \frac{\partial P_t^T}{\partial r_t}}. \tag{10.63}$$

We can simplify a lot of common terms: the reversion speed, κ, in the numerator; and the 'duration', $\frac{\partial P_t^T}{\partial r_t}$, and the volatility of the factor, σ_r, between the numerator and the denominator (this, by the way, is why it didn't really matter whether the one factor was exactly the short rate, as most of the specific features of its process neatly disappear). This finally gives us

$$SR = \lambda. \tag{10.64}$$

We have established that, at least in the simplified, Vasicek-like, setting examined so far, the market price of risk is intimately related to the Sharpe Ratio associated from the invest-long/fund-short strategy described previously. It is important to note that the theoretical Sharpe Ratio from the invest-long/fund-short strategy is independent of the maturity, T, of the 'long' bond in which we invest. Interestingly, we will report in Chapter 25 the empirical result that the Sharpe Ratio is mildly dependent on (slightly declining with) the bond maturity – *which, by the way, implies that also the market price of risk is found to be almost, although not exactly, maturity – in dependent.*[9] We will show in Chapter 12 that this maturity independence is a theoretical requirement on the market price of risk stemming directly from no-arbitrage. This is a nice result.

We will also derive (a long way down the line) that the market price of risk is equal to the volatility of the stochastic discount factor. As the reader may not know yet what the stochastic discount factor is, and is therefore unlikely to have pondered very deeply about its volatility, this equivalence may, at this stage, be

---

[9] Given the nature of our derivation, note it does not necessarily follow that it should be a constant: we have only ascertained that it displays the desired independence from the bond maturity.

a bit underwhelming. It is important, however, to keep what we just obtained in the back of our minds, as it will soon illuminate many dark corners.[10]

10.9 APPENDIX 10A: PROOF THAT
$$r_t = \left\{e^{-\kappa(t-t_0)}\right\}r_0 + \left\{1 - e^{-\kappa(t-t_0)}\right\}\theta + \int_0^t e^{-\kappa(t-s)}\sigma_r dz_s$$

Start from

$$dr_t = \kappa\,(\theta - r_t)\,dt + \sigma_r dz_t. \tag{10.65}$$

Define a new variable, $\tilde{r}_t$,[11]

$$\tilde{r}_t = e^{\kappa t}\,(r_t - \theta). \tag{10.66}$$

Take the differential

$$d\tilde{r}_t = \kappa\tilde{r}_t dt + e^{\kappa t} dr_t. \tag{10.67}$$

Substitute in Equation (10.67) the expression for dr_t given in Equation (10.65):

$$d\tilde{r}_t = \kappa\tilde{r}_t dt + e^{\kappa t}\left[\kappa\,(\theta - r_t)\,dt + \sigma_r dz_t\right]. \tag{10.68}$$

Recognize that

$$r_t = e^{-\kappa t}\,(\tilde{r}_t + \theta). \tag{10.69}$$

Substitute this expression in Equation (10.68):

$$d\tilde{r}_t = \kappa\tilde{r}_t dt + e^{\kappa t}\left[\kappa\,(\theta - r_t)\,dt + \sigma_r dz_t\right]$$
$$= \kappa\tilde{r}_t dt + e^{\kappa t}\left[\kappa\left(\theta - \left(e^{-\kappa t}\,(\tilde{r}_t + \theta)\right)\right)\right)dt + \sigma_r dz_t\right]. \tag{10.70}$$

Make this equation pretty:

$$d\tilde{r}_t = \kappa\tilde{r}_t dt - e^{\kappa t}\kappa e^{-\kappa t}\tilde{r}_t dt + e^{\kappa t}\sigma_r dz_t$$
$$= e^{\kappa t}\sigma_r dz_t. \tag{10.71}$$

---

[10] I will mention in passing just one such dark corner. In the (very interesting) no-too-good-deal approach by Cochrane and Saa-Requejo (1999), two requirements are imposed to obtain the bounds on securities prices. The first is that the stochastic discount factor should be positive (this, as we shall see, just prevents arbitrage). The second is that the variance of the stochastic discount factor should not be 'too high'. This sounds as impressive as opaque: what on earth is the variance of the stochastic discount factor? However, if we take on faith for the moment that the volatility of the stochastic discount factor is just the market price of risk (we show that this is the case in Chapter 13), and that, as we have just seen, the market price of risk is, in turn, related to the Sharpe Ratio, everything begins to fall into place: a no-too-good-deal approach means a no-too-good-Sharpe-Ratio approach, which, in turn, simply means that deals with too high a Sharpe Ratio are just too good to be true. See again, in this respect, the discussion of pseudo-arbitrage (risky arbitrage) in Chapter 2. It is nice to see (again) how far the simple Vasicek model can take us.

[11] The derivation is standard. The result presented here is inspired by the treatment in Cochrane (2001), p. 370.

Integrate both sides:

$$\int_0^t d\tilde{r}_s = \int_0^t e^{\kappa s} \sigma_r dz_s$$

$$= \tilde{r}_t - \tilde{r}_0 = \sigma_r \int_0^t e^{\kappa s} dz_s = \sigma_r \int_0^t e^{\kappa s} dz_s.$$

Substitute back the expression for $r_t = e^{-\kappa t}(\tilde{r}_t + \theta)$ and obtain

$$r_t = \left\{ e^{-\kappa(t-t_0)} \right\} r_0 + \left\{ 1 - e^{-\kappa(t-t_0)} \right\} \theta + \int_0^t e^{-\kappa(t-s)} \sigma_r dz_s.$$

PART III

THE CONDITIONS OF
NO-ARBITRAGE

[Ketchup economists] have shown that two quart bottles of ketchup invariably sell for twice as much as one quart bottle except for deviations traceable to transaction costs.

L. Summers, *On Economics and Finance, 1985*

In this part of the book we look at the conditions of no arbitrage from several different angles.

We start in Chapter 11 with a treatment in a discrete-time, two-state economy. This treatment requires exceedingly little mathematical knowledge. The generality of the result is limited but, hopefully, this is more than compensated by the clarity of intuition that the treatment affords.

In the following chapter we move to a more traditional derivation of the no-arbitrage conditions, based on the construction of a risk-less portfolio. As we do this, we will be a small step away from deriving the Partial Differential Equation that bond prices (and, indeed, all interest-rate sensitive securities) must obey to prevent arbitrage, but we will not cross that particular bridge until Chapter 16. I prefer not to deal with the Partial Differential Equation at this stage in order to keep the focus strictly on the no-arbitrage conditions, which lead to, but do not require, the derivation of the fundamental Partial Differential Equation. As always, we will eclectically jump from a discrete-time to a continuous-time treatment in chase of the simplest and most transparent way to present the derivations.

In Chapter 13 we then look at no-arbitrage from a more abstract point of view, by introducing the concept of the stochastic discount factor. This treatment will give a deeper and more general understanding of no-arbitrage; it will enable the reader to understand the contemporary literature on term-structure modelling; and it will allow the weaving together of concepts introduced in different contexts, or in different treatments of the no-arbitrage conditions. For instance, we shall see that the Sharpe Ratio, the market price of risk, the volatility of the stochastic discount factor (and, for those reader who know some stochastic calculus, the volatility of the change-of-measure-related Radon–Nikodim derivative) are all in essence one and the same thing.

As we shall see, the risk premia attaching to different bonds are directly linked to the conditions of no-arbitrage. Indeed, these conditions can be seen as requirements on the *relative* magnitude of risk premia so that every bond is fairly priced. Note the emphasis on the word 'relative'. In principle, risk premia provide an *absolute* account of the compensation associated with each bond, and we give an idea of how this absolute pricing of risk could be attained in Chapter 15. However, in the approach taken in this book risk premia are mainly observed and measured, not derived from more fundamental quantities (such as the risk aversion of the representative investor). They are 'described', not 'explained', and the only requirement that we shall impose (via the no-arbitrage conditions) is that the *relative* magnitude of risk premia should be 'fairly' apportioned among different bonds. Using Prof. Summers' famous metaphor, no-arbitrage conditions have everything to do with what the fair price of two bottles of ketch-up should be, given the price of one bottle, not with the value of ketch-up.[1] The results that we will derive in Chapter 15 will nonetheless tell us something about the value of ketchup, or, out of metaphor, will enhance the reader's understanding when she looks at the 'descriptions' of the risk premia that we will provide.

Finally, the last chapter of this part of the book will look at the conditions of no-arbitrage when real (inflation-linked) bonds are concerned. This will keep us in good stead when we look at models such as the one by D' Amico, Kim and Wei (which we do in Chapter 31).

---

[1] "The differences [between economics and finance] may be clarified by considering a field of economics that could but does not exist: ketchup economics. There are two groups of researchers concerned with ketchup economics. Some general economists study the market for ketchup as part of the broader economic system. The other group is comprised of ketchup economists located in the Department of Ketchup where they receive much higher salaries than do general economists. [...] General economists are concerned with the fundamental determinants of prices and quantities in the ketchup market. They attempt to examine various factors affecting the supply and demand for ketchup such as the cost of tomatoes, wages, the prices of ketchup substitutes and consumer incomes. [...] The models that are estimated have some success in explaining price fluctuations but there remain puzzles. Ketchup economists reject out of hand much of this research on the ketchup market. [...] They believe that ketchup transaction prices are the only hard data worth studying. Nonetheless the ketchup economists have an impressive research program, focusing on the scope for excess opportunities in the ketchup market. They have shown that two quart bottles of ketchup invariably sell for twice as much as one quart bottle except for deviations traceable to transaction costs, and that one cannot get a bargain on ketchup by buying and combining ingredients once one takes account of transaction costs. [...] Indeed most ketchup economists regard the efficiency of the ketchup market as the best established fact in empirical economics. (Summers, 1985, pp. 633–634) [...] It is unfortunate, therefore, that researchers in economics pay so little attention to finance research, and perhaps more unfortunate that financial economists remain so reluctant to accept any research relating to asset prices and fundamental values" (ibid., p. 634)

CHAPTER 11

No-Arbitrage in Discrete Time

Our discussion will be adequate if it has as much clearness as the subject-matter admits of, for precision is not to be sought for alike in all discussions, any more than in all the products of the crafts.

Aristotle, *Nicomachean Ethics*[1]

I mistrust all systematizers. The will to a system is a lack of integrity.

Nietzsche, *The Twilight of the Idols*[2]

11.1 THE PURPOSE OF THIS CHAPTER

Pasting together as one pleases expectations, risk premia and convexity contributions does not produce a viable description of the evolution of the yield curve. What is missing is the glue (or, rather, the constraint) of no-arbitrage. Why do we need this 'constraining glue'? What is the intuition behind no-arbitrage? Where do these constraints come from? And what terrible things would happen if these constraints were violated? These are the questions that we try to answer in the present chapter.

We want to understand why we need no-arbitrage conditions by using as little mathematics as possible, and using very stylized examples. Generalizations are presented in the next three chapters.[3]

The presentation of no-arbitrage we provide in this chapter puts at centre stage the concept of a 'fair' compensation for risk (the 'market price of risk'). This provides a more solid financial underpinning to the understanding of the no-arbitrage conditions than more elegant, but more abstract, approaches afford. Having said this, we must keep in mind that we often sweep under the capacious risk-premium carpet a multitude of factors – from market segmentation, to regulatory or balance sheet constraints, to imperfect agent–principal relationships – that may stand in the way of the 'fair equilibration' of prices that a perfect market would allow. (See again in this respect Section 6, in Chapter 5, that was actually called 'What Is and What Is Not a *True* Risk Premium'.) So,

---

[1] Section 3, W. D. Ross, translator.   [2] I, 26, Kaufmann and Hollingdale translators.
[3] The treatment in this chapter draws heavily on Fisher (2004), which is strongly recommended.

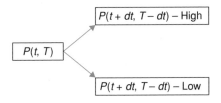

Figure 11.1 The allowed price moves for the example in the text: the bond price can move, with equal probabilities of $\frac{1}{2}$, to an 'up' or 'down' state, in which it will be worth $(P_{t+dt}^{T-dt})_H$ or $(P_{t+dt}^{T-dt})_L$, respectively. The probabilities are in the 'real world'.

the quotes at the beginning of this chapter are meant as a reminder that the elegance, rigour and terseness of no-arbitrage derivations should not make us forget that the matter is, in reality, far messier than the treatment assumes. We should, indeed, strive for as much clearness as the subject matter admits of, but, arguably, no more than that. And, when one comes to the messy subject of human preferences, that great impostor, systematization, should be both cherished and healthily mistrusted.

11.2   TYPE-I ARBITRAGE

Consider the time-t price, P_t^T, of a T-maturity bond. ('T-maturity' means that it will mature T years after t, *not* on calendar date T.) We assume that we know that over the next period, dt, the bond will be found either in a High (H) or a Low (L) state, and that we know the real-world probabilities of these two states. Without loss of generality, we are going to assume that they are $\frac{1}{2}$.

Exercise 25   *Why can we assume that the probabilities are both $\frac{1}{2}$ 'without loss of generality'?*

So, after the move, in the two possible states of the world the bond (which now has only $T - dt$ years to maturity) will become either $(P_{t+dt}^{T-dt})_H$ or $(P_{t+dt}^{T-dt})_L$. See Figure 11.1. The treatment is very similar to what we presented in Section 4.3 of Chapter 4, but in that case we spoke of a bet that paid S_{up} and S_{down} in the two states of the world. If we had a single bond, we could, of course, say that S_{up} and S_{down} are the up and down values of a bond in the *up* and *down* states, respectively, and we would be done. However, when we have several bonds at play, we want to understand how the risk compensation for one bond should relate to the risk compensation for another bond, and there is no obvious way to relate the payoff of the bet in Section 4.3 of Chapter 4 to the maturities of different bonds. This is what we are adding here.

The question we want to ask is the following.

If we knew the prices of the $(T - t)$-maturity bond in these two possible future states (and the probabilities of reaching the two states), what should its price today, P_t^T, be?

One naive way to approach the question is to propose that it should be given by the average (*taken with the real-world probabilities*) of the two future prices, discounted by $\frac{1}{1+r_t dt}$:

$$P_t^T =? = \frac{\frac{1}{2}\left[\left(P_{t+dt}^{T-dt}\right)_H + \left(P_{t+dt}^{T-dt}\right)_L\right]}{1 + r_t dt}, \tag{11.1}$$

where r_t is the risk-less rate. To lighten notation we are going to write

$$\frac{1}{2}\left[\left(P_{t+dt}^{T-dt}\right)_H + \left(P_{t+dt}^{T-dt}\right)_L\right] \equiv \left(P_{t+dt}^{T-dt}\right)_{AVG}. \tag{11.2}$$

We also observe that this average is just the expectation formed at time t of the price of the $(T - t)$-maturity bond. This expectation is more usually written as

$$\frac{1}{2}\left[\left(P_{t+dt}^{T-dt}\right)_H + \left(P_{t+dt}^{T-dt}\right)_L\right] = E_t^{\mathbb{P}}\left[P_{t+dt}^{T-dt}\right], \tag{11.3}$$

where we have appended the superscript, $\mathbb{P}$, to remind ourselves that the expectation was formed using the real-world probabilities. And since we are at it, it is also useful to define another, closely related, quantity, ie, the standard deviation, σ_P^{T-dt} (volatility) of the two prices:

$$\sigma_P^{T-dt} \equiv \frac{1}{2}\left[\left(P_{t+dt}^{T-dt}\right)_H - \left(P_{t+dt}^{T-dt}\right)_L\right]. \tag{11.4}$$

Exercise 26 *Confirm that Equation (11.4) indeed gives the standard deviation.*

With these two pieces of notation under our belts, we can rewrite our first stab at valuation as

$$P_t^T =? = \frac{E_t^{\mathbb{P}}\left[P_{t+dt}^{T-dt}\right]}{1 + r_t dt}. \tag{11.5}$$

As we discussed in Section 4.3 of Chapter 4, this does not look quite right. Just as we don't normally accept to enter a substantial risky bet unless the odds are skewed in our favour (if we are risk averse), why should we accept the (discounted) real-world average price of the two future bond prices as the fair price for the bond today? To enter a risky bet a risk-averse investor requires an inducement. How can we model this?

As we saw in Chapter 4, one way to account for risk aversion is to still use the real-world probabilities, but to pretend that in the two states of the world we actually receive less money ($-a_{t+dt}^{T-dt}$, to be precise) than the bond pays. So we can write

$$P_t^T = \frac{E_t^{\mathbb{P}}\left[P_{t+dt}^{T-dt}\right] - a_{t+dt}^{T-dt}}{1 + r_t dt}, \tag{11.6}$$

where we have adjusted the expectation by a quantity, a_{t+dt}^{T-dt}, that reflects how much the investor requires in order to enter the bet. The attentive reader will immediately notice that there is close link between a_{t+dt}^{T-dt} and the quantity H

introduced in Section 4.3 of Chapter 4. The link will become clearer in what follows, but, for the moment, we simply point out that this quantity, a_{t+dt}^{T-dt}, can depend on time, and *certainly* depends on the residual maturity of the bond.

By the way, when we discuss risk aversion we should consider carefully how a given bond 'fits in' the overall market portfolio of the representative investor: it is not the volatility of the bond in itself that matters, as the analogy with the risky bet may have suggested. What matters in determining the compensation a_{t+dt}^{T-dt} is whether the payoff from the bond occurs in times where our consumption is high or low. (As we have seen, investors pay a lot for securities that pay well in bad states of the world, and little for fair-weather friends.) One way to account for this would be to use a consumption-based equilibrium asset pricing model. However, the main thrust of this book is not the estimation of the risk premium from first principles, such as could be arrived at by assigning a utility function, and by looking at how the payoffs from the bonds co-vary with the investor's consumption.[4] Our risk premium will be derived from combing pricing information and statistical analysis. It will therefore turn out to be 'whatever it is'.

Let's go back to Equation (11.6). Why *subtract* the term a_{t+dt}^{T-dt}? If we are risk averse, we should be willing to pay less than the actuarial (discounted) average, so we *depress* the price by a quantity, a_{t+dt}^{T-dt}, that we expect to be positive. However, given our approach, the sign of the adjustment will be dictated by the market, not by our prejudices.

11.3 BOUNDS TO THE PRICE-CORRECTION TERM: TYPE-I ARBITRAGE

Can we say anything about the range of possible (no-arbitrage) values for a_{t+dt}^{T-dt}?

Suppose that we have skewed the expectation so much that

$$P_t^T < \frac{(P_{t+dt}^{T-dt})_L - a_{t+dt}^{T-dt}}{1 + r_t dt},$$

ie, so much that our price (our expectation) today is less that the worst possible (discounted) value of the bond over the next period. Clearly, this is an arbitrage.

Conversely, if we had chosen a compensation such that, after discounting, the price today is greater than the outcome in the upper state,

$$P_t^T > \frac{(P_{t+dt}^{T-dt})_H - a_{t+dt}^{T-dt}}{1 + r_t dt},$$

we would be paying more than what we could possibly be compensated for, even in the best possible state of the world. 'Going short' the bond is another obvious arbitrage.

These two constraints can be linked together by making use of the other quantity we defined earlier, the standard deviation. Indeed, a bit of algebra then shows that the price adjustment, a_{t+dt}^{T-dt} (that we already expect to be linked to

---

[4] See, however, Chapter 15.

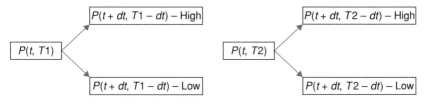

Figure 11.2 The allowed price moves for two bonds of different maturities (T_1 and T_2). The two bonds are shocked by a single source of risk. When bond 1 is in the *High* state, bond 2 is also in the *High* state; and the same applies to the *Low* state. We live in a one-factor world.

the risk premium), must lie within the two bounds

$$-\sigma_P^{T-dt} < a_{t+dt}^{T-dt} < \sigma_P^{T-dt}. \tag{11.7}$$

In words: under penalty of arbitrage, the risk premium can assume a wide range of values, but not any value we like: it must lie between plus and minus the volatility of the $(T - dt)$-maturity bond. Note that this no-arbitrage range *depends on the volatility of the bond in question*.

This is a first constraint we must impose on the possible risk premium. It is often referred to in the literature as 'absence of arbitrage between a bond and the money market account'. As we shall see later, it is not the only one.

Exercise 27 *Derive Equation (11.7).*

11.4 BOUNDS TO THE PRICE-CORRECTION TERM: TYPE-II ARBITRAGE

The first constraint is rather loose. Can we tighten it?

In the previous example, there was just one *up* and one *down* state, corresponding to the two possible realizations of the factor driving the economy. We can generalize the setting, by allowing each bond to be shocked by a number of factors. In our discrete-time description, there will then be one *up* and one *down* state associated with each risk factor.

To see what this entails, take an arbitrary bond. It is intuitive that, by adding as many additional bonds of different maturities as there are driving factors, we can make the portfolio risk-less. For instance, if we think that only one factor can move the yield curve – a 'duration' view of risk – the overall portfolio will be made up of two bonds; if we worry about duration and slope, it will have three bonds; etc. We will show in Chapter 17 how to 'immunize' exactly the bond portfolio against all the risk factors, but for the moment we can derive the result in a baby case, and see where it leads us. It is this ability to create a risk-less portfolio that allows us to obtain an expression for the market price(s) of risk. The reasoning goes as follows.

Let's extend the drawing in Figure 11.1 to the case of two bonds. They have different maturities, but we assume that they are shocked by the same source of risk. Adding more sources of risk would make the algebra and the pictures messier, but the intuition remains the same. The new situation is shown in Figure 11.2.

Now, suppose that we want to build a portfolio, Π, that is not exposed to *the* one source of risk which affects the economy. We try to do this by choosing one unit of the bond that matures at time T_2 (and that for brevity we will call 'bond 2', with a similar short-hand notation for bond 1), and Δ units of bond 1. So, at time t the portfolio is worth Π_t:

$$\Pi_t = \Delta P_t^{T_1} + P_t^{T_2} \tag{11.8}$$

and in the two possible states of the world at time $t + dt$ it will be worth

$$(\Pi_{t+dt})_H = \Delta \left(P_{t+dt}^{T_1-dt}\right)_H + \left(P_{t+dt}^{T_2-dt}\right)_H \tag{11.9}$$

$$(\Pi_{t+dt})_L = \Delta \left(P_{t+dt}^{T_1-dt}\right)_L + \left(P_{t+dt}^{T_2-dt}\right)_L, \tag{11.10}$$

respectively.

If we have indeed managed to insulate the portfolio from risk, then it will have to have the same value no matter what happens (ie, in both states of the world). This means that

$$(\Pi_{t+dt})_H = (\Pi_{t+dt})_L, \tag{11.11}$$

which in turn means that

$$\Delta \left(P_{t+dt}^{T_1-dt}\right)_H + \left(P_{t+dt}^{T_2-dt}\right)_H = \Delta \left(P_{t+dt}^{T_1-dt}\right)_L + \left(P_{t+dt}^{T_2-dt}\right)_L. \tag{11.12}$$

A swift rearrangement of terms gives

$$\Delta = -\frac{\left(P_{t+dt}^{T_2-dt}\right)_H - \left(P_{t+dt}^{T_2-dt}\right)_L}{\left(P_{t+dt}^{T_1-dt}\right)_H - \left(P_{t+dt}^{T_1-dt}\right)_L}. \tag{11.13}$$

But, by looking at Equation (11.4), we recognize that the numerator and the denominator are just the (double of) the bond volatility. Therefore can rewrite the ratio (11.13) in a more elegant way as

$$\Delta = -\frac{\sigma_P^{T_2-dt}}{\sigma_P^{T_1-dt}} \tag{11.14}$$

(where, of course, the factors of $\frac{1}{2}$ cancel out between the numerator and the denominator).

This tells us that, if we go long 1 unit of bond 2 and go short bond 1 by an amount given by the ratio of the two volatilities, we will be insulated against *the* one source of risk we are exposed to. And a moment's reflection convinces us that, indeed, this ratio of volatilities is just what we need: if both bonds are exposed to the same source of risk, and we know how this source of risk impacts their prices, we just have to scale the holding of one bond for the excess volatility of the other, and we are done.

Now, let's compute the expectation of the portfolio at the end of the time interval:

$$\mathbb{E}_t^\mathbb{P}[\Pi_{t+dt}] = \mathbb{E}_t^\mathbb{P}\left[\Delta P_{t+dt}^{T_1-dt} + P_{t+dt}^{T_2-dt}\right]$$

$$= \Delta E_t^\mathbb{P}\left[P_{t+dt}^{T_1-dt}\right] + E_t^\mathbb{P}\left[P_{t+dt}^{T_2-dt}\right]. \tag{11.15}$$

We want to express the expectation in terms of the compensation a_{t+dt}^{T-dt} that we introduced before. To this effect, we first rewrite Equation (11.6) as

$$P_t^T = \frac{\mathbb{E}_t^{\mathbb{P}}\left[P_{t+dt}^{T-dt}\right] - a_{t+dt}^{T-dt}}{1 + r_t dt} \implies \mathbb{E}_t^{\mathbb{P}}\left[P_{t+dt}^{T-dt}\right] = P_t^T(1 + r_t dt) + a_{t+dt}^{T-dt}.$$

(11.16)

Then, substituting what we have obtained into Equation (11.15) we have

$$\mathbb{E}_t^{\mathbb{P}}[\Pi_{t+dt}] = \Delta\mathbb{E}_t^{\mathbb{P}}\left[P_{t+dt}^{T_1-dt}\right] + \mathbb{E}_t^{\mathbb{P}}\left[P_{t+dt}^{T_2-dt}\right]$$
$$= \Delta\left[P_t^{T_1}(1 + r_t dt) + a_{t+dt}^{T_1-dt}\right] + P_t^{T_2}(1 + r_t dt) + a_{t+dt}^{T_2-dt}.$$

(11.17)

However, if the portfolio we constructed was risk-less, and if we do not want to allow the possibility of arbitrage, over the time interval dt it can only earn the risk-less return. This means that we must have

$$\mathbb{E}_t^{\mathbb{P}}[\Pi_{t+dt}] = \left[\Delta P_t^{T_1} + P_t^{T_2}\right](1 + r_t dt).$$

(11.18)

Exercise 28 *Why did we say '... if we do not want to allow the possibility of arbitrage...'?*

Equating Equations (11.17) and (11.18) and cancelling terms leaves us with

$$\Delta a_{t+dt}^{T_1-dt} = -a_{t+dt}^{T_2-dt}.$$

(11.19)

But we have obtained the expression for Δ to be $\Delta = -\frac{\sigma_P^{T_2-dt}}{\sigma_P^{T_1-dt}}$. Therefore we have

$$\frac{a_{t+dt}^{T_1-dt}}{\sigma_P^{T_1-dt}} = \frac{a_{t+dt}^{T_2-dt}}{\sigma_P^{T_2-dt}}.$$

(11.20)

The right-hand side of Equation (11.20) depends only on maturity T_2 and the left hand-side on maturity T_1. Since there was nothing special about these two maturities, and the reasoning must hold for *any* T_1 and T_2, we can impose that the two ratios should be independent of maturity. This means that, for any bond, *the ratio of the risk compensation, a_{t+dt}^{T-dt}, to its volatility, σ_P^{T-dt}, must be the same*. Now, *this* is interesting!

Recall that we said earlier that the bond-specific factor, a_{t+dt}^{T-dt}, that made us willing to 'enter the bond bet' would in general depend on the specific bond in question. But now we also can point to the one feature of the bond it can depend on, namely its volatility. What is so special about volatility? Volatility is special because it is the most natural proxy for risk. Indeed, if our discrete-time universe can be correctly described using a simple *bi*nomial tree[5], then

---

[5] If higher moments of the return distributions mattered for pricing, then our discrete-time tree would have to be tri-, tetra-,..., *n*-nomial. The trade-off between greater generality on the one

variance (and hence volatility) fully describes risk. We have therefore obtained the result that the ratio of the bond-specific factor, a_{t+dt}^{T-dt}, to the bond volatility must be bond- (maturity-) independent.

This is a very important result. Indeed, this ratio is so important that we give it a special symbol, λ_t, and a name, the *market price of risk*:

$$\lambda_t = \frac{a_{t+dt}^{T-dt}}{\sigma_P^{T-dt}}. \tag{11.21}$$

As the notation shows, the market price of risk can depend on calendar time, but it cannot depend on the maturity of any individual bond. If it did, it would mean that we care about price volatility (risk) coming from a bond more than the same amount of price volatility (risk) coming from another. But risk is risk is risk, and the market price of risk is essentially democratic: the price adjustment due to risk aversion for any bond, ie, **its risk premium**, can vary over time, but, at any point in time, but must only be proportional to how risky a bond is. In our economy[6], where 'risk' means 'volatility', this means that it can only be proportional to the volatility of the bond:[7]

$$a_{t+dt}^{T-dt} = \lambda_t \sigma_P^{T-dt}. \tag{11.22}$$

This is the second arbitrage condition we referred to earlier. It is more constraining than the condition coming from forbidding Type-I arbitrage, as it links together the returns from (in the limit) an infinity of bonds. It comes from forbidding free lunches, not by using a given bond and the money-market account (this is what Type-I arbitrage is all about), but by combining all different bonds (and portfolios of bonds) in any clever fashion. Rewarding one bond more than other for reasons other than its riskiness is called Type-II arbitrage.

11.5 A USEFUL REWRITING

Putting the pieces together, we can easily show that absence of arbitrage requires that the expected return on a bond should be written as

$$\frac{\mathbb{E}_t^{\mathbb{P}}\left[P_{t+dt}^{T-dt}\right] - P_t^T}{P_t^T} = \left(r_t + \frac{1}{P_t^T}\lambda_t\sigma_P^{T-dt}\right)dt. \tag{11.23}$$

We can therefore read this equation as saying that the expected return from holding a bond over a time interval dt is given by the sum of the risk-less rate,

---

hand, and elegance and transparency of the treatment on the other, points decisively in the direction the binomial treatment. What about continuous time? If the process for the state variable is shocked by the increments of a Brownian motion, then variance is the only moment that matters (as higher moments are either zero, or can be expressed as functions of the variance), and the limit of a binomial discretization will always converge to the true process.

[6] Why 'in our economy'? The two-state discretization that we have presented is the discrete-time analogue of a diffusion process. If we allowed for jumps the treatment would become more complex.

[7] To be precise, if we require, as we did, a_{t+dt}^{T-dt} to be expressed in units of money, [\$], the Equation (11.22) should be written as $a_{t+dt}^{T-dt} = \lambda_t \sigma_P^{T-dt} dt$.

plus a compensation for risk. This compensation then depends on the common market price of risk, λ_t, and on the volatility of each bond, σ_P^{T-dt}.

We can make a tiny moving around of terms and define a quantity which will prove useful, namely the time-t excess return, xr_t^T, from holding a bond of maturity T:

$$xret_t^T = \frac{\mathbb{E}_t^{\mathbb{P}}\left[P_{t+dt}^{T-dt}\right] - P_t^T}{P_t^T} - r_t dt = \lambda_t \sigma_P^{T-dt} dt. \tag{11.24}$$

It says that the (instantaneous) excess return above the risk-less rate depends on how volatile the bond is times a compensation for risk (the market price of risk) that is the same for all bonds. This is a key quantity, that we will study in detail in Part VI.

11.6 EXTENSION TO MANY FACTORS

So far we have considered the overall volatility of a bond (which may be 'made up of' the volatility of several driving factors, with each factor loading on that bond with different degrees of responsiveness to that source of risk).

This was fine, as long as we considered an economy shocked by a single factor. It would also be perfectly fine if we looked only at one bond in isolation (why?), but this is exactly what we do *not* want to do. However, if we look at a collection of bonds, it is important to distinguish how each bond is exposed to the different risk factors, and at how its volatility is made up of contributions from these various factors. For instance, if the yield curve moves in such a way that it tends to 'pivot around' the 5-year point, a 5-year bond will have no exposure to changes in the slope of the yield curve, and will therefore not be exposed to the 'slope' risk factor. Not so for a 1- or a 10-year bond.

We can make this intuition more precise by denoting by x_i the ith factor that drives the yield curve (for instance, it could be a principal component, or one of the latent factors in the Kim–Wright model), and by σ_{x_i} its volatility. Then it is easy to see (and we shall prove in the Appendix 12A) that Equation (11.23) becomes

$$\frac{\mathbb{E}_t^{\mathbb{P}}\left[P_{t+dt}^{T-dt}\right] - P_t^T}{P_t^T} = \left(r_t + \frac{1}{P_t^T}\sum_i \frac{\partial P_{t+dt}^{T-dt}}{\partial x_i}\lambda_t^i \sigma_{x_i}\right) dt. \tag{11.25}$$

The concept of excess return readily generalizes in this multifactor setting as the sum of individual excess return contributions, $xret_t^T$, each associated with the individual sources of risk:

$$xret_t^T = \frac{\mathbb{E}_t^{\mathbb{P}}\left[P_{t+dt}^{T-dt}\right] - P_t^T}{P_t^T} - r_t dt$$

$$= \sum_i \frac{1}{P_t^T}\frac{\partial P_{t+dt}^{T-dt}}{\partial x_i}\lambda_t^i \sigma_{x_i} dt \equiv \sum_i xr_i^{t,T}. \tag{11.26}$$

As we discussed in Chapter 4, wherever there is uncertainty there is, in principle, a required compensation (a 'market price') for bearing this risk. Here we extend the reasoning by a tiny step, and argue that, wherever there is a market price of risk there is, in principle, an excess return.

Why did we have a single volatility term (σ_P^{T-dt}) in Equation (11.23), and a more complex term $\left(\sum_i \frac{\partial P_{t+dt}^{T-dt}}{\partial x_i} \sigma_{x_i} \right)$ in Equation (11.25)? Because we wrote Equation (11.23) directly in terms of the total bond volatility, while Equation (11.25) is expressed in terms of something more fundamental, ie, the volatilities of the factors. We go from the latter to the former by multiplying each factor volatility (σ_{x_i}) by how much the bond price moves when the factor moves $\left(\frac{\partial P_{t+dt}^{T-dt}}{\partial x_i} \right)$, and adding over these 'duration' terms.

Exercise 29 *Show how the total volatility of a bond, σ_P, is linked to its volatility contributions, σ_{x_i}. Consider both the case when the factors are uncorrelated, and when they are correlated.*

Once again: Equation (11.25) says that the risk adjustment over and above the riskless rate, r_t, is given by the sum of three contributions coming from each risk factor:

- for each risk factor, the term $\frac{\partial P_{t+dt}^{T-dt}}{\partial x_i}$ tells us how the price of the $(T-t)$-maturity bond depends on the ith risk factor – it is a 'duration-like' term, which, in a Vasicek world, is given by the quantity B_t^T discussed at length in Chapter 10;
- λ_t^i is the (time-dependent) compensation per unit risk for the risk introduced by the ith risk factor;
- and σ_{x_i} is the volatility of the ith risk factor.

So, we can understand that by multiplying the risk of the factor (σ_{x_i}) by the sensitivity of the T-maturity bond to that factor $\left(\frac{\partial P_{t+dt}^{T-dt}}{\partial x_i} \right)$, we obtain the risk of the T-maturity bond. Then by multiplying the risk of a bond by the compensation per unit of risk associated with that factor (λ_t^i) we obtain the extra return compensation that the investor will require for bearing the risk *associated with that factor*. Finally, by adding over all the sources of risk (over all the factors), we obtain the total extra return compensation that the investor will require for bearing the risk associated with *all the factors* to which the bond is exposed.

All of this is logical, and it is 'fair'. No-arbitrage conditions are 'fairness' conditions. As long as we ensure that these conditions are satisfied, we can rest assured that no 'unfairness' (no free lunches) will be allowed by our model. Indeed, securities (not just bonds) whose prices satisfies no-arbitrage are said to be 'fairly priced'.

11.7 THE TASK OF THE LONG-TERM BOND INVESTOR

Arguably, the discussion in the preceding text gives us a perspective to analyze the task of the long-term bond investor[8]: in a nutshell, it boils down to identifying at every point in time for which risk the market provides the most handsome compensation. This, of course is made more challenging by the fact that, as we shall see in detail in Part VI, the market prices of risk are not constant over time, but can in general be state dependent. So, a bit more precisely, the task of the bond investor can be described a bit more convincingly as

1. the identification of which sources of risk each bond is exposed to;
2. the determination of the dependence of the various market prices of risk possibly on time, but, more interestingly, on the state of world;
3. the identification of the current state of world;
4. the decision of which risk factors it pays to be exposed to, given the current state of the world;
5. the identification of those bonds that provide the most effective exposure to these risk factors. To the extent that some bonds – or, in general, some assets – may be compensated a bit more handsomely than others to some risk factors, the market price of risk is no longer exactly independent of the specific asset. This can create a tactical investment opportunity. Indeed, one definition of 'smart beta' strategies is the identification of those securities that provide the best exposure – the best (smartest) 'beta' – to a given factor. See Amenc, Goltz and Le Sourd (2017) for a discussion.

---

[8] By 'long-term' I mean here a bond investor who does not rely on her superior ability to guess the direction of rate moves – an investor, that is, who tries to exploit the risk premium (not the expectation or the convexity) part of the yield curve dynamics.

CHAPTER 12

No-Arbitrage in Continuous Time

*As far as the laws of mathematics refer to reality, they are not
certain, and as far as they are certain, they do not refer to reality.*
Albert Einstein, 1956

12.1 THE PURPOSE OF THIS CHAPTER

By moving to continuous time, we present in this chapter a derivation of the
market price of risk that is more general, but in essence very similar, to what
presented in discrete time in the previous chapter. Our construction will lead us
half a step away from obtaining the Partial Differential Equation obeyed by all
bonds (and, indeed, all securities) in the economy. We are not interested (for
now) in deriving and solving the Partial Differential Equation that bond prices
must obey (we will derive this in Chapter 16). However, it is useful to keep the
unity of the underlying argument in mind.

   The discrete-time treatment presented in the previous chapter was simple
and clear enough. Why bother with its continuous-time counterpart? The main
reason for providing a treatment that makes use of elementary stochastic calculus results is to lay the groundwork for the treatment that will be employed
in the next chapter, in which the stochastic discount factor is introduced. As
usual, we will work in the simplest possible setting, where the single factor is
the short rate.

   The main results of this chapter are the derivation of the expression for the
market price of risk, λ_r:

$$\frac{\mu_P - r_t}{\sigma_P} = -\lambda_r, \tag{12.1}$$

and the discussion on what it does (and does not) depend on.

12.2 CONSTRUCTING A RISK-LESS PORTFOLIO:
THE MARKET PRICE OF RISK AGAIN

As we did before, we are going to place ourselves in the simplest possible
continuous-time setting, in which the whole economy is driven by a single

factor. To keep things even simpler, we remain firmly in the furrow histori- cally ploughed by all the early papers on term-structure modelling, and we also assume this single factor to be the short rate.

The results to be derived in this chapter will not depend on the particular (dif- fusive) process followed by our state variable, the short rate: it does not matter, that is, if the process for the short rate is, say, mean-reverting or a geometric Brownian motion. Of course, when set down to obtaining a link (perhaps an analytic formula, if our model assumptions have been kind enough) between bond prices and the short rate, then, of course, specifying the short-rate pro- cess becomes essential. But, as stated previously, this is not the purpose of this chapter.

Therefore, at this stage we simply put down a place-holder for the real-world short-rate process[1]:

$$dr_t = \mu_r(r_t)dt + \sigma(r_t)dz_t \tag{12.2}$$

and briskly write for the process of a bond of maturity T_k

$$\frac{dP_t^{T_k}}{P_t^{T_k}} = \mu_{pk}dt + \sigma_{pk}dz_t. \tag{12.3}$$

Why go through the specification of the short rate process? Why couldn't we have written down Equation (12.3) directly? We could have done so. How- ever, after writing down the process for one particular bond, we would not have known how to write down a consistent process for a bond of different matu- rity. As we shall see, all these bond processes are linked, and the only truly fundamental process is that of the stochastic driver(s): in this case, the short rate.

There is another reason for writing down the process of the short rate as 'primitive' and deriving the process for the bond price as a derived process: by doing so, we stress that the particular form for the process for the bond price in Equation (12.3) (say, the diffusive nature of the process or the number of Brownian shocks by which it is affected) depends on the assumptions we made about the economy, as described (in this case) by the short rate. If we had had, say, two, or seven factors driving the economy, Equation (12.3) would have had more stochastic terms (two or seven, respectively). This is would have mattered, because our strategy in this chapter will be the killing of the stochasticity via some combination of bonds.

So, let's build a portfolio, Π_t, made up of 1 unit of the bond maturing at time T_i and ω units of the bond maturing at time T_j:

$$\Pi_t = P_t^{T_i} + \omega P^{T_j}. \tag{12.4}$$

---

[1] To keep the notation light, we have just written dz_t. In reality we should write $dz_t^{\mathbb{P}}$ to emphasize that we are in the real-world measure.

Let's calculate the increment of the portfolio over a short time dt:

$$d\Pi_t = dP_t^{T_i} + \omega dP^{T_j}$$

$$= P_t^{T_i}\left[\mu_{Pi}dt + \sigma_{Pi}dz_t\right] + \omega P^{T_j}\left[\mu_{Pj}dt + \sigma_{Pj}dz_t\right]$$

$$= \left[P_t^{T_i}\mu_{Pi} + \omega P^{T_j}\mu_{Pj}\right]dt + \left[P_t^{T_i}\sigma_{Pi} + \omega P^{T_j}\sigma_{Pj}\right]dz_t, \qquad (12.5)$$

where in the second line we have used the expression for the price process in Equation (12.3).

This expression holds true for any holding of the j-maturity bond, ω. Now we want to find the special holding, ω^*, that makes the stochastic part of the portfolio equal to zero. This is clearly obtained if we set the term in square brackets that multiplies dz_t equal to zero:

$$P_t^{T_i}\sigma_{Pi} + \omega^* P^{T_j}\sigma_{Pj} = 0. \qquad (12.6)$$

From this it follows that

$$\omega^* = -\frac{P_t^{T_i}\sigma_{Pi}}{P^{T_j}\sigma_{Pj}}. \qquad (12.7)$$

For this skillfully chosen hedge ratio, the portfolio Π_t will be risk-less. Rehearsing a by-now-familiar line of reasoning, if the portfolio is risk-less, *and if we do not want to allow for arbitrage possibilities*, over the next time step it can only earn the risk-less rate. This means that

$$d\Pi_t = \left[P_t^{T_i}\mu_{Pi} + \omega^* P^{T_j}\mu_{Pj}\right]dt = r_t\Pi_t dt$$

$$= r_t\left[P_t^{T_i} + \omega^* P^{T_j}\right]dt. \qquad (12.8)$$

We note in passing that, by the way we have obtained it, Equation (12.8) is immediately linked to the partial differential equation that must be obeyed by any bond (actually, by any security exposed to the same source(s) of risk) if arbitrage is to be avoided. We shall solve this Partial Differential Equation later in the book, but for the moment we focus on a more specific result, relating to the market price of risk.

To see what this result is, we can rearrange terms in such a way that all the T_i-dependent terms are on one side, and all the T_j-dependent terms are on the other. This gives

$$P_t^{T_i}\left(\mu_{Pi} - r_t\right) = \omega^* P_t^{T_j}\left(r_t - \mu_{Pj}\right)$$

$$= P_t^{T_i}\left(\mu_{Pi} - r_t\right) = \frac{P_t^{T_i}\sigma_{Pi}}{P^{T_j}\sigma_{Pj}}P_t^{T_j}\left(\mu_{Pj} - r_t\right)$$

$$= \frac{\mu_{Pi} - r_t}{\sigma_{Pi}} = \frac{\mu_{Pj} - r_t}{\sigma_{Pj}}. \qquad (12.9)$$

We have obtained (again – see Section 11.4) that a certain special ratio must be the same for the two bonds, $P_t^{T_i}$ and P^{T_j} in our portfolio. But there was nothing special about the two bonds that we put in our portfolio. Therefore we can state that the special ratio must be the same for *any* pair of bonds.

This ratio is so important that we give it a special name, the market price of risk, and a special symbol[2], λ_r:

$$\frac{\mu_{P^i} - r_t}{\sigma_{P^i}} = -\lambda_r \quad \text{for any } T_i. \tag{12.10}$$

12.3 INTERPRETATIONS OF THE MARKET PRICE OF RISK

If we had followed a conceptually equivalent but more cumbersome treatment to deal with the case when the economy was shocked by, say, two sources of uncertainty, then there would have been two market prices of risk to compensate investors for bearing the uncertainty associated with the two shocks to the economy. (See Appendix 12A for a proof, or Bolder (2001) for a similar step-by-step derivation.) The essence of the derivation, however, would have remained the same, and so would the 'meaning' of the market price of risk. But how exactly are we to interpret the market price of risk when we have several factors?

From the way we have written it, the market price of risk lends itself to several interpretations. The most natural one is the following: the market price of risk is the extra return over the risk-less rate ($\mu_{P^i} - r_t$) per unit risk (σ_{P^i}) demanded by a risk-averse investor. As we saw in Chapter 10, Section 10.8, this is just the definition of the Sharpe Ratio. This is how much the market compensates the investor for bearing one unit of the risk to which the bond is exposed.

Looking at the market price of risk through the lens of the Sharpe Ratio broadens our horizon, because we don't usually associate Sharpe Ratios to bonds only, but to any strategy or (bundle of) asset(s). Therefore the Sharpe-Ratio/market-price-of-risk parallel alerts us to the fact that Sharpe Ratios should be compared not just across bonds, but across all types of assets.

When we look at the market price of risk as the quantity $\frac{\mu_{P^i} - r_t}{\sigma_{P^i}}$ we stress that any two *bonds* should be fairly and consistently priced – it is a relative type of fairness. When we think of the market price of risk as a Sharpe Ratio, we also compare bonds with, say, equities, or mortgage-backed securities, and we ensure that bonds as an asset class should be fairly priced.[3]

The name 'market price of risk' and its description as the *compensation* for bearing risk is intuitively appealing, but can be a bit misleading. Since we are talking about compensation, the way the problem is framed suggests, if not strictly implies, that the market price of risk should be positive. This,

---

[2] Why $-\lambda_r$ and not just λ_r? It is a convention, needed to obtain a positive risk premium if λ_r is positive and ultimately linked to the fact that as yields and rates go down, prices go up. See Chapter Expectations.

[3] One should always be careful when using Sharpe Ratios across asset classes, however, because the Sharpe Ratio has no understanding of the possible portfolio diversification afforded by a given (type of) security. Sharpe Ratios strictly apply to a one-factor economy, in which every asset is shocked by the same market risk factor.

however, is a prejudice, not a theorem. It is only empirical analysis that will tell us whether the market price of risk is a positive or a negative number.

'Wait a minute,' you may say. 'Why should I have to pay to bear risk? Shouldn't it be obvious that the compensation should be positive?'

The problem with this objection lies in the choice of another loaded word, 'risk'. In reality we should think of bonds, and, indeed, of *any* assets, as a part of a market portfolio. Investors are not forced, guns to their heads, to 'bear the risk' of a portfolio made up only of bonds.[4] A more reasonable 'market portfolio' would contain equities, bonds, and probably lots of other things.

If bonds did particularly well when equities did very poorly, then bonds could have such a diversifying effect that an investor may be willing to accept a negative risk 'premium' as a trade-off against the uncertainty in her whole portfolio. In other words, she may be willing to give up some expected return in order to enjoy a large enough reduction in portfolio variability: that's why, after all, we buy actuarially unfairly priced fire insurance on our house.[5]

Note that the last paragraph started with an '*if*' and was liberally sprinkled with '*may*s' and '*could*s'. This is to emphasize again that only empirical analysis will be able to tell us whether the risk premium is indeed positive. (For the anxious readers, yes it is – we show the evidence in Chapter 25.)

12.4   EXCESS RETURNS

One more observation. We can trivially solve for the real-world drift of the T_i-maturity bond, and rewrite Equation (12.10) as

$$\mu_{Pi} = r_t + \lambda_r \sigma_{Pi} \tag{12.11}$$

From Ito's Lemma, we also know, however (see Equation (12.3)), that, if *the* state variable is the short rate, the price volatility of the *i*th bond is given by

$$\sigma_{Pi} = \frac{1}{P_t^{T_i}} \frac{\partial P_t^{T_i}}{\partial r} \sigma_r \tag{12.12}$$

and therefore

$$\mu_{Pi} - r_t = \frac{1}{P_t^{T_i}} \frac{\partial P_t^{T_i}}{\partial r} \lambda_r \sigma_r. \tag{12.13}$$

---

[4] In the stylized example presented in this chapter the economy was assumed to be shocked by a single source of risk. But this assumption has been made only to unclutter the page and simplify the algebra. In reality several factors will certainly affect the economy as a whole.

[5] Do bonds really have such a powerful diversifying effect? Johnson et al. (2015) provide an excellent discussion of this very important topic. Why is the topic so important? Does it matter whether bonds 'hedge' equity holdings or not, if we only want to hold bonds in our portfolio? It certainly does, because if they do, they will be very sought after by investors with a more balanced portfolio, and will be very 'expensive' from the perspective of the bond-only investor – indeed, their risk premium could in principle even be negative. The important point here is that the market price of bonds does not care how we choose to build our portfolio; it only cares about the market portfolio.

Now, the expected excess return, $xr_t^{T_i}$, for the T_i-maturity bond is a quantity of fundamental importance, which we will discuss at length in Part VI of this book. It can be then defined as

$$xr_t^{T_i} \equiv \mu_{P^i} - r_t = \frac{1}{P_t^{T_i}} \frac{\partial P_t^{T_i}}{\partial r} \lambda_r \sigma_r \qquad (12.14)$$

More generally, if there are n sources of risk, one has

$$xr_t^{T_i} \equiv \mu_{P_i} - r_t = \sum_k \frac{i}{P_t^{T_i}} \frac{\partial P_t^{T_i}}{\partial X_k} \lambda_k \sigma_k, \qquad (12.15)$$

with λ_k and σ_k the market price of risk and the volatility of the kth factor, respectively.

Reverting to the one-factor case, and looking back at Equation (12.13) we see that on the left-hand side we have the expected excess return. Therefore on the right-hand side we have the neat decomposition of the expected excess return from the T_i-maturity bond as the product of three conceptually very different terms:

- a 'duration term', $\frac{1}{P_t^{T_i}} \frac{\partial P_t^{T_i}}{\partial r}$, that tells us how much the T_i-maturity bond changes when the state variable changes;
- a 'compensation term', λ_r, that tells us how large the compensation *per unit risk in the shock factor* is; and
- a 'risk magnitude' term, σ_r, that tells us how volatile *the risk factor* is.

This is very important because excess returns are one of the very few empirical bridges that we can build in order to link the $\mathbb{P}$ and $\mathbb{Q}$ measures. A good proportion of the econometric papers on term empirical term-structure models are devoted to estimating this quantity. And an even greater proportion of the efforts of bond fund managers are devoted to the same worthy goal.

12.5 WHAT THE MARKET PRICE OF RISK CAN DEPEND ON

As we mentioned in the previous section, the market price of risk is the link between the real-world and the risk-neutral (pricing) measure. It specifies and *strongly constrains* the compensation (the relative difference in drifts in going from the real-world to the risk-neutral measure) that can be assigned to bonds of different maturities.

If we derived the market price of risk *ab initio*, ie, by choosing a particular utility function, calibrating it to investors' preferences and risk aversion, and linking it to the prices of bonds, then we could, in principle, arrive at an absolute (as opposed to 'relative') estimate of the market price of risk. In Chapter 15 we sketch how this could be done, but, in our treatment we shall not pursue this route.

In practice, even we do not go down the *ab initio* route, we still need to establish self-consistency requirements: the market price of risk of any given bond in isolation, we say, could be anything. But given the compensation for different sources of uncertainty attaching to this bond, then the compensation for all the other bonds should follow consistently. Why so? Because they are all shocked by the same source(s) of risk, the apportionment of the 'primitive' risk to the various assets depends on their sensitivity (duration) – the term $\frac{1}{P_t^{T_i}} \frac{\partial P_t^{T_i}}{\partial r}$ – and the amount of extra compensation (over the risk-less rate) for a given asset depends only on its apportionment of the systematic risk. As we saw at the end of the previous chapter, the market price of risk is an enforcer of fairness.

The crucial point here is that the market price of risk can depend on time, can depend on the common state variables, but does not depend on the specific features of any particular bond, such as, say, its coupon or maturity. The excess return *can* depend on the bond maturity (after all, it is only reasonable that one should ask for more 'compensation' for bearing the risk associated with a 30-year bond instead of a 6-month Treasury bill); but this maturity dependence can only come via the 'duration' term $\frac{1}{P_t^{T_i}} \frac{\partial P_t^{T_i}}{\partial r}$, that exactly washes away when the expected excess return is divided by the bond volatility.

Recall that risk premia (term premia) are one of our three fundamental building blocks in our description of the yield curve. So, it is important to understand very clearly how we can assign them, and how we cannot. What we have learnt in this chapter is that, if our model of the economy is correct, an investor cannot say 'I kind of fancy 27-year bonds because I was 27 when I met my wife, and therefore I am going to assign a higher price to it'.[6] Or, to be more precise, this romantic investor *could* say so, but if he acted on his fancy, he would find himself at the receiving end of the replication strategy described in this chapter carried out by a more cold-hearted, richer (but possibly unhappily divorced) investor. Therefore, for a model to be worth its salt, the excess returns from *all* the bonds in the economy must be *simultaneously* explained by a common set of risk factors, and by a *consistent* set of model-dependent 'durations'. As we shall see, this is a tall order.

12.6　APPENDIX 12A: THE MARKET PRICE OF RISK AND EXCESS RETURN WITH MANY FACTORS

Suppose that the economy is shocked by n sources of uncertainty (ie, by n 'factors', x_i, $i = 1, 2, \ldots, n$), and that each of these sources of uncertainty

---

[6] As the discussions in the last paragraph of Section 12.1 of this chapter and in Section 5.6 of Chapter 5 make clear, there may be 'messy' reasons why a 27-year-maturity bond may attract a higher-than-fair price than a 26- or a 28-year-maturity bond. Having said that, the age when the investor met his wife is unlikely to be one of these reasons.

follows a simple diffusion of the type

$$dx_i = \mu_i dt + \sum_{k=1,n} \sigma_{ik} dz_k. \tag{12.16}$$

Without loss of generality, we are going to assume that the factors are independent (and so $dz_j dz_k = 0$).

Let us now write P_i as a short-hand notation for $P_t^{T_i}$. Then let the drift of the ith bond be denoted by μ_{pi} and the loading onto the kth factor of the ith bond by σ_{pi}^k, respectively:

$$\frac{dP_i}{P_i} = \mu_{pi} dt + \sum_{k=1,n} \sigma_{pi}^k dz_k. \tag{12.17}$$

As in the one-factor case, we want to create a deterministic portfolio. To do so, we take one unit of bond $n+1$, and a judiciously chosen vector, ω, of n 'other' bonds, whose purpose in life is to kill *all* the stochasticity associated with the $(n+1)$th bond. So, the portfolio, Π, is given by

$$\Pi = P_{n+1} + \sum_{k=1,n} \omega_k P_k. \tag{12.18}$$

Over an infinitesimal time interval dt the change in the portfolio will be given by

$$d\Pi_t = dP_{n+1} + \sum_{k=1,n} \omega_k dP_k. \tag{12.19}$$

If we want every single source of stochasticity to be eliminated, we must have

$$\underbrace{\begin{bmatrix} \sigma_{pn+1}^1 \\ \sigma_{pn+1}^2 \\ \cdots \\ \sigma_{pn+1}^n \end{bmatrix}}_{\vec{s}_{n+1}} = \underbrace{\begin{bmatrix} \sigma_{p1}^1 & \sigma_{p2}^1 & \cdots & \sigma_{pn}^1 \\ \sigma_{p1}^2 & \sigma_{p2}^2 & \cdots & \sigma_{pn}^2 \\ \cdots & \cdots & \cdots & \cdots \\ \sigma_{p1}^n & \sigma_{p2}^n & \cdots & \sigma_{pn}^n \end{bmatrix}}_{\underline{\Sigma}_n} \underbrace{\begin{bmatrix} \omega_1 \\ \omega_2 \\ \cdots \\ \omega_n \end{bmatrix}}_{\vec{\omega}}. \tag{12.20}$$

As long as the matrix Σ_n is invertible (when would it fail to be so?), we can always obtain the vector $\vec{\omega}$ as

$$\vec{\omega} = \underline{\Sigma}_n^{-1} \vec{s}_{n+1}. \tag{12.21}$$

The notation emphasizes that the entries of the vector $\vec{s}_{(n+1)}$ depend on the maturity of the $(n+1)$th bond.

Since with the special vector $\vec{\omega}$ all stochasticity has been eliminated, we have for the now-purely-deterministic increment in the value of the portfolio

$$d\Pi_t = dP_{n+1} + \sum_{k=1,n} \omega_k dP_k$$

$$= \left[\mu_{p_{n+1}} + \sum_{k=1,n} \omega_k \mu_{p_k} \right] dt. \tag{12.22}$$

And since the portfolio is now deterministic, under penalty of arbitrage it can only earn the risk-less rate, r. This implies

$$\mu_{p_{n+1}} + \sum_{k=1,n} \omega_k \mu_{p_k} = r. \tag{12.23}$$

If we denote by $\vec{m}$ the $[n \times 1]$ vector of bond-price drifts, we switch to vector notation and move a few terms around, we have

$$\mu_{p_{n+1}} - r = -\vec{\omega}^{\mathrm{T}} \vec{m}, \tag{12.24}$$

or, equivalently,

$$\mu_{p_{n+1}} - r = -\vec{m}^{\mathrm{T}} \vec{\omega}. \tag{12.25}$$

Substituting the expression obtained in Equation (12.21) for $\vec{\omega}$, one then gets

$$\mu_{p_{n+1}} - r = -\vec{m}^{\mathrm{T}} \left[\underline{\Sigma}_n^{-1} \vec{s}_{n+1} \right] = -\left[\vec{m}^{\mathrm{T}} \underline{\Sigma}_n^{-1} \right] \vec{s}_{n+1}. \tag{12.26}$$

We are now going to define the market-price-of-risk vector, $\vec{\lambda}$, as

$$\vec{\lambda} = -\left[\left(\underline{\Sigma}_n^{-1} \right)^{\mathrm{T}} \vec{m} \right], \tag{12.27}$$

and therefore we can write

$$\mu_{p_{n+1}} - r = \vec{\lambda}^{\mathrm{T}} \vec{s}_{n+1}. \tag{12.28}$$

The important thing to notice is that the vector $\vec{\lambda} = -\left[\left(\underline{\Sigma}_n^{-1} \right)^{\mathrm{T}} \vec{m} \right]$ does not depend in any way on the $(n + 1)$th bond, and would therefore have been the same whatever 'reference' bond we could have chosen. This means that, as in the one-factor case, *it must be maturity-independent (specific-bond independent)*.

Since there was nothing special about the $(n + 1)$th bond, we can relabel it as, say, the generic jth bond, and we have

$$\underbrace{\mu_{p_j} - r}_{xr_t^{T_j}} = \vec{\lambda}^{\mathrm{T}} \vec{s}_j. \tag{12.29}$$

The left-hand side is, of course, the excess return of the generic jth bond. As for the right-hand side, each of the n terms of the vector $\overrightarrow{s}_j$ (say, the kth) is given by

$$s_j^k = \sigma_{P^j}^1 = \underbrace{\frac{1}{P_j} \frac{\partial P_j}{\partial x_k}}_{\text{'Duration' of the } k\text{-th factor}} \sigma_k, \qquad (12.30)$$

where σ_k is the total volatility of the kth factor:

$$\sigma_k = \sqrt{\sum_{i=1,n} (\sigma_{ik})^2}.$$

Putting all the pieces together one finally obtains for the excess return, $xr_t^{T_j}$, of the jth bond:

$$xr_t^{T_j} = \sum_{k=1,n} \underbrace{\frac{1}{P_j} \frac{\partial P_j}{\partial x_k}}_{\text{'Duration' of the } k\text{th factor}} \times \underbrace{\lambda_k}_{\text{market price of risk for factor } k} \times \underbrace{\sigma_k}_{\text{volatility of factor } k} .$$

$$(12.31)$$

CHAPTER 13

No-Arbitrage with State Price Deflators

13.1 THE PURPOSE OF THIS CHAPTER

In this chapter we are going to look at the conditions of no-arbitrage from a more general, but more abstract, perspective – the so-called 'modern' approach. In doing so, we will re-derive the results obtained in Chapter 12 (in particular, the expression for the market price of risk) from a different perspective. In order to build her intuition, the reader may want to look at the results we derive in Chapter 15, but, in case the reader were to find the treatment in that chapter a bit heavy-going, we make the present derivation self-contained.

Why complicate things, when the derivation presented in Chapter 11 was so simple and so intuitively obvious? Mainly for three reasons.

First, the 'modern' approach applies to any asset, and allows us to see bonds as a special case of security that has a particular payoff in some states of the world. When we look at term premia, the concept of securities that perform well or badly in 'states of the world' becomes crucial; for instance, we will be naturally led to ask questions such as: 'Does a bond portfolio perform well or poorly when equities fall or rise? What about inflation?' Therefore, looking at bonds as one *state-dependent* component of the universe of assets available to the investor affords a fruitful perspective.[1]

Second, it is almost impossible to read the contemporary literature on term-structure modelling without a basic understanding of, say, the stochastic discount factor, or of the main properties of the state-price deflator. Studying this chapter won't make the reader an expert in the topic, but will allow her to understand, for instance, the links between the Sharpe Ratio and the volatility of the state-price deflator, why the latter grows at (minus) the short rate and why its volatility is equal to (minus) the market price of risk. Given this bewildering variety of ways of looking at, and talking about, what is essentially the same

---

[1] So, for instance, Cochrane (2001) writes: 'The major advantages of the [stochastic] discount factor [...] approach are its simplicity and its universality. Where once there were three apparently different theories for stocks, bonds, and options, now we see each as a special case of the same theory' (p. xv).

phenomenon, I would therefore like to think that I can serve as a 'liaison officer, making reciprocally intelligible voices speaking provincial languages.'[2]

Third, the derivation in Chapter 12 was predicated on the ability to 'kill' the stochasticity of the portfolio. We achieved this feat by requiring the processes for the driving factor(s) to be Brownian diffusions. However, this condition is not required in order to obtain the no-arbitrage equations. We will show in the text that follows how this is done. Having said this, we will then have to re-introduce the Brownian-diffusion assumption in order to say something specific about the stochastic discount factor (such as finding its drift and volatility).

So, my goal in this chapter is to obtain an expression for the process (the 'drift' and the 'volatility') of the stochastic discount factor that we have introduced in the previous chapter. We will often work in discrete time, and therefore we will derive the process not for the stochastic discount factor, but for a very closely allied quantity, namely the state-price deflator.

The main results of this chapter will be the following.

1. Bond prices can be expressed as expectations of a quantity called the state price deflator. This result will not rely on a Brownian-diffusion assumption.
2. If then we are happy to assume that the state-price deflator follows a diffusion, we will derive that its drift and its volatility are linked to the short rate, and to the market price of risk, respectively.
3. Putting (1) and (2) together, it also means that bond prices fully depend on the (process for) the short rate and on the market price of risk, and nothing else.

13.2   A BIRD'S EYE VIEW OF THE 'TRADITIONAL' AND 'MODERN' APPROACHES

Before delving into the gory details of the derivations, it is useful to have a 30,000-feet view of the (deep) similarities and of the (superficial) differences between the traditional approach to deriving the conditions of no-arbitrage (which leads to a partial differential equation) and the modern way to obtain the same result, which entails the evolution of a special quantity and the integration of a product.

As we mentioned in passing in the previous chapter, the derivation of the no-arbitrage conditions we have presented in the previous chapters (the 'traditional' approach) really boiled down to obtaining a partial differential equation, which we have not solved yet (we shall do so in Chapters 17 and 18), but that we simply used to derive the maturity-independence condition on the market price of risk.

Now, whether we solved it or not, the Partial Differential Equation is still there. Whenever we have a Partial Differential Equation, we solve it by

[2] Dewey, *Experience and Nature*.

imposing the boundary and initial conditions, and by evolving the solution 'from the outside in'. In the case of a bond process, the 'initial' condition (ie, the 'outside') is actually the terminal value of the bond at maturity (which is $1 in every state of the world). So, we know the solution for $t = T$ (with T equal to the bond maturity), and the Partial Differential Equation tells us how to move this solution backwards in time towards today. If we solve the equation numerically using an explicit finite-differences scheme, we really see how the information is literally transported from one time slice to the earlier one.

With the modern approach, we tackle the problem differently. We evolve *forward* in time a special quantity, which we have not defined yet, but which we can think of as the value of a security that pays $1 if a particular state of the world is obtained. Then, to obtain the price today, we integrate the product of the terminal value of this special quantity times the state-dependent payoffs of any security. In particular, for a (discount) bond we multiply the terminal value of the special quantity by the identical unit payment that occurs in every state of the world, and we integrate.

So, in order to obtain the arbitrage-free price of an interest-rate-dependent security, with the traditional approach we take a final payoff, and we move it backwards in time. With the modern approach we move a special quantity forward in time, and then we integrate. The no-arbitrage bit shows up in one case in the instructions on how to take the terminal value backwards, and in the other case in how to move forward the 'special quantity'. (It will turn out that the drift of the special quantity is minus the short rate and its volatility the market price of risk, but we are getting ahead of ourselves.)

Which approach is handier? It is often a matter of habit and of taste. To obtain concrete expressions for bond prices and related quantities given a model, the Partial Differential Equation route is often more convenient; to prove theoretical results, the modern approach can often get us there with more ease or elegance. The reader can decide for herself by going through the derivation of the bond price in the Vasicek model using the modern approach presented in Cochrane (2001)[3], and compare it with the derivation we provide in Chapters 17 and 18.

13.3 PRICING ASSETS: THE BUILDING-BLOCKS APPROACH

Today we are in a given state of the world.[4] The state of the economy can be described by a number of state variables, and we know the value of these state variables today. All of this simply means that we 'know where we stand'.

At a future time τ the state variables will evolve (in general, stochastically) to values that are not known today. Any future combination of the state variables defines a future state of the world. To simplify the treatment (immensely) we

---

[3] See p. 370 and passim.
[4] The treatment in this chapter follows closely Fisher (2004).

suppose that the possible future states are finite in number. We denote the set of all the possible future states at time τ by $\mathcal{S}_\tau$.

Suppose now that we knew the price today of special securities that pay $1 at time τ if a particular future state of the world is realized, and zero in all other states of the world. Suppose also that today we knew the prices today of these special securities for *all* the possible future states of the world at time τ.

These securities are so important that we will give them a special name, state prices, and a special symbol, sp_s. (For reasons we won't go into, these securities are often called Arrow–Debreu prices or Green's functions.[5]) Note that there is a subscript 's' associated with a state price. The subscript identifies the state of the world to which the state price 'refers' – ie, the one and only state in which the state-price security pays $1. One should also specify the time when these 'lottery tickets' pay out, but we will not clutter the notation with the time dependence unless necessary.

Every market could set different prices for these securities, but we can immediately see that their prices should satisfy two requirements:

1. the price of state price securities today should be (strictly) positive: it this were not the case, it is immediate to see how to construct an arbitrage strategy;
2. state prices cannot cost more than $1 today.[6] Again, an obvious arbitrage strategy could be constructed if this were not the case.

So, we have

$$0 < sp_s < 1 \quad \forall s \in \mathcal{S}. \tag{13.1}$$

Now, consider an arbitrary security, which pays out only at time τ. In different states of the world it pays different, *but certain*, amounts. Call *payoff*$_s$ the amount in dollars it pays out in state s. If the state prices are traded in the economy, a moment's reflection shows that, under penalty of arbitrage, its price today, v_0, must be given by

$$v_0 = \sum_{s \in \mathcal{S}} payoff_s \times sp_s. \tag{13.2}$$

It is easy to see that Equation (13.2) reflects a necessary condition for absence of arbitrage. One can also prove that it is a sufficient condition, but we will not

---

[5] For readers who come from a physics background, it is easy to see from the way we have defined them that these securities can be seen as the 'response' of the system to a unit stimulus, – hence the 'Green's function' name. In physics, Green's functions apply to linear systems, for which the superposition principle can be employed. This is the setting that we will build for the pricing of securities.

[6] Actually, if interest rates can be negative, then state prices *could* cost more than $1. Why people would prefer to invest today $1.1 in a security in order to get back $1 if a certain future state of the world is realized and nothing in all other states of the world (rather than putting the same $1.1 under the mattress) is a question that became of topical interest in the mid-2010s.

pursue this route here. For a proof, the reader is referred to Le Roy and Werner (2001) or, for a gentler treatment, Etheridge (2005).

Let's look at the state price, sp_s, a bit more carefully. Its price today reflects two very different pieces of information: it combines the probability of reaching state s and the value to the investor of receiving \$1 if *that* state is reached.

For instance, state s might correspond to 'my house just burnt down'. Unless we live in the house that the first piglet built, the probability of the event should be low, but the value of our receiving a compensation *just when our house has burnt down* can be very high. The price sp_s unhelpfully mixes these two conceptually very different components (the value investors give to \$1 in the s state of the world, and the probability of getting there). Let's therefore separate them out, by defining the probability, p_s, of reaching state s, and the value today, π_s, of \$1 *conditional on state s having been attained*. Then we can write

$$\frac{sp_s}{p_s} = \pi_s. \tag{13.3}$$

The price, v_0, of the security becomes

$$v_0 = \sum_{s \in \mathcal{S}} [payoff_s \times \pi_s] p_s. \tag{13.4}$$

We call the present value of \$1 in state s *conditional on state s having been attained*, ie, the quantity π_s, the *state-price deflator*.

A bit awkwardly, Equation (13.4) can be thought of as being derived from Equation (13.2) after multiplying and dividing by the probability, p_s, of state s:

$$v_0 = \sum_{s \in \mathcal{S}} payoff_s \times sp_s = \sum_{s \in \mathcal{S}} \left[payoff_s \frac{sp_s}{p_s} \right] p_s$$

$$= \sum_{s \in \mathcal{S}} [payoff_s \times \pi_s] p_s. \tag{13.5}$$

Why go through this contortion? Well, whenever we sum over the product of the possible values of a quantity times their probability we are obviously carrying out an expectation. So, the expression we just derived is, of course, exactly the same as Equation (13.4), but it shows directly that today's price is the real-world expectation of the product of the payoff times the state-price deflator.

We saw before that state prices are necessarily positive. But probabilities are positive as well. Therefore, if absence of arbitrage is equivalent to positive state prices,[7] then it is also equivalent to positive state-price deflators.

As we said, Equation (13.4) is written as an expectation (because we multiply the quantities $payoff_s \times \pi_s$ by their probabilities of occurrence, p_s). This

---

[7] Recall that we have not shown the equivalence (ie, that the condition is necessary and sufficient). We have only shown the (easy) necessary part.

means that we have expressed the price of a security today, v_0, as the expectation of its state-dependent payoffs times the state price deflators:

$$v_0 = \mathbb{E}_{t_0}[payoff_s \times \pi_s]. \tag{13.6}$$

Whenever we speak of 'expectations' it is essential to be very clear which 'measure' (probability distribution) we are talking about. Up to this point we have not carried out any fancy transformation of probabilities, and therefore the probabilities in Equation (13.4) are just 'real-world' ('objective', $\mathbb{P}$-measure) probabilities. The point may seem trivial now, but it will become crucial in what follows.

The bottom line is that we can write

$$v_0 = \mathbb{E}_{t_0}^{\mathbb{P}}[payoff_s \times \pi_s]. \tag{13.7}$$

Finally, it is clear that the state-price deflator for a payoff that occurs today should just be $1: \pi_{s_0}(t_0) = 1$ – another trivial observation that will help the algebra that follows. (By the way, s_0 is the one and only state that prevails today: it is the state we are in.)

13.4 A BEAUTIFUL RESULT: THE CHANGE OF MEASURE

13.4.1 Prices as Expectations in the Risk-Neutral Measure – Again

We can re-express the relationships above in an equivalent and very illuminating manner. Here is how we go about it.

Start again from

$$v_0 = \sum_{s \in \mathcal{S}} payoff_s \times sp_s. \tag{13.8}$$

Since this relationships holds for any security, it also holds for the (one-period) security that pays $1 in every possible state of the world. Such a security, as we know well, is a pure discount bond, which is worth

$$P_0^1 = \frac{1}{1 + r_f}, \tag{13.9}$$

with r_f denoting the risk-less rate. Therefore

$$\frac{1}{1 + r_f} = \sum_{s \in \mathcal{S}} 1 \times sp_s = \sum_{s \in \mathcal{S}} (\pi_s) p_s. \tag{13.10}$$

Note again that the last expression is just an expectation (of the state price deflator, π_s). Therefore Equation (13.10) says that that the real-world expectation of the state-price deflator is the risk-less bond.

Now, let's multiply and divide the left-hand side of Equation (13.2) by the same quantity, $\sum_{s \in \mathcal{S}} 1 \times sp_s$ – which we have just seen is equal to $\frac{1}{1+r_f}$. We get:

$$v_0 = \sum_{s \in \mathcal{S}} payoff_s \times sp_s$$

$$= \left(\sum_{s \in \mathcal{S}} sp_s \right) \sum_{s \in \mathcal{S}} payoff_s \times \frac{sp_s}{\left(\sum_{s \in \mathcal{S}} sp_s \right)}$$

$$= \underbrace{\frac{1}{1 + r_f}}_{\sum_{s \in \mathcal{S}}} \sum_{s \in \mathcal{S}} payoff_s \times \frac{sp_s}{\left(\sum_{s \in \mathcal{S}} sp_s \right)}. \tag{13.11}$$

Note, however, that the quantities, ξ_s, given by the relationship

$$\xi_s \equiv \frac{sp_s}{\sum_{s \in \mathcal{S}} sp_s} \tag{13.12}$$

define a set of possible probabilities. How do we know that they do? Because they are all positive, and, by construction add up to 1. This is all we require for a bunch of numbers to be possible probabilities.

Therefore, we can also write that the price, v_0, of a generic security today, is given by

$$v_0 = \frac{1}{1 + r_f} \sum_{s \in \mathcal{S}} payoff_s \times \xi_s, \tag{13.13}$$

which is an expectation with respect to the funny probabilities, ξ_s. More precisely, the equation just derived says that we can also regard the price today as the expectation taken with the funny probabilities, ξ_s, *discounted at the risk-less rate*. With a terminology and notation that is by now familiar, we recognize the 'funny probabilities' as the risk-neutral probabilities, and we can write

$$v_0 = \frac{1}{1 + r_f} \mathbb{E}^{\mathbb{Q}}[payoff]. \tag{13.14}$$

This should be contrasted with the expression for the price today which we obtained before:

$$v_0 = \sum_{s \in \mathcal{S}} [payoff_s \times \pi_s] p_s = \mathbb{E}^{\mathbb{P}}[payoff \times \pi], \tag{13.15}$$

where the expectation was then taken using the real-world probabilities. Equating the two expressions gives

$$\mathbb{E}^{\mathbb{P}}[payoff \times \pi] = \frac{1}{1 + r_f} \mathbb{E}^{\mathbb{Q}}[payoff]. \tag{13.16}$$

Are we really convinced that the expectation taken with respect to the funny probabilities is taken under the risk-neutral measure? Of course it is! Just expand the expectation of the product:

$$v_0 = \mathbb{E}^{\mathbb{P}}[payoff \times \pi] = \mathbb{E}^{\mathbb{P}}[payoff]\mathbb{E}^{\mathbb{P}}[\pi] + \text{cov}(payoff, \pi)$$

$$= \frac{1}{1 + r_f}\mathbb{E}^{\mathbb{P}}[payoff] + \text{cov}(payoff, \pi) \qquad (13.17)$$

and recall what we obtained in Section 13.3 (Equation 13.7), which says (after changing to the new notation) that

$$v_0 = \underbrace{\frac{1}{1 + r_f}\mathbb{E}_0^{\mathbb{P}}[payoff]}_{\text{expectation}} + \underbrace{\text{cov}_t[\pi, payoff]}_{\text{risk premium}}. \qquad (13.18)$$

So, we have

$$v_0 = \underbrace{\frac{1}{1 + r_f}\mathbb{E}_0^{\mathbb{P}}[payoff]}_{\text{expectation}} + \underbrace{\text{cov}_t[\pi, payoff]}_{\text{risk premium}} = \frac{1}{1 + r_f}\mathbb{E}^{\mathbb{Q}}[payoff],$$

$$(13.19)$$

which shows that the measure $\mathbb{Q}$ is indeed the risk-neutral one.

Note the subtle but important difference: with Equation (13.15), the discounting is state specific (this is what the quantities, π_s, the state price deflators, provide: the value today of \$1 *in that state of the world*) and the expectation is with respect to the real-world measure. With Equation (13.14), the discounting is state independent, but the (risk-neutral) probabilities have been deformed in order to compensate for this. For the price today to be the same, the new probabilities will be lower for those states of the world whose value today is high, and vice versa. No wonder that, as we saw in Chapter 4, the risk-neutral probabilities are 'pessimistic'!

13.4.2 The Equivalence of the State-Price Deflator and the Stochastic Discount Factor

One last obvious but important observation.

We have seen that the price of a security today is the $\mathbb{P}$-expectation of the state-price deflator. But, as we shall see in Chapter 15, the same price is given as a $\mathbb{P}$-expectation of the product of the stochastic discount factor, m_s, times the payoff:

$$v_0 = \mathbb{E}^{\mathbb{P}}[payoff_s \times \pi_s] = \mathbb{E}^{\mathbb{P}}[payoff_s \times m_s] \qquad (13.20)$$

with

$$m_s = \beta \frac{u'(c_s)}{u'(c_{s_0})}. \qquad (13.21)$$

We have not shown this to be the case yet, but let's take it on faith for the moment.

Remember, then, that we can write for the risk-neutral ('funny') probabilities

$$\xi_s \equiv \frac{sp_s}{\sum_{s \in \mathcal{S}} sp_s} = \frac{\pi_s p_s}{\sum_{s \in \mathcal{S}} sp_s} = \frac{\pi_s}{\frac{1}{1+r_f}} p_s, \tag{13.22}$$

where we have used again

$$\frac{1}{1+r_f} = \sum_{s \in \mathcal{S}} sp_s \tag{13.23}$$

(see Equation (13.10)).

We can therefore obtain one more important result. Solving for the state-price deflator from the middle term of Equation (13.22), we get

$$\left(\sum_{s \in \mathcal{S}} sp_s\right) \frac{\xi_s}{p_s} = \pi_s \implies \frac{\xi_s}{p_s} = \frac{\pi_s}{\frac{1}{1+r_f}} \tag{13.24}$$

and

$$\frac{\xi_s}{p_s} = \frac{u'(c_s)}{u'\left(c_{s_0}\right)}. \tag{13.25}$$

Both these equations say something very beautiful.

The first interprets the ratio of the risk-neutral (ξ_s) to the real-world (p_s) probabilities as the ratio of the state-specific discount factor (the state-price deflator, π_s) to the average, state-independent discount factor ($\frac{1}{1+r_f}$) – we see the 'pessimistic' probabilities reappearing again.

The second shows that the ratio of the risk-neutral to the real-world probabilities is proportional to the stochastic discount factor, and equal to the ratio of the marginal utilities of consumption.

In principle, if we measure the real-world distribution of prices, and we extract from option prices the risk-neutral distribution, we gain direct access to the stochastic discount factor. Or, alternatively, if we trust our choice and parametrization of the utility function, we can in principle recover one probability distribution from the other. Ross (2011, 2015) shows why in practice there may be many a slip twixt the cup and this particular lip.[8]

13.5 THE PROCESS FOR THE STATE-PRICE DEFLATOR

Up to this point we have made no assumptions about the process driving the asset prices: in particular, its stochastic component could have been made up of jumps, diffusions, infinite-activity processes, you name it. The (very weak) conditions of no-arbitrage obtained so far remain valid, no matter how the state

---

[8] For a nice and clear discussion of the mathematical assumptions underlying the approach by Ross, of a possible inconsistency in the derivation and of the additional hypotheses needed to fix this inconsistency, see Tsui (2013).

price deflators (and hence the bond prices) evolve. Compare and contrast this state of affairs with the treatment in Chapter 12 (the so-called 'Partial Differential Equation approach') where we assumed from the very start that the bond price process was a diffusion: we needed this assumption right from the word 'go', otherwise we could not even have begun to build a *risk-less* portfolio.

Having said this, the conditions of no-arbitrage obtained so far using the state-price deflators, terse and general as they are, do not take us very far. If anything, it is exactly the high degree of generality of the no-arbitrage conditions derived above that stands in the way of making much progress. What do I mean by 'making progress'? For instance, so far we have been talking about the state-price deflators today (relative to payments at a future time). But how will these quantities evolve? It is intuitively obvious that there should be a deterministic component to their evolution, but, as we shall see, there will be a stochastic component as well.

Why should the state-price deflator have a stochastic component? Look at Equation (13.25). Today the state-price deflator is a known function of the time-s consumption (because we know our utility function given the level of consumption today, s_0). But tomorrow the state-price deflator will depend on the marginal utility of consumption evaluated at *tomorrow's* level of consumption – a future level of consumptions that is not known with certainty today. Therefore the state-price deflator is a stochastic quantity, albeit one with a known expectation.

In order to evaluate these two components in the simplest (and most common) setting, we are now going to assume that the state-price deflator follows a diffusion. Since this is the same setting we chose when deriving the no-arbitrage conditions using the Partial Differential Equation approach, we expect some deep conceptual links to appear. As we shall see, we are not going to be disappointed.

How do we translate the diffusive assumption to the state-price-deflator setting? Since, as we have seen, the state-price deflator must be strictly positive, we can write in 'short-hand notation',

$$\frac{d\pi(t)}{\pi(t)} = \mu_\pi dt + \sigma_\pi dz_t. \tag{13.26}$$

The 'drift' and the 'volatility' of the state-price deflator are for the moment just 'place holders', and our notation does not imply that they should be constants. The most important task ahead will be to find concrete expressions for the 'drift' and the 'volatility' of the state-price deflator. Then we will know everything about how it behaves. As we shall see presently, this will also mean that we know everything about how bond prices (and all other prices!) behave.

A brief digression on notation. A state-price deflator depends on three quantities: the time, t, when the conditional value of a unit-payment security is assessed; the 'delivery time', T, ie, the time when the unit payment occurs; and the state of the world, s, in which the unit payment is made. So we should write $\pi_t(s_T)$.

To unclutter our notation in the next section we only keep the dependence on the 'delivery time', T, and write $\pi(T)$. However, in the section where we derive the volatility of the state-price deflator we will have to revert to a fuller notation.

13.6 SPECIAL ASSETS: DISCOUNT BONDS

The treatment so far has been quite general as far as the asset was concerned, apart from requiring that it should pay out only at time τ. Now we want to specialize the discussion to discount bonds, which we denote by $P_{t_0}^T$, where the subscript (t_0) denotes when the bond is evaluated, and the superscript (T) when it pays.

Discount bonds pay \$1 at maturities in every state of the world. Therefore we have

$$P_{t_0}^T = \mathbb{E}_{t_0}^{\mathbb{P}}[\$1 \times \pi(T)] = \mathbb{E}_{t_0}^{\mathbb{P}}[\pi(T)]. \tag{13.27}$$

Since we have set

$$\pi(t_0) = 1 \tag{13.28}$$

we can also write

$$\pi(T) = \frac{\pi(T)}{\pi(t_0)}. \tag{13.29}$$

This may seem an unnecessary complication at this stage, but the more cumbersome notation will come in handy when we look at future times.

This gives us the first important result: *today's price of a T-maturity discount bond is just the expectation (over the states) taken today of the time-T state price deflator.* For those readers who will not skip Chapter 15, Equation (13.27) should be compared with Equation (15.44) in Chapter 15.

Equation (13.27) gives the price of a bond today. More generally, the time-t price of a T-maturity bond, P_t^T, can be written as

$$P_t^T = \mathbb{E}_t^{\mathbb{P}}\left[\$1 \frac{\pi(T)}{\pi(t)}\right]. \tag{13.30}$$

These results are is important in themselves (as they gives us a first link between state price deflators and bond prices); they are also important because they allow us to say something about the *process* for the state-price deflator. This we derive below.

13.7 DERIVING THE DRIFT OF THE STATE-PRICE DEFLATOR

We start from Equation (13.30), which we rewrite as

$$\pi(t)P_t^T = \mathbb{E}_t^{\mathbb{P}}[\pi(T)]. \tag{13.31}$$

(As usual, in arriving at this equation we have taken out of the expectation sign quantities know at the time when the expectation is taken, ie, time t.) Consider the case when we are valuing a one-period bond. Then we have

$$\pi(t)P_t^{t+\Delta t} = \mathbb{E}_t^{\mathbb{P}}[\pi(t+\Delta t)]. \tag{13.32}$$

But, to first order,

$$P_t^{t+\Delta t} = e^{-r_t\Delta t} \simeq 1 - r_t\Delta t \tag{13.33}$$

and therefore

$$\pi(t)(1 - r_t\Delta t) = \mathbb{E}_t^{\mathbb{P}}[\pi(t+\Delta t)]. \tag{13.34}$$

Let's find another expression for the expectation $\mathbb{E}_t^{\mathbb{P}}[\pi(t+\Delta t)]$. To do so, discretize Equation (13.26). We get

$$\pi(t+\Delta t) = \pi(t)(1 + \mu_\pi\Delta t + \sigma_\pi dz_t). \tag{13.35}$$

Taking the expectation one gets

$$\mathbb{E}_t^{\mathbb{P}}[\pi(t+\Delta t)] = \mathbb{E}_t^{\mathbb{P}}[\pi(t)(1+\mu_\pi\Delta t+\sigma_\mu dz_t)] = \pi(t)(1 \mid \mu_\pi\Delta t_t). \tag{13.36}$$

Equating the two expressions we have obtained for $\mathbb{E}_t^{\mathbb{P}}[\pi(t+\Delta t)]$ (Equations (13.34) and (13.36)) we get

$$\mu_\pi = -r_{t_0}. \tag{13.37}$$

So, we have obtained a value for the first 'place holder' for the process of the state price deflator, ie, for its drift: the state price deflator 'grows' in calendar time at the instantaneous rate r_t.

Yes, in calendar time it *grows*, despite the minus sign. Why so? Because one has to be careful in distinguishing between the dependence on the delivery time (T) and on calendar time (t). An expression like

$$\frac{d\pi(t)}{\pi(t)} = -r_t dt + \sigma_\pi dz_t \tag{13.38}$$

shows that the state-price deflator indeed *grows* as a function of calendar time, t, and *decays* as a function of the maturity time, T.

This is what we expect: for a fixed maturity, T, today the state price deflator must be worth less than \$1; and we know that, whatever state of the world will be reached at time T, it will be worth \$1 at that time. So, it grows in calendar time. Conversely, ceteris paribus, if we look at the value of the state price deflator for later and later delivery dates we can readily appreciate that it becomes smaller and smaller with increasing T.

A last comment in ending this section: readers who know a bit of stochastic calculus will clearly see the links between the state-price deflator and the 'change of measure' on the one hand and the Radon–Nykodim derivative on the other. This is an angle that (alas or fortunately, depending on the tastes of the reader) we will not explore in this book.

13.8   THE SHORT RATE AGAIN

The result that we have obtained so far gives another interpretation for the risk-less rate.[9]

In order to see the wood for the trees, we are going to work with power utility functions. To make things even simpler, we are going to assume $\gamma = 1$, which means that we are going to use a logarithmic utility function:

$$u(c_t) = \log(c_t). \tag{13.39}$$

We start from the expression for the price of a Δt-period bond:

$$P_t^{t+\Delta t} = e^{-r_t \Delta t}. \tag{13.40}$$

Next, we use the expression that we derive in Chapter 15 for the stochastic discount factor (specialized to the case of the logarithmic utility function), and write

$$P_t^{t+\Delta t} = \mathbb{E}_t^{\mathbb{P}}\left[\frac{\pi(t+\Delta t)}{\pi(t)}\right] = \mathbb{E}_t^{\mathbb{P}}\left[\frac{e^{-\beta(t+\Delta t)}}{e^{-\beta t}}\left(\frac{c_{t+\Delta t}}{c_t}\right)^{-\gamma}\right]$$

$$= \mathbb{E}_t^{\mathbb{P}}\left[\frac{e^{-\beta(t+\Delta t)}}{e^{-\beta t}}\frac{c_t}{c_{t+\Delta t}}\right] = e^{-\beta\Delta t}\mathbb{E}_t^{\mathbb{P}}\left[\frac{c_t}{c_{t+\Delta t}}\right]. \tag{13.41}$$

We now equate this expression to the expression we obtained before for $P_t^{t+\Delta t}$, to obtain

$$e^{-r_t\Delta t} = e^{-\delta\Delta t}\mathbb{E}_t^{\mathbb{P}}\left[\frac{c_t}{c_{t+\Delta t}}\right]. \tag{13.42}$$

Taking logarithms, this gives

$$r_t \simeq \delta + \frac{1}{\Delta t}\log\left(\mathbb{E}_t^{\mathbb{P}}\left[\frac{c_{t+\Delta t}}{c_t}\right]\right). \tag{13.43}$$

This shows that, *at least with a logarithmic utility function*, the short rate is not just given by the impatience term (the term δ), but also by a component the reflects the *expected* growth in consumption (ie, very broadly speaking, GDP growth) over the next time step. The more we expect the economy to grow, the higher the risk-less rate will be.[10]

Exercise 30 *Re-obtain the same result when the utility function is a power function with $\gamma \neq 1$, (which is trivial), and for a general time-separable utility function (which is more interesting).*

---

[9] This section can be skipped if the reader does not intend to go through the treatment in Chapter 15. It would be a pity, though.

[10] As we shall see in Chapter 15, switching the logarithm of the expectation to the expectation of the logarithm gives rise to a 'convexity' term (see Equation 15.23) that we will associated with 'precautionary saving'. This interpretation, however, is less compelling than the interpretation of the other terms we will present in Chapter 15, and comes about only because of the presence of the volatility term, σ_c^2.

13.9 DERIVING THE VOLATILITY OF THE STATE-PRICE DEFLATOR

We now move to the task of determining the volatility of the state-price deflator. Given the assumptions we have made about its process, and since we know its value today, once we have gathered this piece of information as well we will know everything there is to know about it. And since, via the 'building block approach', once we know how the state-price deflator we know how any security behaves, the size of the gold pot at the end of the rainbow should be clear.

We start from the equation from the bond price that we introduced above:

$$P_t^T = \mathbb{E}_t \left[\frac{\pi(T)}{\pi(t)} \right]. \tag{13.44}$$

Since $P_T^T = 1$, and since the quantity $\pi(t)$ is known at time t (and can therefore be taken out of the expectation) we can write

$$\pi(t) P_t^T = \mathbb{E}_t \left[\pi(T) P_T^T \right]. \tag{13.45}$$

Therefore the expectation of future values of the quantity $\pi(\tau) P_\tau^T$, for any $\tau > t$, is always equal to the value of the quantity today, $P_t^T \pi(t)$. Readers who know some probability at this point become very excited, because they will recognize that Equation (13.45) suggests that $P_t^T \pi(t)$ might be a martingale, but we will not pursue this angle here. The relevant observation for us is that the expectation of the quantity $P_t^T \pi(t)$ does not change when t changes. In particular for $t = t + \Delta t$ we have

$$\pi(t) P_t^T = \mathbb{E}_t \left[\pi(t + \Delta t) P_{t+\Delta t}^T \right] \tag{13.46}$$

Diving both sides by $\pi(t) P_t^T$, pushing inside the expectation sign quantities that we know at time t, and rearranging to make things look prettier, we have

$$1 = \mathbb{E}_t \left[\frac{\pi(t + \Delta t) P_{t+\Delta t}^T}{\pi(t) P_t^T} \right] = \mathbb{E}_t \left[\frac{\pi(t + \Delta t)}{\pi(t)} \frac{P_{t+\Delta t}^T}{P_t^T} \right]. \tag{13.47}$$

From the well-known relationship

$$\mathbb{E}[a \times b] = \mathbb{E}[a]\mathbb{E}[b] + \text{cov}[a, b] \tag{13.48}$$

we then obtain

$$\mathbb{E}_t \left[\frac{\pi(t + \Delta t)}{\pi(t)} \right] \mathbb{E}_t \left[\frac{P_{t+\Delta t}^T}{P_t^T} \right] = 1 - \text{cov} \left[\frac{\pi(t + \Delta t)}{\pi(t)}, \frac{P_{t+\Delta t}^T}{P_t^T} \right]. \tag{13.49}$$

All we are left with is the evaluation of the two expectations and of the covariance. How this is done is shown in the text that follows. But, lest we lose our focus, why go through this? Because the covariance term, as we shall presently see, will give us a term containing the volatility of the state-price deflator, which is what we are looking for.

13.9.1 Evaluation of the Three Terms

In this section, we evaluate, one by one, the three terms that appear in Equation (13.49).

Evaluation of $\mathbb{E}_t \left[\frac{P^T_{t+\Delta t}}{P^T_t} \right]$

To evaluate the first term, recall that we have required the process for the state price deflator to be a simple (geometric) diffusion. Since bond prices must be strictly positive, we must have (from Ito's Lemma)

$$\frac{dP^T_t}{P^T_t} = \mu_P dt + \sigma_P dz_t \tag{13.50}$$

for *some* drift and volatility of the bond price. Note that in the simple case we are looking at the economy is shocked by a single source of uncertainty (we are in a one-factor world), and therefore the term dz_t in expression (13.50) is exactly the same as the term dz_t in process for the state price deflator (see Equation (13.26)). Therefore, discretizing Equation (13.50) one gets for $P^T_{t_0+\Delta t}$:

$$
\begin{aligned}
P^T_{t+\Delta t} &= P^T_t + P^T_t \mu_P \Delta t + P^T_t \sigma_P \Delta z_t \\
&= P^T_t (1 + \mu_P \Delta t + \sigma_P \Delta z_t).
\end{aligned}
\tag{13.51}
$$

Evaluating the expectation then gives

$$\mathbb{E}^{\mathbb{P}}_t \left[\frac{P^T_{t+\Delta t}}{P^T_t} \right] = 1 + \mu_P \Delta t. \tag{13.52}$$

Evaluation of $\mathbb{E}_t \left[\frac{\pi(t+\Delta t)}{\pi(t)} \right]$

Proceeding in a similar manner, we get

$$
\begin{aligned}
\pi^T_{t+\Delta t} &= \pi^T_t (1 + \mu_\pi \Delta t + \sigma_\pi \Delta z_t) \\
&= \pi^T_t (1 - r_t \Delta t + \sigma_\pi \Delta z_t),
\end{aligned}
\tag{13.53}
$$

where in the last line we have made use of the result obtained in the previous section (Equation (13.37): $\mu_\pi = -r$).

Evaluating the expectation gives

$$\mathbb{E}_t \left[\frac{\pi(t+\Delta t)}{\pi(t)} \right] = (1 - r_t \Delta t). \tag{13.54}$$

Evaluation of the Covariance Term

Finally we have to evaluate the covariance term. This is easy:

$$\text{cov}\left[\frac{\pi(t+\Delta t)}{\pi(t)}, \frac{P^T_{t+\Delta t}}{P^T_t}\right]$$

$$= \text{cov}\left[\left(1 - r_{t_0}\Delta t + \sigma_\pi \Delta z_t\right), \left(1 + \mu_P \Delta t + \sigma_P \Delta z_t\right)\right]$$

$$= \text{cov}[\sigma_\pi \Delta z_t, \sigma_P \Delta z_t] = \sigma_\pi \sigma_P \Delta t \tag{13.55}$$

where we have made use of

$$cov[a + bx, c + dy] = cov[bx, dy] = bd\,cov[x, y]. \tag{13.56}$$

The term we are ultimately looking for, ie, the volatility, σ_π, of the state-price deflator, has finally appeared. Now we have all the pieces that we require to obtain an expression for it.

13.9.2 The Link between the Volatility of the State-Price Deflator and the Market Price of Risk

Let's put all the pieces together. One gets

$$\mathbb{E}_t\left[\frac{\pi(t+\Delta t)}{\pi(t)}\right]\mathbb{E}_t\left[\frac{P^T_{t+\Delta t}}{P^T_t}\right] = 1 - cov\left[\frac{\pi(t+\Delta t)}{\pi(t)}, \frac{P^T_{t+\Delta t}}{P^T_t}\right]$$

$$\implies (1 - r_t\Delta t)(1 + \mu_P \Delta t) = -\sigma_\pi \sigma_P \Delta t. \tag{13.57}$$

Recalling then that terms in $(\Delta t)^2$ can be set equal to zero for very small Δt, one finally gets

$$r = \mu_P + \sigma_\pi \sigma_P, \tag{13.58}$$

which can be rearranged to solve for the quantity we were looking for, ie, the volatility of the state-price deflator:

$$\sigma_\pi = -\frac{\mu_P - r}{\sigma_P}. \tag{13.59}$$

This result has two interpretations: the first is that the volatility of the state-price deflator is just equal to (minus) the Sharpe Ratio for a bond. (So, when you read in Cochrane (2001) that to eliminate deals which are 'too good' one must limit the variance of the stochastic discount factor, now you understand where the requirement comes from: he is just asking you not to take very seriously deals with Sharpe ratios that are too good to be true – which is as good a piece of advice as you will probably ever get.[11]).

Second, by comparing the result we have just obtained with the expression for the market price of risk that we derived in the previous chapters, we see

[11] See, eg, Cochrane (2001) and Cochrane and Saa-Requejo (1999).

that the volatility of the stochastic discount factor is just equal to (minus) the possibly-time-and-state-dependent, but-maturity-independent market price of risk:

$$\sigma_\pi = -\frac{\mu_P - r}{\sigma_P} = -\lambda. \tag{13.60}$$

Recall that in the 'traditional' approach we obtained the maturity-independent market price of risk by constructing a risk-less portfolio, a procedure that also requires the shock(s) to the economy to be 'hedgeable' – for instance, increments of Brownian motions. Where has this requirement gone? The equivalence between the two approaches is clearly underpinned by the relationship

$$P_t^T = \mathbb{E}_t \left[\frac{\pi(T)}{\pi(t)} \right], \tag{13.61}$$

which shows that all that there is to know about bond prices comes from the state price deflator.

13.9.3   Where Does the Volatility of Bonds Come from?

Let's put this new knowledge to good use, and let's look, for instance at the volatility of bond prices.

We know that bond prices are, of course, volatile, but where does their volatility 'come from'? From what we have learnt we can immediately say that it does not stem from the volatility of the state-price deflator, because the link between this quantity and bond prices is via an expectation, which 'kills' the volatility of π_s^T.

But, if this is the case, where does the volatility of bond prices come from? It can only come from the drift of the state-price deflator, *which will be stochastic if the short rate is stochastic*. So, when we assign the drift part of the process for the short rate (say, its reversion speed, if any), this will affect the *volatility* of the bond price. The Vasicek model provides a very clear example of this.

Another way to think about this is to look at Equation (13.61), and realize that a bond price is proportional to the time-t expectation of the state-price deflator at time T. Therefore the volatility of a bond price is the volatility of an expectation. For *any* maturity, an expectation today is just a number – which has no volatility. But as we move from today into the future, our expectation will move a lot more for a 30-year bond than for a bond expiring in two days' time. So, it is logical to expect that the volatility of a 30-year bond will be a lot higher than the expectation of a 2-day bond.

What *will* the volatility of the state-price deflator (ie, the market price of risk) affect then? It will affect the expected rate of growth in the real world of the bond price, ie, its excess expected return. Much more about this in the chapters to come.

13.9.4 Summary of Results

In sum, putting the pieces together we have derived for the process of the state-price deflator we can write:

$$\frac{d\pi_t}{\pi_t} = -r_t \, dt - \lambda dz_t. \tag{13.62}$$

We will make use of, and generalize, this relationship when we look at real and nominal rates, and when we extend the approach to the multifactor case in Chapter 34. For the moment, we simply note for future reference that solving Equation (13.62) gives

$$\pi_t = \pi_{t_0} e^{-r_t \tau - \frac{1}{2}\lambda^2 \tau - \lambda\sqrt{\tau}\epsilon}, \tag{13.63}$$

with

$$\tau = t - t_0 \tag{13.64}$$

and

$$\epsilon \sim \mathcal{N}(0, 1). \tag{13.65}$$

This is just a special case of the general result we presented in Chapter 2, with the market price of risk playing the role of the volatility of the process (because it *is* the volatility of the process).

What would this equation look like if we had many factors? Let Λ_t be a vector of market prices of risk. We then state without proof (but giving rise, we think, to little surprise), that we have

$$\pi_t = \pi_{t_0} e^{-r_t \tau - \frac{1}{2}\Lambda_t^{\mathrm{T}}\Lambda_t \tau - \Lambda_t^{\mathrm{T}}\sqrt{\tau}\epsilon}.$$

Finally, we note in closing that now we understand what is meant in term-structure papers, when one reads sentences such as: '...we follow the affine bond pricing literature [...] and specify a nominal pricing kernel.'[12] A nominal pricing kernel is what we have called here the state-price deflator. Specifying the state-price deflator means specifying its process. Specifying its process means assigning the market price of risk. Assigning the market price of risk means describing how it depends on the state variables (or, in general, on macrofinancial variables). Prescribing an *affine* pricing kernel then means imposing that this dependence on the chosen variables of the market price of risk (which contains everything we need to know about the state-price deflator) should be of the affine type. Quite simple, really.

---

[12] Sangvinatsos and Wachter (2006), p. 181.

CHAPTER 14

No-Arbitrage Conditions for Real Bonds

14.1 THE PURPOSE OF THIS CHAPTER

In this chapter we look at the conditions of no-arbitrage for real (inflation-linked) instead of nominal bonds. The formalism learnt in the previous chapter will pay off, because the no-arbitrage conditions will be obtained using the state-price deflator. There are, of course, other ways to obtain the same results, but the route we have followed here will put the reader in good stead to tackle Chapter 31 (devoted to the D'Amico–Kim–Wei model), and the related literature: indeed, virtually all the contemporary literature uses this language, and the reader will not be able to read these interesting works unless she musters the argot.

The plan is to obtain first the no-arbitrage conditions that must be obeyed by *any* (diffusive) model that uses both nominal and real state variables, and then to specialize these conditions to the case of diffusive affine models. One of the by-products of the derivation will be the derivation of the link between break-even inflation and the real-world expectation of inflation.

14.2 THE EXPRESSION FOR THE REAL STATE-PRICE DEFLATOR

As we said, our ultimate goal is to obtain the conditions of no-arbitrage for real bonds, and that we are going to do this by using the state-price-deflator route. Therefore our intermediate goal is to obtain an expression for the time-t value of real state price deflator, $\pi_t^{\mathrm{real},T}$.

Recall first the definitions of nominal state prices and of the nominal state-price deflators: given a set of unit *nominal* payoffs in different states of the world, we introduced two quantities:

- The state prices, sp_s, which were the values today of each of these unit payoffs. This value was obtained by multiplying its probability of reaching each of the possible states by a state-dependent discount factor. Why was the discount factor state dependent? Because, in

general, we value a certain payoff more or less depending on whether
it happens in good or bad times, ie, on the state of the world.

- The state-price deflator, π_s, for a given state was the state price for that state divided by the probability of occurrence of the same state.

We can apply the same reasoning to real bonds. Here is how it works. (To
avoid confusion, we are going to append superscripts the 'nom' and 'real' to
nominal and real quantities, respectively.)

Recall that for a nominal bond we wrote

$$P_{t_0}^{\text{nom},T} = \mathbb{E}_{t_0}^{\mathbb{P}} \left[\frac{\pi_{t_0}^{\text{nom},T}}{\pi_{t_0}^{\text{nom},t_0}} P_T^T \right] = \mathbb{E}_{t_0}^{\mathbb{P}} \left[\pi_{t_0}^{\text{nom},T} \right] \tag{14.1}$$

because $P_T^T = 1$ and we can always set $\pi_{t_0}^{\text{nom},t_0} = 1$. Now we are going to take
a seemingly indirect approach, and think of a 'pure' inflation-linked bond[1] as a
nominal bond whose terminal (time-T) payoff happens to be exactly the cumulative realized appreciation of the price process, $Q_{t_0}^T$. To make our life simple,
we begin by assuming that the inflation is deterministic. (We will relax this
unnecessary assumption in the next section.) This means that for the nominal
price today of a pure inflation-linked bond we are going to write

$$P_{t_0}^{\text{real},T} = \mathbb{E}_{t_0}^{\mathbb{P}} \left[\pi_{t_0}^{\text{nom},T} Q_{t_0}^T \right], \tag{14.2}$$

with

$$Q_{t_0}^T = e^{\int_{t_0}^T i_s ds}, \tag{14.3}$$

where i_s is the inflation at time s and we have set $Q_{t_0} = 1$. Note carefully that
we are making use of the *nominal* state price deflator. (The reader who wants to
refresh her memory about real bonds, real returns and realized inflation might
want to look back at Chapter 4.) But let's keep in mind that our goal is to obtain
an expression for the real (as opposed to nominal) state-price deflator.

Now, *in real terms*, we can write that the future price of a bundle that grows
at the inflation rate is exactly equal to the price of the same bundle today, which,
without loss of generality, we can take equal to $1. So, a security that is worth
$1 today and that, for every $\tau > t_0$, delivers in every state of the world $Q_{t_0}^\tau$ is
always worth $1 *in real terms* at time τ. This means that, for $\tau = T$, we must
also have

$$P_{t_0}^{\text{real},T} = \mathbb{E}_{t_0}^{\mathbb{P}} \left[\pi_{t_0}^{\text{real},T} \times 1 \right]. \tag{14.4}$$

This an expression that now contains the *real* state-price deflator.

Since on the left-hand side of Equations (14.2) and (14.4) we have the same
quantity, ie, the price today, $P_{t_0}^{\text{real},T}$, of a real discount bond of maturity T, we
can equate what is under the expectation sign on the right-hand side of Equations (14.2) and (14.4), and we obtain

$$\pi_t^{\text{real},T} = \pi_t^{\text{nom},T} Q_t^T. \tag{14.5}$$

---

[1] By 'pure' we mean that the real return is zero.

This tells us that the real state-price deflator, $\pi_{t_0}^{\text{real},T}$, is just equal to the nominal state-price deflator, multiplied by the rolled-up price index. This makes sense. For positive inflation, the real state-price deflator is bigger than its nominal counterpart, because it multiplies real future payoffs, which are smaller than the corresponding nominal payoffs. They are smaller exactly by the value of the \$1 rolled-up by inflation.

14.3   THE PROCESS FOR THE REAL STATE-PRICE DEFLATOR

We have obtained an expression for the real state-price deflator. As we did with the nominal state-price deflator, we now want to discover how it evolves.[2] At this point we no longer require the inflation process to be deterministic.

To find an expression for the real state-price deflator, we have to specify clearly which shocks affect the economy, and by which of these shocks the various auxiliary quantities that we are going to use (say, the expected inflation) are affected. Our lives will be made much simpler if we use vector notation, which we have so far only briefly introduced in Chapter 2.[3]

So, we start by saying that the expected inflation, ei_t, is given by

$$dei_t = \mu_{ei}dt + \sigma_t^{ei}dz_t^{ei}. \tag{14.6}$$

Next we stipulate that the real short rate, r_t^R, should also follows a diffusion process, of the form

$$dr_t^R = \mu_{r^R}dt + \sigma_t^{r^R}dz_t^{r^R}. \tag{14.7}$$

Finally, we give an expression for the price process: we write it compactly as

$$\frac{dQ_t}{Q_t} = ei_t dt + \vec{\xi}_t^{\mathsf{T}}\vec{dz}_t + \xi_t^u dz_t^u, \tag{14.8}$$

where the vector $\vec{\xi}_t$ has components

$$\xi_t = \begin{bmatrix} \xi^{ei} \\ \xi^{r^R} \end{bmatrix} \tag{14.9}$$

and $d\vec{z}_t$ is made up of the shocks to the real rate and to the expected inflation:

$$d\vec{z}_t = \begin{bmatrix} dz_t^{ei} \\ dz_t^{r^R} \end{bmatrix}. \tag{14.10}$$

---

[2] The treatment that follows is based in part on Brennan and Xia (2002). This paper also includes an equity stock, S_t, in the economy to which a corresponding price of risk is associated. We do not pursue this route in the treatment that follows.

[3] The reader who needs some 'limbering up' with vector manipulations may want to skim Chapter 17 at this stage.

In addition, the price-level process may also be shocked by a source of risk, dz_t^u, which is orthogonal both to dz_t^{ei} and to $dz_t^{r^R}$. So, for future reference,

$$\mathbb{E}\left[dz^u dz^{ei}\right] = \mathbb{E}\left[dz^u dz^{r^R}\right] = 0. \tag{14.11}$$

As Brennan and Xia (2002) write, 'dz^u, [...] is proportional to the component of the inflation rate, $\frac{dQ_t}{Q_t}$, that is orthogonal to dz.'[4]

It is worthwhile spending a few words on the extra term $\xi_t^u dz_t^u$. The price process is a macroeconomic quantity. We can 'project' it (say, by means of a regression) onto yield-curve variables – ie, variables shocked by the sources of uncertainty that affect yields, $dz_t = \begin{bmatrix} dz_t^{ei} \\ dz_t^{r^R} \end{bmatrix}$. However, there is no a priori reason why all the variability in a macroeconomic variable should be reflected in the variability of yields. Whether yields 'impound' all the information about the economy – both in theory and in practice – is a very important question (the 'spanning' problem) that can only be answered empirically. We will look in detail at this topic in Chapters 27 and 29. For the moment, we simply add a place-holder, the term $\xi^u dz_t^u$, to cater for the possibility that there may be more to life (or, rather, to risk premia) than just yields.

Generalizing the discussion in Chapter 4, we know that, in principle, there are distinct market prices of risk (compensations for risk) associated with each of these sources of risk. We therefore denote by $\overrightarrow{\lambda}$ the (vector) market prices of risk associated with the vector dz:

$$\overrightarrow{\lambda} = \begin{bmatrix} \lambda^{ei} \\ \lambda^{r^R} \end{bmatrix} \tag{14.12}$$

and by λ_u the market price of risk (a single number) associated with the orthogonal source of risk dz_t^u.

Finally, let's move to the process for the nominal state-price deflator. In Chapter 13 we worked in a one-factor world and we obtained that

$$\frac{d\pi^N}{\pi^N} = -r^N dt - \lambda^N dw. \tag{14.13}$$

(See Equation (13.62).) Here we generalize this expression to a multifactor setting, and write

$$\frac{d\pi^N}{\pi^N} = -r^N dt - \left(\overrightarrow{\lambda}^N\right)^{\mathrm{T}} \overrightarrow{dz_t}. \tag{14.14}$$

Note that, given the identification of dz^u as the source of risk orthogonal to the vector $\overrightarrow{dz_t}$ presented earlier, we have not included in the process for the nominal state-price deflator the market price of 'unspanned' risk, λ^u.

---

[4] p. 1206. Note that Brennan and Xia consider an economy where 'there is inflation *and only nominal assets are available for trade.*' (Emphasis added.) Note also that we have changed one of the symbols in the original quote in order to conform with our notation.

We have now described our stylized economy. Our goal, as stated earlier, is to discover how the *real* state-price deflator behaves in this economy. Since we have assumed that everything is a diffusion, we can formally write

$$\frac{d\pi^R}{\pi^R} = \mu_{r^R}dt + \overrightarrow{s}_t^{\mathrm{T}}\overrightarrow{dz}_t + s_t^u dz_t^u, \tag{14.15}$$

where, for the moment, the drift, μ_{r^R}, and the volatilities,[5] $\overrightarrow{s}_t$ and s_t^u are just place-holders. Once we have established expressions for them in terms of the quantities we have assigned to the economy we will know all there is to know about the real state-price deflator. (And, by the way, since real bonds are fully described by the real state-price deflator, we will also know – at least formally – all that there is to know about real bonds.)

After lightening a bit the notation used earlier, we are going to use the relationship derived in Section 14.2:

$$\pi_t^R = \pi_t^N Q_t \tag{14.16}$$

and take the 'differential' to obtain:

$$
\begin{aligned}
d\pi_t^R &= Q_t d\pi_t^N + \pi_t^N dQ_t + d\pi_t^N dQ_t \\
&= Q_t \underbrace{\pi_t^N \left[-r^N dt - \left(\overrightarrow{\lambda}^N \right)^{\mathrm{T}} \overrightarrow{dz} \right]}_{d\pi_t^N} \\
&\quad + \pi_t^N \underbrace{Q_t \left[ei_t dt + \overrightarrow{\xi}^{\mathrm{T}} \overrightarrow{dz} + \xi_u dz_u \right]}_{dQ_t} \\
&\quad + \underbrace{Q_t \left[ei_t dt + \overrightarrow{\xi}^{\mathrm{T}} \overrightarrow{dz} + \xi_u dz_u \right]}_{dQ_t} \underbrace{\pi_t^N \left[-r^N dt - \left(\overrightarrow{\lambda}^N \right)^{\mathrm{T}} \overrightarrow{dz} \right]}_{d\pi_t^R}
\end{aligned}
\tag{14.17}
$$

$$= \pi^R \left[-r_t^N + ei_t - \left(\overrightarrow{\lambda}^N \right)^{\mathrm{T}} \overrightarrow{\xi} \right] dt + \left(\overrightarrow{\xi} - \overrightarrow{\lambda}^N \right)^{\mathrm{T}} \overrightarrow{dz} + \xi_u dz_u, \tag{14.18}$$

where we have substituted the expressions for $d\pi_t^R$ and dQ_t that we obtained before, and we have made use of the orthogonality of $\overrightarrow{dz}$ and dz_u.

Now let's *define* the instantaneous *real* short rate,[6] r_t^R, by

$$r_t^R \equiv r_t^N - ei_t + \left(\overrightarrow{\lambda}^N \right)^{\mathrm{T}} \overrightarrow{\xi} \tag{14.19}$$

---

[5] We say 'volatilities', but remember that $\overrightarrow{s}^{\mathrm{T}}$ is a vector, and s_u a scalar.

[6] This expression differs from the well-known Fisher (1930) relationship, $r_t^R \equiv r_t^N - ei_t$, by the risk-aversion term(s) $\lambda^{\mathrm{T}}\xi$.

and the vector $\overrightarrow{\lambda}^R$ by

$$\overrightarrow{\lambda}^R \equiv \overrightarrow{\lambda}^N - \overrightarrow{\xi} = \begin{bmatrix} \lambda^{ei} - \xi^{ei} \\ \lambda^{r^R} - \xi^{r^R} \end{bmatrix}. \tag{14.20}$$

Then, after putting all the pieces together, we have

$$\frac{d\pi_t^R}{\pi_t^R} = -r_t^R \, dt - \left(\overrightarrow{\lambda}^R\right)^{\mathrm{T}} \overrightarrow{dz}_t + \left(\overrightarrow{\xi}_u\right)^{\mathrm{T}} \overrightarrow{dz}_u. \tag{14.21}$$

Note that in our definition of the real short rate the term $\left(\overrightarrow{\lambda}^N\right)^{\mathrm{T}} \overrightarrow{\xi}$ is added to the difference between the nominal short rate and the expected inflation. This term is made up of products of market prices of risk times volatilities. It is therefore clearly a risk premium. We look at this term in more detail in the text that follows.

Equations (14.14) and (14.21) are the mutually consistent relationships of no-arbitrage that must be obeyed if we want to work with *any* (diffusive) model that uses both nominal and real state variables. These restrictions assume a much more stringent form if we further require that all the variables in our models should be affine. We deal with this in the last section of this chapter. Before that, we are going to address the question of the link between break-even inflation, which we defined in Chapter 4, and various expectations of the growth in the price process.

14.4 THE LINK BETWEEN BREAK-EVEN INFLATION AND INFLATION EXPECTATIONS

Inflation expectations are obviously linked to the break-even inflation that we defined in Chapter 4. As promised, in this section we explore these links more carefully by focussing on how (ie, under which measure) we take the expectation – under the real-world, the risk-neutral or any other measure.

A pure discount inflation-linked bond (ie, a discount *real* bond), of time-t price $P_{t,T}^R$, pays at maturity T the increment of the price level, $\frac{Q_T}{Q_t}$, between times t and T. In Chapter 4 we *defined* the time-t, maturity-T real yield, $y_{t,T}^R$ of a discount real bond, to be given by

$$P_{t,T}^R = e^{-y_t^{\text{real},T} T}, \tag{14.22}$$

with

$$\tau = T - t. \tag{14.23}$$

We also defined the time-t, maturity-T break-even inflation, $BEI_{t,T}$, by the relationship

$$BEI_{t,T} \equiv y_t^{nom,T} - y_t^{\text{real},T}. \tag{14.24}$$

Finally, we defined in the same chapter the expected inflation between time t and time T, I_t^T, by

$$EI_t^T = \frac{1}{T-t}\mathbb{E}\left[\log\left(\frac{Q_T}{Q_t}\right)\right],$$ (14.25)

but, at the time, we were not too precise about the measure used in taking the expectation. Now it's the time to fill this gap by looking at the break-even inflation under different measures.

14.4.1   Inflation Expectation Under $\mathbb{P}$

We begin by calculating the expectation of the inflation under the real-world measure, $\mathbb{P}$; ie, let's evaluate the expectation of $\frac{Q_T}{Q_t}$ under the real-world, $\mathbb{P}$, measure.

To do so, we make use of the result we obtained earlier, namely that

$$P_{t,T}^R = \mathbb{E}^{\mathbb{P}}\left[\mathcal{M}_T^N \frac{Q_T}{Q_t}\right],$$ (14.26)

where $\mathcal{M}_T^N$ is the ratio of the nominal stochastic discount factors:

$$\mathcal{M}_T^N \equiv \frac{\pi^N(T)}{\pi^N(t)}.$$

Then we have

$$\begin{aligned}
P_{t,T}^R &= E^{\mathbb{P}}\left[\frac{Q_T}{Q_t}\mathcal{M}_T^N\right] \\
&= E^{\mathbb{P}}\left[\frac{Q_T}{Q_t}\right]E^{\mathbb{P}}\left[\mathcal{M}_T^N\right] + \text{cov}^{\mathbb{P}}\left[\frac{Q_T}{Q_t}, \mathcal{M}_T^N\right] \\
&= \mathbb{E}^{\mathbb{P}}\left[\frac{Q_T}{Q_t}\right]P_{t,T}^N\left(1 + \frac{\text{cov}^{\mathbb{P}}\left[\frac{Q_T}{Q_t}, \mathcal{M}_T^N\right]}{\mathbb{E}^{\mathbb{P}}\left[\frac{Q_T}{Q_t}\right]P_{t,T}^N}\right),
\end{aligned}$$ (14.27)

where in the last line we have made use of the fact that

$$\mathbb{E}_t^{\mathbb{P}}\left[\mathcal{M}_T^N\right] = P_{t,T}^N$$ (14.28)

and we have written

$$a \times b + \text{cov}(a,b) = a \times b\left(1 + \frac{\text{cov}(a,b)}{a \times b}\right).$$ (14.29)

Taking logarithms of both sides of Equation (14.27) one gets

$$-y_{t,T}^R \tau = \log\left(\mathbb{E}^{\mathbb{P}}\left[\frac{Q_T}{Q_t}\right]\right) - y_{t,T}^N \tau + \log\left(1 + \frac{\text{cov}^{\mathbb{P}}\left[\frac{Q_T}{Q_t}, \mathcal{M}_T^N\right]}{\mathbb{E}^{\mathbb{P}}\left[\frac{Q_T}{Q_t}\right]P_{t,T}^N}\right)$$

(14.30)

with $\tau = T - t$. Therefore we can write

$$y_{t,T}^N - y_{t,T}^R = \frac{1}{\tau} \log \left(\mathbb{E}^{\mathbb{P}} \left[\frac{Q_T}{Q_t} \right] \right) + \frac{1}{\tau} \log \left(1 + \frac{\text{cov}^{\mathbb{P}} \left[\frac{Q_T}{Q_t}, \mathcal{M}_T^N \right]}{\mathbb{E}^{\mathbb{P}} \left[\frac{Q_T}{Q_t} \right] P_{t,T}^N} \right).$$

(14.31)

Recall that we defined the time-t, maturity-T break-even inflation, $BEI_{t,T}$, by

$$BEI_{t,T} = y_{t,T}^N - y_{t,T}^R \ .$$

(14.32)

Then it follows that

$$BEI_{t,T} = \frac{1}{\tau} \log \left(\mathbb{E}^{\mathbb{P}} \left[\frac{Q_T}{Q_t} \right] \right) + \frac{1}{\tau} \log \left(1 + \frac{\text{cov}^{\mathbb{P}} \left[\frac{Q_T}{Q_t}, \mathcal{M}_T^N \right]}{\mathbb{E}^{\mathbb{P}} \left[\frac{Q_T}{Q_t} \right] P_{t,T}^N} \right).$$

(14.33)

Now, in the expression for the expected inflation we had the expectation of the logarithm, and what we have obtained is the logarithm of the expectation. This is only mildly annoying, because we can add and subtract the same quantity, namely $\frac{1}{\tau} \log \left(E^{\mathbb{P}} \left[\frac{Q_T}{Q_t} \right] \right)$, to obtain

$$BEI_{t,T} = \underbrace{\frac{1}{\tau} E^{\mathbb{P}} \left[\log \frac{Q_T}{Q_t} \right]}_{\text{expected inflation}} + \underbrace{\frac{1}{\tau} \left\{ \log \left(\mathbb{E}^{\mathbb{P}} \left[\frac{Q_T}{Q_t} \right] \right) - \mathbb{E}^{\mathbb{P}} \left[\log \frac{Q_T}{Q_t} \right] \right\}}_{\text{convexity}}$$

$$+ \underbrace{\frac{1}{\tau} \log \left(1 + \frac{\text{cov}^{\mathbb{P}} \left[\frac{Q_T}{Q_t}, \mathcal{M}_T^N \right]}{\mathbb{E}^{\mathbb{P}} \left[\frac{Q_T}{Q_t} \right] P_{t,T}^N} \right)}_{\text{risk premium}}.$$

(14.34)

This can be rewritten a bit more neatly as

$$BEI_{t,T} = \mathbb{E}^{\mathbb{P}} \left(I_t^T \right) + \mathcal{P}_{t,T}^{\mathbb{P}} + \text{Ci}_{t,T},$$

(14.35a)

with

$$\mathbb{E}^{\mathbb{P}} \left(I_t^T \right) = \frac{1}{\tau} \mathbb{E}^{\mathbb{P}} \left[\log \frac{Q_T}{Q_t} \right],$$

with

$$\mathcal{P}_{t,T}^{\mathbb{P}} \equiv \frac{1}{\tau} \log \left(1 + \frac{\text{cov}^{\mathbb{P}} \left[\frac{Q_T}{Q_t}, \mathcal{M}_T^N \right]}{\mathbb{E}^{\mathbb{P}} \left[\frac{Q_T}{Q_t} \right] P_{t,T}^N} \right)$$

(14.36)

and with $\mathrm{Ci}_{t,T}$ (the convexity term) given by

$$\mathrm{Ci}_{t,T} \equiv \frac{1}{\tau} \log \left(\mathbb{E}^{\mathbb{P}} \left[\frac{Q_T}{Q_t} \right] \right) - \frac{1}{\tau} \mathbb{E}^{\mathbb{P}} \left[\log \frac{Q_T}{Q_t} \right]. \tag{14.37}$$

So, the break-even inflation is given by the sum of the real-world expectation of inflation ($\mathbb{E}^{\mathbb{P}}(I_t^T)$), plus the inflation risk premium (the term $\mathcal{P}_{t,T}^R$, ie, the risk premium investors demand for bearing real-rate risk), plus a small and 'boring' (convexity) term, $\mathrm{Ci}_{t,T}$. Why 'boring'? Because usually the much bigger and more interesting term is the risk premium, $\mathcal{P}_{t,T}^R$, which has to do with how well a real discount bond performs in states of high or low discounting by the state-price deflator.

14.4.2 Inflation Expectation under $\mathbb{Q}$

Let us now take derive an expression for the expectation of $\frac{Q_T}{Q_t}$ under the risk-neutral measure, $\mathbb{Q}$.

To do so we proceed exactly as before, but now we discount the terminal value of the price process not using the stochastic discount factor, but the quantity $e^{\int_t^T r_s ds}$, ie, the money-market account. So, we write for time-t the price, $P_{t,T}^R$, of a discount real bond:

$$P_{t,T}^R = \mathbb{E}^{\mathbb{Q}} \left[\frac{Q_T}{Q_t} e^{-\int_t^T r_s ds} \right]. \tag{14.38}$$

Then we have

$$
\begin{aligned}
P_{t,T}^R &= \mathbb{E}^{\mathbb{Q}} \left[\frac{Q_T}{Q_t} e^{-\int_t^T r_s ds} \right] \\
&= \mathbb{E}^{\mathbb{Q}} \left[\frac{Q_T}{Q_t} \right] \mathbb{E}^{\mathbb{Q}} \left[e^{-\int_t^T r_s ds} \right] + \mathrm{cov}^{\mathbb{Q}} \left[\frac{Q_T}{Q_t}, e^{-\int_t^T r_s ds} \right] \\
&= \mathbb{E}^{\mathbb{Q}} \left[\frac{Q_T}{Q_t} \right] P_{t,T}^N + \mathrm{cov}^{\mathbb{Q}} \left[\frac{Q_T}{Q_t}, e^{-\int_t^T r_s ds} \right] \\
&= \mathbb{E}^{\mathbb{Q}} \left[\frac{Q_T}{Q_t} \right] P_{t,T}^N \left(1 + \frac{\mathrm{cov}^{\mathbb{Q}} \left[\frac{Q_T}{Q_t}, e^{-\int_t^T r_s ds} \right]}{\mathbb{E}^{\mathbb{Q}} \left[\frac{Q_T}{Q_t} \right] P_{t,T}^N} \right).
\end{aligned}
\tag{14.39}
$$

Taking logarithms of both sides as before one gets

$$
\begin{aligned}
-y_{t,T}^R \tau = {} & \log \left(\mathbb{E}^{\mathbb{Q}} \left[\frac{Q_T}{Q_t} \right] \right) - y_{t,T}^N \tau \\
& + \log \left(1 + \frac{\mathrm{cov}^{\mathbb{Q}} \left[\frac{Q_T}{Q_t}, e^{-\int_t^T r_s ds} \right]}{\mathbb{E}^{\mathbb{Q}} \left[\frac{Q_T}{Q_t} \right] P_{t,T}^N} \right)
\end{aligned}
\tag{14.40}
$$

and therefore

$$y_{t,T}^N - y_{t,T}^R = \frac{1}{\tau} \log \left(\mathbb{E}^{\mathbb{Q}} \left[\frac{Q_T}{Q_t} \right] \right)$$

$$+ \frac{1}{\tau} \log \left(1 + \frac{\text{cov}^{\mathbb{Q}} \left[\frac{Q_T}{Q_t}, e^{-\int_t^T r_s ds} \right]}{\mathbb{E}^{\mathbb{Q}} \left[\frac{Q_T}{Q_t} \right] P_{t,T}^N} \right). \qquad (14.41)$$

From the definition of break-even inflation, we also have

$$BEI_{t,T} = \frac{1}{\tau} \log \left(\mathbb{E}^{\mathbb{Q}} \left[\frac{Q_T}{Q_t} \right] \right)$$

$$+ \frac{1}{\tau} \log \left(1 + \frac{\text{cov}^{\mathbb{Q}} \left[\frac{Q_T}{Q_t}, e^{-\int_t^T r_s ds} \right]}{\mathbb{E}^{\mathbb{Q}} \left[\frac{Q_T}{Q_t} \right] P_{t,T}^N} \right). \qquad (14.42)$$

Note the difference between Equations (14.33) and (14.42).

Proceeding exactly the same way as we did earlier, we are then going to obtain

$$BEI_{t,T} = \mathbb{E}^{\mathbb{Q}} \left(I_t^T \right)$$

$$+ \frac{1}{\tau} \log \left(1 + \frac{\text{cov}^{\mathbb{Q}} \left[\frac{Q_T}{Q_t}, e^{-\int_t^T r_s ds} \right]}{\mathbb{E}^{\mathbb{Q}} \left[\frac{Q_T}{Q_t} \right] P_{t,T}^N} \right) + \text{Ci}_{t,T}^{\mathbb{Q}}, \qquad (14.43)$$

with

$$\text{Ci}_{t,T}^{\mathbb{Q}} \equiv \frac{1}{\tau} \left\{ \log \left(\mathbb{E}^{\mathbb{Q}} \left[\frac{Q_T}{Q_t} \right] \right) - \mathbb{E}^{\mathbb{Q}} \left[\log \frac{Q_T}{Q_t} \right] \right\}, \qquad (14.44)$$

and with

$$\mathbb{E}^{\mathbb{Q}} \left(I_t^T \right) = \frac{1}{\tau} \mathbb{E}^{\mathbb{Q}} \left[\log \frac{Q_T}{Q_t} \right].$$

14.4.3 Inflation Expectation under $\mathbb{T}$

In the two examples so far, we took an expectation of a *discounted* payoff. We had to do so, because we wanted to equate the expectation to a price today. In both cases, the discounting was state dependent. So, for instance, when we took the real-world, $\mathbb{P}$, expectation, in state s at time T the price process was $\frac{Q_T(s)}{Q_t}$, and the state-dependent discount factor was $\mathcal{M}_T^N(s)$. When we took the risk-neutral, $\mathbb{Q}$, expectation, in state s at time T the price process was $\frac{Q_T(s)}{Q_t}$, and the state-dependent discount factor was $e^{-\int_t^T r_u du}$. In both cases, it was the dependence of the discounting on the state of the world that gave rise to the covariance term.

What if we chose to discount by something that, *in nominal terms*, has exactly the same value in all states of the world at time T? Then the expression for the expectation would be nicer, because there would be no covariance term. For lack of a better symbol, let's denote this expectation by $\mathbb{T}$.[7] But we know one such discounting factor, namely, the nominal discount bond that matures exactly at time T and always pays the same amount ($1) at maturity in every state of the world.

So, if we choose to discount the payoff from the discount real bond by a nominal discount bond (instead of the money market account, or the stochastic discount factor) – that is, if we choose as numéraire the nominal discount bond itself, $P_{t,T}^N$ – there will be no covariance term, and the price, $P_{t,T}^R$, of a discount real bond will be just given by

$$
\begin{aligned}
P_{t,T}^R &= \mathbb{E}^{\mathbb{T}}\left[\frac{Q_T}{Q_t}P_{t,T}^N\right] \\
&= \mathbb{E}^{\mathbb{T}}\left[\frac{Q_T}{Q_t}\right]P_{t,T}^N.
\end{aligned} \tag{14.45}
$$

Taking logarithms of both sides one now gets

$$
-y_{t,T}^R\tau = \log\left(\mathbb{E}^{\mathbb{T}}\left[\frac{Q_T}{Q_t}\right]\right) - y_{t,T}^N\tau \tag{14.46}
$$

and therefore

$$
y_{t,T}^N - y_{t,T}^R = \frac{1}{\tau}\log\left(\mathbb{E}^{\mathbb{T}}\left[\frac{Q_T}{Q_t}\right]\right). \tag{14.47}
$$

From the definition of break-even inflation, we then have

$$
BEI_{t,T} = \mathbb{E}^{\mathbb{T}}\left(I_t^T\right) + \text{Ci}_{t,T}^{\mathbb{T}}, \tag{14.48}
$$

with

$$
\text{Ci}_{t,T}^{\mathbb{T}} \equiv \frac{1}{\tau}\left\{\log\left(\mathbb{E}^{\mathbb{T}}\left[\frac{Q_T}{Q_t}\right]\right) - \mathbb{E}^{\mathbb{T}}\left[\log\frac{Q_T}{Q_t}\right]\right\}.
$$

So, if we take the expectation in the measure associated with the T-maturity discount bond, the break-even inflation is simply given by the expected inflation (plus the annoying convexity term).

14.4.4   Inflation Expectations under Different Measures

As Equation (14.32) shows, the break-even inflation is measure independent, because it is just something that we can measure from market prices. Therefore

---

[7] Readers familiar with change-of-measure techniques will recognize that we are working in the 'Terminal', T-maturity, measure – hence the symbol we have chosen. This measure is also called the 'forward measure'.

all three expressions, (Equations (14.33), (14.42) and (14.48)) must all give the same value.

Equating the three expression for $BEI_{t,T}$, we have

$$
\log\left(\mathbb{E}^{\mathrm{T}}\left[\frac{Q_T}{Q_t}\right]\right)
$$

$$
= \log\left(\mathbb{E}^{\mathbb{Q}}\left[\frac{Q_T}{Q_t}\right]\right) + \log\left(1 + \frac{\mathrm{cov}^{\mathbb{Q}}\left[\frac{Q_T}{Q_t}, e^{-\int_t^T r_s ds}\right]}{\mathbb{E}^{\mathbb{Q}}\left[\frac{Q_T}{Q_t}\right] P_{t,T}^N}\right)
$$

$$
= \log\left(\mathbb{E}^{\mathbb{P}}\left[\frac{Q_T}{Q_t}\right]\right) + \frac{1}{\tau}\log\left(1 + \frac{\mathrm{cov}^{\mathbb{Q}}\left[\frac{Q_T}{Q_t}, M_T^N\right]}{\mathbb{E}^{\mathbb{Q}}\left[\frac{Q_T}{Q_t}\right] P_{t,T}^N}\right). \quad (14.49)
$$

We therefore have for the various expectations of inflation:

$$
\mathbb{E}^{\mathrm{T}}\left(I_t^T\right) + \mathrm{Ci}_{t,T}^{\mathrm{T}}
$$

$$
= \mathbb{E}^{\mathbb{Q}}\left(I_t^T\right) + \frac{1}{\tau}\log\left(1 + \frac{\mathrm{cov}^{\mathbb{Q}}\left[\frac{Q_T}{Q_t}, e^{-\int_t^T r_s ds}\right]}{\mathbb{E}^{\mathbb{Q}}\left[\frac{Q_T}{Q_t}\right] P_{t,T}^N}\right) + \mathrm{Ci}_{t,T}^{\mathbb{Q}}
$$

$$
= \mathbb{E}^{\mathbb{P}}\left(I_t^T\right) + \frac{1}{\tau}\log\left(1 + \frac{\mathrm{cov}^{\mathbb{P}}\left[\frac{Q_T}{Q_t}, M_T^N\right]}{\mathbb{E}^{\mathbb{P}}\left[\frac{Q_T}{Q_t}\right] P_{t,T}^N}\right) + \mathrm{Ci}_{t,T}^{\mathbb{P}}. \quad (14.50)
$$

14.5 THE RISK PREMIUM AS A COVARIANCE

Recall that we can write the time-t price of a real or a nominal bond of maturity T as the ratio of the stochastic discount factors, π_T^i and π_t^i, with $i =$ real, nom:

$$
P_t^{\mathrm{real},T} = \mathbb{E}_{t_0}^{\mathbb{P}}\left[\frac{\pi_T^{\mathrm{real},T}}{\pi_t^{\mathrm{real},t}}\right] \quad (14.51)
$$

$$
P_t^{\mathrm{nom},T} = \mathbb{E}_{t_0}^{\mathbb{P}}\left[\frac{\pi_T^{\mathrm{nom},T}}{\pi_t^{\mathrm{nom},t}}\right] = \mathbb{E}_{t_0}^{\mathbb{P}}\left[\frac{\pi_T^{\mathrm{real},T}}{\pi_t^{\mathrm{real},t}}\frac{Q_t^t}{Q_t^T}\right], \quad (14.52)
$$

respectively. In this section we are going to repeat the treatment presented above, but with the risk premium as our focus.

To lighten notation, define as earlier

$$
\mathcal{M}_T^{\mathrm{real}} \equiv \frac{\pi_t^{\mathrm{real},T}}{\pi_t^{\mathrm{real},t}} \quad (14.53)
$$

and

$$\Theta_t^T \equiv \left(\frac{Q_t^T}{Q_t^t} \right)^{-1} .$$ (14.54)

Then we have

$$P_t^{\text{nom},T} = E_t^{\mathbb{P}} \left[\mathcal{M}_T^{\text{real}} \, \Theta_t^T \right] .$$ (14.55)

Using the usual decomposition of the expectation of a product, and proceeding exactly as above but for a nominal bond, we obtain

$$P_t^{\text{nom},T} = \mathbb{E}_t^{\mathbb{P}} \left[\mathcal{M}_T^{\text{real}} \, \Theta_t^T \right] = \mathbb{E}_t^{\mathbb{P}} \left[\mathcal{M}_T^{\text{real}} \right] E_t^{\mathbb{P}} \left[\Theta_t^T \right] + \text{cov} \left(\mathcal{M}_T^{\text{real}}, \Theta_t^T \right) .$$ (14.56)

Taking logarithms of both sides we get

$$\log \mathbb{E}_t^{\mathbb{P}} \left[\mathcal{M}_T^{\text{real}} \, \Theta_t^T \right]$$

$$= \log \left\{ \mathbb{E}_t^{\mathbb{P}} \left[\mathcal{M}_T^{\text{real}} \right] E_t^{\mathbb{P}} \left[\Theta_t^T \right] + \text{cov} \left(\mathcal{M}_T^{\text{real}}, \Theta_t^T \right) \right\}$$

$$= \log \left[\left(\mathbb{E}_t^{\mathbb{P}} \left[\mathcal{M}_T^{\text{real}} \right] \mathbb{E}_t^{\mathbb{P}} \left[\Theta_t^T \right] \right) \left(1 + \frac{\text{cov} \left(\mathcal{M}_T^{\text{real}}, \Theta_t^T \right)}{\mathbb{E}_t^{\mathbb{P}} \left[\mathcal{M}_T^{\text{real}} \right] \mathbb{E}_t \left[\Theta_t^T \right]} \right) \right]$$

$$= \log \mathbb{E}_t^{\mathbb{P}} \left[\mathcal{M}_T^{\text{real}} \right] + \log \mathbb{E}_t^{\mathbb{P}} \left[\Theta_t^T \right] + \log \left(1 + \frac{\text{cov} \left(\mathcal{M}_T^{\text{real}}, \Theta_t^T \right)}{\mathbb{E}_t^{\mathbb{P}} \left[\mathcal{M}_T^{\text{real}} \right] \mathbb{E}_t \left[\Theta_t^T \right]} \right) .$$ (14.57)

After dividing by $T - t$, the log of the expectation of the real stochastic discount factor will give us the real yield:

$$-\frac{1}{T-t} \log \mathbb{E}_t^{\mathbb{P}} \left[\mathcal{M}_T^{\text{real}} \right] = -\frac{1}{T-t} \log P_t^{\text{real},T} = y_t^{\text{real},T} .$$ (14.58)

As above, we would like the expectation of the log of the price level, not the log of its expectation. To get what we want (plus a 'Jensen' correction term), we add and subtract the quantity $\mathbb{E}_t \left[\log \Theta_t^T \right]$, to give:

$$\log \mathbb{E}_t^{\mathbb{P}} \left[\mathcal{M}_T^{\text{real}} \, \Theta_t^T \right] = \log \mathbb{E}_t^{\mathbb{P}} \left[\mathcal{M}_T^{\text{real}} \right] + \mathbb{E}_t^{\mathbb{P}} \left(\log \left[\Theta_t^T \right] \right)$$

$$+ \log \left(1 + \frac{\text{cov} \left(\mathcal{M}_T^{\text{real}}, \Theta_t^T \right)}{\mathbb{E}_t^{\mathbb{P}} \left[\mathcal{M}_T^{\text{real}} \right] E_t^{\mathbb{P}} \left[\Theta_t^T \right]} \right)$$

$$+ \underbrace{\log \mathbb{E}_t^{\mathbb{P}} \left[\Theta_t^T \right] - \mathbb{E}_t^{\mathbb{P}} \left(\log \left[\Theta_t^T \right] \right)}_{\text{convexity}} .$$ (14.59)

Now we divide through by $T - t$, and use the definition of real yield to obtain

$$-\frac{1}{T-t} \log P_t^{\mathrm{nom},T}$$

$$= y_t^{\mathrm{nom},T}$$

$$= y_t^{\mathrm{real},T} + \mathbb{E}^{\mathbb{P}}\left(I_t^T\right) + \log\left(1 + \frac{\mathrm{cov}\left(\mathcal{M}_T^{\mathrm{real}}, \Theta_t^T\right)}{E_t^{\mathbb{P}}\left[\mathcal{M}_T^{\mathrm{real}}\right] E_t^{\mathbb{P}}\left[\Theta_t^T\right]}\right)$$

$$+ \underbrace{\log \mathbb{E}_t^{\mathbb{P}}\left[\Theta_t^T\right] - \mathbb{E}_t^{\mathbb{P}}\left(\log\left[\Theta_t^T\right]\right)}_{\text{convexity}}. \tag{14.60}$$

But we have also obtained earlier that

$$y_t^{\mathrm{nom},T} = y_t^{\mathrm{real},T} + \mathbb{E}^{\mathbb{P}}\left(I_t^T\right) + \mathcal{P}_{t,T} + \mathrm{Ci}. \tag{14.61}$$

Therefore, after equating term by term, we have

$$\mathcal{P}_{t,T} = \log\left(1 + \frac{\mathrm{cov}\left(\mathcal{M}_T^{\mathrm{real}}, \Theta_t^T\right)}{\mathbb{E}_t^{\mathbb{P}}\left[\mathcal{M}_T^{\mathrm{real}}\right] E_t^{\mathbb{P}}\left[\Theta_t^T\right]}\right) \tag{14.62}$$

and

$$\mathrm{Ci} = \log \mathbb{E}_t^{\mathbb{P}}\left[\Theta_t^T\right] - \mathbb{E}_t^{\mathbb{P}}\left(\log\left[\Theta_t^T\right]\right).$$

This is Equation (29) in D'Amico, Kim and Wei (2010).

This equation is very important. It says that the nominal yield differs from the sum of the real yield and the real-world-expected inflation because of two terms: a relatively unimportant one, which comes from the difference between expectations of logs and logs of expectations – it is the usual Jensen convexity term $\log E_t^{\mathbb{P}}\left[\Theta_t^T\right] - E_t^{\mathbb{P}}\left(\log\left[\Theta_t^T\right]\right)$. This is not where the action is.

The important term comes from the covariance contribution, $\log\left(1 + \frac{\mathrm{cov}\left(\mathcal{M}_T^{\mathrm{real}}, \Theta_t^T\right)}{\mathbb{E}_t^{\mathbb{P}}\left[\mathcal{M}_T^{\mathrm{real}}\right] E_t^{\mathbb{P}}\left[\Theta_t^T\right]}\right)$. It is due to the (normalized) covariance between the price process and the real stochastic discount factor. Remember that a real bond is given by an expectation of the real stochastic discount factor. Therefore, in an imprecise but suggestive manner, real stochastic discount factors 'behave' like real bonds.[8]

The risk premium is linked to the variability in real prices, to the variability in the price level, and to the correlation between the two. The reader may want at this point go to the discussion in Section is 15.5 of Chapter 15 on idiosyncratic risk.

---

[8] For instance, as real bonds do, they depend on impatience and aversion to real-rate risk, but do not depend on realized inflation.

14.6   MOVING TO AN AFFINE WORLD

So far, we have kept the diffusive process for the nominal state variable(s) general enough. It is only at this point that we move to a fully affine setting – where by 'fully' I mean that we assume that pretty much everything is an affine function of the chosen mean-reverting state variable(s), x_t. In a nominal-rate world, being in an affine setting means that the (nominal) short rate and (nominal) market price of risk must be affine functions of the state variable(s), ie, that we must set

$$r_t^N = \rho_0^N + \rho_1^N x_t \tag{14.63}$$

$$\lambda_t^N = \lambda_0^N + \lambda_1^N x_t. \tag{14.64}$$

If we want an affine setting also for the mirror real variables, we must have

$$ei_t = \rho_0^{ei} + \rho_1^{ei} x_t \tag{14.65}$$

$$r_t^R = \rho_0^R + \rho_1^R x_t \tag{14.66}$$

$$\lambda_t^R = \lambda_0^R + \lambda_1^R x \tag{14.67}$$

for some p_0, p_1, ρ_0^R, ρ_1^R, λ_0^R and λ_1^R.

Note carefully that, if we work with a single state variable, the 'intercepts' and the slopes in the affine relationships above are just numbers. However, if we have a vector of state variables, $\overrightarrow{x}$, then the quantities subscripted with '1' (such as, say, p_1) become row (transpose) vectors (such as $(\overrightarrow{p}_1)^T$), and Equation, say, (14.65) becomes

$$ei_t = \rho_0^{ei} + \left(\overrightarrow{\rho^{ei}}_1\right)^T \overrightarrow{x}. \tag{14.68}$$

Using Equations (14.19) and (14.63) to (14.67), and after equating constant terms and terms linear in the state variables, a bit of algebra shows that we can determine four of these quantities as

$$\rho_0^R = \rho_0^N - \rho_0^{ei} + \sigma_Q \lambda_0^N \tag{14.69}$$

$$\rho_1^R = \rho_1^N - \rho_1^{ei} + \sigma_Q \lambda_1^N \tag{14.70}$$

$$\lambda_0^R = \sigma_Q - \lambda^N \tag{14.71}$$

and

$$\lambda_1^R = \lambda_1^N. \tag{14.72}$$

This is important: if we want to specify an *affine* model that 'knows' about real and nominal rates, the affine coefficients for the real variables are constrained to be a unique function of the affine coefficients of the nominal rates and market price of risk, and of the volatility of the price level.

14.7 THE MARKET PRICE OF INFLATION RISK – AFFINE MODELS

In the affine approaches, such as the model by D'Amico, Kim and Wei that we examine in Chapter 31, the instantaneous expected inflation is assumed to be an affine function of the state variables, and therefore

$$ei(x_s) = \rho_0^{ei} + \left(\overrightarrow{\rho}_1^{ei}\right)^T x_s. \tag{14.73}$$

Recall that the break-even inflation rate, $BEI_{t,T}$, is defined to be the difference between the nominal and real same-maturity yields (which are also, of course, affine). Then it follows that break-even inflation is affine as well:

$$BEI_{t,T} = y_{t,T}^N - y_{t,T}^R = \alpha_{t,T}^N - \alpha_{t,T}^R + \left(\beta_{t,T}^N - \beta_{t,T}^R\right)^T x_t. \tag{14.74}$$

We have seen that the difference between the break-even inflation and the real-world expectation of the inflation rate from time t to time T, $\mathbb{E}_t^{\mathbb{P}}(I_t^T)$, is the risk premium, $\mathcal{P}_{t,T}$:

$$\mathcal{P}_{t,T} \equiv BEI_{t,T} - \mathbb{E}_t^{\mathbb{P}}\left(I_t^T\right). \tag{14.75}$$

By the way it has been constructed, it is (appropriately) the difference between a $\mathbb{Q}$-measure quantity ($BEI_{t,T}$) and a a $\mathbb{P}$-measure quantity ($\mathbb{E}_t^{\mathbb{P}}(I_t^T)$).

Now, if the instantaneous expected inflation is an affine function of the state variables, so is the inflation rate from time t to time T, I_t^T. We can show this as follows. Starting from Equations (14.25) and (14.3) we have for the expected inflation:

$$\mathbb{E}_t^{\mathbb{P}}\left(I_t^T\right) = \frac{1}{T-t}\mathbb{E}_t^{\mathbb{P}}\left[\int_t^T ei\,(x_s)\,ds\right] \tag{14.76}$$

and therefore

$$\mathbb{E}_t^{\mathbb{P}}\left(I_t^T\right) = \frac{1}{T-t}\mathbb{E}_t^{\mathbb{P}}\left[\int_t^T \rho_0^{ei} + \left(\overrightarrow{\rho}_1^{ei}\right)^T \overrightarrow{x}_s ds\right]$$

$$= \rho_0^{ei} + \frac{1}{T-t}\left(\overrightarrow{\rho}_1^{ei}\right)^T \mathbb{E}_t^{\mathbb{P}}\left[\int_t^T \overrightarrow{x}_s ds\right]. \tag{14.77}$$

However, since our state variables follow a nice mean-reverting process, we can write explicitly today's expectation of their future value as a function of their values today. In the case of a single factor, we recall from Chapter 8 that this expectation is given by a linear (convex) combination of the value of the state variable today and the reversion level:

$$\mathbb{E}_t^{\mathbb{P}}[x_s] = x_t e^{-\kappa(s-t)} + \theta\left(1 - e^{-\kappa(s-t)}\right). \tag{14.78}$$

Using this equation as a guide, generalizing to many variables and remembering Equation (14.73), the reader can easily derive for a multifactor affine model:

$$\mathbb{E}_t^{\mathbb{P}}\left(I_t^T\right) = \alpha_{t,T}^I + \left(\overrightarrow{\beta}_{t,T}^I\right)^T \overrightarrow{x}_t, \tag{14.79}$$

with

$$\alpha_{t,T}^I = \rho_0^{ei} + \frac{1}{T-t} \left(\overrightarrow{\beta}_1^{ei}\right)^{\mathrm{T}} \int_t^T \left(I - e^{-\mathcal{K}s}\right) \overrightarrow{\theta}\, ds \qquad (14.80)$$

$$\overrightarrow{\beta}_{t,T}^I = \int_t^T e^{-(\mathcal{K})^T s} \left(\overrightarrow{\beta}_1^{ei}\right) ds. \qquad (14.81)$$

Exercise 31 *Using Equation (14.78) as a blueprint, derive Equations (14.79) to (14.81).*

Exercise 32 *Specialize Equations (14.80) and (14.81) to the case when the vector is zero ($\overrightarrow{\theta} = \overrightarrow{0}$) and the reversion-speed matrix $\mathcal{K}$ is diagonal. (These, by the way, are the assumptions in the D'Amico–Kim–Wei model that we review in Chapter 31.) If you are not familiar with the exponential of a matrix, you may want to look up some of the results in Appendix 18.A to Chapter 18.*

From what we derived earlier, we can therefore write for the inflation risk premium in an affine setting

$$\mathcal{P}_{t,T} = BEI_{t,T} - \mathbb{E}_t^{\mathbb{P}}\left(I_t^T\right) = y_{t,T}^N - y_{t,T}^R - \mathbb{E}_t^{\mathbb{P}}\left(I_t^T\right) \qquad (14.82)$$

$$= \alpha_{t,T}^N - \alpha_{t,T}^R - \alpha_{t,T}^I + \left(\beta_{t,T}^N - \beta_{t,T}^R - \beta_{t,T}^I\right)^T x_t. \qquad (14.83)$$

Equation (14.82) provides an expression of the market price of inflation risk in terms of real and nominal yields and inflation expectations in a completely affine world. We shall use these results when we look at the D'Amico–Kim–Wei (2010) model.

CHAPTER 15

The Links with an Economics-Based Description of Rates

Financial economists like ketchup economists [...] are concerned with the interrelationships between the prices of different financial assets. They ignore what seems to many to be the more important question of what determines the overall level of prices.

– Summers, 1985, *On Economics and Finance*[1]

15.1 THE PURPOSE OF THIS CHAPTER

If this book were a novel, the risk premium would clearly be one of its central characters, and this chapter would be a pause in the fast-paced plot, where the author takes a breather and regales the reader with illuminating flashbacks about the childhood of the hero. So, this chapter will not change the plot of the book, but will help the reader understand why its main character (the risk premium) behaves the way it does. More specifically, recall that Chapter 11 gave a very 'constructive' derivation of the no-arbitrage conditions, which were obtained by building a very tangible risk-less portfolio, invoking no-arbitrage, and reasoning from there what the ability to do so entailed. Chapter 12 then employed a much more abstract (and general) treatment that starts from the 'virtual' prices that the representative investor would assign to some special hypothetical securities. Finally, we looked at the condition of no-arbitrage with real (inflation-linked) bonds. In all of this, we have strictly engaged in ketchup economics (see the quote by Summers, 1985 that opens the chapter). Now we want to take a brief look at what the price of ketchup should be, not which price two bottles of ketchup should fetch, given the price of one (or three) bottles.

What does this mean in practice? When it comes to risk premia, we can try to establish what consistency relationships they should obey (this is the one-bottle/two-bottles bit); we can describe them empirically; or we can try to explain them – which means, we can try to explain why there should be a risk premium at all, whether it should be positive or negative, how large it should be, to which quantities it may be related, and why so. We shall look at the

---

[1] p. 634.

empirical aspect in Part VI. In this chapter we offer a simple theoretical framework to explain where risk premia may come from. In presenting this explanation, the stochastic discount factor is introduced and quickly takes centre stage. Why the tentative '*may come from*'? Because our explanation implicitly rests on a description of choice behaviour under uncertainty (utility theory) that is well known to have deficiencies. As with any model, it is not surprising that utility theory should be an imperfect model to describe the phenomenon at hand – the phenomenon in this case being how people make choices. However, it is up to the judicious user to choose the extent to which its predictions (and its explanations) can be trusted. As Summers (1985) wrote, '...it may not be possible to construct tractable models that account for ketchup price fluctuations. But this does not establish the perversity of the ketchup market, only the inadequacy of current data, theory and empirical methods.'[2]

The central results of this chapter are that, within the theory,

1. the price of a security (and hence of a bond) can be expressed as expectations of a part that depends only on the security itself (how much it will pay in different states of the world), and a part (the stochastic discount factor (SDF)) that depends only on the investor's attitude to risk and on her impatience.
2. Risk premia stem from the covariance between the stochastic discount factor and the payoff of the security we are valuing.
3. The 'short rate' can be derived, and its fundamental qualitative properties simply explained, by applying the stochastic-discount-factor framework to the case of the risk-less security.
4. The price of a nominal discount bond is simply the expectation of the stochastic discount factor.

For readers who have never encountered utility functions, the treatment in this chapter can be a bit heavy-going. It can be skipped without loss of continuity, but some useful insights would be lost.[3]

15.2   FIRST DERIVATION OF THE SDF

Economic agents like to consume real goods.[4] Unlike Uncle Scrooge, they do not derive intrinsic pleasure from bathing in a vault of gold coins. Therefore we concentrate in what follows on *real* consumption. Then we will move to nominal bonds.

---

[2] p. 634.

[3] For those readers who do not want to miss out on the utility-related fun, but do not want to jump in at the deep end, Hens and Rieger (2010) provide a clear and simple introduction; Gilboa (2010) gives a simple, discursive but deep foundational discussion – with proofs in a web-based appendix; and Binmore (2009) an accessible critical analysis. For those readers who do want to cross all the mathematical *t*s and dot the probabilistic *i*s, Kreps (1988) is a good place to go to.

[4] The treatment in this section follows closely Cochrane (2001), Chapter 1.

We express the agent's liking for real consumption by saying that consumption increases her utility. So, investors try to modify their rate of consumption so as to increase and, if possible, maximize, their lifetime utility. We denote by c_t the consumption at time t and by $u(c_t)$ the utility at time t.

Later on, in order to get some concrete expressions for our results, we will have to assume some specific functional form for the utility function. At that point, we will choose the power (in the limit, log) utility as a simple and useful specification. For the moment, however, we can keep the discussion general.

Investors are assumed to be impatient: everything else being equal, they would rather have a slice of cake today rather than the same slice of cake tomorrow. However, they would be willing to trade a bigger slice of cake in Δt years' time for a slice of cake today. How much bigger? Only the agent can answer this question. Suppose that she says she can trade off an amount $Cake(today + \Delta t)$ of cake tomorrow against an amount $Cake(today)$ of cake today. Then we can define an 'impatience' coefficient, β, such that

$$Cake(today) = \beta \, Cake(today + \Delta t). \tag{15.1}$$

Because of the nature of impatience, β must be smaller than 1 (ie, the future slice must be bigger), and we can therefore write it as

$$\beta = \exp[-\delta \Delta t], \quad \delta > 0. \tag{15.2}$$

The coefficient β (a discounting coefficient) reflects pure impatience. We could make it a lot more complex and interesting. But we won't.

Consider now an investment opportunity (say, equity stock), of time-t price S_t,[5] and a time-separable utility over consumption, C, at time t and time $t + 1$.[6] One unit of stock gives a stochastic payoff, x_{t+1}, at time $t + 1$. The investor can consume at time t and time $t + 1$. Today she has a total wealth, W. She has to decide how much to consume today and how much to invest so that she can consume more at a later time. Given that she has an impatience for consumption, β, the problem she faces is how to maximize her utility over consumption at time t ('today') and time $t + 1$:

$$u(C_t, C_{t+1}) = u(C_t) + \beta E_t[u(C_{t+1})]. \tag{15.3}$$

Note that the expected utility from consumption at time $t + 1$ is discounted (because of impatience) so as to make it comparable with consumption at time t.

---

[5] Here we denote the price of the generic asset by S_t rather than the more customary p_t found in the literature to avoid confusion with bond prices and log bond prices.

[6] Saying that a utility function is time-separable means that the utility from consuming C_1 at time t_1 and C_2 at time t_2 can be nicely decomposed ('separated') into the sum of time-t_1 and time-t_2 components: $u(C_1(t_1), C_2(t_2)) = u(C_1(t_1)) + \beta u(C_2(t_2))$. As assumptions go, it sounds reasonable, but it is not 'innocuous'.

Suppose that she invests a part, aS_t, of her initial wealth at time t in order to invest in the stock, which costs S_t. She is therefore left with only $W - aS_t$ to consume today. So, her utility at time t is given by

$$u(C_t) = u(W - aS_t). \tag{15.4}$$

As we have seen, each unit of stock will pay x_{t+1} at time $t + 1$. So, from buying today a units of stocks the investor will receive ax_{t+1} units at time $t + 1$. Her discounted expected utility derived from consumption at time $t + 1$ therefore is given by[7]

$$\beta E_t[u(ax_{t+1})]. \tag{15.5}$$

So, we have

$$u(C_t, C_{t+1}) = u\underbrace{\left(W - aS_t\right)}_{C_t} + \beta E_t\left[\underbrace{u(ax_{t+1})}_{C_{t+1}}\right]. \tag{15.6}$$

Note that in arriving at Equation (15.6) we have made use of the assumption that the utility is time separable. As assumptions go, it is reasonable, but, as mentioned in footnote 6, not innocuous. Note also that the probability distributions of the return x_{t+1} (ie, the probabilities attaching to each payoff in the various states of the world) are assumed to be known.

The investor wants to determine how much she should invest today (which means forfeiting current consumption) in order to get a units of the expected payoff. This means that the investor wants to determine the optimal investment fraction, a. Recall that the consumption at time t is her initial wealth less what she invested; and that the consumption at time $t + 1$ is whatever the invested fraction of the initial wealth will yield:

$$C_t = W - aS_t$$

$$C_{t+1} = ax_{t+1}. \tag{15.7}$$

Therefore the only quantity the investor can play with to maximize her utility is the amount, a, she invests today. To maximize her utility she must take the derivative with respect to a, and set it to zero.[8] This gives

$$\frac{\partial u(C_t, C_{t+1})}{\partial a} = \frac{\partial u}{\partial C_t}\frac{\partial C_t}{\partial a} + \beta E_t\left[\frac{\partial u}{\partial C_{t+1}}\frac{\partial C_{t+1}}{\partial a}x_{t+1}\right]$$

$$= -u'(C_t)S_t + \beta E_t\left[u'(C_{t+1})x_{t+1}\right]$$

$$= 0. \tag{15.8}$$

---

[7] To keep the notation simple and the equations uncluttered, we have assumed that all of the investor's future income comes from investment: there is no other source of certain time-2 wealth, W_2.

[8] She also has to check the second derivative, to make sure that she has not minimized her utility, or found an inflection point. We take for granted that, being a conscientious investor, she did all of the above.

(This, of course, follows because $\frac{\partial c_t}{\partial a} = -S_t$ and $\frac{\partial c_{t+1}}{\partial a} = x_{t+1}$.) This can be rearranged so as to have the price at time t on the left-hand side:

$$S_t = \frac{\beta \mathbb{E}_t \left[u'(C_{t+1}) x_{t+1} \right]}{u'(C_t)}, \tag{15.9}$$

which we can rewrite more elegantly as

$$S_t = \beta \mathbb{E}_t \left[\frac{u'(C_{t+1})}{u'(C_t)} x_{t+1} \right] = \mathbb{E}_t \left[m_{t+1} x_{t+1} \right], \tag{15.10}$$

with

$$u'(C_t) \equiv \frac{\partial u}{\partial C_t} \tag{15.11}$$

and

$$m_{t+1} = \beta \frac{u'(C_{t+1})}{u'(C_t)}. \tag{15.12}$$

The quantity m_{t+1} is so important that it is given a special name, the *stochastic discount factor* (SDF). It incorporates impatience (via β) and it reflects the trade-off between the marginal utility[9] derived from consuming today when the level of consumption is $W - aS_t$ and the marginal utility of the consumption that the stochastic payoff may provide in the future. It recovers Equation 1.3 in Cochrane (2001).

Equation (15.10) is the starting price of any asset pricing model: it is a relationship that links the price of an asset today (S_t) to what we think it will play in the future (x_{t+1}), to our impatience (β), and to how much we value the smoothing of our consumption over time $\left(\frac{u'(C_{t+1})}{u'(C_t)} \right)$.

Figure 15.1 illustrates the relationship between the stochastic discount factor and the shape of the utility function: the two tangents (drawn for different levels of consumption) are the two marginal utilities of consumption. The stochastic discount factor is interesting because these tangents are different, ie, because at different levels of consumption our utility changes differently. If the utility were a straight line (ie, if investors were risk neutral), the two tangents would lie on the same line, and everything would become simple but boring. See the discussion about risk premia that follow.

15.3 FROM THE SDF TO RISK PREMIA

The equation

$$S_t = \mathbb{E}_t[m_{t+1} x_{t+1}] \tag{15.13}$$

---

[9] The marginal utility is the change in utility when consumption is increased by an infinitesimally small amount, divided by the infinitesmal increase in consumption – so, it is the derivative of the utility function with respect to consumption.

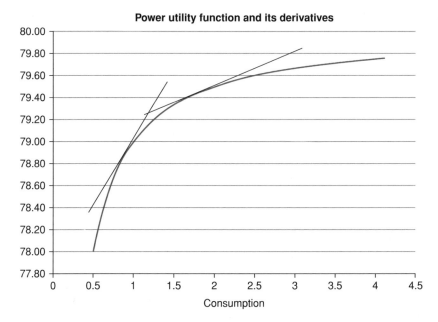

Figure 15.1 A power utility function (see later, $\gamma = 2$) and two tangents (drawn for different levels of consumption). The tangents are the marginal utility of consumption. If the utility were a straight line, the two tangents would lie on the same line. See the discussion about risk premia that follows.

immediately shows, if nothing else, the elegance of the stochastic-discount-factor formalism: the price of a security is neatly decomposed into the expectation of something that depends only on the security in question (x_{t+1}) times something that depends only on the investor's attitude towards risk (m_{t+1}). We can get from it a lot more, however, than aesthetic pleasure.

First of all, consider the well-known relationship that links the expectation of a product to the product of the expectations plus a covariance term:

$$\mathbb{E}[ab] = \mathbb{E}[a]\mathbb{E}[b] + Cov(a, b). \tag{15.14}$$

Applying this to Equation (15.13) gives

$$S_t = \mathbb{E}_t[m_{t+1}x_{t+1}] = \mathbb{E}_t[m_{t+1}]\mathbb{E}_t[x_{t+1}] + Cov_t[m_{t+1}, x_{t+1}]. \tag{15.15}$$

To see what this equation 'means', suppose that a one-period risk-free security is traded in the market. This means that if one invests \$1 at time t, she will certainly receive the gross return, \$$R_f \equiv$ \$$(1 + r_f)$, at time $t + 1$, where r_f is the instantaneous (one-period, really) risk-free rate of return. Applying Equation (15.13) to this case gives

$$1 = \mathbb{E}_t\left[m_{t+1}R^f\right] = \mathbb{E}_t[m_{t+1}]R_f \tag{15.16}$$

where in Equation (15.16) we have taken the gross return out of the expectation because it is known today. Solving for $E_t[m_{t+1}]$ we get

$$\mathbb{E}_t[m_{t+1}] = \frac{1}{R_f}. \tag{15.17}$$

This is a nice result: it says that the expectation of the stochastic discount factor is just the risk-less (deterministic) discount factor.

This also means that Equation (15.15) for a generic asset (not necessarily the risk-less asset) can be rewritten as

$$S_t = \underbrace{\frac{1}{R_f}\mathbb{E}_t[x_{t+1}]}_{\text{expectation}} + \underbrace{\text{cov}_t[m_{t+1}, x_{t+1}]}_{\text{risk premium}}. \tag{15.18}$$

This equation says something very general and very important, namely that the price of a security today is given by the expectation of the payoff discounted at the risk-free rate plus a term that depends on the covariance between the payoff and the stochastic discount factor.

By the way we have obtained this expression, it is clear that the covariance term is the risk premium. Why? Because $\frac{1}{R_f}\mathbb{E}_t[x_{t+1}]$ is the price that the payoff would command if investors were risk neutral.

It is important to stress that nothing in Equation (15.18) implies that the risk premium necessarily should be positive! You may want to ponder this, for instance. In periods of distress equity markets normally do poorly, but bonds tend to perform well. If equities make up a large part of the 'market portfolio', and bonds do well when the market portfolio does poorly (and people feel poor), then bonds would act as 'insurance' and should command a negative risk premium. But this is not what empirical studies tell us. (See Part VI of this book.) This is puzzling, because an asset should have a positive risk premium (a positive Sharpe Ratio) only if it pays well in good states of the world. How can we explain this paradox – if a paradox it is?

To begin with, is it really true that bonds do well when equities (again, taken as a proxy of the market portfolio and hence of how in the aggregate people feel) do poorly? In the decade ending in the late 1990s the correlation between equities and bonds was actually positive. Having a positive risk premium during this period therefore makes sense. It is only in the new millennium that the correlation between equities and bonds has become negative. If the risk premium had remained positive in the new century, *this* would be a conundrum. But can we really know the sign of the risk premium for observations over a period as short as 10–15 years? With difficulty. (See the discussion in Part VI.) However, as we shall discuss, most estimates of the risk premium carried out in the post–Great Recession years point to risk premia that, by historical standards, are unusually low – and perhaps even negative. Is this because investors have observed the 'insurance properties' of bonds, and are therefore ready to give up any risk compensation, or perhaps even to pay an insurance premium?

Within the theory we are looking at, everything hinges on the magnitude and sign of the risk-premium term $\mathrm{cov}_t[m_{t+1}, x_{t+1}]$.

Exercise 33 *Prove that $\frac{1}{R_f}\mathbb{E}_t[x_{t+1}]$ is the price that the payoff would command if investors were risk neutral. Hint: what does the utility function of a risk-neutral investor look like? And, by the way, why is this the case?*

Going back to our derivation, what we have obtained is an absolutely general result: from a model point of view,[10] all the risk premia that we shall encounter are 'ultimately' always due to some covariance between the payoff of the security we are looking at (eg, a real bond or a nominal bond) and the stochastic discount factor – which means between the payoff provided by the security and the trade-off in marginal consumption between today and the uncertain future. Again, what is the intuition? Apart from impatience, the stochastic discount factor depends on the ratio $\frac{u'(C_{t+1})}{u'(C_t)}$, ie, on how much our utility changes for the level of wealth at time $t + 1$ with respect to how much utility changes for the current level of wealth. Now, if investors are not risk neutral, marginal consumption does depend on whether people are doing well or poorly (because reasonable utility functions are concave) and is smaller when we feel rich and larger when we feel poor.

This is really important: if a security pays well in future states of the world when the investor expects to be able to consume little, she will pay a lot for it, driving down the return from the security. Think of the cost of buying fire insurance for your house. Looking at buying insurance as an investment, the associated risk premium is, in general, negative; still, if you own a house fire insurance is a very good investment.

Conversely, investors will pay relatively little (and therefore drive up their expected returns) for those securities that add coals to Newcastle, ie, pay well when the investor is already feeling rich. These results are at the heart of all asset pricing.

Exercise 34 *Specialize Equation (15.15) to the case of a one-period and a two-period discount bond. Why does the covariance term disappear in the former case and what does this disappearing act 'mean'?*

15.4   REAL VERSUS NOMINAL PRICES

Does the expression for the price, S_t, obtained earlier refer to a real or a nominal price? It depends on whether the payoff was expressed in real or nominal terms.

---

[10] Why 'from a model point of view?' Remember the discussion in Chapter 5, where we said that in empirical studies we sweep under the risk-premium carpet *all* deviation from pure expectation, irrespective of whether these deviations are due to risk aversion or not. With very few exceptions all the models we look at in this book understand deviations from expectations only from the perspective of risk aversion and consumption smoothing.

The real price of an asset at any time is just the nominal price divided by the then prevailing price level, Q_t. So, the fundamental pricing equation for a *nominal* asset price,

$$S_t = \mathbb{E}_t \left[\beta \frac{u'(C_{t+1})}{u'(C_t)} x_{t+1} \right] \tag{15.19}$$

becomes for a real and a nominal price

$$\underbrace{\frac{S_t}{Q_t}}_{\text{real price}} = \mathbb{E}_t \left[\beta \underbrace{\frac{u'(C_{t+1})}{u'(C_t)}}_{\text{real sdf}} \underbrace{\frac{x_{t+1}}{Q_{t+1}}}_{\text{real payoff}} \right] \tag{15.20}$$

and

$$\implies \underbrace{S_t}_{\text{nominal price}} = \mathbb{E}_t \left[\beta \underbrace{\frac{u'(C_{t+1})}{u'(C_t)} \frac{Q_t}{Q_{t+1}}}_{\text{nominal sdf}} \underbrace{x_{t+1}}_{\text{nominal payoff}} \right], \tag{15.21}$$

respectively.

15.5 IDIOSYNCRATIC RISK

The results we obtained in the previous section make a lot of intuitive sense. There is, however, a corollary of Equation (15.18) that is less intuitive.

If the payoff of a security is uncorrelated with consumption growth[11] (ie, if the covariance term $cov_t\,[m_{t+1}, x_{t+1}]$ is zero), in the framework we have laid out the return on the security is the same as the risk-less rate. As Cochrane (2001) points out, this remains true even if consumption growth is very volatile, if the securities returns are very volatile, or if the investor is very risk averse.

Seeing that this must be true *within our model* is very easy: if the correlation is zero, the covariance is zero, and the price is just given by discounting the payoff at the risk-less rate: $S_t = \frac{1}{R^f} \mathbb{E}_t\,[x_{t+1}]$. Period.

The more interesting question is whether our modelling of risk aversion has left something important unaccounted for, or of whether this is indeed the way rational investors behave, and prices are formed.[12]

---

[11] Why do we say 'consumption *growth*'? Because for a power or logarithmic utility function the ratio $\frac{u'(c_{t+1})}{u'(c_t)}$ is just equal to $\left(\frac{c_{t+1}}{c_t}\right)^\gamma$, which is exactly the growth in consumption raised to some power γ, which is 1 for a logarithmic utility function. See Section 15.6.

[12] Recall that, for all the sound and fury of the debate between 'classic' and 'behavioural' finance – the former putatively inhabited by rational utility-maximizers, and the latter describing 'real', touchy-feely and possibly irrational individuals –, there is no 'rational' reason why investors should be risk averse. Indeed, for that matter, there is no rational reason why investors *should* prefer more to less. These preferences are both rather commonly observed features of how real investors *behave* faced with choices between less or more, or between certain or uncertain, consumption. The (near) universality of these preferences should not make us conclude that

Whether *this* particular empirical feature (ie, the indifference of investors to volatility of returns as long as this variability is uncorrelated with consumption) is empirically founded or a model fiction is a different matter, which, in principle, could be resolved by careful measurement. This is easier said than done, however, because consumption is not easy to measure, and one must use rather crude proxies.

The corollary about uncompensated-for idiosyncratic risk can be made less counterintuitive by stressing that the idiosyncratic part in the asset return for which the investor is not compensated is, admittedly, variable, but it is ex ante uncorrelated with one's future consumption. The reader may then try to answer the following question: 'Would you prefer to buy for the same price an asset that pays a certain amount, or an asset that will pay a variable amount, but this variability, as long as you can tell today, will not be correlated with the only feature of your portfolio you are interested in, namely the amount of consumption it will allow you to enjoy?'

15.6   THE LINKS BETWEEN THE SDF AND THE RISK-LESS RATE

To get more of a feel for the link between the stochastic discount factor and the risk-less short rate, let's choose a run-of-the-mill utility function, such as the power/logarithmic utility defined by

$$u(C_t) = \frac{C_t^{1-\gamma} - 1}{1 - \gamma} \quad \text{for } \gamma \neq 1 \tag{15.22}$$

$$= \log(C_t) \quad \text{for } \gamma = 1. \tag{15.23}$$

In Equation (15.22) the coefficient γ is called the coefficient of relative risk aversion.[13] The specific functional form for the utility function can be changed

they are rational. All of this is to say that, even in classic choice theory, we cannot pull up a full description of investors' behaviour from the bootstraps of pure rationality. To make progress, we soon have to inject a behavioural component at the heart of the description: investors *like* to consume more; they *dislike* risk; etc. When this is accepted, if a model prediction is strongly at odds with an observed feature, we have two options before us: perhaps investors are behaving irrationally and inconsistently with their true preferences; or perhaps the modelling approach we have chosen is inadequate to capture *all* features of choice under risk. In the latter case, we should rethink the model, or, at least, remain aware of its limitations, not wag a scolding finger in the direction of the non–model-compliant investor and immediately accuse her of 'irrationality'.

[13] In reality, γ has a double life, as it expresses both the investor's aversion to risk – a behavioural response to choices *today* – and, via its inverse $\frac{1}{\gamma}$, the elasticity of intertemporal substitution – linked to the investor dislike to live through feast and famine. This double role has very unpleasant consequences, especially when a utility-maximization approach is used to analyze social problems with risks and benefit extending over extended periods of time. No issue in this respect shows the problem more acutely than the current economics discussion about global warming. Closer to our concerns in this book, this double life of γ becomes relevant if we look at the optimal investment strategies of pension funds.

at little cost, because in this chapter we are interested only in the qualitative predictions afforded by the utility approach. What we *do* require for our derivation is time separability.[14] As mentioned earlier, this means that the utility over consumption at times t_1 and t_2 can be neatly separated into the sum of two utilities, one over consumption at time t_1 and one, after impatience discounting, over consumption at time t_2.[15] And, of course, since we are talking about consumption, the risk-less rate we are referring to, r_t^f, is the real, not the nominal, rate.

15.6.1 The No-Uncertainty Case

Following Cochrane (2001), let's first consider the case when there is no uncertainty in the economy. This means that we don't have to worry about the expectation in the equation $\mathbb{E}_t[m_{t+1}] = \frac{1}{R^f}$ and that we can directly calculate the various derivatives of the utility function that appear in the definitions of the stochastic discount factor (ie, $m_{t+1} = \beta \frac{u'(C_{t+1})}{u'(C_t)}$) using the functional form (15.22). A svelte calculation (and a linearization) then yields

$$r_t^f = \frac{1}{\beta}\left(\frac{C_{t+1}}{C_t}\right)^\gamma - 1. \tag{15.24}$$

Exercise 35 *Derive Equation (15.24).*

This terse little equation packs a lot of information.

First of all, it shows that the more impatient we are (ie, the smaller β is), the higher the risk-less return must be to induce us to postpone consumption.

Second, the higher we expect future consumption to be with respect to present consumption (ie, the higher the ratio $\frac{C_{t+1}}{C_t}$, the higher consumption *growth*), the higher the risk-free rate. Why? Because a high rate of (certain) return will encourage investors to consume less today so as to (invest and) consume more in the future.

---

[14] However, as Cochrane (2001, p. 38), points out, 'state- or time-nonseparable utility [...] complicates the relation between the discount factor and real variables, but does not change [our final result, namely] $p = E[mx]$ or any of the basic structure.'

[15] While common and, at first blush, 'natural', utility functions need not be separable. The main problem with a time-separable utility function is that aversion to risk today, and aversion to unevenness in consumption over time, end up being described by the same parameter. For some problems, this parameter can become a seriously short blanket. One possible way out of this impasse is afforded by a class of Epstein–Zin (1991) utility functions which allow a breaking of this unholy alliance. This can be done by relinquishing the time-separable framework, and by positing that preferences should be defined recursively over current consumption (which is known) and a certainty equivalent, CE, of tomorrow's utility: $U_t = F(c_t, CE(U_{t+1}))$, and $CE(U_{t+1}) = G^{-1}(E_t[G(U_{t+1})])$, with F and G increasing and concave functions. We do not pursue this avenue here. (Incidentally, the recursive nature of the problem greatly increases the complexity of the problem.)

Third, the higher the exponent γ, the higher the risk-less rate. Again, why? Because, as discussed briefly in footnote 13, the utility-function parameter, γ, has a double life. As most readers will be familiar with, it accounts for the investor's aversion to risk today – a behavioural response to choices *today*. But it also describes how investors prefer to avoid feast and famine, and to smooth out their consumption pattern *over time*. One can easily show, in fact, that the parameter γ is linked, via its inverse $\frac{1}{\gamma}$, to the elasticity of *intertemporal* substitution.

What we have just sketched (under conditions of no-uncertainty) is how the short risk-less rate should respond to investors' impatience, and to their desire to smooth consumption over time and to expected future consumption. This is all well and good, but in reality we know that the 'short rate' is manipulated by the central monetary authorities in order to fulfill their price stability (and related) mandates. Does it mean that this analysis would apply only in a world without central banks?

Not really, because we can reverse the arrow of causation and read the same equations backwards: we take the level of rates as exogenous, and derive how economic agents consume and save.[16] So, when rates are (forced to be) high, people have an incentive to save rather than spend, and hence to invest.[17] With high investment, consumption growth should increase. When rates are (forced to be) low everything works in reverse: the incentive to postpone consumption is low, and people spend now rather than later.

15.6.2   Reintroducing Uncertainty

So far we have considered a simplified, no-uncertainty, version of Equation (15.17). We can now switch on uncertainty. To keep matters simple, we are going to assume that consumption growth, ie, the quantity $\frac{C_{t+1}}{C_t}$, is log-normally distributed, with volatility σ_c, and we rewrite the impatience coefficient, β, (which in general depends on the length of the period over which consumption has to be postponed) as follows:

$$\beta \equiv e^{-\delta}. \tag{15.25}$$

Next, we substitute into Equation (15.17) the expression for the expectation of the stochastic discount factor:

$$\mathbb{E}_t\left[m_{t+1}\right] = \frac{1}{R^f} \implies \mathbb{E}_t\left[\beta \frac{u'(C_{t+1})}{u'(C_t)}\right] = \frac{1}{R^f}.$$

---

[16] See Cochrane (2001), p. 15 and Section 2.2, that deal with general equilibrium.
[17] We assume without question here that a dollar saved is a dollar invested.

Then, remembering that, for a normally distributed variable, z, with volatility σ_z, we have[18]

$$\mathbb{E}\left[e^z\right] = e^{E[z] + \frac{1}{2}\sigma_z^2}, \tag{15.26}$$

we finally obtain

$$\log R^f = \log\frac{1}{\beta} + \gamma\mathbb{E}_t\left[\log\frac{C_{t+1}}{C_t}\right] - \frac{\gamma^2}{2}\sigma_c^2. \tag{15.27}$$

Since we know that, for 'small' x, $\log(1+x) \simeq x$, and that $\log\frac{1}{\beta} = -\log \beta = \delta$, we also have

$$r_t^f = \delta + \gamma\mathbb{E}_t\left[\log\frac{C_{t+1}}{C_t}\right] - \frac{\gamma^2}{2}\sigma_c^2, \tag{15.28}$$

where r_t^f is the *real* short rate at time t.

Exercise 36 *Derive Equation (15.28).*

After switching on uncertainty, all the qualitative considerations about the dependence of the short rate on impatience and on (now *expected*) consumption growth that we made in the case of deterministic consumption growth still apply. What about the 'Jensen inequality' term,[19] ie, the term $\frac{\gamma^2}{2}\sigma_c^2$? It comes from the fact that, given the (class of) utility function we have chosen, investors are more 'afraid of' low-consumption states than they are 'happy' in high-consumption states. How can they mitigate the consequences of this state of affairs? By saving. The greater their uncertainty in consumption growth (the term σ_c^2) and their coefficient γ, the more investors want to save, driving the risk-less rate down. It is for this reason that the 'Jensen term' is often referred to as the *precautionary savings* term.[20]

15.6.3 But Does It Work?

We have derived a relationship between the risk-less real rate and consumption growth. Is this relationship borne out in reality? Is it precise enough to be used by policymakers for their rate setting? To answer this question, let's try to gain an order-of-magnitude estimate of the various quantities that enter the expression for the risk-less real rate.

To begin with, since the 'convexity term' ($\frac{\gamma^2}{2}\sigma_c^2$) is small, let's write

$$\rho \equiv \delta - \frac{\gamma^2}{2}\sigma_c^2 \simeq \delta \tag{15.29}$$

---

[18] See Chapter 9, Section 9.3.   [19] We discussed Jensen inequality in Chapter 9.

[20] By the way, this discussion highlights a third role played by the parameter γ, ie, its link to the desire for precautionary savings.

and therefore Equation (15.28) becomes

$$r_t^f \simeq \rho + \gamma \mathbb{E}_t \left[\log \frac{C_{t+1}}{C_t} \right]. \tag{15.30}$$

Define next

$$c_t = \log C_t. \tag{15.31}$$

Then we have (after changing the 'almost equal' sign for the 'equal' sign)

$$r_t^f = \rho + \gamma \left(\mathbb{E}_t [c_{t+1}] - c_t \right). \tag{15.32}$$

Let's rearrange the terms so that c_t is on the left-hand side:

$$c_t = \mathbb{E}_t [c_{t+1}] + \frac{\rho - r_t^f}{\gamma}. \tag{15.33}$$

This makes sense: if impatience is high (ie, if ρ and hence δ are high), a lot will be consumed at time t, and little will be saved for investment. Conversely, if the risk-less real rate is high (which appears with a negative sign), it will pay to delay consumption. The smaller the coefficient γ, which controls how much agents try to smooth their consumption over time, the higher the consumption today.

To make progress, let's assume that the output of the economy, y_t, is equal to consumption,[21] and that actual output can deviate from its optimal equilibrium value, y_t^{nat}.[22] Then the output gap, y_t^{gap}, is simply

$$y_t^{gap} = c_t - y_t^{nat} = y_t - y_t^{nat}. \tag{15.34}$$

Now, since at any point in time output may not be at its natural optimal level, also the short real rate may be at a level other than what would prevail in 'natural' conditions.[23] Call the non-optimal real rate, r_t, and, to emphasize the point, rewrite the optimal ('natural') real rate as $r_t^f = r_t^{f,nat}$. Then from

---

[21] This assumption characterizes the 'baseline' New Keynesian model. See Hamilton, Harris, Hatzious and West (2015), p. 16.

[22] This can happen for a variety of factors. In the Keynesian model, price rigidities are one such factor.

[23] This is how the Federal Market Committee describes the 'natural' or 'neutral' rate: '...The staff presented several briefings regarding the concept of an equilibrium real interest rate – sometimes labeled the "neutral" or "natural" real interest rate, or "r*" – that can serve as a benchmark to help gauge the stance of monetary policy. Various concepts of r* were discussed. According to one definition, short-run r* is the *level of the real short-term interest rate that, if obtained currently, would result in the economy operating at full employment or, in some simple models of the economy, at full employment and price stability....*' (Minutes of the Federal Open Market Committee, held in the offices of the Board of Governors of the Federal Reserve System in Washington, DC, on Tuesday, October 27, 2015, at 10:00 A.M. and continued on Wednesday, October 28, 2015, at 9:00 A.M., emphasis added.)

Equation (15.32) we have for natural real rate of interest

$$r_t^{f,nat} = \rho + \gamma \mathbb{E}_t [\Delta c_{t+1}] = \rho + \gamma \mathbb{E}_t [\Delta y_{t+1}], \tag{15.35}$$

where, applied to any quantity x, the operator Δx gives $x_{t+1} - x_t$.

At any point in time the actual output could be away from its natural level, but over a long period of time there should be no systematic difference between the actual and the natural output level. Therefore in the model of the economy we have been examining the average value of the actual realized real rate is the same as the natural real rate. This gives a way to test whether the approach we have just sketched gives sensible results. This is how it is done.

Let's take $\gamma = 1$ (ie, let's choose a logarithmic utility function), let's accept the approximation $\rho \simeq \delta$ and let's set the average per capita consumption growth to a reasonable 2% per annum. A similarly reasonable value for the impatience coefficient is a few percent; between friends, let's settle for the customary value of $\delta \simeq 0.04$ (see, eg, Hamilton et al. (2015)[24]). This gives for the natural real safe rate an annoyingly high value of 2% + 4% = 6%. After Weil (1989), this implausibly high value for the natural real rate has been referred to as the 'risk-free rate puzzle'.

In a way, complaining that the natural real rate of interest did not come out to be closer to the two-ish percentage points that we were expecting is a bit like complaining that the circus dog did not sing *La Traviata* very well – when, actually, the true wonder was that it could sing at all. Out of metaphor, given the crudeness of the model, and the sweeping assumptions that we have made, it is reassuring that we ended in the right ballpark. However, for those policymakers (such as central bankers) who need to fine tune the economy by turning the target rate dials it would have been more helpful if the agreement had been semiquantitative rather than qualitative.

Can the problem be fixed? Mehara and Prescott (2003) give an extensive survey of the empirical shortcoming of the consumption-based approach to link risk premia to consumption, and it appears unlikely that quick fixes will bring about a good quantitative agreement between predictions and observations. For instance, relinquishing the log-normal assumption for the utility function does not move us in the right direction, because it can be argued that a value of γ of one is probably too low, not too high. Campbell and Cochrane (1995, 1999) suggest an ingenious solution to the puzzle (part of their solution is to recognize that utility should depend not on absolute consumption, but on the change in consumption over the previous period). They do obtain a lower real natural rate, but at the cost of other counterfactual relationships between nominal and real rates. See Canzoneri, Cumby and Diba (2007).

All of this, and lots more, is very well discussed in Hamilton et al. (2015) and Laubach and Williams (2015).

[24] p. 9.

Pursuing this line of inquiry would be very interesting, but would entail too long a detour. Therefore I leave the interested reader with the good references provided in this section, and I continue with the flow of the derivation.

15.7 SDFS IN CONTINUOUS AND DISCRETE TIME

Usually, in this book I tend to play fast and loose between continuous and discrete time. In the case of the stochastic discount factor one has to be a bit more careful than usual, as different definitions apply in the discrete and continuous cases. The reason for this is a bit technical: recall that, in discrete time, we defined the stochastic discount factor by the relationship

$$m_{t+1} = \beta \frac{u'(c_{t+1})}{u'(c_t)}. \tag{15.36}$$

When we move from discrete to continuous time the ratio $\frac{u'(c_{t+1})}{u'(c_t)}$ would become $\frac{u'(c_{t+dt})}{u'(c_t)}$. However, in the limit as dt goes to zero, the ratio is mathematically not well defined.

Exercise 37 *Why? Hint: remember that it is not called* stochastic *discount factor for nothing. Where does the stochasticity come from? If you need another hint, posit for the process for consumption something like $\frac{dc_t}{c_t} = \mu_c dt + \sigma_c dz_t$, and see where this takes you.*

Therefore we write for the continuous-time stochastic discount factor $M_t = \beta u'(c_t)$. Then, if the security provides a stream of payments (dividends), D_{t+s}, from time t to time T, one obtains[25]

$$S_t = \mathbb{E}_t \left[\int_t^T \frac{M_{t+s}}{M_t} D_{t+s} ds \right]. \tag{15.37}$$

One can relate the continuous-time quantities we have introduced as follows. Remember that time-t quantities can be taken in and out of expectation signs as one pleases, and that one can therefore write

$$S_t M_t = \mathbb{E}_t \left[\int_t^T M_{t+s} D_{t+s} ds \right]. \tag{15.38}$$

If we write the impatience term as $\beta_t = e^{-\delta t}$, then the ratio $\frac{M_{t+s}}{M_t}$ becomes

$$\frac{M_{t+s}}{M_t} = \frac{e^{-\delta(t+s)}}{e^{-\delta t}} \frac{u'(c_{t+s})}{u'(c_t)} = e^{-\delta s} \frac{u'(c_{t+s})}{u'(c_t)}. \tag{15.39}$$

Note that in the denominator we have the 'initial' marginal utility of consumption (and we have therefore avoided the problems with $\frac{u'(c_{t\mid dt})}{u'(c_t)}$), and that

---

[25] See Cochrane (2001), p. 30.

the impatience term is given by

$$e^{-\delta s} = \frac{e^{-\delta(t+s)}}{e^{-\delta t}}.$$ (15.40)

This means that

$$M_{t+s} = e^{-\delta(t+s)} u'(c_{t+s})$$ (15.41)

and

$$M_t = e^{-\delta t} u'(c_t).$$ (15.42)

To complicate matters (slightly) the quantity $M_t = \beta u'(c_t)$ is often referred to in the literature as the state price deflator.[26] Whatever the name, this is the quantity that is used to derive the no-arbitrage conditions in continuous time. The starting point is the application of the continuous-time stochastic-discount-factor valuation formula,

$$S_t = \mathbb{E}_t \left[\int_t^T \frac{M_{t+s}}{M_t} x_{t+s} ds \right]$$ (15.43)

to the case of a T-maturity discount bond, for which $x_{t+s} = 0$ for $s < T$, (because we have a single payment at maturity) and $x_{t+T} = 1$. This makes the integral disappear,[27] and we have

$$P_t = \mathbb{E}_t \left[\frac{M_{t+T}}{M_t} \right],$$ (15.44)

which shows that the price of a discount bond is just given by the expectation of the (ratio of) the continuous-time stochastic discount factors.

15.8 A MORE GENERAL RESULT FOR THE SHARPE RATIO

The reader will recall that we obtained in Chapter 8 (see Section 8.8) a very nice and simple result for the Sharpe Ratio in a one-factor (Vasicek-like) world: namely, we derived that the Sharpe Ratio was equal to the market price of risk. We want to obtain a more general result using the stochastic discount factor.[28]

---

[26] See, eg, Fisher (2004), p. 56.

[27] For readers who know how the delta-Dirac distribution, $\delta(t - t_0)$, operates, formally we have
$S_t = \mathbb{E}_t \left[\int_t^T \frac{M_{t+s}}{M_t} x_{t+s} ds \right] = \mathbb{E}_t \left[\int_t^T \frac{M_{t+s}}{M_t} \delta(T - s) ds \right] = \mathbb{E}_t \left[\frac{M_{t+T}}{M_t} \right]$.

[28] In this section we follow Duffee (2010), pp. 5–6, who discusses the topic in far greater detail.

For the Sharpe Ratio, which is defined to be the ratio of the expected one-period excess return to the one-period volatility of strategy i,

$$SR = \frac{\mathbb{E}_t\left[xret^i_{t,t+1}\right]}{\sqrt{\text{var}\left(xret^i_{t,t+1}\right)}},$$ (15.45)

we are going to need the one-period (gross) risk-less rate (to build the *excess* return).[29] We have derived earlier that

$$\mathbb{E}_t\left[\frac{M_{t+1}}{M_t}\right] = \mathbb{E}_t\left[m_{t+1}\right] = \frac{1}{R^f} \implies R^f = \frac{1}{\mathbb{E}_t\left[m_{t+1}\right]}.$$ (15.46)

Consider the case when 'strategy i' is simply investing in the ith bond. Then the (gross) return from strategy i, $ret^i_{t,t+1}$, is given by

$$ret^i_{t,t+1} = \frac{P^i_{t+1}}{P^i_t}.$$ (15.47)

The excess return is then given by

$$xret^i_{t,t+1} = ret^i_{t,t+1} - R^f.$$ (15.48)

Consider then the expectation of the product $m_{t+1}xret^i_{t,t+1}$:

$$\mathbb{E}_t\left[xret^i_{t,t+1}m_{t+1}\right] = \mathbb{E}_t\left[\left(\frac{P^i_{t+1}}{P^i_t} - R^f\right)m_{t+1}\right]$$

$$= \mathbb{E}_t\left[\left(\frac{P^i_{t+1}}{P^i_t}\right)m_{t+1}\right] - R^f\mathbb{E}_t\left[m_{t+1}\right]$$

$$= \frac{1}{P^i_t}\mathbb{E}_t\left[P^i_{t+1}m_{t+1}\right] - 1.$$ (15.49)

(As usual, in the last line we have taken out of t-expectation sign quantities, such as $\frac{1}{P^i_t}$, known at time t.)

Now

$$P^i_{t+1} = \mathbb{E}_{t+1}\left[\frac{M_{t+i}}{M_{t+1}}\right]$$ (15.50)

and we can set $M_t = 1$, so that

$$m_{t+1} = \frac{M_{t+1}}{1} = M_{t+1}.$$ (15.51)

---

[29] Note that we are taking the expectation at time t, ie, a *conditional* expectation. This being the case, the symbol for the Sharpe Ratio should be SR_t, not just SR (which indicates, or at least suggests, an *un*conditional expectation). We write SR to keep notation light.

Then we have

$$
\mathbb{E}_t \left[xret^i_{t,t+1} m_{t+1} \right] = \frac{1}{P^i_t} \mathbb{E}_t \left[P^i_{t+1} m_{t+1} \right] - 1
$$

$$
= \frac{1}{P^i_t} \mathbb{E}_t \left[\mathbb{E}_{t+1} \left[\frac{M_{t+i}}{M_{t+1}} \right] m_{t+1} \right] - 1
$$

$$
= \frac{1}{P^i_t} \mathbb{E}_t \left[\frac{M_{t+i}}{M_{t+1}} M_{t+1} \right] - 1
$$

$$
= \frac{1}{P^i_t} \mathbb{E}_t \left[M_{t+i} \right] - 1 = \left(\frac{1}{P^i_t} P^i_t \right) - 1 = 0. \quad (15.52)
$$

(In the second line we have used the result that $\mathbb{E}_t \left[\mathbb{E}_{t+1} \left[\cdot \right] \right] = \mathbb{E}_t \left[\cdot \right]$.)
Therefore we have derived that

$$
\mathbb{E}_t \left[xret^i_{t,t+1} m_{t+1} \right] = 0. \quad (15.53)
$$

From this it follows that

$$
\mathbb{E}_t \left[xret^i_{t,t+1} \right] = -Cov \left(xret^i_{t,t+1}, m_{t+1} \right) R^f \quad (15.54)
$$

and the expression for the Sharpe Ratio becomes

$$
SR = \frac{\mathbb{E}_t \left[xret^i_{t,t+1} \right]}{\sqrt{Var \left(xret^i_{t,t+1} \right)}} = -R^f \frac{Cov \left(xret^i_{t,t+1}, m_{t+1} \right)}{\sqrt{Var \left(xret^i_{t,t+1} \right)}}
$$

$$
= -R^f Corr \left(xret^i_{t,t+1}, m_{t+1} \right) \sqrt{Var \left(m_{t+1} \right)}. \quad (15.55)
$$

We are almost done. There are (at least) two ways to look at this result. The first is the following: take

$$
SR = -R^f \frac{1}{\sqrt{Var \left(xret^i_{t,t+1} \right)}} Cov \left(xret^i_{t,t+1}, m_{t+1} \right)
$$

$$
= -R^f \frac{1}{\sqrt{Var \, ret^i_{t,t+1}}} Cov \left(ret^i_{t,t+1}, m_{t+1} \right)
$$

$$
= -R^f \frac{1}{\sqrt{Var \left(ret^i_{t,t+1} \right)}} \underbrace{Cov \left(\frac{P^i_{t+1}}{P^i_t}, m_{t+1} \right)}_{\text{risk premium}}. \quad (15.56)
$$

We have learnt in this chapter that the last term is a risk premium. Therefore the term $\frac{1}{\sqrt{Var \left(ret^i_{t,t+1} \right)}} Cov \left(\frac{P^i_{t+1}}{P^i_t}, m_{t+1} \right)$ is a term premium divided by the volatility of the strategy (in our case the bond). The ratio therefore behaves as a market price of risk.

Alternatively, we remember that the 'volatility' (ie, the standard deviation per unit period) of the stochastic discount factor (ie, the term $\sqrt{Var \left(m_{t+1} \right)}$) is the market price of risk, λ_t, (see Chapter 13), and we obtain that

$$
SR = -R^f Corr \left(xret^i_{t,t+1}, m_{t+1} \right) \lambda_t. \quad (15.57)
$$

What about the sign? If the strategy (in this case, the bond) pays well in good times, then the correlation will be negative and the Sharpe Ratio will be positive. In particular, in a one-factor world it will be equal to -1, and we get

$$SR^{1\text{-}fac} = R^f \lambda_t. \tag{15.58}$$

The important thing to note is that, within the theory, we cannot have a strategy that pays well in bad times (provides insurance) *and* has a positive Sharpe Ratio. We cannot, for instance, systematically earn a positive excess return by *buying* fire insurance on all the properties in the United Kingdom. (It is the nice people who insure you against fire, and who pay you a tidy sum in times that are *for you and for them* very bad indeed, who can expect a positive Sharpe Ratio from their business – if they didn't, they would face an existential dilemma.)

Finally, the maximal Sharpe Ratio, $SR^{\max}$, will be given by

$$SR^{\max} = \lambda, \tag{15.59}$$

which is the result we obtained in the Vasicek setting.

PART IV

SOLVING THE MODELS

In this part of the book we apply the model intuition hopefully built with the treatment in Parts I and II and the solid understanding of the conditions of no-arbitrage developed in Part III in order to solve a variety of affine models. By 'solving', we mean finding expressions for bond prices, yields, volatilities, etc, as a function of the parameters of the mean-reverting processes followed by the state variables, and of their initial values.

First we look at the Vasicek model (Chapter 16), and then, in Chapters 17 and 18, we generalize the formalism to the case of several variables.

With the generalizations presented in Chapters 17 and 18, we fulfill two purposes: first, we give the reader the tools to handle virtually any affine model that she may encounter – or, indeed, that she may wish to build herself; second, we introduce the reader to the language needed to read the modern literature on the topic – where, just to be clear, 'modern literature' means the literature written in the last twenty years or so, not in the last six months.

I will not provide the most general solution to the Partial Differential Equations that we shall obtain,[1] but, as usual, I will trade at a very high exchange rate generality for simplicity.

---

[1] For instance, one glaring example of a lack of total generality of the treatment will be that, to obtain the multi-factor solutions, we will require the reversion-speed matrix to be diagonalizable.

CHAPTER 16

Solving Affine Models: The Vasicek Case

The third [rule is] to direct my thoughts in an orderly way; beginning with the simplest objects, those most apt to be known, and
ascending little by little, in steps as it were, to the knowledge of the
more complex.

Descartes (1637, 1968), *Discourse on Method and*
The Meditations[1]

A simple and beautiful theory that agrees pretty well with observation is often closer to the truth than a complicated ugly theory that
agrees better with observation.

S. Weinberg (2014), *To Explain the World: The Discovery of*
Modern Science

16.1 PURPOSE OF THIS CHAPTER

In this chapter I derive, using the simplest and most intuitive route, an expression for bond prices and related quantities (yields, forward rates, their volatilities, etc) in the Vasicek model.

Doing so is in itself character forming. In addition (as the logic is exactly
the same), it also shows clearly the steps that one should follow to obtain the
same results for the more complex models presented in later chapters.

After obtaining an analytic expression for bond prices in the Vasicek model,
we obtain explicit equations for yields, instantaneous forward rates and their
volatilities.

We also discuss under what conditions (ie, for which functional forms of
the market price of risk) the approach remains affine as one moves from the
real-world to the risk-neutral measure.

The chapter does not just present a derivation of analytical results. It also
introduces some issues about model calibration that we will encounter again
with more complex affine models.

---

[1] Translator F. E. Sutcliffe, Penguin Classics.

16.2 THE REPLICATION APPROACH TO SOLVING FOR BOND PRICES: THE VASICEK MODEL

16.2.1 The PDE Satisfied by Bond Prices

I am told that a Japanese proverb goes something like: 'He is a fool who never climbs Mount Fuji; but he is a greater fool who climbs Mount Fuji twice.' I have always liked this proverb, even if I am not one hundred percent sure what it actually means. I take it to suggest that character-forming endeavours are good, but in moderation.

This is therefore the approach that I am going to take to the derivation of the analytical expression for the price of bonds in the Vasicek model: we'll do it once in detail, and we will treasure the wisdom learnt in doing so for future applications.

Despite the fact that a well-known paper[2] shows that there are (at least) three ways to 'solve' for bond prices in the Vasicek model, I will content myself with one, and the simplest one at that. As usual, I will rely on the by-now familiar technique of killing the stochastic part of a portfolio, of observing that we are left with a deterministic quantity, of deducing that it must therefore earn the riskless return, and of deriving the conditions that this implies.

So, let's repeat exactly (but a bit more quickly) the derivation we went through in Chapter 12: we build a portfolio, Π_t, made up of one unit of the bond maturing at time T_i and ω units of the bond maturing at time T_j:

$$\Pi_t = P_t^{T_i} + \omega P^{T_j}. \tag{16.1}$$

We place ourselves in a single-factor economy, and we make the Brownian diffusion assumption; this means that we require that, in the real world, the process for each bond should be given by

$$\frac{dP_t^{T_i}}{P_t^{T_i}} = \mu_{P^i} dt + \sigma_{P^i} dz_t. \tag{16.2}$$

Since we are in a one-factor setting, there is no superscript i decorating the Brownian increment, dz_t: the same shock affects all bonds.

As we saw, the increment of the portfolio over a short time dt is then given by

$$
\begin{aligned}
d\Pi_t &= dP_t^{T_i} + \omega dP^{T_j} \\
&= \left[P_t^{T_i} \mu_{P^i} + \omega P^{T_j} \mu_{P^j} \right] dt + \left[P_t^{T_i} \sigma_{P^i} + \omega P^{T_j} \sigma_{P^j} \right] dz_t. \tag{16.3}
\end{aligned}
$$

---

[2] Rogemar S. Mamon (2004), *Three Ways to Solve for Bond Prices in the Vasicek Model*. The first of the three ways, incidentally, makes use of the distribution of the short rate process; the second tackles the Partial Differential Equation approach by integrating Ordinary Differential Equations (this is the approach we follow); and the third uses the Heath–Jarrow–Morton framework applied in the forward measure.

Now we want to find the special holding, ω^*, that makes the stochastic part of the portfolio equal to zero. This is clearly achieved by setting

$$\omega^* = -\frac{P_t^{T_i}\sigma_{Pi}}{P^{T_j}\sigma_{Pj}}. \tag{16.4}$$

For this skillfully chosen hedge ratio, the portfolio Π_t will be risk-less, and therefore, under penalty of arbitrage, it can earn the risk-less rate only over the next time step. This means that

$$d\Pi_t = \left[P_t^{T_i}\mu_{Pi} + \omega^* P^{T_j}\mu_{Pj}\right]dt = r_t\Pi_t dt$$

$$= r_t\left[P_t^{T_i} + \omega^* P^{T_j}\right]dt. \tag{16.5}$$

Now we can rearrange terms in such a way that all the T_i-dependent terms are on one side, and all the T_j-dependent terms are on the other. This gives (once again)

$$\frac{(\mu_{Pi} - r_t)}{\sigma_{Pi}} = \frac{(\mu_{Pj} - r_t)}{\sigma_{Pj}} = -\lambda_{,} \tag{16.6}$$

with the quantity λ possibly a function of the state variables and of time, but not of maturity. We called this quantity the market price of risk. This is where we got to in Chapter 12. Now we make a few further obvious steps.

First, we drop the superscript i (or j) that identifies the specific maturity, and we rewrite Equation (16.6) as

$$\mu_P = r_t - \lambda\sigma_P. \tag{16.7}$$

What we have on the left-hand side is just the expectation of the increment (the drift) of the bond price. Now, take *some* diffusive process for the short rate, r_t, of the form

$$dr_t = \mu_r dt + \sigma_r dz_t^r. \tag{16.8}$$

We can regard the bond price as a function of the short rate, $P_t^T = P_t^T(r_t)$, and apply Ito's lemma. When we do this we find

$$dP_t^T = \underbrace{\left[\frac{\partial P_t^T}{\partial t} + \frac{\partial P_t^T}{\partial r_t}\mu_r + \frac{1}{2}\frac{\partial^2 P_t^T}{\partial r_t^2}\sigma_r^2\right]}_{\text{bond drift}=\mu_P P}dt + \underbrace{\left[\frac{\partial P_t^T}{\partial r_t}\sigma_r\right]}_{\text{bond volatility}=\sigma_P P}dz_t. \tag{16.9}$$

Therefore, after equating the terms in dt in Equations (16.2) and (16.9), we find that the quantity μ_P is given by

$$\mu_P = \frac{1}{P_t^T}\left[\frac{\partial P_t^T}{\partial t} + \frac{\partial P_t^T}{\partial r_t}\mu_r + \frac{1}{2}\frac{\partial^2 P_t^T}{\partial r_t^2}\sigma_r^2\right]. \tag{16.10}$$

Now we use the market-price-of-risk result in Equation (16.7), we multiply through by P_t^T, and we find

$$\frac{\partial P_t^T}{\partial t} + \frac{\partial P_t^T}{\partial r_t}(\mu_r + \lambda\sigma_r) + \frac{1}{2}\frac{\partial^2 P_t^T}{\partial r_t^2}\sigma_r^2 - P_t^T r_t = 0, \tag{16.11}$$

where we have made use of the fact that

$$\sigma_P = \frac{1}{P_t^T} \frac{\partial P_t^T}{\partial r_t} \sigma_r. \tag{16.12}$$

This means that, if we are interested in prices, the real-world drift of the short rate, μ_r, must be changed into the risk-neutral drift, $\mu_r + \lambda \sigma_r$. We shall denote the risk-neutral drift by $\mu_r^{\mathbb{Q}}$ (ie, with a superscript '$\mathbb{Q}$') to remind ourselves of the transformation:

$$\frac{\partial P_t^T}{\partial t} + \frac{\partial P_t^T}{\partial r_t} \mu_r^{\mathbb{Q}} + \frac{1}{2} \frac{\partial^2 P_t^T}{\partial r_t^2} \sigma_r^2 - P_t^T r_t = 0. \tag{16.13}$$

Equation (16.11) is a Partial Differential Equation that must be solved with the appropriate initial and boundary conditions.

Note that up to this point we have not invoked any special property of bonds in arriving at our Partial Differential Equation – which therefore applies to any instrument whose price depends only on the short rate. It is only now that we require this particular instrument to be a (discount) bond. We do so by imposing the initial condition

$$P_T^T = 1 \tag{16.14}$$

– a condition which simply reflects the fact that, at maturity, any default-free discount bond will pay out exactly \$1.

Note that, so far, we have not made any assumption about the process for the short rate (apart from requiring that it should be a diffusion). Therefore we are not in an affine setting (yet).

16.3   A SPECIAL CASE: AFFINE
TERM STRUCTURES

> What's wrong with that? That's an excellent way to do this: to take a flying guess at it first and then check.
> Richard Feynman – Audio recording of Lecture 8 of *Feynman's Lectures on Physics*, October 20, 1961

As is often done in mathematics, let's start from the solution and work our way backwards. If, as the quote above shows, this was good enough for Feynman, it will certainly be good for us.

What do we mean by 'the solution'? We mean a function of the short rate, r_t, such that, when its appropriate derivatives are inserted in Equation (16.11) and the initial condition (16.14) is satisfied, it will make Equation (16.11) hold true.

What form do we expect for the solution to Equation (16.11)? We note that, apart from the coefficients, we have several first and second derivatives of our solutions adding up the function itself. We know that a self-similar function under differentiation is the exponential. We also know that we must have a dependence on r_t. Finally, we know that, when $t = T$, the unknown function P_t^T must always be equal to 1, and we remember that $e^0 = 1$. We have said nothing so far about the process for the short rate. If the drift and the volatility of the short rate, which appear in Equation (16.11), are simple enough, we can put these hunches, hopes, and pieces of information together and *propose* the following *Ansatz* (which is a far nicer word than 'guess'):

$$P_t^T = e^{A_t^T + B_t^T r}. \tag{16.15}$$

Does it work? And, how simple is 'simple enough'?

To see whether our guess (sorry, *Ansatz*) might work, we take all the required derivatives and obtain the following:

$$\frac{\partial P_t^T}{\partial t} = P_t^T \left(\frac{\partial A_t^T}{\partial t} + \frac{\partial B_t^T}{\partial t} r_t \right) \tag{16.16}$$

$$\frac{\partial P_t^T}{\partial r_t} = P_t^T B_t^T \tag{16.17}$$

$$\frac{\partial^2 P_t^T}{\partial r_t^2} = P_t^T \left(B_t^T \right)^2. \tag{16.18}$$

Therefore, after substituting back into Equation (16.11) we get

$$\frac{\partial P_t^T}{\partial t} + \frac{\partial P_t^T}{\partial r_t} \mu_r^Q + \frac{1}{2} \frac{\partial^2 P_t^T}{\partial r_t^2} \sigma_r^2 - P_t^T r_t = 0$$

$$\implies \left(\frac{\partial A_t^T}{\partial t} + \frac{\partial B_t^T}{\partial t} r_t \right) + B_t^T \mu_r^Q + \frac{1}{2} \left(B_t^T \right)^2 \sigma_r^2 - r_t = 0, \tag{16.19}$$

with the boundary conditions

$$A_T^T = 0 \tag{16.20}$$

$$B_T^T = 0. \tag{16.21}$$

As we said, it is clear that being able to solve relatively easily the Partial Differential Equation (16.19) depends on the functional form for the volatility, σ_r, and the drift, μ_r, of the short rate. If these two quantities had a horribly complex dependence of the state variable (r_t) and/or time, our hopes of solving analytically the Partial Differential Equation (16.19) would be cruelly dashed. Since we have put a lot of work already into all of this, we want to stay the course for as long as possible, and therefore we require the simplest possible behaviour for the drift and variance of the state variable:

$$\mu_r^Q = a + b r_t \tag{16.22}$$

$$\sigma_r^2 = c + f r_t. \tag{16.23}$$

If the drift and the variance of the state variable(s) are a simple affine function of the state variable(s)[3] (in the present case, of the short rate), this

---

[3] What is the difference between 'linear' and 'affine'? The function $f(x) = ax$ is linear and affine, but the function $f(x) = ax + b$ is affine but not linear – because of the constant b. The value of a linear function doubles when the independent variable, the x, doubles; the value of an affine function, in general, does not. A bit more precisely, an affine function is the combination of a linear function (which fixes the origin), with a translation.

specification is important enough to deserve a name, ie, the models compatible with Equations (16.22) and (16.23) are called *affine*.[4]

We note that, despite its simplicity, this choice is rich enough to capture several 'named' models, and a mean-reverting behaviour for the state variable. For instance, the Vasicek model (in which, as we have seen, the short rate is mean reverting):

$$dr_t = \kappa(\theta - r_t)dt + \sigma_r dz_r^t$$ (16.24)

is just a special case of Equations (16.22) and (16.23) with

$$a = \kappa\theta$$ (16.25)

$$b = -\kappa$$ (16.26)

$$c = \sigma_r^2$$ (16.27)

$$f = 0.$$ (16.28)

The Longstaff-and-Schwartz (1992) and the Cox, Ingersoll and Ross (1985a,b) models are shown with similar ease to be affine.

Exercise 38 *Look up the Longstaff-and-Schwartz (1992) and the Cox et al. (1985a,b) models, and work out the constants a, b, c and f in their specifications.*

We go back to the general one-dimensional affine case, and we obtain

$$\frac{\partial A_t^T}{\partial t} + \frac{\partial B_t^T}{\partial t} r_t + B_t^T(a + br_t) + \frac{1}{2}\left(B_t^T\right)^2 (c + fr_t) - r_t = 0.$$ (16.29)

It is now just a matter of collecting terms to obtain

$$\frac{\partial A_t^T}{\partial t} + r_t\left(\frac{\partial B_t^T}{\partial t} - 1\right) + B_t^T(a + br_t) + \frac{1}{2}\left(B_t^T\right)^2(c + fr_t)$$

$$= \frac{\partial A_t^T}{\partial t} + r_t\left(\frac{\partial B_t^T}{\partial t} + bB_t^T - 1 + \frac{1}{2}f\left(B_t^T\right)^2\right) + \frac{1}{2}c\left(B_t^T\right)^2$$

$$+ B_t^T a = 0.$$ (16.30)

Next we employ another of the tricks that we have encountered so far: namely, first we observe that the equation we have obtained must be true for any value of r_t. Then we observe that the right-hand side does not depand on r_t. Therefore we conclude that the coefficient of r_t on the left-hand side must be equal to zero (were it not, we would have to rely on fortuitous cancellations of terms). Therefore, we must have

$$\frac{\partial B_t^T}{\partial t} + bB_t^T + \frac{1}{2}f\left(B_t^T\right)^2 - 1 = 0.$$ (16.31a)

---

[4] We give a more precise definition of affine models in Chapter 18.

Once we have solved this Ordinary Differential Equation for B_t^T, we have to substitute the result (ie, B_t^T) in Equation (16.30), and solve the new resulting Ordinary Differential Equation for A_t^T. This is very good, because we have reduced the problem of solving a Partial Differential Equation to the much simpler problem of solving two Ordinary Differential Equations.

We shall show how to do it in the Vasicek case that immediately follows. For the moment we must stress the logical path that we have followed and the road ahead:

- first we have made an assumption for what the solution may look like if the volatility and the variance of the process for the state variable(s) have an affine form;
- then we have obtained the Ordinary Differential Equations obeyed by the two quantities (A_t^T and B_t^T) that characterize our solution *if the affine assumption holds true*;
- finally, we shall rely on the result that, if we find *one* solution to our general Ordinary Differential Equations satisfying all the boundary and initial conditions, this will be *the* solution to our affine problem.

In the rest of this chapter we find this boundary-and-initial-boundary-conditions-obeying solution for a very special case (the Vasicek case); later chapters we generalize the derivation and the solution to richer models.

Just to repeat the obvious: Equation (16.11) holds for any diffusive process for the short rate; Equation (16.30) holds only for an affine specification for the state variable; and Equation (16.19) is just a hope, that we wrote down before imposing the affine conditions (note that it contains general drifts, μ_r^Q, and volatilities σ_r), and that we obtained using an *Ansatz* solution ($P_t^T = e^{A_t^T + B_t^T r}$) that in reality will hold only if the state variable turns out to be affine (in drift and variance).

16.4 THE VASICEK CASE

For the Vasicek case that we have set out to solve, $d = 0$, and $b = -\kappa$, and therefore Equation (16.31a) reduces to

$$\frac{\partial B_t^T}{\partial t} - \kappa B_t^T - 1 = 0. \tag{16.32}$$

The pleasant feature of this equation is that we have no dependence on the A_t^T term. So, we can solve this part of the equation first, and move to solving the Partial Differential Equation for A_t^T afterwards.

To solve Equation (16.32) we must remember the initial condition $B_T^T = 0$. An obvious guess then suggests

$$B_t^T = -\frac{1 - e^{-\kappa(T-t)}}{\kappa}. \tag{16.33}$$

Direct substitution confirms the correctness of our assumption.

Next we have to

1. make use of Equations (16.25) to (16.28);
2. remember that the coefficient of r_t (ie, the term in square brackets in Equation (16.30)) will be identically equal to zero (this, after all, is how we solved for B_t^T in the first place, and we can therefore save ourselves a lot of algebra); and
3. substitute the expression for B_t^T we have just obtained back into Equation (16.30)

Once we have done this, we obtain

$$\frac{\partial A_t^T}{\partial t} + r_t \left(\frac{\partial B_t^T}{\partial t} - \kappa B_t^T - 1 \right) + \frac{1}{2}\sigma_r^2 \left(B_t^T \right)^2 + \kappa\theta B_t^T$$

$$= \frac{\partial A_t^T}{\partial t} + \frac{1}{2}\sigma_r^2 \left(B_t^T \right)^2 + \kappa\theta B_t^T = 0. \tag{16.34}$$

Recall that we have already obtained the expression for B_t^T (see Equation (16.33)). So, the final expression for A_t^T is obtained by integrating the simple Ordinary Differential Equation (16.34):

$$A_t^T = -\frac{1}{2}\sigma_r^2 \int_t^T \left(B_s^T \right)^2 ds - \kappa\theta \int_t^T B_s^T ds \tag{16.35}$$

to obtain

$$A_t^T = \frac{\left(B_t^T + \tau \right) \left(\kappa^2\theta - \frac{1}{2}\sigma_r^2 \right)}{\kappa^2} - \frac{\sigma_r^2 \left(B_t^T \right)^2}{4\kappa} \tag{16.36}$$

$$B_t^T = -\frac{1 - e^{-\kappa(T-t)}}{\kappa}. \tag{16.37}$$

Exercise 39 *Obtain Equation (16.36) by substituting Equation (16.37) in Equation (16.35), and by evaluating the two integrals. If you get stuck, see Bolder (2001), Section 2.3, or, alternatively, see the solution in a more general, but also more complex, case in Chapter 18.*

Therefore we can conclude that, if

$$\mu_r^Q = a + br_t \tag{16.38}$$

$$\sigma_r^2 = c + dr_t \tag{16.39}$$

and

$$a = \kappa\theta \tag{16.40}$$

$$b = -\kappa \tag{16.41}$$

$$c = \sigma_r^2 \tag{16.42}$$

$$f = 0 \tag{16.43}$$

(the Vasicek model), the bond price is indeed given by

$$P_t^T = e^{A_t^T + B_t^T r_t},$$

(16.44)

with A_t^T and B_t^T given by Equations (16.36) and (16.37).

This concludes our derivation of the analytic expression for the bond price when the short rate follows (in the risk-neutral, $\mathbb{Q}$, measure) a simple mean-reverting process.

16.5 AFFINITY OF THE VASICEK MODEL UNDER $\mathbb{P}$ AND UNDER $\mathbb{Q}$

We have obtained the preceding result under the risk-neutral measure, $\mathbb{Q}$. The model we have solved is patently of the affine form:

$$dr_t = \kappa \left(\theta^\mathbb{Q} - r_t \right) dt + \sigma_r dz_r^t = \mu_r^\mathbb{Q} dt + \sigma_r dz_t$$

$$\Rightarrow \mu_r^\mathbb{Q} = a + br$$

(16.45)

$$\sigma_r^2 = c + f r_t$$

(16.46)

with

$$a = \kappa \theta^\mathbb{Q}$$

(16.47)

$$b = -\kappa$$

(16.48)

$$c = \sigma_r^2$$

(16.49)

$$f = 0.$$

(16.50)

We know that the dynamics for the short rate in the real-world, $\mathbb{P}$, measure is given by

$$dr_t = \kappa \left(\theta^\mathbb{P} - r_t \right) dt + \sigma_r dz_r^t$$

$$= \kappa \left(\theta^\mathbb{Q} - r_t \right) dt - \lambda(r_t)\sigma_r dt + \sigma_r dz_r^t$$

(16.51)

with

$$\mu_r^\mathbb{P} = \kappa \theta^\mathbb{Q} - \kappa r_t - \lambda(r_t)\sigma_r.$$

If the volatility σ_r is a constant, what functional dependence can we give to the market price of risk for the model to remain affine both under $\mathbb{P}$ and under $\mathbb{Q}$?

If, in general, the market price of risk has the affine form

$$\lambda(r_t) = m + g r_t$$

(16.52)

then we have in the Vasicek model

$$\mu_r^\mathbb{P} = \kappa \theta^\mathbb{Q} - \kappa r_t - (m + g r_t)\sigma_r = \kappa \theta^\mathbb{Q} - \kappa r_t - m\sqrt{c} - g\sqrt{c} r_t$$

$$= h + pr$$

(16.53)

with

$$h = \kappa\theta^{\mathbb{Q}} - m\sqrt{c} = \kappa\theta^{\mathbb{Q}} - m\sigma_r \tag{16.54}$$

$$p = -(g\sqrt{c} - \kappa) = -(g\sigma_r + \kappa). \tag{16.55}$$

So, we conclude that the Vasicek model remains affine under $\mathbb{P}$ and under $\mathbb{Q}$ *as long as the market price of risk is at most an affine function of the state variable (the short rate).*

Exercise 40 *Consider the case when the process for the short rate is given by*

$$dr_t = \kappa\left(\theta^{\mathbb{Q}} - r_t\right)dt + \sqrt{r_t}\sigma_r dz_r^t. \tag{16.56}$$

Is this model affine under $\mathbb{Q}$? If it is, which functional dependence of the market price of risk on the state variable preserves affinity across measures? (I guess the second part of the question pretty much gives away the answer to the first, but you may want still to show why the $\mathbb{Q}$-dynamics is indeed affine.)

16.6 OBSERVATIONS ABOUT THE SOLUTION

Now that we have climbed Mount Fuji (once), it is a good time to take a view from the top. The sight is so breathtaking that we shall take it in steps.

16.6.1 Yields

The first observation is that the expression for the yield has a particularly simple and nice form: since we know that

$$y_t^T = -\frac{1}{T-t}\log P_t^T \tag{16.57}$$

we immediately see that

$$y_t^T = \left(\alpha_t^T + \beta_t^T r_t\right) \tag{16.58}$$

where we have defined

$$\alpha_t^T \equiv -\frac{1}{T-t}A_t^T \tag{16.59}$$

and

$$\beta_t^T \equiv -\frac{1}{T-t}B_t^T. \tag{16.60}$$

So, in the Vasicek model (*and, as we shall see, in affine models in general*) yields are just affine functions of the state variable(s) – in this case of the short rate. As an exercise the reader can check that

$$\lim_{T-t\to 0}\beta_t^T = 1 \tag{16.61}$$

and

$$\lim_{T-t\to 0}\alpha_t^T = 0. \tag{16.62}$$

Because of these limits, the yield of the bond of vanishingly short maturity tends to the short rate,

$$\lim_{T-t\to 0} y_t^T = r_t, \tag{16.63}$$

as one would expect.

Therefore it follows that, for affine models, since all yields are affine functions of the state variables, the short rate, which is just a 'special' yield, is also an affine function of the state variables. The result is a tad underwhelming in the case of the Vasicek model, but it is actually very interesting for more general models. All affine models are characterized by the property that the short rate must be an affine function of the state variable. Why are we so concerned about the functional form of the state variable? Because bond prices are given by $\mathbb{Q}$-measure expectations over paths of the short rate.

16.6.2 The Volatility Structure

One of the most important features of a model is its ability to recover the volatilities of yields and forward rates. Why, if we are not interested in derivatives pricing? As we have seen, because of convexity and of risk premia. To see what the Vasicek model says about these quantities, let's derive the volatility of yields first, and then of forward rates.

Equation (16.58) is just what we need for the first task: using Ito's lemma, and neglecting the term in dt we are not interested in, we have

$$
\begin{aligned}
dy_t^T &= \mu_y dt + \frac{\partial y_t^T}{\partial r_t}\sigma_r dz_r^t \\
&= \mu_y dt + \beta_t^T \sigma_r dz_r^t
\end{aligned}
\tag{16.64}
$$

and therefore

$$\sigma_{y_t^T} = \beta_t^T \sigma_r. \tag{16.65}$$

So, we see that the volatility of a τ-maturity yield is just equal to the volatility of the short rate times the term β_t^T. As Figure 16.1 shows, the term β_t^T declines monotonically from the initial value of 1. How quickly it declines is only a function of the reversion speed, κ. Therefore in the Vasicek model the volatilities of yields are a declining function of their maturity, *and the short rate has the highest volatility of all yields* (and, as we shall presently see, of all forward rates). This is a problematic feature of the Vasicek model.

16.6.3 Forward Rates

The problems are every bit as serious when we calculate the volatility of the (instantaneous) forward rates. Recall that instantaneous forward rates, f_t^T, are

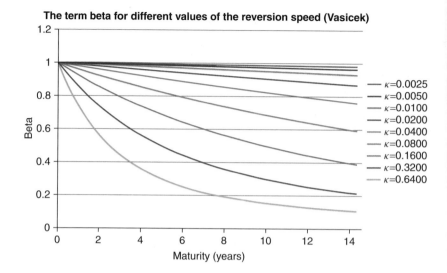

Figure 16.1 The term β_t^T as a function of the maturity $(T - t)$ for different values of the reversion speed from $\kappa = 0.0025$ to $\kappa = 0.64$. A reversion speed, κ, of 0.0025 corresponds to a half-life of more than 250 years, and a reversion speed, κ, of 0.64 corresponds to a half-life of little more than one year.

given by

$$f_t^T = -\frac{\partial}{\partial T} \log P_t^T, \tag{16.66}$$

ie, they are the future borrowing/lending rates that can be 'locked in' given today's bond prices for an infinitesimally short lending/borrowing period. With this definition, in the Vasicek case we get

$$f_t^T = -\frac{\partial}{\partial T} \log P_t^T = -\frac{\partial}{\partial T} \left[A_t^T + B_t^T r_t \right]. \tag{16.67}$$

Let's use Ito's lemma and focus again on the volatility part. We get

$$\sigma_{f_t^T} = -\sigma_r \frac{\partial B_t^T}{\partial T} = \sigma_r e^{-\kappa \tau}. \tag{16.68}$$

The volatilities of instantaneous forward rates of different maturities for reversion speeds ranging from $\kappa = 0.0025$ to $\kappa = 0.64$ are shown in Figure 16.2. We note again the monotonic dependence with maturity for a fixed reversion speed, and with reversion speed for a fixed maturity. The implication that the short rate (ie, the f_t^t instantaneous forward rate) should have the highest volatility of all forward rates is counterfactual, and one of the weaknesses of the simple Vasicek model.

We said that the model implications about the volatility of the short rate are counterfactual. But what do we actually know about the volatility of yields and

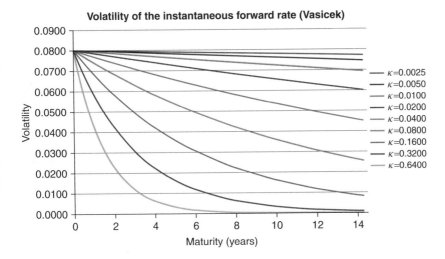

Figure 16.2 The model volatilities of instantaneous forward rates of different maturities for reversion speeds ranging from $\kappa = 0.0025$ to $\kappa = 0.64$.

forward rates? Figures 16.3 and 16.4 answer the question. The figures were obtained using the data provided by the Federal Reserve Board,[5] and show the volatilities of yields and instantaneous forward rates for the period 5 December 1983 to 27 August 2015. The figures clearly show

1. that the volatilities of forward rates peak for maturities between two and four years;
2. that the volatilities of yields (which are averages of forward rates) peak between four and five years; and
3. that the volatility of the short rate is far from being the highest volatility point.

So, the volatility structure implied by the Vasicek model is simple and intuitive, but bears little resemblance with the fine (and, actually, not-so-fine) features of what we know about the volatilities of yields and forward rates. This matters, because, as we have discussed at length in Parts II and III, how well a model apportions term premia and convexity along the yield curve depends crucially on how well it 'understands' the volatilities of yields of different maturities.

Exercise 41 *Using Ito's lemma, obtain the process for an instantaneous forward rate, f_t^T, in a Vasicek world. Does the expression you obtain depend on*

[5] See Gurkaynak, Sack and Wright (2006) for a description of the method used to extract the instantaneous forward rates and the yields – we stress for future reference that, in the terminology of Cochrane and Piazzesi (2004) and Dai, Singleton and Yang (2004), these are 'smooth' forward rates.

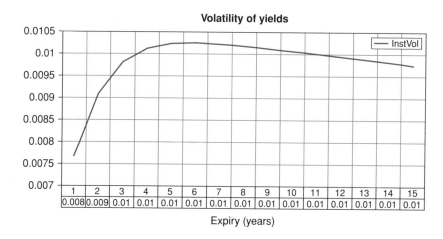

Figure 16.3 The volatilities of yields for maturities out to 15 years for the period 5 December 1983 to 27 August 2015.

the 'distance' of the short rate from the reversion level? Does it depend on the reversion level? Why? Hint: make sure you deal carefully with the usually boring time derivative term in Ito's lemma.

16.6.4   Calibrating to the Volatility Structure: Factorization

We will study in the following how this shortcoming can be fixed. We live with it for the moment, and we ask ourselves how we can calibrate the Vasicek model, ie, how we can determine the values of its parameters (and the initial

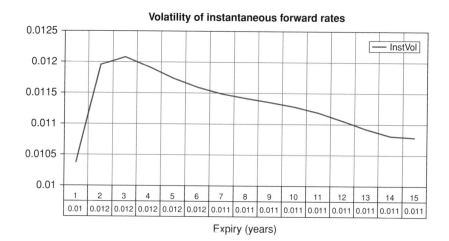

Figure 16.4 Same as Figure 16.3 but for instantaneous forward rates.

value of its state variable). There are, of course, many ways to do so, but I will focus on one particular procedure, *which is transferrable from the Vasicek to the more sophisticated models that are able to capture the volatility structure better.*

The idea starts by noticing that the model volatility structure involves only the volatility of the short rate and the reversion speed (through the quantity B_t^T). As far as volatilities and correlations are concerned, the reversion level plays no role. This feature is very important, because the reverse is not true, ie, the reversion level, *and* the volatility of the short rate *and* the reversion speed all affect the shape of the yield curve. (Why do the volatility and the reversion speed affect the shape of the yield curve? Because the higher the volatility the greater the importance of the convexity term – which pulls yields 'down'; and the greater the reversion speed, the more yields will be 'tucked in', the lower their volatility, and the lesser the importance of the convexity term.) All these terms therefore work together to determine the shape of the yield curve.

This being the case, for a finite maximum maturity of observed yields, different combinations of reversion levels, volatilities and reversion speeds can give rise to fits to the yield curve of very similar quality. How is one to choose among them?

The 'principled' response is to divide and conquer: ie, to calibrate to the volatility structure first – this will determine the volatility of the state variable(s) and the reversion speed(s); and to move then to the fitting of the yield curve, by varying the reversion level, (and, to some extent, the initial value of the short rate, r_{t_0}[6]) but keeping the volatility and the reversion level fixed to the levels determined in the first part of the calibration.

Given the poor recovery of the volatility structure afforded by the Vasicek model, one may well wonder whether these attractive calibration features can yield anything sensible. The good news is that, as anticipated, the same factorization applies to more complex affine models, where the volatility structure *can* be recovered far more realistically.

16.6.5 Fitting to the Yield Curve

The bulk of the weight of fitting to the yield curve (the observed bond prices) rests on the shoulders of the A_t^T term in Equation (16.36) that we reproduce below for ease of reference[7]:

$$A_t^T = \frac{\left(B_t^T - \tau\right)\left(\kappa^2\theta - \frac{1}{2}\sigma_r^2\right)}{\kappa^2} - \frac{\sigma_r^2\left(B_t^T\right)^2}{4\kappa}. \tag{16.69}$$

---

[6] However, for the model to be well specified, this latter quantity cannot be too different from the observed 'short rate' determined by the monetary authorities, such as the Fed fund rates for US$: if the modeller finds a best fit with significantly different values for r_{t_0}, she is probably up to no good.

[7] To simplify notation, in this section, and only in this section, the term B_t^T has the opposite sign to Equation (16.37).

To see this more clearly let's rewrite the bond price as follows:

$$P_t^T = e^{A_t^T - B_t^T r_t}$$

$$= e^{J_\theta + J_{conv}} \tag{16.70}$$

with

$$J_\theta = \theta \left(B_t^T - \tau \right) - B_t^T r \tag{16.71}$$

$$J_{conv} = -\frac{1}{2}\sigma_r^2 \left[\frac{B_t^T - \tau}{\kappa^2} + \frac{\left(B_t^T\right)^2}{2\kappa} \right]. \tag{16.72}$$

The term J_{conv} has been decorated with a subscript 'conv', and, being proportional to one half the square of the volatility, indeed immediately brings to mind a convexity contribution. However, it is important to understand how this comes about.

Consider first the simple expression

$$P(\tau) = e^{-y\tau} \tag{16.73}$$

for some

$$dy = \sigma_y dz. \tag{16.74}$$

As we have seen in Chapter 10, the convexity term is given by

$$\left[\frac{dP(\tau)}{P(\tau)} \right]_{conv} = \frac{1}{2}\sigma_y^2 \tau^2 dt. \tag{16.75}$$

Note that the crude yield model (16.74) can be considered the limit case of the Vasicek model when reversion speed, κ, goes to zero, and therefore $\sigma_r \to \sigma_y$.

Now, we know that, for vanishing κ, the quantity B_t^T behaves like $\tau = T - t$. However, in Equation (16.72) we seem to have terms both in B_t^T and in $\left(B_t^T\right)^2$. To see exactly what happens when the reversion speed goes to zero, we must expand B_t^T to second order, to obtain

$$B_t^T = \frac{1 - e^{-\kappa\tau}}{\kappa} \simeq \frac{1 - \left(1 - \kappa\tau + \frac{1}{2}\kappa^2\tau^2 + ...\right)}{\kappa}$$

$$= \tau - \frac{1}{2}\kappa\tau^2. \tag{16.76}$$

Therefore

$$B_t^T - \tau \simeq -\frac{1}{2}\kappa\tau^2 \tag{16.77}$$

and

$$\frac{B_t^T - \tau}{\kappa^2} \simeq -\frac{1}{2}\frac{\tau^2}{\kappa}. \tag{16.78}$$

This term seems to explode as κ goes to zero for a finite τ, which would not be good. However, consider the term $\frac{(B_t^T)^2}{2\kappa}$. Performing the same expansion, we get

$$\frac{\left(B_t^T\right)^2}{2\kappa} \simeq \frac{1}{2}\frac{\left(\tau - \frac{1}{2}\kappa\tau^2\right)^2}{\kappa} = \frac{1}{2}\frac{\tau^2 + \frac{1}{4}\kappa^2\tau^4 - \kappa\tau^3}{\kappa}$$

$$= \frac{1}{2}\frac{\tau^2}{\kappa} + \frac{1}{8}\kappa\tau^4 - \frac{1}{2}\tau^3 \tag{16.79}$$

and we see that the troublesome terms $-\frac{1}{2}\frac{\tau^2}{\kappa}$ and $\frac{1}{2}\frac{\tau^2}{\kappa}$ exactly cancel out. The remaining terms either do not depend on the reversion speed, κ, or depend on it linearly (and therefore disappear as κ goes to zero).

Which is a long and convoluted way to say that

1. the term $J_{conv} = -\frac{1}{2}\sigma_r^2\left[\frac{B_t^T - \tau}{\kappa^2} + \frac{\left(B_t^T\right)^2}{2\kappa}\right]$ behaves indeed as a convexity term;
2. and, yes, despite the presence of κ and even κ^2 in the denominator, as the reversion speed goes to zero this convexity term does behave properly like the convexity of the simple yield models we have grown up with as children.

What about the term J_θ? For small maturities, the term $\theta(B_t^T - \tau)$ will go to zero (because for small maturities $B_t^T \simeq \tau$ for any reversion speed), and therefore close to expiry the bond price (and the yield) are really not affected by where the reversion level, θ, is. The yields only begin to realize that they have to move towards the reversion level as the 'duration' term B_t^T becomes progressively smaller than τ, giving a bigger and bigger weight to the reversion level. How quickly this 'awakening' occurs depends on the strength of the reversion speed.

Putting the convexity (J_{conv}) and the theta (J_θ) terms together, the yields behaves something like what shown in Figure 16.5, which was obtained with $\theta = 0.045$, $r_0 = 0.02$, $\sigma_r = 0.0120$ and $\kappa = 0.1$.

It is clear that, even for a relatively modest[8] reversion speed ($\kappa = 0.1$) and a high volatility of the short rate ($\sigma_r = 0.0120$) the contribution to the total yield from convexity remains small for maturities under 10 years, and reaches 40 basis points only for 30 years.

Since the convexity term can only 'pull down' the total yield, and since we have discovered that the yield for small maturities has to start from the value 'today' of the short rate, for reversion levels below r_0 the yield curve can only be monotonically downward sloping.

However, if the reversion level is above the current level of the short rate, if the volatility is sufficiently high, we can obtain a 'humped' yield

---

[8] How do we know know that a reversion speed of 0.1 is 'relatively modest'? We can look at the half-life, $H(\kappa)$, which is given by $H(\kappa) = \log(2)/\kappa$. For $\kappa = 0.1$ we get a half-life of almost seven years, which does suggest a rather weak reversion speed.

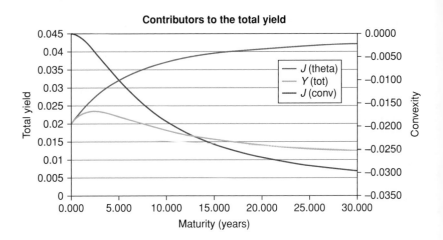

Figure 16.5 The two contributors, J_{conv} and J_θ, to the total yield, $y(tot)$, and the total yield itself for $\theta = 0.045$, $r_0 = 0.02$, $\sigma r = 0.0120$ and $\kappa = 0.1$. Note that the scale for the convexity term is on the right-hand vertical axis.

curve – a shape often encountered in real-life yield curves. See Figure 16.6, obtained with $\theta = 0.045$, $r_0 = 0.02$, $\sigma_r = 0.0080$ and $\kappa = 0.3$.

We can, but *should* we? With this choice of parameters we may well have obtained a better fit to a market yield curve, but we have done serious violence to the Vasicek model: first we have made the short rate move to its reversion level with what Hamlet would probably have called unseemly haste, thereby

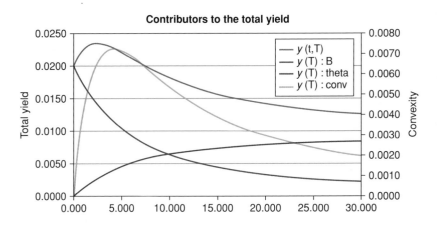

Figure 16.6 Same as Figure 16.5 for $\theta = 0.045$, $r_0 = 0.02$, $\sigma_r = 0.080$ and $\kappa = 0.3$.

raising short-term yields;[9] then we had to 'pump up' the volatility to similarly implausible levels ($\sigma_r = 0.0800$) in order to increase the usually modest convexity contribution and 'turn downwards' the yield curve. In other words, in the terminology of Chapter 1, we have used the Vasicek model as a 'snapshot model' – and a rather poor one at that. This is not how a structural model should be used, and, by forcing this fit, we are certain to throw away what sensible information we could have extracted, with same care and common sense, from the Vasicek model.

What does this sensible information amount to? For instance, for all its limitations, a 'principled' calibration can tell us that, even if the fit to market yield curve may be poor, the 'basis point value' of convexity for 30 years should be of the order of tens of basis points. We don't have to take this answer as gospel, and we should question critically the result, and examine how sensitive it is to our inputs. But, at least, we have something sensible on which to start our analysis. The better-fitting monster shown in Figure 16.6 would suggest instead a value for the volatility of the order of several *hundreds* of basis points – a value that, if taken seriously, would lead us completely astray. The old adage about it being better to be approximately right than exactly wrong comes to mind.

16.7   WHY DO WE CARE ABOUT A HUMPED VOLATILITY CURVE?

As we have discussed previously, the presence of a hump in the volatility curve is in normal market conditions a well established empirical fact. Also implied volatilities clearly point to this feature. (See in this respect the possibly illuminating, but certainly lengthy, discussion in Rebonato (2002).) Let's therefore accept that, at least in normal times, this stylized 'factoid' holds true. True it may be; but is it important? What do we lose if we choose an exponentially decaying instantaneous volatility instead of a humped one? And how bad in practice is it to accept instantaneous volatilities of forward rates that asymptotically go to zero?

Suppose first that we want to price exactly one particular option (a caplet, for simplicity). Then we have to match the integral of the square of the volatility to that expiry with the exponential and humped curves. If we look at the integrated variance, we get the picture in Figure 16.7, where we have calibrated our mean-reverting affine model to get the 10-year caplet exactly the same as with the humped volatility curve.

Note that, in order to get the 10-year caplet exactly priced, all the other options are mispriced: some end up being more expensive and some cheaper

---

[9] Why 'unseemly'? Because if the reversion level were really as high as 0.3, the half-life – ie, the time it would on average take the short rate to halve its current distance from its reversion level – would be as short as 2.3 years, and there would be no statistical problem whatsoever in assessing whether rates follow a unit-root process or not.

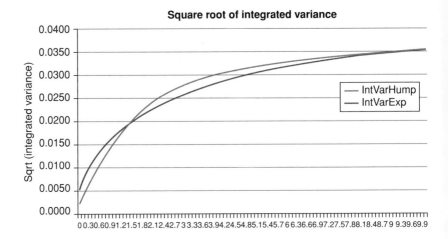

Figure 16.7 The square root of the integrated variance for the exponential (curve labelled IntVarExp) and humped (curve labelled IntVarHump) volatility functions when the 10-year caplet is matched.

than with the humped curve – something which is not obvious just looking at the two instantaneous volatilities, shown in Figure 16.8.

What if, instead of focussing on one particular option, we tried to get the 'best fit' for all the options out to a given horizon[10]? In general, this will work very poorly. We have a short blanket, and either the feet or the head are going to get cold (or the belly, depending on the details). This short blanket is the reason why the users of short-rate–based mean-reverting affine models often end up embracing time dependence with gusto. This, of course, seems to fix the problem as seen from today, but stores up close-to-invisible problems for the future.

As we said many times, pricing interest-rate options is not the concern of this book. However, the caplet pricing example clearly shows how the volatility structure implied by the Vasicek model is seriously wrong (in a humped-volatility world). And we have discussed at length how important recovering ball-park correct yield volatilities is important for convexity and for a structural description of the yield curve. So, caplets or no caplets, we *do* have a problem to fix.

16.8   HOW TO LENGTHEN THE SHORT BLANKET

In sum, we can draw several conclusions from the analysis so far.

First, we have seen that the Vasicek model does not have enough flexibility to reproduce market yield curves well. Rather than chasing an elusive good fit

---

[10] Note that we cannot match options on average for all horizons, because the volatility of OU forward rates goes to zero as their expiry increases, and a different solution is therefore obtained for different horizons.

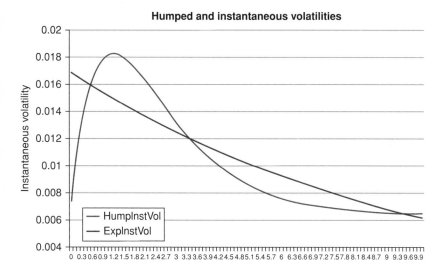

Figure 16.8 The humped and exponential instantaneous volatility functions of the forward rate when the 10-year option is exactly priced.

by letting all the parameters 'run amok' in some non-linear numerical search and hope for the best, one should inject as much information as possible into the reversion speed and volatility parameters from market information about yield volatilities and/or swaption prices. The modeller should then fix these parameters, and use the only parameter left (the reversion level, θ) to fit, as best as she can, the market yield curve. The fit may not be splendid, but at least the model has some meaning.

Second, we have observed that there are serious problems with the term structure of yield (or forward-rate) volatilities, and we have explained why these problems matter. As we shall see, fixing these problems will not prove too difficult (see, for instance, Chapter 30 for a simple solution).

Alas, there is a third problem, which goes back to the modelling choice that requires the market price of risk in the 'classic' Vasicek model to be a constant. But, as we show in Chapter 25, all empirical evidence points to the fact that a constant market price of risk does a very poor job at explaining excess returns. We discuss this evidence at length in Chapter 26, but we can give a sneak preview, and quote Duffee's (2002) result that constant-market-price-of-risk affine models do no better than random walks in accounting for excess returns.

So, we can live with an imperfect, but reasonable, fit to the yield curve; we can fix the term-structure-of-volatility problems; but, if we want to give a structural description of the yield curve, we seem to be fundamentally stumped.[11]

---

[11] A model like the Cox–Ingersoll–Ross does allow for a dependence of the market price of risk on *the* state variable (which is again the short rate). However, the chosen functional dependence is dictated purely by the requirement to keep the model affine, and does not reflect empirical reality any better than the simpler Vasicke model.

Given these problems, one may well wonder whether even a 'principled' approach to term-structure modelling in a Vasicek-like framework can yield anything very interesting. In its simplicity and parsimony the Vasicek model does indeed possess unrivalled elegance. Alas, when one looks at its ability to match empirical evidence, Einstein's reply to Weyl[12] (*"Apart from the [lack of] agreement with reality, it is in any case a superb intellectual performance"*) springs to mind. This would be unfair, and would miss the point.

The important message from this chapter is that the Vasicek model does need fixing, and that we have diagnosed the problems very clearly. The question is whether the therapy can be administered using affine medicines. The answer, as we shall see, is '*yes*'. Weyl's ingenious attempt to unify gravity and electromagnetism turned out to be a dead end. The Vasicek model is anything but.

Furthermore, the factorization into 'volatility-related' parameters and 'yield-curve-shape–related' parameters remains valid also for all the more complex affine models that we shall introduce in the rest of the book exactly to fix the problems that we have identified. We shall see that the divide-and-conquer approach will afford lasting benefits.

This naturally brings us to discussing the affine generalizations alluded to earlier. We undertake this task in Chapters 17 and 18.

---

[12] The comment referred to Weyl's attempt to unify gravitation with electromagnetism. Quoted in Smolin (2006), p. 45.

CHAPTER 17

First Extensions

Matters should be made as simple as possible, but not any simpler.
Attributed to Albert Einstein

I therefore don't have much to say. But I will take a long time anyway.
Richard Feynman, Programme American Physics Society, Annual Meeting, 1950

17.1 THE PURPOSE OF THIS CHAPTER

In this chapter I present a gentle introduction to many-factor affine models. All the results that we obtain in this chapter will be re-obtained with greater elegance and generality in Chapter 18. So, strictly speaking, this chapter is redundant. However, as usual, I have chosen the gradual approach of introducing new concepts (or a new formalism) in the 'friendliest' possible manner, and to build on the intuition that this approach affords for the more general treatment that follows.

Particular care will be devoted to understanding clearly the vector and matrix notation, because it will be used extensively in Chapter 18, and there at a rather brisker pace than here.[1] Given the introductory nature of this chapter, we will carefully decorate matrices with an underscore (like this: $\underline{K}$), and vectors with an arrow (like this: $\vec{x}$). In later chapters we will stick to this convention only when the need for clarity requires it.

17.2 AFFINE MODELS WITH MANY STATE VARIABLES

Consider a set of state variables, x_i, $i = 1, 2, \ldots, N$, which for the moment we leave unspecified. We assume that these variables follow joint mean-reverting diffusive processes of the form

$$d\vec{x} = \underline{K}(\vec{\theta} - \vec{x})dt + \underline{S}d\vec{z}_t. \tag{17.1}$$

---

[1] Some definitions and results have been presented in Chapter 2.

Before we proceed, it is important to understand the notation clearly. As we have explained in Chapter 2, $\vec{a}$ denotes a column vector:

$$\vec{a} = \begin{bmatrix} a_1 \\ a_2 \\ \dots \\ a_N \end{bmatrix}, \tag{17.2}$$

and $\underline{A}$ a matrix:

$$\underline{A} = \begin{bmatrix} a_{11} & a_{12} & \dots & a_{1N} \\ a_{21} & a_{22} & \dots & a_{2N} \\ \dots & \dots & \dots & \dots \\ a_{N1} & a_{N2} & \dots & a_{NN} \end{bmatrix}. \tag{17.3}$$

If $\underline{K}$ is an $[n \times n]$ matrix, and $\vec{\theta}$ an vector, an $[n \times 1]$ vector, an expression like $\underline{K}\vec{\theta}$ (the usual row-by-column matrix multiplication) can be written algebraically as

$$\underline{K}\vec{\theta} = \sum_{j=1}^{N} k_{ij}\theta_j. \tag{17.4}$$

When we add the products of the same-index components of two vectors to obtain a number, as in the expression

$$\sum_i a_i b_i = c, \tag{17.5}$$

we are matrix-multiplying the transpose of the column vector by a column vector (an 'inner product'):

$$[a_1, a_2, \dots, a_n] \begin{bmatrix} b_1 \\ b_2 \\ \dots \\ b_n \end{bmatrix} = \vec{a}^{\mathrm{T}}\vec{b} = c. \tag{17.6}$$

Finally, without loss of generality, we assume in this chapter that all the increments dz_i are orthogonal, ie, that

$$\mathbb{E}[dz_i dz_j] = \delta_{ij}dt \tag{17.7}$$

with δ_{ij} (the Kroeneker delta) equal to 1 if $i = 1$ and zero otherwise.

Why 'without loss of generality'? Because any correlation matrix between the x_is can be recovered, even if the increments, dz_i, are all orthogonal. See later for the $N = 2$ case.

17.2.1 The $N = 2$ Case

Let's go back to Expression (17.1). So as not to miss the wood for the trees, let's consider for simplicity the case $N = 2$. Then we have

$$\begin{bmatrix} dx_1 \\ dx_2 \end{bmatrix} = \begin{bmatrix} \kappa_{11} & \kappa_{12} \\ \kappa_{21} & \kappa_{22} \end{bmatrix} \left(\begin{bmatrix} \theta_1 \\ \theta_2 \end{bmatrix} - \begin{bmatrix} x_1 \\ x_2 \end{bmatrix} \right) dt + \begin{bmatrix} s_{11} & s_{12} \\ s_{21} & s_{22} \end{bmatrix} \begin{bmatrix} dz_1 \\ dz_2 \end{bmatrix}. \quad (17.8)$$

If the reversion-speed matrix is diagonal,

$$\begin{bmatrix} \kappa_{11} & \kappa_{12} \\ \kappa_{21} & \kappa_{22} \end{bmatrix} = \begin{bmatrix} \kappa_{11} & 0 \\ 0 & \kappa_{22} \end{bmatrix}, \quad (17.9)$$

the expression for the drift above factorizes neatly as

$$dx_1 = \kappa_{11}(\theta_1 - x_1)dt \quad (17.10)$$

$$dx_2 = \kappa_{22}(\theta_2 - x_2)dt. \quad (17.11)$$

This shows that, if the reversion speed matrix is diagonal, each state variable is attracted (assuming that each κ_{ii} is positive) to its own reversion level (θ_i), and does not 'feel' what the other state variable is doing.

However, in general, we have for the drift

$$dx_1 = [\kappa_{11}(\theta_1 - x_1) + \kappa_{12}(\theta_2 - x_2)]dt \quad (17.12)$$

$$dx_2 = [\kappa_{21}(\theta_1 - x_1) + \kappa_{22}(\theta_2 - x_2)]dt. \quad (17.13)$$

This shows that the deterministic behaviour of one state variable, say, x_1, is affected not just by how distant it is from its own reversion level, θ_1, but also by how far the other state variable, x_2, is from its own reversion level, θ_2. Look, for instance, at the increment, dx_1, of the first state variable, x_1. Assuming that κ_{11} is positive, we see that the drift of x_1 is made up of a familiar component, $\kappa_{11}(\theta_1 - x_1)$, ie, the attraction to the reversion level, θ_1. However, the drift also contains a component, $\kappa_{12}(\theta_2 - x_2)$, that depends on how far the other state variable is from its own reversion level (θ_2), and the magnitude and sign of the reversion speed κ_{12}. Note that either κ_{11} or κ_{12} could be negative, and yet the joint behaviour of the two state variables could be stable. As a result, for a non-diagonal reversion-speed matrix the resulting dynamics for x_1 and x_2 is far more complex and difficult to visualize than for the simple diagonal case of Equation (17.9). We shall see examples of this in Chapter 33.

Similarly, if the 'volatility' matrix, S, is diagonal then we have

$$\begin{bmatrix} s_{11} & s_{12} \\ s_{21} & s_{22} \end{bmatrix} \begin{bmatrix} dz_1 \\ dz_2 \end{bmatrix} = \begin{bmatrix} s_{11} & 0 \\ 0 & s_{22} \end{bmatrix} \begin{bmatrix} dz_1 \\ dz_2 \end{bmatrix} \quad (17.14)$$

and we can write for the stochastic part of the evolution of the two state variables

$$dx_1 = \ldots dt + s_{11}dz_1$$

$$dx_2 = \ldots dt + s_{22}dz_{12}. \quad (17.15)$$

However, in the general case, we have

$$dx_1 = \ldots dt + s_{11}dz_1 + s_{12}dz_2$$

$$dx_2 = \ldots dt + s_{21}dz_1 + s_{22}dz_2, \tag{17.16}$$

showing that each state variable is affected by both Brownian shocks, dz_1 and dz_2.

As promised earlier, let's calculate the correlation between the two variables. In doing so, recall that we have assumed the Brownian increments to be orthogonal: $\mathbb{E}[dz_i dz_j] = \delta_{ij}dt$. As usual,

$$\rho_{12} = \frac{\mathbb{E}[dx_1 dx_2]}{\sqrt{var_1}\sqrt{var_2}}. \tag{17.17}$$

Let's calculate the numerator first:

$$\mathbb{E}[dx_1 dx_2] = \mathbb{E}[(\ldots dt + s_{11}dz_1 + s_{12}dz_2)(\ldots dt + s_{21}dz_1 + s_{22}dz_2)]$$

$$= (s_{11}s_{21} + s_{12}s_{22})dt. \tag{17.18}$$

Then we have for the variances

$$var_1 = \left[(s_{11})^2 + (s_{12})^2\right]dt \tag{17.19}$$

$$var_2 = \left[(s_{21})^2 + (s_{22})^2\right]dt. \tag{17.20}$$

Putting the pieces together one gets

$$\rho_{12} = \frac{s_{11}s_{21} + s_{12}s_{22}}{\sqrt{(s_{11})^2 + (s_{12})^2}\sqrt{(s_{21})^2 + (s_{22})^2}}. \tag{17.21}$$

We have four numbers with which we have to recover three quantities, var_1, var_1 and ρ_{12}. We can set one of the off-diagonal entries to zero, and still recover an arbitrary exogenous 2×2 covariance matrix. This is normally achieved by means of an upper of lower diagonal matrix, S:

$$\underline{S} = \begin{bmatrix} s_{11} & 0 \\ s_{21} & s_{22} \end{bmatrix}. \tag{17.22}$$

For readers who are familiar with the Choleski decomposition, it is easy to see that this is exactly what we have done. For those readers who are not, we have shown that, in the case of two variables, we can recover exactly the exogenous variances and correlation using a upper or lower diagonal $\underline{S}$, even if the increments dz_i are orthogonal.

17.2.2   An Expression for the Variance for Generic N

We have obtained an expression for the variance when $N = 2$. For future applications it is useful to derive an expression for the instantaneous variance of the vector process, $\vec{x}$ in the general case. To do so, we have to calculate

$\text{var}(x_i) = \mathbb{E}[dx_i dx_i]$. We have seen that, for $N = 2$, we had

$$
\begin{aligned}
var(x_i) &= \mathbb{E}[dx_i dx_i] \\
&= (s_{i1}dz_1 + s_{i2}dz_2)(s_{i1}dz_1 + s_{i2}dz_2) \\
&= \left(s_{i1}^2 + s_{i2}^2\right) dt.
\end{aligned}
\tag{17.23}
$$

This can be expressed in a matrix form by writing for the covariance matrix among the state variables, $\underline{covar}[x]$,

$$
\underline{covar}[x] = d\vec{x}\, d\vec{x}^{\mathrm{T}} =
\begin{bmatrix} dx_1 \\ dx_2 \\ \cdots \\ dx_n \end{bmatrix}
[dx_1, dx_2, \ldots, dx_n]
\tag{17.24}
$$

$$
= \underbrace{\begin{bmatrix} s_{11} & s_{12} \\ s_{21} & s_{22} \end{bmatrix} \begin{bmatrix} dz_1 \\ dz_2 \end{bmatrix}}_{d\vec{x}} \underbrace{\left(\begin{bmatrix} s_{11} & s_{12} \\ s_{21} & s_{22} \end{bmatrix} \begin{bmatrix} dz_1 \\ dz_2 \end{bmatrix} \right)^{\mathrm{T}}}_{d\vec{x}^{\mathrm{T}}}
$$

$$
= \begin{bmatrix} s_{11} & s_{12} \\ s_{21} & s_{22} \end{bmatrix} \begin{bmatrix} dz_1 \\ dz_2 \end{bmatrix} [dz_1, dz_2] \begin{bmatrix} s_{11} & s_{21} \\ s_{12} & s_{22} \end{bmatrix}
$$

$$
= \begin{bmatrix} s_{11} & s_{12} \\ s_{21} & s_{22} \end{bmatrix} \begin{bmatrix} 1 & 0 \\ 0 & 1 \end{bmatrix} \begin{bmatrix} s_{11} & s_{21} \\ s_{12} & s_{22} \end{bmatrix}
$$

$$
= \begin{bmatrix} s_{11} & s_{12} \\ s_{21} & s_{22} \end{bmatrix} \begin{bmatrix} s_{11} & s_{21} \\ s_{12} & s_{22} \end{bmatrix} = \underline{S}\underline{S}^{\mathrm{T}}.
\tag{17.25}
$$

In obtaining the results above we have remembered

1. that terms in dt will disappear when we calculate the product $d\vec{x}\, d\vec{x}^{\mathrm{T}}$, and therefore we have omitted them in the second line;
2. that for any compatible matrices and/or vectors a, b, $(ab)^{\mathrm{T}} = b^{\mathrm{T}}a^{\mathrm{T}}$; and that we have specialized the treatment to the case $N = 2$ after the first line. However, the matrix equation on the right-hand side of Equation (17.25) will apply to any N.

This is the expression for the covariance. Finally, we can easily obtain an expression for the variance of the ith variable, which is given by the appropriate diagonal element of the covariance matrix:

$$
var[x_i] = [\underline{SS}^T]_{ii}.
\tag{17.26}
$$

This, of course, for $N = 2$ reduces to what we have obtained in two lines in Equation (17.23), but we now have a handy expression that will generalize to any dimension. We will need this expression when we look below at exponentially affine models, and when calculate the analytic expression for the covariance.

17.2.3   Stability

If the multivariable system nicely decouples as per Equations (17.10) (ie, in the diagonal reversion-speed-matrix case), it is easy to see that for the system to be stable (not to 'explode') it is enough to require that the two reversion speeds, κ_1 and κ_2, should be positive: if they are, as one state variable is shocked away from its reversion level by the vicissitudes of economic life, it is pulled back to its own reversion speed with a 'spring strength' directly proportional to its own reversion speed. This, after all, is why the behaviour is called 'mean-reverting' (as opposed to 'mean-fleeing').

But how are we to assess the stability of a system like one described by Equations (17.12)? Could some of the elements be negative, and yet the system remain positive? Could perhaps some of the *diagonal* elements be negative?

The answer is given by looking at the eigenvalues of the reversion-speed matrix. Let's assume that the reversion speed matrix can be diagonalized, ie, written in the form

$$\underline{\mathcal{K}} = \underline{a}\,\underline{\Lambda}\,\underline{a}^{-1}, \tag{17.27}$$

where the diagonal matrix, $\underline{\Lambda}$, contains the eigenvalues , $l_{11}, l_{22}, ..., l_{NN}$:

$$\Lambda = \begin{bmatrix} l_{11} & 0 & \dots & 0 \\ 0 & l_{22} & \dots & 0 \\ \dots & \dots & \dots & \dots \\ 0 & 0 & \dots & l_{NN} \end{bmatrix} \tag{17.28}$$

and the matrix $\underline{a}$ contains the eigenvectors of $\underline{\mathcal{K}}$. We show in Appendix 17C that, if the eigenvalues are all positive, then the system is stable.

What do we mean when we say that $\underline{a}$ is the matrix of eigenvectors of $\underline{\mathcal{K}}$, and Λ the matrix of its eigenvalues? Consider the matrix $\underline{a}$ as being made up by stacking column vectors $\overrightarrow{a}_i$, with each $\overrightarrow{a}_i$ containing one eigenvector.

$$\underline{a} = \begin{bmatrix} \uparrow & \uparrow & & \uparrow \\ \overrightarrow{a}_1 & \overrightarrow{a}_2 & \dots & \overrightarrow{a}_n \\ \downarrow & \downarrow & & \downarrow \end{bmatrix}. \tag{17.29}$$

Then we have

$$\underline{\mathcal{K}}\,\overrightarrow{a}_i = l_{ii}\,\overrightarrow{a}_i \quad \text{for any } i. \tag{17.30}$$

This means that, if we consider the reversion-speed matrix, $\underline{\mathcal{K}}$, as an operator that operates on the ith eigenvector, $\overrightarrow{a}_i$, then the effect of the operation is to return the same eigenvector back, multiplied by a constant. This constant, of course, is just the eigenvalue.

As mentioned previously, we can get positive eigenvalues, and hence stability, even if some of the individual reversion speeds, κ_{ij}, are negative – and, indeed, even if some of the diagonal elements, κ_{ii}, are negative. We shall see how very important this will be when we look at the Principal-Component–based affine model presented in Chapter 33.

17.2.4 Changing Variables

One may well say: 'Having stability is all fine and well. However, getting one's head around the deterministic behaviour of the state variables when the reversion-speed matrix is non-diagonal calls for a cold towel around one's forehead. Why don't we introduce new variables such that these have a nice diagonal reversion-speed matrix, and then revert the original variables at the end?'

This is certainly possible. Creating new variables, $\overrightarrow{p}$, means applying a linear transformation to the original variables of the form

$$\overrightarrow{q} = \underline{T}\,\overrightarrow{x} \tag{17.31}$$

or, in algebraic form,

$$q_i = \sum_{j=1}^{N} T_{ij}x_j. \tag{17.32}$$

Such a reversion-speed-diagonalizing transformation can always be found.

Of course, we also know that it is also possible to perform a (different) linear transformation of variables (a rotation) such that the 'volatility' matrix, $\underline{S}$, becomes diagonal:

$$\overrightarrow{p} = \underline{\Omega}\,\overrightarrow{x} \tag{17.33}$$

or, in algebraic form,

$$p_i = \sum_{j=1}^{N} \omega_{ij}x_j. \tag{17.34}$$

(We know that this is possible, because this is exactly what the Principal Component transformation does – see Chapter 6.)

However, we show in Chapter 33 that it is not in general possible to have both the reversion-speed matrix (under $\mathbb{Q}$) *and* the volatility matrix simultaneously diagonal. Which also means that (in the risk-neutral measure) principal components cannot have a nice and simple mean-reverting behaviour with a diagonal reversion-speed matrix. This, as we shall see, is an *a priori* unexpected result with rather deep implications.

These considerations should be kept in mind when we deal with latent models (such as the Kim Wright model discussed in Chapter 31). As we shall see, when we do not know what the variables mean in the first place, we can rotate them to our heart's content (or, rather, to our computational advantage). We can do so either by obtaining a diagonal reversion-speed matrix, or a diffusion matrix. However, we cannot do both at the same time.

17.3 MULTIVARIABLE EXPONENTIALLY AFFINE MODELS

Requiring a mean-reverting behaviour when the reversion speed matrix is diagonal has a clear intuitional appeal. Much of this appeal is, however, lost when the reversion-speed matrix is full, and contains both positive and negative elements. What is the great advantage, then, in requiring our state variables to have this form?

The answer lies in an important theorem, to my knowledge first presented in full generality by Duffie and Kan (1996), which we simply state below without proof. After pole-vaulting over the technical conditions, the theorem says that

1. if the state variables $\vec{x}$ have processes of the form

$$d\vec{x} = \vec{M}\,dt + \underline{S}\,d\vec{z}_t \tag{17.35}$$

   with

$$\vec{M} = \vec{a}_0 + \underline{a}_1\,\vec{x} \tag{17.36}$$

   and *each* component, $[\underline{S}\,\underline{S}^T]_{ii}$, of the variance vector in Equation (17.26) is of the form

$$\text{var}(\vec{x})_i = [\underline{S}\,\underline{S}^T]_{ii} = b_0^i + \left(\vec{b}_1^i\right)^T \vec{x} \tag{17.37}$$

   (where, for each component i, each b_0^i is a scalar and each $\vec{b}_1^i$ is a vector); and

2. if the short rate can be written as an affine combination of the state variables, $\vec{x}$:

$$r = u_r + (\vec{g})^T \vec{x} \tag{17.38}$$

then there exist two quantities, A_t^T and B_t^T, with $A_t^T = f(\underline{K}, \underline{S}, \vec{\theta}, T - t)$ and $B_t^T = g(\underline{K}, \underline{S}, T - t)$, for some functions f and g, such that the bond price, P_t^T, is of the form

$$P_t^T = e^{A_t^T + \left(\vec{B}_t^T\right)^T \vec{x}_t}. \tag{17.39}$$

As for the functions A_t^T and B_t^T, an extension of the derivation we presented in Chapter 16 shows that they are the solutions to the Ordinary Differential Equations

$$\frac{dA_t^T}{d\tau} = -u_r + \left(\vec{B}_t^T\right)^T \underline{K}\vec{\theta} + \frac{1}{2}\left(\vec{B}_t^T\right)^T \underline{S}\,\underline{S}^T \vec{B}_t^T \tag{17.40}$$

$$\frac{d\vec{B}_t^T}{d\tau} = -\vec{g} - \underline{K}^T\left(\vec{B}_t^T\right) \tag{17.41}$$

with initial conditions

$$A_T^T = 0 \tag{17.42}$$

and

$$B_T^T = 0. \tag{17.43}$$

Just as we saw in Chapter 16, in order to derive explicit expressions for the quantities A_t^T and B_t^T one first solves the ordinary differential equation (17.41) for the vector $\vec{B}_t^T$, and then substitutes this result into Equation (17.40).

We give a full derivation of the expressions for A_t^T and B_t^T in the next chapter. For the moment, we simply note that Equation (17.41) is the easier of the two to solve analytically: a glance at it immediately suggests that exponentials will figure prominently. In total generality, one will then have to resort to numerical integration to obtain A_t^T. However, as we shall see, human ingenuity has come up with analytic, if often rather lengthy, expressions for A_t^T for many useful and rich specifications for the process (17.1) for the state variables. And, if one is happy to consider expressions with exponentials of matrices as 'analytic', then virtually all reasonable specifications of the reversion-speed matrix give rise to 'solvable' models. More about this later.

Finally, note carefully the requirement (17.38). It say that, for the model to be affine and to admit exponentially affine solutions of the type (17.39), the short rate must be an affine combination of the chosen state variables. Now, this requirement can be trivial, if one of the state variables is the short rate itself; but it is highly non-obvious for an arbitrary choice of state variables. In particular, if the state variables of choice are latent, this means that they could be 'anything', but only insofar as some affine combination of these variables yields the short rate.

17.4 GENERAL PROPERTIES OF THE SOLUTIONS

17.4.1 Yields and Forward Rates

A few comments are in order about the preceding result.

First, Equation (17.39) immediately shows that the yields, y_t^T, are given by

$$y_t^T = -\frac{1}{T-t} \log P_t^T = -\frac{1}{T-t} \log \left(e^{A_t^T + \left(\vec{B}_t^T\right)^{\mathrm{T}} \vec{x}_t} \right)$$

$$= \left[\alpha_t^T + \left(\vec{\beta}_t^T\right)^{\mathrm{T}} \vec{x}_t \right] \tag{17.44}$$

with

$$\alpha_t^T = -\frac{A_t^T}{T-t} \tag{17.45}$$

$$\beta_t^T = -\frac{B_t^T}{T-t}, \tag{17.46}$$

which means that *all yields are linear (affine) functions of the state variables*. It takes a second to show that so are the forward rates.

Exercise 42 *Derive an expression for the instantaneous forward rates.*

Exercise 43 *Using Ito's Lemma, derive an expression for the volatility of the instantaneous forward rates. Compare and contrast with Equation (16.68) in Chapter 16.*

The second observation is that affine models can have stochastic volatility (because the variance can depend on the state variables, which are, of course, stochastic) but the stochasticity is of a very prescribed form, in the sense that the variance is a deterministic (and linear) function of the state variables. This means that, for the same realization of the state vector, $\vec{x}$, the variance will always be exactly the same.

Next, it is important to observe what the quantities A_t^T and B_t^T do and do *not* depend on. In Equation (17.41) for B_t^T the reversion-level vector is conspicuous by its absence. So, the term B_t^T controls volatility, reversion speed, serial auto-correlation and, therefore, yield volatilities, convexity, etc. Information about swaption implied volatilities or about the covariance matrix among yields can provide information to determine the 'volatilities' in $\underline{S}$, and the reversion speeds in $\underline{K}$.

Both these quantities, the 'volatilities' $\underline{S}$ and the reversion speeds $\underline{K}$, also affect the shape of the yield curve, because they affect (via convexity) its curvature. So, the *level* of the yield curve is determined by the reversion level vector, $\vec{\theta}$, which dominates at short maturities, and enters the expression only for A_t^T (see Equation (17.40)), and by the 'volatilities' $\underline{S}$ and the reversion speeds $\underline{K}$, which affect, via convexity, the long end of the yield curve. However, market quantities such as the yield covariance matrix and swaption volatilities do not depend at all on the reversion-level vector, $\vec{\theta}$. We therefore encounter again the same pleasant factorization that we discussed at length in Chapter 16. All the observations we made there about the joys that flow from splitting the calibration process and the sorrows that attend joint-calibration enterprises remain valid – actually, they are even more important now that the number of parameters has greatly increased. Please, do read again Section 16.6.4.

17.4.2 Distributional Properties

Last, one can obtain that the distribution for the state variables at a future time, T, $\vec{x}_T$, given their value today, $\vec{x}_0$, is just a multivariate Gaussian distribution given by

$$P(x_t|x_0) = \mathcal{N}(\vec{\mu}_t, \underline{\Sigma}_t) \tag{17.47}$$

with

$$\mathbb{E}[\vec{x}_T|\vec{x}_0] = \vec{\mu}_T = e^{-\underline{K}t}\vec{x}_0 + (\underline{I} - e^{-\underline{K}t})\vec{\theta}, \tag{17.48}$$

where $\mathbb{E}[\vec{x}_T | \vec{x}_0]$ is the expectation of the state variables, and the expression for $\underline{\Sigma}$ is derived in Appendix 17B to be given by

$$\underline{\Sigma} = (\underline{G}^{-1})^{\mathsf{T}} \underline{M} \underline{G}^{-1}, \tag{17.49}$$

with

$$\underline{M} = h_{ij} \frac{1 - e^{-(l_i + l_j)u}}{l_i + l_j}, \tag{17.50}$$

with h_{ij} the elements of the matrix $\underline{H}$,

$$\underline{H} = \underline{G}^{\mathsf{T}} \underline{S} \underline{S}^{\mathsf{T}} \underline{G}, \tag{17.51}$$

and with $\{l_i\}$ denoting the eigenvalues of $\underline{K}$. In obtaining this result we have assumed that the reversion speed matrix can be orthogonalized:

$$\underline{K} = \underline{a} \underline{\Lambda} \underline{a}^{-1}. \tag{17.52}$$

17.5   APPENDIX 17A: DERIVATION OF THE VARIANCE OF A ONE-DIMENSIONAL MEAN-REVERTING PROCESS

In this appendix we are going to derive an expression for the variance of a one-dimensional mean-reverting process. The result will be used to extend to the case of a multidimensional mean-reverting process (see Appendix 17B).

Start from

$$dx_t = \kappa(\theta - x_t)dt + \sigma dz_t. \tag{17.53}$$

To simplify the algebra, we are going to set $\theta = 0$. Nothing will hang on this. So we have

$$dx_t = -\kappa x_t dt + \sigma dz_t.$$

Consider the new variable y_t, given by

$$y_t = x_t e^{\kappa t}. \tag{17.54}$$

Then we have

$$
\begin{aligned}
d\left(x_t e^{\kappa t}\right) &= e^{\kappa t} dx_t + d(e^{\kappa t}) x_t \\
&= e^{\kappa t}[-\kappa x_t dt + \sigma dz_t] + \kappa e^{\kappa t} x_t \\
&= e^{\kappa t} \sigma dz_t.
\end{aligned} \tag{17.55}
$$

Integrating both sides from t_0 to t one obtains

$$x_t e^{\kappa t} - x_0 = \sigma \int_{t_0}^{t} e^{\kappa s} dz_s. \tag{17.56}$$

Dividing both sides by $e^{\kappa t}$ one gets

$$x_t = x_0 e^{-\kappa t} + \sigma \int_{t_0}^{t} e^{\kappa(s-t)} dz_s. \tag{17.57}$$

In this case ($\theta = 0$) the expected value of x_t is trivial to calculate, because we know that the expectation of an Ito integral is zero:

$$\mathbb{E}[x_t] = x_0 e^{-\kappa t}. \tag{17.58}$$

To calculate the variance, which is going to be given by

$$var(x_t) = \mathbb{E}\left[x_t^2\right] - (\mathbb{E}[x_t])^2,$$

we are going to need the expectation of x_t^2, ie, we need

$$\mathbb{E}\left[x_t^2\right] = \mathbb{E}\left[\left(x_0 e^{-\kappa t} + \sigma \int_{t_0}^{t} e^{\kappa(s-t)} dz_s\right)^2\right]. \tag{17.59}$$

This is where we are going to make use of the Ito isometry that we have discussed in Chapter 2, and which says that, for any 'nice' function f,[2]

$$\mathbb{E}\left[\left[\int [f(x_t, t) dz_t]^2\right] = \int \mathbb{E}\left[f(x_s, s)^2\right] ds. \tag{17.60}$$

The function in question for our application is, of course, $e^{\kappa(s-t)}$, and therefore we get

$$\mathbb{E}\left[\left(\int_{t_0}^{t} \sigma e^{\kappa(s-t)} dz_s\right)^2\right] = \int \sigma^2 e^{2\kappa(s-t)} ds. \tag{17.61}$$

After integrating, we finally have

$$var(x_t) = \mathbb{E}\left[x_t^2\right] - (\mathbb{E}[x_t])^2$$
$$= \sigma^2 \frac{1 - e^{-\kappa t}}{2\kappa}. \tag{17.62}$$

17.6 APPENDIX 17B: DERIVATION OF THE VARIANCE OF A MULTIDIMENSIONAL MEAN-REVERTING PROCESS

Let

$$d\overrightarrow{x}_t = \underline{K}(\overrightarrow{\theta} - \overrightarrow{x}_t) dt + \underline{S} \overrightarrow{dz}. \tag{17.63}$$

Then

$$P(x_t | x_0) = \mathcal{N}(\overrightarrow{\mu}_t, \underline{\Sigma}_t) \tag{17.64}$$

---

[2] Among the 'niceness' conditions there is, of course, integrability. For our applications, we are not overly worried about the other conditions.

with

$$\vec{\mu}_T = e^{-\underline{\mathcal{K}}t}\vec{x}_0 + (\underline{I} - e^{-\underline{\mathcal{K}}t})\vec{\theta}.$$ (17.65)

We derive the expression for Σ_t. We drop the subscript t in what follows. We assume that the reversion speed matrix can be diagonalized, as in

$$\underline{\mathcal{K}} = \left(\underline{G}^{-1}\right)^{\mathrm{T}}\underline{\Lambda}\underline{G}^{\mathrm{T}}.$$ (17.66)

Generalizing the result obtained in Appendix 17A, it is easy to see that the i, j-th element of Σ_t is given by $[\Sigma]_{ij}$:

$$[\Sigma]_{ij} = \left[\int_0^t e^{-\underline{\mathcal{K}}(t-u)}\underline{S}\underline{S}^T (e^{-\underline{\mathcal{K}}(t-u)})^{\mathrm{T}}du\right]_{ij}.$$ (17.67)

Then we have

$$[\Sigma]_{ij} = \left[(G^{-1})^{\mathrm{T}}\int_0^t e^{-\underline{\Lambda}(t-u)}\underline{H}e^{-\underline{\Lambda}(t-u)}du\, G^{-1}\right]_{ij},$$ (17.68)

where we have used the up-and-down theorem (see Appendix 18B, Section 18.10.1), and

$$\underline{H} = \underline{G}^{\mathrm{T}}\underline{S}\,\underline{S}^{\mathrm{T}}\underline{G}$$ (17.69)

Finally we obtain

$$[\Sigma]_{ij} = \left[(G^{-1})^{\mathrm{T}}\left(\int_0^t \left[e^{-(\lambda_i+\lambda_j)u}h_{ij}\right]du\right)G^{-1}\right]$$ (17.70)

and therefore

$$\underline{\Sigma} = (\underline{G}^{-1})^{\mathrm{T}}\underline{M}\,\underline{G}^{-1}$$ (17.71)

with

$$\underline{M} = h_{ij}\frac{1 - e^{-(\lambda_i+\lambda_j)u}}{\lambda_i + \lambda_j}.$$ (17.72)

17.7 APPENDIX 17C: STABILITY OF THE MEAN-REVERTING SYSTEM

Suppose that we have an n-dimensional system with governing equations of the form

$$d\vec{u}_t = \underline{\mathcal{K}}(\vec{\theta} - \vec{u}_t)\, dt + \underline{S}d\vec{z}.$$ (17.73)

We are going to be interested only in the stability of its deterministic behaviour. Therefore we can write

$$\frac{d\vec{u}_t}{dt} = \underline{\mathcal{K}}(\vec{\theta} - \vec{u}_t).$$ (17.74)

Let's carry out the change of variables

$$(\vec{\theta} - \vec{u}_t) \equiv -\vec{x}_t. \tag{17.75}$$

Then we can write

$$\frac{d\vec{x}_t}{dt} = -\underline{K}\vec{x}_t. \tag{17.76}$$

Let's guess the following solution to this differential equation:

$$\vec{x}_t = e^{-\underline{K}t}\vec{x}_0. \tag{17.77}$$

Then substituting we obtain

$$\frac{d\vec{x}_t}{dt} = -\underline{K}e^{-\underline{K}t}\vec{x}_0 \tag{17.78}$$

and therefore our guess is indeed a solution.

Let's now assume that the reversion-speed matrix, $\underline{K}$, can be diagonalized:

$$\underline{K} = \underline{V}\,\underline{\Lambda}\,\underline{V}^{-1}. \tag{17.79}$$

The matrix $\underline{\Lambda}$ contains the eigenvalues:

$$\underline{\Lambda} = \begin{bmatrix} l_1 & 0 & \dots & 0 \\ 0 & l_2 & \dots & 0 \\ \dots & \dots & \dots & \dots \\ 0 & 0 & \dots & l_n \end{bmatrix}. \tag{17.80}$$

Thanks to the 'up-and-down-theorem' (see Appendix 18B, Section 18.10.1), we then know that we can write:

$$e^{-\underline{K}t} = e^{-(\underline{V}\underline{\Lambda}\underline{V}^{-1})t} = \underline{V}e^{-\underline{\Lambda}t}\underline{V}^{-1}$$

$$= \underline{V} \begin{bmatrix} e^{-l_1 t} & 0 & \dots & 0 \\ 0 & e^{-l_2 t} & \dots & 0 \\ \dots & \dots & \dots & \dots \\ 0 & 0 & \dots & e^{-l_n t} \end{bmatrix} \underline{V}^{-1}. \tag{17.81}$$

From this it is immediate to see that

$$\vec{x}_t = e^{-\underline{K}t}\vec{x}_0 = \vec{x}_t = \underline{V} \begin{bmatrix} e^{-l_1 t} & 0 & \dots & 0 \\ 0 & e^{-l_2 t} & \dots & 0 \\ \dots & \dots & \dots & \dots \\ 0 & 0 & \dots & e^{-l_n t} \end{bmatrix} \underline{V}^{-1}\vec{x}_0.$$

Therefore, in order for the system not to explode as t goes to infinity, it is necessary and sufficient that (the real part of) the eigenvalues should be positive.

CHAPTER 18

A General Pricing Framework

Quand on a pas de charcatère, il faut bien se donner une méthode.[1]
Albert Camus, *La Chute*

18.1 THE PURPOSE OF THIS CHAPTER

This chapter is mathematically more heavy-going and more demanding than the rest of the book. It is also very important. In it we offer a precise definition of what an affine model is, and present a general framework to 'solve' almost any affine model the reader may encounter, or may want to develop herself. By 'solving' we mean obtaining the bond prices, the yields, the forward rates, their volatilities, etc.

For some very simple models, the formalism presented in this chapter may seem like a swatting-a-fly-with-a-cannon exercise. However, the advantage of this general approach becomes clear as soon as a model 'grows up' from being pedagogically simple to being realistically complex. Already in the case of the Doubly-Mean-Reverting Vasicek model obtaining by brute force the expression for the A_t^T term is exceedingly tedious. For more complex models, the unreconstructed brute-force approach can quickly take away the will to live. Since we do not have the moral fiber (the 'charcatère' as Camus would say) to hunt for the similar-yet-slightly-different clever tricks and inspired substitutions that can solve each individual model, we give ourselves an all-purpose method, which lacks elegance, but will never let us down.

The added bonus of the general framework presented in this chapter is that it familiarizes the reader with the formalism used in the current literature, which also eschews 'clever tricks' and embraces general solutions.

Furthermore, as some of the modern programming languages[2] naturally allow matrix manipulation and exponentiation, the modeller is spared the tedious task of littering her code with nested summations, and can almost

[1] If one has no personality, one should get oneself a method.
[2] Notably, MatLab.® See the MatLab® function expm() in particular.

directly 'transliterate' the expressions obtained in this chapter into computer code.

A final comment. As I have done elsewhere in the book, I have relegated the derivations to various appendices, so as not to break the flow of the presentation. However, the reader may want to study the derivations with greater care than she probably gives to the other appendices. This is because learning how to derive the equations that solve the general affine model is one of the main topics of the chapter, not a distraction en route to something else. Nonetheless, the impatient or time-pressed reader can skip to Section 18.4, and look up directly all the results. Needless to say, by doing so she may gain a head-start on the methodical reader, but she will not know how to modify one iota of the solving equations.

18.2   WHAT IS AN AFFINE MODEL?

We have spoken at length of affine models so far, but we have not given a clear definition. It is time to put this straight. Following Cheridito, Filipovic and Kimmel (2007, also 2005), we adopt the following definition. (We change their notation to conform with the symbols used in our work.)

Definition *Consider an N-dimensional vector of state variables, $\overrightarrow{x}_t$. We say that a model of the yield curve is affine if it is a specification of bond prices such that:*

1. *the instantaneous short rate, r_t, is given by an affine function of the state variables,*

$$r_t = u_r + g^T \overrightarrow{x}_t \qquad (18.1)$$

   with u_r a constant;

2. *in the real-world measure, $\mathbb{P}$, the state variables follow a diffusion process:*

$$d\overrightarrow{x}_t = \overrightarrow{\mu}^{\mathbb{P}}\left(\overrightarrow{x}_t\right) + \underline{S}\left(\overrightarrow{x}_t\right) d\overrightarrow{z}_t^{\mathbb{P}} \qquad (18.2)$$

   where $\underline{S}$ is an $N \times N$ matrix;

3. *the instantaneous drift (under $\mathbb{P}$) of the state variables is an affine function of the state variables:*

$$\overrightarrow{\mu}^{\mathbb{P}}\left(\overrightarrow{x}_t\right) = \overrightarrow{a}^{\mathbb{P}} + \underline{b}^{\mathbb{P}}\overrightarrow{x}_t \, ; \qquad (18.3)$$

4. *the elements $[cov]_{ij}$ of the instantaneous covariance matrix are given by an affine function of the state variables:*

$$[cov]_{ij} = \left[\underline{S}\left(\overrightarrow{x}_t\right)\underline{S}\left(\overrightarrow{x}_t\right)^T\right]_{ij} = \alpha_{ij} + \beta_{ij}^T \overrightarrow{x}_t \qquad (18.4)$$

   where β_{ij} is an $N \times 1$ vector for each $1 \leq i, j \leq N$;

5. *there exists a probability measure* $\mathbb{Q}$, *equivalent to* $\mathbb{P}$, *such that the state variables follow a diffusion under* $\mathbb{Q}$ *as well:*

$$d\vec{x}_t = \vec{\mu}^{\,\mathbb{Q}}\left(\vec{x}_t\right) + \underline{S}\left(\vec{x}_t\right) d\vec{z}_t^{\,\mathbb{Q}} \tag{18.5}$$

with the instantaneous drift $\vec{\mu}^{\,\mathbb{Q}}\left(\vec{x}_t\right)$ *given by*

$$\vec{\mu}^{\,\mathbb{Q}}\left(\vec{x}_t\right) = \vec{a}^{\,\mathbb{Q}} + \underline{b}^{\mathbb{Q}}\vec{x}_t. \tag{18.6}$$

6. *Prices of discount bonds,* P_t^T, *are given by*

$$P_t^T = \mathbb{E}^{\mathbb{Q}}\big[e^{-\int_t^T r(\vec{x}_s)ds}\big]. \tag{18.7}$$

In point 5 of this definition we referred to $\mathbb{Q}$ as a measure 'equivalent' to $\mathbb{P}$. Leaving all the technical fine print to one side, this means that events deemed impossible (zero-probability) in one measure are also impossible in any equivalent measure.

As we know well by now, even if bond prices are expressed in the last condition as expectations of the exponential of the path of the short rate, in practice they are obtained as solutions to Partial Differential Equations. It is to the obtainment of these solutions that we turn in the rest of this chapter.

18.3 THE GENERAL STRATEGY

We have n state variables, $x_t^1, x_t^2, \ldots, x_t^n$, which follow a mean-reverting process of the form

$$d\vec{x}_t = \underline{K}\left(\vec{\theta} - \vec{x}_t\right)dt + \underline{S}d\vec{z}_t. \tag{18.8}$$

(In what follows we will often omit the underscore under matrices.)

In this equation we assume that the reversion-speed matrix, K, should be invertible, and that all the Brownian shocks, dz_t^i, $i = 1, 2, \ldots n$ should be independent:

$$\mathbb{E}\left[dz_t^i dz_t^j\right] = \delta_{ij}dt. \tag{18.9}$$

(As usual, the symbol δ_{ij} – the Kroeneker delta – signifies 1 if $i = j$, and 0 otherwise.)

We are now going to require that the short rate should be given by a linear combination (or, rather, should be an affine function of) the state variables:

$$r_t = u_r + \vec{g}^{\,\mathrm{T}}\vec{x}_t. \tag{18.10}$$

Recall that Equation (18.10) does not reflect some deep mathematical or financial theorem. In general, given an arbitrary vector of state variables it is not obvious that the short rate should be an affine function of the same variables.[3]

---

[3] A priori, it is not even obvious that an arbitrary set of variables should fully span the variability of the short rate, let alone do so in an affine manner.

However, an affine model is defined exactly as a model for which Equation (18.10) holds true. So, Equation (18.10) is really a definition.

A couple of words of clarification: $\vec{g}$ is some (column) vector, so $\vec{g}^{\mathrm{T}}$ is a row vector:

$$\vec{g}^{\mathrm{T}} = [g_1, g_2, \ldots, g_n].$$ (18.11)

When we multiply (using the usual matrix multiplication rule) the row vector, $\vec{g}^{\mathrm{T}}$, by the state-variable column vector, $\vec{x}_t$, we just get a number. Which is just as well, because the left-hand side is a scalar (the short rate) and we are adding a scalar (u_r) to the inner product, $\vec{g}^{\mathrm{T}}\vec{x}_t$.[4]

Given these assumptions, we know from the previous chapter that the bond price, $P_t^T = P(\tau)$, will be given by in the rest of the chapter we will drop the underscore for matrices, unless required for clarity.

$$P_t^T = e^{A_t^T + \left(\vec{B}_t^T\right)^{\mathrm{T}}\vec{x}_t},$$ (18.12)

where the quantities A_t^T and $\vec{B}_t^T$ obey the following couple of Ordinary Differential Equations:

$$\frac{dA(\tau)}{d\tau} = -u_r + \vec{B}^{\mathrm{T}}\mathcal{K}\vec{\theta} + \frac{1}{2}\vec{B}^{\mathrm{T}}SS^{\mathrm{T}}\vec{B}$$ (18.13)

$$\frac{d\vec{B}(\tau)}{d\tau} = -\vec{g} - \mathcal{K}^{\mathrm{T}}\vec{B}$$ (18.14)

to be solved with the initial conditions

$$A(0) = 0$$ (18.15)

$$\vec{B}(0) = \vec{0}.$$ (18.16)

Where do these equations come from? We know where they come from because in Chapter 16 we climbed Mount Fuji (once). Indeed, with more factors (as long as each of then follows a Brownian diffusion) the reasoning is exactly the same as in Chapter 16, even if algebraically more tedious: we neutralize the sources of uncertainty (using as many bonds as required); we recognize that the portfolio is now risk-less; we argue that, being risk-less, it must earn the risk-less rate of return; we derive a Partial Differential Equation; we guess a solution; we check that it actually works; etc.

Now, I have never climbed Mount Fuji, but, from the postcards I have seen, it does not look terribly arduous to climb (my apologies to Japanese climbers if this is not the case). The point here is that obtaining the Partial Differential Equation in the multifactor case does not require climbing the

---

[4] The quantity u_r need not be a constant. A function of time would also work here. In general, we caution against an overliberal introduction of time dependence in the quantity u_r. Sometimes, however, a principled and restrained assignment of a simple time dependence *can* be useful to describe over the short horizon a highly structured pattern of expectations of monetary interventions.

Matterhorn (which I have also not climbed, but which, from other postcards I have seen, looks a lot more difficult); it just is a matter of slogging one's way up a mountain which may be two or three times as tall as Mount Fuji, but which presents exactly the same degree and type of climbing difficulty as its one-factor version.

Since we are talking about Mount Fuji $\times$ N (not about the Matterhorn), it is for once fair for me to set as the proverbial exercise to the reader to derive Equations (18.13) to (18.16) in a multifactor case of her choice.

Exercise 44 *Derive Equations (18.13) to (18.16).*

So much for the constitutive equations. But how do we solve them? This is shown in Appendix 18A.

18.4 SUMMARY OF THE EQUATIONS DERIVED IN APPENDIX 18A

Take a process for a vector, $\vec{x}_t$, of generic state variables

$$d\vec{x}_t = \mathcal{K}\left(\vec{\theta} - \vec{x}_t\right)dt + Sd\vec{z}_t \tag{18.17}$$

such that

$$r_t = u_r + \vec{g}^T\vec{x}_t. \tag{18.18}$$

Let also the reversion-speed matrix, $\mathcal{K}$, be invertible, and let it admit diagonalization:

$$\mathcal{K} = L\mathcal{L}L^{-1} \tag{18.19}$$

with its eigenvalues, l_{ii}, on the diagonal of the matrix $\mathcal{L}$,

$$\mathcal{L} = diag\left[l_{ii}\right], \tag{18.20}$$

and its eigenvectors in the matrix L.

Then we show in Appendix 18A of this chapter that the bond price, $P_t^T = P(\tau)$, is given by

$$P_t^T = e^{A_t^T + \left(\vec{B}_t^T\right)^T\vec{x}_t} \tag{18.21}$$

with A_t^T and $\left(\vec{B}_t^T\right)^T$ given by

$$\vec{B}(\tau) = \left(e^{-\mathcal{K}^T\tau} - I_n\right)\left(\mathcal{K}^T\right)^{-1}\vec{g} \tag{18.22}$$

$$\left(\vec{B}_t^T\right)^T = \vec{g}^T\mathcal{K}^{-1}\left[e^{-\mathcal{K}\tau} - I_n\right] \tag{18.23}$$

$$A(\tau) = Int_1 + Int_2 + Int_3 \tag{18.24}$$

and with

$$Int_1 = -u_r T \tag{18.25}$$

$$Int_2 = \vec{g}^{\mathrm{T}} \left(L\mathcal{L}^{-1} D\left(T\right) \mathcal{L}L^{-1} \vec{\theta} - \vec{\theta} \, T \right) \tag{18.26}$$

$$Int_3 = Int_3^a + Int_3^b + Int_3^c + Int_3^d \tag{18.27}$$

$$Int_3^a = \frac{1}{2} \vec{g}^{\mathrm{T}} \mathcal{K}^{-1} L F\left(T\right) \mathcal{L}^{-1} L^{\mathrm{T}} \vec{g} \tag{18.28}$$

$$Int_3^b = -\frac{1}{2} \vec{g}^{\mathrm{T}} \mathcal{K}^{-1} C \left(L^{-1}\right)^{\mathrm{T}} D\left(T\right) \mathcal{L}^{-1} L^{\mathrm{T}} \vec{g} \tag{18.29}$$

$$Int_3^c = -\frac{1}{2} \vec{g}^{\mathrm{T}} \mathcal{K}^{-1} L D\left(T\right) L^{-1} C \left(\mathcal{K}^{\mathrm{T}}\right)^{-1} \vec{g} \tag{18.30}$$

$$Int_3^d = \frac{1}{2} \vec{g}^{\mathrm{T}} \mathcal{K}^{-1} C \left(\mathcal{K}^{\mathrm{T}}\right)^{-1} \vec{g} \, T \tag{18.31}$$

with $M = L^{-1} C \left(L^{-1}\right)^{\mathrm{T}}$, $F = \left[f_{ij} \right]_n$, and

$$f_{ij} = m_{ij} \frac{1 - e^{\left(l_{ii} + l_{jj}\right)T}}{l_{ii} + l_{jj}} \tag{18.32}$$

$$D\left(T\right) = \operatorname{diag} \left[\frac{1 - e^{l_{ii}T}}{l_{ii}} \right]_n \tag{18.33}$$

$$C = SS^{\mathrm{T}}. \tag{18.34}$$

That's it. If one uses a computer package (such as MatLab®) that allows for matrix manipulation and matrix exponentiation, then virtually any affine model (with an invertible and diagonalizable reversion-speed matrix $\mathcal{K}$) can be coded in a few lines. Once this is done, we can obtain from our chosen model anything we want.

18.5   VARIOUS ADDITIONAL RESULTS

Once the expression for the bond price has been obtained, various important results follow without effort.

18.5.1   Expression for the Yield

Since

$$y_t^T = -\frac{1}{T} \log P_t^T \tag{18.35}$$

and

$$P_t^T = e^{A_t^T + \left(\vec{B_t^T}\right)^{\mathrm{T}} \vec{x}_t} \tag{18.36}$$

it immediately follows that

$$y_t^T = \alpha_t^T + \left(\overrightarrow{\beta_t^T}\right)^{\mathrm{T}} \overrightarrow{x}_t \tag{18.37}$$

with

$$\alpha_t^T = -\frac{1}{T} \log A_t^T \tag{18.38}$$

$$\left(\overrightarrow{\beta_t^T}\right)^{\mathrm{T}} = -\frac{1}{T} \log \left(\overrightarrow{B_t^T}\right)^{\mathrm{T}}. \tag{18.39}$$

18.5.2 Expression for the Yield Covariance Matrix and the Yield Volatilities

Since we have

$$y_t^T = \alpha_t^T + \left(\overrightarrow{\beta_t^T}\right)^{\mathrm{T}} \overrightarrow{x}_t \tag{18.40}$$

and since we are looking at a constant-maturity yield[5], it follows with similar ease that

$$dy_t^T = \left(\overrightarrow{\beta_t^T}\right)^{\mathrm{T}} d\overrightarrow{x}_t. \tag{18.41}$$

Substituting the expression for $d\overrightarrow{x}_t$, $d\overrightarrow{x}_t = \mathcal{K}(\overrightarrow{\theta} - \overrightarrow{x}_t)dt + Sd\overrightarrow{z}_t$, and neglecting irrelevant terms in dt, we have

$$dy_t^T = \left(\overrightarrow{\beta_t^T}\right)^{\mathrm{T}} Sd\overrightarrow{z}_t. \tag{18.42}$$

What about the covariance matrix between changes in yields? Each element of the covariance matrix is given by an expectation of the type $\mathbb{E}\left[dy_t^{T_i} dy_t^{T_j}\right]$. This can be written compactly as follows. First collect all the increments in yields in a vector, $\overrightarrow{dy}_t$:

$$\overrightarrow{dy}_t = \begin{bmatrix} dy_t^1 \\ dy_t^2 \\ \dots \\ dy_t^n \end{bmatrix}, \tag{18.43}$$

---

[5] This means that $T - t$ does not change, and therefore the derivatives with respect to time of α_t^T and $\left(\overrightarrow{\beta_t^T}\right)^{\mathrm{T}}$ are zero.

where each dy_t^i is of the form in Equation (18.41). Define β^T as the matrix built by stacking the n row vectors $\left(\vec{\beta}_t^{T_i}\right)^T$. Then the full covariance matrix is then given by the expectation $\mathbb{E}\left[\vec{dy}_t\left(d\vec{y}_t\right)^T\right]$, ie, by

$$\mathbb{E}\left[\vec{dy}_t\left(d\vec{y}_t\right)^T\right] = \underbrace{(\beta)^T\underline{S}\vec{dz}_t}_{\vec{dy}_t}\,\underbrace{\vec{dz}_t^T\underline{S}^T\beta}_{(\vec{dy}_t)^T}$$

$$= (\beta)^T\underline{C}\,\beta\,dt. \tag{18.44}$$

with $\underline{C}$ as before given by

$$\underline{C} = \underline{S}\,\underline{S}^T.$$

Therefore we have for the covariance matrix between changes in yields $y_t^{T_i}$, $i = 1, 2, \ldots, n$:

$$\underline{cov}_y = \mathbb{E}\left[\vec{dy}_t\left(d\vec{y}_t\right)^T\right] = \left(\underline{\beta}\right)^T\underline{C}\,\underline{\beta}_t. \tag{18.45}$$

The volatilities, $\sigma_{y_t^{T_j}}$, of the T_j-maturity yield are then simply given by the square roots of the elements on the diagonal of the covariance matrix, cov_y.

18.5.3 Expression for the Volatility of the Instantaneous Forward Rates

The instantaneous forward rate, f_t^T, is given by

$$f_t^T = -\frac{\partial}{\partial T}\log P_t^T. \tag{18.46}$$

Therefore

$$f_t^T = -\frac{\partial}{\partial T}\left[A_t^T + \left(\vec{B}_t^T\right)^T\vec{x}_t\right] \tag{18.47}$$

and

$$df_t^T = -\frac{\partial}{\partial T}\left[\left(\vec{B}_t^T\right)^T d\vec{x}_t\right]$$

$$= -\frac{\partial}{\partial T}\left[\left(\vec{B}_t^T\right)^T \underline{S}d\vec{z}_t\right] = \left(\vec{b}_t^T\right)^T \underline{S}d\vec{z}_t \tag{18.48}$$

with

$$\left(\vec{b}_t^T\right)^T = -\frac{\partial\left(\vec{B}_t^T\right)^T}{\partial T}. \tag{18.49}$$

Now, $\vec{B}^{\mathrm{T}} = \vec{g}^{\mathrm{T}} \underline{K}^{-1} \left[e^{-\underline{K}\tau} - I \right]$ and therefore

$$-\frac{\partial \left(\vec{B}_t^T \right)^{\mathrm{T}}}{\partial T} = -\frac{\partial}{\partial T} \left(\vec{g}^{\mathrm{T}} \underline{K}^{-1} \left[e^{-\underline{K}T} - I \right] \right)$$

$$= -\frac{\partial}{\partial T} \left(\vec{g}^{\mathrm{T}} \underline{K}^{-1} e^{-\underline{K}T} \right) = -\vec{g}^{\mathrm{T}} \underline{K}^{-1} \frac{\partial}{\partial T} \left(e^{-\underline{K}T} \right)$$

$$= \vec{g}^{\mathrm{T}} \underline{K}^{-1} \underline{K} e^{-\underline{K}T} = \vec{g}^{\mathrm{T}} e^{-\underline{K}\tau}. \tag{18.50}$$

So we have obtained that

$$\left(\vec{b_t^T} \right)^{\mathrm{T}} = \vec{g}^{\mathrm{T}} \underline{K}^{-1} \underline{K} e^{-\underline{K}T} = \vec{g}^{\mathrm{T}} e^{-\underline{K}\tau},$$

and therefore the volatility of the forward rate, $\sigma_{f_\tau^{\mathrm{T}}}$, is given by

$$\sigma_{f_\tau^{\mathrm{T}}} = \vec{g}^{\mathrm{T}} e^{-\underline{K}\tau} \underline{S} \vec{dz}_\tau.$$

From this we can easily calculate the covariance matrix between (changes in) instantaneous forward rates. Proceeding as before, we have to calculate $\mathbb{E}[d\vec{f}_t (d\vec{f}_t)^{\mathrm{T}}]$:

$$\mathbb{E} \left[d\vec{f}_t (d\vec{f}_t)^{\mathrm{T}} \right] = \mathbb{E} \left[\underline{b}^{\mathrm{T}} \underline{S} d\vec{z}_t \left(d\vec{z}_t \right)^{\mathrm{T}} \underline{S}^{\mathrm{T}} \underline{b} \right]$$

$$= \underline{b}^{\mathrm{T}} \underline{S} \, \underline{S}^T \vec{b} = \underline{b}^{\mathrm{T}} C \underline{b}, \tag{18.51}$$

with $\underline{b}^{\mathrm{T}}$ the matrix obtained by stacking the n row vectors $(b_t^{Ti})^T$, and

$$\underline{C} = \underline{S}\,\underline{S}^T. \tag{18.52}$$

As before, the forward-rate volatilities are given by the square roots of the elements on the diagonal of the covariance matrix.

18.6 DERIVATION OF THE MEAN AND VARIANCE OF THE STATE VARIABLES

One of the great advantages of using an affine process for the state variables, as in

$$d\vec{x}_t = \underline{K} \left(\vec{\theta} - \vec{x}_t \right) dt + \underline{S} \vec{dz} \tag{18.53}$$

is that their distribution at a future time, T, given the state vector 'today', is known to be (conditionally) Gaussian:

$$P \left(\vec{x}_T | \vec{x}_0 \right) = \mathcal{N} \left(\vec{\mu}_T, \underline{\Sigma}_T \right). \tag{18.54}$$

We need to find an expression for the expectation vector, $\vec{\mu}_T$, and the (co)variance matrix, $\underline{\Sigma}_T$.

By proceeding exactly as we did to solve for the vector B (ie, by considering the associated homogeneous ODE first, by finding a particular solution for the full ODE then, and, finally, by imposing the initial conditions, $\overrightarrow{x}(0) = \overrightarrow{x}_0$), it is easy to obtain the expectation:

$$\overrightarrow{\mu}_T = e^{-\underline{\underline{K}}T}\overrightarrow{x}_0 + \left(\underline{\underline{I}} - e^{-\underline{\underline{K}}T}\right)\overrightarrow{\theta}. \tag{18.55}$$

Exercise 45 *Derive Equation (18.55).*

This makes perfect sense: we can interpret Equation (18.55) as telling us that the future, time-T, expected values for the state variables are a linear combination of their values today, $\overrightarrow{x}_0$, and their long-term reversion levels, $\overrightarrow{\theta}$, with weights $e^{-\underline{\underline{K}}T}$ and $\left(\underline{\underline{I}} - e^{-\underline{\underline{K}}T}\right)$, respectively. Noting that $e^{-\underline{\underline{K}}T}$ goes to $\underline{\underline{I}}$ as T goes to zero, we see that this is just what we need to satisfy the initial conditions.

Next we derive the expression for Σ_T. We drop the subscript T in what follows.

The matrix $\underline{\underline{\Sigma}}$ is given by

$$\underline{\underline{\Sigma}} = \int_0^T e^{-\underline{\underline{K}}(T-u)}\underline{\underline{S}}\,\underline{\underline{S}}^{\mathrm{T}}\left(e^{-\underline{\underline{K}}(T-u)}\right)^{\mathrm{T}} du. \tag{18.56}$$

Exercise 46 *Why?*

The i, jth element of $\underline{\underline{\Sigma}}$ is given by $[\Sigma]_{ij}$:

$$[\Sigma]_{ij} = \left[\int_0^T e^{-\underline{\underline{K}}(T-u)}\underline{\underline{S}}\,\underline{\underline{S}}^{\mathrm{T}}\left(e^{-\underline{\underline{K}}(T-u)}\right)^{\mathrm{T}} du\right]_{ij}. \tag{18.57}$$

Then, after making use of the orthogonalization of $\underline{\underline{K}}$ (see Equation (18.19)), we have

$$[\underline{\underline{\Sigma}}] = \left[\underline{\underline{L}}\left(\int_0^T e^{-\underline{\underline{\mathcal{L}}}\tau}\underline{\underline{H}}e^{-\underline{\underline{\mathcal{L}}}\tau} d\tau\right)\underline{\underline{L}}^{\mathrm{T}}\right], \tag{18.58}$$

where we have used the up-and-down theorem (see Appendix 18B, Section 18.10.1), and

$$\underline{\underline{H}} = \underline{\underline{L}}^{-1}\underline{\underline{C}}\left(\underline{\underline{L}}^{-1}\right)^{\mathrm{T}}, \tag{18.59}$$

with

$$\underline{\underline{C}} = \underline{\underline{S}}\,\underline{\underline{S}}^{\mathrm{T}}. \tag{18.60}$$

Consider the element $e^{-(l_i+l_j)}h_{ij}$.

The integral $\int_0^T \left[e^{-(l_i+l_j)u} h_{ij} \right] du$ just gives

$$\int_0^T \left[e^{-(l_i+l_j)u} h_{ij} \right] du = \left[\int_0^T e^{-(l_i+l_j)u} du \right] h_{ij} = \frac{1 - e^{-(l_i+l_j)T}}{l_i + l_j} h_{ij}.$$

Therefore it follows that

$$\underline{\Sigma} = LML^{\mathrm{T}}, \tag{18.61}$$

with

$$[M]_{ij} = \frac{1 - e^{-(l_i+l_j)T}}{l_i + l_j} h_{ij}. \tag{18.62}$$

18.7 NOW WE HAVE SOLVED (ALMOST) ANY AFFINE MODEL

The effort put in the derivations presented earlier can finally pay its dividends. As long as the reversion speed matrix, $\mathcal{K}$, is invertible and diagonalizable, we can take virtually any affine model, with any number of factors, linked together via as complex a set of affine relationships as we want, and, by making use of the results presented earlier, we always have at hand a 'solution' for our model. By a 'solution', I don't just mean an analytic expression for the bond price, but also expressions for the model yield covariance matrix, for the model term structure of yield or forward-rate volatilities, for the model-implied convexity or correlation, etc. In short, we have all we need to understand how the model behaves, to calibrate the model, and extract from the model all the answers we may wish about things we do not know. All we have to do to reap this bounty is to recast the model at hand into the framework presented in the preceding sections. This is a mechanical and simple task of 'parameter translation'.

How to carry how this task is shown in detail in the rest of this section. It provides a detailed translation between the parameters that appears in models such as, say, the Doubly-Mean-Reverting Vasicek or the Stochastic-Market-Price-of-Risk model and the parameters that feature in the general formalism presented earlier. As usual, we start from the simple and gradually build up to the complex.

18.7.1 Simple Vasicek

In this case we have

$$dr_t = \kappa \left(\theta - r_t \right) dt + \sigma_r dz_t, \tag{18.63}$$

and therefore trivially

$$\mathcal{K} = \kappa \tag{18.64}$$

$$x(0) = r_0 \tag{18.65}$$

$$S = \sigma_r \tag{18.66}$$

$$\overrightarrow{\theta} = \theta$$

$$u_r = 0, \overrightarrow{g}^{\mathrm{T}} = 1. \tag{18.67}$$

The cannon has succeeded in swatting the first fly. Now things become more interesting.

18.7.2   The Doubly-Mean-Reverting Vasicek Model

As discussed in Chapter 30, the doubly-mean-reverting Vasicek model has the form

$$dr_t = \kappa \left(\theta_t - r_t\right) dt + \sigma_r dw_r \tag{18.68}$$

$$d\theta_t = \alpha \left(\beta - \theta_t\right) dt + \sigma_\theta dw_\theta \tag{18.69}$$

$$\mathbb{E}\left[dw_r dw_\theta\right] = \rho dt. \tag{18.70}$$

To cast it into the mould of the general affine formulation presented in this chapter, we set

$$\overrightarrow{x} = \begin{bmatrix} \theta_t \\ r_t \end{bmatrix}. \tag{18.71}$$

Then we have

$$\mathcal{K} = \begin{bmatrix} \alpha & 0 \\ -\kappa & \kappa \end{bmatrix} \tag{18.72}$$

$$\overrightarrow{\theta} = \begin{bmatrix} \beta \\ \beta \end{bmatrix} \tag{18.73}$$

$$S = \begin{bmatrix} s_{11} & 0 \\ s_{21} & s_{22} \end{bmatrix} \tag{18.74}$$

with

$$s_{11} = \sigma_\theta \tag{18.75}$$

$$s_{21}^2 + s_{22}^2 = \sigma_r^2 \tag{18.76}$$

$$\rho = \frac{s_{11}s_{21}}{\sigma_\theta \sigma_r} = \frac{\sigma_\theta s_{21}}{\sigma_\theta \sigma_r} \implies s_{21} = \sigma_r \rho \tag{18.77}$$

and therefore

$$s_{22}^2 = \sigma_r^2 - \sigma_r^2 \rho^2 = \sigma_r^2 \left(1 - \rho^2\right) \implies s_{22} = \sigma_r \sqrt{\left(1 - \rho^2\right)}. \tag{18.78}$$

As for the vector $\overrightarrow{g}^T$ and the scalar u_r, we clearly have

$$\overrightarrow{g}^T = [0, 1] \tag{18.79}$$
$$u_r = 0.$$

18.7.3 The Trebly-Mean-Reverting Vasicek Model

Let

$$dr_t = \kappa_r [R_t - r_t] dt + \sigma_r dz_t^r \tag{18.80}$$
$$dR_t = \kappa_R [L_t - R_t] dt + \sigma_R dz_t^R \tag{18.81}$$
$$dL_t = \kappa_L [L_\infty - L_t] dt + \sigma_L dz_t^L \tag{18.82}$$
$$E[drdL] = \rho_{rL} \tag{18.83}$$
$$E[drdR] = \rho_{rR} \tag{18.84}$$
$$E[dRdL] = \rho_{RL}. \tag{18.85}$$

Then we have

$$\overrightarrow{x}_t = \begin{bmatrix} L_t \\ R_t \\ r_t \end{bmatrix}$$

$$\mathcal{K} = \begin{bmatrix} \kappa_L & 0 & 0 \\ -\kappa_R & \kappa_R & 0 \\ 0 & -\kappa_r & \kappa_r \end{bmatrix} \tag{18.86}$$

$$\overrightarrow{\theta} = \begin{bmatrix} L_\infty \\ L_\infty \\ L_\infty \end{bmatrix} \tag{18.87}$$

$$\sigma_L^2 = s_{11}^2 + s_{12}^2 + s_{13}^2 \tag{18.88}$$
$$\sigma_R^2 = s_{21}^2 + s_{22}^2 + s_{23}^2 \tag{18.89}$$
$$\sigma_r^2 = s_{31}^2 + s_{32}^2 + s_{33}^2 \tag{18.90}$$
$$\rho_{RL} = \frac{s_{11}s_{21} + s_{12}s_{22} + s_{13}s_{23}}{\sigma_R \sigma_L} \tag{18.91}$$
$$\rho_{rL} = \frac{s_{11}s_{31} + s_{12}s_{32} + s_{13}s_{33}}{\sigma_r \sigma_L} \tag{18.92}$$
$$\rho_{rR} = \frac{s_{21}s_{31} + s_{22}s_{32} + s_{23}s_{33}}{\sigma_r \sigma_R}. \tag{18.93}$$

The system can be recursively solved by choosing

$$S = \begin{bmatrix} s_{11} & 0 & 0 \\ s_{21} & s_{22} & 0 \\ s_{31} & s_{32} & s_{33} \end{bmatrix} \tag{18.94}$$

and solving iteratively:

$$\sigma_L^2 = s_{11}^2 \tag{18.95}$$

$$\sigma_R^2 = s_{21}^2 + s_{22}^2 \tag{18.96}$$

$$\sigma_r^2 = s_{31}^2 + s_{32}^2 + s_{33}^2 \tag{18.97}$$

$$\rho_{RL} = \frac{s_{11}s_{21}}{\sqrt{\sigma_R\sigma_L}} \tag{18.98}$$

$$\rho_{rL} = \frac{s_{11}s_{31}}{\sqrt{\sigma_r\sigma_L}} \tag{18.99}$$

$$\rho_{rR} = \frac{s_{21}s_{31} + s_{22}s_{32}}{\sqrt{\sigma_r\sigma_R}}. \tag{18.100}$$

Finally,

$$u_r = 0 \tag{18.101}$$

$$\vec{g}^{\,\mathrm{T}} = [0, 0, 1]. \tag{18.102}$$

18.7.4   The Stochastic-Market-Price-of-Risk Model

Let the model be

$$dr_t = \kappa_r \left(\theta_t - r_t \right) dt + \sigma_r dz_t^r \tag{18.103}$$

$$
\begin{aligned}
d\theta_t &= \kappa_\theta \left(\Theta^\infty - \theta_t \right) dt + \lambda_t^\theta \sigma^\theta dt + \sigma^\theta dz_t^\theta \\
&= \left[\kappa_\theta \Theta^\infty - \kappa_\theta \theta_t + \lambda_t^\theta \sigma^\theta \right] dt + \sigma^\theta dz_t^\theta
\end{aligned} \tag{18.104}
$$

$$d\lambda_t^\theta = \kappa_\lambda \left(\Lambda^\infty - \lambda_t^\theta \right) dt + \sigma^\lambda dz_t^\lambda \tag{18.105}$$

with

$$E\left[dr d\theta \right] = \rho_{r\theta} \tag{18.106}$$

$$E\left[dr d\lambda \right] = \rho_{r\lambda} \tag{18.107}$$

$$E\left[d\theta d\lambda \right] = \rho_{\theta\lambda}. \tag{18.108}$$

Then, after numbering the state variables as $\lambda_t^\theta = x_t^1$, $\theta_t = x_2^t$ and $r_t = x_3^t$, one has

$$\mathcal{K} = \begin{bmatrix} \kappa_\lambda & 0 & 0 \\ -\sigma_\theta & \kappa_\theta & 0 \\ 0 & -\kappa_r & \kappa_r \end{bmatrix} \tag{18.109}$$

$$\vec{\theta} = \begin{bmatrix} \Lambda^\infty \\ \Theta^\infty + \frac{\sigma_\theta \Lambda^\infty}{\kappa_\theta} \\ \Theta^\infty + \frac{\sigma_\theta \Lambda^\infty}{\kappa_\theta} \end{bmatrix}. \tag{18.110}$$

The affine transformation from the state variables to the short rate is given by

$$u_r = 0 \tag{18.111}$$

$$\overrightarrow{g}^{\mathrm{T}} = [0, 0, 1]. \tag{18.112}$$

For the matrix S one can follow the same procedure shown above for the Trebly-Mean-Reverting Affine model. Indeed, one obtains

$$S = \begin{bmatrix} s_{11} & 0 & 0 \\ s_{21} & s_{22} & 0 \\ s_{31} & s_{32} & s_{33} \end{bmatrix}, \tag{18.113}$$

with

$$s_{11} = \sigma_\lambda \tag{18.114}$$

$$s_{21} = \sigma_\theta \rho_{\lambda\theta} \tag{18.115}$$

$$s_{22} = \sigma_\theta \sqrt{1 - \rho_{\lambda\theta}^2} \tag{18.116}$$

$$s_{31} = \sigma_r \rho_{\lambda r} \tag{18.117}$$

$$s_{32} = \sigma_r \frac{\rho_{\theta r} - \rho_{\lambda\theta}\rho_{\lambda r}}{\sqrt{1 - \rho_{\lambda\theta}^2}} \tag{18.118}$$

$$s_{33} = \sigma_r \sqrt{1 - \rho_{\lambda r}^2 - \frac{(\rho_{\theta r} - \rho_{\lambda\theta}\rho_{\lambda r})^2}{1 - \rho_{\lambda\theta}^2}}. \tag{18.119}$$

18.8 APPENDIX 18A: SOLVING FOR $\overrightarrow{B}(\tau)$ AND $A(\tau)$

Recall that for any affine model, the bond price, $P_t^T = P(\tau)$, will be given by

$$P_t^T = e^{A_t^T + \left(\overrightarrow{B}_t^T\right)^{\mathrm{T}} \overrightarrow{x}_t} \tag{18.120}$$

where the quantities A_t^T and $\overrightarrow{B}_t^T$ obey the following couple of Ordinary Differential Equations:

$$\frac{dA(\tau)}{d\tau} = -u_r + \overrightarrow{B}^{\mathrm{T}} K \overrightarrow{\theta} + \frac{1}{2}\overrightarrow{B}^{\mathrm{T}} S S^{\mathrm{T}} \overrightarrow{B} \tag{18.121}$$

and

$$\frac{d\overrightarrow{B}(\tau)}{d\tau} = -\overrightarrow{g} - K^{\mathrm{T}}\overrightarrow{B}, \tag{18.122}$$

to be solved with the initial conditions

$$A(0) = 0 \tag{18.123}$$

$$\overrightarrow{B}(0) = \overrightarrow{0}. \tag{18.124}$$

The strategy is simple: first we solve the Ordinary Differential Equation for $\vec{B}(\tau)$; then we substitute into Equation (18.13); finally we solve the Ordinary Differential Equation for $A(\tau)$. I show how this is done in detail in what follows.

18.8.1   Solving the ODE for $\vec{B}(\tau)$

The ODE to solve is the following:

$$\frac{d\vec{B}(\tau)}{d\tau} = -\vec{g} - \mathcal{K}^{\mathrm{T}}\vec{B}. \tag{18.125}$$

Equation (18.14) is an inhomogeneous Ordinary Differential Equation (it is inhomogeneous because it has the term $-\vec{g}$). We know[6] that a general solution of this inhomogeneous Ordinary Differential Equation is given by the sum of the solution of the associated homogeneous Ordinary Differential Equation, and any one solution of the inhomogeneous one. (The associated homogeneous Ordinary Differential Equation, you will recall, is the Ordinary Differential Equation obtained by setting the inhomogeneous term, $-\vec{g}$, to zero.)

Solving the Associated Homogeneous ODE

The associated homogeneous Ordinary Differential Equation is given by

$$\frac{d\vec{B}_{\mathrm{hom}}(\tau)}{d\tau} = -\mathcal{K}^{\mathrm{T}}\vec{B}_{\mathrm{hom}}. \tag{18.126}$$

Equation (18.126) screams *"exponential solution"*, because it says that the time derivative of a function is equal to the function itself, times a constant. However, a moment's thought suggests that, if we multiply the exponential[7] by a constant (non–time-dependent) vector, $\vec{H}$, the equation will still be satisfied. Therefore we posit

$$\vec{B}_{\mathrm{hom}} = e^{-\mathcal{K}^{\mathrm{T}}\tau}\vec{H}. \tag{18.127}$$

Indeed, as we take the derivative, we get

$$\frac{d\vec{B}_{\mathrm{hom}}(\tau)}{d\tau} = \frac{d}{d\tau}e^{-\mathcal{K}^{\mathrm{T}}\tau}\vec{H} = -\mathcal{K}^{\mathrm{T}}e^{-\mathcal{K}^{\mathrm{T}}\tau}\vec{H} = -\mathcal{K}^{\mathrm{T}}\vec{B}_{\mathrm{hom}}. \tag{18.128}$$

(Another way to see that we have to multiply $e^{-\mathcal{K}^{\mathrm{T}}\tau}$ by a vector is to notice that $e^{-\mathcal{K}^{\mathrm{T}}\tau}$ is a $[n \times n]$ matrix, which begs to be multiplied by an $[n \times 1]$ vector if the result is to be equated to the left-hand side, which is an $[n \times 1]$ vector.)

---

[6] See, eg, Riley, Hobson and Bence (2006), Chapter 15 in particular, p. 490 and passim.

[7] What we are dealing with here is, of course, the exponent of a matrix. If the reader needs some refreshing of this concept, Appendix 18B presents the fundamental definitions and the results needed for the manipulations ahead.

Finding a Special Solution

Now we have to find any special solution to the inhomogeneous Equation (18.14). Going for the line of least resistance, let's try $\vec{B} = \vec{C}$, where $\vec{C}$ is a constant vector. With this inspired guess we have

$$\frac{d\vec{B}}{d\tau} = \frac{d\vec{C}}{d\tau} = 0 \tag{18.129}$$

and therefore

$$\frac{d\vec{B}(\tau)}{d\tau} = -\vec{g} - \mathcal{K}^{\mathrm{T}}\vec{B} \implies 0 = -\vec{g} - \mathcal{K}^{\mathrm{T}}\vec{C}. \tag{18.130}$$

This means that

$$-\vec{g} = \mathcal{K}^{\mathrm{T}}\vec{C} \tag{18.131}$$

$$\implies \vec{C} = -\left(\mathcal{K}^{\mathrm{T}}\right)^{-1}\vec{g}. \tag{18.132}$$

The General Solution

As advertised, the general solution will be given by the sum of the homogeneous solution plus the special solution we just found. Therefore we get

$$\vec{B}(\tau) = \vec{B}_{\mathrm{hom}}(\tau) + \vec{C}$$
$$= e^{-\mathcal{K}^{\mathrm{T}}\tau}\vec{H} - \left(\mathcal{K}^{\mathrm{T}}\right)^{-1}\vec{g}. \tag{18.133}$$

Imposing the Initial Condition

Finally we have to determine the time-independent vector, $\vec{H}$, that still appears in our general solution. We can do so by imposing Equation (18.16), ie, that $\vec{B}(0) = 0$. We get

$$\vec{B}(0) = e^{-\mathcal{K}^{\mathrm{T}}\tau}\vec{H} - \left(\mathcal{K}^{\mathrm{T}}\right)^{-1}\vec{g} = \vec{H} - \left(\mathcal{K}^{\mathrm{T}}\right)^{-1}\vec{g} = \vec{0} \tag{18.134}$$

and therefore

$$\vec{H} = \left(\mathcal{K}^{\mathrm{T}}\right)^{-1}\vec{g}. \tag{18.135}$$

Putting the pieces together we get

$$\vec{B}(\tau) = e^{-\mathcal{K}^{T}\tau}\left(\mathcal{K}^{\mathrm{T}}\right)^{-1}\vec{g} - \left(\mathcal{K}^{\mathrm{T}}\right)^{-1}\vec{g}$$
$$= \left(e^{-\mathcal{K}^{\mathrm{T}}\tau} - I_n\right)\left(\mathcal{K}^{\mathrm{T}}\right)^{-1}\vec{g}. \tag{18.136}$$

Exercise 47 *Compare Equation (18.136) with the expression for B_t^T obtained in the case of the Vasicek model. What is $\vec{g}$ in that case? What is $\mathcal{K}^T$? And what is $(\mathcal{K}^T)^{-1}$?*

Obtaining the Expression for $\overrightarrow{B}^{\mathrm{T}}$

Recall that the expression for the bond price (Equation (18.12)) requires the transpose of the vector $\overrightarrow{B}$. To obtain this expression we have to remember that, for any two matrices, a and b, and for any invertible matrix, A, we have

$$(ab)^{\mathrm{T}} = b^{\mathrm{T}} a^{\mathrm{T}} \tag{18.137}$$

and

$$\left(A^{\mathrm{T}}\right)^{-1} = \left(A^{-1}\right)^{\mathrm{T}}. \tag{18.138}$$

Exercise 48 *Prove Equations (18.137) and (18.138).*

Proceeding in blocks we have

$$
\begin{aligned}
\overrightarrow{B}^{\mathrm{T}} &= \left[\left(e^{-\mathcal{K}^T \tau} - I_n \right) \left(\mathcal{K}^T \right)^{-1} \overrightarrow{g} \right]^{\mathrm{T}} \\
&= \left[\left(\mathcal{K}^T \right)^{-1} \overrightarrow{g} \right]^{\mathrm{T}} \left[\left(e^{-\mathcal{K}^T \tau} - I_n \right) \right]^{\mathrm{T}} \\
&= \overrightarrow{g}^{\mathrm{T}} \left[\left(\mathcal{K}^T \right)^{-1} \right]^{\mathrm{T}} \left[\left(e^{-\mathcal{K}^T \tau} \right)^{\mathrm{T}} - I_n \right] \\
&= \overrightarrow{g}^{\mathrm{T}} \mathcal{K}^{-1} \left[\left(e^{-\mathcal{K}^T \tau} \right)^{\mathrm{T}} - I_n \right].
\end{aligned}
\tag{18.139}
$$

Next we remember that

$$\left(e^{-\mathcal{K}^T \tau} \right)^{\mathrm{T}} = e^{-\mathcal{K} \tau} \tag{18.140}$$

and we finally have

$$\overrightarrow{B}^{\mathrm{T}} = \overrightarrow{g}^{\mathrm{T}} \mathcal{K}^{-1} \left[e^{-\mathcal{K} \tau} - I_n \right]. \tag{18.141}$$

Exercise 49 *Prove Equation (18.140). Hint: Use the expansion for the exponential of a matrix, and use repeatedly Equation (18.137).*

18.8.2 Solving the ODE for $A(\tau)$

To solve the Ordinary Differential Equation for we have to perform three easy but tedious integrals:

$$
\begin{aligned}
\frac{dA(\tau)}{d\tau} &= -u_r + \overrightarrow{B}^{\mathrm{T}} \mathcal{K} \overrightarrow{\theta} + \frac{1}{2} \overrightarrow{B}^{\mathrm{T}} SS^{\mathrm{T}} \overrightarrow{B} \\
&\Longrightarrow A(\tau) = Int_1 + Int_2 + Int_3
\end{aligned}
\tag{18.142}
$$

with

$$Int_1 = -\int_0^T u_r d\tau \tag{18.143}$$

$$Int_2 = \int_0^T \overrightarrow{B}^{\mathrm{T}} \mathcal{K} \overrightarrow{\theta} \, d\tau \tag{18.144}$$

$$Int_3 = \frac{1}{2} \int_0^T \overrightarrow{B}^{\mathrm{T}} SS^{\mathrm{T}} \overrightarrow{B} \, d\tau \tag{18.145}$$

The strategy is simple: we have to substitute into Int_2 and Int_3 the expression we have just found for $\overrightarrow{B}^T$, and turn the integration handle. We are going to use one result (presented in Appendix 18B): if the matrix $A(t)$ is diagonal, then

$$
\int e^{A(s)}ds = \begin{bmatrix} \int e^{a_{11}(s)}ds & 0 & & 0 & 0 \\ 0 & \int e^{a_{22}(s)}ds & & 0 & 0 \\ \cdots & \cdots & & \cdots & 0 \\ 0 & 0 & & 0 & \int e^{a_{nn}(s)}ds \end{bmatrix}. \quad (18.146)
$$

This is going to be our lifeline in the evaluation of the integrals we need. Since the matrix $\mathcal{K}$ is not, in general, diagonal, we are going to use the up-and-down theorem (also presented in Appendix 18B) which says the following: if the matrix $\mathcal{K}$ can be written as (can be diagonalized as):

$$
\mathcal{K} = L\mathcal{L}L^{-1} \quad (18.147)
$$

with $\mathcal{L}$ a diagonal matrix

$$
\mathcal{L} = \begin{bmatrix} l_{11} & 0 & 0 & 0 \\ 0 & l_{22} & 0 & 0 \\ 0 & 0 & \cdots & 0 \\ 0 & 0 & 0 & l_{nn} \end{bmatrix}. \quad (18.148)
$$

then

$$
e^{-\mathcal{K}\tau} = e^{-L\mathcal{L}\tau L^{-1}} = Le^{-\mathcal{L}\tau}L^{-1} \quad (18.149)
$$

ie, the eigenvector matrices, L and L^{-1}, can be moved from up in the argument of the exponent to down next to the exponential (hence the elegant name 'up-and-down theorem').

Evaluating Int_1

This bit is easy:

$$
Int_1 = -\int_0^T u_r d\tau = -u_r T. \quad (18.150)
$$

By the way, if one really wanted to introduce a short-horizon time dependence to the model, this would be the natural place to do so. For instance, one may believe that the current actions of the monetary authorities are exceptional and that after a short period of time (say, a couple of years) one will revert to normal market conditions. One may want to model this deterministic behaviour by imposing $u_r = u_r(t)$, in which case Equation (18.150) clearly becomes

$$
Int_1 = -\int_{t_0}^T u_r(s)\,ds. \quad (18.151)
$$

Evaluating Int$_2$

We have to evaluate

$$Int_2 = \int_0^T \vec{B}^{\mathrm{T}} \mathcal{K} \vec{\theta} \, d\tau \tag{18.152}$$

Substituting the expression for $\vec{B}^{\mathrm{T}}$ obtained above we get

$$Int_2 = \int_0^T \left[\vec{g}^{\mathrm{T}} \mathcal{K}^{-1} \left[e^{-\mathcal{K}\tau} - I_n \right] \right] \mathcal{K} \vec{\theta} \, d\tau. \tag{18.153}$$

We break this into two parts:

$$Int_2 = Int_2^a + Int_2^b \tag{18.154}$$

with

$$Int_2^a = - \int_0^T \vec{g}^{\mathrm{T}} \mathcal{K}^{-1} \mathcal{K} \vec{\theta} \, d\tau \tag{18.155}$$

and

$$Int_2^b = \int_0^T \vec{g}^{\mathrm{T}} \mathcal{K}^{-1} e^{-\mathcal{K}\tau} \mathcal{K} \vec{\theta} \, d\tau. \tag{18.156}$$

The first bit, Int_2^a, has no dependence on time, and therefore we have

$$Int_2^a = - \int_0^T \vec{g}^{\mathrm{T}} \mathcal{K}^{-1} \mathcal{K} \vec{\theta} \, d\tau = - \int_0^T \vec{g}^{\mathrm{T}} \vec{\theta} \, d\tau = - \vec{g}^{\mathrm{T}} \vec{\theta} \, T. \tag{18.157}$$

To tackle the second integral first we rewrite it as

$$Int_2^b = \vec{g}^{\mathrm{T}} \mathcal{K}^{-1} \int_0^T e^{-\mathcal{K}\tau} \mathcal{K} \vec{\theta} \, d\tau. \tag{18.158}$$

Next we observe that, if the matrix $\mathcal{Z}$ is diagonal, then, the integral $\int_0^T e^{-\mathcal{Z}\tau} d\tau$ is just equal to

$$\int_0^T e^{-\mathcal{Z}\tau} d\tau = \begin{bmatrix} \int_0^T e^{-z_{11}\tau} d\tau & 0 & 0 & 0 \\ 0 & \int_0^T e^{-z_{22}\tau} d\tau & & \\ & & \cdots & \\ & & & \int_0^T e^{-z_{nn}\tau} d\tau \end{bmatrix}. \tag{18.159}$$

Now, in general the matrix $\mathcal{K}$ is *not* diagonal. However, since we have assumed that it is invertible and diagonalizable, it can always be expressed as

$$\mathcal{K} = L\mathcal{L}L^{-1} \tag{18.160}$$

with $\mathcal{L}$ a diagonal matrix

$$\mathcal{L} = \begin{bmatrix} l_{11} & 0 & 0 & 0 \\ 0 & l_{22} & 0 & 0 \\ 0 & 0 & \ldots & 0 \\ 0 & 0 & 0 & l_{nn} \end{bmatrix}. \tag{18.161}$$

But we show in Appendix 18B (the up-and-down-theorem) that

$$e^{L\mathcal{L}L^{-1}} = Le^{\mathcal{L}}L^{-1}. \tag{18.162}$$

Therefore Int_2^b can be rewritten as

$$Int_2^b = \vec{g}^{\mathsf{T}} \mathcal{K}^{-1} \int_0^T e^{-\mathcal{K}\tau} \mathcal{K} \vec{\theta} \, d\tau = \vec{g}^{\mathsf{T}} \mathcal{K}^{-1} \int_0^T e^{-L\mathcal{L}\tau L^{-1}} \mathcal{K} \vec{\theta} \, d\tau$$

$$= \vec{g}^{\mathsf{T}} \mathcal{K}^{-1} \int_0^T L e^{-\mathcal{L}\tau} L^{-1} \mathcal{K} \vec{\theta} \, d\tau$$

$$= \vec{g}^{\mathsf{T}} \mathcal{K}^{-1} \int_0^T L e^{-\mathcal{L}\tau} L^{-1} \mathcal{K} \vec{\theta} \, d\tau$$

$$= \vec{g}^{\mathsf{T}} \left(L\mathcal{L}L^{-1} \right)^{-1} \int_0^T L e^{-\mathcal{L}\tau} L^{-1} L\mathcal{L}L^{-1} \vec{\theta} \, d\tau$$

$$= \vec{g}^{\mathsf{T}} \left(L\mathcal{L}L^{-1} \right)^{-1} L \int_0^T e^{-\mathcal{L}\tau} \mathcal{L}L^{-1} \vec{\theta} \, d\tau$$

$$= \vec{g}^{\mathsf{T}} L\mathcal{L}^{-1} \left[\int_0^T e^{-\mathcal{L}\tau} d\tau \right] \mathcal{L}L^{-1} \vec{\theta}. \tag{18.163}$$

Next we are going to make use of the commutation result that says that, if A is a matrix and $f(A)$ some function of this matrix, then A and $f(A)$ commute, ie:

$$Af(a) = f(A)A. \tag{18.164}$$

This can be applied to $\mathcal{L}$ and $\left[\int_0^T e^{-\mathcal{L}\tau} d\tau \right]$ (which is obviously a function of $\mathcal{L}$), and therefore

$$\left[\int_0^T e^{-\mathcal{L}\tau} d\tau \right] \mathcal{L} = \mathcal{L} \left[\int_0^T e^{-\mathcal{L}\tau} d\tau \right].$$

Inserting back into Equation (18.163) we get

$$Int_2^b = \vec{g}^{\mathsf{T}} L\mathcal{L}^{-1} \left[\int_0^T e^{-\mathcal{L}\tau} d\tau \right] \mathcal{L}L^{-1} \vec{\theta}$$

$$= \vec{g}^{\mathsf{T}} L \left[\int_0^T e^{-\mathcal{L}\tau} d\tau \right] L^{-1} \vec{\theta}.$$

As for the integral $\int_0^T e^{-\mathcal{L}\tau} d\tau$, it is equal to

$$\int_0^T e^{-\mathcal{L}\tau} d\tau = \text{diag}\left[\frac{1 - e^{-l_{ii}T}}{l_{ii}}\right] \equiv D(T) \tag{18.165}$$

and finally

$$Int_2^b = \vec{g}^{\mathrm{T}} L D(T) L^{-1} \vec{\theta} . \tag{18.166}$$

Putting the pieces together we have

$$\begin{aligned} Int_2 &= Int_2^a + Int_2^b \\ &= -\vec{g}^{\mathrm{T}} \vec{\theta} T + \vec{g}^{\mathrm{T}} L \mathcal{L}^{-1} D(T) \mathcal{L} L^{-1} \vec{\theta} \\ &= \vec{g}^{\mathrm{T}} \left(LD(T)L^{-1} \vec{\theta} - \vec{\theta} T \right). \end{aligned} \tag{18.167}$$

Evaluating Integral I_3

Finally we have to evaluate $Int_3 = \frac{1}{2} \int_0^T \vec{B}^{\mathrm{T}} SS^{\mathrm{T}} \vec{B} \, d\tau$. We substitute the expressions we have derived for $\vec{B}$ and $\vec{B}^{\mathrm{T}}$, we note that SS^{T} is a real, symmetric matrix, which we call C, and we proceed as usual by divide-and-conquer:

$$\begin{aligned} Int_3 &= \frac{1}{2} \int_0^T \vec{B}^{\mathrm{T}} SS^{\mathrm{T}} \vec{B} \, d\tau = \frac{1}{2} \int_0^T \vec{B}^{\mathrm{T}} C \vec{B} \, d\tau \\ &= \frac{1}{2} \int_0^T \vec{g}^{\mathrm{T}} \mathcal{K}^{-1} \left[e^{-\mathcal{K}\tau} - I_n \right] C \left[e^{-\mathcal{K}^{\mathrm{T}}\tau} - I_n \right] (\mathcal{K}^{\mathrm{T}})^{-1} \vec{g} \, d\tau \\ &= Int_3^a + Int_3^b + Int_3^c + Int_3^d \end{aligned} \tag{18.168}$$

with

$$Int_3^a = \frac{1}{2} \int_0^T \vec{g}^{\mathrm{T}} \mathcal{K}^{-1} e^{-\mathcal{K}\tau} C e^{-\mathcal{K}^{\mathrm{T}}\tau} (\mathcal{K}^{\mathrm{T}})^{-1} \vec{g} \, d\tau \tag{18.169}$$

$$Int_3^b = -\frac{1}{2} \int_0^T \vec{g}^{\mathrm{T}} \mathcal{K}^{-1} C e^{-\mathcal{K}^{\mathrm{T}}\tau} (\mathcal{K}^{\mathrm{T}})^{-1} \vec{g} \, d\tau \tag{18.170}$$

$$Int_3^c = -\frac{1}{2} \int_0^T \vec{g}^{\mathrm{T}} \mathcal{K}^{-1} e^{-\mathcal{K}\tau} C (\mathcal{K}^{\mathrm{T}})^{-1} \vec{g} \, d\tau \tag{18.171}$$

$$Int_3^d = \frac{1}{2} \int_0^T \vec{g}^{\mathrm{T}} \mathcal{K}^{-1} C (\mathcal{K}^{\mathrm{T}})^{-1} \vec{g} \, d\tau. \tag{18.172}$$

To limber up we proceed in reverse order. The last integral is trivial:

$$\begin{aligned} Int_3^d &= \frac{1}{2} \int_0^T \vec{g}^{\mathrm{T}} \mathcal{K}^{-1} C (\mathcal{K}^{\mathrm{T}})^{-1} \vec{g} \, d\tau = \frac{1}{2} \vec{g}^{\mathrm{T}} \mathcal{K}^{-1} C (\mathcal{K}^{\mathrm{T}})^{-1} \vec{g} \int_0^T d\tau \\ &= \frac{1}{2} \vec{g}^{\mathrm{T}} \mathcal{K}^{-1} C (\mathcal{K}^{\mathrm{T}})^{-1} \vec{g} T. \end{aligned} \tag{18.173}$$

Let's move to the integral Int_3^c. We have

$$Int_3^c = -\frac{1}{2}\int_0^T \vec{g}^{\mathrm{T}}\mathcal{K}^{-1}e^{-\mathcal{K}\tau}C\left(\mathcal{K}^{\mathrm{T}}\right)^{-1}\vec{g}\,d\tau. \tag{18.174}$$

We begin to take out of the integral sign whatever we can:

$$Int_3^c = -\frac{1}{2}\vec{g}^{\mathrm{T}}\mathcal{K}^{-1}\int_0^T e^{-\mathcal{K}\tau}C\left(\mathcal{K}^{\mathrm{T}}\right)^{-1}\vec{g}\,d\tau. \tag{18.175}$$

Next we use the up-and-down theorem to write

$$Int_3^c = -\frac{1}{2}\vec{g}^{\mathrm{T}}\mathcal{K}^{-1}\int_0^T e^{-\mathcal{K}\tau}C\left(\mathcal{K}^{\mathrm{T}}\right)^{-1}\vec{g}\,d\tau$$

$$= -\frac{1}{2}\vec{g}^{\mathrm{T}}\mathcal{K}^{-1}L\left[\int_0^T e^{-\mathcal{L}\tau}d\tau\right]L^{-1}C\left(\mathcal{K}^{\mathrm{T}}\right)^{-1}\vec{g}. \tag{18.176}$$

Since the matrix $\mathcal{L}$ is diagonal the integral is trivial (ie, can be carried out element-by-element), and is given by

$$\left[\int_0^T e^{-\mathcal{L}\tau}d\tau\right] = \mathrm{diag}\left[\frac{1-e^{-l_{ii}T}}{l_{ii}}\right]_n \equiv D(T) \tag{18.177}$$

and therefore we have

$$Int_3^c = -\frac{1}{2}\vec{g}^{\mathrm{T}}\mathcal{K}^{-1}LD(T)L^{-1}C\left(\mathcal{K}^{\mathrm{T}}\right)^{-1}\vec{g}. \tag{18.178}$$

Next we have to tackle the integral Int_3^b. It is almost identical, but it calls for some deft handling of the pesky transposition operator. We have

$$Int_3^b = -\frac{1}{2}\int_0^T \vec{g}^{\mathrm{T}}\mathcal{K}^{-1}Ce^{-\mathcal{K}^{\mathrm{T}}\tau}\left(\mathcal{K}^{\mathrm{T}}\right)^{-1}\vec{g}\,d\tau$$

$$= -\frac{1}{2}\vec{g}^{\mathrm{T}}\mathcal{K}^{-1}C\int_0^T e^{-\mathcal{K}^{\mathrm{T}}\tau}\left(\mathcal{K}^{\mathrm{T}}\right)^{-1}\vec{g}\,d\tau$$

$$= -\frac{1}{2}\vec{g}^{\mathrm{T}}\mathcal{K}^{-1}C\left[\int_0^T e^{-\mathcal{K}^{\mathrm{T}}\tau}d\tau\right]\left(\mathcal{K}^{\mathrm{T}}\right)^{-1}\vec{g}. \tag{18.179}$$

Now,

$$\mathcal{K}^{\mathrm{T}} = \left(L\mathcal{L}L^{-1}\right)^{\mathrm{T}} = \left(L^{-1}\right)^{\mathrm{T}}(L\mathcal{L})^{\mathrm{T}} = \left(L^{-1}\right)^{\mathrm{T}}(\mathcal{L})^{\mathrm{T}}(L)^{\mathrm{T}}$$

$$= \left(L^{-1}\right)^{\mathrm{T}}\mathcal{L}(L)^{\mathrm{T}}. \tag{18.180}$$

where the last line follows because $\mathcal{L}$ is diagonal.

In the integral there also enter the quantities $\mathcal{K}^{-1}$ and $(\mathcal{K}^{\mathrm{T}})^{-1}$, which we can write as

$$\mathcal{K}^{-1} = \left(L\mathcal{L}L^{-1}\right)^{-1} = L\mathcal{L}^{-1}L^{-1} \tag{18.181}$$

and

$$\left(\mathcal{K}^{-1}\right)^{\mathrm{T}} = \left(L\mathcal{L}^{-1}L^{-1}\right)^{\mathrm{T}} = \left(L^{-1}\right)^{\mathrm{T}}\left(L\mathcal{L}^{-1}\right)^{\mathrm{T}} = \left(L^{-1}\right)^{\mathrm{T}}\mathcal{L}^{-1}L^{\mathrm{T}},$$

(18.182)

where we have made use of the fact that, if $\mathcal{L}$ is diagonal, $\mathcal{L}^{-1}$ is diagonal as well.

Substituting all the required pieces and simplifying we get

$$
\begin{aligned}
Int_3^b &= -\frac{1}{2}\vec{g}^{\mathrm{T}}\mathcal{K}^{-1}C\left[\int_0^T e^{-\mathcal{K}^{\mathrm{T}}\tau}d\tau\right]\left(\mathcal{K}^{\mathrm{T}}\right)^{-1}\vec{g} \\
&= -\frac{1}{2}\vec{g}^{\mathrm{T}}\mathcal{K}^{-1}C\left(L^{-1}\right)^{\mathrm{T}}\left[\int_0^T e^{-\mathcal{L}(L)^{\mathrm{T}}\tau}d\tau\right](L)^{\mathrm{T}}\left(L^{-1}\right)^{\mathrm{T}}\mathcal{L}^{-1}L^{\mathrm{T}}\vec{g} \\
&= -\frac{1}{2}\vec{g}^{\mathrm{T}}\mathcal{K}^{-1}C\left(L^{-1}\right)^{\mathrm{T}}D\left(T\right)\mathcal{L}^{-1}L^{\mathrm{T}}\vec{g}.
\end{aligned}
$$

(18.183)

Finally, we have the integral Int_3^a. We have

$$Int_3^a = \frac{1}{2}\int_0^T \vec{g}^{\mathrm{T}}\mathcal{K}^{-1}e^{-\mathcal{K}\tau}Ce^{-\mathcal{K}^{\mathrm{T}}\tau}\left(\mathcal{K}^{\mathrm{T}}\right)^{-1}\vec{g}\,d\tau.$$

(18.184)

Proceeding as earlier we have

$$
\begin{aligned}
Int_3^a &= \frac{1}{2}\vec{g}^{\mathrm{T}}\mathcal{K}^{-1}\int_0^T e^{-L\mathcal{L}\tau L^{-1}}Ce^{-\left(L^{-1}\right)^{\mathrm{T}}\mathcal{L}\tau L^{\mathrm{T}}}\left(L^{-1}\right)^{\mathrm{T}}\mathcal{L}^{-1}L^{\mathrm{T}}\vec{g}\,d\tau \\
&= \frac{1}{2}\vec{g}^{\mathrm{T}}\mathcal{K}^{-1}L\int_0^T e^{-\mathcal{L}\tau}\left[L^{-1}C\left(L^{-1}\right)^{\mathrm{T}}\right]e^{-\mathcal{L}\tau}\mathcal{L}^{-1}L^{\mathrm{T}}\vec{g}\,d\tau.
\end{aligned}
$$

(18.185)

Now, $[L^{-1}C(L^{-1})^{\mathrm{T}}]$ is just some matrix, M: $M = L^{-1}C(L^{-1})^{\mathrm{T}}$, of elements m_{ij}. Therefore

$$Int_3^a = \frac{1}{2}\vec{g}^{\mathrm{T}}\mathcal{K}^{-1}L\left[\int_0^T e^{-\mathcal{L}\tau}Me^{-\mathcal{L}\tau}d\tau\right]\mathcal{L}^{-1}L^{\mathrm{T}}\vec{g}.$$

(18.186)

Since the two matrices $e^{-\mathcal{L}\tau}$ that flank matrix M are diagonal, the integral in the square brackets is just equal to

$$\left[\int_0^T e^{-\mathcal{L}\tau}Me^{-\mathcal{L}\tau}d\tau\right] = F\left(T\right),$$

(18.187)

with $F = [f_{ij}]$, and

$$f_{ij} = m_{ij}\frac{1 - e^{-\left(l_{ii}+l_{jj}\right)T}}{l_{ii}+l_{jj}}.$$

(18.188)

(If the last result is not obvious, see Appendix 18B, Section 18.10.5.) Therefore

$$Int_3^a = \frac{1}{2} \vec{g}^{\mathrm{T}} \mathcal{K}^{-1} L F (T) \mathcal{L}^{-1} L^{\mathrm{T}} \vec{g} . \tag{18.189}$$

18.9   APPENDIX 18B

18.9.1   The Meaning of e^A

If A is an $[n \times n]$ matrix, then e^A is also an $[n \times n]$ matrix, defined to be

$$e^A = I_n + A + \frac{1}{2!} A^2 + \frac{1}{3!} A^3 + \dots . \tag{18.190}$$

If the matrix A is diagonal, $A = \mathrm{diag}[a_{ii}]_n$, then

$$e^A = \begin{bmatrix} e^{a_{11}} & 0 & 0 & 0 \\ 0 & e^{a_{22}} & 0 & 0 \\ \dots & \dots & \dots & 0 \\ 0 & 0 & 0 & e^{a_{nn}} \end{bmatrix} . \tag{18.191}$$

From the definition it is clear that the element-by-element exponentiation is *not* true for a non-diagonal matrix; ie, if A is not diagonal,

$$e^A \neq \begin{bmatrix} e^{a_{11}} & e^{a_{12}} & \dots & e^{a_{1n}} \\ e^{a_{21}} & e^{a_{22}} & \dots & e^{a_{2n}} \\ \dots & \dots & \dots & \dots \\ e^{a_{31}} & e^{a_{32}} & \dots & e^{a_{3n}} \end{bmatrix} . \tag{18.192}$$

Recalling that the if a matrix Λ is diagonal

$$\Lambda = \mathrm{diag}\,[\lambda_{11}, \lambda_{22}, ..\lambda_{nn}] \tag{18.193}$$

then its inverse is just given by

$$\Lambda^{-1} = \mathrm{diag}\left[\frac{1}{\lambda_{11}}, \frac{1}{\lambda_{22}}, ..\frac{1}{\lambda_{nn}}\right] \tag{18.194}$$

we can immediately obtain that, if the matrix A is diagonal, then

$$\left(e^A\right)^{-1} = e^{-A} = \begin{bmatrix} e^{-a_{11}} & 0 & 0 & 0 \\ 0 & e^{-a_{22}} & 0 & 0 \\ \dots & \dots & \dots & 0 \\ 0 & 0 & 0 & e^{-a_{nn}} \end{bmatrix} . \tag{18.195}$$

Exercise 50   *Obtain Equations (18.194) and (18.195).*

(This, by the way, is one of the reasons why, whenever possible, we try to orthogonalize the matrix A, and to make use of the up-and-down theorem presented below – this way, we are left with the exponent of a nice diagonal matrix, which is easy to work with.)

18.10 EXPLICIT CALCULATION OF THE FORMAL SOLUTION $\vec{x}_t = e^{At}\vec{x}_0$

Suppose that we have a solution of an Ordinary Differential Equation of the form

$$\vec{x}_t = e^{At}\vec{x}_0. \tag{18.196}$$

How are we to understand this expression? How are we to calculate the elements, $x_t^1, x_t^2, ..., x_t^n$, of the solution vector, $\vec{x}_t$?

Suppose that the matrix A can be diagonalized and that it has n distinct eigenvalues, $\lambda_a^1, \lambda_a^2, ..., \lambda_a^n$. This means that we can write

$$A = S\Lambda^a S^{-1} \tag{18.197}$$

with

$$\Lambda^a = \begin{bmatrix} \lambda_a^1 & 0 & 0 & 0 \\ 0 & \lambda_a^n & 0 & 0 \\ ... & & ... & \\ 0 & 0 & 0 & \lambda_a^n \end{bmatrix}. \tag{18.198}$$

Substitution of Equation (18.197) into Equation (18.196) gives

$$\vec{x}_t = e^{At}\vec{x}_0 = e^{\left(S\Lambda^A S^{-1}\right)t}\vec{x}_0. \tag{18.199}$$

Remembering the up-and-down theorem, in the case of diagonalizable matrices (see Section 18.10.1), one can write

$$\vec{x}_t = e^{\left(S\Lambda^A S^{-1}\right)t}\vec{x}_0 = Se^{\Lambda^A t}S^{-1}\vec{x}_0. \tag{18.200}$$

Define $\vec{q}$ as

$$\vec{q} = S^{-1}\vec{x}_0. \tag{18.201}$$

This gives

$$\vec{x}_t = Se^{\Lambda^a t}\vec{q}. \tag{18.202}$$

Consider now the term $e^{\Lambda^a t}$:

$$e^{\Lambda^a t} = \sum_{m=0}^{\infty} \frac{(\Lambda^a t)^m}{m!}. \tag{18.203}$$

Recalling that Λ^a is diagonal we have

$$(\Lambda^a)^m = \left(\begin{bmatrix} \lambda_a^1 & 0 & 0 & 0 \\ 0 & \lambda_a^2 & 0 & 0 \\ \cdots & & & \cdots \\ 0 & 0 & 0 & \lambda_a^n \end{bmatrix}\right)^m$$

$$= \begin{bmatrix} \left(\lambda_a^1\right)^m & 0 & 0 & 0 \\ 0 & \left(\lambda_a^2\right)^m & 0 & 0 \\ \cdots & & & \cdots \\ 0 & 0 & 0 & \left(\lambda_a^n\right)^m \end{bmatrix} \tag{18.204}$$

and therefore

$$\sum_{m=0}^{\infty} \frac{(\Lambda^a t)^m}{m!} = \begin{bmatrix} \sum_{m=0}^{\infty} \frac{\left(\lambda_a^1\right)^m t^m}{m!} & 0 & 0 & 0 \\ 0 & \sum_{m=0}^{\infty} \frac{\left(\lambda_a^2\right)^m t^m}{m!} & 0 & 0 \\ \cdots & & & \cdots \\ 0 & 0 & 0 & \sum_{m=0}^{\infty} \frac{\left(\lambda_a^n\right)^m t^m}{m!} \end{bmatrix}$$

$$= \begin{bmatrix} e^{\lambda_a^1 t} & 0 & 0 & 0 \\ 0 & e^{\lambda_a^2 t} & 0 & 0 \\ \cdots & & & \cdots \\ 0 & 0 & 0 & e^{\lambda_a^n t} \end{bmatrix} \equiv D_a. \tag{18.205}$$

Therefore we finally have an explicit expression for the solution vector, $\vec{x}_t$,

$$\vec{x}_t = S e^{\Lambda^a t} \vec{q} = S D_a \vec{q}. \tag{18.206}$$

18.10.1 The Up-and-Down Theorem

Recall that the exponential e^A, of a matrix A, is given by $e^A = I + A + \frac{1}{2}A^2 + \ldots$. Then let U be an $[n \times n]$ orthogonal matrix, ie, a matrix for which

$$UU^T = I_n. \tag{18.207}$$

Let A be an arbitrary $[n \times n]$ matrix.

Consider the expression

$$C = U e^A U^T. \tag{18.208}$$

Expand the exponent to obtain

$$C = U \left[I + A + \frac{1}{2}A^2 + \ldots \right] U^T. \tag{18.209}$$

Expand the expression

$$C = U I U^T + U A U^T + \frac{1}{2} U A^2 U^T + \ldots \tag{18.210}$$

$$= I + U A U^T + \frac{1}{2} U A^2 U^T + \ldots \tag{18.211}$$

where the last line follows because, by orthogonality

$$UU^{\mathrm{T}} = I. \tag{18.212}$$

Consider now the exponential $D = e^{UAU^{\mathrm{T}}}$:

$$D = e^{UAU^{\mathrm{T}}} = I + UAU^{\mathrm{T}} + \frac{1}{2}\left(UAU^{\mathrm{T}}\right)^2 + \dots$$

$$= I + UAU^{\mathrm{T}} + \frac{1}{2}UAU^{\mathrm{T}}UAU^{\mathrm{T}} + \dots$$

$$= I + UAU^{\mathrm{T}} + \frac{1}{2}UAAU^{\mathrm{T}} + \dots$$

$$= I + UAU^{\mathrm{T}} + \frac{1}{2}UA^2U^{\mathrm{T}} + \dots \tag{18.213}$$

Repeating for higher-order terms and comparing Equations (18.213) and (18.211), we can conclude

$$Ue^AU^{\mathrm{T}} = e^{UAU^{\mathrm{T}}}. \tag{18.214}$$

The same result applies to non-orthogonal matrices, as long as matrix inversion replaces transposition:

$$Ze^AZ^{-1} = e^{ZAZ^{-1}}. \tag{18.215}$$

The proof is the same.

18.10.2   Commutation Relationships for A and $f(A)$

When A is a matrix, all functions of A are defined as the corresponding series expansions. So, for instance, e^A is defined to be

$$e^A = I + A + \frac{1}{2!}A^2 + \frac{1}{3!}A^3 + \dots$$

Now, when we have an expression such as Ae^A it 'really' means

$$Ae^A = A\left[I + A + \frac{1}{2!}A^2 + \frac{1}{3!}A^3 + \dots\right]. \tag{18.216}$$

It is clear that, if we had instead e^AA, it would be equivalent to

$$e^AA = \left[I + A + \frac{1}{2!}A^2 + \frac{1}{3!}A^3 + \dots\right]A. \tag{18.217}$$

Multiplying through the two expressions, we see that they are exactly the same.

It is also clear from the derivation that the same reasoning would apply to the power expansion of any function, $f(A)$, ie, and therefore the commutation relationship between A and $f(A)$ holds for any function of A.

18.10.3   Time Derivative of e^{At}

To calculate the time derivative, we first guess a solution, and then check that it is correct.

Let's start with the inspired guess

$$\frac{d}{dt}e^{At} = Ae^{At}.$$ (18.218)

Our guess is equal to

$$Ae^{At} = A\left[I + At + \frac{1}{2}AAt^2 + \dots\right].$$

Next, let's calculate the derivative explicitly:

$$\frac{d}{dt}e^{At} = \frac{d}{dt}\left[I + At + \frac{1}{2}AAt^2 + \frac{1}{3!}AAAt^3\dots\right]$$

$$= A + AAt + \frac{1}{2}AAAt^2\dots$$

$$= A\left[I + At + \frac{1}{2}AAt^2 + \dots\right],$$ (18.219)

which is just what we needed. Should we have written $\frac{d}{dt}e^{At} = Ae^{At}$ or $\frac{d}{dt}e^{At} = e^{At}A$? By the commutation theorem above for matrices, A, and functions of matrices, $f(A)$, we know that it does not matter.

18.10.4   Integral of e^{At}

We want to calculate

$$\int_0^T e^{At}dt.$$ (18.220)

First we substitute inside the integral sign the definition of the exponential of a matrix:

$$\int_0^T e^{At}dt = \int_0^T \left[I + At + \frac{1}{2}AAt^2 + \frac{1}{6}AAAt^3\dots\right]dt.$$ (18.221)

Next we integrate term by term, and we get

$$\int_0^T e^{At}dt = \left[IT + \frac{1}{2}AT^2 + \frac{1}{6}A^2T^3 + \dots\right]$$

$$= A^{-1}\left[AT + \frac{1}{2}A^2T^2 + \frac{1}{6}A^3T^3 + \dots\right],$$ (18.222)

where in going from the second to the last line we have multiplied what is in the square brackets by $I = A^{-1}A$, and we have assumed that the matrix A is invertible. Finally, we recognize that what we have in the square brackets is just $e^{AT} - I$, and therefore we have

$$\int_0^T e^{At}dt = A^{-1}\left(e^{AT} - I\right). \tag{18.223}$$

This expression becomes very simple if the matrix A is diagonal, because then we just have

$$\int_0^T e^{At}dt = \text{diag}\left[\frac{e^{a_{ii}T} - 1}{a_{ii}}\right]. \tag{18.224}$$

18.10.5   Evaluation of the Integral $\left[\int_0^T e^{-\mathcal{L}\tau}Me^{-\mathcal{L}\tau}d\tau\right]$

First of all we recognize that the matrix $e^{-\mathcal{L}\tau}$ is diagonal and therefore, by direct matrix multiplication, we have

$$\left[\int_0^T e^{-\mathcal{L}\tau}Me^{-\mathcal{L}\tau}d\tau\right]_{ij} = \int_0^T \left[m_{ij}e^{-(\lambda_i+\lambda_j)t}\right]dt,$$

where m_{ij} are the elements of M. We therefore want to evaluate the time integral of $m_{ij}e^{(\lambda_i+\lambda_j)t}$:

$$Int = \int_0^T \left[m_{ij}e^{-(\lambda_i+\lambda_j)t}\right]_{ij}dt. \tag{18.225}$$

Since the time integral of a matrix whose elements are time dependent is just given by the matrix with elements given by the integrals, direct integration gives

$$\int_0^T \left[m_{ij}e^{-(\lambda_i+\lambda_j)t}\right]_{ij}dt = \frac{m_{ij}}{\lambda_i + \lambda_j}\left[1 - e^{-(\lambda_i+\lambda_j)T}\right]. \tag{18.226}$$

CHAPTER 19

The Shadow Rate: Dealing with a Near-Zero Lower Bound

19.1 THE PURPOSE OF THIS CHAPTER

In this chapter we discuss how the modelling framework presented in the previous chapters can (must?) be modified when nominal rates are very close to zero. The insight is based on Black's last paper (Black, 1995). The title of the paper (*"Interest Rates as Options"*) clearly suggests that option-like non-linearities enter (and complicate) the treatment of rate-dependent products, such as bonds. (The 'option' in the title, by the way, is the option to put one's money under the mattress if rates became substantially negative, rather than investing it at a certain negative rate of nominal return.)

The chapter starts with a brief descriptions of the macroeconomic implications of close-to-zero rates, of the options open to central banks faced with these macroeconomic conditions, and of the relevance of the attending policy responses (such as 'quantitative easing') for the shape of the yield curve.

From the technical side, first we highlight the technical problems brought about by a zero floor. Then we show that the zero floor affects, albeit to different extents, the whole yield curve, not just the very short end. Indeed, we show that the greatest effect need not be at the shortest-maturity end of the yield curve. Finally, we show how these complications can be easily and effectively overcome using an approximate procedure recently introduced by Wu and Xia (2014). This, of course, is not the only solution that has been proposed to handle the problem, but, as usual, we prefer to look at one model in detail, rather than providing a bird's eye view of the existing approaches. For completeness and guidance, we also provide in the closing section a space-shuttle view of the existing literature on the topic.

Before presenting the computational results, we explain in the opening sections why estimating the 'shadow rate' (ie, the rate that would apply if zero were no lower bound) is important for macroeconomic applications, for predicting excess returns, and in the calibration of affine models.

19.2 MOTIVATION: WHY THE SHADOW RATE MATTERS

When a remarkable degree of prescience, Bomfin (2003a) wrote as early as April 2003:

> Nominal short term interest rates have been low in the United States, so low that some have wondered whether the federal funds rate is likely to hit its lower bound at 0 percent. Such a scenario, which some economists have called the liquidity trap, would imply that the Federal Reserve could no longer lower short-term interest rates to counter any deflationary tendencies in the economy.

We all know that Bomfin's scenario materialized after December 2008 in US$. In Japan a zero-lower bound regime has arguably been in place since the late 1990s. And, in the autumn of 2015, investors paid approximately 30 basis points per annum for the privilege of *lending* money to the Bundesbank. Under these conditions, there can be serious distortions to the shape of the yield curve and to the assessment of macroeconomic quantities (such as the real economic activity) traditionally associated with the slope of the yield curve.

Where do these distortions come from? As Black (1995) says, '[s]ince people can hold currency at a zero nominal rate, the nominal short rate cannot be negative'.[1] Saying that people can hold currency at a zero nominal rate means that they can stuff their bank notes under a mattress (or, more realistically, place them in a vault). In reality, 'storage costs' are not zero, and therefore interest rates can (and have) become slightly negative. However, beyond a certain negative yield level, the ingenuity of the purveyors of safes and vaults, if not of mattresses, would eventually bring to market viable alternatives to making donations to the central bank.

This situation can be modelled as follows.[2] We can set the observed nominal short rate, r_t, to the maximum of a 'shadow rate', ρ_t (to be defined) and zero:

$$r_t = \max[\rho_t, 0].\tag{19.1}$$

We note in passing that this can be equivalently rewritten as

$$r_t = \rho_t + \max[-\rho_t, 0].\tag{19.2}$$

We shall soon see why the second formulation can come in handy.

What is the shadow rate that we have introduced?

We can look at it from several different (but ultimately equivalent) angles. We can regard it as the hypothetical rate at which the market for loanable funds would clear, absent the near-zero bound. Another interpretation is that it would be the 'value of the nominal short-term interest rate that is consistent with the prescription of the policy rule followed by the central bank'.[3] And,

---

[1] p. 1371.
[2] The treatment in this section closely follows Bomfin (2003b).   [3] Bomfin (2003b), p. 4.

for those readers who are familiar with a bit of Keynesian macroeconomics,[4] the shadow rate can also be thought of as the intersection of the IS and LM curves.

The shadow rate can be negative, of course. This turns the well-known blemish associated with Gaussian affine models (ie, the fact that they allow for a negative short rate) into an advantage, as long as we use them to model the *shadow*, and not the observable short, rate. This serendipitous advantage comes, however, at a price.

What is the nature of the problem? Equation (19.1) clearly shows the option interpretation of the market nominal rate, r_t, which becomes the value of a call struck at zero on the shadow rate. Alternatively and equivalently, in the second formulation (Equation (19.2)),[5] the observable short rate, r_t, is expressed as the sum of the shadow rate, ρ_t, and the value of a floor, also struck at zero. Intuitively, 'the floor is akin to an option to switch one's money funds holdings into currency if $\rho(t)$ falls below zero'.[6] Whichever way we look at the new setting, we have an option to deal with. It is the introduction of optionality (ie, non-linearity) in the modelling of the yield curve that creates a problem, as we shall see in the following.

However, let's leave the technical problems to one side for the moment. The inability on the part of the central banks to make rates significantly negative has more serious consequence than forcing the use of Monte Carlo simulations on financial modellers. When the floor in Equation (19.2) is 'in the money' the nominal rate is higher than the rate that would clear the market for loanable funds. This means that firms and individuals borrow less than what is deemed to be socially optimal. It is to restore this socially optional level of borrowing that central banks that are 'stuck at zero' may decide to enter 'unconventional policies' (such as directly or indirectly intervening at the long end of the yield curve). Absent these unconventional policies, the economy may find itself 'trapped' in a low equilibrium, 'where productive activity persistently falls short of the economy's potential'.[7] This is a textbook description of a Keynesian liquidity trap.

---

[4] In the IS-LM model due to Hicks and Hansen the rate of interest is determined by a condition of general equilibrium as the intersection of two curves: the investment/savings (IS) curve, and the liquidity-preference/money-supply (LM) curve. The intersection is typically presented on a graph where, annoyingly, the horizontal axis is usually labelled Y, and represents the national income or the real gross domestic products, while the vertical axis is normally labelled i, and denotes the real interest rate. The point of intersection of the two schedules (the investment/savings and the liquidity/money-supply schedule) represents the short-term equilibrium between the real and the monetary sectors, ie, represents the level of rates for which the product market and the money market will be in equilibrium. For the interested reader there are countless books an macroeconomics that explain this in detail. For a quick an insightful treatment that highlights the links between the micro- and the macroeconomic perspective, see Krugman (undated).

[5] Readers familiar with option pricing can readily see that Equations (19.1) and (19.2) are linked by call-put parity.

[6] Ibid., p. 5.   [7] Ibid., p. 4.

19.3 HOW THE SHADOW RATE AFFECTS THE WHOLE YIELD CURVE

Let's neglect the effect of the shadow rate for a moment. We know (and will discuss at greater length in Part VI[8]) that the time-t instantaneous forward rate of expiry s, $f(t, s)$, is given by

$$f(t, s) = \mathbb{E}_t^{\mathbb{P}}[r(s)] + FWDRP_t^s, \tag{19.3}$$

where $FWDRP_t^s$ is the time-t forward risk premium for expiry s. In words: the forward rate, $f(t, s)$, is equal to the real-world time expectation formed at time t of the value of the short rate at a future time, s, plus a risk premium.

Similarly, we know that a yield, y_t^T, of maturity T is the average of the underlying forward rates. Therefore

$$y_t^T = \frac{1}{T - t} \int_t^T f(t, s) ds \tag{19.4}$$

$$y_t^T = \frac{1}{T - t} \mathbb{E}_t^{\mathbb{P}} \left[\int_t^T r(s) ds \right] + YLDRP_t^T \tag{19.5}$$

where $YLDRP_t^T$ now denotes the T-maturity yield risk premium, and we have introduced the real-world expectation and the associated risk premium.

What happens when we introduce the shadow rate? From the definition of the shadow rate we can also write

$$y_t^T = \frac{1}{T - t} \mathbb{E}_t^{\mathbb{P}} \left[\int_t^T \rho(s) ds \right] + YLDRP_t^T + OPT_t^T, \tag{19.6}$$

where the last term captures the option value associated with the zero floor. We have not given (yet) an explicit expression for this term, but for the moment the important point is that, when the floor 'bites' (ie, when the short rate is not too far from the zero strike), yields of *all* maturities are significantly affected by the option value – and, since the value of an option is always strictly positive, in the presence of a zero floor yields of all maturities will be not just different, but also *higher*.

This has an obvious impact when we calibrate an affine model to market yields. It has even more relevance for the assessment of excess returns and for policymakers: as Bomfin (2003b) says, '[i]nvestors and policymakers alike would be considerably misled if they were to take the positive slope of [the yield curve built without the term OPT_t^T] as an indication that market participants expect that economic activity is likely to increase in the future. In reality, the negative slope of the equilibrium [...] yield curve [built with the term OPT_t^T] suggests that the economy is expected to remain trapped in its low-activity equilibrium well into the future. *Thus we have a situation when an upward sloping (observed) yield curve is signalling expectations of a prolonged slump in the*

---

[8] See Section 23.5 in particular.

economy. This is exactly the opposite of the usual indicator property attributed to the yield curve![9]

The important point in this argument is that the term OPT_t^T can be an increasing function of the yield maturity, T, at least up to a maximum maturity, $\widetilde{T}$. How can this be the case?

Now, in the Black 1995 model (and in producing Figure 1 reported in Bomfin (2003b)) the shadow rate was supposed to be a pure diffusion, without any reversion to a fixed or moving level. As a consequence, in Black's toy model the difference between the market yields and the yields without the option term keeps on growing with yield maturity. This result is a feature of the not-very-realistic pure-diffusion assumption in Equation (19.7). If one inserted a Vasicek-like mean-reversion term to the process of the short rate, *and the reversion level of the short rate were well above zero*, then the effect would not be as pronounced as what Figure 1 in Bomfin (2003b) suggests. However, as we have discussed at length, the level of rates follows an almost-unit-root process (its reversion speed, if any, is very low). The 'tucking-in' effect of a mean-reverting process therefore becomes noticeable only for very long maturities. Which means that the effect can be important at *all* maturities, not just at the short end, because the short rate at a future time τ may well approach zero even if today's forward rate, f_t^τ, is well above this level. We shall discuss this in detail in the last section of this chapter.

19.4 THE MODELLING APPROACH

19.4.1 The Setting

Now that we have appreciated why, in a very-low-rate scenario, the shadow rate can be significantly different from the observed short rate (and, far more important, why it matters), the next question is how to model it.

In his original paper Black (1995) placed himself in the simplest possible setting, and assumed (i) that one single source of uncertainty shocks the economy, and (ii) that the shadow rate follows a simple diffusion, with no reversion speed[10]:

$$d\rho_t = \sigma_\rho dz_t. \tag{19.7}$$

Then, following a line of reasoning similar to what was presented in Chapter 16, one constructs a risk-less portfolio made up of two bonds, one invokes no-arbitrage, and one obtains for the Partial Differential Equation obeyed by the time-t price, P_t^T, of a T-maturity bond:

$$\frac{\partial P_t^T}{\partial t} + \frac{1}{2}\frac{\partial^2 P_t^T}{\partial \rho^2}\sigma_\rho^2 - r_t P_t^T = 0. \tag{19.8}$$

---

[9] Ibid., pp. 8–9, emphasis added.

[10] In keeping with the notation employed in this book, we have slightly changed the notation in Black's (1995) paper and denoted by σ_ρ the volatility of the shadow rate

Exercise 51 *Derive Equation (19.8).*

At first blush Equation (19.8) may seem a special case of the Partial Differential Equations we obtained and solved when dealing with affine models. See, for instance, the derivation in Chapter 16. Note, however, a subtle difference: the second derivative of the bond price is now with respect to the *shadow* rate (not the nominal short rate), but the quantity that multiplies the term P_t^T is still the short rate, r_t. (This must be the case, because, as we discussed in Chapter 16, the term $r_t P_t^T$ 'comes from' making the portfolio risk-less, and from imposing that, under penalty of arbitrage, it must therefore earn the risk-less return.) Since the short rate, as we have seen, can be thought of as an option on the shadow rate, this introduces non-linearities in the problem. It is these non-linearities that, in general, make the nice closed-form affine solution inapplicable in the case of a zero bound and force numerical solutions or Monte Carlo simulations.[11]

Let's be a bit more precise. It still remains true that the time-t value of a T-maturity bond, P_t^T, is given by the $\mathbb{Q}$-expectation of the exponent of the path of the short rate:

$$P_t^T = \mathbb{E}_t^{\mathbb{Q}} \left[e^{-\int_t^T r(s)ds} \right].$$ (19.9)

However, the observed short rate is now given by

$$r_t = \rho_t + \max[-\rho_t, 0]$$ (19.10)

and therefore Equation (19.9) becomes

$$P_t^T = \mathbb{E}_t^{\mathbb{Q}} \left[e^{-\int_t^T [\rho_s + \max(-\rho_s, 0)]ds} \right]$$

$$= \mathbb{E}_t^{\mathbb{Q}} \left[e^{-\int_t^T \rho_s ds} e^{-\int_t^T \max(-\rho_s, 0)ds} \right].$$ (19.11)

If the term $e^{-\int_t^T \max(-\rho_s, 0)ds}$ were equal to 1 (ie, if the shadow rate were always positive) we would of course know how to calculate the expectation: the problem would be exactly what we have solved in the previous chapters, with the shadow rate replacing the 'real' short rate. But, when rates are low, the floor can have a lot of value, and the term $e^{-\int_t^T \max(-\rho_s, 0)ds}$ cannot be neglected. As things stand, there are no exact known solutions. This is where clever tricks come into play.

19.4.2 An Approximate Solution

Wu and Xia (2014) have recently proposed a simple and accurate approximation that makes 'extremely tractable' the non-linear term structure modelling problem that arises with a zero lower bound for rates.

---

[11] Black (1995) shows how a closed-form solution is still possible in the case of a single factor, but the result does not generalize to many factors.

They first slightly generalize the Black setting by requiring that the short rate should be floored not at zero, but at a level $\underline{r}$. Given the level of the rate paid by the Federal Reserve on reserves at the time when they wrote their paper, they set at $\underline{r} = 0.0025$.[12] So they have

$$r_t = \max(\underline{r}, \rho_t), \tag{19.12}$$

with ρ_t denoting the shadow rate, and $\underline{r}$ the lower bound for the observed short rate.[13]

Consider then a generic affine model under $\mathbb{Q}$, with state variables $\vec{x}_t$:

$$d\vec{x}_t = \mathcal{K}^{\mathbb{Q}}(\vec{\theta}^{\mathbb{Q}} - \vec{x}_t)dt + S d\vec{z}_t^{\mathbb{Q}}. \tag{19.13}$$

Discretize it as

$$\vec{x}_{t+1} - \vec{x}_t = \mathcal{K}^{\mathbb{Q}}(\vec{\theta}^{\mathbb{Q}} - \vec{x}_t)\Delta t + S\sqrt{\Delta t}\,\epsilon_{t+1}^{\mathbb{Q}}. \tag{19.14}$$

Reshuffling terms we get

$$\vec{x}_{t+1} = \mathcal{K}^{\mathbb{Q}}\vec{\theta}^{\mathbb{Q}}\Delta t + (I - \mathcal{K}^{\mathbb{Q}}\Delta t)\vec{x}_t + S\sqrt{\Delta t}\,\epsilon_{t+1}^{\mathbb{Q}}. \tag{19.15}$$

Introducing the usual discrete-time notation, this becomes

$$\vec{x}_{t+1} = \mu^{\mathbb{Q}} + \mathcal{R}^{\mathbb{Q}}\vec{x}_t + \Sigma\epsilon_{t+1}^{\mathbb{Q}}, \tag{19.16}$$

with

$$\vec{\mu}^{\mathbb{Q}} = \mathcal{K}^{\mathbb{Q}}\vec{\theta}^{\mathbb{Q}}\Delta t \tag{19.17}$$

$$\mathcal{R}^{\mathbb{Q}} = (I - \mathcal{K}^{\mathbb{Q}}\Delta t) \tag{19.18}$$

$$S\sqrt{\Delta t} = \Sigma. \tag{19.19}$$

Next, let the mapping from the state variables to the shadow rate be given by

$$\rho_t = \delta_0 + \vec{\delta}_1^{\mathsf{T}}\vec{x}_t. \tag{19.20}$$

(As we discussed in previous chapters, this is the mapping that ultimately defines our model as affine. Every affine model specifies one such mapping. See the 'model dictionary' at the end of Chapter 18.) Finally, we assume that the market price of risk, λ_t, should also be an affine function of the state variables:

$$\vec{\lambda}_t = \vec{\lambda}_0 + \underline{\lambda}_1\vec{x}_t. \tag{19.21}$$

---

[12] There is nothing requiring the floor to be non-negative. If one looks at the yields paid in 2015 by German Bunds, a negative floor can actually make great sense. Luckily, in a Gaussian affine setting this creates no problems.

[13] For consistency of notation we are slightly changing the symbols in Wu and Xia (2014), and we denote the shadow rate by ρ_t, rather than by s_t. Also, to conform with the notation introduced in previous chapters, we denote the mapping from the state variables to the shadow rate by $r_t = u_r + g^{\mathsf{T}}x_t$, rather than $r_t = \delta_0 + \delta_1^{\mathsf{T}}x_t$.

This means that in the real-world measure we have

$$\vec{x}_{t+1} = \vec{\mu}^{\mathbb{P}} + \mathcal{R}^{\mathbb{P}} \vec{x}_t + \Sigma \epsilon^{\mathbb{P}}_{t+1} \tag{19.22}$$

with

$$\vec{\mu}^{\mathbb{P}} - \vec{\mu}^{\mathbb{Q}} = \Sigma \vec{\lambda}_0 \tag{19.23}$$

and

$$\mathcal{R}^{\mathbb{P}} - \mathcal{R}^{\mathbb{Q}} = \Sigma \lambda_1. \tag{19.24}$$

Exercise 52 *Derive Equations (19.23) and (19.24).*

Then Wu and Xia (2014) show that the time-t discrete forward rate, $f_{n,n+1,t}$ from time n to time $n + 1$ is given by

$$f_{n,n+1,t} = \underline{r} + \sigma_n^{\mathbb{Q}} g \left(\frac{a_n + b_n^{\mathrm{T}} x_t - \underline{r}}{\sigma_n^{\mathbb{Q}}} \right), \tag{19.25}$$

with the function $g(z)$ given by

$$g(z) = \Phi(z) z + \varphi(z). \tag{19.26}$$

In this equation $\Phi(z)$ and $\varphi(z)$ are the cumulative normal distribution and the normal density, respectively, and $(\sigma_n^{\mathbb{Q}})^2$ is the variance of the shadow rate n periods from time t:

$$\left(\sigma_n^{\mathbb{Q}} \right)^2 = Var \left(\rho_{t+n} \right). \tag{19.27}$$

We will discuss the 'coefficients'[14] a_n and b_n in a moment, but for the moment, note that the quantity $\frac{a_n + b_n^{\mathrm{T}} x_t - \underline{r}}{\sigma_n^{\mathbb{Q}}}$ is a 'normalized' distance, z, of the rate-like quantity $a_n + b_n^{\mathrm{T}} x_t$ from the floor, $\underline{r}$, with the volatility of the shadow rate, $\sigma_n^{\mathbb{Q}}$, acting as normalizer. Figure 19.1 then shows the behaviour of the function $g(\cdot)$ as a function of z. Clearly, as the 'normalized distance' of the shadow rate from the lower bound (ie, the quantity $\frac{a_n + b_n^{\mathrm{T}} x_t - \underline{r}}{\sigma_n^{\mathbb{Q}}}$) becomes large, z becomes large, $\Phi(z)$ approaches 1, $\varphi(z)$ approaches zero, and the function $g(z)$ behaves almost like z – which is what we would expect when rates are high, and the floor does not bite.

When this is the case (ie, when rates are very distant from the lower bound) we expect the shadow-affine model to become virtually indistinguishable from

---

[14] We put the word 'coefficients' under scare quotes because, of course, b_n is a vector, not a number. Now that you have been warned, and reassured, we drop the scare quotes.

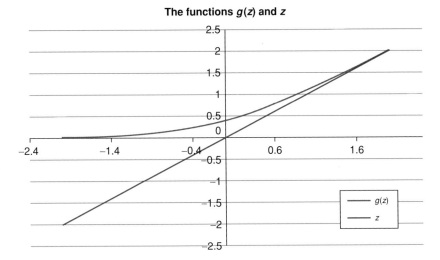

Figure 19.1 The behaviour of the functions $g(z) = \Phi(z)z + \varphi(z)$ and $f(z) = z$ as a function of z. Note that, as the 'distance' z increases (ie, in a high-rate regime), the two functions become almost indistinguishable, and short rate and shadow rate virtually coincide.

a familiar affine model (where the short, not the shadow, rate is an affine function of the state variables). In this situation we would have

$$\lim_{z \to \infty} f_{n,n+1,t} = \lim_{z \to \infty} \left[\underline{r} + \sigma_n^{\mathbb{Q}} g \left(\frac{a_n + b_n^{\mathrm{T}} x_t - \underline{r}}{\sigma_n^{\mathbb{Q}}} \right) \right]$$

$$= \underline{r} + \sigma_n^{\mathbb{Q}} \left(\frac{a_n + b_n^{\mathrm{T}} x_t - \underline{r}}{\sigma_n^{\mathbb{Q}}} \right)$$

$$\Longrightarrow f_{n,n+1,t} = a_n + b_n^{\mathrm{T}} x_t. \tag{19.28}$$

Therefore in this limit the coefficients a_n and b_n must be the same as the coefficients that would obtain from the 'familiar' affine model

$$r_t = \delta_0 + \delta_1^{\mathrm{T}} x_t. \tag{19.29}$$

In general (ie, when we are *not* very far away from the lower bound), Wu and Xia (2014) show that the coefficients a_n and b_n are given by

$$\bar{a}_n = \delta_0 + \delta_1^{\mathrm{T}} J_n \mu^{\mathbb{Q}} \tag{19.30}$$

$$a_n = \bar{a}_n - \frac{1}{2} \delta_1^{\mathrm{T}} J_n \Sigma \Sigma^{\mathrm{T}} J_n^{\mathrm{T}} \delta_1 \tag{19.31}$$

$$b_n^{\mathrm{T}} = \delta_1^{\mathrm{T}} (\mathcal{R}^{\mathbb{Q}})^n \tag{19.32}$$

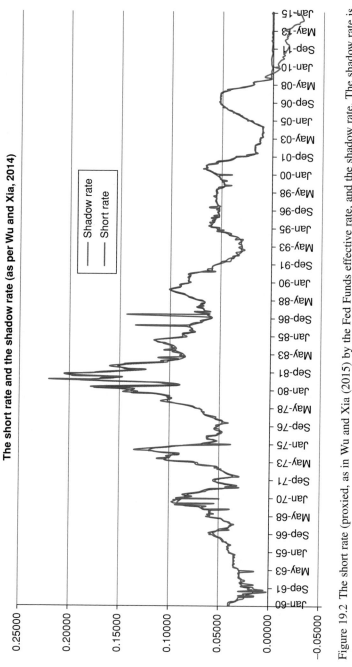

Figure 19.2 The short rate (proxied, as in Wu and Xia (2015) by the Fed Funds effective rate, and the shadow rate. The shadow rate is taken from the file kindly made publicly available by Wu and Xia (2015). Note that the short and shadow rate differ significantly only after 2009.

and

$$J_n = \sum_{j=0,n-1} (\mathcal{R}^{\mathbb{Q}})^j. \tag{19.33}$$

We need one last quantity, namely $\sigma_n^{\mathbb{Q}}$. Luckily, we have posited that the shadow rate should be affine in the state variables. Therefore it is (conditionally) normally distributed, with conditional mean given by

$$E^{\mathbb{Q}}[\rho_{t+n}] = \bar{a}_n + b_n^{\mathrm{T}} x_t \tag{19.34}$$

and conditional variance given by

$$\left(\sigma_n^{\mathbb{Q}}\right)^2 = \mathbb{V}ar(\rho_{t+n}) = \sum_{j=0,n-1} \delta_1^{\mathrm{T}} (\mathcal{R}^{\mathbb{Q}})^j \Sigma \Sigma^{\mathrm{T}} \left((\mathcal{R}^{\mathbb{Q}})^{\mathrm{T}}\right)^j \delta_1. \tag{19.35}$$

Of, course, once we have the (discrete) forward rates, we can reconstruct the (discrete) yield curve, and we can derive everything we may wish about the dynamics in the presence of a zero bound.

19.5 DOES IT MATTER?

19.5.1 The Shadow and Short Rates Compared

With rates as low as they have been in US dollars and in euro after 2009, the answer is, clearly, '*yes, a lot*'. Let's look at Figure 19.2. We have taken the Fed Funds effective rate as a proxy for the short rate.[15] We have also taken the shadow rate calculated and kindly made available in Wu and Xia (2015). In Figure 19.3 we then zoom into the last 10 years.

The shadow and the short rate were virtually indistinguishable before 2009 (and it is amazing that Bomfin (2003b) should have had the inspiration to look into this problem as early as 2003!) However, by early 2014 – when the Fed rate reached and remained at around 25 basis points for the foreseeable near future – the shadow rate had become as low as -3%. Clearly, this makes any assessment of the slope of the yield curve very different from what one would naively read looking at the market yield curve. This matters, because, as we discuss in the Part VI of this book, the magnitude and sign of the slope are simple and robust indicators of expected excess returns. We will explore this angle at length in what follows.

19.5.2 The Effect of the Shadow Rate on Long Yields

We can look at the effect of the shadow rate from a different perspective. Figure 19.4 shows the differences in risk premia for the 5-, 10- and 30-year US Treasury yields obtained using the stochastic-market-price-of-risk model described in Chapter 35, and by imposing that either the shadow rate, or the

---

[15] This is the same choice made by Wu and Xia (2015).

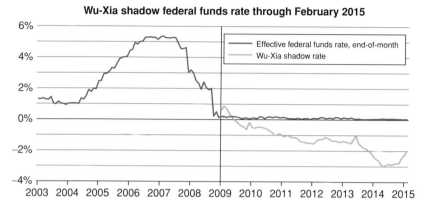

Figure 19.3 Same as Figure 19.2, but zooming in the 2003–2015 period. Note that in early 2014 the shadow rate becomes as low as -3%. *Sources:* Board of Gavernors of the Federal Reserve System and Wu and Xia (2014)

observed short rate, should be affine functions of the state variables. Figure 19.5 then shows the time series of the risk premia for yields of 5-, 10-, 15- and 30-year maturity. As these pictures clearly show, taking the effect of the shadow rate into account does matter a lot.

When the money-under-the-mattress optionality is taken into account, the differences in risk premia are large – at first blush, surprisingly so for long-maturity yields. Before commenting on the size, does the sign make sense?

Consider an observed market yield, y_t^T. Neglecting optionality, this can be written as

$$y_t^T = \mathbb{E}_t^{\mathbb{P}} \left[y_t^T \right] + RP_t^T, \tag{19.36}$$

where $\mathbb{E}_t^{\mathbb{P}}[y_t^T]$ denotes the *real-world* expectation, and RP_t^T the risk premium.

As we have seen, when the optionality is taken into account, we have

$$y_t^T = \mathbb{E}_t^{\mathbb{P}} \left[y_t^T \right] + RP_t^T + OPT_t^T, \tag{19.37}$$

where OPT_t^T is now the value of the floor (in yield terms). Now, the sign of the risk premium is a priori indeterminate, but an option value has to be positive. Since we all agree on the observed market yield, y_t^T, if our expectations do not change, then the risk premium, RP_t^T, must be smaller when the optionality is taken into account. This is indeed what we observe in Figure 19.4.

But why is the change in risk premium so much higher for the 30-year yield – a yield which was for every day in the time series at a much higher level than the short rate and the zero floor? To understand this point, let's neglect convexity, and think of a yield as the average over paths of the average over time of the short rate:

$$y_t^T = \frac{1}{T-t} \mathbb{E}^{\mathbb{Q}} \left[\int_t^T r(s)ds \right]. \tag{19.38}$$

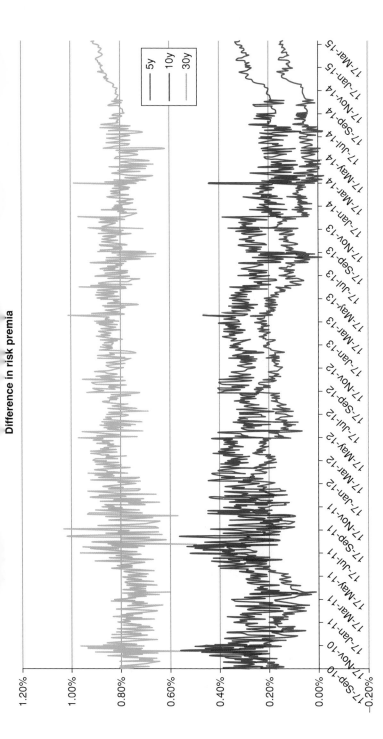

Figure 19.4 Differences in risk premia for the 5-year (bottom line), 10-year (middle line) and 30-year (top line) US Treasury yields obtained using the stochastic-market-price-of-risk model described in Chapter 35, and by imposing that either the shadow rate or the observed short rate should be affine functions of the state variables. A positive value indicates that the risk premium without the shadow rate is higher than it would be with the zero floor.

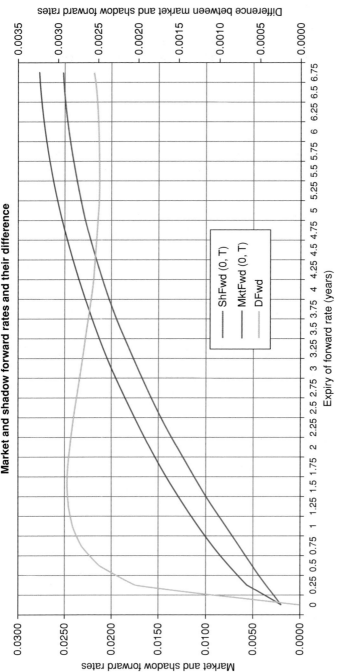

Figure 19.5 The market and shadow forward rates for a hypothetical but realistic yield curve. The volatility of the forward rates was assumed to be given by $\sigma_f(T) = \sigma_0 e^{-\kappa T}$, with $\sigma_0 = 0.014$ and $\kappa = 0.12$. In this part of the study the floor was assumed to be at 20 basis points (this is very close to the value chosen by Wu and Xia (2015) in their study). The bottom blue curve (labelled ShFwd(0,T)) shows the term structure of the shadow forward rates, the middle red (labelled MktFwd(0,T)) displays the term structure of the market forward rates, and the humped green curve (labelled DFwd) indicates the difference between the two curves. Note how the shadow yield curve is *less* steep than the market yield curve. This will influence inferences about excess returns or the phase of the business cycle that can be drawn from the steepness of the yield curve. Choosing a more realistic term (humped) term structure of forward rate volatilities – while retaining approximately the same average volatility – did not materially change the difference between the two forward rate curves or the qualitative conclusions. The axis for

If the shape of the yield curve is upward sloping (as it certainly is in the period covered by the figure) the short rate should revert to a reversion level well above its current level, and the optionality should therefore become less and less valuable. This is true. However, both in the real- and in the risk-neutral world, the reversion speed is very small (once again, this goes back to the quasi-unit-root nature of rate processes). Indeed, Figure 19.4 was produced with a reversion speed (for the reversion level) that gave an half live of almost ten years.

There is therefore a tug-of-war at play: on the one hand, as time passes, uncertainty increases, and all options are worth more and more; on the other hand, the reversion speed should move the short rate away from the zero bound, but can do so only very slowly. The result is what Figures 19.6 and (indirectly) 19.4 show.

Which brings us to our first conclusion: when rates are low (and weakly mean-reverting) the effect of the shadow rate on risk premia is not only large at all maturities, but can actually *increase* with maturity. If and how much it increases depends on a subtle interplay between the current level of each yield (the steepness of the yield curve), its maturity (ie, the 'option expiry), and the strength of the reversion speed for the state variables (which affects the yield volatility). See Figure 19.6 in this respect.

19.5.3 Sensitivity of the Results to the Floor Level

This naturally brings to the fore another question: how sensitive are these results to the level of the floor? We show in Figures 19.7 and 19.8 the time series of the 10- and 30-year risk premium, respectively (again calculated using the stochastic-market-price-of-risk model described in Chapter 35) for values of the floor of 25, −25 and −40 basis points. (By the way, the study by Wu and Xia (2015) referred to a floor of +25 basis points.) As the figures show, the lower the floor, the higher the risk premium. This makes sense: the lower the floor, the less valuable the money-under-the-mattress option, and therefore more of the observed yield can be ascribed to the risk premium (instead of the floor option premium).

In absolute terms, the sensitivity to the level of the floor is modest for the 10-year yield, and becomes significant for the 30-year yield. Compared with the level of the risk premium, however, the impact of the shadow rate remains important for all maturities and for all strike levels.

19.6 A BROADER VIEW OF THE TOPIC

As usual, we have preferred to deal with one approach in some detail, lest we spread ourselves too thin. It is time, however, to put the topic in a wider perspective.

As mentioned, probably the first study in this area (after Black's (1995), that is) is the work by Bomfin (2003a), who used a two-factor shadow-rate model

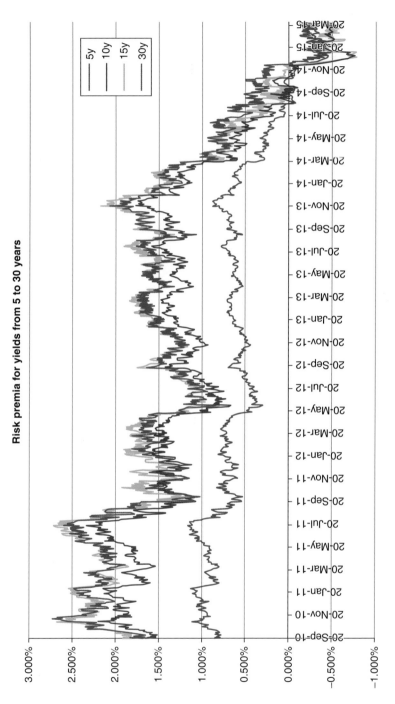

Figure 19.6 Time series of the risk premia from the stochastic-market-price-of-risk model for yields of 5-, 10-, 15- and 30-year maturity. 20 September 2010 to 27 March 2015, US Treasuries.

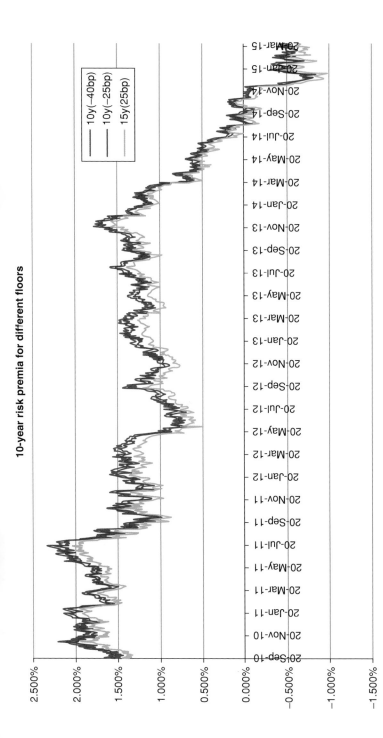

Figure 19.7 Time series for the 10-year risk premia from the stochastic-market-price-of-risk model for value of the floor of −40 basis points (top line), −25 basis point (middle line) and +25 basis points (bottom line).

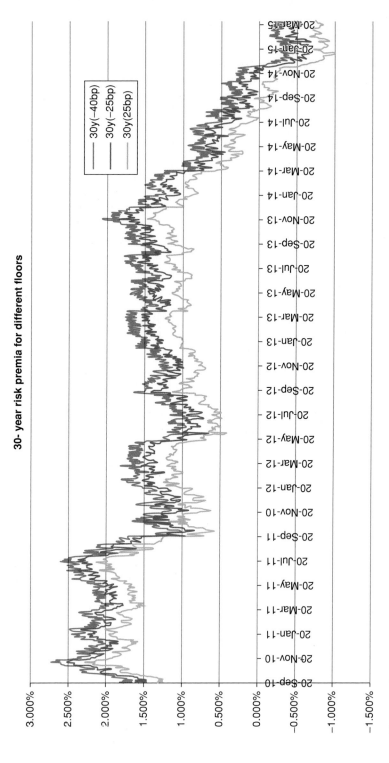

Figure 19.8 Same as Figure 19.7, for the 30-year yield.

to assess the likelihood of the US monetary authorities hitting the zero lower bound. Given the date, this work was certainly prescient.

A currency for which the zero bound has been a reality for a very long time is the Japanese yen. Indeed, between 2004 and 2012 several studies appeared (by Gorovoi and Linetsky (2004), Ueno, Baba and Sakurai (2006), Ichiue and Ueno (2007) and Kim and Singleton (2012)) to study this problem.[16]

Apart from Bomfin (2003a), interest in the zero lower bound for US Treasury rates picks during the Great Repression. Priebsch (2013) places himself in a continuous-time setting and shows how to compute arbitrage-free yields in a multifactor Gaussian setting. His solutions, alas, require numerical integrations. In his treatment, he shows that (i) the approximate approach by Ichiue and Ueno (2013) (which ignores the Jensen inequality) is rather imprecise, and (ii) that by including the second-order term the solution becomes very accurate – and exact for Gaussian models. The insight in Priebsch (2013) is taken up by Bauer and Rudebusch (2016),[17] who move to a discrete setting and, by doing so, avoids the numerical integration in Priebsch (2013).

Some of the best-known studies relating to US Treasuries are those by Ichiue and Ueno (2007), Christensen and Rudebusch (2016) and, in particular by Krippner (2013). The approach by Wu and Xia (2014) discussed in this chapter was developed independently from Krippner's (2013) work, but can be shown to be equivalent, as shown in Krippner (2013). By and large, the consensus for US Treasuries is that in the wake of the Great Recession world shadow-rate Gaussian models make a difference, and give a substantial improvement over non-shadow-rate models. So, for instance, Christensen and Rudebusch (2016) state that

> ... the shadow-rate model provides superior in-sample fit, matches the compression in yield volatility unlike the standard model, and delivers better real-time short rate forecasts. Thus, while one could expect the regular model to get back on track as soon as short- and medium-term yields rise from their current low levels, our findings suggest that, in the meantime, shadow-rate models offer a tractable way of mitigating the problems related to the ZLB constraint on nominal yields. Since shadow-rate models collapse to the regular model away from the ZLB, we recommend their use not only when yields are low, but in general.[18]

Finally, Bauer and Rudebusch (2016) contribute to the field 'by documenting the empirical relevance of the [zero lower bound] and the problems of affine models in this context, [by] showing the fragility of shadow rate estimates, and by estimating the tightness of the [zero lower bound] over time'. From the policy perspective the main contribution by Bauer and Rudebusch (2016) is to relate the various aspects of monetary policy in a [zero lower bound] regime

---

[16] Gorovoi and Linetsky (2004) give an analytic solution for the one-factor model by Ueno et al. (2006). Ichiue and Ueno (2007) and Kim and Singleton (2012) use two-factor models.

[17] See their Appendix D.   [18] p. 25.

using the modal path.[19] Given the asymmetry in the probability distribution of the future short rate (at least during the 2009–2015 period), Bauer and Rudebusch (2016) argue[20] that using the mode rather than that the median or the mean makes sense, and produces estimates for the implied 'lift-off time' from 2009 to 2012 that were at the time 'very closely matched by private-sector and survey forecasts.'[21]

In closing, there is one important word of caution: approaches based on the shadow rate make sense (or, rather, really make a difference) when rates are exceptionally low. When rates are *that* low, the economy is likely to be in a rather exceptional state. However, the estimation of the model parameters is usually made by implicitly enforcing the assumption of stationarity – ie, by assuming that the same parameters apply in the pre- and post-zero-lower-bound period. The ubiquity of the assumption does not make it any more palatable. The situation is made worse when macroeconomic variables are used as state variables in addition to yield-curve-based variables. Bauer and Rudebusch (2016) suggest that regime-switching models could be used, but, to the best of our knowledge, precious little work has been done in this direction (at least as far as the shadow-rate problem is concerned).

---

[19] We discuss why the mode may be more relevant than the mean or the median in Chapter 8.

[20] See their Sections 4.2 and 5.2 in particular. (Section 4.2 looks at the asymmetric distribution of future short rates, and Section 5.2 compares estimates of liftoff made using the mean and the median path.)

[21] p. 23.

PART V

THE VALUE OF CONVEXITY

In this part of the book we look again at convexity. We want to understand if the value of convexity is fairly reflected in the shape of the yield curve. This means that we must first estimate what convexity 'should be' and then compare our theoretical estimates with the market's.

We carry out this comparison from three different angles.

The first (Chapter 20) is model driven, in the sense that we look at the output from affine models to gauge the value of convexity.

The second (dealt with in Chapter 21) is (almost) model agnostic, and looks at what the shape of the yield curve (its 'carry' and its 'roll-down') tells us about what the value of convexity should be.

The third (Chapter 22) is empirical: given what we have learnt about what convexity should be, we explore whether any discrepancies between the theoretical and the observed curvature of the yield curve can be effectively exploited.

As we shall see, extracting the value of convexity boils down to crystallizing the difference between what yield volatilities should be in theory and what they will be in practice. The infinitely wise words of Yogi Berra's that provide the opening quote to Chapter 22 act as a healthy reminder of the width of the chasm that, more often than not, separates theory and reality.

CHAPTER 20

The Value of Convexity

"Right now it's only a notion, but I think I can get money to make
it into a concept, and later turn it into an idea."
A movie producer at a Hollywood party in
Woody Allen's *Annie Hall*[1]

20.1 THE PURPOSE OF THIS CHAPTER

In this chapter we put some flesh around the theoretical bones of Chapter 10.[2]
More precisely, earlier in the book I have argued that convexity is intrinsically
different from risk premia (whose value can be realized with essentially static
strategies). I made the point that the value of convexity can be harvested only
by engaging in a very active hedging strategy, akin to the practice of gamma
trading in the derivatives domain. In this chapter, I provide an expression for
the value of convexity and discuss the actual hedging strategies that must be
established in order to capture the value of convexity.

I do so first by looking at the stylized (and not very realistic) case of
the Vasicek model, and then by employing more general and realistic affine
models. The more general treatment presented in Sections 20.4 and to 20.5
requires some of the formalism and of the vector notation that is introduced in
Chapter 18. The reader who is not familiar with vector notation may want to
go back to Chapter 18 and refresh her memory.

By the end of the chapter we will know what the value of convexity *should*
be, if the model of our choice is correct, and if it has been properly calibrated.
These are big *if*s. We will therefore explore in the next chapter to what extent
we can obtain (quasi-) model-independent results about convexity.

20.2 BREAK-EVEN VOLATILITY – THE VASICEK SETTING

A sketch of the map of the road ahead is as follows. We start by placing ourselves in a Vasicek world. We are going to use two bonds to create a risk-less

---

[1] Quoted in Pinker (2014), p. 36.
[2] This chapter follows closely the treatment in Rebonato and Putyatin (2017).

portfolio – a portfolio, which, as we know, *qua* riskless can only earn the riskless rate. Since, as we also know, working with bond prices is unpleasant, we swiftly change coordinates and work in terms of their yields. This is handy, but conceptually irrelevant.

More importantly, we express the process for these yields in terms of *the single state variable* of our model, and we relate the value of convexity to the yield volatilities (not the volatilities of the state variable(s)). When we have done this we show that, after some clever reshuffling of terms, the volatility of the state variable that drives the whole yield curve determines the ratio of two quantities. The first we interpret as the 'yield give-up' – ie, how much yield the investor must surrender in order to enter the risk-less long-convexity position – and the second as the 'convexity pick-up' – how much she can hope to gain by doing so. (Both quantities, of course, can be positive or negative.) In the second part of this chapter we extend the treatment to many state variables. When we do so, the algebra will become more tedious, but the ideas will not change.

So, to get started, we posit that the short rate, r_t, should follow the Vasicek process

$$dr_t = \kappa \left(\theta - r_t \right) dt + \sigma_r dz_t^r \tag{20.1}$$

where all the symbols have the by-now-familiar meaning. We then know that the bond price, P_t^T, is given by

$$P_t^T = e^{A_t^T + B_t^T r_t} \tag{20.2}$$

and therefore the yield, y_t^T, is simply

$$y_t^T = -\frac{1}{T-t} \log P_t^T = -\frac{1}{T-t} \left(A_t^T + B_t^T r_t \right) \equiv a_t^T + b_t^T r_t \tag{20.3}$$

with

$$a_t^T = -\frac{A_t^T}{T-t} \tag{20.4}$$

$$b_t^T = -\frac{B_t^T}{T-t}. \tag{20.5}$$

The process for the constant-maturity yield is therefore given by

$$dy_t^T = b_t^T dr_t = \left[b_t^T \kappa \left(\theta - r_t \right) \right] dt + b_t^T \sigma_r \, dz_t^r \tag{20.6}$$

$$= \quad [\quad \mu_{y_t^T} \quad] dt + [\sigma_{y_t^T}] \, dz_t^r. \tag{20.7}$$

One important observation is in order: the expression we have just derived refers to a constant-maturity yield, eg, a yield which is always a 10-year yield.[3] In reality, after the time step, dt, the yield will change because it will change residual maturity (it will be a 10-year $-dt$ yield.) We will have to take this

---

[3] This is why we have not included in the expressions terms such as $\frac{\partial a_t^T}{\partial t} dt$ or $\frac{\partial b_t^T}{\partial t} dt$.

into account when we look at our portfolio construction. For the moment, we have determined the process followed by a T-maturity yield because we want to express a bond price as a function of its constant-maturity yield: $P_t^T = P_t^T \left(y_t^T \right)$, plus a time derivative that takes into account the effect of the passage of time on the quantities A_t^T and B_t^T. Using Ito's lemma we obtain for the price process of a generic bond

$$dP_t^T = \frac{\partial P_t^T}{\partial t} dt + \frac{\partial P_t^T}{\partial y_t^T} \mu_{y_t^T} dt + \frac{\partial P_t^T}{\partial y_t^T} \sigma_{y_t^T} dz_t^r + \frac{1}{2} \frac{\partial^2 P_t^T}{\partial \left(y_t^T \right)^2} \sigma_{y_t^T}^2 dt. \quad (20.8)$$

As usual, we now build a risk-less portfolio, Π_t, made up of one unit of bond T_1 ($\omega_1 = 1$) and ω_2 units of bond T_2:

$$\Pi_t = \sum_{i=1,2} \omega_i P_t^{T_i}. \quad (20.9)$$

With some cunning, we can choose the weight ω_2 so as to make the stochastic term dz_t^r disappear:

$$\omega_2 = -\frac{\frac{\partial P_t^{T_1}}{\partial y_t^{T_1}} \sigma_{y_t^{T_1}}}{\frac{\partial P_t^{T_2}}{\partial y_t^{T_2}} \sigma_{y_t^{T_2}}}. \quad (20.10)$$

(See Chapter 16 for an essentially identical derivation at a slightly more leisurely pace.)

Since the terms in dz_t^r have disappeared, the portfolio is now risk-less. Since it is risk-less, under penalty of arbitrage it can only earn the risk-less return

$$d\Pi_t = \Pi_t r_t dt = \sum \omega_i P_t^{T_i} r_t dt. \quad (20.11)$$

Therefore we have

$$d\Pi_t = \sum \omega_i \left[\frac{\partial P_t^{T_i}}{\partial t} + \frac{\partial P_t^{T_i}}{\partial y_t^{T_i}} \mu_{y_t^{T_i}} + \frac{1}{2} \frac{\partial^2 P_t^{T_i}}{\partial \left(y_t^{T_i} \right)^2} \sigma_{y_t^{T_i}}^2 \right] dt$$

$$= \underbrace{\left[\sum \omega_i P_t^{T_i} \right]}_{\text{value of the portfolio}} r_t dt. \quad (20.12)$$

We can rearrange terms to give

$$\sum \omega_i \left[\left(\frac{\partial P_t^{T_i}}{\partial t} + \frac{\partial P_t^{T_i}}{\partial y_t^{T_i}} \mu_{y_t^T} - P_t^{T_i} r_t \right) + \frac{1}{2} \underbrace{\frac{\partial^2 P_t^{T_i}}{\partial \left(y_t^{T_i} \right)^2} \sigma_{y_t^{T_i}}^2}_{\text{convexity}} \right] = 0. \quad (20.13)$$

Up to this point we have not made use of the specific form of the Vasicek model. We have gone through an apparently unnecessarily tortuous route of going from the state variable (r_t) to the yields and from the yields to the bond prices, when we could have applied Ito's lemma directly to the bond-price expression that contains the short-rate state variable. We have chosen to do so, because we wanted to write our results in term of yield volatilities (not of the volatility of a slightly mysterious state variable such as the short rate). Yield volatilities are (almost) market observables, and therefore have a more 'concrete' feel to them than the volatility of the short rate (or of some other – and possibly latent – state variable).

If we want to proceed with the Vasicek model we simply have to remember that the volatility of the T_i-maturity yield is given by

$$\sigma_{y_t^{T_i}} = b_t^{T_i} \sigma_r \qquad (20.14)$$

and therefore

$$\sum \omega_i \left[\left(\frac{\partial P_t^{T_i}}{\partial t} + \frac{\partial P_t^{T_i}}{\partial y_t^{T_i}} \mu_{y_t^{T_i}} - P_t^{T_i} r_t \right) + \frac{1}{2} \frac{\partial^2 P_t^{T_i}}{\partial \left(y_t^{T_i} \right)^2} \underbrace{\left(b_t^{T_i} \right)^2 \sigma_r^2}_{\text{yield variance}} \right] = 0. \qquad (20.15)$$

We can rewrite Equation (20.15) more compactly as

$$C\sigma_r^2 - Y = 0 \qquad (20.16)$$

with C (the 'portfolio convexity') given by

$$C = \frac{1}{2} \sum \omega_i \frac{\partial^2 P_t^{T_i}}{\partial \left(y_t^{T_i} \right)^2} \left(b_t^{T_i} \right)^2 \qquad (20.17)$$

and Y (the "portfolio yield give-up")[4] given by

$$Y = - \sum \omega_i \left(\frac{\partial P_t^{T_i}}{\partial t} + \frac{\partial P_t^{T_i}}{\partial y_t^{T_i}} \mu_{y_t^{T_i}} - P_t^{T_i} r_t \right). \qquad (20.18)$$

This allows us to define a break-even volatility,

$$\sigma_r^2 = \frac{Y}{C}. \qquad (20.19)$$

This quantity has a simple intuitive meaning: if, over the next time interval, the realized volatility is greater than the break-even volatility, a long-convexity portfolio will make money; conversely, if it is lower, the portfolio will lose money. (The reason for choosing C – for 'convexity' – as the symbol for Equation (20.17) is pretty obvious. We will explain in Section 20.6 why we gave the symbol Y, reminiscent of 'yield', to the expression in Equation (20.18).)

---

[4] We explain in Section 20.7 the interpretation of this term.

20.3 PROBLEMS WITH THE VASICEK VERSION
OF THE BREAK-EVEN VOLATILITY

Lord, give me chastity and continence, but not yet.

St Augustine, *Confessions*[5]

In the simple case we studied in the previous section the result was a bit contrived, because, in a Vasicek setting, the only volatility that matters was the volatility of the short rate, and therefore the break-even volatility seemed to be related to the uncertainty in something like the Fed funds. At face value, this is hardly realistic: in reality, what really affects the profitability of the portfolio are the volatilities of very-long-dated yields (or, even more directly, of very-long-maturity bond prices). In the Vasicek model, the volatility of the short rate is linked to the volatilities of the quantities that matter (the yields or bond prices) via the duration terms $\frac{\partial P_t^{T_i}}{\partial y_t^{T_i}}$ and via the term, $b_t^{T_i}$, that translates the volatility of the short rate into the volatility of the appropriate yield. Unfortunately, we have discussed in Chapter 8 (see Section 8.3.4) that the particular (monotonic exponentially decaying) link between the yield volatilities and the volatility of the short-rate state variable is one of the least appealing features of the Vasicek setting.[6] So, to begin with, there is some room for improvement here.

There are other, subtler, problems, however, which are independent of the particular model setting which we may have chosen.

The first is the following. In general, the all-important yield volatilities are determined by the volatility of the factor(s), (σ_r in the Vasicek case). Now, according to the model we use to predict the value of convexity, the volatility is perfectly known, and, over each time step, the state variable exactly delivers the same variance. (Recall that, with Brownian diffusions with non-stochastic volatilities, there are no 'volatility surprises' and the quadratic variation – the 'amount of vibration' – that will be delivered over any time step dt is exactly known and deterministic.) If this is the case, according to the model we have developed over the next time step the delivered variance of the yield is not an uncertain quantity, and the C term should exactly balance the Y term. Therefore no money should ever be made or lost. 'Ah, but this is only what the model says,' the reader may rebut. 'In reality we all known that over any finite interval there will be uncertainty in the realized volatility, so Equation (20.19) is still useful to predict whether our duration-neutral portfolio will make or lose money.'

This is true. However, the moment we say that there is uncertainty, then, if we were purists, we should no longer use the predictions about our break-even variance afforded by Equation (20.19), because these predictions were obtained assuming a deterministic and known volatility.[7] The

---

[5] Vol VIII, 17   [6] See also in this respect Chapter 30.

[7] For those readers who are familiar with option pricing, there is a similar lack of logical consistency in those derivations of the expected profit over a re-hedging period Δt for the holder of a perfectly-delta-hedged option in a deterministic-volatility setting:

$$P\&L = \frac{1}{2}\Gamma S^2 \left(\sigma_{real}^2 - \sigma_{impl}^2\right)\Delta t \qquad (20.20)$$

deterministic-and-known-volatility model *is* still useful, but in a rather heuristic manner, because Equation (20.16) gives the break-even volatility that would apply if there were no uncertainty in the delivered variance.

The second conceptual problem alluded to above is related to the ubiquitous practice of model recalibration. When we calibrate a time-homogeneous term-structure model, first we assume that the volatilities to which the model are calibrated are fully deterministic and constant until the end of the time. When we come back the following day, we discover that the immutable volatilities have changed. Hard-nosed and pragmatic individuals as we are, we admit that the durations and the volatility of the factor(s) we had assumed yesterday to have come down with Moses' tables actually change (a bit) from one time step to the next, and that, by virtue of this change, they imply a different yield volatility than ex ante anticipated. We handle this by the process of periodic recalibration of the model parameters to the changing market conditions.[8]

The logical inconsistency of course comes from the fact that, at the bottom of our heart, today we know full well that tomorrow we will change the model parameters, but today we price and build our replicating portfolio pretending that we never will. In a different (option-related) context (Rebonato, 2002) I likened this behaviour to that of a libertine, who every day promises to mend his ways and retire to a monastery, but only after the next escapade. (This, incidentally, also suggests how St Augustine would have calibrated his affine models.)

So, at least within the confines of our chosen model, Equation (20.19) is a perfectly valid equilibrium condition. However, the moment we use Equation (20.19) as a predictor of the expected profit from a duration-neutral convexity strategy, it is important to understand that we are guilty of a logical inconsistency. We plough ahead nonetheless because, when we use Equation (20.19) for prediction purposes in the context of a convexity strategy, we make the assumption that, even if we used a stochastic volatility model, the true expression for the profit and loss would be sufficiently similar to make the approach useful. This is, after all, the assumption invariably made, but always forgotten, when Equation (20.20) is used in 'gamma trading' with options.

What is far more practically important in order to make the approach useful as a predictor is to create a better link between the volatilities of the state variables and the all-important volatilities of the bond prices – and, this, as we know, is one of the weaknesses of the Vasicek model. Fortunately, in a multifactor case it still remains true that what affects the profitability of the portfolio will be whether the realized volatilities of the yields (and hence of

(In this Equation, S is the underlying, Γ is the gamma of the option from a deterministic-volatility model such as, say, the Black (1976), and σ^2_{real} and σ^2_{impl} are (the squares of) the realized and implied volatilities, respectively.)

[8] Would a stochastic-volatility model help to fix the logical inconsistency? To some extent it would, but only if the model parameters that describe the stochasticity of the volatility (say, the volatility of the volatility) were in turn invariant over time.

the bonds) will be greater or smaller than what predicted by the terms $\left(b_t^{T_i}\right)^2 \sigma_{x_i}^2$. We formalize this intuition more precisely in the next section.

20.4 GENERALIZING TO MANY FACTORS

The generalization from the Vasicek setting to many factors is conceptually straightforward, but notationally a bit heavy-going. As suggested in the introductory section, the reader who is not familiar with matrix notation may want to read again Chapter 18.

Consider a set of $n - 1$ state variables[9], $\overrightarrow{x}_t$, which are assumed to follow a joint mean-reverting processes of the form

$$d\overrightarrow{x}_t = \underline{K}\left(\overrightarrow{\theta} - \overrightarrow{x}_t\right)dt + \underline{S}d\overrightarrow{z}_t \tag{20.21}$$

with

$$E\left[dz_t^i dz_t^j\right] = \delta_{ij}dt. \tag{20.22}$$

(As usual, the symbol δ_{ij} – the Kroeneker delta – signifies 1 if $i = j$, and 0 otherwise.)[10]

Let these state variables be related to the short rate by an affine transformation of the form

$$r_t = u_r + \overrightarrow{g}^{\mathrm{T}}\overrightarrow{x}_t. \tag{20.23}$$

Then we have shown in Chapter 18 that the bond price, $P_t^T = P(\tau)$, will be given by

$$P_t^T = e^{A_t^T + \left(\overrightarrow{B}_t^T\right)^{\mathrm{T}}\overrightarrow{x}_t}. \tag{20.24}$$

In order to mirror the treatment presented in the first part of the chapter, we would like to work in terms of yields. The process for each of these constant-maturity yields can be formally written as

$$dy_k = \mu_{y_k}dt + \left(\overrightarrow{\sigma}^{y_k}\right)^{\mathrm{T}}d\overrightarrow{z}_t. \tag{20.25}$$

Let's derive the expressions for μ_{y_k} and $\left(\overrightarrow{\sigma}^{y_k}\right)^{T}$.

Given the expression preceding for the bond price, remembering the definition

$$y_t^T = -\frac{1}{T-t}\log P_t^T = -\frac{1}{T-t}\left(A_t^T + \left(\overrightarrow{B}_t^T\right)^{\mathrm{T}}\overrightarrow{x}_t\right) \tag{20.26}$$

[9] Why $n - 1$? Because we will need one more bond than factors to build a risk-less portfolio, and we did not want to carry around the ugly $n + 1$ index throughout the chapter. So, we have $n - 1$ factors and n bonds in our risk-less portfolio.

[10] We have used the symbols $\underline{K}$ and $\underline{S}$ for the reversion-speed matrix and the diffusion matrix, repectively, to remind ourselves that they are matrices and not numbers, but from now on we will lighten the notation by dropping the underscores.

and denoting by y_k the T_k-maturity yield, $y_k \equiv y_t^{T_k}$, we easily obtain for a constant-maturity yield

$$dy_k = -\frac{1}{T-t} \left(\overrightarrow{B}_t^{T_k}\right)^{\mathrm{T}} d\overrightarrow{x}_t \qquad (20.27)$$

and therefore

$$dy_k = \left(\overrightarrow{b}_t^{T_k}\right)^{T} \left[K\left(\overrightarrow{\theta} - \overrightarrow{x}_t\right) dt + Sd\overrightarrow{z}_t\right]. \qquad (20.28)$$

So as not to miss the wood for the trees, the reader may want to compare the expression we just obtained with Equation (20.6).

Continuing with the flow of the multivariable derivation, we now have

$$\mu_{y_k} = \left(\overrightarrow{b}_t^{T_k}\right)^{\mathrm{T}} K(\overrightarrow{\theta} - \overrightarrow{x}_t) \qquad (20.29)$$

and

$$\left(\overrightarrow{\sigma}^{y_k}\right)^{\mathrm{T}} = \left(b_t^{T_k}\right)^{\mathrm{T}} S, \qquad (20.30)$$

and therefore the $n-1$ components of the volatility of the kth yield are given by the elements of the vector $\left(\overrightarrow{\sigma}^{y_k}\right)^{\mathrm{T}}$:

$$\left(\overrightarrow{\sigma}^{y_k}\right)^{\mathrm{T}} = \left(b_t^{T_k}\right)^{\mathrm{T}} S. \qquad (20.31)$$

The total volatility of the kth yield, which we denote by σ_k, is then given by

$$\sigma_k^2 = \left(\overrightarrow{\sigma}^{y_k}\right)^{\mathrm{T}} \left(\overrightarrow{\sigma}^{y_k}\right). \qquad (20.32)$$

Just to be clear: each $\left(\overrightarrow{b}_t^{T_k}\right)^{T}$ is a row vector. When a row vector such as $\left(b_t^{T_k}\right)^{\mathrm{T}}$ is multiplied by a matrix, such as S, the result is another row vector, in this case, $\left(\overrightarrow{\sigma}^{y_k}\right)^{\mathrm{T}}$; when this row vector is multiplied by a (column) vector, such as $d\overrightarrow{z}_t$, the result is just a number – in this case the stochastic component of the change of the kth yield.

Looking back at the derivation we obtained in the Vasicek case, we want to derive an expression for the yield volatilities, ie, the multidimensional equivalent of the term $\left(b_t^{T_i}\right)^2 \sigma_r^2$ – see Equation (20.15). To do so, note first that the stochastic part of dy_t^k, $\left(dy_t^k\right)_{stoch}$, is a number given by

$$\left(dy_t^k\right)_{stoch} = \left(b_t^{T_k}\right)^{\mathrm{T}} Sd\overrightarrow{z}_t \qquad (20.33)$$

and so the vector $\left(\overrightarrow{dy_t}\right)_{stoch}$ is just

$$\left(\overrightarrow{dy_t}\right)_{stoch} = \begin{bmatrix} \left(b_t^{T_1}\right)^{\mathrm{T}} Sd\overrightarrow{z}_t \\ \left(b_t^{T_2}\right)^{\mathrm{T}} Sd\overrightarrow{z}_t \\ \dots \\ \left(b_t^{T_n}\right)^{\mathrm{T}} Sd\overrightarrow{z}_t \end{bmatrix}. \qquad (20.34)$$

Therefore the vector $\overrightarrow{(dy_t)}^2 = \overrightarrow{\sigma_y^2}$ is given by

$$
\overrightarrow{(dy_t)}^2 = \overrightarrow{\sigma_y^2} dt =
\begin{bmatrix}
\left(b_t^{T_1}\right)^{\mathrm{T}} S\, d\overrightarrow{z}_t \left(d\overrightarrow{z}_t\right)^{\mathrm{T}} S^{\mathrm{T}} \left(b_t^{T_1}\right) \\
\left(b_t^{T_2}\right)^{\mathrm{T}} S\, d\overrightarrow{z}_t \left(d\overrightarrow{z}_t\right)^{\mathrm{T}} S^{\mathrm{T}} \left(b_t^{T_2}\right) \\
\ldots \\
\left(b_t^{T_n}\right)^{\mathrm{T}} S\, d\overrightarrow{z}_t \left(d\overrightarrow{z}_t\right)^{\mathrm{T}} S^{\mathrm{T}} \left(b_t^{T_n}\right)
\end{bmatrix} dt
$$

$$
=
\begin{bmatrix}
\left(b_t^{T_1}\right)^{\mathrm{T}} SS^{\mathrm{T}} \left(b_t^{T_1}\right) \\
\left(b_t^{T_2}\right)^{\mathrm{T}} SS^{\mathrm{T}} \left(b_t^{T_2}\right) \\
\ldots \\
\left(b_t^{T_n}\right)^{\mathrm{T}} SS^{\mathrm{T}} \left(b_t^{T_n}\right)
\end{bmatrix} dt,
\tag{20.35}
$$

where we made use of the fact that, because of orthogonality,

$$
d\overrightarrow{z}_t \left(d\overrightarrow{z}_t\right)^{\mathrm{T}} =
\begin{bmatrix}
1 & 0 & \ldots & 0 \\
0 & 1 & \ldots & 0 \\
\ldots & \ldots & \ldots & \ldots \\
0 & 0 & \ldots & 1
\end{bmatrix} dt = I_n dt.
$$

Now we have all the pieces in place to generalize to the multifactor case the one-factor Equation (20.15), that we rewrite below for ease of reference:

$$
\sum \omega_i \left[\left(\frac{\partial P_t^{T_i}}{\partial t} + \frac{\partial P_t^{T_i}}{\partial y_t^{T_i}} \mu_{y_t^{T_i}} - P_t^{T_i} r_t \right) + \frac{1}{2} \frac{\partial^2 P_t^{T_i}}{\partial \left(y_t^{T_i}\right)^2} \left(b_t^{T_i}\right)^2 \sigma_r^2 \right]
$$

$$
= 0 \text{ (one factor)}.
\tag{20.36}
$$

We have two tasks at hand: the first is to compute an explicit expression for the time derivative term, $\frac{\partial P_t^{T_i}}{\partial t}$. The other is to obtain the multidimensional equivalent of the single-state-variable equation we obtained for the Vasicek model. To simplify the presentation, we note that in the one-factor case there are four column vector terms, of elements, $\left\{ \frac{\partial P_t^{T_i}}{\partial t} \right\}$, $\left\{ \frac{\partial P_t^{T_i}}{\partial y_t^{T_i}} \mu_{y_t^{T_i}} \right\}$, $\left\{ -P_t^{T_i} r_t \right\}$, and $\left\{ \frac{1}{2} \frac{\partial^2 P_t^{T_i}}{\partial \left(y_t^{T_i}\right)^2} \left(b_t^{T_i}\right)^2 \sigma_r^2 \right\}$, respectively. All these column vectors are pre-multiplied by a row vector of weights $[\omega_1, \omega_2, \ldots \omega_n]$, to give a number. We want to find the multifactor version of these four column vectors.

20.4.1 Calculating the Terms $\vec{c}_1$, $\vec{c}_2$, $\vec{c}_3$ and $\vec{c}_4$

To do so, first we lighten notation by defining the four vectors $\vec{c}_1$, $\vec{c}_2$, $\vec{c}_3$

and $\vec{c}_4$. Let's begin with the first term, $\vec{c}_1 = \begin{bmatrix} \frac{\partial P_t^{T_1}}{\partial t} \\ \frac{\partial P_t^{T_2}}{\partial t} \\ \dots \\ \frac{\partial P_t^{T_n}}{\partial t} \end{bmatrix}$. When we take the time

derivative, the state variables, x_t, do not move, but the quantities A_t^T and B_t^T do move with time. Therefore we have

$$\frac{1}{P_t^{T_i}} \frac{\partial P_t^{T_i}}{\partial t} = \frac{\partial}{\partial t} \left[e^{A_t^T + (B_t^T)^{\mathsf{T}} x_t} \right] = \left(\frac{\partial A_t^{T_i}}{\partial t} + \frac{\partial}{\partial t} \left(B_t^{T_i} \right)^{\mathsf{T}} x_t \right). \tag{20.37}$$

Since we are dealing with an affine model we know that

$$A_t^T + \left(B_t^T \right)^{\mathsf{T}} x_t = -(T-t) y_t^T. \tag{20.38}$$

Therefore

$$\left(\frac{\partial A_t^{T_i}}{\partial t} + \frac{\partial}{\partial t} \left(B_t^{T_i} \right)^{\mathsf{T}} x_t \right) = \frac{\partial}{\partial t} \left[A_t^T + \left(B_t^T \right)^{\mathsf{T}} x_t \right] = -\frac{\partial}{\partial t} \left[(T-t) y_t^T \right]$$

$$= y_t^T + (T-t) \frac{\partial y_t^T}{\partial T}, \tag{20.39}$$

where in the last line we have used time homogeneity:

$$\frac{\partial}{\partial t} = -\frac{\partial}{\partial T}. \tag{20.40}$$

Therefore we have

$$\vec{c}_1 = \begin{bmatrix} \frac{\partial P_t^{T_1}}{\partial t} \\ \frac{\partial P_t^{T_2}}{\partial t} \\ \dots \\ \frac{\partial P_t^{T_n}}{\partial t} \end{bmatrix} = \begin{bmatrix} P_t^{T_1} \left[y_1 - (T_1 - t) \frac{\partial}{\partial T} y_1 \right] \\ P_t^{T_2} \left[y_2 - (T_2 - t) \frac{\partial}{\partial T} y_2 \right] \\ \dots \\ P_t^{T_n} \left[y_n - (T_n - t) \frac{\partial}{\partial T} y_n \right] \end{bmatrix}. \tag{20.41}$$

This is the term that takes care of the passage of time for bonds, and that allows us to work in the remainder with yields which, Dorian Gray–like, never age.

Moving to the drift term we have

$$
\vec{c}_2 = \begin{bmatrix} \frac{\partial P_t^{T_1}}{\partial y_t^{T_1}} \mu_{y_t}^{T_1} \\ \frac{\partial P_t^{T_2}}{\partial y_t^{T_2}} \mu_{y_t}^{T_2} \\ \cdots \\ \frac{\partial P_t^{T_n}}{\partial y_t^{T_n}} \mu_{y_t}^{T_n} \end{bmatrix} = \begin{bmatrix} \frac{\partial P_t^{T_1}}{\partial y_1} \left(b_t^{T_1} \right)^{\mathrm{T}} \left[\mathcal{K} \left(\vec{\theta} - \vec{x}_t \right) dt \right] \\ \frac{\partial P_t^{T_2}}{\partial y_2} \left(b_t^{T_2} \right)^{\mathrm{T}} \left[\mathcal{K} \left(\vec{\theta} - \vec{x}_t \right) dt \right] \\ \cdots \\ \frac{\partial P_t^{T_n}}{\partial y_n} \left(b_t^{T_n} \right)^{\mathrm{T}} \left[\mathcal{K} \left(\vec{\theta} - \vec{x}_t \right) dt \right] \end{bmatrix}
$$

$$
= \begin{bmatrix} -T_1 P_t^{T_1} \left(b_t^{T_1} \right)^{\mathrm{T}} \left[\mathcal{K} \left(\vec{\theta} - \vec{x}_t \right) dt \right] \\ -T_2 P_t^{T_2} \left(b_t^{T_2} \right)^{\mathrm{T}} \left[\mathcal{K} \left(\vec{\theta} - \vec{x}_t \right) dt \right] \\ \cdots \\ -T_n P_t^{T_n} \left(b_t^{T_n} \right)^{\mathrm{T}} \left[\mathcal{K} \left(\vec{\theta} - \vec{x}_t \right) dt \right] \end{bmatrix}. \tag{20.42}
$$

Next we define

$$
\vec{c}_3 = \begin{bmatrix} -P_t^{T_1} r_t \\ -P_t^{T_2} r_t \\ \cdots \\ -P_t^{T_n} r_t \end{bmatrix}; \tag{20.43}
$$

and finally

$$
\vec{c}_4 = \begin{bmatrix} \frac{1}{2} \frac{\partial^2 P_t^{T_1}}{\partial \left(y_t^{T_1} \right)^2} \left(b_t^{T_1} \right)^2 \sigma_r^2 \\ \frac{1}{2} \frac{\partial^2 P_t^{T_2}}{\partial \left(y_t^{T_2} \right)^2} \left(b_t^{T_2} \right)^2 \sigma_r^2 \\ \cdots \\ \frac{1}{2} \frac{\partial^2 P_t^{T_n}}{\partial \left(y_t^{T_n} \right)^2} \left(b_t^{T_n} \right)^2 \sigma_r^2 \end{bmatrix} = \begin{bmatrix} \frac{1}{2} \frac{\partial^2 P_t^{T_1}}{\partial y_1^2} \left(b_t^{T_1} \right)^{\mathrm{T}} SS^{\mathrm{T}} \left(b_t^{T_1} \right) \\ \frac{1}{2} \frac{\partial^2 P_t^{T_2}}{\partial y_2^2} \left(b_t^{T_2} \right)^{\mathrm{T}} SS^{\mathrm{T}} \left(b_t^{T_2} \right) \\ \cdots \\ \frac{1}{2} \frac{\partial^2 P_t^{T_n}}{\partial y_n^2} \left(b_t^{T_n} \right)^{\mathrm{T}} SS^{\mathrm{T}} \left(b_t^{T_n} \right) \end{bmatrix}
$$

$$
= \begin{bmatrix} \frac{1}{2} T_1^2 P_t^{T_1} \left(b_t^{T_1} \right)^{\mathrm{T}} SS^{\mathrm{T}} \left(b_t^{T_1} \right) \\ \frac{1}{2} T_2^2 P_t^{T_2} \left(b_t^{T_2} \right)^{\mathrm{T}} SS^{\mathrm{T}} \left(b_t^{T_2} \right) \\ \cdots \\ \frac{1}{2} T_n^2 P_t^{T_n} \left(b_t^{T_n} \right)^{\mathrm{T}} SS^{\mathrm{T}} \left(b_t^{T_n} \right) \end{bmatrix} = \begin{bmatrix} -\frac{1}{2} P_t^{T_1} \left(B_t^{T_1} \right)^{\mathrm{T}} SS^{\mathrm{T}} B_t^{T_1} \\ -\frac{1}{2} P_t^{T_2} \left(B_t^{T_2} \right)^{\mathrm{T}} SS^{\mathrm{T}} B_t^{T_2} \\ \cdots \\ -\frac{1}{2} P_t^{T_n} \left(B_t^{T_n} \right)^{\mathrm{T}} SS^{\mathrm{T}} B_t^{T_n} \end{bmatrix}, \tag{20.44}
$$

where to obtain the last line we have made use again, but this time in reverse, of the definition

$$
b_t^{T_i} \equiv -\frac{B_t^{T_i}}{T_i}. \tag{20.45}
$$

Now, if we denote the vector of weights by $\vec{\omega}$,

$$\vec{\omega} = \begin{bmatrix} \omega_1 \\ \omega_2 \\ \cdots \\ \omega_n \end{bmatrix} \tag{20.46}$$

the multidimensional equivalent of Equation (20.15) then becomes

$$\vec{\omega}^{\mathrm{T}} \left(\vec{c}_1 + \vec{c}_2 + \vec{c}_3 + \vec{c}_4 \right) = 0. \tag{20.47}$$

Of course, in Equation (20.47) the vector $\vec{\omega}$ contains the optimal weights. How these are determined in the multidimensional case (ie, the multidimensional extension of Equation (20.10)) is shown in Appendix 20A.

20.4.2   Expressing the Convexity in Terms of Yield Volatilities

Our next step is to express the convexity term as a function of the yield volatilities. To do so, consider again the term c_4:

$$\vec{c}_4 = \begin{bmatrix} -\frac{1}{2} P_t^{T_1} \left(B_t^{T_1} \right)^{\mathrm{T}} S S^{\mathrm{T}} B_t^{T_1} \\ -\frac{1}{2} P_t^{T_2} \left(B_t^{T_2} \right)^{\mathrm{T}} S S^{\mathrm{T}} B_t^{T_2} \\ \cdots \\ -\frac{1}{2} P_t^{T_n} \left(B_t^{T_n} \right)^{\mathrm{T}} S S^{\mathrm{T}} B_t^{T_n} \end{bmatrix}. \tag{20.48}$$

Recall that $\left(dy_t^k \right)_{stoch} = \left(b_t^{T_k} \right)^{\mathrm{T}} S d\vec{z}_t$. The term $\left(b_t^{T_k} \right)^{\mathrm{T}} S$ is therefore just a row vector – that we suggestively denote by

$$\left(\vec{\sigma}^{y_k} \right)^{T} S = \begin{bmatrix} \sigma_1^{y_k} & \sigma_2^{y_k} & \cdots & \sigma_n^{y_k} \end{bmatrix}. \tag{20.49}$$

Why 'suggestively'? Because it is a vector made up of the volatility loadings of the T_k-maturity yield onto the orthogonal drivers, $d\vec{z}_t$. Therefore the product

$$\left(b_t^{T_1} \right)^{\mathrm{T}} S S^{\mathrm{T}} \left(b_t^{T_1} \right) = \begin{bmatrix} \sigma_1^{y_k} & \sigma_2^{y_k} & \cdots & \sigma_n^{y_k} \end{bmatrix} \begin{bmatrix} \sigma_1^{y_k} \\ \sigma_2^{T_k} \\ \cdots \\ \sigma_n^{y_k} \end{bmatrix}$$

$$= \sum_{j=1,n} \left(\sigma_j^{y_k} \right)^2$$

is just the (square of the) total volatility of the T_k-maturity yield. This we can more compactly write as $(\sigma^{y_k})^2$:[11]

$$(\sigma^{y_k})^2 \equiv \sum_{j=1,n} \left(\sigma_j^{y_k}\right)^2 . \tag{20.50}$$

Therefore the convexity term c_4 can be written more elegantly and transparently as

$$\overrightarrow{c}_4 = \begin{bmatrix} -\frac{1}{2}T_1^2 P_t^{T_1} (\sigma^{y_1})^2 \\ -\frac{1}{2}T_2^2 P_t^{T_2} (\sigma^{y_2})^2 \\ \dots \\ -\frac{1}{2}T_n^2 P_t^{T_n} (\sigma^{y_n})^2 \end{bmatrix} . \tag{20.51}$$

Therefore, we have obtained that

1. any two deterministic-volatility affine models that recover identically the yield curve and all yield volatilities imply exactly the same value for convexity;
2. if a deterministic-volatility affine model exactly recovers the market prices and the yield volatilities over the next time interval, it will price convexity exactly.

Our next goal will be to obtain a model-independent expression for the other terms ($\overrightarrow{c}_1$, $\overrightarrow{c}_2$ and $\overrightarrow{c}_3$) as well. Before doing so, however, we draw on the approximate results obtained so far to give a suggestive financial interpretation of the 'value of convexity'.

20.5 WHAT TO DO WITH THIS EXPRESSION FOR THE CONVEXITY

It is important to stress that the quantities σ^{y_k} are the yield volatilities *predicted by the model*. And, of course, the convexity contribution to the yield curve we have obtained is the *model-implied* contribution, which is a function, among other things, of what the model thinks the yield volatilities should be.

Now, suppose that our affine model recovers very well our best statistical estimate of the yield covariance matrix. (We shall discuss in Chapter 33 a PCA-based affine model that is constructed to do just that.) With the $\mathcal{K}$ and S matrices thus fitted to the yield covariance matrix, suppose that we determine the remaining degrees of freedom of the model by fitting to the shape of the yield curve out to, say, 10 years.[12] (Why 10 years? Because out to 10 years the convexity contribution to the shape of the yield curve is relatively modest and therefore

---

[11] Here we make use again of the fact that our factors are all orthogonal to each other.

[12] Wait a minute: in the expression for the yield volatilities – and hence for the convexity – we had terms like $\left(b_t^{T_i}\right)^T SS^T \left(b_t^{T_i}\right)$. The volatility matrix is clear to see. But where is the reversion-speed matrix, $\mathcal{K}$? It is embedded in the duration-related terms $\left(b_t^{T_i}\right)^T$.

the market yields tell us little about the *market-implied* convexity.) The 10-to-30-year portion of the model yield curve then tells us what the convexity contribution *should* be (according to the model). If the fit in the 10-to-30-year area is poor, it must mean that the market is assigning a different convexity contribution to the shape of the long end of the yield curve than our model says. Who is right?

There are, of course, many other ways to skin this convexity cat. For instance, once we observe that the fit to the long end is poor, we may want to tinker with the K and S matrices in order to bring about a good fit to the long yields. Once this is done, the model will imply different yield volatilities than those obtained from the statistical covariance matrix. Differences in yield volatilities directly imply different convexity contributions. Again, who is right, the market or the model?

Another cat-skinning idea: if we thought that we could profitably bring swaption-volatility information into play, we could fit the K and S matrices to the full swaption matrices, and, again, compare the model and the market-implied yield volatilities – and, hence, the model and statistical value of convexity. If we think that the future yield volatilities will be higher (lower) than what the market implies we should be long (short) convexity.

And, of course, we can also re-run our model by setting the volatility matrix S to zero (and keeping all the other calibrated degrees of freedom unchanged). The difference between the yields with the volatility switched on and off just gives the value of convexity (in yield terms) as a function of maturity.

Faced with the task of comparing theoretical and empirical prediction for the 'value of convexity' we are confronted with an embarrassment of methodological riches: which of these plausible ways of looking at convexity should we employ? And how should we employ this method in practice? What we need is a framework to simplify the problem, and to extract a few (perhaps one!) clear indictor of the 'value of convexity'. This is the task that we undertake in the next section. Before doing so, however, an important observation about yield volatilities is in order.

20.5.1 An Important Aside

When we obtained the no-arbitrage conditions in Chapter 12, we determined that the drift of the bond prices changed as we moved from the real-world to the risk-neutral measure, but their volatility remained unchanged. The result is general, and for readers familiar with stochastic calculus, it goes back to Girsanov's theorem. The slogan is easy to remember: when we hop across measures, drifts change; volatilities don't.

Like all slogans, uncritical acceptance of what it seems to say brings about the wages of sin. In our case, Girsanov's theorem does not imply that the *yield* volatilities will remain the same across measures. How is that possible? Shouldn't volatilities remain unchanged when we switch from the real-world to the risk-neutral measure?

Recall that in Chapter 8 (see Section 8.8) we made a distinction between completely affine and essentially affine models. In a nutshell, in *completely* affine models the market price of risk is a constant (or, to be more precise, does not depend on the state variables); in *essentially* affine models the market price of risk displays an affine (linear) dependence on the state variables. This makes a big difference. As we saw in Chapter 8, this means that in completely affine models only the reversion level(s) are changed by the change of measure, but in essentially affine models both reversion level(s) (the vector $\overrightarrow{\theta}$) and reversion speed(s) (the matrix $\mathcal{K}$) change. If the reversion speed(s) change(s), then so will the 'tucking in' of the dispersion of the state variables (see the discussion in Chapter 8), and therefore in essentially affine models the volatility of yields will also change. This means that, in general, there will be a difference between the volatility of yields that prevails when investors are risk averse, and the volatility that would be observed if they were risk neutral.

With this important observation out of the way (but firmly lodged somewhere in our prefrontal cortex), we can go back to the task of simplifying the convexity analysis.

20.6 AN INTUITIVE ASIDE: SIMPLIFYING THE ANALYSIS

We have seen that the predicted and realized yield volatilities yield the key to the estimation (and the capture) of the convexity contribution. We are looking for a way to simplify the analysis. We can proceed as follows. Write for each individual yield volatility

$$\sigma^{y_k} = h_k \overline{\sigma}^y \tag{20.52}$$

with[13]

$$\overline{\sigma}^y = \frac{1}{n} \sum_{k=1,n} \sigma^{y_k}. \tag{20.53}$$

With these equations, we still acknowledge that the volatilities of yields of different maturities are all different, but we express them as a fraction (h_k) of their average volatilities, $\overline{\sigma}^y$. So far, we have not sneaked in any assumptions. Our next step, however, will be to argue that what varies will be the average level of volatility (the term $\overline{\sigma}^y$), and not the fractions (h_k). *This* is an assumption. We are making it in order to reduce our analysis of the value of convexity to a single indicator.

Exercise 53 *Argue that the approximation we just made is akin to a first-principal-component simplification of the yield volatilities. Obtain some empirical yield data (perhaps from the excellent source in Gurkaynak, Sack and*

---

[13] We could take the average of volatilities or of variances. The best choice depends on whether we think that volatilities or variances move more closely in parallel.

Wright (2006)), estimate from these data the covariance matrix of yield changes, obtain the principal components, and comment on how good this approximation is.

With this approximation we can then rewrite term c_4 as

$$\vec{c}_4 = (\overline{\sigma}^y)^2 \begin{bmatrix} -\frac{1}{2}T_1^2 P_t^{T_1} h_1^2 \\ -\frac{1}{2}T_2^2 P_t^{T_2} h_2^2 \\ \dots \\ -\frac{1}{2}T_n^2 P_t^{T_n} h_n^2 \end{bmatrix}. \tag{20.54}$$

As anticipated, we now make the assumption that the variances (or the volatilities) move mainly in parallel (ie, that the first principal component of the yield volatilities is strongly dominant, and essentially equivalent to a parallel move of the volatility surface). If this is the case, then the quantities (h_k^2) remain unchanged, and all the variability in yield volatilities is taken up by the term $\overline{\sigma}^y$. This helps the analysis a lot because we can rewrite Equation (20.47) as

$$\vec{\omega}^T \left(\vec{c}_1 + \vec{c}_2 + \vec{c}_3 + \vec{c}_4 \right) = 0$$

$$\implies \vec{\omega}^T \left(\vec{c}_1 + \vec{c}_2 + \vec{c}_3 \right)$$

$$= -\vec{\omega}^T \vec{c}_4 = -(\overline{\sigma}^y)^2 \vec{\omega}^T \begin{bmatrix} -\frac{1}{2}T_1^2 P_t^{T_1} h_1^2 \\ -\frac{1}{2}T_2^2 P_t^{T_2} h_2^2 \\ \dots \\ -\frac{1}{2}T_n^2 P_t^{T_n} h_n^2 \end{bmatrix}. \tag{20.55}$$

Recalling that each term $\vec{\omega}^T \vec{c}_i$, $i = 1, 2, \dots, 4$, is just a number, and that so

is the term $\vec{\omega}^T \begin{bmatrix} -\frac{1}{2}T_1^2 P_t^{T_1} h_1^2 \\ -\frac{1}{2}T_2^2 P_t^{T_2} h_2^2 \\ \dots \\ -\frac{1}{2}T_n^2 P_t^{T_n} h_n^2 \end{bmatrix}$, we then have

$$(\overline{\sigma}^y)^2 = \frac{\vec{\omega}^T \left(\vec{c}_1 + \vec{c}_2 + \vec{c}_3 \right)}{\vec{\omega}^T \begin{bmatrix} -\frac{1}{2}T_1^2 P_t^{T_1} h_1^2 \\ -\frac{1}{2}T_2^2 P_t^{T_2} h_2^2 \\ \dots \\ -\frac{1}{2}T_n^2 P_t^{T_n} h_n^2 \end{bmatrix}}. \tag{20.56}$$

Since the numerator and the denominator are just numbers, we can write these two numbers as

$$Y \equiv \vec{\omega}^T \left(\vec{c}_1 + \vec{c}_2 + \vec{c}_3 \right) \tag{20.57}$$

and

$$C \equiv \vec{\omega}^{\mathrm{T}} \begin{bmatrix} -\frac{1}{2} T_1^2 P_t^{T_1} h_1^2 \\ -\frac{1}{2} T_2^2 P_t^{T_2} h_2^2 \\ \dots \\ -\frac{1}{2} T_n^2 P_t^{T_n} h_n^2 \end{bmatrix}. \tag{20.58}$$

Therefore, in exact analogy to Equation (20.56), we have the neat expression

$$(\overline{\sigma}^y)^2 = \frac{Y}{C}.$$

Indeed, with Equation (20.56) we have re-obtained a (now multi-factor) version of the break-even volatility that we derived in a Vasicek-like setting in Section 20.2.

One more step. If we combine the vectors c_1 and c_3 into a new vector, c_Y, we get:

$$\vec{c}_Y = \vec{c}_1 + \vec{c}_3 = \begin{bmatrix} -P_t^{T_1} y_1 \\ -P_t^{T_2} y_2 \\ \dots \\ -P_t^{T_n} y_n \end{bmatrix} + \begin{bmatrix} P_t^{T_1} r_t \\ P_t^{T_2} r_t \\ \dots \\ P_t^{T_n} r_t \end{bmatrix} = \begin{bmatrix} P_t^{T_1}(r_t - y_1) \\ P_t^{T_2}(r_t - y_2) \\ \dots \\ P_t^{T_n}(r_t - y_n) \end{bmatrix}. \tag{20.59}$$

Each term $(r_t - y_i)$ is the 'funding advantage', ie, the difference between the rate at which we can fund the purchase of a discount bond, (the 'short rate', r_t) and the yield of the bond (y_i). Therefore the 'funding advantage', FA_Π, of the whole portfolio is given by

$$FA_\Pi = \vec{\omega}^{\mathrm{T}} (\vec{c}_1 + \vec{c}_3) = \vec{\omega}^{\mathrm{T}} \begin{bmatrix} P_t^{T_1}(y_1 - r_t) \\ P_t^{T_2}(y_2 - r_t) \\ \dots \\ P_t^{T_n}(y_n - r_t) \end{bmatrix}. \tag{20.60}$$

This quantity tells us whether our portfolio has what in trading parlance is called a positive or negative 'carry'.

What about the term $\vec{\omega}^{\mathrm{T}} \vec{c}_2$? A glance at $\vec{c}_2$,

$$\vec{c}_2 = \begin{bmatrix} -T_1 P_t^{T_1} \left(b_t^{T_1} \right)^{\mathrm{T}} \left[\mathcal{K} \left(\vec{\theta} - \vec{x}_t \right) \right] \\ -T_2 P_t^{T_2} \left(b_t^{T_2} \right)^{\mathrm{T}} \left[\mathcal{K} \left(\vec{\theta} - \vec{x}_t \right) \right] \\ \dots \\ -T_n P_t^{T_n} \left(b_t^{T_n} \right)^{\mathrm{T}} \left[\mathcal{K} \left(\vec{\theta} - \vec{x}_t \right) \right] \end{bmatrix}, \tag{20.61}$$

immediately shows this is a 'drift term'. More precisely, it is a term that tells us in which direction the yields are headed over the next time interval because of expectations: the factors we have chosen as state variables for our affine model will deterministically revert towards their reversion levels (these are the terms $[\mathcal{K}(\vec{\theta} - \vec{x}_t)]$); these factor moves are then translated into yield moves via the 'duration-related' terms, $(b_t^{T_i})^{\mathrm{T}}$.

It is important to understand that this drift term has nothing to do with (or, rather, has a very indirect bearing on) what a statistical analysis would tell us about the mean-reversion or otherwise of the bond yields: all our analysis, based on replicating and hedging, is firmly embedded in the risk-neutral (pricing, $\mathbb{Q}$-) measure, and the drift term is intimately related to the no-arbitrage conditions that our model embeds. Of course, the profitability of the portfolio will depend on this drift term as well, but it is more difficult to interpret intuitively: we will include it in our analysis, but we will park it to one side when we give in the next section a suggestive graphical interpretation of a convexity strategy.

Going back to the break-even volatility, expression (20.56) is just what we were looking for: a simple quantity, easy to monitor and easy to understand, that can tell us what the yield volatilities should be over the next time interval for the convexity to be fairly priced. It also lends itself to a nice, if approximate, graphical interpretation, that we discuss below.

20.7   A GRAPHICAL INTERPRETATION

As discussed, let us park to one side for the moment the drift term $\vec{c}_2$. Then consider the following very stylized example: enter a naive long-convexity strategy, whereby the investor is long 50 units of the 30-year bond, long 50 units of the 10-year bond and short 100 units of the 20-year bond. For simplicity, let's unrealistically assume that the strategy is cash neutral (ie, that the portfolio costs zero to set up.)

For a typical shape of the yield curve, which tends to be concave at the long end (and so with the 20-year yield higher than the average of the 10- and 30-year yields), the strategy will have a negative funding advantage. We call this 'negative carry' the *yield give-up*.

At the same time, the portfolio will be long convexity (because convexity grows more than linearly with maturity, and therefore the average of the 10- and 30-year convexity will be higher than the convexity of the 20-year bond). The portfolio will display a 'convexity pick-up'. The interplay between the two is shown in Figure 20.1.

Is this convexity pick-up enough to compensate for the yield give-up? Within the simplifications we have made to arrive at this picture, this will depend on the realized volatility over the next (re-hedging) interval, as shown in Figure 20.2.

Nirvana, of course, is found in the top right corner, where the investor can find a positive convexity pick-up and a positive funding advantage (and, presumably, world peace and a cure for the common cold). Hell is in the bottom left corner, where the portfolio has negative carry *and* a negative convexity pick-up (and the investor is forced to watch endless repeats of *Celebrity Chefs*).

We stress that the analysis presented here is suggestive rather than exact. In particular, the interpretation of the yield give-up given above is incomplete. We show in the next chapters how to make this intuitive more precise. As we do so, we will begin turn the notion/concept/idea in the quote that opens the

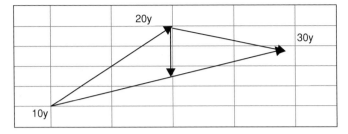

Figure 20.1 The 'yield give-up' (shown by the vertical downward-pointing arrow) from the stylized strategy discussed in the text for the case of a positive-convexity strategy, and with a typical (concave) shape of the yield curve. The funding advantage is a convex combination of the funding advantages of the different constituent bonds. The holdings in the bonds of different maturities cannot all have the same sign if one wants to immunize against the factor uncertainty. See Equation (20.10) for a low-dimensional example. Therefore the portfolio funding advantage (its yield give-up) can, in general, have either sign. For the case depicted in the figure and the stylized example discussed in the text, it must be negative.

chapter into something that will not only enhance our understanding, but can also actually be used in practice.

$$
\begin{bmatrix}
\quad & \textbf{Yield Give-Up} > 0 & \textbf{Yield Give-Up} < 0 & \quad \\
C > 0 & \text{Enter strategy if} & \sigma^2 > \frac{Y}{C} < 0 \Rightarrow & \\
& \sigma^2 > \frac{Y}{C} > 0 & \textbf{always enter the strategy} & \\
& & & \\
C < 0 & \sigma^2 < \frac{Y}{C} < 0 \text{ (impossible)} & \text{Enter reverse strategy if} & \\
& \Rightarrow \textbf{never enter the strategy} & \sigma^2 < \frac{Y}{C} > 0 &
\end{bmatrix}
$$

Figure 20.2 The optimal strategy in the four possible configurations corresponding to convexity pick-up positive or negative, and yield give-up positive or negative.

20.8 APPENDIX 20A

We are looking for the vector of weights, $\vec{\omega}$, that will make our portfolio of bonds riskless. Recall that, in order to 'kill' $n - 1$ sources of risk, we are going to need n bonds. This will give $n - 1$ equations for n unknowns. Therefore our optimal-weight solution will only be determined to within a scaling factor. Without loss of generality we therefore impose that

$$
\sum_{i=1,n} \omega_i = 1. \tag{20.62}
$$

Now, for each source of risk, j, $j = 1, 2, \ldots n - 1$, we must have

$$\sum_{i=1,n} \frac{\partial P_i}{\partial x_j} \omega_i = 0. \tag{20.63}$$

Now, split the sum $\sum_{i=1,n}$ into a sum over the first $n - 1$ terms, $\sum_{i=1,n-1}$, plus the nth term. Because of Equation (20.62), this is equivalent to

$$\sum_{i=1,n-1} \left[\frac{\partial P_i}{\partial x_j} - \frac{\partial P_n}{\partial x_j} \right] \omega_i = - \frac{\partial P_n}{\partial x_j}. \tag{20.64}$$

This can be written as

$$A \vec{\omega} = \vec{b}, \tag{20.65}$$

with A an $[(n - 1) \times (n - 1)]$ matrix, given by

$$A = \begin{bmatrix} \frac{\partial P_1}{\partial x_1} - \frac{\partial P_n}{\partial x_1} & \frac{\partial P_2}{\partial x_1} - \frac{\partial P_n}{\partial x_1} & \cdots & \frac{\partial P_{n-1}}{\partial x_1} - \frac{\partial P_n}{\partial x_1} \\ \frac{\partial P_1}{\partial x_2} - \frac{\partial P_n}{\partial x_2} & \frac{\partial P_2}{\partial x_2} - \frac{\partial P_n}{\partial x_2} & \cdots & \frac{\partial P_{n-1}}{\partial x_2} - \frac{\partial P_n}{\partial x_2} \\ \cdots & & \cdots & \cdots \\ \frac{\partial P_1}{\partial x_{n-1}} - \frac{\partial P_n}{\partial x_{n-1}} & \frac{\partial P_2}{\partial x_{n-1}} - \frac{\partial P_n}{\partial x_{n-1}} & \cdots & \frac{\partial P_{n-1}}{\partial x_{n-1}} - \frac{\partial P_n}{\partial x_{n-1}} \end{bmatrix}, \tag{20.66}$$

and $\vec{\omega}$ and $\vec{q}$ are $[(n - 1) \times 1]$ vectors, given by

$$\vec{\omega} = \begin{bmatrix} \omega_1 \\ \omega_2 \\ \cdots \\ \omega_{n-1} \end{bmatrix} \quad \vec{q} = \begin{bmatrix} -\frac{\partial P_n}{\partial x_1} \\ -\frac{\partial P_n}{\partial x_2} \\ \cdots \\ -\frac{\partial P_n}{\partial x_{n-1}} \end{bmatrix}. \tag{20.67}$$

Therefore the optimal weights are obtained as

$$\vec{\omega} = A^{-1} \vec{q}. \tag{20.68}$$

CHAPTER 21

A Model-Independent Approach to Valuing Convexity

I have not failed. I have just found 10,000 ways that won't work.[1]
— Thomas A. Edison

I refuse to recognize that there are impossibilities. I cannot discover that anyone knows enough about anything on this earth definitely to say what is and what is not possible.
— Henry Ford

21.1 THE PURPOSE OF THIS CHAPTER

The 'value of convexity' (ie, the difference between the market yields and the yields that would prevail in the absence of convexity) is substantial, as Figure 21.1 clearly shows.[2] Yet one finds in the literature relatively little discussion of the fair value of convexity.

Of course, speaking of fairness makes reference to a modelling approach, and, probably herein lies the problem: in studies of this type, one always tests a joint hypothesis, that the convexity is correctly priced *and* the model correctly specified. Given the great uncertainty in model specification, any possible rejection must therefore always include a caveat of particularly lurid health warnings.

It is for this reason that we adopt in this chapter a quasi-model-agnostic approach. By this we mean that we do place ourselves in an affine-modelling framework, but we make our results as independent as possible from the specifics of any affine model (such as the number of factors, or the nature of the state variables – latent, specified, yield-curve-based, macroeconomic, etc). We

---

[1] Apparently, Thomas Edison tested close to 2,000 different materials before finding something suitable for the filament of a light bulb. The happy ending of the story is that, eventuually, he did. There aren't quite as many affine models (I think) whose performance one can test in the quest for the convexity prize, but perhaps the model-agnostic approach presented in this chapter is the closest one can get to the convexity equivalent of the tungsten wire.

[2] I am indebted for the idea behind this chapter to the insight of Dr Putyatin. I have also benefitted from discussions with Mr Saroka. The treatment in this chapter is based on Rebonato and Putiatyn (2017).

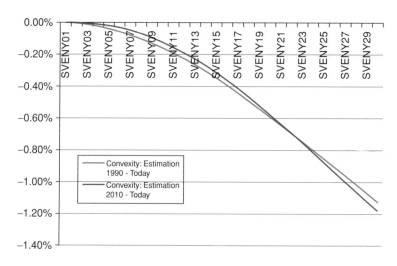

Figure 21.1 The value of convexity, ie, the difference between the market yields and the yields that would prevail in the absence of convexity, as estimated in August 2015 using the Rebonato, Saroka, Putiatyn (2017) model, for yields ranging from 1 year (point labelled SVEN01), to 29 years (point labelled SVEN29). The estimates of convexity from this model are reliable because the model accurately recovers (by construction) the volatilities of all yields. The two curves show that the 'value of convexity' is modestly affected by the precise choice of the historical period during which the yield volatilities are calculated, and to which the model is calibrated. The blue curve shows the value of convexity when the yield volatilities are estimated using data from 1990 to 2015. The red shows the same quantity using data from the start of the post-Great- Recession period to 2015.

only require that *some* affine model should exist, capable of recovering the market yield curve and yield covariance matrix with the precision required by our study. We show in Chapter 33 that at least one such model exists, and we then rely in our reasoning on a simple equivalence result that we state and briefly prove in Section 2.

We put our quasi-model-agnostic methodology to the test by examining whether it is possible to systematically make money by means of a trading strategy based on immunizing against the exposure to 'level' and 'slope' risk, on estimating the yield volatility over the next time interval, and on comparing this estimate with the volatility 'implied' by the curvature in the yield curve. On purpose, we do not employ a sophisticated volatility estimate, because we want to ascertain whether easily available information about future volatility is correctly embedded in the shape of the yield curve.

As we show in Section 4, the convexity-induced downward curvature of the yield curve is analogous to an 'option premium' (in the form of a 'yield give-up') that an investor has to pay to go long convexity. Exactly as in option trading, the long-convexity investor will be compensated for this 'yield cost' by making money during her re-hedging activity ('buying low' and 'selling high'). If the realized volatility of yields matched on average the 'implied volatility' embedded in the shape of the yield curve, there would be no money to be made from being either long or short convexity.

By looking at 30 years of data, we find that neither strategy of being systematically long or short convexity (and immunized against 'level' and 'slope' risk) would have been profitable. However, a conditional strategy that carefully looks at the difference between the 'implied' and the statistically estimated volatilities would have identified extended periods during which the convexity was not correctly priced (by which we mean that it was possible to make money by being long or short convexity, while remaining hedged against the yield curve factors).

Next, we explain the residuals from the strategy, that is to say, we try to explain the failures to capture all of the theoretically available mispricings: were the failures due to our misestimation of the future volatility? Or where they due to our inability to immunize the portfolio exactly against the first-order ('duration') exposure? As we shall see, since convexity is, quite literally, a second-order effect, many first-order confounding factors stand in the way of capturing its value, and it is essential to examine carefully what the source of errors may be. Which is a roundabout way of saying that 'monetizing' the value of convexity is not easy, and only rather specialized investors can engage in the strategies required to capture it – which, after all, may be the explanation of why *some* value can still be found. Indeed, in his attempts to extract the elusive elixir of the convexity value from the dry stone of the yield curve curvature, this writer has often felt he had to avail himself of a Thomas-Edison–Henry-Ford-like resilience and optimism (as revealed by the quotes that open the chapter).

21.2 EQUIVALENT AFFINE MODELS

The results of this section are discussed at greater length and from a more general perspective in Section 33.2. In this section we simply state that, under mild conditions, all affine models that produce *exactly* the same yield curve and the same covariance matrix display an exactly identical dynamic behaviour. In particular, they will predict exactly the same yield volatilities and the same convexity.

The reasoning goes as follows. Let $\{m_1\}$ and $\{m_2\}$ be two time-homogeneous, non-stochastic-volatility, essentially affine models with an invertible mapping from state variables to yields. Their state variables, $\{x_1\}$ and $\{x_2\}$, can be very different, and either both or neither could include macro variables. The two models will be said to be "equivalent" if they produce today *exactly* the same yield curve and the same yield covariance matrix.

Since the two equivalent models are affine, and we have assumed invertibility, it is always possible to write for the market yields:

$$y_t = A_1 x_1^t \tag{21.1}$$

and

$$y_t = A_2 x_2^t.$$ (21.2)

We then show in Section 32.2 that, given two equivalent models,

- the initial conditions are the same (thanks to invertibility, the two models produce the same time-t_0 yield curve by definition of equivalent models);
- the drift of yields or forward rates under $\mathbb{Q}$ is the same, because – this is the essence of the Heath–Jarrow–Merton (1989) result – the no-arbitrage drift is purely a function of the forward rate covariance matrix (which is identical for the two models today by the equivalence assumption, and in the future by time-homogeneity);
- the stochastic evolution is the same also because of the assumed equivalence (same covariance matrix) and time-homogeneity.

From this it follows that the evolution of the yield curve under $\mathbb{Q}$ is, in absolutely all its aspects, exactly the same for any two equivalent models.

It is possible to show that, under the preceding assumptions, the two equivalent essentially affine models behave identically also under the objective ($\mathbb{P}$) measure, but we do not need this result here.

The upshot of all of this is that, as long as the mild conditions about invertibility and non-stochastic volatility given earlier are satisfied, all conclusions we draw about one equivalent model exactly extend to any other equivalent model.

This is interesting, because principal-components–based affine models (such as the model discussed in Chapter 33) can be made to recover both the market yield curve and the covariance matrix with arbitrary precision (and greater ease than most other models). As a consequence, at least one model capable of recovering the initial yield curve and covariance matrix (and hence yield volatilities) to arbitrary accuracy exists.

Why does this matter? Because we show in Section 3 that in an affine setting the 'value of convexity' depends only on the correct recovery of the volatilities of all yields. We therefore obtained our convexity results with a model such as the one in Chapter 33 in the back of our mind. However, our results will not depend on the specific parametrization of this 'class-representative' model, or on its choice of state variables, and will in this sense be quasi-model-agnostic.

21.3 THE EXPRESSION FOR CONVEXITY IN AN AFFINE SETTING

Picking up the thread of the derivation presented in the previous chapter, recall that we placed ourselves in the usual affine setting. More precisely, we considered a set of $n - 1$ state variables,[3] $\overrightarrow{x}_t$, following a joint mean-reverting processes of the form

$$d\overrightarrow{x}_t = \underline{K}(\overrightarrow{\theta} - \overrightarrow{x}_t)dt + \underline{S}d\overrightarrow{z}_t \tag{21.3}$$

with

$$E\left[dz_t^i dz_t^j\right] = \delta_{ij}dt, \tag{21.4}$$

with δ_{ij} denoting the Kroeneker delta. We imposed that these state variables should be related to the short rate by an affine (linear) transformation of the form

$$r_t = u_r + \overrightarrow{g}^{\mathrm{T}}\overrightarrow{x}_t. \tag{21.5}$$

We then obtained in the previous chapter (see Equations (20.39) and passim) that, after choosing the optimal weights, $\overrightarrow{\omega}$, we could write for the portfolio of first-order-neutralized bonds

$$\overrightarrow{\omega}^{\mathrm{T}}\left(\overrightarrow{c}_1 + \overrightarrow{c}_2 + \overrightarrow{c}_3 + \overrightarrow{c}_4\right) = 0 \tag{21.6}$$

with the four vectors, $\overrightarrow{c}_1$, $\overrightarrow{c}_2$, $\overrightarrow{c}_3$, and $\overrightarrow{c}_4$, given by

$$\overrightarrow{c}_1 = \begin{bmatrix} \frac{\partial P_t^{T_1}}{\partial t} \\ \frac{\partial P_t^{T_2}}{\partial t} \\ \dots \\ \frac{\partial P_t^{T_n}}{\partial t} \end{bmatrix} = \begin{bmatrix} P_t^{T_1}\left[y_1 + (T_1 - t)\frac{\partial}{\partial T}y_1\right] \\ P_t^{T_2}\left[y_2 + (T_2 - t)\frac{\partial}{\partial T}y_2\right] \\ \dots \\ P_t^{T_n}\left[y_n + (T_n - t)\frac{\partial}{\partial T}y_n\right] \end{bmatrix}; \tag{21.7}$$

$$\overrightarrow{c}_2 = \begin{bmatrix} \frac{\partial P_t^{T_1}}{\partial y_t^{T_1}}\mu_{y_t^{T_1}} \\ \frac{\partial P_t^{T_2}}{\partial y_t^{T_2}}\mu_{y_t^{T_2}} \\ \dots \\ \frac{\partial P_t^{T_n}}{\partial y_t^{T_n}}\mu_{y_t^{T_n}} \end{bmatrix} = \begin{bmatrix} -T_1 P_t^{T_1}\left(b_t^{T_1}\right)^{\mathrm{T}}\left[K(\overrightarrow{\theta} - \overrightarrow{x}_t)dt\right] \\ -T_2 P_t^{T_2}\left(b_t^{T_2}\right)^{\mathrm{T}}\left[K(\overrightarrow{\theta} - \overrightarrow{x}_t)dt\right] \\ \dots \\ -T_n P_t^{T_n}\left(b_t^{T_n}\right)^{\mathrm{T}}\left[K(\overrightarrow{\theta} - \overrightarrow{x}_t)dt\right] \end{bmatrix}; \tag{21.8}$$

$$\overrightarrow{c}_3 = \begin{bmatrix} -P_t^{T_1}r_t \\ -P_t^{T_2}r_t \\ \dots \\ -P_t^{T_n}r_t \end{bmatrix}; \tag{21.9}$$

---

[3] Why $n - 1$? Because with $n - 1$ factors we will need a portfolio of n bonds to neutralize the sources of risk associated with the state variables, and we did not want to write a lot of superscripts of summations as $n + 1$. Sometimes one has to choose where to be elegant.

and finally

$$\vec{c}_4 = \begin{bmatrix} \frac{1}{2}\dfrac{\partial^2 P_t^{T_1}}{\partial\left(y_t^{T_1}\right)^2}\left(b_t^{T_i}\right)^2\sigma_r^2 \\[2mm] \frac{1}{2}\dfrac{\partial^2 P_t^{T_2}}{\partial\left(y_t^{T_2}\right)^2}\left(b_t^{T_i}\right)^2\sigma_r^2 \\[2mm] \cdots \\[2mm] \frac{1}{2}\dfrac{\partial^2 P_t^{T_n}}{\partial\left(y_t^{T_n}\right)^2}\left(b_t^{T_i}\right)^2\sigma_r^2 \end{bmatrix} = \begin{bmatrix} -\frac{1}{2}P_t^{T_1}\left(B_t^{T_1}\right)^{\mathrm{T}}SS^{\mathrm{T}}B_t^{T_1} \\[2mm] -\frac{1}{2}P_t^{T_2}\left(B_t^{T_2}\right)^{\mathrm{T}}SS^{\mathrm{T}}B_t^{T_2} \\[2mm] \cdots \\[2mm] -\frac{1}{2}P_t^{T_n}\left(B_t^{T_n}\right)^{\mathrm{T}}SS^{\mathrm{T}}B_t^{T_n} \end{bmatrix}. \tag{21.10}$$

The term c_4 contains the convexity term, and we chose to express it as a function of yield volatilities. After defining the vector

$$\left(\vec{\sigma}^{y_k}\right)^T = \begin{bmatrix} \sigma_1^{y_k} & \sigma_2^{y_k} & \cdots & \sigma_n^{y_k} \end{bmatrix}, \tag{21.11}$$

made up of the volatility loadings of the T_k-maturity yield onto the orthogonal drivers, $d\vec{z}_t$, we notice that the variance of the kth yield

$$\left(\sigma^{y_k}\right)^2 = \left(b_t^{T_1}\right)^{\mathrm{T}}SS^{\mathrm{T}}\left(b_t^{T_1}\right)$$

$$= \begin{bmatrix} \sigma_1^{y_k} & \sigma_2^{y_k} & \cdots & \sigma_n^{y_k} \end{bmatrix}\begin{bmatrix} \sigma_1^{y_k} \\ \sigma_2^{T_k} \\ \cdots \\ \sigma_n^{y_k} \end{bmatrix} = \sum_{j=1,n}\left(\sigma_j^{y_k}\right)^2 \tag{21.12}$$

is just the (square of the) sum of the volatility contributions from the different factors to the T_k-maturity yield:

$$\left(\sigma^{y_k}\right)^2 \equiv \sum_{j=1,n}\left(\sigma_j^{y_k}\right)^2. \tag{21.13}$$

Therefore the convexity term c_4 can be written more elegantly and transparently as

$$\vec{c}_4 = \begin{bmatrix} -\frac{1}{2}T_1^2 P_t^{T_1}\left(\sigma^{y_1}\right)^2 \\[2mm] -\frac{1}{2}T_2^2 P_t^{T_2}\left(\sigma^{y_2}\right)^2 \\[2mm] \cdots \\[2mm] -\frac{1}{2}T_n^2 P_t^{T_n}\left(\sigma^{y_n}\right)^2 \end{bmatrix}. \tag{21.14}$$

The vector $\vec{c}_4$ is one of the building blocks we were looking for: each of its elements gives the convexity contribution to a different-maturity yield in the case of a multifactor affine model purely as a function of the yield volatilities, σ^{y_i}, and of the bond prices, $P_t^{T_i}$. Recall that we concluded that

1. any two deterministic-volatility affine models that recover identically the yield curve and all yield volatilities imply exactly the same value for convexity;

2. if a deterministic-volatility affine model exactly recovers the market prices and the yield volatilities over the next time interval, it will price convexity exactly.

What we would like to obtain is an expression for the profitability of the full portfolio, not just of its convexity component, as a function of market observables. This we obtain in the rest of the chapter.

21.4 AN EXPRESSION FOR THE THEORETICAL CONVEXITY OF THE PORTFOLIO

As promised, in this section we no longer neglect any terms. In particular, we do not make the constant-maturity-yield approximation.

So far we have worked in term of yields in order to arrive at a simple intuitive expression for the 'value of' convexity and of the break-even volatility. To proceed, we now work directly with bond prices. Give our working assumptions, the bond price, $P_t^T = P(\tau)$, is given by

$$P_t^T = e^{A_t^T + \left(\overrightarrow{B}_t^T\right)^{\mathrm{T}} \overrightarrow{x}_t} \tag{21.15}$$

where A_t^T and $\overrightarrow{B}_t^T$ have the usual meaning. Given the dynamics in Equations (21.3) to (21.5), Ito's lemma for the differential of the bond price gives

$$dP_t^T = \frac{\partial P_t^T}{\partial t} dt + \left(\mathrm{grad}\, P_t^T\right)^{\mathrm{T}} d\overrightarrow{x} + \underbrace{\frac{1}{2} \mathrm{Tr}\left[S^{\mathrm{T}} B_t^T \left(B_t^T\right)^{\mathrm{T}} S\right]}_{\text{convexity}} dt. \tag{21.16}$$

The symbol $(\mathrm{grad}\, P_t^T)^{\mathrm{T}}$ denotes the (transpose of the) gradient of the bond price with respect to the state variables. The quantity $\mathrm{grad}\, P_t^T$ is a column vector whose components are given by

$$\mathrm{grad}\, P_t^T = \begin{bmatrix} \frac{\partial P_t^T}{\partial x_1} \\ \frac{\partial P_t^T}{\partial x_2} \\ \cdots \\ \frac{\partial P_t^T}{\partial x_n} \end{bmatrix}. \tag{21.17}$$

Of course, $(\mathrm{grad}\, P_t^T)^{\mathrm{T}}$ is a row vector and, as usual, $(\mathrm{grad}\, P_t^T)^{\mathrm{T}} d\overrightarrow{x}$ is just a number.

As for the expression $\mathrm{Tr}[S^{\mathrm{T}} B_t^T (B_t^T)^{\mathrm{T}} S]$, it denotes the trace – ie, the sum of the diagonal elements – of the matrix $[S^{\mathrm{T}} B_t^T (B_t^T)^{\mathrm{T}} S]$. The convexity term assumes such a simple form, of course, because we have assumed our factors to be orthogonal. As we have shown in Chapter 18, there is no loss of generality in doing so.

The term $\frac{1}{2}\text{Tr}[S^T B_t^T (B_t^T)^T S]dt$ is the convexity term we are interested in.

Exercise 54 *Verify that Equation (21.16) indeed holds. The only slightly tricky bit is the term $\frac{1}{2}Tr[S^T B_t^T (B_t^T)^T S]$. To obtain this term, here are a few hints: start from Equation (21.3); write the expression for Ito's lemma for several correlated variables, each of volatility σ_i; express σ_i as a function of the elements of the matrix S; and make use of the orthogonality $\mathbb{E}[dz_t^i dz_t^j] = \delta_{ij} dt$.*

Let $\{w_i\}$ denote the weights that ensure that the portfolio is first-order immunized, ie, does not change value, to first order, when the factors move. As usual, we have n bonds and $n-1$ risk factors. As we have seen in the previous chapter, for immunization to hold the weights must satisfy the equation

$$\sum_{i=1,n} \left(w_i \frac{\overrightarrow{\partial P_t^{T_i}}}{\partial x_k} \right) = \overrightarrow{0}. \tag{21.18}$$

Let's pause for a second here: the right-hand side is a (zero) column vector. The left-hand side is the sum of n column vectors; thus

$$\begin{bmatrix} w_1 \frac{\partial P_t^{T_1}}{\partial x_1} \\ w_1 \frac{\partial P_t^{T_1}}{\partial x_2} \\ \cdots \\ w_1 \frac{\partial P_t^{T_1}}{\partial x_{n-1}} \end{bmatrix} + \begin{bmatrix} w_2 \frac{\partial P_t^{T_2}}{\partial x_1} \\ w_2 \frac{\partial P_t^{T_2}}{\partial x_2} \\ \cdots \\ w_2 \frac{\partial P_t^{T_2}}{\partial x_{n-1}} \end{bmatrix} + \cdots + \begin{bmatrix} w_n \frac{\partial P_t^{T_n}}{\partial x_1} \\ w_n \frac{\partial P_t^{T_n}}{\partial x_2} \\ \cdots \\ w_n \frac{\partial P_t^{T_n}}{\partial x_{n-1}} \end{bmatrix} = \begin{bmatrix} 0 \\ 0 \\ \cdots \\ 0 \end{bmatrix}. \tag{21.19}$$

To be totally comfortable with this expression, consider any row, say, the second. The equation in the second row says that

$$\sum_{i=1,n} w_i \frac{\partial P_t^{T_i}}{\partial x_2} = 0, \tag{21.20}$$

ie, that the portfolio must be immunized against changes in the second stochastic factor. The other rows then repeat the same conditions for the remaining $n-2$ factors.

To lighten notation we now introduce the vector $\overrightarrow{\xi}$, of $n-1$ components:

$$\xi_k = \sum_{i=1,n} w_i \frac{\partial P_t^{T_i}}{\partial x_k}.$$

As usual, with these special weights the portfolio has become risk-less, and, under penalty of arbitrage, can therefore only grow at the risk-less rate of return,

r_t. This gives the usual equation

$$\sum_{i=1,n} w_i dP_t^{T_i}$$

$$= \sum_{i=1,n} \left(w_i \frac{\partial P_t^{T_i}}{\partial t} dt + \left(\overrightarrow{\xi} \right)^{\mathrm{T}} d\overrightarrow{x} + \frac{1}{2} w_i \mathrm{Tr} \left[S^{\mathrm{T}} B_t^{T} \left(B_t^{T} \right)^{\mathrm{T}} S \right] dt \right)$$

$$= r_t \left[\sum_{i=1,n} w_i P_t^{T_i} \right] dt. \tag{21.21}$$

Since we have established that

$$\sum_{k=1,n} \left(\overrightarrow{w_i \frac{\partial P_t^{T_i}}{\partial x_k}} \right) = \overrightarrow{0} \tag{21.22}$$

we have ensured by Equation (21.18) that the term $\sum_{i=1,n} \left(\overrightarrow{w_i \frac{\partial P_t^{T_i}}{\partial x_k}} \right)^{\mathrm{T}} d\overrightarrow{x}$ will

be zero for any possible $d\overrightarrow{x}$. Therefore we have

$$\sum_{i=1,n} w_i \left(\frac{\partial P_t^{T_i}}{\partial t} + \frac{1}{2} \mathrm{Tr} \left[S^{\mathrm{T}} B_t^{T} \left(B_t^{T} \right)^{\mathrm{T}} S \right] \right) = r_t \left[\sum_{i=1,n} w_i P_t^{T_i} \right]. \tag{21.23}$$

For reasons that will become clear in a minute, we are now going to multiply and divide the left-hand side by $P_t^{T_i}$. Then, after moving across the equal sign the right-hand term in Equation (21.23), we obtain

$$\sum_{i=1,n} \omega_i \left(\frac{1}{P_t^{T_i}} \frac{\partial P_t^{T_i}}{\partial t} - r_t + \frac{1}{2} \frac{1}{P_t^{T_i}} \mathrm{Tr} \left[S^{\mathrm{T}} \left(B_t^{T} \right) \left(B_t^{T} \right)^{\mathrm{T}} S \right] \right) = 0 \tag{21.24}$$

with the new weights, $\{\omega_i\}$, given by

$$\left\{ w_i P_t^{T_i} \right\} = \{\omega_i\}. \tag{21.25}$$

We now define for compactness the matrix D, given by

$$D = \sum_{i=1,n} \omega_i \left(B_t^{T_i} \right) \left(B_t^{T_i} \right)^{\mathrm{T}}. \tag{21.26}$$

Let's be clear about the meaning of this expression. For a given maturity, T_i, (B_t^{T}) is an $(n-1) \times 1$ vector, and therefore the product $(B_t^{T_i})(B_t^{T_i})^{\mathrm{T}}$ is an $(n-1) \times (n-1)$ matrix, indexed by the maturity, T_i. This means that there is one such matrix for every maturity, T_i. We then add up these matrices, each weighted by its own maturity-specific weight, ω_i, and we obtain the matrix D. So, just as the vector $\sum_{k=1,n} \left(w_i \overrightarrow{\frac{\partial P_t^{T_i}}{\partial x_k}} \right)$ was the sum of n vectors, so the matrix D is the sum of n matrices.

Using this sum of matrices, we have the nice and compact expression for the overall convexity of the portfolio, $\mathcal{CP}$, which we can write as

$$\mathcal{CP} = \frac{1}{2}\mathrm{Tr}\left[S^\mathrm{T} D S\right] = \sum_{i=1,n} \omega_i \left(r_t - \frac{1}{P_t^{T_i}} \frac{\partial P_t^{T_i}}{\partial t} \right). \tag{21.27}$$

We note that the expression obtained so far is still model-dependent.

21.5 THEORETICAL CONVEXITY AS A FUNCTION OF MARKET OBSERVABLES

21.5.1 Theoretical Portfolio Convexity as a Function of Forward Rates

Recall that, for a time-homogeneous model, the instantaneous forward rate is given by

$$f_t^T = -\frac{\partial \log P_t^T}{\partial T} = \frac{\partial \log P_t^T}{\partial t} = \frac{1}{P_t^{T_i}} \frac{\partial P_t^{T_i}}{\partial t}, \tag{21.28}$$

where the last line follows from time-homogeneity (ie, from $-\frac{\partial}{\partial T} = \frac{\partial}{\partial t}$) We can therefore simplify the expression for $\mathcal{CP}$ obtained in the previous section (Equation (21.27)), to obtain

$$\mathcal{CP} = \frac{1}{2}\mathrm{Tr}\left[S^\mathrm{T} D S\right] = -\sum_{i=1,n} \omega_i \left(f_t^{T_i} - r_t \right). \tag{21.29}$$

This expression is very interesting because, apart from the weights, ω_i, the remaining terms on the right-hand side are completely model independent and can be directly read from the shape of the yield curve today. What we would now like to do is to express the left-hand term, which is just the convexity term, as a function of the shape of the yield curve. If we managed to do so, we would have found what the shape of *today's* yield curve 'says' the convexity of the delta-neutralized portfolio 'should be'. This would establish a link between the shape of the yield curve and the volatility of yields, that we explore more fully below.

Exercise 55 *Here is a little paradox. Equation (21.27) gives (correctly) the convexity of the delta-neutralized portfolio. Convexity is additive. Yet the individual terms $\left[r_t - \frac{1}{P_t^{T_i}} \frac{\partial P_t^{T_i}}{\partial t} \right] = \left[r_t - f_t^{T_i} \right]$ do not give the convexity of the individual component bonds. Why?*

21.5.2 The Portfolio Time Decay as a Function of 'Carry' and 'Roll-Down'

We now fulfill another of our promises, ie, we express the terms in Equation (21.27) in terms of quantities ('carry' and 'roll-down') which can be 'read' from today's yield curve. We shall find that the quantities that we find form a prominent part of market lore, and greatly enhance the financial intuition above the value of convexity.

To do so, consider again the term $\frac{1}{P_t^{T_i}}\frac{\partial P_t^{T_i}}{\partial t}$. We know, that, given our model assumptions, we have

$$P_t^T = e^{A_t^T + \left(\overrightarrow{B}_t^T\right)^{\mathrm{T}}\overrightarrow{x}_t} \tag{21.30}$$

and therefore

$$
\begin{aligned}
\frac{1}{P_t^T}\frac{\partial P_t^T}{\partial t} &= \frac{\partial \log P_t^T}{\partial t} = \frac{\partial}{\partial t}\left[A_t^T + \left(\overrightarrow{B}_t^T\right)^{\mathrm{T}}\overrightarrow{x}_t\right] \\
&= \frac{\partial A_t^T}{\partial t} + \left[\frac{\partial\left(\overrightarrow{B}_t^T\right)}{\partial t}^{\mathrm{T}}\overrightarrow{x}_t\right].
\end{aligned} \tag{21.31}
$$

Now, we also know that the yield of a bond is given under the affine-model assumption by

$$y_t^T = -\frac{1}{T-t}\log P_t^{T_i} = -\frac{1}{T-t}\left[A_t^T + \left(\overrightarrow{B}_t^T\right)^{\mathrm{T}}\overrightarrow{x}_t\right] \tag{21.32}$$

and therefore

$$-(T-t)y_t^T = A_t^T + \left(\overrightarrow{B}_t^T\right)^{\mathrm{T}}\overrightarrow{x}_t. \tag{21.33}$$

Let's differentiate both sides with respect to t. We get

$$y_t^T - (T-t)\frac{\partial y_t^T}{\partial t} = \frac{\partial A_t^T}{\partial t} + \left[\frac{\partial\left(\overrightarrow{B}_t^T\right)}{\partial t}^{\mathrm{T}}\overrightarrow{x}_t\right]. \tag{21.34}$$

However, because of the time-homogeneity assumption, we also know that

$$\frac{\partial y_t^T}{\partial t} = -\frac{\partial y_t^{T_i}}{\partial T} \tag{21.35}$$

and therefore, putting all the pieces together, we get

$$y_t^T + (T-t)\frac{\partial y_t^T}{\partial T} = \frac{1}{P_t^T}\frac{\partial P_t^T}{\partial t}. \tag{21.36}$$

Looking at Equation (21.27), we can immediately see that the expression just derived is exactly equal to the portfolio convexity, $\mathcal{C}\mathcal{P}$:

$$\mathcal{C}\mathcal{P} = \frac{1}{2}\mathrm{Tr}\left[S^\mathsf{T}DS\right] = -\sum_{i=1,n}\omega_i\left(\frac{1}{P_t^{T_i}}\frac{\partial P_t^{T_i}}{\partial t} - r_t\right) \tag{21.37}$$

$$= -\sum_{i=1,n}\omega_i\left[\left(y_t^{T_i} - r_t\right) + (T_i - t)\frac{\partial y_t^{T_i}}{\partial T_i}\right]. \tag{21.38}$$

The two terms on the right-hand side are well known to traders: the quantity $(y_t^{T_i} - r_t)$ tells the investor how much a given bond 'carries' (ie, how much extra yield it returns above the funding cost, r_t) – and therefore the term $\sum_{i=1,n}\omega_i(y_t^{T_i} - r_t)$ tells the trader how much the whole portfolio 'carries'.

The term $\frac{\partial y_t^{T_i}}{\partial T}$ is also part of the traders' lore: it is the 'roll-down', ie, the change in yield as the maturity changes by a small amount, multiplied by the duration of the bond (recall that the weight ω_i 'contains' the bond price, and that the duration of a discount bond is given by

$$\frac{dP_t^T}{dy_t^T} = -P_t^T(T - t). \tag{21.39}$$

Why is this quantity interesting? Suppose for a moment that we can neglect convexity and expectations. Then, the only reason why a yield curve should be upward sloping (or, more generally, not flat) is because of risk (term) premia. Therefore the roll-down is a first stab at assessing the expected excess returns that can be extracted by investing long and funding short. We will discuss this in detail in Chapters 23 and 24.

Putting the pieces together we therefore have

$$\mathcal{C}\mathcal{P}_{theor} = \frac{1}{2}\mathrm{Tr}\left[S^\mathsf{T}DS\right] = -\left[Carry + Roll\right] \tag{21.40}$$

where

$$Carry = \sum_{i=1,n}\omega_i Carry_i \tag{21.41}$$

$$Roll = \sum_{i=1,n}\omega_i Roll_i \tag{21.42}$$

and

$$Carry_i = y_t^{T_i} - r_t \tag{21.43}$$

$$Roll_i = (T_i - t)\frac{\partial y_t^{T_i}}{\partial T}, \tag{21.44}$$

ie, the portfolio convexity is equal to the opposite of the sum of the portfolio carry and roll-down. Note that we have appended the subscript '*theor*' to the symbol, for the portfolio convexity, $\mathcal{CP}_{theor}$, in order to emphasize that this is what is convexity *should* be.

21.6 WHAT THESE RESULTS IMPLY

Equation (21.40) is very important, and it is worthwhile pausing for a second to understand its power, and its limitations.

The quantity on the left-hand side of Equation (21.40), $\frac{1}{2}\text{Tr}[S^T DS]$, is the theoretical portfolio convexity. Once again, this is what the convexity *should* be. This quantity enjoys two important features.

First, it seems to be very model-dependent, containing as it does the 'durations' $B_t^{T_i}$ – see Equation (21.26) – and the 'volatility' matrix, S. Second, it depends on what bonds will do over the next time step (on their volatility, and hence on the absolute magnitudes of their future moves). A reasonable estimate for this quantity can be obtained by looking at how bonds have behaved in the recent past, ie, by estimating their volatility. We can estimate this quantity either directly, or by calibrating a model to yield volatilities (covariances), and then letting the calibrated model tells what it thinks the fair value should be for a quantity like $\frac{1}{2}\text{Tr}[S^T DS]$. So far, so easy.

The 'magical' thing is that this model-dependent, time-series-estimated quantity must always be equal to an exquisitely model-independent, cross-sectional, quantity, $-[Carry + Roll]$ – a quantity, that is, that we can readily calculate from the observed yield curve today without knowing anything about its history (or, indeed, without knowing how to spell 'model').

Here is another piece of magic. Take *any* time-homogeneous affine model,[4] which has been calibrated to fit perfectly the shape of the yield curve out to extremely long maturities. It will always produce the same value for the theoretical convexity. This means that for such a model the duration terms $B_t^{T_i}$ and the volatility matrix, S, will combine to give exactly the same value for $\frac{1}{2}\text{Tr}[S^T DS]$.

Exercise 56 *Why did we write 'out to extremely long maturities'?*

It also follows from this that any model calibrated to fit perfectly the shape of the yield curve out to extremely long maturities *will imply the same volatility for the portfolio of bonds which is specified by the weights* $\{\omega_i\}$.

All of this almost sounds too 'magical' to be true, and, indeed, in this fundamentalist version, the statement is *not* strictly true. The model, that we have tried to throw out of the window, unfortunately comes limping back through the back door because of the weights, ω_i, that enter the construction of the 'duration-neutralized' portfolio. Surely, to duration-neutralize a portfolio of bonds we are going to need a model. Or do we? We show in Section 21.8 that, if the variables x_i are taken to be principal components, the immunizing weights can be readily estimated using model-agnostic statistical techniques.

---

[4] For a discussion of why the model must have time-homogeneous parameters see Section 21.9.

More precisely: a well-calibrated model which uses the quantities x_i as state variables will have to return as hedge parameters exactly the statistically estimated eigenvectors of the yield covariance matrix.

We still seem to have one term, ie, the quantity $\frac{1}{2}\mathrm{Tr}\left[S^{\mathrm{T}}DS\right]$, that depends on the model (recall that the matrix D is a function of the model-dependent duration vectors $B_t^{T_i}$). However, we show in the next section that also this quantity can be estimated without direct reference to any model. If this is the case, we can bypass the model step altogether. We can assess, that is, what the fair value of convexity should be without making reference to any specific model. We show how this is done in the next section.

21.7   LINKING THE TERM $\frac{1}{2}$TR[$S^{\mathrm{T}}DS$] WITH YIELD VOLATILITIES

Let's now look directly at the convexity term $\frac{1}{2}\mathrm{Tr}\left[S^{\mathrm{T}}DS\right]$. Recall that the matrix D was defined to be given by

$$D = \sum_{i=1,n} \omega_i \left(B_t^{T_i}\right)\left(B_t^{T_i}\right)^{\mathrm{T}}. \tag{21.45}$$

Consider now the volatility of a yield, $y_t^{T_i}$, which, for brevity, we have denoted in this section as y_i. Then, using Ito's lemma, we have

$$\left(\sigma_{y_i}\right)^2 = \sum_{k=1,n} \left(\frac{\partial y_i}{\partial x_k}\sigma_k\right)^2, \tag{21.46}$$

where σ_{y_i} is the volatility of the T_i-maturity yield, σ_k is the volatility of the kth factor, and we have made use of the orthogonality of the chosen factors.

However, we know that

$$y_i = \alpha_t^{T_i} + \left(\beta_t^{T_i}\right)^{\mathrm{T}} x_t \tag{21.47}$$

with

$$\alpha_t^{T_i} = -\frac{1}{T_i - t}A_t^{T_i} \tag{21.48}$$

$$\beta_t^{T_i} = -\frac{1}{T_i - t}B_t^{T_i} \tag{21.49}$$

and $A_t^{T_i}$ and $B_t^{T_i}$, as usual, enter the pricing formula for a bond:

$$P_t^{T_i} = e^{A_t^{T_i} + \left(B_t^{T_i}\right)^{\mathrm{T}} x_t}. \tag{21.50}$$

Now it is just a matter of recalling the definition of the matrix D, and that the durations that enter the matrix D are given by

$$\frac{1}{\partial P_t^{T_i}}\frac{\partial P_t^{T_i}}{\partial x_k} = \left[\left(B_t^{T_i}\right)^{\mathrm{T}}\right]_k. \tag{21.51}$$

Next, write

$$\frac{\partial P_t^{T_i}}{\partial x_k} = \frac{\partial P_t^{T_i}}{\partial y_t^{T_i}} \frac{\partial y_t^{T_i}}{\partial x_k} \tag{21.52}$$

and use Equation (21.47).

Putting the pieces together it is now a simple matter to show that

$$\frac{1}{2}\mathrm{Tr}\left[S^{\mathrm{T}}DS\right] = \frac{1}{2}\sum w_i \left(T_i - t\right)^2 \sigma_{y_i}^2. \tag{21.53}$$

Exercise 57 *Fill in the missing steps required to obtain this result.*

So, we have equated the term $\frac{1}{2}$Tr[$S^{\mathrm{T}}DS$] to a simple function of the yield volatilities. To the extent that we can measure the volatilities of the various yields in the portfolio, we have therefore moved another step towards making the expression for the convexity model independent.

Putting together the results obtained so far we have found

$$\mathfrak{CP}_{theor} = \frac{1}{2}\mathrm{Tr}\left[S^{\mathrm{T}}DS\right] \tag{21.54}$$

$$\frac{1}{2}\mathrm{Tr}\left[S^{\mathrm{T}}DS\right] = -\left[Carry + Roll\right]$$

$$\frac{1}{2}\mathrm{Tr}\left[S^{\mathrm{T}}DS\right] = \frac{1}{2}\sum w_i \left(T_i - t\right)^2 \sigma_{y_i}^2 \tag{21.55}$$

and therefore

$$\frac{1}{2}\sum w_i \left(T_i - t\right)^2 \sigma_{y_i}^2 = -\left[Carry + Roll\right]$$

$$= \frac{1}{2}\sum w_i \left(T_i - t\right)^2 \sigma_{y_i}^2 = -\sum_{i=1,n}\omega_i Carry_i - \sum_{i=1,n}\omega_i Roll_i$$

$$= \frac{1}{2}\sum w_i \left(T_i - t\right)^2 \sigma_{y_i}^2 = -\sum_{i=1,n}\omega_i \left[\left(y_t^{T_i} - r_t\right) + \left((T_i - t)\frac{\partial y_t^{T_i}}{\partial T}\right)\right]. \tag{21.56}$$

The important observation is that, apart from the weights, all the quantities in the preceding expression can be either read from the shape of the market yield curve – the quantities on the right-hand side – or empirically calculated – the yield volatilities on the left-hand side. Apart from the weights, ω_i, there are no model parameters left.

The equation just obtained is an equilibrium relationship, which tells us how the yields in our economy *should* behave. To derive it we placed ourselves in a deterministic-volatility affine framework, and obtained the quantities that appear in Equation (21.56). The unobservable model parameters (such as its reversion-speed matrix, or the volatility of the unspecified factors) have disappeared from the equation. We don't even have to specify what the state variables are, or how many state variables the model has, as long as we can assume that the market yield curve and the covariance matrix have been recovered accurately during the calibration phase. So, the only condition the approach presented so far requires is the existence of *some* affine model that can recover the market yield curve and the covariance matrix sufficiently well. As we said, we know that Principal-Component–based affine models, such as the one presented in Chapter 33, enjoy these properties.

We only have to remove model dependence from the immunizing weights, and we are done. This we accomplish in the next section.

21.8   MAKING THE WEIGHTS (ALMOST) MODEL INDEPENDENT

The apparent model-dependence of the weights somewhat spoils the very nice results that we obtained in the previous section. However, we can make progress also here.

So far, the immunizing weights are, of course, model dependent because the weights ω_i depend on the 'factor durations', $\frac{\partial P_t^{T_i}}{\partial x_k}$. If we want to obtain these from the chosen affine model, they will depend on the reversion-speed matrix (although it can easily be shown that they do not depend on the factor volatilities). However, suppose that we choose as our factors principal components. Then we have

$$d\overrightarrow{y} = V d\overrightarrow{x} \tag{21.57}$$

where V is the matrix of eigenvectors of the yield covariance matrix.

As usual, to build intuition and to keep the wood firmly in sight amidst the oak trees, let's look at the one-factor case, and let's go back to Equation (20.10) in Chapter 20 that we obtained in that setting:

$$\omega_2 = -\frac{\frac{\partial P_t^{T_1}}{\partial y_t^{T_1}} \sigma_{y_t^{T_1}}}{\frac{\partial P_t^{T_2}}{\partial y_t^{T_2}} \sigma_{y_t^{T_2}}}. \tag{21.58}$$

Taking the derivatives

$$\frac{\partial P_t^{T_i}}{\partial y_t^{T_1}} = P_t^{T_i}(T_i - t) \tag{21.59}$$

and remembering that in a one-factor setting the volatility, $\sigma_{y_t^{T_i}}$, of the T_i-maturity yield is simply given by

$$\sigma_{y_t^{T_i}} = \frac{\partial P_t^{T_i}}{\partial r} \sigma_r, \tag{21.60}$$

the expression for *the* weight, ω_2, can be rewritten as

$$\omega_2 = -\frac{\frac{\partial P_t^{T_1}}{\partial y_t^{T_1}}\sigma_{y_t^{T_1}}}{\frac{\partial P_t^{T_2}}{\partial y_t^{T_2}}\sigma_{y_t^{T_2}}} = \frac{P_t^{T_1}(T_1-t)\frac{\partial P_t^{T_1}}{\partial r}\sigma_r}{P_t^{T_2}(T_2-t)\frac{\partial P_t^{T_2}}{\partial r}\sigma_r} = \frac{P_t^{T_1}(T_1-t)\frac{\partial P_t^{T_1}}{\partial r}}{P_t^{T_2}(T_2-t)\frac{\partial P_t^{T_2}}{\partial r}}. \qquad (21.61)$$

Note that the volatility of the factor has disappeared (has been cancelled out). In order to calculate the weight ω_2, the only quantities that we do not have are therefore the 'factor durations', $\frac{\partial P_t^{T_i}}{\partial r}$ – which, of course, in the multifactor case generalize to $\frac{\partial P_t^{T_i}}{\partial x_k}$.

Let's go back to the multifactor case. The generalized durations will still depend only on the reversion speeds, and not on the factor volatilities. But, if we choose principal components as state variables, using Equation (21.57) we can empirically obtain the derivatives of the yields with respect to the factors by looking up the appropriate element of the matrix V: this is because the derivative of the i-maturity yield with respect to the kth factor, $\frac{\partial y_t^{T_i}}{\partial x_k}$, is just given by the i, k element of the V matrix:

$$\frac{\partial y_t^{T_i}}{\partial x_k} = (V)_{ik}. \qquad (21.62)$$

Why so? Because, by definition as principal components, we have

$$\vec{y} = \underline{V}\vec{x}. \qquad (21.63)$$

What we actually need to plug into Equation (21.61) is $\frac{\partial P_t^{T_i}}{\partial x_k}$, not $\frac{\partial y_t^{T_i}}{\partial x_k}$. But this is easily obtained:

$$\frac{\partial P_t^{T_i}}{\partial x_k} = \frac{\partial P_t^{T_i}}{\partial y_t^{T_i}}\frac{\partial y_t^{T_i}}{\partial x_k} = -(T_i-t)P_t^{T_i}(V)_{ik}. \qquad (21.64)$$

Summarizing: we have obtained that

$$\sum_{k=1,n}\left(\overrightarrow{\omega_i\frac{1}{P_t^{T_i}}\frac{\partial P_t^{T_i}}{\partial x_k}}\right) = \vec{0}. \qquad (21.65)$$

(Note that for convenience we have switched to the weights $\{\omega_i\}$.) Since, as we have seen,

$$\frac{\partial P_t^{T_i}}{\partial x_k} = -(T_i-t)P_t^{T_i}(V)_{ik}^{T} \qquad (21.66)$$

we have

$$\sum_{k=1,n}\left(\overrightarrow{\omega_i(T_i-t)(V)_{ik}^{T}}\right) = \vec{0}. \qquad (21.67)$$

Just to be clear, the expression on the left-hand side is a sum of vectors:

$$
\begin{bmatrix} \omega_1 \tau_1 \,(V)^{\mathrm{T}}_{11} \\ \omega_1 \tau_1 \,(V)^{\mathrm{T}}_{21} \\ \cdots \\ \omega_1 \tau_1 \,(V)^{\mathrm{T}}_{n-1,1} \end{bmatrix}
+
\begin{bmatrix} \omega_2 \tau_2 \,(V)^{\mathrm{T}}_{12} \\ \omega_2 \tau_2 \,(V)^{\mathrm{T}}_{22} \\ \cdots \\ \omega_2 \tau_2 \,(V)^{\mathrm{T}}_{n-1,2} \end{bmatrix}
+ \cdots +
\begin{bmatrix} \omega_n \tau_n \,(V)^{\mathrm{T}}_{1n} \\ \omega_n \tau_n \,(V)^{\mathrm{T}}_{2n} \\ \cdots \\ \omega_n \tau_n \,(V)^{\mathrm{T}}_{n-1,n} \end{bmatrix}
=
\begin{bmatrix} 0 \\ 0 \\ \cdots \\ 0 \end{bmatrix}
\tag{21.68}
$$

with

$$
\tau_i = (T_i - t). \tag{21.69}
$$

Without loss of generality we can set $\omega_1 = 1$, and therefore

$$
\begin{bmatrix} \omega_2 \tau_2 \,(V)^{\mathrm{T}}_{12} \\ \omega_2 \tau_2 \,(V)^{\mathrm{T}}_{22} \\ \cdots \\ \omega_2 \tau_2 \,(V)^{\mathrm{T}}_{n-1,2} \end{bmatrix}
+ \cdots +
\begin{bmatrix} \omega_n \tau_n \,(V)^{\mathrm{T}}_{1n} \\ \omega_n \tau_n \,(V)^{\mathrm{T}}_{2n} \\ \cdots \\ \omega_n \tau_n \,(V)^{\mathrm{T}}_{n-1,n} \end{bmatrix}
=
\begin{bmatrix} -\tau_1 \,(V)^{\mathrm{T}}_{11} \\ -\tau_1 \,(V)^{\mathrm{T}}_{21} \\ \cdots \\ -\tau_1 \,(V)^{\mathrm{T}}_{n-1,1} \end{bmatrix}.
\tag{21.70}
$$

The immunizing weights are therefore obtained by a matrix inversion:

$$
\overrightarrow{\omega} = A^{-1} \overrightarrow{q}. \tag{21.71}
$$

(Recall that we have derived in Appendix 20A of Chapter 20 the expression for the matrix A.)

These are the statistically determined weights we were looking for.

We stress the two levels of assumptions used in the derivation.

Up to the determination of the weights, we only required the setting to be that of a deterministic-volatility time-homogeneous affine model capable of recovering well the yield curve and the covariance matrix. *Any* affine model that produces these results will do.

For the determination of the weights we have then required the affine model to use principal components as its state variables, and we have used the equivalence results in Section 21.2. We have used the empirical eigenvectors to determine the weights that immunize the portfolio. This is not an inconsistency, because a Principal-Component–based affine model can always be constructed to have exactly these empirical eigenvectors as the corresponding 'durations'.

21.9   HOW GENERAL ARE THE RESULTS?

We have shown something that, at first blush, seems a bit extraordinary. Let's look at the result again:

$$
\frac{1}{2} \sum w_i \,(T_i - t)^2 \, \sigma_i^2 = -[Carry + Roll]. \tag{21.72}
$$

As we said, this equation is telling us something very profound (and, one might say, even a bit 'magical') about the relationship between the shape of the yield curve (the right-hand side of the equation, a purely *cross-sectional* type of information fully determined by *today's* shape of the yield curve), and the volatility of bonds (the left-hand side of the equation, that we obtain from *time series* analysis). How can it work?

Suppose that we have two parallel universes. In both worlds investors have exactly the same views about volatility, have the same risk aversion, believe exactly in the same model, but with one difference. In Universe 1 investors believe that in 20 years' time the monetary authorities will cut rates aggressively. In Universe 2 investors have no such belief. All investors share all other expectations (ie, all expectations for the behaviour for the short rate out to 20 years in the future).

Of course, the yield curve seen by investors in Universe 1 will look very different at the long end from the yield curve seen by investors in Universe 2. Therefore the right-hand side of Equation (21.72) will be different in the two universes. But the left-hand side, which depends only on the volatilities (about which the investors in the two universes agree), must be the same. How can it be?

The explanation of this little paradox is that we have introduced a lack of time homogeneity in Universe 1, because we said that the investors in this universe had beliefs that depended on calendar time (not just on maturity). When we took derivatives with respect to time (and we argued that $\frac{\partial}{dt} = -\frac{\partial}{dT}$) we were invoking time homogeneity, ie, that all the equations depend on $(T - t)$, and not on t and T separately.

So, for our results to hold, we must live in a universe where only time to maturity matters, not calendar time. This is good and bad.

It is bad, because in the real world we often *do* have the belief that we live in 'exceptional times' (think of the extraordinarily accommodative monetary conditions of the early 2010s, of September 2008, or Volker's fight against inflation, ...).

It is not so bad, because usually these beliefs are limited to the near future, and, for short maturities, convexity matters very little.

21.10 MODEL-BASED OR EMPIRICAL?

We have shown how the convexity term can be expressed as a function of quantities that can be read off today's yield curve, and of weights. These weights can be either obtained from a model, or determined empirically. Which route is better?

Let's think for a moment at how we would calibrate our model if we were interested in estimating the value of convexity. To fix the ideas, let's assume that we have chosen principal components as our state variables. Then we would calibrate our model in order to recover as best we can (and, in Chapter 33, we show that our best is indeed very good) the yield covariance matrix, and its diagonal elements in particular. This, in turn, means that we will have created a matrix of model eigenvectors V, ie, a matrix of model loadings from the yields onto the factors, that closely resembles its empirical counterpart. If we are interested purely in convexity, going through the tortuous model route does not bring very obvious advantages. (The situation may change, of course, if we want to consider at the same time expectations, convexity and term premia.)

Therefore the analysis presented in this chapter shows that (under the assumption that *some* affine process drives the yield curve, and that this process is *time homogeneous*) we can estimate the value of convexity from two sets of quantities:

1. a first set (carry and roll-down), which we can directly read off from cross-sectional information (ie, from the shape of today's yield curve);
2. a second set, which we can estimate from yield volatilities and from the empirical 'hedge ratios', ie, from the empirically determined sensitivities of the yields to changes in the chosen factors. We can in general obtain these sensitivities via regressions, but, as we have seen, if the chosen factors are principal components, then we have a particularly nice expression for the weights in terms of the eigenvector matrix, V.

Choosing the right 'patch' of relevant data to estimate the covariance matrix (and hence the principal components) is not a trivial task, but the problem does not disappear if we entrust to a model (that somehow will also have to be calibrated to an appropriate patch of relevant data) the task of determining the portfolio weights.

Looked at from this perspective, there seems to be little that a model can tell us about convexity, which is not available in the cross-sectional information about today's yield curve, and about yield volatilities – two quantities we would strive to calibrate or affine model to anyhow. However, this cross-sectional-plus-time-series information can only tell us about the *instantaneous* value of convexity. This is useful in order to tell us whether convexity is fairly priced today, and can therefore give us trading suggestions. However, it cannot give us 'integrated' quantities, such as the convexity contribution to the T-maturity market yield. This is the function of model as 'integrators' that we discuss in our concluding Chapter 36 (see Section 36.1.6 in particular).

CHAPTER 22

Convexity: Empirical Results

In theory, there is no difference between theory and practice. In practice, there is.

Yogi Berra

22.1 THE PURPOSE OF THIS CHAPTER

In the approach taken in this book, we model the yield curve by decomposing its shape into an expectations term, a term-premia component and a convexity contribution. This decomposition is universally, if not always explicitly, accepted in the literature. However, far less attention has been devoted to the study of the third contributor (convexity) than to the other two – or, for that matter, than to liquidity (see, eg, Fontaine and Garcia (2012)) or even to the effect of the zero bound (see, eg, Wu and Xia (2014)). An early classic paper by Brown and Schaefer (2000) discussed the qualitative effect of convexity on the long end of the yield curve and provided some semi-quantitative estimates of the magnitude of the effect. However, we are not aware of a quantitative study of whether convexity is 'fairly' priced in the most liquid government bond market, ie, Treasuries. This is surprising, because the 'value of convexity' (ie, the difference between the market yields and the yields that would prevail in the absence of convexity) is substantial, as Figure 22.1 clearly shows. In this chapter we try to fill this empirical gap.[1]

Of course, speaking of fairness makes reference to a modelling approach, and, probably herein lies the problem: in studies of this type, one always tests a joint hypothesis, that the convexity is correctly priced *and* the model correctly specified. Given the great uncertainty in model specification, any possible rejection must therefore always include a caveat with particularly lurid health warnings.

It is for this reason that we adopt in the analysis that follows the quasi-model-agnostic approach described in Chapter 21. By this we mean that we do place ourselves in an affine-modelling framework, but we make our results

---

[1] It is a pleasure to thank Dr Vlad Putiatyn for discussions and help with the computations.

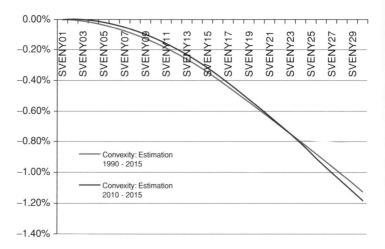

Figure 22.1 The value of convexity, ie, the difference between the market yields and the yields that would prevail in the absence of convexity, as estimated in August 2015 using the Rebonato, Saroka, Putiatyn (2017) model, for yields ranging from 1 year (point labelled SVEN01), to 29 years (point labelled SVEN29). The estimates of convexity from this model are reliable because the model accurately recovers (by construction) the volatilities of all yields. The two curves show that the 'value of convexity' is modestly affected by the precise choice of the historical period during which the yield volatilities are calculated, and to which the model is calibrated.

as independent as possible from the specifics of any affine model (such as the number of factors, or the nature of the state variables – latent, specified, yield curve–based, macroeconomic, etc). We only require that *some* affine model should exist, capable of recovering the market yield curve and yield covariance matrix with the precision required by our study. We know that at least one such model exists (we discuss it in Chapter 33), and we then rely in our reasoning on a simple equivalence result that we state and briefly prove in Section 33.2 of Chapter 33.

We put our quasi-model-agnostic methodology to the test by examining whether it is possible systematically to make money by means of a trading strategy based on immunizing against the exposure to 'level' and 'slope' risk, on estimating the yield volatility over the next time interval, and on comparing this estimate with the volatility 'implied' by the curvature in the yield curve. On purpose, we do not employ a sophisticated volatility estimate, because we want to ascertain whether easily available information about future volatility is correctly embedded in the shape of the yield curve.

As we have discussed, the convexity-induced downward curvature of the yield curve is analogous to an 'option premium' (in the form of a 'yield give-up') that an investor has to pay to go long convexity. Exactly as in option trading, the long-convexity investor will be compensated for this 'yield cost' by making money during her re-hedging activity ('buying low' and 'selling high'). If the realized volatility of yields matched on average the 'implied volatility' embedded in the shape of the yield curve, there would be no money to be made from being either long or short convexity. By looking at 30 years of data, we find that neither the strategy of being systematically long or the strategy of being always short convexity would have been profitable. However, a *conditional* strategy, ie a strategy that looks at the difference between the 'implied' and the statistically estimated volatilities, would have identified extended periods during which the convexity was not correctly priced (by which we mean that it was possible to make money by being long or short convexity, while remaining hedged against the yield curve factors).

Finally, we explain the residuals from the strategy, that is to say, we try to explain the failures to capture all of the theoretically available mispricing: were the failures due to our misestimation of the future volatility? Or where they due to our inability to immunize the portfolio exactly against the first-order ('duration') or second-order ('slope') exposure?

22.2 THE STRATEGY: A REMINDER

To refresh our memory, we start by recalling the approach that we followed with the model-agnostic strategy.

In the previous chapter we first built a 'duration-neutral' portfolio (more about this later), by choosing suitably chosen weights, ω_i, for the three bonds in the portfolio.[2] Once this portfolio was built, we obtained that the theoretical portfolio convexity, CP_{theor}, was given by

$$CP_{theor} = \frac{1}{2}\mathrm{Tr}[S^T DS] = -[Carry + Roll].$$ (22.1)

On the right-hand side we have two terms, the 'carry' and 'roll-down' that depend only on the shape of today's yield curve:

$$Carry = \sum_{i=1,n} \omega_i Carry_i,$$ (22.2)

$$Roll = \sum_{i=1,n} \omega_i Roll_i$$ (22.3)

with

$$Carry_i = y_t^{T_i} - r_t,$$ (22.4)

$$Roll_i = (T_i - t)\frac{\partial y_t^{T_i}}{\partial T}.$$ (22.5)

The right-hand side of Equation (22.1) is the theoretical portfolio convexity, ie, what its convexity *should* be, given today's shape of the yield curve. Pursuing the option analogy presented in Chapter 10, we can call this term the

---

[2] Since we are using *three* bonds to form the risk-less portfolio, we are immunizing against *two* sources of risk. The term 'duration' must therefore be understood in this generalized sense.

'implied' convexity. As the preceding equations show, this implied portfolio convexity can be extracted from cross-sectional information. More precisely, we showed that the theoretical portfolio convexity is equal to (minus) the sum of the portfolio carry and roll-down.

We can look at the same quantity, the portfolio convexity, from a different angle. Since the convexity of a portfolio is additive, if we can calculate the convexity of each bond, $Conv_i$, and we know the weights for each portfolio constituent, we can immediately calculate the yield-volatility-dependent convexity of the whole portfolio:

$$CP = \sum_i \omega_i Conv_i = \frac{1}{2} \sum_i \omega_i T_i^2 \sigma_i^2. \tag{22.6}$$

Where do the yield volatilities, σ_i, come from? They could be the outputs of a calibrated model, in which case we would be calculating what the model says the volatility should be. But they could simply come from our statistical estimation of the future yield volatilities, in which case we would be looking at what our empirical evidence says the future yield volatility should be.

If we pursue the second route, ie, if we use our statistical estimates of the yield volatilities in a predictive mode, we obtain our best guess of what the 'realized' convexity over the next time step should be. We can compare this quantity with the 'implied' convexity, ie, the theoretical portfolio convexity that we can read from the carry and the roll-down. The language of 'realized' and 'implied' convexities has not been chosen carelessly, because the parallels with the practice of 'gamma trading' with options after delta hedging run deep. If this is not clear, please re-read Chapter 10.

Now, let's denote statistically estimated volatilities by $\widehat{\sigma}_i$; more precisely, let $\widehat{\sigma}_i$ be our best time-t estimate of the volatility of the ith yield over the next time step, obtained using all the history up to time t that we consider relevant.[3] Then we can define the prediction of the next-step portfolio convexity, CP_{pred}, by

$$CP_{pred} = \frac{1}{2} \sum_i \omega_i T_i^2 \widehat{\sigma}_i^2. \tag{22.7}$$

The difference between the theoretical and the predicted portfolio convexity will be our trading signal, S:

$$S = CP_{pred} - CP_{theor} = \underbrace{\frac{1}{2} \sum_i \omega_i T_i^2 \widehat{\sigma}_i^2}_{CP_{pred}} - \underbrace{\frac{1}{2} \text{Tr}[S^T DS]}_{CP_{theor}}$$

$$= \frac{1}{2} \sum_i \omega_i T_i^2 \widehat{\sigma}_i^2 + \underbrace{[Carry + Roll]}_{-CP_{theor}}. \tag{22.8}$$

---

[3] Usually, 'all the history up to time t that we consider relevant' will be the most recent history up to time t. This, however, need not be the case, as we could apply 'importance weights' of our choice, on the basis of our identification of sets of 'similar' patches of past history. See Rebonato and Denev (2013) on this topic.

When the signal is positive we expected the future 'realized' volatility portfolio to be higher than what is baked into the yield curve, and we will buy a duration-hedged *long*-convexity portfolio. When the signal is negative, we will do the opposite. The results discussed in the rest of this chapter report the outcome of this trading strategy. Before doing so, however, we must discuss a couple of practical implementation points.

22.3 SETTING UP THE STRATEGY

22.3.1 Determining the Optimal Weights

In Chapter 21 we showed how to choose the portfolio weights so as to be, at least in theory, perfectly immunized against shocks to as many principal components as one may wish. As we have shown in Appendix 20A in Chapter 20, the optimal weights in this perfectly hedged portfolio come from the solution of a linear problem, ie, from a matrix inversion: typically we have

$$A \vec{x} = \vec{y} \tag{22.9}$$

with a known vector, $\vec{y}$, and A a matrix of known coefficients, and we are looking (we are solving) for the unknown vector, $\vec{x}$:

$$\vec{x} = A^{-1}\vec{y}. \tag{22.10}$$

As anybody who has used matrix-inversion solutions knows very well, few solutions can be more practically imperfect than some of the perfect solutions found by inverting these linear systems. The reason for their imperfection is not that these solutions do not deliver what is written on the tin, but that on the same tin there is a lot of fine print about poorly conditioned systems and almost-colinearity which is rarely read.

In practice, this means that in our case it is not uncommon to find highly leveraged solutions with very large and positive weights on some bonds offset by similarly large and negative weights on other bonds. These leveraged portfolios are not just impractical to put in place in practice. (If this were the only problem, we could still look at the strategy with the 'perfect' solution as a theoretical indicator of the 'fairness' of the yield curve curvature: we would not become richer, but at least somewhat wiser.) The problem is that these very positive and very negative positions act as noise-and-small-errors amplifiers, making the detection of the trading signal all but impossible.

There are at least two ways to deal with the stiffness of the matrix-inversion solutions for the application at hand. The first goes under the name of Singular Value Decomposition.[4] It is a beautiful approach, which naturally generalizes

---

[4] A good description of Singular Value Decomposition can be found Section 8.18.3 of Riley, Hobson and Bence (2006). A very insightful tutorial with a nice discursive description of the technique is presented in Baker (2005, 2013).

Principal Component Analysis. The other approach, which we have followed in our study, works as follows.

Given a number of bonds (typically three, but sometimes four), we determine at time t the portfolio weights that minimize the portfolio variance given the actual yield curve moves experienced in the n days before time t. These minimum-variance weights are obtained by a simple, low-dimensionality non-linear search. The number of days, n, was chosen in our study to be 300 business days, and the optimal weights – and, more importantly, the results of the strategy – turned out to be largely insensitive to the exact choice.

22.3.2   Estimating the Yield Volatilities

The other crucial input for the strategy are the predictive volatilities of the yields. The 'noddy' choice of calculating the standard deviation of the daily or weekly changes using a fixed-length window, and equal weights is, of course, always available. Recall, however, that we are interested in what the volatility *has been* only to the extent that it can predict what the volatility *will be* over the next step.

Now, if we use a fixed-length, equal-weight window, we are between the Scylla of a noisy but responsive estimator (if we use a short window), and the Charybdis of a stable-but-sluggish-to-respond estimator (if we use a long window).

This matters for our strategy. Suppose that we have just entered an unexpectedly volatile period. Ex ante, we had no way to predict when the unexpected would happen. However, as soon as, say, Lehman has defaulted, or the attacks of September 11 have happened, we would like our model to know *immediately* that the future volatility is likely to be much higher than what we had estimated when the sky was still blue and cloudless. Such an immediate update of the volatility is unlikely to happen with a long fixed window, as it will take many days of the new excited regime to move significantly the volatility needle. (See Figure 22.3.) As we underestimate the future volatility, but the market does not, during this period we are likely to remain stubbornly short convexity. If we do, we will be severely (to be precise: quadratically) punished for our sluggishness in updating the volatility.

The standard solution to this problem is to use a volatility estimator of the Generalized Auto Regressive Conditional Heteroscedasticity (GARCH) family.[5] In one of its simplest incarnations, the prediction of the variance, σ_i^2, of the a yield, y, at time $i\Delta t$ for time $(i+1)\Delta t$ is given by

$$\sigma_i^2 = a\sigma_{i-1}^2 + b\left(\Delta y_{i-1}^2\right) + c\widehat{\sigma}^2 + \epsilon_i. \tag{22.11}$$

[5] The literature on (G)ARCH models is immense. I simply mention here some of the original papers, such as Engle (1982), and Engle and Bollerslev (1986). A simple how-to-do-it description of the GARCH(1,1) model – the one most commonly used in practice – is provided in Hull (2014). McNeil, Frey and Embrechts (2015) – see their Chapter 4 in particular – give a discussion of GARCH models with a good blend of theory and applications.

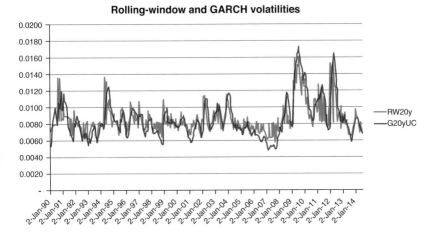

Figure 22.2 A comparison of a rolling-window and a GARCH estimate for the volatility of the 20-year US\$ yield. The estimate obtained using a rolling window is shown by the curve labelled RW20y. The estimate obtained using the GARCH model is shown by the curve labelled G20yUC. Data from Gurkaynak, Sack and Wright (2006). The absolute yield volatility is on the y-axis.

This can be interpreted as saying that the time-i variance, σ_i^2, is a linear combination of the previous-time variance, σ_{i-1}^2, of the square of the change in the underlying[6], Δy_{i-1}^2, and of the long-term unconditional sample variance, $\widehat{\sigma}^2$. The last term, ϵ_i, is the usual iid residual noise.[7] For the stability of the system, the coefficients a, b and c have to be positive.

One can get far more sophisticated estimates of the predictive volatility. However, we have found that Equation (22.11) provides a good trade-off of simplicity, stability, transparency and responsiveness.

To show the point, Figure 22.2 provides a comparison of a rolling-window and a GARCH estimate for the volatility of the 20-year yield. At first blush, the two curves look quite similar. However, careful analysis shows that the rolling-window estimate lags the GARCH estimate, and that it does so in a more pronounced manner when large spikes in volatility occur. This means that the convexity trader who used the naive volatility estimate would be caught napping just when it matters most. The effect is clearly shown in Figure 22.3, which encompasses the unexpected rate hike by the Fed in February 1994.

In sum: all the results that we report in the rest of this chapter were obtained using a GARCH estimate of volatility as per Equation (22.11), and with the

---

[6] This can be roughly interpreted as the 'realized quadratic variation of the yield'.

[7] Note that, when one estimates the Ordinary Least Squares coefficients of the regression the product of the coefficient, c, and of the long-term unconditional sample variance, $\widehat{\sigma}^2$, will appear as a single intercept.

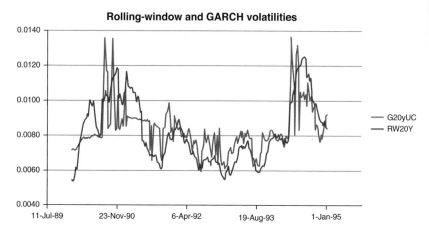

Figure 22.3 A subset of the same data as in Figure 22.2. Note how the lag in the rolling-window volatility estimate is worse in the aftermath of spikes in volatility.

weights derived from the non-linear, minimum-variance, 300-day optimization described in the previous subsection.

Finally, it is important to stress that, *if* we are indeed immunized against the duration shocks to which the portfolio is exposed, and *if* we do guess correctly the future volatilities of the constituent yields, then it does not matter *why* the curve does not have the 'correct' curvature – eg, because of market segmentation, of regulatory constraints or distortions, or of an incorrect estimation by the market of the future volatility: whatever the cause of the 'miscurvature' may be, we should still make money. This is the good news.

The bad news is that what we are trying to capture is a second-order effect. This means that even relatively small residual first-order ('duration') exposures can overwhelm and mask the effect we are trying to capture. Our 'delta-hedging' must therefore be very accurate.

22.4   RESULTS

22.4.1   Is the Yield Curve Fairly Curved?

In the first part of this section we report the results from engaging over a 35-year period in three typical convexity strategies, namely the strategies based on

- a portfolio made up of 5-year, 10-year and 30-year bonds (Portfolio 5–10–30);
- a portfolio made up of 10-year, 20-year and 30-year bonds (Portfolio 10–20–30);
- a portfolio made up of 5-year, 15-year and 30-year bonds (Portfolio 5–15–30).

Figure 22.4 The cumulative profit from the convexity strategy with Portfolio 5–10–30.

In the test we notionally traded each portfolio with weekly intervals, rebalancing (duration-neutralizing) our portfolio at the end of every week, and accumulating the profits and losses obtained at the end of each rebalancing week. The duration neutralization was carried out by determining the weights of the minimum-variance portfolio as described in the previous section. The estimates of the volatility were obtained using the GARCH method, also discussed in the previous section.

The cumulative profits made from the three strategies are shown in Figures 22.4, 22.5 and 22.6 for portfolios made up of 5-year-/10-year-/30-year bonds, 10-year-/20-year-/30-year bonds and 5-year-/15-year-/30-year bonds, respectively. We call these portfolios the 5–10–30, 10–20–30 and 5–15–30

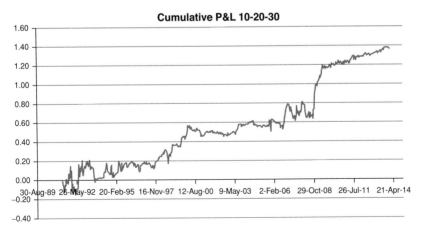

Figure 22.5 Same as Figure 22.4 for Portfolio 10–20–30.

Figure 22.6 Same as Figure 22.4 for Portfolio 5–15–30.

portfolios. Figures 22.7, 22.8 and 22.9 then show the weights of the bonds of maturity other than 30 years for the same portfolio. For all the strategies the holding in the 30-year bond was always normalized to 1.

It is important to pause briefly to explain what is shown in Figures 22.7 to 22.9. The two lines show the amounts of 5-year and 10-year bonds needed to insulate the portfolio against yield curve moves, *conditional on the position in the 30-year bond being equal to* +1. We note that during the period under analysis this duration-neutral portfolio is sometimes obtained by being long the

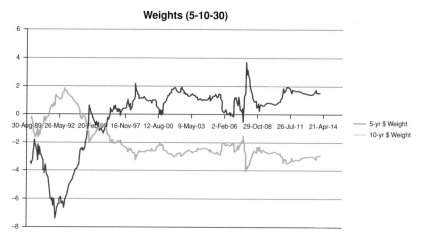

Figure 22.7 The weights of the 5-year and of the 10-year bonds throughout the strategy needed to immunize the portfolio against level and slope changes. The weight of the 30-year bond was always taken to be 1.

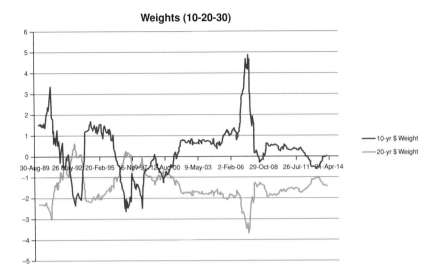

Figure 22.8 The weights of the 10-year and of the 20-year bonds throughout the strategy needed to immunize the portfolio against level and slope changes. The weight of the 30-year bond was always taken to be 1.

5-year and 30-year bond and short the 10-year bond, and sometimes by being long the middle and long bond and (very) short the short-maturity bond. Which combination is preferred depends on how the slope and curvature exposures are immunized against by the minimum-variance algorithm.

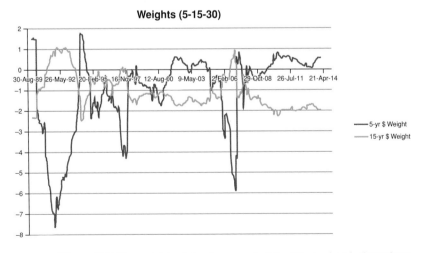

Figure 22.9 The weights of the 5-year and of the 15-year bonds throughout the strategy needed to immunize the portfolio against level and slope changes. The weight of the 30-year bond was always taken to be 1.

Table 22.1 *The Sharpe Ratios for the three strategies, over the whole sample (second column), over the first and second halves of the sample (third and fourth columns) and over the post-2008, strong-signal period (right-hand-side column).*

	Sharpe Ratio (whole)	Sharpe Ratio (1st half)	Sharpe Ratio (2nd half)	Sharpe Ratio (post-2008)
5-10-30	0.58	0.52	0.63	1.21
10-20-30	0.45	0.32	0.58	0.93
5-15-30	0.61	0.52	0.70	1.41

The first observation is that the weights are well-behaved, and their magnitude intuitively understandable. So, for instance, the magnitude of the weight in the 5-year bond tends to be large because of the short duration of the bond: for a given shock, 'more of' the 5-year bond is needed to duration-hedge the corresponding movement in the 30-year bond. It is also clear that the changes in the weights tend to be strongly anticorrelated.

The second observation is that the three strategies are all overall profitable, with a Sharpe Ratio for the whole sample ranging between 0.45 and 0.61. For the strong-signal, post 2008 part of the sample the Sharpe Ratios are considerably higher, ranging from 0.9 to 1.4. See Table 22.1.

Broadly speaking, we recognize three distinct periods of similar length (approximately 10 years): during the first period the strategy is somewhat profitable; during the second it 'treads water'; during the third it is clearly profitable. We look at these differences in Sharpe Ratios in the following section.

22.4.2   Why Are the Strategies Not *Always* Profitable?

A priori, there are two reasons why the money-machine may fail to work: either because the yield curve curvature was 'fair'[8]; or because we did something wrong. In order to understand the reason(s) for the different profitabilities of the strategies, we therefore begin by looking at the strength of our signal. If we make money when the signal is strong, and we fail to make money when it is weak, it would be prima facie evidence that we are indeed capturing phases of different 'curvature fairness'; if the strength of the signal failed to have much of an explanatory power, it would suggest that we are guilty of either of the two capital sins highlighted earlier (failure to duration-hedge, or errors in guessing the volatility).

Figures 22.10 and 22.11 show the cumulative profit from the three strategies together with the signal and the absolute value of the signal, respectively.

---

[8] If this was the case, *and the strategy correct*, we should report a zero profit, but never a loss (apart from transaction costs, that we did not include in the study anyhow).

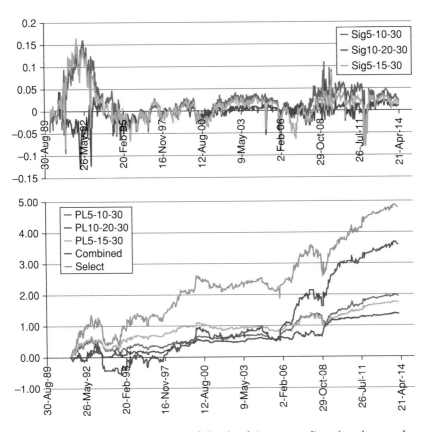

Figure 22.10 The strength of the signal (upper panel) against the cumulative P&L for the various strategies. The construction of the curves labelled 'Combined' and 'Select' is explained in the text.

In the same picture we also report the cumulative profits and losses (P&Ls) obtained following two slightly more robust strategies: in the curve labelled 'Select' we show the combined cumulative profit made by trading only when the three strategies are all concordant (ie, when they all suggest to be either long or short convexity); in the curve labelled 'Combined' we show the cumulative profit made by adding up the three strategies. In all cases we expect a large and positive slope when the absolute value of the signal is large.

The two figures convey a complex message. Looking at the more recent (post-2008) period, it is clear that there is indeed a positive correlation between the money made and the strength of the signal. The failure to make money in the period than ends in 2008 can also be explained by looking at the weakness of the signal. It is the earliest period, when the signal is strongest, yet relatively little money is made (and sometimes money is lost) that requires some explaining. What might have gone wrong?

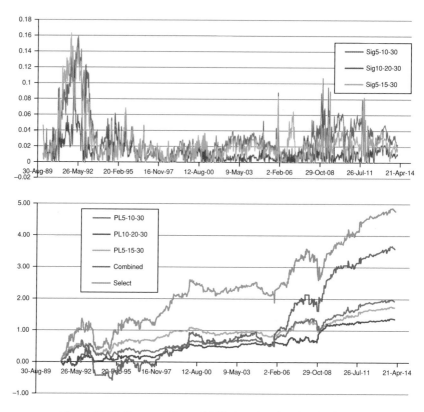

Figure 22.11 Same as Figure 22.10, but showing the absolute value of the signal.

Just to be clear. There can be three reasons for not making money at every time step.

1. The yield curve is fairly curved – if this is why we don't make money, then the strength of the signal should be small when the cumulative P&L remains flat. We can test this.
2. We are not really duration-immunized. In this case we have an unwanted residual exposure to the level, slope or curvature. We can test by regressing the daily P&L against changes in the three Principal Components.
3. We are bad at predicting the future yield volatilities. We can test this as well: if this is why we do not make money, we would get a significant R^2 from regressing the convexity-attributable P&L (the stripped P&L) against the difference between the predicted and the realized convexity.

All these are explanations are testable. Which one is true? We try to answer this question in the next subsection.

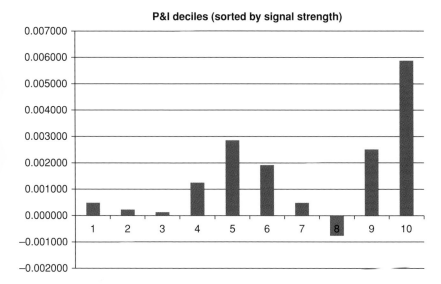

Figure 22.12 Each bar represents the average P&L in the corresponding decile. The deciles were obtained by sorting the (signed) realized P&L by (absolute) signal strength.

22.4.3 Is the Strength of the Signal Correlated with the Money Made?

We start by looking at whether the absence of profit on a particular trading period is simply due to the fact that there is no money to be made, ie, to the fact that curve is fairly curved. If this were the case we would observe a strong correlation between the profit actually made and absolute value of the signal strength (the absolute value, because we don't care whether the signal is positive or negative, as long as it is loud and clear). To test this we sorted the realized (signed) P&L by the strength of the absolute signal. Then we took the average of the P&L in each decile, and we plotted it in Figure 22.12. If there were a clear relationship between signal strength and P&L made, we would expect a graph monotonically increasing with the decile.

The picture is a bit more complex. As Figure 22.12 shows, when the signal is weak, indeed, we make very little money (see the first three deciles). Also, the last decile has the largest average, and the average P&L in last two deciles are in the top three averages. This 'impressionistic' depiction of the dependence can be made more precise by regressing the average P&L in each decile against the decile. The results of this regression are shown in Figure 22.13, which also displays the trend line and a respectable, but not very exciting, R^2 of almost 30%.

Clearly, the signal *is* informative, but there is a lot more than signal strength contributing to the realized P&L. We try to understand what this 'a lot more' is in the next two sub-sections.

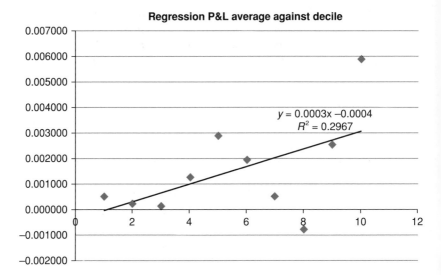

Figure 22.13 The average P&L in each decile plotted against the decile. The figure also shows the trend line and the R^2 statistic.

22.4.4   Explaining the Residuals – Residual Exposure?

The first candidate explanation for the observed lack of strong correlation between signal strength and profit made is the possible failure to immunize against the duration exposure to the first and second principal components. (Recall that the portfolio has a residual exposure to the third principal component that cannot be addressed by throwing three bonds into the mix. Why not use four? Because we find that the outcome becomes less stable – we are 'over-fitting'.[9]) If indeed we were failing to immunize properly, we would observe significant coefficients in the regression of P&L changes against changes in the level, slope and curvature of the three-bond yield curve of interest.

What we find is that the coefficients, reported in Tables 22.2 to 22.4, are rarely significant, and the R^2 for the more volatile residual exposure (ie, the exposure to the changes in level) is close to non-existent. There is a relatively high R^2 coefficient (27.26%) and significant slope and intercept coefficients for the 10–20–30 portfolio, but the exposure is to the least volatile of the three factors, ie, the curvature.

The same message is clearly shown in Figures 22.14, 22.15 and 22.16, which display again the cumulative P&L from the various strategies and the cumulative P&L explained by their residual duration exposure. The only noteworthy

---

[9] 'Overfitting' in this context means that by increasing the number of bonds in the portfolio from three to four we are reducing the error, Err_{in}, in the training set (the 300 days we use to determine the optimal weights), but we increase the error, Err_{out}, in the prediction set. See 00 for a very nice discussion of the capital sin of overfitting.

Table 22.2 *The R^2 statistic, the intercept (a) and the slope (b) of the regression, with the standard error of the estimates in parentheses, for the regression of the P&L changes against changes in level for the three strategies.*

Level	R^2	a	b
Port 5–10–30	0.429%	0.0017 (0.0007)	1.2519 (0.5671)
Port 10–20–30	1.044%	0.0011 (0.0006)	−1.7764 (0.5144)
Port 5–15–30	0.011%	0.0015 (0.0006)	0.1989 (0.5574)

Table 22.3 *Same as Table 22.2 for changes in slope.*

Slope	R^2	a	b
Port 5–10–30	14.43%	0.0015 (0.0006)	8.3794 (0.6069)
Port 10–20–30	10.77%	0.0011 (0.0006)	−1.7764 (0.5144)
Port 5–15–30	3.639%	0.0014 (0.0007)	3.999 (0.6121)

Table 22.4 *Same as Table 22.2 for changes in curvature.*

Curvature	R^2	a	b
Port 5–10–30	13.61%	0.0016 (0.0007)	8.6202 (0.6461)
Port 10–20–30	27.26%	0.0011 (0.0005)	−7.6940 (0.6589)
Port 5–15–30	0.541%	0.0015 (0.0006)	1.3552 (0.5468)

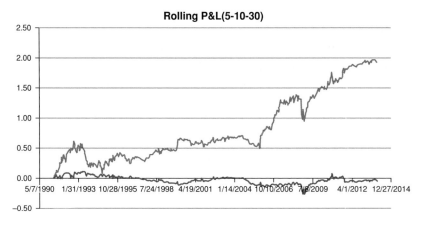

Figure 22.14 The cumulative P&L from the 5–10–30 strategy and the cumulative P&L explained by the residual duration exposure.

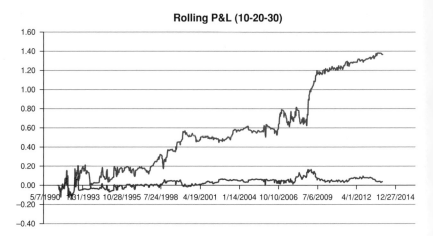

Figure 22.15 Same as Figure 22.14 for the 10–20–30 strategy.

feature is the strong correlation between the residual 'delta' exposure and the strategy P&L at the beginning of the period for the 10–20–30 strategy. The period, however, is short, and the effect overall insignificant. It is probably this short period that accounts for the relatively high R^2 against slope and curvature for the 10–20–30 strategy.

Overall, one can clearly say that our minimum-variance portfolio did a good job at neutralizing the portfolio against first-order exposure. Therefore, our failure always to correlate the strength of the signal with the P&L made cannot be laid at the door of a residual delta exposure.

We therefore explore in the next subsection the last possible source of error, ie, the poor prediction of the future volatility.

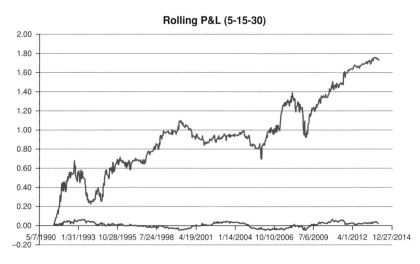

Figure 22.16 Same as Figure 22.14 for the 5–15–30 strategy.

22.4.5 Explaining the Residuals – Wrong Volatility Estimate?

The second possible explanation for the difference between the P&L actually made and the prediction of the P&L that we would make is our failure to guess the realized volatility correctly. To test this possibility we took the daily realized profit or loss made by deploying our agnostic convexity strategy, and we stripped out the first-order contributions coming from the change in yield.[10] The reasoning then goes as follows. First we regress the stripped P&L (as defined earlier) against the difference between the model-implied portfolio convexity and the realized convexity.

The model-implied convexity is given by

$$\mathfrak{CP}_{theor} = -[Carry + Roll]. \tag{22.12}$$

This is the model-independent quantity (the 'implied convexity') that can be read off the yield curve. We can write it as $\frac{1}{2} \sum \omega_i \widehat{\sigma}_i^2 T_i^2$, but this is just the definition of an implied volatility, σ_i.

The realized convexity is given by $\frac{1}{2} \sum \omega_i \Delta y_i^2 T_i^2$, where Δy_i is the observed change in the ith yield. Therefore, as a first step, we regress the stripped P&L against $\frac{1}{2} \sum \omega_i (\Delta y_i^2 - \widehat{\sigma}_i^2) T_i^2$.

When we carry out the regression of the stripped P&L against the difference between the implied and realized convexity, for all portfolios we get an R^2 of almost 1, and a slope and intercept statistically indistinguishable from 1 and zero, respectively. Since looking at straight lines is not very exciting, we do not show a picture of the relevant scatterplot, but let's keep this result in the back of our minds.

With this reassuring result about the effectiveness of our stripping procedure, we now consider the differences between the predicted and realized convexity. More precisely we regress the stripped profit against the difference between the *realized* convexity, $\frac{1}{2} \sum \omega_i (\Delta y_i^2 - \widehat{\sigma}_i^2) T_i^2$, and the *predicted* convexity, $\frac{1}{2} \sum \omega_i (\Delta y_i^2 - \widetilde{\sigma}_i^2) T_i^2$, and look at the deterioration of the R^2 from the value of almost 1 that we obtained before. Any reduction in R^2, or any statistically significant deviations of the intercept and slope from (0,1) would indicate how much of the deviation of the stripped cumulative profit from the signal strength is due to our volatility misestimation.

The results of this regressions are shown in Table 22.5 and in Figure 22.17 for the 5–15–30 strategy.

It is clear from the figure that most of the time there is a positive relationship between the difference in convexities and the stripped P&L, but that this relationship is occasionally spoiled when large moves occur (when the stripped P&L is large). These large unexpected moves deteriorate the significance of the

---

[10] The stripped P&L, $SP\&L_i$, for bond i was calculated as $SP\&L_i = Dur_i \Delta y_i$. The stripped P&L for the portfolio, $SP\&L$, was then calculated as $SP\&L = \sum_i \omega_i SP\&L_i = \sum_i \omega_i Dur_i \Delta y_i$.

Table 22.5 *The R^2 statistic, the intercept (a) and the slope (b) of the regression, with the standard error of the estimates in parentheses, for the regression of the 'stripped' P&L changes against the difference between the predicted and realized portfolio convexity.*

	R^2	a	b
Port 5–10–30	17.38%	0.0000 (0.0000)	0.9687 (0.0629)
Port 10–20–30	16.07%	−0.0001 (0.0000)	1.0970 (0.0756)
Port 5–15–30	18.69%	0.0000 (0.0000)	1.0120 (0.0628)

slope (and intercept) coefficients in the regression. This is the main reason why we do not make money over every rebalancing period.

So, the picture that is conveyed by this analysis is the following.

1. Usually, one can predict fairly accurately the volatility that will be realized over the next time step. In these conditions the agnostic convexity strategy as implemented has good predictive power – by which we mean that it identifies correctly whether the yield curve is fairly curved or not. If it is not, in these conditions the strategy is profitable.
2. Not surprisingly, the GARCH volatility estimation does not provide us with a crystal ball. When moves of unexpected size occur, the strategy ceases to work as predicted – it may fail, or it may 'work too well', depending on the size of the move, and on whether the strategy was long or short convexity before the unexpected-size move.
3. There is an intrinsic asymmetry (skewness) to the P&L profile from the strategy. Consider the case first when the investor is long convexity before the move. A loss will be made if the realized move is

Stripped P&L vs difference in convexity

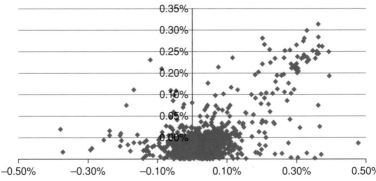

Figure 22.17 A scatterplot of the differences between the predicted and realized portfolio convexity against the 'stripped' P&L (on the *x*-axis). See the text for a precise description.

'too small', and an unexpectedly large gain will be made if the move is exceptionally large. However, if the investor is *long* convexity, the maximum loss that can be incurred is the 'theta decay' over the time step (which will occur for a zero move in yields); the gain is unlimited with the size of the move. The reverse occurs is the strategy is short convexity.

22.5 CONCLUSIONS

In the previous chapter we proposed a criterion based on cross-sectional information (the 'carry' and 'roll-down' of a suitably immunized portfolio) to determine whether the market yield curve displayed 'too much' or 'too little' curvature. (As we discussed, the term *'suitably* immunized' that we sneaked in the previous section reintroduces some model dependence in the choice of the portfolio weights; however, we based our immunization strategy on the minimization of the portfolio variance, making the whole approach as model independent as possible.)

In order to test the validity of our criterion, we set in place a trading strategy, that we discussed in this chapter. Like all *trading* strategies its purpose is, of course, to make money. However, our main focus in this chapter was not to become inordinately rich, but to validate our insight, and to discover its limitations.

The results have been positive. The strategy was overall profitable; with some exceptions (that we discussed) it was more so when the signal was strong; we were able to explain the imperfect correlation between the strength of the signal and the money made by the strategy in terms of (i) the residual (delta) exposure inherent in our portfolio and (ii) the errors we made in predicting the variance over the next time step: our GARCH crystal ball was evidently good, but a bit cloudy at times.

Finally we noticed that, despite the asymmetry of the P&L profile from a long-convexity position, the strategy does not generate much skewness, because it recommends to be opportunistically long or short convexity. The profile is, of course fat-tailed (ie, displays a higher kurtosis that a normal distribution would). This will come as no surprise to anyone familiar with the profits, losses and 'carry' of long- and short-gamma strategies based on options.

PART VI

EXCESS RETURNS

In this part of the book we look at whether any excess returns can be reaped by bearing 'duration' risk – or, for that matter, any other yield curve–related risk. If the price of a risky bond reflects a compensation (a premium) over the actuarial expectation of its payoff, then investing in a long bond while financing the position by borrowing at the risk-less short rate should, in the long run, earn a positive compensation – an 'excess return'.[1] Is this true? If it is, what does the magnitude compensation depend on? What risks are investors paid to bear? Are there no-peek-ahead variables that can tell us when it is a good idea to engage in the buy-long–fund-short strategy?

These are the questions we look at in this part of the book. They have obvious practical relevance. Their answers can also tell us something very important about such fundamental issues as the (local) expectation hypothesis, (ie, the statement that forward rates are unbiased[2] predictors of future rates – and Figure 23.1 explains what we mean when we say that a predictor is biased or unbiased), term premia, whether expectations of long-term inflation are 'well-anchored', and the market price of risk in general.

The empirical estimation of excess returns is also extremely important for a *structural* modelling of the yield curve, because excess returns are directly related to the market price of risk, and the market price of risk is the bridge between the real-world and the risk-neutral description of rates. Structural models are the (sometimes oddly shaped) vessels into which the empirical information about excess returns can be poured.

So, Chapter 23 defines precisely the topic at hand, and introduces the standard notation that will be encountered in the literature. It does so by looking at nominal and real returns. Chapter 24 derives some important implications

---

[1] As we shall see, as it stands this statement is a bit of an oversimplification. The important question is whether the payoffs of bonds are high in 'good' states of the world – in other words, whether bonds 'diversify' the market portfolio. See in this respect the discussion in Section 5.7.

[2] Saying that something is an unbiased predictor of something else does not mean that it is a *good* predictor. It simply means that there is no systematic bias in the predictions it makes. Figure 23.1 illustrates this point.

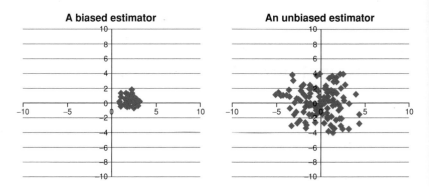

Figure 23.1 The predictions of a biased and of an unbiased estimator. In both cases the 'true' quantity being estimated had the value (0,0). The obvious point is that 'unbiased' does not automatically mean 'accurate', and that, in this particular example, any one prediction produced by a biased estimator may well be more likely to be close to the 'target' than the prediction from an unbiased one. Yet, the average of the high-variance unbiased estimator will be closer to the true value than the average of the lower-variance biased estimator.

of the definitions provided in Chapter 23. In Chapter 25 we present our own empirical results on excess results for nominal and real bonds. Chapters 26 and 27 review the recent literature in the area. Next, Chapter 28 looks at different possible explanations of why the return-predicting factor(s) that we identify – such as the slope – should predict at all. Finally, in Chapter 29 we revisit an important topic touched upon in Chapter 27, namely the number and nature of the variables needed to 'span' (account for) the observed excess returns.

CHAPTER 23

Excess Returns: Setting the Scene

> If the attractiveness of an economic hypothesis is measured by the number of papers which statistically reject it, the expectations theory of the term structure is a knockout.
>
> Froot (1989)

23.1 THE PURPOSE OF THIS CHAPTER

In this chapter we define precisely the local expectation hypothesis and excess returns, and we present several convenient expressions for this latter quantity. We do so both for nominal and for real returns. We show how the existence (or otherwise) of systematic excess returns from the strategy of 'investing long and funding short' is linked to the validity of the (local) expectation hypothesis.

23.2 THE (LOCAL) EXPECTATION HYPOTHESIS

As Sangvinatsos (2008) points out in his helpful review paper, the expectation hypothesis has spawned an immense literature, as the tongue-in-cheek quote by Froot that opens the chapter indicates. This is not surprising, because the expectation hypothesis relates to the evolution of yields, and is of direct relevance for the investment decisions of firms, for monetary policy, for portfolio allocation, and, less directly but not less importantly, for derivatives pricing and hedging. Above all, as Sangvinatsos (2008) says, the expectation hypothesis matters for our economic understanding.

Given its importance, researchers have begun looking into its validity as early as the late 1930s (see, eg, Macaulay (1938), Hicks (1939) and Lutz (1940)).[1] Not surprisingly, the definition of the hypothesis provided in these early days (when Arbitrage Theory and stochastic discount factors were

---

[1] For a discussion of the economic relevance of the local expectation hypothesis (ie, its links with the marginal utility of consumption, utility functions, etc) see, eg, Gilles and Leroy (1986). The authors present a simplified version of the work by Cox, Ingersol and Ross by placing themselves in a discrete-time setting, and avoiding stochastic calculus. It is still not very easy going.

decades in the making) bears little apparent resemblance to the 'modern' definition. As Sangvinatsos (2008) says, '[t]hese [early versions of the hypothesis] were developed as a need of understanding the returns and yields on long versus short-term bonds, and the time series movements of the term structure. Later, researchers developed theoretical models that give rise to some of the hypothesized equations associated with the expectations hypothesis'.

Despite the apparent differences, the underlying concept (and, more importantly, the underlying economic concern) can be expressed in terms of the Local (or Pure) Expectation Hypothesis, and the Weak Expectation Hypothesis. Confusion is created because some authors speak of *the* Expectation Hypothesis with any qualification when they refer to the weak version, and other authors when they mean the local variety.[2]

The first (local) version can be equivalently stated by saying that

1. the expected returns that can be reaped by systematically investing in a long-maturity bond and funding its purchase with a short maturity bond are zero;
2. the expected return from investing for one year in bonds of any maturity is the same as the spot yield on a 1-year bond;
3. the yield (or forward) term premia are zero;[3]
4. the forward rates are an unbiased predictors of future rates.

The Weak Expectation Hypothesis states that

1. the expected returns that can be reaped by systematically investing in a long-maturity bond and funding the purchase with a short-maturity bond are constant;
2. yield (or forward) term premia are constant.

So, according to the (weak) expectation hypothesis 'there are no particularly good times to invest in long-term bonds relative to short-term bonds, nor are there particularly bad times. Long-term bonds will always offer the same expected return.'[4]

Let's go back to the Local Expectation Hypothesis, with which we shall mainly concern ourselves. The fourth definition clearly justifies the 'expectation' monicker, but does not immediately show why the validity or otherwise of the hypothesis should be so important. The first definition clearly shows why it matters (it does, right?), but does not make clear why the hypothesis should be referred to as an 'expectation' conjecture. In Section 24.2.2 we show the link between the transparent but puzzling formulation and the opaque but interesting one. In a nutshell, before the proof, here is the statement: if 'forward rates come true' (ie, if, on average, the *future* spot rate at time τ will be equal to *today's*

---

[2] To add to the confusion, some authors refer to the Strong Expectation Hypothesis as the hypothesis that risk premia are zero, and take the Weak Expectation Hypothesis to mean that they are constant.

[3] See later for a definition of term premia.   [4] Sangvinatsos and Wachter (2005), p. 179.

forward rate of expiry τ) no money will (on average) be made by the buy-long–fund-short strategy. (Lest we get too demoralized, no money will be lost either, apart from the transaction costs paid to brokers, but they have children to feed as well.)

Exercise 58 *Show that the first and the second definitions of the local expectation hypothesis are equivalent.*

The expectation hypothesis that, according to Froot, has won a badge of honour for the number of statistical rejections is the local one. Modern studies (see, eg, Duffee (2002)) suggest that also the Weak Expectation Hypothesis should be rejected but, by Froot's criterion, it is truly in a different league. In what follows, unless we explicitly state otherwise, we will deal only with the local version.

Verbal definitions are suggestive, but notoriously imprecise. Can we give a mathematical definition? Here is one (of many). Let ret_t^n be the return reaped at time $t + 1$ by investing at time t for 1 period into the n-year maturity bond:

$$ret_{t \to t+1}^n = P_{t+1}^{n-1} - P_t^n.$$

Let bor_t be the borrowing cost that we incur from time t to time $t + 1$ in order to finance the purchase the time-t purchase of the n-maturity bond. The borrowing cost is known with certainty at time t, but the return is not, because it will depend on the future realization of the bond that was bought at time t, ie, on the future price P_{t+1}^{n-1}. So, at time time t we can only speak of the *expectation* of the difference between the return, $ret_{t \to t+1}^n$, and the borrowing cost, bor_t. We define the time-t expected *excess* return, $\mathbb{E}_t[xret_{t \to t+1}^n]$, the expectation of the difference between the two:

$$\mathbb{E}_t\left[xret_{t \to t+1}^n\right] = \mathbb{E}_t\left[ret_{t \to t+1}^n - bor_t\right]. \tag{23.1}$$

The Local Expectation Hypothesis then states that the expectation $\mathbb{E}_t[xret_{t \to t+1}^n] = \mathbb{E}_t[ret_{t \to t+1}^n - bor_t]$ is zero. (By the way, in which measure are we taking the expectation? In the real-world measure, of course!)

This is nice, because, once we provide an expression for the borrowing cost in terms of market observables, this definition will also give us a way to test the Local Expectation Hypothesis.

23.3 WHAT ONE REALLY TESTS FOR WHEN ONE TESTS THE (L)EH

Every study of excess returns (or any identification of a return-predicting factor) is, in passing, also a test of the Local Expectation Hypothesis. However, as Fontaine and Garcia (2015) point out, one must keep in mind that this is a *joint* test: of the expectation hypothesis and of the hypothesis that investors are rational and form expectations based on the best available information (and update their prior beliefs as good Bayesian agents). To see why this is the case we follow Fontaine and Garcia (2015).[5]

So far we have only introduced the real-world (data-generating, $\mathbb{P}$) measure and the pricing (risk-neutral, $\mathbb{Q}$) measure. As we discuss in Chapter 28, it is also useful to introduce the subjective probability, $\mathbb{S}$, that reflects an investor's beliefs. This may, but need not, coincide with the 'objective' real-world probability $\mathbb{P}$.

Let's denote by $xret_t^{(n)}$ the *excess* return from investing at time t in the n-maturity bond. Suppose that we assume that the Local Expectation Hypothesis holds true. Then, we can apply the pricing equation that we derived in Chapter 15 to the excess return, to obtain

$$E_t^{\mathbb{S}}\left[m_{t+1} xret_t^{(n)}\right] = 0. \qquad (23.2)$$

(Comparing with Equation (15.12) In Chapter 15, the right-hand side is equal to zero because we are looking at *excess* returns, ie, at returns over the riskless rate of return.) Note that we are taking the expectation under the subjective measure, $\mathbb{S}$.

Next we are going to use the covariance formula,

$$E_t^{\mathbb{S}}\left[m_{t+1} xret_t^{(n)}\right] = E_t^{\mathbb{S}}[m_{t+1}] E_t^{\mathbb{S}}\left[xret_t^{(n)}\right] + \mathrm{cov}_t^{\mathbb{S}}\left[m_{t+1}, xret_t^{(n)}\right] = 0 \qquad (23.3)$$

and we divide through by $E_t^{\mathbb{S}}[m_{t+1}]$ to obtain

$$E_t^{\mathbb{S}}\left[xret_t^{(n)}\right] + \frac{\mathrm{cov}_t^{\mathbb{S}}\left[m_{t+1}, xret_t^{(n)}\right]}{E_t^{\mathbb{S}}[m_{t+1}]} = 0. \qquad (23.4)$$

Finally we add and subtract the expectation of the excess return under the real-world measure, $\mathbb{P}$, and we get

$$E_t^{\mathbb{P}}\left[xret_t^{(n)}\right] = \left(E_t^{\mathbb{P}}\left[xret_t^{(n)}\right] - E_t^{\mathbb{S}}\left[xret_t^{(n)}\right]\right) - \underbrace{\frac{\mathrm{cov}_t^{\mathbb{S}}\left[m_{t+1}, xret_t^{(n)}\right]}{E_t^{\mathbb{S}}[m_{t+1}]}}_{\text{risk premium}}.$$

$$(23.5)$$

Now, as we know from Chapters 13 and 15, the last term is the risk premium, ie, the quantity we shall painfully try to estimate in the following chapters. However the risk premium is 'all there is' to the expectation of the excess return *only if we assume that the subjective probabilities and the real-world probabilities coincide (ie, that the term $E_t^{\mathbb{P}}[xret_t^{(n)}] - E_t^{\mathbb{S}}[xret_t^{(n)}]$ is zero)*. If the subjective measure ($\mathbb{S}$) is different from the objective measure ($\mathbb{P}$), then an extra term (ie, the term $E_t^{\mathbb{P}}[xret_t^{(n)}] - E_t^{\mathbb{S}}[xret_t^{(n)}]$) will contribute to the excess return. What we measure (with difficulty), however, is just the left-hand side, $E_t^{\mathbb{P}}[xret_t^{(n)}]$. We cannot know just from our observations whether what we measure is due

---

[5] See p. 479 and passim in particular.

to the risk premium only, the difference in expectations only, or some mixture of the two. This is what we mean when we say that, when we look for non-zero excess returns, we jointly test the assumptions that the local expectation hypothesis holds and that investors are rational and efficiently avail themselves of all the available information.

Now, the foundations of post-Lucas economics have been firmly laid on the assumption of Bayesian investors who update their expectations in the most rational possible manner. Therefore, expectations may ex post well turn out to bear little resemblance to reality, but, ex ante – ie, when they were formed – they were as good as they could have been, and, since *everybody* is a rational Bayesian agent, the investor's measure was the same as the econometrician's.

This orthodox view is widely held among professional economists. However, one should at least acknowledge the existence of some dissenting voices. One strand of criticism places the emphasis on the difference between the subjective measure ($\mathbb{S}$) and the objective measure ($\mathbb{P}$). It goes as follows.

From the mid-1980s, this line of argument goes, rates have declined to an unprecedented extent – so much, actually, that this secular decline in rates could not have been predicted by the investors who lived through this once-in-a-century event. So, handsome excess returns were indeed reaped by investors who 'went long duration' (bought long-maturity bonds funded at the short end of the yield curve), but not because of any risk premium. The real reason was that *rates fell more than anyone could have predicted*, and therefore investors were continually surprised. $\mathbb{S}$-measure expectations, the proponents of this view claim, were (systematically and biasedly) wrong.

It is difficult (although not impossible) to test this alternative reading of what happened.[6] We will revisit these points in Chapter 28, where the differences between the subjective and the real-world probability measures will come to the fore. However, it is important to keep these *caveats* in mind before ploughing through the treatment of excess returns.

23.4 DEFINING EXCESS RETURNS

We now move to providing a general expression for nominal excess returns, and we specialize it to several important cases.

23.4.1 General Exact Results

At time 0, we start with nothing. We buy $\left(\frac{1}{P_0^N}\right)$ units of P_0^N, ie, of the N-maturity bond[7]. This would cost us \$1, which we do not have. Therefore we sell $\left(\frac{1}{P_0^n}\right)$

---

[6] One way to look at whether this explanation holds is to look at the frequency decomposition of the excess returns. If the major spectral component came from the lowest frequencies (ie, from a trend-like contribution), then the wrong-expectations view would be corroborated. Instead Hatano (2016) finds that the bulk of the spectral contribution to excess returns comes from much shorter, business-cycle-like, frequencies.

[7] Note that the superscript denotes the *residual* maturity of the bond, reckoned from the time in the subscript.

units of P_0^n, ie, the n-maturity bond. This provides us with \$1 in cash, with which we can finance our purchase. Our zero-cost initial portfolio, Π_0, is given by

$$\Pi_0(\tau, N, n) = \left(\frac{1}{P_0^N}\right) P_0^N - \left(\frac{1}{P_0^n}\right) P_0^n = 0, \tag{23.6}$$

where the quantities in large parentheses are the notionals of the two bonds.

We now move to time τ (with $\tau \leq n$), when both positions are unwound. From the long position we receive $\left(\frac{1}{P_0^N}\right) P_\tau^{N-\tau}$. To buy back the short position we must pay $\left(\frac{1}{P_0^n}\right) P_\tau^{n-\tau}$. Therefore the time-$\tau$ portfolio, Π_τ, will be worth

$$\Pi_\tau(\tau, N, n) = \left(\frac{1}{P_0^N}\right) P_\tau^{N-\tau} - \left(\frac{1}{P_0^n}\right) P_\tau^{n-\tau} . \text{ exact} \tag{23.7}$$

We therefore define the quantity $\Pi_\tau - \Pi_0 = \Pi_\tau$ to be the τ-period excess return from investing in the N-period bond and financing it with the n-period bond, $xret(\tau, N, n)$:

$$xret(\tau, N, n) \equiv \Pi_\tau(\tau, N, n). \tag{23.8}$$

This is an exact and general expression. We specialize it and obtain approximate expressions for it in what follows.

23.4.2 Special Cases

Two special cases are often considered in the literature.

Case $\tau = n$

In this case we assume that we have financed the purchase of the N-period bond by shorting a bond that will mature exactly at the end of the investment horizon, ie, $\tau = n$. In this case the cost from selling the τ-period bond and buying back for par at maturity (at time $\tau = n$), ie, the funding cost of the strategy, is known at the outset. Clearly this is what we called in the previous section the known borrowing cost. Expression (23.7) then becomes

$$xret(\tau, N, \tau) = \left(\frac{1}{P_0^N}\right) P_\tau^{N-\tau} - \left(\frac{1}{P_0^n}\right) \quad \text{exact} \tag{23.9}$$

because, when $\tau = n$, $P_\tau^{n-\tau} = P_\tau^{\tau-\tau} = 1$.

Case $\tau = n = 1$

In this case we still assume that $n < N$, and that the investment period is equal to the maturity of the financing bond ($n = \tau$), but we also add the requirement that the investment period should be exactly 1 year ($\tau = 1$). Then we simply have

$$xret(1, N, 1) = \left(\frac{1}{P_0^N}\right) P_1^{N-1} - \left(\frac{1}{P_0^1}\right) . \text{ exact} \tag{23.10}$$

To lighten notation, we often write in the following $xret(1, N, 1) = xret_{t+1}$.

23.4.3 Approximate Results for the $\tau = n = 1$ Case

In the case when $\tau = n = 1$ we can write for each term of the form P_t^T

$$P_t^T = e^{-y_t^T T} \simeq 1 - y_t^T T + \ldots \tag{23.11}$$

and therefore, after expanding the exponential to first order and neglecting products of yields, we have

$$xret_{t+1} \simeq \underbrace{\left(1 + y_0^N N\right)}_{\left(\frac{1}{P_0^N}\right)} \underbrace{\left(1 - y_1^{N-1} [N - 1]\right)}_{P_\tau^{N-\tau}} - \underbrace{\left(1 + y_0^1\right)}_{\left(\frac{1}{P_0^n}\right)}$$

$$= y_0^N N - y_1^{N-1}[N - 1] - y_0^1. \tag{23.12}$$

If we define

$$p_t^T = \log P_t^T \tag{23.13}$$

we have

$$xret_{t+1} \simeq p_1^{N-1} - p_0^N - y_0^1. \tag{23.14}$$

Finally, in order to conform with the discrete-time notation usually used in the literature, we rewrite the last expression as

$$xret_{t+1}^n \simeq p_{t+1}^{n-1} - p_t^n - y_t^1. \tag{23.15}$$

This is the expression almost universally used in the literature on empirical excess returns (see, eg, Cochrane and Piazzesi (2004, 2005)), so it is good to be familiar with it.

Which excess returns should we use, the exact or the approximate? Exact must be better than approximate, right? Well, yes and no. Indeed, if we are interested in the total return from the buy-long–fund-short strategy, the exact return *has* to be better. However, it will contain a contribution from convexity as well – recall that we are long the long bond, and therefore the portfolio will be long convexity. If what we are interested in is just the excess return due to the term premium, the approximate expression, which linearizes the returns, is a bit better. In reality, for maturities up to 10 years the difference is minuscule, but one may want to be a bit more careful if one is dealting with 30-year returns. In general, we lose little sleep because of this fine feature.

23.5   EXPRESSING EXCESS RETURNS AS A FUNCTION OF FORWARD RATES

We have seen in Chapter 2 that the log bond price of an n-period discount bond can be written as

$$p_t^n = - \left(\sum_{i=1,n} f_t^i \right).$$
(23.16)

That being the case, the excess return rx_{t+1}^n can also be written as

$$xret_{t+1}^n = p_{t+1}^{n-1} - p_t^n - y_t^1$$
$$= \sum_{i=2,n} f_t^i - \sum_{i=2,n} f_{t+1}^{i-1} = \sum_{i=2,n} \left(f_t^i - f_{t+1}^{i-1} \right).$$
(23.17)

This expression shows that the excess return reaped by engaging in the 'carry' trade with the n-maturity bond can be expressed as the sum of $(n-1)$ terms. Each term is the difference between today's forward rate for maturity i (f_t^i) and the forward rate in one year's time with the maturity decreased by one year (f_{t+1}^{i-1}).

Radwanski (2010) then defines forward premia, fpr_{t+1}^n, as

$$fpr_{t+1}^n \equiv f_t^n - f_{t+1}^{n-1}$$
(23.18)

and therefore

$$xret_{t+1}^n = \sum_{i=2,n} fpr_{t+1}^i.$$
(23.19)

Why is it useful to express the excess returns this way? Consider the expression $xret_{t+1}^n = p_{t+1}^{n-1} - p_t^n - y_t^1$. As Equation (23.17) clearly shows, the excess return on the 3-year bond 'contains' also the excess return on the 2-year bond; the excess return on the 4-year bond 'contains' also the excess returns on the 2-year bonds and the 3-year bond; and so on. Therefore the decomposition afforded by Equation (23.17) gives a 'cleaner' decomposition of excess returns – where by 'cleaner' we mean that we can look at the individual forward risk premia in isolation. This is particularly important when we look at the principal components obtained from the covariance matrix of excess returns, ie, when we try to ascertain if excess returns of different maturities all move in the same direction, or whether some increase when others decrease. See in this respect Radwanski (2010), Sections 2.1 and 2.3.1.

23.6   EXCESS RETURNS WITH REAL RATES

So far we have been dealing with nominal rates, ie, with bonds that promise (and, at least in this book, deliver) a future payment which is certain in dollar terms. Buying a risk-less nominal bond does not imply, however, that we have any certainty about what we shall get at maturity in real (consumption) terms.

Fortunately, as we have seen in Chapters 4 and 14, in several important currencies there exist bonds that pay a real return. More precisely, they promise (and deliver) a certain real yield plus an inflation component.

As we discussed in Chapter 4, it is important to remember that, despite the inflation proofing, also these bonds are not risk-less. Admittedly, these real bonds are insulated from inflation risk. However, one second after we have bought a 5-year inflation-linked bond, the market may decide that it is willing to grant a higher real yield to the holders of inflation-linked bonds. Therefore, if we sell the real bond we just bought, we will get less than what we paid. To the extent that inflation risk is greater (or more worrisome) than real-rate risk, we may want to treat inflation-linked bonds as 'almost risk-less' – and, perhaps, we may want to neglect the real-rate risk premium tout court. However, if we do so, we must realize that this is because of our modelling choice, not because the uncertainty in the real rate of return shouldn't give rise to an associated risk premium.[8]

We now derive an expression for the excess returns of real (inflation-protected) discount bonds. As usual, we shall neglect those pesky complications due to indexation lags.

At time t_0 we invest \$1 in an N-maturity inflation-linked discount bond, that promises to pay, in nominal terms, a real yield $y^R_{t,N}$ plus inflation indexation at time N. This means that its price, $P^R_{t,N}$, at time t is given by

$$P^R_{t,N} = e^{-y^R_{t,N}N}. \tag{23.20}$$

Today we buy $\frac{1}{P^R_{t,N}}$ units of this real bond. This means that, at, time t_0, the long (investment) position is worth \$1.

We fund this long position by shorting $\frac{1}{P^R_{t,n}}$ units of a real bond of maturity $n < N$. Our portfolio, $\Pi(t_0)$, is therefore worth zero to start with.

One time unit goes by. As our original portfolio was worth zero, the return from the portfolio, $\Delta\Pi(t_0 \to t_1)$, will just be equal to the value of the portfolio at time 1, ie, $\Pi(t_1)$. The long position will be worth

$$\frac{Q_{t+1}}{Q_t} \frac{1}{P^R_{t,N}} P^R_{t+1,N-1} \tag{23.21}$$

and the short position will be worth

$$-\frac{Q_{t+1}}{Q_t} \frac{1}{P^R_{t,n}} P^R_{t+1,n-1}. \tag{23.22}$$

---

[8] We shall see in Chapter 25 that, at least in the last two decades, real-rate risk premia have actually dominated inflation risk premia. This makes sense, as inflation during this period was successfully brought under control. It would have been interesting to carry out a similar attribution of the total risk premium in the 1970s, when inflation was high, and difficult to control. Unfortunately for the researcher, but fortunately for the issuing Debt Management Offices of Western countries, inflation-linked instruments, such as Treasury Inflation Protected Securities (TIPS), were not available at the time.

(As usual, Q_t denotes the price level at time t.) Therefore the value of the portfolio at time 1, $\Pi(t_1)$ will be given by

$$\Pi(t_1) = \frac{Q_{t+1}}{Q_t} \left[\frac{1}{P_{t,N}^R} P_{t,N-1}^R - \frac{1}{P_{t+1,n}^R} P_{t+1,n-1}^R \right]. \quad \text{(exact)} \quad (23.23)$$

This is an exact result. Note the small difference between the analogous result for nominal bonds coming from the common indexation term, $\frac{Q_{t+1}}{Q_t}$.

As usual, we can express any real price as

$$P_{t,N}^R = e^{-y_{t,N}^R N}; \quad (23.24)$$

linearize the exponentials, $(e^x \simeq 1 + x)$; define real log prices, $p_{t,N}^R$, as

$$p_{t,N}^R = \log P_{t,N}^R = -y_{t,N}^R N; \quad (23.25)$$

and finally obtain

$$\Pi(t_1) = \frac{Q_{t+1}}{Q_t} \left[p_{t+1,N-1}^R - p_{t,N}^R - \left(p_{t+1,n-1}^R - p_{t,n}^R \right) \right] \quad \text{(linearized)}$$

$$(23.26)$$

or, equivalently,

$$\Pi(t_1) = \frac{Q_{t+1}}{Q_t} \left[y_{t,N}^R N - y_{t+1,N-1}^R (N-1) \right.$$

$$\left. + y_{t+1,n-1}^R (n-1) - y_{t,n}^R n \right]. \quad \text{(linearized)}$$

In real terms, the expressions obtained are exactly the same as what we got in the case of nominal bonds (with R, of course, replaced by N). In nominal terms, we have the additional inflation indexation, $\frac{Q_{t+1}}{Q_t}$, pre-multiplying what is in the square brackets.

Finally, we define the nominal excess return from the real portfolio, $xret_{t+1}^R$ (*nom*), as the money return from the real portfolio, which is the same as the nominal value of the real portfolio at time t_1:

$$xret_{t+1}^R(nom) \equiv \frac{Q_{t+1}}{Q_t} \left[\frac{1}{P_{t,N}^R} P_{t,N-1}^R - \frac{1}{P_{t+1,n}^R} P_{t+1,n-1}^R \right]. \quad \text{(exact)} \quad (23.27)$$

$$xret_{t+1}^R(nom) \quad (23.28)$$

$$\equiv \underbrace{\frac{Q_{t+1}}{Q_t}}_{\text{infl. indexation}} \left[p_{t+1,N-1}^R - p_{t,N}^R - \underbrace{\left(p_{t+1,n-1}^R - p_{t,n}^R \right)}_{\text{funding cost}} \right] \quad \text{(linearized)}$$

$$(23.29)$$

$$xret_{t+1}^R(nom) \equiv \frac{Q_{t+1}}{Q_t} \left[y_{t,N}^R N - y_{t+1,N-1}^R (N-1) \right.$$

$$\left. + y_{t+1,n-1}^R (n-1) - y_{t,n}^R n \right]. \quad \text{(linearized)}$$

The real excess return from the real portfolio, $xret_{t+1}^R$ (real), is then just given by

$$xret_{t+1}^R(\text{real }) \equiv \left[\frac{1}{P_{t,N}^R} P_{t,N-1}^R - \frac{1}{P_{t+1,n}^R} P_{t+1,n-1}^R \right] \quad (\text{exact}) \quad (23.30)$$

$$xret_{t+1}^R(\text{real }) \equiv \left[p_{t+1,N-1}^R - p_{t,N}^R - \left(p_{t+1,n-1}^R - p_{t,n}^R \right) \right]. \quad (\text{linearized})$$
$$(23.31)$$

Note that, unless we are in a period of raging inflation, for investment (holding) periods no longer than, say, one year, the real and the nominal excess returns from the real portfolios will differ by a few percentage points – which, given the noise in the statistical estimates of these returns, is the last worry that should keep us awake at night.[9]

These are the expressions that we will use for the empirical estimations discussed in the following chapters.

23.7 EXCESS RETURNS: LINKS WITH CARRY, ROLL-DOWN AND RELATED MARKET LORE

Practitioners often think of excess returns in terms of 'carry', roll-down' and related quantities. We have already encountered these quantities in our discussion of convexity. (See Section 23.7.) In this section we revisit these concepts from an excess-returns perspective.

We start from the definition of the instantaneous excess return, $xret_t$, for the strategy consisting of investing at time t in a T-maturity bond, P_t^T, financing the purchase at the short rate (the term $P_t^T r_t dt$), and selling the bond at time $t + dt$ at a price P_{t+dt}^{T-dt}:

$$xret_t = \frac{P_{t+dt}^{T-dt} - P_t^T - P_t^T r_t dt}{P_t^T} = \frac{P_{t+dt}^{T-dt} - P_t^T}{P_t^T} - r_t dt. \quad (23.32)$$

We can write the future price, P_{t+dt}^{T-dt}, as

$$P_{t+dt}^{T-dt} = P_t^{T-dt} + dP_t^{T-dt}. \quad (23.33)$$

It is important to pause for a second on this term: we are saying that P_{t+dt}^{T-dt} will be equal to the evolution of today's price of a $(T - dt)$-maturity bond. We are not specifying the process for the T-maturity bond that we bought at time t, because we are not interested in what T-maturity bonds will do over the time step dt. This is so because we will be holding a $(T - dt)$-maturity bond at disposal time. In other words, we are looking at the evolution *of a constant-maturity bond*. This will be relevant when, in a few lines, we look at the application of Ito's lemma.

[9] If we truly wanted to treat the term $\frac{Q_{t+1}}{Q_t}$ properly, we would in general be faced with seasonality issues, which, for our purposes, are really an unnecessary complication.

To use Ito's lemma, we are going to express the price of a bond in terms of its yield. In general, we can always write

$$P_t^{T-dt} = e^{-y_t^{T-dt}[(T-dt)-t]} \tag{23.34}$$

and

$$P_t^T = e^{-y_t^T(T-t)}. \tag{23.35}$$

Rearranging Equation (23.32) we have

$$xret_t = \frac{P_{t+dt}^{T-dt}}{P_t^T} - 1 - r_t dt = \frac{P_t^{T-dt} + dP_t^{T-dt}}{P_t^T} - 1 - r_t dt. \tag{23.36}$$

Writing the excess return this way allows us to express it in terms of quantities we know today, $(P_t^{T-dt}, P_t^T$ and $r_t)$ and one stochastic quantity, dP_t^{T-dt}, that we don't know at time t. For this quantity we are going to use Ito's lemma. So we have

$$dP_t^{T-dt} = \left[\frac{\partial P_t^{T-dt}}{\partial t} + conv \right] dt + \frac{\partial P_t^{T-dt}}{\partial y_t^{T-dt}} dy_t^{T-dt}. \tag{23.37}$$

The term $\frac{\partial P_t^{T-dt}}{\partial t}$ requires some little care: here we are not taking the derivative with respect to time of a bond that will change maturity by an amount dt as time ticks forward. Instead, we are looking at a bond of constant maturity $T - dt$. Therefore $\frac{\partial P_t^{T-dt}}{\partial t} = 0$.

As for the term $\frac{\partial P_t^{T-dt}}{\partial y_t^{T-dt}}$, we have from Equation (23.34) that

$$\frac{\partial P_t^{T-dt}}{\partial y_t^{T-dt}} = -(T - t - dt)P_t^{T-dt}. \tag{23.38}$$

If, in addition, we neglect convexity, putting the pieces together we can write

$$dP_t^{T-dt} = -P_t^{T-dt} \left[(T - t - dt)dy_t^{T-dt} \right]. \tag{23.39}$$

Therefore we have

$$P_{t+dt}^{T-dt} = P_t^{T-dt} + dP_t^{T-dt} = P_t^{T-dt} \left(1 - (T - t - dt)dy_t^{T-dt} \right).$$

In order to put some flesh on the Ito's bones, we must say something about the process for the yield. As usual, we prescribe for it a diffusive behaviour:

$$dy_t^{T-dt} = \mu_t^{T-dt} dt + \sigma_t^{T-dt} dz_t^{\mathbb{P}}. \tag{23.40}$$

Therefore

$$\mathbb{E}_t^{\mathbb{P}} \left[dy_t^{T-dt} \right] = \mu_t^{T-dt} dt. \tag{23.41}$$

But since

$$xret_t = \frac{P_{t+dt}^{T-dt}}{P_t^T} - 1 - r_t dt \qquad (23.42)$$

we have

$$\mathbb{E}_t^{\mathbb{P}}[xret_t] = \mathbb{E}_t^{\mathbb{P}}\left[\frac{P_t^{T-dt}}{P_t^T} \left(1 - (T-t-dt)dy_t^{T-dt}\right) - 1 - r_t dt \right]$$

$$= \mathbb{E}_t^{\mathbb{P}}\left[\frac{e^{-y_t^{T-dt}(T-t-dt)}}{e^{-y_t^T(T-t)}} \left(1 - (T-t-dt)dy_t^{T-dt}\right) - 1 - r_t dt \right]$$

$$= \frac{e^{-y_t^{T-dt}(T-t)}e^{+y_t^{T-dt}dt}}{e^{-y_t^T(T-t)}} \left(1 - (T-t-dt)\mu_t^{T-dt}dt\right) - 1 - r_t dt$$

$$= e^{-\left(y_t^{T-dt}-y_t^T\right)(T-t)}e^{+y_t^{T-dt}dt} \left(1 - (T-t-dt)\mu_t^{T-dt}dt\right)$$
$$- 1 - r_t dt.$$

where in the third line we have used Equation (23.41).

So, up to this point we have obtained that

$$\mathbb{E}_t^{\mathbb{P}}[xret_t] = e^{-\left(y_t^{T-dt}-y_t^T\right)(T-t)}e^{+y_t^{T-dt}dt} \left(1 - (T-t-dt)\mu_t^{T-dt}dt\right)$$
$$- 1 - r_t dt. \qquad (23.43)$$

Note that up to this point, apart from neglecting convexity, we have made no approximations or assumptions (other than the diffusive assumption for the yield).

For reasons that we will explain later, let's make at this point the important assumption that over the investment period, dt, all yields are expected (under the real-world measure, $\mathbb{P}$) to remain at their current level. This means that all drifts (and, in particular, the drift μ_t^{T-dt}) must be zero. If this is the case we have

$$\mathbb{E}_t^{\mathbb{P}}[xr_t] = e^{-\left(y_t^{T-dt}-y_t^T\right)(T-t)}e^{y_t^{T-dt}dt} - 1 - r_t dt. \qquad (23.44)$$

We now proceed to expanding all the exponentials, to get[10]:

$$e^{-\left(y_t^{T-dt}-y_t^T\right)(T-t)} \simeq 1 - \left(y_t^{T-dt} - y_t^T\right)(T-t) \qquad (23.45)$$

and

$$e^{y_t^{T-dt}dt} \simeq 1 + y_t^{T-dt}dt. \qquad (23.46)$$

Therefore we are left with

$$\left(1 - y_t^{T-dt}\tau - y_t^T\tau\right)\left(1 + y_t^{T-dt}dt\right) - 1 - r_t dt \qquad (23.47)$$

---

[10] In general, we can safely expand exponentials when their argument is 'small'. But this is always the case in the expression we are looking at because $(T-t)$ may well be large, but the difference between two yields of infinitesimally small difference in maturity, $(y_t^{T-dt} - y_t^T)$, will always be infinitesimally small; and because y_t^{T-dt} may well be large, but the term it multiplies, dt, is by definition, infinitesimally small.

where we have called

$$\tau = T - t. \tag{23.48}$$

Multiplying through, and neglecting, because much smaller, all the terms in which two yields are multiplied together, we have

$$\mathbb{E}_t^{\mathbb{P}}[xret_t] = \left(1 - \left[y_t^{T-dt} - y_t^T\right]\tau\right)\left(1 + y_t^{T-dt}dt\right) - 1 - r_t dt$$

$$\simeq \underbrace{\left(y_t^{T-dt} - r_t\right)dt}_{\text{carry}} + \underbrace{\left(y_t^T - y_t^{T-dt}\right)(T - t)}_{\text{roll-down}}. \tag{23.49}$$

Let's look at the two terms: the first, which in market lore is known as the 'carry' or the 'funding advantage', reflects the difference between the funding cost, $r_t dt$, and the investment yield, $y_t^{T-dt}dt$. Even with the two approximations that we have made (no convexity and zero drift for the bond), and which we discuss later, this is, however, not the whole story: there is also the term $y_t^T - y_t^{T-dt}$, which quantifies by how much the yield is expected to decline (increase) – and hence the price to increase (fall) – if the yield curve does not change shape between time t and time $t + dt$. The curve not changing shape is, of course, tantamount to saying that the real-world expectation for the $(T - dt)$-maturity yield does not change. One can suggestively think of the yield 'rolling down' the yield curve (if the yield curve is upward-sloping), hence the name 'roll-down' for the term $(y_t^T - y_t^{T-dt})(T - t)$.

A last comment: the expression we have just derived is the expected return from investing at time t in a T maturity bond, where the expectation is taken at time t. This expectation is a quantity known at time t. Indeed, we have expressed it as a function of quantities (yields) which are all known at time t. Compare this expression with Equation (23.12) for the realized (not expected!) return, which we reproduce below for ease of comparison, after changing $y_t^1 \to r_t$, $dt \to 1$, $N \to T - t$ and $N - 1 = T - dt$:

$$xret_{t+1} = y_t^T(T - t) - y_{dt}^{T-dt}[T - t - dt] - r_t dt.$$

This can be rewritten as

$$xret_{t+1} = \underbrace{\left(y_t^T - y_{t+dt}^{T-dt}\right)(T - t)}_{\text{roll-down}} + \underbrace{\left(y_{t+dt}^{T-dt} - r_t\right)dt}_{\text{carry}}. \tag{23.50}$$

where we have given again the carry and roll-down interpretation to the two terms. These two terms, however, are slightly different. Comparing the result we just obtained with Equation (23.49), in fact, we note that we now have the *future* yield, y_{t+dt}^{T-dt}, in the roll-down term (instead of today's yield, y_t^{T-dt}) and the same *future* yield, y_{t+dt}^{T-dt}, in the carry term (again, instead of today's yield, y_t^{T-dt}). This shows that (with the yield-don't-change assumption we have made) taking expectations has the effect of replacing a future – and therefore today-unknown – quantity, y_{t+dt}^{T-dt}, with a quantity known today, y_t^{T-dt}.

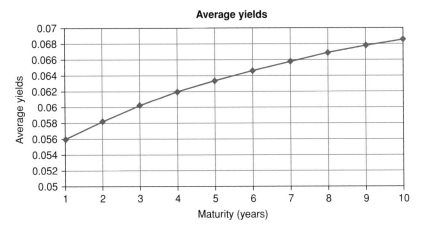

Figure 23.2 The average of the zero-coupon yields for US Treasury from August 1971 to July 2014 for maturities ranging from 1 to 10 years. Data from Gurkaynak, Sack and Wright (2007). See the text for a discussion.

23.8 WHY 'CARRY' AND 'ROLL-DOWN' MATTER

The derivation presented in the previous section for the excess return as a function of 'carry' and 'roll-down' was predicated on the bold assumptions that, in the real-world measure, yields would not change from time t to time $t + dt$. We can, of course, assume anything we like; but why should we be at all interested in results obtained from this very strong assumption?

Consider the following situation. The economy is, more or less, in a 'normal' state – in the sense that all the yield-curve and non–yield-curve variables that describe the state of the economy are not too far from their ($\mathbb{P}$-measure) reversion level. Expectations, in this setting, should produce an approximately flat shape for the yield curve. Let's also focus on yields below, say, 10 years – for which we know that convexity plays a limited role. If, in these conditions, we observe an upward-sloping yield curve (a curve, that is, that has a positive carry and roll-down), its steepness can come only from risk premia. In these conditions carry and roll-down (an upward-sloping yield curve) must be a reflection of a positive compensation for risk.

Of course, nobody knows whether, at any one point in time, the market indeed thinks that the economy truly is in a steady-as-she-goes state. However, when we average over many decades of realized rates, expectation of up-and-down moves should 'wash out', and (apart from convexity) the slope of the average yield curve should give us a rough-and-ready proxy for the magnitude of the unconditional risk premium. It is in this sense that I like to refer to carry and roll-down as the poor man's way of estimating the (unconditional) risk premium.

Figure 23.2 shows what we get when we carry out this exercise: a monotonically increasing 'average' yield curve that starts a little above 5.50% and ends a bit below 7.00%. Unless, throughout these decades, investors always expected rates to 'go up',[11] this steepness of the yield curve constitutes prima facie evidence that the unconditional risk premium is non-zero, and is positive. The skepticism aired in Section 23.3 therefore finds a simple, far-from-conclusive, but nonetheless intriguing rebuttal in these findings.

---

[11] By the way, in the sample under consideration rates started at round 6% and ended well below 1% – so rates actually *declined*.

CHAPTER 24

Risk Premia, the Market Price of Risk and Expected Excess Returns

> A common mistake that people make when trying to design something completely foolproof is to underestimate the ingenuity of complete fools.
>
> – Douglas Adams, *Mostly Harmless*

24.1 THE PURPOSE OF THIS CHAPTER

In this chapter we tease out some of the consequences of the dry definitions provided in the previous chapter. In particular, we

1. prove that if 'forward come true' then the invest-long–fund-short strategy will, on average, reap no profits;
2. derive an expression for the difference between the market yields and the 'actuarially expected' yields;
3. spell out the precise link between excess returns, the market price of risk and risk premia;
4. discuss again why looking at the 'yields-do-not-move' assumption is interesting and important; and
5. revisit the distinction between the real-world and the subjective probabilities (this is a topic to which we will return in greater detail in Chapter 28).

What do we mean by 'actuarially expected yields'? We mean that we take the expectation over (minus) the exponential of the paths of the short rate in the real-world measure. This gives us the 'virtual' bond prices that investors would demand if they did not care for risk. From these 'virtual' actuarial bond prices (ie, the bond prices that would prevail if investors did not care about risk) we derive 'virtual' actuarial yields, which we can compare with the market ($\mathbb{Q}$-measure) yields.

Understanding of all this will put us in good stead to discuss the literature that we present in the remaining chapters of this part of the book.

24.2 DECOMPOSING AND INTERPRETING THE APPROXIMATE EXCESS RETURNS

24.2.1 The 'Carry' Description

If we discretize the results obtained at the end of the previous chapter we see that the realized (approximate) excess return can be decomposed as follows:

$$
\begin{aligned}
xret_{t+1} &= p_{t+1}^{n-1} - p_t^n - y_t^1 \\
&= -y_{t+1}^{n-1}(n-1) + y_t^n(n) - y_t^1 \\
&= \left(y_t^n - y_{t+1}^{n-1}\right)(n-1) + \left(y_t^n - y_t^1\right).
\end{aligned}
\tag{24.1}
$$

Looking at the last line, we find two familiar terms.

The first term is the change between the time-t n-year yield and the value of the $(n-1)$-year yield at time-$(t+1)$, all multiplied by the $(n-1)$ duration. *It is the roll-down term.*

The second term is the difference between the funding cost (y_t^1) of the strategy and the yield of the long bond (y_t^n), enjoyed for one year. *It is the carry term.*

With the long/short strategy we always enjoy the carry term, ($y_t^n - y_t^1$). So, the excess return always has a certain component ($y_t^n - y_t^1$). With an upward-sloping curve, this component ($y_t^n - y_t^1$) is positive. It is 'wind in the sail' for the excess return.

Whether the long/short strategy is overall profitable or not (ie, whether the excess return is positive or negative), then depends on the behaviour of the $(n-1)$-maturity yield, y_{t+1}^{n-1} over the investment horizon.

24.2.2 The 'Forwards-Come-True' Condition

In general, the risky long/short strategy will make more money (the excess return will be more positive), the lower the time-$(t+1)$ yield of maturity $(n-1)$ (because the lower the yield, the higher the price at which we can sell the bond). And we already know that, with an upward sloping yield curve, the excess return is already boosted by the carry term, ($y_t^n - y_t^1$). What is the level of the time-$(n-1)$ yield such that the excess return is exactly zero? (We know that, if it is lower than that, the risky strategy will make money, and the excess return will be positive.)

The answer is that if 'forwards come true' (ie, if *future* rates equal today's *forward* rates) the two terms in Equation (24.1) exactly add up to zero, and the excess return will be zero. This can be seen as follows.

At time t the only uncertain quantity in the expression for the excess return is the term y_{t+1}^{n-1}. Let's therefore look at the future (ie, time $t+1$) value, $[y_{t+1}^{n-1}]_{break-even}$, of this yield that would make the (approximate) excess return exactly equal to zero. From Equation (24.1) one gets

$$xret_{t+1} = 0$$

$$\implies \left[y_{t+1}^{n-1}\right]_{break-even} = \frac{y_t^n n - y_t^1}{n - 1}. \tag{24.2}$$

Consider now the time-t forward (not future!) bond, FP_t^{n-1}:

$$FP_t^{n-1} = \frac{P_t^n}{P_t^1} = e^{-y_t^n n + y_t^1}. \tag{24.3}$$

The time-t forward yield, Fy_t^{n-1}, of a $(n-1)$-maturity bond is therefore given by

$$Fy_t^{n-1} = \frac{y_t^n n - y_t^1}{n - 1}. \tag{24.4}$$

But this is exactly the expression we found for the break-even value of the future yield that would make the excess return exactly equal to zero (see Equation (24.2)).

In sum: if the future yield, y_{t+1}^{n-1}, is exactly equal to today's forward yield, Fy_t^{n-1}, then the long/short strategy breaks even; if it is lower (higher), the excess return is positive (negative).

Which gives the result we were after: *if forward rates 'come true', the 'carry' strategy of investing long and funding short neither makes nor loses money.*

This is a very simple, but very important result. Why so? Because, naively, one might argue: "Of course I can expect to make money in an upward-sloping yield curve if I invest, say, at 6% and fund myself at 2%!" Not so. If forward rates come true (and rates will indeed climb as much as the upward sloping yield curve at investment time implied) no money at all will be made. Expectations – or, rather, the realization of expectations – do matter.

24.3 FROM EXCESS RETURNS TO THE MARKET PRICE OF RISK

24.3.1 Market Yields versus Expected Yields

It is very important to understand clearly the link between term premia and expected excess returns.[1]

To establish this link, we start by assuming that the economy is shocked by n factors, x_i, $i = 1, 2, \ldots, n$. Next, we use the definition of expected return earned

---

[1] A note on terminology: as a rule, we use the terms 'risk premia' and 'term premia' interchangeably. Normally, we prefer the expression 'risk premia', because it stresses that it is a compensation for bearing *risk*. However, when we want to emphasize that we are interested in how this extra compensation depends on the maturity of the bond we invest in, as we do in this section, we prefer to use the expression '*term* premium'.

from time t to time $t + dt$ from entering the carry strategy with a T-maturity bond, $\mathbb{E}^{\mathbb{P}}[ret_t^T]$:

$$\mathbb{E}^{\mathbb{P}}\left[ret_t^T\right] = \mathbb{E}^{\mathbb{P}}\left[\frac{dP_t^T}{P_t^T}\right] = \left[r_t + \sum_{i=1,n} \frac{1}{P_t^T}\frac{\partial P_t^T}{\partial x_i}\lambda_i\sigma_i\right]dt, \qquad (24.5)$$

where λ_i and σ_i are the market price of risk and volatility associated with the ith factor, respectively. As for the term $\frac{1}{P_t^T}\frac{\partial P_t^T}{\partial x_i}$, it is the responsiveness of the t-maturity bond to the ith factor – a 'duration' term. In an affine setting this is equal to (minus) the usual $(B_t^T)^{\mathrm{T}}$ term. We will call this term the duration associated with the ith term, and denote it as $Dur_i(T, t)$:

$$Dur_i(T, t) \equiv \frac{1}{P_t^T}\frac{\partial P_t^T}{\partial x_i}.$$

Equation (24.5) gives the expected return earned at time t over an infinitesimal interval dt. Suppose that, after time dt, we continue the carry (invest-long–fund-short) strategy with the same bond, which will now have maturity $T - dt$. Actually, let's continue to do so until the expiry of the bond. This means that, if we want the total expected return, we must integrate the instantaneous expected return from today (time 0) to the expiry of the bond. We have

$$\int_0^T \mathbb{E}_s^{\mathbb{P}}\left[\frac{dP_s^{T-s}}{P_s^{T-s}}\right] = \mathbb{E}_0^{\mathbb{P}}\left(\int_0^T\left[r_s + \sum_{i=1,n}Dur_i(T - s, s)\lambda_i(s)\sigma_i(s)\right]ds\right).$$

$$(24.6)$$

Two observations. First, there is an expectation sign on the right-hand side of the equation, even if we are dealing with a time integral because the integral is over the path of short rate and over the market price of risk, both of which can be a function of the state variables. Note carefully that in this expression the short rate evolves as prescribed by the parameters of its *real-world* process.

Second, we have made use of the tower law to transform the integral of expectations on the right-hand side into today's expectation of the integral.[2]

When we do the same on left-hand side we have

$$\int_0^T \mathbb{E}_s^{\mathbb{P}}\left[\frac{dP_s^{T-s}}{P_s^{T-s}}\right] = \mathbb{E}_0^{\mathbb{P}}\left(\int_0^T\left[\frac{dP_s^{T-s}}{P_s^{T-s}}\right]ds\right).$$

Neglecting convexity, we equate what is under the expectation signs, and obtain

$$\int_0^T\left[\frac{dP_s^{T-s}}{P_s^{T-s}}\right] \simeq \int_0^T d\log P_s^{T-s} = \left[\log P_s^{T-s}\right]_0^T = 0 - \log P_0^T,$$

$$(24.7)$$

---

[2] The tower law says that $\mathbb{E}_0[\mathbb{E}_1[x_t]] = \mathbb{E}_0[x_t]$.

and therefore

$$\mathbb{E}_s^{\mathbb{P}} \left[\frac{dP_s^{T-s}}{P_s^{T-s}} \right] = -\log P_0^T. \tag{24.8}$$

Using the right-hand side of Equation (24.6) and recalling that

$$-\log P_0^T = y_0^T \times T$$

we can then write

$$y_0^T = \frac{1}{T} \mathbb{E}^{\mathbb{P}} \left(\int_0^T \left[r_s + \sum_{i=1,n} Dur_i(T - s, s)\lambda_i(s)\sigma_i(s) \right] ds \right). \tag{24.9}$$

Recall that (apart from convexity) on the left-hand side we have a market yield. To make this totally clear we write it as $(y_0^T)^{\mathbb{Q}}$. *Modulo* convexity, the yield, $(y_0^T)^{\mathbb{P}}$, that would obtain if investors were indifferent to risk would obviously be

$$\left(y_0^T \right)^{\mathbb{P}} = \frac{1}{T} \mathbb{E}^{\mathbb{P}} \left(\int_0^T r_s ds \right). \tag{24.10}$$

Therefore we define for the yield term premium, TPY_t^T, associated with the T-maturity bond to be

$$TPY_t^T \equiv \left(y_0^T \right)^{\mathbb{Q}} - \left(y_0^T \right)^{\mathbb{P}}$$

$$= \frac{1}{T} \mathbb{E}^{\mathbb{P}} \left(\int_0^T \left[\sum_{i=1,n} Dur_i(T - s, s)\lambda_i(s)\sigma_i(s) \right] ds \right). \tag{24.11}$$

Note that the yield term premium depends on the *a series of* durations from time 0 to time T.

Exercise 59 *Show that, if we are in a one-factor world, if the market price of risk is a constant, and if the volatility is a constant, then the yield term premium, TPY_t^T, is given by*

$$TPY_t^T = \lambda \sigma \frac{T}{2}. \tag{24.12}$$

Exercise 60 *This is a bit trickier.* **Continue to neglect convexity.** *Derive the conditions under which the relationship*

$$\left(y_0^T \right)^{\mathbb{Q}} > \left(y_0^T \right)^{\mathbb{P}}$$

implies

$$\mathbb{E}^{\mathbb{P}} \left[xret_{t,t+dt}^T \right] > 0.$$

*In other words: if today's term premium is positive, can one always rest assured that today's **instantaneous** expected excess return will be positive?*

Exercise 61 *We know that the market price of risk can depend on calendar time and on the value of the state variables, but not on any specific feature of a given bond, such as its coupon or its maturity. Suppose that we live in a universe in which bonds of all maturities and a single equity stock are traded. In this universe long-maturity bonds happen to provide an excellent hedge against movements in equity prices. Short-maturity bonds provide no such hedge. Investors in this universe therefore 'like' long bonds because of their portfolio diversifying properties, and, ultimately, their nice effects on consumption. Could in this universe bonds of different maturities command a different risk premium? The market price of risk can depend on lots of complicated state variables, but 'bond maturity' is not a state variable. How could this effect be captured in the framework we are working in? Can it be captured at all? If you find a way to fix this problem, do you find your 'fix' satisfactory?*

24.4 THE LINK BETWEEN EXCESS RETURNS AND TERM PREMIA

So far, so good. We now want to establish a more direct link between the expected excess returns, the term premia and the market price of risk.

Let's look again at the expression for the expected one-period excess return – as usual, neglecting convexity. We have seen that the one-period excess return from investing at time t in the N-year bond is given by

$$xret_{t+1}^T \simeq p_{t+1}^{n-1} - p_t^n - y_t^1 \tag{24.13}$$

with the log-price, p_t^n, defined by

$$p_t^n \equiv \log P_t^{T_n}. \tag{24.14}$$

Therefore the excess return that one can expect at time t (at the start of the trade) is given by

$$\mathbb{E}_t[xret_{t+1}] = \mathbb{E}_t\left[p_{t+1}^{n-1} - p_t^n - y_t^1\right] = \mathbb{E}_t\left[p_{t+1}^{n-1}\right] - p_t^n - y_t^1. \tag{24.15}$$

Therefore, neglecting as usual convexity and using Equation (24.9),[3] we can write for p_t^n and p_{t+1}^{n-1}:

$$\log P_t^T = p_t^T = -\mathbb{E}_t^{\mathbb{P}}\left(\int_t^T \left[r_s + \sum_{i=1,n} Dur_i(s)\lambda_i(s)\sigma_i(s)\right] ds\right) \tag{24.16}$$

---

[3] We have changed the $\simeq$ sign into an $=$ sign to keep notation light, but convexity is still missing from the reasoning.

and

$$\log P_{t+1}^{T-1} = p_{t+1}^{T-1} = -\mathbb{E}_{t+1}^{\mathbb{P}} \left(\int_{t+1}^{T} \left[r_s + \sum_{i=1,n} Dur_i(s)\lambda_i(s)\sigma_i(s) \right] ds \right),$$
(24.17)

respectively.

Next, we bring all the terms in Equation (24.15) obtained for the expected excess return inside the time-t expectation:

$$\mathbb{E}_t \left[xret_{t+1}^T \right] = \mathbb{E}_t \left[p_{t+1}^{n-1} - p_t^n - y_t^1 \right].$$
(24.18)

Now it is just a matter

- of substituting Equations (24.16) and (24.17) into Equation (24.18);
- of recalling that

$$\mathbb{E}_t[\mathbb{E}_t[\ldots]] = \mathbb{E}_t[\ldots]$$
(24.19)

and that[4]

$$\mathbb{E}_t[\mathbb{E}_{t+1}[\ldots]] = \mathbb{E}_t[\ldots];$$
(24.20)

- of discretizing the integrals (eg, $\int_t^T r(s)ds \simeq \sum r_i \Delta t$), with $\Delta t = 1$; and
- of recognizing that, in our discretized setting,

$$r(t) = y_t^1$$
(24.21)

to obtain

$$\mathbb{E}_t^{\mathbb{P}} \left[xret_{t+1}^T \right] = \sum_{i=1,n} Dur_i(t,T)\lambda_i(t)\sigma_i.$$
(24.22)

In words: under the assumptions and with the approximations we have used in this section, the one-period expected excess return is equal to the sum over factors of the products of the market price of risk times the volatility of the factor times the duration of the T-maturity bond (the bond we invested in) *at the start of the investment period.*

Exercise 62 *Go through all the steps in the bullet points above and derive Equation (24.22). It is a bit tedious, but it will be good for you.*

Exercise 63 *Show that, if we had funded the purchase of the T-maturity bond with a τ-maturity bond (with $1 < \tau < T$), if we lived in a one-factor world, and if the market price of risk and the volatility were constant, then Equation (24.22) would become $\mathbb{E}_t[rx_{t+1}] = \lambda \sigma_x[Dur^T(t) - Dur^\tau(t)]$.*

---

[4] This property of nested expectations is referred to as the tower law. See, eg, Brezeźniak and Zantawniak (1999).

24.5 THE LINK BETWEEN TERM PREMIA AND EXPECTED EXCESS RETURNS

So far we have established that the yield term premium is given by

$$TPY_t^T \equiv \frac{1}{T-t} \mathbb{E}_t^{\mathbb{P}} \left(\int_t^T \left[\sum_{i=1,n} Dur_i(T-s,s)\lambda_i(s)\sigma_i(s) \right] ds \right)$$

(24.23)

and that the instantaneous excess return is given by

$$\mathbb{E}_t^{\mathbb{P}} \left[xret_t^T \right] = \sum_{i=1,n} Dur_i(T-t,t)\lambda_i(t)\sigma_i(t).$$

(24.24)

Therefore it follows that

$$TPY_t^T \equiv \mathbb{E}_t^{\mathbb{P}} \left(\frac{1}{T-t} \int_t^T xret_s^{T-s} ds \right).$$

(24.25)

This says that the yield risk premium today from investing in the T-maturity bond is equal to the expectation (over paths) of the average (over shrinking maturities) risk premium.

Exercise 64 *Show that, if we are in a one-factor world, if the market price of risk is a constant, and if the volatility is a constant, then the expected excess return from entering the carry strategy with a T-maturity bond, $\mathbb{E}_t^{\mathbb{P}} \left[rx_t^T \right]$, is given by*

$$\mathbb{E}_t^{\mathbb{P}} \left[xret_t^T \right] = \lambda \sigma T.$$

(24.26)

So, in this simple setting, the expected instantaneous excess return should scale linearly with the maturity of the (discount) bond. This scaling property is a simple feature of empirical excess-return studies that can be easily checked.

Exercise 65 *Show that, in the same one-factor world,*

$$TPY_t^T = \lambda \sigma \frac{T}{2}$$

(24.27)

and therefore

$$TPY_t^T = \frac{\mathbb{E}_t^{\mathbb{P}} \left[xret_t^T \right]}{2}.$$

(24.28)

The result of Exercise 65 (ie, that, under the stated assumptions, the n-maturity term premium should be half the expected excess return for the same-maturity carry strategy) can be tested empirically as follows.

First, let's assume that, over many business cycles $\mathbb{P}$-measure expectations of changes in rates should average approximately zero. Then (leaving convexity to one side), the average steepness of the yield curve should just reflect the term premium. We can get a rough estimate of the average steepness of the yield curve (in the $\mathbb{Q}$-measure, of course) by calculating for each maturity

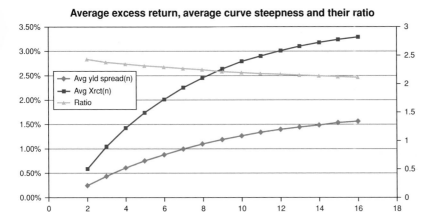

Figure 24.1 The average steepness of the yield curve obtained by calculating for different bond maturities the time-averages of the differences $y_t^{(n)} - y_t^{(1)}$ (blue curve with diamond-shaped markers), the time-average of excess returns for different maturities (red curve with square markers, both on the left-hand axis), and the ratio between the two (green curve with triangular markers, right-hand axis). Note how close the ratio is to the value of 2 (see the text as to why this should approximately be the case). Data from Gurkaynak, Sack and Wright (2007).

the time-averages of the differences $y_t^{(n)} - y_t^{(1)}$. We use the data from 1971 to 2015 provided in Gurkaynak, Sack and Wright (2007) to do so. These are the diamonds labelled "Avg yld spread(n)" in Figure 24.1. For each maturity, these are our estimates of the term premia, TPY_t^n, ie, of the left-hand side in Equation (24.28).

What about the average excess return? To obtain a similarly quick-and-dirty estimate we can time-average from the same reference historical record, and over the same period, the excess returns for each maturity. These are the squares labelled Avg Xret(n) in Figure 24.1. The values for both quantities are displayed on the left-hand vertical axis.

Finally we can take the ratio between the two. If the aforementioned assumptions above do not do too much violence to economic reality we should have

$$\frac{\mathbb{E}_t^{\mathbb{P}}\left[xret_t^T\right]}{TPY_t^T} = 2. \tag{24.29}$$

This ratio of these two quantities is then shown as the triangles, unsurprisingly labelled as Ratio in the figure (right-hand vertical axis).

What *is* surprising (given the crudeness of the approximations) is how close the empirical ratio is to the theoretical value of 2. Indeed, neither the term premium nor the excess returns grow linearly with maturity (as Equations (24.26) and (24.27) suggest they should), but they fail to do so almost exactly at the same rate.

Table 24.1 *The data in Figure 24.1 in tabular form.*

Maturity	Avg yield spread(n)	Avg Xret(n)	Ratio
2	0.0024	0.0059	2.43
3	0.0044	0.0105	2.38
4	0.0061	0.0143	2.35
5	0.0075	0.0175	2.32
6	0.0088	0.0203	2.30
7	0.0100	0.0227	2.27
8	0.0110	0.0247	2.25
9	0.0119	0.0265	2.22
10	0.0127	0.0279	2.20
11	0.0134	0.0292	2.18
12	0.0140	0.0302	2.17
13	0.0145	0.0311	2.15
14	0.0149	0.0319	2.14
15	0.0153	0.0325	2.13
16	0.0156	0.0331	2.12

These results (also presented in tabular form in Table 24.1) should give us food for thought when we look at the empirical studies discussed in the next chapters.

24.6 RECONCILING RESULTS

A moment's thought shows that both the result that we obtained for the term premium (Equation (24.11)) and the result we obtained for the expected instantaneous excess return (Equation (24.22)) make perfect sense: in the term premium we have the expectation of the *average* of the quantity $\int_t^T \lambda(s) \sigma Dur(s) ds$, because we can notionally think of repeating the one-period strategy with a bond that becomes of shorter and shorter maturity (and hence of shorter and shorter duration) as the strategy is rolled over period after period. But when we look at the *one-period* expected excess return, we experience the duration only at the start of the strategy.

One more observation. Suppose that, in our simple one-factor universe, all of the steepness of the yield curve is due to term premia – that is to say, that convexity still plays no role at all, and that, in the long run, expectations of rate changes average to zero. Then, if the simple model sketched in the previous section is correct, the expected excess return for strategies that employ bonds of different maturities (say, investing at time t in a 2-, 5- and 10-year bonds) should scale exactly with the duration of each bond. And if the expectation of the excess returns correctly reflects the actual returns, then the actual profits or losses from the same strategies should also scale with the maturity of each strategy. But do they? This is another testable hypothesis – it is a test of how much the bond market behaves as a one-factor market as far as risk premia are concerned. We will look at this question in more detail in the next chapters.

24.7 EXPECTED VERSUS REALIZED EXCESS RETURNS

In this section we try to answer the following question. Suppose that we have observed a long history of bond prices, and of excess returns. With these data we have calibrated our affine model – which means that we have determined its real-world parameters and the market price of risk. Our model then tells us today what the instantaneous expected return should be over the next time interval. Day after day we compare the prediction with what is realized. We build a history of differences between the expected and realized one-period returns. If the average of this quantity is statistically indistinguishable from zero, we can feel reasonably happy. But what can we conclude if it is not equal to zero?

The reasoning goes as follows. We have obtained an expression for the expected excess return, which we reproduce below in the one-period-bond-funding case for ease of reference[5]:

$$\mathbb{E}_t^{\mathbb{P}}\left[xret_{t+1}^T\right] = \mathbb{R}_t^{\mathbb{P}}\left[p_{t+1}^{n-1} - p_t^n - y_t^1\right]. \tag{24.30}$$

The realized excess return, $Real\left[xret_{t+1}^T\right]$, will instead be

$$Real\left[xret_{t+1}^T\right] = p_{t+1}^{n-1} - p_t^n - y_t^1. \tag{24.31}$$

Therefore the difference, $\Delta xret_{t+1}^T$, between the expected and the realized excess return is just given by

$$\Delta xret_{t+1}^T = \mathbb{E}_t^{\mathbb{P}}\left[p_{t+1}^{n-1}\right] - p_{t+1}^{n-1}, \tag{24.32}$$

where the last line follows because p_t^n and y_t^1 are known quantities at time t (we know today how much we paid for the long bond, and our funding costs), and can therefore be first taken out of the expectation and then cancelled out.

Equivalently, we also note from Equation (24.22) that, in a one-factor case, we can also write

$$\Delta xret_{t+1}^T = \underbrace{\lambda\sigma_x Dur^T(t)}_{\mathbb{E}_t^{\mathbb{P}}\left[xret_{t+1}^T\right]} - \underbrace{\left(p_{t+1}^{n-1} - p_t^n - y_t^1\right)}_{\text{realized xret}}. \tag{24.33}$$

To lighten notation, lets's denote the future realized excess return, $(p_{t+1}^{n-1} - p_t^n - y_t^1)$, by g_{t+1}^{n-1}:

$$p_{t+1}^{n-1} - p_t^n - y_t^1 \equiv g_{t+1}^{n-1}.$$

So, we have

$$\Delta xret_{t+1}^T = \underbrace{\lambda\sigma_x Dur^T(t)}_{\text{expected xret}} - \underbrace{g_{t+1}^{n-1}}_{\text{realized xret}}.$$

---

[5] In order not to mix-and-match different notations, we assume $T = n$; so, for instance, $xret_{t+1}^T$ is the excess return earned by investing from time t to time $t+1$ in the bond which originally has a maturity $T = n$, and whose log-price is p_t^n.

Now, for any single strategy started at a generic time t, the difference $\Delta xret_{t+1}^T$ could be (almost) anything. But what is the *expectation* of this difference? Obviously, if we take the expectation over the strategies in the same real-world measure, whichever way we look at it, we get

$$\mathbb{E}_t^{\mathbb{P}}\left[\Delta xret_{t+1}^T\right] = \mathbb{E}_t^{\mathbb{P}}\left[\mathbb{E}_t^{\mathbb{P}}\left[p_{t+1}^{n-1}\right] - g_{t+1}^{n-1}\right] = 0 \qquad (24.34)$$

and

$$\mathbb{E}_t^{\mathbb{P}}\left[\Delta xret_{t+1}^T\right] = \mathbb{E}_t^{\mathbb{P}}\left[\lambda\sigma_x Dur^T(t) - g_{t+1}^{n-1}\right] = 0. \qquad (24.35)$$

By confining our analysis to the one-and-only real-world measure, we have made our system, if not foolproof, certainly inconsistency-proof. However, mindful of Douglas Adams' warning about something-proof systems, let's look at these relationships a bit more carefully.

The first of these two equalities holds as long as the two nested expectations on the right-hand side ($\mathbb{E}_t^{\mathbb{P}}[\mathbb{E}_t^{\mathbb{P}}[g_{t+1}^{n-1}]]$) are taken in the same measure, because then $\mathbb{E}_t^{\mathbb{P}}[\mathbb{E}_t^{\mathbb{P}}[g_{t+1}^{n-1}]] = \mathbb{E}_t^{\mathbb{P}}[g_{t+1}^{n-1}]$. This seems to be almost too obvious to state: if there were a systematic difference between realized and expected excess returns, we should revise our expectations.

But suppose for a moment that, for some reason, investors formed their expectations about the future path of rates in a systematically wrong way, by misinterpreting the statistical information available to all and sundry in the representative past data.[6] If that were the case, the expectation of the profitability of the buy-long–fund-short strategy would indeed be taken in the correct real-world measure, but the investor's expectations would be formed in a 'wrong' (subjective) real-world measure – call it $\mathbb{S}$.[7] If we make this distinction, we would have

$$\mathbb{E}_t^{\mathbb{P}}\left[\Delta xret_{t+1}^T\right] = \mathbb{E}_t^{\mathbb{P}}\left[\mathbb{E}_t^{\mathbb{S}}\left[p_{t+1}^{n-1}\right] - g_{t+1}^{n-1}\right] \neq 0 \qquad (24.36)$$

as it would no longer be the case that

$$\mathbb{E}_t^{\mathbb{P}}\left[\mathbb{E}_t^{\mathbb{S}}\left[p_{t+1}^{n-1}\right]\right] = \mathbb{E}_t^{\mathbb{P}}\left[p_{t+1}^{n-1}\right]. \qquad (24.37)$$

Let me make a contrived example just to stress the point: suppose that, for some bizarre reason, investors ignored evidence to the contrary and consistently and wrongly formed their real-world expectations of future rates believing that rates will always climb from their present value to 50%. Then it is obvious that the buy-long–fund-short strategy would end up being a licence to print money, and that the difference between the expected and the realized excess returns

---

[6] This is not so far-fetched: after all, *today* we make use of 50 years' worth of data. Thirty or forty years ago investors did not have the same wealth of relevant information. See the discussion in Chapter 28.

[7] We have already discuss the difference between the subjective and the objective measures in Section 23.3. We will explore further the difference between the 'objective' real-world distribution (also called the 'data-generating' measure), $\mathbb{P}$, and the subjective distribution, $\mathbb{S}$, in Chapter 28. See also Piazzesi, Salomao and Schneider (2013).

would be mainly due to the repeated formation of the crazy rate expectations, not to the existence of any risk premium.

Now, it is not reasonable to assume that investors keep on believing that rates will always climb to 50%, even if they never do. However, as we discussed in the previous chapter, if one looks at the history of rates in most developed economies from the early 1990s onward, one observes a continuous and unprecedented decline. When I took my first mortgage I was paying a rate of interest of 17%, but, as of this writing, UK short rates hover around zero. One may argue that the secular decline in rates, and the accompanying 'defeat of inflation', that occurred in these three decades were largely unanticipated. In this view, estimates of the level of rates were continuously revised, but investors kept on being surprised that rates could go *so* low. The expectations of investors, in this description of what happened from the 1990s to the second half of the 2010s, were systematically wrong (biased).

Looking closer to home, I show in Figures 24.2 and 24.3 the predictions about the future level of rates made by the 18 members of the FOMC from January 2012 to September 2015. It is important to be clear about what the figures show. Each committee member is asked to express a view about the most likely realization of the Fed Funds rate at the end of the year when the prediction is made, at the end of the following three years, and 'in the long term'. Each prediction is a 'blue dot'.

In Figure 24.2, these predictions are then averaged, and they are organized by date when the prediction is made, and by final projection date. These are the lines shown in Figure 24.2. Then Figure 24.3 shows the expected path of the Fed Funds rate projected from different dates. The striking feature from both figures is that the predictions of the economists who arguably have the best information in the world about the state of the US economy were not just wrong (we *are* all human after all) but also systematically biased. Almost every single one of the 16 probability updates made in this period would have been in the same direction! And, these revisions were not just about the short-term unfolding of the resolution of the Great Recession: also the (average of the) long-term rate projections steadily declined over the same period from 4.21% to 3.46%. Clearly, any inferences about the effectiveness of an excess-return-predicting factor during the 2010–2016 period would be contaminated by the fact that during this period the expectations turned out to be systematically wrong. By going 'long duration' an investor would have made (a lot of) money during this period, not because she was collecting a handsome risk premium, but because rates always turned out lower than expected. We shall revisit this important point in the rest of the book.

In reality, nobody can know what the 'market's expectations' truly are, and a five-year snapshot, suggestive as it may be, is not enough to conclude that expectations can be *systematically* biased over a statistically significant period. A week may be a long time in politics, but five years is a short time in excess-return studies. As a consequence, it is not easy to pursue this line of enquiry in a systematic, non-impressionistic way. The point in discussing this example in

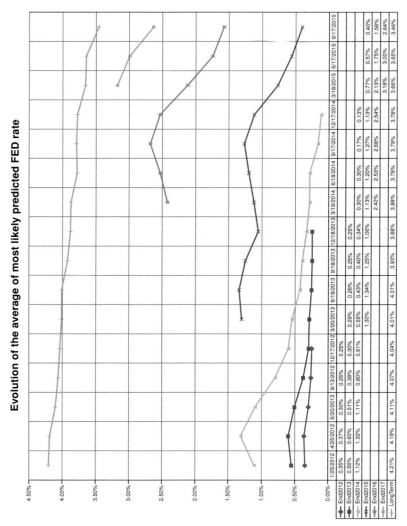

Figure 24.2 For each meeting date of the FOMC (shown at the bottom of the figure) each point represents the average of the most likely rate, as predicted by the 18 members of the committee, for the short rate at the end of (i) the year when the question was posed; (ii) at the end of the following year; (iii) at the end of the year after that; and (iv) in the 'long term'. Clearly, the prediction made in mid-December about the most likely rate that will prevail at the end of the year when the question is posed has virtually zero standard deviation: all the members always correctly predicted it at all

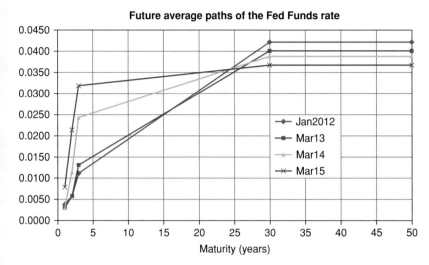

Figure 24.3 The future average paths of the Fed Funds rate, as predicted on several dates approximately one year apart. The last two points (corresponding to the 30- and 50-year maturities) correspond to the 'long-term' projections. *Two* points have been shown on the graph to avoid giving the impression that the yield curve should be extrapolated upwards.

some detail was to show in a real-life case how expectations which are wrong *in the same direction* for an extended period of time can contaminate excess return results relative to the same period.

In general, what one can say is that, everybody, equipped with a long enough time series of past returns and patience to match, can measure the profit from the buy-long–fund-short strategy. Now, *if* our model is passably correct, *if* past information is representative of the future, and *if* the expectations formed by the market participants are 'correct' (in the sense of being unbiased given the available information), then the ex ante expectations of the excess return, given by Expression (24.22), should on average equal the ex post profits from the buy-long-fund-short strategy. But if they do not, there can, in principle be several culprits, and we should not eliminate some characters a priori from the police line-up.

The first suspect is, of course, our model specification, and, in particular, our assumptions about the functional dependence of the market price of risk on the state variables. This means that we would have

$$\mathbb{E}_t^{\mathbb{P}}\left[\Delta xret_{t+1}^T\right] \neq \mathbb{E}_t^{\mathbb{P}}\left[\underbrace{\lambda\sigma_x Dur^T(t)}_{\text{model-dependent term}} -g_{t+1}^{n-1}\right]. \tag{24.38}$$

So, this explanation for the systematic difference between the expected and the realized excess return lays the blame at the door of our faulty model specification – say, the wrong market price of risk. Note that we have the same superscript, $\mathbb{P}$, on both sides of the equation.

However, logically, the reason for a disagreement could be different: it may be the case that our specification of the market price of risk (and of the volatility of the factor) was correct, but the investors' expectations were not unbiased – which means that the investors' expectations were not consistent with the expectations we take when we estimate the difference between the realized and the excess returns. In that case, the non-zero expectation of the difference between expected and realized returns would be due to the two 'different' $\mathbb{P}$ measures, $\mathbb{P}$ and $\mathbb{S}$:

$$\mathbb{E}_t^{\mathbb{P}} \left[\mathbb{E}_t^{\mathbb{S}} \left[p_{t+1}^{n-1} \right] \right] \neq \mathbb{E}_t^{\mathbb{P}} \left[p_{t+1}^{n-1} \right]. \tag{24.39}$$

The issue of whether investors incorporate 'efficiently' new information into prices is a vexed one. In the case of equities, the most famous study arguing that investors over-react is probably Shiller's 1981 paper, aptly titled "Do Stock Prices Move Too Much To Be Justified by Subsequent Changes in Dividends?" (The answer, in case you wondered, was 'yes'.) Shiller (1979) asks the same question about Treasury bonds in "The Volatility of Long-term Interest Rates and Expectations Models of the Term Structure". He does not provide conclusive evidence that bond investors certainly over-react, but instills sufficient doubt in a reasonable mind that the over-reaction case cannot be dismissed out of hand: let's say that the evidence he produces is of the on-the-balance-of-probability, not beyond-all-reasonable-doubt, type. And in Chapter 28 we present a simple model that shows that many regularities in the dependence of excess returns on the slope of the yield curve could be explained if investors guessed correctly the future direction of the short rate intended by the central banks, but over-reacted.

Departures from rationality are not the only possible explanations, though. Perhaps investors are free from estimation biases, but, as mentioned earlier, in the past they simply did not have the wealth of empirical information we can now avail ourselves of, and their estimate were therefore statistically poor. This is the explanation offered by Piazzesi, Salomao and Schneider (2013). See in this respect the discussion in Section 28.4 of Chapter 28.

In any case, the important point here is that, if we are interested in a *structural* explanation of the yield curve dynamics, and we are faced with a discrepancy between expected and realized excess returns, we should keep an open mind as where this discrepancy comes from.

24.8 FORWARDS-COME-TRUE VERSUS YIELDS-DON'T-MOVE: ROLL-DOWN AGAIN

Let's move to a different, but related, topic.

We have seen that if forwards 'come true', then the excess returns are zero. For forwards to come true, yields have to evolve in a particular way; ie, as we have seen, future yields have to become today's forward yields. But, of course, in reality they don't have to. What if instead yields didn't move at all; ie, what if, for any maturity n, the yield at time $t + 1$ of then-residual maturity n, $y_{t+1}^{(t+1)+n}$, were the same as the time-t yield of the same residual maturity, y_t^{t+n}:

$$y_{t+1}^n = y_t^n? \tag{24.40}$$

If this were true, in, say, one year's time the n-maturity yield that today has value y_t^n will have the same value as *today's* $(n - 1)$-maturity yield y_t^{n-1}. The yield curve, in other words, would never change shape.

Let's look at the expression for the excess return again:

$$xret_{t+1} = \left(y_t^n - y_{t+1}^{n-1}\right)(n - 1) + \left(y_t^n - y_t^1\right). \tag{24.41}$$

Then, if yields did not move, we would have

$$xret_{t+1} = \left(y_t^n - y_t^{n-1}\right)(n - 1) + \left(y_t^n - y_t^1\right). \tag{24.42}$$

As we have seen in the previous chapter, the excess return is then just equal to the sum of two terms:

- the carry term, $(y_t^n - y_t^1)$, which we have already seen;
- and a 'roll-down' term, which is equal to the slope of the time-t yield curve, times the $(n - 1)$-duration.

The 'carry' term is obvious enough: it reflects our 'funding advantage', ie, the fact that we borrow at y_t^1 but invest at y_t^n. But why is the roll-down term interesting? Why should we pay attention to what happens to excess returns if this particular future realization of the future yields were to materialize?

Let's neglect convexity for the moment.[8] Then, apart from expectations, the steepness in the yield curve *can come only from term premium*. In this special setting, the roll-down component of the excess return earned when yields do not change would therefore just be equal to the risk premium (again, apart from convexity and expectations). As we said in the previous chapter, one can think of the roll-down as the poor-man's estimate of the one-period excess return – and that is why the carry and roll-down are important quantities for investors. All of which can be pithily summarized in these two slogans.

A world in which forwards come true is of relevance to those who hedge, and engage in relative pricing.

A world in which same-maturity yields do not change is of relevance to those who invest, and who engage in the extraction of the risk premia.

As for all slogans, what they leave out is as important as the grain of truth they contain.

---

[8] We have neglected convexity anyhow, because in all the approximate expressions used in this section we have retained only linear terms.

24.9   WHEN TO INVEST

Of course, investors would like to commit their money to a fund-short–invest-long strategy

1. at those points in time when the expected excess returns are highest; and
2. at any point in time, in those securities that offer the highest expected excess return.

To understand when these conditions are met (ie, when it is good to invest), one possible strategy is to look cross-sectionally (at each point in time) at the expected excess returns for all maturities, and estimate where the highest excess return can be expected.

Another is to look across time for correlations between high excess returns and some exante-observable variables: perhaps one can expect higher excess return when the yield curve is steeply upward sloping (ceteris paribus, this, after all, is the suggestion of the roll-down term); or perhaps when yields are high, or low; or perhaps when the curve is inverted, or flat.

Combining cross-sectional and time-series information one would like to arrive at conclusions such as: "At any point in time, short/long/belly bonds/… offer on average better expected extra returns; and, for all bonds, the best excess returns can be expected when the yield curve is steep/flat/inverted/…"

These conditions for investing can, of course, be more complex: perhaps one should invest, say, in long bonds when the curve is steep and in short bonds when it is flat. And, of, course, one can try to explain the time-varying magnitude of the excess returns also by looking at variables other than the shape of the yield curve – say, at expected inflation, or at some measure of economic activity.

In any case, the quantity which is statistically examined (usually, regressed) against the chosen explanatory variables is the excess return. Most often, because of the ease with which it can be interpreted, it is the approximate expression (24.1) which is used in statistical studies, but this is not important. What matters for investors is to have a quantity, the (approximate or exact) excess return, that contains the information about the term premium that they try to harvest.

CHAPTER 25

Excess Returns: Empirical Results

Gregory (Scotland Yard detective): "Is there any other point to which you would wish to draw my attention?"
Holmes: "To the curious incident of the dog in the night-time."
Gregory: "The dog did nothing in the night-time."
Holmes: "That was the curious incident."

Sir Arthur Conan Doyle, "Silver Blaze", in
The Memoirs of Sherlock Holmes

25.1 THE PURPOSE OF THIS CHAPTER

In this chapter we present the salient features of empirical estimations of the term premia for nominal and real bonds that we have conducted using the data made available by the Fed.

For both nominal and real bonds we comment on their Sharpe Ratios, and we regress the excess returns on a small number of a-priori-chosen yield-curve–based regressors: the first few principal components (or their proxies), 'carry and roll-down', and all the forward rates in the problem. (We look at predictive regressions using macroeconomic variables as regressors in the next chapter.) Using as regressors all the forward rates in the problem constitutes the maximal (most general) set of yield-curve–based regressors. Barring information not contained in the prices, this regression must give the highest explanatory power of the observed excess returns. It is also the most vulnerable to over-fitting.[1] Therefore we pay a lot of attention to (i) how *much* worse the more austere and parsimonious regressors perform with respect to the maximal set

---

[1] For a very clear and good discussion of how to recognize and avoid the perils of overfitting see Abu-Mustafa, Magdon-Ismail and Lin (2012), their Chapter 4 in particular. Strictly speaking, the book in question is about 'theoryless' learning (ie, learning purely from data). However, many of the results and considerations about overfitting, data snooping, training versus testing, etc apply to theory-driven learning as well. I highly recommend the book, which deserves careful reading. Their Figure 5.3 (in the chapter about data snooping), for instance, has given me food for thought for many hours.

of yield-curve regressors and (ii) how stable the predictions from the maximal set are.

Our conclusion will be that, both for nominal and for real rates, the second principal component by itself strikes a very good compromise between explanatory power (measured in terms of R^2), parsimony and robustness when yield-curve–only regressors are used. As this conclusion is somewhat at odds with the most recent findings, we carefully compare our results with the recent literature in the next chapter.

25.2   UNDERSTANDING THE EMPIRICAL SETTING

25.2.1   The Empirical Questions

When we undertake empirical investigations of excess returns we normally try to answer two very important, and very different, questions. One is a question of dependence; the other is a question about the nature of the risk compensation. We explain what this means in this subsection.

From the previous chapter recall that we have for the instantaneous expected return from investing in the T-maturity bond

$$\frac{\mathbb{E}_t^{\mathbb{P}}\left[P_{t+dt}^{T-dt}\right] - P_t^T}{P_t^T} = r_t + \frac{1}{P_t^T}\left(\sum \frac{\partial P_{t+dt}^{T-dt}}{\partial x_i}\lambda_t^i(\overrightarrow{x})\sigma_{x_i}\right)dt. \quad (25.1)$$

The n model factors, $\overrightarrow{x}$, could be latent variables, macro-economic quantities or identifiable statistical quantities. In principle, each source of risk has a potential market price of risk associated with it. It must be stressed that in a structural description $\{\overrightarrow{x}\}$ is the set of variables required to describe the prices of bonds *and* the market price of risk. For instance, everybody agrees that the first three principal components account in a very satisfactory manner for changes in the observed market yields. However, Cochrane and Piazzesi (2005, 2008) and Adrian, Crump and Moench (2013) argue that the market price of risk depends on principal components as high as the fifth.[2] We will discuss in what follows whether this finding is 'robust', but the general point about the need for the model variables to span *all* relevant uncertainty does not change.

Each market price of risk could therefore in principle be of the form

$$\lambda_t^i = \lambda_t^i(x_1, x_2, \ldots, x_n, t). \quad (25.2)$$

---

[2] More precisely, they argue that one can obtain better predictions of excess returns if one uses principal components as high as the fifth.

If we want to remain in a tractable affine setting, this general dependence can be written as[3]

$$\vec{\lambda} = \vec{\lambda}_0 + \underline{\underline{\Lambda}}\,\vec{x}. \tag{25.3}$$

Of course, this affine modelling choice is dictated by our desire for analytic tractability, not by any fundamental understanding of the nature of the relationship $\lambda_t^i = \lambda_t^i(x_1, x_2, \ldots, x_n, t)$ between the market prices of risk and the state variables: apart from generic first-order-expansion considerations (such as '*every function in a sufficiently close neighbourhood of a point behaves like a straight line*'), there is no fundamental reason for requiring a linear dependence of the market price of risk on the state variables.

There are two pieces of information that we would like to extract from an empirical study of excess returns:

1. *What does the market price of risk depend on?* In other words, what is the nature of the dependence in Equation (25.2)? This could be relatively easy or very tricky depending on our choice of 'co-ordinates'. What do we mean by this? Suppose that the market piece of risk depends on the slope of the yield curve. If we have chosen principal components as our state variable ($x_1 = x_{PC1}$, $x_2 = x_{PC2}$, ..., $x_n = x_{PCn}$), and we interpret the second principal component as the slope, this means that

$$\lambda_t = \lambda_t(x_1, x_2, \ldots, x_n, t) = \lambda(x_{PC2}). \tag{25.4}$$

This is easy and 'natural'. Suppose, however, that we have chosen as state variables, say, the short rate and its stochastic reversion level ($x_1 = r, x_2 = \theta$.) Then unscrambling the slope dependence of the market price of risk from these variables will be less straightforward – although in principle exactly equivalent.

Exercise 66 *Suppose that we define as 'slope' the difference between the 10-year and the 1-year yields. If we choose the short rate and its stochastic reversion level as state variables, show, at least formally, how you could express the slope as a function of these two state variables.*

Exercise 67 *Suppose now that we have empirically determined that the curvature of the yield curve contributes to the explanation of excess returns. We define a proxy for the curvature as the sum of the 1-year and 10-year yields minus twice the 5-year yield. Could you now express the curvature as a function of the short rate and reversion level state variables? What if we had chosen the first two principal components as state variables?*

---

[3] As we shall discuss in detail (see Chapter 35) this is not the only option, as the market price of risk could be turned into an additional state variable, with its own independent source of stochasticity and its own mean-reverting behaviour. This qualification, as we shall see, is not 'innocuous'.

2. *What do investors seek compensation for?* This is not self-evident. The excess return that we measure with the invest-long–fund-short ('carry') strategy is, in principle, made up of the contribution from all the sources of uncertainty that affect the yield curve (and the market price of risk itself!). See Equation (25.1). To some extent we may be able to decompose the all-in excess return that we measure: if we think in terms of principal components, for instance, we shall see that investors appear to seek compensation for the level risk; or, after inflation was brought under control in developed markets after the 1990s, it appears that investors wanted to be compensated for uncertainty in the real yield far more than for uncertainty in future inflation. However, it should be kept in mind that the estimation of excess returns is a tricky business to begin with, and trying its decomposition does not make it any easier.

25.2.2   A Very Important Caveat on Spanning

When we undertake empirical studies of excess returns we typically regress the excess return for an investment horizon (the y, left-hand, variable) against a set of explanatory regressors (the vector of x, right-hand variables). We then repeat the same for all the investment horizons using the same regressors, and try to establish the significance of the regression coefficients.

So we have

$$xret_i^{(n)} = \alpha^{(n)} + \left(\vec{\beta}^{(n)}\right)^{\mathrm{T}} \vec{x_i} + \epsilon_i, \tag{25.5}$$

where $xret_i^{(n)}$ is the excess return from investing at time i in the n-maturity bond (a scalar), $\alpha^{(n)}$ is a maturity-dependent intercept, $\vec{\beta}^{(n)}$ is is a maturity-dependent vector of 'slope' coefficients, and $\vec{x_i}$ denotes the value of the vector of regressors at time i. Of course, if there are p regressors, the dimensions of $\vec{\beta}^{(n)}$ and $\vec{x_i}$ are $(p, 1)$. As usual, when we multiply the transpose of $\vec{\beta}^{(n)}$ by the p-vector, $\vec{x_i}$, we obtain a number. The term ϵ_i is the error (the residual). Needless to say, we would love the residuals to be independent and identically distributed. For ease of statistical analysis we would love them even more if they were normally distributed, but this is not something we have much control over.

Now, how do we choose the explanatory variables (the regressors)? Suppose that we are interested in a *predictive* regression. When the analysis of excess returns is approached from a statistical angle, lags of the explanatory variables are often used. When this choice is made, the size of the matrix of regression coefficients can quickly become extravagantly large. See the comments in Chapter 1. When we want to use the empirical information as the input for an affine model, it is far more common to make use of contemporaneous information only. So, if we look in an affine-modelling setting at the excess return from time t to time $t + 1$ we will use only information available at time t.

Now something really important comes up. (For a nice discussion of this important point see Ludvigson and Ng (2009). We also revisit this topic in Chapter 29.) We may have established that some macroeconomic quantities (say, inflation or the real economic activity) have ex ante explanatory power for predicting excess returns. It would be logical to add these variables to the set of the state variables of our affine model, in addition to the usual yield curve variables (such as, say, the short rate, or some principal components). Let's call the macro variable $\{x_{macro}\}$, and the yield curve–related variable $\{x_{yc}\}$. To both sets of variables (the macros variables and the yield curve variables) we can assign the customary mean-reverting behaviours, and the appropriate market prices of risk.

Now, since our model is affine we know that we can always write

$$P_t^T = e^{A_t^T + (B_{yc}^{t,T})^{\mathrm{T}} x_{yc} + (B_{macro}^{t,T})^{\mathrm{T}} x_{macro}}. \tag{25.6}$$

Yields will therefore have the form

$$\overrightarrow{y}_t^T = \overrightarrow{\alpha}_t^T + \left(\beta_{yc}^{t,T}\right)^{\mathrm{T}} \overrightarrow{x}_{yc} + \left(\beta_{macro}^{t,T}\right)^{\mathrm{T}} \overrightarrow{x}_{macro}$$

$$= \overrightarrow{y}_t^T = \overrightarrow{\alpha}_t^T + \left(\beta^{t,T}\right)^{\mathrm{T}} \overrightarrow{x}, \tag{25.7}$$

with

$$\left\{\overrightarrow{x}\right\} = \left\{\overrightarrow{x}_{macro}\right\} \cup \left\{\overrightarrow{x}_{yc}\right\}. \tag{25.8}$$

Note that on the left-hand side of Equation (25.7) we have a vector of yields, and that this vector will contain as many elements as the combined vector $\{\overrightarrow{x}\}$. As long as the system is invertible, one can always write

$$\overrightarrow{y}_t^T - \overrightarrow{\alpha}_t^T = \left(\beta^{t,T}\right)^{\mathrm{T}} \overrightarrow{x}$$

$$\implies \overrightarrow{x} = \left(\left(\beta^{t,T}\right)^{\mathrm{T}}\right)^{-1} \left(\overrightarrow{y}_t^T - \overrightarrow{\alpha}_t^T\right). \tag{25.9}$$

But this means that, whatever the choice of state variables, and no matter how many macrovariables we had decided to include in our description, in a simple affine setting we could just as well have used yields as state variables. There-fore, *even if we enrich our affine model with macro variables, it can know only about the excess return predictability that is embedded in the yield curve.* We capture this insight in the following pithy slogan:

A (simple) affine model knows only about what yields know about.

We will revisit this important point in detail in the next chapter and in Chap-ter 29. For the moment it is essential to keep in mind that, once we pour the empirical information about excess return into the affine-modelling container, some of it may be forced to spill out. Out of metaphor, whatever predictable information cannot be embedded in the present and past forms of the yield curve cannot be captured by any (simple) affine model.[4]

25.2.3   The Methodological Dilemma

In principle, when it comes to carrying out estimates of excess returns we have three options:

1. using non-overlapping returns, each with a 'long' investment horizon, say, 1 year. For, say, 50 years' worth of data, this would give us 50 independent observations;
2. using non-overlapping returns, each with a 'short' investment horizon (say, 1 month). For the same 50 years' worth of data, this would give us 600 independent observations;
3. using overlapping returns (say, 1-month returns), with an long investment horizon of, say, 1 year. With 50 years' worth of data, this would give us 600 highly correlated observations.

Drawing a lot of far-reaching conclusions from 50 data points is clearly risky. This seems to leave the option of using either short investment horizons and non-overlapping returns, or long investment horizons and overlapping returns.

What is the problem with using overlapping returns? Clearly, it is that the residuals from two consecutive data points are obviously correlated. The pitfalls arising from the lack of independence in the residuals are well discussed in any elementary text on econometrics. Unfortunately, as Britten-Jones, Neuberger and Nolte (2011) point out, when there is a strong autocorrelation pattern induced by the overlapping scheme,

> '[i]t is now well known that commonly used methods to deal with the autocorrelation are inadequate and can lead to misleading estimates of the confidence interval associated with coefficients estimated from finite samples[5]. Despite this, many studies still resort to standard inference techniques, such as applying White or common Newey–West standard errors within an overlapping regression framework.'[6]

It would seem, then, that we would be better off using short-horizon returns. But this is not without problems, either. The shorter the horizon, the worse the signal-to-noise ratio of each observation – ie, the greater the measurement

---

[4] We will explain in detail in the following what we mean by 'simple'.

[5] For a clear and simple discussion of the problems arising in linear regressions when the residual are either non-homoskedastic (non-constant variance) or serially correlated, see, eg, Dougherty (1992), Chapter 7, Sections 7.5 to 7.9 in particular: 'The consequences of autocorrelation are somewhat similar to those of heteroskedasticity. The regression coefficients remain unbiased, but they become inefficient and their standard errors are estimated worngly [if the standard techniques are used], probably being biased downwards', p. 218.

[6] p. 2. See references in their footnote 1 in this respect.

Table 25.1 *Sharpe Ratios for the excess return strategy described in Section 25.2 applied to US Treasuries during the 1955–2014 period, subdivided (i) into different chronological sub-periods, (ii) into periods of recessions or expansions, and (iii) during tightening cycles. Note how the Sharpe Ratios are very negative when the curve is flat to inverted (during the tightening cycles), and very positive during recessions (when the curve tends to be steeply upward sloping). Adapted from Naik, Nowobilski and Page (2016).*

	2-year	5-year	10-year
Full Sample	0.20	0.20	0.16
1955–1986	0.04	−0.01	−0.07
1987–2014	0.59	0.56	0.49
Recession	0.82	0.72	0.59
Expansion	0.01	0.06	0.05
1st half Expansion	0.52	0.50	0.45
2nd half Expansion	−0.61	−0.50	−0.48
Tightening Cycles			
1979:Q3–1981:Q2	−1.06	−1.13	−1.23
1993:Q3–1995:Q1	−0.79	−0.86	−0.86
2004:Q2–2006:Q2	−1.52	−0.90	−0.50

error.[7] It is for this reason that Cochrane and Piazzesi (2005) warn us that 'to see the core results you must look directly at the one-year horizon' and claim that using monthly horizons 'completely misses the single factor representation' (the 'tent') that constitutes the main finding of their study.

What is one to do then?

We present and compare in the rest of the chapter the results from several methodological choices, but we can already say that a very useful approach is the one introduced by Britten-Jones et al. (2011), who show how to use overlapping, long-horizon data and still obtain robust and believable confidence intervals. See Villegas (2015) for a nice discussion exactly in this context.

25.3 UNCONDITIONAL RESULTS: NOMINAL BONDS

Before trying to predict excess returns, it pays to take a close look at how big and significant they are. To this effect we report in Table 25.1 the Sharpe Ratios obtained by engaging in the buy-long–fund-short strategy over different periods.

[7] As a rule of thumb, if we assume that the underlying process is a simple diffusion, the nuisance random term scales as the square root of the horizon, $\Delta\tau$, and the deterministic term (that we are looking for) scales linearly with $\Delta\tau$.

As Table 25.1 shows, the unconditional Sharpe Ratio from a carry strategy of 'investing long and funding short' is positive (and so, therefore, is the risk premium).[8] The Sharpe Ratio is mildly dependent (declining) with the investment maturity; the magnitude of the *unconditional* risk premium shows some dependence on the periods used in the estimation, but (as long as each period spans one or more business cycles) the qualitative picture is fundamentally robust.

The conditional information is far richer, and more interesting: Sharpe ratios are much higher during recessions; they are above average during the first half of economic expansions; and they become very negative in the latter phases of expansions. Note from the bottom three rows of Table 25.1 that they are very negative throughout all the major tightening cycles represented in the 1955–2013 period.

This clear business-cycle dependence is partly (but not fully) embedded in yield curve return-predicting factors, of which the yield-curve slope is the best known and the most intuitively understandable. This makes sense: during recessions central banks cut the short-term rates and yield curves become steeper; in the second phase of an expansion, the monetary authorities 'pull away the punch bowl', begin to raise rates, and generate a flatter or even inverted yield curve.[9]

There is a vibrant debate at the moment as to whether more complex, but still yield-curve-based, return-predicting factors have a greater return-predicting power than the slope. We explore in detail several facets of this debate in the following chapters, but it is important to stress already at this stage that Ludvigson and Ng (2009) show that there is a substantial portion of predictability that is not efficiently captured within an affine setting in present or past yield curve information.[10] This extra predictability is revealed by macro-economic factors, of which real-growth indicators appear to be the most important, followed by inflation indicators. Adding the macro factors increases the R^2 by approximately 10%. We discuss this in detail in Chapter 27.

Work by Cieslak and Povala (2010a, 2010b) (and, indirectly, by Radwanski (2010)) then suggests that the yield- curve-based and the macro factors interact via a co-integration relationship (say, between the level of rates and expected inflation, or the level of rates and real economic activity), and that it is the 'distance' between the two that matters. For instance, Radwanski (2010) says that '[s]ometimes, expected inflation is further below the level [of rates] than implied by the long-run relation. In other words, market prices are seemingly below fundamentals, which results in a correction during which excess returns are realized.'[11] We discuss this as well in Chapter 27.

---

[8] This, of course, assumes that investors' expectations were not systematically wrong for more than 50 years.

[9] It must be stressed again that 'just' investing at a high long-dated yield and funding at a low short-dated yield is no guarantee for making money, as the expectation-related steepness of the yield curve must also be taken into account: as we know well, if on average 'forward rates come true' no money will be made or lost.

[10] The next chapter will make clear what is meant by *'efficiently* captured'.   [11] p. 3.

Finally, if the simple picture of the excess returns as a compensation for 'risk' holds true, we should expect to find a positive relationship between excess returns and expected volatility. Alas, empirical evidence fails to detect this feature[12]. After fitting models of this type to four decades' worth of data, Duffee (2002) finds that yield forecasts produced by a constant-λ affine model are even a bit worse than those predicted by assuming that yields follow a random walk.[13] This is, to say the least, disconcerting. We therefore explore this feature in what follows. Before that, however, we present our own results.

25.4 REGRESSION RESULTS: NOMINAL BONDS

25.4.1 1- to 10-Year Returns

To start with, we look at long holding nominal discount bonds for long investment periods (1 year, to be precise), for maturities up to and including 10 years.[14] We do not push the maturities any further because doing so would significantly reduce the number of observations. We look both at overlapping (1 month) and non-overlapping strategies.

Mindful of the dangers of regressor-fishing so eloquently described in the quote that opens this chapter (and of the equally eloquent, if slightly more technical, warnings in Bailey and de Prado (2014) and in Abu-Mostafa et al. (2012)), we have limited ourselves to a small number of 'natural regressors':

1. the forward rates themselves;
2. a small number of true principal components;
3. an equally small number of 'simplified' principal components; the simplified principal components were taken to be the level of the yield curve (proxied by the average of the yields), and its slope (proxied by the longest-maturity yield minus the 1-year yield); plus
4. carry and roll-down.

---

[12] See, eg, Table I on p. 410 in Duffee (2002). Work by Chan et al. (1992) and Andersen and Lund (1997) suggests that volatility *is* linked to the slope of the yield curve, but, when it comes to excess returns, slope does not seem to proxy for volatility.

[13] Duffee (2002), p. 406.

[14] A remark on terminology: to be precise we should say, for instance, 'the one-year return on the n-year bond'. However, unless otherwise stated, we always hold the investment for 1 year. Therefore, for the sake of brevity we prefer to say the 'n-year return', by which we mean the return on investing in the n-year bond over the 1-year holding period. It is important to keep in mind that we have four 'periods':

- the maturity of the bond we invest in;
- the maturity of the bond with which we fund the trade;
- the holding period, ie, for how long we hold the trade (as we said, usually one year);
- how frequently we enter a new trade (often every month, giving rise to 11 overlapping investment periods for a holding period of one year, but sometimes every 3, 6 or 12 months.)

We have always taken the maturity of the funding bond equal to the holding period for nominal bonds. Not so for real bonds.

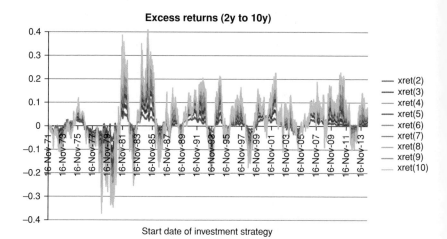

Figure 25.1 The returns for the excess returns strategies (nominal US$ Treasuries) for maturities from 2 to 10 years from 16 August 1971 to 16 July 2013 (the starting dates of the 12-month strategies on the *x*-axis). Data from Gurkaynak et al. (2006).

We use as our source the data made available by the Fed, and described in Gurkaynak, Sack and Wright (2006). For maturities up to 5 years, this means that we have access to data going back to the early 1960s. For 10-year maturities, a continuous record is available only from 1971 onwards.

First of all, we show in Figure 25.1 the excess returns themselves (overlapping returns).

The most obvious observation is that excess returns are very variable, ranging from −30% to more than +50% – this is why we say that we are trying to detect the strength and direction of a gentle breeze in the middle of a raging storm.

Second, we note from Table 25.2 that the excess returns are, on average, positive, ranging from 104 (117) basis points per annum for the 3-year strategy, to 281 (328) basis points per annum[15] for the 10-year for the 1971–2014 period. So, the unconditional risk premium appears to be positive. What is more interesting is that returns per unit of duration are remarkably stable, but the Sharpe Ratios are not, and they decline with maturity. This indicates that the bond price volatility does not scale linearly with bond maturity: long-dates yields, in other words, are not *that* much less volatile than short-dates yields. See also Shiller (1979) in this respect.

Why should long-dated bonds have lower Sharpe Ratios than shorter-dated ones? Perhaps they provide a better diversification against equity moves (in which case they would act as better 'insurance' against market risk, and

---

[15] The numbers in parentheses refer to non-overlapping strategies.

Table 25.2 *Excess returns for the excess returns strategies for maturities from 2 to 10 years, (column Returns), excess returns per unit of duration and Sharpe Ratios (columns Returns/Duration and Sharpe Ratios) for the same strategies, with monthly overlaps. The number in parentheses display the same quantities for non-overlapping investment periods.*

	Returns	Returns/Duration	Sharpe Ratios
3y	0.0104 (0.0117)	0.0035 (0.0039)	29.59%
4y	0.0143 (0.0159)	0.0036 (0.0040)	25.98%
5y	0.0176 (0.0195)	0.0035 (0.0039)	23.53%
6y	0.0204 (0.0228)	0.0034 (0.0038)	21.52%
7y	0.0228 (0.0257)	0.0033 (0.0037)	19.67%
8y	0.0249 (0.0283)	0.0031 (0.0035)	17.97%
9y	0.0267 (0.0307)	0.0030 (0.0034)	16.51%
10y	0.0281 (0.0328)	0.0028 (0.0033)	15.37%

command a smaller – or perhaps even negative – risk premium). What we find is (i) that the correlation between equities and bonds is by and large positive up to the end of the 1990s, and then becomes negative and (ii) that there is little difference between the equity diversification offered by short-maturity and long-maturity bonds. So, the equity-diversification explanation does not seem to be very compelling to explain the difference in Sharpe Ratio between different-maturity bonds. What we *do* find is a positive correlation (at all maturities, but stronger at short maturities) between the ex post Sharpe Ratio and the bond-equity correlation. For instance, there is a correlation of 37% between the 2-year realized Sharpe Ratio and the bond–equity correlation. As one would expect, the dependence is positive (high correlation, poor diversification, higher Sharpe Ratio).

25.4.2 Effectiveness of Various Regressors

Next we look at the effectiveness of the various regressors.

When we use as regressors the first three principal components, we find R^2 statistics monotonically increasing from 9.11% for the 2-year strategy to 15.31% and 20.50% for the 5-year and 10-year strategies, respectively (overlapping returns).

If we use only the second principal component as regressor on the same set of data, we get R^2 statistics of 4.88% for the 2-year strategy, 12.48% for 5 years and 19.39% for 10 years. So, the extra predictive power from using the first and the third principal components is negligible for the 10-year strategy, and modest for 5 years.

These findings are clearly shown in Figure 25.2, which shows the actual excess returns for the 10-year strategy (monthly overlapping returns), and the

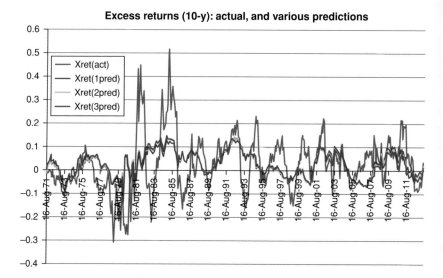

Figure 25.2 The excess returns for the 10-year strategy: the actual excess returns (blue line), and the predictions obtained using as regressors the second principal component only (curve labelled Xret(1pred)), the first two principal components (curve labelled Xret(2pred)), and the first three principal components (curve labelled Xret(3pred)).

predicted excess returns obtained using as regressors the first principal component only (curve labelled Xret(1pred)), the first two principal components (curve labelled Xret(2pred)), and the first three principal components (curve labelled Xret(3pred)). Clearly, adding more principal components to the slope adds little, if anything.

In order to comment on the significance of the coefficients, we now look at non-overlapping investment periods.

With three principal components the R^2 statistic for non-overlapping investment periods is 6.78% for 2 years, 10.99% for 5 years and 19.81% for 10 years. At the 95% confidence level, only the slope coefficients for excess returns from 5 to 10 years are significant.

When only the slope (the second principal component) is used as regressor for non-overlapping investment periods, we get an R^2 statistic of 2.73% for 2 years, 10.45% for 5 years and 19.33% for 10 years. Once again, for long maturities, the improvement from adding the first and third principal components is close to non-existent.

Next, we look at the stability of the results by analyzing 6-month overlapping returns with the second principal component only, and with the first three principal components. The R^2 statistics are quite similar, with values of 3.78%, 10.80 and 17.80% for the 2-, 5-year and 10-year strategies.

Is using a true second principal components rather than a simple-minded proxy such as the difference between the 10-year and the 1-year yield important? Using again non-overlapping periods, we find that using the true second principal component does make a significant difference, because the maximum R^2 for the 10-year strategy using the simple proxy for the slope becomes as low as 13.62% (a statistically significant difference). As in the case of the 'proper' second principal component, only the regression coefficient for maturities of 5 years or more are significant at the 95% level.

What about carry and roll-down? As we discussed in Chapter 23 (see Section 23.7), carry and roll-down can be regarded as the 'poor man's proxy' for the slope returning factor. How much poorer is the user of this proxy?

Perhaps surprisingly[16], also carry and roll-down, even when taken together, do not do as well as the second principal component *by itself*, producing a maximum R^2 for the 10-year strategy of 14.91%. With non-overlapping returns, the 95% significance threshold for the coefficients of carry and roll-down is crossed only for the 10-year return.

25.4.3 5-Year Returns: Comparison with Cochrane–Piazzesi (2005)

In this sub-section we focus on 5-year returns.[17] The reason for doing so is that this will enable us to compare our findings with the results by Cochrane and Piazzesi (2005), and by Dai, Singleton and Yang (2004), which are discussed in detail in the next chapter.

First we carry out the same investigation procedure carried out by Cochrane and Piazzesi (2005), with a slightly different length of data (we use more data), and a different data source.

When we look at the full sample at our disposal, and, as Cochrane and Piazzesi do, use the five forward rates as regressors, the R^2 statistics that we find are significantly lower than those found by Cochrane and Piazzesi, ranging from 13% (2-year) to 18.85% (10-year). However, when we restrict the attention to the shorter period used in the Cochrane–Piazzesi regression, we obtain similar R^2 statistics, ranging from 29.2% for the 2-year excess returns to 32.1% for the 5-year excess returns. We stress that the data we and Cochrane and Piazzesi (2005) use are different. See the discussion of this point in Chapter 26.

What is perhaps more surprising is that the shape of the return-predicting factor is very different: instead of finding the 'tent' that Cochrane and Piazzesi (2005) identify, we discover a 'bat', as shown in Figure 26.7.

At first blush, the two analyses seem to produce very different answers. We discuss in detail the equivalence (or otherwise) of the 'tent' or 'bat' solution in the next chapter.

---

[16] We say 'surprisingly' because one would think that a high slope would be naturally associated with high carry and roll-down.

[17] For the avoidance of doubt, here and in what follows we refer to the returns from investing in the n-year bond, funding with the 1-year bond, and unwinding the position after one year as the 'n-year returns'.

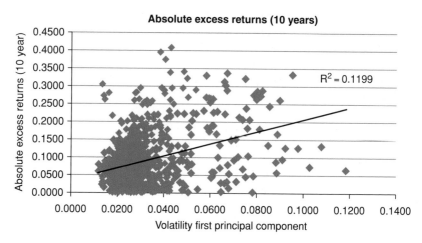

Figure 25.3 The 10-year absolute excess returns (*x*-axis) against the volatility of the yield curve (*y*-axis), proxied by the volatility of the first principal component.

25.5 WHERE HAS THE VOLATILITY GONE?

As we said, Duffee (2002) claims to find no dependence of risk premia on volatility. The account of this empirical result therefore has some elements of Sherlock Holmes' dog-that-didn't-bark-in-the-night story, and prompts the questions: 'Where has the volatility gone?' If risk premia are a compensation for uncertainty, and volatility is a reasonable proxy for uncertainty, shouldn't there be *some* dependence on the volatility of something? Why does the volatility dog remain silent?

When we looked at volatility as a regressor we found very similar results. Very simplistically, first we calculated a no-peek-ahead estimate of the volatility of the first three principal components at the start of the investment period by using a 25-day, rolling-window estimate with equal weights; and then we created the 'volatility of the yield curve' by taking the square root of the sum of the three volatilities. This is our yield-curve–volatility proxy.[18]

When this volatility proxy was used as a regressors to predict the excess returns, the intercept and slope coefficients was not significant, and the R^2 was statistically indistinguishable from zero. However, when the *absolute value* of the excess returns is regressed against the volatility of the first principal component, the R^2 becomes a more respectable 12.0%, and both intercept and slope are statistically significant.

This makes sense, and Figure 25.3 explains what is happening: in the presence of a state-dependent term premium, by itself volatility fails to have any

---

[18] In reality, we observe that this proxy is very closely correlated – nay, almost identical – to the volatility of the first principal component.

explanatory power, as Duffee (2002) observed. However, once the slope of the yield curve determines whether the excess return is expected to be positive or negative, the volatility does contribute (a bit) to the explanation of the magnitude of the return. This ties in well with the empirical findings discussed so far: the slope determines the 'compensation' (positive or negative as it might be) per unit risk; what investors are compensated for is then the volatility of the yield curve level.

If this interpretation is correct, then we should find the volatility to be significant *when added to* the slope regressor. Indeed, when we regress excess returns against the volatility of the first principal component (a good proxy for the 'volatility of the yield curve'), with Duffee we find a pitiful R^2, and insignificant regression coefficients. Interestingly, however, when the volatility is added as a regressor to the slope, the R^2 is statistically significantly higher than the R^2 obtained from the three principal components only, and its regression coefficients is also significant.

Figure 25.3 suggests what is happening: the volatility of the yield curve is an imperfect but meaningful predictor of the magnitude (the absolute value) of the excess returns (positive or negative as these may be). It affects excess returns both when they are positive and when they are negative. In the presence of a state-dependent term premium, it is therefore clear that, *by itself*, volatility will fail to display any explanatory power, as Duffee (2002) observed *because it will dampen or amplify (by becoming smaller or larger, respectively) both positive and negative excess returns*. By looking at Figure 25.3 we now understand better the results in Duffee (2002), and we can qualify them. The volatility dog in the opening quote does bark, but it is of little use as a guard dog, because it barks both at its master and at the night burglars (or, out of metaphor, at positive and negative excess returns).

25.6 REGRESSION RESULTS: REAL BONDS

Estimating excess returns in general is really hard; when it comes to real bonds the task verges on 'mission impossible', because data series are much shorter (TIPS, unlike nominal Treasuries, were first issued relatively recently), and the price time series may be contaminated from the liquidity factor discussed in the last section of Chapter 4.[19] Also, the brevity of the historical record makes using non-overlapping periods close to impossible. If this were not enough, during the relatively short period when reliable observations can be made, we have had one perfect-storm event (the Lehman default) right in the middle, and very unusual monetary conditions thereafter. Apart from this, the conditions for econometric analysis are perfect.

Despite this strong health warning, we nonetheless present results on excess returns from TIPS, because we believe that tentative and caveated information is better than no information at all.

---

[19] See also the discussion in Chapter 31.

25.7   THE DATA

We use the data on real bonds kindly provided by the Fed in the electronic file associated with the paper by Gurkaynak, Sack and Wright (2000). The reader is referred to their paper for the description of how they distilled they discount bond prices from the traded prices of coupon-bearing TIPS. (The procedure is broadly based on the same Nelson–Siegel (1987) method used for nominal yields.)

With an excess-return strategy one has to fund a long-dated bond with a short-dated one. Unfortunately, at the start of issuance, the shortest maturity TIPS bond had five years to maturity, and the universe of investable bonds was rather limited. For this reason we start our analysis in 2004, when shorter-maturity bonds became available.

Furthermore, at the short end of the maturity spectrum prices are contaminated by inflation-seasonality effect, and therefore we have chosen not to fund with bonds of maturity shorter than three years.

Our universe of investable and funding TIPS therefore spans little more than 10 years (to be precise, from 2 June 2004 to 24 June 2014), for the 3-to-20-year maturity spectrum.

25.8   THE REAL EXCESS RETURNS

We regressed the real excess returns calculated as described in Chapter 24. More precisely, the excess returns were regressed against the first three principal components obtained from orthogonalizing the (level) covariance matrix of real yields.

To give a qualitative feel for the excess returns Figure 25.4 shows the time series of the excess returns for the 17 maturities under considerations. Figures 25.5 and 25.6 show the average excess returns and the Sharpe Ratios, respectively, as a function of the maturity of the investment bonds. Note that, once again, we find declining Sharpe Ratios as a function of maturities, as we found for nominal Treasuries.

To appreciate the nature of the dependence of the real excess returns on various possible regressors, we begin by showing in Figure 25.7 the time series of the average *real*[20] excess return (maturities 4 to 20 years) from funding with a three-year real bond for the period from 2 June 2004 to 24 June 2014, and the second principal component over the same period.

The most noteworthy feature is the magnitude of the returns associated with the Lehman events. Anybody who invested in real bonds for a year with a holding period ending right after the Lehman default would have experienced a substantial loss (this is the dip to -10% in the middle of the graph). Similarly, anyone who had started the yearly investment in any of the long real bonds

---

[20] As discussed in Section 23.6 of Chapter 23, the nominal excess return would only differ by a multiplicative factor of $(1 + X)$, with X equal to the yearly inflation.

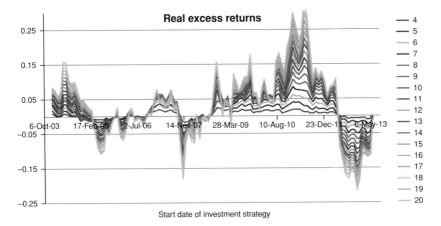

Figure 25.4 The time series the 17 *real* excess returns (maturities 4 to 20 years) from funding with a three-year real bond for the period from 2 June 2004 to 24 June 2014. The date on the *x*-axis show the start of the 12-month investment period. Data from Gurkaynak et al. (2006).

immediately after this pronounced swoon would have made a very large profit (this is the peak above 10% approximately one year thereafter).

Clearly, the profits and losses from this extraordinary, and extraordinarily large, event have little to do with the risk premium effect that we are looking at, and can therefore pollute the estimate. Just another *caveat*.

We go into finer detail with Figure 25.8, which shows the real excess return from investing in the 20-year real bond and the predicted real excess returns obtained from using the first, the second, the third and the first three principal components together as regressors. (Similar results hold for other maturities.)

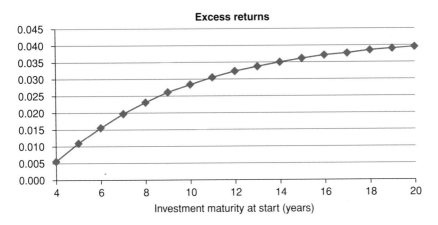

Figure 25.5 The average real excess returns from the investing in real bonds as described in the text as a function of the maturity of the investment bonds.

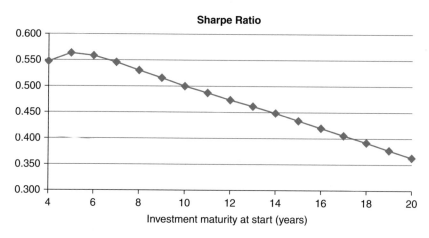

Figure 25.6 The Sharpe Ratios from the investing in real bonds as described in the text as a function of the maturity of the investment bonds.

It is clear that the first and third principal components provide virtually no explanation, either in isolation, or combined with the slope component. The second principal component provides instead a good ex ante prediction of excess returns. For greater clarity, it is shown by itself against the real excess returns in Figure 25.9.

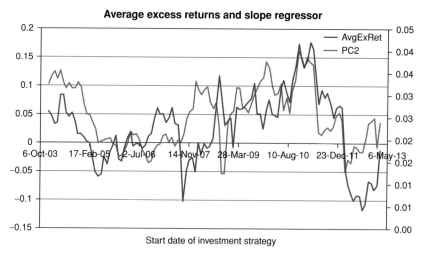

Figure 25.7 The time series the average *real* excess returns (maturities 4 to 20 years) from funding with a three-year real bond for the period from 2 June 2004 to 24 June 2014, and of the second principal component over the same period. The date on the *x*-axis shows the start of the 12-month investment period.

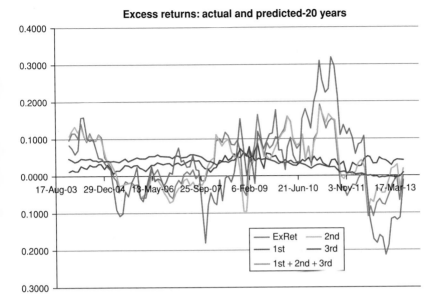

Figure 25.8 The real excess return from investing in the 20-year real bond and the predicted real excess returns obtained from using the first, the second, the third and the first three principal components as regressors (jointly or severally). The date on the x-axis shows the start of the 12-month investment period.

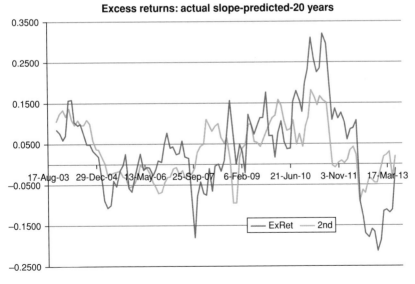

Figure 25.9 The real excess return from investing in the 20-year real bond and the predicted real excess returns obtained from using the second principal components as regressor. The date on the x-axis shows the start of the 12-month investment period.

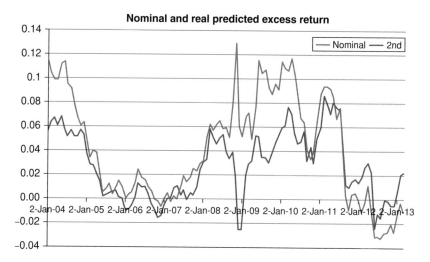

Figure 25.10 The predicted nominal (blue curve) and real (red curve) 10-year risk premia for the data discussed in the text.

It is reassuring that the prediction does *not* do a good job chasing the large positive and negative returns associated with the exceptional Lehman event. (If it had, it could have indicated that the regression coefficients had been severely biased by this exceptional event.)

As for the regression coefficients, we find that, in single regressions, the second principal coefficient is very significant (and so is the intercept), and the first and the third principal components are not. In a joint regression, the slope is very significant, the third is not, and the first is borderline significant at the 95% confidence level.

The R^2 statistics from regressing against the slope only is 39.1%, and from regressing against the first three principal components is little different (43.9%).

For the sake of parsimony, and guided by the results obtained for nominal rates, we therefore identify the slope as the robust and significant predictor of real excess returns.

25.9 EXTRACTING THE REAL-RATE RISK PREMIUM

If we trust both the estimate of the nominal risk premia obtained in the first part of this chapter, and, notwithstanding the health warnings luridly posted in the previous section, the estimate of the real risk premia discussed immediately above we can try and estimate the inflation risk premium in nominal bonds.

To fix our ideas we focus on the 10-year yields, nominal and real.

First, we take the regression coefficients obtained from nominal bonds using the nominal slope (second principal component) as regressor, and we construct the predicted nominal risk premium. This is shown as the blue curve in Figure 25.10.

Table 25.3 *The coefficients from the regression of the real and nominal excess returns (10-year) against the respective second principal components. The numbers in parentheses display the standard errors.*

	Nominal	Real
Intercept	−0.108(0.020)	−0.075(0.017)
Slope	−4.242(0.541)	−4.023(0.674)

Next we take the regression coefficients obtained from real bonds using the real slope (second principal component) as regressor, and we construct the predicted real risk premium. This is the red curve in the same figure.

The two curves display a very clear and strong correlation (80.8%). This makes perfect sense, because the nominal risk premium should contain the real risk premium as one of its components, and because we have seen in Chapter 5 that changes in nominal yields are 'driven by' changes in real rates, not in inflation expectations.

If we can trust the results of our regression studies, we find in these results corroborating evidence of the statement that, during the 2004–2014 period, the predominant component of the nominal risk premium comes from the real component. This makes sense, since all central banks had brought inflation firmly under control during the period we are considering. Investors, it would seem, in the first decades of the twenty-first century did not care much about inflation risk, but *did* care about real-rate risk. I note in passing that the degree of confidence placed by investors in the central bankers' ability to keep inflation under control is all the more remarkable, if one thinks of the magnitude and unprecedented nature of the Quantitative Easing operations entered by the Fed in the first half of the 2010s.

It must be stressed that the strong coincidence of the two curves shown in Figure 25.10 is particularly encouraging when we remember that it was obtained using different regressors, and that the two sets of data have been obtained from the analysis of totally non-overlapping sets of instruments (Treasuries and TIPS).

This encouraging congruence of the two analyses is reinforced when we look at Table 25.3, which shows the regression coefficients from the nominal and real regressions.

Note that the two intercepts and the two slopes are very similar (indistinguishable within standard error), and that the numbers that refer to the nominal returns just 'tell the same story' as the real coefficients, but in a more pronounced manner. Again, these results were obtained using different data.

What about the two spikes, upward for the nominal and downward for the real predicted risk premia? They are clearly related to the Lehman events: during the crisis there was a flight to liquidity and nominal Treasuries rose in price

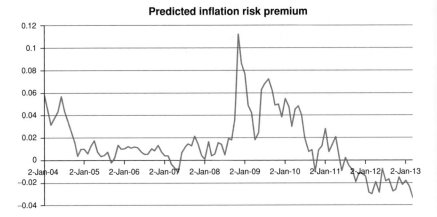

Figure 25.11 The predicted inflation (and liquidity) 10-year risk premium, obtained as the difference of the curves shown in Figure 25.10. The dates on the x-axis show the beginning of the investment period.

as everything else fell. All investment strategies ending or starting right after or right before this watershed event clearly bear its hallmark.

25.10 ESTIMATING THE INFLATION PREMIUM IN NOMINAL BONDS

With the information we have gathered we can try to extract the inflation risk premium in nominal bonds. If we make the joint assumptions

- that investors seek the same real-rate compensation in nominal and real bonds, and
- that the risk premium we have extracted from real bonds is predominantly due to real-rate – not liquidity – risk

then we can take the difference between the all-in nominal risk premium (made up of a real-rate and inflation component) and the real-bond risk premium (which 'contains' only the real risk premium). We do so with some trepidation, because taking the difference of two noisy and highly correlated quantities of similar magnitude can be a recipe for statistical disaster.[21] What we obtain is shown in Figure 25.11.

If we are to trust this quantity – and excluding the spike in the middle of the time series due to the Lehman event, as discussed earlier – Figure 25.11 points to a steadily declining compensation in nominal bonds for bearing inflation risk. Lest we read too much in this picture, we stress that the intercept in the regression is associated with a greater statistical uncertainty than the slope

---

[21] Why so? Because, if $y = a - b$, then $Var(y) = Var(a) + Var(b) - 2Cov(a, b)$. Note that the error can be very high as a fraction of the average magnitude of y.

Table 25.4 *The coefficients from the regression of the real excess returns (10-year) against the real second principal component (Slope 1) and the VIX (Slope 2). The numbers in parentheses display the standard errors.*

	Regression Coefficient
Intercept	−0.107(0.0195)
Slope 1	−3.962(0.6405)
Slope 2	+0.001(0.0004)

coefficient, and therefore our estimates of changes in inflation risk premium are more trustworthy than estimates of its absolute level.

25.10.1 Isolating the Liquidity Component

Emboldened by the plausibility of these result, we may try to correct for the liquidity effect by using, as we did in Chapter 5, the VIX as a proxy for conditions of market turmoil. We therefore ran a bivariate regression of the real excess return against the real second principal component and the VIX.

The regression coefficients are shown in Table 25.4.

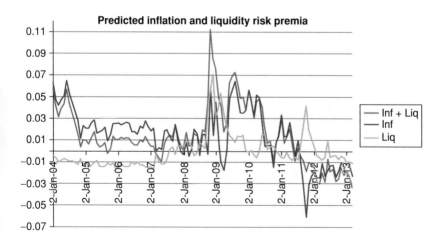

Figure 25.12 The total inflation risk premium for nominal bonds displayed in Figure 25.11 (curve labelled Inf+Liq) and the 'pure' inflation risk premium (curve labelled Inf). The liquidity risk premium of real bonds is also shown (curve labelled Liq). The dates on the *x*-axis show the beginning of the investment period.

Given this decomposition, we can now subtract from the all-in nominal risk premium only the true real-risk component (because we assume that only the less-liquid TIPS attract compensation for liquidity risk). By doing so, we can the extracted 'pure' inflation risk premium in nominal bonds and compare this quantity with the inflation risk premium estimated previously when we neglected the liquidity risk premium of real bonds. These quantities are shown in Figure 25.12.

The analysis yields again sensible results: in particular, note from Figure 25.12 how the liquidity component greatly reduces the 'inflation' risk premium of nominal bonds around the Lehman events.

We also note that the simple liquidity proxy we have chosen does not do such a good job at creating an estimate of the pure inflation risk premium of nominal bonds during the European peripheral-sovereign crisis of the summer of 2012. This happens because the VIX index responded greatly to these events, but the liquidity of the US-based TIPS was barely affected. Perhaps one could look for a better proxy for TIPS-specific illiquidity (such as the US$ LIBOR/OIS or the Treasury/US$ swap spread). However, lest we torture the data until they confess what we expected from the start, we prefer to leave the analysis at this point.

CHAPTER 26

Excess Returns: The Recent Literature – I

It is a capital mistake to theorize before one has data. Insensibly one begins to twist facts to suit theories, instead of theories to suit facts.
Sir Arthur Conan Doyle, "A Scandal in Bohemia",
The Adventures of Sherlock Holmes

The experiments are so sophisticated these days that they can match the theory almost perfectly.
A former colleague at the high-flux research nuclear reactor at the Institut Laue Langevin (Grenoble), commenting on the power of the local experimental facilities.

26.1 THE PURPOSE OF THIS CHAPTER

We have presented in the previous chapter the results of some basic regressions to explain excess returns. We looked at nominal and real excess returns. What we found is broadly in line with earlier work by Fama and Bliss (1987) and Campbell and Shiller (1991) (discussed in Section 26.2), but seems to be at odds with the more recent findings. To understand the origin of these differences, in this chapter we look in considerable detail at the results obtained by Cochrane and Piazzesi (2005). We do so because their work has become the standard against which subsequent regression studies (such as those by Cieslak and Povala (2010a, 2010b), Ludvigson and Ng (2009), and Radwanski (2010) examined in the next chapter) have pitted themselves. Once these literature results have been presented, we will try in Chapter 28 to reconcile, to the extent possible, the traditional, slope-based, results (we include ours in the traditional class) with the new findings.

We devote a lot of time to understanding the empirical findings well, because we think that a solid anchor with empirical reality is essential, lest we get carried away by the beauty of the models and confuse what the world should look like (if the models were true) with how the world actually behaves. Hence the first quote.

Furthermore, newer-generation affine models are endowed with such richness and flexibility that they can now perform tricks and stunts totally beyond the capabilities of the early-generation models. This is good and bad, as richer models must be kept in check by correspondingly richer and more 'constraining' empirical evidence. Hence the second quote.

26.2   THE EARLY WORK

Before the work by Cochrane and Piazzesi in the mid-2000s the conventional wisdom was that the best yield-curve–based predictor of bond excess return was the yield-curve 'slope'. These were the conclusions reached both by Fama and Bliss (1987) and by Campbell and Shiller (1991). More precisely, in Fama and Bliss (1987) the return-predicting factor for the n-maturity excess return was defined as the difference between the n-year forward rate and the 1-year excess return. Therefore, strictly speaking, a different return-predicting factor was applied to each individual excess return (The different slopes, of course, are very similar, so it would not be difficult to construct a common factor out of the n highly correlated ones.)

Similar considerations apply to the Campbell and Shiller (1991) study, in that they used (different) yield spreads as return-predicting factors. For future discussion, we present in some detail the work by Campbell and Shiller (1991), who conducted their investigation as follows.

First they regressed the differences between the time-$(t + 1)$, $(n - 1)$-maturity yield and the time-t, n-maturity yield (the left-hand variable) against the time-t differences between the n-maturity yield and the funding rate, y_t^1 (the right-hand variables):

$$y_{t+1}^{n-1} - y_t^n = \alpha_n + \beta_n \frac{y_t^n - y_t^1}{n - 1}. \tag{26.1}$$

This regression is interesting because Campbell and Shiller show that, if the expectation hypothesis holds, then all the slope coefficients, β_n, must be statistically indistinguishable from 1.

Exercise 68   *Show why this should be the case.*

Exercise 69   *Specify a regression which uses forward and future rates to test the expectation hypothesis. Argue whether the test provides a necessary or a necessary and sufficient condition for the expectation hypothesis to apply.*

From the Table 10.3 in Campbell and Shiller (1991) one can then construct Table 26.1.

Now, if the expectation hypothesis held, when the slope of the yield curve is positive, the long-maturity yield is expected to rise (and hence bond price to fall) by the exact amount that 'penalizes' the investor for the 'funding advantage' – ie, the term $y_t^n - y_t^1$. The empirical results by Campbell and Shiller (in particular, the significantly negative β regression coefficients) show that with

Table 26.1 *The non-intercept regression coefficients β_n as in Equation (26.1). The integer n denotes the maturity (in months) of the yield at the beginning of the investment period. The holding period in the study by Campbell and Shiller (1991) was one month. The bottom row shows the standard error for each coefficient. All the coefficients are significantly different from 1 (the value that would apply if the expectation hypothesis held). Note also that, for maturities longer than 3 months, all the coefficients are significantly negative, indicating that the slope is a significant regressor of excess returns.*

n (months)	2	3	6	12	24	48	120
β_n	0.003	−0.145	−0.835	−1.435	−1.448	−2.262	−4.226
standard error	(0.191)	(0.282)	(0.442)	(0.599)	(1.004)	(1.458)	(2.076)

an upward sloping yield curve long-maturity yields are expected to fall (and hence bond prices to rise), adding to, rather than detracting from, the 'funding advantage'. This is, of course, contrary to the expectation hypothesis, and indicates that bond excess returns should be proportional to the steepness of the yield curve.

In sum: looking at the results in Fama and Bliss (1987) and in Campbell and Shiller (1991), one can say that, before the work by Cochrane and Piazzesi (2004, 2005) the consensus was that, give or take some marginal details, a slope-like factor was the best predictor of bond excess returns.

26.3 COCHRANE AND PIAZZESI (2005)

With their often-quoted 2005 work, Cochrane and Piazzesi changed the slope-related received wisdom presented in the previous section. In their work, they claimed to have identified a unique set of factors such that

1. 'the *same* linear combination of forward rates predicts bond returns at all maturities'[1];
2. their *p*-values are much smaller and the R^2 much higher (almost double) than what was found by Fama, Bliss, Shiller and Campbell;
3. they 'drive out individual forward or yield spreads in multiple regressions'[2].

So, what does this factor looks like? Figure 26.1 shows the loadings β from regressing the yearly excess returns for maturities from 2 to 5 years (monthly overlapping), onto the five forward rates at the start of the investment period.

---

[1] p. 138, emphasis in the original.
[2] p. 138. 'Driving out' forward rates and yield spreads means that, once their factor is accounted for, the slope and spreads cease to be significant. So, they are truly subsumed in, not additional to the Cochrane–Piazzesi factor.

(Clearly, the first forward rate is a spot rate, but, with Cochrane and Piazzesi and the rest of the literature, we will refer to all the rates as 'forward rates'.)

More precisely, using the notation introduced in the previous chapters, and remembering that, for yearly horizons, the forward rate, $f_t^{(n)}$, is given by the difference of the log prices

$$f_t^{(n)} = p_t^{(n-1)} - p_t^{(n)}, \tag{26.2}$$

we have for the excess return, $rx_{t+1}^{(n)}$,

$$
\begin{aligned}
rx_{t+1}^{(n)} &= p_{t+1}^{(n-1)} - p_t^{(n)} - y_t^{(1)} \\
&= \left(p_{t+1}^{(n-1)} - p_t^{(n-1)} \right) - \underbrace{\left(p_t^{(n)} - p_t^{(n-1)} \right)}_{-f_t^{(n)}} - y_t^{(1)}
\end{aligned}
$$

$$\Rightarrow rx_{t+1}^{(n)} = \left(p_{t+1}^{(n-1)} - p_t^{(n-1)} \right) + \left(f_t^{(n)} - y_t^{(1)} \right) \tag{26.3}$$

The regression then is

$$rx_{t+1}^{(n)} = \beta_0^{(n)} + \beta_1^{(n)} y_t^{(1)} + \beta_2^{(n)} f_t^{(2)} \cdots + \beta_5^{(n)} f_t^{(5)} + \epsilon_{t+1}^{(n)}, \tag{26.4}$$

where the maturity index n ranges from 2 to 5 (clearly, as we are funding the position with the 1-year bond, the 1-year excess return is always exactly zero).

As Figure 26.1 (top panel) shows, the coefficients $\beta_i^{(n)}$, $i = 1, 2, \ldots, 5$, trace a shape that, without a greater strain on one's imagination than what is required to discern in the configurations of the night stars lions, rams and scales, can be interpreted as a tent. The same plot also justifies the claim that *the same function of forward rates forecasts holding period returns at all maturities. Longer maturities just have greater loadings on this same function.*[3]

It is precisely the regularity of the tent shape that motivates the restricted regression which Cochrane and Piazzesi carry out as a next step. More precisely, they proceed as follows.

First they define the average (averaged over maturities) excess return, $\overline{rx}_{t+1}$,

$$\overline{rx}_{t+1} = \frac{1}{4} \sum_{n=2}^{5} rx_{t+1}^{(n)}. \tag{26.5}$$

Next they carry out the regression of the average excess returns against the same explanatory (x, right-hand) variables:

$$\overline{rx}_{t+1} = \gamma_0 + \gamma_1 y_t^{(1)} + \gamma_2 f_t^{(2)} \cdots + \gamma_5 f_t^{(5)} + \overline{\epsilon}_{t+1}. \tag{26.6}$$

Finally, having fixed the coefficients $\{\gamma\}$ from this stage, they carry out a restricted regression of the individual excess returns, where the regression is constructed in such a way to preserve the qualitative shape of the factor, but

---

[3] p. 142. Emphasis in the original.

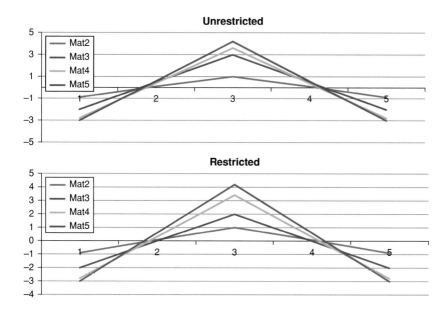

Figure 26.1 Regression coefficients for the 'restricted' (Equation (26.7)) and 'unrestricted' (Equation (26.4)) regression of one-year excess returns on 1–5-year forward rates (reproduced from Figure 1 in Cochrane and Piazzesi 2005). The legend shows the maturity of the bond whose excess return is being calculated. See the text for the description of the construction of the restricted coefficients.

allows for different maturity-dependent loadings, labelled n, onto the same tent-like factor:

$$rx_{t+1}^{(n)} = b^{(n)} \left(\gamma_0 + \gamma_1 y_t^{(1)} + \gamma_2 f_t^{(2)} \cdots + \gamma_5 f_t^{(5)} \right) + \varepsilon_{t+1}^{(n)}. \tag{26.7}$$

The coefficients of the restricted regression are shown in the bottom panel of Figure 26.1.

As Cochrane and Piazzesi point out, restricting the coefficients 'does little damage' to the economic and statistical significance of the predictive regression.

The findings by Cochrane and Piazzesi are very intriguing. These are just a few of the obvious questions that they raise:

1. Is the tent shape robust across sub-periods and across different data sets?

2. Is the tent-shaped return-predicting factor in some way similar to the traditional slope factor? Is it adding something to the slope explanation, or is it telling an altogether different story?

3. Can one give an economic interpretation to the tent factor? Can one link it to the business-cycles periodicity, or to macroeconomic variables?

4. Are the differences in prediction between the tent and the slope return-predicting factor robust? (By posing this question we ask whether the 'extra information' in the tent factor performs well out-of-sample.)
5. It is common knowledge that three principal components describe the yield curve very accurately. How can it be that five principal components are needed in order to account for the excess returns?

We will try to answer these questions in the rest of this chapter and in the next one.

26.4   CRITICAL ASSESSMENT OF THE COCHRANE–PIAZZESI RESULTS

In the rest of this chapter we take a critical look at the results of Cochrane and Piazzesi (2005). We do so because, as mentioned in the first section of this chapter, they have assumed a benchmark status when it comes to predictive regressions of excess returns.

We carry out our analysis along several different lines:

1. we look at the robustness of the tent *shape*;
2. we look at how economically different tent-based and bat-based predictions of excess returns are;
3. we look at how economically different tent-based and slope-based predictions of excess returns are;
4. we look at the relative robustness of the tent predictions versus the slope predictions. (This is different from the analysis carried out in point 1, which looked at the robustness of the *shape*. Here we look at the robustness of the *predictions*.)

We stress that we deal with (at least) two different main topics: we look at whether the difference in shapes of the bat and tent regression patterns are robust (our conclusion will be that we should not worry too much about the optical appearance of the regressors); and we look at whether the more complex return-predicting factors (bats or tents as they may be) tell a different economic story than the slope. Here our conclusions will be far more nuanced, and will be fully articulated only after the empirical results discussed in the next chapter.

26.5   ROBUSTNESS OF THE TENT SHAPE: TENTS VERSUS BATS

Dai, Singleton and Yang (2004), Rebonato (2014) and Villegas (2015) raise some doubts about the robustness of the tent shape, and show that almost arbitrary choices about the interpolation method used to obtain the forward rates can alter – significantly – the loadings on the regressors.

'Altering the loading on the regressors' means that the magnitudes and the signs of the coefficients in the linear combination of forward rates that make up the return-predicting factor (the coefficients $\{\beta_i^{(n)}\}$ in Equation (26.4)) change significantly with the choice of interpolation method. More precisely, Dai et al. (2004) draw attention to the fact that almost arbitrary choices about the interpolation method used to obtain the forward rates from the 'virtual' discount bonds[4] can alter the loadings on the regressors – and significantly so. The Cochrane tent disappears, and the pattern that Dai et al. (2004) (and we) find resembles more the wings of a gliding animal, which we choose to call a bat.

Dai et al. (2004) find these findings disturbing because 'even small measurement errors, in the presence of highly correlated forward rates, can lead to large differences in fitted projection coefficients'.[5] In particular, Dai et al. (2004) conclude that 'in projections of excess returns onto forward rates, the data based on the relatively choppy forward curves will give rise to projection coefficients that are "biased" in the direction of having a tent-like shape'.

Furthermore, the 'choppy' forward rates produce a tent, while the smooth ones produce a bat-like pattern. I don't know whether much can be read into this, but, as Dai et al. (2004) point out, if anything, market practitioners prefer to build their curves so as to produce smooth rather than jagged forward rates.

Cochrane and Piazzesi (2004) then provide a rebuttal, which is centred on the claim that the smoothness of the Nelson–Siegel procedure irons away not just noise, but also information.

Villegas (2015) elaborates along these lines. Interestingly, she starts from a set of data that produces a bat pattern (top right panel in Figure 26.2), and then adds a small amount of uninformative noise to the data. When the regression is run on the original signal plus noise the original tent often mutates into a bat. Dai et al. (2004) obtain similar results, which they shown in the bottom right panel in Figure 26.2.

How can such optically different patterns of regressors arise from very similar (and similarly well fitting) sets of input data? The answer becomes apparent if we look at Figure 26.3, which shows the very highly correlated regressors used to obtain the two patterns of coefficients. For regressors as close to colinearity as these, swapping any two regressors (say, applying to the fifth forward rate the β coefficient for, say, the second forward rate) has a relatively small effect. Since all patterns (tents, bats and slopes) display some positive and some negative coefficients, switching from one shape to the other by swapping coefficients is very easy, and the loss in predictive power should not be too great. The big 'optical' differences in shapes can therefore be misleading, as the different patterns could actually try to convey very similar 'stories'. We try to unravel in

---

[4] 'Absent a formal economic model, a definitive choice among these methods seems infeasible. Which method one chooses in practice will likely depend on one's prior about the smoothness of the zero and forward rate curves [. . .].' Dai et al. (2004), p. 4.

[5] ibid, p. 7.

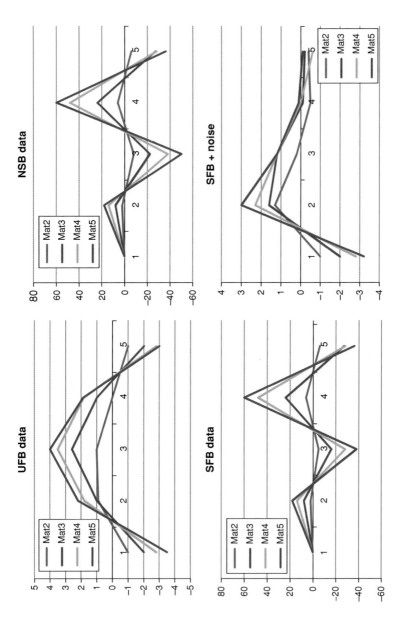

Figure 26.2 The $\{\beta_i^{(n)}\}$ coefficients over the sample period 1970–2000 obtained by Dai et al. (2004) for four different data sources: NSB refers to the Nelson–Siegel–Bliss ((Nelson and Siegel, 1987)) interpolation method, UFB and SFB to the Unsmoothed (Fama and Bliss, 1987) and Smoothed Fama–Bliss interpolation and FW to the Fisher–Wagoner interpolation. See Bliss (1997) for a detailed description of these methods. The legend identifies the maturity of the discount bonds used as regressors.

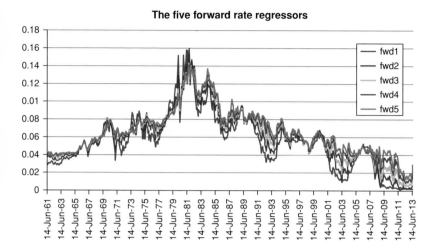

Figure 26.3 The five forward rates used as regressors in the excess return study. The forward rate shown were obtained from a 'smooth' interpolation method (namely, the Nelson–Siegel). Note the high degree of correlation among the regressors.

what follows what this story may be. As we shall see, the underlying story is strongly – but not fully – slope-related.

The validity of this explanation is reinforced by looking at Figure 26.4, which shows the predicted 5-year excess return obtained with the properly determined regression coefficients (curve labelled Original) and the predicted excess returns predicted by keeping the same regression coefficients, but

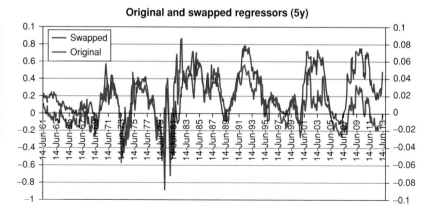

Figure 26.4 The predicted 5-year excess return obtained with the properly determined regression coefficients (curve labelled Original) and the predicted excess returns predicted by keeping the same regression coefficients, but swapping two random forward rates (curve labelled Swapped).

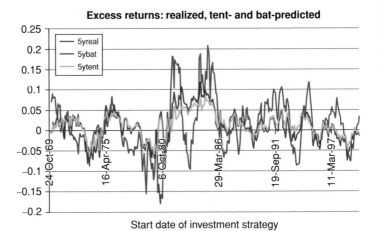

Figure 26.5 Comparison of the predictions of the excess returns produced by our regression with the Cochrane–Piazzesi predictions (and with the real excess return) (April 1970 to December 2000). The date on the *x*-axis show the date of the start of the strategy.

swapping two random forward rates (curve labelled Swapped). So, to be clear, the picture was obtained by using the regression coefficient obtained for the second forward rate and using it for the fourth, and vice versa. After swapping the two forward rates, the original 'bat-like' pattern becomes a slope pattern.

26.6 THE LINK BETWEEN THE TENT AND THE BAT FACTORS: CONSTRAINED REGRESSIONS

We hand-wavingly argued that, when the regressors are as highly correlated as the forward rates used by Cochrane and Piazzesi, switching any two around (and perhaps gently adjusting the coefficients) should have a small effect on the quality of the prediction. If this were the case one should not lose too much sleep over the exact shape of the pattern of the regressors. In this and the next subsection, we substantiate this claim.

We start by discussing how different tents and bats really are. More precisely, we show that, irrespective of whether we use the bat coefficients or Cochrane's tent coefficients, we get an extremely similar prediction of excess returns (see Figure 26.5). Indeed, we find that the correlation between the excess returns produced by the two analyses is as high as 84.7%. The coefficient becomes even higher (90.3%) if the analysis is restricted to the period during which the Cochrane and Piazzesi regression were obtained.

Our analysis was carried out as follows. First, we took the exact coefficients of the Cochrane–Piazzesi (2005) regression from the technical appendix to their

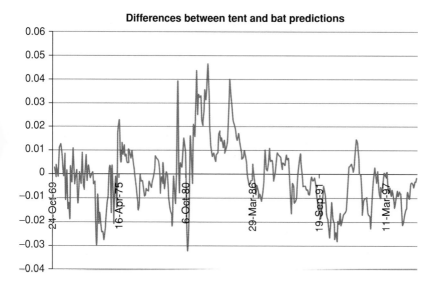

Figure 26.6 The differences between the tent and the bat predictions of excess returns for the portion of data to which the Cochrane–Piazzesi model was fitted.

paper, predicted the 5-year excess returns with these coefficients, and compared these results with the prediction produced by our 'bat' regression.

We display the results in Figure 26.5, which clearly shows that the match is not just at the level of R^2 (perhaps one prediction could do well in one part of the data series, and another might perform better in another part), but is *local*, ie, the two predictions are very close *everywhere*.

Figure 26.6 then shows the differences between the two predictions for the period over which the Cochrane–Piazzesi model was fitted. The average difference is minute, ie, 7 basis points. At first blush, it is difficult to detect much structure in these 'differences in residuals'.

26.6.1 Constrained Regression: The Investigation Methodology

In order to look more carefully into the differences, we mimicked the Cochrane and Piazzesi (2005) study by using the Gurkaynak, Sack and Wright (2006) data provided daily by the Federal Reserve Board. As in Cochrane and Piazzesi (2004, 1008), we used overlapping 1-year returns periods, with reinvestment every month. We used data spanning exactly the same period used in the Cochrane and Piazzesi sample. This gave us 351 (non-independent) observations. We regressed these excess returns against the five forward rates defined by our five-year horizon (the first rate is clearly a spot rate). We stress again that the Nelson–Siegel procedure to obtain yields and forward rates gives what Dai et al. (2004) and Cochrane and Piazzesi (2004) call 'smooth' fits.

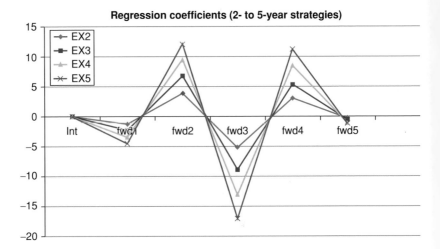

Figure 26.7 Slope regression coefficients on the forward rates. The curves labelled Exn, with $n = 2, 3 \ldots, 5$, denote the coefficients on the excess returns from investing in bonds on maturity n. We call this shape the 'bat' pattern.

The bat shape for the loadings on the linear forward rate regressors obtained by running a linear regression of the excess returns against the five forward rates is shown in Figure 26.7. This shape is qualitatively similar to what Dai et al. (2004) find.

As we have been discussing, clearly this shape is at first blush very different from the tent pattern. In order to see how significant this difference is, we impose that the return-predicting factor should have the forward rates arranged in a tent-like shape. We do so by requiring that the return-predicting factor should be given by

$$RPF_{tent} = \alpha_0 + \sum_{k=1}^{5} \alpha_k f_k \qquad (26.8)$$

with

$$\alpha_1 = -(k_1)^2 \qquad (26.9)$$

$$\alpha_2 = (k_2)^2 \qquad (26.10)$$

$$\alpha_4 = (k_4)^2 \qquad (26.11)$$

$$\alpha_5 = -(k_5)^2 \qquad (26.12)$$

$$\alpha_3 = \max\{\alpha_4, \alpha_2\} + (k_3)^2. \qquad (26.13)$$

The constraints that we impose ensure that the 'pegs' of the tent (loadings α_1 and α_5) should have a negative value, that the points next to the pegs (loadings α_2 and α_4) should be positive, and that the tent apex (loading α_3) should be the highest point. As for the parameter α_0, we imposed that it should equal to the intercept obtained from the unconstrained linear regression. There is nothing fundamental about this choice of constraints, apart from the requirement that the resulting pattern should be approximately tent-like. See Figure 3 in Cochrane and Piazzesi (2005) for a comparison.

To avoid doubt, we stress that we still impose that the dependence of the excess returns on the forward rates should be linear, but we restrict the space of the solution coefficients to be of the form specified in Equations (26.8) to (26.13). When we speak in the text that follows of the 'non-linear' solution we therefore refer to the search method, not to the nature of the dependence, which remains linear.

Given the assumptions we made, the non-linear (the shape-constrained) solution must be worse (in sum-of-squares terms) than the linear solution. The interesting question is how much worse.

26.6.2 Constrained Regression: Results

To answer this question we ran a non-linear unconstrained optimization over the five parameters $\{k\}$. We did so both on each individual return and on the stacked returns. In the latter case we found a 'global' best result, and in the former case five sets of optimal loadings.

When we then ran our constrained optimization, in all cases we obtained (by construction) an approximate tent-like pattern, an example of which is shown in Figure 26.8. The figure clearly shows the similarity between the Cochrane–Piazzesi and the shape-constrained solutions. Optical similarity tells only part of the story, however. We therefore look at the correlation between the Cochrane–Piazzesi and the shape-constrained predictions of excess returns, and between the bat and the shape-constrained predictions: these turned out to be 96.64%, and 99.74%, respectively for the 5-year excess returns. Clearly, at least with these 'smooth' data, the three descriptions are 'telling the same story'.

We show the two sets of coefficients in Table 26.2.

Finally, we note that, when the shape-constrained regression coefficients are used instead of the 'proper' bat regressors, the R^2 statistic decreases by a minuscule (and statistically insignificant) amount from 32.07% to 31.91%.

Villegas (2015) follows a very similar procedure, and she finds an even closer match between the predicted average excess return using unconstrained or constrained coefficients. See Figure 26.9. The tent shape she obtains using her procedure (see Figure 26.10) is even closer to the original Cochrane–Piazzesi tent than the 'forced' tent we obtain, and shown in Figure 26.8.

In sum: when smooth data are used, the two return-predicting factors not only give a very similar *global* set of errors; the prediction errors are also *locally* almost indistinguishable: this is attested by correlations between the

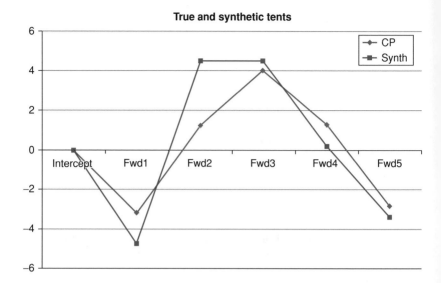

Figure 26.8 The coefficients (loadings on the first five forward rates) from the constrained regression (curve labelled Synth) and from the Cochrane–Piazzesi regression (curve labelled CP). Note the approximate tent shape of the shape-constrained regression. The data for the CP curve were taken from the technical appendix in Cochrane and Piazzesi (2005). The shape of the tent looks somewhat different because we have included the intercept (first point on the *x*-axis).

various predictions ranging between 96.64% and 99.74%. We can therefore draw the first conclusion: if we use smooth data, the difference in terms of prediction between the tent and the bat pattern is economically and statistically insignificant.

Table 26.2 *The regression coefficients for the 5-year excess returns from the Cochrane–Piazzesi (2005) technical appendix (column labelled CP), and the regression coefficients obtained using the shape-constrained procedure described in the text (column labelled Synth).*

	CP	Synth-Constr
Intercept	−0.0489	−0.0772
Fwd1	−3.21	−4.80
Fwd2	1.24	4.47
Fwd3	4.11	4.48
Fwd4	1.25	0.15
Fwd5	−2.83	−3.41

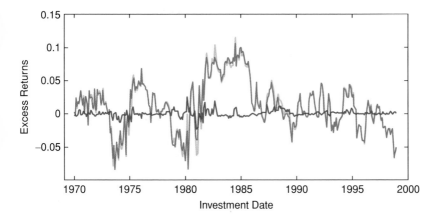

Figure 26.9 The predicted average excess return using unconstrained or constrained coefficients obtained by Villegas (2015) using a procedure similar to the one described in the text. See Villegas (2015) for details. The red curve shows the difference between the constrained and the unconstrained predictions. These differences are even smaller than the ones we find. The data used were the smooth forward rates obtained from the Nelson–Siegel procedure (as calculated in Gurkaynak et al., 2006, 2007).

26.6.3 Constrained Regression: First Conclusions

We are therefore lead to the first conclusion: despite their optically very different shape, tents and bats are in predictive terms very similar. How can this be? As we anticipated in the previous subsection, it is because the regressors are (i) highly co-linear (very strongly correlated) and (ii) both positive and

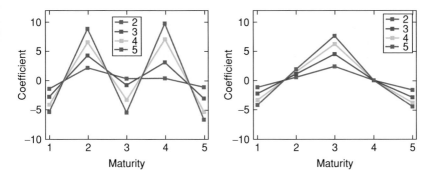

Figure 26.10 The unconstrained regression coefficients obtained by Villegas (2015) using the same data as in Figure 26.9, and the constrained coefficients obtained along similar lines to what is described in the text. Note how the Cochrane-Piazzesi tent is even more closely recovered. For comparison with Figure 26.8, note that the intercept is not reported.

negative. Therefore switching and rearranging the right-hand variables one can easily obtain either a tent or a bat.

The important message for now is that we should not get too hung up between the bat and the tent shapes, as they both require five forward rates for their construction. The more interesting question, which we try to answer in the next chapter, is whether we actually need five factors when traditional wisdom suggests that three factors do a very good job at describing both levels and changes in yields (see Chapter 7). If we find that five factors are indeed statistically better then three, it would also be interesting to understand how much the extra factors 'buy' us in terms of predictive ability.

26.7   THE LINK BETWEEN THE TENT AND THE SLOPE FACTORS

In this subsection we want to show that a tent shape in forward-rate space is very similar to a slope shape in yield space.

26.7.1   Tent versus Slope Shape Similarity: The Investigation Methodology

We start from the observation that the slope *in yield space* is an important return predicting factor. Yields are averages of forward rates:

$$y_k = \frac{1}{T_k} \sum_{j=1}^{k} f_j \tau_j \quad k = 1, \ldots N \tag{26.14}$$

$$\tau_j = T_j - T_{j-1}. \tag{26.15}$$

To lighten notation, we assume in the following that $\tau_j = 1$ for all js, and we set $N = 5$. Then we have

$$y_k = \frac{1}{k} \sum_{j=1}^{k} f_j. \tag{26.16}$$

The slope return-predicting factor for the n-maturity excess return for the investment periods starting at time i, rpf_i^n, can be written as

$$rpf_i^n = Dur^n slope_i, \tag{26.17}$$

where, based on our regressions, we have assumed that the return-predicting factor can be expressed as a common slope factor times the duration, Dur^n, of the underlying, n-maturity, bond.[6]

---

[6] Nothing hangs on this exact relationship, which we enforce to simplify notation. Our results follow as long as the dependence on the maturity of the excess return is smooth and monotonic.

The common slope factor is given (by definition of principal components) by

$$slope_i = \sum_{k=1}^{5} \gamma_k y_k^i. \tag{26.18}$$

Given our assumption of the importance of the slope as a return-predicting factors we write for the excess return, $rx_{i,i+1}^n$,

$$rx_{i,i+1}^n = a_0 + a \times rpf_i^n = a \times Dur^n slope_i$$

$$= a \times Dur^n \sum_{k=1}^{5} \gamma_k y_k^i. \tag{26.19}$$

Finally, substituting from Equation (26.16) we have

$$rx_{i,i+1}^n = a \times Dur^n \sum_{k=1}^{5} \gamma_k y_k^i$$

$$= a \times Dur^n \sum_{k=1}^{5} \frac{\gamma_k}{k} \sum_{j=1}^{k} f_j^i. \tag{26.20}$$

Collecting terms gives

$$rx_{i,i+1}^n =$$

$$f_1^i \left[a \times Dur^n \left(\gamma_1 + \frac{\gamma_2}{2} + \frac{\gamma_3}{3} + \frac{\gamma_4}{4} + \frac{\gamma_5}{5} \right) \right] \tag{26.21}$$

$$f_2^i \left[a \times Dur^n \quad \left(\frac{\gamma_2}{2} + \frac{\gamma_3}{3} + \frac{\gamma_4}{4} + \frac{\gamma_5}{5} \right) \right] \tag{26.22}$$

$$f_3^i \left[a \times Dur^n \quad \left(\frac{\gamma_3}{3} + \frac{\gamma_4}{4} + \frac{\gamma_5}{5} \right) \right] \tag{26.23}$$

$$f_4^i \left[a \times Dur^n \quad \left(\frac{\gamma_4}{4} + \frac{\gamma_5}{5} \right) \right] \tag{26.24}$$

$$f_5^i \left[a \times Dur^n \quad \left(\frac{\gamma_5}{5} \right) \right]. \tag{26.25}$$

Alternatively, we can regress directly the excess return on the forward rates, obtaining

$$rx_{i,i+1}^n = b_0 + \sum_{k=1}^{5} b_k f_k^i, \tag{26.26}$$

which implies

$$b_k = a \times Dur^n \sum_{s=1}^{k} \frac{\gamma_s}{s} \tag{26.27}$$

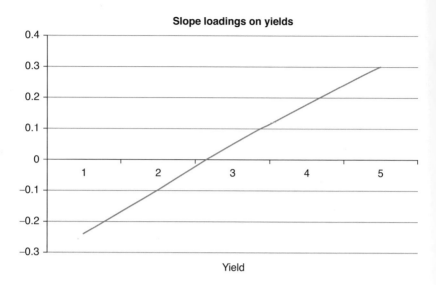

Figure 26.11 The return-predicting factor in yield space obtained by *imposing* that it should have a slope shape.

We can now answer the following question: what do these relationships imply for the regression coefficients b_i when the γs are slope-like loadings in yield space as shown in stylized form in Figure 26.11?

26.7.2 Tent versus Slope Shape Similarity: Results

The corresponding regression coefficients b_i on the forward rates, as given by Equation (26.27) – ie, the loadings onto the forward rates when regression coefficients on the yields are arranged as a slope, are shown in Figure 26.12. While the recovery of the tent is not perfect, it is clear that a tent-like solution is closely linked to the slope being the single most important explanatory principal component. We stress that to keep the argument simple and 'clean' we have not 'optimized' over the loadings γ consistent with a slope interpretation: we just took a straight line.

It is not difficult to understand why a slope-in-yields factor must bring about positive and negative loadings on the forward rates: one just has to look again at Figure 26.3, which shows the regressors, ie, the forward rates. It is clear that they are very highly correlated. If, indeed, the second principal component of the yields covariance matrix (the slope) is an important explanatory variable, the positive and negative weights on yields will result in positive signs for the loadings on some of the forward rates, and negative signs on the loadings for some other forward rates. Whether the positive and negative loadings then conjure the shape of a bat or of a tent (or some other jagged shape) matters relatively little. As we shall see in the next chapter, this alternation of negative and

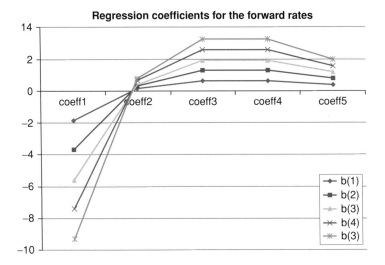

Figure 26.12 The corresponding regression coefficients b_i on the forward rates, as given by Equation (26.27) – ie, the loadings onto the forward rates when regression coefficients on the yields are forced to trace the shape of a slope.

positive signs may show something very important about the aptness of forward rates to span effectively the uncertainty in excess returns.

26.8 EXPLORING THE ECONOMIC ROBUSTNESS OF TENT VERSUS SLOPE PREDICTIONS

So far we have shown that there are virtually no differences between tent- and bat-shaped return-predicting factors; and that there are some, but rather small, differences between the slope-based factor one the one hand and the tent or bat factor on the other.

These differences may be small, but are they robust? Are they significant? And where do they 'come from'? We try to answer the latter questions in the next chapter, and the former immediately below.

26.8.1 Tent versus Slope Robustness: Methodology

We answer the robustness question in steps. First, we quantify how different the time series of the tent and of the slope regressor really are.[7] To do this, we created time series from the early 1960s to 2014 of the Cochrane–Piazzesi tent return-predicting factor, and of the slope factor that we estimated as described in

---

[7] This seems to be generally accepted as true: 'Importantly, the factor has a low correlation with the standard principal components of yields' (Cieslak and Povala, 2010a, p. 5).

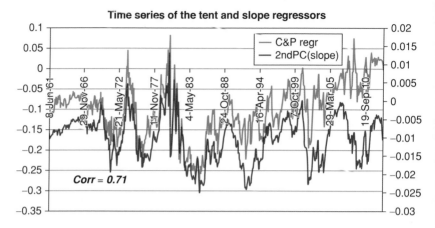

Figure 26.13 The time series of the tent and the slope return-predicting factor from the early 1960s to 2014.

Chapter 25. The two time series are shown in Figure 26.13. As one can readily see, they are very similar indeed (the correlation between the two is 71%) – and, as discussed, this puts into question the received wisdom that the slope and the tent are intrinsically different. This observation in itself, however, still does not answer the question as to whether the (small) differences are significant.

To answer the significance question, we first regressed the Cochrane–Piazzesi tent factor against our slope (second-principal-component) factor; then we looked at the residuals (ie, what is left over when we project one factor onto the other); and, finally, we looked at whether these residuals (the 'difference' between the two factors) had any explanatory powers for the excess returns left over.

We do find (in-sample) that the slope and intercept are significant, but the additional explanatory power (R^2) they provide (0.017) is minute.

There is no question, of course, that, given the data used by Cochrane and Piazzesi, their tent return-predicting factor provide the best in-sample account for the excess returns. The difference, in sample, is not huge, but statistically significant. The tent return-predicting factor seems to be telling a rhyming, but not an identical, story to the one recounted by the slope regressor. But are these differences – and hence the tent-based predictions – robust? Would we do better out of sample if we used the slope or the tent-return predicting factor?

To answer this question we compare the slope and the Cochrane–Piazzesi, tent-shaped return-predicting factor as follows. First we calculate the best regression coefficients for the 5-year excess returns using the full sample and the two different sets of regressors (which we shall henceforth call tent and slope for brevity). With these coefficients we estimate the R^2 coefficient, which, for future reference, we recall is defined as follows:

$$R^2 = 1 - \frac{SS_{res}}{SS_{tot}} \tag{26.28}$$

with

$$\bar{y} = \frac{1}{n} \sum_{i=1,n} y_i \tag{26.29}$$

$$SS_{tot} = \sum_{i=1,n} (y_i - \bar{y})^2 \tag{26.30}$$

$$SS_{res} = \sum_{i=1,n} (y_i - f_i)^2 \tag{26.31}$$

and

$$f_i = \alpha_0 + \sum_{k=1,n_{reg}} \beta_k x_i. \tag{26.32}$$

As usual, the $\{x_i\}$ are the n_{reg} regressors, α_0 is the intercept of the regression, and the quantities $\{\beta_k\}$ are the n_{reg} slope coefficients of the regression. This is all very standard, but we will use this expression in a slightly novel way in a moment.

Next we estimate the slope and tent regression coefficients for the first and the second halves of the sample.

Finally we predict the 5-year excess returns in the first half of the sample using the coefficients estimated using the second half, and vice versa. We do so both for the slope and tent regressors. The results are shown in Figures 26.14 and 26.15.

26.8.2 Tent versus Slope Robustness: Results

The figures show something very striking: the slope predictor seems *in sample* to be somewhat less powerful than the tent regressors ($R^2_{sl} = 0.15$, $R^2_{tent} = 0.19$). Since we have five tent regressors against one slope regressor, in itself this is no big surprise. However, out-of-sample the slope predictor is much more robust than the tent one, providing an acceptable guess for the excess returns when the parameters estimated in the first half are used in the second half, and vice versa.

The tent predictors, on the contrary, predict rather poorly out of sample, especially when the first-half coefficients are used to predict the second-half returns. This is borne out quantitatively by the R^2 statistics, which declines from 0.15 to 0.014 for the slope regressor, but from 0.1884 to -1.81 for the tent. (Yes, the R^2 statistic *can* become negative when one looks outside the sample over which the regression coefficients have been optimized – this is the reason why we showed earlier the full expression for the R^2. For a discussion of out-of-sample R^2 in the context of excess returns, see Campbell and Thompson (2008).)

The findings are summarized in Table 26.3.

The careful reader can guess from this table that the over-good R^2 entry obtained with the tent regressor for the first half of the data (entry C&P

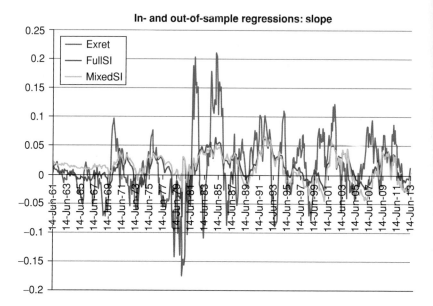

Figure 26.14 The observed excess returns (10-year maturity) (curve labelled Exret) and their predictions using the slope as regressor and in-sample data (curve labelled FullSl), or using the regression coefficients estimated with the first half of the data to estimate the second half, and the coefficients estimated with the second half of the data to predict excess returns in the first half (curve labelled MixedSl).

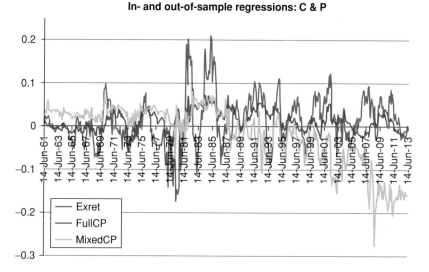

Figure 26.15 Same as Figure 26.14, but using as predictor the Cochrane–Piazzesi return-predicting factor.

Table 26.3 *The R^2 statistics for the slope and tent regressors calculated and used consistently over the full sample (entries on the row Whole sample are under the columns Slope (full) and C&P (full); the R^2 statistics for the slope and tent regressors calculated and used consistently over the first half of the sample (entries on the row First half are under the columns Slope (mixed) and C&P (mixed); the R^2 statistics for the slope and tent regressors calculated and used consistently over the second half of the sample (entries on the row Second half are under the columns Slope (mixed) and C&P (mixed); and the R^2 statistics for the slope and tent regressors use for predictions over the full sample using coefficients estimated in the 'wrong' halves of the sample, as discussed in the text (entries on the row Whole sample are under the columns Slope (mixed) and C&P (mixed).*

R^2	Slope (full)	Slope (mixed)	C&P (full)	C&P (mixed)
Whole sample	0.1525	0.014	0.1884	-1.81
First half	0.2014	–	0.3830	–
Second half	0.0772	–	0.1440	–

(full) – First half) portends trouble for the second half – exactly because, by being *so* good (over 38%) it is likely to be due to non-repeatable overfitting.

Does the puny out-of-sample R^2 entry obtained with the slope regressor ($R^2 = 0.014$) indicate that the slope estimator may be robust, but almost useless for predictive purposes? Such a conclusion would probably be too harsh, because in reality one would not use data collected between 1961 and 1987 to predict excess returns in, say, 2014.

26.8.3   Tent versus Slope Robustness: Conclusions

We can therefore draw the very important conclusion that using the simple slope regressor rather than the tent regressor does not entail a great deterioration in predictive power in-sample, but performs more robustly out of sample – which is exactly what one would want from a predictor. However, this still does not necessarily mean that one can find no yield-curve–based predictive information beyond what is 'contained' in the second principal component. It may just mean that we are 'projecting' the available information into an inappropriate set of coordinates, the forward rates. Remembering how highly correlated forward rate are, it is not a priori surprising that this may be the case.

This point is sufficiently important that it is worthwhile repeating, qualifying and expanding it.

First, we have shown that the tent-based return predicting factor (with its fine-tuning of cancelling loadings on highly correlated forward rates) does not perform very well out of sample. We have not discussed in detail the results obtained with a bat-shaped return-predicting factor, but they lead to the same conclusion.

Second, we have not shown that there are no informative predictors out there (perhaps using a combination of yield curve and macrofinancial explanatory variables) that can perform robustly better than the slope return predicting factor. We have just shown that, out of sample, the tent (or bat) predictor is not one of these better predictors.

Third, whether the inability of a many-forward-rates yield-curve–based return predicting factor to perform well out of sample displays an in-principle or an in-practice limitation is another important question that needs answering.

We will revisit these very important points in depth in the next chapter, when we discuss whether macroeconomic information adds predictive power to the estimation of bond excess returns, and to what extent the macro information can be *effectively* projected onto (can be *effectively* 'spanned by') yield-curve variables.

CHAPTER 27

Excess Returns: The Recent Literature – II

I hope that [my] accounts of other people's work will be accurate, but they will assuredly be selective.

Bernard Williams[1]

Let me only say that what econometrics – aided by electronic computers – can do, is only to push forward by leaps and bounds the line of demarcation from where we have to rely on our intuition and sense of smell.

Ragnar Frish, Nobel Prize Lecture, June 1970

27.1 THE PURPOSE OF THIS CHAPTER

We have presented in detail in the previous chapter the results on the tent-shaped bond-return-predicting factor obtained by Cochrane and Piazzesi (2005). We have also discussed their robustness and the extent to which the tent factor is equivalent to other return-predicting factors. We did so in some detail because the Cochrane-Piazzesi tent has achieved a benchmark status in predictive regressions of bond risk premia.

A lot of very interesting work has been produced in the wake of the paper by Cochrane and Piazzesi (2005). We present the results of three interesting papers in this by-now-crowded field because of their complementary aims: the first (Radwanski, 2010) tries to give an economic interpretation to the tent; the second (Ludvigson and Ng, 2009) shows what yield-curve–based return-predicting factors are, by design, forced to miss; the third (Cieslak and Povala, 2010a, 2010b) explain why tents, slopes and bats look as they do, what they miss, and what else is required to obtained the best prediction of risk premia. We provide a simple reinterpretation of the results of Cieslak and Povala (2010a, 2010b) that has helped us, and hopefully will help the reader, understand how their return-predicting factor is constructed, and why it works so well.

We will also try to answer an outstanding question: why should it be the case that principal components as high as the fifth should be necessary for predicting

---

[1] *Ethics and the Limits of Philosophy*, p. 3.

bond returns, when conventional wisdom suggests that three components do an extremely good job at explaining the yield curve?

Apart from the intrinsic interest, the chapter is very important because of the implications it has for affine modelling. These implications are spelled out in Sections 27.4 and 27.5, in Chapter 29, and in the rest of the book.

27.2 THE WORK OF RADWANSKI (2010)

27.2.1 Features and Highlights of the Radwanski Results

The Cochrane–Piazzesi return-predicting factor (which requires five principal components to describe four excess returns)[2] may well have a high R^2, but, as far as economic interpretation goes, it leaves a bit to be desired. Guns to our heads, we could easily enough spin stories as to why the level and the slope of the yield curve may be linked to excess returns. If we thought that the gun was actually loaded, we may perhaps even come up with an explanation as to why the curvature may explain excess returns. But do we even know what the fourth and fifth principal components look like – let alone explain why they should be part of a return-predicting factor?

This is the gap Radwanski's paper attempts to fill, by trying to give an economic interpretation to the tent-shaped Cochrane–Piazzesi return-predicting factor.

It does so by looking at the class of explanatory variables (return-predicting factors) which use only information embedded in the yield curve. It finds two variables that, taken together, not only have the same explanatory power as the Cochrane–Piazzesi factor, but actually *behave* (almost exactly) like the Cochrane–Piazzesi factor. The beauty of the approach is that the two Radwanski explanatory variables are interpretable: the first is the first principal components extracted from the covariance matrix of nominal rates; the second is (a proxy for) the one-year-ahead inflation expectation.

Possibly the most interesting feature of Radwanski's work is that it is the 'distance' between the two variables, not the level of either variable in isolation, that has predictive power. We shall see in detail how this comes about, but this result, as we shall see, is a precursor of the conclusions drawn by Cieslak and Povala (see Section 27.5).

The careful reader may well object that, surely, the inflation expectation is a macro variable, and therefore the Radwanski's explanatory variables cannot all be said to be extracted from the yield curve. In reality, Radwanski uses

---

[2] Strictly speaking, the Cochrane–Piazzesi return-predicting factor is made up of forward rates, not of principal components. However, the latter are linear combinations of the former, and we are using *linear* regressions to obtain our predictions. Therefore we can use as regressors forward rates, principal components, yields or any linear combination of these yield-curve variables and we will obtain different regression coefficients, but exactly the same predictions, the same residuals and the same R^2.

the projection onto the yield curve of the one-year-ahead inflation expectation. It is this projection, as we shall see, that bears a passing resemblance to the Cochrane–Piazzesi tent factor. Whether this – admittedly unexpected – family resemblance points to a deep similarity, or is a consequence of their use of quasi-colinear right-hand variables when a slope-like regressor is highly significant is a different matter, which we will address in the next chapter.[3]

A few more observations.

First, as we said, Radwanski shows that his economically interpretable *and yield curve–based* return-predicting factor behaves similarly to Cochrane–Piazzesi's. Separately, Ludvigson and Ng (2009) show that, when it comes to predicting excess returns, yield curve–based factors do not seem to tell the full explanatory story. It therefore follows that the Radwanski factor is almost certain to leave some explanation by the wayside.[4]

Second, Ludvigson and Ng (2009) show that real-growth macro variables, not inflation-related factors, have the greatest explanatory power of excess returns. Again, if the Radwanski factor is indeed a close equivalent of the Cochrane–Piazzesi factor, and the former is a good proxy for expected inflation, then it follows that the lion's share of what a Cochrane–Piazzesi-like factor leaves out is the explanatory power provided by real-growth variable. Furthermore, since, as we explain in Section 27.3, for five forward rates the Cochrane–Piazzesi unrestricted regression is equivalent to the most general forward-rate-based regression, it would seem that the part of the predictability that is left out by any yield-curve–based regressor is that related to the real-growth variables. More about this later.

27.2.2 The Methodology and Results

Radwanski (2010) expresses the excess return as a function of the forward premia. These are defined as follows: using the customary notation, and since $f_t^1 = y_t^1$, one has:

$$xret_{t+1}^{(n)} = p_t^{(n-1)} - p_t^{(n)} - f_t^1$$

$$\implies xret_{t+1}^{(n)} = \sum_{i=2}^{n} \left(f_t^i - f_{t+1}^{i-1} \right).$$

The realized forward premium for maturity k then is defined to be

$$fpr_t^{(k)} \equiv f_t^i - f_{t+1}^{i-1} \qquad (27.1)$$

---

[3] Saying that a set of n regressors, $\{x_i^t\}$, $i = 1, 2, ..., n$, is colinear means that it is possible to find n constants, $\{d_i\}$, *not all equal to zero*, such that $\sum_{i=1}^{n} d_i x_i^t \simeq 0$. Of course, if the sum is exactly zero, $\sum_{i=1}^{n} d_i x_i^t = 0$, then the regressors are linearly dependent, and the matrix $X^T X$ is not invertible. For a simple discussion of how to deal with colinear regressors, see Burke (2010), pp. 9–10.

[4] Why 'almost' certain? Because it is conceivable that, say, real-growth may be imperfectly spanned by the yield curve variables, but that inflation expectation could be totally reflected in the shape of the yield curve. This is possible, but somewhat stretched.

and therefore

$$xret_{t+1}^{(n)} = \sum_{i=2}^{n} fpr_t^{(i)}. \tag{27.2}$$

Radwanski then constructs the covariance matrix of the changes in realized forward premia, orthogonalizes it to obtain the principal components, and obtains that the first factor (the usual "level") accounts for 90% of the variability, and the slope-looking second factor for 6%. We stress that these are the principal components of the excess returns, not of the yields.

The results are similar to Cochrane–Piazzesi's (although somewhat less dramatic), and justify the claim that what investors get compensated for is yield curve–level risk. For the rest of the analysis *Radwanski then focusses on explaining the first principal component of the excess returns, not the whole excess return.* The difference is admittedly small, but the merit of this choice is not obvious.

So, this is what Radwanski actually does. First, he defines as the 'CP first factor', F_{t+1}^1, the linear combination of the first five forward rates that best explains the first principal component of forward premia (where 'best' has to be understood in a Ordinary Least Squares-regression sense):

$$F_{t+1}^1 = \alpha_0 + \alpha_1 f_t^1 + \ldots + \alpha_5 f_t^5 + \epsilon_{t+1}. \tag{27.3}$$

The correlation between the CP first factor and Cochrane and Piazzesi's 'full' factor is 99.84%.[5] Radwanski then notes that (either) factor has clear business-cycle properties, assuming a low value at the beginning of recessions and rising sharply throughout their continuation and resolution.

The second step in the procedure is the construction of the yield curve–based inflation proxy, which Radwanski builds as follows. First he takes the difference in log price level,

$$\pi_{t+1} \equiv \log (CPI_{t+1}) - \log (CPI_{t+1}) = \log \left(\frac{CPI_{t+1}}{CPI_t} \right) \simeq \frac{CPI_{t+1} - CPI_t}{CPI_t},$$

and he regresses it against the same five forward rates used in the regression (27.3):

$$\pi_{t+1} = \delta_0 + \delta_1 f_t^1 + \ldots + \delta_5 f_t^5 + \eta_{t+1}. \tag{27.4}$$

By construction, this factor is the projection onto the yield curve of the expected inflation. As the author admits, the R^2 of the regression is high (above 40%), but only three of the regressors are statistically significant. However, Radwanski adds, 'using all five forward rates makes it easier to compare the inflation forecasting factor to the CP factor'.[6] More about this later. For the moment we note that the $\{\delta\}$ regressors arrange themselves in the pattern of an inverted tent, strongly reminiscent of the Cochrane–Piazzesi tent (although, admittedly, upside down).

---

[5] Once again, this begs the question why this extra step is introduced, but we shall leave it at that.
[6] p. 15.

Radwanski therefore defines the IE_t (*Inflation Expectation*) factor as[7] 'the linear combination of forward rates, which contains all the information about one-year-ahead inflation revealed by the term structure, and that can be extracted by means of a linear regression'.[8]

Radwansky finds 'striking similarities between the CP and the IE factors'. Not only is the shape of one almost a mirror image of the shape of the other, but also their time series properties are closely related at the business-cycle frequency, even if not so over a short horizon: '[a] rise in IE is almost always associated with a fall in CP. However, the correlation is only -0.19'. Radwanski explains how it is possible to have similarity at low frequency, and yet a low correlation by noting that the CP factor is strongly mean-reverting, while the IE factor appears to be almost unit-root (non-mean-reverting). In this sense, it would be a contributor to the quasi-unit-root behaviour of the first principal component of forward rates, which should plausibly contain expected inflation as an important component. (This, after all, is in essence the Fisher hypothesis.) We note in passing that this difference between signals with similar low-frequency components, but different high-frequency behaviour is at the base of the treatment by Cieslak and Povala (2010a, 2010b) reviewed in Section 27.5.

This brings Radwanski to focus on the relationship between the level of forward rates and (his proxy for) expected inflation, and argues that excess returns should depend on the 'distance' of one quantity from the other because

> [i]f prices were "too high" with respect to fundamentals, either the fundamentals should be expected to improve, or prices to fall.[9] [...] Since expected inflation is persistent [shows little, if any, mean-reversion], IE summarizes well expected inflation for some years in the future. Sometimes, expected inflation is further below the level than implied by the long-run relation. In other words, market prices of bonds are seemingly below fundamentals, which results in a correction during which excess bond returns are realized.[10]

We shall revisit in the section (29.5) devoted to the work of Cieslak and Povala (2010a, 2010b) the explanation of bond premia as originating from deviations in a cointegration relationship – in the case of Cieslak and Povala between a long-term, secular, component and a higher frequency, cyclical component, in the case of Radwanski between the expected inflation and the level of yields.

It is on the basis of this intuition that Radwanski runs a regression of the CP first factor, F_{t+1}^1 (see Equation (27.3)), against expected inflation, EI_t, and

---

[7] p. 16.

[8] Could one do better if one looked at past values of realized inflation? Yes, one could: including in the regression an autoregressive term (ie, a term in the latest value of the realized inflation) $\pi_{t+1} = a_0 + a_1\pi_t + a_2 IE_t + \eta'_{t+1}$ increases the R^2 by 16–18%. This result should be compared with the findings by Ludvigson and Ng (2010) discussed in Section 27.3, where they show that the yield curve does not contain all the predictive information about excess returns. For our purposes, we can regard the IE_t factor as 'a projection of the agents' information set on the interest rates' (p. 17).

[9] p. 18.   [10] p. 3.

a level-of-nominal-forward-rates factor, L_t:

$$F_{t+1}^1 = \kappa_0 + \kappa_1 L_t + \kappa_2 IE_t + \xi_{t+1}. \tag{27.5}$$

By definition, the new factor, which is totally built from combinations of yield curve quantities linearly related to each other, cannot 'beat' the Cochrane–Piazzesi regression. However, it performs 'almost as well as the CP factor [with] [t]he differences in R^2 [..] between zero and two percentage points only'.

It is important to point out the neither the inflation expectation factor, IE_t, nor the level factor, L_t, are significant, or produce a meaningful R^2, when used in isolation as explanatory variables in a univariate regression.[11] Removing either factor from the regression leads to a severe omitted-variable bias, and indicates that it is the *distance* between the two that matters for excess returns, not whether either, or both, are at a high or low level. Indeed, the correlation between the level and the expected-inflation proxy is 0.73 (full sample), high enough for the omission of either variable to be important.[12]

---

[11] The reported R^2 are 3% for the level factor, and 1% for the inflation-expectation factor over the full sample.

[12] What is the omitted-variable bias? Suppose that the true model is

$$y_t = a_0 + a_1 x_1^t + a_2 x_2^t + e_t$$

but we fail to include the variable x_2^t from our set of regressors, and we estimate instead

$$y_t = b_0 + b_1 x_1^t + u_t.$$

We can express the omitted variable x_2^t as a linear function of the included variable, x_1^t:

$$x_2^t = c_0 + c_1 x_1^t + w$$

and notionally we can estimate the coefficients c_0 and c_1 by Ordinary Least Squares regression. (I say 'notionally' because usually we do not know that we have omitted a variable.) This means that in the univariate regression we are actually estimating the effect on the quantity y both of the variable x_1 and of the projection of the variable x_2 onto x_1:

$$y_t = a_0 + a_1 x_1^t + a_2 \left(c_0 + c_1 x_1^t \right) + \varepsilon_t = \underbrace{(a_0 + a_2 c_0)}_{f_0} + \underbrace{(a_1 + a_2 c_1)}_{f_1} x_1^t + \varepsilon_t.$$

Now, when no variables are excluded, and all the conditions for the validity of Ordinary Least are met, we know that the estimated values, $\widehat{a}_i$, for the true coefficient, a_i, are such that $\mathbb{E}\left[\widehat{a}_i\right] = a_i$. However, it is easy (if a bit messy) to obtain that the expectation of $\widehat{b}_1$, $\mathbb{E}\left[\widehat{b}_1\right]$, is now given by

$$\mathbb{E}\left[b_1\right] = a_1 + a_2 \frac{\sigma_{12}}{\sigma_1^2}$$

Therefore the regression estimate of the 'slope' of x_1 in the mis-specified model, f_1, is linked to the regression estimate of the 'slope' of x_1 in the correct model, a_1, by

$$f_1 = a_1 + a_2 \frac{\widehat{Cov}\left(x_1, x_2\right)}{\widehat{Var}\left(x_1\right)}.$$

This means that the coefficient of the included variable is in general biased; that we do not know whether it is biased upwards or downwards; and that this bias will not disappear no matter how large a sample we employ – the larger the sample, the more precise our error. For an excellent discussion of the omitted-variable bias, see Angrist and Pischke (2015), their Section 2.3, pp. 68–74.

In sum, for our purposes the work by Radwanski can be summarized as possible:

1. the Cochrane-Piazzesi return-predicting factor is shown to behave almost exactly as the combination of two regressors, the level of yields and a yield-based proxy for expected inflation;
2. what explains excess returns is the 'distance' between the two factors; neither factor is significant in isolation;
3. the shape of the Cochrane-Piazzesi tent appears to be inherited by the similar (but inverted) shape for the inflation proxy.

27.2.3 Comments and Conclusions

A few comments about these results.

First of all, the economic 'explanation' of the shape of the Cochrane–Piazzesi tent only kicks the can one rather short step down the road. Admittedly, it is true that the important expected inflation factor has an inverted tent shape (and therefore this is where the Cochrane-Piazzesi tent is likely to have inherited its shape from). However, this *gives an interpretation for* the tent shape, but does not explain it. The questions still remain: "Why should the expected inflation be explained by an inverted tent of forward rates?" and 'Why should the distance between the inflation proxy and the level of rates be a predictor of excess returns?"

More fundamentally: since, as we have seen in the previous chapter, with highly colinear regressors little should be read in the exact shape, the real question is not whether the regressors arrange themselves in a tent, a bat or a slope pattern. Rather, we should ask ourselves why the fourth and fifth principal components should convey predictive information about expected inflation. The Radwanski 'explanation' of the shape is then made even more dubious when one notices that only three of the five inverted-tent coefficients are statistically significant (two, when we use our data set).

However, the work by Radwanski does make a useful explanatory contribution by arguing that a well-defined and easy to proxy macroeconomic variable – namely their projection of the expected inflation on the yield curve – is closely related to the Cochrane–Piazzesi tent. This important piece of information was absent in the Cochrane–Piazzesi (2005) work, and in this sense the work by Radwanski goes some way towards interpreting, if not explaining, the Cochrane–Piazzesi results. So, Radwanski suggests a plausible link between bond risk premia and inflation, but leaves unanswered the question as to why information about this macroeconomic factor should be embedded in very high principal components.

Second, the author states (repeatedly) that the excess returns are unlikely to be due to market inefficiencies. He says, for instance: 'Since both level and expected inflation are formed using market prices, it is very unlikely that irrationality or inefficiency played a role in observed predictability patterns.'[13] However, his own explanation of term premia invokes divergences from 'fundamentals'. Perhaps he means that these divergences are short lived, and therefore the inefficiencies do not persist for long. However, in his explanation risk premia are proportional to deviations of the level of rates from the expected inflation, and excess returns are made in the process of 'catching up': as he puts it, 'market prices of bonds are *seemingly below the fundamentals*, which results in a correction, during which high excess bond returns are realized.'[14] And again: 'The level and expected inflation can be a priori suspected to contain important information on bond risk premia, because while the latter variable summarizes the expectations of real cash flows to the bondholders, the former controls for the general level of bond prices. *If prices are "too high" with respect to the fundamentals, either the fundamentals should be expected to improve, or prices to fall.*'[15] It is difficult not to read this statement in an inefficiency light. We shall revisit this inefficiency-based explanation in Chapter 28.

The most interesting contribution of the Radwanski paper, however, lies in the cointegration interpretation of the risk factor. As Radwanski clearly says, it is neither the expected inflation, nor the level of rates that has explanatory power, but the distance between the two. This insight is important and useful, and will be significantly expanded by Cieslak and Povala (2010a, 2010b) – see Section 27.5. As it happens, their account will also give an explanation (of sorts) to the bat or tent shapes of the return-predicting factor – although not one that Cochrane, Piazzesi or Radwanski would have predicted.

27.3 THE WORK OF LUDVIGSON AND NG (2009)

27.3.1 Main Results

When it comes to the prediction of bond risk premia, the prevailing – or, perhaps, one should say 'the easiest' – approach builds return-predicting factors directly derived from the yield curve: quantities, that is, such as forward rates, yields, principal components, etc.[16]

Ludvigson and Ng (2009) take a different approach and, extending early work by Ang and Piazzesi (2003), ask two related questions:

---

[13] p. 2.   [14] p. 3, emphasis added.   [15] p. 16, emphasis added.

[16] If we take a macroeconomic quantity, we project it (by means of an Ordinary Least Squares regression) onto the time-t yield curve, and we use the resulting combination of yield-curve quantities as return-predicting factors, we are still using a yield curve–based approach, because we are using only that part of the dynamics of the macroeconomic variable that is projected onto the forward rates. So, one should not be fooled when an author such as Radwanski (2010) dubs his predicting factors 'expected inflation' – what he actually uses (and he is very clear about this) is the *projection of* expected inflation onto the forward rates. This point about projections is very important, both from the practical and the theoretical points of view, because we can ask two very distinct questions: (1) are the variations in a certain quantity *in principle* spanned by a set of variables (such as forward rates)? and (2) are the variations in a certain quantity *effectively* spanned by the same set of variables? We will discuss this point in detail in Section 27.4.

1. Can movements in bond risk premia be related to cyclical macroeconomic activity?
2. Do macro fundamentals contain information about risk premia not embedded in bond market data?

Note that the two questions are not equivalent. If the answer to the second is 'no', it can still be the case that bond risk premia are related to cyclical macroeconomic activity, but this information would be reflected in the shape (and possibly the history) of the yield curve. If the answer were 'no', it would follow that we would be wasting time parsing through noisy and messy macro data because the yield curve would contain all there is to know about what we are interested in. (As we shall see, matters are not quite as clear-cut, because issues of *effectiveness* of spanning are intertwined with issues of in-principle ability to span. But we are getting ahead of ourselves – see the following section.)

As for the first question there are strong a priori reasons why the answer may be 'yes': for instance, that investors want to be compensated for risks associated with recessions; and, surely, buyers of fixed rate bonds should demand some compensation for bearing inflation risk.

These are certainly plausible 'hunches', and, as the quote that opens the chapter reminds us, we certainly want to use econometric tools in order to 'push forward by leaps and bounds the line of demarcation from where we have to rely on our intuition and sense of smell'. Unfortunately, previous studies of the predictive power of macro indicators produced indifferent results – and Ludvigson and Ng (2009) mention a few of the reasons, such as noise in the data, revisions in the macroeconomic data, lack of synchronicity, lags, etc.

To get around these problems, Ludvigson and Ng apply Principal Components Analysis to 132 measures of economic activity, and create a handful of factors that they use as regressors to explain excess returns.

In order to see whether these factors have additional explanatory power, the Authors take the Cochrane and Piazzesi tent regressor (which *in sample* cannot be beaten using yield curve–only variables) as a benchmark, and look at whether they can improve on its predictions by adding their carefully constructed factors.

Their results are as follows:

1. Bond returns are predictable by macro fundamentals.
2. The maximum predictive power is for 2 years, with an R^2 of 26%.
3. This is less than the R^2 of the Cochrane–Piazzesi factor, but more than the R^2 produced by the Fama and Bliss (1987) factor.
4. The macro fundamentals have strong out-of-sample predictive power.
5. The estimated macro factors contain substantial extra information on top of what is contained in the Cochrane–Piazzesi tent. More precisely, with (hopefully) obvious notation, if we symbolically denote by $\{CP\}$ the Cochrane–Piazzesi risk predicting factor, and by $\{CP \cup Macro\}$ the combination of the Cochrane–Piazzesi and the macro factors,

Ludvigson and Ng find $R^2_{\{CP \cup Macro\}} = 44\%$ to be compared with $R^2_{\{CP\}} = 31\%$.

What are the important macro factors? After many appropriate caveats about the dangers of overinterpreting the factors, Ludvigson and Ng report that the most important one is a 'real-activity' factor, which displays high correlation with real output and employment, and low correlation with the level of prices or with financial variables (such as yields or equity prices). The second most important factor can then be interpreted as an 'inflation' factor, highly correlated with measures of prices.[17]

In concordance with the empirical studies by other researcher, Ludvigson and Ng find that bond returns are high in recessions, when economic growth is slow or negative, and low during expansions. More precisely they state that

> ...the cyclical behaviour of the risk-premium component, both in yields and in returns, depends importantly on whether predictive information contained in the estimated factors is included when forecasting excess bond returns. When the information in the macro factors is ignored, both return and yield risk premia are virtually acyclical, exhibiting a correlation with real industrial production that is close to zero.[18] This is true even if CP_t [the Cochrane–Piazzesi factor] is used as a predictor variable for returns.[19]

They add that when macro information is neglected

> ...too much of the business cycle variation in long-term yields is attributed to expectations of future nominal interest rates, and too little is attributed to changes in the compensation for bearing risk...[20]

One observation is in order. When looking at 5-year returns the Cochrane–Piazzesi factor is made up of a combination of five forward rates. Any linear combination of five forward rates would give exactly the same R^2 as the (unrestricted) tent factor. In particular, principal components are one such linear combination. But we know well that, if we have n variables and we use n principal components, we have a description of the dynamics of the original variables which is exactly equivalent to the one afforded by the original five forward rates. Therefore, if the Cochrane–Piazzesi factor does not tell the full predictive story, neither could five principal components – or, for that, matter, any other linear combination of forward rates. It also follows that, when Ludvigson and Ng show that $R^2_{\{CP \cup Macro\}} > R^2_{\{CP\}}$, they also show that macro variables contain explanatory power that is not present in *any* linear combination of the five time-t yield-curve-based forward rates (or yields or log prices).

---

[17] To ascertain the interpretation of the factors, Ludvigson and Ng ran the univariate regressions of each macroeconomic series on each principal component. So, the '"real" factor was labeled as such because it has a high explanatory power for real quantities (eg, Industrial Production)' (Fontaine and Garcia, 2008, p. 24).

[18] Cfr our findings about the slope as rate-predicting factor.

[19] p. 5030.   [20] ibid.

27.3.2 The Spanning of Yield Curve Factors Revisited: Implication for Affine Models

This brings us to the important point of the spanning of the yield curve factors. Arguably the main result obtained by Ludvigson and Ng (2009) is that

> measures of real activity and inflation in the real economy captured by estimated factors contain economically meaningful information about future bond returns that is not contained in [the Cochrane-Piazzesi factor], and therefore not contained in contemporaneous spreads, or even yield factors estimated as the principal components of the yield covariance matrix.[21]

In short: there is more to bond-return prediction than what is captured by the Cochrane–Piazzesi factor, or by any other yield-curve–based factor which uses linear combinations of the same variables.

Now, a defining feature of affine models is that yields should be a linear (actually, affine) function of the n state variables, x_t, whatever the nature of these state variables. In the terminology adopted so far this means:

$$y_t = \alpha + \beta x_t. \tag{27.6}$$

Therefore, as long as the β matrix is invertible, we can always write

$$\beta^{-1}(y_t - \alpha) = x_t \tag{27.7}$$

and therefore

$$x_t = -\beta^{-1}\alpha + \beta^{-1}y_t$$
$$\implies x_t = c + \beta^{-1}y_t \tag{27.8}$$

with

$$c = -\beta^{-1}\alpha. \tag{27.9}$$

This means that, under the invertibility assumption, we can always express the vector of state variables, x_t, as an affine function of the n yields.

But if this is the case, from the conceptual point of view then we can just as well use yields as state variables. And this is true irrespective of whether the original state variables, x_t, were yield curve observables (say, principal components), macroeconomic variables (say, inflation or real economic activity) or even latent variables.

It follows that, according to these affine models, non-yield-based variables can contain no information useful for predicting bond excess return other than what is embedded in the yields.

However, the empirical conclusions quoted earlier seem to indicate very clearly that this is not the case, ie, that yield-curve–only variables miss an important portion of the bond predictability. It would therefore seem to

[21] p. 5047.

follow that there is an intrinsic limitation in the predictive capabilities of the commonly used affine yield curve models.

This conclusion is sobering, to say the least. Are there some ways to escape from the fetters this conclusion seems to impose on affine yield cure modelling? Indeed there are. Let's look at some of these escape routes.

One way to avoid the strictures of these conclusions is to invoke unspanned stochastic volatility models. We will not pursue this line of argument, but the reader is referred to Collin-Dufresne and Goldstein (2002).

Another way is to invoke factors that have a small effect on today's cross section of yields, but have a substantial forecasting power for future yields. See Duffee (2008) in this respect. We explore this possibility in the next section, by linking it to the next 'escape route'.

Possibly the most interesting avenue is the following. Recall that in Equations (27.6) to (27.9) we required invertibility of the matrix β. Now, in affine models where the forecastability of bond returns is fully embedded in the yields (ie, essentially affine models for which the market price of risk is a deterministic function of the state variables), it is implicitly assumed that, given n state variables, x_t, there are exactly n yields that are measured without error. (We prove this in the next section.) The other yields may (and in general will) have measurement errors. It is thanks to the exact recovery of n yields that, using the invertibility of the matrix β, we can go back and forth between the state variables and the yields. Ang, Piazzesi and Dong (2007) suggest a model when *all* yields contain measurement error. If this is the case, we can go back and forth (by matrix inversion) between 'wrong' yields (ie, true yields plus their measurement errors) and state variables, but not between the correct yields and the state variables.

This escape route seems appealing; however, looking at how closely present-day affine models recover the yield curve (see in this respect the results in Part VII), the claim that these tiny measurement errors should be able to explain so much seems at first blush indigestible. In Ludvigson and Ng's words, '[i]t remains an open question as to whether a plausibly calibrated model of measurement error can account for the quantitative findings reported here.'[22]

We shall revisit this important point when we discuss the work by Cieslak and Povala (2010a, 2010b) – see Section 27.5 –, but for the moment we stress that the argument just presented required that the forecastability of bond returns should be fully embedded in the yields. As we shall see, this assumption in not innocuous.

27.4   YIELD-CURVE SPANNING: WHY ONE MAY NEED FIVE FACTORS AFTER ALL

Before looking at the work of Cieslak and Povala, we shall make more precise the conclusions we have just reached about what is needed in order to explain

---

[22] p. 5048.

bond returns – and about what apparently is *not* sufficient for the task. Recall that we have also left unexplained the question of why as many as five factors (forward rates, principal components, yields, whatever) seem to be necessary in order to predict as best as one can excess returns. *This*, not the tent-like shape of the return-predicting factor, is one of the more startling results by Cochrane and Piazzesi (and by Adrian, Crump, and Moench, 2013).

The argument we present is simple, but a bit subtle. It deserves close attention. To help the reader follow the flow, we break it into digestible bits.

27.4.1 The Essentially Affine Description

Suppose that we start with n state variables, x_t^i, $i = 1, 2, \ldots, n$. Since three principal components have until recently been thought to be all that is needed to describe the dynamics yield curve, we shall start with $n = 3$, but nothing hangs on this.

Under the real-world measure we have, as usual,

$$dx_t = \mathcal{K}^{\mathbb{P}} \left(\theta^{\mathbb{P}} - x_t \right) dt + S dz. \tag{27.10}$$

Let's suppose now that the market price of risk vector, λ, is an affine function of the state variables:

$$\lambda_t = \lambda_0 + \Lambda x_t. \tag{27.11}$$

This assumption, common as it is, has deep consequences. It means that, yes, the market price of risk is stochastic, but that it inherits all of its stochasticity from the stochasticity of the state variables. Once these assume a certain value, then the market price of risk is fully determined: in this setting, it is a *deterministic* function of *stochastic* variables.

Finally, if we live in an affine world we know that the short rate must be an affine function of the state variables:

$$r_t = u_r + g^{\mathrm{T}} x_t. \tag{27.12}$$

Let's use this information.

We know that bond prices are given by the discounted expectation, under $\mathbb{Q}$, of the path of the short rate. If we know how to evolve the state variables in the risk-neutral measure, $\mathbb{Q}$, then at each time step we can convert from the state variables to the short rate via Equation (27.12). Given the value of the short rate, we can construct its whole path; we can then average over paths, ie, take the discounted expectation – that's the bond price. So, as we have seen in Part III, to get the bond price we just have to evolve the state variables under the risk-neutral measure, $\mathbb{Q}$.

However, we can follow an equivalent, but slightly less direct route: we can use for the evolution of the state variables the parameters that apply under the real-world measure, $\mathbb{P}$, and add explicitly the compensation for risk:

$$dx_t = \mathcal{K}^{\mathbb{P}}(\theta^{\mathbb{P}} - x_t)dt + Sdz + S\lambda_t dt$$
$$= \mathcal{K}^{\mathbb{P}}(\theta^{\mathbb{P}} - x_t)dt + Sdz + S(\lambda_0 + \Lambda x_t)dt, \qquad (27.13)$$

where we have made use of the essentially affine assumption (Equation (27.11)) in the second line.

It does not take much to see that the terms $S\lambda_0$ and $S\Lambda x_t$ can be absorbed into a new reversion speed matrix and reversion level vector. Equation (27.10) can therefore be recast in the form

$$dx_t = \mathcal{K}^{\mathbb{Q}}\left(\theta^{\mathbb{Q}} - x_t\right)dt + Sdz. \qquad (27.14)$$

(See Chapter 33 for the details. Even better, please derive the expressions for $\mathcal{K}^{\mathbb{Q}}$ and $\theta^{\mathbb{Q}}$ yourself.)

Of course, we know that we do not have to perform the *Gedanken* 'Monte Carlo' evolution described earlier, and that we can directly value bond prices today by calculating

$$P_0^T = \exp^{A_0^T + \left(\vec{B}_0^T\right)^{\mathrm{T}}\vec{x}_0}, \qquad (27.15)$$

where A_0^T and $\vec{B}_0^T$ are functions of $\mathcal{K}^{\mathbb{Q}}$ and $\theta^{\mathbb{Q}}$. Thanks to this affine representation of bond prices, we can always recover exactly as many yields as state variables. More precisely, we can always find three initial values for the $n = 3$ state variables, x_0^i, $i = 1, 2, 3$, such that $n = 3$ yields are exactly recovered. Doing so is easy: we know that

$$y_0^T = \alpha_0^T + \left(\vec{\beta}_0^T\right)^{\mathrm{T}}\vec{x}_0$$

with

$$\alpha_0^T = -\frac{1}{T}A_0^T \qquad (27.16)$$

and

$$\vec{\beta}_0^T = -\frac{1}{T}\vec{B}_0^T. \qquad (27.17)$$

Therefore we can stack the n state variables in a vector and write

$$\vec{y}_0^T - \vec{\alpha}_0^T = \left(\beta_0^T\right)^{\mathrm{T}}\vec{x}_0$$
$$\Rightarrow \vec{x}_0 = \left(\left(\beta_0^T\right)^{\mathrm{T}}\right)^{-1}\left[\vec{y}_0^T - \vec{\alpha}_0^T\right]. \qquad (27.18)$$

So, n yields are exactly recovered. And, as we have seen, since the original state variables are linked to these n yields by an affine transformation, we can just as well work with the n chosen yields as state variables.

27.4.2 Switching to Yields as State Variables

It is important to stress that these chosen yields will be perfectly recovered, but that all the other yields only to within measurement error. In this description, some yields are more equal than others, in the sense that n yields (the only ones to be exactly recovered) play the role of state variables. To stress their privileged status we will denote them by the symbol $\widetilde{y}_t$.

In our setting it follows that the (essentially affine) market price of risk, which we had expressed as in Equation (27.11), can be rewritten as

$$\lambda_t = \widetilde{\lambda}_0 + \widetilde{\Lambda}\widetilde{y}_t. \tag{27.19}$$

It may seem awkward to write it this way, but we can certainly do so.

27.4.3 Augmenting the State Vector

Suppose now, however, that the market price of risk *cannot* be expressed as an affine function of the special-yields state variables. This means that we must write it as

$$\lambda_t = \widetilde{\lambda}_0 + \underline{\widetilde{\Lambda}\widetilde{y}_t} + \underline{R}\,w_t, \tag{27.20}$$

where w_t are m new variables that are orthogonal to the special yields, $\widetilde{y}_t$, (or to the original x_t, it doesn't matter – if they are orthogonal to one set of variables they can be made orthogonal to the others). Being orthogonal in this context means that if we run a regression

$$w_t^i = w_0^i + \left(w_1^i\right)^{\mathrm{T}}\widetilde{y}_t \tag{27.21}$$

the intercepts, w_0^i, and the slopes, w_1^{T}, are statistically zero.

If this is the case then the pricing equation for the state variables under $\mathbb{Q}$ becomes

$$
\begin{aligned}
d\widetilde{y}_t &= \mathcal{K}_y^{\mathbb{P}}\left(\theta_y^{\mathbb{P}} - \widetilde{y}_t\right)dt + S_y dz + S_y\lambda_t dt \\
&= \mathcal{K}_y^{\mathbb{P}}\left(\theta_y^{\mathbb{P}} - \widetilde{y}_t\right)dt + S_y dz + S_y\left(\widetilde{\lambda}_0 + \widetilde{\Lambda}\widetilde{y}_t + Rw_t\right)dt.
\end{aligned} \tag{27.22}
$$

Now, the terms $S_y\widetilde{\lambda}_0$ and $S_y\widetilde{\Lambda}\widetilde{y}_t$ can be absorbed into the new, $\mathbb{Q}$-measure, reversion level vector and reversion speed matrix exactly as before, but not so for the term $S_y Rw_t$: one can now only write

$$d\widetilde{y}_t = \mathcal{K}_y^{\mathbb{Q}}\left(\theta_y^{\mathbb{Q}} - \widetilde{y}_t\right)dt + S_y dz + S_y Rw_t dt. \tag{27.23}$$

This implies that, in order to account for the new source of uncertainty that affects the evolution of the reference yields, one has to augment the state vector from n to $n+m$, ie, to augment the original state variables with the new unspanned variables w_t:

$$\{x_t\}_n \Longrightarrow \left\{x_t'\right\}_{n+m} = \{x_t\}_n \cup \{w_t\}_m. \tag{27.24}$$

This means that to describe the evolution of the $n = 3$ special yields over the next time steps we have to enrich our state vector from $\{x_t\}_n$ to $\{x_t'\}_{n+m} = \{x_t\}_n \cup \{w_t\}_m$.

Once we have augmented the state vector from $\{x_t\}_n$ to $\{x_t'\}_{n+m}$, we can absorb the troublesome term $S_y R w_t dt$ into a new reversion speed matrix and a new reversion speed level. And, of course, with the augmented set of state variables, the specification of the market price of risk has become essentially affine again!

27.4.4   Switching Back to an 'Augmented' Set of Yields as State Variables

We are not finished, however. There is one more important twist to this tedious argument of insidious intent.

Using our augmented state vector $\{x_t'\}_{n+m}$ we can write again

$$P_0^T = \exp^{A_0^T + \left(\vec{B}_0^T\right)^T \vec{x}_0}. \tag{27.25}$$

This being the case, by an inversion similar to Equation (27.18), we can obtain again $n + m$ 'special' yields, where 'special' means again that they will be *exactly* priced, and that they can be promoted to the the status of state variables.

How do we know that this is always possible? We know because we can always invert the yield equation as we did in Equation (27.18) and obtain initial values for the variables x and w such that $n + m$ yields are exactly recovered. Therefore, exactly as we did before, we can choose $n + m$ 'special yields' (which will be exactly recovered, with no measurement error) to act as new state variables.

What is the difference? Aren't we back to where we started? Not really.

The difference is that the market price of risk is now an affine function of the augmented state variables – if we want, of the augmented yields. We have transformed a problem with n yield state variables and an unspanned market of risk, to a problem with $n + m$ yield state variables and a fully spanned market price of risk (and therefore we are back to working with an essentially affine, purely-yield-curve–based model.)

But, one may object, surely this must be a 'trick'. New-generation affine models price the *whole* yield curve (not just the special yields) extremely well. Didn't the original, n-variable problem, give almost exactly the same value for the 'new yields' that we have added as the augmented model? Yes, *almost* exactly, but not precisely so. Can such small errors in pricing make such a big difference in predictability? Yes, they can: remember what Cochrane and Piazzesi and Ludvigson and Ng suggested, that there may be lurking out there extra factors that may have a very limited effect on today's yields, but a big effect in predicting bond returns.

27.4.5 The Subtle Role of 'Measurement Error'

Isn't it strange that that should be the case? Isn't it strange, that is, that small measurement errors – small errors, that is, in the pricing of the m 'new' bonds – could account for so much? The problem is not really with the small bond-pricing errors: after all, we know that, by using more and more state variables (for instance, more and more principal components) we can recover exactly more and more market yields. The real problem is that, once we have chosen the perfectly priced $n + m$ (not n!) yields as explanatory variables, we are faced with the task of regressing the excess returns on this augmented (and now possibly rather large) set of state variables. Alas, when we choose yields (even the augmented yields) as state variables, we are choosing a very poor set of explanatory variables (of 'coordinates') to describe excess returns. Since all yields are strongly correlated, to 'pick up' information that was orthogonal to the original n yields and contained in the additional (but highly correlated) m yields, the loadings of the return-predicting factor must really amplify small intra-yield differences. No surprise, then, that both tents and bats have such wild shapes, with large positives and large negatives! This, by the way, is where tents, bats and slopes come from! But this amplification of small differences is a statistical nightmare, because of the 'known statistical problems that arise when using linear combinations of multiple forward rates, such as the sensitivity to small measurement errors'.[23]

What if we had used principal components as the original state variables, ie, linear combination of yields that are built to be orthogonal to each other? Suppose that n (the original number of principal components) was chosen to be 3, and m (the number of additional principal components) to be 2. Wouldn't the fourth and fifth principal components, which are orthogonal to the first three important components, pick up exactly the bond return predictability that we are looking for? In principle they would, but the problem now is that the estimation of high-order principal components is easily contaminated by noise, and that they have much less stable loadings (a much less stable shape) than the first three.

27.4.6 Spanning in Principle versus Spanning in Practice

From this argument it follows that one can look at the spanning problems from two different angles.

From one angle one can claim that, *no matter how many yields one looks at*, there is information about excess returns that is not contained in these yields. In this view, the impossibility is, so to speak, irreducible. If this view is correct, there is something deeply inadequate about affine modelling.

Alternatively one can argue that, admittedly, three yields do not contain all the available information about excess returns, but more yields *in principle* could – and the preceding argument shows how they could be constructed. However, *in practice* these $n + m$ yields do not predict well, because they

---

[23] Cieslak and Povala (2010a), p. 3.

constitute a very poor set of coordinates onto which to project the excess return information: in an $n + m$-dimensional space, the forward-rate 'axes' are almost co-linear, and a small measurement error can translate into a large difference in the resulting projections onto the coordinate axes. And, as we argued, despite being orthogonal, principal components do not fare much better, because, for yield-curve–related problems, noise easily contaminates the components of order higher than three: even if we use principal components, the problems stemming from the strong correlation between the original variables do not completely go away.

It is important to note that in this view essentially affine modelling with yield-curve–based variables is in (practical) troubles, but not affine modelling *tout court*: there is nothing stopping us from using a market price of risk of the form (27.20), and using the yield-curve–related and macro quantities as state variables, without translating them onto the equivalent special-yields coordinates. Indeed we shall present in Chapter 35 a model that, albeit in reduced form, reflects exactly this approach.

So, yes, we may well need five factors, but projecting these factors onto lots of highly colinear forward rates, or lots of difficult-to-estimate principal components, is not a good idea. No surprise then, that, as we saw in Section 26.8, the Cochrane–Piazzesi factor turned out to be not so robust out of sample! The idea of choosing an augmented state vector (ie, of using five instead of three forward rates) is correct, but their choice of coordinates poor. As Cieslak and Povala (2010a) point out, 'although the CP [Cochrane and Piazzesi] factor captures an important element of the risk premium, its coefficient estimates are noisy, creating a wedge between in- and out-of-sample forecasts'.[24]

Switching to principal component coordinates does not improve much on the situation – after all, high-order principal components are just 'wild' linear combination of many positive and negative yields; the higher the order, the more the oscillations between positive and negative signs in the loadings.

What are we to do then? The next section can give us a god idea about how to proceed. It is important to stress, however, that we are finally understanding why we may need more than three yield-curve variables if we want to explain not just today's yield curve, but also bond excess returns.

27.5   THE WORK OF CIESLAK AND POVALA

27.5.1   The Set-Up and Main Features

The literature surveyed in the previous sections makes clear that there are two sources of predictability of excess returns:

1. one is linked to the information that can be extracted from the yield curve; the earlier studies by Fama, Bliss, Shiller and Campbell, and the more recent work by Cochrane, Piazzesi and Radwanski all fall in this category;

---

[24] p. 32.

2. one is linked to the information that can be extracted from macro variables; as we explained the information in the latter is not fully spanned by the information retrievable from the former.

Cieslak and Povala (2010a, 2010b) ask whether these two domains can be united in a coherent framework.

Their approach rests on their claim that interest rates move on two different frequencies: a slow and persistent component, made up of

- 'adjustments in short rate expectations that may take decades to unfold'; this component, in the view of the authors, is highly persistent (has very low reversion speed), and is 'linked economically and statistically with the shifting long-run mean of inflation and savings rate';[25]
- and short-lived fluctuations with a quick reversion speed and which are specific to each maturity; these higher-frequency fluctuations are called 'cycles'.

As a proxy for the persistent component the authors choose weighted moving averages either of core inflation or of the savings rate. Then they operationally define the cycles as the stationary deviations in the long-term relationship between the level of yields and the slowly moving (persistent) factor. Cycles, as we shall see, play an important role in explaining excess returns, because they are highly significant predictors of yield changes.

Given their definition as the deviations of two (as we shall see, co-integrated) variables, cycles play a very similar role to the factors identified by Radwanski (2010). With a very broad brush, the intuition, once again, is that a higher value of the cycle (of the deviation) today will lead to lower yields next month, and hence to higher excess returns. We shall comment in what follows on how deeply this analogy can be pushed.

When cycles are used to predict excess returns, Cieslak and Povala find a much higher degree of predictability (a much higher R^2) than previously reported in the literature – so high, indeed, that they claim that their findings set a new benchmark for bond returns predictability. Let's look at the argument and the methodological set-up more precisely.

27.5.2 The Investigation Methodology and Results

Cieslak and Povala start from the definition of yields as the $\mathbb{P}$-measure (real-world) expectation of the future path of the short rate plus a risk premium component. In discrete time this means:

$$y_t^{(n)} = \underbrace{\frac{1}{n}\mathbb{E}^{\mathbb{P}}\left[\sum_{i=0}^{n-1} r_{t+i}\right]}_{\text{expectation}} + \underbrace{rpy_t^{(n)}}_{\text{risk premium}} . \tag{27.26}$$

[25] p. 1.

In keeping with their two-frequency description of the economy, the authors then posit that the short rate should evolve as the sum of a highly persistent (actually, unit-root) component, τ_t, and a quickly-mean-reverting $AR(1)$ component, x_t, with autoregression coefficient ϕ_x:

$$r_t = \rho_0 + \overbrace{\underbrace{\rho_\tau \tau_t}_{\text{unit-root part}} + \underbrace{\rho_x x_t}_{\text{AR(1) part}}}^{\text{two factors differing in persistence}} . \tag{27.27}$$

Given the value of the short rate at time t, we can easily write the expression for its value i periods ahead:

$$r_{t+i} = \rho_0 + \rho_\tau \tau_{t+i} + \rho_x x_{t+i}. \tag{27.28}$$

But, since the quickly mean-reverting component follows an $AR(1)$ process, we can write for the quickly mean-reverting part

$$x_{t+1} = \mu_x + \phi_x x_t + \sigma_x \epsilon^x_{t+1}. \tag{27.29}$$

By iterating and by direct substitution into Equation (27.26) one gets

$$y_t^{(n)} = \underbrace{b_0^{(n)} + b_\tau^{(n)} \tau_t + b_x^{(n)} x_t +}_{\text{expectation}} \underbrace{rpy_t^{(n)}}_{\text{risk premium}} \tag{27.30}$$

$$y_t^{(n)} = \underbrace{b_0^{(n)} + b_\tau^{(n)} \tau_t}_{\text{persistent component}} + \underbrace{b_x^{(n)} x_t + rpy_t^{(n)}}_{\text{transitory component}} \tag{27.31}$$

with

$$b_\tau^{(n)} = \rho_\tau \tag{27.32}$$

and

$$b_x^{(n)} = \frac{1}{n} \rho_x \frac{\phi_x^n - 1}{\phi_x - 1}. \tag{27.33}$$

Cieslak and Povala therefore define as the maturity-dependent cycle the quantity $\tilde{c}_t(n)$, given by

$$\tilde{c}_t^{(n)} \equiv b_x^{(n)} x_t + rpy_t^{(n)}. \tag{27.34}$$

It is important to note that the contributions to the cycles from the risk premia and the expectation components vary with maturity. So, for instance, the risk premium for $n = 1$ is, of course, 0, and its associated cycle purely captures changes in short-rate expectations. However, things change as the maturity increases: because of its fast mean-reversion, the contribution from the $AR(1)$ process, ie, the coefficient $b_x^{(n)}$, becomes smaller and smaller, expectations become less and less important and risk premia contribute more and more. This makes intuitive sense: we do not expect investors to have particularly strong views about the short rate in, say, ten years' time; nor do we expect risk premia to be major contributors to the two-year yield.

What about the persistent component? This is linked by Cieslak and Povala to the time series of inflation, CPI_t, which is assumed to follow

$$CPI_t = \tau_t^{CPI} + CPI_t^c, \tag{27.35}$$

where CPI_t^c denotes a cyclical contribution to inflation, and τ_t^{CPI} a persistent (no-mean-reversion) inflation time-varying endpoint:[26]

$$\tau_t^{CPI} = \tau_{t-1}^{CPI} + \epsilon_t^\tau. \tag{27.36}$$

A proxy for this persistent endpoint, τ_t^{CPI}, can be created as weighted moving average of past inflation data:

$$\tau_t^{CPI} = \frac{\sum_{i=0}^{t-1} v^i CPI_{t-i}}{\sum_{i=0}^{t-1} v^i}. \tag{27.37}$$

(In Equation (27.37) the weight parameter, v, is set to 0.987, and the sum runs over 120 monthly observations. It can be shown that the estimator (27.37) is optimal and maximally robust when one wants to estimate a parameter, but one is uncertain about the true data-generating process, and wants to make sure that the estimator is robust across different models. See, in this respect, Evans, Honkapohja and Williams (2010) for a precise discussion, or Evans and Honkapohja (2009) for a more general account.)

Operationally, the cycles are therefore obtained as follows. First yields are regressed against the *contemporaneous* persistent component calculated as per Equation (27.37):

$$y_t^{(n)} = b_0^{(n)} + b_\tau^{(n)} \tau_t + \epsilon_t^{(n)}. \tag{27.38}$$

Looking at Equations (27.31) and (27.34), it is clear that what has been 'left over' in the regression (27.38) is just the cycle, $c_t^{(n)}$. Therefore the cycle is calculated as the 'residual'[27]

$$c_t^{(n)} = y_t^{(n)} - \left[b_0^{(n)} + b_\tau^{(n)} \tau_t \right]$$

$$= y_t^{(n)} - \left[b_0^{(n)} + b_\tau^{(n)} \left(\frac{\sum_{i=0}^{t-1} v^i CPI_{t-i}}{\sum_{i=0}^{t-1} v^i} \right) \right]. \tag{27.39}$$

As mentioned in the previous section, cycles represent deviations from the long-term relationship between yields and the slow-moving component of inflation. It is just as well then that statistical tests strongly reject the hypothesis that cycles may be unit root (ie, have zero reversion speed).

---

[26] We appended a superscipt CPI to the quantity τ_t to indicate that the persistent component was estimated using inflation data. A parallel treatment can be carried out using as the macroeconomic variable the savings rate. Cieslak and Povala show that qualitatively the final results are little changed by the precise choice of the persistent variable.

[27] To be precise, one should distinguish between the 'true' (and unknown) coefficients a and b in the regression $y = a + bx + \epsilon$, and their estimated counterparts, $\hat{a}$ and $\hat{b}$. To keep the notation light we will not make this distinction, but please don't tell your econometrician friends.

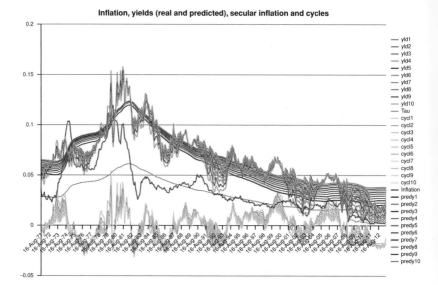

Figure 27.1 Inflation, yields (real and predicted), secular inflation and cycles. The top jagged lines (labelled yld1 to yld10) show the time series of the market yields from the early 1970s to the mid-2010s; the blue jagged line labelled Inflation shows the yearly inflation over the same period; the smooth pink line labelled Tau shows the long-term inflation, calculated using Equation (27.37); the smooth lines labelled predy1 to predy10 show the yield predicted by the terms $b_0^{(n)}$ and $b_\tau^{(n)} \tau_t$ in regression (27.38); and the lines at the bottom of the graph labelled cycl1 to cycl10 show the cycles calculated using Equation (27.39).

Figure 27.1 shows what the cycles look like. More precisely, the top jagged lines (labelled yld1 to yld10) show the time series of the market yields from the early 1970s to the mid-2010s; the blue jagged line labelled Inflation shows the yearly inflation over the same period; the smooth pink line labelled Tau shows the long-term (secular) inflation, calculated using Equation (27.37); the smooth lines labelled predy1 to predy10 show the yield predicted by the terms $b_0^{(n)}$ and $b_\tau^{(n)} \tau_t$ in regression (27.38); and the lines at the bottom of the graph labelled cycl1 to cycl10 show the cycles calculated using Equation (27.39). Note how smooth the predicted yields are, and how jagged – and strongly mean-reverting – the cycles.

Why are cycles important? Because, in the authors' model, cycles are highly significant predictors of yield changes. To show that this is indeed the case, the authors carry another regression, this time using as left-hand variable the time-t change in the n-maturity yield, $\Delta y_t^{(n)}$, against the *previous-time* values of the cycle, $c_{t-\Delta t}^{(n)}$, of the persistent component, $\tau_{t-\Delta t}$, and of the the yield change, $\Delta y_{t-\Delta t}^{(n)}$,

$$\Delta y_t^{(n)} = a_0 + a_c c_{t-\Delta t}^{(n)} + a_y \Delta y_{t-\Delta t}^{(n)} + a_\tau \tau_{t-\Delta t} + \epsilon_{t+1}. \tag{27.40}$$

When they do so, they find that the (negative) coefficient a_c associated with the cycles is highly significant.[28] It is the statistical significance of the negative coefficient that suggests the interpretation offered in the previous section, according to which a *higher* value of the cycle at time $t - \Delta t$ is associated with a *lower* value for the yield at time t, and hence to a *higher* excess return.

This intuition is made precise with the following analysis of excess returns. After estimating the cycles using Equation (27.39), these are now 'known quantities'. As we have seen, cycles are maturity dependent. Six of these maturity-dependent cycles (ie, those associated with maturities of 1, 2, 5, 7, 10 and 20 years) are then used as regressors to explain excess returns:

$$xret_{t+1}^{(n)} = \delta_0 + \sum_{i=1,6} \delta_i c_t^{(i)} + \epsilon_{t+1}^{(n)}. \tag{27.41}$$

To establish a fair horse race, Cieslak and Povala also use the six forward rates of maturities of 1, 2, 5, 7, 10 and 20 years as alternative regressors. This is therefore an extended Cochrane–Piazzesi model. They find that in all samples 'and across all maturities, cycles give much stronger evidence of predictability than do forward rates',[29] a conclusion that is not changed by choosing different maturities, or increasing the number of forward rates. More precisely, the R^2 obtained using cycles varies from 0.43 to almost 0.60 for the whole-sample studies, to be contrasted with an R^2 ranging from (approximately) 0.20 to 0.30 when forward rates are used.

These R^2 are very impressive – perhaps too much so. To see whether overfitting may be at play, Cieslak and Povala carry out a very powerful test, using a restricted return-predicting factor. This is how they do it.

27.5.3 The Link with Forward-Rate-Based RPFs

Using six regressors may seem extravagant. So as not to miss the wood for the trees, and (changing metaphor) to make the horse race with the Cochrane–Piazzesi thoroughbred even fairer, Cieslak and Povala set up a restricted cycle-based return-predicting factor, and pit it against the Cochrane–Piazzesi restricted factor. As usual, the tent factor is used as the benchmark to 'beat', but, as we shall see the conclusions they draw will apply just as well to other factors (like the slope or the bat).

To perform the comparison Cieslak and Povala therefore define a single forecasting factor, $\widehat{cf}$, which they build as follows.

---

[28] The reader should be careful here: the regression in Equation (27.39) is carried out against the *same-time* values of the persistent component, τ_t. The predictive regression in Equation (27.40) links changes in yields at time t to cycles (and changes in yields, and changes in the persistent variable, τ) at time $t - \Delta t$.

[29] p. 13.

They start from the definition of the maturity-dependent cycle in Equation (27.34):

$$\widetilde{c}_t^{(n)} \equiv b_x^{(n)} x_t + rpy_t^{(n)}. \tag{27.42}$$

Recall that the 'composition of' (the information conveyed by) the cycle depends on its maturity, with the cycle for $n = 1$ containing no information about risk premia (because $rpy_t^{(1)} = 0$), and a lot of information about expectations. As a consequence $\widetilde{c}_t^{(1)}$ 'captures variation[s] in short rate expectations $(b_x^{(1)} x_t)$, but not in premia.[30] [...] Therefore a natural way to decompose the transitory variation in the yield curve into the expectations part and the premium part is by estimating[31]

$$xret_{t+1}^{(n)} = \alpha_0 + \alpha_1^{(n)} c_t^{(1)} + \alpha_2^{(n)} c_t^{(n)} + \epsilon_{t+1}^{(n)} \quad n \geq 2.' \tag{27.43}$$

Next Cieslak and Povala look at the average excess returns, $\overline{xret}_{t+1}$, (averaged over maturities), and use as regressors to predict the average excess returns (i) the expectation-only-related factor, $c_t^{(1)}$, and (ii) the average, $\overline{c}_t$, of the maturity-dependent cycle factors, $c_t^{(i)}$, $i = 2, 3, \ldots, n$:

$$\overline{xret}_{t+1} = \gamma_0 + \gamma_1 c_t^{(1)} + \gamma_2 \overline{c}_t + \overline{\epsilon}_{t+1}. \tag{27.44}$$

This is their single forecasting factor, $\widehat{cf}_t$:

$$\widehat{cf}_t \equiv \gamma_0 + \gamma_1 c_t^{(1)} + \gamma_2 \overline{c}_t. \tag{27.45}$$

Once the Cieslak-and-Povala single forecasting factor is built, they pit it against the restricted single-tent factor built by Cochrane and Piazzesi. When they do so, once again, they find that the cycle-based factor, $\widehat{cf}$, explains a lot more than the restricted tent factor. (The R^2 coefficients they find range from a minimum of 0.41 (2-year maturity) to a maximum of 0.56 (15-year maturity).) What is more interesting, however, is the discussion of *why* forward-rate-based regressions encounter some intrinsic limitations.

27.5.4   Intrinsic Limitations of Forward-Rate-Based Factors

To see the gist of the argument, following Cieslak and Povala (2010a, 2010b) we write the Cochrane–Piazzesi-factor-based regression as

$$\overline{xret}_{t+1} = \gamma_0 + \sum_{i=1,5} \gamma_i f_t^{(i)} + \overline{\epsilon}_{t+1}. \tag{27.46}$$

We want to translate the tent into the Cieslak and Povala vocabulary of cycles and persistent components. To do so, they first make use of the regression (34.38a)

$$y_t^{(n)} = b_0^{(n)} + b_\tau^{(n)} \tau_t + \epsilon_t^{(n)} \tag{27.47}$$

---

[30] p. 8.   [31] p. 14.

of the definition of yield, $y_t^{(n)}$,

$$y_t^{(n)} = -\frac{1}{n} p_t^{(n)} \tag{27.48}$$

and of the definition of forward rate, $f_t^{(n)}$,

$$f_t^{(n)} = p_t^{(n-1)} - p_t^{(n)} \tag{27.49}$$

to obtain

$$\overline{xret}_{t+1} = \gamma_0 + \tau_t \left(\sum_{i=1,m} \overline{\gamma}_i \right) + \tau_t \left(\sum_{i=1,m} \widetilde{\gamma}_i c_t^{(i)} \right) + \overline{\epsilon}_{t+1}, \tag{27.50}$$

with

$$\overline{\gamma}_i = \gamma_i \left[i b_\tau^{(i)} - (i-1) b_\tau^{(i-1)} \right] \tag{27.51}$$

and

$$\widetilde{\gamma}_i \begin{cases} = i(\gamma_i - \gamma_{i+1}) & \text{for } 1 < i < m \\ = i\gamma_i & \text{for } i = m \end{cases}. \tag{27.52}$$

Exercise 70 *Prove Equation (27.50).*

To repeat: Equation (27.50) is just the Cochrane–Piazzesi restricted tent, after the coordinates are changed from forward rates to cycles and persistent component. This part of the exercise is analogous to the translation we carried out when we moved from the forward-rate to the yield coordinates.

It is then easy to show that, if the coefficients γ_i in the tent regression approximately add up to 1 (as they do), then so will the coefficients $\overline{\gamma}_i$. And, incidentally, this will also apply to any return-predicting-factor (such as the slope or the bat!) that has roughly equal and offsetting coefficients on the various forward rates.

However, what Cieslak and Povala have shown is that, *by itself*, the persistent component, τ_t, plays a negligible role in predicting returns. Therefore, if this result holds, the coefficient $\left(\sum_{i=1,m} \overline{\gamma}_i \right)$ of τ_t should be close to zero. Therefore

> the OLS [Ordinary Least Square regression] tries to remove the common τ_t from forward rates, while preserving a linear combination of the cycles. Thus, forecasting returns with forward rates embeds an implicit restriction on the slope [ie, non-intercept] coefficients: γ_i's are constrained by the dual role of removing the persistent component and minimizing the prediction error of excess returns using the cycles.[32] [...] As a consequence [...] the commonly used forward rate factor is, to a good approximation, a constrained linear combination of interest rate cycles. The constraint is introduced by the persistence of yields.[33]

---

[32] p. 18.   [33] p. 2.

This gives another perspective as to why forward rates may be an 'awkward' set of variables onto which to project term premia.

27.5.5   Implications for Term-Structure Models

The message from investigations like those of Cochrane and Piazzesi[34] is that in order to model the evolution of the yield curve under $\mathbb{P}$ and under $\mathbb{Q}$, one needs

- return-forecasting factors (such as the tent) which do nothing to price better the cross section of market yields, but are essential to describe the market price of risk;
- yield-curve factors (such as the first three principal components), which are essential to fit to prices, but close-to-useless to predict returns.[35]

According to Cieslak and Povala what one needs are instead three factors (two for the risk premium, and one for the expectation):

$$y_t^{(n)} = A^{(n)} + B_\tau^{(n)} \tau_t^{CPI} + B_r^{(n)} c_t^{(1)} + B_x^{(n)} \widehat{cf}_t + e_t^{(n)}. \qquad (27.53)$$

This regression explains on average 99.68% of the variation in yields for all maturities out to 20 years (with a minimum explained variance of 98.8% for the 20-year yield, and 100% – by construction – for the 1-year yield.) As one should expect given their interpretation, the loadings (regression coefficients) onto the regressor $c_t^{(1)}$ (the 'fast cycle') decline with maturity; the slow-moving ('secular') factor τ_t^{CPI} has a level effect; and the regression coefficients of the factor $\widehat{cf}_t$ become larger as the maturity increases. As Cieslak and Povala (2010) say, their approach 'relies on extending the information set [...] to contain both yields and [the persistent component] τ_t. Models that exploit only yield curve information to represent pricing factors [...] are likely to miss the importance of disentangling the different factor frequencies.'[36] The important thing to note is that the Cieslak–Povala approach describes the variability in market yields as well as three principal components, but predicts excess returns much better than three, or five (or, for that matter, twenty) principal components can. This is important.

27.5.6   Re-Interpretation of the Cieslak–Povala RPF: Conditional Slope and Level

Let's look in some detail at the restricted Cieslak and Povala return-predicting factor. We can write it as follows:

$$\overline{xret}_{t+1} = \gamma_0 + \gamma_1 c_t^{(1)} + \gamma_2 \bar{c}_t + \overline{\epsilon}_{t+1}^{(n)}. \qquad (27.54)$$

---

[34] The Cochrane–Piazzesi model is not unique in this respect. Other recent approaches, such as, for instance, the model by Adrian, Crump, and Moench (2013) discussed in Chapter 34, reach similar conclusions.

[35] In passing, we remark that if the return-predicting factor is the second principal component this harsh dichotomy is too harsh.

[36] p. 23.

It is important for the future discussion to note that, when the regression is carried out on US\$ and GBP data, the coefficient γ_1 (ie, the loading onto the short cycle) turns out to be significantly negative, the coefficient γ_2 (ie, the loading onto the average cycle) is significantly positive and $|\gamma_2| > |\gamma_1|$. For reasons that will become apparent in a few lines, we prefer to work with positive coefficients and we introduce γ_3:

$$\gamma_3 = -\gamma_1. \tag{27.55}$$

With uncanny foresight we also choose to write

$$\gamma_2 = \gamma_3 + \Delta\gamma, \tag{27.56}$$

with $\Delta\gamma > 0$ because $|\gamma_2| > |\gamma_1|$.

With these two definitions we therefore have

$$\overline{xret}_{t+1} = \gamma_0 - \gamma_3 c_t^{(1)} + (\gamma_3 + \Delta\gamma)\bar{c}_t + \bar{\epsilon}_{t+1}^{(n)}. \tag{27.57}$$

Next, recall that the two cycles are given by the residuals of the regression of the 1-year yield and average yield against the slowly moving inflation proxy, τ_t:

$$c_t^{(1)} = y_t^{(1)} - \left[b_0^{(1)} + b_\tau^{(1)}\tau_t\right] \tag{27.58}$$

and

$$\bar{c}_t = \bar{y}_t - \left[\widehat{b}_0 + \widehat{b}_\tau \tau_t\right], \tag{27.59}$$

respectively.

Substituting these expressions into Equation (27.57) gives

$$\overline{xret}_{t+1} = \gamma_0$$

$$+ \gamma_3 \left\{ \underbrace{\left(\bar{y}_t - y_t^{(1)}\right)}_{\text{actual slope}} - \left[\underbrace{\left(\widehat{b}_0 + \widehat{b}_\tau \tau_t\right) - \left(b_0^{(1)} + b_\tau^{(1)}\tau_t\right)}_{\text{regression-predicted slope}}\right] \right\}$$

$$+ \Delta\gamma \left[\underbrace{\bar{y}_t}_{\text{actual level}} - \underbrace{\left(\widehat{b}_0 + \widehat{b}_\tau \tau_t\right)}_{\text{regression-predicted level}} \right]$$

$$+ \bar{\epsilon}_{t+1}^{(n)}. \tag{27.60}$$

Exercise 71 *Derive Equation (27.60).*

Let's look carefully at the various terms for a moment, beginning from the quantities in curly brackets. The first, $\left(\bar{y}_t - y_t^{(1)}\right)$, is just a reasonable proxy for the observed yield-curve slope at time t. Then the terms $\left(\widehat{b}_0 + \widehat{b}_\tau \tau_t\right)$ and $\left(b_0^{(1)} + b_\tau^{(1)}\tau_t\right)$ are the CPI-regression–based predictions of the average yield and the 1-year yield, respectively. Therefore the difference $\left(\widehat{b}_0 + \widehat{b}_\tau \tau_t\right) - \left(b_0^{(1)} + b_\tau^{(1)}\tau_t\right)$ is just the regression-predicted slope. This means that the quantity in curly brackets is the difference between the real slope and the regression-predicted slope.

Moving to the term in square brackets that multiplies $\Delta\gamma$, $\bar{y}_t$ is an obvious proxy for the level of the yield curve, and the quantity $\left(\widehat{b}_0 + \widehat{b}_\tau \tau_t\right)$ is, by definition, the regression-based prediction of the same quantity. The square bracket in the third line of Equation (27.60) therefore contains the difference between the actual yield-curve level and the level prediction by the regression. We call in the following the distances of level and slope from their local regression-predicted values the 'conditional' distances.

This simple rearrangement therefore shows that in the Cieslak and Povala restricted factor no single 'typical' slope or typical 'level' of the yield curve is a significant predictor of excess returns: there are instead conditional 'typical' levels and slopes of the yield curve associated with any value of the slow-moving inflation proxy, τ_t. Indeed, from Equation (27.60) we see that, if the long-term expected inflation, τ_t, is high, then the level of the yield curve should be high – as shown by the term $\left(\widehat{b}_0 + \widehat{b}_\tau \tau_t\right)$. Then, if we rewrite $\left(\widehat{b}_0 + \widehat{b}_\tau \tau_t\right) - \left(b_0^{(1)} + b_\tau^{(1)} \tau_t\right)$ as $\left(\widehat{b}_0 - b_0^{(1)}\right) + \left(\widehat{b}_\tau - b_\tau^{(1)}\right)\tau_t$, and we remember that $\widehat{b}_\tau - b_\tau^{(1)}$ is negative, we see just as easily that the regression predicts that the slope should be low when the long-term inflation is high.

This allows us to understand very clearly the Cieslak and Povala return-predicting factor: we expected a high excess return (the return predicting factor is high)

- when the actual slope of the yield curve is higher than what it 'should be' (given the regression prediction);
- when the actual level of the yield curve is higher than what it 'should be' (again, given the regression prediction).

This interpretation gives an interesting twist to the slope (and level) interpretation and significance. Whether we expect to make money by engaging in the carry trade does not depend on whether the slope of the yield curve is higher or lower than a fixed reference level, but whether it is higher or lower than the *inflation-predicted slope*. And the same applies to the level – which by itself, as we remember well, is not a statistically significant predictor.

One last observation: the actual and predicted slope are strongly co-integrated, and so are the actual and predicted yield-curve levels.[37] So, when 'rates are higher than they should be' they will, on average, come down, and the carry strategy will make money; and when the yield curve is 'steeper than it should be', it will on average flatten, and this will also make money for the fund-short, invest-long carry strategy.

---

[37] *Very* imprecisely, we say that two variables are co-integrated when their difference displays a mean-reverting behaviour (ie, the difference does not wander off to plus or minus infinity). A bit (but not much) more precisely, take two variables, which in isolation are not stationary. If there is a linear combination of these two variables that is stationary, then the two original variables are said to be co-integrated.

It all makes perfect sense, and we now intuitively understand why the Cieslak and Povala return-predicting factor can perform so much better than the slope or the Cochrane–Piazzesi factor: because it contains information about the *conditional* slope and level that the yield-curve–based approaches do not have.

27.6 RELATED WORK

As usual, I have preferred to deal in some detail with a few representative studies in the topic at hand (excess returns in the present case), rather than skim over the surface of the vast literature. A few pointers to related work would, however, not go amiss. The reader may also want to compare the findings reported below with the discussion of the literature on the spanning problem in Section 27.4.

First of all, the discussion in Chapter 25 of this book has been devoted to the *empirical* estimation of excess returns. In Chapters 26 and 27 we have looked at the predictions of excess returns from affine models but one may expect that adding the no-arbitrage information models 'know about' may improve the quality of the model predictions over the purely statistical ones. (This assumes, of course, that the models are flexible enough to incorporate in their parametrization all the relevant econometric information – such as, say, the dependence of excess returns on the slope of the yield curve). Joslin, Le and Singleton (2013) provide a sobering rebuttal of this view in their aptly named paper, "Why Gaussian Macro-Finance Models Are (Nearly) Unconstrained Factor-VARs." The main conclusion they draw is that 'canonical MTSMs [macro-dynamic term structure models][38] typically do not offer any new insights into economic questions regarding the historical distribution of macros variables and yields [and hence excess returns], over and above what one can learn from economics-free factor VAR [Vector Auto-Regression models]'.[39] They note, however, that

> [w]hen the no-arbitrage structure of a [macro-dynamic term structure model] is combined with over-identifying restrictions[40] on the parameters governing the physical [$\mathbb{P}$-measure] distribution of [the state variables], their dynamic properties within a [macro-dynamic term structure model] and its factor-VAR counterpart may differ. It then becomes an empirical question as to whether any such differences are economically significant.[41]

---

[38] Loosely speaking, a macrodynamic term structure model is model that includes among its state variables both macrofinancial quantities (such as inflation) and yield-curve variables (for instance, yields or combinations thereof, such as Principal Components).

[39] p. 605.

[40] When the restriction imposed on a model (such as, for instance, the conditions of no-arbitrage) are just enough to determine the model parameters, the restrictions are said to be 'just-identifying'. If, after the desired restrictions are imposed, there still are free model parameters left, then the restrictions are said to be under-identifying. If the model parameters cannot, in general, exactly satisfy all the imposed restrictions, then they are said to be 'over-identifying'.

[41] pp. 616–617.

They also point out that a common 'over-identifying restriction' is the imposition that the reversion-speed matrix in the real-world measure, $\mathcal{K}^{\mathbb{P}}$, should be diagonal. Indeed, Diebold and Li (2006) find that imposing this restriction on yield-curve-based term-structure models improves out-of-sample forecasts of bond yields. This restriction will be reconsidered in Chapter 33.

Duffee (2010) looks at the maximum Sharpe Ratios predicted by multi-factor Gaussian term structure models for excess returns, and finds that they are 'astronomically high'. This is worrying, because '[f]lexibility and overfitting go hand-in-hand.[42] Estimated models may be uncovering sample-specific patterns instead of the true data-generating process. [...] Large Sharpe Ratios are evidence of overfitting.'[43] He tries to overcome this problem by imposing constraints on the maximum Sharpe Ratios. He finds that doing so has two main effects. First, models than do not incorporate these Sharpe Ratio constraints imply than investors may have been smarter than perhaps they actually were, in the sense that according to the implausibly-high-Sharpe-Ratio models 'investors anticipated much of the decline in bond yields from the end of 1988 through the end of 2000; [...] For reasonable Sharpe Ratios, little to none of this drop was expected.'[44] The second effect of constraining the maximum Sharpe Ratio is that the predictability of excess returns of short-dated bonds is significantly reduced – more so than the predictability of long bonds is reduced. Duffee's observation about how much of the drop in yields is predicted by a model is very important because of the secular and unprecedented decline in yields from the late 1980s to the late 2010s. Clearly, a 'dumb' strategy of always being long long-maturity bonds and funding at the short end of the yield curve would have been profitable, irrespective of any term premium.

Finally, Cochrane (2015) provides an interesting perspective on the Cieslak-Povala results. The main virtue of the approach, he claims, comes from the de-trending of the fall in yields Duffee (2010) refers to above afforded by a macrofinancial quantity that also fell dramatically during the same period. Now, the level of rates and inflation are obviously linked. However, Cieslak and Povala find a similar (and high) R^2 when their 'predictive residual' is formed by regressing yields against the savings rate – and it is far more difficult to image a direct economic link between yields and savings. This reinforces the claim that 'any' smooth time series that happened to decline (for economically related or independent reasons) during the same period would have produced a similar de-trending. We discuss this point in Chapter 29, where we review the topic of spanning.

---

[42] See Abu-Mostafa, Magdon-Ismail and Lin (2012), Chapters 2 and 4 in particular, on this important point.

[43] p. 1.   [44] p. 3.

CHAPTER 28

Why Is the Slope a Good Predictor?

"Anything that happens, happens.
Anything that, in happening, causes something else to happen,
causes something else to happen.
Anything that, in happening, causes itself to happen again, happens
again.
It doesn't necessarily do it in chronological order, though."
–Douglas Adams, *Mostly Harmless*

28.1 THE PURPOSE OF THIS CHAPTER

We have seen in the previous chapters that the slope is one of the most important return-predicting factors. There may be (slightly) more powerful predictors, but we have made the case that the slope tells a substantial part of the story. We stress that we do not claim that the slope is the only predictor. In this chapter we simply argue that it explains an important part of the observed return predictability. Even as they propose the tent-shapes return-predicting factor, Cochrane and Piazzesi (2004) agree on this point. Cieslak and Povala (2010a, 2010b) implicitly qualify the importance of the slope predictor by making it conditional (on where it 'should be' given the long-term inflation) – see the interpretation we give in Equation (27.56). And we have also shown that bat-like or tent-like return-predicting factors or 'conditional slopes' can be interpreted as 'refinements' of the slope predictor.[1] In sum: from the empirical perspective, we can confidently say that the (unconditional) slope still remains an important factor to predict excess returns.[2] What we have not answered is the all-important question of why this should be the case.

---

[1] In addition to Cochrane and Piazzesi (2004, 2005) and Radwanski (2010), Hellerstein (2011) also finds a tent-shaped factor in a number of currencies, Garcia and Luger (2102) find a tent-shaped factor after constructing an equilibrium model of the term structure of interst rates (see their figure 2 on p. 1032), and, as we discuss later, Xiong and Yan (2010) do so by introducing heterogeneity in expectations.

[2] Bauer and Hamilton (2015) argue that the slope is *the* one and only robust predictor of excess returns. See the discussion in Section 29.3.

In this chapter we present four possible explanations for this empirically observed regularity. In a nutshell,

- the first suggests that 'we now know' what earlier investors could not have known (for instance, because their record of data was shorter, or their statistical methods less powerful);
- the second points to the possibility that the risk aversion of investor may depend on business-cycle–related economic conditions;
- the third accounts for the slope dependence by invoking heterogeneous beliefs associated with different cohorts of (smart and noise) traders and wealth fluctuations between the two classes; and
- the fourth possible explanation is that investors guess (on average) correctly the direction of rate moves, but over-react. By doing so, upward-sloping curve become 'too' steep, and so do downward-sloping yield curves.

We also present wider empirical evidence about excess returns and return-predicting factors – evidence that looks beyond the narrow history of bond prices, in the direction of the real economy.

28.2   WHAT DOES *NOT* QUALIFY
AS AN EXPLANATION

The first thing to explain is why anything needs explaining in the first place. Surely, one is tempted to say, if I can invest in a 10-year bond at 6% and fund myself for one year at 1%, I *must* be making money? And isn't the difference between the 10-year and the 1-year rates just the slope of the yield curve? The case is open and shut. Or is it?

As I have argued in previous chapters, *just* because long-dated yield (the yield at which we invest) is higher than short-dated one (the yield at which we fund ourselves) it does not mean that there is any money to be made. Recall from Section 24.2.2 that, if 'forwards come true' the long-duration strategy will not reap any profits, no matter how steep the yield curve is (ie, no matter how great the funding advantage – the difference between the investment yield and the funding rate – is). By 'forwards come true', remember, I mean that *future* short rate will follow the path (at least on average) traced by today's instantaneous *forward* rates. It is the expectation hypothesis again.

So, if the (positive or negative) steepness of the yield curve were all due to expectations, and if the expectations were (on average) correct, there would be no money to be made from the invest-long/fund-short strategy.

Of course, if one looked at the forward portion of the yield curve, say, five years in the future, and one systematically observed an upward-sloping forward yield curve, a far more convincing case could be made that this steepness may be due to risk premia – it is difficult to believe, after all, that investors should consistently have precise expectations about changes in rates five years or more in the future. But this is a different argument.

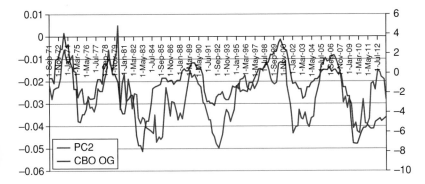

Figure 28.1 The time series of the second principal component from yield curve levels (left-hand y-axis, curve labelled PC2) and of the output gap (right-hand y-axis, curve labelled CBO OG) from the early 1970s to the mid-2010s.

28.3 EXCESS RETURNS, THE SLOPE AND THE REAL ECONOMY

Let us look at the significance of the slope from a different perspective: let us ask ourselves, that is, what aspects of the real economy may make the curve upward or downward sloping. There is a large body of research in this area, and here we only want to give a flavour of the arguments.

Let us take an indicator of real economic activity, namely the output gap. This is defined as the estimated difference between the potential and the actual GDP. A positive output gap indicates overutilization of the production capabilities of the economy, and vice versa for a negative gap.

Now, if the gap is positive, monetary authorities will tend to increase rates to cool the economy. They will signal their intentions, and the investors will incorporate these signals in the formation of their expectations about the path of future rates.[3] If this is the case, there should be a positive correlation between the slope of the yield curve and the output gap. We can test whether this is indeed the case.

Figure 28.1 shows the time series of the second principal component (roughly speaking, minus the yield curve slope) and of the output gap from the early 1970s to the mid-2010s. There is a clear relationship between the two quantities, and, indeed, the correlation of coefficient is a respectable 52%. (Both the intercept and the slope of the regression, by the way, are very highly

---

[3] By the way, the signals communicated by the central bankers are just one channel from the output gap to the investors' expectations. It is not that the output-gap statistics are secret, and investors have to rely only on the central banks' forward guidance: they can observe themselves the output gap using a Bloomberg terminal and form their own independent views about the actions of the monetary authorities. I am just trying to keep the story simple here.

significant.) This is in comforting agreement with work by Rudebusch and Wu (2008) and Bauer and Rudebusch (2010).

This sounds promising. 52% is the correlation we have obtained with just one regressor. When they decide their policy, central bankers do not just look at the output gap, but at a number of macroeconomic indicators. Surely, if we use a higher number of macroeconomic regressors – and check in a disciplined way that they are all significant and that we are not overfitting – we will explain more and more of the slope (which, in turn, we know significantly explains excess returns). If we did so, would we have come closer to understanding why the slope predicts excess returns? Would we have uncovered a deeper, macroeconomic, explanation for the slope-related statistical predictability of excess returns?

As things stand, not really. The output gap may well suggest to central bankers whether rates should be raised or lowered (thus steepening or flattening the yield curve). But if investors read, on average, the intentions of the monetary authorities correctly, then we are back to expectations. Yes, the curve may well become upward or downward sloping, but, in the little model depicted so far, this steepness is only due to expectations. And, as we argued in the previous section, if forwards come true (if the $\mathbb{P}$-measure expectations are realized), no excess return will be reaped from a buy-long/fund-short strategy.

More generally, we saw in Chapter 25 that, historically, the excess returns from the invest-long/fund-short strategy strongly depend on the phase of the business cycle. Recall, for instance, that Sharpe Ratios were positive in recessions, close to zero during expansions, and *very negative* during the second phase of expansions. (See again Table 25.1 in Chapter 25.) Now, during recessions monetary authorities typically cut the short rates, thereby creating an upward sloping yield curve. Similarly, during expansions, and, more precisely, during the *latter* phases of expansions, when the time has come to remove the punch bowl, central banks usually raise the short rates, and create a flat or even downward-sloping yield curve. And we observe that the Sharpe Ratios strongly depend on these different phases of the business cycle.

However, the yield curve assumes these shapes in recessions and expansion (upward- and downward-sloping, respectively) partly in expectation of future actions of the monetary authorities: if we *expect* rates to be, say, progressively lifted to cool the economy, yields (which, to a first approximation[4], are averages over these future expected paths) will increase with maturity. And vice versa when the economy is sputtering and needs the tonic of lower rates. But, in itself, this does *not* point to the steepness of the yield curve ('carry' and 'roll-down') as the explanation of the sign and magnitude of the excess returns. To repeat again: *no matter how steep the yield curve*, if 'forwards come true' – ie, if the *future* rates will exactly trace the path implied by today's *forward* rates – the invest-long/fund-short strategy will on average neither make nor lose any money. We are still in need of an explanation of why the slope of the yield curve has predictive power for excess returns.

---

[4] We say 'to a first approximation' because we are neglecting convexity.

Of course, if, say, investors were more risk averse in bad economic environments (in environments, that is, when rates are cut and the curve becomes steeper), this *could* provide an explanation. But, if this explanation were correct, the output gap, or the phase of the business cycle, or the slope of the yield curve would be a concomitant occurrence, not a cause, of the excess returns. Indeed, this explanation of the predictive power of the slope of the yield curve in terms of a concomitant increase in risk aversion is probably the one more commonly encountered in the literature,[5] probably because it avoids bringing into play either a subjective measure different from the objective measure or systematic errors in prediction – two concepts that are given enthusiastic endorsement by behavioural finance economists, and a similarly cold shoulder by rational-expectation-based economists.

To summarize: so far we have understood what does *not* qualify as an explanation for the dependence of excess returns on the slope of the yield. We have also proposed one mechanism that could explain the slope-dependence of excess returns and is fully compatible with (i) rational expectations and (ii) knowledge of the correct real world measure, $\mathbb{P}$: in this account investors simply become more risk averse in periods of economic distress.

In the remainder of the chapter we look at explanations that, in one respect or another, depart from either, or both, of the two assumptions that follow (ie, the perfect rationality of the expectations formed by investors, and the availability of a conditionally correct real-world distribution).

To understand the first of these alternative possible explanations of the predictive power of the slope we have to revisit a probability measure, which is neither the 'real-world', nor the risk-neutral measure: namely, the *subjective* measure.[6]

28.4 THE DATA-GENERATING, SUBJECTIVE AND RISK-NEUTRAL MEASURES

So far we have implicitly (and reasonably) assumed that investors form expectations on the basis of the same information available to the statistician or econometrician. But what if the forecasters had in the historical past 'interpreted' the statistical information with what we recognize today to be some bias? As Piazzesi, Salomoao and Schneider (2013) suggest,

> ...investors' historical predictions of excess returns may have been different from predictions found in today's statistical analysis. Investors may have not recognized the same patterns that we see today with the benefit of hindsight, at least not to the same extent...

So, in this description of the world, investors of yesteryears were simply not blessed with the abundance of statistical information we now possess, and

---

[5] See, eg, Campbell and Cochrane (1995/1999) for excess returns in the equity market; Bansal and Yaron (2004) and Gabaix (2012), who both look at this problem while trying to resolve a number of asset pricing puzzles; and Wachter (2006), who focusses on interest rates.

[6] See also the discussion of the subjective measure in Section 23.3.

therefore drew worse conclusions. In this view, the biasedness of the forecast is a small-sample problem, and, to explain the bias, we do not need to invoke any cognitive bias or bounded rationality.

However, there is a similar, but importantly different, explanation for the biasedness of expectations formed in the past, which points not to the paucity of the then-available information, but to systematic biases (say, over-reaction) which were *and still are* present in the expectation-formation process.

Piazzesi et al. (2013) pursue this line of reasoning by pointing to another possible explanation for the predictability linked to the risk-predicting factors, namely what they call 'risk assessment'. In this view, investors predict correctly (ie, unbiasedly and consistently with all the available statistical information) the regularities that the econometrician records (and that we have reported in previous chapters). However, in some states of the world they may perceive the fund-short/invest-long trade riskier than in other states of the world. Or they may simply be more risk averse in these states of the world. This, after all, is exactly the meaning of an expression for the market price of risk like

$$\lambda_t = \lambda_0 + \lambda_1 X_t: \tag{28.1}$$

when the factor, X_t, (the slope) is high (and λ_1 is positive) the compensation for bearing risk becomes higher.

Why should that be the case? If, as we have sketched earlier, the slope is high when things are bad (think of the rate-cutting programmes engaged in by the Fed in the wake of the 1998 Long-Term Capital Management crisis, of the 2001 bursting of the dot.com bubble, of the September 11 events or of the 2008 Lehman default – think, that is, of the 'Greenspan put'), then it is reasonable that investors should have felt a tad more cautious when these darkest of clouds were gathering over their heads. 'Feeling a tad more cautious' means that the compensation for risk should increase in these turbulent times (see Equation (28.1)); and since the turbulent times are linked (via 'Greenspan-put-like' policies) to steep upward-sloping yield curves, the shape of the yield curve becomes the tangible epiphany of the investors' behavioural response to turmoil.

As we mentioned in the previous section, in the literature this explanation has been the favoured one – partly because it 'rescues' the rationality of investors' formation of expectations.[7] The risk-assessment explanation, however, may be more economical, but is not the only possible alternative. We have mentioned the 'today-we-know-better' explanation. We present in what follows an explanation of the dependence of excess returns on the slope of the yield

---

[7] See, in this respect, Campbell and Cochrane (2005)(on the stock market), Bansal and Yaron (2004), Wachter (2006) (on interest rates) and Gabaix (2012) (for a resolution of a number of asset-pricing puzzles).

As Piazzesi et al. (2013) put it, '[m]ost quantitative asset pricing studies focus exclusively on risk assessment as the reason for predictability. They assume that investors' historical predictions were identical to (in-sample) predictions made today from statistical models. By construction, this approach rules out beliefs as a reason for predictability.'

curve based on the heterogeneity of beliefs, and an explanation based on an over-reaction argument. Before that, however, let's pause for a moment in order to understand the importance of what may otherwise seem to be hair splitting.

28.5 DOES IT MATTER?

> Nobody goes there anymore. It's too crowded!
> –*Attributed to Yogi Berra, about his favourite restaurant*

Deciding which explanation is correct can make for an exciting discussion in the senior common room of a Financial Economics department. But, from an investment perspective, does it matter which picture of the world is more correct? It certainly does. To see why, let's take the explanations in turn.

If today we are all smarter and wiser than investors were in the past (because today we know more about the behaviour of rates than earlier investors did and we can analyse data with fancier econometric techniques), we *could* make money, but only if a time machine could transport us to, say, the early 1980s. However, those naive days are, alas, gone. Today, we are *all* smarter, and therefore we will not make similar mistakes. The exceptional returns are in our historical record as a vestigial reminder of a more naive past, but there no longer are any exceptional returns to be made today. In this view, the fund-short/invest-long investment strategy would join the many 'anomalies' that, once discovered, are washed away by the efficiency of the market.

If the predictability comes from risk assessment, yes, there is extra expected return to be made in some (pretty scary) states of the world. However, unless we think that the market's assessment of how risky the future looks is wrong, or we are just more brave-hearted than the average investor, there is no *risk-adjusted* return to be made: from a Sharpe Ratio perspective, if investors have become more risk averse, they will require a higher return to make them accept the bearing of risk.

If, however, there are systematic and persistent cognitive biases in the expectation-formation process[8], then matters can look different. If *we* are statistically savvy and cooled-headed (or simply unencumbered by the institutional constraints that may fetter the large market investors), then we *can* make money.

There is a corollary to all of this. If the risk-assessment explanation is not the main part of the story (the people-become-more-cautious-in-scary-times explanation), then we have to distinguish between

- the probability distribution of asset returns (the 'measure') that is available to the econometrician (or, at least, to *today's* econometrician)[9];

---

[8] Cognitive biases are not enough. There must also be institutional constraints of such a nature as to hinder the efficiency-enforcing action of pseudo-arbitrageurs. See, in this respect, Shleifer and Vishny (1997) and Shleifer (2000).

[9] This measure is often referred to as the 'data-generating measure'.

- the subjective probability distribution generated by the forecasts of the (cognitively biased or ignorant) investors; and
- the risk-neutral distribution that we observe in the prices.

In the rest of this chapter we therefore look at the subjective probability, at the econometrician's (data-generating) distribution, and at the risk-neutral distribution. So do Piazzesi et al. (2013), and their Figure 2 is particularly illuminating in this respect.[10] These researchers take the now-we-know-better route. In Section 28.7 we take the persistent-cognitive-bias route. Despite the different starting points, we reach, as we shall see, similar conclusions. In particular, Piazzesi et al. (2013) find that 'survey forecasts of interest rates are made as if both the level and the slope of the yield curve are more persistent than under common statistical models'.[11]

What does this mean? Recall that the term 'persistent' refers to the effect of a random shock. If a process is highly persistent, it means that the effect of a shock is not 'mean-reverted' back to a stable reversion level with great speed. High reversion speed therefore means low persistence, and vice versa. As we shall see, we can explain (a lot of) the empirical evidence about return predictability by positing that investors 'overreact' in their assessment of how long and how far a tightening or easing cycle will go. This means that investors, in the simple model we present in Section 28.6, see a weaker speed of mean reversion in the process that drives rates, and hence, in agreement with Piazzesi et al. (2013), in their subjective distribution they see a higher persistence than in the statistical measure.

If the description of the world in the model presented in Section 28.7 is correct, then there *is* still money out there to be made. If the view of Piazzesi et al. is correct, there would have been an opportunity to make money in the past for a time-machine-transported econometrician, but these past opportunities are now all too clear for everyone to see. Much as the diners of Yogi Berra's restaurant ('Nobody goes there anymore. It's too crowded!'), present-day investors can all see the great deals that were available (but at the time not visible) to the early customers of the *Steep Yield Curve* restaurant, but today can only patronize an overcrowded establishment with indifferent courses.

So, there is great theoretical and practical interest in determining whether an over-reaction model or a now-we-know better explanation accounts more convincingly for the stylized features of excess returns that we have discussed in previous chapters. Before doing so, however, we present another possible explanation.

28.6 WHY IS THE SLOPE SIGNIFICANT? A HETEROGENEOUS-EXPECTATIONS MODEL

Xiong and Yan (2010) present a dynamic equilibrium model of the bond market in which agents form different expectations about future macroeconomic

---

[10] p. 13.   [11] p. 1.

variables. These agents are no armchair philosophers, but want to trade against each other on the basis of their views. By doing so they become rich or poor (rich*er* or poor*er*) depending on the relative correctness of their views.

The heterogeneity of beliefs, and the attending trading actions, have several interesting consequences: they provide a mechanism through which the Expectation Hypothesis may fail; they amplify price volatility (and, incidentally, impart to the term structure of volatilities the humped shaped discussed in Chapter 30.[12]); and they give rise to time-dependent bond risk premia. Regarding the last finding, the authors show that the model explains 'the ability of the tent-shaped linear combination of forward rates to predict bond returns'.[13]

We will not go into the details of the model, but simply sketch the reasoning with a broad brush. The focus of our discussion will be on providing an intuitive understanding of why heterogeneous beliefs can give rise to a dependence on the slope.

In the economy described by Xiong and Yan (2010) there is a single consumption good, whose aggregate endowment (ie, how much of it investors have in the aggregate) follows a geometric diffusion with volatility σ_D. The price level (for which an index such as the CPI can be a good proxy) follows the process

$$\frac{dCPI_t}{CPI_t} = i_t dt, \tag{28.2}$$

where i_t is the inflation rate. Inflation follows a mean-reverting process:

$$di_t = \kappa_i (\theta_t - i_t) dt + \sigma_i dz_t^i. \tag{28.3}$$

The instantaneous reversion level, θ_t (which we call the inflation target) is in turn mean-reverting with its own constant long-term reversion level, $\bar{\theta}$:

$$d\theta_t = \kappa_\theta (\bar{\theta} - \theta_t) dt + \sigma_\theta dz_t^\theta. \tag{28.4}$$

This inflation target is unobservable. We have seen variations of this model in Chapter 4, and we will explore its analytical properties in detail in Chapter 30.

Investors monitor a visible signal, which they believe to be correlated with *the* significant macroeconomic in the economy, which is assumed to be the inflation target, θ_t. In reality what they observe is just pure noise. In the economy there is also a smart econometrician who realizes that the visible signal is not informative, but who, being an academic, does not have enough money to affect the market by taking positions.

As mentioned earlier, the heterogeneity of beliefs has several effects: on the equilibrium asset prices, on the asset price dynamics and on the variance of the investors' beliefs – as compared with the variance of the smart-but-poor econometrician's beliefs. The authors show that, if the average of the beliefs of the two groups happens to be equal to the belief of the econometrician at

---

[12] See their Fig. 1 on p. 1450.

[13] p. 1434. We note in passing that the model by Xiong and Yan (2010) can also account for a Campbell-and-Shiller–like dependence of bond premia on the slope of the yield curve. See their p. 1435, and their Section 3.4.2, p. 1451 and passim.

time 0, then the future average belief will always keep track of the econometrician's beliefs. This result is not obvious, and is very useful because it allows the authors to disentangle the various contributions of belief heterogeneity to what is empirically observed. So, by choosing the parameters of the investors' beliefs to be such as to match the econometrician's, they can 'isolate belief-dispersion effects from other learning-related effects, such as those caused by erroneous average beliefs and underestimation of risk'.[14]

After imposing the market equilibrium (under reasonable conditions of completeness), Xiong and Yan cast the problem in the form of an affine model, where the factors are the current inflation rate and the investors' beliefs about the inflation target. (As usual, both beliefs and target inflation are supposed to be mean-reverting.)

From this the authors derive the state-price density (see Chapter 13). As we know, its volatility is given by the market price of risk. This is made up of two components: the first (the boring one) is just a constant and comes from the uncertainty in the aggregate endowment of the consumption good; the second (where the action is) is time dependent, and proportional to the difference between the econometrician's estimate of the reversion level and the wealth-weighted average of the beliefs about the reversion level held by the two cohorts of investors. Therefore, when the average of the beliefs does not magically add up to the econometrician's beliefs, the bond risk 'premium varies over time with the relative wealth fluctuation across the two groups of investors'.[15]

And now (finally) to the intuitive explanation of the slope dependence. To understand the explanation, we must keep in mind that the average belief of the market is wealth weighted. Again, this means that, as one cohort of investors becomes more successful in trading, it captures a larger share of the market. Prices therefore reflect more and more the expectations of the successful cohort. Now, suppose that the weighted average of beliefs above the target rate is above the econometrician's. This means that in the aggregate investors believe that inflation will rise more than the econometrician does, and are therefore more pessimistic about assets that are negatively correlated with instantaneous inflation. Investors do not like these assets; they sell them, and, in the eyes of the econometrician, they become 'cheap' – ie, they acquire high-risk premia. From this the slope-dependence of the term premium naturally follows. As the authors say,

> ...Suppose that the wealth-weighted average belief about the future short rates is higher than the econometrician's belief. On the one hand, this implies that investors discount long-term bonds more heavily, which leads to higher long-term bond yields and so [a steeper yield curve]; on the other hand, it also implies that the long-term bond prices appear "cheap"from the econometrician's point of view—i.e., the long-term bond prices are expected to rise and

---

[14] p. 1441. Their Section 2.4 shows that this result is not obvious.   [15] p. 1447.

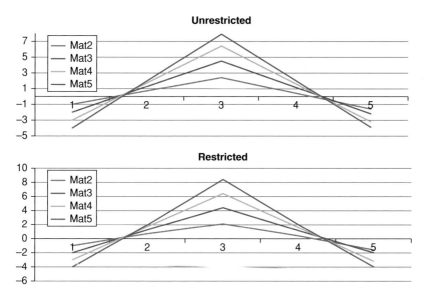

Figure 28.2 The shape of the return-predicting factors (unrestricted, top panel, and restricted, bottom panel, obtained by Xiong and Yan (2010) after running many simulations of their economy and then regressing the excess returns on the forward rates. Note the obvious similarity with the Cochrane–Piazzesi (2005) tent.

bond yields are expected to fall. Taken together, a high wealth-weighted average belief implies both [a steep yield curve] and falling long-term bond yields in the future.[16]

So, the slope dependence is accounted for. What about the tent? When the authors run many simulations of their economy and then regress the excess returns on the forward rates they find a pattern very similar to Cochrane and Piazzesi's tent. See Figure 28.2. But why should this be the case? Here the argument is a bit more complex, and heavily relies on the humped shape of the term structure of forward-rate volatilities, with a hump around three years. According to the authors, the shape of the Cochrane and Piazzesi return-predicting factor can be accounted for because, if the 'three-year forward rates increases more than the one-year and five-year forward rates, [t]his leads to a higher value of the tent-shaped factor since it has a high loading on the three-year forward rate but low loadings on the one- and five-year forward rates'.

There is no doubt that the model of Xiong and Yan produces a tent-shaped return-predicting factor. As for the account they provide of this qualitative shape, when we look at excess returns for maturities longer than five years

[16] p. 1451–1452. To avoid confusion, I have changed the authors' terminology from 'larger yield spreads' to 'steeper yield curve'.

and run regressions with more than five forward rates, we find ('bat-like') patterns more complex than a simple tent. This makes us a bit tentative about the explanation of the tent provided by the authors. In any case, we have shown (see Section 26.6) that tents and bats are not as different as their shape would at first blush suggest, and that they are not *that* different from the slope return-prediciting factor. The upshot of the study by Xiong and Yan is therefore that heterogeneity of beliefs can also provide an explanation for the power of slope-like return-predictive factors.

So, heterogeneity of beliefs is at the root of the explanation offered by Xiong and Yan for the predictive power of the slope. In the next section we look at another – and simpler – possible explanation.

28.7 WHY IS THE SLOPE SIGNIFICANT? AN OVER-REACTION MODEL

We have seen that two of the best established empirical facts about term premia are (i) that their magnitude depends on the slope of the yield curve (Fama and Bliss (1987), Duffie (2002), Adrian et al. (2013), etc) and (ii) that what investors seek compensation for is level risk. It is (perhaps) intuitively clear why investors should seek compensation about *level* risk. But the question at the heart of this chapter is why the magnitude of the risk compensation should depend on the slope of the yield curve.

In this section we present a simple model to explain the predictive power of the yield-curve slope. The model's success in explaining this feature (and some additional empirical facts) does not imply, of course, that we have identified *the* reason for these empirical regularities. However, since the candidate explanation that we present is both simple and testable, it is worthwhile considering it when trying to explain the problem at hand.

The intuition is simple. We assume that central monetary authorities revise periodically their expectations about how they will adjust the target rates. In our model investors correctly predict the direction of the changes in monetary policy. However, they systematically overestimate the magnitude of the policy revision. We show that this feature immediately generates the desired dependence of risk premia on the slope of the yield curve *even if investors are risk neutral*.[17] So overreaction gives rise to a market price of risk whose magnitude and sign depend on the slope of the yield curve – which is exactly what is empirically found.

The very crude model we present gives predictions of the correct order of magnitude, and the results are very robust to different reasonable changes in

---

[17] The issue of investor's over-reaction to economic news is a long-standing, and vexed, one. The classic work in this area is Shiller's who finds evidence of over-reaction to changes in fundamentals ('excessive volatility'). See Shiller (1979) for a discussion of over-reaction in the context of interest rates and Shiller (1981) for a similar analysis of equity volatility.

We do not revisit this issue, but simply assume that some degree of over-reaction indeed exists.

the model parameters – ie, they do not depend on a precise fine-tuning of the model features. Before presenting the model, we note that it is a small variation on a well-rehearsed theme, ie, the over-reaction of prices in general, and bond prices in particular, to news.[18] A Shiller clearly put it as early as 1979

> Models which represent long-term interest rates as long averages of expected short-term interest rates imply, because of the smoothing implicit in the averaging, that long rates should not be too volatile. The volatility of actual long-term interest rates, as measured by the variance of short-term holding yields on long-term bonds, appears to exceed limits imposed by the models. Such excess volatility implies a kind of forecastability for long rates. Long rates show a slight tendency to fall when they are high relative to short rates rather than rise as predicted by expectation models.'[19]

28.8   THE MODEL IN DETAIL

28.8.1   The Actions of the Central Bank

The behaviour of the monetary authorities is modelled as follows.

At time t_0 the central bank intends to move over time the target rate, r_t,[20] from its present value, r_0, towards some long-term reversion level, θ_0, at a certain speed, κ_0. The intended path of the target rate is described by the deterministic part of an Ornstein–Uhlenbeck process:

$$r_t|r_{t_0} = r_0 e^{-\kappa_0 \tau} + \theta_0 \left(1 - e^{-\kappa_0 \tau}\right) \tag{28.5}$$

with

$$\tau = t - t_0. \tag{28.6}$$

The central banks revises its intended policy at regular intervals, Δt. We take $\Delta t = 1$ year. A policy revision means

- a change in the long-term reversion level of the short rate (a change in θ);
- a change in today's target rate (a change in r_{t_0}); and
- a change in how quickly the target rate should go from today's level to its long-term level (a change in κ).

To be clear: at a generic time t_0 the average (across voting members) of the cluster of 'blue dots' in the right-hand section of the document published by the Fed on that date is a good proxy for the long-term reversion level of the short rate; the current 'Fed Funds rate' is a good proxy for today's level of the short rate; and as for the speed of adjustment from the market visible Fed Fund rate

---

[18] See, eg, Shiller (1979, 1981).   [19] Shiller (1979), p. 1190.
[20] We make no distinction in our model between the target rate and the short rate. We use the two terms interchangeably.

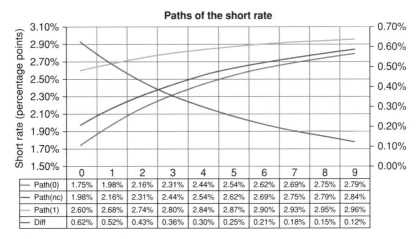

Figure 28.3 The path of the short rate over the next nine years intended by the central bank at time t_0 (Path0); the path for the short rate at time t_1 (ie, one year later) if the central bank had not 'changed its mind' – ie, if it still maintained the same reversion level and reversion speed that it had at time t_0; (Path(nc)), the updated path for the short rate at time 1 (Path1) (all on the left-hand y-axis), and the difference between the future path intended at time t_0 (Path(fwd)) and the actually chosen path at time 1 (Path1) (on the right-hand y-axis).

and the long-term level, they can be gauged, imperfectly but reasonably, from the location of the medians of the blue dots for different horizons.

Figure 28.3 shows a few intended paths of the target rate.

The innovations (the changes in the parameters θ and κ, and in the spot target rate r_0) are drawn from a log-normal distribution, with zero drift and volatilities σ_r, σ_θ, and σ_κ. In order to mimic central-bank behaviour, the Brownian shocks are serially correlated, with a coefficient of auto-correlation equal to ρ: this tries to capture the observation that an up revision in the target rate is more likely to be followed by an up revision than by a down move. As we shall see, this feature has important consequences.

In our simulation, we describe the yield curve by 11 regularly spaced zero-coupon yields, of maturity from 0 to 10 years. We note that, if there were no revisions to the monetary policy, the time-$t + 1$ expectation of the target rate at time $N - 1$ would be equal to the time-t expectation of the rate at time N.

From Equation (28.5), the average path out to time T, $\langle r_{t_0}^T \rangle$, of the short rate expected at time t_0 by the central bank is given by

$$\langle r_{t_0}^T \rangle = \frac{1}{T} \int_0^T r_s ds = \theta + (1 - e^{-\kappa T}) \frac{r_0 - \theta}{\kappa T}. \tag{28.7}$$

28.8.2   The Investors' Expectations

At each time interval, and just before the central bank adjusts the short rate, investors make revisions both to the short rate and to the reversion level, θ.

We have two versions of the model: in the first, investors correctly predict the short rate that the central bank will announce; in the other they make their predictions with a random error. In both versions of the model, investors also correctly predict the direction of the change in reversion level and the speed of adjustment. However, they over-react. This means that if $\Delta\theta_{CB}^t$ is time-t revision in ultimate reversion level of the central bank, the investors' revisions will be $K\Delta\theta_{CB}^t$, with $K > 1$. For the sake of simplicity we do not analyze the case of over-reaction in the estimate of the reversion speed.

In our simple model investors do not seek any compensation for bearing level risk (they are risk-neutral). If investors correctly predicted the change in reversion level intended by the central bank, their reversion level would therefore change at each revision time by exactly $\Delta\theta_{CB}^t$. Instead, because of overreaction, it changes to $K\Delta\theta_{CB}^t$. We want to see whether this over-reaction feature makes the slope a predictor of excess returns.

28.8.3   The Bond Price Formation

Once we have these ingredients, it is easy to calculate the Vasicek-like bond prices by taking the suitable expectations in the risk-neutral measure – at least as long as we assume that, at each point in time, investors believe that the model parameters, κ, σ and θ, will not change. To be precise, in our world κ and σ are constant, but the reversion level does change. So, the true model is a doubly mean-reverting Vasicek model of sorts (see Chapter 30), but investors form prices at time t using a Vasicek model with the parameters they estimate at time t. We also note that, since our investors are risk neutral, expectation in the risk-neutral measure are the same as expectations in the real-world measure.

Within this model, we could easily compute bonds and yields using the necessary closed-form expressions. However, doing so would also introduce convexity effects, in which we are not interested. Therefore we equate the *convexity-adjusted market yield* with the average of the short rate in the investor measure. (We do not call this measure the 'risk-neutral measure' because it differs from the objective ($\mathbb{P}$) measure because of over-reaction, not because of risk aversion. See in this respect the discussion in Section 5.6.)

Given the friendly assumptions we have made, working out the path-averaged value of the short rate (and hence the yield) is easy, and it is given by

$$y_t^T = \theta_t^Q + \frac{1 - e^{-\kappa\tau}}{\kappa\tau}\left(r_t - \theta_t^Q\right),$$ (28.8)

with

$$\tau = T - t.$$ (28.9)

Exercise 72 *Derive Equation (28.8).*

As we know, this is equivalent to calculating a bond price as

$$P_t^T = e^{\mathbb{E}_t^{\mathbb{Q}}\left[-\int_t^T r_s ds\right]} \tag{28.10}$$

instead of

$$P_t^T = \mathbb{E}_t^{\mathbb{Q}}\left[e^{-\int_t^T r_s ds}\right]. \tag{28.11}$$

The difference between the two expressions, as we have discussed at length, is just the convexity contribution, that we neglect in this context.

28.8.4   The Excess Returns

The strategy we consider consists of investing at time t in a T-maturity bond, funding the purchase at the 1-year bond, and unwinding the portfolio after 1 year. We calculate the time-t excess returns from the T-maturity strategy, $rx_{t\to t+1}^T$, as

$$xet_t^T = p_{t+1}^{N-1} - p_t^N - y_t^1, \tag{28.12}$$

where, as usual, p_t^T denotes the log-bond-price:

$$p_t^T = \log P_t^T, \tag{28.13}$$

This gives

$$xret_{t\to t+1}^T = -y_{t+1}^{N-1}(N-1) + y_t^N N - y_t^1. \tag{28.14}$$

Finally, we define the slope of the yield curve at time t, sl_t, simply as the difference between the 10-year yield and the short rate. As discussed in the next section, this will be our right-hand-side variable in the regression of excess returns.

28.8.5   The Simulations

We set up simulations in which the system described in Section 28.2 is evolved over 1,000 years. If there were no revisions to the central bank's policy, the future value of the short rate τ periods ahead projected from time t would be equal to the value of the short rate $\tau - 1$ periods ahead projected from time $(t + 1)$. Forwards rates (which would now be equal to future rates) would 'come true'. As we know, in this setting no extra returns could be made.

Note that forward rates need not be equal to conditional expectations of future rates even if the investors are risk neutral, because we have posited overreaction. So, with an upward-sloping yield curve, the forward rates will on average be above the corresponding future rates, and vice versa with a downward-sloping yield curve.

Figure 28.4 A typical simulation of the target rate and the long-term rate chosen by the bank over the full 1,000-year period. A coefficient of serial correlation ρ of 0.64 was used for the simulation.

The bank applies revisions to these reference values, and the revisions, Δr_t and $\Delta \theta_t$, are assumed to be given by

$$\Delta r_t = \sigma_r \sqrt{\Delta t} \epsilon_t^r \qquad (28.15)$$

and

$$\Delta \theta_t = \sigma_\theta \sqrt{\Delta t} \epsilon_t^\theta. \qquad (28.16)$$

The time interval is always 1 year, and ϵ^σ and ϵ^θ are drawn independently of each other. However, each draw is serially correlated:

$$\epsilon_t^i = \rho \epsilon_{t-1}^i + \sqrt{1 - \rho^2} \eta_t^i \qquad i = r, \theta, \quad \eta_\epsilon^i \sim \mathcal{N}(0, 1). \qquad (28.17)$$

The 'volatilities' for the short rate and the reversion level were chosen to be 0.0040 and 0.0012, respectively.

Figures 28.4 and 28.5 display the target rate and the long-term rate chosen by the bank over the full 1,000-year period, and over a time span of 60 years. From the latter graph one can see the tightening and easing cycles with durations of many years, and the secular change in the long-term reversion level. A coefficient of serial correlation ρ of 0.64 was used for the simulation.

A typical evolution of the 10-year yield in the $\mathbb{P}$ ('central-bank') world and in the $\mathbb{Q}$ ('risk-neutral', over-reacting) world is shown in Figure 28.6. In this figure the over-reaction factor (K) was set to 1.6.

In order to see more clearly the difference between the $\mathbb{P}$ (real-world) and $\mathbb{Q}$ (risk-neutral) measures, Figure 28.7 then shows the slope of the yield curve, again for an amplification factor of 1.6.

We are now in a position to test our hypothesis. We do so by regressing the average excess returns, $\overline{xret}_{t \to t+1}$, (averaged across maturities) against the yield curve slope, sl_t, calculated as the difference between the 10-year and the 1-year

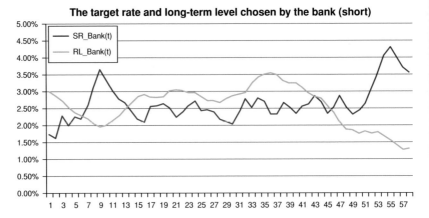

Figure 28.5 The first 60 years of the time series in Figure 28.4. Note the tightening and easing cycles and the slow secular change in the long-term rate.

yields at the time when the investment strategy was put on. Our model therefore is

$$\overline{xret}_{t\rightarrow t+1} = \alpha + \beta \times sl_t + \epsilon_t. \tag{28.18}$$

We also investigated the forward-rate–based regression

$$\overline{xret}_{t\rightarrow t+1} = a + b_1 \times f_t^1 + b_3 \times f_t^3 + b_5 \times f_t^5 + \eta_t, \tag{28.19}$$

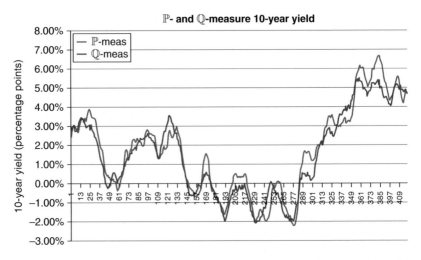

Figure 28.6 Simulated history of the 10-year yield in the $\mathbb{P}$ (real-world) and $\mathbb{Q}$ (risk-neutral) measures for an over-reaction factor, K, of 1.6. The risk-neutral measure is the measure of the over-reacting investor.

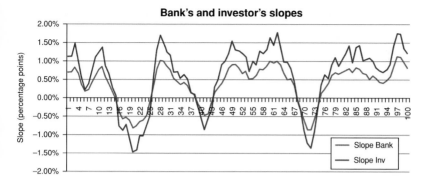

Figure 28.7 Simulated time history of the slope of the yield curve in the $\mathbb{P}$ (real-world, curve labelled Slope Bank) and $\mathbb{Q}$ (risk-neutral, curve labelled Slope Inv) measures.

where f_t^i, $i = 1, 3, 5$ denote the 1-year, 3-year and 5-year-expiry, 1-year forward rates, respectively.

First of all, we checked the obvious, namely, that, if investors guess on average correctly the direction and magnitude in the changes in monetary policy, then the regression 'beta' and intercept are zero. In our setting, this means that we set the amplification factor, K, to 1 for this batch of simulations. What we expected turned out to be indeed the case in this entry-level test, as neither slope nor intercept turned out to be statistically significant.

Next we switched on the coefficient of serial correlation, setting to a value of $\rho = 0.64$. The unconditional excess return was still equal to zero, but, interestingly enough, now the slope and the forward-rate–based factors are both significant predictors with an R^2 of approximately 0.15. For future reference, we note that the pattern of the forward-rate regressors is almost a straight line (a 'slope' with opposite signs at the two ends).

As a third experiment, we put the serial correlation coefficient to zero, and the over-reaction parameter, K, to 1.6. The slope and the forward-rate regressors are, predictably, significant, with an R^2 of approximately 0.23. The forward-rate regressors are still arranged in a straight line (a slope).

When both the over-reaction ($K = 1.6$) and the serial correlation coefficient ($\rho = 0.60$) are switched on all the regressors are strongly significant, and the R^2 is very high (approximately 0.60). The regressors are still in a slope-pattern.

As a last twist to the tale, we allow for a small mistake (white noise, on top of the over-reaction) in the investor's prediction of where the short rate will be set. (The noise was given by $0.0008 \times \epsilon(0, 1)$.) There was a small deterioration in the R^2 (that now ranges between 0.45 and 0.50), but the interesting twist is that the forward rates are now arranged in the shape of a tent! In all of these permutations of parameters, the unconditional excess returns from the carry (buy-long/fund-short) strategy are always statistically indistinguishable from zero – as they should be.

The salient results are shown in Table 28.1.

Table 28.1 *The R^2 and the shape of the forward-rate regressors for different combinations of the model parameters. The symbol ρ denotes the coefficient of serial correlation in the central bank's innovation process for the short rate and K is the coefficient of over-reaction (K = 1 means no over-reaction).*

Combination of coefficients	R^2, shape of forward-rate regressors
$\rho = 0.00$, $K = 1.0$	0.00, no shape
$\rho = 0.64$, $K = 1.0$	0.15, slope
$\rho = 0.00$, $K = 1.6$	0.23, slope
$\rho = 0.64$, $K = 1.6$	0.60, slope
$\rho = 0.64$, $K = 1.6$, uncertain r_t	0.45, tent

28.8.6 Summary of Results

In this chapter we have presented a simple model to explain the widely documented success of the slope of the yield curve to predict excess returns. We stress that in our model investors are risk neutral, and therefore do not require a compensation for bearing risk. Indeed, the *unconditional* carry strategy (invest long/fund short) is not profitable in any of the permutations of model parameters.

We have shown that if investors 'over-react' (ie, guess the correct sign, but overestimate the magnitude of the changes of the central bank's revisions to the path of the short rate),

1. term premia become state dependent;
2. there is predictability in the differences between forward rates and realized future rate;
3. the slope of the yield curve becomes a significant predictor of excess returns.

To our surprise, we also found that the same three results apply if we assign serial correlation to the central bank's innovation, and *we assume that investor form prices with a constant-parameter Vasicek model*. This is, of course, strictly speaking logically inconsistent, but the practice of continuous recalibration of in-theory-constant model parameters is universally adopted in the not-so-distant field of derivatives modelling.

CHAPTER 29

The Spanning Problem Revisited

29.1 THE PURPOSE OF THIS CHAPTER

This is a short but important chapter. It brings together several strands of empirical and theoretical evidence to answer two questions: first, what type of variables are required to predict future yields or excess returns; and, second, whether affine models are *in principle* up to this predictive task. The first is an empirical/econometric question, the second a theoretical/modelling one.

We bring together evidence and arguments developed in the previous chapters of this part of the book, and broaden considerably the discussion by including several recent contributions to the debate.

29.2 WHAT IS THE SPANNING PROBLEM?

This chapter is about the so-called spanning problem. It is therefore important to be clear what we are talking about.

Informally speaking, a set of variables, $\{x\}$, 'span' another set of variables, $\{y\}$, if the variables in $\{y\}$ can be fully accounted for (explained, 'spanned') by $\{x\}$. What does this mean?

Suppose that we are interested in explaining the cross-sectional changes in a set of market yields $\{y\}$. Let's call this our 'target set'. Let's take a few yields, $\{x\}$, as our explanatory variables. We want to see whether we can explain the yield changes $\{y\}$ by means of the few selected yields, $\{x\}$. So, for instance, we know that to predict excess returns all we have to predict are changes in yields. We also know that the level of the yield curve has hardly any predictive power for yield changes. So, the time series of any one single yield will not even begin to span the observed yield changes.

Suppose then that we take two yields. With these we can already create a yield-curve slope of sorts. As we well know, we can now explain a fair bit of excess return.

We saw in Part VI that the second principal component has a better predicting factor than a simple-minded difference between a long and a short yield. And we also saw that recent research has suggested that other combinations of yields may have even better predicting power. (See Chapters 26 and 27.) Creating these more powerful return-predicting factors requires more $\{x\}$ variables. So, more yields explain (span) the yield changes better.

It comes to a point, however, when adding even more yields to the set of $\{x\}$ variables does not improve our predictive power. This does not automatically mean, however, that no better prediction of yield changes could be made. Perhaps there are other variables – say, the *volatility* of yields, or some well-chosen macrofinancial quantities – that could unlock some more predictive power: that is to say, that could span more efficiently the target variables, $\{y\}$.

In the context of term-structure modelling the spanning problem is therefore tantamount to finding which $\{x\}$ variables can best explain excess returns. As we shall see, there is an empirical and a theoretical angle to this problem.

29.3   THE EMPIRICAL SPANNING PROBLEM

To fix ideas we concentrate on the prediction of excess returns.[1] One part of the spanning problem is clearly empirical, and boils down to answering the following questions:

1. Does the knowledge of yields and combinations of yields *at time t* give us robust predictive power about the excess returns from investing in a carry strategy from time t to time $t + 1$?
2. Can we find variables other than yields and combinations of yields that add explanatory power to the yield-based information set?

As we have amply documented, the answer to the first question is a resounding 'yes'. Yields may not impound all the available information about excess returns, but certainly tell an important part of the story. Fama and Bliss (1987), Campbell and Shiller (1991), Cochrane and Piazzesi (2004), Cieslak and Povala (2010a), Radwanski (2010), Ludvigson and Ng (2009) – and, to my knowledge, anyone who has worked on the matter – agree on this. Whether the 'combination of yields' endowed with the greatest and the most robust predictive powers is the simple slope, the tent, the bat, the principal components or some other configuration is an important, but different, question.

What about the second question? Do non–yield-curve variables contain information useful for predicting future yields?

As we have seen in Chapter 27, Ludvigson and Ng (2009) answer affirmatively, and point to composite quantities related to real economic activity and inflation as the additional variables that complement the yield-only information. So do Joslin, Priebsch and Singleton (2014), who find that adding some

---

[1] It should be clear that focussing on the market price of risk or, given the market yields, on the $\mathbb{P}$-measure expectations of yields would be totally equivalent. It should also be just as clear that predicting excess returns is exactly the same as predicting future yields. After all, in the expression for the excess return the only quantity that we do not know is 'tomorrow's' yield y_{t+1}^{n-1}.

measure of economic growth and inflation to the first three principal components increases the predictive power of the latter.

Radwanski (2010) and Cieslak and Povala (2010a, 2010b) reach similar conclusions, but the results are more nuanced. One way to interpret the work by Cieslak and Povala, for instance, is to recognize that the 'distance' between where yields are and where they 'should be' has predictive power for excess returns. In the previous sentence 'where yields should be' in turn refer to the level that they 'should' assume given the current level of inflation or real economic activity. This appropriate level is determined by regressing them on the (non-yield) regressors. Both Radwanski (2010) and Cieslak and Povala (2010a,a) implicitly posit that yields are not always 'where they should be', but that they quickly discover the error of their ways, and revert (perhaps with overshoot) to their natural level. This, of course, is the underpinning of the 'over-reaction' model explored in Chapter 28.

Apart from this subtle twist, the conclusion one can draw from these studies is univocal: yes, when it comes to predicting excess returns, non-yield variables add predictive power to yield-only variables.

Bauer and Hamilton (2015) agree that '[a] consensus has recently emerged that a number of variables in addition to the level, slope, and curvature of the term structure can help predict interest rates and excess bond returns'.[2] They nonetheless raise a dissenting voice. They argue that the statistical tests that have been used to reach this broad consensus have been vitiated by 'very large size distortions from a previously unrecognized problem arising from highly persistent regressors and correlation between the true predictors and lags of the dependent variable'.[3] They re-examine the evidence using tests that, they claim, are statistically more robust and reach the conclusion that 'the current consensus is wrong', in the sense that only yield-curve variables (in particular, the slope and level of the yield curve) can robustly predict excess bond returns (and hence future yields).[4]

What is one to make of these sobering claims? As Cochrane (2015) points out, Bauer and Hamilton (2015) raise two distinct points: they calculate that the estimates of the macrofinancial variables are greatly reduced out of sample – this is an *empirical* issue; and they find that the marginal increase in explanatory power, as translated in the increase in the R^2 statistic,[5] is statistically insignificant – this is an *econometric* issue. Cochrane (2015) then comments

---

[2] p. 1.   [3] Ibid.

[4] One of the procedures that Bauer and Hamilton (2015) employ is remarkably simple. Following suggestions by Ibragimov and Mueller (2010), they split the sample into two sub-sets, and they separately estimate the regression coefficients relating to the full set of putatively predicting variables on both sub-samples. They then perform a simple significance t-test on the coefficients in the two sub-samples. When they do this they find that only level and slope pass the test. Note the similarity between this test and the procedure we describe in Section 26.8.

[5] In the original 1985–2008 sample, the R^2 almost doubles by adding macro variables, but with the bootstrap procedure by Bauer and Hamilton (2015), it increases only from 0.30 to 0.37. See their Table 4.

that, using exactly the same data employed by Bauer and Hamilton, he finds that 'the slope [. . .] has some ability to forecast bond excess returns, a standard result, with a 0.18 R^2, a standard value'.[6] He notices that 'growth and inflation on their own do absolutely nothing to forecast returns'.[7] However, considering all the regressors (the three principal components and the macrofinancial variables together) not only makes the economic activity and inflation variables significant, but also increases both the coefficients and the significance of the first two principal components. So far, everything tallies with what we have learnt in the previous chapters about co-integration relationships between the *conditional* slope and the *conditional* level.

But now comes the surprise, in two pieces: first, Cochrane includes among the regressors a linear trend (the last two rows in his Table 1). When he does this, Cochrane finds that the R^2 skyrockets to 64%. Next Cochrane takes out the third principal component *and both macroeconomic variables*, and yet his R^2 (with the trend regressor retained) remains at a staggering 62%!

How can we explain this finding? Cochrane argues that 'the inflation was just proxying (and poorly) for detrending of the level and slope factors'. This observation resonates nicely with the puzzling finding that the Cieslak and Povala results (and, in particular, their R^2) was little changed when the savings rate (which bear very little economic relationship to inflation) was substituted for the inflation proxy.

Where does this leave us? The middle of the Cochrane (2015) paper goes more deeply into the econometric weeds than the readers of this book have been taught how to wade through. However, Cochrane captures the intuition very clearly as follows:

> The point is not whether a trend or long-run inflation is the "right" forecaster. The point is that inflation helps yields to forecast returns by removing a very slowly moving component of yields. [. . .] What's the problem? Well, clearly, *lots of other variables have trends.* If this is a pre-2000 vs post-2000 variable, we can think of hundreds of other variables that are larger pre-2000 and post-2000. [. . .] In my east and west of Mississippi example, we can think of lots of other variables that have that pattern. A variable that moves more frequently has a more distinct pattern. One can be more sure that this variable, and only this variable, could have entered correctly on the right hand side [ie, could have been a significant regressor]. [. . .] Really, the problem is, that we could have found so many other similar variables. If the data had a significant V shaped pattern, we could have found that. [. . .] That's the sense in which it is "easy" to find these results. [. . .] Traditionally, the main guard against this king of fishing has been an economic interpretation of the forecasting variable. But that discipline is dying out, with the results that we have hundreds of claimed forecasting variables.[8]

Interesting as this debate is, we leave it at that. The important point is that empirically we can state very confidently that yield curve variables matter; and,

---

[6] p. 3.   [7] Ibid.   [8] Ibid., p. 6 and p. 13, emphasis in the original.

with a quiver of hesitation in our voice, we can propose that macrofinancial quantities matter as well.

29.4 THE THEORETICAL SPANNING PROBLEM

So much for the empirical/econometric part of the question. What about the modelling/theoretical aspect?

Another long quote (by Ludvigson and Ng (2009) this time) frames the question more eloquently than I possibly could. If we accept that there are non–yield curve factors that have predictive power for excess returns, this seems to create problems for

> ... unrestricted (and commonly employed) affine term structure models, where the forecastability of bond returns [...] is completely summarized by the cross-section of yields [...]. In such models, [...] yields [...] are linear functions of the K state variables. Thus, assuming that the matrix that multiplies the state vector in the affine function for log bond yields is invertible, we can express the vector of K state variables as an affine function of K bond yields. *It follows that bond yields themselves can serve as state variables and will contain any forecasting information that is in the state variables, regardless of whether these state variables are observable macro variables or treated as latent factors* [...].[9] ...

It is important to stress that in the previous section we discussed a feature of reality ('Do excess returns depend on macrofinancial variables?'). Now we are addressing a modelling question: *assuming that macrofinancial variables do matter*, can affine models handle this?

What is the way out of the existential dilemma described by Ludvigson and Ng?

In Section 27.4 we argued that, yes, one *could* in principle invert the matrix that map from macro state variables to yields and use these yields (that we dubbed 'special') as the new state variables. However, we said, given how strongly correlated yields are, it may not be a good idea to do so in practice. Personally, I like to project points onto nice orthogonal axes, not onto axes arranged at impossibly squinty angles, even if the squinty-angle axes do 'span the space'. Incidentally, this interpretation could explain why three principal components could account well for ($\mathbb{Q}$ measure) prices, but more forward rates (or principal components) seem to be needed to predict excess returns. It could also explain why the exact configuration of these numerous return-predicting factors (tents, bats, slopes, etc) can be so dependent on the vagaries of the input data: in this explanation, once the 'easy' projection onto the slope and level has been sorted out, the vestigial signal from the macro variables is imprecisely projected onto additional regressors which are either highly correlated (if yields) or unstable (if principal components beyond the third).

---

[9] See in this respect our detailed discussion in Section 27.4.

Second, measurement errors should not be dismissed lightly. It is true that modern affine models produce very tight fits to market prices, and therefore pricing errors are small. However, *exactly because of the almost-colinearity of the yields*, it is not obvious how small pricing errors in the $\mathbb{Q}$ measure may translate into predictions in the $\mathbb{P}$ measure.

A third possible line of resolution of the spanning conundrum points to term structure models with unspanned stochastic volatility. (See Collin-Dufresne and Goldstein, 2002.) We do not pursue this line of enquiry here, but see Ludvigson and Ng (2009).[10]

In sum: it is fair to say that macro variables are likely to have predicting power for excess returns. After the work by Bauer and Hamilton (2015) we are a bit less sure about this than we were before, but, to put a half-full-glass gloss on their findings, their work has weakened our confidence in the predictive power of macro variables, but has not conclusively proven that macro variables have no predictive power.

If we accept that the dependence on macrofinancial variables is real and significant, we seem to have then reached the conclusion that 'traditional' affine models are not well set up to handle this state of affairs. This can be either because they *intrinsically* miss something (say, unspanned stochastic volatility); or because *in practice* the yield curve projections become progressively unreliable as the number of yields or principal components increases.

What modelling choices are therefore available?

29.5   THE MODELLING CHOICES TO HANDLE THE SPANNING PROBLEM

In Chapter 27 we alluded to a stochastic-market-price-of-risk model (that we develop fully in Chapter 35). The approach is strongly reduced-form, but it is simple and intuitive. It explicitly forces the model to have a market price of risk which is correlated with (but not deterministically dependent on) the slope state variable, and which has a residual degree of variability not spanned by the yield curve variables. The model is silent about what these sources of unspanned variability are (and in this sense it is reduced-form), but captures in a simple – albeit rather ad hoc – way the essence of the problem.

Could this reduced-form model be recast in a yield-only-state-variables formulation? Of course it could (since the mapping matrix is invertible). But why mess things up on purpose when we have a nice choice of coordinates to work with? The resulting projections onto yields would be very imprecise, and, above all, unreliable out-of-sample. So, this model is viable in a world where high-order principal components (or many yields) are in principle capable, but in practice ill-suited, to impounding the information in macro variables.

There is a related but theoretically-more-solidly-grounded approach, by Joslin et al. (2014). The idea is the following.

---

[10] p. 5048. See ibid for a discussion of Duffee's (2008) work.

They start from the same conclusions that we drew:

> First, output, inflation, and other macroeconomic risks are not linearly spanned by the information in the yield curve. Second, the unspanned components of many macro risks have predictive power for excess returns (risk premiums) in bond markets, over and above the information in the yield curve. Third, the cross section of bond yields is well described by a low-dimension set of risk factors.

How do Joslin et al. manage to account for all these features in an affine framework? To start with, they collect their state variables in a vector Z that 'contains' all the risks in the economy – those that can be mapped onto yield curve variables, and the non–yield-curve-spanned ones, if any. In our terminology (Joslin et al. work in discrete time, so their notation is different) this means

$$dZ_t = \mathcal{K}^{\mathbb{P}}\left(Z_t - \theta^{\mathbb{P}}\right)dt + Sdz_t^{\mathbb{P}}. \tag{29.1}$$

Let's split the state variables into a vector, $\mathcal{P}_t$, of yield curve variables, and macroeconomic variables, $\mathcal{M}_t$. We do *not* assume that the macroeconomic variables can be deterministically spanned by the yield curve variables. This means that in the projection

$$\mathcal{M}_t = \gamma_0 + \gamma_1 \mathcal{P}_t + OM_t \tag{29.2}$$

the residual, OM_t, is not identically zero. This is in turn means that knowing the value of the combination of yields $\mathcal{P}_t$ does not tell us everything there is to know about excess returns. For clarity, we can write Equation (29.1) as

$$\begin{bmatrix} d\mathcal{P}_t \\ d\mathcal{M}_t \end{bmatrix} = \begin{bmatrix} \mathcal{K}_{\mathcal{P}\mathcal{P}}^{\mathbb{P}} & \mathcal{K}_{\mathcal{P}\mathcal{M}}^{\mathbb{P}} \\ \mathcal{K}_{\mathcal{M}\mathcal{P}}^{\mathbb{P}} & \mathcal{K}_{\mathcal{M}\mathcal{M}}^{\mathbb{P}} \end{bmatrix} \left(\begin{bmatrix} \theta_{\mathcal{P}}^{\mathbb{P}} \\ \theta_{\mathcal{M}}^{\mathbb{P}} \end{bmatrix} - \begin{bmatrix} \mathcal{P}_t \\ \mathcal{M}_t \end{bmatrix} \right) dt$$
$$+ \begin{bmatrix} S_{\mathcal{P}\mathcal{P}} & S_{\mathcal{P}\mathcal{M}} \\ S_{\mathcal{M}\mathcal{P}} & S_{\mathcal{M}\mathcal{M}} \end{bmatrix} \begin{bmatrix} dz_t^{\mathcal{P}} \\ dz_t^{\mathcal{M}} \end{bmatrix}. \tag{29.3}$$

Then Joslin et al. impose that the market price of risk, λ_t, should be an affine function of the extended variables, Z_t:

$$\lambda_t = \lambda_{0,Z} + \lambda_{1,Z}Z_t. \tag{29.4}$$

This makes their approach essentially affine. So far, everything looks pretty standard. Note, in particular, that real-world expectations of (portfolios of) yields, $\mathcal{P}_t$, depend on the full set of variables $\{Z_t\} = \{\mathcal{P}_t\} + \{\mathcal{M}_t\}$.

At this point, however, they impose that in the risk-neutral measure, $\mathbb{Q}$, the portfolios of yields should follow a mean-reverting process of the form

$$d\mathcal{P}_t = \mathcal{K}_{\mathcal{P}}^{\mathbb{Q}}\left(\mathcal{P}_t - \theta_{\mathcal{P}}^{\mathbb{Q}}\right)dt + S_{\mathcal{P}\mathcal{P}}dz_t^{\mathbb{Q}}. \tag{29.5}$$

It is essential to note that there are no 'mixed' terms (such as, eg, $\mathcal{K}_{\mathcal{P}\mathcal{M}}^{\mathbb{Q}}$ or $S_{\mathcal{P}\mathcal{M}}$) in the $\mathbb{Q}$-measure dynamics of the market yields. This implies

1. that the yields will be an affine function of the $\mathcal{P}_t$ variables only:

$$y_t^T = \alpha_t^T + \left(\beta_t^T\right)^T \mathcal{P}_t; \tag{29.6}$$

2. and that also the short rate will be an affine function of the subset, $\mathcal{P}$, of variables that map exactly onto the yields:

$$r_t = \xi_{0,y} + (\xi_{1,y})^T \mathcal{P}_t. \tag{29.7}$$

After some clever rotation we can think of these $\mathcal{P}$-variables as principal components, if we so wish. Without loss of generality we will do so in what follows.

What about the market price of risk? This is how Joslin et al. square the circle. If we assume that we know the real-world drifts for the $\mathcal{P}$-variables (not an innocuous assumptions), then the market price of risk for the principal components, $\Lambda_\mathcal{P}(Z_t)$, will depend on the whole set of variables, Z_t, and will be given by the (scaled) difference between the real-world and risk-neutral drifts of the principal components:

$$\Lambda_\mathcal{P}(Z_t) = S_{\mathcal{PP}}^{-1} \left[\mu_\mathcal{P}^\mathbb{P}(Z_t) - \mu_\mathcal{P}^\mathbb{Q}(Z_t) \right], \tag{29.8}$$

with $\mu_\mathcal{P}^\mathbb{P}(Z_t)$ coming from Equation (29.3) and $\mu_\mathcal{P}^\mathbb{Q}(Z_t)$ from Equation (29.5). The important thing to note is that the $\mathbb{P}$-measure drift of the $\mathcal{P}$-variables, $\mu_\mathcal{P}^\mathbb{P}(Z_t)$ (and hence their real-world expectations), depends on the full set of yield-curve ($\mathcal{P}_t$) and macrofinancial ($\mathcal{M}_t$) variables, and is given (to first order) by

$$\mu_\mathcal{P}^\mathbb{P}(Z_t) = \mathcal{K}_{\mathcal{PP}}^\mathbb{P} \left(\theta_\mathcal{P}^\mathbb{P} - \mathcal{P}_t \right) + \mathcal{K}_{\mathcal{PM}}^\mathbb{P} \left(\theta_\mathcal{M}^\mathbb{P} - \mathcal{M}_t \right), \tag{29.9}$$

not just by

$$\mu_\mathcal{P}^\mathbb{P}(Z_t) = \mathcal{K}_{\mathcal{PP}}^\mathbb{P} \left(\theta_\mathcal{P}^\mathbb{P} - \mathcal{P}_t \right). \tag{29.10}$$

To stress the point, this means that expectations of yields and excess returns depend on the full set of yield curve and macroeconomic variables.

Now, bond prices are expectations of (a function of) the short rate. Note that bond prices depend only on $\mathcal{P}$-variables. This part of the modelling set-up reflects the fact that market yields are well described by a (small number of) principal components. (This is Joslin et al.'s third point.)

However, as Equation (29.8) shows, the market price of risk can now depend on the full set of yield and macro variables, without affecting bond prices (once the $\mathbb{Q}$-dynamics for the short rate are assigned via Equation (29.7)). So, $\mathbb{P}$-measure expectations depend on Z_t (predictions of yields depend on Z_t, expected excess returns depend on Z_t, etc); but market prices only depend on $\mathcal{P}_t$. This squares the circle.

There are obvious similarities between the model by Joslin et al. and the stochastic-market-price-of-risk reduced-form approach we present in Chapter 35. Their model lends itself to more direct econometric specification, but the motivation for the approach and the spirit of the solution they offer is exactly the same.

Joslin et al. conclude with the following words, which clearly indicate why so much work still remains to be done in this field, (and why the field is so exciting):

> Unspanned macro risks, particularly real economic risks, have large effects on forward term premiums over short- to medium-time horizons. What are the sources of these unspanned risks? On the other hand, a substantial portion of the variation in long-dated forward term premiums is attributable to economic factors that are orthogonal to both spanned and unspanned output and inflation. What is the nature of these risks that are so important in Treasury markets and yet are orthogonal to growth and inflation? [...] Our modelling framework provides a means to systematically examine these possibilities within arbitrage-free dynamic term structure models.

As the authors say, the means to tackle these questions are indeed offered, but the answers are as elusive as ever: for all its elegance and cleverness, the approach by Joslin et al., *in itself*, still does not give us any clearer answers as to the ultimate source of excess returns than, say, the reduced-form model we present in Chapter 35. In particular, the reader should not forget that, in the way it has been presented here, their procedure still relies on the estimation of the real-world properties of the principal components – the most important of which, as we know, displays a quasi-unit-root behaviour.

PART VII

WHAT THE MODELS TELL US

Models are to be used, not believed.
— Henri Theil, *Principles of Econometrics*

Our mistake is not that we do not our theories too seriously, but that we do not take them seriously enough.
— Steven Weinberg[1]

In this part of the book we look in detail at what a number of significant Gaussian affine models tell us about expectations, risk premia and the behaviour of the yield curve in general. Some of the models are well known; some are introduced here for the first time.

Our intention is not to present an encyclopaedia of models. Rather, we want to discuss the strengths and the shortcomings of a handful of models, each of which is a salient representative of an interesting class. In a way, each model we present in this part of the book tries to answer the questions left open by the Vasicek approach that we have examined in detail in Parts I to II of this book.

As explained in the Introduction, we do not consider affine models as (just) mathematical entities endowed with formal properties (axioms and theorems). Rather, we look at them as restricted-view windows on the financial reality we would like to understand. Therefore the calibration of a model, and its congruence with the empirical evidence about how yields behave, take centre stage in this part of the book.

Broadly speaking, we will look at two classes of models – which, for lack of a better description, we will refer to as the 'financial-story' and the 'statistically motivated' models. With the first class, one starts from a simplified picture of how the world works (a 'financial story'), and one translates as best one can this picture into a set of relationships among the chosen variables: a simple model. One then makes the model speak (ie, one extracts predictions from the model), and compares the model predictions with reality. If the match is acceptable,

---

[1] Quoted in Tegmark (2015), p. 20.

this is corroborating evidence that the financial story we started with was not entirely fanciful, and we can use the model for predictions about quantities that we would like to know, but cannot observe – such as for instance, the risk premium.

When one finds wanting some model-predicted features of reality that are considered important, one cautiously enriches the model by adding some missing elements of realism (or bells and whistles) to the original financial story. The 'evolution' from the Doubly Mean-Reverting Vasicek model (presented in Chapter 30) to the Stochastic-Market-Price-of-Risk model (see Chapter 35) is an example of this process of 'enrichment'.

Statistically motivated models are somewhat different. Here the interpretation of the variables (and the attending 'financial story') recedes into the background, and models become devices that enforce no-arbitrage on statistically-estimated quantities. The 'modern-school' models described in Chapters 31 and 34 fall in this category.

The tension between the 'financial-story' and the 'statistically motivated' schools of modelling, and the discussion of their relative strengths and weaknesses, are two of the most important and recurring themes of this book. More about this in the closing chapter.

Another important and recurrent topic covered in this part of the book is the process of calibration: the set of procedures, that is, that enable the model user to find the parameters that characterize each particular model. As we are not interested in 'snapshot' models, and we deal with financially grounded models, we always strongly constrain in our calibration the values the model parameters can assume. This means that we never 'throw in the mix' uninterpreted factors with their attending retinue of parameters begging to be estimated just to get a better fit. If we so did, we would indeed obtain, by construction, a better fit – but we would be none the wiser as to how the world works.

Once gain, to avoid misunderstanding: with our calibration we never want to find the unconstrained set of parameters that best recover the market quantities to which the model is fitted. What we want to see is whether there exists a set of parameters congruent with the financial story we started with, and such that the model outputs are not violently at odds with the corresponding empirical quantities. If the fit is good, we are, of course, happy, but obtaining a tight fit at all costs is not our purpose. With Weinberg,[2] we want to take our models seriously, in the sense that we want to use them to understand reality better, not as glorified interpolation devices.

We shall see that this constrained approach to model calibration (the approach, that is, in which the values of the model parameters consistent with the financial story can be assigned a priori) becomes difficult, if not impossible, when we deal with the 'modern' school of modelling. This is because with these models the financial interpretation of the state variables is often tenuous or altogether absent. As we shall see, this can create problems.

---

[2] See the second quote that opens this part of the book.

CHAPTER 30

The Doubly Mean-Reverting Vasicek Model

30.1 THE PURPOSE OF THIS CHAPTER

We have seen in Chapter 8 that the Vasicek model has some very appealing features (its simplicity, parsimony and intuitional appeal being three of the most obvious ones), but that it also has some significant, and unavoidable, drawbacks. The first problem that springs to mind is the monotonically decaying nature of the term structure of volatility (see Equation (8.39)), but, as we have seen in Part VI of this book, when we look at risk premia more, and arguably more important, shortcomings come to the fore.

In this chapter we try to fix at least the problems connected wih the term structure of volatilities. We do so by enriching the Vasicek model with a simple twist: the short rate still reverts to the reversion level with a constant reversion speed; however, the reversion level itself is not fixed, as it follows a simple mean-reverting behaviour – this time to a fixed reversion level. The 'improvement' brought about by allowing the reversion level of the short rate to be stochastic is aimed at taking care of the poor recovery of the term structure of volatilities afforded by the simple Vasicek model. There is a lot more work to be done, but this is a first step in the right direction.

Adding a mean-reverting reversion level does not just produce a better fit to the term structure of volatilities. We show that this simple addition also makes the model financially richer and more convincing. Indeed, with this simple 'twist' this model can be interpreted as a version of the macrofinancial and monetary-economics models discussed in Chapter 3. Finally, we highlight in the last section which problems this approach still leaves unsolved, and which models can offer further improvements.

To be clear: the model we present in this chapter is not *the* solution to the problems that afflict affine models. In particular, this is the only model we discuss to be almost exclusively rooted in the $\mathbb{Q}$ (pricing) measure. However, it shows one direction in which one set of improvements can be made. The model presented in Chapter 35, which straddles the physical ($\mathbb{P}$) and risk-neutral ($\mathbb{Q}$) measures, is its natural extension.

30.2 THE DOUBLY MEAN-REVERTING VASICEK MODEL

The doubly mean-reverting Vasicek (DMRV) model that we present in this section is a variation of a model introduced by Hull and White in the mid-1990s (Hull and White, 1994).[1] These are its constitutive equations in the $\mathbb{Q}$ (pricing) measure:

$$dr_t = \kappa_r(\theta_t - r_t)dt + \sigma_r dz_r \tag{30.1}$$

$$d\theta_t = \kappa_\theta(r_\infty - \theta_t)dt + \sigma_\theta dz_\theta \tag{30.2}$$

$$\mathbb{E}[dz_r dz_\theta] = \rho dt \tag{30.3}$$

The behaviour makes sense: the short rate still moves stochastically around a reversion level, but this level is not constant. A cursory look at yields in the 1970s and in the 2010s shows that this is not such a bad idea.

Casual inspection also suggests that the level to which the short rate reverts does not wander aimlessly to infinity, but is in turn 'anchored' to some long-term level. (We feel some degree of physical discomfort as we make these qualitative and rather hand-waving considerations, because we are glossing here over the distinction between the $\mathbb{P}$ and the $\mathbb{Q}$ measure. More about this later.)

Apart from being generically plausible, a model such as the one described by Equations (30.1) to (30.3) can be seen as an incarnation of the macrofinancial and monetary-economics-inspired models discussed in Chapter 3, which the reader is invited to re-read at this point. It is a particularly simple example of this class, in that there is no description of the reversion of the short rate to the target rate (a reversion which is assumed to be instantaneous). As discussed in Chapter 3, unless one is interested in the behaviour of very-short-maturity yields, this is a reasonable approximation.

We also recall for future discussion that in Chapter 3 we had suggested that the reversion speeds of the short rate to the target rate, κ_r, of the target rate to the local reversion level, κ_{TR}, and of the local reversion level to the 'secular' reversion level, κ_θ, should satisfy the relationships[2]

$$\kappa_r >> \kappa_{TR} > \kappa_\theta. \tag{30.4}$$

In general, the shape of the yield curve will depend on all the model parameters (and on the initial values of the state variables), with the two reversion speeds (κ_r and κ_θ) and the two volatilities (σ_r and σ_θ) affecting via the convexity contribution the long end of the yield curve. As we discussed in the case

---

[1] Variants of the two-factor mean-reverting model presented in this chapter are also discussed in Balduzzi, Das and Foresi (1998), Babbs and Nowman (1999), Bomfin (2003a, 2003b).

[2] We have imposed the relationship $\kappa_r > \kappa_\theta$ on the basis of our financial interpretation of the 'meaning' of the state variables. Dai and Singleton (2000) present corroborating empirical evidence, and state that 'consistent with with analysis of a central tendency factor in Andersen and Lund (1997) and Balduzzi et al. (1996), we find that the short rate tends to mean-revert relatively quickly to a factor that itself has a relatively slow rate of mean reversion to its own constant long-term mean' (p. 1971). The 'central tendency' they refer to is the variable θ in our approach.

of the simple Vasicek model, for a finite maximum maturity, several combinations of reversion levels and convexity can produce very similar-quality fits to a given finite-maturity yield curve: high volatilities and low reversion speeds 'pull down' (because of convexity) the long end of the yield curve, while a high reversion level of reversion level, r_∞, pulls it upwards. These two different yield-curve-shape-affecting mechanisms therefore engage in an unseemly tug of war.

If we just use the model in a 'snapshot' manner this is of little concern. But this multiplicity of possible solutions matters a lot if we are interested in the dynamic properties of the model.

In order to escape from this impasse we employ in what follows a divide-and-conquer calibration procedure. We are helped in this by a nice decomposition of the parameter set into a 'volatility subset' (κ_r, κ_θ, σ_r, ρ and σ_θ), a 'yield-curve shape' subset[3] (mainly r_0, r_∞ and θ_0, but, to a lesser extent, also the parameters in the 'volatility subset'). As we show in the text that follows, the volatilities of, and the correlations among, rates are affected only by the 'volatility subset'. Once this subset is fixed using volatility information, the parameters of the 'yield-curve shape' subset can be determined, keeping the volatility-subset parameters fixed, and thereby avoiding the tug of war referred to earlier.

30.3 BOND PRICES AND PROPERTIES OF THE SOLUTION

Since the model falls squarely in the affine class, we know that the expression for the bond price is given by

$$P_t^T = e^{A_t^T + B_t^T r_t + C_t^T \theta_t}. \tag{30.5}$$

The explicit expressions for the quantities A_t^T, B_t^T and C_t^T are given in Chapter 18.[4]

The short rate is a Gaussian normal variable, with mean and variance given by

$$\mathbb{E}_0[r_t] = r_0 e^{-\kappa_r t} + \frac{\kappa_r(\theta_0 - r_\infty)}{\kappa_r - \kappa_\theta} \left(e^{-\kappa_\theta t} - e^{-\kappa_r t} \right)$$
$$+ r_\infty \left(1 - e^{-\kappa_r t} \right) \tag{30.6}$$

and

$$\text{var}(r_t) = p + q + s \tag{30.7}$$

---

[3] Strictly speaking, this subset contains both parameters and initial values of the state variables.

[4] For a nice discussion of the properties of the Doubly Mean-Reverting Vasicek model, of its calibration to swaption prices and yield volatilities, of its application to 'repressed markets', of its eigenstructure and for approximate closed-form expressions when the volatility of the short rate is time dependent, see Erekhinskiy (2013).

with

$$p = \left(\frac{\kappa_r \sigma_\theta}{\kappa_r - \kappa_\theta}\right)\left[\frac{1 - e^{-2\kappa_\theta t}}{2\kappa_\theta} + \frac{1 - e^{-2\kappa_r t}}{2\kappa_r} - \frac{2\left(1 - e^{-(\kappa_r + \kappa_\theta)t}\right)}{\kappa_r + \kappa_\theta}\right]$$

(30.8)

$$q = \frac{\sigma_r^2\left(1 - e^{-2\kappa_r t}\right)}{2\kappa_r}$$

(30.9)

$$s = \frac{\rho\sigma_r\sigma_\theta}{\kappa_r - \kappa_\theta}\left[\frac{1 - e^{-(\kappa + \kappa_\theta)t}}{\kappa_r - \kappa_\theta} - \frac{1 - e^{-2\kappa t}}{2\kappa_r}\right].$$

(30.10)

Exercise 73 *Derive Equations (30.6) and (30.7).*

Exercise 74 *Looking at Equation (30.7), discuss what happens when $\kappa_\theta = \kappa_r$.*

Exercise 75 *Show that the expectation at time t_0 of the long-term short rate is given by*

$$\lim_{t \to \infty} \mathbb{E}_0[r_t] = r_\infty.$$

(30.11)

Exercise 76 *Derive the expression for the asymptotic variance of the short rate, $\lim_{t \to \infty} var[r_t]$.*

Exercise 77 *Show that the 'long yield', y_∞, in the Doubly Mean-Reverting Vasicek model is given by*

$$y_\infty = r_\infty - \left[\frac{\sigma_r^2}{2\kappa_r^2} + \frac{\sigma_\theta^2}{2\kappa_\theta^2} + \rho\frac{\sigma_r\sigma_\theta}{\kappa_r\kappa_\theta}\right]$$

(30.12)

Recognize the 'meaning' of the various terms in the square brackets. In particular, explain why y_∞ is not identical to (more precisely, is lower than) r_∞.

30.4 THE VOLATILITY OF THE INSTANTANEOUS FORWARD RATE

Given the definition of the instantaneous forward rate, f_t^T, given in Chapter 2, it is easy to derive that in the Doubly Mean-Reverting Vasicek model it is given by

$$f_t^T = -\frac{\partial}{\partial T}\ln P_t^T = \phi_t^T + b_t^T r_t + c_t^T \theta_t$$

(30.13)

with

$$\phi_t^T = -\frac{\partial A_t^T}{\partial T}$$

$$b_t^T \equiv -\frac{\partial B_t^T}{\partial T}$$

(30.14)

$$c_t^T \equiv -\frac{\partial C_t^T}{\partial T}.$$

(30.15)

Simple calculations give for b_t^T and c_t^T, respectively

$$b_t^T = e^{-\kappa_r(T-t)} \qquad (30.16)$$

$$c_t^T = \kappa \left\{ \frac{e^{-\kappa_\theta(T-t)} - e^{-\kappa_r(T-t)}}{\kappa_r - \kappa_\theta} \right\}. \qquad (30.17)$$

Exercise 78 *Derive Equations (30.16) and (30.17). Hint: the quickest way is to use the expression for B_t^T derived in the general affine setting in Chapter 18, Section 18.2, to consult the dictionary that translates the quantities of the general model into the specific parameters of the Doubly Mean-Reverting Vasicek model, and take the necessary derivatives.*

Proceeding as in Chapter 8, we can write for the volatility, $\sigma_{f_t^T}$, of the constant-maturity instantaneous forward rate, f_t^T

$$df_t^T = [\ldots]dt + b_t^T \sigma_r dz_r + c_t^T \sigma_\theta dz_\theta.$$

Exercise 79 *Why did we say 'constant-maturity'? What extra term would have appeared if we had followed a forward rate through its life?*

Then the application of Ito's lemma gives for the time-t volatility, $\sigma_{f_t^T}$, of the forward rate, f_t^T, expiring at time T:

$$\sigma_{f_t^T} = \sqrt{\left(b_t^T \sigma_r^t\right)^2 + \left(c_t^T \sigma_\theta^t\right)^2 + 2b_t^T c_t^T \rho \sigma_\theta^t \sigma_r^t}. \qquad (30.18)$$

Note that, as anticipated earlier, the volatility of forward rates (and hence of swaptions or of yields) depends only on the volatility-subset of parameters (of course, the terms b_t^T and c_t^T depend on κ and α). This pleasant feature is the key to the decomposition of the fitting procedure advocated in the previous section.

Now, one of the most firmly established facts about the volatilities of forward rates is that they are not monotonically declining (as the Vasicek model requires), but display a 'hump' for maturities ranging from 6 to 24 months. This is reflected both in the shape of implied volatilities of caplets, in the instantaneous volatilities that can be estimated from them (see Rebonato, 2002[5]), and from direct estimation of yield and forward-rate volatilities.

We saw in Chapter 8 (see Section 8.3 in particular) that the Vasicek model is intrinsically unable to recover this feature. The Doubly Mean-Reverting Vasicek model looks more promising, or, at least, richer. At this stage it is not clear, however, whether the extra richness of the Doubly Mean-Reverting Vasicek model is enough (or, rather, is 'of the right type') to account for the observed term structure of volatilities. Furthermore, the time-dependent reversion level is a latent variable, whose volatility and reversion speed are neither easy to get an intuitive feel about, nor simple to estimate statistically. Might we get similar-quality fits to the term structure of volatilities (by which we mean the yield covariance matrix or the swaption matrix) with radically different combinations of parameters? We answer this question in the next section.

---

[5] See Chapters 6 and 8 in particular.

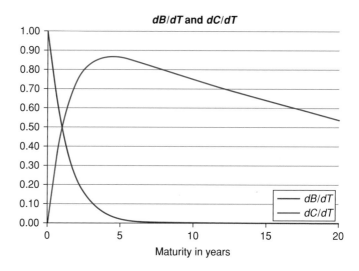

Figure 30.1 The terms $b_t^T \equiv \frac{\partial B_t^T}{\partial T}$ and $c_t^T \equiv \frac{\partial C_t^T}{\partial T}$ as a function of the residual time to maturity for a high reversion speed, κ_r, of 0.7513 and a reversion speed of the reversion level, κ_θ, of 0.03325.

30.5 THE BUILDING BLOCKS

In order to understand the qualitative behaviour of the volatility of the forward rate, it is useful to look one by one at the individual components.

We start from the term b_t^T. This has the simplest behaviour, as it is always monotonically decreasing, starting from an initial value of 1 for a vanishingly short forward-rate expiry (as it should, because in this case its volatility must coincide with the volatility of the short rate, σ_r). The smaller the reversion speed of the short rate, the slower the decay as a function of residual time to maturity. See Figure 30.1, which displays the term $b_t^T \equiv \frac{\partial B_t^T}{\partial T}$ as a function of the residual time to maturity for a high reversion speed, κ, of 0.75.

The term c_t^T has a more complex behaviour, because, for reasonable parameters, it starts from zero, reaches a maximum, and then exponentially decays with a speed dictated by the reversion speed of the reversion level. See Figure 30.1, which displays $c_t^T \equiv \frac{\partial C_t^T}{\partial T}$ as a function of the residual time to maturity for a reversion speed, κ_θ, of 0.033. Note that this function by itself displays some of the qualitative features of a forward-rate term-structure-of-volatility function, namely the presence of a 'hump' in normal market conditions.[6]

When the two functions are combined using Equation (30.18), the behaviour for the term structure of volatilities becomes richer. An example is given in Figure 30.2.

[6] For a detailed discussion of the origin and implications of the hump, see Rebonato (2002).

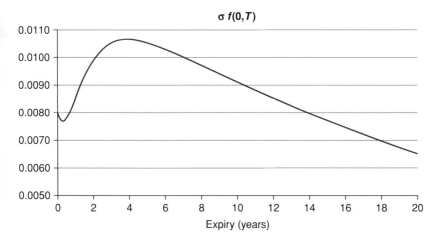

Figure 30.2 The reference term structure of forward-rate volatility, obtained with a volatility for the short rate, σ_r, of 80 basis points; a volatility for the reversion level, σ_θ, of 121 basis points, a reversion speed for the short rate, κ_r, of 0.7513; and a reversion speed for the reversion level, κ_θ, of 0.0333. The expiry in years of the forward rate is shown on the x-axis.

We note that in Figure 30.2 a small initial 'dip' in the volatilities for very short expiries is visible (a dip which is not observed in the term structure of forward-rate volatilities) This dip is, of course, due to the contribution to the total volatility that comes from the interaction of the two components, b_t^T and c_t^T. Now, this dip is emphatically not observed in the empirical data about discrete-tenor forward-rate volatilities. This 'small dip' disappears when we move from instantaneous to finite-tenor forward rate – the more quickly, the longer the tenor. A rather pronounced dip, however, persists even with 3- or 6-month tenors. What features of the model make this dip worse, and what do we have to do to make it disappear altogether?

Figure 30.3 shows what we should *not* do: it has been obtained keeping the other parameters unchanged, but reducing the reversion speed for the short rate, κ_r, to the still high, but lower level of 0.2. As Figure 30.3 shows, the dip has now increased. This allows us to draw a first conclusion: the counterfactual dip is associated with relatively low values for the reversion speed, κ_r, of the short rate to the instantaneous reversion level, θ_t. Which is just as well, as we concluded in Chapter 3 that the reversion speed, κ_r, should have a rather high value.

Going back to the original parameters, increasing the volatility of the short rate (say, setting $\sigma_r = 0.0140$) also moves us in the wrong direction – in the sense that the dip becomes more pronounced. This is shown in Figure 30.4.

This suggests that, in order to recover the correct qualitative shape of the term structure of forward-rate volatilities, we have two avenues open to us: the

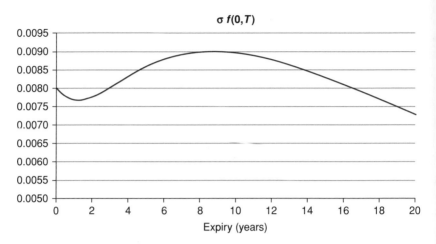

Figure 30.3 Same parameters as in Figure 30.2, but now the reversion speed of the short rate, κ_r, has been reduced to 0.2. The expiry in years of the forward rate is shown on the x-axis.

first is to set the volatility of the short rate much, much lower than the volatility of the reversion level (say, setting $\sigma_r = 0.00140$; see Figure 30.5); the second is to increase the reversion speed of the short rate, κ_r. Which route should we take?

The price to pay if we follow the first is that, by setting the volatility of one of the two state variables to a very low level, we are effectively 'wasting' one state variable and end up working with a one-factor model.

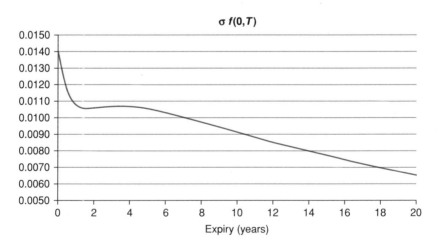

Figure 30.4 Same as base-case parameters, but the volatility of the short rate has now been increased to $\sigma_r = 0.0140$. The expiry in years of the forward rate is shown on the x-axis.

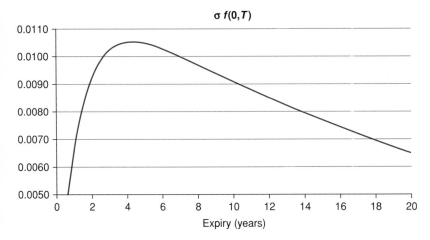

Figure 30.5 Same parameters as base case, but now with a low volatility for the short rate ($\sigma_r = 0.0014$). The expiry in years of the forward rate is shown on the x-axis.

The second alternative (increasing the reversion speed, κ_r) is more appealing, because, from the financial story spun in Chapter 3, we do expect $\kappa_r \simeq \kappa_{TR}$, ie, the reversion speed of the short rate, to be similar to the (high) reversion speed of the target rate.

If we really want a model which truly has two factors (and therefore a volatility of the short rate of, say, at least one half to one quarter of the volatility of the reversion level) and which has reversion speeds consistent with the financial story in Chapter 3, we are therefore naturally led to split not too unevenly the total volatility between the short rate and the reversion level, and to choose a reversion speed for the short rate, κ_r, much higher than the reversion speed for the reversion level, κ_θ. See Figure 30.6. We stress that we like this route not just because 'it fis the market well', but because it chimes well with the 'financial story' that underpins the model. See again Equation (30.4) and the discussion in Chapter 3.

The short-expiry behaviour is still not perfect, but we must keep in mind that

1. we are looking at the volatilities of *instantaneous* forward rates here (and, as we said, that the volatilities *discrete* forward rates would 'smooth out' to some extent the initial dip);
2. market-observed implied volatilities are root-mean-squared averages of the instantaneous volatility, and therefore the dip will be quickly absorbed for all but the shortest expiries; and
3. it may not be unreasonable to preserve a small increase in implied volatilities for extremely short-dated options to cater for 'surprises' (ie, for unexpected events that might generate short-term uncertainty

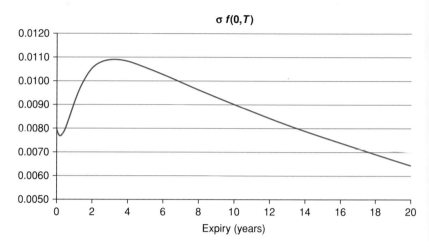

Figure 30.6 Same parameters as the base case, but now with $\kappa_r = 1$. The expiry in years of the forward rate is shown on the x-axis.

in the actions of the monetary authorities – actions that would plausibly affect the very short end of the yield curve).

Exercise 80 *We have worked with instantaneous forward rates. Obtain the expression for finite-tenor forward rates, $F_t^{T,T+\tau}$, and comment on what happens to the 'dip'.*

30.6   INITIAL CONCLUSIONS

So far we have shown that, if we want to recover the well-established humped behaviour for the volatility of the forward rates using a doubly mean-reverting Vasicek model such as the one in Equations (30.1) to (30.3), we are naturally led to embrace either of two choices (or a judicious combination of both):

1. either we set an extremely *and permanently low* volatility for the short rate, we work with what is effectively a one-factor model, and we accept that the short-rate stochastic dynamics is essentially there for decoration purposes;
2. or we work with a proper two-factor model, in which case the reversion speed for the short rate must be much higher than the reversion speed of the instantaneous reversion level.

The first option has unpleasant consequences that go beyond the offence it causes to our aesthetic sense. Recall in fact the shape of the function c_t^T, which goes to zero at the origin. (See again Figure 30.17). This means that, if we put *all* the burden of the recovery of the humped term structure of volatilities on the shoulders of the reversion-level factor, the volatility of the forward rate of vanishingly short expiries has to go exactly to zero. This is not reasonable.

A non-negligible volatility for forward rates of very short expiries can therefore only come from a non-zero volatility of the short rate. For this non-negligible volatility not to 'spoil' the term structure of volatilities, the effect of this volatility component will have to be neutralized rather quickly, because we want the pleasant behaviour of the function c_t^T to take over. The natural way to do so is with a high reversion speed of the short rate, κ_r.

As we shall see, this has important implications for the magnitude of convexity.

Exercise 81 *We have not considered yet the effect of the correlation parameter, ρ, on the qualitative shape of the term structure of forward-rate volatilities. Establish some reasonable bounds for this quantity by keeping the constraints on σ_r, σ_θ, κ_r and κ_θ obtained previously, and imposing that the resulting term structure of forward-rate volatilities should be humped. A very good discussion of the impact of the correlation parameter, ρ, on the term structure of volatilities is presented in Erekhinskiy (2013), Section 3.3 in particular.*

30.7 QUALITY OF THE FIT

As a next step, we move to fitting the model parameters to the volatility structure and to the shape of the yield curve. As the reader knows well by now, we are not interested in fitting at all costs the observed market yields or their volatilities as snugly as possible. We do not want to use the model, to go back to the nomenclature introduced in Chapter 1, in a 'snapshot mode'. We are interested in fits that are consistent with the financial story that underpins the model, and with a plausible economic interpretation of the yield curve. The discussion presented in the previous section shows that it should be possible to recover the salient qualitative features of the term structure of forward-rate volatilities. We now want to look at the degree of quantitative agreement. As explained earlier, the actual fitting procedure is carried out in two stages: to the volatility structure first, and to the yield curve then.

30.7.1 Calibrating the Model to the Volatility Structure

In order to fit to the volatility structure we look at the recovery of the market swaption matrix.[7]

The parameters we could optimize over are the two volatilities (σ_r and σ_θ), the two reversion speeds (κ_r and κ_θ); and the correlation, ρ. We do not leave these quantities unconstrained, but we require that they should obey the relationships we have established in Section 30.4. These constraints are required in

---

[7] We could have looked at the recovery of the yield covariance matrix. However, this quantity contains little information about the volatility of forward par rates. Therefore taking into account the information from the swaption matrix introduces a 'basis' (the difference between the volatility of forward Treasury par rates, and the volatility of LIBOR-based forward swap rates), but makes the fit more interesting and more demanding.

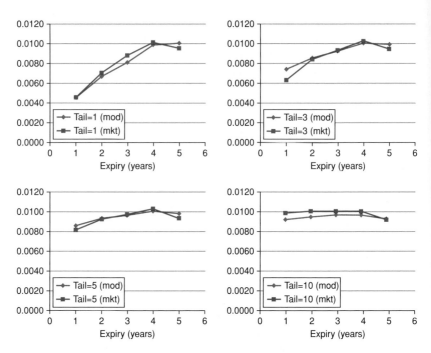

Figure 30.7 The fit to the whole $ swaption matrix on a typical day in the first half of 2012 obtained with $\kappa_r = 0.751$, $\kappa_\theta = 0.033$, $\sigma_\theta = 0.0122$ and $\sigma_r = 0.0099$ (and, as imposed, $\rho = 0.4$). The labels Tail$n$, with $n = 1$, 3, 5 and 10 in the four panels denote the maturity of the underlying swap rate; mod and mkt denote the model and market values for the absolute swaption volatilities. The expiry of the swaption in years is shown in all cases on the x-axis.

order to recover (i) the gist of our financial story and (ii) a model shape for the term structure of forward-rate volatilities consistent with what observed in the market (at least in normal times). So we require $\kappa_r > k_\theta$ and $\sigma_\theta > \sigma_r$. As for the correlation ρ, in our calibration procedure it was not optimized over, but set to 0.4.[8]

The quality of the resulting fit to the whole $ swaption matrix on a typical day in the first half of 2012 is shown in Figure 30.7. The best fit was obtained with $\kappa_r = 0.751$, $\kappa_\theta = 0.033$, $\sigma_\theta = 0.0122$ and $\sigma_r = 0.0099$ (and, as imposed, $\rho = 0.4$).

It is interesting to pause and consider the relative magnitude of the two reversion speeds obtained by the fit to the swaption matrix. They differ by an order of magnitude. The picture that the fitting conveys is the following: the short rate reverts quickly to the instantaneous reversion level. The instantaneous

---

[8] How did we choose this magic value? By looking at the effect of the correlation coefficient on the qualitative shape of the term structure of forward-rate volatilities. See also Erekhinskiy (2013), Section 3.3.

reversion level, however, reverts very slowly to its own long-term level of attraction. What the fit produces is indeed consistent with the discussion in Naik (2002) and in Chapter 3. This is good.

In the model under consideration, the quasi-unit-root nature of rates behaviour is therefore due to the low reversion speed of the reversion level, θ_t, to its own very-long-term reversion level, r_∞. Rates, in this picture, ultimately gravitate towards a stable long-term level, but they can wonder with great freedom around this level. After taking care of all the *mutandis* that need to be mutated when we switch between measures, a casual inspection of a long time series of bond yield suggests that this is not an outlandish picture of the behaviour of yield curves.

Exercise 82 *Consider a yield of maturity τ. Show that, to second order in τ, its volatility, $\sigma_{y(\tau)}$, is given by*

$$\sigma_{y(\tau)} = \sigma_r \sqrt{1 + \left(\frac{\kappa \tau}{2}\right)^2 \left(\frac{\sigma_\theta}{\sigma_r} - 1\right)}.$$

Comment on what the result shows about whether, for short-but-not-so-short maturity (ie, to second, not to first, order) the yield volatility will be increasing or decreasing with maturity. What relationship between the volatilities σ_r and σ_θ must be satisfied for the second-order approximation of the yield variance to be positive? For the volatility as a function of maturity to be increasing? Which parameter that you may have expected to play a role is missing in the second-order result? How will it make an appearance in higher-order terms? Under what conditions does a hump appear?

Going back to the quality of the fit, we note the closeness of the fit is not sufficient for derivatives-pricing purposes. However, the model, simple as it is, has the ability to capture well the essential features of the swaption matrix. As the volatilities of yields of different maturities are well recovered, we can also have confidence that the estimation of the value of convexity (see the discussion in Chapter 21) will also be captured in a satisfactory manner.

30.7.2   Calibrating the Model to the Yield Curve

With the volatility parameters fixed after the first stage of the calibration as described earlier, we move to the fitting of the reversion level of the reversion level (r_∞) and of the initial values of the two state variables, the short rate (r_0) and the instantaneous reversion level (θ_0). If the model has to make sense, the initial value of the short rate must be very close to 'today's' level of Fed fund rate. Therefore we constrain the quantity r_0 to lie in the close neighbourhood of the current Treasury 'short rate'. We are therefore effectively left with only two degrees of freedom (r_∞ and θ_0) to fit the whole yield curve.

Despite this Spartan parsimony, there is some scope for flexibility in the yield curve shapes that one can obtain. For instance, if today's short rate (r_0)

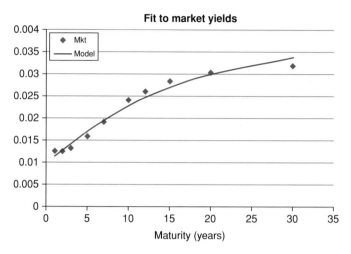

Figure 30.8 The fit to the yields for the same day used for the swaption fit. The continuous curve shows the model yields (curve labelled Model) and the dots the market yields (curve labelled Mkt). The fit was carried out using information about bond prices only out to 20 years. The 30-year yield is therefore a model prediction.

were at a low level, the instantaneous reversion level (θ_0) at a high level, and the reversion level of the reversion level (r_∞) at an intermediate level, the yield curve could assume a humped shape. Also a V-shaped yield curve, similar to what was observed in the US Treasury market in early 2001, could be obtained by reversing the relative positioning of the quantities r_0, θ_0 and r_∞.

The success of this fitting enterprise clearly depends on the received shape of the market yield curve, but the inability to recover much more complex shapes should be seen as a virtue, not a drawback, of the model. This is so, because, by its inability to fit, the model can alert the modeller that something important (probably liquidity, or market segmentation, or a complex pattern of short-term expectations) has been left out the picture offered by the model.

Figure 30.8 shows the quality of the fit to the market yield curve for the same day for which the swaption fit discussed earlier was carried out. Note that the fit was carried out using information about bond prices only out to 20 years. The 30-year yield is therefore a model prediction, that can be (rather favourably) compared with the observed market yield.

We stress that it is possible to obtain a much closer fit to the yield curve by optimizing blindly over all the model parameters. However, this choice of parameters would fail to recover the yield volatilities (and the swaption matrix), and would therefore give no reliable information about, say, the value of convexity. Since with the calibration procedure we have carried out we *can* say something meaningful about convexity, we turn to this topic in the next section.

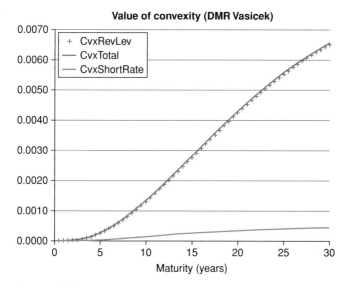

Figure 30.9 The total value of convexity (to continuous curve, labelled CvxTotal) for different maturities (on the *x*-axis, in years), split into the component from the short rate (continuous curve labelled CvxShortRate) and the component from the reversion level (curve labelled CvxShortRate).

30.8 THE VALUE OF CONVEXITY

The parameters determined in the swaption part of the fitting procedure imply a certain value of convexity for all maturities. The overall contribution of convexity to the level of yields comes from the yield variability from the stochasticity of both state variables. So, we have a short-rate component to the convexity contribution and a corresponding contribution from the reversion level.

This value of convexity is most simply estimated by setting all the volatilities to zero (while leaving the other degrees of freedom unchanged), recalculating the model yield curve, and taking the difference between the two yield curves.

The outcome from this procedure is shown in Figure 30.9, which splits the contribution to convexity arising from the two state variables.

The first observation is that for long maturities the contribution of convexity to the observed market yields is important: for the yield curve that prevailed in the early 2010s, for instance, the 'all-in' 30-year yield was about 300 basis points, and the convexity contribution approximately 65. (Without convexity, remember, yields would be *higher*). At the long end of the yield curve this is not a 'small correction'.

The split of this significant convexity contribution to the observed market yields is every bit as interesting as its overall magnitude. It is easy to see that the lion's share of the convexity contribution comes from stochasticity of the reversion level, not of the short rate. This may at first blush seem surprising, given the relatively small difference between the two volatilities: $\sigma_\theta = 0.0122$ and $\sigma_r = 0.0099$. Recall, however, that the contribution to the yield volatility from one state variable depends both on the volatility of the state variable, *and on its reversion speed*. The higher the reversion speed, the more the evolution that state variable will be 'tucked in' and will hug its reversion level, the more muted the associated long-term variability. Indeed, when we look at the values for the reversion speeds obtained during the swaption optimization, we find a difference of one order of magnitude ($\kappa_r = 0.751, \kappa_\theta = 0.033$), which explains the radically different contributions to the convexity from the two state variables.

30.9   WHAT HAPPENED TO THE $\mathbb{P}$-MEASURE?

All the treatment presented in this chapter was firmly embedded in the risk-neutral ($\mathbb{Q}$) measure. What happened to our desire to attain a *structural* understanding of the yield curve, an understanding, that is, that straddles the real-world and the risk-neutral measures?

We do not deal with the $\mathbb{P}$-measure dynamics in this chapter, because we need to understand first some of the problems encountered when working 'across measures' with traditional affine models. These are best introduced by looking at the models discussed in Chapters 31 and 33. The solutions to these common problems proposed in Chapter 35 can then be most naturally grafted on top of the DMRV model.

CHAPTER 31

Real Yields, Nominal Yields and Inflation: The D'Amico–Kim–Wei Model

"He had been told that when looking for a good oracle, it was best to find the oracle that other oracles went to."
– Douglas Adamas, *Mostly Harmless*

31.1 THE PURPOSE OF THIS CHAPTER

In this chapter we look in detail at the Kim–Wright (2005) model, and at its natural successor, the D'Amico, Kim and Wei (2010) model. Both are very good examples of latent-variable models, and they attempt to give a coherent account of both nominal and real rates (and, to some extent, even of liquidity).

One of the tasks for which this class of models can be used is the prediction of future yields and future inflation. Hence the first reason for the oracular reference in the quote that opens the chapter. As predicting yields is only a quarter of a tiny step away from predicting excess returns, these models also produce predictions for risk premia and yield expectations. These we analyze in the last part of the chapter. The main results are that "a large portion of the decline in long-term yields and distant-horizon forward rates since the middle of 2004 [is due] to a fall in term premiums", and that "about two-thirds of the decline in nominal term premium owes to a fall in real term premiums, but estimated compensation for inflation risk has diminished as well".

This is interesting in itself. Apart from the specific findings, the Kim–Wright model provides a blueprint for the latent-variable approaches discussed further in Chapter 34. It is important to become familiar with this approach, because it is very common in the modern term-structure literature. See, in this respect, the references quoted in Section 31.10.

Finally, the Kim–Wright model and its cousins are frequently referred to by central banks, and are used by policymakers as one of the tools to assess the magnitude and sign of the risk premium, the extent to which inflation expectations are 'well-anchored'[1], etc. So, whatever the merits of the model, in itself this is a powerful reason for going to the oracle others oracles go to. The last

---

[1] See, eg, Gospodinov and Wei (2015).

section of the chapter mentions a few of the currently most popular (first-order) oracles.

31.2 EMPIRICAL FINDINGS ABOUT INFLATION

The modelling approaches presented in this chapter attempt to account for some empirical facts about nominal rates, real rates and liquidity that we summarize in this section.

First of all, recall from Chapter 14 that we defined the time-t, maturity-T break-even inflation, $BEI_{t,T}$, as the difference between the the time-t, maturity-T nominal and real yields[2]:

$$BEI_{t,T} = y_{t,T}^N - y_{t,T}^R. \tag{31.1}$$

We also obtained in the same chapter that the expected realized inflation from time t to time T, $EI_{t,T}^{\mathbb{P}}$, is related to the break-even inflation, $BEI_{t,T}$, by the relationship

$$BEI_{t,T} = EI_{t,T}^{\mathbb{P}} + \mathcal{P}_{t,T}, \tag{31.2}$$

where $\mathcal{P}_{t,T}$ is the time-t, maturity-T inflation risk premium.

D'Amico et al. (2010) start their study by running a regression of the time-t, 10-year-maturity break-even inflation against three nominal yields, namely the 3-month, 2-year and 10-year yields:

$$BEI_{t,10} = \alpha + \beta_1 y_{t,0.25}^N + \beta_2 y_{t,2}^N + \beta_3 y_{t,10}^N. \tag{31.3}$$

Now, if market real yields did not incorporate any liquidity distortions, they would be a reflection of the underlying true real yields. Nominal yields, in turn, would be just the sum of expected inflation plus the inflation risk premium (which together make up the break-even inflation), plus the real yield. Therefore one would expect a high R^2 in the regression of break-even inflation against the nominal-yield regressors.

If, however, the yields from the inflation-linked bonds were affected by factors other than the real yields (such as liquidity) that do not affect – or affect to a more limited extent[3] – the nominal yields, then the R^2 would be low.

The results from the regression show that all the regressors (and the intercept) are highly significant (the level of yields do contain information about the level of break-even inflation), but the R^2 is low (about 32%). This leads D'Amico et al. (2010) to conclude that "a large part in variation in break-even inflation cannot be explained by factors underlying the nominal interest rate variations.[4]

---

[2] Here and in what follows, the superscripts N and R denote 'nominal' and 'real' quantities, respectively.

[3] For a discussion of liquidity, see Section 32.5 in Chapter 32, and Fontaine and Garcia (2008).

[4] p. 4.

Next D'Amico et al. (2010) carried out a joint Principal Component Analysis of nominal and TIPS yields.[5] We have shown in Chapter 7 that three factors account for more than 97% of the variation in nominal yields. However, if the 5-, 7- and 10-year TIPS yields are added to the nominal yields, D'Amico et al. (2010) find that an extra principal component is needed to account for the same level of variance. Again, this suggests that there is 'something more' to the dynamics of the TIPS yields – something that is not reflected in the dynamics of the nominal yields.

Finally, D'Amico et al. also note that the third principal component extracted from combined nominal and TIPS yields is poorly correlated with any of the nominal principal components.

Putting all these pieces of circumstantial evidence together, the authors conclude that the extra variability must come from a liquidity factor, which was larger in the early years of TIPS issuance, and then progressively decreased in importance as the market matured.

In addition to various pieces of anecdotal evidence to buttress their liquidity case D'Amico et al. (2010) also observe, that (if the inflation risk premium is relatively small and constant) the break-even inflation should be closely related to inflation expectations. Now, nobody knows what the market 'expects' about inflation, but one can look at the results of survey inflation forecasts. The authors report that the TIPS break-even inflation was below the inflation forecasts "almost all the time before 2004.[6] In the absence of a liquidity factor, a break-even inflation *below* expectation would imply a negative (and highly volatile) risk premium – while all empirical research suggests that it should be relatively low and slow-varying.

Of course, a liquidity factor would push TIPS prices down and TIPS yields up, and would reduce the estimated break-even inflation – see Equation (31.1).

In sum: D'Amico et al. (2010) build a case for the need to add a liquidity factor to the three factors used by Kim and Wright (2005) to account for nominal and real rates. This they do in a latent-variable, affine framework that we discuss in the rest of the chapter.

31.3 THE NO-ARBITRAGE RELATIONSHIPS

In Chapter 14 we derived an expression for the real and nominal market prices of risk and for the real and nominal short rate, that we reproduce below for ease of reference.[7]

---

[5] Usually, we speak interchangeably of real yields and of yields from index-linked bonds (such as the *T*reasury *I*nflation *P*rotected *S*ecurities – TIPS, for short). However, we are exploring here the possibility that the yields of the traded TIPS may reflect factors (such as liquidity) other than real rates, and we must therefore carefully distinguish between TIPS yields and real yields.

[6] p. 6.

[7] Useful discussions with, and comments from, Dr Naik Vasnt and Dr Vlad Putyatin are gratefully acknowledged.

Call the chosen state variables, x_t. Recall that in Chapter 14 we obtained that the process of the real stochastic discount factor was given by

$$\frac{d\pi_t^R}{\pi_t^R} = -r_t^R dt - (\lambda^R)^{\mathrm{T}} dz_t + (\xi^u)^{\mathrm{T}} dz_t^u, \tag{31.4}$$

with the real short rate given by

$$r_t^R \equiv \underbrace{r_t^N - ei_t + (\lambda^N)^{\mathrm{T}}\xi}_{-\mu_{\pi^R}}, \tag{31.5}$$

and where

- r_t^N denotes the nominal short rate,
- ei_t is the expected inflation,
- λ^N is the vector of market prices of risk associated with the shocks to the nominal yield curve, and
- ξ is the volatility vector of the price process.

Then, changing notation to conform with the D'Amico et al. symbols, we have

$$\mu_{\pi^R} = ei_t - r_t^N - (\lambda^N)^{\mathrm{T}}\sigma_Q, \tag{31.6}$$

with

$$\sigma_Q = \xi. \tag{31.7}$$

These results are general. Now we introduce the affine assumption. More specifically, we first require that the (nominal) short rate, the (nominal) market price of risk and the nominal state-price deflator should all be affine functions of the state variable(s):

$$r_t^N = \rho_0^N + \left(\rho_1^N\right)^{\mathrm{T}} x_t \tag{31.8}$$

$$\lambda_t^N = \lambda_0^N + \left(\lambda_1^N\right)^{\mathrm{T}} x_t \tag{31.9}$$

$$\pi_t^N = \rho_0^{\pi^N} + \left(\rho_1^{\pi^N}\right)^{\mathrm{T}} x_t. \tag{31.10}$$

Then we make same affine requirement for inflation and for the associated real-rate quantities. This gives

$$ei_t = p_0 + (p_1)^{\mathrm{T}} x_t \tag{31.11}$$

$$r_t^R = \rho_0^R + \left(\rho_1^R\right)^{\mathrm{T}} x_t \tag{31.12}$$

$$\pi_t^R = \rho_0^{\pi^R} + \left(\rho_1^{\pi^R}\right)^{\mathrm{T}} x_t \tag{31.13}$$

$$\lambda_t^R = \lambda_0^R + \left(\lambda_1^R\right)^{\mathrm{T}} x_t. \tag{31.14}$$

The coefficients for the nominal and real short rate cannot be arbitrary, however, because of Equation (31.5) that links the two quantities. Therefore, using

Equations (31.6) and (31.8) to (31.14), and equating constant terms and terms linear in the state variables, we can determine four of the quantities as

$$\rho_0^R = \rho_0^N - p_0 + \left(\lambda_0^N\right)^{\mathrm{T}} \sigma_Q \qquad (31.15)$$

$$\rho_1^R = \rho_1^N - p_1 + \left(\lambda_1^N\right)^{\mathrm{T}} \sigma_Q \qquad (31.16)$$

$$\lambda_0^R = \sigma_Q - \lambda^N \qquad (31.17)$$

and

$$\lambda_1^R = \lambda_1^N. \qquad (31.18)$$

It is important to note that the no-arbitrage conditions and the affine assumption imply that the real market price of risk must track the (stochastic) nominal market price of risk[8], with a constant offset given by Equation (31.17).

Exercise 83 *Derive the last four equations. Careful: our expressions are slightly different from what is found in D'Amico et al. because they define the price process as $d(\log Q_t) = ei_t dt + \xi_t^T dz_t + \xi^u dz_t^u$ while we write $\frac{dQ_t}{Q_t} = ei_t dt + \xi_t^T dz_t + \xi^u dz_t^u$. Two two specifications differ by a convexity term.*

In sum: we reached the conclusion that, if we want to specify an *affine* model both for real and for nominal rates, the affine coefficients for the real variables are constrained to be some specified functions of the affine coefficients of the nominal rates and market price of risk, and of the volatility of the price level.

31.3.1 What the No-Arbitrage Relationships Really Imply

The results we have just obtained are very important, and it is worthwhile pausing for a moment.

Let's start from the nominal rates. Suppose that we want to price nominal bonds. Within an affine setting, we begin by assuming that there is a set of variables, x_t, such that nominal bonds are obtained as follows. We start from

$$dx_t = \mathcal{K}_N^{\mathbb{P}} \left(\theta_N^{\mathbb{P}} - x_t\right) dt + S_N \lambda_t^N dt + S_N dz_t$$

$$= \mathcal{K}_N^{\mathbb{Q}} \left(\theta_N^{\mathbb{Q}} - x_t\right) dt + S_N dz_t, \qquad (31.19)$$

where, as usual, in the second line the nominal market prices of risk have been absorbed in the $\mathbb{Q}$-measure nominal reversion-speed matrix and in the $\mathbb{Q}$-measure nominal reversion level, $\theta_N^{\mathbb{Q}}$. The affine assumption then means that the nominal short rate, r_t^N, must be expressible as an affine function of the state variables:

$$r_t^N = \rho_0^N + \rho_1^N x_t, \qquad (31.20)$$

---

[8] The nominal market price of risk is, of course, stochastic because it is an affine function of the state varibales: it is a *deterministic* function of the *stochastic* state variables.

and (if the market price of risk also is an affine of the state variables) that the nominal bond prices can be obtained as the $\mathbb{Q}$-measure expectation of the exponential of the path of the nominal short rate:

$$P_{t,T}^N = \mathbb{E}^{\mathbb{Q}}\left[e^{-\int_t^T r_s^N ds}\right], \tag{31.21}$$

where we have slightly changed the expression for the bond price (which we usually denote by P_t^T) in order to make room for a superscript, i, $i = R, N$, to keep track of whether we are dealing with nominal (superscript N) or real (superscript R) bonds. We shall use the same superscript convention for yields, and for all bond-related quantities.

So far, so familiar. Let's suppose that we are now interested in real, not nominal, bond prices, but that we want to use the same state variables, x_t, to describe them. Then we could, of course, write

$$\begin{aligned}
dx_t &= \mathcal{K}_R^{\mathbb{P}}\left(\theta_R^{\mathbb{P}} - x_t\right) dt + S_R \lambda_t^R dt + S_R dz_t \\
&= \mathcal{K}_R^{\mathbb{Q}}\left(\theta_R^{\mathbb{Q}} - x_t\right) dt + S_R dz_t.
\end{aligned} \tag{31.22}$$

In an affine setting we would posit:

$$r_t^R = \rho_0^R + \rho_1^R x_t, \tag{31.23}$$

and everything would flow exactly as before, to obtain

$$P_{t,T}^R = \mathbb{E}^{\mathbb{Q}}\left[e^{-\int_t^T r_s^R ds}\right]. \tag{31.24}$$

Of course, the reversion speeds and the reversion levels under $\mathbb{P}$ would be different in the nominal and real cases, as would the market prices of risk; however, if we are interested either in real bonds only, then the affine coefficients, $\rho_0^R, \rho_1^R, \lambda_0^R, \lambda_1^R$ that link the short rate and the market price of risk (and, of course, the stochastic discount factor) to the state variables could be, so to speak, anything.

But let's suppose that we want simultaneously to model both nominal and real bonds, still using the same set of variables. All of a sudden, a number of self-consistency issues arise. Take for instance the equation

$$r_t^R = r_t^N - ei_t + (\lambda^N)^{\mathrm{T}}\xi. \tag{31.25}$$

Suppose that we have estimated to our heart's content – perhaps using nominal excess return studies – the functional dependence of the nominal market price of risk, λ^N, on the state variables. Let's also suppose that we have estimated the volatility of the price process, ξ. Once we have done this, as soon as we model the nominal and real short rate together, we clearly see that the expected inflation is totally determined by Equation (31.25). This already tells us that the coefficients that relate the real short rate, the inflation expectations and the nominal market price of risk to the state variable must obey one set of constraints. In general, the constraints on the affine coefficients expressed in

Equations (31.6) and (31.8) stem from the self-consistency conditions of which Equation (31.25) is one example.

The important point here is that the joint estimation of real and nominal rates with the same state variables requires far more delicate handling than what is required for the modelling of either set of rates in isolation. And, as we shall see, the calibration issues become correspondingly more demanding,

31.4 THE ASSUMPTIONS ABOUT THE PROCESS FOR THE STATE VARIABLES

Let's go back to the D'Amico et al. (2010) model.

As we have seen, if we have a nominal and a real short rate, r^i, $i = R, N$, we can always write

$$P_{t,T}^i = E^{\mathbb{Q}} \left[e^{-\int_t^T r^i(s)ds} \right] \qquad i = R, N. \tag{31.26}$$

Assume now that the chosen state variables follow in the real world a process of the type[9]

$$dx_t = \mathcal{K} (\theta - x_t) dt + S dz_t \tag{31.27}$$

Then given the treatment presented in Chapters 16 to 18, we know straight away that, once we have make this affine assumption, we can write

$$P_{t,T}^i = e^{A_{t,T}^i + \left(B_{t,T}^i \right)^{\mathrm{T}} x_t}, \tag{31.28}$$

where the differential equations and the initial conditions that we derived in Chapter 18 apply. As usual, as we move from the real-world to the risk-neutral measure, the reversion level vector and the reversion speed matrix have to be adjusted to account for state-dependent risk aversion.

The nominal and real yields, $y_{t,T}^i$, take the form

$$y_{t,T}^i = \alpha_{t,T}^i + \left(\beta_{t,T}^i \right)^{\mathrm{T}} x_t \tag{31.29}$$

with

$$\alpha_{t,T}^i = -\frac{1}{T-t} A_{t,T}^i \tag{31.30}$$

and

$$\beta_{t,T}^i = -\frac{1}{T-t} B_{t,T}^i. \tag{31.31}$$

Of course, a model is specified only once specific values are assigned for the placeholders in Equation (31.27). Recall that D'Amico et al. (2010) do not

---

[9] To remain consistent with the notation used in this book we have slightly changed the notation in Kim and Wright (2005) and D'Amico et al. (2010): their reversion-level vector, μ, is our θ, and their matrix Σ is our matrix S. Also, for consistency their quantities $a_{t,T}^i$ and $b_{t,T}^i$ (Equations (22) and (23) in Kim and Wright (2005)) have been changed to $\alpha_{t,T}^i$ and $\beta_{t,T}^i$.

refer to a financial 'story' and want to employ latent variables. Without loss of generality, they therefore make the following choices:

$$\theta = \begin{bmatrix} 0 \\ 0 \\ 0 \end{bmatrix} \tag{31.32}$$

$$\mathcal{K} = \begin{bmatrix} k_{11} & 0 & 0 \\ 0 & k_{22} & 0 \\ 0 & 0 & k_{33} \end{bmatrix}. \tag{31.33}$$

Then they require that

$$S = \begin{bmatrix} 0.01 & 0 & 0 \\ \Sigma_{21} & 0.01 & 0 \\ \Sigma_{31} & \Sigma_{32} & 0.01 \end{bmatrix}. \tag{31.34}$$

Why 'without loss of generality?' Because, as we will discuss in Chapter 33, it is always possible to orthogonalize either $\mathcal{K}$ or S. What is not possible, under $\mathbb{Q}$, is to have both $\mathcal{K}$ and S diagonal. Here D'Amico et al. (2010), choose to diagonalize the reversion-speed matrix, rather then the 'volatility' matrix, under $\mathbb{P}$.

What about the zero reversion-level vector? Since we are dealing with latent variables, any rigid offset can also be absorbed in a suitable variable redefinition, and therefore this choice, too, causes no violence to generality.

31.5 INFLATION EXPECTATIONS AND RISK PREMIA

Recall from Chapter 4 that, modulo a convexity term, we obtained for the price process, Q_t:

$$\log\left(\frac{Q_T}{Q_t}\right) = \int_t^T ei_s ds + \int_t^T \sigma_{i,N} dz_s + \int_t^T v_i dw_s \tag{31.35}$$

where the first shock is affected by nominal rates and inflation ($\sigma_{i,N} dz$), and one orthogonal to it ($v_i dw$). The second shock is typically introduced to account for short-run inflation variations not captured ('spanned') by movements in the yield curve.

Taking expectations and dividing by $(T - t)$ we defined for the time-t expected inflation per unit time over the period $[t, T]$, EI_t^T:

$$EI_t^T = \frac{1}{T - t} \mathbb{E}_t \left[\log\left(\frac{Q_T}{Q_t}\right) \right] = E_t \left[\int_t^T ei_s ds \right]. \tag{31.36}$$

If we make the assumption that the expected inflation is an *affine* function of the state variables introduced earlier,

$$ei(x_t) = \rho_0^{ei} + \left(\rho_1^{ei}\right)^{\mathrm{T}} x_t, \tag{31.37}$$

we can calculate the expectation $\mathbb{E}_t \left[\int_t^T ei_s ds \right]$. To do so,

- first we interchange the expectation and the integration:

$$\mathbb{E}_t \left[\int_t^T ei_s ds \right] = \int_t^T \mathbb{E}[ei_s] ds; \tag{31.38}$$

- next we write

$$\mathbb{E}[ei_s] = \rho_0^{ei} + \left(\rho_1^{ei} \right)^{\mathrm{T}} E[x_s | x_t]; \tag{31.39}$$

- then we substitute the expression for the expectation $\mathbb{E}[x_s | x_t]$:

$$\mathbb{E}[x_s | x_t] = x_t e^{-\mathcal{K}(s-t)} + \left(I - e^{-\mathcal{K}(s-t)} \right) \theta; \tag{31.40}$$

- finally we substitute back into $\int_t^T \mathbb{E}[ei_s] ds$ and integrate to obtain

$$EI_t^T = \alpha_{t,T}^{EI} + \beta_{t,T}^{EI} x_t \tag{31.41}$$

with

$$\alpha_{t,T}^{EI} = \rho_0^{ei} + \frac{1}{T-t} \left(\rho_0^{ei} \right)^{\mathrm{T}} \left[\int_t^T \left(I - e^{-\mathcal{K}(s-t)} \right) ds \right] \theta \tag{31.42}$$

and

$$\beta_{t,T}^{EI} = \frac{1}{T-t} \left[\int_t^T \left(e^{-\mathcal{K}^T(s-t)} \right) ds \right] \rho_1^{ei}. \tag{31.43}$$

Remember that we *defined* the time-t, maturity-T break-even inflation, BEI_t^T, to be given by

$$BEI_t^T = y_{t,T}^N - y_{t,T}^R \tag{31.44}$$

and that we *derived* that

$$BEI_t^T = EI_t^T + \mathcal{P}_t^T, \tag{31.45}$$

where $\mathcal{P}_t^T$ is the inflation term premium.

It then immediately follows that, in the D'Amico et al. model, both break-even inflation and the inflation risk premium are affine functions of the state variables:

$$BEI_t^T = \left(\alpha_{t,T}^N - \alpha_{t,T}^R \right) + \left(\beta_{t,T}^N - \beta_{t,T}^N \right)^{\mathrm{T}} x_t \tag{31.46}$$

and

$$\mathcal{P}_t^T = \left(\alpha_{t,T}^N - \alpha_{t,T}^R - \alpha_{t,T}^{EI} \right) + \left(\beta_{t,T}^N - \beta_{t,T}^N - \beta_{t,T}^{EI} \right)^{\mathrm{T}} x_t. \tag{31.47}$$

31.6 ADDING LIQUIDITY

In addition to the variables $\{x_t\}$, D'Amico et al. (2010) include a liquidity factor. They do so as follows.

First, they distinguish between the TIPS real yields, $y_{t,T}^R$ (the quantities we have been working with so far, but which are now 'hidden' variables), and the

TIPS actual yields, $y_{t,T}^{TIPS}$ (which we can measure, but which are also affected by liquidity). More precisely, they begin by writing

$$y_{t,T}^{TIPS} = y_{t,T}^R + L_{t,T}^{stoch} \tag{31.48}$$

with

$$L_{t,T}^{stoch} = \frac{1}{T-t} \log E_t^{\mathbb{Q}} \left[e^{-\int_t^T (r_s^R + l_s)ds} \right] - y_{t,T}^R \tag{31.49}$$

and with l_s representing the instantaneous liquidity spread.

Why did we append the superscript '*stoch*' to the $L_{t,T}$ term? Because D'Amico et al. (2010) distinguish between a stochastic liquidity factor (the quantity $L_{t,T}^{stoch}$ defined in Equation (31.49)), and a deterministic component, $L_{t,T}^{det}$, to reflect the deterministic change in liquidity between the first issuance of TIPS and approximately 2004 – by which time the TIPS market had fully matured, and liquidity had significantly improved. We do not analyze this aspect[10]; however, we stress that by following this modelling route a decline in the magnitude of the liquidity premium is to some extent backed into the model.[11]

As we are in an affine universe, it will come to no surprise that we are now going to posit

$$l_t = \gamma^T x_t + \widetilde{\gamma}\widetilde{x}_t, \tag{31.50}$$

where γ is a (3×1) vector, $\widetilde{\gamma}$ is a constant and $\widetilde{x}_t$ is a new (liquidity) variable that follows a simple Vasicek-like process:

$$d\widetilde{x}_t = \widetilde{\kappa}(\widetilde{\mu} - \widetilde{x}_t) + \widetilde{\sigma}dB_t. \tag{31.51}$$

As for the Brownian shock dB_t, it is assumed to be independent of the shock vector, dz_t, that affects the state variables, x_t.

As we have introduced a new factor that carries uncertainty with it, we must also add a liquidity risk premium, $\widetilde{\lambda}_t$, that, also unsurprisingly, we assume to be affine in the liquidity variable, $\widetilde{x}_t$:

$$\widetilde{\lambda}_t = \widetilde{\lambda}_0 + \widetilde{\lambda}_1^T x_t. \tag{31.52}$$

31.7 THE PARAMETER ESTIMATION PROCEDURE AND RESULTS

One of the great advantages of the affine assumptions made throughout is that we 'only' have to estimate the process for the driving variables, and the loadings from the driving variables and the 'primitive' derived variables.

---

[10] See, however, p. 12 in their paper.

[11] To be precise, the deterministic component L_t^{det} is maturity-independent (it depends only on calendar time) and has the shape of a backward 'S', a shape conferred to it by the functional form $L_t^{det} = \frac{c_1}{2}[1 - \tanh(c_2(t - c_3))]$.

From the discussion in the previous section it follows that the real-world quantities for the process for the state variables that need estimating are

1. the non-zero elements of the reversion-speed matrix, $\mathcal{K}$, under $\mathbb{P}$;
2. the non-zero elements of the volatility matrix, S;
3. the reversion speed, $\widetilde{\kappa}$, and the volatility, $\widetilde{\sigma}$, of the liquidity factor.

In principle, if these real-world quantities could be reliably estimated, and if these estimates were augmented with price information, the parameters that characterize the affine mapping from the state variables to the market price of risk parameters could be estimated.

However, the authors are well aware that "the standard technique of estimating [the model] using only nominal and TIPS yields and inflation data for a relative short period of 1990–2007 will almost surely run into small sample problems" and they conclude that "variables like $\mathcal{K}$ and Λ^N may not be reliably estimated."

Therefore D'Amico et al. augment the yield data with survey data, which are taken to be noisy estimates of the corresponding $\mathbb{P}$-measure quantities. However, as they are at pains to point out, they do not directly include inflation survey data in their information set, and use the survey information only to gently 'guide' the estimation of the parameters. They do so because they want to understand how well the model performs in extracting inflation expectations (and hence inflation risk premia).

Including the survey data, their vector of observable quantities, Y_t, is given by

$$Y_t = \left[q_t, \left\{ y_{t,T_i}^{TIPS} \right\}_{i=1,7}, \left\{ y_{t,T_j}^N \right\}_{j=3}, \{f_k\}_{k=1,3} \right]^{\mathrm{T}} \qquad (31.53)$$

with

$$q_t \equiv \log Q_t \qquad (31.54)$$

and Q_t, as usual, denotes the price level at time t.

The specific estimation procedure is based on an application of the Kalman filter, whose detailed mechanics need not concern us here. What is important is that D'Amico et al. (2010) allow for several nested versions of their more general model formulation, one of which (version NL – for 'No Liquidity' – in their paper) does not have the TIPS liquidity factor.

After the parameters have been estimated, all models (including the NL version) return a very persistent factor (ie, a factor with very low reversion speed, and a half-life of approximately 13 years). All the models also produce a similar, and very good, fit to nominal yields and survey forecasts of nominal short-maturity rates. This is noteworthy, because the model parameters are fixed by the calibration procedure, and the model only has the initial values of the state variables (three quantities in the NL version) to fit the nominal yield curve (and do lots besides).

However, the no-liquidity NL version of the model produces, especially in the first part of the sample, large pricing errors for the TIPS yields and fails to resolve the paradox of the 'negative inflation risk premium' mentioned in Section 31.2.

When liquidity-aware versions of the models are employed, the fit to TIPS yield becomes good throughout the sample (this is good, but, of course, there are also more fitting parameters). Furthermore, as one would expect, the liquidity premium estimated using the richer versions of the model declines markedly in the second half of the sample – this chimes well with what one can expect to have happened as the market matured. Recall, however, that this 'prediction' becomes somewhat less impressive when we recall that a deterministic declining liquidity component was built into the model via the deterministic component, $L_{t,T}^{\mathrm{det}}$ discussed earlier.

Finally, it is important to stress for the future discussion that the model was calibrated using data spanning the 1990–2007 period – a reasonable compromise between quantity and relevance of data. The 1990–2007 parameters were then kept fixed in the 2008–2014 part of the sample. Alas, as (bad) luck would have it, 2008 was not just any year, and the appropriateness of parameters estimated before the Great Recession for the post-2009 period is debatable. More about this later.

These results are interesting and encouraging. To understand better the nature of the solution the model provides, we analyze in detail in the rest of the chapter the predictions about nominal risk premium and rates expectations. We do so using the simpler, and considerably simpler-to-estimate, NL version of the model (for which the results of our calculations closely match the data kindly made available by the authors). This should be acceptable, as nominal yields and survey forecasts of nominal rates are well recovered also by the no-liquidity model version. Before doing so, however, it is important to understand better the challenge of the empirical estimation of the parameters. We do so by looking at the cum-liquidity version of the model.

31.7.1   The Difficulty of Parameter Estimation

We know that the breakeven inflation is defined to be

$$BEI_t^T = y_{t,T}^N - y_{t,T}^R \tag{31.55}$$

and that we *derived* that it is given by

$$BEI_t^T = EI_t^T + \mathcal{P}_t^T + L, \tag{31.56}$$

where L denotes the liquidity contribution. Suppose that we are interested in inflation expectations. (This, by the way, is not a purely academic concern: in early 2016 a marked fall in break-even inflation was observed. The Fed officials were keenly interested in whether the fall was due to a decline in long-term inflation expectations, in whether the liquidity or the risk premium were responsible for the fall, and in whether the inflation expectations had remained 'well-anchored'.[12] Given the 'early-rate-lift-off' conditions prevailing at the time, the monetary policy implication were obvious.)

Now, one can argue that, by adding information from inflation swaps, one can bring into play a set of market observables that are affected by the same inflation expectations and risk premia, but not – or, at least, not to the same extent – by liquidity.[13] Let's accept this as true.

With a clever set of regressions, one can therefore separate the differential effect of liquidity on break-even inflation and the inflation swap rate. However, short of introducing extra information from, say, excess return studies, one cannot decompose the contributions from inflation risk premia and expectations. Nonetheless, an affine model such as the D'Amico et al. claims that it can accomplish this feat. This clearly prompts one to ask: where does the extra information come from? How can the model be so clever?

The answer, of course, is that the extra 'something' comes from the cross-sectional information from bond prices, and from the no-arbitrage restrictions. The cross-section bond price information comes into play during the calibration of the model to the yield curve, when one set of parameters is observed to do a better job at recovering the yield curve than another one. The no-arbitrage conditions that we discussed in Section 31.3 then place strong restrictions on the parameters (for instance, by requiring that the real and nominal market prices of risk can differ only by a constant offset).

In theory this is all well and good. But do cross-sectional bond prices and no-arbitrage provide in practice the correct type of information to extract such fine features? *Especially when one is using latent variables*, how confident is one that a very different set of parameters may not have given a slightly worse, but still acceptable, fit? The very different set of parameters, of course, may matter very little as far as the fitting of the yield curve is concerned, but could produce very different predictions for other quantities, which we cannot observe, but in which we are interested – such as inflation expectations. See in this respect the discussion in Section 1.5, and Figure 1.2 in particular.

And as for the extra information provided by the no-arbitrage conditions, the reader is referred again to the brief discussion in Section 27.6 of the paper by Joslin, Le and Singleton (2013) whose very title, "Why Gaussian Macro-Finance Models Are (Nearly) Unconstrained Factor-VARs," suggests that, *by themselves,* no-arbitrage conditions add very little predictive power.

All of this is to say that, the more a model purports to predict fancy things that we cannot see, the more it is essential to check that it predicts well the

---

[12] As it happens, in an at-the-time influential study Gospodinov and Wei (2015) used an affine setting to argue that the observed fall in breakeven inflation was due mainly to a deterioration in liquidity.

[13] Why so? Because inflation swaps ae unfunded instruments in zero net supply. If, in a situation of market distress (poor liquidity), investors only want to hold on to nominal Treasury bonds, and try to lighten their balance sheets by selling everything else, this will automatically depress the yield of nominal bonds, increase the yield of real bonds and reduce the break-even inflation. The *mid* inflation swap rate, on the other hand, may well remain relatively unaffected.

less-fancy things that we can observe. This is what we shall do with gusto in the rest of the chapter.

31.8 NOMINAL AND REAL RATE EXPECTATIONS AND RISK PREMIA

31.8.1 Full-Sample Analysis

We show in Figures 31.2 to 31.5 the time series (1990 to 2014) of the observable nominal yield, and the estimated term premium and rate expectation for the 1-, 3-, 5- and 10-year nominal yields. For clarity of exposition we refer to the 1990–2007 fitting period as Period I, and the 'extrapolated', 2008–2014 as Period II.

For maturities up to three years (see Figures 31.2 and 31.3) the changes in nominal yields are driven in Period I by changes in expectations, and in Period II by changes in the risk premium. This is defensible, at least to the extent that one believed that the post-2009 Fed commitment to low rates for a very extended period was at the time fully accepted by the market. (It is slightly puzzling, if this explanation is valid, that the expectation of the 1-year yield should display more variability in Period II than the expectation of the 3-year yield, but the difference is, admittedly, small). However, this switch in the driving factor of market yields from expectations to risk premia is also uncomfortably associated with the end of the period over which the model has been fitted, raising the question of whether the model performs well in-sample, and not as well out-of-sample. This nagging worry is made more troublesome by the 'regime-switching' nature of the last year (2008) in the calibration set.

The bottom half of Figure 31.3 then displays the term premium, the level of the yield curve and its slope, proxied by the average of the yields, and the difference between the 10-year and the 1-year yield, respectively. Note that in the in-sample Period I the estimated term period is strongly correlated with the level of the yield curve. It is more difficult to disentangle the slope and level dependence in the second half, as the two quantities become extremely correlated. See Figure 31.1. For the January 2103–September 2014 period the correlation between the simple level and slope proxies is as high as 98%.

The term premium steadily decreases from 1990 to 2104; however, a small but interesting increase in risk premium occurs in May 2013. We discuss this feature at length in what follows.

As we move the analysis to the 5-year yield (see Figure 31.4), we notice the same strong dependence of changes in the nominal yields on the estimated expectations in Period I, and a switch-over to a strong dependence on changes in the risk premium in Period II, with expectations now remaining almost constant.

It is only when we look at the time series of the 10-year nominal yield (see Figure 31.5) that we observe a more balanced contribution between expectations and term premia throughout the fitted history. Unfortunately, the counterfactual dependence of the term premium on the level of the yield curve still

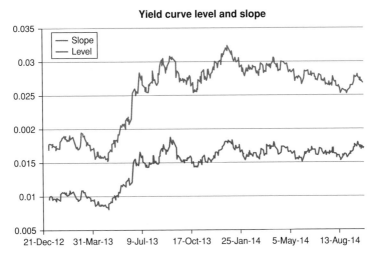

Figure 31.1 The level and the slope of the yield curve, proxied by the average of the yields, and the difference between the 10-year and the 1-year yield, respectively, from 2013 to summer 2014. Note how strongly correlated these two quantities have become in this period – since in normal times they are reasonable proxies for the first and second principal components they are close to uncorrelated. The strong correlation observed in the early 2010s is highly atypical, and is due to the exceptional monetary conditions prevailing at the time.

applies. For the 5-year yield, for instance, over the whole sample the correlation between the estimated term premium and the level of the yield curve and the term premium is as high as 91.8%, but the correlation with the slope is a negative −0.05! As we shall see, the picture changes in the more recent part of the data.

31.8.2 Prediction of Nominal and Real Excess Returns

It is obviously important to analyze how well the model predicts excess returns. Following a study by Qu (2015), we look at the excess returns not from discount bonds, but from several well-known nominal and real bond indices (the Barclays bond total-return indices). For each index (including the all-bond index), Qu calculates the one-year excess return as

$$xret_t^i = \log\left(prc_{t+1}^i\right) - \log\left(prc_t^i\right) - y_t^1, \tag{31.57}$$

where prc_t^i denotes the time-t price of the ith index, and, as usual, y_t^1 signifies the funding rate.

Qu (2015) uses the D'Amico–Kim–Wei model as calibrated in the paper described earlier, and, on any given investment, date regresses the excess returns against the model-produced state-dependent market prices of risk for 2, 5 and 10 years at the beginning of the investment period. Each set of

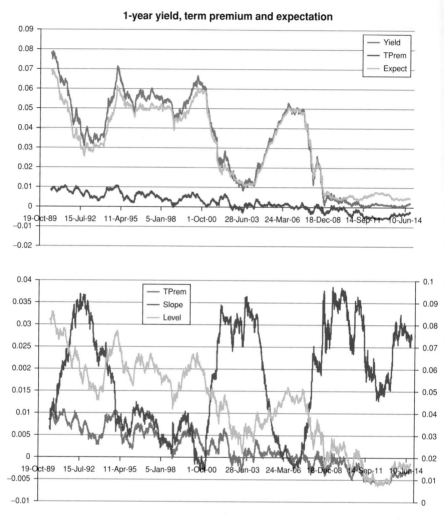

Figure 31.2 Time series (1990–2014) of the observable nominal yield, and the estimated term premium and rate expectation for the 1-year nominal yields (top panel) and the term premium, the level of the yield curve and its slope, proxied by the average of the yields, and by the difference between the 10-year and the 1-year yield, respectively (bottom panel). The y-axis for the slope is on the right-hand side of the graph.

regression coefficients uses 10 years worth of data. So, for instance, the prediction of excess return made on 1 January 2003 for the period 1 January 2003–31 December 2003 will use regression coefficients determined using the period 1 January 1993–1 January 2003. This ensures no peeking ahead.

In the study a different set of regression coefficients is determined for each index maturity. However, one of the indices refers to the universe of all the

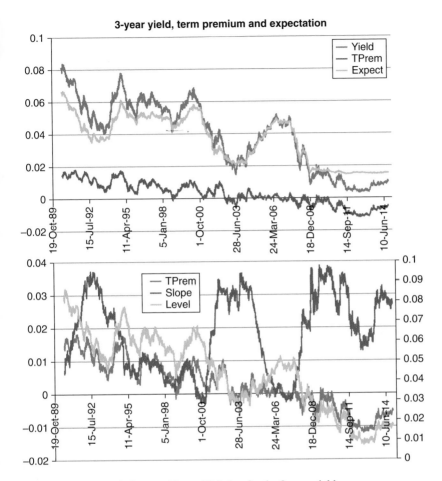

Figure 31.3 Same as Figure 31.2, but for the 3-year yield.

bonds, and is therefore very similar to the average excess return reported in Part VI of this book.

The historical and predicted excess returns for the all-bond nominal index is shown in Figure 31.6. The predicted excess returns were obtained using as right-hand variables in the predictive regression the three market prices of risk and the D'Amico–Kim–Wei liquidity factor. Figure 31.7 displays the same information, but for inflation-linked securities (TIPS).

Qu (2015) also performs regressions using the D'Amico–Kim–Wei liquidity variable as an additional explanatory (right-hand) variable. The results of these regressions are shown in Figures 31.8 and 31.9. The bottom panel of the figures (labelled SPX Sector) also show the results of the regressions of the total return from the S&P equity index (column labelled SPTR) and its sector components.

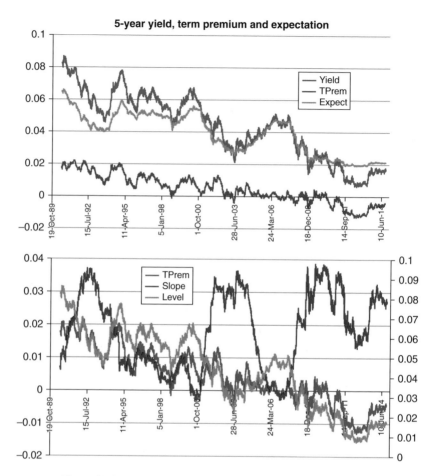

Figure 31.4 Same as Figure 31.2, but for the 5-year yield.

These data suggest several interesting observations.

First of all, over this relatively short period (approximately 10 years) the explanatory power (measured in terms of R^2) is very high, reaching 0.65 and 0.45 for the nominal and real indices, respectively. The degree of explanatory power is certainly flattered by the relatively short investigation period, but it remains impressive.

Second, the coefficients, apart from being all significant, 'make sense':

- when looked at across regressors, they have opposite signs, as we have argued in Part VI they should if one wants to capture a slope-like predicting factor;
- when looked at across maturities, they have the same sign for all index maturities;
- when looked at across nominal and real indices, same regressors have the same signs for nominal and for real, confirming the findings

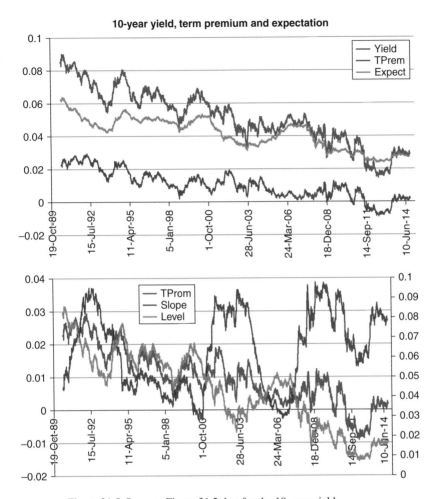

Figure 31.5 Same as Figure 31.2, but for the 10-year yield.

discussed in Chapter 5 that, during the period under analysis, the nominal risk premium is 'driven' by the real excess return;

- when looked at across bond (nominal and real) and equity indices, each block of non-intercept coefficients has the opposite sign: say, positive slopes for the regression of nominal and real bond returns against the 2-year market price of risk, and negative slope for the regression of the S&P excess returns against the same variables;

- the regression finds the opposite sign for the regression coefficients of nominal and S&P excess returns against the D'Amico–Kim–Wei liquidity factor;

- the regression finds the same sign for the regression coefficients of real and S&P excess returns against the D'Amico–Kim–Wei liquidity factor.

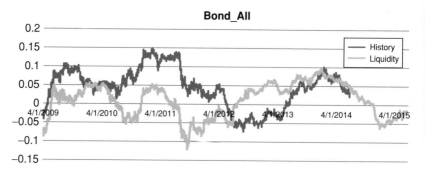

Figure 31.6 The realized excess return for the all-bond nominal index (blue curve labelled History) and the prediction from the regression (green curve labelled Liquidity) for the period 2008–2014 (for the realized returns) and 2015 (for the predictions).

Qu also shows that adding to the D'Amico–Kim–Wei liquidity factor the VIX index as an additional regressor adds very little to the explanatory power, generates difficult-to-interpret regression coefficients and gives rise to regression coefficients that are either outright statistically insignificant or borderline.

In sum: the relatively short history puts the high return predictability obtained using the D'Amico–Kim–Wei model in perspective, and cautions against making an outright comparison with, say, the Cochrane–Piazzesi or the Cieslak–Povala results reported in Chapter 27. However, the results are certainly very interesting. We therefore look at them in more detail in the next subsections.

31.8.3   Analysis of the May–September 2013 Events

We have discussed in chapter 5 the events linked to Bernanke's 'tapering talk' in May 2013, and the subsequent clarification of the true meaning of his words

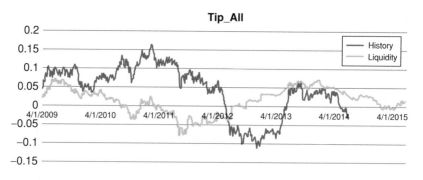

Figure 31.7 Same as Figure 31.6, but for TIPS.

			Beta			Std Error			
		R2	Const	2Y	5Y	10Y	Const	2Y	5Y	10Y
Bond Index	All	0.55	0.56	(3.41)	4.24	(1.65)	0.09	0.50	0.64	0.26
	3-5Yrs	0.54	0.45	(2.59)	3.25	(1.29)	0.07	0.40	0.51	0.21
	7-10Yrs	0.55	0.65	(3.93)	4.89	(1.90)	0.10	0.56	0.71	0.29
	>10Yrs	0.48	0.68	(4.26)	5.25	(2.00)	0.13	0.76	0.96	0.39
	1-5Yrs	0.52	0.35	(2.01)	2.54	(1.01)	0.06	0.32	0.40	0.17
	5-10Yrs	0.56	0.64	(3.83)	4.78	(1.87)	0.09	0.54	0.69	0.28
	>15Yrs	0.48	0.71	(4.51)	5.55	(2.11)	0.13	0.80	1.01	0.40
	3-7Yrs	0.56	0.52	(3.01)	3.78	(1.50)	0.08	0.44	0.56	0.23
	1-10Yrs	0.57	0.50	(2.97)	3.72	(1.47)	0.07	0.42	0.54	0.22
	5-15Yrs	0.55	0.65	(3.93)	4.89	(1.91)	0.10	0.57	0.72	0.29
	>5Yrs	0.52	0.67	(4.13)	5.12	(1.98)	0.11	0.63	0.80	0.32
Tip Index	All	0.38	0.28	(1.96)	2.34	(0.84)	0.21	1.19	1.53	0.63
	7-10Yrs	0.37	0.36	(2.44)	2.95	(1.08)	0.23	1.26	1.62	0.67
	1-5Yrs	0.21	0.16	(1.05)	1.28	(0.47)	0.14	0.79	1.01	0.42
	5-10Yrs	0.35	0.34	(2.29)	2.76	(1.01)	0.22	1.25	1.60	0.66
	>15Yrs	0.41	0.36	(2.77)	3.25	(1.11)	0.29	1.63	2.09	0.85
	3-7Yrs	0.28	0.24	(1.55)	1.88	(0.69)	0.19	1.05	1.34	0.55
	1-10Yrs	0.31	0.26	(1.70)	2.07	(0.76)	0.18	1.02	1.31	0.54
	5-15Yrs	0.37	0.36	(2.44)	2.94	(1.08)	0.23	1.29	1.65	0.68
	>5Yrs	0.40	0.34	(2.45)	2.91	(1.03)	0.25	1.40	1.80	0.74
SPX Sector	SPTR	0.28	(2.40)	13.19	(17.18)	7.10	0.68	3.77	4.83	1.99
	SPTRTELs	0.14	(1.86)	10.43	(13.52)	5.60	0.61	3.33	4.29	1.78
	SPTRUTIL	0.09	(1.24)	7.17	(9.25)	3.81	0.58	3.22	4.13	1.71
	SPTRMATR	0.10	(1.82)	10.54	(13.56)	5.53	0.04	5.28	6.75	2.78
	SPTRINDU	0.22	(2.59)	14.30	(18.59)	7.67	0.83	4.63	5.93	2.45
	SPTRINFT	0.19	(1.81)	9.54	(12.60)	5.31	0.80	4.43	5.68	2.34
	SPTRHLTH	0.48	(1.76)	9.59	(12.63)	5.21	0.46	2.54	3.25	1.34
	SPTRFINL	0.37	(5.37)	29.50	(38.11)	15.64	1.00	5.62	7.18	2.95
	SPTRENRS	0.08	(1.30)	8.13	(10.32)	4.15	0.75	4.17	5.34	2.21
	SPTRCONS	0.25	(0.88)	4.87	(6.46)	2.69	0.40	2.25	2.88	1.18
	SPTRCOND	0.41	(3.09)	16.18	(21.37)	8.98	0.68	3.79	4.85	2.00

Figure 31.8 The results of the regression of the excess returns from the nominal and real Barclays total-return indices between 2003 and 2014. The column labelled R2 reports the R^2 statistic; the column labelled Const the intercept in the regression; the columns labelled 2Y2, 5Y and 10Y the slopes in the regression of the excess returns against the 2-, 5- and 10-year model-produce market price of risk. The next three columns report the associated standard errors. Adapted from Qu (2015).

in September of the same year. In a nutshell, the market interpreted Chairman Bernanke's May pronouncement as implying that rates would be rising earlier than expected; and investors were then partly, but not totally, reassured that rates would remain low for a long time in September of the same year.

It is useful to look at Figures 31.10 to 31.13 in light of this background information. These figures simply 'zoom in' the 2013–2014 period in order to focus clearly on what happened during this very interesting period.

Looking at Figure 31.11, we note first that the 3-year market yield climbs significantly after May 2013, and stabilizes and partially retraces its step only after September. However, the model-extracted expectation remains absolutely flat during this period – even flatter than the expectations for the 1-year yield. (Not even the most aggressive interpretations of the May taper talk suggested moves in the Fed funds within one year – so this behaviour is somewhat puzzling.)

			Beta					Std Error				
		R2	Const	2Y	5Y	10Y	Liq	Const	2Y	5Y	10Y	Liq
Bond Index	All	0.65	0.68	(4.11)	5.12	(1.98)	(0.04)	0.08	0.47	0.60	0.25	0.01
	3-5Yrs	0.56	0.48	(2.77)	3.48	(1.38)	(0.01)	0.07	0.37	0.47	0.20	0.00
	7-10Yrs	0.64	0.78	(4.69)	5.84	(2.26)	(0.04)	0.10	0.53	0.68	0.28	0.01
	>10Yrs	0.63	0.91	(5.67)	7.01	(2.66)	(0.08)	0.12	0.70	0.88	0.36	0.01
	1-5Yrs	0.53	0.37	(2.11)	2.66	(1.06)	(0.01)	0.05	0.30	0.38	0.16	0.00
	5-10Yrs	0.63	0.75	(4.47)	5.57	(2.17)	(0.03)	0.09	0.51	0.66	0.27	0.01
	>15Yrs	0.62	0.96	(5.95)	7.36	(2.79)	(0.08)	0.13	0.74	0.94	0.38	0.01
	3-7Yrs	0.59	0.57	(3.30)	4.14	(1.63)	(0.02)	0.07	0.41	0.52	0.22	0.01
	1-10Yrs	0.63	0.57	(3.34)	1.18	(1.64)	(0.02)	0.07	0.39	0.51	0.21	0.01
	5-15Yrs	0.63	0.77	(4.61)	5.74	(2.23)	(0.04)	0.10	0.54	0.70	0.29	0.01
	>5Yrs	0.64	0.84	(5.14)	6.38	(2.45)	(0.05)	0.10	0.59	0.75	0.31	0.01
Tip Index	All	0.45	0.15	(1.21)	1.40	(0.48)	0.04	0.21	1.17	1.50	0.61	0.01
	7-10Yrs	0.43	0.24	(1.69)	2.01	(0.73)	0.04	0.22	1.25	1.60	0.65	0.01
	1-5Yrs	0.50	0.02	(0.21)	0.23	(0.08)	0.05	0.13	0.70	0.90	0.37	0.01
	5-10Yrs	0.44	0.19	(1.41)	1.67	(0.60)	0.05	0.22	1.21	1.55	0.63	0.01
	>15Yrs	0.42	0.27	(2.24)	2.59	(0.86)	0.03	0.30	1.70	2.17	0.88	0.02
	3-7Yrs	0.49	0.07	(0.56)	0.63	(0.22)	0.05	0.17	1.95	1.22	0.50	0.01
	1-10Yrs	0.47	0.11	(0.84)	0.99	(0.36)	0.05	0.17	1.95	1.22	0.50	0.01
	5-15Yrs	0.44	0.22	(1.61)	1.91	(0.69)	0.04	0.23	1.27	1.62	0.66	0.01
	>5Yrs	0.43	0.22	(1.74)	2.03	(0.70)	0.04	0.25	1.42	1.81	0.74	0.01
SPX Sector	SPTR	0.38	(2.89)	16.08	(20.79)	8.47	0.16	0.62	3.46	4.43	1.82	0.04
	SPTRTELs	0.16	(2.04)	11.48	(14.83)	6.09	0.06	0.60	3.27	4.22	1.75	0.03
	SPTRUTIL	0.11	(1.43)	8.29	(10.65)	4.34	0.06	0.58	3.22	4.11	1.69	0.03
	SPTRMATR	0.28	(2.60)	15.21	(19.39)	7.73	0.25	0.84	4.68	5.99	2.46	0.04
	SPTRINDU	0.32	(3.18)	17.80	(22.98)	9.32	0.19	0.78	4.33	5.55	2.28	0.05
	SPTRINFT	0.37	(2.47)	13.44	(17.47)	7.15	0.21	0.72	4.01	5.14	2.11	0.03
	SPTRHLTH	0.53	(2.01)	11.06	(14.47)	5.90	0.08	0.44	2.45	6.54	1.29	0.02
	SPTRFINL	0.47	(6.16)	34.17	(43.95)	17.84	0.25	0.91	5.12	6.54	2.68	0.07
	SPTRENRS	0.13	(1.68)	10.39	(13.14)	5.22	0.12	0.71	3.93	5.04	2.08	0.04
	SPTRCONS	0.33	(1.13)	6.36	(8.33)	3.40	0.08	0.39	2.17	2.77	1.13	0.02
	SPTRCOND	0.52	(3.68)	19.70	(25.77)	10.64	0.19	0.61	3.38	4.33	1.78	0.04

Figure 31.9 Same as Figure 31.8, but with the liquidity D'Amico–Kim–Wei factor added as a right-hand (explanatory) variable. Adapted from Qu (2015).

If we focus on the 10-year yield, the split between expectations and term premia is even more puzzling, because the model implies that immediately after the taper testimony the expectations slightly *decreased*. As for the September rectification by the Fed (which arguably should have lowered rate expectations), it has no visible effect on the model-extracted yield expectation. The bottom panel of the same figure shows that the term premium, which clearly accounts for the lion's share of the observed changes in the 10-year nominal yield, is very strongly correlated with the slope proxy for the yield curve. (The correlation between the term premium and the slope over this limited period is 99.1%.) This observation will be very important for future discussion – see, in particular, Section 35.2.

Similar considerations apply to the other intermediate yields.

31.9 CONCLUSIONS

To begin with the positive features of the D'Amico–Kim–Wei model, the most noteworthy one is its ability to fit nominal yields very well even in its simplest (no-liquidity, NL) incarnation. This is no mean feat because the numerous parameters are kept fixed at the values estimated in the pre-2008 period, and

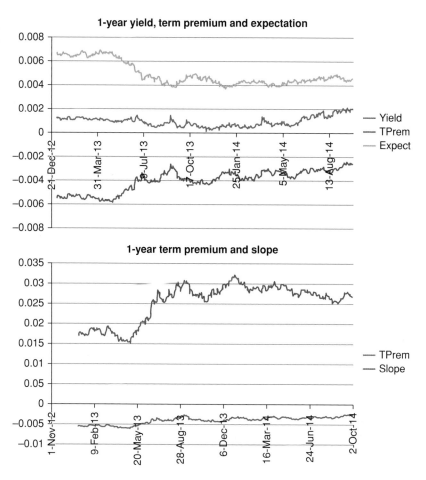

Figure 31.10 Same as Figure 31.2, but with data limited to the January 2013–September 2014 period.

the only degrees of freedom left to achieve the high-quality fit are the initial values of the three state variables of the restricted NL version.

Similarly encouraging is the good fit to real yields attained by the non-restricted versions of the model. The contention that the mispricing of real yields with the restricted version of the model is due to the neglect of the liquidity component is convincing.

The increase in liquidity 'discovered' by the non-restricted versions of the model is therefore encouraging. However, not too much should probably be made of this feature, as it is mainly due to the deterministic liquidity term, $L_{t,T}^{det}$, that firmly 'guides' the discovery.

Over a relatively short period (2003–2014), the Kim–Wright model successfully produces good predictions of excess returns both for nominal and for real

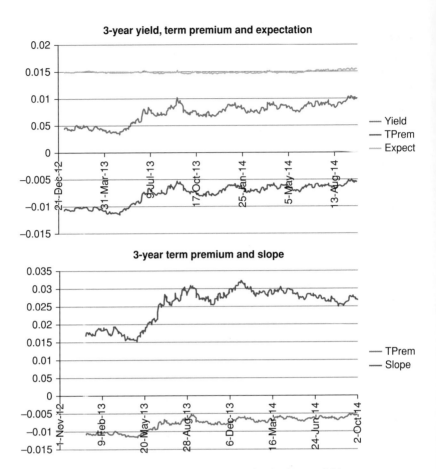

Figure 31.11 Same as Figure 31.10, but for the 3-year yield.

Treasuries. The adjective 'good' should be understood not just in terms of the predictive R^2, or of the significance of the regression coefficients, but of the overall plausibility of the financial 'story' produced by the 'story-less' (latent-variable) D'Amico–Kim–Wei model.

Other aspects of the model are less compelling. In particular, the confidence that can be placed on the reliability of the estimates of the more opaque quantities (the various term premia and expectations) is rather limited. There are two reasons for this:

1. The counterfactual dependence of the risk premium on the level and not the slope. (This result should be compared with the empirical analysis presented in Part VI.)
2. The difficult-to-understand apportionment of the observed changes in yields during a period (May 2013–September 2013) when plausible accounts of the market reactions to the Fed announcements would point to an increase first, and a decrease then, of expectations.

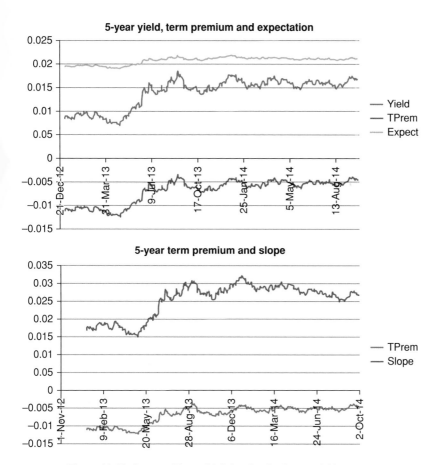

Figure 31.12 Same as Figure 31.2, but for the 5-year yield.

As we shall see, the second problem is shared by all but one of the modelling approaches that we review in the following. The first is not, and therefore a bit more troubling.

Going back to the interpretation of the yield rises in 2013 as being due almost exclusively to changes in term premia (with virtually no changes in expectations), we may have an explanation for this puzzling performance of the D'Amico–Kim–Wei model. As these puzzling predictions are shared by other modelling approaches that we review in detail in the following, we postpone the discussion of this point to later parts of the book (see Chapter 35 in particular).

31.10 RELATED WORK

One of the results of the model of D'Amico et al. (2010) discussed in this chapter is the decomposition of the yield curve into a real and a nominal component, and of the break-even inflation into inflation expectation and risk premium.

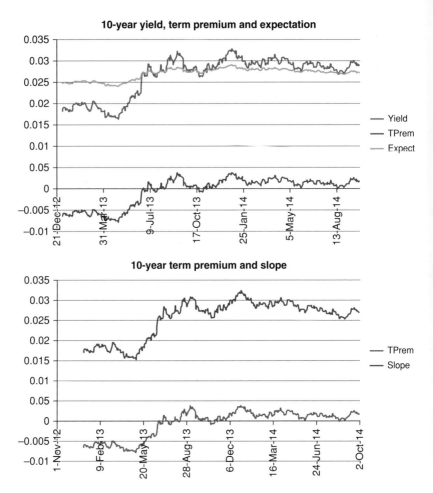

Figure 31.13 Same as Figure 31.2, but for the 10-year yield.

These decompositions have been looked at in a number of recent papers, such as the work by Abraham, Adrian, Crump and Moench (2015), who focus on the nominal/real split; Chen, Liu and Cheng (2010), who look at the term structure of inflation risk premia and of Gospodinov and Wei (2015), who extract inflation expectations using information from nominal and real Treasury bonds, inflation swaps and inflation options. Regarding this latest work, it is worth noting that they also look at the liquidity contributions to TIPS yields, and conclude that, when liquidity is taken into account, 'breakeven inflation is largely driven by a significant liquidity premium' and 'U.S. inflation expectations appear to be anchored and stable over time'. (See, in particular their Figure 31.7.) If correct, these conclusions are somewhat surprising, considering that at the time of their writing realized inflation was falling, or remaining at historically atypically low levels, in most of the developed world.

There is a vast literature devoted to the attempt to decompose the break-even inflation into a ($\mathbb{P}$-measure) inflation expectation and a risk premium. In addition to the works quoted earlier, the reader is referred to Christensen, Lopez and Rudebusch (2010); Grishencko and Huang (2013); Haubrig, Pennacchi and Ritchken (2012) (who use information from inflation swaps); Hördal and Tristani (2012); Joyce, Lidholt and Sorensen (2010) (who look at the UK nominal and real yield curves); and Kitsul and Wright (2013) (who analyse, as Gospodinov and Wei (2015) do, the information embedded in inflation options).

Finally, Fleckenstein, Longstaff and Lustig (2010, 2014) look at the 'quasi-arbitrage' of purchasing an inflation-linked TIPS bond, selling a (strip of) Treasuries, and entering an inflation swap. They find that TIPS are 'mispriced' (too 'cheap') with respect to Treasuries to the tune of $20 per $100 notional. This price 'error' cannot be accounted for, the authors claim, by counterparty credit risk, repo effects, financing costs, collateral value, or any frictions (including the obvious ones, such as bid-offer spreads, or less obvious ones, such as small differences in tax treatment). This, they claim, is a 'major puzzle to classical asset pricing theory'.

CHAPTER 32

From Snapshots to Structural Models: The Diebold–Rudebusch Approach

32.1 THE PURPOSE OF THIS CHAPTER

In the previous chapter we have seen the strengths and weaknesses of latent-variables models. Starting with this chapter we return to specified-variable models.[1] We do so by looking in some detail at the approach by Diebold and Rudebusch (2013)[2], who take a 'snapshot model'[3] and turn it into a dynamic affine model whose state variables can be interpreted as proxies for the Principal Components.

Since we know a lot about principal components, and they afford a ready intuition in terms of level, slope and curvature of the yield curve, this is very desirable, and facilitates the calibration of the model. Indeed, this insight will be the motivation for the Principal Component–based model presented in the next chapter. As we shall see in the next chapter, however, the transition from state variables that 'look a bit like principal components' to state variables that are exactly principal components is not all plain sailing.

We stress that in this chapter we give only a partial account of the Diebold–Rudebusch approach – in particular, we do not cover the important aspect of the statistical estimation of the model. This is a pity because, as Diebold and Rudebusch, say, their model

> blends two important and successful approaches to yield curve modelling: the [...] empirically based and the no-arbitrage theoretically based one. Yield curve models in both traditions are impressive successes, albeit for different reasons. Ironically, both approaches are equally impressive failures, and for the same reasons, swapped. That is, models in the [statistical] tradition fit and

---

[1] Arguably, the doubly mean-reverting Vasicek model discussed in Chapter 30 is a hybrid model, in that, strictly speaking, the short rate and its reversion level (the 'target rate', in the interpretation afforded in Chapter 3) are not observable. However, if we want the model to be financially motivated rather than a fitting device, we should interpret the state variables as proxies for observable rates (such as, say, the Fed Funds rate and the target rate).

[2] The work presented in Diebold and Rudebusch (2013) builds on earlier work by Christensen, Diebold and Rudebusch (2011).

[3] We defined snapshot models in the Introduction. See also the beginning of the next section.

forecast well, but they [...] may admit arbitrage possibilities, while the models in the arbitrage-free tradition are theoretically rigorous insofar as they enforce absence of arbitrage, but they may fit and forecast poorly.[4]

The model presented in this chapter, the authors continue, 'bridges the divide with a [statistically]-inspired model that enforces absence of arbitrage'.[5]

So, our sin of omission, when we fail adequately to cover in this chapter the statistical (parameter-estimation) aspect of the model, is not a minor blemish, as it fails to do full justice to an important aspect of the Diebold–Rudebusch approach. Since, however, the econometric aspect is very well covered in the book by Diebold and Rudebusch, brevity and a tight focus on the book narrative have recommended the skewed treatment we present below.

32.2 TURNING A SNAPSHOT MODEL INTO A DYNAMIC MODEL

Recall that in the Introduction we defined 'snapshot models' as cross-sectional devices to *interpolate* prices or yields of bonds that we cannot observe, given a set of prices or yields that we can observe. Snapshot models are not designed to explain the evolution of the yield curve, and their coefficients are, in general, not endowed with any financial or economic meaning. Snapshot models never trade off an ounce of fitting power for a pound of financial reasonableness – quite simply, because they do not know what financial reasonableness means.

The Nelson–Siegel (1987) model is certainly one of the most popular snapshot models and (in its Neslon–Siegel–Svensson incarnation) it is indeed the model used by the Fed to generate the data we have used in our studies of convexity and excess returns. (See Gurkaynak, Sack and Wright (2000, 2006).) In its simplest formulation, the time-t, T-expiry instantaneous forward rates, f_t^T, are given by

$$f_t^T = \beta_1^t + \beta_2^t e^{-\lambda \tau} + \beta_3^t \lambda e^{-\lambda \tau}, \tag{32.1}$$

with $\tau = T - t$. From the forward rates it is easy to obtain bond prices (see Chapter 2), and from these yields. The model parameters are then varied until the best possible fit is obtained between observed market prices and the corresponding model prices.

A brief comment on notation: the functional form above is characterized by four parameters, $\beta_1^t, \beta_2^t, \beta_3^t$ and λ. (Of course, there are no state variables.) I have appended a superscript 't' to three of them $(\beta_1^t, \beta_2^t, \beta_3^t)$ but not to the fourth (λ) simply to indicate that these quantities have been determined, as shown later, by fitting to the time-t yield curve. In the Nelson–Siegel approach, so is the parameter, λ, but in the Diebold–Rudebusch approach it is kept constant. The reason for this asymmetry will become apparent in the following. No dynamic interpretation should be given to these parameters – not at this stage, at least.

---

[4] Diebold and Rudebusch (2013), p. 76.   [5] Ibid., p. 76.

It is easy to show that, given the instantaneous forward rates in Equation (32.1), the corresponding yields, $(y_t^T)^{NS}$, are given by

$$(y_t^T)^{NS} = \beta_1^t + \beta_2^t \left(\frac{1 - e^{-\lambda\tau}}{\lambda\tau} \right) + \beta_3^t \left(\frac{1 - e^{-\lambda\tau}}{\lambda\tau} - e^{-\lambda\tau} \right). \qquad (32.2)$$

Exercise 84 *Derive Equation (32.2).*

Despite its unashamedly ad hoc nature, the Nelson–Siegel specification enjoys some promising features, which create an intriguing, albeit at this stage rather tenuous, link with financial reality. First of all, the two limiting values for the bond prices (namely, $\lim_{T \to t} P_t^T = 1$ and $\lim_{(T-t) \to \infty} P_t^T = 0$) are recovered for any choice of the parameter set $\{\beta_1^t, \beta_1^t, \beta_1^t, \lambda\}$.

Second, recall that

$$\lim_{T \to t} f_t^T = r_t. \qquad (32.3)$$

Then it is easy to show that, again for any choice of the parameter set $\{\beta_1^t, \beta_1^t, \beta_1^t, \lambda\}$,

$$\lim_{T \to t} \left(y_t^T\right)^{NS} = \lim_{T \to t} f_t^T = r_t. \qquad (32.4)$$

This says that the limit of the yields produced by the Nelson–Siegel model approaches the short rate, as it should, as the residual maturity goes to zero.

Finally, the limit of the infinite-maturity yield, $\lim_{(T-t) \to \infty} (y_t^T)^{NS}$, is a constant, given by

$$\lim_{(T-t) \to \infty} \left(y_t^T\right)^{NS} = \beta_1^t. \qquad (32.5)$$

This chimes well with what we derived in Chapter 8, where we showed that the yield curve it produces tends to a long-term constant. It's not much, but it's a start.

Exercise 85 *Prove properties (32.3) to (32.5).*

Finally, the Nelson–Siegel curve, despite its simplicity, is empirically observed to fit a wide variety of yield curves surprisingly well. Readers interested in understanding why such a simple functional form can perform so well are referred to the original paper by Nelson and Siegel (1987) and to the discussion in Diebold and Rudebusch (2013).[6]

So far, despite the asymmetry in the superscript notation, we have taken λ to be a fitting parameter on the same footing as the $\{\beta\}$ parameters. However, let's set the λ parameter to a fixed value, whose interpretation will be discussed later. Then we are left with the three parameters $(\beta_1^t, \beta_1^t, \beta_1^t)$ to fit the time-t yield curve. As we are not ashamed to state the obvious, we want to point out that, since yield curves change day after day, so will the optimal fitting parameters $\{\beta_1^t, \beta_2^t, \beta_3^t\}$ – but not λ.

---

[6] See p. 25.

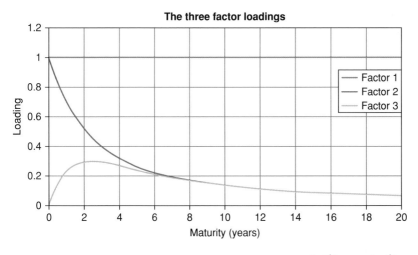

Figure 32.1 The factor loadings (the 'parameters') 1, ($\frac{1-e^{-\lambda\tau}}{\lambda\tau}$) and ($\frac{1-e^{-\lambda\tau}}{\lambda\tau}$ − $e^{-\lambda\tau}$) for a lambda of 0.7308.

If we look at the fitting exercise in this light, the time-t yield, y_t^{T},[7] can be seen as the result of multiplying three *fixed* quantities, 1, $\left(\frac{1-e^{-\lambda\tau}}{\lambda\tau}\right)$ and $\left(\frac{1-e^{-\lambda\tau}}{\lambda\tau}\right.$ − $e^{-\lambda\tau}$), by three *time-varying quantities*, β_1^t, β_2^t and β_3^t. In this interpretation, the coefficients $\left\{\beta_1^t, \beta_2^t, \beta_3^t\right\}$ (but not λ!) have become dynamic *variables*, and 1, $\left(\frac{1-e^{-\lambda\tau}}{\lambda\tau}\right)$ and $\left(\frac{1-e^{-\lambda\tau}}{\lambda\tau} - e^{-\lambda\tau}\right)$ have become *parameters*.

This interpretation could seem a bit contrived and unexciting, were it not for the fact that the three now-fixed 'parameters', 1, $\left(\frac{1-e^{-\lambda\tau}}{\lambda\tau}\right)$ and $\left(\frac{1-e^{-\lambda\tau}}{\lambda\tau} - e^{-\lambda\tau}\right)$, lend themselves to an interesting interpretation, suggested by Figure 32.1.[8]

The first loading is just a constant. Looking at Equation (32.2), this means that any shock to the first 'variable', β_1^t, will be transmitted equally to all the yields.

The second loading decays rapidly, with a 'half-life' of approximately 2.15 years. Looking at Equation (32.2), one can see that shocks to the second 'variable', β_2^t, will mainly affect the short maturity yields, and will have a negligible effect on the longest maturities.

Finally, the third loading has a humped shape, with a shallow maximum around 2.5 years. From Equation (32.2) this indicates that shocks to the third 'variable', β_3^t, will have no effect at the very short end, a decaying effect at the long end, and a maximum impact for intermediate-maturity yields (in the 2-to-5-year region).

---

[7] In the following we drop the superscript *NS* that denotes the yields produced by the Nelson–Siegel model.

[8] For readers comparing our results with those in Diebold and Rudebusch (2013), p. 28, it should be noted that their decay constant ($\lambda = 0.0609$) takes months, not years, as the unit of time – and therefore the dimensions of their λ are months^{-1}, not years^{-1}.

Diebold and Rudebusch $(2013)^9$ give another interpretation to the three loadings. Note that β_1^t moves yields in a parallel fashion (and therefore changes the *level* of the yield curve); that β_2^t changes the *slope* of the yield curve; and that β_3^t creates a hump in the yield curve (and therefore changes its *curvature*). The suggestive choice of words ('level', 'slope' and 'curvature') points to an obvious similarity between shocks to the variables, $\{\beta_1^t, \beta_2^t, \beta_3^t\}$, and shocks to the three first principal components. All of the sudden the rather artificial decomposition of the Nelson–Siegel snapshot model begins to look very interesting.

Before one gets carried away too much by this similarity, note however (i) that the 'slope factor' has the same sign for all yields, while the second principal component moves yields on opposite sides of the 'pivot point' in opposite directions; (ii) that the first true principal component is not a constant as a function of yield maturity (it actually resembles a combination of the Diebold–Rudebusch first and third factors, β_1^t and β_3^t); (iii) that the Nelson–Siegel loadings are not orthogonal, as true principal components should be (they cannot be, as they are all positive). To refresh her memory, the reader may want at this point to revisit the discussion of the empirical features of principal components presented in Chapter 7.

This decomposition carries out a good change of coordinates (from yields to the variables $\{\beta\}$) that readily lends itself to statistical estimation. As we said in the opening section, we do not pursue this route, which is well covered in Diebold and Rudebusch (2013), but we note that, at the very least, the treatment so far has provided us with a very useful statistical model of the yield curve. It remains to be seen if it can be turned into an arbitrage-free model, and an affine one at that.

Finally, we note that shocks to the short rate (which, as Equation (32.4) shows, is the limit of the yield of vanishingly short maturity) are just given by the sum of shocks to the first and second variables:

$$dr_t = d\beta_1^t + d\beta_2^t \tag{32.6}$$

because the impact of the loadings on the three factors for zero maturity are 1, 1 and 0, respectively. This relationship will become important when we turn this dynamic description of the yield curve into a no-arbitrage, affine model. This we do in the next section.

32.3   TURNING A DYNAMIC MODEL INTO A NO-ARBITRAGE AFFINE MODEL

So far we have turned a snapshot model into a model with an associated dynamics. However, as discussed in Part I of this book, it is not enough to cobble together plausible but disjointed building blocks to obtain an arbitrage-free model. And, if we want to make sure that an arbitrage-free model belongs to

---

[9] See p. 29.

the affine family, we must at least impose that some affine combination of the chosen state variables should give the short rate.

So, how can the suggestive statistical model sketched in the previous section be turned into an affine arbitrage-free model? We refer the reader to the derivation in Diebold and Rudebusch (2013), but, in a nutshell, the strategy they employ is the following.[10]

They start from three variables, which they would like to behave like the variables, $\{\beta_1^t, \beta_2^t, \beta_3^t\}$ discussed earlier. Since no respectable variable in the financial literature has ever been called β, they call the new variables x_i. They would like these variables to display a mean-reverting behaviour, with a reversion-speed matrix, $\mathcal{K}$, a reversion-level vector, $\vec{\theta}$, and a volatility matrix, S.[11] So, as usual, we have:

$$ d\vec{x} = \mathcal{K}\left(\vec{\theta} - \vec{x}\right)dt + Sd\vec{z}. \tag{32.7} $$

Then Diebold and Rudebusch look at the family of arbitrage-free affine models in the taxonomy provided by Duffie and Kan (1996), and pick the family member that most closely resembles the dynamic factors described above. More precisely, if the reversion-speed matrix, $\mathcal{K}$, is chosen to be[12]

$$ \mathcal{K} = \begin{bmatrix} 0 & 0 & 0 \\ 0 & \lambda & -\lambda \\ 0 & 0 & \lambda \end{bmatrix} \tag{32.8} $$

and if, inspired by Equation (32.6), the mapping from the state variables to the short rate is given by[13]

$$ r_t = x_1^t + x_2^t, \tag{32.9} $$

then we know (see Chapter 18) that the bond price, P_t^T, is given by

$$ P_t^T = e^{A_t^T + \left(\vec{B}_t^T\right)^T \vec{x}_t} \tag{32.10} $$

with

$$ \left(\vec{B}_t^T\right)^T = \begin{bmatrix} 1 & \frac{1-e^{-\lambda\tau}}{\lambda\tau} & \frac{1-e^{-\lambda\tau}}{\lambda\tau} - e^{-\lambda\tau} \end{bmatrix} \tag{32.11} $$

---

[10] See Sections 3.2 to 3.3, pp. 62–78.

[11] We have slightly changed the notation in Diebold and Rudebusch in order to conform to the notation adopted in the rest of the book. So, their X_i are our x_i, and their matrix Σ is our matrix S.

[12] We note in passing that we obtained in Chapter 7 (see Section 7.2.3 in particular) that the reversion-speed matrix in the real-world measure, $\mathbb{P}$, had the form $\mathcal{K} = \begin{bmatrix} \epsilon & 0 & 0 \\ 0 & a & -b \\ 0 & 0 & c \end{bmatrix}$, with $\epsilon << \min(|a|, |b|, |c|)$. Not quite the same, but a passable resemblance. Note, however, that the reversion speed matrix in Equation (32.8) applies to the pricing, $\mathbb{Q}$, measure. We will discuss in detail in Chapter 33 how an affine the market price of risk changes the form of the $\mathbb{P}$-measure reversion-speed matrix.

[13] This means that, using the notation in Chapter 18, $u_r = 0$, and $\vec{g}^T = [1, 1, 0]$.

and

$$\tau = T - t. \qquad (32.12)$$

As we have seen in Chapter 18, the expression for the arbitrage-free yields turns out to be

$$y_t^T = x_1^t + x_2^t \left(\frac{1 - e^{-\lambda \tau}}{\lambda \tau} \right) + x_3^t \left(\frac{1 - e^{-\lambda \tau}}{\lambda \tau} - e^{-\lambda \tau} \right) + \alpha_t^T. \qquad (32.13)$$

Exercise 86 *Derive Equations (32.10) and (32.13). Hint: From Chapter 18 look at the expression for the bond price for a general affine model, substitute Equation (32.8) for the reversion-speed matrix, and derive the expression for bond price and for the yields.*

A few observations are in order.

First note that, in order to pick out the strongest family resemblance between the NS-inspired dynamic model described Section 32.2, and the arbitrage-free affine models in the Duffie and Kan (1996) family tree, the first row of the reversion-speed matrix, $\mathcal{K}$, is zero. This means that the first factor (the first 'pseudo-principal-component') experiences no mean reversion at all and is a unit-root process. Given the hardly detectable reversion speed of the true first principal component uncovered, at least in the $\mathbb{P}$ measure, by statistical studies (see the discussion in Chapter 7) this is not an unreasonable choice.[14]

Second, we saw in Chapter 7 that the orthogonalization of the market yield covariance matrix, Σ, yields

$$\Sigma = V \Lambda V^{\mathrm{T}} \qquad (32.14)$$

and therefore

$$\overrightarrow{y} = V \overrightarrow{x}^{pc}, \qquad (32.15)$$

where we have appended the superscript pc to indicate that these are the true, not the proxy, principal components. Stating the obvious, as long as the covariance matrix is constant, this relationship must be true not just today, but at any time.

Now, let's pursue the analogy of the state variables with the principal components, and, for simplicity, let's deal with just three yields, of which we choose the first one to be the short rate. We can always construct from the Diebold–Rudebusch model three vectors, $\overrightarrow{u}_1$, $\overrightarrow{u}_2$ and $\overrightarrow{u}_3$, given by

$$\overrightarrow{u}_1 = \begin{bmatrix} 1 \\ 1 \\ 1 \end{bmatrix}, \overrightarrow{u}_2 = \begin{bmatrix} \frac{1-e^{-\lambda \tau_1}}{\lambda \tau_1} \\ \frac{1-e^{-\lambda \tau_2}}{\lambda \tau_2} \\ \frac{1-e^{-\lambda \tau_3}}{\lambda \tau_3} \end{bmatrix}, \overrightarrow{u}_3 = \begin{bmatrix} \frac{1-e^{-\lambda \tau_1}}{\lambda \tau_1} - e^{-\lambda \tau_1} \\ \frac{1-e^{-\lambda \tau_2}}{\lambda \tau_2} - e^{-\lambda \tau_2} \\ \frac{1-e^{-\lambda \tau_3}}{\lambda \tau_3} - e^{-\lambda \tau_3} \end{bmatrix}. \qquad (32.16)$$

---

[14] Technically, however, the reversion-speed matrix, $\mathcal{K}$, ceases to be invertible, and therefore the simple and handy derivations presented in Chapter 18 do not apply. As a computational trick, one can introduce a small reversion speed, ϵ, as element k_{11}, derive the equations as usual, and then take the limit as ϵ goes to zero.

If the parallel with principal components is to be pursued, one should have

$$\vec{y}_t = U\vec{x}_t \qquad (32.17)$$

with

$$U = \begin{bmatrix} \uparrow & \uparrow & \uparrow \\ \vec{u}_1 & \vec{u}_2 & \vec{u}_3 \\ \downarrow & \downarrow & \downarrow \end{bmatrix}. \qquad (32.18)$$

In the Diebold–Rudebusch model this relationship is always exactly satisfied. Indeed, if the first yield is the short rate, $\tau_1 = 0$, and we have that

$$\frac{1 - e^{-\lambda \tau_1}}{\lambda \tau_1} = 1 \qquad (32.19)$$

and

$$\frac{1 - e^{-\lambda \tau_1}}{\lambda \tau_1} - e^{-\lambda \tau_1} = 0. \qquad (32.20)$$

It follows that

$$U = \begin{bmatrix} 1 & 1 & 0 \\ 1 & \frac{1-e^{-\lambda \tau_2}}{\lambda \tau_2} & \frac{1-e^{-\lambda \tau_2}}{\lambda \tau_2} - e^{-\lambda \tau_2} \\ 1 & \frac{1-e^{-\lambda \tau_3}}{\lambda \tau_3} & \frac{1-e^{-\lambda \tau_3}}{\lambda \tau_3} - e^{-\lambda \tau_3} \end{bmatrix}$$

and the first element of the $\vec{y}$ vector (the short rate) is always exactly recovered as

$$y_1 = r_t = \begin{bmatrix} 1 & 1 & 0 \end{bmatrix} \begin{bmatrix} x_1^t \\ x_2^t \\ x_3^t \end{bmatrix} = x_1^t + x_2^t. \qquad (32.21)$$

(See Equation (32.9).) But, thanks to Equation (32.13), the identity also automatically applies to the other yields, for which we have

$$y_2 \simeq \begin{bmatrix} 1 & \frac{1-e^{-\lambda \tau_2}}{\lambda \tau_2} & \frac{1-e^{-\lambda \tau_2}}{\lambda \tau_2} - e^{-\lambda \tau_2} \end{bmatrix} \begin{bmatrix} x_1^t \\ x_2^t \\ x_3^t \end{bmatrix} \qquad (32.22)$$

and

$$y_3 \simeq \begin{bmatrix} 1 & \frac{1-e^{-\lambda \tau_3}}{\lambda \tau_3} & \frac{1-e^{-\lambda \tau_3}}{\lambda \tau_3} - e^{-\lambda \tau_3} \end{bmatrix} \begin{bmatrix} x_1^t \\ x_2^t \\ x_3^t \end{bmatrix}. \qquad (32.23)$$

This is all well and good. However, the yields must also be recovered as minus the logarithm of a bond price, P_t^T, divided by $T - t$. Fortunately, looking at Equations (32.10) and (32.13) we note that indeed they always do. One very pleasing feature of the Diebold–Rudebusch approach is therefore that these two separate routes of obtaining yields (either as $\vec{y}_t = U\vec{x}_t$ or as $y_t^i = -\frac{1}{T_i - t} \log P_t^{T_i}$) always exactly converge.

It may seem that we have made unnecessarily heavy weather to clarify an obvious point. Not so: we shall show in the next chapter, in which we work with 'true' principal components, that ensuring this convergence is not trivial, and requires some careful handling.

In sum: the interpretation of the variables $\{x\}$ as principal components is not skin-deep, but captures some important features that one would like to find in a principal component–inspired model. If it looks like a duck, it walks like a duck, and it talks like a duck, we should conclude that it is a duck. Or is it?

32.4   ARE THE VARIABLES REALLY PRINCIPAL COMPONENTS?

There is no question that the specification of the reversion-speed matrix (Equation (32.8)) proposed by Diebold and Rudebusch is the one that most closely resembles (actually, perfectly coincides with) the dynamic Nelson–Siegel model described in Section 32.2. However, the precise functional form of this model was not derived on the basis of some profound theoretical derivation. Rather, it came from a clever transformation of a snapshot model, whose variables ended up lending themselves to a serendipitous interpretation as quasi-principal components.

This observation prompts two possible lines of development.

First, if a modeller thought the unit-root assumption for the first quasi-principal component too drastic, one could easily add a (small) reversion-speed element, κ_{11}, turning the reversion-speed matrix, $\mathcal{K}$, into

$$\mathcal{K} = \begin{bmatrix} \kappa_{11} & 0 & 0 \\ 0 & \lambda & -\lambda \\ 0 & 0 & \lambda \end{bmatrix}. \tag{32.24}$$

The resulting no-arbitrage affine model would no longer be *exactly* equivalent to the dynamic Nelson–Siegel model, but, as just discussed, there is no fundamental reason why one should require that it should be so.

The second, (and perhaps the more interesting) development is the following. As we have seen, one of the more appealing features of the dynamic Nelson–Siegel model was that its variables lent themselves to an interpretation as quasi-principal components. But, if this is the case, why not work *exactly* with principal components as state variables, rather than with their proxies? If we did so, we could make use of the wealth of information we have accumulated about these quantities, and we could test with confidence whether our variables do behave as they should.

This is the avenue we explore in the next chapter. As we shall show, turning quasi-principal components into *true* principal components in a no-arbitrage affine setting is not a trivial matter – which only goes to show, if further proof were needed, that life is never quite as easy as one initially thinks.

A couple more observations. As we discussed earlier, Diebold and Rudebusch pick the dynamics of their chosen state variables on the basis of an interpretation of their 'meaning' and of what we called the family resemblance with the models in the Duffie and Kan (1996) family. This pins down uniquely the reversion-speed matrix, $\mathcal{K}$, in the $\mathbb{Q}$ measure. Now, if we want to interpret the variables $\{x\}$ as quasi-principal components, their $\mathbb{P}$-measure dynamics should be statistically determinable. In particular, for the interpretation to hold, their S volatility matrix should be (close to) diagonal. As for the $\mathbb{P}$-measure reversion-speed matrix, $\mathcal{K}^{\mathbb{P}}$, it should be whatever comes out from the econometric analysis. As Diebold and Rudebusch make clear in the opening chapters, we *do* know a lot about the $\mathbb{P}$-measure behaviour of the principal components – such as their degree of persistence[15]– and this is precisely one of the features that make their approach more appealing than latent-variables models. Indeed, we have examined in detail the $\mathbb{P}$-measure mean-reverting behaviour of the principal components in Chapter 7.

For the sake of simplicity let's assume that, in the real-world ($\mathbb{P}$) matrix, the reversion-speed matrix, $\mathcal{K}^{\mathbb{P}}$, should be diagonal,

$$\mathcal{K}^{\mathbb{P}} = \begin{bmatrix} \kappa_{11}^{\mathbb{P}} & 0 & 0 \\ 0 & \kappa_{22}^{\mathbb{P}} & 0 \\ 0 & 0 & \kappa_{33}^{\mathbb{P}} \end{bmatrix}, \tag{32.25}$$

with $\kappa_{11}^{\mathbb{P}} << \kappa_{22}^{\mathbb{P}} < \kappa_{33}^{\mathbb{P}}$ to reflect the persistence findings reported in Diebold and Rudebusch (2013). (We know from Chapter 7 that imposing a diagonal form to the real-world matrix $\mathcal{K}^{\mathbb{P}}$ is not quite right, but nothing in the following argument hangs on this particular form for the $\mathbb{P}$-measure reversion-speed matrix, $\mathcal{K}^{\mathbb{P}}$.)

Now, once the reversion-speed matrix under $\mathbb{Q}$ (32.8) is chosen, and the $\mathcal{K}^{\mathbb{P}}$ matrix turns out to be whatever we estimate, the affine market price of risk, $\Lambda = \Lambda_0 + \Lambda_1 x$, is fully specified. It would be an incredible fluke (or a convincing sign of the existence of a Benevolent Higher Being) if the 'implied' market price of risk so obtained turned out to bear more than a passing resemblance to the market price of risk that can be estimated from excess-return studies.

To repeat this point: as we have seen in Part VI, from Fama and Bliss (1987) onwards we know that the slope of the yield curve 'contains' a lot, if not all, of the return-predicting factor. But if this is the case, and if the second state variable of the Diebold–Rudebusch approach is to be interpreted as a 'yield curve slope', then the matrix Λ_1 should have the form

$$\Lambda_1 = \begin{bmatrix} 0 & \lambda_{21}^1 & 0 \\ 0 & \lambda_{22}^1 & 0 \\ 0 & \lambda_{23}^1 & 0 \end{bmatrix}. \tag{32.26}$$

---

[15] As we explained in Chapter 10, the degree of persistence of a process is related to its reversion speed (if any): the weaker the reversion speed, the more a shock will persist in the future. For a very strong reversion speed, the process quickly reverts to the reversion level and the shock is soon 'forgotten'; with zero reversion speed, a shock is for life, not just for Christmas.

It is most unlikely that the market-price-of-risk matrix Λ_1 obtained as the 'difference' between the $\mathbb{P}$- and $\mathbb{Q}$-measure reversion-speed matrices will look similar to the market-price-of-risk matrix Λ_1 obtained from statistical analysis of excess return. In general, it is easy to see that there is a tension (bordering on incompatibility) between (i) the $\mathbb{Q}$-measure reversion-speed matrix, $\mathcal{K}$, Diebold and Rudebusch choose, (ii) the empirical market-price-of-risk matrix, Λ_1, that reflects some well-established facts about excess returns, (iii) a statistically determined reversion-speed matrix, $\mathcal{K}^{\mathbb{P}}$, and (iv) the interpretation of the state variables as (quasi) principal components. Once the market price of risk is made to depend in a *specified* (affine) manner on the state variables, the modeller loses the ability to assign the nature of the variables *and* their $\mathbb{Q}$-measure reversion-speed matrix, $\mathcal{K}$. (This may well be one of the reasons why latent-variables affine term structure models are currently very popular.)

This tension is not unique to the Diebold–Rudebusch approach, and resurfaces in all the approaches that Saroka (2014) dubs 'specified-variables', and in the constraints highlighted in Joslin, Singleton and Zhu (2011). And as we discuss at length in Chapter 33, the problem is not solved (if anything is made more acute) if one moves from quasi- to exact principal components.

For all this, the model presented by Diebold and Rudebusch is very appealing, useful, simple and clearly presented. It does not solve all the problems, but, then again, neither does general relativity.

32.5 DEALING WITH LIQUIDITY

32.5.1 On-the-Run, Off-the-Run Bonds

Liquidity is a topic that transcends the Diebold–Rudebusch model – to be more precise, that has little to do with the model we have been looking at in this chapter. The reason for dealing with it here is that the general approach to deal with liquidity presented by Fontaine and Garcia (2008) is grafted on top of the Diebold–Rudebusch model.

To start with: what is liquidity? A textbook definition usually makes reference to the ability to sell (or buy) a position without 'moving its price'. [16] Discussing what 'moving its price' means would bring in a host of microstructural issues that are really beside the point here. In general 'liquidity hinges in large part on whether specialised dealers ("market-makers") respond to temporary imbalances in supply and demand by stepping in as buyers (or sellers) against trades sought by other market participants'.[17]

Since we are dealing with default-free government bonds, for our purposes the most immediate manifestation of differential liquidity is in the

---

[16] So, for instance, Fender and Lewrisk say that '[m]arkets are liquid when investors are able to buy or sell assets with little delay, at low cost and at a price close to the current market price'. Fender and Lewrisk (2015), p. 98.

[17] Fender and Lewrisk (2015), p. 97.

on-the-run/off-the-run spread. This is the difference in yields between otherwise almost identical bonds that differ only in the date of their issuance (not in their maturity!). For reasons that we will briefly touch upon in the text that follows, newly issued ('on-the-run') Treasury bonds are deemed to be more desirable than otherwise identical bonds that have been issued in the past. This means that they cost more (yield less) than their off-run counterparts.

The difference in yields (the on-the-run/off-the-run spread) is normally worth just a few basis points, but in periods of market distress can become as large as 75 basis points.

Why should newly minted bonds be more desirable? In normal market conditions Treasury bonds are used by traders and arbitrageurs in the US repurchase (repo) market to obtain the funding needed for their activities.[18] If this is what drives the 'value of liquidity', one would expect that the on-the-run premium should share a common component with the risk premia observed in other markets (such as the credit or the equity markets). This is indeed what Fontaine and Garcia (2008) find. More precisely, as they say,

> liquidity value affects the cross-section of risk premia at quarterly and annual horizons. An increase in the value of liquidity predicts lower risk premia for on-the-run and off-the-run bonds but higher risk premia on LIBOR loans, swap contracts and corporate bonds. Moreover, the measured impact is pervasive through crisis and normal times. [...] [L]iquidity value varies with changes in aggregate uncertainty, measured from S&P500 options, and with changes in monetary stance, measured from bank reserves and monetary aggregates. These linkages are consistent with the theory and suggest that different securities serve, in part, and to varying degrees, to fulfill investors' uncertain future needs for cash.[19]

Note that during periods of crisis Fontaine and Garcia find that the risk premia for off- and on-the-run Treasury bonds are lowered – when the going gets *really* tough, that is, the importance of subtle differences in liquidity recedes in the background, and, compared with everything else, a US Treasury bond is a US Treasury bond is a US Treasury bond.

32.5.2 The Modelling Approach

When it comes to the treatment of the on-the-run/of-the-run liquidity component, here is an important technical difference: one can no longer make use of the bootstrapped virtual discount bonds that are otherwise universally used in empirical studies in general, and in those which focus on excess return in particular. The reason is clear: this 'pre-processing [of] the data wipes out the most accessible evidence on liquidity, that is the on-the-run-premium'.[20] Therefore, Fontaine and Garcia have to take the hard route, and work with the nitty-gritty details of each individual bond.

---

[18] Fisher (2002) presents an excellent discussion of this market.
[19] p. 1.   [20] p. 4.

They start with three latent state variables, x_t.[21] Of, course, little changes if the state variables are interpreted as pseudo-principal components. As in the Diebold–Rudebusch model the short rate is written as

$$r_t = x_t^1 + x_t^2 \tag{32.27}$$

(see Equation (32.6)) and the reversion speed matrix, $\mathcal{K}^{\mathbb{Q}}$, has the form

$$\mathcal{K}^{\mathbb{Q}} = \begin{bmatrix} 0 & 0 & 0 \\ 0 & \lambda & -\lambda \\ 0 & 0 & \lambda \end{bmatrix}. \tag{32.28}$$

(This is just Equation (32.8).) As we obtained previously, we then have for the yields

$$y_t^T = x_1^t + x_2^t \left(\frac{1 - e^{-\lambda\tau}}{\lambda\tau} \right) + x_3^t \left(\frac{1 - e^{-\lambda\tau}}{\lambda\tau} - e^{-\lambda\tau} \right) + \alpha_t^T. \tag{32.29}$$

Next, in order to facilitate the estimation process, Fontaine and Garcia discretize the fundamental SDE: from

$$d\overrightarrow{x}_t = \mathcal{K}^{\mathbb{Q}} \left(\theta^{\mathbb{Q}} - x_t \right) dt + S dz_t \tag{32.30}$$

they obtain

$$(x_t - \overline{x}) = \Phi (x_{t-1} - \overline{x}) + \Gamma \epsilon_t, \tag{32.31}$$

with

$$\Phi = e^{-\mathcal{K}^{\mathbb{Q}} \Delta t} = e^{-\frac{\mathcal{K}^{\mathbb{Q}}}{12}} \tag{32.32}$$

and the covariance matrix, Γ, given by

$$\Gamma = \int_0^{\Delta t = \frac{1}{12}} e^{-\mathcal{K}^{\mathbb{Q}} s} S S^T e^{-\mathcal{K}^{\mathbb{Q}} s} ds. \tag{32.33}$$

Exercise 87 *Derive Equations (32.32) and (32.33) and relate the discrete-time parameters Φ, Γ and $\overline{x}$ to the corresponding quantities in the continuous-time treatment. Hint: See the equations in Section 18.5.2 in Chapter 18. How do expressions (32.32) and (32.33) simplify if the time interval Δt becomes very small? What is the quantity that determines when 'very small' is 'small enough'?*

The state variables x_t are meant to describe the term structure dynamics of perfectly liquid bonds. In addition, Fontaine and Garcia introduce a new latent state variable, L_t, that will account for the liquidity. Also this variable is assigned a mean-reverting behaviour. In a discrete setting this translates to

$$\left(L_t - \overline{L} \right) = \phi (x_{t-1} - \overline{x}) + \sigma^l \epsilon_t^l. \tag{32.34}$$

---

[21] To conform with the notation in this book the state variables (which are denoted by F_t in Fontaine and Garcia (2008)) have been renamed x_t.

The liquidity innovations ϵ_t^l are assumed to be uncorrelated with the innovations, ϵ_t, that drive the term structure.

Given this setting, it is easy to use the general dictionary presented in Chapter 18 and to obtain the prices of discount bonds including the liquidity factor. From these we know from Chapter 2 how to obtain the time-t price, $\widetilde{PC}_t^T$, of a perfectly liquid T-maturity coupon bond from the prices of the pure discount bonds:

$$\widetilde{PC}_t^T = \left[\sum_{i=1,N} coup_i \times P_t^{T_i} \right] + 1 \times P_t^{T_N}. \tag{32.35}$$

To this liquidity-naive expression Fontaine and Garcia add a liquidity contribution, $\zeta(L_t, Z_{n,t})$, to obtain the all-in price:

$$PC_t^T = \left[\sum_{i=1,N} coup_i \times P_t^{T_i} \right] + 1 \times P_t^{T_N} + \zeta\left(L_t, Z_{n,t}\right), \tag{32.36}$$

where $Z_{n,t}$ is a shorthand notation for the important characteristics of the bond, namely, coupon, maturity *and age*.

So, in the approach by Fontaine and Garcia, their 'specification of the liquidity factor is based on a latent factor common to all bonds but with loadings that vary with a bond's maturity and age'.[22] More precisely, following work by Warga (1992), they write

$$\zeta\left(L_t, Z_{n,t}\right) = L_t \times \beta_{M} e^{-\frac{1}{\kappa} age_{n,t}}, \tag{32.37}$$

where the parameter β_{M_n} describes the average liquidity premium within maturity group, M, κ controls the decay of the liquidity premium as the age of the nth bond, $age_{n,t}$, increases. (The variable $age_{n,t}$ is zero at the time of issuance.) So, immediately after issuance the liquidity premium for a bond in the Mth maturity group is just β_M. A 30-year bond will on average command a different liquidity premium than a 2-year bond, and this is what the factor β_M controls. In addition, at different times the market liquidity will vary *for all bonds* – for instance, it will be very large in times of turmoil. This is captured by the factor, L_t. Omitting the liquidity term will push into the pricing errors the systematic dependence of each bond on its own characteristics (age, maturity band) and on the general market conditions.

32.5.3 The Results

Not surprisingly, when the augmented model is used for Treasury bonds, the fit to their prices is much better than for the corresponding liquidity-agnostic model. This, of course, is to be expected because the simpler model is nested as a special case of the liquidity-enriched model. However, statistical tests show

[22] p. 9.

that the improvement is not due to overfitting, but really captures something that had been left by the wayside before.[23] What was this 'something'? The main results are as follows.

1. The important decay parameter, κ, that determines for how long a newly isued bond remains on-the-run was estimated to be 0.74. This is a fast reversion speed, which implies a reduction by half in the liquidity premium after approximately half a year.
2. Increases in the liquidity factor obviously lead to lower expected excess returns for on-the-run bonds. The more interesting finding is that Fontaine and Garcia also find a negative relationship between liquidity and expected excess returns on the off-the-run bonds. As mentioned in the opening section, this can be interpreted as showing that in periods of distress, when the liquidity premium increases most, off-the-run bonds become close substitutes for on-the-run bonds, and behave much more like recently issued bonds than, say, corporate bonds or swap rates: 'although off-the-run bonds demand higher [transaction] costs, they can be readily converted into cash via the repo market. This is especially true relative to other asset classes'.[24]
3. Fontaine and Garcia find that '[t]he impact of liquidity on excess returns is economically significant: a one-standard deviation shock to liquidity lowers excess returns by 47 and 350 basis points for maturities of two and ten years respectively'.[25]
4. Looking back at the empirical results by Ludvigson and Ng (2009) discussed in Chapter 27 – recall that Ludvigson and Ng looked at the power of macrofinancial variables to predict bond excess returns – Fontaine and Garcia find that the liquidity factor is correlated with the "inflation" factor, the "financial" factor, and, interestingly, with the factor linked to monetary aggregates and bank reserves, but not with the "real" factor (which was the dominant one in the work of Ludvigson and Ng).
5. The authors find that liquidity factor they estimate makes on-the-run (and off-the-run) bonds very expensive during periods of market turmoil. This fits in well with our intutitve understanding of what liquidity is about, and confirms that the factor they have estimated does behave as we would expect. (The use the implied volatility of options on the S&P 500 index as proxy for aggregate market uncertainty.)

32.5.4   Conclusions

In their study, Fontaine and Garcia look at markets other than the US Treasury market, such as the corporate bond or the swaps markets. Beyond the specific findings mentioned earlier, they point out that 'financial assets are in part valued

---

[23] See the discussion on their p. 16.   [24] p. 18, ibid.   [25] p. 18, ibid.

for the monetary services they render. Investors consider the relative ease of converting financial investments back to cash before deciding their porftolio allocation.'

These liquidity considerations are by and large absent from the treatment presented elsewhere in this book – a treatment focussed, as we explain in the Introduction, on expectations, risk premia and convexity. The aforementioned conclusions therefore serve as an important reminder that liquidity – the ability to convert 'financial investments back to cash' – plays an additional important role in determining the equilibrium price of an asset in general, and of a bond in particular. The treatment presented in the closing pages of this chapter has shown how this component can be modelled and accounted for. Of course, it is appealing and general enough to be applied to modelling approaches other than Diebold and Rudebusch's.

CHAPTER 33

Principal Components as State Variables of Affine Models: The PCA Affine Approach

Molti giorni e molte avventure dovevano passare prima che Cadmo
e Armonia celebrassero le loro nozze.[1]

R. Calasso, *Le Nozze di Cadmo e Armonia*

33.1 THE PURPOSE OF THIS CHAPTER

In the previous chapter we explained why it is desirable to use principal components as state variables of a no-arbitrage model – in a nutshell, because doing so would allow us to marry the two successful yield curve modelling traditions mentioned in the extended quote by Diebold and Rudebusch (2013)[2], namely the statistical and the no-arbitrage schools. As we discussed, the first line of research is stronger at prediction and fitting, but lacks a solid theoretical grounding, in that it cannot guarantee absence of arbitrage. The second carefully crosses all the theoretical ts and dots the no-arbitrage is, but often leaves a lot to be desired when it comes to fitting and predicting. The approach by Diebold and Rudebusch (2013) presented in the previous chapter can be seen as a valiant attempt at bridging this gap.

In this chapter we continue this enterprise by presenting another reason why principal-components-based affine models are a bit 'special'. We do so by looking in detail at another Gaussian affine model that uses as state variables principal components. Unlike the Diebold model discussed in the previous chapter, the model presented here does not use proxies, but the proper principal components. Using principal components will allow us to draw on the extensive related econometric knowledge. Embedding the principal components in the setting of a no-arbitrage model can then put our theoretical worries to rest and ensure easy analytical tractability. As we shall see, there are, however, some difficulties in doing so.

---

[1] 'Many days had to elapse and many vicissitudes came to pass before Cadmus and Harmonia could celebrate their marriage', p. 429.

[2] See Chapter 32, Section 32.1.

To get a flavour for these difficulties, recall from the discussion in the Introduction that it is always the case that for exponentially affine models yields should have the very simple form

$$\overrightarrow{y}_t^T = \overrightarrow{u}_t + U\overrightarrow{x}_t. \tag{33.1}$$

Now, in what we called specified-variable approaches, the modeller assigns a priori the link between the state variables and the yields. When the specified variables are chosen to be principal components, then the matrix U in Equation (33.1) will be the matrix V in Equation (6.5) of Chapter 6[3] in the following:

$$\overrightarrow{x} = V^T\overrightarrow{y}. \tag{33.2}$$

As mentioned previously, working with principal components as state variables is a great advantage, because of the richness of empirical information that has been accumulated about them, and of the ready intuition that they afford. As we explained in the Introduction, however, the luxury of working with a priori specified variables comes with a price. For the dynamics of the pre-specified state variables to be consistent with absence of arbitrage and with the specification imposed by Equation (33.2), some constraints will have to be satisfied.

These constraints will be derived in the body of the chapter, but we can already anticipate some of the more surprising and far-reaching constraints. The reasoning goes as follows.

We start as usual from

$$dx_t = \mathcal{K}(\theta - x_t)dt + Sdz_t.$$

If the state variables, $\{x_t\}$, have to be interpreted as principal components, then clearly the 'volatility' matrix, S, will have to be diagonal[4]. However, once this specification is imposed, it will turn out that, in the risk-neutral measure, the reversion speed matrix, $\mathcal{K}$, cannot be diagonal as well. This means that, under the risk-neutral measure, each principal component cannot simply revert to its own reversion level, but is simultaneously attracted to and repulsed by the other state variables.

As a result of this, the resulting ($\mathbb{Q}$-measure) dynamics of the yield curve is surprising complex. This means that we can either have a very simple volatility matrix S, as one does with the PC Affine model, or a very simple reversion-speed matrix, $\mathcal{K}$, as one does with, say, the Kim–Wright model; alas, one cannot have both.

But there is more. As we saw in the case of the Diebold–Rudebusch (2013) model (see Chapter 32), if the no-arbitrage conditions determine the shape of

---

[3] What happens to the vector $\overrightarrow{u}_t$? When we obtain the principal components by orthogonalizing the covariance matrix of *changes* in yields, we really have $d\overrightarrow{x} = V^T d\overrightarrow{y}$. We will show the vector $\overrightarrow{u}_t$ has to be specified using information other than what is embedded in the covariance matrix.

[4] The diagonal elements, in passing, are equal to the square roots of the eigenvalues, which makes the calibration to variances extremely easy, but this bit is not essential to the reasoning.

the reversion-speed matrix in the $\mathbb{Q}$ measure, then the market price of risk is uniquely specified by the reversion-speed matrix in the objective (real-world) $\mathbb{P}$ measure; or, conversely, the $\mathbb{P}$-measure is uniquely determined once the no-arbitrage conditions are imposed and the market price of risk is made to display the *empirical* features determined, say, by statistical estimation of excess returns. But both the dependence of excess returns on the state variables (say, on the slope) and the real-world reversion speed are 'facts of nature'. Will nature be kind enough to be consistent with our model?

This chapter shows that these results are more general than one might suppose, because we prove early in the chapter that all 'equivalent' essentially affine models share exactly the same features that we identify for the principal component–based affine models (as we explain in the text that follows, roughly speaking two affine model are said to be equivalent if they produce exactly the same yield curve and covariance matrix.)

So what?, the reader may retort. Why should be so concerned about problems generated by principal component–based affine models (and their equivalent class)? Simply because they can recover the market yield curve and covariance matrix, not only more easily, but also more accurately than virtually any other model. So, to the extent that a non-principal component–based essentially affine model is different (in the recovery of market observables), it is also (slightly) 'wrong'. More about this later.

These considerations suggest that the marriage of the statistical and the arbitrage-free approach, while possible, will prove no more straightforward that the nuptials of Cadmus and Harmonia, referred to in the opening quote to this chapter.

33.2   WHY PC-BASED MODELS ARE SPECIAL (AGAIN)

> *All animals are equal, but some animals are more equal than others.*
> George Orwell, *Animal Farm*

In this section I want to explain why all affine models may well be in some sense equal, but principal components–based affine models are more equal than others. We start by stating (and sketching the proof for) an apparently tangential result.

Let $\{m_1\}$ and $\{m_2\}$ be two time-homogeneous, non-stochastic-volatility, essentially affine models with an invertible mapping from state variables to yields. Their state variables, $\{x_1\}$ and $\{x_2\}$, can be very different, and either, both or neither could include macro variables. The two models will be said to be "equivalent" if they produce *exactly* the same yield curve and the same covariance matrix.

Since the two equivalent models are affine, and we have assumed invertibility, it is always possible to write for the market yields:

$$y_t = A_1 x_1^t \tag{33.3}$$

and

$$y_t = A_2 x_2^t. \tag{33.4}$$

Consider now the Partial Differential Equation that governs the evolution of the yields. We don't need to know its form, but only that its solution is unique given the same initial conditions, the same drifts and the same covariance structure.

But, given two equivalent models,

- the initial conditions are the same (the two models produce the same time-t yield curve by definition of equivalent models);
- the drift of yields or forward rates under $\mathbb{Q}$ is the same, because – this is the essence of the famous Heath–Jarrow–Merton (1989) result – the no-arbitrage drift is purely a function of the forward rate covariance matrix (which is identical for the two models today, and in the future by time-homogeneity);
- the stochastic evolution is the same also because of equivalence (same covariance matrix) and time-homogeneity.

From this it follows that the evolution of the yield curve under $\mathbb{Q}$ is, in absolutely all its aspects, exactly the same for any two equivalent models.

But there is more. If the two models are essentially affine, presented with the same econometric information about the dependence of excess returns on (linear combinations of) yields, they will produce the same dependence of the market price of risk on the yields. Hence, also the evolution under $\mathbb{P}$ is exactly the same.

So, as long as the mild conditions above about invertibility and non-stochastic volatility are satisfied, all conclusions we draw about one equivalent model exactly extend to any other equivalent model.

Why is this interesting? Because principal components–based affine models can be made to recover both the market yield curve and the covariance matrix with arbitrary precision (and greater ease than most other models). Therefore any 'strange behaviour' we associate with principal-component-based models will be exactly shared by all models that recover as well the initial market yield curve and covariance matrix.

It also follows that, if the principal-component–based model recovered the exogenous market inputs perfectly, any model that behaved differently could only do so because of 'pricing errors'. If the pricing errors are optically 'small', then a qualitatively different behaviour can only arise from these 'small' pricing errors. (I have put the word 'small' in scare quotes twice, because of the discussion in Section 27.4.5 – please re-read it in the not-too-distant future, and possibly before you have forgotten what this section was about.)

Why go on about his? Because we shall derive some unexpected results concerning principal component–based models (and about their reversion-speed matrix under $\mathbb{Q}$, in particular). The constraints we find on this quantity will have to reappear, after some linear transformation of variables,[5] in all equivalent essentially affine models. The constraints may be less transparent, but they will not go away. So anything we learn about principal component–based affine models applies to all affine models that recover the yield curve and the covariance matrix as well. Non-principal-components–based affine models may well produce different results, but the origin of these differences must be traced back to (probably 'small') differences in fitting to the market yield curve or covariance matrix. And, most likely than not, these differences will be pricing mistakes. No wonder that principal-component-based affine models are more equal than other affine models!

33.3 SPECIFIED-VARIABLE MODELS REVISITED

In the previous chapter we discussed the interesting variation on the well-rehearsed theme of affine term structure, which has recently been introduced by Christensen, Diebold and Rudebusch (2011), and developed in Diebold and Rudebusch (2013). As we have seen, these researchers show how to turn the 'static' (curve-fitting) Nelson and Siegel (1987) model into a dynamic, arbitrage-free affine model.[6] To the extent that the coefficients of the Nelson–Siegel model generate a close match to the observed term structure – and it is well known that they do – the dynamic Nelson–Siegel formulation automatically ensures an easy calibration to the market bond prices. This is in itself a desirable result.

We have seen that there is, however, a more important positive feature to their approach: Diebold and Rudebusch (2013) in fact show that, perhaps surprisingly, after a clever transformation the factors of the associated affine model lend themselves to an appealing interpretation as principal components. If one can identify the factors as principal components (or their proxies) one can draw on a wealth of econometric[7] and macrofinancial[8] studies to constrain their behaviour, and guide the parameter estimation ('calibration') process.

The appeal of this approach naturally raises the question of whether it is possible to assign a Gaussian affine behaviour *exactly* to the principal components, rather than to some proxies, and, at the same time, comply with the conditions of no-arbitrage.

The idea of harnessing together two of the most commonly used workhorses of term-structure modelling – principal component analysis and affine (mean-reverting) modelling – is natural enough, and indeed has been exploited, more or less directly, in some recent approaches. (See, eg, Joslin, Ahn Le and Singleton (2013), Joslin, Singleton and Zhu (2011), Joslin, Priebsh and Singleton

---

[5] This, by the way, is why we require an invertible mapping from state variables to yields.
[6] See also Ungari and Turc (2012) for a closely related treatment.
[7] For an early study relating to Treasuries, see Litterman and Scheinkman (1991).
[8] See, eg, Duffee (2002), Fama and Bliss (1987), Fama and French (1989, 1993) and the references in Joslin, Priebsch and Singleton (2014).

(2014) and references therein). The model presented in this chapter is in this line of research. More precisely, we go back to the classification by Dai and Singleton (2000) presented in the Introduction. They show that, if N factors, $\vec{x}_t,$[9] follow a diffusive process of the form

$$d\vec{x}_t = \vec{a}\left(\vec{x}_t\right)dt + \underline{b}\left(\vec{x}_t\right)d\vec{z}_t \qquad (33.5)$$

with

$$a\left(\vec{x}_t\right) = \vec{a}_0 + \vec{a}_1\vec{x}_t, \qquad a_0 \in R^N, a_1 \in R^{N \times N}$$

$$\underline{b}\left(\vec{x}_t\right)\underline{b}\left(\vec{x}_t\right)^T = \underline{b}_0 + b_1\vec{x}_t, \qquad b_0 \in R^{N \times N}, b_1 \in R^{N \times N \times N} \quad (33.6)$$

and if the short rate, r_t, can be written as a linear combination of these N factors plus a constant,

$$r_t = c_0 + \vec{c}_1^T\vec{x}_t \qquad (33.7)$$

then bond prices, P_t^T, can be written as exponentially affine functions of the factors,

$$P_t^T = e^{A_t^T + \left(\vec{B}_t^T\right)^T\vec{x}_t}. \qquad (33.8)$$

Following the notation in Dai and Singleton (2000), we focus in what follows on models for which $b_1 = 0$, in which case the factors follow an N-dimensional mean-reverting (Ornstein-Uhlenbeck) process.

Apart from the short-rate requirement that $r_t = c_0 + \vec{c}_1^T\vec{x}_t$ the factors can, up to this point, be totally general. However, as mentioned in Section 33.1, given the exponentially affine nature of the bond pricing function, it is always the case that

$$\vec{y}_t^T = \vec{u}_t + \underline{U}_t\vec{x}_t. \qquad (33.9)$$

Saroka (2014) presents a general expressions for the admissible parameters of the N-dimensional Ornstein–Uhlenbeck process for the factors of pre-specified models, ie, when the loadings $\vec{u}_t$ and $\underline{U}_t$ are assigned a priori. In this chapter we make use of these results for the special case when the factors are chosen to be principal components.

In so doing we discover some interesting results: indeed, we show in Section 33.5 that it is possible to specify *an infinity* of term-structure models such that

- the driving factors are principal components;
- they follow (under $\mathbb{P}$ and under $\mathbb{Q}$) a mean-reverting (generalized Ornstein–Uhlenbeck) dynamics;
- an arbitrary exogenous covariance matrix among N yields can always be exactly recovered (and hence so are all the observed eigenvalues and eigenvectors);

---

[9] See Section 33.5.3 for a description of our notation.

- an arbitrary exogenous yield curve (also defined by N yields) is exactly recovered;
- no-arbitrage is satisfied.

Accomplishing this, however, imposes some important constraints on the mean-reverting dynamics, the reason for which is rather subtle. An intuitive explanation of what these constraints entail goes along the following lines.

33.3.1   Parameter Constraints for PCA Prespecified Models

First of all, it is well known that, given an N-dimensional Ornstein–Uhlenbeck process, expressing *either* the diffusion *or* the 'reversion-speed' matrix in diagonal form is always possible (and, indeed, straightforward).[10] The associated 'rotation of axes' has no economic significance, and all the 'invariants'[11] – bond prices, short rate, etc – are recovered. However, we show that an affine model in which both the diffusion matrix, S, *and* the $\mathbb{Q}$-measure reversion-speed matrix, $\mathcal{K}$, are diagonal is not compatible with absence of arbitrage.

This is somewhat surprising, and economically significant: if we want the factors to be principal components, the diffusion matrix must be diagonal. We show in what follows that the reversion-speed matrix cannot be diagonal as well, *and that some of its elements must be negative and of the same order of magnitude as the positive ones.*

This matters: if the reversion-speed matrix is forced to contain large non-diagonal negative elements, the outcome is a rather 'complex' $\mathbb{Q}$-measure *deterministic* dynamics (even for asymptotically stable systems): each principal component not only reverts to its own fixed reversion levels, but is also attracted to, *and repulsed by*, the other dynamically moving principal components. Therefore the principal components state variables (and hence yields, to which they are linked via an affine transformation) are forced to follow a complex *deterministic* evolution: it is complex, because in this evolution a reversion level is not approached with a monotonic first derivative (a 'decaying-exponential' approach), but with over- and/or undershoots during which the first derivative can change sign. This evolution may well be asymptotically stable, but can easily produce complex deterministic oscillations of the $\mathbb{Q}$-expectations of yields many years into the future.

We find that the 'impossibility results' and the constraints they impose raise some interesting questions about what an affine description of the yield curve in terms of principal components entails – for instance, the interplay between the

---

[10] Cheridito, Filipovic and Kimmel (2010) show that, under loose conditions, it is possible to diagonalize the diffusion matrix using a regular, but not necessarily orthogonal, transformation – see their Theorem 2.1 and Corollary 2.2.

[11] Invariants are defined in Cheridito, Filipovic and Kimmel (2010). Roughly speaking, they are 'co-ordinate independent' quantities. The term is borrowed from physics, where quantities like the (space or space–time) coordinates of two points depend on the frame of reference, but the (space or space–time) distance between the two is an invariant.

persistence of yields, the risk premia, and the 'complexity of the yield curve, or the ability to detect unit-root behaviour for rates and principal components with reasonable-size samples'. And, as we argued in the previous section, these conclusions must also apply to all equivalent models. We touch on these aspects in the concluding section of this chapter.

33.4 OUR STRATEGY TO LINK THE ℙ- AND ℚ-MEASURES

In this chapter we link the ℙ and ℚ-measures as follows.

1. We start by determining the measure-invariant model parameters (the coefficients of the diagonal diffusion matrix) using real-world volatility data;
2. keeping these data fixed, we determine the measure-dependent reversion-speed matrix in the ℚ measure by *cross-sectional* fitting to the whole covariance matrix and by imposing the smoothness requirements that we describe later;
3. with this information, we carry out a cross-sectional fit to the yield curve to determine the reversion-level vector in the ℚ measure;
4. we then make use of the results of the empirical study of excess returns discussed in Chapter 25, and we establish (by multivariate regression) a link between these excess returns and our state variables;
5. as a next step, we determine (see Section 33.7) the shape of the dependence of the reversion-level vector and the reversion-speed matrix (in the ℙ measure) on the market prices of risk associated with our model and our chosen state variables – in order to accommodate the empirical findings in Duffee (2002) and the results of our own studies; at this point we allow for the market price of risk to depend in an affine manner on the state variables (ie, we require our model to be essentially affine);
6. finally, we specialize the results in point 5 above so as to reflect the particular dependence determined in our empirical estimation of excess returns.

We stress that the last step is quite general, and does not rely on the specific empirical findings of our statistical estimation. For instance, a Cochrane–Piazzesi-like return-predicting factor (see Cochrane and Piazzesi (2005, 2008))[12] or a slope factor (as in Duffee, 2002) can be readily accommodated by our methodology.

---

[12] To accommodate exactly the Cochrane–Piazzesi 'tent' factor, five principal components would have to be used. Conceptually, our approach extends without difficulty to as many factors as desired. The uniqueness of parameters in the calibration phase may disappear if too many factors are used.

So, for the avoidance of doubt: we start from the $\mathbb{Q}$-measure and determine by cross-sectional fit to bond prices the $\mathbb{Q}$-measure model parameters; we carry out a statistical estimate of excess returns; with this information we distill the $\mathbb{P}$-measure model parameters.

33.5   THE SET-UP

33.5.1   Notation

As usual, the time-t price of a discount bond of maturity T is denoted by P_t^T, and its yield by y_t^T. The time-t value of the short rate is denoted by r_t.

We describe the time-t discrete yield curve by an $[N \times 1]$ vector of yields, $\overrightarrow{y_t}$, of elements $y_t^{T_i}$, $i = 1, 2 \ldots N$ The elements of the vector $\overrightarrow{y_t}$ are ordered with increasing maturity ($T_j > T_k$ if $j > k$).

33.5.2   The Geometry (Kinematics) of the Problem

Consider the following dynamics for the component yields of the $N \times 1$ vector $\overrightarrow{y}$:

$$\overrightarrow{dy} = \overrightarrow{\mu}_y dt + \underline{\sigma} \overrightarrow{dw}^{\mathbb{Q},\mathbb{P}} \tag{33.10}$$

with $\overrightarrow{dw}^{\mathbb{Q},\mathbb{P}}$ denoting the vector of Brownian shocks in the real-world ($\mathbb{P}$) or in the risk-neutral ($\mathbb{Q}$) measure, with

$$\underline{\sigma} = \text{diag}\,[\sigma_1, \sigma_2, \ldots, \sigma_n] \tag{33.11}$$

$$E\left[\overrightarrow{dw}\,\overrightarrow{dw}^{\mathsf{T}}\right] = \underline{\rho} dt \tag{33.12}$$

and with the drift term μ_y reflecting the no-arbitrage conditions when $\overrightarrow{dw}^{\mathbb{Q},\mathbb{P}} = \overrightarrow{dw}^{\mathbb{Q}}$, and the real-world dynamics when $\overrightarrow{dw}^{\mathbb{Q},\mathbb{P}} = \overrightarrow{dw}^{\mathbb{P}}$.

Thee covariance matrix among the yields is given by

$$E\left[\overrightarrow{dy}\,\overrightarrow{dy}^{\mathsf{T}}\right] = \underline{\sigma}\,\underline{\rho}\,\underline{\sigma}^{\mathsf{T}} = \underline{\Sigma}_{mkt} dt. \tag{33.13}$$

This quantity is an exogenous market observable, which we assume to be known and constant. This is one of the key quantities that we would like our model to reproduce. We know that it is important that a model should do so, because the covariance matrix is linked to the convexity contribution to the shape of the yield curve, and to the apportionment of the risk premia among different yields.

The real symmetric matrix $\underline{\Sigma}_{mkt}$ can always be diagonalized to give

$$\underline{\Sigma}_{mkt} = \underline{\Omega}\,\underline{\Lambda}\,\underline{\Omega}^{\mathsf{T}} \tag{33.14}$$

with

$$\underline{\Lambda} = \text{diag}\,[\lambda_1, \lambda_2, \ldots, \lambda_N] \tag{33.15}$$

and with $\underline{\Omega}$ an orthogonal matrix:

$$\underline{\Omega}\,\underline{\Omega}^{\mathrm{T}} = \underline{I}. \tag{33.16}$$

If the exogenous matrix $\underline{\Sigma}_{mkt}$ is positive definite, all the eigenvalues λ_i are positive.

Given this diagonalization, we can define the principal components, $\overrightarrow{x}$, by

$$\overrightarrow{y}_t = \overrightarrow{\overline{y}} + \underline{\Omega}\,\overrightarrow{x}_t, \tag{33.17}$$

where $\overrightarrow{\overline{y}}$ is a *constant* vector.

Recall that an affine model is defined by requiring that the short rate should be an affine function of the state variables, and by assigning the affine coefficients (the loadings). This means that we must have

$$r_t = u_r + \overrightarrow{g}^{\mathrm{T}}\overrightarrow{x}. \tag{33.18}$$

Equation (33.18) is important because it must be satisfied if the model is to be affine. It is not a theorem – it is a wish. As usual, there is no a priori reason why the short rate should be an affine function of our chosen state variables. If it is – or, more realistically, if it reasonable to assume that it is – then we can proceed with our affine treatment.

33.5.3 The Dynamics of the Problem

We impose that the principal components, $\overrightarrow{x}_t$, should follow a mean-reverting diffusion of the form:

$$d\overrightarrow{x}_t = \underline{K}\left(\overrightarrow{\theta} - \overrightarrow{x}_t\right) dt + \underline{S}\overrightarrow{dz} \tag{33.19}$$

and we now choose the Brownian increments, $\overrightarrow{dz}$, to be orthogonal:

$$E\left[\overrightarrow{dz}\,\overrightarrow{dz}^{\mathrm{T}}\right] = \underline{I}dt. \tag{33.20}$$

As usual, we refer to $\underline{K}$ as the reversion-speed matrix, to $\underline{S}$ as the diffusion matrix, and to $\overrightarrow{\theta}$ as the reversion-level vector. For reasons that will become apparent in the following, we require the matrix $\underline{K}$ to be invertible and full rank.[13] Since we want to interpret the factors, $\overrightarrow{x}_t$, as principal components, we require the matrix $\underline{S}$ to be diagonal:

$$\underline{S} = \mathrm{diag}\,[s_1, s_2, \ldots s_N] \tag{33.21}$$

and we impose

$$s_i = \sqrt{\lambda_i}, \tag{33.22}$$

where $\{\lambda_i\}$ are the eigenvalues of the market covariance matrix (33.14).

---

[13] Saroka (2014) shows how the full-rank requirement can be relaxed.

For the reasons discussed in the introductory section, we would also like the reversion-speed matrix, $\underline{\mathcal{K}}$, to be diagonal, but, at this stage, we do not know whether this is possible (once a diagonal form is imposed for the diffusion matrix) – indeed, we shall see that it is not.

Absence of arbitrage then imposes that

$$P_t^T = E^{\mathbb{Q}}\left[e^{-\int_t^T r_s ds}\right] \tag{33.23}$$

and therefore, because of (33.18), we have

$$P_t^T = E^{\mathbb{Q}}\left[e^{-\int_t^T (u_r + \vec{g}^{\,\mathrm{T}}\vec{x}_s)ds}\right]. \tag{33.24}$$

33.5.4 Solution

We have shown in Chapter 18 that[14] (see also Dai and Singleton (2000)) that the solution to Equation (33.24) is given by

$$P_t^T = \exp^{A_t^T + \left(\vec{B}_t^T\right)^{\mathrm{T}}\vec{x}_t}, \tag{33.25}$$

with the vector $\vec{B}_t^T$ and the scalar A_t^T satisfying the Ordinary Differential Equations (with $\tau = T - t$)

$$\frac{dA_\tau}{d\tau} = -u_r + \left(\vec{B}_\tau\right)^{\mathrm{T}}\underline{\mathcal{K}}\vec{\theta} + \frac{1}{2}\left(\vec{B}_\tau\right)^{\mathrm{T}}\underline{SS}^{\mathrm{T}}\vec{B}_\tau \tag{33.26}$$

$$\frac{d\vec{B}_\tau}{d\tau} = -\vec{g} - \underline{\mathcal{K}}^{\mathrm{T}}\vec{B}_\tau \tag{33.27}$$

with boundary conditions

$$\vec{B}(\tau = 0) = 0, \quad A(\tau = 0) = 0. \tag{33.28}$$

As we have seen, the solution for $\vec{B}_\tau$ is given by[15]

$$\vec{B}_\tau^{\mathrm{T}} = \vec{g}^{\,\mathrm{T}}\mathcal{K}^{-1}\left[e^{-\mathcal{K}\tau} - I_n\right]. \tag{33.29}$$

Not every square matrix can be diagonalized. In what follows, we consider the case in which the matrix $\underline{\mathcal{K}}$ has n distinct and real eigenvalues. When both these conditions are satisfied, the matrix $\underline{\mathcal{K}}$ can always be diagonalized, and the diagonalizing matrix is real. Again, we refer the reader to Saroka (2014) for a more general treatment. We find little difference between the solutions we obtain assuming diagonalization and the more general treatment.

If one diagonalizes the reversion-speed matrix, $\underline{\mathcal{K}}$, one obtains:

$$\underline{\mathcal{K}} = \underline{a}\,\Lambda_{\mathcal{K}}\underline{a}^{-1} \tag{33.30}$$

---

[14] All the proofs are presented in the Appendices 33A and 33B.

[15] An equivalent solution can be written in the form $\vec{B}_\tau = -\int_0^\tau e^{-\underline{\mathcal{K}}\tau}\underline{\Omega}\vec{e}_1 d\tau$. This allows the handling of more general settings. We do not pursue this route here, but the reader is referred to Saroka (2014).

with

$$\underline{\Lambda}_{\mathcal{K}} = \text{diag}[l_j], \quad j = 1, 2, \dots, N. \tag{33.31}$$

For the stability of the resulting dynamic system, we require the N real eigenvalues l_j to be positive.[16] One can then derive (see Appendix 33A)

$$\vec{B}_\tau = -a \, \text{diag} \left[\frac{1 - e^{-l_j \tau}}{l_j} \right] a^{-1} \vec{\omega}_1. \tag{33.32}$$

Once the vector $\vec{B}_\tau$ has been obtained, the scalar A_τ can be obtained by integrating Equation (33.26), to give

$$A_\tau = \int_0^\tau \left[-u_r + \left(\vec{B}_\tau \right)^{\mathrm{T}} \underline{K} \vec{\theta} + \frac{1}{2} \left(\vec{B}_\tau \right)^{\mathrm{T}} \underline{SS}^{\mathrm{T}} \vec{B}_\tau \right] d\tau. \tag{33.33}$$

In the case we consider, the integral can be carried out analytically, and the resulting expression is also given in Appendix A.

33.5.5 Necessary Conditions for Identifiability

As mentioned previously, we now want to explore what constraints the identification of the factors as principal components imposes on the $\mathbb{Q}$-measure reversion-speed measure K. In particular, we would like to see whether the choice of principal components as state variables admits a diagonal reversion-speed matrix, $\underline{K}$. We call this the 'identifiability problem' (we choose this name because we want to see whether we can find a reversion-speed matrix such that the factors can be identified as principal components. As we shall see, the answer is 'yes, but'.)

From the no-arbitrage dynamics (33.19), and the solution (33.25), the yields vector, $\vec{y}_t$, has the expression

$$\vec{y}_t = \vec{\alpha} + \underline{\beta}^{\mathrm{T}} \vec{x}_t \tag{33.34}$$

with

$$\vec{\alpha} = - \begin{bmatrix} \frac{A_{\tau_1}}{\tau_1} \\ \frac{A_{\tau_2}}{\tau_2} \\ \dots \\ \frac{A_{\tau_N}}{\tau_N} \end{bmatrix} \tag{33.35}$$

---

[16] Strictly speaking, the eigenvalues, $\{l_j\}$, need not be real. They could be complex, as long as their real part is positive. We do not pursue this avenue here.

and

$$\beta^T = - \begin{bmatrix} \dfrac{\left(\vec{B}_{\tau_1}\right)^T}{\tau_1} \\ \dfrac{\left(\vec{B}_{\tau_2}\right)^T}{\tau_2} \\ \cdots \\ \dfrac{\left(\vec{B}_{\tau_N}\right)^T}{\tau_N} \end{bmatrix}. \tag{33.36}$$

Recall now that we have required the particular portfolios of yields to be principal components. If this is the case, for identifiability of the factors with principal components, Equation (33.17) must also hold:

$$\vec{y}_t = \vec{y} + \underline{\Omega}\,\vec{x}_t. \tag{33.37}$$

For Equations (33.17) and (33.34) to be compatible for an arbitrary vector $\vec{x}_t$, one must therefore have

$$\underline{\Omega} = \underline{\beta}^T \tag{33.38}$$

and

$$\vec{y} = \vec{\alpha}, \tag{33.39}$$

If the first yield is chosen to be the short rate, from Equations (33.17) and (33.34) it also follows that[17]

$$\tilde{y}_1 = -\frac{A(+0)}{+0} \tag{33.40}$$

$$\tilde{y}_k = -\frac{A(\tau_k)}{\tau_k}, \quad k = 2, 3, \ldots, N. \tag{33.41}$$

In sum: if the vector $\vec{y}$ is chosen as per Equations (33.40) and (33.41), the time-0 discrete yield curve is automatically and exactly recovered for any reversion-level vector, $\vec{\theta}$. (We discuss in the calibration section how a 'good' choice for the vector $\vec{\theta}$ can be arrived at.)

Note then from Equation (33.32) that the vector $\vec{B}_\tau$ (and hence the vector $\vec{\beta}_\tau$) are a function of the reversion speed, $\underline{K}$. This means that if we can find a reversion-speed matrix, $\underline{K}$, such that Equation (33.38) is also satisfied, we can rest assured that the chosen yields will have a (discrete) model covariance matrix automatically identical to the exogenously assigned matrix, Σ_{mkt}.

Assuming that a solution satisfying (33.38) and (33.39) can indeed be found, the extreme ease with which this usually nettlesome joint calibration problem (to the yield curve and to the covariance matrix) can be tackled clearly shows at least one advantage from identifying the vector $\vec{x}_t$ with the principal components. We therefore turn in the next section to showing that the identification is indeed possible.

---

[17] The notation $(+0)$ means that we approach 0 from above.

Before that, we note in passing that the first element of the vector $\overrightarrow{y}$ is at this point indeterminate, ie, any value can be chosen for it, and all N yields can be recovered exactly.[18] This can be seen as follows. Recall that the bond price is given by

$$P_t^T = e^{A_i^T + \left(\overrightarrow{B}_i^T\right)^{\mathrm{T}} \overrightarrow{x}_t}$$

(33.42)

But we have from the preceding that

$$\alpha_i = -\frac{A_i}{\tau_i}$$

(33.43)

and $\overrightarrow{y} = \overrightarrow{\alpha}$ (with $A_i \equiv A_t^{T_i}$). Therefore $A_i = -\tau_i \widetilde{y}_i$, and $A_1 = -\tau_1 \widetilde{y}_1$ in particular. We know, however, that

$$\lim_{\tau \to 0} \frac{A(\tau)}{\tau} = 0$$

(33.44)

$$\lim_{\tau \to 0} \frac{B(\tau)}{\tau} = 1$$

(33.45)

and therefore we see from Equation (40) that any value can be assigned to $\widetilde{y}_1$, while retaining the property that the infinitesimally short yield be given by

$$\lim_{(T-t) \to 0} y_t^T = r_t.$$

(33.46)

33.6 THEORETICAL RESULTS

33.6.1 Impossibility of Identification When $\mathcal{K}$ Is Diagonal

What does all of this imply about the reversion-speed matrix, $\underline{\mathcal{K}}$? In particular, can $\underline{\mathcal{K}}$ be diagonal?

To answer these questions, we start from Equation (33.38). Recalling that $\underline{\Omega}$ is an orthogonal matrix, it is clear that one must have

$$\underline{\beta}\underline{\beta}^{\mathrm{T}} = \underline{I}.$$

(33.47)

To prove that the reversion-speed matrix $\mathcal{K}$ cannot be diagonal when the state variables are principal components, we proceed by *reductio ad absurdum*, ie, we show that, given Equation (33.47) and the identification of the state variables as principal components, an impossibility arises.

So, let's assume that $\mathcal{K}$ is diagonal and the state variables independent. In this case, for dynamic stability the diagonal elements of the reversion-speed martix must be positive. This means that, for any i, we must have $\kappa_{ii} > 0$. Note, however, even if some κ_{ii} were negative, the ratio $\frac{1-e^{-\kappa_{ii}\tau_1}}{\kappa_{ii}}$ would always be

---

[18] However, all the yield-recovering solutions associated with different values of $\overrightarrow{y}_1$ will imply different model parameters: we will show in the following how this indeterminacy can be resolved.

positive. In this setting it is then straightforward to show that the matrix $\underline{\beta}$ is given by[19]

$$
\underline{\beta} = \begin{bmatrix} \frac{1}{\tau_1}\left[\frac{1-e^{-\kappa_{11}\tau_1}}{\kappa_{11}}g_1, \frac{1-e^{-\kappa_{22}\tau_1}}{\kappa_{22}}g_2, \dots, \frac{1-e^{-\kappa_{NN}\tau_1}}{\kappa_{NN}}g_N\right] \\ \frac{1}{\tau_2}\left[\frac{1-e^{-\kappa_{11}\tau_2}}{\kappa_{11}}g_1, \frac{1-e^{-\kappa_{22}\tau_2}}{\kappa_{22}}g_2, \dots, \frac{1-e^{-\kappa_{NN}\tau_2}}{\kappa_{NN}}g_N\right] \\ \dots \\ \frac{1}{\tau_N}\left[\frac{1-e^{-\kappa_{11}\tau_N}}{\kappa_{11}}g_1, \frac{1-e^{-\kappa_{22}\tau_N}}{\kappa_{22}}g_2, \dots, \frac{1-e^{-\kappa_{NN}\tau_N}}{\kappa_{NN}}g_N\right] \end{bmatrix}, \tag{33.48}
$$

with g_j the N elements of the vector $\overrightarrow{g}$ in Equation (33.18). For compactness we write $\beta_{ij} = h_{ij}g_j$, with $h_{ij} = \frac{1}{\tau_i}\frac{1-e^{-\kappa_{jj}\tau_i}}{\kappa_{jj}}$.

Consider now $\gamma \equiv \underline{\beta}\,\underline{\beta}^{\mathsf{T}}$. Take a generic off-diagonal element $\gamma[r,s]$, $r \neq s$. For identifiability (ie, if our state variables were really principal components), we should have

$$
\left[\overrightarrow{\beta}\,\overrightarrow{\beta}^{\mathsf{T}}\right]_{rs} = 0, \quad r \neq s. \tag{33.49}
$$

In reality we have

$$
\gamma[r,s] = \sum_j \beta_{rj}\beta_{sj}^{\mathsf{T}} = \sum_j \beta_{rj}\beta_{sj} = \sum_j h_{rj}g_j h_{sj}g_j = \sum_j h_{rj}h_{sj}(g_j)^2. \tag{33.50}
$$

But these terms cannot possibly be zero for $r \neq s$, because, for any j, $(g_j)^2 > 0$, *and all the terms* $h_{sj} = \frac{1-e^{-\kappa_{jj}\tau_s}}{\kappa_{jj}}$ *are strictly positive.* Therefore the matrix $\mathcal{K}$ cannot be diagonal.

We can summarize the first result as follows.

Conclusion *If the factors* $\overrightarrow{x}_t$ *are principal components, absence of arbitrage is not compatible with a diagonal reversion-speed matrix, $\mathcal{K}$, under $\mathbb{Q}$*

33.6.2 What Does It Mean to Require that the Factors $\overrightarrow{x}_t$ Should Be Principal Components?

An important observation is in order. What exactly does it mean to require that the factors $\overrightarrow{x}_t$ should be principal components? Now, at time t_0 it is always possible to choose the initial values of the factors, $\overrightarrow{x}_0$, in such a way that

$$
\overrightarrow{y}_0 = \overrightarrow{y} + \underline{\Omega}\,\overrightarrow{x}_0. \tag{33.51}
$$

Consider, however, future, time-t, values of the state vector, $\overrightarrow{x}_t$, which has been evolved according to the arbitrage-free equations that lead to

$$
P_t^T = \exp^{A_t^T + \left(\overrightarrow{B}_t^T\right)^{\mathsf{T}}\overrightarrow{x}_t}. \tag{33.52}
$$

---

[19] Given the decoupling of the variables in this setting, each term $\frac{1-e^{-\kappa_{ii}\tau_j}}{\kappa_{ii}}$ is simply a 'Vasicek'-like term.

The time-t yields are always given by

$$y_t^T = -\frac{1}{T-t} \log P_t^T = -\frac{1}{T-t} \left[A_t^T + \left(\vec{B}_t^T \right)^{\mathrm{T}} \vec{x}_t \right]. \tag{33.53}$$

This is true for any affine model and any set of state variables. However, the factors, $\vec{x}_t$, will be principal components only if it is also true that, *for any future time $\tau > t$,*

$$\vec{y}_t = -\frac{1}{T-t} \left[A_t^T + \left(\vec{B}_t^T \right)^{\mathrm{T}} \vec{x}_t \right] = \vec{\bar{y}} + \underline{\Omega} \vec{x}_t, \tag{33.54}$$

ie, if

$$-\frac{1}{T-t} A_t^T = \vec{\bar{y}} \tag{33.55}$$

and

$$-\frac{1}{T-t} \left(\vec{B}_t^T \right)^{\mathrm{T}} = \underline{\Omega} \tag{33.56}$$

for the same constant vector, $\vec{\bar{y}}$, and for the same matrix, $\underline{\Omega}$, that we chose at time t_0.

If both these conditions are not satisfied, the factors will still evolve in an arbitrage-free manner, will still have a diagonal volatility matrix, S, but will no longer be principal components. This means that we no longer know the wealth of empirical statistical information that we do know about real principal components, and that we can no longer build the future covariance matrix virtually by inspection. And this was, after all, the purpose of our enterprise.

This is a very strong requirement – a requirement that will be satisfied only if the reversion-speed matrix satisfies the conditions that are derived in the following subsection.

33.6.3 Constraints on $\mathcal{K}$ for Identifiability

We have ascertained that, if the factors $\vec{x}_t$ are principal components in the sense explained previously (and we want to preclude the possibility of arbitrage), the matrix $\mathcal{K}$ cannot be diagonal. This raises the question of whether absence of arbitrage is compatible with *some* reversion-speed matrix, $\underline{\mathcal{K}}$, for factors $\vec{x}_t$ that behave like principal components.

The answer is affirmative. More precisely, in Appendix 33A we prove the following.

Proposition *Given N yields as previously, let the reversion speed matrix, $\mathcal{K}$, be diagonalizable as in*

$$\underline{\mathcal{K}} = \underline{a}\underline{\Lambda}_{\mathcal{K}}\underline{a}^{-1} \tag{33.57}$$

$$\underline{\Lambda}_{\mathcal{K}} = diag[l_j] \tag{33.58}$$

with the eigenvalues $\{l_j\}$ distinct and real. Let $\underline{F}$ be the $[N \times N]$ matrix of elements $[F]_{ji}$ given by

$$[F]_{ji} = \frac{1 - e^{-l_{jj}\tau_i}}{l_{jj}\tau_i}. \tag{33.59}$$

Take any set of yield maturities τ_2, τ_3, .., τ_N and any set of eigenvalues l_1, l_2, ..., l_N as long as they re all distinct, real and positive (so as to ensure stability of the dynamic system)[20]. Then, if the variables x_t are to be interpreted as principal components, the mapping

$$r_t = u_r + \overrightarrow{g}^{\mathrm{T}} \overrightarrow{x}_t \tag{33.60}$$

must be of the form

$$\overrightarrow{g} = \underline{\Omega}^{\mathrm{T}} \overrightarrow{e} \tag{33.61}$$

with

$$\overrightarrow{e} = \left(\underline{F}^{\mathrm{T}}\right)^{-1} \overrightarrow{1}, \tag{33.62}$$

and the reversion-speed matrix, $\underline{K} = \underline{K}(\overrightarrow{l})$, must be given by

$$\underline{K} = \underline{\Omega}^{\mathrm{T}} \underline{F} \, \underline{\Lambda}_{\underline{K}} \underline{F}^{-1} \underline{\Omega} \tag{33.63}$$

so that

$$\underline{\beta} \, \underline{\beta}^{\mathrm{T}} = \underline{I}. \tag{33.64}$$

It is important to pause for a moment. Suppose that we had chosen to work with N principal components as state variables. We have established that, given an exogenous (empirical) matrix of covariance eigenvalues, Ω, given N arbitrary positive real numbers (the eigenvalues $\{l_j\}$), the reversion-speed matrix, $\underline{K}$, is fully determined.

To stress the point again: we have no control over the yield covariance matrix Ω: once we have measured the volatility of, and correlation among, the yields, it is what it is. We have then proven that we can arbitrarily pick N (real, distinct, positive) numbers out of thin air, and the reversion-speed matrix, $\underline{K}$, in the affine setting (33.19) is fully determined via Equation (33.63).

This result is very important, because it shows that, for any reversion-speed vector, $\overrightarrow{\theta}$, it is possible to find an N-tuple infinity of possible solutions (each indexed by the distinct eigenvalues, $\{l_j\}$, $j = 1, 2, \ldots N$) such that

1. any exogenous discrete yield curve is perfectly recovered (condition (33.39)), and
2. any discrete exogenous covariance matrix is exactly recovered (condition (33.63)).

---

[20] Saroka (2014) shows that the result can be generalized to the case when the eigenvalues are real, positive but not distinct. We do not pursue this angle here because, apart from numerical issues (arising from matrix inversion), the same-eigenvalue case can be approximated arbitrarily closely by having two or more eigenvalues becoming closer and closer. Saroka (2014) also deals with the case in which the eigenvalues are imaginary, but with positive real part.

As we shall see, each choice for the eigenvalues $\{l_j\}$ gives rise to a very different model behaviour. It also gives rise to different values for the yields and covariance matrix elements other than those associated with the N reference yields. We discuss in what follows some criteria to strongly bound the acceptable values for the eigenvalues $\{l_j\}$. These criteria will also give a precise meaning to the idea of 'behaviour complexity' which has so far been repeatedly, but hand-wavingly, mentioned.

33.6.4 What the $\mathbb{Q}$-measure Reversion-Speed Matrix Affects

In the approach we present in this chapter we require the observed yields to be rotated in such a way as to obtain orthogonal principal components. Once this 'rotation of axes' has been made, it permeates every aspect of the resulting mean-reverting dynamics. This is obvious enough, if one looks at Equations (33.32) and (33.36), that play a central role in determining the prices and yields of bonds, and in ensuring the orthogonality. But the rotation of axes imposed by the principal-component interpretation of the factors also affects, in a less obvious way, the admissible reversion-speed matrices, which, we recall, are given by

$$\underline{\mathcal{K}} = \underline{\Omega}^{\mathrm{T}} \underline{F} \, \Lambda_{\mathcal{K}} \underline{F}^{-1} \underline{\Omega}. \tag{33.65}$$

This link between the reversion-speed matrix and the particular rotation singled out by $\underline{\Omega}$ entails a rather complex mean-reverting deterministic dynamics. This can be see as follows.

Once the state variables have been chosen to be principal components, and they have been assigned a mean-reverting behaviour as in Equation (33.19), the conditions of no-arbitrage only leave as 'degrees of freedom' the N eigenvalues, $\{ \overrightarrow{l} \}$, of the reversion-speed matrix, and, as we have seen, require the $\underline{\mathcal{K}}$ matrix to be non-diagonal. Furthermore, for the non-diagonal terms of $\overrightarrow{\beta} \, \overrightarrow{\beta}^{\,T}$ to be zero, the negative entries of the reversion-speed matrix must be large enough to cancel completely the contributions coming from the positive-sign reversion speeds (see Equation (33.64)). So, the negative entries of the reversion-speed matrix (which can give rise to a locally mean-fleeing behaviour) are not a 'small correction', but must be of the same order of magnitude as the positive matrix elements.

It is this feature (and the locally mean-fleeing behaviour between some state variables that it implies) that causes the behaviour complexity:[21] these positive and negative reversion speeds simultaneously generate attraction to, and *significant* repulsion from, the various state variables and their fixed reversion levels. The overall system *is*, of course, asymptotically stable (because we have

---

[21] For the moment we call a deterministic behaviour 'complex' if, in the absence of stochastic shocks, the expectation of the state variables approaches the relative reversion levels with a non-monotonic behaviour. The larger the amplitude of these oscillations is, and the more numerous the oscillations are, the more complex the resulting behaviour. See the results in Section 33.9.

required all the eigenvalues l_k to be real and positive[22]), but, as shown in detail later, given a set of initial conditions, $\overrightarrow{x}_0$, for the state variables, the *deterministic* path to their equilibrium can easily display an oscillatory behaviour, with over- and undershoots of their reversion levels. A similar deterministic oscillatory behaviour is inherited by the yields, which are a linear (affine, really) combination of the factors.

So, we can assign and recover exactly an exogenous (discrete) covariance matrix and we can assign and recover exactly an exogenous (discrete) time-0 yield curve. However, once no-arbitrage is enforced, we can only imperfectly specify the values of the non-reference covariance-matrix elements; and we can only imperfectly specify how the short rate will evolve from 'here to there'. For large eigenvalues of the reversion-speed matrix (which, we recall, can be arbitrarily assigned under the only constraint that they should be positive and distinct) there can be significant overshoots *and* undershoots, *even if all the N reference 'market' yields are exactly recovered* – the larger the trace of the $\underline{\underline{K}}$ matrix, the 'wilder' the over- and undershootings in between the 'nodes' of the market yields.

Figure 33.1 shows a clear example of this behaviour. To understand the three lines in the figure, consider the first yield, which is just the short rate. The time-0 $\mathbb{Q}$-measure expectation over the paths of the short rate out to a given maturity, T, is straightforwardly related to the time-0 yield of a discount bond of that maturity:

$$y_0^T = -\frac{1}{T} \log E^{\mathbb{Q}} \left[e^{-\int_0^T r_s ds} \right]. \tag{33.66}$$

Neglecting for the moment convexity effects (which anyhow play a very small role for maturities out to five years), one can approximately write

$$y_0^T \simeq E^{\mathbb{Q}} \left[\frac{1}{T} \int_0^T r_s ds \right]. \tag{33.67}$$

Therefore, simply by averaging out to a horizon T the values of the short rate along a deterministic path, one can immediately (if approximately) relate the path of the short rate to the current model yield curve. At the reference points, by construction, one will observe a perfect match between the market and the model yields (again, within the limits of the approximation given earlier); in between the reference points, however, every choice of eigenvalues will determine, by affecting the path of the state variables to their reversion levels, the values of the intermediate-maturity yields. The observed market yields therefore behave as fixed 'knots' through which the yield curve has to move: how smoothly it goes from point to point will depend on the eigenvalues of the reversion speed matrix. This is clearly shown in Figure 33.1.

The three lines in Figure 33.1 show the averages of the short rate out to five years for the eigenvalues of the reversion-speed matrix used in the case study

---

[22] As far as stability is concerned, we could allow imaginary eigenvalues with a positive real part. We do not explore this route, for which we see little a priori justification.

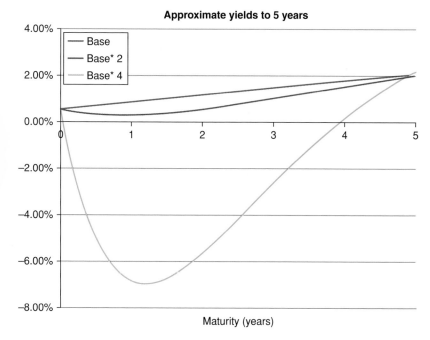

Figure 33.1 The averages of the short rate out to five years for the three cases discussed in the text, namely, for the eigenvalues of the reversion-speed matrix used in the case study (curve labelled Base); for eigenvalues twice as large (curve labelled Base*2); and for eigenvalues four times as large (curve labelled Base*4). In all cases, to within the accuracy of the approximation, the average of the short rate out to five years is indeed 2.00% (the exogenously assigned 'market' today's value of the 5-year yield).

(top curve labelled Base); for eigenvalues twice as large (middle curve labelled Base*2); and for eigenvalues four times as large (bottom curve labelled Base*4). In all cases, to within the accuracy of the convexity approximation, the average of the short rate out to five years is indeed 2.00% (the exogenously assigned 'market' value of y_0^2); however, intermediate yields can assume values which strongly depend on the eigenvalues of the reversion-speed matrix. The larger these eigenvalues, the more 'complex' the behaviour in between the 'knots'.

This interpretation also makes more precise the concept of 'complexity' for the yield behaviour, to which we have frequently alluded to earlier: for instance, as in the case of splines, the integral of the non-convexity–induced curvature of the model yield curve between reference points can be taken as a measure of complexity.

Similar considerations apply to the interpolated covariance matrix. Also in this case, the choice of the eigenvalues $\{\overrightarrow{l}\}$ strongly influences the values of the 'interpolated' covariance elements. Indeed, some choices for the vector $\overrightarrow{l}$ can

Square root of model covariance matrix

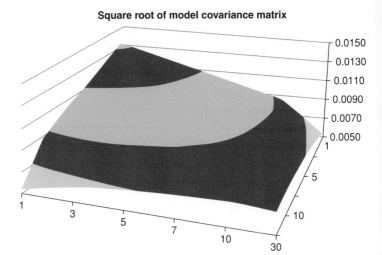

Square root of market covariance matrix

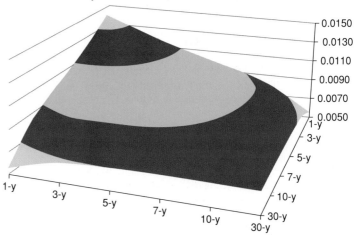

Figure 33.2 The square root of the entries of the model (top panel) and market (bottom panel) covariance matrix for yields from 1 to 30 years for the optimal choice of the eigenvalues { $\vec{l}$ }. (Note that the intervals along the x- and y-axes are not equally spaced – units in years.)

even produce negative correlations for yields in between the exactly recovered covariances.

Figure 33.2 shows the square root of the entries of the model (top panel) and market (bottom panel) covariance matrix for yields from 1 to 30 years obtained with the optimal choice of the eigenvalues { $\vec{l}$ }.[23] The overall quality of the

---

[23] Unless otherwise stated, in all our calibration studies we used $N = 3$, ie, three yields, and three principal components.

fit for the interpolated and extrapolated covariance matrix is excellent, with a maximum error of 6 basis points (in units equivalent to absolute volatility) and an average absolute error of 1.5 basis points (in the same units).

One might think that, since the values of the covariance matrix in correspondence with the reference yields are exactly recovered by construction, the errors in interpolation (and possibly extrapolation) should be small. If this were true, little information about the eigenvalues $\{\vec{l}\}$ could be gleaned from the non-reference covariance elements. This is not the case, as displayed clearly in Figure 33.3, which shows that an injudicious (but, at first blush, reasonable) choice of eigenvalues $\{\vec{l}\}$ can give extrapolated covariance elements wrong by a factor of 5 (even if the covariance elements among the reference yields are still exactly recovered)!

This dependence of the 'intermediate' yields and of the 'intermediate' covariance matrix elements on the eigenvalues $\{\vec{l}\}$ is not a drawback, but one of the most appealing features of the model. As we shall show in the calibration section (33.9) this set of dependences will provide very useful guidance to determine the acceptable values of the eigenvalues $\{\vec{l}\}$.

33.7 MOVING FROM THE $\mathbb{Q}$- TO THE $\mathbb{P}$-MEASURE

We want to show in this section how the model behaviour can be specified both in the $\mathbb{Q}$ (risk-neutral) and in the $\mathbb{P}$ (data-generating) measures.

Let's go back to the $\mathbb{Q}$-measure dynamics (33.19) – which we rewrite here for ease of reference:

$$d\vec{x}_t = \underline{K}\left(\vec{\theta} - \vec{x}_t\right)dt + \underline{S}\vec{dz}_t^{\mathbb{Q}}. \tag{33.68}$$

As discussed in Section 33.2, we can assign to the market price of risk, $\vec{T}_t$, any of the many affine forms discussed in the literature, as long as it is nested in the following general formulation:

$$\vec{T}_t = \vec{q}_0 + \underline{R}\vec{x}_t. \tag{33.69}$$

For instance, if we embraced the Duffee (2002) specification (according to which the magnitude of the market price of risk depends on the slope of the yield curve) we would have[24] for the matrix $\underline{R}$

$$\underline{R} = \begin{bmatrix} 0 & a & 0 \\ 0 & b & 0 \\ 0 & c & 0 \end{bmatrix}. \tag{33.70}$$

---

[24] This is not strictly correct. We find that the single regressor that most effectively explains excess returns is the second principal component from the orthogonalization of the covariance matrix of yields (not yield differences). The second factor of our model is the second principal component from the orthogonalization of the covariance matrix of yield *differences*. After the required transformation is applied, the matrix $\underline{R}$ is similar to, but no longer exactly equal to, the simple single-column matrix displayed in Equation (33.70).

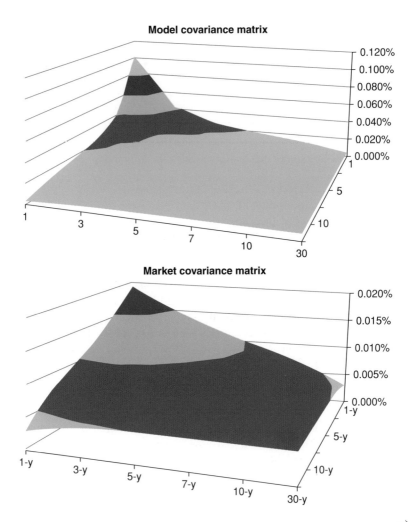

Figure 33.3 Same as Figure 33.2 for a poor choice of the eigenvalues $\{\vec{l}\}$. Note that the covariance matrix elements between each reference yield are still exactly recovered.

In general, for *any* specification of the dependence of the market price of risk on the state variables, we have

$$d\vec{x}_t = \underline{\mathcal{K}}\left(\vec{\theta} - \vec{x}_t\right) dt + \underline{S}\vec{dz} + \underline{S}\left(\vec{q}_0 + \underline{\mathcal{R}}_t\vec{x}_t\right) dt. \tag{33.71}$$

Under $\mathbb{P}$ the dynamics are

$$d\vec{x}_t = \underline{\mathcal{K}}^{\mathbb{P}}\left(\vec{\theta}^{\mathbb{P}} - \vec{x}_t\right) dt + \underline{S}\vec{dz}, \tag{33.72}$$

with

$$\underline{\mathcal{K}}^{\mathbb{P}} = \underline{\mathcal{K}} - \underline{S}\underline{\mathcal{R}} \tag{33.73}$$

and

$$\vec{\theta}^{\,\mathbb{P}} = \left(\underline{\mathcal{K}} - \underline{S}\underline{\mathcal{R}}_t\right)^{-1}\left(\underline{\mathcal{K}}\vec{\theta} + \underline{S}\vec{q}_0\right) \tag{33.74}$$

Exercise 88 *Derive Equations (33.73) and (33.74).*

Equations (33.73) and (33.74) define the reversion-speed matrix and the reversion-level vector, respectively, as a function of the corresponding $\mathbb{Q}$-measure quantities, and of the market-price-of risk vector, $\vec{q}_0$, and matrix, $\underline{\mathcal{R}}$, respectively. We show in the next section how we propose to estimate these quantities.

As we mentioned in the case of the Diebold–Rudebusch (2013) model discussed in Chapter 32, once we assign – for instance on the basis of the empirical excess-return studies presented in Part VI – the form of the matrix (33.70), the real-world reversion-speed matrix is fully specified. Does it correspond to the empirically observed one? The question is not easy to answer, because the real-world estimation of a full reversion-speed matrix is a very complex task. The nagging consistency issue, however, does not go away. Hiding behind the difficulty to estimate the reversion speed matrix in the real world is not a very satisfactory answer. The question remains: if the statistical estimate of the real-world reversion-speed matrix were inconsistent with no-arbitrage and the empirically estimated excess return matrix, what would have to give? The N eigenvalues of the $\mathbb{Q}$-measure version speed matrix provide far too little flexibility to ensure the squaring of this particular circle. These issues are further explored in the next section.

33.8 ESTIMATING THE PARAMETERS OF $\vec{q}_0$ AND $\underline{\mathcal{R}}$

As shown in Part VI, using 50 years of data from the database provided by the Federal Reserve Board of Washington, DC Gurkaynak, Sack and Wright (2006), we have statistically estimated the excess returns from holding bonds up to 10 years. We have regressed these excess returns against our state variables, ie, the principal components. If we call $\overrightarrow{xret}$ the vector of excess returns, the Ordinary Least Squares estimation gives

$$\overrightarrow{xret}_t = \vec{a} + \underline{b}\vec{x}_t + \epsilon_t, \tag{33.75}$$

where ϵ_t is fitting error at time t. This is our statistical estimation of the dependence of the excess returns on the state variables. (For simplicity in what follows we consider as many excess returns as factors in the model, but this setting could be easily generalized.) We can look at the same dependence from the model point of view. In one dimension, we know that

$$\mathbb{E}^{\mathbb{P}}\left[\frac{dP_t^T}{P_t^T}\right] = r_t + \frac{1}{P_t^{T_i}}\frac{\partial P_t^{T_i}}{\partial x}s\,dt \tag{33.76}$$

and therefore we have for the excess return

$$\mathbb{E}^{\mathbb{P}}\left[\overrightarrow{xret_t}\right] = \mathbb{E}^{\mathbb{P}}\left[\frac{dP_t^T}{P_t^T} - r_t\right] = \frac{1}{P_t^{T_i}}\frac{\partial P_t^{T_i}}{\partial x}s\lambda(x)dt, \tag{33.77}$$

where s is the volatility of the single factor, x_t.

When we have several factors, Equation (33.77) for the excess return vector generalizes to

$$\mathbb{E}^{\mathbb{P}}\left[\overrightarrow{xret_t}\right]dt = \mathbb{E}^{\mathbb{P}}\left[\overrightarrow{\frac{dP_t^T}{P_t^T} - r_t dt}\right] = \underline{Dur}\,\underline{S}\left[\underbrace{\overrightarrow{q}_0 + \underline{\mathcal{R}}\,\overrightarrow{x}_t}_{\text{mpr vector}}\right]dt, \tag{33.78}$$

where

$$[Dur]_{ij} = \frac{1}{P_t^{T_i}}\frac{\partial P_t^{T_i}}{\partial x_j}. \tag{33.79}$$

Exercise 89 *Derive Equation (33.78).*

Now that we have obtained an expression for the excess returns as understood by the model, and as estimated by our regression, we can equate the coefficients of Equations (33.75) and (33.78) to obtain

$$\overrightarrow{a} = \underline{Dur}\,\underline{S}\,\overrightarrow{q}_0 \tag{33.80}$$

and

$$\underline{b} = \underline{Dur}\,\underline{S}\,\underline{\mathcal{R}} \tag{33.81}$$

and therefore

$$\overrightarrow{q}_0 = \left(\underline{Dur}\,\underline{S}\right)^{-1}\overrightarrow{a} \tag{33.82}$$

$$\underline{\mathcal{R}} = \left(\underline{Dur}\,\underline{S}\right)^{-1}\underline{b}. \tag{33.83}$$

Since

$$\frac{1}{P_t^{T_i}}\frac{\partial P_t^{T_i}}{\partial x_j} = \frac{\partial \log P_t^{T_i}}{\partial x_j} \tag{33.84}$$

and recalling that

$$P_t^T = \exp^{A_t^T + \left(\overrightarrow{B}_t^T\right)^{\mathsf{T}}\overrightarrow{x}_t} \tag{33.85}$$

we have

$$\underline{Dur} = \left(\underline{B}_t\right)^{\mathrm{T}} \tag{33.86}$$

and therefore

$$\vec{q}_0 = \left(\left(\underline{B}_t\right)^{\mathrm{T}} \underline{S}\right)^{-1} \vec{a} \tag{33.87}$$

$$\underline{\mathcal{R}} = \left(\left(\underline{B}_t\right)^{\mathrm{T}} \underline{S}\right)^{-1} \underline{b}. \tag{33.88}$$

Note that the 'duration' matrix $(\underline{B}_t^T)$ clearly depends on the maturity of the yield under consideration; so does the matrix of regression coefficient, $\underline{b}$, and the vector of 'intercepts', $\vec{a}$. However, the market price of risk must be independent of the maturity of the yields. Therefore the maturity dependence in $\underline{b}$ and $\vec{a}$, on the one hand, and on the 'duration' matrix $(\underline{B}_t^T)$ on the other must neatly cancel out. This means that, within the precision of the statistical estimate of the regressors, the market price of risk vector and matrix, $\vec{q}_0$ and $\underline{\mathcal{R}}$, must be independent of the N yields used in the regression. *This condition imposes an internal consistency check on the model and on the statistical estimates of the coefficients in the excess return regression.*

The results derived so far complete the formal specification of the model. For a given set of exogenous market yields and covariance matrix, we have a $(2N + 1)$-ple infinity of solutions (each exactly recovering the reference exogenous yield and covariance elements), parametrized by the vector $\vec{l}$ (the eigenvalues of the reversion-speed matrix), the vector $\vec{\theta}$, and the first element of the vector $\vec{y}$. Each of these solutions gives rise to economically different behaviours for important quantities such as the market price of risk. The next section shows the criteria on the basis of which the number of degrees of freedom, or their acceptability range, can be reduced virtually to zero. We call this part of the project the 'calibration of the model'.

33.9 CALIBRATION OF THE MODEL

33.9.1 Cross-Sectional Fit to Yields

If N principal components are chosen as state variables, one can easily show that, for any choice of the eigenvalues, $\{\vec{l}\,\}$, and of the 'level' constant, u_r, the values of N market yields can always be exactly recovered, if so desired, without error by a suitable choice of the initial values, $\vec{x}_0$, of the state variables. Indeed, assuming invertibility, one has

$$\vec{y}_0 = \vec{\alpha} + \underline{\beta}^{\mathrm{T}} \vec{x}_0 \Longrightarrow \vec{x}_0 = \left(\underline{\beta}^{\mathrm{T}}\right)^{-1} \left(\vec{y}_0 - \vec{\alpha}\right). \tag{33.89}$$

Of course, one can also choose to achieve a least-square fit for all yields. See later.

Furthermore, since the state variables are principal components, it is well known that as few as three can recover the trace of the yield covariance matrix to a high level of accuracy. Furthermore, since the yield covariance matrix is given by

$$
cov[dy] = \mathbb{E}\left[d\overrightarrow{y}_t \left(d\overrightarrow{y}_t \right)^{\mathrm{T}} \right] = \underline{\beta}^{\mathrm{T}} \begin{bmatrix} \lambda_1^2 & 0 & \dots & 0 \\ 0 & \lambda_2^2 & \dots & 0 \\ \dots & \dots & \dots & \dots \\ 0 & 0 & \dots & \lambda_N^2 \end{bmatrix} \underline{\beta},
$$

(33.90)

it is clear that N eigenvalues can always be chosen so that the exogenous covariance matrix elements referring to the reference yields are always exactly recovered.

33.9.2   Estimating the Values of the Eigenvalues $\overrightarrow{l}$

As we have shown earlier, the model recovers exactly N exogenous market yields, and the N variances of the same yields. As shown later, this does not mean, however, that the yields or the covariance elements 'in between' the reference maturities will be similar to the corresponding market quantities. We therefore choose the eigenvalues of the $\mathbb{Q}$-measure reversion speed matrix in such a way that the covariance matrix and the yield curve in between the reference yields should be closely recovered. Since both the market yields curves and the market covariance matrix tend to be smooth, this is effectively achieved by imposing a smoothness requirement in the optimization. This helps determine the eigenvalues $\{l_i\}$, that, in our model, uniquely determine the reversion-speed matrix, $\underline{\mathcal{K}}$.

33.9.3   Estimating the 'Level' Constant, u_r

As shown earlier, the smoothness (interpolation) constraint leaves one degree of freedom. The natural market quantity to fix this degree of freedom is the yield of the consol, or some similar long-term $\mathbb{Q}$-measure quantity. (The quantity, $k_\infty^{\mathbb{Q}}$, that in Joslin, Singleton and Zhu (2011) plays the same role as our u_r, is described by them as 'proportional to the risk-neutral long-term mean of the short rate $r_\infty^{\mathbb{Q}}$'.)

33.10   CALIBRATION RESULTS

We show in this section the result obtained by calibrating the model using the procedure described earlier to Treasury data provided by the Federal Reserve Board (Gurkaynak et al., 2006) for the period 1990–2014. Qualitatively similar results were obtained using a longer data sets (extending back to the late 1970s).

However we used the shorter time window of 24 years in order to avail ourselves of information about the 20-year yields, useful for assessing the quality of the model-suggested extrapolations. We used 5 and 10 years for the intermediate and long yield maturities, respectively.

After using covariance information from the period 1990–2014, the eigenvalues of the $\mathbb{Q}$-measure reversion-speed matrix, $\mathcal{K}^{\mathbb{Q}}$, that gave rise to the smoothest model covariance matrix turned out to be

$$
\begin{bmatrix}
\text{Eigenvalues of } \mathcal{K}^{\mathbb{Q}} \\
l_1 = 0.03660 \\
l_2 = 0.63040 \\
l_3 = 0.63036
\end{bmatrix}.
\tag{33.91}
$$

The reversion-speed matrix in the $\mathbb{Q}$-measure was obtained from Equation (33.63), and turned out to be as follows:

$$
\mathcal{K}^{\mathbb{Q}} =
\begin{bmatrix}
-0.1880 & 1.0187 & -3.0499 \\
-0.2229 & 0.7731 & -4.2299 \\
0.0242 & -0.0304 & 0.7123
\end{bmatrix}.
\tag{33.92}
$$

As anticipated, note the presence of large and negative reversion speeds, also on the main diagonal.

With this reversion-speed matrix the model covariance matrices, and the difference between the model and the empirical covariance matrices, were calculated. The results are shown in Figure 33.4. The high quality of the fit in between reference points is evident.

To assess the ability of the model to predict quantities it has not been calibrated to, the empirical and model yield volatilities out to 20 years are shown in Figure 33.5. We stress that the volatilities beyond 10 years are extrapolated by the model.

Figure 33.6 shows the observed and fitted yield curves on randomly selected dates between 1990 and 2014. The same model parameters were used for all the fits, and only the state variables were changed. The yields for the key maturities are, of course, perfectly recovered. It is interesting to note, however, that the intermediate and the extrapolated yields (ie, the yield beyond 10 years) are also well recovered.

Note that the same parameters are used throughout, and that yields beyond 10 years are extrapolated.

After empirical estimation of the regression matrix of excess returns we were able to estimate the $\mathbb{P}$-measure reversion levels, and the trace of the matrix. See Equations (33.73) and (33.74). To show the robustness of the procedure, we present the estimates obtained for three different subsections of the data. Observe that all the parameters remain reasonably stable, with the possible exception of the reversion level of the first factor in the first half of the sample.

Model COV

0.000124	0.000118	0.000112	0.000106	0.000101	0.000096	0.000092	0.000088	0.000085	0.000082
0.000118	0.000136	0.000140	0.000136	0.000130	0.000124	0.000118	0.000112	0.000107	0.000102
0.000112	0.000140	0.000148	0.000147	0.000142	0.000136	0.000130	0.000124	0.000119	0.000115
0.000106	0.000136	0.000147	0.000148	0.000145	0.000141	0.000136	0.000131	0.000126	0.000122
0.000101	0.000130	0.000142	0.000145	**0.000144**	0.000141	0.000138	0.000134	0.000130	0.000127
0.000096	0.000124	0.000136	0.000141	0.000141	0.000140	0.000138	0.000135	0.000132	0.000130
0.000092	0.000118	0.000130	0.000136	0.000138	0.000138	0.000137	0.000135	0.000133	0.000131
0.000088	0.000112	0.000124	0.000131	0.000134	0.000135	0.000135	0.000134	0.000133	0.000132
0.000085	0.000107	0.000119	0.000126	0.000130	0.000132	0.000133	0.000133	0.000133	0.000132
0.000082	0.000102	0.000115	0.000122	0.000127	0.000130	0.000131	0.000132	0.000132	**0.000131**

Mkt COV

0.000124	0.000121	0.000113	0.000107	0.000101	0.000096	0.000091	0.000088	0.000085	0.000085
0.000121	0.000140	0.000141	0.000135	0.000128	0.000122	0.000116	0.000112	0.000108	0.000105
0.000113	0.000141	0.000148	0.000146	0.000141	0.000135	0.000129	0.000124	0.000120	0.000116
0.000107	0.000135	0.000146	0.000147	0.000145	0.000140	0.000136	0.000131	0.000127	0.000123
0.000101	0.000128	0.000141	0.000145	**0.000144**	0.000142	0.000138	0.000134	0.000131	0.000127
0.000096	0.000122	0.000135	0.000140	0.000142	0.000141	0.000138	0.000136	0.000133	0.000129
0.000091	0.000116	0.000129	0.000136	0.000138	0.000138	0.000137	0.000136	0.000133	0.000131
0.000088	0.000112	0.000124	0.000131	0.000134	0.000136	0.000136	0.000135	0.000133	0.000131
0.000085	0.000108	0.000120	0.000127	0.000131	0.000133	0.000133	0.000133	0.000133	0.000132
0.000082	0.000105	0.000116	0.000123	0.000127	0.000129	0.000131	0.000131	0.000132	**0.000131**

Error

0.000000	−0.000002	−0.000001	0.000000	0.000000	0.000000	0.000000	0.000000	0.000000	0.000000
−0.000002	−0.000004	−0.000001	0.000001	0.000002	0.000002	0.000001	0.000000	−0.000001	−0.000003
−0.000001	−0.000001	0.000000	0.000001	0.000001	0.000001	0.000001	0.000000	−0.000001	−0.000002
0.000000	0.000001	0.000001	0.000001	0.000001	0.000000	0.000000	0.000000	0.000000	−0.000001
0.000000	0.000002	0.000001	0.000001	**0.000000**	0.000000	0.000000	0.000000	0.000000	0.000000
0.000000	0.000002	0.000001	0.000000	0.000000	−0.000001	−0.000001	0.000000	0.000000	0.000000
0.000000	0.000001	0.000001	0.000000	0.000000	−0.000001	−0.000001	0.000000	0.000000	0.000000
0.000000	0.000000	0.000000	0.000000	0.000000	0.000000	0.000000	0.000000	0.000000	0.000000
0.000000	−0.000001	−0.000001	0.000000	0.000000	0.000000	0.000000	0.000000	0.000000	0.000000
0.000000	−0.000003	−0.000002	−0.000001	0.000000	0.000000	0.000000	0.000000	0.000000	**0.000000**

Figure 33.4 Model (Model COV) and market (MKT COV) covariance matrices, and the error (market - model). The rows and columns correspond to maturities from 1 to 10 years. Note that the errors are exactly zero for all the covariance elements associated with the reference yields (ie, not just for the diagonal – variance – elements).

This is probably due to the quasi-unit-root nature of the first principal component.

$$
\begin{bmatrix}
\text{Data sample} & \theta_1^{\mathbb{P}} & \theta_2^{\mathbb{P}} & \theta_3^{\mathbb{P}} & \text{Trace } (\mathcal{K}^{\mathbb{P}}) \\
\text{1990–2002} & 0.0958 & 0.0090 & -0.0073 & 3.78 \\
\text{2002–2014} & 0.0367 & 0.0115 & -0.0057 & 3.62 \\
\text{1990–2014} & 0.0380 & 0.0132 & -0.0055 & 3.11
\end{bmatrix}
$$

Once the term premia have been estimated, we can calculate the deterministic evolution of the reference yields under both measures from 'today's' yield curve (30 January 2014). This is shown in Figure 33.7.

Note that under the risk-neutral measure the asymptotic yield curve is almost exactly flat. This should indeed be the case: apart from convexity effects (whose magnitude is estimated in the text that follows), all factors will ultimately reach their reversion levels, and in the $\mathbb{Q}$ measure no term premia can steepen the yield curve. As a consequence, apart from convexity terms, under $\mathbb{Q}$ the curve will evolve deterministically to a flat shape.

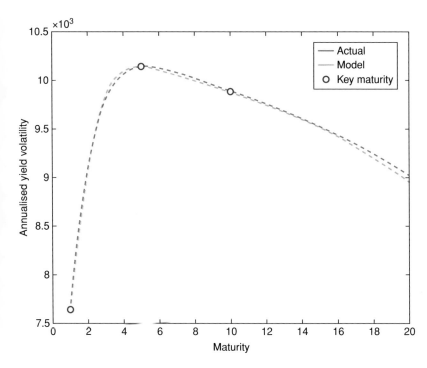

Figure 33.5 Model and empirical yield volatilities. Volatilities beyond 10 years are extrapolated. The red dots indicate the volatilities of the reference maturitities.

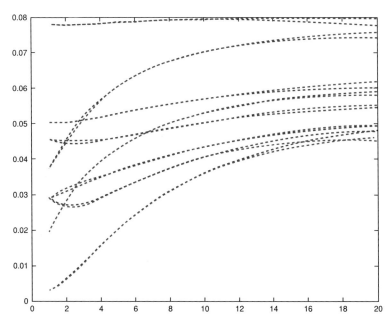

Figure 33.6 Fitted and empirical yield curves for random dates between 1990 and 2014.

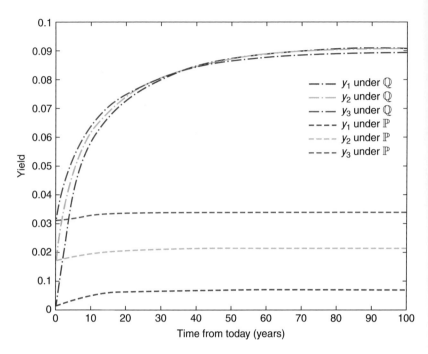

Figure 33.7 The deterministic evolution of the reference yields under $\mathbb{Q}$ (solid lines) and under $\mathbb{P}$ (dashed lines). The yield curve is flat if the three lines (which correspond to three different maturities) are superimposed.

The magnitude of the convexity term is shown in Figure 33.8, which shows yields and value of convexity for different eigenvalues of the mean-reversion speed matrix $\mathcal{K}$. Dashed lines represent the yield curves, and dash-and-dot lines represent the yield curves without the convexity term. The colours correspond to different eigenvalues of $\mathcal{K}$: blue – (0.02; 0.2; 0.5), green – (0.03; 0.3; 0.6), red – (0.04; 0.4; 0.7).

We see that it is possible to obtain very similar fits on the reference portion of the yield curve with different eigenvalues of $\mathcal{K}$, but the consequences for extrapolation are very different. We emphasize, however, that, despite the similar quality of the fit for the yields, *the fit to the full covariance matrix produced by the three sets of eigenvalues was very different*. This stresses again the importance of making use of the full covariance matrix information in the fitting phase.

Finally we show in Figure 33.9 the time series of the 10-year yield observed in the market ('yield under $\mathbb{Q}$'), and the yield that would have been observed if investors had the same expectations, but were risk-neutral ('yield under $\mathbb{P}$'). In the same figure we also show the term premium (red line), which is the difference between the two yields. The average risk premium for the last 24 years averages around 3%, which compares well

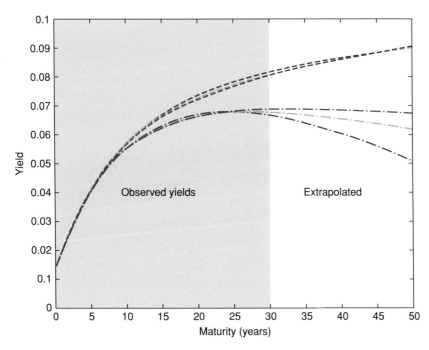

Figure 33.8 Yields and values of convexity for different eigenvalues of the mean-reversion speed matrix $\mathcal{K}$. Dashed lines represent the yield curves, and dash-and-dot lines represent the yield curves without the convexity term. The colours correspond to different eigenvalues of $\mathcal{K}$: blue – (0:02; 0:2; 0:5), green – (0:03; 0:3; 0:6), red – (0:04; 0:4; 0:7).

with our empirical estimates of unconditional excess returns for the 10-year maturity.

33.11 GENERALIZABLE RESULTS ON TERM PREMIA FROM A PC-BASED AFFINE MODEL

As we indicated in the first part of this chapter, principal component–based affine models are particularly interesting because whatever conclusion we draw about them applies to all the members of their equivalence class, and because they can be made to recover the market yield curve and covariance matrix arbitrarily well. So, what are these generalizable conclusions?

We know that, if a model is affine (and invertible), then the yields can be expressed as an affine function of the state variables:

$$\overrightarrow{y}_t = \underline{\beta}^{\mathrm{T}} \overrightarrow{x}_t + \overrightarrow{\alpha}, \tag{33.93}$$

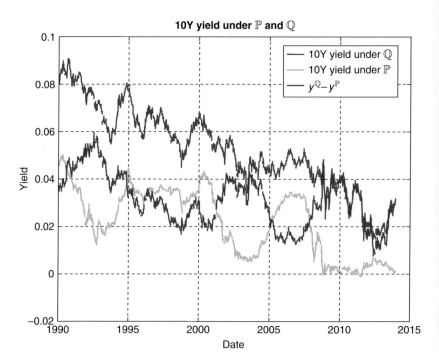

Figure 33.9 Observed 10-year zero coupon yield (blue), the '$\mathbb{P}$' 10-year zero-coupon yield (green) and the term premium (red).

with $\underline{\beta}^{\mathrm{T}}$ some function of the reversion-speed matrix under $\mathbb{Q}$,

$$\underline{\beta}^{\mathrm{T}} = f\left(\mathcal{K}^{\mathbb{Q}}; T - t\right).\tag{33.94}$$

If the chosen state variables are principal components, then we also know that

$$d\overrightarrow{y}_t = \underline{\Omega}d\overrightarrow{x}_t,$$

with $\underline{\Omega}$ the orthogonal matrix given by the orthogonalization of the covariance matrix of yield changes. Therefore

$$\overrightarrow{y}_t = \overrightarrow{\tilde{y}} + \underline{\Omega}\overrightarrow{x}_t,\tag{33.95}$$

with $\overrightarrow{\tilde{y}}$ an 'integration constant' vector.

For both of these relationships to hold for any value of $\overrightarrow{x}_t$, we must have

$$\overrightarrow{\alpha} = \overrightarrow{\tilde{y}}\tag{33.96}$$

and

$$\underline{\beta}^{\mathrm{T}} = \underline{\Omega}.\tag{33.97}$$

As we have seen this implies that

$$\underline{\Omega}\,\underline{\Omega}^{\mathrm{T}} = I \Longrightarrow \underline{\beta}\,\underline{\beta}^{\mathrm{T}} = I.\tag{33.98}$$

We have also obtained that, if the reversion-speed matrix under $\mathbb{Q}$, $\mathcal{K}^{\mathbb{Q}}$, is diagonalizable as

$$\underline{\Lambda}_{\mathcal{K}} = \text{diag}[l_1, l_2, \ldots l_N], \qquad \{l_j\} > 0 \tag{33.99}$$

and the state variables are indeed principal components, then $\mathcal{K}^{\mathbb{Q}}$ must be given by

$$\mathcal{K}^{\mathbb{Q}} = \underline{\Omega}^{\mathrm{T}} \underline{F} \underline{\Lambda}_{\mathcal{K}} \underline{F}^{-1} \underline{\Omega} \tag{33.100}$$

with

$$F_{ij} = \frac{1 - e^{-l_j \tau_i}}{l_j \tau_i}. \tag{33.101}$$

So, in a nutshell, the reversion-speed matrix under $\mathbb{Q}$ is fully specified by the N (real, positive, but otherwise arbitrary) eigenvalues of the diagonalizing matrix, $\underline{\Lambda}_{\mathcal{K}}$.

Now, suppose that the reversion-speed matrix under $\mathbb{P}$ has been econometrically estimated. For simplicity, we can assume that it is diagonal, but nothing hangs on this. The important point is that the reversion-speed matrix under $\mathbb{P}$ 'is what it is', and it is not in our gift to modify it as we please. It is an 'experimental fact', or a 'fact of nature', over which we have no control. If we assume for simplicity that it is diagonal then, for $N = 3$, we have

$$\mathcal{K}^{\mathbb{P}} = \begin{bmatrix} \kappa_{11} & 0 & 0 \\ 0 & \kappa_{22} & 0 \\ 0 & 0 & \kappa_{33} \end{bmatrix}. \tag{33.102}$$

Let's also assume that the market price of risk depends on the second state variable (the 'slope'), and that investors only get compensated for level risk. Again, the argument does not depend on these choices, which are made only for the sake of simplicity – the important fact is that these, too, are empirical observations about how investors react, and upon which we have control. Then, for an essentially affine model, we have for the market price of risk vector, $\overrightarrow{T}$,

$$\overrightarrow{T} = \overrightarrow{q}_0 + \underline{R} \overrightarrow{x}_t \tag{33.103}$$

with (for $N = 3$)

$$\overrightarrow{T} = \overrightarrow{q}_0 + \underbrace{\begin{bmatrix} 0 & a & 0 \\ 0 & b & 0 \\ 0 & c & 0 \end{bmatrix}}_{\underline{R}} \overrightarrow{x}_t \quad \text{(return-predicting factor = slope)}$$

$$\tag{33.104}$$

$$\vec{T} = \vec{q}_0 + \underbrace{\begin{bmatrix} 0 & a & 0 \\ 0 & 0 & 0 \\ 0 & 0 & 0 \end{bmatrix}}_{\underline{R}} \vec{x}_t \quad \text{(compensation only for level risk)}.$$

(33.105)

From all of this it follows that

$$d\vec{x}_t = \mathcal{K}^{\mathbb{Q}} \left(\vec{\theta} - \vec{x}_t \right) dt + \underline{S} \vec{dz} \quad [\underline{S} \text{ diagonal}] \tag{33.106}$$

$$d\vec{x}_t = \mathcal{K}^{\mathbb{P}} \left(\vec{\theta} - \vec{x}_t \right) dt + \underline{S} \vec{dz} + \underline{S} \left(\vec{q}_0 + \underline{R} \vec{x}_t \right) dt \tag{33.107}$$

and

$$\mathcal{K}^{\mathbb{Q}} = \mathcal{K}^{\mathbb{P}} + \underline{S} \vec{T}$$

$$= \begin{bmatrix} \kappa_{11} & 0 & 0 \\ 0 & \kappa_{33} & 0 \\ 0 & 0 & \kappa_{33} \end{bmatrix} + \begin{bmatrix} s_{11} & 0 & 0 \\ 0 & s_{22} & 0 \\ 0 & 0 & s_{33} \end{bmatrix} \begin{bmatrix} 0 & a & 0 \\ 0 & 0 & 0 \\ 0 & 0 & 0 \end{bmatrix}$$

$$\implies \mathcal{K}^{\mathbb{Q}} = \begin{bmatrix} \kappa_{11} & s_{11}a & 0 \\ 0 & \kappa_{33} & 0 \\ 0 & 0 & \kappa_{33} \end{bmatrix}.$$

So, this is the only possible form of the reversion-speed matrix under $\mathbb{Q}$ compatible with the assumed 'experimental' facts

1. that the reversion-speed matrix under $\mathbb{P}$ is diagonal;
2. that the slope is a good return-predicting factor; and
3. that investors mainly seek compensation for level risk.

If we had assumed different risk preferences, or a different reversion-speed behaviour in the objective measure, we would have found a different form for $\mathcal{K}^{\mathbb{Q}}$, but, once again, the gist of the argument would not change.

Let's now choose principal components as state variables. Since we have found that in the risk-neutral measure the reversion-speed matrix must be of the form

$$\mathcal{K}^{\mathbb{Q}} = \underline{\Omega}^{\mathrm{T}} \underline{F} \, \underline{\Lambda}_{\mathcal{K}} \underline{F}^{-1} \underline{\Omega}, \tag{33.108}$$

this now raises an interesting question.

Conventional wisdom tells us that three principal components do a splendid job at describing the evolution of market yields. So, let's stick with our choice of $N = 3$. Then from points 1, 2 and 3 above we get a matrix of the form

$$\mathcal{K}^{\mathbb{Q}} = \begin{bmatrix} \kappa_{11} & s_{11}a & 0 \\ 0 & \kappa_{33} & 0 \\ 0 & 0 & \kappa_{33} \end{bmatrix}. \tag{33.109}$$

We can now ask: is it possible to find three positive real numbers (the eigenvalues $[l_1, l_2, l_3]$ of the reversion-speed diagonal matrix, $\underline{\Lambda}_{\mathcal{K}}$,) such that the reversion-speed matrix from the equation

$$\mathcal{K}^{\mathbb{Q}} = \underline{\Omega}^{\mathrm{T}} \underline{F} \underline{\Lambda}_{\mathcal{K}} \underline{F}^{-1} \underline{\Omega} \tag{33.110}$$

assumes the form of Equation (33.109)?

The answer is a firm 'no'. Why so? Because we have seen (from Equation (33.29)) that

$$\overrightarrow{\beta_\tau}^{\mathrm{T}} \propto (\mathcal{K}^{\mathbb{Q}})^{-1} \left[e^{-\mathcal{K}\tau} - I_n \right]. \tag{33.111}$$

If this is the case, for the conditions $\beta\beta^{\mathrm{T}} = I$ and $\overrightarrow{\beta_\tau}^{\mathrm{T}} \propto (\mathcal{K}^{\mathbb{Q}})^{-1}[e^{-\mathcal{K}\tau} - I_n]$ to hold simultaneously, as we explained some of the off-diagonal elements of β, and hence of $\mathcal{K}^{\mathbb{Q}}$, must be 'large' and negative. But this does not happen to be compatible with

$$\mathcal{K}^{\mathbb{Q}} = \begin{bmatrix} \kappa_{11} & s_{11}a & 0 \\ 0 & \kappa_{33} & 0 \\ 0 & 0 & \kappa_{33} \end{bmatrix}, \tag{33.112}$$

which depends on empirical and behavioural regularities, and with the stability of $\mathcal{K}^{\mathbb{Q}}$ (its eigenvalues must be positive).

I stress that what we cannot say is something like: 'Let's start from $\mathcal{K}^{\mathbb{Q}}$ and derive what $\mathcal{K}^{\mathbb{P}}$, or the market price of risk $\overrightarrow{T} = \overrightarrow{q}_0 + \mathcal{R} \overrightarrow{x}_t$, or the eigenvector matrix $\underline{\Omega}$ should be.' It would be a bit like tinkering with the charge of the electron to salvage the results of a wonky experiment. We have to play with the cards Nature had dealt us, not with the cards we wish we had received.

And now comes the really interesting bit. We have derived these results for affine models which use principal components as state variables. Perhaps, one may say, this was not such a good choice of state variables, and we will be luckier if we choose different drivers for the yield curve. But the conclusions reached in the opening sections of this chapter show that these constraining results apply to all models equivalent (in the sense of Section 33.2) to the principal component–based essentially affine model we have presented in this chapter.

The point is important, and it pays to repeat it. In general, we have shown that it would be an incredible fluke if nature were so kind as to accommodate the strictures of the model under consideration: on the one hand, from experimental information we know that the reversion-speed matrix should look something like the one in Equation (33.112); on the other hand, affine models with principal components as state variables are incapable of recovering a reversion-speed matrix with this structure. Which means that, indeed, nature is not unreasonably kind. More disturbingly, even if differently specified affine equivalent models may look different, this 'tension' between facts of nature and what the model allows does not go away.

If we are interested in a *structural* affine description of the yield curve, we seem to have a pretty big problem on our hands.

33.12   THE EXISTENTIAL DILEMMA

Let's review the reasoning so far.

In essentially affine models the market price of risk vector ($\overrightarrow{T}$) is a deterministic (affine) function of the state variables: $\overrightarrow{T} = \overrightarrow{q}_0 + \underline{R}\,\overrightarrow{x}_t$. Whatever the stochastic variables, the reversion speed matrix under $\mathbb{Q}$, $\mathcal{K}^{\mathbb{Q}}$, is given by $\mathcal{K}^{\mathbb{Q}} = \mathcal{K}^{\mathbb{P}} + \underline{S}\,\overrightarrow{T}$. Therefore we have

$$\overrightarrow{T} = \overrightarrow{q}_0 + \underline{R}\,\overrightarrow{x} \implies \mathcal{K}^{\mathbb{Q}} = \mathcal{K}^{\mathbb{P}} + \underline{S}\left(\overrightarrow{q}_0 + \underline{R}\,\overrightarrow{x}\right). \tag{33.113}$$

This is totally general for essentially affine models.

When the state variables are principal components, we then showed that there are constraints on the possible shape of the risk-neutral reversion-speed matrix, $\mathcal{K}^{\mathbb{Q}}$:

$$\mathcal{K}^{\mathbb{Q}} = \underline{\Omega}\,\underbrace{{}^{\mathrm{T}}\underline{F}\,\Lambda_{\mathcal{K}}\underline{F}^{-1}}_{\text{dependent on } \{l_i\}}\,\underline{\Omega}. \tag{33.114}$$

We argued that this creates a problem for all essentially affine models equivalent to the principal components–based essentially affine model.

What exactly is the problem? In a nutshell it is the following. On the one hand we have obtained that, if the state variables are principal components, then the reversion-speed matrix is 'complex', by which we mean that it must have large positive and negative entries. This is a mathematical result.

We also know that the $\mathbb{Q}$-measure reversion-speed matrix is linked to its $\mathbb{P}$-measure counterpart by a simple transformation:

$$\mathcal{K}^{\mathbb{Q}} = \mathcal{K}^{\mathbb{P}} + \underline{S}\,\overrightarrow{T}, \tag{33.115}$$

where $\underline{S}$ is a 'volatility' diagonal matrix with positive entries (it is diagonal, because we are dealing with principal components, and its entries are positive because they are the square roots of the eigenvalues of the covariance matrix.)

For a given 'volatility' matrix, and given a market price of risk, the $\mathbb{P}$-measure reversion-speed matrix is fully determined; and, conversely, for a given $\mathbb{P}$-measure reversion-speed matrix, the market price of risk is uniquely pinned down.

Next, we empirically observe that, given what we know about the first-order dependence of the market price of risk on the principal components state variables, no combination of eigenvalues $[l_1, l_2, \ldots l_N]$ manage to produce a simple shape for the $\mathbb{P}$-measure reversion-speed matrix.

One may object that it may be difficult to estimate the reversion-speed matrix in the real-world measure, especially because the first principal component is close to being unit root. True. However, the disturbing bit is that the constraints that determine the complex shape of the reversion-speed matrix in the risk-neutral world, ie, the equation

$$\mathcal{K}^{\mathbb{Q}} = \underline{\Omega}^{\mathrm{T}}\underline{F}\,\Lambda_{\mathcal{K}}\underline{F}^{-1}\underline{\Omega},$$

is compatible only with a very limited and 'artificial' set of combinations of risk aversion patterns and $\mathbb{P}$-measure dynamics for the reversion-speed matrix.

So, essentially affine models with principal components as state variables seem to have some intrinsic limitations in describing the risk-neutral and real-world dynamics. If we add to this the 'equivalence result' obtained earlier, the finding becomes even more worrying.

Did we go wrong, or, rather, too hastily somewhere? To start with, this result relied on the market price of risk being an affine function of the state variables (ie, on the modelling framework being *essentially* affine.) If the market price of risk itself became a stochastic state variable, then the realization of the "other" (yield-curve–based) state variables would not uniquely pin down its value. Therefore the constraints $\mathcal{K}^{\mathbb{Q}} = \mathcal{K}^{\mathbb{P}} + \underline{S}\left(\vec{q}_0 + \underline{\mathcal{R}}\,\vec{x}\right)$ on the reversion-speed matrix would no longer apply, because one would now have

$$\mathcal{K}^{\mathbb{Q}} = \mathcal{K}^{\mathbb{P}} + \underline{S}\left(\vec{b}_0 + \underline{G}\,\vec{x} + \epsilon\right), \tag{33.116}$$

with $\{\vec{b}_0, \underline{G}\}$ the regression coefficients ('intercept' and 'slope') of the market price of risk on the state variables, and with the 'residuals' ϵ not containing the variability in the market price of risk not explained by the yield-curve state variables. So, if the variability is significant enough, the reversion-speed matrix under $\mathbb{Q}$ would no longer necessarily have the form

$$\mathcal{K}^{\mathbb{Q}} = \begin{bmatrix} \kappa_{11} & s_{11}a & 0 \\ 0 & \kappa_{33} & 0 \\ 0 & 0 & \kappa_{33} \end{bmatrix}, \tag{33.117}$$

and non-zero, large and possibly negative elements could appear instead of the zeros. All of this, while retaining the dependence of the market price of risk on the *yield curve* variables of choice (such as, for instance, the slope).

So, essentially affine models with principal components as state variables could still work as long as the market price of risk were not a deterministic function of the principal components. These considerations will motivate the stochastic-market-risk affine model presented in Chapter 35.

Where could this 'extra stochasticity' for the market price of risk come from?

Recall from Chapter 27 the Ludvigson and Ng observation that macroeconomic variables add information to the market price of risk that is not contained in yield-curve variables. We also argued in Section 27.4 and passim that these informative macroeconomic variables could *in principle* always be projected onto additional yields. (Please read the argument carefully again, because it was rather subtle.) However, given the high colinearity of yields, what is possible in theory may not be such a good idea in practice: if something depends on two very different quantities (say real growth and the level of savings), it is not clever to use as state variables two highly correlated quantities (say, the

3- and 5-year yields) onto which the original variables may well project, but in an exceedingly awkward way.[25]

Principal components, one may rebut, are orthogonal to each other, and do not suffer from colinearity. True, but if, as we argued, one indeed needs as many as five to describe both the $\mathbb{P}$ and $\mathbb{Q}$ dynamics, the problem of determining stable loadings on the high components does not disappear. In a finite sample, noise always plagues the estimates of high principal components – the higher the components, the greater the problem.

Let's try to be a bit more precise. When we (very successfully) fit the reversion-speed matrix $\mathcal{K}^Q$ to the exogenous covariance matrix using the smoothness criterion described in Section 33.9, we empirically observe that we can obtain virtually identical results with optically very different distributions across the matrix $\mathcal{K}^Q$ of the positive and negative elements. In other words, lack of similarity of the entries of two matrices, $\mathcal{K}^{aQ}$ and $\mathcal{K}^{bQ}$, each associated with very optically different sets of eigenvalues $\{l_i\}^a$ and $\{l_i\}^b$, does not necessarily entail noticeable differences in the dynamic behaviour of the yields. So, even if the matrices $\mathcal{K}^Q$ we can obtain by varying the eigenvalues $\{l_i\}$ do not optically 'look like' the nice matrix (33.112), the resulting differences in yield behaviour may be very small.

We can therefore argue that we can still use an affine modelling framework as long as we use principal components as *some* of the state variables, to which we add some orthogonal non–yield-curve variables to provide additional information to the market price of risk. Admittedly, the slope by itself (a yield curve variable) seems to tell a lot of the market-price-of-risk-dependence story. However, the previous paragraph suggests that we should not automatically interpret 'large' positive and negative elements as 'economically important'.

Alternatively, we can take a short-cut: instead of using some orthogonal macrofinancial variables as additional state variables, we could insert an ad hoc degree of stochasticity to the market price of risk. As mentioned, this is indeed what we shall do in Chapter 35.

We do not pursue the additional-macroeconomic-variables route in this book. However, we strongly invite the reader to work on the project outlined in the following Exercise.

Exercise 90 *Explain why the Cieslak–Povala 1-year cycle, $c_t^{(1)}$, can be interpreted as a proxy for the short real rate.*

Exercise 91 *Re-read Section 27.4 in Chapter 27. Then construct an affine model that uses as state variables the Cieslak-Povala inflation proxy (τ_t); the Cieslak–Povala 1-year cycle, $c_t^{(1)}$, as a proxy for the short real rate; and the reduced return-predicting factor, $\widehat{cf}_t$, as a proxy for the risk premium. (By the way, to motivate your efforts, Cieslak and Povala (2010a) report that, when*

---

[25] This, by the way, is why physicists like to describe coupled systems of two particles using centre-of-mass coordinates, where one coordinate describes where the combined 'blob' is, and the second the distance between the two particles.

these variables are used in a same-time (non-predictive) cross-sectional regression, they recover the market yields with an R^2 greater than 98%.) Write the equations for the state variables under $\mathbb{P}$ and under $\mathbb{Q}$, and provide an expression for all the quantities in $\overrightarrow{T} = \overrightarrow{q}_0 + \underline{R}\,\overrightarrow{x}_t$. Where would you find the elements in the vector $\overrightarrow{q}_0$ and the matrix $\underline{R}$? (Hint: look carefully at the regression for $\widehat{cf}_t$.) Finally, use the 'dictionary' in Chapter 18 to solve the model. Explain how you would fit to the yield curve and to the covariance matrix.

33.13 APPENDIX 33A: PROOF OF THE CONSTRAINTS ON THE REVERSION-SPEED MATRIX $\mathcal{K}^{\mathbb{Q}}$[26]

33.13.1 Preliminaries

Recall that a defining property of a generic affine model is that the short rate should be expressible as an affine function of the state variables:

$$r_t = u_r + \overrightarrow{g}^{\mathrm{T}}\overrightarrow{x}_t. \tag{33.118}$$

We express the vector $\overrightarrow{g}$ as a function of the matrix of the eigenvectors of the yield covariance matrix, $\underline{\Omega}$, as

$$\overrightarrow{g} = \underline{\Omega}^{\mathrm{T}}\overrightarrow{e} \tag{33.119}$$

for some vector $\overrightarrow{e}$ to be determined.

Recall also that we have obtained

$$\left(\overrightarrow{B}_{\tau_i}\right)^{\mathrm{T}} = \overrightarrow{g}^{\mathrm{T}}\mathcal{K}^{-1}\left[e^{-\mathcal{K}\tau_i} - I_n\right]. \tag{33.120}$$

Now, define vectors $\overrightarrow{\beta}_i^{\mathrm{T}}$, such that

$$\overrightarrow{\beta}_i^{\mathrm{T}} \equiv -\frac{\left(\overrightarrow{B}_{\tau_i}\right)^{\mathrm{T}}}{\tau_i}. \tag{33.121}$$

With these vectors build the matrix, $\underline{\beta}^{\mathrm{T}}$, obtained by stacking the row vectors $\overrightarrow{\beta}_i^{\mathrm{T}}$:

$$\underline{\beta}^{\mathrm{T}} = \begin{bmatrix} \overrightarrow{\beta}_1^{\mathrm{T}} \\ \overrightarrow{\beta}_2^{\mathrm{T}} \\ \cdots \\ \overrightarrow{\beta}_n^{\mathrm{T}} \end{bmatrix}. \tag{33.122}$$

---

[26] This elegant derivation was provided by Dr Lyashenko (2015, private communication). It is both simpler and more general than the derivation presented in Rebonato, Saroka and Putyatin (2017). Thank you.

Since each row vector, $\vec{\beta}_i^{\mathrm{T}}$, is given by the corresponding row vector $\vec{B}_i^{\mathrm{T}}$ divided by τ_i, the quantity in (33.122) is a matrix, made up of stacked row vectors, the ith of which is given by

$$\vec{\beta}_i^{\mathrm{T}} = -\frac{\left(\vec{B}_{\tau_i}\right)^{\mathrm{T}}}{\tau_i} = \begin{bmatrix} -\dfrac{\left(\vec{B}_{\tau_1}\right)^{\mathrm{T}}}{\tau_1} \\ -\dfrac{\left(\vec{B}_{\tau_2}\right)^{\mathrm{T}}}{\tau_2} \\ \cdots \\ -\dfrac{\left(\vec{B}_{\tau_N}\right)^{\mathrm{T}}}{\tau_N} \end{bmatrix} = -\vec{g}^{\mathrm{T}}\mathcal{K}^{-1}\frac{1}{\tau_i}\left[e^{-\mathcal{K}\tau_i} - I_n\right].$$

(33.123)

From the body of the chapter we know that, for identifiability of the chosen state variables as principal components, we have to impose

$$\underline{\vec{\beta}}\,\underline{\vec{\beta}}^{\mathrm{T}} = \underline{I}.$$

(33.124)

Recall that for matrix the eigenvectors of the yield covariance matrix, Ω, we have

$$\underline{\Omega}^{\mathrm{T}}\,\underline{\Omega} = \underline{I}.$$

(33.125)

Therefore

$$\underline{\Omega}^{\mathrm{T}} = \underline{\vec{\beta}}.$$

(33.126)

Multiply both sides of (33.126) by $\underline{\Omega}$, to obtain

$$\underline{\Omega}\,\underline{\Omega}^{\mathrm{T}} = \underline{I} = \underline{\Omega}\,\underline{\vec{\beta}} = \begin{bmatrix} \vec{\xi}_1 & \vec{\xi}_2 & \cdots & \vec{\xi}_N \end{bmatrix}$$

(33.127)

with

$$\vec{\xi}_j = \underline{\Omega}\underbrace{\left(-\frac{1}{\tau_j}(\mathcal{K}^{\mathrm{T}})^{-1}\left[e^{-\mathcal{K}\tau_i} - I_n\right]\vec{g}\right)}_{\underline{\vec{\beta}}}$$

$$= -\frac{1}{\tau_j}\underline{\Omega}(\mathcal{K}^{\mathrm{T}})^{-1}\left[e^{-\mathcal{K}\tau_i} - I_n\right]\underline{\Omega}^{\mathrm{T}}\vec{e},$$

(33.128)

where the last line follows from Equation (33.119).

33.13.2   Some Ancillary Results

For any $N \times 1$ vector $\vec{e}$,

$$\vec{e} = \begin{bmatrix} e_1 \\ e_2 \\ \cdots \\ e_N \end{bmatrix}$$

(33.129)

define

$$
Diag\left[\vec{e}\right] = \begin{bmatrix} e_1 & 0 & \dots & 0 \\ 0 & e_2 & 0 & 0 \\ \dots & \dots & \dots & \dots \\ 0 & 0 & 0 & e_N \end{bmatrix}.
$$

(33.130)

With this definition it is simple to show that, for any two $\vec{e}$ vectors and $\vec{v}$, one has

$$
Diag\left[\vec{e}\right]\vec{v} = Diag\left[\vec{v}\right]\vec{e}.
$$

(33.131)

From this it follows that, for any $N \times N$ matrices A, B, C and for any vector $\vec{e}$ one has

$$
\left[ADiag\,(B_{j1})C\vec{e} \quad ADiag\,(B_{j2})C\vec{e} \quad \dots \quad ADiag\,(B_{jN})C\vec{e}\right]
$$
$$
= ADiag\,[C\vec{e}]B.
$$

33.13.3   The Derivation of the Main Result

We are going to apply these results to Equation (33.128). Before doing so, however, we use the assumption that the reversion-speed matrix is diagonalizable:

$$
\mathcal{K}^{\mathrm{T}} = b\mathcal{L}b^{-1}.
$$

(33.132)

With this we get

$$
I = \left[\vec{\xi}_1 \quad \vec{\xi}_2 \quad \dots \quad \vec{\xi}_N\right]
$$
$$
= \left[\tfrac{1}{\tau_1}\underline{\Omega}(\mathcal{K}^{\mathrm{T}})^{-1}\left[I - e^{-\mathcal{K}\tau_1}\right]\underline{\Omega}^{\mathrm{T}}\vec{e}, \quad \tfrac{1}{\tau_2}\underline{\Omega}(\mathcal{K}^{\mathrm{T}})^{-1}\left[I - e^{-\mathcal{K}\tau_2}\right]\underline{\Omega}^{\mathrm{T}}\vec{e}, \right.
$$
$$
\left. \dots \quad \tfrac{1}{\tau_N}\underline{\Omega}(\mathcal{K}^{\mathrm{T}})^{-1}\left[I - e^{-\mathcal{K}\tau_N}\right]\underline{\Omega}^{\mathrm{T}}\vec{e}\right]
$$
$$
= \left[\underline{\Omega}bDiag\left[\tfrac{1-e^{-l_{jj}\tau_1}}{l_{jj}\tau_1}\right]b^{-1}\underline{\Omega}^{\mathrm{T}}\vec{e}, \quad \underline{\Omega}bDiag\left[\tfrac{1-e^{-l_{jj}\tau_2}}{l_{jj}\tau_2}\right]b^{-1}\underline{\Omega}^{\mathrm{T}}\vec{e}, \right.
$$
$$
\left. \dots \quad \underline{\Omega}bDiag\left[\tfrac{1-e^{-l_{jj}\tau_N}}{l_{jj}\tau_N}\right]b^{-1}\underline{\Omega}^{\mathrm{T}}\vec{e}\right].
$$

(33.133)

Using the results obtained above we can write

$$
I = \underline{\Omega}bDiag\left[b^{-1}\underline{\Omega}^{\mathrm{T}}\vec{e}\right]F^{\mathrm{T}}
$$

(33.134)

with

$$
F[i, j] = \frac{1 - e^{-l_{jj}\tau_i}}{l_{jj}\tau_i}.
$$

(33.135)

From this we can solve for the reversion-speed eigenvector matrix b:

$$
b = \underline{\Omega}^{\mathrm{T}}\left(F^{\mathrm{T}}\right)^{-1}\left(Diag\left[b^{-1}\underline{\Omega}^{\mathrm{T}}\vec{e}\right]\right)^{-1}.
$$

(33.136)

We can substitute this into Equation (33.132) to obtain

$$\mathcal{K}^{\mathrm{T}} = \underbrace{\left[\underline{\Omega}^{\mathrm{T}}\left(F^{\mathrm{T}}\right)^{-1}\left(Diag\left[b^{-1}\underline{\Omega}^{\mathrm{T}}\overrightarrow{e}\right]\right)^{-1}\right]}_{b}[\mathcal{L}]$$

$$\times \underbrace{\left[\underline{\Omega}^{\mathrm{T}}\left(F^{\mathrm{T}}\right)^{-1}\left(Diag\left[b^{-1}\underline{\Omega}^{\mathrm{T}}\overrightarrow{e}\right]\right)^{-1}\right]^{-1}}_{b^{-1}}$$

$$= \underline{\Omega}^{\mathrm{T}}\left(F^{\mathrm{T}}\right)^{-1}\mathcal{L}F^{\mathrm{T}}\underline{\Omega}. \tag{33.137}$$

(in deriving the last line we have made use of the fact that

$$\left[\Omega^{\mathrm{T}}\left(F^{\mathrm{T}}\right)^{-1}\left(Diag\left[b^{-1}\underline{\Omega}^{\mathrm{T}}\overrightarrow{e}\right]\right)^{-1}\right]^{-1} = Diag\left[b^{-1}\underline{\Omega}^{\mathrm{T}}\overrightarrow{e}\right]F^{\mathrm{T}}\Omega \tag{33.138}$$

and that $\mathcal{L}$ and commute $Diag\left[b^{-1}\underline{\Omega}^{\mathrm{T}}\overrightarrow{e}\right]$ (because they are both diagonal). Finally, this gives

$$\underline{\mathcal{K}} = \underline{\Omega}^{\mathrm{T}}\underline{F}\underline{\mathcal{L}}\underline{F}^{-1}\underline{\Omega}, \tag{33.139}$$

which concludes the derivation of the necessary conditions to be satisfied by the reversion-speed matrix if the state variables are principal components. We still need a condition on the vector $\overrightarrow{e}$ in Equation (33.119):

$$\overrightarrow{g} = \underline{\Omega}^{\mathrm{T}}\overrightarrow{e}. \tag{33.140}$$

33.13.4   The Conditions on the Vector $\overrightarrow{e}$

Comparing Equation (33.139),

$$\underline{\mathcal{K}} = \Omega^{\mathrm{T}}\underline{F}\underline{\mathcal{L}}\underline{F}^{-1}\underline{\Omega}, \tag{33.141}$$

and Equation (33.132)

$$\mathcal{K}^{\mathrm{T}} = b\mathcal{L}b^{-1} \tag{33.142}$$

one finds

$$b = \underline{\Omega}^{\mathrm{T}}\left(\underline{F}^{\mathrm{T}}\right)^{-1}. \tag{33.143}$$

To get the condition on vector $\overrightarrow{e}$, substitute this expression for b in Equation (33.134):

$$I = \underline{\Omega}bDiag\left[b^{-1}\underline{\Omega}^{\mathrm{T}}\overrightarrow{e}\right]F^{\mathrm{T}}$$

$$= \underline{\Omega}\,\underline{\Omega}^{\mathrm{T}}\left(\underline{F}^{\mathrm{T}}\right)^{-1}Diag\left[\underline{F}^{\mathrm{T}}\underline{\Omega}\underline{\Omega}^{\mathrm{T}}\overrightarrow{e}\right]F^{\mathrm{T}}$$

$$\Longrightarrow I = \left(\underline{F}^{\mathrm{T}}\right)^{-1}Diag\left[\underline{F}^{\mathrm{T}}\overrightarrow{e}\right]F^{\mathrm{T}}. \tag{33.144}$$

Now multiply from the left by $\underline{F}^{\mathrm{T}}$ and from the right by $(\underline{F}^{\mathrm{T}})^{-1}$. This gives

$$I = Diag\left[\underline{F}^{\mathrm{T}}\vec{e}\,\right]. \tag{33.145}$$

This implies that

$$\underline{F}^{\mathrm{T}}\vec{e} = \begin{bmatrix} 1 \\ 1 \\ \cdots \\ 1 \end{bmatrix} \equiv \vec{1}. \tag{33.146}$$

(The symbol $\vec{1}$ signifies a vector of 1s.) Finally we have

$$\vec{e} = \left(\underline{F}^{\mathrm{T}}\right)^{-1}\vec{1}. \tag{33.147}$$

Thus means that in the formulae

$$r_t = u_r + \vec{g}^{\mathrm{T}}\vec{x}_t, \tag{33.148}$$

$$\vec{g} = \underline{\Omega}^{\mathrm{T}}\vec{e} \tag{33.149}$$

one must have

$$\vec{e} = \left(\underline{F}^{\mathrm{T}}\right)^{-1}\vec{1} \tag{33.150}$$

$$r_t = u_r + \left(\underline{\Omega}^{\mathrm{T}}\left(\underline{F}^{\mathrm{T}}\right)^{-1}\vec{1}\right)^{\mathrm{T}}\vec{x}_t. \tag{33.151}$$

33.14 APPENDIX 33B: SWITCHING REGRESSORS

Define first

$$\Sigma_{mkt}^{ij} = cov\left[dy_i, dy_j\right] \quad \text{differences} \tag{33.152}$$

Diagonalize to obtain

$$\Sigma_{mkt}^{ij} = \Omega\Lambda\Omega^{\mathrm{T}}. \tag{33.153}$$

Let x denote the principal components from orthogonalizing the covariance matrix of yield *differences*. Given

$$y = \widetilde{y} + \Omega x \tag{33.154}$$

we have

$$x = \Omega^{\mathrm{T}}(y - \widetilde{y}) \tag{33.155}$$

Let now P be the covariance matrix of yield levels:

$$P^{ij} = cov[y_i, y_j] \quad \text{levels} \tag{33.156}$$

Diagonalize to obtain

$$P^{ij} = V\Lambda_{lev}V^{\mathrm{T}}. \tag{33.157}$$

Let ξ denote the principal components from orthogonalizing the covariance matrix of yield *levels*. We have

$$y = V\xi. \tag{33.158}$$

Therefore, by equating the expressions for y, we have

$$\tilde{y} + \Omega x = V\xi \tag{33.159}$$

and, solving for ξ,

$$\xi = V^{\mathrm{T}}(\tilde{y} + \Omega x). \tag{33.160}$$

Consider now the regression of excess returns for bond of maturity k from time i to time $i + \tau$, xr, on the principal components obtained from levels:

$$\mathbb{E}\left[xr_i^k | \xi_{i1}, \xi_{i2}, \dots \xi_{ip}\right] = b_0^k + b_1^k \xi_{i1} + b_2^k \xi_{i2} + \cdots + b_p^k \xi_{ip}$$
$$= xr(t_i) = b_0 + b\xi_i(t_i). \tag{33.161}$$

We want the regression coefficients of excess returns for bond of maturity k from time i to time $i + \tau$, xr, on the principal components obtained from differences:

$$\mathbb{E}\left[xr_i^k | x_{i1}, x_{i2}, \dots x_{ip}\right] = a_0^k + a_1^k x_{i1} + a_2^k x_{i2} + \cdots + a_p^k x_{ip}$$
$$= xr(t_i) = a_0 + ax_i(t_i). \tag{33.162}$$

Using Equation (33.160) one can then translate the empirically determined regression coefficients matrix b based on level-PC regressors, to the regression coefficients matrix based on differences-PC regressors, as required by the model:

$$a_0 = b_0 + bV^{\mathrm{T}}\tilde{y} \tag{33.163}$$
$$a = bV^{\mathrm{T}}\Omega. \tag{33.164}$$

CHAPTER 34

Generalizations: The Adrian–Crump–Moench Model

34.1 THE PURPOSE OF THIS CHAPTER

In this chapter we generalize the treatment in Chapters 32 and 33. As the reader will recall, in those chapters we played match makers, trying to unite the statistical and the no-arbitrage research strands when the state variables were chosen to be (proxies of) the yield principal components.

The generalization presented in this chapter follows the treatment in Adrian, Crump and Moench (2013), who

1. choose some linear combination of yields as state variables;
2. impose that bonds should be priced as expectations of the state-price-deflator (doing so ensures absence of arbitrage);
3. enforce the affine assumption for the yields and the market price of risk;
4. express the excess returns in terms of the affinely constrained state-price deflator;
5. recast the resulting equations in such a form that they lend themselves to an econometric estimation of the parameters of the process for these state variables; and
6. establish a connection between the parameters of the statistical models and the 'yield coefficients' of the underlying exponentially affine model.

The heart of this procedure is point 5 (the econometric estimation). By carrying out this estimation, the authors are able to determine the state-dependent market price of risk, which constitutes the key 'structural' bridge between the real-world and risk-neutral measures in their explanatory view of yield curve dynamics.

We report and comment on the estimates of the term premia in the closing sections of the chapter, and we revisit the issue of under what conditions expected excess returns are the same as term premia. Finally, we discuss what happens when they are not.

We stress that, besides being of intrinsic interest, the model by Adrian et al. (2013) can also be seen as a representative instance of similar modelling approaches, such as the one in Ang and Piazzesi (2003).

34.2   THE STRATEGY BEHIND THE
ADRIAN–CRUMP–MOENCH MODEL

One of the most important features of the approach is by Adrian, Crump and Moench (2013) is that a 'traditional' affine model has demurely receded in the background. By 'traditional' I mean a model that starts from a financial 'story' (see, eg, Section 3.2); adds a clear identification of the 'meaning' of the state variables (by stipulating that they should be, say, the principal components or the target rate); and provides a specification of their dynamics motivated by the financial identification of the variables, and by our understanding of how the world works.

To give a couple of concrete examples of these traditional, specified-variables models, suppose we choose the principal components as our state variables; then their volatility matrix should be diagonal, and the entries on the diagonal should be related to the eigenvalues of the covariance matrix. Or, to give another example, if the state variables are the short rate and the target rate, then, as discussed in Section 4.2, the former should revert to the latter with a high reversion speed, etc.

At the opposite end of the spectrum we have latent-variable models, which totally dispense with an identification of the state variables – think, for instance, of the Kim–Wright model that we reviewed in Chapter 31. However, at least in the incarnations we have looked at so far, even these latent-variable approaches are introduced by starting from a precise specification of the mean-reverting dynamics for the (latent) state variables, such as the Equations (31.8) to (31.18) in Chapter 31. Since the variables are latent, the model parameters – say, the reversion speeds, or the volatilities – are at the start of the procedure pure 'place-holders'. However, the idea is to put specific values into the place-holders by bringing statistical, survey and cross-sectional information into play.

The approach by Adrian et al. (2013), which is typical of much modern work in affine models, is a bit different, in that it mixes some features of the latent- and specified-variables methods. Admittedly, it starts from identifiable state variables, but the authors are rather casual about what these variables should be, as they simply gesture to some linear combinations of yields, which, they say, could, but need not, be principal components.

The salient feature of the variables they choose is not their interpretability (and the modelling guidance that interpretability affords), but their statistical estimability. A good model, in their approach, is a linear model that can be easily estimated (in their case, by linear regressions but, in general, by any statistical technique, such as Kalman or particle filters).[1]

So, the authors start from a number of observable variables, X_t, and estimate, by regressing their time-$t + 1$ values on their time time-t levels, the parameters

---

[1] To be precise, Adrian et al. (2013, p. 12) say that 'our approach does not require pricing factors to be linear combinations of yields but can also be readily applied to models that use observable (and economically interpretable) pricing factors such as macroeconomic variables'.

of their AR(1) process. See Equation (34.1). Then they enrich and constrain the statistical estimation that constitutes the backbone of their empirical work with the no-arbitrage conditions and the affine assumption. In particular, it is at this point that they make use of the statistically estimated values for the discrete-time process for the state variables determined in the first part of their procedure.

From these they directly derive recursive relationships for the quantities A_t^T and B_t^T in $P_t^N = e^{A_t^T + (B_t^T)^\top X_t}$, without ever going through the explicit solution of the continuous-time differential equations we discussed in Chapter 18.

The 'model', of course, is still present, but has been nudged into the background. The (constrained) estimation takes centre stage – and, indeed, the title of their paper is not, say, "An Exciting New Model of the Term Structure", but "Pricing the Term Structure with Linear Regressions".

The difference with more traditional approaches is not fundamental, but the shift of emphasis is significant, and representative of modern affine modelling. (Again, see Ang and Piazzesi (2003) for a comparison.) We shall discuss in the final chapter the strengths and weaknesses of this way of doing things.

Perhaps because of this semi-agnostic stance, the whole approach turns out to be rather complex, and is made up of two separate components, that come together in their Section 2.4: this is the authors' particular version of the marriage of the no-arbitrage and statistical traditions Diebold and Rudebusch mention in their work.

Lest we miss the wood for the tree, it is useful to sketch in what follows the general strategy they employ.

34.3 A HIGH-LEVEL DESCRIPTION OF THE MODEL

Adrian et al. (2013) require that the state variables, X_t, that describe their economy, should be a linear combination of observable yields,[2] and that they should follow a mean-reverting (in discrete time, a multivariate $AR(1)$)[3] process:

$$X_{t+1} = \mu + \Phi X_t + \upsilon_{t+1}, \tag{34.1}$$

where the shocks that affect the economy are normally distributed,[4] with zero mean and covariance matrix Σ:

$$\upsilon_{t+1} \sim \mathcal{N}(0, \Sigma). \tag{34.2}$$

Next they require that the pricing kernel (the state price deflator) should be exponentially affine, and that the market price of risk should be affine. The main

---

[2] As we said, their linear combination of choice could, but need not, turn the yields into principal components.

[3] See Appendix 2 in Chapter 2 for some elementary properties of AR(1) processes.

[4] It is more correct to say that the shocks that affect the economy are *conditionally* normally distributed, where the conditioning is on the past and present realizations of the state variables. It is for this reason that the authors write $\upsilon_{t+1}|\{X_s\}_{s=0}^{s=t} \sim \mathcal{N}(0, \Sigma)$.

result of the first part of their paper (their Equation (12)) is then a statistically estimable expression for the excess returns in terms of the parameters of the $AR(1)$ process for the state variables and of the pricing kernel. The affine modelling assumptions provide constraints for the estimation.

Next, the authors notice that, as we have seen in Chapter 18, from the same affine assumptions it follows that bond prices are exponentially affine in the state variables:

$$P_t^T = e^{A_t^T + (B_t^T)^\mathsf{T} X_t}. \tag{34.3}$$

This allows them to derive a model-based expression for the excess returns, as a function of the current and lagged quantities A_t^T and B_t^T, and of the state variables X_t. This is their Equation (21).

The authors then equate the expression for excess returns in terms of the statistical quantities estimated in part one of their work (their Equation (12), with the expression for the excess returns implied by the model (their Equation (21)), to obtain a recursive linear relationship for the bond pricing parameters (their Equations 25 to 28).

What is new in their approach? One (rather technical) difference is that the recursion relationships derived as sketched earlier are not imposed in the statistical estimation phase.[5] As they say, this allows them 'to derive simple regression-based estimators for all model parameters whereas both [Joslin, Singleton and Zhu] and [Hamilton and Wu] require numerical optimization for a subset of the parameters in their models'.[6] Useful stuff, to be sure, but not really fundamental.

The second novel feature is subtler, but more interesting: as we shall derive, in exponentially affine models serially uncorrelated yield pricing errors give rise to autocorrelation in return pricing errors.[7] (See their Equation (29) and our Equation (34.39).) Alternatively, one could have no autocorrelation in return pricing errors but a correlation in yield pricing errors. Both quantities, however, cannot be simultaneously serially uncorrelated. The question then is: which independence assumption is empirically more palatable?

Procedures like the one proposed by Joslin, Singleton and Wu, assume (for computational reasons) that yield pricing errors are (conditionally) independent of lagged values of yield pricing errors. This implies that return pricing errors become serially correlated. Is this good or bad? Adrian et al. (2013) claim[8] that their empirical analysis shows that 'there is a strong level of serial correlation in yield fitting errors while there is little to no autocorrelation in return pricing errors'.

---

[5] Compare and contrast with the approach by Joslin, Singleton and Zhu (2011), or Hamilton and Wu (2012).

[6] p. 11.

[7] The return pricing error is the part of the difference between the expected and the experienced excess return which is independent of the shocks affecting the economy. See Equation (34.31).

[8] p. 26.

So, once again, the originality of the Adrian–Crump–Moench approach does not lie is a particularly clever 'model', in a compelling financial 'story' or in an inspired choice of state variables – as mentioned, they are actually somewhat lackadaisical about the exact specification of what their state variables, X_t, 'really mean'. Their innovation lies in the link between the statistical estimation of the model parameters and the no-arbitrage conditions in an affine setting.

One important question, that we will address in the last section of this chapter, is whether this different (and certainly statistically rather complex) estimation procedure yields results for, say, term premia or the market price of risk, different from what simpler, and more traditional, procedures afford. As we shall see, the (somewhat surprising) answer is that the differences in prediction of risk premia originating from a variety of prima facie very different models are surprisingly muted. Whether all these models therefore point to the same correct answer, or whether they are all similarly 'wrong' is, of course, a different question, that we try to address in the last chapters of this book.

34.4 STATE-PRICE DEFLATORS: GENERALIZING THE RESULTS

In what follows we guide the reader through the derivation presented by Adrian et al. (2013). In essence, their treatment is quite similar to what we presented in previous chapters, and does not involve any new concepts. However, some of their choices of definitions are somewhat idiosyncratic, and this can create some confusion.

In order to understand the approach taken by Adrian et al. (2013) it is useful to review and generalize the discussion about state-price deflators presented in Chapter 13. Recall that we established in Chapter 13 that enforcing absence of arbitrage is tantamount to requiring that the time-t_0 price of a T-maturity bond should be given by the $\mathbb{P}$-measure expectation of the state-price deflator:[9]

$$P_{t_0}^T = \mathbb{E}_{t_0}^{\mathbb{P}} \left[\pi^T(s) \right], \tag{34.4}$$

where $\pi^T(s)$ is the state-price deflator at time T in state s, and the expectation is taken over the states at time T. As for the state-price deflator, $\pi^T(s)$, recall that it is the value today of receiving \$1 at time T (the state price, $sp_{s(T)}$), conditional on state s having being attained at time T:

$$\pi^T(s) = \frac{sp_{s(T)}}{p_{s(T)}}, \tag{34.5}$$

where $p_{s(T)}$ is the probability of attaining state $s(T)$ at time T.

As we have seen in Chapter 13, this relationship assumes this particularly simple form because the payoff of a discount bond at maturity is exactly \$1 in every state of the world. More generally, one can express the value today, V_{t_0},

---

[9] As usual, we assume $\pi^{t_0}(s) = 1$. See Chapter 13.

of any generic security as an expectation over the state-dependent values of this security at time T:

$$V_{t_0} = \mathbb{E}_{t_0}^{\mathbb{P}} \left[V^T(s) \pi^T(s) \right] \tag{34.6}$$

Since Equation (34.6) is totally general, one can also express the price today of a T-maturity bond as the expectation of the state-price deflators for payoffs at time τ, times a special security: the future, time-τ, state-dependent value of a bond with $T - \tau$ years to expiry:

$$P_{t_0}^T = \mathbb{E}_{t_0}^{\mathbb{P}} \left[\pi^\tau(s) P_\tau^{T-\tau}(s) \right], \tag{34.7}$$

where the expectation is now taken over the states at time τ, with $t_0 < \tau < T$.

Note that the superscript $T - \tau$ for the bond under the expectation sign signifies that the discount bond which today has T years to maturity, will mature in $T - \tau$ years at time τ. The reader should make herself happy that Equation (34.7) is just a special case of Equation (34.6).

Why writing the price today of a T-maturity bond this way? Because Equation (34.7) is often used for estimation purposes in statistical studies. To see how this comes about, we choose, as it is customary in econometric studies, time units such that the time interval (the 'time step') τ is just 1, and the maturity T becomes N in these units. In this case we have

$$P_t^N = \mathbb{E}_t^{\mathbb{P}} \left[\pi_{t+1} P_{t+1}^{N-1} \right], \tag{34.8}$$

where we have dropped the dependence on the states to lighten notation. For ease of reference, apart from the different choice of symbol for the state-price deflator, we note that, with this choice of time units, this is Equation (3) in Adrian et al. (2013).[10]

Next, we recall that we have seen in Chapter 13 that, in a one-factor world, the future value of the state-price deflator is given by

$$\pi_t = \pi_{t_0} e^{-r_{t_0}\tau - \frac{1}{2}\lambda^2\tau - \lambda\sqrt{\tau}\epsilon}, \tag{34.9}$$

with

$$\tau = t_0 - t \tag{34.10}$$

and

$$\epsilon \sim \mathcal{N}(0, 1). \tag{34.11}$$

In the unit-time-step setting just examined, this would become

$$\pi_{t+1} = e^{-r_t - \frac{1}{2}\lambda^2 - \lambda\epsilon}, \tag{34.12}$$

where we have set $\pi_{t_0} = 1$.

In Chapter 13 we looked at the simple case when the economy was shocked by a single source of uncertainty. We now assume multiple possible shocks,

---

[10] Note also that Adrian et al. (2013) refer to the state-price deflator as the 'pricing kernel'.

which we still require to have zero mean, but which can have a covariance structure characterized by a covariance matrix, Σ_t. If the vector $\overrightarrow{X}$ denotes the *observable* state variables,[11] we have seen in Chapter 2 that in discrete time a mean-reverting (Ornstein–Uhlenbeck) process becomes

$$\overrightarrow{X}_{t+1} = \overrightarrow{\mu} + \underline{\underline{\Phi}}\,\overrightarrow{X}_t + \overrightarrow{v}_{t+1}. \tag{34.13}$$

This means that

$$\overrightarrow{v}_{t+1} \sim \mathcal{N}\left(0, \Sigma_t\right). \tag{34.14}$$

Once again: what are these variables $\overrightarrow{X}_t$? As we have seen, Adrian et al. (2013) state that they 'use linear combinations of log yields (such as principal components)'.[12] For the sake of concreteness, we shall refer to these variables as principal components in what follows, but different choices could be possible. As we said, whatever they are chosen to be, the main virtue of the chosen variables is not that they should be interpretable, but that they should lend themselves to statistical estimation. In this light, principal components will do nicely, but other combinations of yields would do just as well.

Let's go back to the derivation. In the multifactor setting at hand the single market price of risk of Chapter 13 will then become a vector, $\overrightarrow{\lambda}$, and Equation (34.12) generalizes to

$$\pi_{t+1} = e^{-r_t - \frac{1}{2}\left(\overrightarrow{\lambda}_t\right)^{\mathrm{T}} \overrightarrow{\lambda}_t - \left(\overrightarrow{\lambda}_t\right)^{\mathrm{T}} \Sigma^{-\frac{1}{2}} \overrightarrow{v}_{t+1}}, \tag{34.15}$$

where we have set again $\pi_{t_0} = 1$.[13]

One small observation: in the derivation that we presented in Chapter 13, we saw that the 'volatility' of the state-price deflator was just given by the market price of risk, which therefore multiplies in Equation (34.12) a shock of unit variance. At first blush, the multivariate expression in Equation (34.15) appears different, because the 'volatility vector' (λ^T) multiplies a seemingly more complicated quantity, $\Sigma^{-\frac{1}{2}} v_{t+1}$. However, note that the term $\Sigma^{-\frac{1}{2}}$ exactly 'cancels out' the term $\Sigma^{\frac{1}{2}}$ that comes from using v_{t+1} (which has covariance Σ) instead of ϵ_{t+1} (which has the identity matrix as covariance matrix) as the shocks. Therefore, expression (34.15) is indeed a perfectly legitimate multifactor generalization of expression (34.12). The reason for writing the 'volatility' term in this more awkward fashion will be clear in the following.

Exercise 92 *Derive carefully the generalization (34.15).*

It is important to stress that, up to this point, we have generalized to many driving variables the results obtained in Chapter 13; we have moved to discrete

---

[11] It is important that they should be observable, because the authors will soon proceed to their econometric estimation.

[12] Adrian et al. (2013), p. 6.

[13] We drop the vector and matrix symbols in what follows.

time steps; and we have introduced some slightly different notation; however, we have not added anything conceptually new.

Let's go back to the by-now-familiar linearized expression for the excess returns, $xret_{t+1}^{N-1}$, from investing over one period in the originally-N-maturity bond:

$$xret_{t+1}^{N-1} = \log P_{t+1}^{N-1} - \log P_t^N - r_t \qquad (34.16)$$

(See Equation 23.15) We can rewrite this expression as

$$r_t = -xret_{t+1}^{N-1} + \log \frac{P_{t+1}^{N-1}}{P_t^N}. \qquad (34.17)$$

Now, from this equation we have that

$$e^{-r_t} = e^{xret_{t+1}^{N-1} - \log \frac{P_{t+1}^{N-1}}{P_t^N}} = \frac{P_t^N}{P_{t+1}^{N-1}} e^{xret_{t+1}^{N-1}}. \qquad (34.18)$$

Substituting this expression for e^{-r_t} into the equation for the state-price deflator (Equation (34.15)), we have

$$\pi_{t+1} = e^{-r_t - \frac{1}{2}\lambda^T\lambda - \lambda^T\Sigma^{-\frac{1}{2}}v_{t+1}}$$

$$= \left[\frac{P_t^N}{P_{t+1}^{N-1}} e^{xret_{t+1}^{N-1}} \right] e^{-\frac{1}{2}\lambda^T\lambda - \lambda^T\Sigma^{-\frac{1}{2}}v_{t+1}}$$

$$= \frac{P_t^N}{P_{t+1}^{N-1}} e^{xret_{t+1}^{N-1} - \frac{1}{2}\lambda^T\lambda - \lambda^T\Sigma^{-\frac{1}{2}}v_{t+1}}. \qquad (34.19)$$

This expression is finally ripe for substitution into the expression for the bond price, which is the expectation of the time-$t+1$ state-price deflator times the future bond (Equation (34.8)):

$$P_t^N = \mathbb{E}_t^{\mathbb{P}} \left[\pi_{t+1} P_{t+1}^{N-1} \right]. \qquad (34.20)$$

This gives

$$P_t^N = \mathbb{E}_t^{\mathbb{P}} \left[\pi_{t+1} P_{t+1}^{N-1} \right]$$

$$= \mathbb{E}_t^{\mathbb{P}} \left[\underbrace{\left(\frac{P_t^N}{P_{t+1}^{N-1}} e^{xret_{t+1}^{N-1} - \frac{1}{2}\lambda^T\lambda - \lambda^T\Sigma^{-\frac{1}{2}}v_{t+1}} \right) P_{t+1}^{N-1}}_{\pi_{t+1}} \right]$$

$$= P_t^N \mathbb{E}_t^{\mathbb{P}} \left[e^{xret_{t+1}^{N-1} - \frac{1}{2}\lambda^T\lambda - \lambda^T\Sigma^{-\frac{1}{2}}v_{t+1}} \right], \qquad (34.21)$$

where the terms P_{t+1}^{N-1} in the numerator and the denominator have been cancelled out, and the term P_t^N, which is known at time t, has been taken out of the time-t expectation.

Dividing by P_t^N both sides of the last equation finally gives

$$1 = \mathbb{E}_t^{\mathbb{P}} \left[e^{xret_{t+1}^{N-1} - \frac{1}{2}\lambda^{\mathsf{T}}\lambda - \lambda^{\mathsf{T}}\Sigma^{-\frac{1}{2}}v_{t+1}} \right], \tag{34.22}$$

which is Equation (7) in Adrian et al. (2013). We note for future reference that the quantity $u \equiv \Sigma^{-\frac{1}{2}} v_{t+1}$ is distributed like a multivariate standard-normal distribution:

$$u \sim \mathcal{N}(0, I).$$

34.5 ESTABLISHING AN EXPRESSION FOR THE EXCESS RETURNS

So far we have done little apart from reshuffling terms and extending the notation to deal with many factors. We still have two tasks ahead of us.

First, we want to relate Equation (34.22) to quantities that can be estimated via linear regression, because this is what econometricians do for a living.

Second, we want to relate these econometrically estimable quantities to the coefficients of an exponentially affine model, because this is what modellers do for *their* living.

It is in this sense that the authors' strategy can be seen as another incarnation of the marriage of the modelling and the statistical strands of research that we have dealt with in the context of principal components in Chapters 32 and 33. The parallel is made stronger by the authors' choice for observable state variables of some 'linear combination of log yields (such as principal components)'.[14]

So, in order to make progress, Adrian et al. (2013) make two assumptions: first, they require that the excess returns, $xret_{t+1}^{N-1}$, and the innovations that shock the economy, v_{t+1}, should be jointly normally distributed. Second, they impose that the market price of risk should be an affine function of the state variables[15]:

$$\overrightarrow{\lambda}_t = \underline{\Sigma}^{-\frac{1}{2}} \left(\overrightarrow{\lambda}_0 + \underline{\lambda}_1 \overrightarrow{X}_t \right). \tag{34.23}$$

(Note the presence of the 'awkward' term $\underline{\Sigma}^{-\frac{1}{2}}$, but this is of no consequence, because it multiplies the vectors $\overrightarrow{\lambda}_0$ and $\underline{\lambda}_1 \overrightarrow{X}_t$.)

Keeping these two assumptions in mind, first we recall[16] that

$$\mathbb{E}_t^{\mathbb{P}} \left[e^{-\frac{1}{2}\lambda^{\mathsf{T}}\lambda - \lambda^{\mathsf{T}}\Sigma^{-\frac{1}{2}}v_{t+1}} \right] = 1. \tag{34.24}$$

(This follows because $\overrightarrow{v}_{t+1} \sim \mathcal{N}(0, \Sigma_t)$, not $\overrightarrow{v}_{t+1} \sim \mathcal{N}(0, 1)$.)

---

[14] Ibid., p. 6.

[15] This is the another example of unconventional definition: normally the market price of risk is expressed as $\lambda_t = (\lambda_0 + \lambda_1 X_t)$, without the term $\Sigma^{-\frac{1}{2}}$ in front. Of course, there is no deep difference, because the term $\Sigma^{-\frac{1}{2}}$ will be absorbed by the 'coefficients', λ_0 and λ_1; however, this perfectly legitimate definition can create some confusion.

[16] See Chapter 2.

Next, since $xret_{t+1}^{N-1}$ and u are jointly normally distributed, consider $\mathbb{E}_t^{\mathbb{P}}[e^a e^b]$, with

$$a \equiv xret_{t+1}^{N-1} - \frac{1}{2}\lambda^{\mathrm{T}}\lambda \tag{34.25}$$

and

$$b \equiv \lambda^{\mathrm{T}}\Sigma^{-\frac{1}{2}}v_{t+1} = \lambda^{\mathrm{T}}u. \tag{34.26}$$

With this notation we can rewrite Equation (34.22) as

$$1 = \mathbb{E}_t^{\mathbb{P}}\left[e^{xret_{t+1}^{N-1} - \frac{1}{2}\lambda^{\mathrm{T}}\lambda - \lambda^{\mathrm{T}}\Sigma^{-\frac{1}{2}}v_{t+1}}\right] = \mathbb{E}_t^{\mathbb{P}}\left[e^{a-b}\right].$$

Therefore we have

$$
\begin{aligned}
1 &= \mathbb{E}_t^{\mathbb{P}}\left[e^a e^{-b}\right] \\
&= e^{\mathbb{E}_t^{\mathbb{P}}\left[\left(xret_{t+1}^{N-1} - \frac{1}{2}\lambda^{\mathrm{T}}\lambda\right)\right]} e^{\mathbb{E}_t^{\mathbb{P}}\left[\left(-\lambda^{\mathrm{T}}\Sigma^{-\frac{1}{2}}v_{t+1}\right)\right]} \\
&\quad \times e^{\frac{1}{2}var\left[xret_{t+1}^{N-1} - \frac{1}{2}\lambda^{\mathrm{T}}\lambda\right]} e^{\frac{1}{2}var\left[-\lambda^{\mathrm{T}}u\right]} e^{covar\left[xret_{t+1}^{N-1}, -\lambda^{\mathrm{T}}u\right]} \\
&= e^{\mathbb{E}_t^{\mathbb{P}}\left[xret_{t+1}^{N-1}\right]} e^{-\frac{1}{2}\lambda^{\mathrm{T}}\lambda} e^{\left[-\lambda^{\mathrm{T}}u\right]} e^{\frac{1}{2}var\left[xret_{t+1}^{N-1}\right]} e^{\frac{1}{2}var\left[\lambda^{\mathrm{T}}u\right]} e^{covar\left[xret_{t+1}^{N-1}, -\lambda^{\mathrm{T}}u\right]} \\
&= e^{\mathbb{E}_t^{\mathbb{P}}\left[xret_{t+1}^{N-1}\right]} e^{-\frac{1}{2}\lambda^{\mathrm{T}}\lambda} e^{\frac{1}{2}var\left[xret_{t+1}^{N-1}\right]} e^{+\frac{1}{2}\lambda^{\mathrm{T}}\lambda} e^{-covar\left[xret_{t+1}^{N-1}, -\lambda^{\mathrm{T}}u\right]} \\
&= e^{\mathbb{E}_t^{\mathbb{P}}\left[xret_{t+1}^{N-1}\right]} e^{\frac{1}{2}var\left[xret_{t+1}^{N-1}\right]} e^{-covar\left[xret_{t+1}^{N-1}, -\lambda^{\mathrm{T}}u\right]} \\
&= e^{\mathbb{E}_t^{\mathbb{P}}\left[xret_{t+1}^{N-1}\right] + \frac{1}{2}var\left[xret_{t+1}^{N-1}\right] - covar\left[xret_{t+1}^{N-1}, -\lambda^{\mathrm{T}}u\right]}.
\end{aligned}
\tag{34.27}
$$

In case you forgot, the last line was equal to what we started from, ie, $\mathbb{E}_t^{\mathbb{P}}[e^a e^{-b}]$. (See the first line of Equation (34.27).) For the quantity in the last line to be equal to one, the argument of the exponent in the last line must be equal to zero, and therefore

$$\mathbb{E}_t^{\mathbb{P}}\left[xret_{t+1}^{N-1}\right] + \frac{1}{2}\mathrm{var}\left[xret_{t+1}^{N-1}\right] - \mathrm{cov}\left[xret_{t+1}^{N-1}, \lambda^{\mathrm{T}}u\right] = 0$$

$$\implies \mathbb{E}_t^{\mathbb{P}}\left[xret_{t+1}^{N-1}\right] = \mathrm{cov}_t\left[xret_{t+1}^{N-1}, \lambda^{T}\Sigma^{-\frac{1}{2}}v_{t+1}\right] - \frac{1}{2}\mathrm{var}_t\left[xret_{t+1}^{N-1}\right]. \tag{34.28}$$

To lighten notation we define

$$\left(\beta_t^{N-1}\right)^{T} = \mathrm{cov}_t\left[xret_{t+1}^{N-1}, v_{t+1}^{\mathrm{T}}\right]\Sigma^{-\frac{1}{2}} = \mathrm{cov}_t\left[xret_{t+1}^{N-1}, u^{\mathrm{T}}\right]. \tag{34.29a}$$

Then after remembering that, for two random variables, x and y, and a constant a, $cov\,[x, ay] = acov\,[x, y]$, we use Equation (34.23), and we write

$$\mathbb{E}_t^{\mathbb{P}}\left[xret_{t+1}^{N-1}\right] = \left(\beta_t^{N-1}\right)^{T}(\lambda_0 + \lambda_1 X) - \frac{1}{2}var_t\left[xret_{t+1}^{N-1}\right]. \tag{34.30}$$

At this point we distinguish between the excess return that we expected at time t, $\mathbb{E}_t\left[xret_{t+1}^{N-1}\right]$, and the excess return that we actually achieved, $xret_{t+1}^{N-1}$.

The difference between the two is the *unexpected* excess return. This is clearly a stochastic term. Its stochasticity will come both from the sources of uncertainty that shock the chosen state variables, v_{t+1}, and possibly from other sources as well. However, to the extent that our expectations are unbiased, the difference will contain no deterministic term. (If we knew that it would, we should have changed our expectation at time t.) We therefore write this unexpected return as

$$xret_{t+1}^{N-1} - \mathbb{E}_t^{\mathbb{P}}\left[xret_{t+1}^{N-1}\right] = \underbrace{\left(\gamma_t^{N-1}\right)^T v_{t+1}}_{\text{shocks to the state variables}} + \underbrace{\xi_{t+1}^{N-1}}_{\text{orthogonal shocks}}$$

$$= \left(\gamma_t^{N-1}\right)^T \Sigma^{\frac{1}{2}} u + \xi_{t+1}^{N-1}, \tag{34.31}$$

where ξ_{t+1}^{N-1} is assumed to be orthogonal to v_{t+1}.[17] Substituting Equation (34.31) into Equation (34.29a) we get

$$\left(\beta_t^{N-1}\right)^T = \text{cov}_t\left[\left(\gamma_t^{N-1}\right)^T \Sigma^{\frac{1}{2}} u, u^T\right] = \mathbb{E}_t^{\mathbb{P}}\left[\left(\gamma_t^{N-1}\right)^T \Sigma^{\frac{1}{2}} u u^T\right]$$

$$= \left(\gamma_t^{N-1}\right)^T \Sigma^{\frac{1}{2}} \tag{34.32}$$

and therefore

$$\gamma_t^{N-1} = \Sigma^{-\frac{1}{2}} \beta_t^{N-1}. \tag{34.33}$$

Finally, we can substitute the expression for γ_t^{N-1} just derived into the equation for the difference between the realized and the expected excess return (Equation (34.31)), to obtain

$$xret_{t+1}^{N-1} - \mathbb{E}_t^{\mathbb{P}}\left[xret_{t+1}^{N-1}\right] = \underbrace{\left(\beta_t^{N-1}\right)^T \Sigma^{-\frac{1}{2}} v_{t+1}}_{\text{shocks to the state variables}} + \underbrace{\xi_{t+1}^{N-1}}_{\text{orthogonal shocks}} .$$

$$\tag{34.34}$$

Again, Equation (34.34) simply decomposes the unexpected return into a component that is perfectly correlated with the innovations that shock the state variables used to describe the economy, v_{t+1}, and a component that is totally independent from it.

Recall again that the (linearized) excess return, $xret_{t+1}^{N-1}$, is given by

$$xret_{t+1}^{N-1} = \log P_{t+1}^{N-1} - \log P_t^N - r_t.$$

[17] Throughout the book, in order to help the reader I have tried as much as possible to retain the same notation as in the original papers. However, in this case the symbol for the error is e_t^{N-1}, which I found too confusing, especially if one drops the subscript. So, please beware, my ξ_t^{N-1} is Adrian et al.'s (2013) e_t^{N-1}.

Therefore the unexpected excess return is given by

$$xret_{t+1}^{N-1} - \mathbb{E}_t^{\mathbb{P}} \left[xret_{t+1}^{N-1} \right]$$

$$= \left[\log P_{t+1}^{N-1} - \log P_t^N - r_t \right]$$

$$- \left(\mathbb{E}_t^{\mathbb{P}} \left[\log P_{t+1}^{N-1} \right] - \mathbb{E}_t^{\mathbb{P}} \left[\log P_t^N \right] - r_t \right) \tag{34.35}$$

$$= \log P_{t+1}^{N-1} - \mathbb{E}_t^{\mathbb{P}} \left[\log P_{t+1}^{N-1} \right], \tag{34.36}$$

where the last line follows because $\log P_t^N$ is a known quantity at time t, and can therefore be taken out of the expectation operator, $\mathbb{E}_t^{\mathbb{P}} [\cdot]$.

What does this tell us? That, in order to calculate the difference between the excess return that we expected at time-t, $\mathbb{E}_t^{\mathbb{P}} \left[xret_{t+1}^{N-1} \right]$, and the excess return that we actually achieved, $xret_{t+1}^{N-1}$, we simply have to evaluate the difference between the log price that will prevail at time $t + 1$, $\log P_{t+1}^{N-1}$, and its time-t expectation.

Mirroring the preceding derivation, we then find that

$$\log P_{t+1}^{N-1} - \mathbb{E}_t \left[\log P_{t+1}^{N-1} \right] = \left(\beta_t^{N-1} \right)^T \Sigma^{-\frac{1}{2}} v_{t+1} \tag{34.37}$$

and therefore

$$\left(\gamma_t^{N-1} \right) = \Sigma^{-\frac{1}{2}} \left(\beta_t^{N-1} \right). \tag{34.38a}$$

Therefore we have for the unexpected returns

$$rx_{t+1}^{N-1} - \mathbb{E}_t \left[rx_{t+1}^{N-1} \right] = \underbrace{\left(\beta_t^{N-1} \right)^T \Sigma^{-\frac{1}{2}} v_{t+1}}_{\text{priced return innovation}} + \underbrace{\xi_{t+1}^{N-1}}_{\text{return pricing error}}. \tag{34.39}$$

It is important to look at Equation (34.39) carefully. The term $\left(\beta_t^{N-1} \right)^T \Sigma^{-\frac{1}{2}} v_{t+1}$ is what Adrian et al. (2013) call the 'priced return innovation'. This means that the excess return is stochastic, but part of the stochasticity is explained by the variability in the state variables (v_{t+1}), via the 'sensitivity', $\left(\beta_t^{N-1} \right)^T$ – hence the label 'priced' to the return innovation.

Not all of the excess returns is explained, however, by the variability in the state variables. What is left over, ie, the term ξ_t^{N-1}, is the return pricing error. One can think of Equation (34.39) simply as a decomposition of the 'residual' (the term $rx_{t+1}^{N-1} - \mathbb{E}_t \left[rx_{t+1}^{N-1} \right]$) into two orthogonal components: the first is the projection onto the axes that underlie the state variables, and hence v_{t+1}; and other is whatever is left over. Why bother with this decomposition? As we shall see, because one can impose serial independence either to $\left(\beta_t^{N-1} \right)^T v_{t+1}$ or to ξ_t^{N-1}, but not to both. More about this later.

At this point Adrian et al. (2013) assume that the return pricing errors, ξ_t^{N-1}, are (conditionally) serially independent, (and normally distributed, with variance σ^2). As we discussed in Section 2, this is an important assumption – an assumption that, the authors claim, is well supported by their empirical findings.

Finally, we can substitute and rearrange the terms in Equation (34.39) to obtain

$$xret_{t+1}^{N-1} = ExpRet + Conv + PricedRetIn + RetPricingError \quad (34.40)$$

with the term $ExpRet$ given by (see Equation (33.78))

$$ExpRet = \left(\beta_t^{N-1}\right)^{\mathrm{T}} (\lambda_0 + \lambda_1 X_t), \quad (34.41)$$

the convexity adjustment, $Conv$, given by

$$Conv = -\frac{1}{2} \left[\left(\beta_t^{N-1}\right)^{\mathrm{T}} \Sigma \left(\beta_t^{N-1}\right) + \sigma^2 \right], \quad (34.42)$$

the priced return innovation, $PricedRetIn$, given by

$$PricedRetIn = \left(\beta_t^{N-1}\right)^{\mathrm{T}} v_{t+1}, \quad (34.43)$$

and, finally, the return pricing error, $RetPricingError$, given by

$$RetPricingError = \xi_{t+1}^{N-1}. \quad (34.44)$$

A few comments are in order.

First, the contribution $ExpRet$ to the excess return reflects what we can expect ex ante the excess return to be, given the value at time t of the state variables, which in turn determine the market price of risk, $\lambda_0 + \lambda_1 X_t$.

Next, we have decomposed in Equation (34.39) the difference between the realized and expected excess return into a priced return innovation, $\left(\beta_t^{N-1}\right)^T v_{t+1}$, and an independent component, ξ_t^{N-1}.

Finally, why isn't $\mathbb{E}_t \left[xret_{t+1}^{N-1} \right]$ just equal to the term $ExpRet$? Because, when we calculate the expectation we also have a convexity contribution. This is made up of all the contributions to the volatility of the excess return, both the one which is associated with the uncertainty in the state variables, $\left(\beta_t^{N-1}\right)^T \Sigma \left(\beta_t^{N-1}\right)$, and the one that is totally independent of it, σ^2. See again Equation (34.39).

Exercise 93 *Derive Equations (34.38a) and (34.40).*

Excess returns can be measured. Therefore the left-hand side of Equation (34.40) can be assumed to be known. As a consequence, the parameters on the right-hand side of the same equation can, in principle, be estimated. We will not go into the details of the econometric estimation of the parameters that characterize the state variables and the market price of risk,[18] but we provide a sketch in the next section.

---

[18] See Section 2.2 in Adrian et al. (2013).

34.6 THE ESTIMATION PROCEDURE

How are the model parameters going to be estimated? Recall that we have to estimate the parameters of the process of the state variables, $\overrightarrow{X}_t$, ie, the (discretized) quantities $\overrightarrow{\mu}$, $\underline{\Phi}$ and $\overrightarrow{v}_{t+1}$ in

$$\overrightarrow{X}_{t+1} = \overrightarrow{\mu} + \underline{\Phi}\,\overrightarrow{X}_t + \overrightarrow{v}_{t+1}. \tag{34.45}$$

In addition we have to estimate the parameters of the affine specification of the market price of risk:

$$\overrightarrow{\lambda}_t = \underline{\Sigma}^{-\frac{1}{2}} \left(\overrightarrow{\lambda}_0 + \overrightarrow{\lambda}_1 \underline{X}_t \right). \tag{34.46}$$

A few reminders and observations. First, just to be clear, in the continuous-time description we are more familiar with the quantities $\overrightarrow{\mu}$, $\underline{\Phi}$ and $\overrightarrow{v}_{t+1}$ correspond to

$$\overrightarrow{\mu} = \underline{K}\,\overrightarrow{\theta}\,dt, \tag{34.47}$$

$$\underline{\Phi} = \left(I - \underline{K}dt \right) \tag{34.48}$$

and

$$\overrightarrow{v}_{t+1} = \underline{S}\sqrt{dt}\,\overrightarrow{\epsilon}_t \tag{34.49}$$

in

$$d\overrightarrow{X}_{t+1} = \underline{K} \left(\overrightarrow{\theta} - \overrightarrow{X}_t \right) dt + \underline{S}d\overrightarrow{z}_t. \tag{34.50}$$

Second, the quantity $\underline{\Sigma}$ that appears in Equation (34.46) is the covariance matrix of the innovations $\overrightarrow{v}_{t+1}$ in Equation (34.45):

$$\overrightarrow{v}_{t+1} \sim \mathcal{N}(0, \Sigma). \tag{34.51}$$

Third, the estimation procedure suggested by Adrian et al. is extremely simple, in that it only calls for a linear regression. This should be contrasted with other common approaches, which make use of more complex, and computationally demanding, techniques such as Kalman filtering, particle filtering, etc. How do they get away with this? A simple Ordinary Least Square approach is good enough because Adrian et al. assume that the state variables – say, the principal components, or more generally, the chosen combination of yields – are known and observed. Therefore they do not have to be imputed via filtering or other inversion techniques. This is a bonus.

So, the first step of the estimation procedure is the determination via Ordinary Least Squares of the process parameters $\overrightarrow{\mu}$, $\underline{\Phi}$ and $\overrightarrow{v}_{t+1}$ in Equation (34.45).

As a preparation to the second step of the procedure we stack the excess returns obtained for maturity N and time t into a matrix $N(mat) \times N(days)$.

When this stacking is done, the excess returns are regressed against (i) a constant, α; (ii) the lagged state variables, X^-; and (iii) the contemporaneous innovations to the pricing factors, V:

$$xret = \alpha + \beta^{\mathrm{T}}V + \gamma X^- + E. \tag{34.52}$$

Why did Adrian et al. choose this set of regressors? Because the analysis that led to Equation (34.40) showed that excess returns depend both on the state variables, via the essentially affine assumption and the expression for the expected excess return: $ExpRet = \left(\beta_t^{N-1}\right)^{\mathrm{T}}(\lambda_0 + \lambda_1 X_t)$; and on the 'priced' innovations, via the term $PricedRetIn = \left(\beta_t^{N-1}\right)^{\mathrm{T}} v_{t+1}$. The first contribution is obvious; the second perhaps less so.

This part of the procedure determines the parameters α, β and γ. (Note that the set of regressors V are obtained from the innovations (the 'residuals') of Equation (34.45).)

Looking back to Equation (34.40), we now recognize that the vector λ_0 and the matrix λ_1 are 'contained' in the terms α and γ. (They better be: if the market price of risk does not appear in the excess returns, where can it show up?) More precisely, λ_0 can be determined from recognizing that α (the 'intercept') must related to the constant term in Equation (34.40), ie, to $\left(\beta_t^{N-1}\right)^{\mathrm{T}}\lambda_0 - \frac{1}{2}\left[\left(\beta_t^{N-1}\right)^{\mathrm{T}}\Sigma\left(\beta_t^{N-1}\right) + \sigma^2\right]$.

Adrian et al. (2013) give in their Equations (16) and (17) the somewhat messy, but conceptually simple, expressions for λ_0 and λ_1.

This concludes the statistical estimation of excess returns. We comment on the first step of the procedure later in the chapter.

34.7 ESTABLISHING A LINK WITH THE AFFINE MODEL: THE DISCOUNT FACTOR

Now comes the link with the affine model. If the observable state variables follow the usual affine process, and satisfy the affine conditions, we know that

$$\log P_t^N = A^N + \left(\vec{B}^N\right)^{\mathrm{T}} \vec{X}_t + u_t^N. \tag{34.53}$$

The last term in the equation, u_t^N, is the 'measurement error', ie, the difference between the true (log) price, P_t^N, and the model (log) price for the discount bond, $\log \left(P_t^N\right)_{model} = A^N + \left(\vec{B}^N\right)^{\mathrm{T}} \vec{X}_t$. To avoid confusion, it is important to remember that we have three different 'residuals' or errors:

- the 'measurement error', u_t^N, that we have just defined, ie, the difference between the model and the market log price of the N-maturity bond;
- the residual, v_{t+1}, in the regression of X_{t+1} on its lagged variable, X_t, in the $AR(1)$ process $X_{t+1} = \mu + \Phi X_t + v_{t+1}$ – these are best thought of as the innovations in the state variables;

- the residual, ξ_{t+1}^{N-1}, is what is left over after expressing the excess return as a function of the expected excess return, the convexity adjustment, the priced return innovation: see Equation (34.40).

We can now use the expression derived for the log price into the definition of the excess return for the T-maturity bond, which we report below for ease of reference:

$$xret_{t+1}^{N-1} = \log P_{t+1}^{N-1} - \log P_t^N - r_t. \tag{34.54}$$

After direct substitution, we get

$$xret_{t+1}^{N-1} = \left[A^{N-1} + \left(B^{N-1} \right)^{\mathrm{T}} X_{t+1} + u_t^{N-1} \right] \tag{34.55}$$

$$- \left[A^N + \left(B^N \right)^{\mathrm{T}} X_t + u_t^N \right] \tag{34.56}$$

$$- r_t. \tag{34.57}$$

Now, recall that we assumed that

$$X_{t+1} = \mu + \Phi X_t + v_{t+1} \tag{34.58}$$

and that the first step of the proposed procedure[19] was the statistical estimation of the model parameters, μ and Φ. Therefore these two quantities are (assumed to be) known at this stage. Equation (34.57) then suggests an obvious recursive relationship. Indeed, let's start by proxying the short rate by the return on the 1-period bond

$$r_t = - \left(A^1 + \left(B^1 \right)^{\mathrm{T}} X_t - u_t^1 \right). \tag{34.59}$$

With this identification Adrian et al. (2013) can express Equation (34.57) purely as a function of the values of the state variables at time t, X_t, and equate the model-linked expression for the excess return with the corresponding expression that was used for the econometric estimation, Equation (34.40). Doing so obtains

$$A^{N-1} + \left(B^{N-1} \right)^{\mathrm{T}} \underbrace{\left(\mu + \Phi X_t + v_{t+1} \right)}_{X_{t+1}} - \left[A^N + \left(B^N \right)^{\mathrm{T}} X_t \right]$$

$$+ A^1 + \left(B^1 \right)^{\mathrm{T}} X_t + \left[u_{t+1}^{N-1} - u_t^N + u_t^1 \right]$$

$$= \left(\beta_t^{N-1} \right)^{\mathrm{T}} \left(\lambda_0 + \lambda_1 X_t + v_{t+1} \right)$$

$$- \frac{1}{2} \left[\left(\beta_t^{N-1} \right)^{\mathrm{T}} \Sigma \left(\beta_t^{N-1} \right) + \sigma^2 \right] + \xi_{t+1}^{N-1}. \tag{34.60}$$

---

[19] See p. 1 and p. 4 in Adrian et al. (2013).

This relationship must always be true, for any value of X_t and of v_{t+1}. Therefore one gets

$$\left(B^{N-1}\right)^{\mathrm{T}} = \left(\beta_t^{N-1}\right)^{\mathrm{T}}, \tag{34.61}$$

which gives rise to the following recursive relationships:

$$A^N = A^{N-1} + \left(B^{N-1}\right)^{\mathrm{T}}(\mu - \lambda_0)$$
$$+ \frac{1}{2}\left[\left(B^{N-1}\right)^{\mathrm{T}}\Sigma B^{N-1} + \sigma^2\right] - A^1 \tag{34.62}$$

$$\left(B^N\right)^{\mathrm{T}} = \left(B^{N-1}\right)^{\mathrm{T}}(\Phi - \lambda_1) - \left(B^1\right)^{\mathrm{T}} \tag{34.63}$$

to be started with

$$A^0 = 0 \tag{34.64}$$

$$\left(B^0\right)^{\mathrm{T}} = 0. \tag{34.65}$$

Finally one gets

$$\underbrace{\left[u_{t+1}^{N-1} - u_t^N + u_t^1\right]}_{\text{bond measurement errors}} = \underbrace{\xi_{t+1}^{N-1}}_{\text{excess return residual}}. \tag{34.66}$$

34.8 SOME OBSERVATIONS

A couple of observations are in order. First, in moving from Equation (34.57) to Equation (34.60) one has to use the estimated parameters, μ and Φ (a vector and a matrix, respectively) of the process for the state variables, X_t. These are linear combinations of yields. No matter how we scramble yields, we cannot escape the fact that they display a quasi-unit-root behaviour (loosely speaking, a mean-reverting behaviour with exceedingly weak mean reversion). This feature does not go away by linearly combining the yields. As we saw in the case of the Vasicek model, estimating the reversion level and the reversion speed of this quasi-unit-root process is extremely arduous, and, when the reversion speed is so weak virtually every sample becomes 'small'.[20] The more complex multivariate setting of the Adrian et al. approach camouflages, but does not solve, this problem.

Second, as mentioned before, Equation (34.66) implies that if the (log) yield pricing errors (the terms u_t^N) are independent and identically distributed variables, then the return pricing errors (the quantities ξ_t^{N-1}) are cross-sectionally and serially correlated. As Adrian et al. (2013) say, '[l]ikelihood-based estimation approaches for affine term structure models typically assume serially uncorrelated yield pricing errors and, thus, implicitly assume return pricing errors to be serially correlated.'[21] They continue,

---

[20] Recall that Diebold and Rudebusch boldly set the reversion speed of the first principal component to zero. See Chapter 32.

[21] p. 10.

'We think that this is an undesirable assumption and indeed our empirical results suggest that there is a strong level of serial correlation in yield fitting errors[22] while there is little to no autocorrelation in return pricing errors.'[23]

34.9   RESULTS

34.9.1   Full-Sample Analysis

In this section we present the results produced by the Adrian–Crump–Moench procedure. These days, high-quality fitting to the yield curve is achieved with little effort by almost all the new-generation models. Therefore we do not dwell on this aspect. By 'results' we refer instead to the term premia – or, equivalently, to the expectation under the real-world measure $\mathbb{P}$ of the future path of rates, as the sum of the two components (expectations plus risk premia) adds up, modulo convexity, the the observed market yield.[24]

Let us start from the term premia.[25] The time series of the term premia for maturities 1 to 10 years from 30 June 1961 to 30 September 2014 estimated using the approach described above is shown in Figure 34.1 (bottom panel) alongside a time series of the nominal yields for the same maturities (top panel).

The first noteworthy feature is the great degree of variation of the term premia, and their overall dependence on the level of rates. So, for instance, in the late 1970s–early 1980s, when Treasury yields were around 15%, the 10-year term premia were of the order of 4-to-5%; in the 1960s and in the first half of the 2000s (when rates were in the 2-to-3% region), term premia were barely positive.

Let's look a bit more carefully at this dependence of the term premia on the level of rates and, more generally, on the shape of the yield curve.

Figure 34.2 shows the average of the risk premia from 1- to-10-year maturities plotted alongside the slope of the yield curve (where, in this context, the slope is simply the difference between the 10-year and the 1-year yield) for the period 30 June 1961 to 30 September 2014. There is a clear correlation between the two quantities, which is borne out by a correlation coefficient of 36.9% for

---

[22] Saying that there is 'a strong correlation in yield fitting errors' means that if the model predicts at time τ the bond of maturity N is, say, cheap (model yield above the market yield), then it is more likely to predict that the same bond will be cheap than expensive (model yield below the market yield) at time $\tau + 1$.

[23] p. 12.

[24] Strictly speaking, this is not quite true, because the model yields do not exactly match the market yields – this is what the term u_t^N in Equation (34.53) is all about; however, the pricing errors are so small in comparison to the effects we are looking at, that they can be safely neglected: 'The ACM model fits the data extremely well, allowing us to decompose yields without concerns about measurement error.' Adrian et al. (2013, p. 1).

[25] The discussion that follows based on the results produced by Adrian et al. (2013), and kindly made available in electronic form in Federal Reserve Bank of New York (2014). Their analysis in turn uses the same source data (Gurkaynak, Sack and Wright (2007)), that we, too, have used for the original results presented in this book.

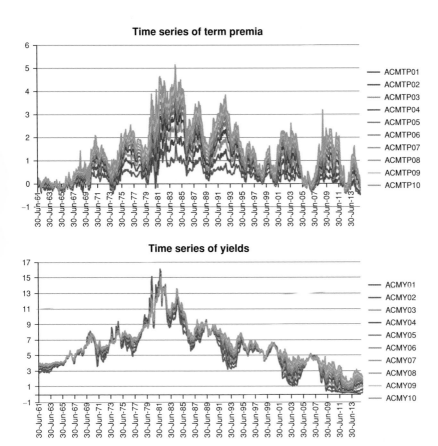

Figure 34.1 The time series of the term premia for maturities 1 to 10 years from 30 June 1961 to 30 September 2014 estimated using the approach by Adrian et al. (2013) (top panel) and a time series of the nominal yields for the same maturities (bottom panel). The y-axis is in percentage points – so a number like, say, 6 means 0.06.

the levels, and 72.1% for the differences. Given the empirical work presented in Part VI of this book (and in the copious references there mentioned) this should come as no surprise.

What is in less good agreement with the empirical evidence presented in Part VI is the strong dependence of the average (across maturities) of the term premia on the level of the yield curve (proxied by the simple arithmetic average of the first 10 yields). The correlation coefficient is 66.1% for the levels and 30.0% for the differences. See Figure 34.3.

Not surprisingly, when we carry out a bivariate regression of the average term premia estimated by Adrian et al. (2013) against the level and the slope of the yield curve, defined as previously, we find that level and slope explain almost all of the term premium: the R^2 of the regression is as high as 97.2%,

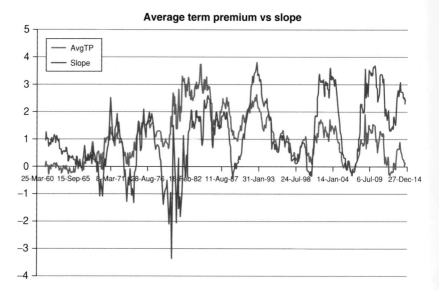

Figure 34.2 The average of the term premia from 1- to 10-year maturities (blue line) and the slope of the yield curve (red line) for the period 30 June 1961 to 30 September 2014. The slope is simply defined as the difference between the 10-year and the 1-year yield).

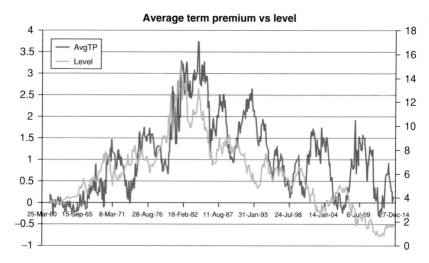

Figure 34.3 The average of the term premia from 1- to 10-year maturities (blue line, right-hand axis) and the level of the yield curve (green line, left-hand axis) for the period 30 June 1961 to 30 September 2014. The level is simply defined as the arithmetic average of the 10 yields.

Table 34.1 *The intercept (α) and the slope coefficients (β_{sl} and β_{lev}) in the regression of the 10-year excess return, $xret_{10}$, against the slope and level of the yield curve: $xret_{10} = \alpha + \beta_{sl}slope + \beta_{lev}level$. The entries in the second and third rows of the second and fourth columns give the ± 2 standard deviation confidence intervals for the two slopes, β_{sl} and β_{lev}. The entries in the fifth to seventh rows give the t and the R^2 statistics.*

	-2σ	Estimate	$+2\sigma$
α		-1.509 (0.018)	
β_{sl}	0.5775	0.5878	0.5598
β_{lev}	0.3111	0.3156	0.3201
t-stat (slope)		637.0	
t-stat (level)		11, 455.3	
R^2		97.2%	

and both 'betas' and the intercept are extremely statistically significant (with t-statistics for the betas of 637 (slope) and 11,455 (level). See Table 34.1.

Why did we say that the regression results are not surprising? Because within the model the term premium is an affine function of the state variables, and these are chosen to be the principal components. More precisely, we established in Chapter 24 that the time-t expected excess return for maturity T, $\mathbb{E}_t^{\mathbb{P}}\left[xret_{t+1}^T\right]$, is equal to the product of the market price of risk times the 'duration', times the volatility (matrix) of the factor(s). In the one-factor case this is given by

$$\mathbb{E}_t^{\mathbb{P}}\left[xret_{t+1}^T\right] = \lambda Dur^T(t)\sigma_x. \tag{34.67}$$

But, if the market price of risk is a *deterministic* function of the state variables, then all of the *expected* excess return is explained by the time-t realization of the state variables. It is therefore reassuring – but nothing more than reassuring – that the model does not place undue loading onto the third principal component. See in this respect Figure 34.4.

Equation (34.67) does not tell us that *all* of the excess return that will actually obtain from time t_i to time t_{i+1} can be explained by the state variables: the 'residual' may be very large indeed, and, over a one-year horizon, may well swamp the expectation part. However, Equation (34.67) does tell us what we can ex ante expect.

34.9.2 Analysis of the May–September 2013 Events

Let us examine the behaviour of the term premium (and hence of the yield expectations) more closely by focussing on the 'laboratory test case' of the tapering-talk period of summer 2013. (See Chapter 5 for a detailed discussion of what happened in this period.)

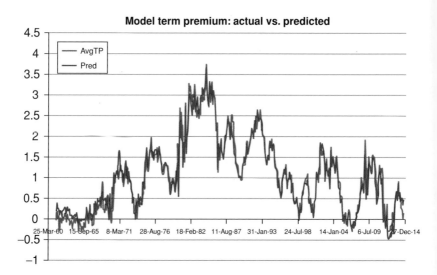

Figure 34.4 The time series of the average term premia estimated using the ACM procedure, and predicted by the slope and curvature of the yield curve.

Figures 34.5 to 34.8 show the observed market yields, the term premia, the expectation components (ie, the difference between the two) and the slope of the yield curve (proxied by the 10-year minus 1-year yield) from January 2013 to September 2014 for the 1-year, 3-year, 5-year and 10-year yields.

Starting from the 1-year market yield we notice that after the 22 May testimony by the then-chairman Bernanke the yield, if anything, declined slowly. Admittedly, not even the most hawkish interpreters read Bernanke's 'tapering' words at the time to mean to that the Fed rate would begin to climb *within one year*. However, there is no reason to believe that the market should have revised *downwards* its expectations about the path of the short rate over the next 12 months. Therefore, from the observation that the 1-year market yield declined, it is not unreasonable to ascribe this small fall in the observed yield to a decline in the term premium *over the next 12 months*: perhaps investors became even less uncertain than they had been before the testimony that rates would not be raised within one year. This decrease in uncertainty may well have reduced the risk premium. So far, so (apparently) good.

Let's move to the opposite end of the maturity spectrum, ie, to the 10-year yield. The market 10-year yield markedly increased. After parsing the observed market yield into its expectation and risk premium components, we observe that almost all of the increase in the 10-year yield is ascribed by the Adrian–Crump–Moench model to an increase in term premium. Exactly as we saw in the case of the D'Amico–Kim–Wei model discussed in Chapter 31, the $\mathbb{P}$-measure expectation of the future path of the short rate produced by the Adrian–Crump–Moench model, if anything, *declines* from May to November 2013.

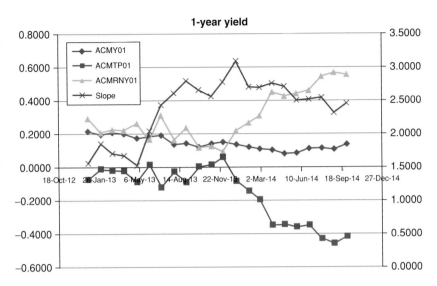

Figure 34.5 The observed market 1-year yield (curve labelled ACMY01), the term premium (curve labelled ACMTP01), the expectation components (ie, the difference between the two) (curve labelled ACMRN01) and the slope of the yield curve (proxied by the 10-year minus 1-year yield) (curve labelled Slope) from January 2013 to September 2014. Note that the values for the slope must be read on the y-axis on the right. Both y axes are in percentage points.

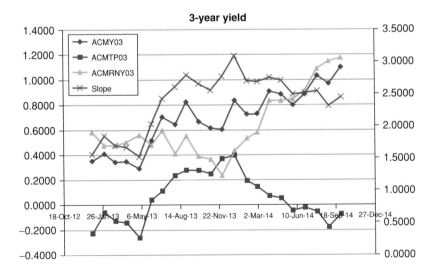

Figure 34.6 Same as above for the 3-year yield.

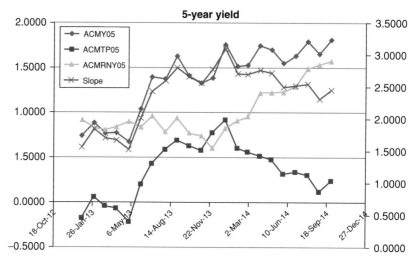

Figure 34.7 Same as above for the 5-year yield.

This does not make a lot of sense in the context of a reasonable interpretation of the events in 2013.

Admittedly, the less-than-crystal-clear May pronouncements by the Fed chairman may have created some degree of uncertainty, and this may have increased the risk compensation. However, the uncertainty was about how quickly rates would begin to go *up*. It is difficult to rationalize *flat-to-declining* expectations.

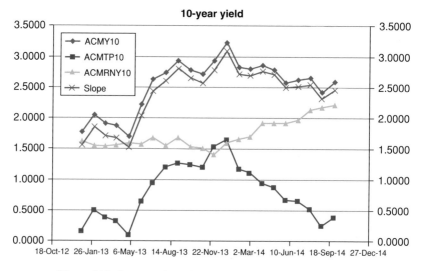

Figure 34.8 Same as above for the 10-year yield.

Similarly, in the early autumn of 2013 Chairman Bernanke 'clarified' in a dovish direction the meaning of his earlier tapering talk. This may have reduced or increased uncertainty, depending on one's take on the clarity of his utterances. However, expectations should have certainly declined after the rectification. According to the model, they strongly increased throughout the latter part of 2013 and well into 2014.

What can account for this behaviour? Two features are most striking when one looks carefully at Figure 34.8: first, the extremely high correlation between the slope and the level of the 10-year yield – this is obvious enough, since the short rate is pinned.

The second feature, namely, the very strong correlation between the slope and the term premium, is more interesting. Why is this happening? Because, according to the model, the market price of risk is a deterministic function of level and slope, and as the slope increases first and then decreases, the term premium must follow this roller-coaster. Owing to the model-induced deterministic link between the market price of risk and the slope of the yield curve, the market-price-of-risk tail therefore vigorously wags the expectation dog.

The behaviour of the expectations and term premia for the 3- and 5-year yields can then be readily understood as intermediate cases between the two yields just examined.

These observations bring to the fore some important and general considerations that we discuss in the concluding chapters of the book.

34.10 CONCLUSIONS

The Adrian–Crump–Moench model shares many of the positive features of the D'Amico–Kim–Wei model, and some of its potential problems.

Starting with the good news, the quality of the fit to the nominal yield curve is very good. As in the case of the D'Amico–Kim–Wei model, this is obtained by varying the state variables, and not the model parameters. This is good.

However, as in the case of the D'Amico–Kim–Wei model, the 'drivers' of risk premia seem to be mis-specified, because we discover a much stronger correlation between the estimated term premia and the level, rather than the slope, of the yield curve. This is not what the empirical evidence surveyed, and independently obtained, in Part VI tells us: as we have seen, the level of the yield curve has very little, if any, predictive power of excess returns. However, according to the Adrian et al. (2013) model, it should predict *even better than the slope*.

Also the 'deconstruction' of the model decomposition of the observed market yield into expectation and risk premium during the May–October 2013 test case leaves a lot to be desired – or, at least, to be explained. As we have seen in the discussion so far, this is not unique to the model we have examined in this chapter. We will revisit this point in the last chapters of the book.

CHAPTER 35

An Affine, Stochastic-Market-Price-of-Risk Model

A well-known scientist (some say it was Bertrand Russell) once gave a public lecture on astronomy. He described how the earth orbits around the sun and how the sun, in turn, orbits around the center of a vast collection of stars called our galaxy. At the end of the lecture, a little old lady at the back of the room got up and said: "What you have told us is rubbish. The world is really a flat plate supported on the back of a giant tortoise." The scientist gave a superior smile before replying, "What is the tortoise standing on?" "You're very clever, young man, *very* clever," said the old lady. "But it's turtles all the way down!"

Stephen Hawking, *A Brief History of Time*, 1988

35.1 THE PURPOSE OF THIS CHAPTER

If one uses a structural affine model to describe the yield curve, one has to establish an affine relationship between the state variables and the market price of risk. In non-trivial cases (ie, if the affine relationship is not just a constant), the resulting behaviour for the market price of risk is stochastic – because the state variables are stochastic. However, if the values of the state variables are known (in statistical parlance, if one conditions on a particular set of values for the state variables), there can be one and only one possible value for the market price of risk.

So, for instance, if one of the state variables is the slope of the yield curve, and, on the basis of our regression studies, we impose a deterministic (affine) relationship between market price of risk and the yield curve slope, then the instantaneous expected excess return will always be exactly the same whenever the slope has a certain value.

In this chapter[*] we break the deterministic link between the market price of risk and the return-predicting factor. We do so by introducing a model that enforces the regularities uncovered by the empirical investigation on average, but not at each point in time. We argue that this will result in a more realistic decomposition of the observed market yields into an expectation and a risk-premiumcomponent.

---

[*] This chapter is based on Rebonato (2017).

35.2 WHY DO WE NEED ANOTHER AFFINE MODEL?

Let us try to be more precise. As we have seen in previous chapters, empirical regression studies suggest that excess returns should be linearly related to the slope of the yield curve. (As we have seen, the story may be more complex, but this is a good starting point.) Let's therefore take the slope as our return-predicting factor. When the outputs of these regression studies are fed into an affine model[1] they impose a 'hard' deterministic relationship between the risk premium and the slope. This can be undesirable. If the yield curve is steep, the risk premium predicted by an essentially affine model thus calibrated to the outputs of these regression studies will *have* to be high. Given this high estimate of the risk premium, for a given observed (market) nominal yield, the imputed expectation of yields may turn out to be implausibly low.

This is exactly what was happening, for instance, in 2013–2014: at the time the Fed was committed to keeping short rates exceptionally low for an unknown, but considerable, length of time. As the economy was beginning to recover, the expectation was, however, being formed of higher future rates.

Now, in normal market conditions, this would be reflected in the expectation that the short rate would be increased soon. Importantly, in normal market conditions, longer-maturity forward rates would display a more muted expected increase. Taken together, a larger increase in yields at the short than at the long end would usually correspond to a *flattening* of the yield curve.

This is indeed borne out by the yield history we have been working with. And in the long-term relationship between slope and expected excess returns to which an affine model is calibrated, flat yield curves are typically associated with low excess returns (and with the beginning of a tightening cycle – see the data in Table 25.1 of Chapter 25). This yield-curve–flattening behaviour in the presence of tightening expectations could not, however, be realized in 2013–2014, because of the commitment made by the monetary authorities to keep the short rate low for an extended period. During this special period, an expectation of future higher rates could only reveal itself as a *steepening* of the yield curve (because the short rate was 'pinned').

Therefore, given the market-visible nominal yields (about which everybody must agree), the steepened-by-expectations yield curve would be associated (by empirical analysis or by a calibrated model) with a particularly high term premium. The 'balancing item' (ie, the expectation of the future paths of the short rate) would end up being implausibly low.

Let's look at the same problem from a similar angle. Figure 35.1 shows the time series from May 2013 to July 2014 of the 10-year nominal, real and inflation expected excess returns. These were obtained from the regression coefficients of realized excess returns against the ex ante slope of the curve, following the methodology described in Chapter 23.

---

[1] See, for instance, the procedure described in Sections 33.7 and 33.8 of Chapter 33.

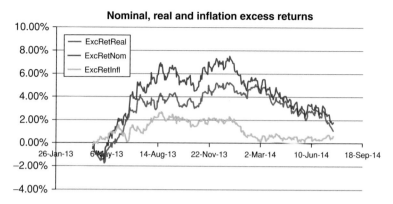

Figure 35.1 The time series of the nominal, real and inflation excess returns from May 2013 to July 2014 obtained from the regression coefficients of excess returns against the slope of the yield curve. The surprising behaviour of the risk premium for the 10-year yield discussed in the text (which implies strongly negative rate expectations) stems from the high steepness of the yield curve in late 2013, which, in turn, suggests (on the basis of past occurrences of steep yield curves) implausibly high excess returns.

The most noteworthy feature is the very high term premium for the 10-year predicted by these regression. In early 2014, for instance, it was close to 8% – and this at a time when the 10-year nominal yield was less than 3.00%. If this risk premium were taken seriously, it would imply an expectation for the 10-year yield of −4.5%! What was going wrong? Figure 35.2 explains the surprising result by showing both the 10-year and the 2-year rate (in the top panel) and, in the bottom panel, the slope of the yield curve (proxied by the difference between the 10-year and the 2-year yields) during the same period.

As is apparent, the maxima in the slope and in the predicted excess return almost coincide: once again, the regression model suggests that such high excess returns should be expected because the curve is so steep, *and in the past steep yield curves were associated with different (ie, recessionary) phases in the business cycle.* But the curve in 2013 was so steep because the short-term rates were pinned at zero by the Fed's accommodative monetary policies. Needless to say, any affine model with a market price of risk deterministically linked to the same slope return-predicting factor will in essence return the same answer.

In this chapter we try to fix this problem by breaking the rigid deterministic link between the market price of risk and the combination of state variables that make up the return-predicting factor. While the breakage of the rigid link is clearly desirable, we would not want to throw away the baby with the bath water, or, out of metaphor, we would not want to discard the empirical statistical regularities, which clearly point to a positive correlation between the slope of the yield curve and the expected excess returns. In other terms, we would still

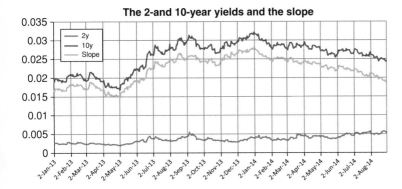

Figure 35.2 The 10-year and the 2-year rate (top panel) and the slope of the yield curve (proxied by the difference between the 10-year and the 2-year yields) during 2013 and 2014. The date of the maximum in the slope curve approximately coincides with the date of the maximum of the predicted excess return curve. Data from Gurkaynak et al. (2007).

like the slope/excess-return relationship to be recovered *on average*, but not in a hard deterministic manner.

We try to achieve both these feats by assigning a stochastic, mean-reverting behaviour to the market price of risk. So, at any given point in time, the curve could be steep, yet the market price of risk could be low (or even negative). The positive relationship between the expected excess returns and the slope of the yield curve should only be an average property of the model. And, in a perfect world, if one ran a real-world simulation of, say, 50 years of yield curve realizations and regressed excess returns against the model yield curve slope, one would like to find an R^2 of about 0.20–0.40 (not 0.98, and not 0.002!).

35.3 ANOTHER JUSTIFICATION FOR A STOCHASTIC-MARKET-PRICE-OF-RISK MODEL

Let's go back to Chapter 27, in which we discussed the number and type of variables needed to span the yield curve uncertainty in the $\mathbb{P}$ and $\mathbb{Q}$ measures.

As the reader will recall, we there argued that, if the return-predicting-factor is a function of yield-curve variables (linear combinations of yields), one can always go from the $\mathbb{P}$- to the $\mathbb{Q}$-measure description simply by changing the reversion level (vector) and the reversion speed (matrix). With the by-now-familiar notation, if the market price of risk can be written as $\lambda_t = \lambda_0 + \Lambda x_t$, we can always write

$$dx_t = \mathcal{K}^{\mathbb{P}} \left(\theta^{\mathbb{P}} - x_t \right) dt + S dz + S \lambda_t \, dt$$
$$= \mathcal{K}^{\mathbb{P}} \left(\theta^{\mathbb{P}} - x_t \right) dt + S dz + S \left(\lambda_0 + \Lambda x_t \right) dt. \tag{35.1}$$

If this is the case, the equations that govern the $\mathbb{Q}$-measure dynamics of the state variables can be recast in the form

$$dx_t = \mathcal{K}^{\mathbb{Q}} \left(\theta^{\mathbb{Q}} - x_t \right) dt + S\, dz. \tag{35.2}$$

This, after all, is what an essentially affine model is all about.

We also argued that, for n factors, n exogenous market yields can always be exactly recovered, and we switched to these n 'reference' yields, $\widetilde{y}_t$, as state variables. We therefore wrote the market price of risk as

$$\overrightarrow{\lambda}_t = \overrightarrow{\lambda}_0 + \widetilde{\Lambda} \overrightarrow{\widetilde{y}}_t. \tag{35.3}$$

As we said, it may seem awkward to write it this way, but we can certainly do so, and we are still firmly in an essentially affine setting. (Since we are carrying around enough symbols, we will drop the vector notation in the following.)

However, matters do not seem to be so simple if the market price of risk is made to depend on some non–yield-curve (macrofinancial) variables:

$$\lambda_t = \widetilde{\lambda}_0 + \widetilde{\Lambda} \widetilde{y}_t + Rw_t, \tag{35.4}$$

where w_t are m new variables that are orthogonal to the special yields, $\widetilde{y}_t$.

In this apparently more complex case we were therefore led to write

$$
\begin{aligned}
d\widetilde{y}_t &= \mathcal{K}_y^{\mathbb{P}} \left(\theta_y^{\mathbb{P}} - \widetilde{y}_t \right) dt + S_y dz + S_y \lambda_t\, dt \\
&= \mathcal{K}_y^{\mathbb{P}} \left(\theta_y^{\mathbb{P}} - \widetilde{y}_t \right) dt + S_y dz + S_y \left(\widetilde{\lambda}_0 + \widetilde{\Lambda} \widetilde{y}_t + Rw_t \right) dt.
\end{aligned}
\tag{35.5}
$$

As we observed, the terms $S_y \widetilde{\lambda}_0$ and $S_y \widetilde{\Lambda} \widetilde{y}_t$ can be absorbed into the new, $\mathbb{Q}$-measure, reversion level vector and reversion speed matrix exactly as before, but, if we want to work with the reference yields $\widetilde{y}_0$, not so for the term $S_y Rw_t$: one can now only write

$$d\widetilde{y}_t = \mathcal{K}_y^{\mathbb{Q}} \left(\theta_y^{\mathbb{Q}} - \widetilde{y}_t \right) dt + S_y dz + S_y Rw_t\, dt. \tag{35.6}$$

This implies that, in order to account for the new source of uncertainty that affects the evolution of the reference yields, one has to augment the state vector from n to $n + m$, ie, to augment the original state variables with the new unspanned variables w_t:

$$\{x_t\}_n \Longrightarrow \{x_t'\}_{n+m} = \{x_t\}_n \cup \{w_t\}_m. \tag{35.7}$$

This also means that, for a given configuration of the yield-curve variables $\{x_t\}_n$, the market price of risk is not fully determined by the original n yields: its realization will also depend on the time-t values of the macrofinancial variables w_t.

In Chapter 27 we went on to argue that it was possible to recast the problem in terms of $(n + m)$ 'special yields', and that, with this augmented set of variables, the formulation

$$dx_t = \mathcal{K}^{\mathbb{Q}} \left(\theta^{\mathbb{Q}} - x_t \right) dt + S\, dz \tag{35.8}$$

could always be recovered. Recall, however, that we had some misgivings about the wisdom to do so in practice, essentially because of colinearity problems (see the discussion that follows). In this chapter we therefore take a different tack: *the stochastic-market-price-of-risk approach introduced in this chapter can be regraded as a reduced-form model to handle the situation where the market price of risk is affected by variables other than yield curve ones.* Instead of using the fully-specified model described by

$$d\widetilde{y}_t = \mathcal{K}_y^{\mathbb{Q}} \left(\theta_y^{\mathbb{Q}} - \widetilde{y}_t \right) dt + S_y dz + S_y R w_t \, dt \tag{35.9}$$

we subsume the stochasticity in the market price of risk not captured by the yield-curve variables in an additional stochastic component to the market price of risk of the form $\sigma_\lambda \, dz_t^\lambda$:

$$d\lambda_t^\theta = \kappa_\lambda \left[\widehat{\lambda} - \lambda_t^\theta \right] dt + \sigma_\lambda \, dz_t^r. \tag{35.10}$$

We stress again that the dependence of the market price of risk on the 'extra' (macrofinancial) variables is not irreducible. As we have shown in Sections 27.4.4 and 27.4.5, it is *in theory* possible to use an augmented set of yield curve variable, ie, $n + m$ reference yields, in terms of which the market price of risk becomes essentially affine again. However, what is in theory possible is not always in practice desirable: by using as state variables $n + m$ yields, we are projecting the macrofinancial information (orthogonal by construction to the original n yield variables) onto m additional yields which *will be very highly correlated with the original ones.* This is not an attractive perspective.

In short: one can look at the model presented in this chapter as the poor-man's version of a full yield curve-plus-macrofinancial-variables specification of the market price of risk – or (and this sounds a lot better) as a fast-and-frugal heuristic to simplify an otherwise very complex estimation problem.

35.4 THE MODEL

Given the discussion in the previous section, the model is as follows:

$$dr_t^{\mathbb{Q}} = \kappa_r^{\mathbb{P}} \left[\theta_t - r_t \right] dt + \sigma_r \, dz_t^r \tag{35.11}$$

$$d\theta_t^{\mathbb{Q}} = \kappa_\theta^{\mathbb{P}} \left[\widehat{\theta}_t^{\mathbb{P}} - \theta_t \right] dt + \lambda_t^\theta \sigma_\theta \, dt + \sigma_\theta \, dz_t^\theta \tag{35.12}$$

$$d\lambda_t^\theta = \kappa_\lambda \left[\widehat{\lambda} - \lambda_t^\theta \right] dt + \sigma_\lambda \, dz_t^\lambda \tag{35.13}$$

where, as usual, $dr_t^{\mathbb{Q}}$ and $d\theta_t^{\mathbb{Q}}$ denote the increments of the short rate and of its own instantaneous reversion level (the 'target rate'), $\widehat{\theta}_t^{\mathbb{P}}$ is the reversion level of the target rate; λ_t^θ is the stochastic market price of risk; $\widehat{\lambda}$ denotes the reversion level of the market price of risk; σ_r, σ_θ and σ_λ are the volatilities of the short rate, the target rate and of the market price of risk, respectively; and the increments dz_t^r, dz_t^θ and dz_t^λ are suitably correlated (see later). The model is fully specified once the initial state (r_0, θ_0 and λ_0^θ) is given.

To simplify the analysis, we assume that investors seek compensation only for the uncertainty about the long-term reversion level. Therefore the model assumes that both the risk associated with uncertainty in the short rate and in the market price of risk are not incorporated in the prices. More about this later. It is for this reason that the reversion speed, $\kappa_r^{\mathbb{P}}$, of the short rate is the same in the real-world and in the risk-neutral measures. Also, in Equation (35.12) we have the long-term reversion level, $\widehat{\theta}_t^{\mathbb{P}}$, of the 'target rate' (θ_t) in the real-world measure. The increment $d\theta_t^{\mathbb{Q}}$ is then in the risk-neutral measure because we are adding the risk compensation, $\lambda_t^{\theta} \sigma_{\theta}$. Indeed, we could equivalently have written

$$d\theta_t^{\mathbb{Q}} = \kappa_{\theta}^{\mathbb{P}} \left[\widehat{\theta}_t^{\mathbb{Q}} - \theta_t\right] dt + \sigma_{\theta}\, dz_t^r \tag{35.14}$$

with

$$\widehat{\theta}_t^{\mathbb{Q}} = \frac{\sigma_{\theta}}{\kappa_{\theta}^{\mathbb{P}}} \lambda_t^{\theta}. \tag{35.15}$$

This immediately tells us that the higher the volatility of the target rate (σ_{θ}, the source of uncertainty for which, in our model, investors seek compensation), the higher the risk-adjusted reversion level of the target rate. This makes sense. Also, the lower the reversion speed of the target rate to its reversion level, the more the target rate will be allowed to wander, creating uncertainty for the bond holders, who will ask for more yield compensation (ie, for a higher risk premium). This also makes sense.

The model can be easily solved analytically – the constitutive equations and their solutions are given in Chapter 18, Section 18.7.4 in particular. What remains to be done is understanding how the model actually behaves, and how well it describes what we know about the yield curve. This we do in Section 35.6, after a brief detour.

35.5   IN WHICH MEASURE(S) ARE WE WORKING?

Before delving into the behaviour of the model, it is worthwhile commenting on the measures to which the preceding equations apply.[2] There is no real difficulty in the argument, but some subtlety is required, and it may be a good idea to take the cold towel out of the cooler bag.

To start with, we have assumed that there is no risk premium associated with the short rate (ie, with the shocks dz_t^r). Given the financial story we have proposed in Chapter 3, and the high reversion speed and low volatility that we expect for the story to hold, this is acceptable.

We have also discussed the two equations for the reversion level in the $\mathbb{P}$ and in the $\mathbb{Q}$ measures, and this is therefore pretty clear as well. But what about the equation for the market price of risk? Rather coyly, we have not appended any superscripts there. To which measure does Equation (35.13) refer?

To answer the question recall that in general the excess return from a T-maturity bond can be expressed as the sum of the products of duration (sensitivity) terms ($\frac{1}{P_t^T} \frac{\partial P_t^T}{\partial x_i}$) – one for each source of risk – times the difference

---

[2] Discussions with Dr Vasant Naik are gratefully acknowledged.

between the risk-neutral and the real-world drift for the corresponding risk factor:

$$\mathbb{E}\left[xret_t^T\right] = \sum_i \frac{1}{P_t^T} \frac{\partial P_t^T}{\partial x_i} \left(\mu_{x_i}^{\mathbb{Q}} - \mu_{x_i}^{\mathbb{P}}\right). \tag{35.16}$$

This is clearly equal to

$$\mathbb{E}\left[xret_t^T\right] = \sum_i \frac{1}{P_t^T} \frac{\partial P_t^T}{\partial x_i} \lambda_t^{x_i} \sigma_{x_i}. \tag{35.17}$$

As usual, the bond price is going to be an (affine) function of the state variables, and, in our model, one of these state variables happens to be market price of risk itself. So, when, say, $x_k = \lambda$, we really have

$$\mathbb{E}\left[xret_t^T\right]_\lambda = \frac{1}{P_t^T} \frac{\partial P_t^T}{\partial \lambda} \lambda^\lambda \sigma_\lambda, \tag{35.18}$$

where the left-hand side represents the contribution to the expected excess return coming from the uncertainty in the market price of risk[3]. On the right-hand side of Equation (35.18) we then have three quantities: the first, $\frac{1}{P_t^T} \frac{\partial P_t^T}{\partial \lambda}$, is the (percentage) sensitivity of the bond price to the market price of risk; this is easy to understand: as the market price of risk increases, the bond price will decrease to induce the investor to enter the risky bet.

The third term, σ_λ, is also easy to understand, as it reflects our uncertainty in the market price of risk.

The middle term, λ^λ (which looks like a typo, but which isn't) requires a bit of attention: it is the market price of risk associated with the market price of risk. In slightly less tongue-twisting terms, it is, as usual, a compensation per unit risk, where the 'risk' in question now refers to the uncertainty in the market price of risk. Recall that investors are in principle 'entitled' to ask compensation for any source of uncertainty that can affect bond prices. Whether they do or don't is then an empirical question.

Now, if we extract the reversion level of the market price of risk, $\widehat{\lambda}_t$, from bond prices and volatilities, this quantity will be in the risk-neutral measure. This does not pose any problems if we 'just' want to price bonds. But if we want to arrive at expectations about yields in the real world, we *do* have a problem, as these will depend on the real-world (not the risk-neutral) reversion level of the market price of risk. Now, if the 'market price of risk of the market price of risk' is a constant, the real-world reversion level of the market price of risk (let's call it $\widehat{\lambda}_t^{\mathbb{P}}$) will be linked to the risk-neutral one, $\widehat{\lambda}_t$, by the usual relationship:

$$\widehat{\lambda}_t = \widehat{\lambda}_t^{\mathbb{P}} + \frac{\sigma_\lambda \lambda^\lambda}{\kappa_\lambda}. \tag{35.19}$$

---

[3] Or, more precisely, to the part of the uncertainty in the market price of risk that is not spanned by the other state variables.

If we really trust the model, after calibrating the model to the yield covariance structure we may have a sporting chance of estimating the volatility, σ_λ, and the reversion speed, κ_λ, of the market price of risk. However, how can we estimate the market price of risk of the market price of risk, λ^λ (especially given that we have another risk premium term, $\lambda_t^\theta \sigma_\theta$, thrashing around in the model)?

Of course, one can always carry out a decomposition such as the one shown above for the reversion level, and write

$$d\lambda_t^{\theta Q} = \kappa_\lambda \left[\widehat{\lambda}_t^{\mathbb{P}} - \lambda_t \right] dt + \sigma_\lambda \lambda^\lambda dt + \sigma_\lambda \, dz_t^r, \tag{35.20}$$

but is clear that we have just temporarily kicked our problem into the weeds, not solved it. As the quote that opens this chapter reminds us, it's turtles (or market prices of risk) all the way down!

As ultimately one has to rest the mother turtle on *something*, in our treatment we are going to assume that the market price of risk of the market price of risk is 'small enough' to be neglected, and that therefore the reversion levels of the market price of risk in the two measures should be close enough to be, for practical purposes, indistinguishable.[4] This will give us a way to anchor an important model parameter in the calibration phase. More about this below.

35.6 THE QUALITATIVE BEHAVIOUR OF THE MODEL

In this section we want to get a feel for the qualitative behaviour of the model, and to check whether it does behave as advertised.

To start with, Figure 35.3 shows one typical evolution over a 30-year horizon of the three state variables with the following choice of parameters: $r_0 = -0.0042, \theta_0 = 0.0344, \lambda_0 = 0.0744, \kappa_r = 0.3437, \kappa_\theta = 0.085, \kappa_\lambda = 0.2816, \sigma_r = 0.0050, \sigma_\theta = 0.0157, \sigma_\lambda = 0.1200, \widehat{\theta}_t^{\mathbb{P}} = 0.0350, \widehat{\lambda}_t = 0.1287, \rho_{r\theta} = 0.6, \rho_{r\lambda} = -0.05, \rho_{\theta\lambda} = 0.64$. (Unless otherwise stated, the same correlation parameters are used throughout this chapter.)

We can see from Figure 35.3 that, as it should, the short rate (blue line) is strongly attracted to the target rate (red line), while, over a single 30-year evolution, the target rate is not visibly tethered to its long-term reversion level: it display what, at first blush, would appear a close-to-unit-root behaviour. Also the market price of risk (the green curve labelled 'lambda') can wonder rather freely about its own reversion level.

One of the distinguishing features of the approach presented here is its in-principle ability to generate a positive correlation between the slope of the yield

---

[4] In the rare modelling settings when the market price of risk is allowed to be stochastic, the assumption that no risk premium should attach to uncertainty in its future value is, to my knowledge, almost universally adopted. So, for instance, Cieslak and Povala (2010a, 2010b) present a simple model in which the market price of risk follows an AR(1) process and state: 'Suppose that investors require compensation for facing shocks to trend inflation and the real factor, and that bond premiums at all maturities vary with a single factor x_t, *whose own shocks are not priced*' (p. 7, emphasis added).

Figure 35.3 A typical evolution over a 30-year horizon of the three state variables: the short rate (blue line, labelled $r(t)$), the target rate (red line, labelled $theta(t)$) and the market price of risk (the green curve labelled 'lambda')

curve and the market price of risk. Can the model actually fulfill this promise with a reasonable set of parameters?

This is indeed the case. *As Figures (35.4) and (35.5) show, one of the most appealing features of the model is that, for a suitable choice of the correlation matrix among the three state variables, the model can easily produce a strong positive stochastic relationship between the slope of the yield curve and the market price of risk.*

(The slope of the yield curve was proxied as earlier by the difference between the short rate and the reversion level). At any point in time, the market price of risk can be high or low even if the slope is low or high, respectively. However,

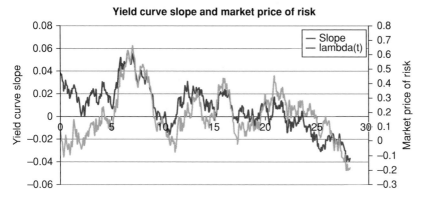

Figure 35.4 A time series of the slope of the yield curve (blue line labelled 'slope') and the market price of risk (green line labelled $lambda(t)$), showing a strong positive stochastic relationship between the two quantities. The slope was taken to be the difference between the 10-year and the 1-year yields.

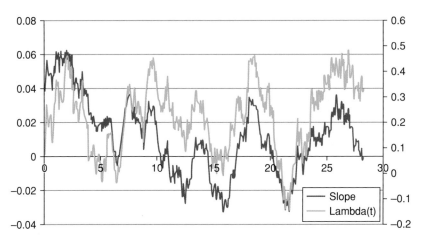

Figure 35.5 Same as Figure 35.4 for a different realization of the state variables.

the positive relationship between the market price of risk and the slope is on average recovered.

More precisely, as for the reversion speed and volatility of the market price of risk, the higher its volatility, and the lower its reversion speed, the greater its potential for assuming values other than what implied by the deterministic dynamics, and to break the deterministic relationship between excess returns and the return-predicting factor.

The behaviour of the model therefore appears to be sensible and appealing. Is reality kind enough to let itself be reasonably well described by the model? We answer this question in the next section.

35.7   CALIBRATION OF THE MODEL

As explained in Chapter 30, we employ a divide-and-conquer strategy, whereby we calibrate separately first to the degrees of freedom that control the covariance matrix (or the swaption prices), and then to those that affect the shape of the yield curve. As we know, the latter set of parameters (ie, the reversion levels and the initial values of the state variables) have no effect on the model covariance structure, and the former only have a modest effect (through convexity) on the shape of the yield curve.

So, starting with the covariance structure, we argued in Chapter 3 that, for the model to make financial sense, we should have a high reversion speed of the short rate to the target rate, $\kappa_r^{\mathbb{P}} > \kappa_r^{\theta}$, and a lower volatility for the short rate than for the target rate, $\sigma_r < \sigma_\theta$. A priori, we cannot say much about the relative volatility of the market price of risk and of the target rate, and we will therefore let the calibration to the yield covariance matrix give us some guidance. Note, however, that the market price of risk, which is a Sharpe Ratio–like

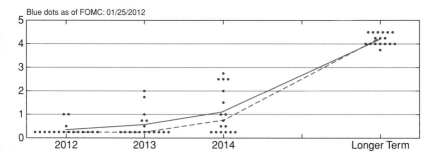

Figure 35.6 Overview of FOMC participants' assessments of appropriate monetary policy in the second half of 2014.

quantity (see the discussion in Chapter 8, Section 8), is one order of magnitude larger than a typical rate, and therefore, in order to produce a meaningful dispersion, its absolute volatility should turn out to be significantly larger than the volatilities of the short rate or of the target rate.

Let's move to the parameters which affect the shape of the yield curve.

Let's look again at Equation (35.12):

$$d\theta_t^{\mathbb{Q}} = \kappa_\theta^{\mathbb{P}} \left[\widehat{\theta}_t^{\mathbb{P}} - \theta_t \right] dt + \lambda_t^\theta \sigma_\theta \, dt + \sigma_\theta \, dz_t^r. \tag{35.21}$$

If we only look at market prices we cannot disentangle $\widehat{\theta}_t^{\mathbb{P}}$ and λ_t^θ: this can be seen easily by rewriting Equation (35.12) as

$$d\theta_t^{\mathbb{Q}} = \kappa_\theta^{\mathbb{P}} \left[\widehat{\theta}_t^{\mathbb{P}} + \frac{\lambda_t^\theta \sigma_\theta}{\kappa_\theta^{\mathbb{P}}} - \theta_t \right] dt + \sigma_\theta dz_t^r$$

$$\implies d\theta_t^{\mathbb{Q}} = \kappa_\theta^{\mathbb{P}} \left[\widehat{\theta}_t^{\mathbb{Q}} - \theta_t \right] dt + \sigma_\theta \, dz_t^r, \tag{35.22}$$

with

$$\widehat{\theta}_t^{\mathbb{Q}} = \widehat{\theta}_t^{\mathbb{P}} + \frac{\lambda_t^\theta \sigma_\theta}{\kappa_\theta^{\mathbb{P}}}. \tag{35.23}$$

So, even if we have determined in the first phase of the calibration $\kappa_\theta^{\mathbb{P}}$ and σ_θ, there is an infinity of couples $\{\widehat{\theta}_t^{\mathbb{P}}, \lambda_t^\theta\}$ that give exactly the same $\widehat{\theta}_t^{\mathbb{Q}}$, and hence the same market bond prices.

With all the treatments covered so far in the book, we have broken this impasse by bringing in information about excess returns. On this occasion we want to make use of the direct real-world information about $\widehat{\theta}_t^{\mathbb{P}}$ that we can glean from the forward guidance provided by the Fed.[5] For our purposes the right-hand panel of Figure 35.6 (labelled Longer Run) serves our purposes well,

---

[5] This is not the only possible source of real-world expectations. See, eg, Christensen and Kwan (2014), who discuss the expectations of federal funds rates from different surveys and from the FOMC participants' funds rate projections.

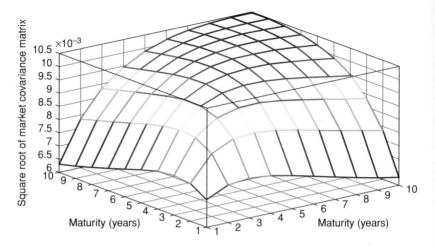

Figure 35.7 The market US$ covariance matrices for yields from 1 to 10 years, sampled over 2000 business days, before and up to September 2014.

as it embodies the expectations of the FOMC participants of the long-term level of the target rate. *We therefore require the real-world long-term reversion level, $\widehat{\theta}_t^{\mathbb{P}}$, to be located in the neighbourhood of this real-world expectation.*

This strategy should be contrasted with the more usual approach, which consists of subtracting from the visible yields today's deterministic estimate of the excess return – which, as discussed, in market conditions such as those prevailing in the early 2010s can give an implausibly low for estimate of the market expectations.

Finally, the considerations about the market price of risk presented in Chapter 8 (see Equation (8.4) in particular) can also give us an idea about the reversion level to which the market price of risk should be attracted – and this should not be too different from the Sharpe Ratio for the long-bond strategy. This is another anchor that we can use to guide the optimization process. Finally, our task is simplified to no end by our assumption that the 'market price of risk of the market price of risk' is zero. (See again the discussion in Section 35.5 of this chapter.)

35.8 CALIBRATION RESULTS

As mentioned earlier, the first quantity to which we want to calibrate our model is the yield covariance structure. Figures 35.7 and 35.8 show the market and the model yield covariance matrices for yields from 1 to 10 years (US$, market covariance matrix sampled over 2000 business days, before and up to September 2014) and Figures 35.9 and 35.10 show the same quantities for matrices for yields from 1 to 20 years. The model yield covariance matrix was obtained

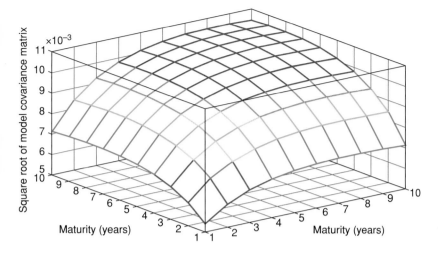

Figure 35.8 The model yield covariance matrices for yields form 1 to 10 years obtained with the parameters reported in the text.

with a constrained choice of parameters, and the optimal set of volatility and reversion speeds obtained using yields of maturities out to 10, 20 and 30 years were as follows:

	10-year	20-year	30-year
σ_r	0.0051	0.0050	0.0055
σ_θ	0.0161	0.0157	0.0153
σ_λ	0.1200	0.1200	0.1200
κ_r	0.4105	0.3437	0.2737
κ_θ	0.1001	0.0850	0.0667
κ_λ	0.4224	0.2816	0.2816

As Figures 35.7 to 35.10 show, the fit, while not spectacularly good, is satisfactory, and suggests that the model can do an acceptably good job at accounting for convexity, and at apportioning risk premia across the yield curve.

A sample of 32 paths showing the evolution over 10 years for the market price of risk with the parameters obtained in the calibration to the covariance matrix are then shown in Figure 35.11 ($\widehat{\lambda}_t = 0.1287$, $\lambda_0 = 0.0744$, $r_0 = -0.0042$, $\theta_0 = 0.0344$, $\widehat{\theta}_t^{\mathbb{P}} = 0.0350$). These paths give a clear indication of the range of values that the stochastic market price of risk can attain.

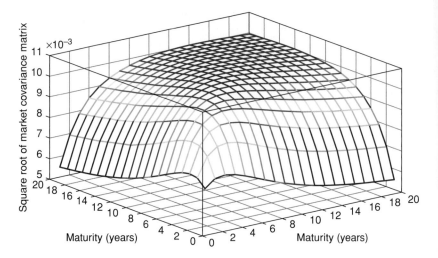

Figure 35.9 The market US$ covariance matrices for yields from 1 to 20 years, sampled over 2000 business days, before and up to September 2014.

The fits to the yield curve obtained by keeping the reversion-speed matrix and the volatility matrix fixed to the values obtained in the calibration to the covariance matrix, and by varying the initial state vector, $\vec{x}_0$, and the reversion levels, $\widehat{\theta}_t^{\mathbb{P}}$ and $\widehat{\lambda}$, are shown in Figures 35.12, 35.13 and 35.14. (The US$ curve used was the Treasury curve for May 2014.) The quality of the fit is very

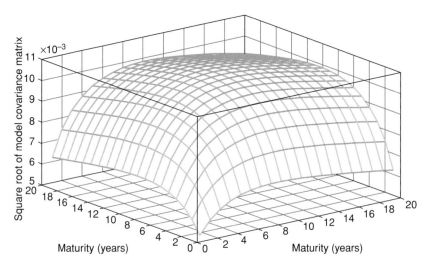

Figure 35.10 The model yield covariance matrices for yields from 1 to 20 years obtained with the parameters reported in the text.

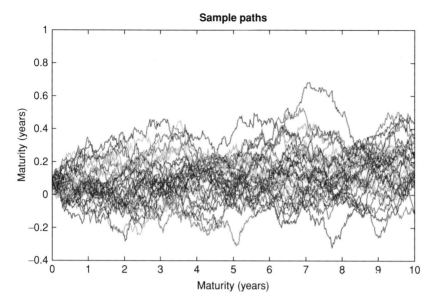

Figure 35.11 A sample of 32 paths showing the evolution over 10 years for the market price of risk. Model parameters as in the text.

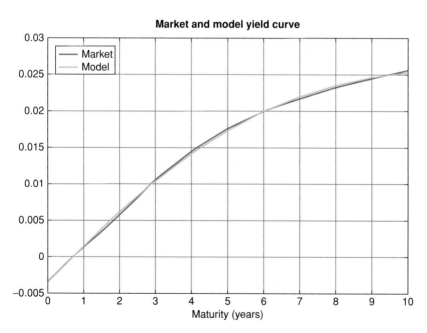

Figure 35.12 The fit to the yield curve out to 10 years obtained by keeping the reversion-speed matrix and the volatility matrix fixed to the values obtained in the calibration to the covariance matrix, and by varying the initial state vector, $\overrightarrow{x}_0$, and the reversion levels, $\widehat{\theta}_t^{\mathbb{P}}$ and $\widehat{\lambda}_t$ (September 2014).

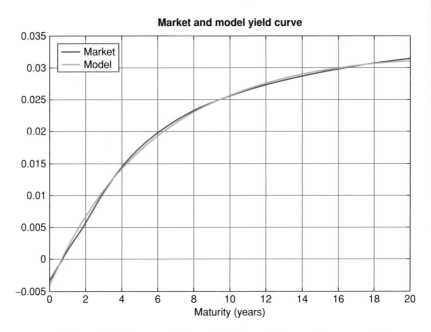

Figure 35.13 Same as Figure 35.12, but with maturities extended out to 20 years.

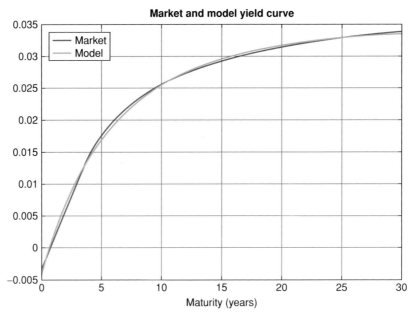

Figure 35.14 Same as Figure 35.12, but with maturities extended out to 30 years.

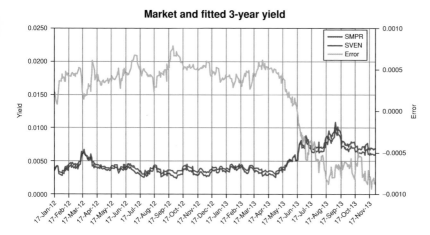

Figure 35.15 Time series of the 3-year yields (market, red curve, labelled SVEN and model, blue curve, labelled SMPR), from January 2012 to December 2013. The values for the yields are on the left-hand vertical axis. The errors are shown by the green curve (right-hand vertical axis).

good.[6] We obtained similar-quality fits for all the US$ Treasury yield curves we examined in 2013–2014.

Snapshot fits are impressive, but they do not tell us much about the consistency of the quality of the fits to the shape of the yield curve. Figures 35.15, 35.16 and 35.17 therefore show the time series of the market and model 3-, 5- and 10-year yields, together with the pricing error. As these figures clearly show, the good fits shown in Figures 35.12, 35.13 and 35.14 were no fluke, and were representative of the ability of the model to capture very well the shape of the yield curve, at least during the period under investigation.

Finally, Figure 35.18 shows the model yield curves obtained by directly fitting the model using market yields out to 30 years (red curve labelled Fit30), and by fitting the model using market yields out to 20 years (blue curve labelled Fit20), *and by extrapolating the model curve from 20 to 30 years*. Note that the model does not do anything 'silly'.

35.9 COMMENTS ON THE SOLUTION

A few comments are in order.

First of all, it may seem that, once the fit to the covariance matrix has been carried out, one has five degrees of freedom to fit the yield curve. Remembering Johnny von Neumann's trunk-wiggling elephant on page 13, this may strike one as quite a lot. However, this embarrassment of parameter riches can be substantially reduced as follows.

---

[6] The hawk-eyed reader may wonder why the 'market' yields for very short maturities – to which our model fits very well – is as negative as −40 basis points. The reason is that at the very short end we fitted our model making use of the shadow rate discussed in Chapter 19.

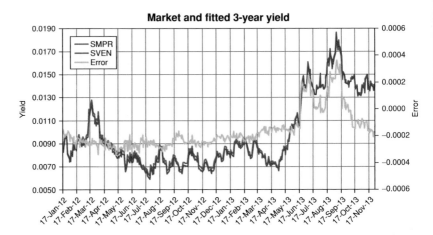

Figure 35.16 Same as Figure 35.15, but for the 5-year yields.

First, the initial value of the short rate must be very close to the observable Fed funds rate, which virtually 'kills' one degree of freedom.[7]

Second, as mentioned earlier, we have an idea from the central bank forward guidance of the real-world reversion level, $\widehat{\theta}_t^{\mathbb{P}}$ (this, as discussed, can be provided by the blue dots in the right-hand panel of Figure 35.6); this is a powerful constraint on the plausible values of this parameter.

Third, as mentioned earlier, we have derived in Chapter 8 that the reversion level of the market price of risk should be approximately equal to the Sharpe ratio from bearing 'duration risk'. This, in turn, is available from the empirical studies we present in Chapter 25. This gives us another anchor in the calibration.

As a result of these 'priors' (some of which are rather sharply peaked), the behaviour of the parameters is tightly disciplined, and we are left with a far more limited ability to create nonsense than the original number of free parameters may have made us fear.

What about the solution itself? The first observation is that, in the neighbourhood of the parameters space that we have restricted as previously there lies an acceptable simultaneous solution both to the yield curve and to the covariance matrix. We also find the predictions about the magnitude of the expectation and risk-premium contribution to the observed market yields eminently reasonable – indeed, as we shall discuss, more convincing that the estimate produced by the more complex models discussed in Chapters 31 and 33.

The reason for this greater plausibility is to be found in the breakage of the deterministic link between the slope of the yield curve and the market price of risk enforced by other models. Without our imposing that this should be the

---

[7] In the presence of a hard zero-bound (about which the model knows nothing about) one may wish to adopt, as we did, a slightly negative 'shadow rate', as discussed in Christensen and Rudebusch (2016). See also Chapter 19.

Figure 35.17 Same as Figure 35.15, but for the 10-year yields.

case (today's value of the market price of risk, λ_0, is one of the parameters we do not tamper with), we find the result that today's level of the market price of risk is significantly below its reversion level (and very significantly below the historical Sharpe Ratio).

As for the reversion level of the market price of risk (which was also left unconstrained in the optimization), this turned out to be ($\widehat{\lambda} = 0.128$) towards

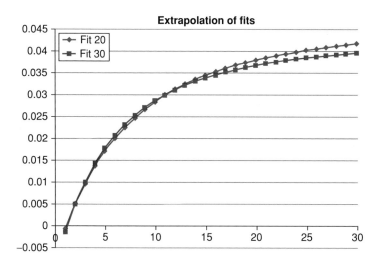

Figure 35.18 The model yield curves obtained by directly fitting the model using market yields out to 30 years (red curve labelled Fit30), and by fitting the model using market yields out to 20 years (blue curve labelled "Fit20"), and by extrapolating the model curve from 20 to 30 years. Note that the model remains well-behaved.

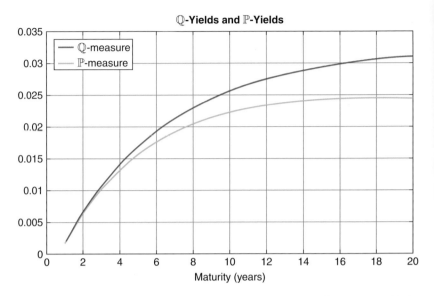

Figure 35.19 The best-fit model yield curve (labelled ℚ-measure) with the parameters discussed in the text, and the best-fit yield curve after subtracting the term premia. The best-fit model yield curve (labelled Q-measure), and the best-fit yield curve after subtracting the term premia. The difference between the two curves represents the yield term premium. This suggests that in May 2014 the yield term premium for bearing 20-year duration risk was a rather miserly 50 basis points.

the lower end of historical estimates of the Sharpe Ratio for the 'long-duration' bond-holding strategy. This could well be consistent with the mid-2010s idea of a 'New Normal', according to which real returns in all asset classes, and in fixed-income products in particular, will, on the secular horizon, turn out to be lower than they have been in the past. See in this respect Figure 35.19, which shows the best-fit model yield curve (labelled ℚ-measure), and the best-fit yield curve after subtracting the term premia (May 2014).

35.10   TERM PREMIA IN THE STOCHASTIC-MARKET-PRICE-OF-RISK MODEL

Figure 35.19 provides a one-day snapshot of the risk-neutral (ℚ-measure) yield curve and of the (ℙ-measure) yield curve that would prevail if investors were not risk averse (and hence, by subtraction, of the term premium).[8]

In Figures 35.20 and 35.21 we present a time series of the term premia for various maturities (out to 10 years) from September 2010 to September 2014.

---

[8] Discussion with Dr Putyiatin, and the results of his calcualtions are gratefully acknowldged.

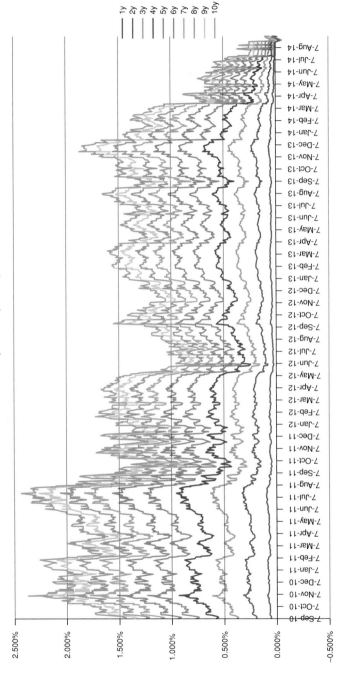

Figure 35.20 Time series of the term premia for yields from 1 year to 10 years obtained with the stochastic-market-price-of-risk model described in the text, from September 2010 to September 2014.

Figure 35.21 Time series of the term premia for the 10-year yield obtained with the stochastic-market-price-of-risk model described in the text, from September 2010 to September 2014.

We observe an obvious monotonic decrease in the yield risk premia with yield maturity, and of the cross-sectional variation in term premium, a clear compression from 2010 to 2014.

Figures 35.20 and 35.21 were obtained by using in the calibration only the 'terminal' (right-most) blue dot on the Fed chart in Figure 35.6. In order to check the robustness of the results, we show in Figure 35.22 the estimates of the risk premia obtained by using the information about the expected path of the short rate (in the real-world measure) that can be gleaned from all the dots in the blue dots communications. More precisely, we fitted a mean reverting process to the median of the blue dots, and extrapolated to infinite time. As one can see, the results are qualitatively identical, and quantitatively very close. This bodes well.

Next we focus on the expectations of various yields (namely, the 2-, 3-, 5- and 10-year yields) in the immediate aftermath of the Bernanke May 2013 announcement discussed at length in previous chapters, and after the 'clarification' in the autumn of 2013. See Figures 35.23 and 35.24. It is clear that, unlike most of the affine models examined so far, the stochastic-market-price-of-risk model explains the corresponding changes in the observed market yields as a clear increase at the beginning of the 'tapering tantrum' and as a clear decrease after the clarification. This chimes in well with an intuitive understanding of plausible market reactions to the testimony by the then-chairman Bernanke, and to the subsequent clarification.

Finally, we show in Figure 35.25 the risk premia for the 5-year and 10-year yields and a simple proxy for the slope of the yield curve (we used again in this

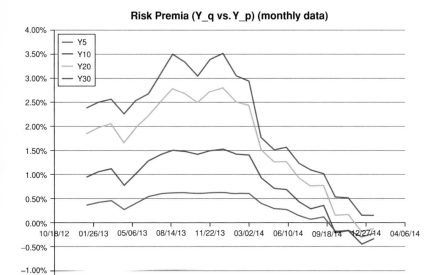

Figure 35.22 Time series of the risk premia for the 5-, 10-, 20- and 30-year yields obtained with the stochastic-market-price-of-risk model described in the text and using the mean-reverting information about the path of the short rate contained in all the dots in the Fed guidance, from August 2013 to January 2015. The top, second, third and bottom curves correspond to the 30-, 20-, 10y- and 5-year time series of the risk premium, respectively.

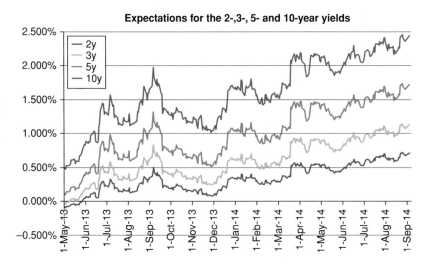

Figure 35.23 Time series of the term premia for the 2-, 3-, 5- and 10-year yields from 1 year to 20 years obtained with the stochastic-market-price-of-risk model described in the text, from September 2010 to September 2014.

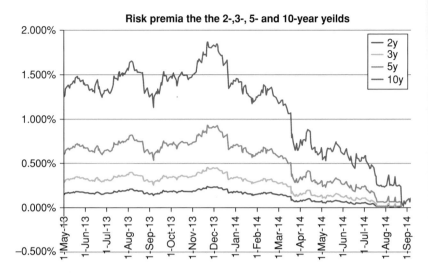

Figure 35.24 Same as Figure 35.23 for the associated risk premia.

case the difference between the 10-year and the 1-year yields). There is a very clear link between the slope proxy and the risk premia (the correlation between the 10-year risk premium and the slope proxy, for instance, is 52%). It is very however important to stress that, unlike what we did with the Kim–Wright, the

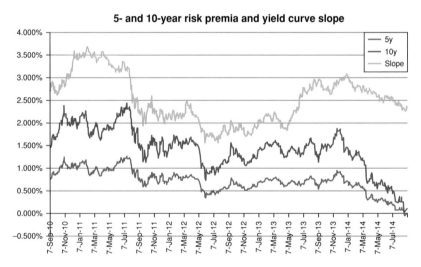

Figure 35.25 Time series of the term premia for the 5- and 10-year risk premia obtained with the stochastic-market-price-of-risk model described in the text, and a simple proxy of the slope of the yield curve (taken to be the difference between the 10-year and the 1-year yield), from September 2010 to September 2014.

PC Affine and the Adrian-Crump-and-Munch models, *excess-return informa-tion is not directly input into this model.* Therefore the slope dependence of the risk premia is not baked into the model, and naturally drops out of the interplay between observed market yields and real-world expectations (as reflected in the 'blue dots').

In sum: we have constructed a model designed to break the rigid determin-istic link between the market price of risk and the return predicting factor, but capable of retaining the statistical link between the slope and the market price of risk. The resulting model does a very good job at fitting the yield curve, and an acceptable job at recovering the yield covariance matrix. What matters most, the risk premia we extract from this analysis seem more reasonable than the corresponding quantities estimated with the much-more-lavishly parametrized Kim–Wright or the PC Affine models.

CHAPTER 36

Conclusions

If all we ever did was wind and unwind the tangled threads of learning without ever getting any further – then what an unhappy fate we would have![1]

Herder

The men of experiment are like the ant, they only collect and use; the reasoners resemble spiders, who make cobwebs out of their own substance. But the bee takes a middle course: it gathers its material from the flowers of the garden and of the field, but transforms and digests it by a power of its own. Not unlike this is the true business of philosophy.

Sir Francis Bacon, Novum Organon

Computers are useless. They only give us answers.

Picasso

36.1 WHAT HAVE WE LEARNT?

36.1.1 The Road Followed

By the end of a book, the writer is pretty tired, and the reader rarely feels much perkier. Therefore I will try to keep these concluding remarks short, sweet and to the point.

We have looked at affine yield curve modelling from a structural perspective. We started from a really beautiful and simple model (the Vasicek model), that we liberally employed to build our intuition about the workings of more complex affine models. We examined carefully up to which point this entry-level approach could take us in our structural understanding.

Alas, when we looked at the recent empirical information about excess returns and term premia, we concluded that, for all its elegance and beauty, we had to graft a pretty substantial extension onto the Vasicek structure. Above all, we decided that for a model to be worth its predictive salt it would have to

---

[1] Herder (1773, 2008), p. 4.

have a non-constant market price of risk. More precisely, as a bare minimum, the market price of risk would have to be state-dependent, and would have to capture the dependence of the expected excess returns on the slope of the yield curve (and perhaps on more exotic return-predicting factors).

We therefore gathered the tools to analyze, and perhaps even build, new models that could incorporate this evidence. We clambered with greater determination than elegance over the analytical and notational difficulties of the more modern approaches, and we compared their predictions about term premia and rate expectations with what has been found empirically in the last 10-or-so years. What did we find?

36.1.2 The Case for the Prosecution: Models As Regurgitators

We found that, after a considerable investment, these more complex models were able to 'play back to us', sometimes fluently, but, more often than not, rather haltingly, the empirical facts about excess returns that were fed into them in the calibration phase. In particular, we noticed that, despite greatly different choices for state variables and calibration methods, all these models gave very similar predictions of risk premia and expectations. And these predictions, we also found, were very similar to those produced by purely statistical models, which knew nothing about no-arbitrage.

This put a first unsettling thought in our minds: if the quality of a model is assessed on the basis of its ability to recover the empirical information which has been fed into it, why not use directly the statistical information? What is the model *adding*?[2]

Our misgivings seemed to be confirmed by the paper by Joslin, Anh Le and Singleton (2013), whose title ("Why Gaussian Macro-Finance Models Are (Nearly) Unconstrained Factor-VARs") apparently says it all[3]: as we discussed in Section 27.6, the paper (and Joslin, Singleton and Zhu (2011)) showed that, unless additional 'over-identifying' restrictions are imposed, the addition of the conditions of no-arbitrage, does (virtually) nothing to improve the predictive abilities of a statistical approach. Since one of the 'selling points' of models is the provision of a no-arbitrage framework to complement the raw information provided by statistical analysis, these finding did not bode well for their predictive ability.

A similarly unsettling feeling was left in our minds when we looked at convexity. First we obtained what convexity should be worth according to a well-calibrated model. (See Chapter 20.) But then we saw that the theoretical value of convexity could be obtained following an almost-completely-model-agnostic route, a route that made almost exclusive use of statistically determined

---

[2] This, by the way, is the question raised by Diebold and Rudebusch (2013) in the section they provocatively title "Is Imposition of "No-Arbitrage" Useful?", see p. 16 and passim.

[3] A similar conclusion is reached in Joslin et al. (2011).

quantities. (See Chapter 21.) Once again, a (rather complex) model *could* be made to reproduce these results. Indeed, it could. But what was it *adding*?

In the quote at the beginning of Chapter 32, Diebold and Rudebusch spoke of a marriage of the statistical and modelling traditions. This is all well and good, but what exactly, a cynic may say, are the affine models bringing to the wedding party? Should the statistical-approach bride consult a good family lawyer and insist on a strong pre-nup?

36.1.3   The Case for the Defence: Models as Enforcers of Parsimony

The first reason why relying *only* on statistical information is unsatisfactory even if we are just interested in predicting goes back to the over-liberal parametrization of unconstrained statistical models. Models are useful not just because they tell us what the phenomenon at hand depends on, but also which variables it does *not* depend on. Absent a model, the econometrician is faced with a bewildering number of state variables, and their lags, as potentially 'significant regressors'.

If this agnostic econometrician is not guided by a picture of 'how the world works', yet she wants the statistical description to be sufficiently rich to capture the complexity of the yield curve dynamics, she is quickly faced with a very large number of parameters waiting to be estimated – and we have mentioned in Chapter 32 how the number of parameters to be estimated can quickly grow to ridiculous levels. A model, with its simplified picture of the workings of the economy (and, yes, with its prejudices), can enforce some drastic and principled pruning.

Take, for instance, the modelling of the dependence of the market price of risk on the state variables. Absent any theoretical or empirical information, the market price of risk could depend on all the state variables, and on their lags. And things do not get any better if, as it is common to do in the recent literature, the state variables are assumed to be latent. This is the stuff of a principled econometrician's nightmares.

Fortunately, there is another way – a way in which models play an important part. Every structural model makes some simplifying assumptions about the market price of risk; it implies some testable model properties (eg, when excess returns should be large or small); and it lays itself open to empirical testing. So, for instance, in approaches such as the one by Cochrane and Piazzesi (2005, 2008) or in the one by Cieslak and Povala (2010a, 2010b) the market price of risk is made to depend on one single (carefully chosen) combination of forward rates (plus, in the case of the Cieslak and Povala (2010a, 2010b) model, on a reasonable proxy for a macroeconomic quantity). In other approaches (see, eg, Duffee (2002)), the market price of risk is linked to the slope of the yield curve. And in the Vasicek model, of course, it is simply a constant. In comparison with the pure statistical analyses, these specifications have an almost Spartan simplicity. It is exactly thanks to their pared-down nature that empirical analysis and hypothesis testing can tell us something much more meaningful about the significance and the robustness of these voluntarily restricted descriptions of the functional form of the market price of risk.

So, the first virtue of a structural model is the ability it affords to reduce the number of parameters that need estimation and to constrain the signs and relative magnitudes of those parameters that are left. If the model we chose fails to predict excess returns (as a constant-market-price-of-risk model would), then we have at least learnt something – in this case that the market price of risk cannot be independent of the state of the world.

But there is more. Most of the interesting features of yield curve dynamics (say, the reversion level in the real world or the deviations from the local expectations hypothesis[4]) are very hard to estimate statistically. Take again excess returns. With the long investment horizons needed to obtain meaningful return information,[5] either we have to use overlapping data, or we are left with very few data points. After running a number of fancy statistical tests, we may then well find statistical significance for some of our regressors. But, if we do not understand *why* these combinations of yields or forward rates should be able to predict excess returns, it is difficult to 'trust' the results of our regression analysis even if they have passed the standard battery of statistical tests.[6]

This matters a lot. One thing is to make investment decisions on the basis of the statistical result that, somewhat mysteriously, excess returns are linked to, say, the slope of the yield curve; another is to make the same investment decision, after linking the slope of the yield curve to, say, some business-cycle properties that help us understand *why* the slope dependence of excess returns might occur.

So, these are the first two reasons why structural "interpretable" models that straddle the $\mathbb{P}$- and $\mathbb{Q}$-measures can help. First, they can guide the

---

[4] In this context the validity of the local expectation hypothesis is tantamount to asking the questions: 'Are forward rates unbiased predictors of future rates?' Do forward rates 'come true' (on average)?

[5] Cochrane and Piazzesi (2005, p. 139), for instance, justify their use of monthly overlapping yearly returns because, they claim, estimating one-month (non-overlapping) returns is just not good enough. This is because, they say, 'to see the effect [they discover] you must look directly at the one-year horizon' and one-months returns 'completely miss the single factor representation' that they uncover because the noise (that roughly scales as the square root of time step) overwhelms the signal (that grows roughly linearly in the time step).

[6] As we all know, if we throw 20 uncorrelated regressors at a 'left-hand' variable, at the 5% confidence level one regressor will, on average, show up as significant. This would not be so terrible if the literature reported all the battery of tests that turn out negative, but this is rarely the case – regrettably, but understandably so: to my knowledge, Michelson has been the only scientist who got a Nobel Prize for *not* finding an effect (in his case, the ether). This selection bias is, however, pernicious, as the American Statistical Association (1997) clearly warns (guideline #8): 'Running multiple tests on the same dataset at the same stage of an analysis increases the chance of obtaining at least one invalid result. Selecting one "significant" result from a multiplicity of parallel tests poses a grave risk of an incorrect conclusion. *Failure to disclose the full extent of the tests and their results in such a case would be highly misleading.*' (emphasis added), quoted in Bailey and de Prado (2014), p. 95. See on this very important point the excellent discussion in Abu-Mostafa, Magdon-Ismail and Lin H-T (2012).

statistical estimation task by stating which variables the market price of risk should depend on, and by specifying the nature of the dependence. Second, by providing, as sometimes they do, an explanation of why certain regularities occur, they engender the confidence we need in order to act on the basis of the statistically informed projections.[7]

One should not assume, of course, that, just because we have attached the label 'model' to our prejudices about how the world works, the explanation (or rationalization) offered by a model automatically becomes true. But a good model lays itself open to empirical testing and, if we have a receptive mind, may even upset our preconceived notions.

36.1.4   The Case for the Defence: Models as Enforcers of Cross-Sectional Restrictions

Let me move to the second reason why structural models can be useful.

Suppose that we have full faith in the statistical significance of the regressors we have chosen to account for, say, excess returns. Even so, the regression parameters we have estimated will in reality still have very large uncertainty bars – which means that they are informationally meaningful, but very noisy.

Suppose that, on the basis of these statistically-significant-but-imperfect estimates, we want to predict the risk premia for the 3-, 5- and 10-year-maturity bonds. (Perhaps we have obtained from survey data the market real-world expectations about the future path of rates[8], and we want to see what today's yields 'should be', given the risk premia we have estimated).

Now, our statistical estimates have been obtained from time series of market yield data that (presumably) impounded the no-arbitrage conditions (which, as we have seen in Chapters 11 to 14, are just restrictions on how risk premia are 'fairly' apportioned to bonds of different maturities). However, our noisy statistical estimates do not *directly* 'know about' no-arbitrage. In the presence of unavoidable *and large* measurement error, the projections of term premia for different-maturity yields may not be compatible with absence of arbitrage. If we embed the statistical information into a model that knows about no-arbitrage, one would hope that we may be able to improve our predictions, by making sure that they reflect not only the imperfectly-estimated statistical regularities, but also the additional information about differences in yields brought about by enforcing absence of arbitrage. This is (in part) what is meant in the literature when people speak about 'imposing cross-sectional restrictions': no-arbitrage condition link yields of different maturities at the same point in time (and in this sense they are cross-sectional) and complement this with time-series information about excess returns, yields, etc.

---

[7] To be precise, specified-variable models and macrofinancial models afford this explanatory bonus. Latent-variable models do not.

[8] Of course, we also have to throw convexity into the pot.

Admittedly, the work by Joslin et al. (2013) pours some cold water on these hopes, and suggests that, as far as prediction goes, no-arbitrage *by itself* does not add much to what is uncovered by statistical analysis. However, besides imposing no-arbitrage, financially motivated models also impose additional constraints, and in doing so suggest the possible ranges for their various parameters. This helps the statistical estimation immensely.

This way of looking at models – the models-as-statistical-regularizers view – can be seen as a special case of statistical shrinkage in a direction reflecting prior views.[9] For readers familiar with Bayesian thinking, the prior views with which the 'raw' estimate is blended can either be diffuse, or informative. In the case at hand, what a model suggests in general, and the constraints of absence of arbitrage in particular, can be seen as the highly informative prior views which the solution should be 'encouraged' to take into account when confronted with the rude reality of evidence.

One important *caveat*. There is no such thing as model-free conditions of no-arbitrage – or to be more precise, the model-independent condition of no-arbitrage are so loose as to provide hardly any cross-sectional restriction at all.[10] A violation of arbitrage for, say, the Cox–Ingersoll–Ross model can cease to be a free lunch in the Vasicek model. So, 'informative' no-arbitrage conditions depend on the model we have chosen. The restrictions no-arbitrage models impose on the excess returns from bonds of different maturities (because this is what no-arbitrage conditions ultimately do) are therefore useful only if the model is (approximately) true. If, for tractability, laziness or ignorance, our model is so 'stylized' as to miss essential ingredients of the dependence of term premia on the state variables, then the extra conditions the model imposes on the 'naive' statistical projections may well be cross-sectionally very restrictive, but they may also do more harm than good.[11]

This is the reason why in this book I devote so much importance to the discussion of what we 'now know' about the market price of risk, and to how efficiently different models are able to reflect this information.

36.1.5 The Case for the Defence: Models as Revealers of Forward-Looking Informations

Models which are fitted to market information can also helpful because, by virtue of being fitted to *today's* yield curve and *today's* covariance matrix, they

---

[9] For an early discussion of shrinking techniques in statistical estimation, see Stein (1956).

[10] For instance, if we accept that rates cannot be negative, any model will prescribe that a discount bond of maturity T_1 must be worth more than a discount bond of maturity T_2 if $T_1 < T_2$. We don't go very far – we do not impose very 'biting' cross-sectional restrictions – with the condition of no-arbitrage of this type.

[11] In a similar vein, Diebold and Rudebusch (2013) write: '[A] misspecified model may be internally consistent (free from arbitrage) yet have little relationship to the real world, and hence forecast poorly [...]. [I]mposition of no-arbitrage on a misspecified model may actually *degrade* empirical performance' (p. 17, emphasis in the original).

know about the *forward-looking* information embedded in the prices of the relevant instruments. Using our historical record, we may well estimate, say, the volatilities of yields of different maturities. But this does not mean that these historically based estimates of volatilities are slavishly used by the forward-looking market participants to arrive at prices, especially when structural breaks occur – ie, when, arguably, we need most the help from models. The shape of the yield curve in the days after Lehman's default provides a vivid case in point.

This matters a lot if one is interested in conditional information. In general, any assessment of 'value' in the yield curve comes from the interplay between what the 'market thinks' and how reality will unfold. A purely statistical approach, based, in however sophisticated a way, on the assumption that the future looks like the past, implicitly enforces the assumption that the world will keep on behaving as it did in the 'training set'. The market is not constrained by such fetters, and can adjust 'its views' in a far more complex manner.

When looked at from this perspective, the output from models calibrated to market prices can therefore differ from the output from statistical analyses for two reasons, one bad and one good.

The bad recovery failure stems from the model inability to account for some established empirical features: a constant volatility for the state variables, or a state-independent market price of risk are two obvious examples of model shortcomings.

The 'good' failure to produce the same predictions for market observables (say, yield volatilities) as suggested by a backward-looking statistical analysis is that the market-calibrated model may know something that the econometric analysis does not. This 'something' is the market (measure-adjusted) forward-looking estimates of the same quantities.

Of course, we don't have to believe that either the market is right, or that the statistical estimates tell the truth. When it comes to predictions, this is where the judgement of the modeller comes to the fore. And it is for this reason that much of current affine modelling tries to combine the modelling and the statistical strands of research. As Diebold and Rudebusch (2013) eloquently put it, the modern approach 'blends two important and successful approaches to yield curve modelling: the [...] empirically based and the no-arbitrage theoretically based one'.[12]

36.1.6   The Case for the Defence: Models as Integrators

It is very conceptually instructive and practically useful to have a decomposition of the term structure of yields in terms of expectations, term premia and convexity contribution. Consider, however, what happened when we looked at excess returns, at the market price of risk and at the difference between the real

---

[12] p. 76.

market yield and the yield that would prevail if investors were risk-neutral – that it to say, the yield term premium. We soon found out (see Sections 24.3 to 24.5) that it is in general not easy to go from the expected excess return today (the *current* value of the market price of risk) to the desired yield term premium. The reason is simply that the yield today contains information about all the possible future paths of the market price of risk out to maturity and that a non-constant market price of risk is in general a function of the future and stochastic state variables. As we saw in Chapter 24, if the state variables today are a long way from their reversion level, *today's* value of the market price of risk and the yield term premium may even have the opposite sign!

Something similar can be said about convexity: if we are interested about the convexity contribution to a T-maturity yield, what matters is not the volatility today of a T-maturity yield, but how its volatility will evolve throughout its life. It is not easy to go from the quantity we can measure (the volatility of yield today) to the average quantity we are interested in (the convexity contribution to a yield). See in this respect the discussion in the last paragraph of Section 21.10.

So, this is another application where models come to the fore: as prices are expectations of exponential functions of the path of the state variables, and yields are immediately obtainable from prices, models provide the 'integrated' information we are interested in. And, to boot, if we had the good taste to use a solvable affine model, the answer is analytic.

36.1.7 The Case for the Defence: Models as Enhancers of Understanding

Important as they are, these various reasons why models are not redundant, but complement statistical information are only a (small) part of the story of why models matter. There is, I believe, far more to model building than the regularization of noisy inputs, the enforcement of parsimony, the revelation of forward-looking information and the ease with which we can obtain some integrated quantities of interest. And there certainly is more to models, I believe, than enforcement of no-arbitrage. It all goes back to Picasso's quote at the beginning of this chapters: questions can often be more useful than answers to further our understanding. And models allow us to pose questions that statistical analysis by itself cannot suggest. How so?

The main reason is that structural models afford an *understanding* of what drives the yield curve that is very difficult for a purely statistical analysis to provide. Statistical information is essentially associative, and does not lend itself readily to a causal interpretation. Yet the human mind readily works in a causal mode, but often falters when presented with association-based information.[13]

---

[13] Rebonato and Denev (2013, p. 13) vividly discuss the different cognitive responses of a risk modeller faced with the same information, but presented in an association-based mode in one case (via a correlation matrix) and in a causality-based mode in the other (via a Bayesian net). See also Pearl (2009) for a thorough discussion of this point.

Faced with empirical findings, we naturally like to build explanations ('financial stories'). These causal accounts – these 'models' – allow us to make sense of reality, to sieve the noise from the signal, and to understand the inadequacies of our current thinking. These causal accounts are dynamic, because they naturally point to the direction in which the model should be enriched. And these causal explanations naturally beg new questions: *why* is the slope (or the tent, or the bat) a significant predictor of bond excess returns? *Why* do investors value liquidity? *Why* should the market price of risk depend on the state of the world? *What* does absence of arbitrage ultimately rest on? And so on.

An answer to a question often has the form of a 'story'. Of course, when this story-telling is undisciplined, we are in the land of blogs, op-eds and television talking heads – a strange, yet infinitely comforting, land, where every new piece of empirical evidence is always explained (away) by the idea we had before the new piece of information became available. Comforting as they are, these pseudo-explanations are of little, if any, value and help. However, if the 'stories' are made to yield testable predictions (and, of course, if we do carry out the necessary tests), then we have powerful tools to enhance our understanding. By weaving statistical information with the causal structure afforded by a model we can try to be, in short, like Bacon's bees, neither like his spiders nor his ants.

This is more true than ever when our models suggest answers that are difficult to understand or to reconcile with our expectations, or with empirical evidence. Nothing stimulates thought and fosters progress more keenly than a recalcitrant piece of statistical evidence or a 'paradox'. After all, it was after observing the predictive deficiencies of the early constant-market-price-of-risk that researchers began thinking about what was missing – namely the state-dependence of the market price of risk. And it was the puzzling finding that principal-components as high as the fifth may have explanatory power when it comes to excess returns that made us think more deeply about spanning variables in affine models, about macrofinancial versus yield curve–based return-predicting factors, about the theoretical but not practical equivalence of the two descriptions, etc.

Even the findings by Joslin et al. (2013) about the quasi-equivalence of macrofinance term structure models and statistical (VAR-based) approaches do not imply that term-structure models 'are of little value for understanding the risk profiles of portfolios of bonds'. This is because, as the Authors point out, '[r]estrictions on risk premiums in bond markets typically amount to constraints across $\mathbb{P}$ and $\mathbb{Q}$ distributions of [the state variables], and such constraints cannot be explored outside of a term structure model that (implicitly or explicitly) links these distributions. Moreover, the presence of constraints on risk premiums will in general imply that [Maximum Likelihood] estimates of the $\mathbb{P}$ distribution of yields within a [term structure model] are more efficient than those from its corresponding factor-VAR'.[14]

---

[14] p. 617. The last point is (to some extent) related to the 'regularization' effect of models discussed earlier.

More generally, the main virtue of models is the power they confer on their thoughtful users to engage in a critical analysis of what the model may be lacking, and of how it should be improved. When we look at modelling from this perspective, currently we are probably in the midst of one of the more vibrant phases in the many-decades-old history of affine term-structure modelling. I hope that this book has given the reader an exciting introduction to this lively field, and the desire to learn more about it. Indeed, as Herder said, '[i]f all we ever did was wind and unwind the tangled threads of learning without ever getting any further – then what an unhappy fate we would have!'

References

Abraham MT, Adrian T, Crump RK, Moench E. (2015). *Decomposing Nominal and Real Yield Curves*. Staff Report No. 570, Federal Reserve Bank of New York.

Abu-Mostafa Y, Magdon-Ismail M, Lin H-T. (2012). *Learning from Data – A Short Course*. AML.

Acemoglu D. (2008). *Introduction to Modern Economic Growth*. Princeton University Press, Princeton, NJ.

Adrian T, Crump RK, Mills B, Moench E. (2014). *Treasury Term Premia: 1961–Present*. Liberty Street Economics, Federal Reserve Bank of New York, May 12, 2014. Data available at www.newyorkfed.org/research/data_indicators/term_premia.html (Accessed 27 January 2015).

Adrian T, Crump RK, Moench E. (2013). *Pricing the Term Structure with Linear Regressions*. Federal Reserve Bank of New York, Staff Report No. 340, August 2008, revised 2013. Available at www.newyorkfed.org/research/staff_reports/sr340.pdf (Accessed 15 October, 2014).

Ahn D, Dittmar RF, Gallant AR. (2002). *Quadratic Term Structure Models: Theory and Evidence*. Review of Financial Studies, 15, 243–288.

Amenc N, Goltz F, Le Sourd V. (2017). The EDHEC European ETF and Smart Beta Survey 2016, EDHEC Risk Institute Publication, May 2017.

American Statistical Association. (1997). Ethical Guidelines, Guideline No. 8.

Andersen TG, Lund J. (1997). *Estimating Continuous-Time Stochastic Volatility Models of the Short-Term Interest Rate*. Journal of Econometrics, 77, 343–377.

Anderson N, Breedon F, Deacon M, Derry A, Murray G. (1996). *Estimating and Interpreting the Yield Curve*. Series in Financial Economics and Quantitative Analysis. John Wiley & Sons, Chichester.

Ang A, Dong S, Piazzesi M. *No-Arbitrage Taylor Rules* (September 2007). NBER Working Paper No. w13448. Available at https://ssrn.com/abstract=1017771

Ang A, Piazzesi M. (2003). *A No-Arbitrage Vector Autoregression of Term Structure Dynamics with Macroeconomic and Latent Variables*. Journal of Monetary Economics, 50, 745–787.

Angrist JD, Pischke J-S. *Mastering 'Metrics: The Path from Cause to Effect*. Princeton University Press, Princeton, NJ.

Babbs S, Nowman B. (1999). *Kalman Filtering of Generalized Vasicek Term Structure Models*. Journal of Financial and Quantitative Analysis, 34, 115–30.

Bailey DH, de Prado ML. (2014). *The Deflated Sharpe Ratio: Correcting for Selection Bias, Backtest Overfitting, and Non-Normality*. Journal of Portfolio Management, Special 40th Anniversary Issue, November 2014, 94–118.

Balduzzi P, Das SR, Foresi S, Sundaram RK. (1996). *A Simple Approach to Three Factor Affine Term Structure Models*. Journal of Fixed Income, 6, 43–53.

Ball C, Torous W. (1983). *Bond Price Dynamics and Options*. Journal of Financial and Quantitative Analysis, 18, 517–531.

Baker K. (2005, 2013). *Singular Value Decomposition Tutorial*. Working Paper, Ohio State University. Available at www.ling.ohio-state.edu/~kbaker/pubs/Singular_Value_Decomposition_Tutorial.pdf (Accessed 2 October 2014).

Bain K, Howell P. (2003, 2009). *Monetary Economics: Policy and Theoretical Basis*. Palgrave Macmillan, London.

Balduzzi P, Das S, Foresi S. (1998). *The Central Tendency: A Second Factor in Bond Yields*. The Review of Economics and Statistics, 80, 62–72.

Bansal R, Yaron A. (2004). *Risks for the Long Run: A Potential Resolution of Asset Pricing Puzzles*. Journal of Finance, 59, 1481–1509.

Bauer MD, Hamilton JD. (2015). *Robust Risk Premia*. Federal Reserve Bank of San Francisco Working Paper, September 2015. Available at http://econweb.ucsd.edu/~jhamilto/bh_robust.pdf (Accessed 27 November 2015).

Bauer MD, Rudebusch GD. (2016). *Monetary Policy Expectations at the Zero Lower Bound*. Journal of Money, Credit, and Banking 48(7), October, pp. 1439–1465.

Bernanke BS. (2013). *The Economic Outlook*. Testimony before the Joint Economic Committee, US Congress, Washington, DC, May 22, 2013. Available at www.federalreserve.gov/newsevents/testimony/bernanke20130522a.htm (Accessed 11 November 2014).

Binmore K. (2009). *Rational Decisions*. Princeton University Press, Princeton, NJ.

Black F (1976). *The Pricing of Commodity Contracts*. Journal of Financial Economics, 3, 167–179.

Black F. (1995). *Interest Rates as Options*. The Journal of Finance, 50, 1371–1376.

Black F, Derman E, Toy W. (1990). *A One-Factor Model of Interest Rates and Its Application to Treasury Bond Options*. Financial Analysts Journal, 24–32.

Bliss R. (1997). *Testing Term Structure Estimation Models*. Advances in Futures and Options Research, 9, 197–231.

Bolder DJ. (2001). *Affine Term-Structure Models: Theory and Implementation*. Bank of Canada Working Paper 2001–15. Available at www.bankofcanada.ca/wp-content/uploads/2010/02/wp01-15a.pdf (Accessed 11 August 2017).

Bomfin AN, (2003a). *Monetary Policy and the Yield Curve*. Working Paper, Board of Governors of the Federal Reserve System, Washington, DC.

Bomfin AN, (2003b). *"Interest Rates as Options:" Assessing the Markets' View of the Liquidity Trap*. Working Paper, Board of Governors of the Federal Reserve System, Washington, DC. Available at www.federalreserve.gov/pubs/feds/2003/200345/200345pap.pdf (Accessed 31 March 2015).

Boswell J. (1992, 1791). *The Life of Samuel Johnson, LL D*. Everyman's Library, London.

Brace A, Gatarek D, Musiela M. (1997). *The Market Model of Interest-Rate Dynamics*. Mathematical Finance, 7(2), 127–147.

Brayton F, Laubach T, Reifschneider D. (2014). *Optimal-Control Monetary Policy in the FRB/US Model*. FEDS Notes, Board of Governors of the Federal Reserve System, 21 November, 2014. Available at www.federalreserve.gov/econresdata/notes/feds-notes/2014/optimal-control-monetary-policy-in-frbus-20141121.html (Accessed 15 September 2015).

Brennan MJ, Xia Y. (2002). *Dynamic Asset Allocation under Inflation*. Journal of Finance, 57(3), 1201–1238.

Brezeźniak Z, Zastawniak T. (1999). *Basic Stochastic Processes*. Springer-Verlag, Berlin.

Britten-Jones M, Neuberger A, Nolte I. (2011). *Improved Inference in Regression with Overlapping Observations*. Warwick Business School Working Paper, FERC, CoFE, 26 January, 2011.

Brown RH, Schaefer SM. (2000). *Why Long Term Forward Interest Rates (Almost) Always Slope Downwards*. London Business School Working Paper. Available at http://citeseerx.ist.psu.edu/viewdoc/download?doi=10.1.1.196.7176&rep=rep1&type=pdf (Accessed 26 January, 2015).

Buraschi A, Jiltsov A. (2005). *Inflation Premia and the Expectation Hypothesis*. Journal of Financial Economics, 75, 429–490.

Burke O. (2010). More Notes for Least Squares, University of Oxford, lecture notes. Available at www.stats.ox.ac.uk/~burke/Linear%20Models/LS%20notes.pdf (Accessed 28 July 2015).

Calasso R. (1988, 2007). *Le Nozze di Cadmo e Armonia*. 12th edn. Adelphi, Milano.

Campbell JY, Cochrane J. (1995, 1999). *By Force of Habit: A Consumption-Based Explanation of Aggregate Stock Market Behavior*. NBER Working Paper 4995 and Journal of Political Economy, 107(2), 205–251.

Campbell JA, Lo A, McKinley C. (1996). *The Econometrics of Financial Markets*. Princeton University Press, NJ.

Campbell JY, Perron P. (1991). *What Macroeconomists Should Know about Unit Roots*. NBER Macroeconomics Annual, 6, 141–201. Available at http://nrs.harvard.edu/urn-3:HUL.InstRepos:3374863 (Accessed August 2, 2011).

Campbell JY, Shiller R. (1991). *Yield Spreads and Interest Rate Movements: A Bird's Eye View*. Review of Economic Studies, 58, 495–514.

Campbell JY, Thompson SB. (2008). *Predicting Excess Stock Returns Out of Sample: Can Anything Beat the Historical Average?* Review of Financial Studies, 21(4), 1509–1531.

Canzoneri MB, Cumby RE, Diba BT. (2007). *Euler Equations and Money Market Interest Rates: A Challenge for Monetary Policy Models*. Journal of Monetary Economics, 54, 1863–1881.

Chan KC, Karoly A, Logstaff FA, Sanders AB. (1992). *An Empirical Comparison of Alternative Models of the Short-Term Interest Rate*. Journal of Finance, 47, 1209–1227.

Chandler D. (1987). *Introduction to Modern Statistical Mechanics*. Oxford University Press, Oxford.

Chatfield C. (1989). *The Analysis of Time Series: An Introduction*, 4th edn. Chapman and Hall, London.

Chatfield C. (2003). *The Analysis of Time Series: An Introduction*. CRC Texts in Statistical Science, Chapman & Hall, London.

Chatfield C, Collins AJ. (1980, 1989). *Introduction to Multivariate Analysis*. Chapman and Hall, London.

Chen X, Sun Z, Yao T, Yu T. (2014). *In Search of Habitat*. Working Paper, Shangai University of Finance and Economics. Available at https://editorialexpress.com/cgi-bin/conference/download.cgi?paper_id=1625&db_name=AFA2015 (Accessed 11 February 2016).

Chen R-R, Liu B, Cheng X. (2010). *Pricing the Term Structure of Inflation Risk Premia: Theory and Evidence from TIPS*. Journal of Empirical Finance, 17, 702–721.

Cheridito P, Filipovic D, Kimmel RL. (2007). *Marekt Price of Risk Specifications for Affine Models: Theory and Evidence*. Journal of Financial Economics, 123–170, also (2005), Working Paper, Princeton University. Available at www.princeton.edu/˜dito/papers/mprSept14_05.pdf (Accessed 14 January 2016).

Cheridito P, Filipovic D, Kimmel RL. (2010). *A Note on the Dai-Singleton Canonical Representation of Affine Term Structure Models*. Mathematical Finance, 2(3), 509–519.

Christensen JHE, Diebold FX, Rudebusch GD. (2011). *The Affine Arbitrage-Free Class of Nelson Siegel Term Structure Models*. Journal of Econometrics, 164, 4–20.

Christensen JHE, Kwan S. (2014). *Assessing Expectations of Monetary Policy*. FRBSF Economic Letter, 2014–27, September 8, 2014.

Christensen JHE, Lopez JA, Rudebusch GD. (2010). *Inflation Expectations and Risk Premiums in an Arbitrage-Free Model of Nominal and Real Bond Yields*. Journal of Money, Credit and Banking, 42, 367–394.

Christensen JHE, Rudebusch GD. (2016). *Modelling Yields at the Zero Lower Bound: Are Shadow Rates the Solution?* In Dynamic Factor Models (Advances in Econometrics, Vol. 35), ed. by Eric Hillebrand and Siem Jan Koopman, Emerald Publishing Group, pp. 75–125.

Cieslak A, Povala P. (2010a). *Understanding Bond Risk Premia*. Working Paper, Kellogg School of Management, Northwestern University and University of Lugano. Available at www.gsb.stanford.edu/sites/default/files/documents/fin_01_11_Cieslak Anna.pdf (Accessed 5 May 2015).

Cieslak A, Povala P. (2010b). *Expected Returns in Treasury Bonds*. Working Paper, Northwestern University and Birbeck College. Review of Financial Studies.

Clarida R, Gali J, Gertler M. (2000). *Monetary Policy Rules and Macroeconomic Stability: Evidence and Some Theory*. Quarterly Journal of Economics, CXV, (1), 147–180.

Cochrane JH. (2001). *Asset Pricing*. Princeton University Press, Princeton, NJ, and Oxford.

Cochrane JH. (2015). *Comments on "Robust Risk Premia" by Michael Bauer and Jim Hamilton*. Working Paper, University of Chicago, November 2015. Available at http://faculty.chicagobooth.edu/john.cochrane/research/Papers/bauer_hamilton_comments.pdf (Accessed 27 November 2015).

Cochrane JH, Piazzesi M. (2004). *Reply to Dai, Singleton and Yang*. Working Paper, University of Chicago. Available at http://faculty.chicagobooth.edu/john.cochrane/research/papers/dsy.pdf (Accessed 25 February 2015).

Cochrane JH, Piazzesi M. (2005). *Bond Risk Premia*. American Economic Review, 95(1), 138–160. See also www.aeaweb.org/aer/data/mar05_app_cochrane.pdf (Accessed 25 November, 2014) for technical details and the regression coefficients.

Cochrane JH, Piazzesi M. (2008). *Decomposing the Yield Curve*. University of Chicago and NBR Working Paper, March 2008.

Cochrane JH, Saa-Requejo J. (1999). *Beyond Arbitrage: Good-Deal Asset Bounds in Incomplete Markets*. Working Paper, January 26, 1999, Graduate School of Business, University of Chicago.

Collin-Dufresne P, Goldstein RS. (2002). *Do Bonds Span the Fixed Income Markets? Theory and Evidence for Unspanned Stochastic Volatility*. Journal of Finance, 57, 1685–1730.

Cox J, Ingersoll J, Ross S. (1985a). *An Intertemporal General Equilibrium Model of Asset Prices*, Econometrica, 53, 363–384.

Cox J, Ingersoll J, Ross S. (1985b). *A Theory of the Term Structure of Interest Rates.* Econometrica, 53, 385–408.

Dai Q, Singleton KJ, Yang W. (2004). *Predictability of Bond Risk Premia and Affine Term Structure Models.* Working Paper, Stern School of Business.

Dai Q, Singleton KJ. (2000). *Specification Analysis of Affine Term Structure Models.* Journal of Finance, 55(5), 1943–1978.

D'Amico S, Kim DH, Min Wei. (2010). *Tips from TIPS: The Informational Content of Treasury Inflation Protected Security Prices.* Working Paper, Finance and Economics Discussion Series, Federal Reserve Board, Washington, DC. Available at www.federalreserve.gov/pubs/feds/2010/201019/201019pap.pdf (Accessed 13 November 2014).

Davies H, Green D. (2010). *Banking on the Future: The Fall and Rise of Central Banking.* Princeton University Press, Princeton, NJ, and Oxford.

Descartes R. (1637, 1968). *Discourse on Method and The Meditations, Trans.* FE Sutcliffe. Penguin Classics, London.

Diamond PA. (1999). *What Stock Market Returns to Expect for the Future?*, Working Paper, Center for Retirement Research, Boston College. Available at http://economics.mit.edu/files/637 (Accessed 10 June 2015).

Diebold FX, Li C. (2006). *Forecasting the Term Structure of Government Bond Yields.* Journal of Econometrics, 130, 337–364.

Diebold FX, Rudebusch GD. (2013). *Yield Curve Modelling and Forecasting: The Dynamic Nelson–Siegel Approach.* Princeton University Press, Princeton, NJ, and Oxford.

Dougherty C. (1992). *Introduction to Econometrics.* Oxford University Press, Oxford and New York.

Duffee GR. (2002). *Term Premia and Interest Rate Forecasts in Affine Models.* Journal of Finance, LVII, (1), 405–443.

Duffee GR. (2008). *Information in (and Not in) the Term Structure.* Working Paper, Haas School of Business, University of California, Berkeley.

Duffee GH. (2010). *Sharpe Ratios in Term Structure Models.* Working Paper, Johns Hopkins University. Available at www.econ2.jhu.edu/People/Duffee/duffeeSharpe.pdf (Accessed 16 December 2015).

Duffie D, Kan R. (1996). *A Yield-Factor Model of Interest Rates.* Mathematical Finance, 6(4), 379–406.

Ellenberg J. (2014). *How Not to Be Wrong: The Hidden Maths of Everyday Life.* Penguin Books (Allen Lane), London.

Engle RF. (1982). *Autoregressive Conditional Heteroskedasticity with Estimates of the Variance of United Kingdom Inflation.* Econometrica, 50, 987–1008.

Engle RF, Bollerslev T. (1986). *Modelling the Persistence of Conditional Variances.* Econometric Reviews, 5, 1–50.

English WB, Lopez-Salido D, Tetlow R. (2013). *The Federal Reserve's Framework for Monetary Policy: Recent Changes and New Questions.* Federal Reserve Board, Finance and Economics Discussion Series 2013–76. Available at www.federalreserve.gov/pubs/feds/2013/201376/index.html. (Accessed 15 September 2015).

Epstein LG, Zin SE. (1991). *Substitution, Risk Aversion, and the Temporal Behaviour of Consumption and Asset Returns: An Empirical Analysis.* Journal of Political Economy, 99(21), 263–279.

Erekhinskiy A. (2013). *A Model for Interest Rates in Repressed Markets.* Thesis for MSc in Mathematical Finance, Oxford University, 18 April, 2013.

Etheridge A. (2005). *A Course in Financial Calculus*. Cambridge: Cambridge University Press.

Evans MDD. (1998). *Real Rates, Expectations and Inflation Risk Premia*. Journal of Finance, 53(1), 167–218.

Evans GW, Honkapohja S. (2009). *Learning and Macroeconomics*. Annual Review of Economics, 1, 421–449.

Evans GW, Honkapohja S, Williams N. (2010). *Generalized Stochastic Gradient Learning*. International Economic Review, 51, 237–262.

Fama E, Bliss R. (1987). *The Information in Long-Maturity Forward Rates*. American Economic Review, 77, 680–692.

Fama E, French K. (1989). *Business Conditions and Expected Returns on Stocks and Bonds*. Journal of Financial Economics, 25, 23–49.

Fama E, French K. (1993). *Common Risk Factors in the Returns on Stocks and Bonds*. Journal of Financial Economics, 33, 3–56.

Federal Reserve Board. (2014). www.federalreserve.gov/monetarypolicy/files/fomcprojtabl20140618.pdf (Accessed 12 August 2014).

Federal Reserve Bank of New York. (2014). www.newyorkfed.org/research/data_indicators/term_premia.html (Accessed 7 November 2014).

Fender I, Lewrisk U. (2015). *Shifting Tides: Market Liquidity and Market-Making in Fixed Income Instruments*. BIS Quarterly Review, March 2015.

Fisher, I. (1930). *The Theory of Interest*. Macmillan, New York.

Fisher M. (2002). *Special Repo Rates: An Introduction*. Federal Reserve Bank of Atlanta, Economic Review, 27–43, Available at www.frbatlanta.org/research/publications/economic-review/2002/q2/vol87no2_special-repo-rates.aspx (Accessed 6 August 2015).

Fisher M. (2004). *Modeling the Term Structure of Interest Rates: An Introduction*. Federal Reserve Bank of Atlanta, Economic Review, 41–62. Available at www.frbatlanta.org/research/publications/economic-review/2004/q3/vol89no3_modeling-term-structure-of-interest-rates.aspx (Accessed 6 August 2015).

Fisher M, Nychka D, Zervos D. (1995). *Fitting the Term Structure of Interest Rates with Smoothing Splines*. Finance and Economics Discussion Series Paper No. 95–1, Federal Reserve Board.

Fleckenstein M, Longstaff FA, Lustig H. (2010, 2014). *Why Does the Treasury Issue TIPS? The TIPS-Treasury Bond Puzzle*. NBER Working Paper No. 16358, September 2010, and Journal of Finance, 69, 2151–2197.

Fontaine J-S, Garcia R. (2008). *Bond Liquidity Premia*. Working paper, University of Montreal and EDHEC Business School. www.rmi.nus.edu.sg/_files/events/paper/Bond%20Liquidity%20Premia.pdf (Accessed 5 May 2015).

Fontaine J-S, Garcia R. (2012). *Bond Liquidity Premia*. Review of Financial Studies, 25(4), 1207–1254.

Fontaine J-S, Garcia R. (2015). *Recent Advances in Old Fixed-Income Topics: Liquidity, Learning, and the Lower Bound*. In Pietro Veronesi (ed.), *Handbook of Fixed Income*. John Wiley & Sons, Chichester.

Froot KA. (1989). *New Hope for the Expectations Hypothesis of the Term Structure of Interest Rates*. Journal of Finance, 44, 283–305.

Gabaix X. (2012). *Variable Rare Disasters: An Exactly Solved Framework for Ten Puzzles in Macro-Finance*. Quarterly Journal of Economics, 127(2), 645–700.

Garcia R, Luger R. (2102). *Risk Aversion, Intertemporal Substitution, and the Term Structure of Interest Rates*. Journal of Applied Econometrics, 27, 1013–1036.

Gilboa I. (2010). *Rational Choice*. MIT Press, Cambridge, MA, and technical appendices available at http://mitpress.edu/rationalchoice.

Gilles C, Leory SF. (1986). *A Note on the Local Expectation Hypothesis: A Discrete-Time Exposition*. Journal of Finance, 41(4), 975–979.

Gorovoi V, Linetsky V. (2004). *Black's Model of Interest Rates as Options, Eigenfunction Expansions, and Japanese Interest Rates*. Mathematical Finance, 14(1), 49–78.

Gospodinov N, Wei B. (2015). *A Note on Extracting Inflation Expectations from Market Prices of TIPS and Inflation Derivatives*. Working Paper, Federal Reserve Bank of Atlanta, November 2015.

Grishencko OV, Huang J-Z. (2013). *Inflation Risk Premium: Evidence from the TIPS Market*. Journal of Fixed Income, 22, 5–30.

Gurkaynak RS, Sack B, Wright JH. (2000). *The TIPS Yield Curve and Inflation Compensation*. Working Paper No. 2000-05, Federal Reserve Board, Washington, DC, Division of Research & Statistics and Monetary Affairs. Data available at www.federalreserve.gov/pubs/feds/2008/200805/200805abs.html (Accessed 26 February 2016).

Gurkaynak RS, Sack B, Wright JH. (2006). *The US Treasury Yield Curve: 1961 to the Present*. Working Paper No. 2006-28, Federal Reserve Board, Washington, DC, Division of Research & Statistics and Monetary Affairs.

Gurkaynak RS, Sack B, Wright JH. (2007). *The US Treasury Yield Curve: 1961 to the Present*. Journal of Monetary Economics, 54, 2291–2304. Data available at www.federalreserve.gov/econresdata/researchdata/feds200805.xls (Accessed 27 January 2015) and www.federalreserve.gov/pubs/feds/2006/200628/200628 abs.html (Accessed 20 September 2014).

Hamilton JD. (1994). *Time Series Analysis*. Princeton University Press, Princeton, NJ.

Hamilton JD, Harris ES, Hatzious J, West KD. (2015). *The Equilibrium Real Funds Rate: Past, Present and Future*. NBER Working Paper No. 21476, Issued in August 2015. Available at www.nber.org/papers/w21476 (accessed 3 November 2015).

Hamilton JD, Wu C. (2012). *Identification and Estimation of Affine-Term-Structure Models*. Journal of Econometrics, 168, 315–331.

Hamilton JD, Wu JC. (2012). *Effectiveness of Alternative Monetary Policies in a Zero Lower Bound Environment*. Journal of Money, Credit, and Banking, 44, 346.

Hansen LP, Sargent TJ. (2008). *Robustness*. Princeton University Press, Princeton, NJ, and Woodstock, UK.

Harrison JM, Kreps DM. (1979). *Martingales and Arbitrage in Multiperiod Securities Markets*. Journal of Economic Theory, 20(3), 381–408.

Hatano Taku. (2016). *Investigation of Cyclical and Unconditional Excess Return Predicting Factors*. St Catherine's College, University of Oxford, thesis submitted in partial fulfillment of the MSc in Mathematical Finance.

Haubrig JG, Pennacchi G, Ritchken P. (2012). *Inflation Expectations, Real Rates, and Risk Premia: Evidence from Inflation Swaps*. Review of Financial Studies, 25, 1588–1629.

Hazlitt W. (2000). *On Reason and Imagination*. in *The Fight and Other Writings*, Penguin Classics, London.

Heath D, Jarrow RA, Merton R. (1989). *Bond Pricing and the Term Structure of Interest Rates: A New Methodology*. Working Paper (revised edition), Cornell University.

Heath D, Jarrow RA, Merton R. (1992). *Bond Pricing and the Term Structure of Interest Rates: A New Methodology*. Econometrica, 61(1), 77–105.

Hellerstein R. (2011). *Global Bond Risk Premiums*. Federal Reserve Bank of New York Staff Report No. 499, June. Available at www.nyfedeconomists.org/research/staff_reports/sr499.pdf (Accessed 4 June 2015).

Hens T, Rieger MO. (2010). *Financial Economics: A Concise Introduction to Classical and Behavioral Finance*. Springer-Verlag, Heidelberg, Berlin.

Herder JG. (1773, 2008). *Shakespeare*, trans. (G. Moore). Princeton University Press, Princeton, NJ, and Oxford.

Hicks JR. (1937). *Mr Keynes and the "Classics."* Econometrica, 2(April), 147–159.

Hicks JR. (1939). *Value and Capital*. Oxford University Press, Oxford.

Hördal P, Tristani O. (2012). *Inflation Risk Premia in the Term Structure of Interest Rates*. Journal of the European Economic Association, 10, 634–657.

Hull J. (2014). *Options, Futures and Other Derivatives*. 9th edn., Prentice Hall, Englewood Cliffs, NJ.

Hull J, White A. (1990). *Pricing Interest-Rate Derivative Securities*. Review of Financial Studies, 3(4) 573–592.

Hull J, White A. (1994). *Numerical Procedures for Implementing Term Structure Models II: Two-Factor Models*. Journal of Derivatives, Winter, 37–48.

Ibragimov R, Mueeler UK. (2010). *t-Statistic Based Correlation and Heterogeneity Robust Inference*. Journal of Business and Economic Statistics, 28, 453–468.

Ichiue H, Ueno Y. (2007). *Equilibrium Interest Rates and the Yield Curve in a Low Interest Rate Environment*. Working Paper 2007-E-18, Bank of Japan.

Jackson K. (2015). *And All That Jazz*. Review of *Fracture: Life and Culture in the West, 1919–1938*, by Philipp Blom. In *Literary Review*, August 2015, 8–9.

Jensen JLWV. (1906). *Sur les fonctions convexes et les inégalités entre les valeurs moyennes*. Acta Mathematica, 30, 175–193.

Johnson N, Naik V, Page S, Pedersen N, Sapra S. (2015). *The Stock-Bond Correlation*. Journal of Investment Strategies, 4(1), 3–18.

Joslin S, Anh Le, Singleton KJ. (2013). *Why Gaussian Macro-Finance Models Are (Nearly) Unconstrained Factor-VARs*. Journal of Financial Economics, 109(3), 604–622.

Joslin S, Priebsch, M, Singleton KJ. (2014). *Risk Premiums in Dynamic Term Structure Models with Unspanned Macro Risks*. Journal of Finance, LXIX(3), 1197–1233.

Joslin, S, Singleton KJ, Zhu H. (2011). *A New Perspective on Gaussian Dynamic Term Structure Models*. The Review of Financial Studies, 24, 926–970.

Joyce M, Kaminska I, Lildholdt P. (2008). *Understanding the Real Rate Conundrum: An Application of No-Arbitrage Finance Models to the UK Real Yield Curve*. Bank of England Working Paper No. 358, December 2008. Available at www.bankofengland.co.uk/research/Documents/workingpapers/2008/wp358.pdf (Accessed 27 January 2015).

Joyce M, Lidholt P, Sorensen S. (2010). *Extracting Inflation Expectations and Inflation Risk Premia from the Term Structure: A Joint Model of the UK Nominal and Real Yield Curves*. Journal of Banking and Finance, 34, 281–294.

Judd, JP, Rudebusch GD. (1998). *Describing Fed Behaviour*. FRSBF Economic Letter, December.

Karatzas I, Shreve SE. (1988). *Brownian Motion and Stochastic Calculus*. Springer-Verlag, Berlin.

Kim DH. (2007). *Challenges in Macro-Finance Modelling*. BIS Working Paper No. 240, December 2007.

Kim DH, Singleton KJ. (2012). *Term Structure Models and the Zero Bound: An Empirical Investigation of Japanese Yields*. Journal of Econometrics, 170(1), 32–49.

Kim DH, Wright JH. (2005). *An Arbitrage-Free Three-Factor Term Structure Model and Recent Behavior of Long-Term Yields and Distant-Horizon Forward Rates*. Finance and Economics Discussion Series, Division of Statistics and Monetary Affairs, Federal Reserve Board, Washington, DC, 2005–33. Available at www. federalreserve.gov/pubs/feds/2005/200533/200533pap.pdf (Accessed 13 November 2014).

Kitsul Y, Wright JH. (2013). *The Economics of Option-Implied Inflation Probability Density Functions*. Journal of Financial Economics, 110, 696–711.

Klebaner F. (2005). *Introduction to Stochastic Calculus with Application*. Imperial College Press, London.

Kreps DM. (1988). *Notes on the Theory of Choice*. Westview Press, Boulder, CO.

Krippner L. (2013). *Measuring the Stance of Monetary Policy in Zero Lower Bound Environments*. Economics Letters, 118(1), 135–138.

Krugman P. (undated). *There's Something About Macro*. Available at http://web.mit. edu/krugman/www/islm.html (Accessed 3 July 2015).

Lam KS. (2015). *Topics in Contemporary Mathematical Physics*. 2nd edn. World Scientific, Singapore and London.

Laubach T, Williams JC. (2015). *Measuring the Natural Rate of Interest Redux*. Federal Reserve Bank of San Francisco, Working Paper Series, Working Paper 2015–16, October 2015. Available at www.frbsf.org/economic-research/publications/ working-papers/wp2015-16.pdf (Accessed 3 November 2015).

LaWare F. (1993). Minutes of the meeting of the Federal Open Market Committee held on May 18, 1993. Available at www.federalreserve.gov/monetarypolicy/files/ FOMC19930518meeting.pdf (Accessed 26 October 2014).

Lengwiler Y. (2004). *Microfoundations of Financial Economics: An Introduction to General Equilibrium Asset Pricing*. Princeton University Press, Princeton, NJ and Oxford.

Le Roy SF, Werner J. (2001). *Principles of Financial Economics*. Cambridge: Cambridge University Press.

Litterman R, Scheinkman J. (1991). *Common Factors Affecting Bond Returns*. Journal of Fixed Income, 1(1), 54–61.

Longstaff FA, Schwartz ES. (1992). *Interest Rate Volatility and the Term Structure: A Two-Factor General Equilibrium Model*. Journal of Finance, 47(4), 1259–1282.

Ludvigson SC, Ng S. (2009). *Macro Factors in Bond Risk Premia*. Review of Financial Studies, 22, 5027–5067. Available at http://rfs.oxfordjournals.org/content/22/ 12/5027.abstract (Accessed 6 May 2015).

Lutz FA. (1940). *The Structure of Interest Rates*. The Quarterly Journal of Economics, 55, 36–63.

Macaulay FR. (1938). *Some Theoretical Problems Suggested by the Movements of Interest Rates, Bond Yields, and Stock Prices in the United States Since 1856*. NBER Working Paper Series, New York, 1938.

Mamon RS. (2004). *Three Ways to Solve for Bond Prices in the Vasicek Model*. Journal of Applied Mathematics and Decision Sciences, 8(1), 1–14.

Markowitz HM. (1959, 1991). *Portfolio Selection*. Blackwell, Oxford.

Mayer J, Khairy K, Howard J. (2010). *Drawing an Elephant with Four Complex Parameters*. American Journal of Physics, 78(6), 648–649.

McNeil A, Frey R, Embrechts P. (2015). *Quantitative Risk Management: Concepts, Techniques and Tools*. Princeton University Press, Princeton, NJ.

Mehara R, Prescott EC. (2003). *The Equity Premium in Retrospect*. In G Constantinides, M. Harris, and R. Stultz R (eds.), Handbook of the Economics of Finance, Vol. 1B, 889–938. Elsevier, Amsterdam.

Naik V. (2002). *Modelling the Yield Curve with Dynamic Interest Rate Targets*. Working Paper.

Nawalka SK, Rebonato R. (2011). *What Interest Models to Use? Buy Side Versus Sell Side*. Journal of Investment Management, 9(3), 5–18.

Nelson CR, Siegel AF. (1987). *Parsimonious Modeling of Yield Curves*. Journal of Business, 60, 473–489.

Pearl J. (2009). *Causality*. 2nd edn. Cambridge University Press, Cambridge.

Pearson ND, Sun T-S. (1994). *Exploiting the Conditional Density in Estimating the Term Structure: An Application to the Cox, Ingersoll and Ross Model*. The Journal of Finance, XIXL(4), 1279–1304.

Pettofrezzo AJ, (1966), Reprinted 1978. *Matrices and Transformations*. Dover Publications, mineola, NY.

Piazzesi M. (2010). *Affine Term Structure Models*, In *Handbook of Financial Econometrics*. Elsevier, Philadelphia.

Piazzesi M, Salomao J, Schneider M. (2013). *Trend and Cycle in Bond Premia*. Working Paper, Stanford University, December 2013. Available at http://web.stanford.edu/~piazzesi/trendcycle.pdf. (Accessed 24 February 2015).

Piazzesi M, Swanson ET. (2008). *Futures Prices as Risk-Adjusted Forecasts of Monetary Policy*. Journal of Monetary Economics, 55, 677–691.

Pinker S. (2014). *The Sense of Style*. Allen Lane, London.

Priebsch MA. (2013). *Computing Arbitrage-Free Yields in Multi-Factor Gaussian Shadow-Rate Term Structure Models*. Finance and Economics Discussion Series, Federal Reserve Board, Washington, DC. Available at www.federalreserve.gov/pubs/feds/2013/201363/201363pap.pdf (Accessed 26 November 2015).

Qu W. (2015). *Does the Kim-Wright Risk Premium Tell Us Anything about Investing?*, Working paper, PIMCO, August 2015.

Radwanski JF. (2010). *Understanding Bond Risk Premia Uncovered by the Term Structure*. Working Paper, Vienna Graduate School of Finance, Vienna University of Economics, (VGSF). Available at www.wu.ac.at/ruw/other/vgsf/students/Radwanski10Bonds.pdf (Accessed 5 May 2015).

Rebonato R. (2000). *Volatility and Correlation: The Perfect Hedger and the Fox*. John Wiley & Sons, Chichester.

Rebonato R. (2002). *Modern Pricing of Interest-Rate Derivatives: The LIBOR Market Model and Beyond*. Princeton University Press, Princeton, NJ.

Rebonato R. (2014). *Why Does the Market Price of Risk Depend on the Slope of the Yield Curve?*, International Journal of Theoretical and Applied Finance and ssrn working paper. Available at http://papers.ssrn.com/sol3/papers.cfm?abstract_id=2518985. (Accessed 5 May 2015).

Rebonato R. (2015). *Return-Predicitng Factors for US Treasuries: On the Similarity of 'Tents' and 'Bats'*. International Journal of Theoretical and Applied Finance, 18(4), 1–14.

Rebonato R. (2017). *Affine Models with Stochastic Market Price of Risk*. International Journal of Theoretical and Applied Finance, 20(4), 1750027-1-1750027-38.

Rebonato R, Denev A. (2013). *Portfolio Management under Stress*. Cambridge University Press, Cambridge.

Rebonato R, Putyatin V, Saroka V. (2014). *A Study of Excess Returns in US Treasuries: In- and Out-of-Sample Stability*. Quantitative Finance.

Rebonato R, Saroka I, Putyatin V. (2017). *A Principal-Component-Based Affine Term Structure Model*. Submitted for publication to. Applied Mathematical Finance. Available at http://papers.ssrn.com/sol3/papers.cfm?abstract_id=2451130.

Riley KF, Hobson MP, Bence SJ, *Mathematical Methods for Physics and Engineering*. Cambridge University Press, Cambridge.

Rosenberg JV, Maurer S. (2008). *Signal or Noise? Implications of the Term Premium for Recession Forecasting*. Federal Reserve Bank of New York, Working Paper, July 2008. Available at www.newyorkfed.org/research/epr/08v14n1/0807rose.pdf (Accessed 22 October 2014).

Ross SA. (2011). *The Recovery Theorem*. National Bureau of Economic Research Working Paper. Available at www.nber.org/papers/w17323 (Accessed 11 June 2015).

Ross SA. (2015). *The Recovery Theorem*. Journal of Finance, 70(2), 615–648.

Rudebusch GD, Sack BP, Swanson ET. (2007). *Macroeconomic Implications of Changes in Term Premium*. Federal Reserve Bank of St Louis, Review, July/August, 89(4), 241–270.

Rudebusch GD, Wu T. (2008). *A Macro-Finance Model of the Term Structure, Monetary Policy, and the Economy*. Economic Journal, 118, 906–926.

Sangvinatsos A. *The Expctation Hypothesis*. Working Paper, University of Southern California & Stern Business School, New York University. Available at http://pages. stern.nyu.edu/˜sternfin/asangvin/ExpHyp.pdf (Accessed 31 October 2014).

Sangvinatsos A, Wachter JA. (2005). *Does the Failure of the Expectations Hypothesis Matter for Long-Term Investors?* The Journal of Finance, LX(1), 179–230.

Saroka I. (2014). *Arbitrage-Free Modelling of Affine Principal Components of the Yield Curve*. Oxford University, thesis for MSc in Mathematical Finance.

Schaefer SM. (1977). *The Problem with Redemption Yields*. Financial Analyst Journal, 33(4), 59–67. Available at www.jstor.org/discover/10.2307/ 4478054?sid=21105764005313&uid=70&uid=2129&uid=2&uid=3738032&uid=4 (Accessed 2 February 2015).

Sharpe WF. (1966). *Mutual Fund Performance*. Journal of Business, 39, 119–138.

Sharpe WF. (1994). *The Sharpe Ratio*. The Journal of Portfolio Management, 21(1), 49–58.

Shiller RJ. (1979). *The Volatility of Long-term Interest Rates and Expectations Models of the Term Structure*. Journal of Political Economy, 87(61), 1190–1218.

Shiller RJ. (1981). *Do Stock Prices Move Too Much to Be Justified by Subsequent Changes in Dividends?* American Economic Review, 71, 421–435.

Shleifer A. (2000). *Inefficient Markets – An Introduction to Behavioural Finance*. Clarendon Lectures in Economics. Oxford University Press, Oxford.

Shleifer A, Vishny R. (1997). *The Limits of Arbitrage*. Journal of Finance, 52, 35–55.

Shlens J. (2009). *A Tutorial on Principal Component Analysis*. Working paper, Centre for Neural Science, New York University. Available at www.cs.uu.nl/docs/ vakken/ddm/texts/Normal/pca.pdf (Accessed 26 September 2014).

Smolin L. (2006). *The Trouble with Physics*. Allen Lane, London.

Stein C. (1956). *Inadmissibility of the Usual Estimator for the Mean of a Multivariate Distribution*. Proceedings Third Berkeley Symposium on Mathematical Statistics and Probability, 1, 197–206.

Summers L. (1985). *On Economics and Finance*. The Journal of Finance, 40(3), 633–635.

Svensson LEO. (1997). *Inflation Targeting as a Monetary Policy Rule*. Journal of Monetary Economics, 43, 655–679.

Svensson LEO. (1999). *Inflation Forecast Targeting: Implementing and Monitoring Inflation Targets*. European Economic Review, 41, 1111–1146.

Taylor JB. (1993). *Discretion versus Policy Rules in Practice*. Carnegie-Rochester Series on Public Policy, 39, 195–214.

Tegmark M. (2015). *Our Mathematical Universe*. Penguin Press, Allen Lane, London.

Tsui HM. (2013). *Ross Recovery Theorem and Its Extension*. Thesis submitted in partial fulfillment of the MSc in Mathematical Finance, Oxford University.

Ueno Y, Baba N, Sakurai Y. (2006). *The Use of the Black Model of Interest Rates as Options for Monitoring the JGB Market Expectations*. Working Paper 2006-E-15, Bank of Japan.

Ungari S, Turc J. (2012). *Macro-Financial Model*. Working Paper SocGen Cross Asset Quant Research, 19 October 2012.

Vasicek O. (1977). *An Equilibrium Characterization of the Term Structure*. Journal of Financial Economics, 5, 177–188.

Vayanos D, Vila JL (2009). *A Preferred-Habitat Model of the Term Structure of Interest Rates*. Working Paper, W15487, NBER.

Villegas D. (2015). *Bond Excess Returns Predictability and the Expectation Hypothesis*. thesis submitted in partial fulfillment of the requirements for the M.Sc. in Mathematical Finance, University of Oxford, Hillary Term, 2015.

Wachter J. (2006). *A Consumption-Based Model of the Term Structure of Interest Rates*. Journal of Financial Economics, 79, 365–399.

Weil P. (1989). *The Equity Premium Puzzle and the Risk-Free Rate Puzzle*. Journal of Monetary Economics, 24, 401–421.

Wu JC, Xia FD. (2014). *Measuring the Macroeconomic Impact of Monetary Policy at the Zero Lower Bound*. Working Paper, Chicago Booth and NBER, Available at http://faculty.chicagobooth.edu/jing.wu/research/pdf/wx.pdf (Accessed 31 March 2015).

Wu JC, Xia FD. (2015). *Shadow Federal Funds Rate*. Available at www.frbatlanta.org/cqer/researchcq/shadow_rate.aspx (Accessed 2 April 2015).

Xiong W, Yan H. (2010). *Heterogeneous Expectations and Bond Markets*. The Review of Financial Studies, 23(4), 1433–1466.

Index

Note: page numbers followed by *f* or *t* respectively indicate figure or table.